- **Be sure each promo piece can be used in more than one situation.**

- **Negotiate with your clients for 100 or 200 printed pieces of the brochure you photographed for them and use them as promo pieces by adding a name label.**

- **Join your local photo association and negotiate with local camera stores and photo labs for a members-only discount on their services and products.**

- **Contact your local business association and offer to trade photo services for their mailing list.**

- **Buying mailing lists from companies can be less expensive than researching and maintaining your own.**

- **Hire your local Girl Scout troop to put together your mailings. They could use the extra money and it will cost you less money than hiring someone for the job.**

For more information on self-promotion in photography, read Maria Piscopo's article on page 5.

1993 Photographer's Market

Distributed in Canada by McGraw-Hill,
300 Water Street,
Whitby Ontario L1N 9B6.
Also distributed in Australia by Kirby Books, Private Bag No. 19, P.O. Alexandria NSW 2015.

Managing Editor, Market Books Department:
Constance J. Achabal; Assistant Managing
Editor: Glenda Tennant Neff

This 1993 hardcover edition of Photographer's
Market features a "self-jacket" that eliminates
the need for a separate dust jacket. It provides
sturdy protection for your book while it saves paper, trees and energy.

International Standard Serial Number
0147-247X
International Standard Book Number
0-89879-583-4

1993
Photographer's Market

Where & How to Sell Your Photographs

Edited by
Michael Willins

Assisted by
Pat Beusterien

Writer's
Digest
Books

Cincinnati, Ohio

Contents

Important Information on Market Listings

- *The majority of markets listed in this book are those which are actively seeking new freelance contributors. Some important, well-known companies which have declined complete listings are included within their appropriate section with a brief statement of their policies. In addition, firms which for various reasons have not renewed their listings from the 1992 edition are listed in the " '92-'93 Changes" lists at the end of each section.*
- *Market listings are published free of charge to photography buyers and are not advertisements. While every measure is taken to ensure that the listing information is as accurate as possible, we cannot guarantee or endorse any listing.*
- Photographer's Market *reserves the right to exclude any listing which does not meet its requirements.*
- *Although every buyer is given the opportunity to update his listing information prior to publication, the photography marketplace changes constantly throughout the year and between editions. Therefore it is possible that some of the market information will be out of date by the time you make use of it.*
- *Market listings new to this edition are marked with an asterisk. These new markets are often the most receptive to new freelance talent.*
- *This book is edited (except for quoted material) in the masculine gender because we think "he/she," "she/he," "he or she," "him or her" in copy is distracting.*

Key to Symbols and Abbreviations

🍁 *Canadian Markets*
‡ *Markets located outside the United States and Canada*
■*Audiovisual Markets*
*New Listings
NPI no payment information given
SASE self-addressed stamped envelope
IRC International Reply Coupon, for use on reply mail in markets outside of your own country
Ms, Mss manuscript(s)
© *copyright*
FAX facsimile transmission
(for definitions and abbreviations relating specifically to the photographic industry, see the glossary in the back of the book.)

From the Editor

In recent years the field of photography has almost resembled the United States' Gold Rush of the 1800s. Equipped with everything from top quality lenses and heavy duty tripods to point-and-shoot cameras, photographers worldwide are battling to carve a niche for themselves in the industry. Everywhere aspiring photographers prepare their submissions and make frequent pilgrimages to post offices, dropping off packages that, hopefully, will help them strike it rich.

If you are one of the many photographers eager to sell photos, the *1993 Photographer's Market* can help you. By studying the listings in this book and following the advice of professionals who appear in feature articles and Close-ups, photographers of any level can sell their images.

This directory contains around 2,500 potential buyers for your work and over 450 listings are new this year. Because of the sagging economic times this year's edition includes an article called Cost-Effective Self-Promotion, which can help you promote your work without breaking your budget. Another feature piece, Minimizing the Risks of Freelancing, offers advice to keep you from getting taken by unscrupulous clients.

Along with those two feature stories there are several major changes in the book that are designed to help you in your pursuit of image sales. For those of you who are new to the field of photography, in the back of this book there is a First Markets Index which contains over 600 listings (an increase of around 400 from last year). These markets encourage newer, lesser-known photographers to submit work. In the past this list only included the names of low-paying or no-paying markets, but this year high-paying and middle-of-the-road markets also are included.

As you flip through these pages you may also notice two new symbols located before some listings. The maple leaf (✿) has been used to designate Canadian markets, while the double dagger (‡) is used for listings outside the United States and Canada. As in past years, the asterisk (*) appears before all new listings and a black square (■) has been used to indicate markets that seek various types of audiovisual materials.

As always, we try to provide as much detail as possible about each listing, particularly when it comes to payment and terms. You will notice that some of the markets contain the code "NPI," which stands for "No payment information given." All of the codes listed above should make your search for markets easier as you try to sell your work.

You will quickly realize while reading the listings that the markets have vastly different wants and needs. The article How to Use Your Photographer's Market can help you understand the contents of these markets and guide you in your pursuit of sales.

The 13 Close-up articles once again feature some of photography's top professionals who offer advice to people wanting to sell images. One of the world's best travel photographers, Lisl Dennis, explains how the industry became so crowded with aspiring artists and she outlines her key to success in the future. As our stock section Close-up subject, Canadian stock agency owner Gerry Boudrias reflects on the photographer-client relationship. Pulitzer-prize winning photographer Anthony "Kal" Roberts describes his modus operandi when it comes to shooting work for record companies and his methods would serve you well if you are interested in that field.

Photographers Nancy Clendaniel, Ron Austing, Mark Chester, Melvin Grier and Laurance Aiuppy share their experiences in creating images and they offer tips to less-seasoned artists who are trying to succeed in this highly competitive business. Publisher Tom Hamilton and photo editors Kathy Getsey, Ted Matthews and Christopher Bain explain the ins and outs of getting published and they paint pictures of the type of photographers with whom they want to work.

We have used the Business of Photography article and the introductions preceding each section as forums for new information regarding industry trends. The stock agency category, for example, outlines the controversy surrounding CD-Rom technology. The debate regarding the purchase of The Image Bank by Eastman Kodak also is included in the stock section. Insurance concerns for professionals and new copyright problems have been discussed in the Business of Photography.

All of the updates and changes in this year's book have been made with you, the reader, in mind. Everything from the 35 sample photos, which show you the kind of photos buyers have recently purchased, to the Glossary located in the back has been included to better service your needs.

Although we expect these changes to make it easier for you to sell images, your work is just beginning. We can't stand looking over your shoulder pointing to listings that best suit your style and we can't be there every time you have a concern about normal business practices. Scouring through the listings and learning everyday business practices are tedious tasks, but when all the work is done you almost certainly will reap the benefits of your efforts.

You will have tearsheets containing your photos as they appear in magazines, posters, greeting cards or whatever. Those tearsheets then can be shown to potential clients to let them know you have been published and are serious about your work. You also will earn income from your images and you will know your efforts were worth it.

The markets are out there. All you have to do is find them. . . . That's why we're here.

How to Use Your Photographer's Market

You're probably sitting at home in your most comfortable chair preparing to flip through these pages and find every photobuyer who ever purchased one-time rights to an image. Hoping to turn exposed film into a profit, you are eager to find those markets which will buy and publish your work. You may be a professional trying to strengthen your already established list of clients or you may be a beginner with faith in your "photographic eye."

Whatever your interests, this year's *Photographer's Market* can help you sell your work. While the listings provide you with contacts, payment structures and helpful tips, there are other features in the book that are just as important.

If sales are floundering because you can't seem to sell yourself or your work to potential buyers, the upfront piece entitled Cost-Effective Self-Promotion by Maria Piscopo can get you going. The Business of Photography section offers information on insurance, taxes and copyright and there are several sample forms which can help you maintain a professional relationship with clients. An article at the end of the section, Minimizing the Risks of Freelancing by John Nash, also can add to your business savvy.

The 13 close-up subjects tell you the positives and negatives of freelancing and they give advice that can help you succeed in the photo industry. If you are uncertain about your abilities and just want to test the waters, flip to the contests located in the Resources section. There also are numerous workshops listed if you want to hone your photographic skills. Reading section introductions can improve your knowledge about the various industries represented throughout the book. The key, however, is knowing where to begin and what to look for when reviewing listings.

Where to begin

With around 2,500 listings to review, it is easy to get lost when searching for a place to start. The first step is to thin out those sections which are of little or no use to you. If, for example, you are a professional who only wants to shoot product shots, there is little sense in spending all your time pouring over editorial listings. Advertising, Public Relations and Audiovisual Firms would be a natural for you as would Art/Design Studios, Businesses/ Organizations and Stock Agencies.

If you are a beginner wanting to build a portfolio start with the Publications section, which includes consumer magazines, newspapers, special interest publications and trade publications. This, however, does not mean that other sections should be ignored, just prioritized. Most sections of the book contain markets whose needs "cross over."

For all newer or lesser-known photographers it is a good idea to use the First Markets Index in the back of the book. The index, which contains over 600 buyers, is divided into categories to save you time in finding the markets you're interested in. This list used to contain only low-paying or non-paying markets. It now includes buyers at all points of the payscale and these listings contain the phrase, "Interested in receiving work from newer, lesser-known photographers."

While payment is important for any businessperson, don't judge markets solely on the aspect of money. Through negotiations you may find that those payments are not set in stone. You also may find that one buyer who pays $500 for a magazine cover photo only buys one or two shots each year. On the other hand, a buyer who pays $35 for a magazine cover shot might buy 50 images annually. Obviously the odds of selling your work are greater if you contact markets which buy a lot of images. When reviewing the listings it is important to know how many photos a buyer purchases from freelancers each year. This usually is stated in this manner: "Uses 70 photos/issue; 80 percent supplied by freelancers." The numbers will change, but you get the idea. Some markets did not provide any payment information and those listings contain the code "NPI," which stands for "No payment information given."

While you are reading the book take a good look at this year's sample photos. These images are examples of the kind of photos buyers have purchased in the past and the cutline information will help you better understand the freelancing process. The captions also will explain the strengths of the photos and, in some cases, background information about images.

Probably the most important thing to remember when preparing to submit photos to a buyer is to know what the buyer wants. There is no sense in wasting time, effort and money submitting work to buyers who aren't interested in the subject matter. Each listing tells you what topics the buyer is interested in. In many cases a query letter and a stock photo list can give a book publisher or a paper product company a good idea what you have to offer. If they are interested in your list of photos, they may ask you to submit the work for a closer review.

This brings up another important point. Most listings have information regarding the submission process. Some may want to see unsolicited submissions along with a query letter. Others may just want photographers to submit stock photo lists. Follow these instructions so that your first contact with a buyer is the right one.

One final note, if you have a problem with the book or don't understand something, don't hesitate to contact us. Through the suggestions and advice of our readers we are able to improve the book and make future editions even more useful.

Cost-Effective Self-Promotion

by Maria Piscopo

Today, you don't have the luxury of being just a photographer; you must operate like a photography business. All successful businesses have a written marketing plan and photographers should be no exception. There are four basic areas to consider when you write a plan to achieve cost-effective and successful promotion of your photography: personal selling, publicity, direct mail and advertising. It is important to understand how closely the four work together and how poorly each works alone.

Imagine that an umbrella containing these four sections is your overall marketing strategy. One-half or even two-thirds of the umbrella will not work as well as the whole umbrella. You won't stay dry in the rainstorms of a changing economy and marketplace.

What will it cost? Plan on spending about 10-15 percent of your projected gross sales on self-promotion. This means that to plan on making $50,000 in total sales, you will need to spend between $5,000 and $7,500 per year on self-promotion. This will cover all of the "tools" we will discuss, such as portfolios, promo pieces and direct mail.

Finding clients

Before you start self-promotion, identify the types of clients you want to attract. When you begin looking for clients, you can't ask the question, "What do I do as a photographer?" because the answer is "everything." You can't sell to everyone! At least not at the same time. This need for targeting does not mean you will be locked into one type of photography. In fact, it doesn't matter how diverse your work is. Prospective clients willl only buy your work if it suits their needs.

The simplest targeting is to separate products and people. Within product photography there are many target areas and possible clients, such as computers, electronics, food, fashion accessories, medical products and catalogs. People photography can be geared to service firms such as banking, computer software, insurance, medical and financial services. In the end, you can target as many areas as you like, but you must keep them separate. However, you would be well-served by identifying the growth markets such as healthcare and travel/leisure. It's a good idea to look for new clients who buy photography to promote their goods and services and will continue to do so for years to come.

In our search for clients, we must first find the name of the firm—the "lead." Let's look in some obvious places:

1. Trade directories list the names, addresses and phone numbers of the firm. Some of your best bets are *Photographer's Market, Standard Directory of Advertisers, Adweek Directory of Advertising Agencies, Design Firm Directory* or your county chamber of commerce.

2. Local library reference sections will have directories and many other sources on file. You can literally walk into your library and ask "Where can I find the names of food service firms based in this area?" No matter what you are looking for, someone has already done the work for you and all you have to do is look it up.

Maria Piscopo from Costa Mesa, California, has been an art/photo rep since 1978. She sells to corporations, ad agencies and design firms. Piscopo teaches at the Art Center College of Design, the PHOTO Conferences and the VICOM Conference in Canada. She writes on marketing and managing for Rangefinder, Confetti and other photo-industry magazines. Her book, The Photographer's Guide to Marketing and Self-Promotion, was published by Writer's Digest Books. She is a member of the Visual Artists Association, National Speakers Association and the Society of Photographers & Artists Reps.

3. Daily newspapers are full of leads if you learn how to read them carefully. Look in the business sections for new products, services, mergers, etc. and you will find clients who need photography for new promotional material.

4. Industry trade shows are a great place to gather leads as well as view firms' current brochures and other literature that use photography.

5. Business publications frequently list potential clients. An article on the "Top Publicly Held Firms" is an excellent source for annual report photography. Almost every city has a business journal that compiles this information and publishes an annual book of lists.

6. Membership directories you receive when you join associations are all you need for portfolio appointments or a mailing list. One step better, you can go to the regular meetings and meet potential clients face-to-face. Of course, you are not "selling" at this stage, but only gathering leads and information to use later on. One of the secrets to successfully selling your photography with the minimum investment of time is to establish relationships with this type of "networking" before you start selling to them.

While seeking clients, we often focus on ourselves without looking at the client's needs. You'll find that clients are looking for more value for their photography dollar. Beyond creativity and technical expertise (composition, lighting) you will have to demonstrate flexibility, professionalism, good communication and business skills. Combining these qualities and targeting specific areas will result in successfully finding new photography clients.

Personal selling

The most effective, but most time-consuming area of the marketing umbrella is personal selling. Unlike direct mail, advertising and public relations, personal, one-to-one contact is the goal of selling. Also, since selling takes more time than money, it is the best place to start and run your photography business on a small budget.

Your selling efforts can reach more people and be more effective by fortifying them with "nonpersonal" marketing such as direct mail, advertising and public relations. Once a buyer has been exposed to who you are and what you can do for them through your advertising and mailings, they will be more likely to meet with you when you call for an appointment. The reverse is also true. Once you have shown your portfolio, your ads and mailings will help them remember you when they have a job. Always plan for a full marketing plan for the best results.

Phone calls and portfolio presentations have been the most traditional (and least expensive) methods of marketing photography. But it would be a mistake to consider the portfolio presentation the first step. The most successful approach to selling your photography consists of several steps.

Qualifying the prospect

This is simply a matter of determining the name of the person who has the authority and responsibility to purchase photography. Remember that the client is the contact, not the company, and it is very common for any given company to have more than one buyer. Check by job title. Agencies have art directors, corporations have marketing and public relations directors. This is a critical step, you want to be sure to approach the correct person and avoid a lot of wasted time and energy. The end result could be one company, but three contacts and three prospective clients!

Approach the prospective client

You only have one chance for a first impression, so make it a good one. You may decide to send several direct mail promotions before calling. Are you sure this prospect has been getting your advertising and public relations efforts? Once you decide to approach the prospective client, it is important to establish a personal relationship. In the end, people buy photography from people they feel they know and it is for this reason you want to begin by meeting face-to-face and showing samples of your work. You are just as important to selling your photography as your portfolio. Be sure to get information whenever you can't get an appointment. For example, ask "Who else buys photography?"; "When is a good time to call back?"

The portfolio presentation

The time is most productively spent if you have done all your homework and can fulfill two criteria. One, does this person buy the kind of photography you sell? Two, will this person get to know you and your work? It is important during the presentation to talk about who you are, what you do and how all of this relates to the prospective client. Be sure the presentation leaves a very clear visual impression of your work. Remember, showing "everything" you do will only confuse the buyer. Someone can like your work but never consider working with you because you don't do what they need. Ever hear "nice portfolio" and wonder why you never got called back? This means showing 10 to 15 photographs that display your expertise at photographing what they need. In the end, what you do as a photographer is much less important than what your client needs.

Concluding the presentation is very simple, but often is the most overlooked area in the selling of photography. It is as simple as coming to some kind of agreement with the client as to what happens next. Ask about upcoming jobs you could bid on. Agree to get together in two months to show an updated portfolio. Whatever you do, don't leave until you have come to some kind of conclusion. This step will increase the number of jobs you get from portfolio presentations because it provides for the next step.

Follow-up

Follow-up is when portfolio presentations turn into jobs. The most work a successful photographer gets is after the sixth contact with a client. Remember, these people don't know who you are until they have heard from you or seen your name six times! By reaching a conclusion and getting information you will have something important to say when you call back. Remember, always do what you say you will do. If you have promised to call back in two weeks, do it!

Most photographers don't do enough follow-up and lose the equity built up from advertising, direct mail, public relations and selling. If you don't have the time for a phone call, then drop a note in the mail. It is your job to keep in touch and turn prospects into clients, it is not the client's responsibility. It is a lot easier and cheaper to keep clients than to find new ones; don't forget about current and past clients! Good follow-up habits will insure your success. Good marketing will increase your chances for success. No marketing will insure the lack of success.

Public relations

Public relations is the most inexpensive promotion for photographers. You can't buy it! You submit your story with a press release and hope to get the information published. Unlike buying an ad, you should submit to all the media, client and nonclient. The "word of mouth" benefit from getting published anywhere outweighs the fact that the publication isn't targeted to your particular clients. Besides, you can always reprint any publicity and mail it to the clients on your mailing list.

Because you can't guarantee the publicity like buying an ad, public relations does not work by itself. It works best in conjunction with other marketing tools such as selling, advertising and direct mail. The press release is a standardized form of communicating some "newsworthy" item to the editors of publications read by the people in your target market. It should be sent to the editors of your client media, local newspaper and photography magazines. The goal of public relations is repeated exposure of your name and firm. A prospective client may see your ad, receive your direct-mail promotion, see your portfolio, then read about you in the paper. That's four exposures or contacts you have made by having a full umbrella!

Here are some examples of "newsworthy" items:

- You participate in community or industry groups.
- You win an award for your photography.
- You begin a big, important job.
- You successfully complete a big, important job.
- You add personnel to your staff.
- You expand with additional services for clients.
- You relocate your studio.
- You celebrate your anniversary.

The first example leads to a second important area of public relations that could be the key to cost-effective promotion. Networking! Every industry has professional associations or organizations. Photographers have peer groups like Professional Photographers of American (PPA) and American Society of Magazine Photographers (ASMP). Networking in these groups is important for the development of good business practices and educational opportunities. They often provide referral networks for job leads as well as discounts on advertising and other programs.

Your clients' organizations also can provide a fertile ground for your marketing efforts. Membership in these trade or industry groups offers numerous benefits to photographers — personal contact at meetings with potential clients, inexpensive advertising in newsletters, free listings in membership directories, publication of your press releases in association newsletters and opportunities to participate in awards programs.

Direct mail

Mailings are another form of advertising very popular with photographers and photo buyers. If you can clearly identify your client base, such as advertising agencies with food clients or computer manufacturers, then direct mail is a good tool for marketing. Costs for direct mail (in addition to the postage) vary with the quantity. Your per-piece cost could range from 50 cents to $1.50 depending on size, shape and format.

Don't be dissuaded from direct mail because some clients tell you they throw mailers away. If 90 percent of your clients toss out your piece, you should be ecstatic! That means 10 percent have responded, about three times higher than the average response. But direct mail is becoming more and more sophisticated with elements of design and copy becoming necessary, not optional.

There are four important factors that will determine the success of your direct mail:

1. The mailing list must be current and be in the name of the client or buyer for the firm with which you wish to work.

2. The mailing list must include people who buy the kind of photography you want to produce. If you can't clearly identify potential clients by what they buy, such as food or fashion photography, then you'll find it difficult to be successful with direct mail. Display ads might be a better buy. To further use the "umbrella" concept of marketing and to tie your advertising into your direct mail, acquire a mailing list from the business where you advertise.

3. Some kind of response mechanism (such as an 800 phone number or reply card) is essential to the success of your direct mail. It's impossible to call everyone you mail to, so ask people to call you!

4. A regular schedule of mailings is very important to build the exposure you need. As with display advertising, "one-shot" mailings do not work as well as a regular schedule of mailings that are planned around your other efforts, such as ads and press releases. Don't forget about the visual impression you must make! A buyer will need to see your logo, company name and any other visual message you want to communicate six to sixteen times before they recognize who you are and what you can do for them.

Advertising

Because advertising is the most expensive form of self-promotion, it should be done wisely and well. Advertising is a "nonpersonal" form of marketing because it is designed to reach very large groups of people all at once without your personal time and attention. When you can't pinpoint your buyers, such as when you have a very distinct style, buying a display ad in a creative source book is needed.

Source book ads will cost $2,500 and up per year and you must plan on being in the same directory for three to five years in a row to see if it is really working for you. Publication advertising will cost from $250-$2,500 and up per ad depending on the ad size and the magazine circulation.

The best reason to advertise is that you have so many potential clients, it is more efficient to advertise to all of them at once then to call them one at a time! For a photographer with a unique style, it's more efficient to expose thousands of people to that style so they can contact you when they have a project. It's difficult, if not impossible, to call art directors and ask, "What are your needs for stylish images?"

With a distinct specialty, your photography display ad allows thousands of clients to see the work and indentify themselves as potential clients. Photography clients look at ads to find something they don't already have. Your objectives for the ad are to give clients a strong and distinct impression and to ask people to respond to the ad.

For maximum cost-effectiveness and return on your investment, be sure to build in the "umbrella" factor. Add people who respond to your ad to your mailing list. Make your advertising work with your direct mail and selling, not independent of them! Always be certain you are reaching the right audience. If you do wedding and portrait photography, buy display ads in consumer publications such as community newspapers and magazines. Find out when these publications plan special articles, such as "How To Plan Your Wedding," so you can take advantage of the extra interest in that issue.

Commercial photographers must advertise where their specific buyers can be found: advertising directories and magazines for the advertising photographer; corporate publications for the corporate/industrial photographer.

Referral networks

Once you've completed your marketing strategy, you can always add to these efforts by building a referral network. A referral network is a group of people you can count on to refer work to you. They could be other designers whose work compliments yours. They are often good clients who act as advocates and are willing to tell their friends about you and your work. They could even be people in the community who don't buy from you, but they can influence the people that do. You are probably already getting referrals from these people, but it's time you set them up as an official network.

Go through this checklist to develop and maintain your referral network:
• Set up a mailing list of all of the people who have referred work to you. A photographer in business for more than three years should be able to identify at least six to twelve people who refer to them. Even if they have only done it once or twice, add them to the list to see if you could increase the number of referrals. The more the better! You probably already have them on a mailing list of clients and prospective clients. They should get all the same promotion any other client gets plus some extra attention.

At least six times per year, send them some kind of personal promo piece designed to "keep in touch." It could be a postcard from an out-of-town trip. It could be a personal letter. It should feature your photography and be more of a greeting card than a hard-sell piece. It should have some kind of hand-written note to let this person know you took the time and care to send this to them.

● Many times when we get a call for an assignment, we are so thrilled to get a job we forget to ask where it came from! On the estimate form you use when quoting a job, add the question, "Who referred you?" Get all the information you can about how this job came to your door and about the person who made that happen. You want them to do it again! Add this person to your referral network mailing list if they're not already on it.

● Immediately send a thank you note to the person who referred work to you. Don't wait to find out whether you got the job or not, just do it! This is not the kind of chore to put off or to schedule for another day. To make sure it becomes a habit and to make it easy, keep correspondence materials available.

Planning ahead

How do you promote yourself to new clients and create work for your current clients at the same time? Is "feast or famine" the only way? How do you manage in the most cost-effective way possible? Planning ahead plays a big part in the ongoing success of your photography business. Once you have a plan for selling, advertising, direct mail campaigns, publicity and networking, you're ready to plan a schedule to make it happen.

The real key to marketing and self-promotion is to make these "noncreative" tasks a natural element of your day rather than something to do when there is nothing else to do! After you have written your plan, transfer every self-promotion chore to your calendar. Schedule every press release and mailing as though it were a job for a client. Give every part of your plan a day and a time to work on it. Be sure to break it down into manageable pieces that can be easily scheduled into your work day. For example, rather than scheduling "produce portfolio for portrait clients" you would divide it up into "create self-assignments," "research portfolio formats," "find lab for making prints." Don't forget to schedule time off, trips to conferences and networking.

With a framework and structure to your daily, weekly and even monthly calendar, you'll always have two important things. One, you'll have a much better and more efficient scheduling of incoming work when you know what's already on the calendar. Two, you'll always be busy with projects and activities. You'll stay happy, creative and motivated. Clients will notice this in everything from your voice when you answer the phone to the quality and frequency of your contact with them. This will actually encourage clients to call you with their jobs. As everyone knows, "When you want something done, give it to a busy person!"

When a paying job comes along, you can always reschedule the self-assignment or that day off you planned. But, if it is not there on your calendar staring back at you, you probably would never get around to it. The problem with not scheduling is that you'll do the work that's in front of you (not necessarily the most important) and it will expand to fit the time you give it.

Writing your plan for maximum cost-effectiveness will take time, patience and practice to work. It's all up to you to make it better for yourself. These ideas for promotion will allow you to be both productive and profitable as a photographer.

The Business of Photography

Operating any business is not a simple task. It's especially difficult if clients are acquired through the mail or over the telephone as is the case for many freelance photographers. Not only do photographers have to cultivate new clients, via direct mail, advertising and other self-promotional tools (see page 5 for Maria Piscopo's article on self-promotion), but they also must find time to shoot photos. Often photographers can't balance these various business aspects and they quickly find themselves overwhelmed and discouraged.

This section in *Photographer's Market* is a guide to help photographers succeed as business people. Along with new information on copyright and insurance, there are several sample forms, provided by the American Society of Magazine Photographers (ASMP), which should serve as a foundation for daily operation. The forms, however, are meant to be used as guidelines and should be tailored to suit artists' specific needs. Some of the forms mention "no alteration" of photographs, which is an important clause to include now that so many technological advances are being made in photography. Although the ability to alter images is not new, a computer can quickly turn them into something unrecognizable.

Prior to setting up your business, it's best to take the time to talk with other photographers about their business practices. What system of financial recordkeeping have they adopted? What types of insurance do they carry? What type of photo filing system have they found works best? Seek out any professional photography associations in your town or look into taking a small business course at the local community college. The more knowledge you are armed with beforehand, the more business-related problems you'll be able to trouble-shoot effectively. There may come a time when you will want to consult a professional—whether it is a lawyer for contract counseling, or an accountant to help with your finances—to take advantage of their expertise. Such guidance can be invaluable in preventing disaster in some important aspect of your business.

At the end of this section there is an important article by John Nash, starting on page 29, which provides ways to avoid troublesome clients who knowingly break the laws regarding copyright infringement or respond too slowly when returning images or paying for photo usage.

Copyright/rights

While altering photographs is something photographers should guard against, they should also keep in mind that this technology can be used as a bargaining tool when talking to prospective clients who want to buy all rights to photos (see list of image rights in this subsection).

There are certain terms photo buyers use when they seek ownership of copyrights. The most common terms are "work for hire" and "all rights." However, the basic concept can come in many other disguises as well. These include: "buyout," "unlimited use," "world rights," "in perpetuity" and "no right of reversion," just to name a few. "Exclusive rights" also may be a signal that the client really wants all rights, but this is a term that can usually be negotiated for limited periods, such as one year.

Many times, especially in advertising, a client wants to buy all rights to images because he doesn't want to take the chance that the photographer will sell the image to a competitor for a similar campaign. But from a photographer's standpoint, losing the copyright to a photograph means he has lost future sales.

It is understandable for a client not to want a photo he purchased to be used in a competitor's ad. Skillful negotiation usually can result in an agreement between the photographer and the client that says the image(s) will not be sold to a competitor, but could be sold to other industries, possibly offering regional exclusivity for a stated time period as well.

Many photographers ask,"This photograph of a Mercedes sitting on the beach at sunset isn't going to be used by anyone except Mercedes. Why should I care if they own all the rights?" Maybe that sunset is the most dazzling sunset ever captured on film and another company wants to use it as a backdrop for an ad. With the types of computer manipulation that exist today the Mercedes can be extinguished from the photograph and another car or image can be put in its place. This means protecting your resale rights is more important than ever.

The area of copyrights is one in which photographers can never be too careful, since it involves a complex set of terms and considerations that are frequently misunderstood by photographers and photo buyers alike. Even a knowledgeable photographer will find himself at risk when dealing with a misinformed or intentionally deceptive client. So, it's essential not only to know your rights under the Copyright Law but also to make sure that every photo buyer you deal with understands them.

A 1989 Supreme Court decision involving the question of copyright ownership has reaffirmed the rights of all creative, people, including photographers, under the Copyright Law of 1976. Also, an amendment to the law is still in progress. Two results of the decision are: 1) a clarification, that a creator cannot unknowingly lose the copyright to his work, and 2) a reaffirmation, that the Copyright Law provides a 35-year time limit on the ownership. These results mean that ownership of copyrights can be transferred only in a written agreement, and when it is assigned in writing, the copyright will revert to the creator or his estate in 35 years.

Here is a list of image rights typically sold in the marketplace:

• One-time rights. These photos are "leased" on a one-time basis; one fee is paid for one use.

• First rights. This is generally the same as purchase of one-time rights though the photo-buyer is paying a bit more for the privilege of being the first to use the image. He may use it only once unless other rights are negotiated.

• Serial rights. The photographer has sold the right to use the photo in a periodical. It shouldn't be confused with using the photo in "installments." Most magazines will want to be sure the photo won't be running in a competing publication.

• Exclusive rights. Exclusive rights guarantee the buyer's exclusive right to use the photo in his particular market or for a particular product. A greeting card company, for example, may purchase these rights to an image with the stipulation that it not be sold to a competing company for a certain time period. The photographer, however, may retain rights to sell the image to other markets. Conditions should always be in writing to avoid any misunderstandings.

• Promotion rights. Such rights allow a publisher to use the photographer's photo for promotion of a publication in which the photo appeared. The photographer should be paid for promotional use in addition to the rights first sold to reproduce the image. Another form of this—agency promotion rights—is common among stock photo agencies. Likewise, the terms of this need to be negotiated separately.

• Work for hire. (See sidebar in this section for detailed definition.)

• All rights. This involves selling or assigning all rights to a photo for a specified period of time. This differs from work for hire, which always means the photographer permanently surrenders all rights to a photo and any claims to royalties or other future compensation. Terms for all rights—including time period of usage and compensation—should only be negotiated and confirmed in a written agreement with the client.

Copyright protection

Here are a few basic practices you can implement to ensure protection of your copyright. Primarily, you should mark each of your images with a copyright notice—copyright, copr. or ©—plus the year of creation as well as the name of the owner, which in most cases is the creator. Since the © symbol is universally accepted in most countries and it is becoming more common for photographers to work with clients overseas, it is best to settle on this designation as you establish your routine practices.

According to the Buenos Aires Convention, which covers many Western Hemisphere countries, copyright notices should also include the notation "All rights reserved." However, all rights are automatically reserved under U.S. Copyright Law. For convenience, you can have rubber stamps made or use a computer software package to create labels for your images. Such labeling is preferable to handmarking, since handwritten notices—especially those done in ink—can sometimes become unreadable or bleed through into printed images. If clients ever advise you not to include copyright information on your slides or prints, take this as a warning sign and do not do business with them.

In the event that you have to file suit against a photo buyer for copyright infringement, copyright registration is ordinarily necessary if you are a U.S. citizen. To do this, you should write to the Copyright Office of the Library of Congress, Washington DC 20559. Request the form titled Form VA (works of visual arts).

Obviously, registering photos can be expensive if you have a large number of images. So you may wish to decide which images are most valuable to you in terms of future resale

---

Work for hire definition:

Under the Copyright Act of 1976, section 101, a "work for hire" is defined as:

"(1) a work prepared by an employee within the scope of his or her employment; or (2) a work . . .
- *specially ordered or commissioned for use as a contribution to a collective work**
- *as part of a motion picture or audiovisual work**
- *as a translation*
- *as a supplementary work**
- *as a compilation*
- *as an instructional text*
- *as a test*
- *as answer material for a test*
- *or as an atlas*

. . . if the parties expressly agree in a written instrument signed by them that the work shall be considered a work made for hire."

NOTE: The asterisk (*) denotes categories within the Copyright Law which apply to photography.

---

value—as well as those most likely to be infringed—and register only those to keep down costs.

As a quick reference, here are several areas that are helpful to remember when dealing with questions of copyright and rights:
- contracts
- licensing
- setting value and prices for images
- keeping records of all correspondence and submissions
- enforcement of rights

A valuable tool for any photographer trying to deal with all the copyright language and various forms of the photography business is the *SPAR* Do-It-Yourself Kit*. This survival package includes sample forms, explanations and checklists of all terms and questions a photographer should ask himself when negotiating a job and pricing it. It's available from SPAR, the Society of Photographer and Artist Representatives, Inc., Suite 1166, 60 E. 42nd St., New York NY 10165, (212)822-1415. Price: $50 plus $3 shipping and handling. New York state residents pay in-state tax of $4.37.

Pricing and negotiating

Pricing follows closely on the heels of usage and rights as these areas are intimately related for photographers. As one formula promoted by industry professionals has proclaimed, "Copyright is the key to usage, and usage is the key to pricing."

Many of the markets listed in *Photographer's Market* quote specific dollar amounts for buying single stock images or payment on assigned work. (A code—NPI, for "no payment information given"—is inserted into listings which haven't provided any figures.) Whether the payment you are offered compensates you fairly for the work you have done, your overhead and the rights the client wants to purchase are important questions to ask yourself before you agree to do business with the client. Asking this question is especially critical when a client asks you to do work for hire or to transfer all rights to an image.

Some photographers—at least in the area of assignment work—work on a day rate, or sometimes a half-day rate. For instance, editorial photographers will typically quote fees in the low hundreds, while advertising and corporate shooters may quote fees upward into the low thousands. But all photographers have been finding that the day rate by itself is incomplete. As a result, they now will also bill the client for the number of finished pictures and rights the client wishes to purchase, as well as additional expenses such as equipment rental or hiring assistants. (See the following Sample Invoice and Estimate Confirmation forms.)

Typically, the photographer's strategy in such a case is to hold to the fee for the shoot as a basic, guaranteed rate. All other charges are negotiable, but the shoot fee remains fixed or the photographer does not do the work. When the client suggests a lower price, the photographer can then review the costs with the client and make adjustments in the complexity of the shoot's elements, the number of final shots or the usage. But the photographer does not just unconditionally lower his price. Accordingly, the photographer helps the client to get most if not all of what he wants at the price he wants, while ensuring that he will still get his base rate—which should include some profit.

An important advantage to breaking down the price for the client in this way is that it heads off the client coming back later and saying "Can you throw in one more print?" or trying to use the image in other ways not discussed. When negotiating the shoot, terms and price, it's a good idea to talk through all of the client's possible uses for the image. Then, you can either quote a higher price upfront if more usage is involved, or charge an extra fee later if the client requests additional usage or more images down the road.

The times of doing business on a handshake are fading fast and it's important for any photographer to protect himself against unnecessary lawsuits. Using a Terms & Conditions form, like the policies beginning on page 16, can guarantee that the buyer knows what he is getting and the photographer understands his responsibilities. Forms like this should accompany an estimation/confirmation letter so that any conflicts can be settled before a job is underway. Similar Terms & Conditions can be formulated to accompany other forms, such as invoices or delivery memos. ASMP published the Terms & Conditions on the backs of invoices and other forms.

The sample "Editorial Assignment Invoice," "Editorial Assignment Estimate/Confirmation," "Terms & Conditions," and "Model Release" in this year's edition of *Photographer's Market*, beginning on page 18, were reprinted from FORMS, produced by the American Society of Magazine Photographers. To order copies of FORMS write to ASMP, 419 Park Avenue South, New York NY 10016, (212)889-9144. Price: $19.95 plus $2 shipping and handling. New York state residents must pay sales tax.

In terms of selling images from your stock to various companies or publications, as you would be doing with many of the listings in *Photographer's Market*, it's best to study a cross-section of prices that other businesses of these types are paying for photos as well as the rights they are buying. Then, before contacting any of these prospects, you will already be screening out some markets that do not meet your requirements for sales potential. Whether you decide to accept lower payment rates for your stock will have a great deal to do with other motives you may have, such as getting published, gathering photo credits or getting your foot in the door with a client. However, it is generally best for your long-term career strategy if you avoid underpricing too much in the beginning and try to establish a more consistent, accurate system for arriving at a fair value for your work.

Special markets, such as galleries and stock photo agencies, typically charge photographers a commission—from 20 to 50 percent—for displaying or representing their images. In these markets, payment on sales comes from the purchase of prints by gallery patrons, or from royalties on the rental of photos by clients of stock photo agencies. Accordingly, pricing formulas should be developed depending on your costs and current price levels in those markets, as well as on the basis of submission fees, commissions and other administrative costs charged to the photographer.

Financial recordkeeping

You won't know whether your business is making a profit unless you keep accurate financial records that allow you to determine profits and losses quickly. Browse around office supply stores to determine the type of ledger you feel can suit your business needs. Ideally, a ledger should include spaces for information such as job number, date of assignment, client name, expenses incurred, sales taxes and payments due. For tax purposes, be sure to retain all business receipts, invoices and cancelled checks to support ledger entries. For convenience, file these records in an envelope by month—it will be less time consuming when filling out income-tax forms each year. Using computer software which performs electronic spreadsheet functions is also a good way to organize your accounting records. If you set up basic ledgers on computer, then you can input sales, expenses and tax information daily, weekly or monthly, as needed.

Another business necessity you will want to look into is designing and printing business forms. These forms are useful when selling stock photography as well as when shooting on assignment. For assignment work such forms should include columns for estimating services, assignment confirmation, and delivery of photos and invoicing. Photographers selling from stock will be concerned with delivery of photos and invoicing. When sending photos out in the marketplace be sure to itemize what images are being sent so the photo buyer and you will have a record. Business forms can be reproduced quickly and inexpensively at most quick-print services.

Also, either by purchasing or having access to a desktop publishing system and laser printer, you can design and produce forms specifically for your needs. With this kind of

TERMS & CONDITIONS

1. "Photograph(s)" means all photographic material furnished by Photographer hereunder, whether transparencies, negatives, prints or otherwise.

2. Except as otherwise specifically provided herein, all photographs and rights therein, including copyright, remain the sole and exclusive property of Photographer. Any additional uses require the prior written agreement of Photographer on terms to be negotiated. Unless otherwise provided herein, any grant of rights is limited to one (1) year from the date hereof for the territory of the United States.

3. Client assumes insurer's liability (a) to indemnify Photographer for loss, damage, or misuse of any photograph(s), and (b) to return all photographs prepaid and fully insured, safe and undamaged, by bonded messenger, air freight, or registered mail, within thirty (30) days after the first use thereof as provided herein, but in all events (whether published or unpublished) within _____ after the date hereof. Client assumes full liability for its principals, employees, agents, affiliates, successors and assigns (including without limitation messengers and freelance researchers) for any loss, damage, or misuse of the photographs. Client will supply Photographer with two free copies of each use of the photographs.

4. Reimbursement by Client for loss or damage of each original transparency shall be in the amount of One Thousand Five Hundred Dollars ($1,500), or such other amount set forth next to said item on the front hereof. Reimbursement by Client for loss or damage of each other item shall be in the amount set forth next to said item on the front hereof. Photographer and Client agree that said amount represents the fair and reasonable value of each item, and that Photographer would not sell all rights to such item for less than said amount.

5. Photographer's copyright notice "©[YEAR OF FIRST PUBLICATION] [PHOTOGRAPHER'S NAME]" must accompany each use as an adjacent credit line. Invoice amount will be tripled if said credit is not provided.

6. Client will not make or permit any alterations, additions, or subtractions in respect of the photographs, including without limitation any digitalization or synthesization of the photographs, alone or with any other material, by use of computer or other electronic means or any other method or means now or hereafter known.

7. Client will indemnify and defend Photographer against all claims, liability, damages, costs, and expenses, including reasonable legal fees and expenses, arising out of any use of any photographs for which no release was furnished by Photographer, or any photographs which are altered by Client. Unless so furnished, no release exists. Photographer's liability for all claims shall not exceed in any event the total amount paid under this invoice.

8. Client assumes full risk of loss or damage to materials furnished by client hereunder and warrants that said materials are adequately insured against such loss or damage. Client shall indemnify Photographer against all claims, liability, damages and expenses incurred by Photographer in connection with any third party claim arising out of use of said material hereunder.

9. All expense estimates are subject to normal trade variance of 10%.

10. Time is of the essence for receipt of payment and return of photographs. No rights are granted until timely payment is made.

11. Client may not assign or transfer this agreement or any rights granted hereunder. This agreement binds and inures to the benefit of Photographer, Client, Client's principals, employees, agents and affiliates, and their respective heirs, legal representatives, successors and assigns. Client and its principals, employees, agents and affiliates are jointly and severally liable for the performance of all payments and other obligations hereunder. No amendment or waiver of any terms is binding unless set forth in writing and signed by the parties. However, the invoice may reflect, and Client is bound by, oral authorizations for fees or expenses which could not be confirmed in writing because of immediate proximity of shooting. This agreement incorporates by reference Article 2 of the Uniform Commercial Code, and the Copyright Act of 1976, as amended.

12. Except as provided in (13) below any dispute regarding this agreement shall be arbitrated in [PHOTOGRAPHER'S CITY AND STATE] under rules of the American Arbitration Association and the laws of [STATE OF ARBITRATION]. Judgment on the arbitration award may be entered in any court having jurisdiction. Any dispute involving $ _____ [LIMIT OF LOCAL SMALL CLAIMS COURT] or less may be submitted without arbitration to any court having jurisdiction thereof. Client shall pay all arbitration and court costs, reasonable legal fees, and expenses, and legal interest on any award or judgment in favor of Photographer.

13. Client hereby expressly consents to the jurisdiction of the Federal courts with respect to claims by Photographer under the Copyright Act of 1976, as amended.

14. In the event a shoot extends beyond eight (8) consecutive hours, Photographer may charge for such excess time of assistants and freelance staff at the rate of one-and-one-half their hourly rates.

15. Reshoots: Clients will be charged 100% fee and expenses for any reshoot required by Client. For any reshoot required because of an act of God or the fault of a third party, Photographer will charge no additional fee and Client will pay all expenses. If Photographer charges for special contingency insurance and is paid in full for the shoot, Client will not be charged for any expenses covered by insurance. A list of exclusions from such insurance will be provided on request.

16. Cancellations and postponements: Client is responsible for payment of all expenses incurred up to the time of cancellation, plus 50% of Photographer's fee. If notice of cancellation is given less than two (2) business days before the shoot date, Client will be charged 100% fee. Weather postponements: Unless otherwise agreed, Client will be charged 100% fee if postponement is due to weather conditions on location and 50% fee if postponement occurs before departure to location.

Reprinted from FORMS with permission of the American Society of Magazine Photographers, Inc. (ASMP).

EDITORIAL ASSIGNMENT INVOICE

TO:

INVOICE #:
INVOICE DATE:
JOB #:
EDITOR:
STORY SLUG:

SS/FED. ID#:

DESCRIPTION/RIGHTS GRANTED/PERIOD OF USE

FEES

Photography Fees @ $ per day   _____
Prep Days @ $ per day   _____
Travel/Weather Days @ $ per day   _____
Usage Fees and Space Rates   _____
                                              $ _____

EXPENSES

Assistants and Crew   _____
Film and Polaroids   _____
Photo Lab   _____
Locations   _____
Telephone   _____
Rentals and Props   _____
Shipping and Messengers   _____
Transportation   _____
Meals and Lodging   _____
Miscellaneous   _____
                                  $ _____

Subtotal   _____
Sales Tax   _____
Less Advance   _____
Total Amount Due $ _____

Time is of the essence for payment which is due upon receipt. Granting of right of usage is contingent upon full payment and is subject to the terms and conditions on the reverse side. Balance is subject to monthly rebilling charges applied thereafter. Adjustment of amount, or terms, must be requested within 14 days of invoice date. All expenses are subject to normal trade variance of 10% from estimated amounts.

EDITORIAL ASSIGNMENT
ESTIMATE/CONFIRMATION

TO:

DATE:

JOB #:

EDITOR:

STORY SLUG:

SS/FED. ID#:

ASSIGNMENT DESCRIPTION/RIGHTS GRANTED/PERIOD OF USE

FEES

Photography Fees @ $ per day   _____

Prep Days @ $ per day   _____

Travel/Weather Days @ $ per day   _____

Usage Fees and Space Rates   _____

$ _____

EXPENSES

Assistants and Crew   _____

Film and Polaroids   _____

Photo Lab   _____

Locations   _____

Telephone   _____

Rentals and Props   _____

Shipping and Messengers   _____

Transportation   _____

Meals and Lodging   _____

Miscellaneous   _____

$ _____

Subtotal _____

Sales Tax _____

Total Estimated Fees and Expenses _____

Cash Deposit Required Prior to Start of Assignment $ _____

ACKNOWLEDGED AND ACCEPTED   DATE

PLEASE SIGN AND RETURN ONE COPY

Usage is limited to that specified above and is subject to all terms and conditions on the reverse side. Unless otherwise agreed to in writing, the Photographer retains ownership of all photographs resulting from this assignment. Additional usage requires negotiation of additional fees. Time in excess of a normal working day will be pro-rated and billed on an hourly basis as overtime. Payment of invoices regarding this assignment will be due upon receipt.

system, you can produce master forms to be duplicated or print them out for each client or sale. Not only does use of a business form help you keep track of your work, it presents a more professional appearance to the photo buyer who will perceive you as being organized and dependable.

Depending upon the size of your business and your sales volume, you may find professional assistance indispensable when it comes to accounting and preparing taxes. Many photographers do their own bookkeeping in the beginning and delegate these tasks as they become more successful and involved in other aspects of their business. However, some photographers will — right from the beginning — at least have their records reviewed periodically by experts to ensure their accuracy. Whenever possible, try to find someone who works primarily with creative people or similar small business operators. Such specialists are often more familiar with the needs and problems of business people such as photographers, as well as any laws governing them.

Such review — whether done by you or by an expert — is important, too, for the overall financial health of your business. Looking closely at your costs and cash flow helps you to identify both profitable and unprofitable areas of your business. In particular, a good rule of thumb is that earnings should be in the range of 25 to 40 percent of your billings. If not, then it would be helpful to go back and study your records to see where you may need to cut costs or raise prices.

For any specific questions about starting up or maintaining your business, contact the following: American Society of Magazine Photographers (ASMP), 419 Park Ave. S., New York NY 10016, (212)889-9144; Service Corps of Retired Executives Association (SCORE) at Suite 5900, 409 Third St. SW, Washington DC 20024-2314, (202)205-6762. SCORE is a 12,000-member group of business men and women who provide free management assistance to those requiring expert advice.

Taxes

Whether you're a freelance photographer or a fulltime studio owner, taxes are an inevitable part of the territory for you as an operator of a small business. The various types of taxes — income, payroll, social security and sales tax — all have a great deal of impact on your costs of doing business, and so must be considered as you are developing your pricing formulas. Accordingly, to keep your business profitable in both the short and the long term, it's best to learn what taxes are in effect in the area where you market your work and how to keep track of all tax-related information. It's also your responsibility.

Changes in the law

Once again, we want to remind you of one such change in federal tax law which is favorable to photographers and other creative people. This is the revision of the 1986 tax reform bill, the Technical Corrections Act. Under this revision, which just became effective on 1988 returns, photographers can now deduct any expenses accumulated in the production of images, within the same calendar year as they were produced. Previously, these expenses had to be spread out over a number of years until the image logged a profit. Without this revision, bookkeeping would have become unmanageable beyond a point for most photographers. The revision also relieved stock photographers, in particular, of the burden of projecting what the sales for certain images would be in the current year.

Another important related change under the 1986 Act has been a confusing new classification for individuals who incorporate as businesses. This is the Personal Service Corporation, or PSC classification. In most cases, individuals who incorporate their businesses in a number of professional areas automatically become classified as PSC's, and they are taxed at a very high rate of 34 percent. Though photography is not one of the professions that come under this category and is exempt from this tax rate, many individual photographers who incorporate have still been led to think that they must file as PSC's. As a result, the IRS has had to review claims by photographers and set some clearer guidelines.

Even though incorporated photographers were considered exempt from the PSC rate, they apparently qualified for another high tax rate. The catch was that according to UNI-CAP rules—the guidelines established under the original 1986 Act—incorporated photographers had been classified as manufacturers, and as such, were required to assign higher value to their inventories. Of course, this would often result in these photographers having to pay higher taxes. Lobbying efforts which led to the 1988 repeal of the UNICAP rules as they apply to photographers also made photographers effectively exempt from taxes on verifiable creative expenses. In other words, incorporated photographers are free of the obligation to both taxes. Nonetheless, all photographers are still subject to a number of taxes of which they must have a clear understanding and plan for accordingly.

Self-employment tax

If you are a freelancer—whether you have a primary source of income and photography serves as a sideline or photography is your fulltime pursuit—it's important to beware of higher tax rates on self-employment income. All income you receive without taxes being taken out by an employer qualifies as self-employment income. Normally, when you are employed by someone else, your income is taxed at a lower rate and the employer shares responsibility for the taxes due. However, when you are self-employed, even if only part-time, you are taxed at a higher rate on that income, and you must pay the entire amount yourself. This also applies to social security tax.

Freelancers frequently overlook self-employment and social security taxes and fail to set aside a sufficient amount of money. They also tend to forget state and local taxes are payable. If the volume of your photo sales reaches a point where it becomes a substantial percentage of your income, then you are required to pay estimated tax on a quarterly basis. This requires you to project what amount sales you expect to generate in a three-month period. However burdensome this may be in the short run, it works to your advantage in that you plan for and stay current with the various taxes you are expected to pay.

Many other deductions can be claimed by self-employed photographers. It's in your best interest to be aware of them. Examples of 100 percent deductible claims include production costs of resumes, business cards and brochures; photographer's rep commissions; membership dues; costs of purchasing portfolios and educational/business-related magazines and books; insurance, legal and professional services; and office expenses. Be aware that if you take a client out to dinner or treat him to some form of entertainment as a business investment, you may only deduct 80 percent of the costs. Making the photographer pay more out-of-pocket for meals and entertainment is the IRS's way of reducing abuses which have occurred.

Other deductions

Additional deductions may be taken if your office or studio is home-based. The catch here is that your work area can be used only on a professional basis; your office can't double as a family room after hours. The IRS also wants to see evidence that you use the work space on a regular basis via established business hours and proof of actively marketing your work. If you can satisfy these criteria then a percentage of mortgage interests, real estate taxes, rent, maintenance costs, utilities, and homeowner's insurance, plus office furniture and equipment, can be claimed on your tax form at year's end. (Furniture and equipment can be depreciated over a seven-year period.) To figure the percentage of your home or apartment that is used for business, divide the total floor space of your home or apartment (e.g., 4,000 sq. ft.) by the percentage used for business (e.g., 400) to get your answer (10 percent). Next, divide your total home expenses (e.g., $1,000) by 10 percent, and you've got your deductible total of $100.

Be aware that the above-mentioned deductions are only available to "professional" photographers, not hobbyists. According to hearsay, anyone who deducts for use of home facilities and equipment automatically runs a higher risk of being audited, especially if the individual is late in filing. The burden of proof will be on you if the IRS questions any deductions claimed. To maintain professional status in the eyes of the IRS you will need to show a profit for three years out of a five-year period. If you are working out of your home, be sure to keep separate records and bank accounts for personal and business finances, as well as a separate business phone. Since the IRS can audit tax records as far back as seven years, it's vital to keep all paperwork related to your business. This includes invoices, vouchers, expenditures and sales receipts, canceled checks, deposit slips, register tapes and business ledger entries for this period.

Tax deferments

Fulltime photographers—especially those who have a high sales volume—may be interested in investments as a tax shelter for their income. However, as experts in the industry have noted, you should avoid deferring income in this way for the foreseeable future since tax rates are quite likely to rise. In the long run, such tax deferments would result in higher business taxes. So, it's advisable that if you are already doing this, or have considered it, you should consult with a tax advisor or investment counselor to get complete, accurate information about such shelters.

Sales tax

Sales taxes are deceptively complicated and need special consideration. For instance, if you are working in more than one state, use models or work with reps in one or more states, or work in one state and store equipment in another, you may be required to pay sales tax in each of the states that apply. In particular, if you are working with an out-of-state stock photo agency which has clients over a wide geographic area you will need to explore your tax liability with a tax professional.

As with all taxes, sales taxes must be reported and paid on a timely basis to avoid audits and/or penalties. In regard to sales tax, you should:

1) Always register your business at the tax offices with jurisdiction in your city and state.
2) Always charge and collect sales tax on the full amount of the invoice, unless an exemption applies.
3) If an exemption applies because of resale, you must provide a copy of the customer's resale certificate.
4) If an exemption applies because of other conditions, i.e., selling one-time reproduction rights or working for a tax-exempt, nonprofit organization, you must also provide documentation.

Background information and assistance

In general, to plan properly for your taxes—especially when the size of your business and volume of sales increase—you should seek out the advice of an accountant or a tax expert. As suggested before, it's best to work with someone familiar with the needs and concerns of small business people, particularly photographers. You can also obtain more background information about federal taxes and any recent changes in tax law for small business operators by contacting a local branch of the IRS. You can request a number of booklets which provide specific information on allowable deductions and rate structures. These include: 334—Tax Guide for Small Business; 463—Travel, Entertainment and Gift Expense; 505—Tax Withholding and Estimated Tax; 525—Taxable and Nontaxable Income; 533—Self-Employment Tax; 535—Business Expenses; 538—Accounting Periods and Methods; 587—Business Use of Your Home; 910—Guide to Free Tax Services; 917—Business Use of Car. Order by phone at (800)829-3676.

Insurance—business and personal

Taxes are not the only responsibility that self-employed photographers must take for themselves. Setting up proper, comprehensive insurance coverage on their business and themselves is also an important task. When deciding on the types of insurance—liability, property, health, disability and life—and the amounts of coverage, it's best to look carefully at your needs and at which companies can provide you with the best policies.

Policies are not all the same and it's important to make sure every aspect of your business is covered. After examining his policy, a photographer who works out of his home may be surprised to find out that his home owner insurance does not cover his equipment. Separate coverage for a business owner is needed to guarantee that all phases of operation are covered.

Generally it's a good strategy to set up your business coverage with two main areas in mind—liability and property protection. Liability coverage aides you in the event a client or other individual is injured or suffers property damage as a result of using your products or services. Insurance for your equipment will cover you in the case of loss from fire, water damage, theft, vandalism, or for other stipulated reasons. It's important to read your policy closely and know what is covered. Some photographers find out too late that their property is covered only in the office, not out in the field. There also is the possibility that certain pieces of equipment, such as cameras, are covered in the case of theft, but a computer may not be included in the policy.

In order to safeguard against property loss many photographers find it helpful to keep some equipment in a different location. Duplicate transparencies of top images can be made and kept in a safety deposit box. The same storage procedure can be used for backup computer files or b&w and color print negatives. Other storage spaces can be used for larger pieces of equipment. Taking such precautions can insure that, if a disaster strikes at the office, all is not lost. Fireproof safes can protect equipment from fire damage, but film may melt inside during a sweltering blaze.

Worker's compensation, which applies to anyone you hire, is another form of insurance that is indispensable if you grow beyond being your only employee. This is available through most state governments or private insurance companies. In general, liability insurance covers members of the general public; worker's compensation insures employees. "Grey" areas come into the picture in many states because it's sometimes hard to determine according to labor and tax laws whether models, set builders or any other subcontractors are "employees." Therefore, a blend of liability coverage and worker's compensation should protect you in most cases.

Health and disability insurance are important to freelance photographers as well. With the high cost of hospitalization, health coverage is vital. You can't afford to live without it. Many professional or trade organizations such as the American Society of Magazine Photographers (ASMP) or Advertising Photographers of America (APA) offer health/disability packages to members. In some cases, a policy is even included as a membership benefit. But, in order to qualify for disability coverage, you will need to accumulate a track record of sales so the insurance agent can calculate an income-average measure to determine the appropriate amount of coverage for you.

When you select a disability plan, first consider how long you could survive on your income—should a long-term injury occur—before you would need to rely on disability payments. Self-employed photographers will ideally want to have three to four months worth of "liquid" income accrued, such as cash-value life insurance, money-market accounts or savings accounts that can be dipped into in an emergency.

Since you don't want to go bankrupt paying insurance premiums for every potential disaster, you will want to first determine what misfortunes you can afford to pay out-of-pocket. In other words, protect yourself from losses that would be "catastrophic" to you.

It's important to "shop around" until you find an agent with whom you're comfortable, and one who is well versed in the professional needs of photographers. Check with other photographers, or call some photography trade groups for recommendations of agents in your area. These groups will also be able to assist you in determining your insurance needs and recommend companies which offer specialized coverage to photographers. Also, take the time to carefully read all policy clauses to be certain you get the insurance coverage you need. Finally, when you're researching companies to do business with, select those licensed to do business in your state.

Model and property releases

Photographers should be attuned to the need for obtaining model and property releases. Such a release gives the photographer the right to use, sell and publish the photo in editorial or advertising matter without fear of demands for additional financial compensation or

---

ADULT RELEASE

In consideration of my engagement as a model, and for other good and valuable consideration herein acknowledged as received, I hereby grant to _____ ("Photographer"), his/her heirs, legal representatives and assigns, those for whom Photographer is acting, and those acting with his/her authority and permission, the irrevocable and unrestricted right and permission to copyright, in his/her own name or otherwise, and use, re-use, publish, and re-publish photographic portraits or pictures of me or in which I may be included, in whole or in part, or composite or distorted in character or form, without restriction as to changes or alterations, in conjunction with my own or a fictitious name, or reproductions thereof in color or otherwise, made through any medium at his/her studios or elsewhere, and in any and all media now or hereafter known for illustration, promotion, art, editorial, advertising, trade, or any other purpose whatsoever. I also consent to the use of any printed matter in conjunction therewith.

I hereby waive any right that I may have to inspect or approve the finished product or products and the advertising copy or other matter that may be used in connection therewith or the use to which it may be applied.

I hereby release, discharge and agree to save harmless Photographer, his/her heirs, legal representatives and assigns, and all persons acting under his/her permission or authority or those for whom he/she is acting from any liability by virtue of any blurring, distortion, alteration, optical illusion, or use in composite form, whether intentional or otherwise, that may occur or be produced in the taking of said picture or in any subsequent processing thereof, as well as any publication thereof, including without limitation any claims for libel or invasion of privacy.

I hereby warrant that I am of full age and have the right to contract in my own name. I have read the above authorization, release, and agreement, prior to its execution, and I am fully familiar with the contents thereof. This release shall be binding upon me and my heirs, legal representatives, and assigns.

_____	_____
DATE	NAME
_____	_____
WITNESS	ADDRESS

Reprinted from FORMS with permission of the American Society of Magazine Photographers, Inc. (ASMP).

legal reprisals. In this age of stock photo sales, it is unknown whether the photo buyer will use the image for editorial or advertising use. It is wise to have model releases on file; their existence may gain you additional sales from buyers who prefer the work they use to be model-released. The images can't ever be used in such a way as to embarrass or insult the subject, however.

Usually photo rights purchased for editorial use (i.e., public education purposes) are free from the need for a model release. Such markets include newspapers, textbooks, filmstrips, encyclopedias or magazines. An exception to this, however, is when the photo is used for a cover illustration. Photos used for advertising purposes always need model releases. If photographing children, remember that the guardian also must sign before the release is legally binding. Also, be aware that laws governing the use of releases vary from state to state.

Lawyers also are advising photographers to obtain property releases, especially if recognizable property—including pets—will be used for advertising purposes. Government property, facilities, park lands and so on also fall under this requirement. Since it is unclear exactly when property releases are needed in every case, it would be wise for your own protection to obtain one every time you shoot.

Additional samples of release forms can be found in *Professional Business Practices in Photography*, published by American Society of Magazine Photographers.

Filing prints and transparencies

Each photographer must work out his own system of coding and filing images according to what is best for his needs. You will want to talk to different photographers, first, to see what method of photo filing and retrieval works for them. You can also refer to books such as *Sell & Resell Your Photos* and *How to Shoot Stock Photos*, published by Writer's Digest Books, for good information on filing methods.

Transparencies can be coded by a letter that would stand for a general topic, such as "A" for aviation subjects, "B" for medical shots, "C" for children, and so on. Within these areas, simply assign a numerical code to each transparency. Rohn Engh, author of *Sell & Re-Sell Your Photos*, says the key to easy retrieval also lies in setting up a good 3×5 index card system that catalogs cross-over subjects, such as pediatric shots of medical personnel and children interacting. When you receive a photo request, it will be much easier to find the requested photo when you simply have to refer to your catalog system rather than rifle through large numbers of images. For easy storage, invest in some 20-slide capacity 35mm transparency sleeves (or whatever size image sleeve your work requires), then store those in a notebook by subject letter, and within the sleeve itself by image number.

A slight variation of this coding can be used for black-and-white prints. You would still use the letter code "A", for instance to represent aviation subjects. The next number, however, would denote how many rolls of film have been shot in that subject heading, and the third number would represent which frame on a given roll of film was exposed. Such a coding system would read as A-35-26: "A" for aviation, "35" meaning this was the 35th roll of film shot, and "26" denoting the image to be pulled from the file is on the 26th frame. Black-and-white prints can be stored in a manila folder marked with this coding number, and a photocopy of that picture taken from the contact sheet. This latter step will help to more quickly identify the print in the folder, and if the folder is empty, will let you know at a glance what image to make more copies of. Cross referencing via 3×5 cards is important, too.

If you want to adapt the coding system previously described, you can use a numerical coding system in which "1" stands for negatives, "2" for transparencies, "3" for prints, etc. In this case 2-A-24 would stand for an aviation transparency assigned the number 24 for filing purposes. Don't forget the 3×5 card system here either. Many photographers are finding that use of a computer to store their image codes and captions is very helpful.

Software packages which enable you to set up your coding in a label format have also become available. With these packages, labels can be printed from the computer and in turn, attached to your prints or slides.

If you are interested in going this route you will want to refer to Engh's book, which contains a chapter on use of the computer in a photography business. You will also want to watch photography publications for information they carry about the best computers for photography-related business uses, as well as talk to other photographers about their good—or not-so-good—experiences with different computer models.

Use of a computer can also help you track images submitted to photo buyers for consideration, and record which ones have been purchased and how much was paid for them. The process of tracking photos also can be accomplished manually by maintaining separate 'project' folders that let you review the status of submissions easily. Your payment ledger can be a useful tool here as well. All you need to note is the date photo submissions were sent out, when they were returned, and when payment was made. The photo's code can be entered in the ledger, thereby providing handy information about the status of a specific image.

Once you get a system of photo filing and retrieving adapted to your special needs, the time investment needed to maintain and add to the system can be done easily and with a limited time expenditure.

Cover letters/queries/resumes

The cover letter and query letter are slightly different approaches to the same goal—making a photo sale. You, as the photographer, use either of these "vehicles" as a means to convince the photo buyer that your photography will enhance his product or service. Be sure to have the point you wish to make clearly in mind before you begin writing.

A proper cover letter should include an itemization of what photos you are submitting and caption information pertinent to each image. Photo captions should explain who, what, where, why and how. Try to avoid offering "when" information so you don't date your image(s). Also, be sure to make clear what rights you are offering for sale, and where you can be reached during the day if the photo buyer wishes to reach you via phone or mail. Keep your cover letter brief and concise.

If you want to send a query letter, try to limit it to one page. In publishing, the purpose of the query letter is to propose a photo story idea or a photo/text package. Make the story idea sound exciting, yet maintain an overall business tone in the proposal. This is also an excellent time to provide a bit more information about your photographic specialty; such material will establish credibility prior to your requesting an assignment from the photobuyer. In the query letter you can either request the photo buyer's permission to shoot the assignment for his consideration, submit stock photos, or ask to be considered for an upcoming assignment.

Quite a few of the listings in *Photographer's Market* will be looking to buy stock photos for their future use, and will ask that photographers submit a stock photo list. A stock list is simply a summary of all the photos you have available on different subject matter or regions, whether black and white or color, in print or transparency form, and so on. You can either submit a stock list with your query letter to a market or send one when it is specifically recommended in a listing as the main method of contact.

Some photo buyers may ask you to shoot on speculation. Though this implies some interest on their part, if the material isn't used, you aren't compensated for your time and materials. If, however, you are hired on assignment and the material isn't used, you will sometimes be paid a "kill fee." Such a fee generally amounts to one-fourth to one-third of the agreed upon assignment fee. Be sure to negotiate the kill fee prior to taking an assignment.

Resumes also may be sent with your query letter to give the photo buyer more indepth information about your skills and previous experience. The resume should be attractive, and as complete as possible. Be sure to highlight past accomplishments beginning with photo experience (specify whether it's industrial, advertising, editorial, etc.) If you have any staff photo experience, include it, plus any photography-related education (including workshops attended), shows or exhibitions held, or awards and achievements earned in the photographic field. Professional memberships also are good to list.

Mailing photo submissions

Before sending photo submissions out into the marketplace, be sure to stamp each print or transparency with your copyright notice, and a "Return to: (your name, address, phone number) and an identifying number" (see the section "Filing prints and transparencies" for more information). The address and identifying number will assist both you and the photobuyer in locating any images which may be misplaced. Also, as mentioned earlier, computer software packages are available that help in both organizing images and printing out labels for them.

To ensure your images' safe arrival—and return—pay attention to the way you package them. Insert 8 × 10 black-and-white photos into an 8½ × 11 plastic jacket; transparencies should be stored in protective vinyl pages. Most camera stores carry these in a variety of format sizes. Never submit photos in mounted glass—the glass can break. Also, do not send slides in the "little yellow boxes"—many photo buyers consider them an inconvenience and will not even look at the slides.

Another highly recommended practice which helps to ensure the safe handling and return of your photos is the inclusion of a delivery memo. This is a form that summarizes the number and type of photos (slides or prints) and specifies the terms under which you are making the photos available. In particular, you can specify the value of the photos if they are damaged or lost. Then, by signing and returning a copy, the photo buyer confirms both the safe arrival of the images and his acceptance of the terms. Or if he declines to accept the photos on those terms, he simply returns the photos. Sample memos can be found in the previously mentioned book by the American Society of Magazine Photographers, *Professional Business Practices in Photography*.

Be sure to include a return mailing label, adequate postage and an envelope with your submission. If you include a manila envelope, also pack two cardboard sheets to stiffen the envelope so your images aren't damaged. You can also buy heavy-weight insulated envelopes that are reusable. These can be purchased at most office-supply or stationery stores.

Send your submissions via first class mail. The service is quicker and handling tends to be less rough. Many photographers also use certified mail. Though a certified package travels a bit slower than first class mail because it is logged in at each enroute destination, it is much easier to trace in the event of a mishap. Also, to ensure the safe arrival of your submission, we recommend making a quick address check by phone. We make the effort to update all addresses every year, but businesses still move and go out of business after press time. Many photo buyers discourage phone calls, but your address check can be handled by a firm's receptionist without having to disturb the photo buyer.

There are still other ways to safeguard against losing an irreplaceable image; some involve a little pre-planning. When submitting black-and-white prints, never send out the negatives. If a photo buyer is interested in purchasing your image, but doesn't like a technical flaw such as contrast, offer to send a reprint. Transparencies are a bit trickier. It is ideal to send out dupes with an offer to send the original if the other party is interested in purchasing rights to the image. Some labs can produce high-quality dupes, though you may want to decide which are your most valuable (marketable) images since this can become costly. If you're shooting an image that you feel is going to be marketable, expose multiple images—in-camera dupes— (if this is possible) at the time you shoot your original. Using this method, you retain other "original" images should one be lost.

As more businesses and publications start to use facsimile transmission (fax) machines, more photographers have begun to submit trial images or proofs of assignments to clients by fax. We have added fax numbers to many of the listings in the various sections. However, since faxes are more or less considered a priority form of communication, it's advisable in terms of business etiquette not to use a fax to contact a listing until you have established a working relationship with them.

Agents and reps

Another avenue that some photographers take in promoting themselves as they become more established is to work through an agent or photographer's representative, or "rep." This can be especially valuable for photographers who are involved in highly competitive markets such as advertising and art/design studios or who want to branch out on a regional or national basis. The primary value of having a rep is that it frees the photographer to spend as much of his time as possible shooting or planning for work.

Since some photographers are less comfortable with the marketing and negotiating aspects of their business, using a rep can be very attractive. However, many photographers either like to rep themselves, or split the repping duties with another person. It's quite common with husband and wife photography teams that either or both of them will handle repping for their business. Of course, one big plus to keeping it "in the family" is that you don't have to pay out the rep's commission every time you make a sale.

Photographer/rep relationships are of a limited nature and end for various reasons. So it's important when planning to work with a rep to consider also how you will handle the eventual termination. Such relationships are usually governed by a contract, which should include not only compensation for sales but also terms for severance. Also, the procedure for letting go of the rep—even if it's basically "at will"—needs to be spelled out. If you are not willing or able to offer a severance package, or you wish to reserve the right of termination on your terms, then having the agreement in writing will help to limit your liability when a rep presses the issue legally. For additional information—as well as names and addresses—on photo reps, see Writer's Digest Books' newest market book title, *A Guide to Literary Agents and Art/Photo Reps*.

Minimizing the Risks of Freelancing

by John G. Nash

This is probably not what you want to hear, but it should be said, and right up front: freelance photography is a risky business. It is one of the few jobs I know where workers routinely make substantial investments of time and money before being paid, even without promise of future payment. The risks are particularly high when doing business by mail and with clients you've never met.

Now that I've fulfilled my obligation to properly caution aspiring freelancers, let me hasten to add that I would not trade this line of work for any other career. The fact that I have survived in a field characterized by over-supply and high risks is attributable, not only to a modest degree of photographic talent, but also to a fair amount of business savvy. Let me begin to share some of that knowledge with you.

It is true today, has been for more than a decade, and almost certainly will remain thus for the foreseeable future: *freelance photography is essentially a buyers' market.* A legion of eager "photographers," outfitted with automated cameras that make it possible for almost anyone to make an occasional sellable image, has flooded the publications market, driven down prices and set the stage for buyers dictating terms unheard of in any other profession. It is now virtually standard practice for clients to require "contributors" to submit their work on "speculation." "Spec" means the photo editor will review images, but makes no commitment to use any of them, pay even a token amount for the photographer's trouble, nor take reasonable care of work while it is in his custody. To succeed in such an environment, we must learn how to minimize the risks. This can be accomplished by carefully picking new markets, making thoughtful analysis of subsequent business relations with those selections, and by then making necessary changes to a list of core clients. Let's take a look at how each of those tasks can be handled, even when there is no personal contact between the photographer and client.

Finding markets

Of course, the best way to pick ethical clients is from personal recommendations by colleagues. Unfortunately, because this business has become so exceptionally competitive, even your best friend may be reluctant to offer advice that could help you compete with him. So if you can't get reliable references, you must pick markets by yourself.

Most freelancers start their search right here in this reference volume. Although the staff has exercised great care to ensure that the listings are accurate, it is not reasonably possible for them to include any sort of ethics measure. You must develop that on your own, with the understanding that most successful freelancers have had to work with the less desirable, riskier markets while getting started. It seems to be part of one's "dues."

John G. Nash is a freelance writer and photographer from Homosassa, Florida. He writes primarily about three subjects: travel, photography and philately and has worked with a collection of notable clients, including the Chicago Tribune, Washington Post, Parade *and the* Atlanta Journal-Constitution.

First, as you scan the market listings in this book, don't be overly impressed with large circulation figures and do not be blinded by prestigious names. Some of the smallest publications are the best clients. Several of the best-known publications are patently unethical in relations with freelance photographers. What you should look for are "indicators" that can help you pick the better markets.

If a market you've heard of is not listed, it is probably because they don't buy freelance photographs, or they are so unethical that the staff has refused to give them exposure in this publication. The more desirable markets will present the following information:

1. They buy a large and specified number of images from freelancers (e.g., "Uses approximately 80 photos per issue. 95 percent assigned to freelance photographers.").

2. A specific range of fees paid for use of photography and *when* they will pay those fees (e.g., "Pays on acceptance . . . . Uses 35mm, 2¼ × 2¼ and 4 × 5 transparencies. Pays $125-300 inside; $700 cover; $450 table-of-contents.").

3. They report back to you in less than four weeks on whether they plan to use your images. My top clients report in less than two weeks.

4. They outline the sort of photography they are seeking (e.g., "Need photos of healthy and happy couples, in their 50s, having fun."). The more professional clients also will offer to send you guidelines for contributing photographers.

5. The "rights" they expect to obtain (e.g., "all," "one-time," "first serial," etc.).

Caution signs

Here are a few things to watch for in eliminating potential markets from serious consideration, or at least in relegating them to the bottom of the barrel. Be wary of sending anything other than one query letter with tearsheets, or perhaps a few *duplicate* slides or proof prints to markets that do any of the following:

1. Admit to routinely requiring "all rights" to your photography (unless they are also willing to pay significantly more for that unusual agreement and you are prepared to forfeit future income from the image).

2. Pay "on publication," or worse, "several weeks after publication," particularly if they do not specify when publication occurs. A publisher may hold your photographs for a year before they are used and you receive your first check. During that unacceptably long time, editorial plans may change, or the editor may be replaced. If your photos have not been lost over the months, you might get them back—only to discover that the market for them went away because the subject grew stale, or perhaps another magazine ran a similar set of photos. Can you imagine how your photo supply store would react if you told them you will take that new 4 × 5 view camera, but pay them only if and when it is used? No ethical publisher should hold your work for more than a few weeks, unless you have agreed to such, and unless you have been paid a reasonable, nonrefundable amount "on account."

3. Establish general rates for photography as being "negotiable," or perhaps as varying between wide limits (e.g., "$25-150). You can bet the fee you may be offered under such conditions will be closer to the lower end of that range than the top. And your ability to "negotiate" by letter or telephone, especially once you've gone to the expense and trouble of selecting, packaging and providing some of your finest work, is severely limited. Editors sense that "hungry" photographers frequently will accept ridiculously low fees, rather than turn down much-needed credit lines, or possibly alienate a potential market even though not recovering the out-of-pocket expenses already spent.

4. Offer little or no guidance concerning the type of photography they want to see. If they don't know, your chance of satisfying them is too small to be worth the effort. Worse, they might be merely "fishing," or trying to see what is out there. You almost certainly will lose money dealing with that kind, even if you do make an occasional $35 sale.

5. Don't require new photographers to submit samples of published work, resumes, business cards, or other evidence of success. This may sound self-defeating to those who haven't yet achieved many credits, but it is a valid test of ethical behavior, because the better markets have no need to spend the extra time and effort required to work with unknown and unproved solicitors.

Unfortunately, even after applying this selection criteria, we freelancers can still run afoul of undesirable clients. Here I am writing about client ethics as though I know most if not all the answers, yet I was recently victimized by another amoral editor. In order to attempt to break in with the travel editor of a major newspaper, I agreed to send her a specified selection of photographs applicable to travel stories about the American Southeast. Against my nagging better judgment, I sent those images without a contract, without advance payment and with no assurance of eventual use. When the photography was returned (via uninsured mail) in about three weeks, it was with a cheerful and encouraging note telling how "very impressed" the editor was with the work, but "it just isn't *exactly* what I'm looking for at the moment." She wondered if I could please send other pages of slides? Sadly, I did.

When those also were returned without apparent or reported use, and without any payment, I decided to take a closer look at the images before refiling them. What I found was significant evidence that many of the images had apparently been selected by someone at the paper, removed from the page in which they were shipped and quite possibly copied. I will, of course, attempt to learn if any of those images appear in that newspaper, but short of subscribing to the publication (which would add insult to financial injury) I likely will never know if one or more of my images was used, perhaps served as the basis and inspiration for a reshoot, or possibly has a new life as an electronically-altered copy. Of course, that editor gets nothing more from this photographer unless she pays my contractual price up front, and she has been tactfully so advised. I don't expect to get any business from her under my stipulated conditions, but then I can't afford her kind of business.

Significant evidence

The lesson learned from this experience is that there are indicators as to a client's ethics hidden in the way they have handled photographs returned as "unused," and therefore unpaid. Here are a few things to look for:
• New, grease-pencil marks on slide pages, especially where such might indicate selection of specific images.
• Any new notations or marks made on slide frames or in the borders of prints.
• Evidence of newly applied wax, tape or other temporary adhesives anywhere on slides or prints.
• Fingerprints, smears or scratches on photos. I assume you never ship your work with such marks.
• Slide mounts that have been opened (slits in the mount; cracked plastic mounts; exchanged mounts; slides upside down, off center or reversed in mounts).

Manhandling

In the same low class with a client who would steal work is the one who loses or damages images and then refuses to pay the photographer for that loss. Too many publishers appear to believe that it is normal practice for the photographer to accept all risks for damage or loss of photography in the care of the client. If you send them *unsolicited* work, they are probably correct, but several important legal decisions have established that if the client requested the work, they are almost certainly liable for its safe care, use and return.

Even some of what might otherwise appear to be excellent markets are so careless in handling submitted photography they should be dropped, except under the most unusual circumstances. One of my better clients, for example, routinely damages slides by careless handling when making color separations. I continue with them because they pay well and quickly, and because the particular photos have almost no possible use outside of that one, specialized magazine.

Contract protection

It is always advisable to have a written contract and a downpayment before sending valuable work to a new client. I recently agreed to furnish the editor of a "new, regional magazine, paying top dollar for photography" with a selection of images created especially to fit his detailed requirements. I obtained no contract and no advance payment. I felt such a request might jeopardize a new and seemingly lucrative account, by offending the client.

Although I started my usual, tactful follow-up procedures ten days after I'd sent the registered and insured package, I was unable to reach the editor or anyone else in a position of responsibility in the company. Reluctant to act as if the sky was falling (even though my staff and I had invested 100 manhours, and around $1,200 in other direct costs), I waited another two weeks before initiating the sort of documentary correspondence usually required in any legal action to recover expenses. The publisher was eventually served a notice to appear in court, but didn't. Although the judge found in my favor, I never collected a cent. The client had skipped town, left no forwarding address, nor was there any sign of what had happened to the 36 original slides I had sent them. The only protection in dealing with such unestablished publishers, is a contract with a healthy payment *up front*.

Some guidelines

There are four cardinal rules that should help any freelancer to significantly reduce the risks inherent in this wonderful, but sometimes frustrating business.

1. Pick your potential clients with studied care. Start with the cream of the crop. Lower your standards and expectations only when unsuccessful with the top of the order. Accept the fact that risk increases as you go down the list and tailor your actions accordingly.

2. Once you make contact with a new client who appears interested in using your work, attempt to reach an agreement in writing concerning, not only what you are to deliver, but also what and when the client is to pay. Ideally, this is enough in advance to cover your out-of-pocket expenses. Also, the contract should cover the important area of liability for damage or loss of photography.

3. Keep reasonably close tabs on all submissions, while bearing in mind that some editors are working with hundreds of similar submissions, and could understandably become disenchanted with a photographer who calls every day to check on the status of a submission. If you see an indication that the publication might be closing its doors, initiate rapid action to recover your photography or to gain an offsetting legal award.

4. Inspect all returned work for signs of suspicious behavior by the client. Tactfully drop any that you suspect of unethical practices. "Tactfully" because your conclusions could be faulty and you might find it necessary or desirable to do business with that same client in the future.

The Markets

Advertising, Public Relations and Audiovisual Firms

When it comes to finding work in advertising, there are two facts for photographers that couldn't be more clear. First, the big jobs of old are scarce and second, in order to succeed you must have a marketable style. Unlike the 1980s when advertising agencies and public relations firms had more business than they could handle, the present economy mandates a closer look at the bottom line. Large ad campaigns could be placed on the endangered species list and tightening ad budgets have limited profits for photographers.

When bidding on jobs for advertising firms, a well-established, top-quality photographer could very well lose a job to another photographer who has less experience and talent but charges less. Some ad agencies are not willing to spend a little more money for quality and experience. Instead, they are glued to the bottom line and, unless photographers are willing to adhere to those cost restraints, they will end up with few jobs and a limited income.

Richard Weisgrau, executive director of the American Society of Magazine Photographers (ASMP), says photographers should note the trend of re-running advertising campaigns. If this continues or expands, the photo industry could suffer because those regurgitated campaigns take jobs away from photographers. To survive the lean times many photographers have chosen to couple their advertising work with other types of businesses. Some shoot editorial assignments or work for paper product companies, others have found stock to be a savior.

Develop better, fresher images

Though on the surface this sounds quite bleak, this is not to say that opportunity no longer exists in these markets. More than ever, advertising and PR agencies are placing a premium on top-notch skills, creativity and professionalism. In fact, these markets are already full of photographers who possess these qualities. But always in demand is the photographer who is not just good and does not just imitate but can take an ordinary subject or message and communicate it in a fresh, attention-getting way.

In this year's edition of *Photographer's Market* the two Close-up subjects discuss ways to succeed in the photography field. As a San Francisco-based marketing consultant, Deanne Delbridge knows how to spark creativity in photographers and she shares some of her ideas and observations on page 54. On page 90, Nancy Clendaniel, a photographer from Renton, Washington, explains her modus operandi when shooting images.

Economic changes

Some listings which have been in the book for several editions may now be absent because of any of a number of the financial or competitive reasons described above. For instance, they may have been driven out of business or snapped up in a corporate takeover. Others have chosen not to renew their listings because of being flooded with inappropriate or unprofessional submissions. However, many of the listings which have returned, as well as the numerous new listings, have taken more time to point out their very specific needs. So it pays you, the photographer, to pay close attention to those guidelines and needs and provide them only with what they indicate.

The payment structure

A number of factors go into how advertising, public relations and audiovisual firms determine their rates of payment for photography. For instance, it may depend upon the client's budget, the type of shoot (studio or location), the type of usage and rights being purchased, or the photographer's talent and experience.

We have made the attempt to obtain more specific information from listings about the rates of payment. However, some firms will still only discuss those terms with the photographer during negotiations. Accordingly, we have inserted a new code—NPI, for "no payment information given"—into listings that did not offer specific figures.

Also, we have included more detail about the rights a firm usually purchases. Advertising agencies, in particular, have tended to purchase all rights or assign work only on a "work-for-hire" basis. Since work for hire is a serious issue for all photographers to consider (see Copyright/rights, in the Business of Photography, on page 11), it is important that you look closely for this information in the listings.

Once again, audiovisual markets are included among the listings for advertising and PR firms. These include a number of production houses as well as advertising or PR agencies with in-house production units. For easy recognition, any listing with various kinds of audiovisual, film or video needs has been marked with a special AV symbol—a black square—before the listing's name. Listings with these symbols may also include detailed descriptions under the subheading, Audiovisual Needs. Many ad agencies, PR firms and AV production companies hire locally- or regionally-based freelancers, and this information is included in listings where it applies.

Alabama

■**BARNEY & PATRICK INC.**, 300 St. Francis St., Mobile AL 36602. (205)433-0401. Ad agency. Vice President/Associate Creative Director: George Yurcisin. Types of clients: industrial, financial, medical, retail, fashion, fast food, tourism and food services.
Needs: Works with 1-3 freelance photographers/month. Uses photographers for consumer magazines, trade magazines, direct mail, brochures, P-O-P displays, audiovisuals, posters and newspapers.
Audiovisual Needs: Works with freelance filmmakers to produce TV and audiovisuals.
Specs: Uses 8×10 and 11×17 glossy b&w prints; 35mm, 2¼×2¼, 4×5 and 8×10 transparencies; 16mm, 35mm film and videotape.
First Contact & Terms: Arrange a personal interview to show portfolio or query with samples and list of stock photo subjects. Provide resume, business card, brochure, flyer or tearsheets to be kept on file for possible future assignments. Does not return unsolicited material. Reports as needed. NPI; payment "varies according to budget." Pays net 30. Buys all rights. Model release required.

■**BARRY HUEY, BULLOCK & COOK, ADVERTISING, INC.**, Suite 400, 3800 Colonnade Pkwy., Birmingham AL 35243. (205)969-3200. FAX: (205)969-6464. Ad agency. Art Directors: Mike Macon/Melanie Townsend. Estab. 1972. Types of clients: retail, food and sporting goods. Client list provided on request.
Needs: Works with 6-10 freelance photographers/month. Uses photographers for consumer magazines, trade magazines, P-O-P displays, catalogs, posters and audiovisuals. Subjects include fishing industry and water sports.
Audiovisual Needs: Uses AV for product introductions, seminars and various presentations.
Specs: Uses 5×7 b&w; 35mm, 4×5 and 8×10 transparencies.
First Contact & Terms: Submit portfolio for review. Provide resume, business card, brochure, flyer or tearsheets to be kept on file for possible future assignments. Works on assignment basis only. Pays $50-400/b&w photo; $85-3,000/color photo; $500-1,600/day; $150-20,000/job. Payment is made on

acceptance plus 60 days. Buys all rights. Model release and captions preferred.
Tips: Prefers to see "table top product with new, exciting lighting."

■**J.H. LEWIS ADVERTISING, INC.**, 1668 Government St., Mobile AL 36604. (205)476-2507. President: Larry Norris. Creative Directors, Birmingham office: Spencer Till. Mobile office: Ben Jordan and Helen Savage. Ad agency. Uses billboards, consumer and trade magazines, direct mail, foreign media, newspapers, P-O-P displays, radio and TV. Serves industrial, entertainment, financial, agricultural, medical and consumer clients. Commissions 25 photographers/year.
Specs: Uses b&w contact sheet and 8×10 b&w glossy prints; uses 8×10 color prints and 4×5 transparencies; produces 16mm documentaries.
First Contact & Terms: NPI. Pays per job, or royalties on 16mm film sales. Buys all rights. Model release preferred. Arrange a personal interview to show portfolio; submit portfolio for review; or send material, "preferably slides we can keep on file," by mail for consideration. SASE. Reports in 1 week.

Alaska

THE NERLAND AGENCY, (formerly Nerland/Mystrom & Associates), 808 E St., Anchorage AK 99501. (907)274-9553. Ad agency. Art Director: Hans Aune. Types of clients: retail, hotel, restaurant, fitness, healthcare. Client list free with SASE.
Needs: Works with 1 freelance photographer/month. Uses photographers for consumer magazines, trade magazines, direct mail and brochures and collateral pieces. Subjects include Alaskan scenic shots.
Specs: Uses 11×14 matte b&w prints; 35mm, 2¼×2¼ and 4×5 transparencies.
First Contact & Terms: Query with samples. Provide resume, business card, brochure, flyer or tearsheets to be kept on file for possible future assignments. Does not return unsolicited material. Pays $500-700/day or minimum $100/job (depends on job). Pays on receipt. Buys all rights or one-time rights. Model release and captions preferred.
Tips: Prefers to see "high technical quality (sharpness, lighting, etc). All photos should capture a mood. Simplicity of subject matter. Keep sending updated samples of work you are doing (monthly). We are demanding higher technical quality and looking for more 'feeling' photos than still life of product."

Arizona

*■**ARIZONA CINE EQUIPMENT INC.**, 2125 E. 20th St., Tucson AZ 85719. (602)623-8268. AV firm. Estab. 1972. Types of clients: industrial and retail.
Needs: Works with 6 photographers, filmmakers and/or videographers/month. Uses photos for audiovisual.
Audiovisual Needs: Uses slides, film and videotape.
Specs: Uses color prints; 35mm, 4×5 transparencies.
First Contact & Terms: Query with resume of credits. Query with list of stock photo subjects. Send unsolicited photos by mail for consideration. Query with samples. Works with freelancers on assignment only. Keeps samples on file. SASE. Reports in 3 weeks. Pays $15-30/hour; $250-500/day; or per job. Pays on receipt of invoice. Buys all rights; negotiable. Model/property release required; captions preferred. Credit line sometimes given.

CHARLES DUFF ADVERTISING AGENCY, Dept. PM, P.O. Box 34820, Phoenix AZ 85067-4820. (602)285-1660. Ad agency. Creative Director: Trish Spencer. Client list provided on request with SASE.

 The asterisk before a listing indicates that the market is new in this edition. New markets are often the most receptive to freelance submissions.

Needs: Works with 2-3 freelance photographers/month. Uses photographers for consumer and trade magazines, direct mail, P-O-P displays, catalogs. Subjects include: horses, dogs, cats and livestock.
Specs: Uses 8×10 b&w and color prints; 35mm, 4×5 transparencies. "Would prefer 4×5 but can accept any size transparency."
First Contact & Terms: Send unsolicited photos by mail for consideration. Provide resume, business card, brochure, flyer or tearsheets to be kept on file for possible future assignments. SASE. Reports in 1 month. Pays $25-50/b&w photo; $100-300/color photo. Pays on receipt of invoice. Buys one-time rights. Model release preferred.
Tips: Prefers to see horses. Send samples of work for review.

■**FARNAM COMPANIES, INC.**, Dept. PM, 2nd Fl., 301 W. Osborn, Phoenix AZ 85013-3928. (602)285-1660. Inhouse ad agency. Creative Director: Trish Spencer. Types of clients: animal health products, primarily for horses and dogs; some cattle.
Needs: Works with 2 freelance photographers/month. Uses photographers for direct mail, catalogs, consumer magazines, P-O-P displays, posters, AV presentations, trade magazines and brochures. Subject matter includes horses, dogs, cats, farm scenes, ranch scenes, cowboys, cattle and horse shows. Occasionally works with freelance filmmakers to produce educational horse health films and demonstrations of product use.
Specs: Uses 8½×10 glossy b&w and color prints; 35mm, 2¼×2¼ and 4×5 transparencies; 16mm and 35mm film and videotape.
First Contact & Terms: Arrange a personal interview to show portfolio. Query with samples. Send unsolicited photos by mail for consideration. Provide resume, business card, brochure, flyer or tearsheets to be kept on file for possible future assignments. Works with freelance photographers on assignment basis only. SASE. Reports in 2 weeks or per photographer's request. Pays $25-75/b&w photo; $50-300/color photo. Pays on publication. Buys one-time rights. Model release required. Credit line given whenever possible.
Tips: "Send me a number of good, reasonably priced for one-time use photos of dogs, horses or farm scenes. Better yet, send me good quality dupes I can keep on file for *rush* use. When the dupes are in the file and I see them regularly, the ones I like stick in my mind and I find myself planning ways to use them. We are looking for original, dramatic work. We especially like to see horses, dogs, cats and cattle captured in artistic scenes or poses. All shots should show off quality animals with good conformation. We rarely use shots if people are shown and prefer animals in natural settings or in barns/stalls."

JOANIE L. FLATT AND ASSOC. LTD, Suite 2, 623 W. Southern Ave, Mesa AZ 85210. (602)835-9139. FAX: (602)835-9597. PR firm. CEO: Maggie Bruce. Types of clients: service, educational, insurance companies, developers, builders and finance.
Needs: Works with 2-3 photographers/month. Uses photographers for consumer magazines, brochures and group presentations. Subject matter varies.
Specs: Vary depending on client and job.
First Contact & Terms: Query with list of stock photo subjects. Provide resume, business card, brochure, flyer or tearsheets to be kept on file for possible future assignments. Works with local freelance photographers only. Does not return unsolicited material. Reports in 3 weeks. NPI. Photographer bids a job in writing. Payment is made 30 days after invoice. Buys all rights and sometimes one-time rights. Model release required. Captions preferred. Credit line given if warranted depending on job.

■**PAUL S. KARR PRODUCTIONS**, 2949 W. Indian School Rd., Phoenix AZ 85017. (602)266-4198. Contact: Kelly Karr. Film & tape firm. Types of clients: industrial, business and education. Works with freelancers on assignment only.
Needs: Uses filmmakers for motion pictures. "You must be an experienced filmmaker with your own location equipment, and understand editing and negative cutting to be considered for any assignment." Primarily produces industrial films for training, marketing, public relations and government contracts. Does high-speed photo instrumentation. Also produces business promotional tapes, recruiting tapes and instructional and entertainment tapes for VCR and cable. "We are also interested in funded co-production ventures with other video and film producers."
Specs: Uses 16mm films and videotapes. Provides production services, including inhouse 16mm processing, printing and sound transfers, scoring and mixing and video production, post production, and film-to-tape services.

The code NPI (no payment information given) appears in listings that have not given specific payment amounts.

First Contact & Terms: Query with resume of credits and advise if sample reel is available. NPI. Pays/job; negotiates payment based on client's budget and photographer's ability to handle the work. Pays on production. Buys all rights. Model release required.
Tips: Branch office in Utah: Karr Productions, 1045 N. 300 East, Orem UT 84057. (801)226-8209. Contact: Mike Karr.

WALKER AGENCY, #160, 15855 N. Greenway Hayden Loop, Scottsdale AZ 85260-1726. (602)483-0185. FAX: (602)948-3113. Marketing communications. President: Mike Walker. Estab. 1982. Types of clients: banking, marine industry and outdoor recreation products.
Needs: Works with 2 photographers/month. Uses photographers for consumer magazines, trade magazines, posters and newspapers. Subjects include outdoor recreation scenes: fishing, camping, etc. "We also publish a newspaper supplement 'Escape to the Outdoors' which goes to 11,000 papers."
Specs: Uses 8×10 glossy b&w print with borders; 35mm, 2¼×2¼, 4×5 and 8×10 transparencies.
First Contact & Terms: Query with resume of credits; query with list of stock photo subjects; provide resume, business card, brochure, flyer or tearsheets to be kept on file for possible future assignments. Reports in 1 week. Pays $25/b&w or color photo; $150-500/day; also pays per job. Pays on receipt of invoice. Buys all rights; other rights negotiable. Model and property release required.
Tips: In portfolio/samples, prefers to see a completely propped scene. "There is now more opportunity for photographers within the Advertising/PR industry."

Arkansas

BLACKWOOD, MARTIN, AND ASSOCIATES, P.O. Box 1968, 300 First Pl., Fayetteville AR 72702. (501)442-9803. Ad agency. Creative Director: Gary Weidner. Types of clients: food, financial, medical, insurance, some retail. Client list provided on request.
Needs: Works with 3 freelance photographers/month. Uses photographers for direct mail, catalogs, consumer magazines, P-O-P displays, trade magazines and brochures. Subject matter includes "food shots—fried foods, industrial."
Specs: Uses 8×10 high contrast b&w prints; 35mm, 4×5 and 8×10 transparencies.
First Contact & Terms: Arrange a personal interview to show portfolio; query with samples; provide resume, business card, brochure, flyer or tearsheets to be kept on file for possible future assignments. Works with freelance photographers on assignment basis only. Does not return unsolicited material. Reports in 1 month. NPI. Payment depends on budget—"whatever the market will bear." Buys all rights. Model release preferred.
Tips: Prefers to see "good, professional work, b&w and color" in a portfolio of samples. "Be willing to travel and willing to work within our budget. We are using less b&w photography because of newspaper reproduction in our area. We're using a lot of color for printing."

■**WILLIAMS/CRAWFORD/PERRY & ASSOCIATES, INC.,** (formerly Williams/McIntosh & Associates, Inc.) P.O. Box 789, Ft. Smith AR 72901. (501)782-5230. FAX: (501)782-6970. Creative Director: Jim Perry. Estab. 1983. Types of clients: financial, healthcare, manufacturing, tourism. Examples of ad campaigns: Touche-Ross, 401K and Employee Benefits (videos); Cummins Diesel engines (print campaigns); and Freightliner Trucks (sales promotion and training videos).
Needs: Works with 2-3 freelance photographers—filmmakers—videographers/month. Uses photographers for consumer magazines, trade magazines, direct mail, P-O-P displays, catalogs, posters, newspapers and audiovisual uses. Subjects include: people, products and architecture. Reviews stock photos, film or video of healthcare and financial.
Audiovisual Needs: Uses photos/film/video for 30-second video and film TV spots, 5-10-minute video sales, training and educational.
Specs: Uses 5×7, 8×10 b&w prints; 35mm, 2¼×2¼ and 4×5 transparencies.
First Contact & Terms: Query with samples, provide resume, business card, brochure, flyer or tearsheets to be kept on file for possible future assignments. Works with freelancers on assignment basis only. Cannot return material. Reports in 1-2 weeks. Pays $500-1,200/day. Pays on receipt of invoice and client approval. Buys all rights (work-for-hire). Model release required; photo captions preferred. Credit line given sometimes, depending on client's attitude (payment arrangement with photographer).
Tips: In freelancer's samples, wants to see "quality and unique approaches to common problems." There is "a demand to separate themselves with the use of fresh graphics and design solutions." Freelancers should "expect to be pushed to their creative limits, to work hard and be able to input ideas into the process, not just be directed."

California

ADVANCE ADVERTISING AGENCY, #202, 606 E. Belmont, Fresno CA 93701. (209)445-0383. Ad and PR agency and Graphics Design Firm. Manager: Martin Nissen. Types of clients: Industrial, commercial, retail, financial. Examples of recent projects: Investors Thrift (Direct Mail); Windshield Repair Service (radio, TV, newspaper); and Mr. G's Carpets (Radio, TV, Newspaper).
Specs: Uses color and b&w prints.
First Contact & Terms: Send unsolicited photos by mail for consideration; provide business card, brochure, flyer to be kept on file for possible future assignments. Keeps samples on file. Reports in 1-2 weeks. NPI; payment negotiated per job. Pays 30 days from invoice. Buys all rights. Model release required. Credit line given.
Tips: In samples, looks for "not very abstract or overly sophisticated or 'trendy.' Stay with basic, high quality material." Advises that photographers "consider *local* market target audience."

■**AIRLINE FILM & TV PROMOTIONS,** 13246 Weidner, Pacoima CA 91331. (818)899-1151. President: Byron Schmidt. Types of clients: major film companies.
Audiovisual Needs: Works with 4-5 freelance photographers/month. Uses freelance photographers for films and videotapes. Subjects include publicity and advertising.
Specs: "Specifications vary with each production." Uses 8×10 color prints; 35mm transparencies; VHS videotape.
First Contact & Terms: Provide resume, business card, self-promotion piece or tearsheets to be kept on file for possible future assignments. Works on assignment only. Does not return unsolicited material. Payment varies per assignment and production: pays $250-500/b&w photo; $500-1,000/job. Pays on acceptance. Buys all rights. Model release required. Credit line sometimes given. Looks for work that shows "imagination."

AUSTIN ASSOCIATES, Suite 600, 2055 Gateway Pl., San Jose CA 95111. (408)453-7776. Ad agency. Art Director: Meri Duffy. Serves high technology clients.
Needs: Works with 3 photographers/month. Uses work for billboards, consumer magazines, trade magazines, direct mail, P-O-P displays, newspapers. Subject matter of photography purchased includes: table top (tight shots of electronics products).
Specs: Uses 8×10 matte b&w and color prints; 35mm, 2¼×2¼, 4×5 or 8×10 transparencies.
First Contact & Terms: Arrange a personal interview to show portfolio, send unsolicited photos by mail for consideration; provide resume, business card, brochure, flyer or tearsheets to be kept on file for possible future assignments. Works on assignment basis only. Does not return unsolicited material. Reports in 3 weeks. Pays $500-2,500/job. Pays on receipt of invoice. Buys all rights (work-for-hire). Model release required, captions preferred.
Tips: Prefers to see "originality, creativity, uniqueness, technical expertise" in work submitted. There is more use of "photo composites, dramatic lighting, and more attention to detail" in photography.

BENNETT, ALEON, AND ASSOCIATES, Suite 212, 13455 Ventura Blvd., Sherman Oaks CA 91423. (818)990-8070. President: Aleon Bennett. Types of clients: finance, industrial.
Needs: Works with varied number of freelance photographers/month. Uses photographers for trade magazines and newspapers.
Specs: Uses b&w prints.
First Contact & Terms: Query with resume of credits. Does not return material. NPI. Pays per photo. Pays on acceptance. Buys all rights. Model release required; captions preferred.

■**WALT DISNEY HOME VIDEO,** 500 S. Buena Vista St., Burbank CA 91521-7026. (818)562-3640. Vice President Creative Services: Randall Erickson.
Needs: Uses photographers for brochures, P-O-P materials and presentations.
Specs: Uses 8×10 glossy b&w prints and color prints; also 35mm, 4×5 or 8×10 transparencies.
First Contact & Terms: Arrange a personal interview to show portfolio; provide resume, business card, self-promotion piece or tearsheets to be kept on file for possible future assignments. Works with local freelancers only; interested in stock photos/footage. SASE. Pays $35-50/color photo; $1,200-1,500/day; $500-1,000/job. Pays "with purchase order and invoice." Buys all rights.

■ *The solid, black square before a listing indicates that the market uses various types of audiovisual materials, such as slides, film or videotape.*

Tips: "We do not use a lot of photography. Mostly we need product photography for brochures, video cassette packages and point of purchase materials."

■**DOCUMENTARY FILMS**, Box 97, Aptos CA 95001. (408)688-6632. Producer: M.T. Hollingsworth. AV firm. Estab. 1966. Serves clients in schools, colleges, universities, foreign governments and service organizations. Produces motion pictures.
Needs: Language arts, nature, marine science, physical education, anthropology, dance and special education; 16 mm film material at all stages of production. Film length requirements: 10, 15 and 20 minutes. Prefers 16mm color prints and camera originals.
Audiovisual Needs: Produces 16mm originals, color print work, color internegative and release prints. Interested in stock footage. Film scripts considered.
First Contact & Terms: NPI. Pays royalties by mutual agreement depending on production stage at which film is submitted. "Royalties for a film treatment. If the concepts are good, and the resulting film successful, the royalties will pay much more than single use rates." Buys all film distribution rights. Model release and captions required. Send material by mail for consideration. "On first submission, send prints, *not originals*, unless requested." SASE. Reports in 2 weeks.
Tips: "For films: have a specific market in mind. Send enough footage to show continuity, significant high points of action and content, personalities. Film should be clearly identified head and tails. Any accompanying sound samples should be in cassettes or ¼-inch reels clearly identified including proposed background music. We look for originality of concept, technical quality of craftmanship, creative and artistic elements, meticulous attention to detail. We do not use isolated single photos. Photos must tell a story which might become the basis or the idea on which to hang a film."

■**HAYES ORLIE CUNDALL INC.**, 46 Varda Landing, Sausalito CA 94965. (415)332-7414. FAX: (415)332-5924. Executive Vice President and Creative Director: Alan W. Cundall. Ad agency. Estab. 1991. Uses all media except foreign. Types of clients: industrial, retail, fashion, finance, computer and hi-tech, travel, healthcare, insurance and real estate. Examples of recent campaigns: West Coast Life (trade ads to insurance agents); and Ross Hospital (newspaper and magazine campaign on drugs and alcohol). Works with 1 freelance photographer/month on assignment only.
First Contact & Terms: Provide resume, business card and brochure to be kept on file for future assignments. "Don't send anything unless it's a brochure of your work or company. We keep a file of talent—we then contact photographers as jobs come up." NPI. Pays on a per-photo basis; negotiates payment based on client's budget, amount of creativity required and where work will appear. "We abide by local photographer's rates." Model release required; photo captions preferred.
Tips: "Most books are alike. I look for creative and technical excellence, then how close to our offices; cheap vs. costly; personal rapport; references from friends in agencies who've used him/her. Call first. Send samples and resume if I'm not able to meet with you personally due to work pressure. Keep in touch with new samples." Produces occasional audiovisual for industrial and computer clients; also produces a couple of videos a year.

THE HITCHINS COMPANY, 22756 Hartland St., Canoga Park CA 91307. (818)715-0510. Ad agency. President: W.E. Hitchins. Estab. 1985. Types of clients: industrial, retail (food) and auctioneers.
Needs: Uses photographers for trade magazines, direct mail and newspapers.
Specs: Uses b&w and color prints. "Copy should be flexible for scanning."
First Contact & Terms: Provide resume, business card, brochure, flyer or tearsheets to be kept on file for possible future assignments. Works on assignment only. Cannot return material. NPI. Pays on receipt of invoice (30 days). Rights purchased "varies as to project." Will negotiate with photographer not willing to sell all rights. Model release required.
Tips: Wants to see shots of people and products in samples.

■**BERNARD HODES ADVERTISING**, 11755 Wilshire Blvd., Los Angeles CA 90025. (310)575-4000. Ad agency. Creative Directors: Steve Mitchell and Michelle Skerry. Produces "recruitment advertising for all types of clients."
Needs: Works with 1 freelance photographer/month. Uses photographers for billboards, trade magazines, direct mail, P-O-P displays, brochures, catalogs, posters, newspapers, AV presentations and internal promotion. Also works with freelance filmmakers to produce TV commercials, training films (mostly stills).
First Contact & Terms: Query with samples "to be followed by personal interview if interested." Does not return unsolicited material. Reporting time "depends upon jobs in house; I try to arrange appointments within 3 weeks-1 month." NPI. Payment "depends upon established budget and subject." Pays on acceptance for assignments; on publication per photo. Buys all rights. Model release required.

Tips: Prefers to see "samples from a wide variety of subjects. No fashion. People-oriented location shots. Nonproduct. Photos of people and/or objects telling a story—a message. Eye-catching." Photographers should have "flexible day and ½ day rates. Must work fast. Ability to get a full day's (or ½) work from a model or models. Excellent sense of lighting. Awareness of the photographic problems with newspaper reproduction."

■**INTERNATIONAL VIDEO NETWORK,** 2242 Camino Ramon, San Ramon CA 94583. (510)866-1121. Director of Marketing Communications: Katie Jahnes. Estab. 1985. "Looking for transparencies on travel destinations; also freelance producers wishing to make travel videos for our company."
Needs: "Releasing 10-15 new titles a year." Uses photographers for videotapes and video jacket photos.
Specs: Uses transparencies and videotape. Contact for video needs.
First Contact & Terms: Provide query with stock photo list; provide resume, business card, self-promotion piece or tearsheets to be kept on file for possible future assignments. "I am interested in stock photos of travel destinations." Reports in 1 month. Pays $350-400/color photo. Pays on acceptance. Buys one-time rights. Captions and model releases preferred.

*■**THE KLINGER GROUP,** #101, 6330 Variel, Woodland Hills CA 91367. (818)887-9874. President: Sherry Klinger. Estab. 1983. Types of clients: industrial, fashion, retail, food, corporate and entertainment. Examples of recent projects: Eugene Lang's "I Have a Dream Program"; Rachel Perry Skin Care; and Summa Medical Group.
Needs: Works with 1 photographer and/or videographer/month. Uses photos, slides and videotape for trade magazines, direct mail, catalogs, newspapers and audiovisual. Subject depends on project.
First Contact & Terms: Query with resume of credits. Provide resume, business card, brochure, flyer or tearsheets to be kept on file for possible future assignments. Works on assignment only. Keeps samples on file. SASE. Reports in 1 month. NPI; "payment depends on job and client." Buys all rights; negotiable. Model/property release required; captions preferred. Credit line "sometimes given depending on where photo is being placed."

■**MARKEN COMMUNICATIONS,** Suite 130, 3600 Pruneridge, Santa Clara CA 95051. President: Andy Marken. (408)296-3600. FAX: (408)296-3803. Ad agency and PR firm. Estab. 1977. Production Manager: Leslie Posada. Types of clients: furnishings, electronics and computers. Examples of recent ad campaigns include: Burke Industries (resilient flooring, carpet); Boole and Babbage (mainframe software); Maxar (PCs).
Needs: Works with 3-4 freelance photographers/month. Uses photographers for trade magazine, direct mail and catalogs. Subject matter includes product/applications.
Audiovisual Needs: Slide presentations and sales/demo videos.
Specs: Uses color and b&w prints; 35mm, 2¼×2¼ and 4×5 transparencies.
First Contact & Terms: Arrange a personal interview to show portfolio, query with samples or submit portfolio for review. "Call." Works with freelancers on an assignment basis only. SASE. Reports in 1 month. Pays $50-1,000/b&w photo; $100-1,800/color photo; $50-100/hour; $500-1,000/day; $200-2,500/job. Pays 30 days after receipt of invoice. Model release required. Credit line given "sometimes."

■**WARREN MILLER ENTERTAINMENT,** 505 Pier Ave., P.O. Box 536, Hermosa Beach CA 90254. (310)376-2494. FAX: (310)374-4042. Production Manager: Don Brolin. Motion picture production house. Buys 5 films/year.
Subject Needs: Works with 5-20 freelance photographers/month. Uses photographers for outdoor cinematography of skiing (snow) and other sports. Also travel, documentary, promotional, educational and indoor studio filming. "We do everything from TV commercials to industrial films to feature length sports films."
Audiovisual Needs: Uses 16mm film. "We purchase exceptional sport footage not available to us."
First Contact & Terms: Filmmakers may query with resume of credits and sample reel. "We are only interested in motion picture-oriented individuals who have practical experience in the production of 16mm motion pictures." Works on assignment only. SASE. Reports in 1 week. Pays $150-200/day. Also pays by the job. Pays on receipt of invoice. Buys all rights. Credit line given.
Tips: Looks for technical mastering of the craft and equipment—decisive shot selection. "Make a hot demo reel and be a hot skier; be willing to travel."

■**MORRIS MEDIA,** #105, 2730 Monterey St., Torrance CA 90503. (213)533-4800. Contact: Operations Manager.
Needs: Uses 4-6 freelancers per month to produce slide sets and videotapes. Subjects vary according to projects.
Specs: Uses b&w and color prints, any size and format; 35mm and 2¼×2¼ transparencies; and ¾" and 1" NTSC videotape.
First Contact & Terms: Submit portfolio/demo tape by mail. Query with samples. Provide resume and list of stock photo subjects with business card, self-promotion piece or tearsheets to be kept on file for possible future assignments. Works with local freelancers on assignment only. Interested in

stock photos; subjects vary. Cannot return materials. Reports in 1 week. NPI; payment negotiable. Pays on publication/delivery. Buys all rights (work-for-hire). Captions preferred; model release required. Credit line given.

Tips: "Submit enough material initially to get acquainted." In samples/demos, wants to see creativity and fee range indicated.

*■NEW & UNIQUE VIDEOS, 2336 Sumac Dr., San Diego CA 92105. (619)282-6126. FAX: (619)283-8264. AV firm. Director of Acquisitions: Candace Love. Estab. 1981. Types of clients: industrial, financial, fashion, retail and special interest video distribution. Examples of recent projects: "Ultimate Mountain Biking," Raleigh Cycle Co. of America (special interest video); "John Howard's Lessons in Cycling," John Howard (special-interest video); and "Battle at Durango: First-Ever World Mountain Bike Championships," *Mountain & City Biking Magazine* (special interest video).

Needs: Works with 2-6 photographers and/or videographers/year. Subjects include: mainly cycling and sports; anything that fits as "new and unique" in special interest realm. Reviews stock photos: cycling, sports, comedy, romance, "new and unique."

Audiovisual Needs: Uses videotape.

Specs: Uses VHS videotape, ¾" and Betacam SP.

First Contact & Terms: Query with list of stock photo (video) subjects. Works on assignment only. Keeps samples on file. SASE. Reports in 3 weeks. NPI; payment always negotiated." Pays on acceptance. Buys exclusive and nonexclusive rights. Model/property release preferred. Credit line given.

Tips: In samples looks for "originality, good humor and timelessness. We are seeing an international hunger for action footage; good wholesome adventure; comedy, educational, how-to—special interest. The entrepreneurial, creative and original video artiste—with the right attitude—can always feel free to call us."

■ON-Q PRODUCTIONS INC., 618 E. Gutierrez St., Santa Barbara CA 93103. (805)963-1331. President: Vincent Quaranta. Estab. 1984. Producers of multi-projector slide presentations and computer graphics. Buys 100 freelance photos/year; offers 50 assignments/year. Uses photos for brochures, posters, audiovisual presentations, annual reports, catalogs and magazines. Types of clients: industrial, fashion and finance.

Needs: Scenic, people and general stock.

Specs: Uses 35mm, 2¼ × 2¼ and 4 × 5 transparencies.

First Contact & Terms: Provide stock list, business card, brochure, flyer or tearsheets to be kept on file for possible future assignments. Pays $100 minimum/job. Buys rights according to client's needs. Model releases and captions required.

Tips: Looks for stock slides for AV uses.

PHOTEC, P.O. Box 20328, Long Beach CA 90801. Assignment photography and stock photo agency. Manager/Owner: Steve Potter. Estab. 1964. Clients: industrial, commercial, marine, maritime, public services, high-tech R&D, manufacturing, training, publishers and licensing agencies.

Needs: Uses photography stock for consumer and trade magazines, direct mail, catalogs, posters, signage, brochures, annual reports and manuals. Subjects: Boat living (people live-aboards); boats in design, manufacture and use; high-tech/aerospace technology and equipment. Interested in reviewing photos of marine living and cruising, boats in design, manufacture and use; boat operating, navigating and maintenance.

Specs: Uses 8 × 12 glossy b&w and color prints; 35mm, 120mm and 4 × 5 transparencies, S-VHS videotape.

First Contact & Terms: Interested in receiving work from newer, lesser-known photographers "if they are talented, well trained. (No portrait, school, editorial or 'papparazi' types.") Query with resumé of credits and education, list of photo subjects, samples, business card, brochure and flyer/tearsheets. SASE. NPI. Pays via contract agreement only. Rights must be negotiable. Model/property release required for people and with privately owned boats/equipment. Photo captions preferred; include "who, what, when, where, why and how." Credit line usually given.

Tips: "Technical photographic capabilities in all formats, knowledge of boats and operating uses and an artistic sense are essential, but you should be more technical than 'arty.' Also, know graphics methods/limitations, 'state-of-the-art' photo technology, films and materials." Sees a trend toward PC-CD-electronic scanning/storage/repro technology development; cost-effective equipment and training, i.e., hi-resolution and continuous tone/color eq. and transmission; and facsimilie (Fax) at reasonable cost.

■**BILL RASE PRODUCTIONS, INC.**, 955 Venture Court, Sacramento CA 95825. (916)929-9181. Manager/Owner: Bill Rase. Estab. 1965. AV firm. Types of clients: industry, business, government, publishing and education. Produces filmstrips, slide sets, multimedia kits, motion pictures, sound-slide sets, videotapes, mass cassette, reel and video duplication. Photo and film purchases vary.
Needs: "Script recording for educational clients is our largest need, followed by industrial training, state and government work, motivational, etc." Freelance photos used sometimes in motion pictures. No nudes. Color only. Vertical format for TV cutoff only. Sound for TV public service announcements, commercials, and industrial films. Uses stock footage of hard-to-find scenes, landmarks in other cities, shots from the 1920s to 1980s, etc. Special subject needs include 35 mm and ¾-inch video shot of California landmark locations, especially San Francisco, Napa Valley Wine Country, Gold Country, Lake Tahoe area, Delta area and Sacramento area. "We buy out the footage—so much for so much," or ¾-inch video or 35 mm slides. Uses 8 × 10 prints and 35mm transparencies.
First Contact & Terms: NPI. Payment depends on job, by bid. Pays 30 days after acceptance. Buys one-time rights or all rights; varies according to clients needs. Model release required. Query with samples and resume of credits. Freelancers within 100 miles only. Does not return samples. SASE. Reports "according to the type of project. Sometimes it takes a couple of months to get the proper bid info."
Tips: "Video footage of the popular areas of this country and others is becoming more and more useful. Have price list, equipment list and a few slide samples in a folder or package available to send."

■**TAMARA SCOTT PRODUCTIONS**, 19062 Two Bar Rd., Boulder Creek CA 95006. (408)338-9683.
Needs: Uses freelance photographers for filmstrips, slide sets, multimedia productions, films and videotapes.
First Contact & Terms: Submit portfolio by mail; query with samples, resume and photo stock list; provide resume, business card, self-promotion piece or tearsheets to be kept on file for possible future assignments. Works on assignment only; interested in stock photos/footage. Does not return unsolicited material. Reports "as needed." Pays $25-75/hour, $25-2,500/b&w photo; $25-2,500/color photo; $25-500/hour; $200-2,500/day. Pays upon payment from client. Buys one-time rights, exclusive product rights or all rights. Model release required. Credit line given.
Tips: Looks for special effects, business portraiture, poster, greeting card and postcard imagery. "Submit samples to keep on file."

EDGAR S. SPIZEL ADVERTISING AND PUBLIC RELATIONS, C-31, 2610 Torrey Pines Rd., La Jolla CA 92037-3445. Ad agency and PR firm. President: Edgar S. Spizel. Types of clients: retail, finance, hotels, developers, arts, TV and radio.
Needs: Works with 2 freelance photographers/month. Uses photographers for consumer and trade magazines, direct mail, P-O-P displays, posters, signage and newspapers. Subjects include people, buildings, hotels, apartments, interiors.
Specs: Uses 8 × 10 glossy b&w and color prints; 35mm, 2¼ × 2¼, 4 × 5 transparencies.
First Contact & Terms: Send unsolicited photos by mail for consideration; provide resume, business card, brochure, flyer or tearsheets to be kept on file for possible future assignments. Works with freelance photographers on an assignment basis only. Does not return unsolicited material. NPI; pays by the hour, day, or job. Pays on acceptance. Buys all rights. Model release required. Credit line sometimes given.

■**RON TANSKY ADVERTISING CO.**, Suite 111, 14852 Ventura Blvd., Sherman Oaks CA 91403. (818)990-9370. FAX: (818)990-0456. Ad agency and PR firm. Consulting Art Directors: Van Valencia, Norm Galston. Estab. 1976. Serves all types of clients.
Needs: Works with 2 freelance photographers/month. Uses photographers for billboards, consumer and trade magazines, direct mail, P-O-P displays, brochures, catalogs, signage, newspapers and AV presentations. Subjects include "mostly product—but some without product as well." Special subject needs include consumer electronics, nutrition products and over-the-counter drugs.
Audiovisual Needs: Works with freelance filmmakers to produce TV commercials.
Specs: Uses b&w or color prints; 2¼ × 2¼, 4 × 5 transparencies; 16mm and videotape film.
First Contact & Terms: Query with resume of credits; provide resume, business card, brochure, flyer or tearsheets to be kept on file for possible future assignments. SASE. Payment "depends on subject and client's budget." Pays $50-250/b&w photo; $100-1,500/color photo; $500-1,500/day; $100-1,500/ complete job. Pays in 30 days. Buys all rights. Model release required.
Tips: Prefers to see "product photos, originality of position and lighting" in a portfolio. "We look for creativity and general competence, i.e., focus and lighting as well as ability to work with models." Photographers should provide "rate structure and ideas of how they would handle product shots." Also, "Don't use fax unless we make request."

■DANA WHITE PRODUCTIONS, INC., 2623 29th St., Santa Monica CA 90405. (310)450-9101. FAX: (310)450-9101. AV firm. President: Dana White. Estab. 1977. Types of clients: corporate and educational. Examples of recent productions: MacMillan-McGraw-Hill (textbook illustrations); Pepperdine University (awards banquets, tribute to winners); St. Joseph Center (homelessness, multi-image).
Needs: Works with 2-3 freelance photographers/month. Uses photographers for catalogs, audiovisual and books. Subjects include: people, products and architecture. Interested in reviewing 35mm stock photos.
Audiovisual Needs: Uses all AV formats; also slides for multi-image slide shows using 1-9 projectors. "Photographer must be able to work well on his own and shoot to the style of our company."
Specs: Uses b&w prints; 35mm, 2¼×2¼ transparencies.
First Contact & Terms: Interested in receiving work from newer, lesser-known photographers. Arrange a personal interview to show portfolio; query with samples, past credits. Works with freelancers on assignment only. Cannot return material. Report time depends on schedule. Pays $20-150/hour; $50-1,200/day; $25-100/color photo. Pays on acceptance and receipt of invoice. Buys one-time rights, exclusive product rights and all rights; negotiable, usually share in rights. Model release required; property release preferred for company logos and ID's. Credit line given sometimes.
Tips: In freelancer's portfolio or demos, wants to see "quality of composition, lighting, saturation, degree of difficulty and importance of assignment." The trend is toward "more video, less AV." To break in, freelancer should "diversify, negotiate, get the job. Don't get stuck in a fixed way of doing things. Work flexibly with producers."

■WILSON & WILSON, 970 Arnold Way, San Jose CA 95128-3476. (408)271-7900. FAX: (408)292-9595. Ad agency, PR firm. Art Director: Erica K. Wilson. Types of clients: industrial, finance, business to business, high-tech and distribution companies.
Needs: Works with 2-3 freelance photographers/month. Uses photographers for trade magazines, direct mail, catalogs, posters, newspapers, trade shows and annual reports. Subjects include: technology, real estate. Reviews stock photos on technology and real estate, also b&w people shots.
Audiovisual Needs: Uses photos for slide shows, training and sales video.
Specs: Uses 3×5 to 11×16 (depends on job), glossy b&w prints; 35mm, 4×5 transparencies; 1″ videotape.
First Contact & Terms: Query with samples, provide resume, business card, brochure, flyer or tearsheets to be kept on file for possible future assignments, "follow with phone call for portfolio review." Keeps samples on file. Reports as needed. Pays $70-120/hour; $750-1,200/day; photographer's quote. Rights negotiable. Model release and photo captions preferred. Credit line sometimes given depending upon job.
Tips: In portfolio, wants to see "technical proficiency, ability to *show product* creatively. Variety preferred." One trend is that "Standards are continually improving." To break in with this firm, "flexibility is important. Be able to contribute to creative process. Have ability to work with tight deadlines."

■WINMILL ENTERTAINMENT, 813 N. Cordova St., Burbank CA 91505. (818)954-0065. President/Creative Director: Chip Miller. Motion picture, music video, commercial, and promotional trailer film production company. Types of clients: entertainment, motion picture, TV and music.
Needs: Works with 2-6 freelance photographers/month. Uses freelancers for TV, music video, motion picture stills and production.
First Contact & Terms: Provide business card, resume, references, samples or tearsheets to be kept on file for possible future assignments. NPI; payment negotiable "based on project's budget."
Tips: Wants to see minimum of 12 pieces expressing range of studio, location, style and model-oriented work. Include samples of work published or commissioned for production.

Los Angeles

BEAR ADVERTISING, 1424 N. Highland, Los Angeles CA 90028. (213)466-6464. Vice President: Bruce Bear. Ad agency. Uses consumer magazines, direct mail, foreign media, P-O-P displays and trade magazines. Serves sporting goods, fast foods and industrial clients. Works with 4 freelance photographers/month on assignment only.
Needs: Prefers to see samples of sporting goods, fishing equipment, outdoor scenes, product shots with rustic atmosphere of guns, rifles, fishing reels, lures, camping equipment, etc.
Specs: Uses b&w and color photos.
First Contact & Terms: Call to arrange interview to show portfolio. Provide business card and tearsheets to be kept on file for possible future assignments. SASE. Reports in 1 week. Pays $150-250/b&w photo; $200-350/color photo. Pays 30 days after billing to client. Buys all rights.

THE GARIN AGENCY, Suite 614, 6253 Hollywood Blvd., Los Angeles CA 90028. (213)465-6244. Ad agency. Contact: Art Director. Estab. 1980. Types of clients: financial.
Needs: Works with freelance photographers occasionally. Uses photographs for direct mail and catalogs.
Specs: Uses any size b&w prints.
First Contact & Terms: Query with samples. Works on assignment only. Reports in 1 month. NPI. Pays on acceptance. Buys all rights. Model release required. Credit line not given.

GORDON GELFOND ASSOCIATES, INC., Suite 350, 11500 Olympic Blvd., Los Angeles CA 90064. (213)478-3600. FAX: (213)477-4825. Ad agency. Art Director: Barry Brenner. Types of clients: retail, financial, hospitals and consumer eletronic.
Needs: Works with 1-2 photographers/month. Uses freelance photographers for billboards, consumer magazines, trade magazines, direct mail and newspapers. Subject matter varies.
Specs: Uses b&w and color prints; 35mm, 2¼ × 2¼ and 4 × 5 transparencies.
First Contact & Terms: Arrange a personal interview to show portfolio, send unsolicited photos by mail for consideration, submit portfolio for review. Provide resume, business card, brochure, flyer or tearsheets to be kept on file for posssible future assignments. Works with local freelance photographers on assignment basis only. Does not return unsolicited material. Reports ASAP. NPI. Pays by the job. Payment is made 30 days after receipt of invoice. Buys all rights. Model release required. Credit line sometimes given.
Tips: Preferred subjects, styles in portfolio or samples depends on assignment. "Works within a budget."

■**MYRIAD PRODUCTIONS,** Suite 402, 1314 N. Hayworth Ave., Los Angeles CA 90046. (213)851-1400. President: Ed Harris. Primarily involved with sports productions and events. Photographers used for portraits, live-action and studio shots, special effects photos, advertising, illustrations, brochures, TV and film graphics, theatrical and production stills. Works with freelance photographers on assignment only basis.
Specs: Uses 8 × 10 b&w glossy prints, 8 × 10 color prints and 2¼ × 2¼ transparancies.
First Contact & Terms: Provide brochure, resume and samples to be kept on file for possible future assignments. NPI. Credit line sometimes given. Buys all rights. Send material by mail for consideration. Does not return unsolicited material. Reporting time "depends on urgency of job or production."
Tips: "We look for an imaginative photographer, one who captures all the subtle nuances, as the photographer is as much a part of the creative process as the artist or scene being shot. Working with us depends almost entirely on the photographer's skill and creative sensitivity with the subject. All materials submitted will be placed on file and not returned, pending future assignments. Photographers should not send us their only prints, transparencies, etc. for this reason."

San Francisco

■**ANDERSON, ROTHSTEIN, FUQUA INC.,** (formerly Anderson/Rothstein, Inc.), 28 Geary St., San Francisco CA 94108. (415)394-8000. FAX: (415)495-0319. Ad agency. Creative Director: Tom Livingston. Estab. 1982. Types of clients: food service and consumer.
Needs: Works with 5-6 freelance photographers/filmmakers/videographers/month. Uses photographers for consumer, trade magazines, direct mail, P-O-P displays, catalogs, posters, newspapers, signage and audiovisual. Subjects include: food.
Audiovisual Needs: Occasionally uses 35mm slides for slide shows; infrequent need for film and videotape.
Specs: Uses b&w prints, any format or size. Uses 2¼ × 2¼, 4 × 5 and 8 × 10 transparencies.
First Contact & Terms: Arrange personal interview to show portfolio. Provide resume, business card, brochure, flyer or tearsheets to be kept on file for possible future assignments. Cannot return material. Reports as needed. Usually pays $1,000-2,000/day; specific terms negotiable. Buys all rights (work-for-hire) and one-time rights. Credit line sometimes given.

■**ARNOLD & ASSOCIATES PRODUCTIONS, INC.,** 2159 Powell St., San Francisco CA 94133. (415)989-3490. President: John Arnold. Types of clients: Fortune 500.
Needs: Works with 4 freelance photographers/month. Uses photographers for multimedia productions. Subjects include: national trade shows, permanent exhibits and national TV commercials.
Specs: Uses 35mm transparencies; 35mm film; U-matic ¾" and 1" videotape.
First Contact & Terms: Query with resume. Works with freelancers by assignment only. Does not return unsolicited material. Reports in 2 weeks. Pays $300-1,200/day. Pays net 20 days. Buys all rights. Model release and captions required.

Tips: "We produce top-quality, award-winning productions working with top professionals able to provide highest quality work." Wants to see dramatic lighting, creative composition and sense of style in photos submitted.

PINNE/HERBERS ADVERTISING INC., 200 Vallejo St., San Francisco CA 94111. (415)956-4210. Creative Director: Jim Hall. Art Directors: Pierre Jacot, Jim Temple, Hank Kosinski and Greg Clow. Ad agency. Uses all media including radio and TV. Serves clients in electronics, finance, banking, software and hardware and transportation.
Specs: Uses transparencies and prints; contact sheet OK. "Do not send originals unsolicited." Model release required.
First Contact & Terms: Call to arrange an appointment or submit portfolio by mail if out of town. Reports in 5 days. SASE. NPI. Model release required.
Tips: "Out of town talent should not send original material unless requested." Photographers should "be realistic as to whether his/her style would be applicable to our client list. If so, call for an appointment. It's a waste of both our time for me to say, 'that's beautiful work, but we can't use that type.'"

PURDOM PUBLIC RELATIONS, 395 Oyster Point, San Francisco CA 94080. (415)588-5700. PR firm. Estab. 1965. President: Paul Purdom. Types of clients: industrial and financial. Examples of recent PR campaigns: Sun Microsystems, Varian Associates, Calma Co. (all showing computers and instruments systems in use).
Needs: Works with 4-6 freelance photographers/month. Uses photographers for trade magazines, direct mail and newspapers. Subjects include industrial and scientific topics.
Specs: Uses 35mm and 2¼ × 2¼ transparencies; film: contact for specs.
First Contact & Terms: Query with resume of credits, list of stock photo subjects. Provide resume, business card, brochure, flyer or tearsheets to be kept on file for possible future assignments. Works on assignment only. Does not return unsolicited material. Reports as needed. Pays $50-150/hour, $400-1,500/day. Pays on receipt of invoice. Buys all rights. Model release preferred.

■**VARITEL VIDEO**, 350 Townsend St., San Francisco CA 94107. (415)495-3328. Vice President of Marketing and Sales: Lori Anderson. Production Manager: Blake Padilla. Types of clients: advertising agencies.
Needs: Works with 10 freelance photographers/month. Uses freelance photographers for filmstrips, slide sets and videotapes. Also works with freelance filmmakers for CD Rom, Paint Box.
Specs: Uses color prints; 35mm transparencies; 16mm, 35mm film; VHS, Beta, U-matic ¾" or 1" videotape. Also, D2.
First Contact & Terms: Provide resume, business card, self-promotion piece or tearsheets to be kept on file for possible future assignments. Does not return unsolicited material. Reports in 1 week. Pays $50-100/hour; $200-500/day. Pays on acceptance. Rights vary.
Tips: Apply by resume and examples of work to Julie Resing.

*■**WINKLER MCMANUS**, Suite 1600, 150 Spear St., San Francisco CA 94105. (415)957-0242. FAX: (415)495-7118. Ad agency. Senior Art Director: Floyd Yost. Estab. 1980. Types of clients: Industrial and business to business. Examples of recent projects: Improve Your Image, (Sony computer products) and MX Open (new automated control of paper making).
Needs: Works with 3-4 photographers/videographers/month. Uses photos for billboards, trade magazines and direct mail.
Audiovisual Needs: Uses videotape.
Specs: Uses 35mm, 2¼ × 2¼, 4 × 5, 8 × 10 transparencies and ½" videotape.
First Contact & Terms: Arrange personal interview to show portfolio. Works with freelancers on assignment only. Samples kept on file. SASE. Reports only when interested. Pays $1,500-15,000/job. Pays 30-60 days after receipt of invoice. Buys one-time rights; negotiable. Model and/or property release required. Credit line not given.
Tips: Seeks photos of "all subjects, people, products, sheet metal, places and food. Lighting is number one, but also look for new ideas that can be used for exsisting clients. Keep calling until you get in to see us."

Colorado

■**BROYLES ALLEBAUGH & DAVIS, INC.**, 8231 E. Prentice Ave., Englewood CO 80111. (303)770-2000. Executive Art Director: Kent Eggleston. Ad agency. Types of clients: business-to-business, industrial, financial, health care, high-tech, travel and consumer firms.

Needs: Works with approximately 25 freelance photographers/year on assignment only basis. Uses photographers for consumer and trade magazines, direct mail, P-O-P displays, brochures, catalogs, posters, newspapers, AV presentations and TV.
First Contact & Terms: Arrange interview to show portfolio. NPI; negotiates payment according to job.

■FRIEDENTAG PHOTOGRAPHICS, 356 Grape St., Denver CO 80220. (303)333-7096. Manager: Harvey Friedentag. AV firm. Estab. 1957. Serves clients in business, industry, government, trade and union organizations. Produces slide sets, motion pictures and videotape. Works with 5-10 freelancers/month on assignment only. Provide flyer, business card and brochure and nonreturnable samples to show to clients. Buys 1,000 photos and 25 films/year.
Needs: Business, training, public relations and industrial plants showing people and equipment or products in use.
Audiovisual Needs: Uses freelance photos in color slide sets and motion pictures. No posed looks. Also produces mostly 16mm Ektachrome and some 16mm b&w; ¾" and VHS videotape. Length requirement: 3-30 minutes. Interested in stock footage on business, industry, education, recreation and unusual information.
Specs: Uses 8×10 glossy b&w prints; 8×10 glossy color prints; transparencies; 35mm or 2¼×2¼ or 4×5 color transparencies.
First Contact & Terms: Send material by mail for consideration. SASE. Reports in 3 weeks. Pays $300/day for still; $500/day for motion picture plus expenses, or $25/b&w photo or $50/color photo. Pays on acceptance. Buys rights as required by clients. Model release required.
Tips: "More imagination needed, be different and above all, technical quality is a must. There are more opportunities now than ever, especially for new people. We are looking to strengthen our file of talent across the nation."

*■MERIWETHER PUBLISHING LTD., 885 Elkton Dr., Colorado Springs CO 80907. (719)594-4422. Editor: Arthur Zapel. "We create our own products—books, filmstrips or videotapes."
Needs: "Use very few—most is done in house. Uses photographers and/or videographers for slide sets and videotapes. We specialize in subjects relating to theater arts. We would consider any how-to photos or videotapes on acting, stage lighting or set design."
Specs: Uses 35mm transparencies; also "standard VCR videotapes."
First Contact & Terms: Query with resume; provide business card, self-promotion piece or tearsheets to be kept on file for possible future assignments. Works with freelancers on assignment only. SASE. Reports in 3 weeks. NPI; payment negotiable. Pays on acceptance. Buys one-time rights. Captions preferred; model releases required. Credit line given.
Tips: "Provide a marketable concept relating to our product line. We look for how-to photography about theater arts. Videotapes will be as important as books for publishers."

■TRANSTAR PRODUCTIONS, INC., Suite C, 9520 E. Jewell Ave., Denver CO 80231. (303)695-4207. Contact: Doug Hanes. Motion picture and videotape production. Serves clients in business and industry. Produces 16mm films, ¾", Betacam and 1" video-tapes, multiprojector slide shows and sound tracks. Also offers Betacam SP video editing suite and ¼" multi-track sound studio.
Audiovisual Needs: Looking for freelance photographers, writers and film production personnel experienced in a variety of film and video areas.
First Contact & Terms: Send resume and/or material before phone contact. Previous sales experience very helpful. "Know the business of film production." NPI; by the job, or per day. Pays negotiable rates; 50% of expenses up front; balance upon delivery of approved product.

Connecticut

■AV DESIGN, 1823 Silas Deane, P.O. Box 588, Rocky Hill CT 06067. (203)529-2581. FAX: (203)529-5480. President: Joseph Wall. Types of clients: Industrial, finance, manufacturers, insurance and lecturers. Examples of ad campaigns: Pirelli Armstrong and Stanley Hardware, (multi-image presentations); also, Heublein, (product photography).

The First Markets Index preceding the General Index in the back of this book provides the names of those companies/publications interested in receiving work from newer, lesser-known photographers.

Audiovisual Needs: Works with 3 freelance photographers/month. Uses photographers for slide sets, multimedia productions and videotapes. Subjects include industrial—manufacturing.
Specs: Uses 8×10 b&w and color prints; 35mm, 2¼×2¼ and 4×5 transparencies.
First Contact & Terms: Query with samples, resume or stock photo list. Works with local freelancers on assignment basis only; interested in stock photos/footage. Reports in 1 month. NPI; payment varies according to client's budget. Pays on acceptance. Buys all rights. Captions and model release preferred.

■**CORP VIDEO CENTER**, 307 Atlantic St., Stamford CT 06901. (203)965-0444. Operations/Facilities Manager: Ted Eland. Examples of recent productions: "GE Monogram Kitchen", (still photography and video); "Electronic Information Systems (still photography).
Needs: Uses photographers for videotapes. Subjects include: corporate, industrial and live-action videos.
Specs: Uses ¾" Beta or 1" videotape.
First Contact & Terms: Provide resume, business card, self-promotion piece or tearsheets to be kept on file for possible future assignments; provide demo reel. Works on assignment only. Pays $250-400/day or by project. Pays on booking—within 2-4 weeks of acceptance. Buys "unlimited" rights. Model releases required. Credit lines sometimes given depending on client and project.
Tips: "Since our freelancers represent us when doing a job, appearance, timeliness, and flexibility are important."

■**DISCOVERY PRODUCTIONS**, 1415 King St., Greenwich CT 06831-2519. (203)531-6288. Proprietor: David Epstein. PR/AV firm. Serves educational and social action agencies. Produces 16mm and 35mm documentary, educational and industrial films.
Needs: Buys 2 films annually.
First Contact & Terms: Query first with resume of credits. Provide resume to be kept on file for possible future assignments. Works with up to 2 freelance photographers/month on assignment only. Pays 25-60% royalty. Pays on use and 30 days. Buys all rights, but may reassign to filmmaker. Model release required.
Tips: Possible assignments include research, writing, camera work or editing. "We would collaborate on a production of an attractive and practical idea."

*■**DONAHUE ADVERTISING & PUBLIC RELATIONS, INC.**, 227 Lawrence St., Hartford CT 06106. (203)728-0000. FAX: (203)247-9247. Ad agency and PR firm. Creative Director: Rob Saetens. Estab. 1980. Types of clients: industrial and high-tech.
Needs: Works with 1-2 photographers and/or videographers/month. Uses photos for trade magazines, catalogs and posters. Subjects include: products.
Audiovisual Needs: Uses videotape—infrequently.
Specs: Uses 8×10 matte and glossy color or b&w prints; 4×5 transparencies.
First Contact & Terms: Contact through rep. Arrange personal interview to show portfolio. Send unsolicited photos by mail for consideration. Provide resume, business card, brochure, flyer or tearsheets to be kept on file for possible future assignments. Keeps samples on file. Cannot return material. Reports in 1-2 weeks. Pays $1,200-1,500/day. Pays on receipt of invoice with purchase order. Buys all rights. Model/property release required. Credit line not given.

THE MORETON AGENCY, P.O. Box 749, East Windsor CT 06088. (203)627-0326. Ad agency. Art Director: Roy Kimball. Types of clients: industrial, sporting goods, corporate and consumer.
Needs: Works with 3-4 photographers/month. Uses photographers for consumer and trade magazines, direct mail, catalogs, newspapers and literature. Subject matter includes people, sports, industrial, product and fashion.
Specs: Uses b&w prints; 35mm, 2¼×2¼, 4×5 and 8×10 transparencies.
First Contact & Terms: Provide business card, brochure, flyer or tearsheets to be kept on file for possible future assignments. Works with freelance photographers on assignment only. Does not return unsolicited material. Pays $800-1,500/day; other payment negotiable. Buys all rights. Model release required. Credit line negotiable.

■**PRAXIS MEDIA, INC.**, 18 Marshall St., South Norwalk CT 06854. (203)866-6666. FAX: (203)853-8299. President & Creative Director: Chris Campbell. Estab. 1981. Serves corporate/industrial clients. Produces children's and other home video products. Examples of recent clients: American Express, AT&T, IBM, Random House and NFL Properties.

Needs: Works with 1-2 freelance photographers/month. Uses photographers for slide sets, multimedia productions and videotapes. Subjects include corporate primarily, some entertainment/music.
Audiovisual Needs: Uses slides, video and computer graphics.
First Contact & Terms: Provide resume, business card, self-promotion piece or tearsheets to be kept on file for possible future assignments. Works with local freelancers only; works with freelancers by assignment only. SASE. Reports in 2-3 weeks. Pays $250-1,000/day; $250-2,500/job. Pays via 45 day payment policy. Buys all rights.
Tips: Looks for a "creative eye," with good composition and lighting. "Follow up on calls—we normally hire local photographers/videographers."

Delaware

■LYONS MARKETING COMMUNICATIONS, 715 Orange St., Wilmington DE 19801. (302)654-6146. Ad agency. Senior Art Director: Erik Vaughn. Types of clients: consumer, corporate and industrial.
Needs: Works with 6 freelance photographers/month. Uses photographers for consumer and trade magazine ads, direct mail, P-O-P displays, catalogs, posters and newspaper ads. Subjects vary greatly. Some fashion, many "outdoor-sport" type of things. Also, high-tech business-to-business.
Specs: Format varies by use.
First Contact & Terms: Query with resume of credits and list of stock photo subjects. Provide resume, business card, brochure, flyer or tearsheets to be kept on file for possible future assignments. SASE. Reports in 3 weeks. Pays $1,000/day. Payment varies based on scope of job, abilities of the photographer. Pays on publication. Rights purchased vary. Model release required; captions preferred. Credit line given depending on job.
Tips: "We consider the subjects, styles, and capabilities of the photographer. Rather than guess at what we're looking for, show us what you're good at and enjoy doing. Be available on a tight and changing schedule; show an ability to pull together the logistics of a complicated shoot."

District of Columbia

■HILLMANN & CARR INC., 2121 Wisconsin Ave. N.W., Washington DC 20007. (202)342-0001. Art Director: Michal Carr. Estab. 1975. Types of clients: corporations, industrial, government, associations and museums.
Audiovisual Needs: Uses photographers for multimedia productions, films and videotapes. "Subjects are extremely varied and range from the historical to current events. We do not specialize in any one subject area. Style also varies greatly depending upon subject matter."
Specs: Uses 35mm transparencies; 16mm and 35mm film.
First Contact & Terms: Provide resume, business card, self-promotion pieces or tearsheets to be kept on file for possible future assignments. Works on assignment only. Does not return unsolicited material. "If material has been unsolicited and we do not have immediate need, material will be filed for future reference." NPI; payment and rights negotiable. Captions preferred; model releases required.
Tips: Looks for photographers with multi-image experience and artistic style. "Quality reproduction of work which can be kept on file is extremely important."

■WORLDWIDE TELEVISION NEWS (WTN), Suite 300, 1705 DeSales St. NW, Washington DC 20036. (202)835-0750. FAX: (202)887-7978. Bureau Manager, Washington: Paul C. Sisco. AV firm. Estab. 1952. "We basically supply TV news on tape, for TV networks and stations. At this time, most of our business is with foreign nets and stations." Buys dozens of "news stories per year, especially sports."

Can't find a listing? Check at the end of each market section for the " '92-'93 Changes" lists. These lists include any market listings from the '92 edition which were either not verified or deleted in this edition.

Subject Needs: Generally hard news material, sometimes of documentary nature and sports.
Audiovisual Needs: Produces motion pictures and videotape. Works with 6 freelance photographers/
month on assignment only.
First Contact & Terms: Send name, phone number, equipment available and rates with material by
mail for consideration. Provide business card to be kept on file for possible future assignments. Fast
news material generally sent counter-to-air shipment; slower material by air freight. SASE. Reports
in 2 weeks. Pays $100 minimum/job. Pays on receipt of material; nothing on speculation. Video rates
about $400/half day, $750/full day or so. Negotiates payment based on amount of creativity required
from photographer. Buys all video rights. Dupe sheets for film required.

Florida

*BEBER SILVERSTEIN & PARTNERS, 3361 SW Third Ave., Miami FL 33145. (305)856-9800. FAX:
(305)854-1932. Ad agency. Associate Creative Director: Joe Perz. Estab. 1975. Types of clients: industrial, financial, fashion, retail and food. Examples of recent projects: Florida Power and Light and
First Florida Bank.
Needs: Works with 6-10 freelance photographers/filmmakers/videographers/month. Uses photos for
billboards, consumer magazines, trade magazines, direct mail, P-O-P displays, posters and newspapers.
Specs: Uses any size or finish color or b&w prints; 2¼×2¼, 4×5 or 8×10 transparencies and ¾″ or
½″ film.
First Contact & Terms: Submit portfolio for review. Query with samples. Works with freelancers on
assignment only. Samples kept on file. Does not return unsolicited material. Reports only if like work.
Pays $200-5,000/job. Pays in 30-60 days. Buys all rights and rights for usage over specific time; negotia-
ble. Model and/or property release required. Credit line given sometimes, depending on price of
photography.

■STEVEN COHEN, 4800 NW 96th Dr., Coral Springs FL 33076-2447. (305)346-7370. Contact: Steven
Cohen. Examples of productions: TV commercials, documentaries, 2nd unit feature films and TV
series - 2nd unit.
Needs: Uses film and videotapes.
Specs: Uses 16mm, 35mm film; 1″, ¾″ U-Matic and ½″ VHS, Beta videotape.
First Contact & Terms: Query with resume, provide business card, self-promotion piece or tearsheets
to be kept on file for possible future assignments. Works on assignment only. Cannot return material.
Reports in 1 week. NPI. Pays on acceptance or publication. Buys all rights (work-for-hire). Model
releases required. Credit line given.

COLEE SARTORY, Suite 405, 631 US Hwy. #1, North Palm Beach FL 33408. (407)844-7000. Ad
agency. Art Director: Don Bolt. Types of clients: industrial, finance, residential.
Needs: Works with 2-3 photographers/month. Uses photographers for trade magazines, newspapers,
brochures. Subjects include residential, pertaining to client.
Specs: Uses b&w and color prints; 35mm, 2¼×2¼ and 4×5 transparencies.
First Contact & Terms: Arrange a personal interview to show portfolio, submit portfolio for review;
provide resume, business card, brochure, flyer or tearsheets to be kept on file for possible future
assignments. Works with local freelance photographers on an assignment only. Pays $50-100/hour and
$250-1,000/day. Pays on receipt of invoice. Buys all rights. Model release required.

COVALT ADVERTISING AGENCY, 12907 N.E. 7th Ave., P.O. Box 610578, North Miami FL 33161.
(305)891-1543. Ad agency. Creative Director: Fernando Vasquez. Types of clients: industrial, retail,
finance.
Needs: Works with 2 freelance photographers/month. Uses photographers for billboards, consumer
and trade magazines, direct mail, P-O-P displays and posters. Subjects include product/still life.
Specs: Uses b&w and color prints and 35mm transparencies.
First Contact & Terms: Arrange a personal interview to show portfolio. Provide resume, business
card, brochure, flyer or tearsheets to be kept on file for possible future assignments. Works with local
freelance photographers on assignment only. Does not return unsolicited material. Reports in 2 weeks.
Pays $150 minimum/job. Pays on receipt of invoice. Buys all rights. Model release required.

CREATIVE RESOURCES, INC., 2000 S. Dixie Highway, Miami FL 33133. (305)856-3474. FAX:
(305)856-3151. Chairman and CEO: Mac Seligman. Estab. 1970. PR firm. Handles clients in travel
(hotels, resorts and airlines). Buys 10-20 photos/year. Photos used in PR releases. Works with 1-2
freelance photographers/month on assignment only.

Specs: Uses 8×10 glossy prints; contact sheet OK. Also uses 35mm or 2¼×2¼ transparencies and color prints.

First Contact & Terms: Provide resume to be kept on file for possible future assignments. Query with resume of credits. Pays $50 minimum/hour; $200 minimum/day; $100/color photo; $50/b&w photo. Negotiates payment based on client's budget. For assignments involving travel, pays $60-200/day plus expenses. Pays on acceptance. Buys all rights. Model release preferred. No unsolicited material. SASE. Reports in 2 weeks. Most interested in activity shots in locations near clients.

RICH FIELD ADVERTISING AGENCY, 2050 Spectrum Blvd., Ft. Lauderdale FL 33309. (305)938-7600. FAX: (305)938-7775. Inhouse ad agency for Personnel Pool of Americas, Inc. Advertising Supervisor: Daniel Cooper. Estab. 1946. Types of clients: temporary services.

Needs: Works with 2 photographers/month. Uses photographers for consumer magazines, trade magazines, direct mail, posters, newspapers and signage. Subjects include "People Helping People®." Reviews stock photos of people.

Specs: Uses color prints; 35mm, 2¼×2¼, 4×5 transparencies.

First Contact & Terms: Query with resume of credits; send unsolicited photos by mail for consideration. Works with local freelancers only. Cannot return material. Reports in 3 weeks or "as needed." Pays $1,000-1,500/day; other payment "depends on what service I'm going after." Pays on receipt of invoice. Buys all rights; "total buy-out only." Model release and photo captions required. Credit line given sometimes, "depending on usage."

■**LEON SHAFFER GOLNICK ADVERTISING, INC.**, 2817 E. Oakland Park Blvd., Ft. Lauderdale FL 33306. (305)563-5000. FAX: (305)564-9057. Ad agency. President: Leon S. Golnick. Estab. 1945. Types of clients: financial and automotive.

Needs: Works with 2 photographers/month. Uses photographs for trade magazines and newspapers. Subjects include: models and background.

Audiovisual Needs: Uses slides.

Specs: Variable according to project.

First Contact & Terms: Provide resume, business card, brochure, flyer or tearsheets to be kept on file for possible future assignments. Works on assignment only. Keeps samples on file. SASE. Reports as needed. NPI. Does not pay on regular schedule. Rights negotiable. Model release required; photo captions preferred. Credit line given.

HACKMEISTER ADVERTISING & PUBLIC RELATIONS, INC., Suite 205, 2727 E. Oakland Park Blvd., Ft. Lauderdale FL 33306. (305)568-2511. Ad agency and PR firm. Estab. 1979. President: Dick Hackmeister. Serves industrial, electronics manufacturers who sell to other businesses.

Needs: Works with 1 freelance photographer/month. Uses photos for trade magazines, direct mail, catalogs. Subject needs include electronic products.

Specs: Uses 8×10 glossy b&w and color prints and 4×5 transparencies.

First Contact & Terms: "Call on telephone first." Does not return unsolicited material. Pays by the day and $200-2,000/job. Buys all rights. Model release and captions required.

Tips: Looks for "good lighting on highly technical electronic products—creativity."

RONALD LEVITT ASSOC. INC., 141 Sevilla, Coral Gables FL 33134. (305)443-3223. PR firm. President: Ron Levitt. Types of clients: corporate, fashion, finance.

Needs: Works with 3-4 freelance photographers/month. Uses photos for consumer and trade magazines, direct mail, newspapers and brochures.

Specs: Uses b&w and color prints; 35mm transparencies.

First Contact & Terms: Arrange a personal interview to show a portfolio. Provide resume, business card, brochure, flyer or tearsheets to be kept on file for possible future assignments. Works with freelance photographers on assignment only. Reports immediately. Pays $75 minimum/hour; $600 minimum/day. Pays on receipt of invoice. Buys all rights. Model release required; captions preferred. Credit line sometimes given.

■**MYERS, MYERS & ADAMS ADVERTISING, INC.**, 938 N. Victoria Park Rd., Ft. Lauderdale FL 33304. (305)523-0202. Ad agency. Creative Director: Virginia Sours-Myers. Estab. 1986. Types of Clients: industrial, retail, fashion, finance, marine, restaurant, medical and real estate.

Needs: Works with 3-5 photographers, filmmakers and/or videographers/month. Uses photographers for billboards, consumer magazines, trade magazines, direct mail, P-O-P displays, catalogs, newspapers and audiovisual. Subjects include: marine, food, real estate, medical and fashion. Wants to see "all subjects" in stock images and footage.

Often in advertising a photographer is called upon to shoot handsome photos of products. This photo of a laboratory counter-timer, purchased by Hackmeister Advertising and Public Relations Company, Ft. Lauderdale, Florida, was used to accompany a press release concerning this piece of equipment.

© Hackmeister Advertising & Public Relations

Audiovisual Needs: Uses photos/film/video for slide shows, film and videotape.
Specs: Uses all sizes b&w/color prints; 35mm, 2¼ × 2¼, 4 × 5 transparencies; 35mm film; 1″, ¾″, but to review need ½″.
First Contact & Terms: Provide resume, business card, brochure, flyer or tearsheets to be kept on file for possible future assignments. Works with freelancers on assignment basis only. Cannot return material. Reports as needed. Pays $50-200/hour; $800-2,500/day; $50-10,000/job. Buys all rights (work-for-hire) and 1 year's usage. Credit line given sometimes, depending on usage.
Tips: "We're not looking for arty-type photos or journalism. We need photographers that understand an advertising sense of photography: good solid images that sell the product." Sees trend in advertising toward "computer-enhanced impact and color effects. Send samples, tearsheets and be patient. Please don't call us. If your work is good we keep on file and as a style is needed we will contact the photographer. Keep us updated with new work. Advertising is using a fair amount of audiovisual work. We use a lot of stills within our commercials. Make portfolio available to production houses."

*■NISSEN ADVERTISING, 1037 S. Florida Ave., Lakeland FL 33803. (813)688-7078. FAX: (813)682-0695. Ad agency. Creative Services Director: Melanie Drake. Estab. 1971. Types of clients: industrial, financial, retail and food. Examples of recent projects: Newcomer Guide, First National Bank (Florida attractions).
Needs: Works with 3 photographers, filmmakers and/or videographers/month. Uses photos for billboards, consumer and trade magazines, direct mail, P-O-P displays, catalogs, posters, newspapers. Subjects include: people, products and places.
Audiovisual Needs: Uses slides and videotape.
Specs: Uses color and b&w prints, all sizes; 35mm, 2¼ × 2¼, 4 × 5 transparencies; 16 or 35mm film; 1″ or ½″ Betacam videotape.
First Contact & Terms: Arrange personal interview to show portfolio. Query with list of stock photo subjects. Provide resume, business card, brochure, flyer or tearsheets to be kept on file for possible future assignments. Works on assignment only. Keeps samples on file. Cannot return material. Reports in 3 weeks. Pays $75-175/hour; $600-1200/day; $200-5,000/job; $20/color photo; $15/b&w photo. Pays net 30 days. Buys all rights. Model/property release required. Photo captions preferred. Credit line sometimes given.
Tips: Looks for strong lighting, dramatics and angles.

PRODUCTION INK, 2826 NE 19 Dr., Gainesville FL 32609. (904)377-8973. FAX: (904)373-1175. Ad agency, PR firm. President: Terry Van Nortwick. Types of clients: hospital, industrial, computer.
Needs: Works with 1 freelance photographer/month. Uses photographs for ads, billboards, trade magazines, catalogs and newspapers. Reviews stock photos.
Specs: Uses b&w prints and 35mm, 2¼ and 4×5 transparencies.
First Contact & Terms: Arrange personal interview to show portfolio; submit portfolio for review; provide resume, business card, brochure, flyer or tearsheets to be kept on file for possible future assignments. Keeps samples on file. NPI. Pays on receipt of invoice. Buys all rights. Model release required. Credit line sometimes given; negotiable.

*■TEL—AIR INTERESTS, INC., 1755 NE 149th St., Miami FL 33181. (305)944-3268. AV firm. Production Manager: Marlinda Jester. Serves clients in business, industry and government. Produces filmstrips, slide sets, multimedia kits, motion pictures, sound-slide sets and videotape. Buys 10 filmstrips and 50 films/year.
Specs: Uses b&w prints and 8×10 matte color prints; also 35mm transparencies.
First Contact & Terms: Arrange a personal interview to show portfolio or submit portfolio for review. SASE. Reports in 1 month. Pays $100 minimum/job. Pays on production. Buys all rights. Model release required, captions preferred.

Georgia

■FRASER ADVERTISING, Suite 110, 2531 Center West Pkwy., Augusta GA 30901. (404)737-6219. Ad agency. President: Jerry Fraser. Estab. 1980. Types of clients: automotive, industrial, manufacturing, residential.
Needs: Works with "possibly one freelance photographer every two or three months." Uses photographers for consumer and trade magazines, catalogs, posters, and AV presentations. Subject matter: "product and location shots." Also works with freelance filmmakers to produce TV commercials on videotape.
Specs: Uses glossy b&w and color prints; 35mm, 2¼×2¼ and 4×5 transparencies; videotape and film. "Specifications vary according to the job."
First Contact & Terms: Provide resume, business card, brochure, flyer or tearsheets to be kept on file for possible future assignments. Works with freelance photographers on assignment only. Does not return unsolicited material. Reports in 1 month. NPI; payment varies according to job. Pays on publication. Buys one-time and all rights; negotiable. Model release required.
Tips: Prefers to see "samples of finished work—the actual ad, for example, not the photography alone. Send us materials to keep on file and quote favorably when rate is requested."

■PAUL FRENCH & PARTNERS, INC., 503, Gabbettville Rd., LaGrange GA 30240. (706)882-5581. Contact: Gene Ballard. AV firm. Estab. 1969. Types of clients: industrial, corporate.
Needs: Works with freelance photographers on assignment only basis. Uses photographers for filmstrips, slide sets, multimedia. Subjects include: industrial marketing, employee training and orientation, public and community relations.
Specs: Uses 35mm and 4×5 color transparencies.
First Contact & Terms: Query with resume of credits; provide resume to be kept on file for possible future assignments. Pays $75-150 minimum/hour; $600-1,200/day; $150 up/job, plus travel and expenses. Payment on acceptance. Buys all rights, but may reassign to photographer after use.
Tips: "We buy photojournalism . . . journalistic treatments of our clients' subjects. Portfolio: industrial process, people at work, interior furnishings product, fashion. We seldom buy single photos."

■GRANT/GARRETT COMMUNICATIONS, (formerly Garrett Communications), P.O. Box 53, Atlanta GA 30301. (404)755-2513. FAX: (404)755-2513. Ad agency. President/Owner: Ms. Ruby Grant Garrett. Estab. 1979. Types of clients: technical. Examples of ad campaigns: Simons (help wanted); CIS Telecom (equipment); Anderson Communication (business-to-business).

■ *The solid, black square before a listing indicates that the market uses various types of audiovisual materials, such as slides, film or videotape.*

Needs: Uses photographers for trade magazines, direct mail and newspapers. Interested in reviewing stock photos/video footage of people at work.
Audiovisual Needs: Uses stock video footage.
Specs: Uses 4×5 b&w prints; VHS videotape.
First Contact & Terms: Interested in receiving work from newer, lesser-known photographers. Query with resume of credits, query with list of stock photo subjects; provide resume, business card, brochure, flyer or tearsheets to be kept on file for possible future assignments. Works with freelancers on an assignment basis only. SASE. Reports in 1 week. NPI; pays per job. Pays on receipt of invoice. Buys one-time and other rights; negotiable. Model/property release required; photo captions preferred. Credit line sometimes given, depending on client.
Tips: Wants to see b&w work in portfolio.

Idaho

CIPRA AD AGENCY, 314 E. Curling Dr., Boise ID 83702. (208)344-7770. Ad agency. President: Ed Gellert. Estab. 1979. Types of clients: industrial and retail.
Needs: Works with 1 freelance photographer/month. Uses photos for trade magazines. Subjects include: electronic, industrial and scenic. Reviews general stock photos.
Specs: Uses matte and glossy 4×5, 8×10, 11×14, color, b&w prints; also 35mm and 4×5 transparencies.
First Contact & Terms: Provide resume, business card, brochure, flyer or tearsheets to be kept on file for possible future assignments. Usually works with local freelancers only. Keeps samples on file. Cannot return material. Reports as needed. Pays $75/hour. Pays on publication. Buys all rights. Model release required.

Illinois

BRAGAW PUBLIC RELATIONS SERVICES, Suite 807, 800 E. Northwest Hwy., Palatine IL 60067. (708)934-5580. PR firm. Contact: Richard S. Bragaw. Estab. 1981. Types of clients: professional service firms, high-tech entrepreneurs.
Needs: Works with 1 freelance photographer/month. Uses photographers for trade magazines, direct mail, brochures, newspapers, newsletters/news releases. Subject matter "products and people."
Specs: Uses 3×5, 5×7 and 8×10 glossy prints.
First Contact & Terms: Provide resume, business card, brochure, flyer or tearsheets to be kept on file for possible future assignments. Works with freelance photographers on assignment basis only. SASE. Pays $25-100/b&w photo; $50-200/color photo; $35-100/hour; $200-500/day; $100-1,000/job. Pays on receipt of invoice. Buys all rights. Model release preferred. Credit line "possible."
Tips: "Execute an assignment well, at reasonable costs, with speedy delivery."

JOHN CROWE ADVERTISING AGENCY, 1104 S. 2nd St., Springfield IL 62704. (217)528-1076. President: Bryan J. Crowe. Ad agency. Uses photos for billboards, consumer and trade magazines, direct mail, newspapers, radio and TV. Serves clients in industry, commerce, aviation, banking, state and federal government, retail stores, publishing and institutes. Works with 1 freelance photographer/month on assignment only.
First Contact & Terms: Send material by mail for consideration. Provide letter of inquiry, flyer, brochure and tearsheet to be kept on file for future assignments. Pays $50 minimum/job or $18 minimum/hour. Payment negotiable based on client's budget. Buys all rights. Model release required. SASE. Reports in 2 weeks.
Specs: Uses 8×10 glossy b&w prints; also uses color 8×10 glossy prints and 2¼×2¼ transparencies.

CS&A ADVERTISING, 207 Landmark Dr., Normal IL 61761. (309)452-0707. Ad agency. Senior Art Director: Jeff Bernius. Types of clients: industrial, finance, most often business-to-business type.
Needs: "We have an in-house photo studio. We freelance hard to get locations—off season—metro locations." Uses photographers for trade magazines, direct mail and P-O-P displays. Particular metro buildings and skylines, people shots and situations.
Specs: Uses 4×5 transparencies.
First Contact & Terms: Provide resume, business card, brochure, flyer or tearsheets to be kept on file for possible future assignments. "We will use freelance if we can't get what we want from stock or if pricing is similar." Does not return unsolicited material. Reports in 2 weeks. Pays per b&w photo

Close-up

Deanne Delbridge
Creative and Marketing Consultant
San Francisco

© Bill Zemanek

Photographers who want to sell their images better listen when Deanne Delbridge speaks. A creative and marketing consultant for many pro photographers, Delbridge became involved with photography when she signed on as the West Coast agent for the Creative Black Book. While with Creative Black Book, she saw many photographers poorly marketing their talents and, a few years later, she went on her own to help photographers better sell themselves and their images.

"I would see portfolios from excellent photographers and they were just dreadful . . . and their promotions were all different sizes and typefaces," says Delbridge, who learned her marketing skills while in the investment business. "There was nothing cohesive about their presentation. They had no understanding of how to speak the language of the marketplace."

As Delbridge began advising photographers, she realized that, while many were talented with a camera, they still needed a personal vision to enhance their work.

"There was no soul in visual arts and advertising," says Delbridge, remembering the commercial photography of the late 1970s. "There was just showing an image and putting words with it to sell a product."

Times have changed and photographers should realize while an image can carry several messages, everything works best when they find themselves.

"Most people are trying to work from the outside rather than from the inside," states Delbridge. "Because of television, we have these ideas of perfection, the ideas that we're somehow inadequate, that we have to create this thing that's beyond ourselves. It's not true. The most brilliant ideas are the simple ones that come from the creator's own life. You don't need any more than your own life to come up with wonderful ideas. Everyone can learn to develop their creativity. It's not something that belongs only to a chosen few."

Of course, creativity does not happen automatically, notes Delbridge. "That's why taking time to play with your own vision, your personal work, is an extremely important part of your weekly work. The market now offers the opportunity to get back to what you enjoy doing instead of what you feel compelled to do to make money," she says.

In her lectures, Delbridge teaches students how to acquire, and in some cases re-acquire, creativity. "Creative burnout happens when you don't take the time to play or explore your own personal vision. If you don't play enough, you'll lose your passion."

Often individuals get trapped into thinking, "We're too old, too young, too busy or too stupid to innovate," says Delbridge. "You have to be willing to go into the danger area . . . reach into the void every day. Even if it's for some little job, you must remember that nothing is insignificant when you put it out there in the world. There isn't one visual you do that doesn't affect people in some way."

After all, it was the vastness of the western United States, portrayed in photos, that impressed former President Theodore Roosevelt so much that he created the world's first national park, she says. Delbridge also notes the present rise in social and environmental responsibility of corporate photography, one of her current lecture subjects.

"Remember all the predictions of doom and gloom about the environment?" asks Delbridge. "That's not a holocaust that's going to happen. It's here. The rivers are running green, red and yellow. The air's already bad. The animals are disappearing. The ozone is going . . . We're sitting in the pollution and leftovers from having created industries and technology and now it's the artist who's going to have to bring the humanness back into this."

Delbridge points out that several large companies already promote their environmental concerns rather than their products, a movement photographers should note. "First, ads sold products, then feelings and now sociological and educational ideas," she says.

Although Delbridge feels that photographers should make others aware of concerns in the world, she reiterates her belief that if photographers want to sell anything, they first must know themselves.

"Martha Graham said, 'No one can do it the way you can do it and that's why it's important that you do it and not give up,' and I agree with that," says Delbridge. "If you block your feelings, the work will never exist through any other medium. The world will never have it. It is not your business to determine how good it is, nor how valuable, nor how it compares with other expressions. It is your business to keep it yours, clearly and directly."

— Michael Whye

Photographer Cheryl Maeder, of San Francisco, California, was interested in improving her portfolio and she turned to Deanne Delbridge for help. The two reorganized Maeder's work, which includes this shot for a 1990 fashion spread in **SF Moda** *Magazine.*

© Cheryl Maeder

$25-450; per color photo $250-850; by the hour $40-85; by the day, $500-1,000. "Payment is made after all invoices are returned." Model release required; captions preferred.
Tips: Prefers to see buildings and people, construction, seasonal; unique angles and styles, no special effects industrial.

■**DATA COMMAND INC.,** 119 S. Schyler Ave., P.O. Box 548, Kankakee IL 60901. (815)933-7735. FAX: (815)935-8577. Director, Product Development: Aggie Posthumus. Estab. 1981. Types of clients: educational market (early childhood, K-12).
Needs: Works with 3-4 freelance photographers/year. Uses photographers for multimedia productions. Subjects: product shots; photos also used for packaging/teachers' manuals..
Specs: Uses 5×7 glossy b&w prints, various sizes glossy color prints; also 35mm color transparencies; 35mm film.
First Contact & Terms: Provide resume, business card, self-promotion piece or tearsheets to be kept on file for possible future assignments. Works with freelancers by assignment only; interested in stock photos/footage. SASE. Reports in 2 weeks. Pays by the job or by royalty; also pays $25-150/b&w photo; $50-250/color photo. Pays on acceptance. Buys all rights and exclusive rights in intended market. Captions preferred; model release required. Credit line sometimes given.
Tips: There is an increasing interest in educational use of computer graphics and computer-enhanced illustrations. Call and establish relationship. "The most recent photographer I spoke with usually comes to mind first."

■**EGD & ASSOCIATES, INC.,** 1801 H Hicks Rd., Rolling Meadow IL 60008. (708)991-1270. FAX: (708)991-1519. Ad agency. Vice President: Kathleen Dorn. Estab. 1970. Types of clients: industrial, retail, finance. Example of ad campaigns: Gould, Bostick and Jiffy Print.
Needs: Works with 7-8 freelance photographers—videographers/month. Uses photographers for billboards, consumer magazines, trade magazines, direct mail, P-O-P displays, catalogs and audiovisual. Subjects include: industrial products and facilities. Reviews stock photos/video footage of 'creative firsts.'
Audiovidual Needs: Uses photos/video for slide shows and videotape.
Specs: Uses 4×5, 8×10 b&w/color prints; 35mm, 2¼×2¼, 4×5, 8×10 transparencies; videotape.
First Contact & Terms: Arrange personal interview to show portfolio; provide resume, business card, brochure, flyer or tearsheets to be kept on file for possible future assignments. Works with local freelancers on assignment basis only. Cannot return material. Reports in 1-2 weeks. NPI; pays according to "clients budget." Pays on 30 days of invoice. Model release required. Credit line sometimes given; credit line offered in lieu of payment.
Tips: Sees trend toward "larger budget for exclusive rights and creative firsts. Contact us every six months."

■**GOLDSHOLL DESIGN AND FILM,** Dept. PM, 420 Frontage Rd., Northfield IL 60093. (708)446-8300. Contact: Deborah Goldsholl. AV firm. Serves clients in industry and advertising agencies. Produces filmstrips, slide sets, multimedia kits, corporate brochures, merchandising material, and motion pictures. Works with 2-3 freelance photographers/month on assignment only basis. Buys 100 photos, 5 filmstrips and 25 films/year.
Needs: General subjects. No industrial equipment. Length requirement: 30 seconds to 30 minutes. Reviews stock footage.
Specs: Uses 16 and 35mm industrial, educational, TV, documentaries and animation. Uses contact sheet or 35mm, 2¼×2¼, 4×5 or 8×10 transparencies.
First Contact & Terms: Query with resume. SASE. Reports in 1 week. Provide letter of inquiry and brochure to be kept on file for future assignments. NPI. Pays by the job or by the hour; negotiates payment based on client's budget, amount of creativity required from photographer, photographer's previous experience/ reputation. Pays in 30 days. Buys all rights. Model release required.

■**LEADER ADVERTISING AGENCY, INC.,** 2311 W. 22nd St., Oak Brook IL 60521. (708)654-3188. Ad agency. Art Director: Mike Zagorski. Estab. 1970. Types of clients: medical. Examples of recent clients: JC Penney, A.B. Dick, St. Joseph's Hospital.
Needs: Works with 1-2 freelance photographers. Uses photographs for trade magazines, direct mail, catalogs, posters and newspapers. General subject matter and people. Reviews stock photos of models.
Audiovisual Needs: Uses slides.
Specs: Uses b&w and color prints; no format preference.
First Contact & Terms: Query with list of stock photo subjects. Send unsolicited photos by mail for consideration. Query with samples. Keeps samples on file. Cannot return material. Reports in 1-2 weeks. NPI. Pays on acceptance. Buys first rights. Model/property release preferred. Credit line given.
Tips: Wants to see "clean shots of models in current styles" in samples. Observes that "business is slowing down."

■**MOTIVATION MEDIA, INC.**, 1245 Milwaukee Ave., Glenview IL 60025. (708)297-4740. FAX: (708)297-6829. AV firm. Vice President of Producer Services: Peter Tanke. Estab. 1969. Types of clients: industrial, financial, fashion, retail, medical, "all kinds."
Subject Needs: Works with 1-3 freelancers per month. Uses photos for new product announcements, corporate use.
Audiovisual Needs: Typically uses slides, film and videotape of all specifications.
First Contact & Terms: Interested in receiving work from newer, lesser-known photographers. Provide resume to be kept on file for possible future assignments. Arrange interview to show portfolio. Pays $400-700/day, or per job "as negotiated." Buys one-time rights normally; negotiable. Pays on receipt of invoice. Model and/or property release required. Reports in 1 month. No credit given. SASE.
Tips: Interested in photos of people and products. "Be negotiable and multi-talented, versatile, able to photograph in all formats and adapt to many lighting situations; be willing to travel. We see a trend toward more emphasis on people photography."

OMNI ENTERPRISES, INC., 430 W. Roosevelt Rd., Wheaton IL 60187. (708)653-8200. FAX: (708)653-8218. Contact: Steve Jacobs. Ad agency and consultants. Estab. 1962. Uses photos for consumer and trade magazines, direct mail, newspapers and P-O-P displays. Types of clients: business, industrial, area development, economic development and financial. Examples of recent projects: employee orientation campaign, Overton Gear & Tool Corp. (AV and trade ads); Perfection Equip. Co. (capabilities brochure); technical/medical brochures, Med-Tek Corp (direct mail).
Needs: Needs photos of "all varieties—industrial and machine products and human interest." Works with an average of 3 freelance photographers/month on assignment only. Buys 100 photos annually. Prefers to see composites in b&w and color.
Specs: Uses 5×7 and 8×10 b&w glossy prints. Also uses 8×10 color glossy prints, 2¼×2¼, 4×5 and 8×10 transparencies.
First Contact & Terms: Provide resume, flyer, business card, brochure, composites and list of equipment to be kept on file for possible future assignments. Call for an appointment. Buys one-time, second (reprint) rights or all rights. Model release required. Pays $50-500/b&w photo; $100-750/color photo; $50-150/hour; $400-1,500/day. SASE.
Tips: In portfolio or samples, wants to see "creative composition; technical abilities, i.e., lighting, color balance, focus and consistency of quality. We need to see samples and have an idea of rates. Because we are loyal to present suppliers, it sometimes takes up to 6 months or longer before we begin working with a new photographer."

■**VIDEO I-D, INC.**, 105 Muller Rd., Washington IL 61571. (309)444-4323. President: Sam B. Wagner. Types of clients: health, education, industry, cable and broadcast.
Needs: Works with 5 freelance photographers/month to shoot slide sets, multimedia productions, films amd videotapes. Subjects "vary from commercial to industrial—always high quality."
Specs: Uses 35mm transparencies; 16mm film; U-matic ¾" and 1" videotape.
First Contact & Terms: Provide resume, business card, self-promotion piece or tearsheets to be kept on file for possible future assignments; "also send video sample reel." Works with freelancers on assignment only, "somewhat" interested in stock photos/footage. SASE. Reports in 3 weeks. Pays $8-25/hour; $65-250/day. Pays on acceptance. Buys all rights. Model release required. Credit line sometimes given.
Tips: Sample reel—indicate goal for specific pieces. "Show good lighting and visualization skills. Be willing to learn. Show me you can communicate what I need to hear — and willingness to put out effort to get top quality."

Chicago

■**AGS & R COMMUNICATIONS**, 314 W. Superior, Chicago IL 60010. (312)649-4500. Senior Vice President: Gary J. Ballenger. Types of clients: advertising, Fortune 1000 and Fortune 500 corporate and industrial companies.
Needs: Works with freelance photographers monthly depending on work load. Uses photographers for original slide and multimedia productions. Subjects include: portrait, table top, talent, 35mm pin-registered photo sequences and 4×5 and 8×10 color transparencies, and product shots.
Specs: Uses 5×7 and 8×10 b&w and color prints; 35mm, 2¼×2¼, 4×5 or 8×10 transparencies; 16mm or 35mm film; VHS, Beta, U-matic ¾", 1" videotape.
First Contact & Terms: Provide resume, business card, self-promotion piece or tearsheets to be kept on file for possible future assignments. "Do not call, please." Works with freelancers by assignment only; interested in stock photos/footage. SASE. Reports in 1-2 weeks. Pays 30 days after completion

from invoice. Payment negotiable; $275-600/day. Model release required. Credit line sometimes given.
Tips: "You must have good people skills, be dependable and have strong skills in slide market."

■**DARBY MEDIA GROUP,** 4015 N. Rockwell St., Chicago IL 60618. (312)583-5090. Production Manager: Dennis Cyrier. Types of clients: corporate and agency.
Needs: Uses photographers for filmstrips, slide sets, multimedia productions, videotapes, print and publication uses.
First Contact & Terms: Provide resume, business card, self-promotion piece or tearsheets to be kept on file for possible future assignments. Works on assignment only; interested in stock photos/footage. NPI. Payment is made to freelancers net 30 days. Captions preferred; model release required.

■**DAVIS HARRISON ADVERTISING,** Suite 1400, 333 N. Michigan Ave., Chicago IL 60601. (312)332-0808. FAX: (312)332-4260. Ad agency. Creative Supervisor: Bob Dion. Estab. 1982. Types of clients: agricultural, consumer, retail and business-to-business. Examples of recent projects: "Armorcote" for Cook Composites (advertisement); "Rawhide Dog Chews" for Pet-Ag (catalog); and "Florish" for Abbott (brochure).
Needs: Works with 2 freelance photographers/month. Uses photographs for consumer and trade magazines, direct mail, posters and collateral. General subject matter. Reviews stock photos; subject varies according to need.
Audiovisual Needs: Uses slides and videotape.
Specs: Uses 35mm, 2¼×2¼, 4×5, 8×10 transparencies and ¾" Betacam videotape.
First Contact & Terms: Interested in receiving work from newer, lesser-known photographers. Arrange personal interview to show portfolio. Send unsolicited photos by mail for consideration. Works on assignment only. Keeps samples on file. Cannot return material. Reports in 1 month. Pays $80-350/b&w photo; $250-450/color photo; $600-1,700/day. Pays on receipt of invoice. Buys exclusive product rights; rights negotiable. Model and property releases required. Credit line not given.
Tips: "Send great samples periodically, then call."

DRUCILLA HANDY CO., #505, 333 N. Michigan Ave., Chicago IL 60601. (312)704-0040. PR firm. Executive Vice President: Susanne Wren. Handles public relations campaigns for home furnishings and products, retail, building products, other consumer products and services.
Needs: Works with one freelancer every two months. Uses photos for newspapers.
Specs: Uses 2¼×2¼ and 4×5 transparencies.
First Contact and Terms: Query with resume of credits. Works on assignment only. Does not return unsolicited material. Reports in 2 weeks. Pays $500-1,200/day "depending on assignment from client." Pays on receipt of invoice. Buys all rights. Model release and photo captions preferred. Credit line given sometimes, depending on magazine.
Tips: "Query first; mention other public relations firms and clients that you have worked with."

*****GARFIELD-LINN & COMPANY,** 142 E. Ontario Ave., Chicago IL 60611. (312)943-1900. Executive Art Director: Ralph Woods. Ad agency. Types of clients: Serves a "wide variety" of accounts; client list provided upon request.
Needs: Number of freelance photographers used varies. Works on assignment only. Uses photographs for billboards, consumer and trade magazines, direct mail, brochures, catalogs and posters.
First Contact & Terms: Arrange interview to show portfolio and query with samples. NPI. Payment is by the project; negotiates according to client's budget.

KEROFF & ROSENBERG ADVERTISING, 444 N. Wabash Ave., Chicago IL 60611. (312)321-9000. Ad agency. Art Directors: Bernie Kanuza and Norbert Shimkus. Estab. 1972. Types of clients: fashion, consumer products, banking, real estate, hotels. Examples of ad campaigns: Prudential (corporate campaign for real estate division); Marriott Hotels (ad and collateral); Centel Cellular (car phone ad campaign); Urban Shopping Centers (fashion ads for major centers in Chicago and Boston).
Needs: Uses 5 freelance photographers/month. Uses photographers for consumer magazines, trade magazines, posters and newspapers. Interested in reviewing stock photos/film or video footage (nothing specific at this time).

 The asterisk before a listing indicates that the market is new in this edition. New markets are often the most receptive to freelance submissions.

Specs: Uses b&w and color prints; 2¼×2¼, 4×5 transparencies.

First Contact & Terms: Query with resume of credits, or list of stock photo subjects; send unsolicited photos by mail for consideration; provide resume, business card, brochure, flyer or tearsheets to be kept on file for possible future assignments. Works with freelancers on assignment basis only. Reports in 1 month. Pays $200-1,000/day; pays by the project (including model, film etc.). Pays 30 to 60 days after invoice. Buys all rights. Model release required; photo captions preferred. Credit line given sometimes, depending on uniqueness of material.

Tips: Looks for "fashion (people, models and clothes), real estate (interiors and exteriors), table-top product shots." Freelancers wanting to break in with the company should "start with one project on a project basis, if work is good we would continue to use. We tend to work with same sources to provide consistency for quality; we work with different people at different budget levels." Trends in ad photography include "more lifestyle, less posed shots for fashion but with good attitude. All photography must be simple and graphic."

■**LADD YOUNG & LARAMORE,** 200 W. Superior, Chicago IL 60610. (312)335-1100. FAX: (312)335-0111. Ad agency. President: Robert Ladd. Estab. 1957. Types of clients include industrial, financial, food and healthcare. Examples of recent campaigns: "100th Anniversary DM," Union Tank Car Co. (12 calendars); "Tri-Tips Introduction," E.W. Kneip (packaging ads); and "Food Editors Campaign," NutraSweet (collateral).

Needs: Works with 3 freelance photographers/month. Uses photographs for consumer, trade magazines, direct mail, posters, newspapers, audiovisual and packaging. Reviews stock photos of transportation subjects.

Audiovisual Needs: Uses slides and film.

Specs: Uses 4×5 color and b&w prints; also ½" and ¾" videotape.

First Contact & Terms: Arrange personal interview to show portfolio; submit portfolio for review; provide resume, business card, brochure, flyer or tearsheets to be kept on file for possible future assignments. Works with freelancers on assignment only. Keeps samples on file. SASE. Reports in 3 weeks. Pays $1,000-3,000/day. Pays on receipt of invoice. Buys one-time and all rights; negotiable. Model and/or property release required usually for technical subjects. Credit line given sometimes, for collateral work mostly.

Tips: Wants to see "use of natural light, and natural people" in samples.

QUALLY & COMPANY, INC., Suite 2502, 30 E. Huron, Chicago IL 60611. (312)944-0237. Ad agency and graphic design firm. Creative Director: Robert Qually. Types of clients: finance, package goods and business-to-business.

Needs: Uses 4-5 freelance photographers/month. Uses photographers for billboards, consumer and trade magazines, direct mail, P-O-P displays, posters and newspapers. "Subject matter varies, but is always a 'quality image' regardless of what it portrays."

Specs: Uses b&w and color prints; 35mm, 2¼×2¼, 4×5 and 8×10 transparencies.

First Contact & Terms: Query with samples or submit portfolio for review. Provide resume, business card, brochure, flyer or tearsheets to be kept on file for possible future assignments. Works with local freelance photographers on assignment only. Does not return unsolicited material. Reports in 2 weeks. NPI. Payment depends on circumstances. Pays on acceptance or net 45 days. Rights purchased depend on circumstances. Model release required. Credit lines sometimes given, depending on client's cooperation.

WUNDERMAN KATO JOHNSON CHICAGO, 1 S. Wacker Dr., Chicago IL 60601. (312)329-1105. Senior Art Director: Steve Wheeler. Creative Director: Alan Blose. Ad agency. Types of clients: consumer, business-to-business, retail, industry, travel, etc.

Needs: Works with 2-5 photographers/month. Uses photos for direct mail, brochures, consumer and trade print, sales promotion and TV.

First Contact & Terms: Call for appointment to show portfolio. NPI; payment based on client's budget and the job. Reports as needed.

Tips: Looks for b&w prints, transparencies and printed samples; show style.

Indiana

■**CALDWELL-VAN RIPER,** 1314 N. Meridian, Indianapolis IN 46202. (317)632-6501. Executive Creative Directors: Bryan Hadlock, John Bugg. Ad agency. Uses photos for billboards, consumer and trade magazines, direct mail, foreign media, newspapers, P-O-P displays, radio and TV. Serves all types of clients. Works with 2-5 freelance photographers/month on assignment only basis. Provide brochure or samples to be kept on file for future assignments.

Specs: Uses b&w photos and color transparencies. Uses filmmakers for TV spots, corporate films and documentary films.
First Contact & Terms: Arrange a personal interview to show portfolio or submit portfolio for review. SASE. Reports in 1 week. Pays $200-2,000/hour, day and job. Negotiates payment based on client's budget. Model release required. Buys all rights.

■**KELLER CRESCENT COMPANY,** 1100 E. Louisiana, Evansville IN 47701. (812)426-7551 or (812)464-2461. Manager Still Photography: Cal Barrett. Ad agency, PR and AV firm. Uses billboards, consumer and trade magazines, direct mail, newspapers, P-O-P displays, radio and TV. Serves industrial, consumer, finance, food, auto parts, dairy products clients. Types of clients: Old National Bank, Community Coffee and Eureka Vac's.
Needs: Works with 2-3 freelance photographers/month on assignment only basis.
Specs: Uses 8×10 b&w prints; 35mm, 4×5 and 8×10 transparencies.
First Contact & Terms: Query with resume of credits, list of stock photo subjects; send material by mail for consideration. Provide business card, tearsheets and brochure to be kept on file for possible future assignments.Prefers to see printed samples, transparencies and prints. Does not return unsolicited material. Pays $200-2,500/job; negotiates payment based on client's budget, amount of creativity required from photographer and photographer's previous experience/reputation. Buys all rights. Model release required.

■**OMNI COMMUNICATIONS,** 655 W. Carmel Dr., Carmel IN 46032. (317)844-6664. Senior President: Winston Long. AV firm. Types of clients: industrial, corporate, educational, governmental and medical.
Needs: Works with 6-12 freelance photographers/month. Uses photographers for AV presentations. Subject matter varies. Also works with freelance filmmakers to produce training films and commercials.
Specs: Uses b&w and color prints; 35mm transparencies; 16mm and 35mm film and videotape.
First Contact & Terms: Provide resume, business card, brochure, flyer or tearsheets to be kept on file for possible future assignments. Works with freelance photographers on assignment basis only. Does not return unsolicited material. NPI. Pays on acceptance. Buys all rights "on most work; will purchase one-time use on some projects." Model release required. Credit line given "sometimes, as specified in production agreement with client."

Iowa

*■**PHOENIX ADVERTISING CO.,** W. Delta Park, Hwy. 18 W., Clear Lake IA 50428. (515)357-9999. FAX: (515)357-5364. Ad agency. Estab. 1986. Types of clients: industrial, financial and consumer. Examples of recent projects: "Western Tough," Bridon (print/outdoor/collateral); "Blockbuster," Video News Network (direct mail, print); and "Blue Jeans," Clear Lake Bank & Trust (TV/print/newspaper).
Needs: Works with 2-3 photographers or videographers/month. Uses photos for billboards, consumer and trade magazines, direct mail, P-O-P displays, catalogs, posters, newspapers, signage, audiovisual uses. Subjects include: people/products. Reviews stock photos and/or video.
Audiovisual Needs: Uses slides and videotape.
Specs: Uses 8×10 color and b&w prints; 35mm, 2¼×2¼, 4×5, 8×10 transparencies; ½" or ¾" videotape.
First Contact & Terms: Contact through rep. Submit portfolio for review. Provide resume, business card, brochure, flyer or tearsheets to be kept on file for possible future assignments. Works on assignment only. Keeps samples on file. SASE. Reports in 3 weeks. Pays $1,000-10,000/day. Pays on receipt of invoice. Buys first rights, one-time rights, all rights and others; negotiable. Model/property release required. Credit line sometimes given; no conditions specified.

Kansas

MARKETAIDE, INC., P.O. Box 500, Salina KS 67402. (913)825-7161. Production Manager: Eric Lamer. Creative Director: Ted Hale. Ad agency. Uses all media. Serves industrial, retail, financial, agribusiness and manufacturing clients.

Needs: Needs photos of banks, agricultural equipment, agricultural dealers, custom applicators and general agricultural subjects.
First Contact & Terms: Call to arrange an appointment. Provide resume and tearsheets to be kept on file for possible future assignments. Reports in 3 weeks. SASE. Buys all rights. "We generally work on a day rate ranging from $200-1,000/day." Pays within 30 days of invoice.
Tips: Photographers should have "a good range of equipment and lighting, good light equipment portability, high quality darkroom work for b&w, a wide range of subjects in portfolio with examples of processing capabilities." Prefers to see "set-up shots, lighting, people, heavy equipment, interiors, industrial and manufacturing" in a portfolio. Prefers to see "8 × 10 minimum size on prints, or 35mm transparencies, preferably unretouched" as samples.

PAT PATON PUBLIC RELATIONS/PATON & ASSOCIATES, INC., P.O. Box 7350, Leawood KS 66207. (913)491-4000. Contact: N.E. (Pat) Paton, Jr. Ad agency. Estab. 1956. Clients: medical, financial, home furnishing, professional associations, vacations resorts.
Needs: Works on assignment only. Uses freelancers for billboards, consumer and trade magazines, direct mail, newspapers, P-O-P displays and TV.
First Contact & Terms: Call for personal appointment to show portfolio. NPI. Payment negotiable according to amount of creativity required from photographer.

Kentucky

■**BARNEY MILLERS INC.,** 232 E. Main St., Lexington KY 40507. (606)252-2216. FAX: (606)253-1115. Chairman: Harry Miller. Estab. 1922.
Needs: Works with 3-4 freelance photographers/month. Uses photographers for video transfer, editing and titling. Types of clients: retail, legal and government. Examples of recent projects: Bluegrass AAA (internal training); Bank One (internal training); and Renfro Valley (television promotion).
Specs: Uses b&w and color prints; 35mm transparencies; 8mm, super 8, 16mm and 35mm film.
First Contact & Terms: Arrange a personal interview to show portfolio or submit portfolio by mail. Provide resume, business card, self-promotion piece or tearsheets to be kept on file for possible future assignments. Works with local freelancers only; interested in stock photos/footage. SASE. Reports in 1 week. Pays $35-200/hour. Pays on acceptance. Captions preferred. Credit line given if desired.

*■**KINETIC CORPORATION,** 240 Distillery Commons, Louisville KY 40206. (502)583-1679. FAX: (502)583-1104. Director of Creative Service: Stephen Metzger. Estab. 1968. Types of clients: industrial, financial, fashion, retail and food.
Needs: Works with freelance photographers and/or videographers as needed. Uses photos for audiovisual and print. Subjects include: location photography.
Audiovisual Needs: Uses photos for slides and videotape.
Specs: Uses varied sizes and finishes color and b&w prints; 35mm, 2¼ × 2¼, 4 × 5, 8 × 10 transparencies; and ¾" Beta SP videotape.
First Contact & Terms: Provide resume, business card, brochure, flyer or tearsheets to be kept on file for possible future assignments. Works with local freelancers only. Keeps samples on file. SASE. Reports only when interested. Pays $100-200/hour; $750-1,000/day. Pays within 30 days. Buys all rights. Model and/or property release required.

Louisiana

RICHARD SACKETT EXECUTIVE CONSULTANTS, Suite 3400, 101 Howard Ave., New Orleans LA 70113. (504)522-4040. Ad agency. Creative Director: Matt Spisak. Types of clients: industrial, optical, retail, real estate, hotel, shopping center management, marine. Client list free with SASE.
Needs: Works with 3 photographers/month. Uses photographers for billboards, consumer and trade magazines, direct mail, P-O-P displays, posters, newspapers. Subject matter includes merchandise, places, scenery of the city, scenery of the sites of construction, mood photos and food.
Specs: Uses 35mm, 4 × 5 and 8 × 10 transparencies.
First Contact & Terms: Arrange a personal interview to show portfolio; send unsolicited photos by mail for consideration. Works with freelance photographers on an assignment basis only. SASE. Reports in 1 week. Pays $600-1,000/day and $3,000-40,000/job. Pays on publication or on receipt of

invoice. Buys all rights. Model release required. Credit line given when appropriate.

Maryland

■BARRETT ADVERTISING, Suite 300, Thanner Building, 1615 York Rd., Lutherville MD 21093. (301)828-8686. FAX: (301)296-9359. Ad agency. President: Rich Barrett. Estab. 1969. Types of clients: business-to-business for high-tech and industrial clients. Example of ad campaign: The Racal Corporation, (Reaching Beyond Today's Standards).
Needs: Uses approximately 5-8 freelance photographers/month for billboards, trade magazines, direct mail, P-O-P displays, catalogs, posters, newspapers and trade shows. Interested in reviewing stock photos of industrial subjects.
Specs: Uses b&w and color prints, any size or format; 35mm, 2¼ × 2¼, 4 × 5 and 8 × 10 transparencies; also film. "Call for specs on film and videotape."
First Contact & Terms: Arrange a personal interview to show portfolio, query with list of stock photo subjects; provide resume, business card, brochure, flyer or tearsheets to be kept on file for possible future assignments. Works with freelancers on an assignment basis only. Does not return unsolicited material. Reports in 3 weeks. NPI. Pays on receipt of invoice. Buys one-time rights. Model release required. Credit line given "depending on price."

Massachusetts

BUYER ADVERTISING AGENCY, INC., (formerly Elbert Advertising Agency, Inc.), 85 Wells Ave., Newton MA 02159. (617)969-4646. Production Manager: Gary Taitz. Ad agency. Uses all media. Serves clients in fashion and industry.
Needs: Needs photos of food, fashion and industry; and candid photos. Buys up to 600 photos/year.
First Contact & Terms: Call to arrange an appointment, submit portfolio, or send mailer. Reports in 1 week. SASE. Pays $25 minimum/hour.
Specs: Uses 5 × 7, 8 × 10 semigloss b&w prints; contact sheet OK. Also uses color prints; and 35mm, 2¼ × 2¼, 4 × 5 and 11 × 14 transparencies.

*■CRAMER PRODUCTION CENTER, 355 Wood Rd., Braintree MA 02184. (617)849-3350. FAX: (617)849-6165. Film/video production company. Operations Manager: Maura MacMillan. Estab. 1982. Types of clients: industrial, financial, fashion, retail and food. Examples of recent projects: "What's a Lechmere," Lechmere (video wall/point-of-purchase); "Walktoberfest," National Diabetes (PSA broadcast); and Pepsi/Red Sox campaign, Cuneo Sullivan Dolabany (broadcast spot).
Audiovisual Needs: Works with 3-8 freelance filmmakers and/or videographers/month for P-O-P displays and audiovisual. Subjects include: industrial to broadcast/machines to people. Reviews stock film or video footage. Uses film and videotape.
First Contact & Terms: Send demo of work, ¾" or VHS videotape. Query with resume of credits. Works on assignment only. Keeps samples on file. Reports in 1 month. Pays $175-560/day, depending on job and level of expertise needed. Pays 30 days from receipt of invoice. Buys all rights. Model/property release required. Credit line sometimes given, depending on how the program is used.
Tips: Looks for experience in commercial video production. "Don't be discouraged if you don't get an immediate response. When we are have a need, we'll call you."

*FOREMOST FILMS & VIDEO, INC., 7 Regency Dr., Holliston MA 01746. (508)429-8046. FAX: (508)429-3848. Video production/post production multi-media company. President: David Fox. Estab. 1983. Types of clients: industrial and corporate. Examples of recent projects: Health Awareness Video, Marlboro Hospital; State Mutual Speakers, State Mutual Companies; and Metrowest Momentum, Metrowest Chamber of Commerce.
Needs: Works with 2-4 freelance photographers/videographers/month. Varied subjects. Reviews area footage.
Audiovisual Needs: Typically uses slides and videotape.
Specs: Uses 35mm transparencies, slides and ½", SVHS and all formats and standards of videotape.
First Contact & Terms: Arrange personal interview to show portfolio; provide resume, business card, brochure, flyer or tearsheets to be kept on file for possible future assignments. Works on assignment only. Keeps samples on file. Cannot return material. Reports in 1 month. NPI; payment depends on project, person's experience to match project—fee is negotiated. Pays within 30 days. Buys all rights;

negotiable. Model/property release required. Credit line sometimes given depending on situation and client.
Tips: Looks for style, abilities, quality and commitment and availability in reviewing freelancer's work. "We are expanding our commercial photography and audiovisual areas, including multimedia. We see a trend toward inclusion of photos with computer graphics and video. We tend to have more need in springtime and fall, than other times of the year. We're very diversified in our services—projects come along and we use people on an as-need basis."

MDK, 800 Statler Bldg., Boston MA 02116. (617)482-0309. Ad agency. Production Manager: Mike Stankiewiz.
Needs: Works with 2-4 freelance photographers/month. Uses photographers for billboards, consumer and trade magazines, direct mail, P-O-P displays, brochures, catalogs, posters, signage, newspapers, AV presentations, packaging, and press releases. Subject needs "too varied to list one particular type. About 70% industrial, 25% consumer/retail, 5% PR." Also works with freelance filmmakers to produce TV commercials, industrial films, P-O-P film loops.
Specs: Uses 8 × 10 RC and glossy b&w prints; 4 × 5, 8 × 10 color transparencies for studio work; 16mm, 35mm and videotape film.
First Contact & Terms: Arrange a personal interview to show portfolio. Works with freelance photographers on assignment basis only. Pays $60-150/hour, $600-3,000/day or $100-2,500/photo. Pays on acceptance. Buys all rights. Model release required. Credit line "usually not" given.
Tips: In a portfolio, prefers to see "cross section of types of photography that the photographer feels he/she handles most easily. Photographers are matched by their strong points to each assignment. Keep agency updated as to new projects."

MILLER COMMUNICATIONS, INC., Dept. PM, 607 Boylston, Copley Sq., Boston MA 02116. (617)536-0470. Supervisor: Nancy Milka. PR firm. Handles high technology/computer accounts, computer communication. Photos used in press kits, consumer and trade magazines.
Needs: Most interested in editorial type: photographs, head shots, creative product shots, user shots, equipment, and press conference coverage.
Specs: Uses contact sheet; also 2¼ × 2¼ transparencies or color contact sheet and negatives.
First Contact & Terms: Commissions 10 photographers/year. Pays $75 minimum/half day. Buys all rights. Model release preferred.
Tips: "Select a product the agency is representing and make up a portfolio showing this particular product from the simplest photography to the most sophisticated image-builder. Photographers we need must be thinkers, philosophers, not impulsive types who take 600 slides from which we can select 1 or 2 good pictures."

■**TR PRODUCTIONS,** 1031 Commonwealth Ave., Boston MA 02215. (617)783-0200. Executive Vice President: Ross P. Benjamin. Types of clients: industrial, commercial and educational.
Needs: Works with 1-2 freelance photographers/month. Uses photographers for slide sets and multimedia productions. Subjects include: people shots, manufacturing/sales and facilities.
Specs: Uses 35mm transparencies.
First Contact & Terms: Provide resume, business card, self-promotion piece or tearsheets to be kept on file for possible future assignments. Works with local freelancers by assignment only; interested in stock photos/footage. Does not return unsolicited material. Reports "when needed." Pays $500-1,000/day. Pays "14 days after acceptance." Buys all AV rights.

Michigan

■**CREATIVE HOUSE ADVERTISING, INC.,** Suite 301, 30777 Northwestern Hwy., Farmington Hills MI 48334. (313)737-7077. Sr. Vice President/Executive Creative Director: Robert G. Washburn. Ad agency. Uses photos for brochures, catalogs, annual reports, billboards, consumer and trade magazines, direct mail, newspapers, P-O-P displays, radio and TV. Serves clients in retailing, industry, finance and commercial products.
Needs: Works with 4-5 freelance photographers/year on assignment only. Uses b&w and color prints, and transparencies. Also produces TV commercials (35mm and 16mm film) and demo film to industry. Does not pay royalties. Buys all rights. Model release required.
First Contact & Terms: Arrange personal interview to show portfolio; query with resume of credits, samples, or list of stock photo subjects; submit portfolio for review ("Include your specialty and show your range of versatility"); or send material by mail for consideration. Provide resume, business card, brochure, flyer and anything to indicate the type and quality of photos to be kept on file for future assignments. Local freelancers preferred. SASE. Reports in 2 weeks. Pays $100-200/hour or $800-

1,600/day; negotiates payment based on client's budget and photographer's previous experience/reputation. Pays in 1-3 months, depending on the job.

DALLAS C. DORT AND CO., 900 Northbank Center, Flint MI 48502. (313)238-4677. FAX: (313)238-5671. Creative Director: Gretchen Tambellini. Estab. 1972. Ad agency. Uses all media except foreign. Serves food, health care, retail, government, travel, automotive, and publishing clients. Works on assignment only, approximately 10 times/year.
Needs: Uses b&w prints. Also uses color prints and film. Specifications for each per assignment.
First Contact & Terms: Submit portfolio. Send resume and samples to be kept on file for possible future assignments. SASE. Reports in 2 weeks. NPI. Buys all rights. "We outline the job to the photographer, he quotes on the job and it is billed accordingly."

EXPOtacular INDUSTRIES LTD., #546, 29555 Northwestern Hwy., Southfield MI 48034. (313)355-0189. FAX: (313)355-0189. Display builder. President: Bob Molner. Types of clients: industrial, community service, charitable, environmental, institutional, religious and political.
Needs: Uses up to 3 freelancers per month. Uses photographers for displays for trade shows, expositions, etc. Subjects include human interest, industrial processing.
Specs: Uses 16 × 20 and larger matte b&w or color prints; 35mm, 2¼ × 2¼, 4 × 5 and 8 × 10 transparencies.
First Contact & Terms: Query with list of available subject matter. Works with freelancers on an assignment basis only. SASE. Reports in 1-2 weeks. Pays $100/color photo; $50/b&w photo; other rates subject to negotiation. Pays on acceptance or upon approval by exhibitor. Usually buys all rights, but other rights or usage fees negotiable. Model release required; photo captions preferred. Credit line given sometimes, depending on negotiation.
Tips: In freelancer's samples, looks for "human interest and involvement, dramatic, eye-catching potential, and pertinence to exhibitors display and selling needs." To contact, "send name, address, phone, and subjects specialty/specialties with non-returnable printed sample if available. Otherwise hold sample for our request."

■PHOTO COMMUNICATION SERVICES, INC., P.O. Box 508, Acme MI 49610. (616)938-5694. Commercial/Illustrative and AV firm. President: M'Lynn Hartwell Jackson. Estab. 1970. Types of clients: commercial/industrial, fashion, food, general, human interest. Examples of recent projects: Harper & Row, internal corporate AV communications; Zondervan Family Bookstores, a semiannual AV production for vendor recruitment/sales promotion; and General Electric Corp.
Needs: Works with variable number of freelance photographers/month. Uses photos for catalogs, P-O-P displays, AV presentations, trade magazines and brochures. Photographers used for a "large variety of subjects." Sometimes works with freelance filmmakers.
Audiovisual Needs: Primarily needs 35mm slides for industrial multi-image; also video and some film.
Specs: Uses 8 × 10 gloss and semigloss b&w and color prints (or larger); 35mm, 2¼ × 2¼, 4 × 5 and 8 × 10 transparencies; 16mm film; VHS/SVHS and ¾″ videotape.
First Contact & Terms: Query with resume of credits, samples or list of stock photo subjects. Works with freelance photographers on assignment basis only. SASE. Reports in 1 month. Pays $25-150/hour, $100-1,000/day, or private negotiation. Pays 30 days from acceptance. Rights negotiated. Model release required. Credit line given "whenever possible."
Tips: Looks for professionalism in portfolio or demos. "Be professional and to the point. If I see something I can use I will make an appointment to discuss the project in detail. We also have a library of stock photography and can be reached on the (Compuserve 76360, 113) or MCI mail (ID 247-7996) via your computer or Western Union Easylink (62909611) or (616)676-2429, Photo Communication Services private Electronic Mail System." Foresees growth of video, especially 'video walls,' but slowdown of multi-image.

ROSS ROY, INC., 100 Bloomfield Hills Parkway, Bloomfield Hills MI 48304. (313)433-6000. Ad agency. Contact: Art Director. Types of clients: Chrysler, K-Mart, FTD, Ameritech, La-Z-Boy, State of Michigan.
Needs: Uses freelance photographers for billboards, consumer and trade magazines, P-O-P displays, catalogs, posters, and newspapers. Subjects include retail, corporate, fashion, automotive, product.
Specs: Uses 8 × 10, 11 × 14 matte b&w prints; "all formats" transparencies.
First Contact & Terms: Arrange a personal interview to show portfolio; provide resume, business card, brochure, flyer or tearsheets to be kept on file for possible future assignments. Works with freelance photographers on assignment only. Does not return unsolicited material. Pays $250-1,500/ b&w photo; $300-2,500/color photo; $750-2,000/day. Pays on receipt of invoice. Buys all rights. Model release required.

Tips: Prefers to see lighting, design and a sense of style and individuality. Contact Jean Oliveri for list of art directors; contact art directors individually for interview, or send tearsheets, flyers, etc. if out-of-town. "We use photography extensively, but tend to use mostly local for advertising; out-of-town (location) for automotive. Be persistent in calling to set up the initial contact, but don't be pesky. Work looks best as a combination of laminated tearsheets and mounted transparencies."

■**SOUNDLIGHT PRODUCTIONS**, 1915 Webster, Birmingham MI 48009. (313)642-3502. FAX: (313)642-3502. Contact: Terry Keth Luke. Estab. 1972. Types of clients: corporations, industrial, businesses, training institutions, astrological and spiritual workshops and books, and fashion magazines. Examples of productions: "Heavytruck Computer Stories," Rockwell International; and "What Can It Do?" Arcade Machine.
Needs: Works with 2-3 freelance photographers/month. Subjects include city people in activities, business activities, industrial, scenics landscapes, animals, travel sites and activities, dance and models (glamour and nude). Reviews stock photos, film or video.
Audiovisual Needs: Uses freelance photographers for slide sets, multimedia productions and videotapes.
Specs: Uses 8×10 b&w prints, 5×7 and 8×10 glossy color prints, 35mm color slides; VHS, U-matic ¼" and SVHS videotape.
First Contact & Terms: Query with resume. Send stock photo list. Provide resume, slides, business card, self-promotion piece or tearsheets to be kept on file for possible future assignments. Works on assignment only. May not return unsolicited material. Reports in 2 weeks. Pays $5-100/b&w and color photo; $10-100/hour; $50-750/day; $2,000 maximum/job; sometimes also pays in "trades." Pays on publication. Buys one-time rights and various negotiable rights; depends on use. Model release required, for models and advertising people. Captions preferred; include "who, what, where." Credit line sometimes given.
Tips: In portfolios or demos, looks for "unique lighting, style, emotional involvement; beautiful, artistic viewpoint." Sees trend toward "more use of video, and manipulated computer images." To break into AV work, "join AV organizations, shoot stills of productions, volunteer your help, etc.".

■**WALLER, COOK & MISAMORE ADVERTISING & PUBLIC RELATIONS**, Suite 100, 3001 Orchard Vista Dr. SE, Grand Rapids MI 49456. (616)940-0900. Ad agency. Art Director: Scott Scheerhorn. Types of clients: industrial, business-to-business. Client list free with SASE.
Needs: Works with 4-5 freelance photographers/month. Uses photographers for trade magazines, direct mail, P-O-P displays, catalogs, posters, AV presentations, case history articles. Subjects include products, illustrative, facilities, etc.
Specs: Uses all sizes b&w and color prints; 35mm, 2¼×2¼, 4×5, 8×10 transparencies, "all depending on situation."
First Contact & Terms: Query with resume of credits and samples; provide resume, business card, brochure, flyer or tearsheets to be kept on file for possible future assignments. Works with freelance photographers on assignment only. Does not return unsolicited material. Reports in 1 week. Pays $50-200/hour; $300-1,500/day; $150/b&w photo; $600/color photo. Pays within 30 days. Buys all rights. Model release required.
Tips: Prefers to see industrial, products. "Please send letter, credentials, and samples printed if available."

Minnesota

*■**AMERICAN INTERNATIONAL MEETING MAKERS CORP. (AIMM)**, Suite 201, 2901 Metro Dr., Minneapolis MN 55425. (800)356-2466. FAX: (612)854-0547. AV firm. Director of Reservation Operations: Gary Duncan. Estab. 1984. Types of clients: industrial, financial, fashion, retail, food, associations and government. Examples of recent proejcts: National Hockey League (All Star game and Stanley Cup); American College Healthcare Executives (Annual Congress); and Citicorp (new identity campaign).
Needs: Works with 5-6 photographers, filmmakers and/or videographers/month. Uses photos for audiovisual. Varied subject matter.
Audiovisual Needs: Uses slides, film, videotape and audio only.
Specs: Uses 35mm transparencies, ¾" Beta videotape.
First Contact & Terms: Send unsolicited photos by mail for consideration. Provide resume, business card, brochure, flyer or tearsheets to be kept on file for possible future assignments. Works on assignment only. Keeps samples on file. SASE. Reports in 3 weeks. NPI: "payment negotiated." Buys first rights, one-time rights and all rights; negotiable. Model/property release required for human subjects, corporate logo. Photo captions preferred. Credit line sometimes given, depending on use.

Tips: Sees trends toward computer enhancement.

■BUTWIN & ASSOCIATES ADVERTISING, INC., 8700 Westmoreland Ln., Minneapolis MN 55426. (612)546-0203. Ad agency. President: Ron Butwin. Estab. 1977. Types of clients: industrial, retail, corporate.
Needs: Works with 1-2 freelance photographers/month. Uses photographers for billboards, direct mail, catalogs, newspapers, consumer magazines, P-O-P displays, posters, AV presentations, trade magazines, brochures and signage. Uses "a wide variety" of subjects and styles.
Audiovisual Needs: Works with freelance filmmakers to produce TV commercials and training films.
Specs: Uses all sizes b&w or color prints; 35mm and 2¼×2¼, 4×5 and 8×10 transparencies; 16mm film and videotape.
First Contact & Terms: Interested in receiving work from newer, lesser-known photographers. Provide resume, business card, brochure, flyer or tearsheets to be kept on file for possible future assignments. Does not return unsolicited material. NPI. Usually buys all rights. Model release required. Credit line sometimes given.

■CARMICHAEL-LYNCH, INC., 800 Hennepin Ave., Minneapolis MN 55403. (612)334-6000. Ad agency. Executive Creative Director: Jack Supple. Send info to: Cathy Dalager, Art Buyer. Types of clients: recreational vehicles, food, finance, wide variety. Client list provided on request.
Needs: Uses "maybe 8" freelance photographers/month. Uses photographers for billboards, consumer and trade magazines, direct mail, P-O-P displays, brochures, posters, newspapers, and other media as needs arise. Also works with freelance filmmakers to produce TV commercials.
Specs: Uses b&w and color prints; 35mm, 2¼×2¼, 4×5 and 8×10 transparencies; 16mm and 35mm film and videotape.
First Contact & Terms: Provide resume, business card, brochure, flyer or tearsheets to be kept on file for possible future assignments; submit portfolio for review; arrange a personal interview to show portfolio; works with freelance photographers on assignment basis only. Reports in 1 week. Pay depends on contract; $400-2,500/day; $200-2,500/job. Pays on acceptance. Buys all rights or one-time rights, "depending on agreement." Model release required.
Tips: "Be close at hand (Minneapolis, Detroit, Chicago). In a portfolio, we prefer to see the photographer's most creative work—not necessarily ads. Show only your most technically, artistically satisfying work."

*EMC PUBLISHING, 300 York Ave., St. Paul MN 55101. (612)771-1555. VP/Editorial Director: Wolfgang S. Kraft. Types of clients: teachers at secondary and university levels.
Needs: Uses photos for textbooks.
Specs: Uses 5×7 b&w prints; 35mm, 2¼×2¼ and 4×5 transparencies.
First Contact & Terms: Query with stock photo list. Works with freelancers on assignment only; interested in stock photos/footage. Does not return unsolicited material. Reports according to project. NPI. Payment depends on number of photos. Buys all rights. Captions and model releases preferred. Credit line given.
Tips: "Find out about publisher's materials and then submit list of photos available. Portfolio or samples have to fit into our publishing plans."

MARTIN-WILLIAMS ADVERTISING INC., 10 S. 5th St., Minneapolis MN 55402. (612)340-0800. FAX: (612)342-9716. Ad agency. Production Coordinator/Buyer: Lyle Studt. Estab. 1947. Types of clients: industrial, retail, fashion, finance, agricultural, business-to-business and food. Client list free with SASE.
Needs: Works with 6-12 photographers/month. Uses photos for billboards, consumer and trade magazines, direct mail, catalogs, posters and newspapers. Subject matter varies.
Specs: Uses 8×10 and larger b&w and color prints; 35mm, 2¼×2¼, 4×5 and 8×10 transparencies.
First Contact & Terms: Arrange a personal interview to show portfolio; provide resume, business card, flyer or tearsheets to be kept on file for possible future assignments. Works with freelance photographers on an assignment basis only. SASE. Reports in 2 weeks. Payment individually negotiated. Pays $500-2,000/b&w photo; $500-2,400/color photo; $100-250/hour; $1,200-2,000/day; $600-$10,000/complete job. Pays on receipt of invoice. Buys one-time rights or all rights. Model and property releases required.
Tips: Looks for "high quality work, imagination."

MEDIAWERKS, 1400 Homer Rd., Winona MN 55987. (507)454-1400. Ad agency. Creative Director: Rich Hultman. Estab. 1975. Types of clients: industrial, retail, fashion, finance and landscape.
Needs: Works with 4 freelance photographers/month for billboards, consumer and trade magazines, direct mail, P-O-P displays, catalogs, posters, signage and newspapers. Subjects include fashion, tabletop, and industrial.

Specs: Uses b&w and color prints, and transparencies; all sizes.
First Contact & Terms: Send unsolicited photos by mail for consideration. Provide resume, business card, brochure, flyer or tearsheets to be kept on file for possible future assignments. Works with freelance photographers on assignment basis only. Does not return unsolicited material. Pays $200-400/b&w photo; $400-700/color photo; $50-100/hour; $500-1,000/day. Pays on receipt of invoice. Buys exclusive product rights and one-time rights. Model release required.
Tips: Prefers to see fashion, tabletop photos, stock, industrial, outdoor environment, archival."Submit samples of best work which includes approximate costs and type of involvement."

PIERCE THOMPSON & ASSOCIATES, INC., 8100 26th Ave. S., Bloomington MN 55425. (612)854-7131. Chairman and CEO: R.P. Thompson. President: Kimberley Thompson-Benike. Types of clients: industrial, retail, financial, construction, medical, communications and insurance.
Needs: Works with 1-2 freelance photographers/month. Uses photographers for trade magazines, annual reports and publicity. Subject matter includes people, events, buildings and offices.
Specs: Uses 4×5 and 8×10 glossy b&w prints.
First Contact & Terms: Provide resume, business card, brochure, flyer or tearsheets to be kept on file for possible future assignments. Works with local freelancers on assignment basis only. Does not return unsolicited material. NPI. Payment negotiable per hour, day, job or photo. Buys all rights. Model release required; captions preferred. Credit line given "at times."
Tips: "Send me information and rates."

■**WORLD WIDE PICTURES,** 1201 Hennepin Ave., P.O. Box 59235, Minneapolis MN 55459. (612)338-3335. FAX: (612)338-3029. Film and video firm. Marketing Communications Specialist: Nancy Hagberg. Estab. 1952. We serve the religious community and many others through advertising. Example of recent production: "The Crusade Story," Billy Graham Evangelistic Association.
Needs: Works with 5-10 photographers/filmmakers/videographers/month. Uses photographers for consumer magazines, trade magazines, direct mail, P-O-P displays, catalogs, posters, newspapers and audiovisual uses. Subjects include: evangelism and pubicity shots of film actors/actresses. Reviews stock photos, film or video.
Audiovisual Needs: Slides/videotape. Uses 8×10 b&w and color prints; 35mm transparencies; ½", ¾" and 1" videotape.
First Contact & Terms: Query with resume of credits; provide resume, business card, brochure, flyer or tearsheets to be kept on file for possible future assignments. Works with freelancers on assignment only. SASE. Reports in 3 weeks. NPI. Payment varies depending on job. Buys one-time and all rights. Model release preferred. Credit line given depending on project.
Tips: Sees trend toward computer graphics.

Missouri

AARON D. CUSHMAN AND ASSOCIATES, INC., Suite 900, 7777 Bonhomme, St. Louis MO 63105. (314)725-6400. Executive Vice President/General Manager: Joseph B. McNamara. PR, marketing and sales promotion firm. Types of clients: real estate, manufacturing, travel and tourism, telecommunications, consumer products, corporate counseling.
Needs: Works with 3-5 freelance photographers/month. Uses photographers for news releases, special events photography, and various printed pieces. More news than art oriented.
First Contact & Terms: Call for appointment to show portfolio. Pays $50-100/b&w photo; $50-250/color photo; $50-100/hour; $350-750/day.
Tips: "We are using increasing amounts of architecturally oriented and consumer product-related stills."

EVERETT, BRANDT & BERNAUER, INC., 1805 Grand Ave., Kansas City MO 64108. (816)421-0000. Contact: James A. Everett. Ad agency. Types of clients: construction, finance, auto dealership, agribusiness, insurance accounts.
Needs: Works with 1-2 freelance photographers/month on assignment basis only. Uses photos in brochures, newsletters, annual reports, PR releases, AV presentations, sales literature, consumer and trade magazines. Buys 25 photos./year.
Specs: Uses 5×7 b&w and color prints; transparencies.
First Contact & Terms: Arrange a personal interview to show portfolio. Provide resume and business card to be kept on file for possible future assignments. Prefers to work with local freelancers. SASE. Reports in 1 week. NPI; negotiates payment based on client's budget and amount of creativity required from photographer. Buys all rights. Model relese required.

Tips: "We have a good working relationship with three local photographers and would rarely go outside of their expertise unless work load or other factors change the picture."

*GGH&M ADVERTISING, Suite 136, 11500 Olive Blvd., St. Louis MO 63141. (314)991-5311. FAX: (314)991-5260. Ad agency. Contact: Art Director. Estab. 1968. Types of clients: retail, fashion and finance. Client list free with SASE.
Needs: Works with 2-3 photographers/month. Uses photos for consumer and trade magazines, posters and newspapers. Subjects include products to fashion shots.
First Contact & Terms: Interested in receiving work from newer, lesser-known photographers. Query with samples and outline of experience. Provide business card or flyer to be kept on file for possible future assignments. Works with freelance photographers on assignment only. SASE. NPI. Pays by the job. Buys all rights; rights negotiable. Model and property releases required. Photo captions required.
Tips: "More responsibility rests with photographer to suggest ideas, handle props and model accessories."

GEORGE JOHNSON ADVERTISING, Suite 221, 13523 Barrett Pkwy. Dr., Ballwin MO 63021-3800. (314)822-0553. President/Creative Director: George Johnson. Ad agency. Uses all media except foreign. Types of clients: real estate, financial and social agencies.
Needs: Works with 2 freelance photographers/month on assignment only basis.
First Contact and Terms: Provide resume and flyer to be kept on file for possible future assignments. Buys 50 photos/year. Pays $10-50/hour; negotiates payment based on client's budget and amount of creativity required. Pays in 60 days. Prefers to see working prints of typical assignments and tearsheets (application). Submit material by mail for consideration.

KUPPER PARKER COMMUNICATIONS INC., (formerly Parker Group, Inc.), 6900 Delmar, St. Louis MO 63130. (314)727-4000. FAX: (314)727-3034. Advertising, public relations and direct mail firm. Creative Director: Peter A.M. Charlton; Associate Creative Directors: Mark K. Ray, Rick Riley; Senior Art Directors: Deborah Boggs, Michael Smith; Art Directors: Brenda Clark, William Tuttle, Jeff Twardoski, Anthony Patti; Graphic Designers: Lisa Taylor, John Mank. Estab. 1992. Types of clients: retail, fashion, automobile dealers, consumer, broadcast stations, health care marketing, sports and entertainment, busines-to-business sales and direct marketing.
Needs: Works with 12-16 freelance photographers/month. Uses photographers for billboards, consumer magazines, trade magazines, direct mail, P-O-P displays, catalogs, posters, signage and newspapers.
First Contact & Terms: Query with resume of credits or with list of stock photo subjects. Provide resume, business card, brochure, flyer or tearsheets to be kept on file for possible future assignments. Works on assignment only. Does not return unsolicited material. Reports in 2 weeks. Pays $50-2,500/ b&w photo; $250-5,000/color photo; $50-300/hour; $400-2,500/day. Buys one-time rights, exclusive product rights, all rights, and limited-time or limited-run usage. Pays upon receipt of client payment. Model release required; captions preferred.

■PREMIER FILM, VIDEO AND RECORDING, 3033 Locust, St. Louis MO 63103. (314)531-3555. Contact: Bob Heuermann. Types of clients: educational, social service and religious organizations.
Audiovisual Needs: Works with various number of freelance photographers/month. Uses photographers for filmstrips, slide sets, multimedia productions, films and videotapes.
Specs: Uses any size color prints; 35mm transparencies; reduction prints Super 8, 16mm, 35mm film; VHS, Beta, U-matic ¾" videotapes.
First Contact & Terms: Provide resume, business card, self-promotion piece or tearsheets to be kept on file for possible future assignments, "include letter with name, address and phone number." Works on assignment only. SASE. Reports "ASAP." Pays $2.50-250/b&w photo, $5-300/color photo, $5-16.50/ hour, $40 minimum/day and $150-1,600/job. Pays on acceptance. Buys one-time, exclusive product and all rights; flexible. Credit line sometimes given.
Tips: "Nearly 100% of our freelance photographers are St. Louis residents." Looks for clean, traditional work with "integrity of reproduction, artistry, simplicity and especially beauty. To make best impression, be clean-cut in all presentations."

The code NPI (no payment information given) appears in listings that have not given specific payment amounts.

Nebraska

■**J. GREG SMITH**, Suite 102, 1004 Farnam, Burlington on the Mall, Omaha NE 68102. (402)444-1600. Art Director: Karen Kowalski. Ad agency. Types of clients: finance, banking institutions, national and state associations, agriculture, insurance, retail, travel.
Needs: Works with 10 freelance photographers/year on assignment only basis. Uses photographers for consumer and trade magazines, brochures, catalogs and AV presentations. Special subject needs include outer space, science and forest scenes.
First Contact & Terms: Arrange interview to show portfolio. Pays $500/color photo; $60/hour; $800/day; varies/job. Buys all rights, one-time rights or others, depending on use. Looks for "people shots (with expression), scenics (well known, bright colors)."
Tips: Considers "composition, color, interest, subject and special effects when reviewing a portfolio or samples."

■**SWANSON, RUSSELL AND ASSOCIATES**, 1222 P St., Lincoln NE 68508. (402)475-5191. Executive Vice President/Creative Services: Brian Boesche. Ad agency. Types of clients: primarily industrial, financial and agricultural; client list provided on request.
Needs: Works with 10 freelance photographers/year on assignment only basis. Uses photographers for consumer and trade magazines, direct mail, brochures, catalogs, newspapers and AV presentations.
First Contact & Terms: Query first with small brochure or samples along with list of clients freelancer has done work for. NPI. Negotiates payment according to client's budget. Rights are negotiable.

Nevada

■**DAVIDSON & ASSOCIATES**, 3940 Mohigan Way, Las Vegas NV 89119. (702)871-7172. President: George Davidson. Full-service ad agency. Types of clients: beauty, construction, finance, entertainment, retailing, publishing, travel.
Needs: Photos used in brochures, newsletters, annual reports, PR releases, AV presentations, sales literature, consumer magazines and trade magazines.
First Contact & Terms: Arrange a personal interview to show portfolio, query with samples, or submit portfolio for review; provide resume, brochure and tearsheets to be kept on file for possible future assignments. Offers 150-200 assignments/year. Pays $15-50/b&w photo; $25-100/color photo; $15-50/hour; $100-400/day; $25-1,000 by the project. Pays on production. Buys all rights. Model release required.

■**TRI VIDEO TELEPRODUCTION—LAKE TAHOE**, P.O. Box 8822, Incline Village NV 89452-8822. (702)323-6868. Director: Jon Paul Davidson. Estab. 1978. Types of clients: corporate, documentary and government. Examples of recent projects: Grand Marnier Chefs Ski Race Western Regionals (publicity).
Needs: Uses 3-4 freelance photographers/year. Uses photographers and videographers for publicity photography on the set. Subjects include video documentary, educational, motivational; b&w publicity photos.
Specs: Uses 5×7 SWG finish b&w prints; ¼" U-matic videotape; 1" and Betacam.
First Contact & Terms: Interested in receiving work from newer, lesser-known photographers. Provide resume, business card, self-promotion piece or tearsheets to be kept on file for possible future assignments. Works with freelancers by assignment only. Does not return unsolicited material. Reports in 1 week. NPI. Pays by the hour and day. Pays on acceptance. Buys all rights; negotiable. Model and property releases required. Credit line given.
Tips: "We work in several cities—mostly western. We would like to know competent people for production assistance. In reviewing samples, we look for good clean composition, proper exposure—nothing exotic. We are seeing much greater video use by corporate clients. Publicity photos are always needed. Photographers interested in making the transition from film to videography should proceed with care. Composition is the same, electronics aren't!"

New Hampshire

LEGASSE ASSOCIATES, P.O. Box 99, Westminster St., Walpole NH 03608-0099. (603)756-4781. Advertising agency. Art Director: Phil Thomsen. Types of clients: industrial, real estate, business-to-business. Clients list free for SASE.
Needs: Uses photographers for consumer magazines, trade magazines, direct mail, P-O-P displays, catalogs and newspapers. Subjects include studio still life of product; location shots of real estate; stock photo/location of outdoor scenes.
Specs: Uses 8×10 and 11×14 matte or glossy finish b&w prints; 35mm, 2¼×2¼, 4×5 and 8×10 transparencies.
First Contact & Terms: Arrange a personal interview to show portfolio. Query with resume of credits, list of stock photo subjects or samples. Provide resume, business card, brochure, flyer or tearsheets to be kept on file for possible future assignments. SASE. Pays $350-750/day or /job. Pays on receipt of invoice. Buys all rights. Model release required.
Tips: Prefers to see "studio still life; dramatic lighting; metal; architectural."

■**PORRAS & LAWLOR ASSOCIATES**, 15 Lucille Ave., Salem NH 03079. (603)893-3626. FAX: (603)898-1657. Ad agency, PR and AV firm. Contact: Victoria Porras. Estab. 1980. Types of clients: industrial, educational, financial and service. Examples of recent projects: "You Can Get There from Here", MBTA; "Annual Giving", N.E. Telephone.
Needs: Works with 1-2 freelance photographers/month. Uses photographs for direct mail, catalogs, posters, signage and audiovisual uses. Subjects include: people and studio photography.
Specs: Uses all glossy and matte color and b&w prints; 35mm transparencies.
First Contact & Terms: Interested in receiving work from newer, lesser-known photographers.Query with resume of credits, list of stock photo subjects and samples; provide resume, business card, brochure, flyer or tearsheets to be kept on file for possible future assignments. Works with local freelancers, on assignment only. Pays $800-1,500/day; $200-800/color photo; $150-500/b&w photo. Pays on receipt of invoice. Buys one-time and exclusive product rights; negotiable. Model release preferred; photo captions preferred.
Tips: In sample, looks for "Product photography, people, architectural, landscape, or other depending on brochure or promotion we are working on. We don't buy photos too often. "We use photographers for product, architectural or diverse brochure needs. We buy stock photography for interior graphic projects and others—but less often." To break in with this firm, "stay in touch, because timing is essential."

■**STILLPOINT INTERNATIONAL**, P.O. Box 640, Walpole NH 03608. (603)756-9281. FAX: (603)756-9282. Publisher. Managing Editor: Charmaine Wellington. Estab. 1980. Types of clients: environmental, health and self-development.
Needs: Uses photos for direct mail, catalogs, bookcovers and posters. Subjects include: nature, people in interrelation with nature, animals, plant life. Interested in reviewing stock photos/on nature and environment. "We are willing to work with new artists eager for exposure. Understand our needs: the environment and humanity's impact on it. Although down-to-earth and pragmatic, not new-age, our goal is to explore the spiritual connection between humanity and nature."
Specs: Uses 3×5 or larger b&w prints and color photos.
First Contact & Terms: Interested in receiving work from newer, lesser-known photographers. Query with list of stock photo subjects; query with samples; provide resume, business card, brochure, flyer or tearsheets to be kept on file for possible future assignments. Works with freelancers on an assignment only. Reports in 1-2 weeks. NPI. Pays on per job basis. Contact for payment figures. Buys one-time and all rights; negotiable. Model/property release preferred. Credit line given.
Tips: In freelancer's color samples, wants to see "book covers, effective use of color and subject matter to translate essence of book"; 1" b&w samples for magazine scenes depicting both the beauty and devastation of the planet (especially forest related) as well as people in interrelation with the natural world, animals and the plant world." To break in, "keep trying and price work within range of small publisher."

New Jersey

■**AM/PM ADVERTISING, INC.**, 196 Clinton Ave., Newark NJ 07108. (201)824-8600. FAX: (201)824-6631. Ad agency. President: Robert A. Saks. Estab. 1962. Types of clients: food, pharmaceuticals and health and beauty aids.

Needs: Works with 6 freelance photographers/month. Uses photographs for consumer magazines, trade magazines, direct mail, P-O-P displays, catalogs, posters, newspapers and audiovisual. Subjects include: fashion, still-life and commercials. Reviews stock photos of food and beauty products.
Audiovisual Needs: "We use multi-media slide shows and multi-media video shows."
Specs: Uses 8 × 10, color and/or b&w prints; 35mm, 2¼ × 2¼, 4 × 5, 8 × 10 transparencies; 8 × 10 film; broadcast videotape.
First Contact & Terms: Arrange personal interview to show portfolio. Send unsolicited photos by mail for consideration. Provide resume, business card, brochure, flyer or tearsheets to be kept on file for possible future assignments. Works on assignment only. Keeps samples on file. Reports in 1-2 weeks. Pays $150/hour; $1,000-2,000/day; $1,000-2,000/job; $1,000/color photo; $500/b&w photo. Pays on receipt of invoice. Buys one-time rights. Model release required; photo captions preferred. Credit line sometimes given depending upon client and use.
Tips: In portfolio or samples, wants to see originality. Sees trend toward more use of special lighting.

ARDREY INC., 505 Main St., Metuchen NJ 08840. (908)549-1300. PR firm. Office Manager: Lisa Fania. Types of clients: industrial. Client list provided on request.
Needs: Works with 10-15 freelance photographers/month throughout US. Uses photographers for trade magazines, direct mail, brochures, catalogs, newspapers. Subjects include trade photojournalism.
Specs: Uses 4 × 5 and 8 × 10 b&w glossy prints; 35mm, 2¼ × 2¼ and 4 × 5 transparencies.
First Contact & Terms: Provide resume, business card, brochure, flyer or tearsheets to be kept on file for possible future assignments. Works with freelance photographers on assignment basis only. SASE. Pays $150-450/day; "travel distance of location work—time and travel considered." Pays 30-45 days after acceptance. Buys all rights and negatives. Model release required.
Tips: Prefers to see "imaginative industrial photojournalism. Identify self, define territory you can cover from home base, define industries you've shot for industrial photojournalism; give relevant references and samples. Regard yourself as a business communication tool. That's how we regard ourselves, as well as photographers and other creative suppliers."

THE BECKERMAN GROUP, 35 Mill St., Bernardsville NJ 07924. (201)766-9238. Ad agency. Contact: Ilene Beckerman. Types of clients: industrial. Client list free with SASE.
Needs: Works with 3 photographers/month. Uses photos for catalogs, posters, corporate internal organs and brochures. Subject matter includes table top.
Specs: Uses b&w prints and 2¼ × 2¼ transparencies.
First Contact & Terms: Arrange a personal interview to show portfolio; provide resume, business card, brochure, flyer or tearsheets to be kept on file for possible future assignments. Works with freelance photographers on assignment only. Does not return unsolicited material. Reports as needed. Payment negotiable; maximum $1,500/day. Pays on receipt of invoice. Buys all rights. Model release required.
Tips: Looks for "the ability to think conceptually and solve a problem in a strong fresh way."

■**CREATIVE ASSOCIATES,** 626 Bloomfield Ave., Verona NJ 07044. (201)857-3444. AV firm. Producer: Harrison Feather. Estab. 1975. Types of clients: industrial, cosmetic and pharmaceutical.
Needs: Works with 1-2 photographers—filmmakers—videographers/month. Uses photographers for trade magazines and audiovisual uses. Subjects include product and general environment. Reviews stock photos or videotape.
Audiovisual Needs: Uses photos/video for slides and videotape.
Specs: 35mm, 4 × 5 and 8 × 10 transparencies; Betacam videotape.
First Contact & Terms: Provide resume, business card, brochure, flyer or tearsheets to be kept on file for possible future assignments. Works on assignment only. SASE. Reports as needed. Pays $500-1,000/day; $1,500-3,000/job. Pays on publication. Buys all rights. Model release required. Photo captions preferred. Credit line sometimes given, depending on assignment.

■**CREATIVE PRODUCTIONS, INC.,** 200 Main St., Orange NJ 07050. (201)676-4422. Contact: Gus Nichols. AV producer. Types of clients: industry, advertising, pharmaceuticals and business. Produces film, video, slide presentations, multimedia programs and training programs. Works with freelance photographers on assignment only basis. Provide resume and letter of inquiry to be kept on file for future assignments.
Subject Needs: Subjects include: sales training, industrial and medical topics. No typical school portfolios that contain mostly artistic or journalistic subject matter. Must be 3:4 horizontal ratio for film, video and filmstrips; 2:3 horizontal ratio for slides.
Specs: Uses color prints, slides and transparencies. Produces video and 16mm industrial, training, medical and sales promotion films. Possible assignments include shooting "almost anything that comes along—industrial sites, hospitals, etc." Interested in some occasional stock footage.

First Contact & Terms: Query first with resume of credits and rates. SASE. Reports in 1 week. NPI. Payment negotiable based on photographer's previous experience and client's budget. Pays on acceptance. Buys all rights. Model release required.
Tips: "We would use freelancers out-of-state for part of a production when it isn't feasible for us to travel, or locally to supplement our people on overload basis."

DIEGNAN & ASSOCIATES, Box 343 Martens, Lebanon NJ 08833. President: N. Diegnan. Ad agency/PR firm. Types of clients: industrial, consumer.
Needs: Commissions 15 photographers/year; buys 20 photos/year from each. Local freelancers preferred. Uses billboards, trade magazines, and newspapers.
Specs: Uses b&w contact sheet or glossy 8×10 prints. For color, uses 5×7 or 8×10 prints; also 2¼×2¼ transparencies.
First Contact & Terms: Arrange a personal interview to show portfolio. SASE. Reports in 1 week. NPI. Negotiates payment based on client's budget and amount of creativity required from photographer. Pays by the job. Buys all rights. Model release preferred.

■**IMAGE INNOVATIONS, INC.,** Suite 201, 29 Clyde Rd., Somerset NJ 08873. (908)873-0700. President: Mark A. Else. AV firm. Types of clients: business, industry and government. Examples of productions: Warner-Lambert Co. and Johnson & Johnson-ARC.
Audiovisual Needs: Uses photographers for videotapes, multi-image and slide/sound, print.
Specs: Produces 35mm slides and video.
First Contact & Terms: Query with resume of credits. Works on assignment only. Provide resume and tearsheets to be kept on file for future assignments. Pays $300-600/day; $300 minimum/job. Pays 30 days after billing. Buys one-time rights. Model release required; captions optional. Works with talent in New York metropolitan area only.
Tips: "Uses photographers who are conceptually creative and can execute their ideas into a clear, concise, and interesting visual. We like to see samples that will reflect the photographers technical as well as creative abilities, regardless of the medium (b&w/color etc.)" Likes to see "true sense of professionalism and good work. Experience in the field is not always a deciding factor in determining freelance work."

■**INSIGHT ASSOCIATES,** 333 Rt., 46 W., Bldg. A, Fairfield NJ 07004. (201)575-5521. President: Raymond Valente. Types of clients: major industrial companies.
Needs: Works with 4 freelancers/month. Uses freelancers for filmstrips, slide sets, multimedia productions, videotapes and print material—catalogs. Subjects include: industrial productions. Examples of production: Matheson (safety), Witco Corp. (corporate image), Volvo (sales training), P.S.E.&G.
Specs: Uses 35mm, 2¼×2¼ and 4×5 transparencies.
First Contact & Terms: Arrange a personal interview to show portfolio. Interested in stock photos/footage. SASE. Reports in 1 week. Pays $450-750/day on acceptance. Buys all rights. Model releases preferred. Credit line given.
Tips: "Freelance photographers should have knowledge of business needs and video formats. Also,versatility with video or location work. In reviewing a freelancer's portfolio or samples we look for content appropriate to our clients' objectives. We are seeing a heavy swing from slides to video production. Still photographers interested in making the transition into film and video photography should learn the importance of understanding a script."

■**INTERNATIONAL MEDIA SERVICES, INC.,** 718 Sherman Ave., Plainfield NJ 07060. (201)756-4060. AV firm/independant film and tape production company/media consulting firm. President/General Manager: Stuart Allen. Types of clients: industrial, advertising, print, fashion, broadcast and CATV.
Needs: Works with 0-25 freelance photographers/month; "depending on inhouse production at the time." Uses photographers for billboards, direct mail, catalogs, newspapers, consumer magazines, P-O-P displays, posters, AV presentations, trade magazines, brochures, film and tape. Subjects range "from scenics to studio shots and assignments"—varies with production requirements. Also works with freelance filmmakers to produce documentaries, commercials and training films.
Specs: Uses 8×10 glossy or matted b&w and color prints; 35mm, 2¼×2¼ and 8×10 transparencies; 16mm, 35mm film and ¾-1" videotape.
First Contact & Terms: Provide resume, business card, brochure, flyer or tearsheets to be kept on file for possible future assignments. Query with resume of credits. Query with list of stock photo subjects. Arrange a personal interview to show portfolio. SASE. Reporting time "depends on situation and requirements. We are not responsible for unsolicited material and do not recommend sending same. Negotiated rates based on type of work and job requirements." Usually pays $100-750/day, $25-2,500/job. Rights negotiable, generally purchases all rights. Model release required; captions preferred. Credit line given.

Tips: "Wants to see a brief book containing the best work of the photographer, representative of the type of assignment sought. Tearsheets are preferred but must have either the original or a copy of the original photo used, or applicable photo credit. Send resume and sample for active resource file. Maintain periodic contact and update file."

■**JANUARY PRODUCTIONS**, P.O. Box 66, 210 6th Ave., Hawthorne NJ 07507. (201)423-4666. FAX: (201)423-5569. President: Allan W. Peller. Estab. 1973. AV firm. Types of clients: schools, teachers and public libraries. Audience consists of primary, elementary and intermediate-grade school students. Produces filmstrips. Subjects are concerned with elementary education—science, social studies, math and conceptual development.
Audiovisual Needs: Uses 35mm transparencies for filmstrips and pictures (slides) of products for company catalogs.
First Contact & Terms: Call or send resumé/samples of work, etc. to Karen Neulinger, Art Director. SASE. NPI. Payment amounts "depend on job." Buys all rights.
Tips: Wants to see "clarity, effective use of space, design, etc. It helps our business to show pictures of the products we produce in our catalogs. The more pictures we have in them, the better they look and it helps to sell the product."

*■**KJD TELEPRODUCTIONS, INC.**, 30 Whyte Dr., Voorhees NJ 08043. (609)751-3500. FAX: (609)751-7729. AV firm. President: Larry Scott. Estab. 1989. Types of clients: industrial, fashion, retail and food. Examples of recent projects: Marco Island Florida Convention, ICI Americas (new magazine show); "Kid Stuff," Whyte Light Syndications (TV broadcast); and "Rukus," Merv Griffin Productions (TV broadcast).
Needs: Works with 2 photographers, filmmakers and/or videographers/month. Uses photos for trade magazines and audiovisual.
Audiovisual Needs: Primarily videotape, also slides and film.
Specs: Uses ½", ¾", Betacam/SP 1" videotape. Send unsolicited photos by mail for consideration. Works on assignment only. Keeps samples on file. Reports in 1 month. Pays $50-300/day. Pays on acceptance. Buys first rights. Model/property release required. Credit lines sometimes given.
Tips: "We are seeing more use of freelancers, less staff. Be visible!"

LOHMEYER SIMPSON COMMUNICATIONS, (formerly Adler, Schwartz, Inc.), 14 Pine St., Morristown NJ 07960. (201)267-0400. Purchasing Manager: Tony Grasso. Ad agency. Uses all media. Types of clients: automotive, electronic and industrial.
Needs: Works with freelance photographers on assignment only basis. Uses photos for cars, people, fashion and still life.
First Contact & Terms: Provide business card and tearsheets to be kept on file for possible future assignments. Model release required. Buys all rights, but may reassign to photographer. Negotiates payment based on client's budget, amount of creativity required, where the work will appear and photographer's previous experience and reputation. Pays $1,000/b&w photo; $2,000/color photo; or $2,000/day. Call to arrange an appointment. "Show samples of your work and printed samples." Reports in 2 weeks.
Specs: Uses semigloss prints and transparencies. Model release required.
Tips: "Interested in cars (location/studio), still life (studio), location, editorial and illustration."

*PRINCETON PARTNERS ADVERTISING**, 2 Research Way, Princeton NJ 08540. (609)452-8500. FAX: (609)452-7212. Ad agency. Director of Creative Services: Paul Schindel. Estab. 1965. Types of clients: industrial, financial, fashion, retail.
Needs: Works with 3 freelance photographers/month. Uses photos for billboards, consumer and trade magazines, direct mail, P-O-P displays, newspapers and signage.
Specs: Uses color and b&w prints; 35mm, 2¼×2¼, 4×5 and 8×10 transparencies.
First Contact & Terms: Contact through rep. Arrange personal interview to show a portfolio. Submit portfolio for review. Query with samples. Provide resume, business card, brochure, flyer or tearsheets to be kept on file for possible future assignments. Works on assignment only. Keeps samples on file. SASE. Reports in 1-2 weeks. Pays $150-2,500/day; $150-2,500/job. Pays on receipt of invoice. Buys all rights; negotiable. Model/property release required. Credit line not given.

The asterisk before a listing indicates that the market is new in this edition. New markets are often the most receptive to freelance submissions.

*■SORIN PRODUCTIONS, INC.,** 4400 Rt. 9 South, Freehold NJ 07728. (908)462-1785. President: David Sorin. Type of client: corporate.

Needs: Works with 2 freelance photographers/month. Uses photographers for slide sets, multimedia productions, films and videotapes. Subjects include people and products.

Specs: Uses b&w and color prints; 35mm and 2¼×2¼ transparencies.

First Contact & Terms: Query with stock photo list. Provide resume, business card, self-promotion piece or tearsheets to be kept on file for possible future assignments. Works with freelancers by assignment only; interested in stock photos/footage. Does not return unsolicited material. Reports in 2 weeks. NPI. Pays per piece or per job. Pays on acceptance. Buys all rights. Captions and model releases preferred. Credit line given by project.

New Mexico

MEDIAWORKS, 4002 Silver Ave. SE, Albuquerque NM 87108. (505)266-7795. President: Al Costanzo. Ad agency. Types of clients: retail, industry, politics, government, law. Produces overhead transparencies, slide sets, motion pictures, sound-slide sets, videotape, print ads and brochures.

Needs: Works with 1-2 freelance photographers/month on assignment only basis. Buys 70 photos and 5-8 films/year. Health, business, environment and products. No animals or flowers. Length requirements: 80 slides or 15-20 minutes, or 60 frames, 20 minutes.

Specs: Produces ½" and ¾" video for broadcasts; also photos b&w or color prints and 35mm transparencies, "and a lot of 2¼ transparencies and some 4×5 transparencies."

First Contact & Terms: Arrange personal interview or query with resume. Provide resume, flyer and brochure to be kept on file for possible future assignments. Prefers to see a variety of subject matter and styles in portfolio. Does not return unsolicited material. Pays $40-60/hour, $350-500/day, $40-800/ job. Negotiates payment based on client's budget and photographer's previous experience/reputation. Pays on job completion. Buys all rights. Model release required.

New York

■AUTHENTICATED NEWS INTERNATIONAL, 34 High St., Katonah NY 10536-1117. (914)232-7726. Managing Editor: Mr. Sidney Polinsky. Types of clients: book publishers, media, newspapers, etc.

Needs: Works with approximately 25 freelance photographers/month. Uses photographers for slide sets. Also uses high-quality slides for posters.

Specs: Uses 8×10 glossy b&w prints; 35mm, 2¼×2¼ and 4×5 transparencies.

First Contact & Terms: Query with samples or resume. Interested in stock photos/footage. SASE. Reports in 1 month. Pays 50% commission to photographers. Pays on acceptance. Buys one-time rights. Captions and model release required. Credit line given.

*■DON BOSCO MULTIMEDIA,** P.O. Box T, 475 North Ave., New Rochelle NY 10802. (914)576-0122. FAX: (914)654-0443. Production Director: John Thomas. Types of clients: educational. Recent projects include: self-publishing/marketing subjects.

Needs: Works with 1 photographer, filmmaker and/or videographer/year; "varies greatly." Uses photos for direct mail, catalogs and audiovisual. Subjects include: product for photography, educational/ religious for video.

Audiovisual Needs: Uses slides, film and videotape.

Specs: Uses 5×7 glossy color and b&w prints; ¾" SP U-Matic videotape.

First Contact & Terms: Provide resume, business card, brochure, flyer or tearsheets to be kept on file for possible future assignments. Works with local freelancers only. Keeps samples on file. SASE. Reports in 1 month. Pays $50-100/hour; $300-550/day. Pays on receipt of invoice. Buys all rights; negotiable. Model/property release preferred. Credit line not given.

Tips: "As an AV educational/religious publisher we are looking for adolescent and family subjects in primarily realistic styles." Sees trend to, "unfortunately, a great deal of stock photography. Be on time, reliable, and affordable. Don't let client stop you from using your imagination. The photographer instincts are better; sometimes clients need gentle persuasion. Try it your way and theirs."

C. L. & B. ADVERTISING, INC., 100 Kinloch Commons, Manlius NY 13104-2484. (315)682-8502. FAX: (315)682-8508. Advertising, public relations and research. President: Richard Labs. Creative Director: Adam Rozum. Types of clients: industrial, fashion, finance.
Needs: Works with 4-6 freelance photographers/year. Uses photos for billboards, consumer and trade magazines, P-O-P displays, catalogs and newspapers. Subject matter includes industrial, consumer, models, location and/or studio.
Specs: Uses all formats.
First Contact & Terms: "Send bio and proof sheet (if available) first; we will contact you if interested." Works on assignment only. Also uses stock photos. Does not return unsolicited material. Pays $25-2,500/photo. Pays in 30 days. Buys all rights. Model release required. Credit line seldom given.
Tips: "We review your work and will call if we think a particular job is applicable to your talents."

WALTER F. CAMERON ADVERTISING, 275 Broad Hollow Rd., Melville NY 11747. (516)752-1515. FAX: (516)752-1525. Ad agency. Art Director: Neil Channon. Types of clients: retail, trade and corporate. Client list free with SASE.
Needs: Uses photographers for consumer magazines, trade magazines, catalogs and newspapers. Subject matter varies from time to time; furniture settings, cars, product shots, on-location shots.
Specs: Uses 4×5 or 8×10 b&w and color glossy prints.
First Contact & Terms: Arrange a personal interview to show portfolio; submit portfolio for review; provide resume, business card, brochure, flyer or tearsheets to be kept on file for possible future assignments. Works with freelance photographers on assignment only. Pays per hour or $700/day. Pays within 30 days of invoice. Buys all rights. Model release required; captions preferred.

■EDUCATIONAL IMAGES LTD., P.O. Box 3456, West Side Station, Elmira NY 14905. (607)732-1090. AV publisher. Executive Director: Dr. Charles R. Belinky. Types of clients: educational market, grades 6-12 and college; also serves public libraries, parks and nature centers. Produces filmstrips, slide sets, and multimedia kits.
Needs: Works with 12 freelance photographers/year. Subjects include a heavy emphasis on natural history, ecology, anthropology, conservation, life sciences. Also is interested in other subjects especially chemistry, physics, astronomy, math. "We are happy to consider any good color photo series on any topic that tells a coherent story. We need pictures and text."
Specs: Uses videotape; also buys any size transparencies, but 35mm preferred. Will consider buying photo collections, any subject, to expand files. Will also look at prints, "if transparencies are available."
First Contact & Terms: Buys 200-400 photos/year; film and video are "open." Buys all rights, but may reassign to photographer. Pays $150 minimum/job, or on a per-photo basis. Query with resume of credits; submit material by mail for consideration. Prefers to see 35mm or larger transparencies and outline of related text in portfolio. Reports in 1 month. SASE. Captions required; prefers model release.
Tips: "Write for our catalog. Write first with a small sample. We want complete or nearly complete AV programs—not isolated pictures usually. Be reliable. Follow up commitments on time and provide only sharp, well-exposed, well-composed pictures. Send by registered mail."

*■FINE ART PRODUCTIONS, 67 Maple St., Newburgh NY 12550. (914)561-5866. Ad agency, PR firm and AV firm. Director: Richie Suraci. Estab. 1989. Types of clients: industrial, financial, fashion, retail, food—all industries. Examples of recent projects: "Great Hudson River Revival," Clearwater, Inc. (folk concert, brochure); feature articles, Hudson Valley News (newspaper); and "Wheel and Rock to Woodstock," MS Society (brochure).
Needs: Uses photos for billboards, consumer and trade magazines, direct mail, P-O-P displays, catalogs, posters, newspapers, signage and audiovisual. Reviews stock photos.
Audiovisual Needs: Uses slides, film (all formats) and videotape.
Specs: Uses color and b&w prints, any size or finish; 35mm, 2¼×2¼", 4×5, 8×10 transparencies; film, all formats; and ½", ¾" or 1" beta videotape.
First Contact & Terms: Submit portfolio for review. Query with resume of credits. Query with list of stock photo subjects. Send unsolicited photos by mail for consideration. Query with samples. Provide resume, business card, brochure, flyer or tearsheets to be kept on file for possible future assignments.

Can't find a listing? Check at the end of each market section for the " '92-'93 Changes" lists. These lists include any market listings from the '92 edition which were either not verified or deleted in this edition.

Keeps samples on file. SASE. Reports in 1 month or longer. NPI: "All payment negotiable relative to subject matter." Pays on acceptance, publication or on receipt of invoice; "varies relative to project." Buys first, one-time and all rights; negotiable. Model/property release required. Photo captions required; include basic information. Credit line sometimes given, "depending on project or if they want it."

Tips: Looks for "all subjects, styles and capabilities."

HARRINGTON ASSOCIATES INC., 57 Fairmont Ave., Kingston NY 12401-5221. (914)331-7136. FAX: (914)331-7168. PR firm. President: Gerard Harrington. Estab. 1988. Types of clients: industrial, high technology, retail, fashion, finance, transportation, architectural, artistic and publishing.
Needs: Number of photographers used on a monthly basis varies. Uses photos for consumer magazines, trade magazines, P-O-P displays, catalogs and newspapers. Subjects include: general publicity including head shots and candids. Also still lifes.
Specs: Uses b&w prints, any size and format. Also uses 4×5 color transparencies; and ¾ inch videotape.
First Contact & Terms: Interested in receiving work from newer, lesser-known photographers. Provide resume, business card, brochure, flyer or tearsheets to be kept on file for possible future assignments. Works with freelancers on assignment only. Does not return unsolicited material. Reports only when interested. NPI; payment negotiable. Pays on receipt of invoice. Buys all rights; negotiable. Model release and photo captions required. Credit line given whenever possible, depending on use.

■HART/CONWAY CO., INC., 387 E. Main, Rochester NY 14604. (716) 232-2930. Ad agency. Estab. 1924. Print Production: Jackie Pike. Types of clients: automotive, industrial, retail, public transit, finance, recreational.
Needs: Works with 2-3 freelance photographers/month. Uses photographers for consumer magazines, trade magazines, direct mail, newspapers and audiovisual. Subjects include: people and props (table top).
Audiovisual Needs: Uses freelance filmmakers to produce industrial productions, (5-15 minutes) and television spots (15- and 30-second).
Specs: Uses b&w and color prints; 2¼×2¼, 4×5 transparencies.
First Contact & Terms: Query with list of stock photo subjects. Provide resume, business card, brochure, flyer or tearsheets to be kept on file for possible future assignments. Works with freelancers on assignment only. Cannot return material. Reports in 1 week. Pays $40-2,500/b&w photo; $100-5,000/color photo; $25-250/hour; $400-1,800/day; $50-10,000/complete job. Buys one-time rights. Model release required; photo captions preferred. Credit line sometimes given, depending on usage/money.

KOPF, ZIMMERMANN, SCHULTHEIS, 35 Pinelawn Rd., Melville NY 11747. (516)293-6115. Ad agency. Art Directors: Evelyn C. Rysdyk and Art Zimmermann. Estab. 1980. Types of clients: industrial (high-tech, medical, computers, software, etc.), business-to-business and consumer.
Needs: Works with 4 freelance photographers/month. Uses photos for billboards, consumer and trade magazines, catalogs, posters, newspapers. Subjects include: still life (technical products), office situations with models. Examples of ad campaigns: Philips Medical Systems and North Fork Bank.
Specs: Uses 35mm, 2¼×2¼, 4×5 and 8×10 transparencies.
First Contact & Terms: Interested in receiving work from newer, lesser-known photographers. Query with samples; provide resume, business card, brochure, flyer or tearsheets to be kept on file for possible future assignments. Works with freelance photographers on assignment only. Does not return unsolicited material. Pays $200-3,000/b&w photo; $200-5,000/color photo; $800-2,000/day; $200-5,000/job. Pays on receipt of invoice. Buys all rights; negotiable. Model/property release and photo captions required.
Tips: Prefers to see creative still life work and good people shots (annual report type); printed samples. Looks for good technical skills. Special note: "Show us something innovative. Fine art techniques also accepted." Seeks to work with "professionals only." Sees a trend in greater "use of highly creative, stylized, even gritty work."

McANDREW ADVERTISING CO., P.O. Box 254, 2125 St. Raymond Ave., Bronx NY 10462. (212)892-8660. Ad agency, PR firm. Contact: Robert McAndrew. Estab. 1961. Types of clients: industrial and technical. Examples of recent projects: Electronic Devices, Inc. (ad campaign); Yula Corp. (new photo series, brochure, trade show); and American Steam Timer Corp. (new product brochure).
Needs: Works with 1 freelance photographer/month. Uses photos for trade magazines, direct mail, brochures, catalogs, newspapers. Subjects include industrial products.
Specs: Uses 8×10 glossy b&w or color prints; 4×5 or 8×10 transparencies.
First Contact & Terms: Interested in working with newer, lesser-known photograhers. Provide resume, business card, brochure, flyer, tearsheets or non-returnable samples to be kept on file for possible future assignments. Works with local freelancers only. Reports as needed. Pays $45-100/b&w

© Will Faller

Photographer Will Faller, Tillson, New York, sees Vincent Tese, New York state's Director of Economic Development, as a powerful and prestigious political leader. When Faller was hired by Harrington Associates Inc., a public relations firm in Kingston, New York, he placed Tese behind a Times Square restoration model to depict him as a "roll-up-your-sleeves-and-get-it-done type of bureaucrat." This striking image was bought by Crain Communications Inc. for a profile in a national magazine.

photo; $85-200/color photo; $500-700/day. Pays in 60 days. Buys all rights and exclusive product rights. Model/property release required; captions preferred.
Tips: Photographers should "let us know how close they are, and what their prices are. We look for photographers who have experience in industrial photography." In samples, wants to see "sharp, well-lighted" work.

MCCUE ADVERTISING & PR INC., 91 Riverside Dr., Binghamton NY 13905. (607)723-9226. Ad agency and PR firm. President: Donna McCue. Types of clients: industrial, retail, all types.
Needs: Works with 5 freelance photographers/month. Uses photos for consumer and trade magazines, direct mail, P-O-P displays, catalogs, signage and newspapers.
Specs: Uses 8×10 prints; 35mm, 4×5 transparencies.
First Contact & Terms: Provide resume, business card, brochure, flyer or tearsheets to be kept on file for possible future assignments. Does not return unsolicited material. Reports when assignment comes up. NPI; payment negotiable. Pays in 30 days. Buys all rights. Model release required. Credit line sometimes given.

■NATIONAL TEACHING AIDS, INC., 1845 Highland Ave., New Hyde Park NY 11040. (516)326-2555. FAX: (516)326-2560. AV firm. President: A. Becker. Estab. 1960. Types of clients: schools. Produces filmstrips.
Needs: Science subjects; needs photomicrographs and space photography. Buys 20-100 photos/year.
Specs: Uses 35mm transparencies.
First Contact & Terms: Does not return unsolicited material. Pays $50 minimum. Buys one-time rights; negotiable.

■ORGANIZATION MANAGEMENT, 7 Heather Lane, Gloversville NY 12078. (518)725-9714. President: Bill Dunkinson. Ad agency and PR firm. Types of clients: construction, credit and collections, entertainment, finance, government, publishing and travel accounts.
Needs: Photos used in brochures, newsletters, annual reports, PR releases, sales literature, consumer and trade magazines. Buys 200 photos/year.
Specs: Uses 5×7 and 8×10 glossy, matte and semigloss prints. NPI. Pays per job. Negotiates payment based on client's budget, amount of creativity required, where work will appear and photographer's previous experience/reputation. Credit line sometimes given.
First Contact & Terms: No unsolicited material. Works with freelance photographers on assignment only; local freelancers preferred. Freelance filmmakers may query for assignment. SASE. Reports in 2 weeks.

PRO/CREATIVES, 25 W. Burda Pl., New City NY 10956-7116. President: David Rapp. Ad agency. Uses all media except billboards and foreign. Types of clients: package goods, fashion, men's entertainment and leisure magazines, sports and entertainment.
Specs: Send any size b&w prints. For color, send 35mm transparencies or any size prints.
First Contact & Terms: Submit material by mail for consideration. Reports as needed. SASE. NPI. Negotiates payment based on client's budget.

■RONAN, HOWARD, ASSOCIATES, INC., 11 Buena Vista Ave., Spring Valley NY 10977-3040. (914)356-6668. Contact: Howard A. Ronan. Ad agency and PR firm. Uses direct mail, foreign media, newspapers and trade magazines. Serves clients in audiovisual media, motion picture services, video support equipment, portable power units, motion picture cameras, electronic components.
Specs: Uses b&w glossy prints; also transparencies and paper prints.
First Contact & Terms: Query first with resume of credits. Works with 1-2 freelance photographers/ month on assignment only. Buys 50-100 photos/year. Pays per photo, $25-40/hour in photographer's studio or $250-400/"shoot" on location plus travel expenses. Negotiates payment based on client's budget.
Tips: Extra sharp details on products are always the assignment. "Photographers must have new, or rebuilt to 'new' performance-ability cameras, high-powered (not the average strobe) strobes and other lights for location shooting, a full range of lenses including lenses suitable for macro, and must understand how to shoot color under fluorescents without going green. Be able to shoot client executives and have them show up with good 'head and shoulders' detail when reproduced in printed media."

JACK SCHECTERSON ASSOCIATES, 5316 251st Place, Little Neck NY 11362. (718)225-3536. FAX: (718)423-3478. Ad agency. President: Jack Schecterson. Estab. 1967. Types of clients: industrial and consumer.
Needs: Uses photographers for consumer and trade magazines, packaging, product, design, direct mail, P-O-P displays, brochures, catalogs, etc.
Specs: Uses b&w or color prints; 35mm, 2¼×2¼, 4×5 and 8×10 transparencies.
First Contact & Terms: Send resume, business card, brochure, flyer or tearsheets to be kept on file for possible future assignments. Does not return unsolicited material. Works on assignment only. Reporting time "subject to job time requirements." NPI. Pays according to client's budget. Buys all rights. Model release and captions required.

■TOBOL GROUP, INC., 33 Great Neck Rd., Great Neck NY 11021. (516)466-0414. FAX: (516)466-0776. Ad agency/design studio. President: Mitch Tobol. Estab. 1981. High-tech, industrial, business-to-business and consumer. Examples of ad campaigns: Weight Watchers, (in-store promotion); Eutectic & Castolin; Mainco (trade ad); and Light Alarms.
Needs: Works with up to 4 photographers/videographers/month. Uses photographers for billboards, consumer magazines, trade magazines, direct mail, P-O-P displays, catalogs, posters, newspapers and audiovisual. Subjects are varied; mostly still-life photography. Reviews business-to-business and commercials' video footage.

Audiovisual Needs: Uses videotape.

Specs: Uses 4×5, 8×10, 11×14 b&w prints; 35mm, 2¼×2¼ and 4×5 transparencies; and ½″ videotape.

First Contact & Terms: Send unsolicited photos by mail for consideration. Query with samples. Provide resume, business card, brochure, flyer or tearsheets to be kept on file for possible future assignments: follow-up with phone call. Works on assignment only. SASE. Reports in 3 weeks. Pays $100-10,000/job. Pays net 30. Rights purchased depend on client. Model release required. Credit line sometimes given, depending on client and price.

Tips: In freelancer's samples or demos, wants to see "the best they do—any style or subject as long as it is done well. Trend is photos or videos to be multi-functional. Show me your *best* and what you enjoy shooting. Get experience with existing company to make the transition from still photography to audiovisual."

■**UNISOURCE**, 363 DeGraw St., Brooklyn NY 11231. (718)643-2800. FAX: (718)643-2804. Ad agency, PR firm. Vice Pres./Client Services: Val Reisig. Vice Pres./Art Director: Don James. Estab. 1970. Types of clients: industrial, technical.

Needs: Works with 6-10 freelance photographers/month. Uses photographers for trade magazines, direct mail, catalogs, signage, literature and PR. Subjects include: machinery.

Audiovisual Needs: Uses freelancers to produce slides, film and videotape.

Specs: Uses 8×10 b&w prints; 4×5, 8×10 transparencies; film and videotape.

First Contact & Terms: Arrange a personal interview to show portfolio; query with resume of credits; submit portfolio for review; provide resume, business card, brochure, flyer or tearsheets to be kept on file for possible assignments. Works with freelance photographers on assignment basis only. Does not return unsolicited material. NPI. Pays per photo, per job. Pays on receipt of invoice. Buys all rights. Model release required.

Tips: Prefers to see industrial, plant photography, studio work—all subjects. Amateurism is discouraged. "Impress us with talent, experience and offer value."

■**VISUAL HORIZONS**, 180 Metro Park, Rochester NY 14623. (716)424-5300. FAX: (716)424-5313. AV firm. President: Stanley Feingold. Types of clients: industrial.

Audiovisual Needs: Works with 2 freelance photographers/month. Uses photographers for AV presentations. Also works with freelance filmmakers to produce training films.

Specs: Uses 35mm transparencies and videotape.

First Contact & Terms: Provide resume, business card, brochure, flyer or tearsheets to be kept on file for possible future assignments. Works on assignment only. Reports as needed. NPI. Pays on publication. Buys all rights. Model release and captions required.

WALLACK & WALLACK ADVERTISING INC., 33 Great Neck Rd., Great Neck NY 11021. (516)487-3974. VP/Creative: Shelly Burn Wallack. Types of clients: fashion, industrial.

Needs: Works with 5-6 freelance photographers/year. Uses photographers for direct mail, catalogs, P-O-P displays, posters, trade and consumer magazines and brochures. Subject needs "very clean, graphic look. Black and white important."

Specs: Uses 11×14 b&w prints; 2¼×2¼, 4×5 and 8×10 transparencies.

First Contact & Terms: Provide resume, business card, brochure, flyer or tearsheets to be kept on file for future assignments. Works with freelancers on assignment only. SASE. Pays $75-750/ b&w photo; $150-750/color photo; $350-1,800/day. Buys all rights. Written release required.

Tips: Prefers to see "what the photographer wants to shoot—his specialty, not a little of everything" in a portfolio.

HAROLD WARNER ADVERTISING, INC., 232 Delaware Ave., Buffalo NY 14202. (716)852-4410. FAX: (716)852-4725. Ad agency. Art Director: William Walsh. Estab. 1945. Types of clients: industrial. Previous/current clients: "We are the agency for 40 clients—all industrial."

Needs: Works with 3-4 photographers/month. Uses photographers for trade magazines, direct mail and catalogs. Subjects are varied—but all industrial. Reviews stock photos.

Audiovisual Needs: Uses 4×5 to 20×24 glossy and matte b&w and color prints; 35mm, 2¼×2¼, 4×5 and 8×10 transparencies.

First Contact & Terms: Arrange personal interview to show portfolio. Query with resume of credits. Query with list of stock photo subjects. Provide resume, business card, brochure, flyer or tearsheets to be kept on file for possible future assignments. Works with freelancers on assignment only. Reports "as needed." Pays $500-800/day; specific rates negotiable. Pays on acceptance. Buys all rights. Model release required; photo captions preferred. No credit line given.

Tips: "Freelancers are few and far between who can deal with mundane, industrial topics such as machines and machine parts. Our work is largely industrial advertising, so we look for freelancers who can show experience and ability to shoot industrial subjects imaginatively."

WOLF MANSFIELD BOLLING ADVERTISING INC., 40 Fountain Plaza, Buffalo NY 14202. (716)853-1200. Ad agency. Art Director: Janet Slonim. Types of clients: Consumer.
Needs: Works with 2 freelance photographers/month. Uses photographers for direct mail, catalogs, newspapers, consumer magazines, P-O-P displays, posters, AV presentations, trade magazines and brochures. Needs product, situation and location photos. Also works with freelance filmmakers for TV commercials and training films.
Specs: Uses 11×14 b&w and color prints; 35mm, 2¼×2¼, 4×5 and 8×10 transparencies; 16mm film and videotape.
First Contact & Terms: Arrange a personal interview to show portfolio or query with resume of credits. Works with freelance photographers on assignment only. Does not return unsolicited material. Reports in 2 weeks. Pays $50-150/hour; $450-1,500/day. Pays 1 month after acceptance. Buys all rights. Model release required.
Tips: In a portfolio, prefers to see transparencies and printed materials.

■**ZELMAN STUDIOS, LTD.**, 623 Cortelyou Rd., Brooklyn NY 11218. (718)941-5500. AV firm. General Manager: Jerry Krone. Estab. 1966. Types of clients: industrial, retail, fashion, public relations, fund raising, education, publishing, business and government.
Needs: Works on assignment only. Uses photographers for slide sets, filmstrips, motion pictures and videotape. Subjects include: people, machines and aerial.
Specs: Produces Super 8, 16mm and 35mm documentary, educational and industrial films and slide/sound shows. Uses 8×10 color prints; 35mm transparencies.
First Contact & Terms: Interested in receiving work from newer, lesser-known photographers. Query with samples; send material by mail for consideration; submit portfolio for review; provide resume, samples and calling card to be kept on file for possible future assignments. Pays $50-100/color photo. Pays $250-800/job. Pays on acceptance. Buys all rights. Model release required; property release preferred; captions preferred.

New York City

■**ALDEN GROUP-PUBLIC RELATIONS DIVISION**, 535 5th Ave., New York NY 10017. (212)867-6400. Public Relations Director: Laura Baddish. Estab. 1955. PR firm. Photos used in newspapers, trade publications and general media. Types of clients: chemicals, health care, food/beverage, home furnishings, manufacturing and travel/resorts. Examples of ad campaigns: Gucci Eyewear (fashion), Sharp Watches (popular priced value). Most interested in product publicity by assignment; event/area coverage by assignment; portraits for publicity use; occasional use of models/props.
Audiovisual Needs: Assigns AV projects to filmmakers for industrial and commercial films.
Specs: Uses glossy b&w prints. For color, uses glossy prints and transparencies; contact sheet and negatives OK.
First Contact & Terms: "Write first; describe your area of specialization and general abilities; access to models, props, studio; area/event/people coverage; equipment used; time and fee information; agency/commercial experience; and location and availability." SASE. Reports in 1 month or less. NPI. Buys all rights. Model release required.
Tips: "Work through our director." Also, "be able to respond quickly."

■**ANITA HELEN BROOKS ASSOCIATES**, 155 E. 55th St., New York NY 10022. (212)755-4498. Contact: Anita Helen Brooks. PR firm. Types of clients: beauty, entertainment, fashion, food, publishing, travel, society, art, politics, exhibits and charity events.
Needs: Photos used in PR releases, AV presentations, consumer magazines and trade magazines. Buys "several hundred" photos/year. Most interested in fashion shots, society, entertainment and literary celebrity/personality shots.
Specs: Uses 8×10 glossy b&w prints; contact sheet OK. For color uses 8×10 glossy prints; contact sheet OK.
First Contact & Terms: Provide resume and brochure to be kept on file for possible future assignments. Query with resume of credits. No unsolicited material; does not return unsolicited material. Works on assignment only. Pays $50 minimum/job; negotiates payment based on client's budget. Credit line given. Model release preferred.

■**COX ADVERTISING**, 379 W. Broadway, New York NY 10012. (212)334-9141. FAX: (212)334-9179. Ad agency. Associate Creative Directors: Marc Rubin and Beth Anderson. Types of clients: industrial, retail, fashion and travel.

Needs: Works with 2 freelance photographers—videographers/month. Uses photographers for billboards, consumer magazines, trade magazines, direct mail, P-O-P displays, catalogs, posters, newspapers, signage and audiovisual. Reviews stock photos or video.
Audiovisual Needs: Uses photos for slide shows; also uses videotapes.
Specs: Uses 16×20 b&w prints; 35mm, 2¼×2¼, 4×5 and 8×10 transparencies.
First Contact & Terms: Arrange personal interview to show portfolio. Works on assignment only. Cannot return material. Reports in 1-2 weeks. Pays minimum of $1,500/job; higher amounts negotiable according to needs of client. Pays within 30-60 days of receipt of invoice. Buys all rights when possible. Model release required. Credit line sometimes given.

■**RICHARD L. DOYLE ASSOC., INC.**, 15 Maiden Lane, New York NY 10038. (212)349-2828. FAX: (212)619-5350. Ad agency. Client Services: R.L. Stewart, Jr. Estab. 1979. Types of clients: primarily in insurance/financial services and publishers. Client list free with SASE.
Needs: Works with 5-6 freelance photographers/month. Uses photographers for consumer and trade magazines, direct mail, newspapers, audiovisual, sales promotion and annual reports. Subjects include people—portrait and candid.
Audiovisual Needs: Typically uses prepared slides—in presentation formats, video promotions and video editorials.
Specs: Uses b&w and color prints; 35mm and 2¼×2¼ transparencies.
First Contact & Terms: Query with resume of credits and samples. Prefers resume, business card, brochure, flyer or tearsheets to be kept on file for possible future assignments. SASE. Reports in 2 weeks. NPI. Pays on acceptance or receipt of invoice. Buys all rights. Model release required; captions required.
Tips: Prefers to see photos of people; "good coverage/creativity in presentation. Be perfectly honest as to capabilities; be reasonable in cost and let us know you'll work *with us* to satisfy the client. Trends include more imaginative settings and composition in normally mundane situations."

■**JOHN EMMERLING INC.**, 135 E. 55th St., New York NY 10022. (212)751-7460. Creative Director: Art Gilmore. Types of clients: magazines. Examples of recent projects: "Powerful People" for *Readers' Digest*, (magazines, newspapers, radio, TV); "Unconventional Wisdom" for *Newsweek*, (magazines, newspapers, posters); "Rewards of Money" for *Money Magazine*, (magazines, newspapers, radio).
Needs: Works with 5 photographers and videographers/month. Uses photographs for billboards, consumer and trade magazines, direct mail, P-O-P displays, posters, newspapers, audiovisual and other. Subjects include: reportage, people, still life.
Audiovisual Needs: Uses slides, film and videotape.
Specs: Uses b&w prints; 35mm, 2¼×2¼, 4×5 and 8×10 transparencies; 35mm film; 1″, ¾″, ½″ videotape.
First Contact & Terms: Contact through rep. Arrange personal interview to show portfolio. Submit portfolio for review. Provide business card, brochure, flyer or tearsheets to be kept on file for possible future assignments. Keeps samples on file. Cannot return material. Reports only as needed. NPI. Pays on receipt of invoice. Rights negotiable. Model release required. Credit line sometimes given depending upon fee schedule.
Tips: Looks for original work.

■**KEYSTONE PRESS AGENCY, INC.**, 202 East 42nd St., New York NY 10017. (212)924-8123. Managing Editor: Brian F. Alpert. Types of clients: book publishers, magazines and major newspapers.
Needs: Uses photographers for slide sets. Subjects include photojournalism.
Specs: Uses 8×10 glossy b&w and color prints; 35mm and 2¼×2¼ transparencies.
First Contact & Terms: Interested in stock photos/footage. Does not return unsolicited material. Reports upon sale. NPI; payment is 50% of sale per photo. Captions required. Credit line given.

KOEHLER IVERSEN ADVERTISING, 71 W. 23rd St., New York NY 10010. FAX: (212)645-6451. Ad agency. Creative Director: W. Peter Koehler. Estab. 1977. Types of clients: industrial, health care and pharamceutical.
Needs: Works with 2 photographers/month. Uses freelance photographers for trade magazines, direct mail, catalogs and newspapers. Subjects include people/corporate.
Specs: Uses b&w and color prints; 35 mm, 2¼×2¼ transparencies.
First Contact & Terms: Interested in receiving work from newer, lesser-known photographers. Query with samples, submit portfolio for review. Provide resume, business card, brochure, flyer or tearsheets to be kept on file for possible future assignments. Works with freelance photographers on assignment only. Does not return unsolicited material. NPI. Pays by the job or per photo. Payment made "30 days from receipt of invoice." Buys all rights. Model and property releases required.
Tips: Looks for "originality, composition and lighting" in work. Sees trends in increasing competition and flexible rates.

*■LIPPSERVICE, 305 W. 52nd St., New York NY 10019. (212)956-0572. Celebrity consulting firm. President: Ros Lipps. Estab. 1985. Types of clients: industrial, financial, fashion, retail, food; "any company which requires use of celebrities." Examples of recent projects: "Remembering Felicia," Judy Kreston and David Lahm (cabaret action, tribute to Felicia Sanders); also projects for United Way of Tri-State and CARE.

Needs: Works with 6 freelance photographers and/or videographers/month. Uses photographers for billboards, trade magazines, P-O-P displays, posters, audiovisual. Subjects include: celebrities.

Audiovisual Needs: Uses videotape.

Specs: Uses videotape.

First Contact & Terms: Provide resume, business card, brochure, flyer or tearsheets to be kept on file for possible future assignments. Works on assignment only. Keeps samples on file. Cannot return material. Reports in 3 weeks. NPI; pays per job. Rights purchased depend on job; negotiable. Model/property release required. Credit line given.

Tips: Looks for "experience in photographing celebrities. Contact us by mail only."

■MARSDEN, 30 E. 33 St., New York NY 10016. (212)725-9220. Vice President/Creative Director: Stephen Flores. Types of clients: corporate, nonprofit, Fortune 500.

Needs: Works with 2-3 photographers/month. Uses photographers for filmstrips, slide sets, multimedia productions, films and videotapes. Subjects include industrial, technical, office, faces, scenics, special effects, etc.

Specs: Uses 35mm, 2¼×2¼, 4×5 and 8×10 transparencies; 16mm film; U-matic ¾", 1" and 2" videotapes.

First Contact & Terms: Query with samples or a stock photo list. Provide resume, business card, self-promotion piece or tearsheets to be kept on file for possible future assignments. Works with local freelancers only; interested in stock photos/footage. "We call when we have a need—no response is made on unsolicited material." Pays $25-1,000/color photo; $150-600/day. Pays on acceptance. Buys one-time rights. Model release preferred. Credit line rarely given.

■MATTHEW-LAWRENCE ADVERTISING & SALES PROMOTION INC., 322 8th Ave., New York NY 10011. (212)929-1313. FAX: (212)929-1396. Ad agency. President: Larry Danziger. Types of clients: industrial, fashion and finance. Examples of ad campaigns: Monsanto (ads and promotion programs); Dupont (collateral material and videos); and Federal Express (collateral materials).

Needs: Works with 2-3 freelance photographers/filmmakers/videographers per month. Uses photographers for consumer magazines, trade magazines, direct mail, P-O-P displays and audiovisual. Reviews stock photos and video.

Audiovisual Needs: Video.

Specs: Uses any size of format b&w prints; 35mm, 2¼×2¼, 4×5 and 8×10 transparencies; also VHS videotape.

First Contact & Terms: Arrange personal interview to show portfolio. Provide resume, business card, brochure, flyer or tearsheets to be kept on file for possible future assignments. Work with freelancers on assignment only. Reports in 1-2 weeks. Pays $250-1,000/day. Pays on receipt of invoice. Buys all rights (work-for-hire). Model release required. Credit line sometimes given.

Tips: In freelancer's portfolio or demos, wants to see fashion and reportage.

MIZEREK ADVERTISING, 48 E. 43rd St., New York NY 10017. (212)986-5702. President: Leonard Mizerek. Estab. 1974. Types of clients: Fashion, jewelry and industrial.

Needs: Works with 2 freelance photographers/month. Uses photographs for trade magazines. Subjects include: still life and jewelry. Reviews stock photos of creative images showing fashion/style.

Specs: Uses 8×10 glossy b&w prints; 4×5 and 8×10 transparencies.

First Contact & Terms: Submit portfolio for review. Provide resume, business, card, brochure, flyer or tearsheets to be kept on file for possible future assignments. SASE. Reports in 2 weeks. Pays $1,000-1,500/day; $300-800/job; $500/color photo; $150/b&w photo. Pays on acceptance. Buys all rights; negotiable. Model release required. Credit line sometimes given.

Tips: Looks for "clear product visualization. Must show detail and have good color balance. Sees trend toward "more use of photography and expanded creativity."

*■MOLINO + ASSOCIATES, INC., Suite 2404, 245 Fifth Ave., New York NY 10016. (212)689-7370. FAX: (212)689-7448. PR firm. Production Manager: Debra Fisher. Estab. 1989. Types of clients: nonprofit health care. Recent projects include General Motors Cancer Research Foundation, The Hebrew Home for the Aged at Riverdale and American Association for Cancer Research.

Needs: Works with 1-2 freelancers/month. Uses photos for direct mail, posters, newspapers and audiovisual. Subjects include: health care for the elderly.
Audiovisual Needs: Uses slides, film and videotape—"all, but not too often—once or twice a year."
Specs: Uses 5×7 and 8×10 color and b&w prints; 35mm transparencies.
First Contact & Terms: Interested in receiving work from newer, lesser-known photographers. Submit portfolio for review. Provide resume, business card, brochure, flyer or tearsheets to be kept on file for possible future assignments. Works with local freelancers only. Keeps samples on file. SASE. Reports in 1-3 weeks. Pays $500-1,000/day; $12-16/b&w photo. Pays on receipt of invoice. Buy all rights and others; negotiable. Model release required for caregivers and patients. Photo captions preferred. Credit line sometimes given: "If the photo is used on an invitation, no; if in a brochure, yes."
Tips: Wants to see "subjects—people, styles—realistic. Capabilities: showing personality of subjects through lighting, etc. Mainly photos are used for fundraising and/or informational brochures. Photographer has to be good with people he/she's photographing—especially old people, have a good eye for composition and lighting."

■**RUTH MORRISON ASSOCIATES**, 19 West 44th St., New York NY 10036. (212)302-8886. FAX: (212)302-5512. PR firm. Account Executive: Gail Hulbert. Estab. 1972. Types of clients: specialty foods, housewares, home furnishings and general business.
Needs: Works with 1-2 freelance photographers—videographers/month. Uses photographers for consumer magazines, trade magazines, P-O-P displays, posters, newspapers, signage and audiovisual.
Audiovisual Needs: Uses photos and videotape.
Specs: Specifications vary according to clients' needs. Typically uses b&w and transparencies.
First Contact & Terms: Arrange personal interview to show portfolio. Provide resume, business card, brochure, flyer or tearsheets to be kept on file for possible future assignments. Works with freelancers on assignment only. Reports "as needed." Pays $100-1,000 depending upon client's budget. Rights negotiable. Credit line given sometimes, depending on use.

MOSS & COMPANY, INC., 49 W. 38th St., New York NY 10018. (212)575-0808. Executive Art Director: Anthony Micale. Ad agency. Serves clients in consumer products, manufacturing, utilities, insurance and packaged goods. Annual billing: $10,000,000.
Needs: Works with 2-3 freelance photographers/month. Uses photographers for billboards, consumer and trade magazines, direct mail, TV, brochures/flyers and newspapers.
First Contact & Terms: Call for appointment to show portfolio. Negotiates payment based on client's budget: $300-3,000/job; $600/b&w photo; $2,000/color photo. Prefers to see samples of still life and people.
Tips: "Photographer must be technically perfect with regard to shooting still life and people."

*■**TOM NICHOLSON ASSOCIATES, INC.**, 295 Lafayette St., 8th Fl., New York NY 10012. (212)274-0470. FAX: (212)274-0380. AV firm. Estab. 1987. Types of clients: industrial and financial. Examples of recent projects: "Citibank IdeaBank," Citibank, N.A.; "Sailing," IBM Corp.; Shopper's Express, Whittle Communications; (all interactive computer programs).
Needs: Works with 1 freelance photographer/filmmaker/videographer/month. Uses photographers for audiovisual and interactive computer programs (multimedia). Subjects include scenes, nature. Reviews stock photos "on project basis only."
Audiovisual Needs: Uses slides, film and videotape as part of computer interactive programs; broad range of subject matter.
Specs: Uses b&w and color prints; 35mm transparencies; ¾" or 1" Beta videotape.
First Contact & Terms: Provide resume, business card, brochure, flyer or tearsheets to be kept on file for possible future assignments. Works on assignment only. Keeps samples on file. Cannot return material. Reports in 3 weeks. NPI. Pays on receipt of invoice. Buys all rights and one-time rights; negotiable. Credit line sometimes given.
Tips: Sees a "need for broad-based material in larger quantity on videodisk and computer."

NOSTRADAMUS ADVERTISING, #1128A, 250 W. 57th, New York NY 10107. (212)581-1362. Ad agency. President: Barry Sher. Estab. 1974. Types of clients: politicians, nonprofit organizations and small businesses.
Needs: Uses freelancers occasionally for consumer magazines, trade magazines, direct mail, catalogs and posters. Subjects include: people and products.
Specs: Uses 8×10 glossy b&w and color prints; 8×10 transparencies.
First Contact & Terms: Provide resume, business car, brochure. Works with local freelancers only. Cannot return material. Pays $50-100/hour. Pays 30 days from invoice. Buys all rights (work-for-hire). Model release required. Credit line sometimes given.

RICHARD H. ROFFMAN ASSOCIATES, Suite 6A, 697 West End Ave., New York NY 10025. (212)749-3647. Contact: Vice President. Estab. 1962. PR firm. Types of clients: all types of accounts, "everything from A to Z." Free client list available with SASE.
Needs: Photos used in public relations, publicity and promotion. Works with about 3 freelance photographers/month on assignment only.
First Contact & Terms: Provide resume, flyer, business card or brochure to be kept on file for possible future assignments. Buys about 40 photos annually. Negotiates payment based on client's budget, amount of creativity required, where work will appear and photographer's previous experience/reputation. Pays $10-20/hour; $50-100/day; $50-100/job; $35/b&w photo; $85/color photo. Pays on delivery. Submit model release with photo.
Tips: "Nothing should be sent except a business card or general sales presentation or brochure. Nothing should be sent that requires sending back, as we unfortunately don't have the staff or time. We have assignments from time to time for freelancers."

■**PETER ROGERS ASSOCIATES,** 355 Lexington Ave., New York NY 10017. (212)599-0055. FAX:(212)682-4309. Ad agency. Art Director: Tracy. Estab. 1977. Types of clients: retail, fashion and package goods. Examples of ad campaigns: "Images," Judith Leiber, spreads (magazine); "International Salons," Vidal Sassoon, TV and print; and "La Prairie," La Prairie, ads and PR.
Needs: Works with 10-20 freelancers/month. Uses photographers for trade magazines, consumer magazines, P-O-P displays, posters, signage and audiovisual. Subjects include: people and still life photos. Reviews video footage; beauty and fashion subject matter.
Audiovisual Needs: Uses film and videotape.
Specs: Uses b&w prints; 35mm and 8 × 10 transparencies; 35mm and 16mm film and ¾" videotape. Corporate images.
First Contact & Terms: Arrange personal interview to show portfolio. Send unsolicited photos by mail for consideration. Query with samples. Submit portfolio for review. Provide resume, business card, brochure, flyer or tearsheets to be kept on file for possible future assignments. Works on assignment only. SASE. Reports in 2 weeks. NPI. Payment depends on artist and job. Pays on receipt of invoice. Buys one-time rights and all rights; one-year buyout. Model release required. Credit line sometimes given.
Tips: In freelancer's work, wants to see "high style, editorial style, best quality, unique and well done technically. Trend is toward more informality, more dynamic. Be persistent, be cooperative, have a concept behind your work, and show intelligence. Also note, videotapes are made with stills all the time."

SCHORR, HOWARD AND MEGILL, 770 Lexington Ave., New York NY 10021. (212)935-5555. Principal: Martha Megill. Types of clients: industrial.
Needs: Works with 1-3 freelance photographers/month. Uses photographers for trade magazines. Subject matter includes manufacturing operations.
Specs: Uses b&w prints, 35mm and 2¼ × 2¼ transparencies (film and contact sheets).
First Contact & Terms: Provide resume, business card, brochure, flyer or tearsheets to be kept on file for possible future assignments. Works on assignment only. Does not return unsolicited material. Reports in 1 week. Pays $500-1,500/day. Pays on receipt of invoice. Buys all rights. Model release required.
Tips: Wants to see in portfolio or samples "solid industrial photography experience, particularly in manufacturing processes and operations." To break in, "send b&w and color samples of industrial work. Send brochure, flyer, tearsheets; follow up with call."

■**SPENCER PRODUCTIONS, INC.,** 234 5th Ave., New York NY 10001. General Manager: Bruce Spencer. Estab. 1961. PR firm. Types of clients: business, industry. Produces motion pictures and videotape.
Needs: Satirical approach to business and industry problems. Freelance photos used on special projects. Length: "Films vary—from a 1-minute commercial to a 90-minute feature." Works with 1-2 freelance photographers/month on assignment only. Buys 2-6 films/year.
Specs: 16mm color commercials, documentaries and features.
First Contact & Terms: Interested in receiving work from newer, lesser-known photographers. Provide resume and letter of inquiry to be kept on file for possible future assignments. Query with samples and resume of credits. "Be brief and pertinent!" SASE. Reports in 3 weeks. Pays $50-150/color and b&w photos (purchase of prints only; does not include photo session); $5-15/hour; $500-5,000/job; negotiates payment based on client's budget. Pays a royalty of 5-10%. Pays on acceptance. Buys one-time rights and all rights; negotiable. Model/property release and captions required.
Tips: "Almost all of our talent was unknown in the field when hired by us. For a sample of our satirical philosophy, see paperback edition of *Don't Get Mad . . . Get Even* (W.W. Norton), by Alan Abel which we promoted, or *How to Thrive on Rejection* (Dembner Books, Inc.) or rent the home video *Is There Sex After Death?*, an R-rated comedy featuring Buck Henry."

∎**LEE EDWARD STERN COMMUNICATIONS**, Suite 2302, 450 7th Ave., New York NY 10123. (212)564-4250. Contact: Marilyn. PR firm; also provides editorial services. Types of clients: industrial, publishing, financial. Client list free with SASE.
Needs: Works with 1-2 freelance photographers/year. Uses photographers for brochures, annual reports, news coverage. Subject needs vary—people, plants, equipment, destination shots. Also works with freelance filmmakers to produce TV news clips, industrial films.
First Contact & Terms: Provide resume, business card, brochure, flyer or tearsheets to be kept on file for possible future assignments. Works with freelancers on assignment only. Pays $350 minimum/day. Pays after receiving client payment. Rights purchased vary. Model release required. Credit line sometimes given.

∎**TALCO PRODUCTIONS**, 279 E. 44th St., New York NY 10017. (212)697-4015. President: Alan Lawrence. Vice President: Marty Holberton. Estab. 1964. Public relations agency and TV and audiovisual production firm. Types of clients: industrial, education, fashion, labor, political and nonprofit organizations. Produces motion pictures and videotape.
Needs: Buys "a few" photos/year; does subcontract short sequences at distant locations.
Audiovisual Needs: 16mm and 35mm film, all professional videotape formats; documentaries, industrials, public relations. Filmmaker might be assigned "second unit or pick-up shots."
First Contact & Terms: Provide resume, flyer or brochure to be kept on file for possible future assignments. Prefers to see general work or "sample applicable to a specific project we are working on." Works on assignment only. Payment negotiable according to client's budget and where the work will appear. Pays on acceptance. Buys all rights. Model release required.
Tips: Filmmaker "must be experienced—union member is preferred. We do not frequently use freelancers except outside the New York City area when it is less expensive than sending a crew." Query with resume of credits only—don't send samples. "We will ask for specifics when an assignment calls for particular experience or talent." Returns unsolicited material (unread) if SASE included. Reports in 3 weeks.

AL WASSERMAN COMPANY, (formerly Newmarks Advertising Agency), % Merling Marx & Seidman, 5th Floor, 440 Park Ave S., New York NY 10016. Ad agency. Owner: Al Wasserman. Estab. 1991. Types of clients: industrial, finance, business-to-business, real estate, recruitment and fitness.
Needs: Uses freelance photographers for consumer and trade magazines, direct mail, catalogs, posters and newspapers. Subjects include fitness and sports.
Specs: Uses 8×10 glossy b&w prints; 35mm, 2¼×2¼, 4×5, 8×10 transparencies.
First Contact & Terms: Query with photocopies of samples. Provide resume, business card, brochure, flyer or tearsheets to be kept on file for possible future assignments. Works on assignment only. Does not return unsolicited material. Reports in 1 week. Pays $350-900/b&w photo; $350-900/color photo; $500-1,500/day; and $750-5,000/job. Pays on acceptance and receipt of invoice. Buys one-time rights or all rights. Model release required; captions preferred. Credit line sometimes given.
Tips: Looks for originality. Send nonreturnable samples such as Xerox prints or shots.

North Carolina

CLELAND, WARD, SMITH & ASSOCIATES, Suite 520, Tobacco Square Bldg., 836 Oak St., Winston-Salem NC 27101. (919)723-5551. Ad agency. Production Manager: James K. Ward. Types of clients: primarily industrial and business-to-business.
Needs: Uses photographers for trade magazines, direct mail, brochures and catalogs. Subjects include: "product shots or location shots of plants, offices, workers and production flow; also technical equipment detail shots."
Specs: Uses 8×10 b&w and color prints and transparencies.
First Contact & Terms: Arrange a personal interview to show portfolio. Works on assignment only. Does not return unsolicited material. NPI; payment negotiable. Pays on acceptance. Buys all rights. Model release required.
Tips: Prefers to see "innovation—not just execution. We are not dazzled by pretty color. How the shot tells the story of the product is the important part."

*∎EPLES ASSOCIATES, 4819 Park Rd., Charlotte NC 28209. (704)522-1220. Graphics Manager: Erin Minton. Estab. 1968. Types of clients: industrial and others.
Needs: Works with 2-4 freelance photographers and/or videographers/month. Subjects include: photojournalism.
Audiovisual Needs: Uses slides and videotape.
Specs: "Specifications depend on situation."
First Contact & Terms: Works on assignment only. NPI. Pays on receipt of invoice. Buys various rights. Model/property release required. Credit line sometimes given, "depends on client circumstance."

∎IMAGE ASSOCIATES, 4314 Bland Rd., Raleigh NC 27609. (919)876-6400. FAX: (919)876-7064. AV firm. Estab. 1984. Creative Director: John Wigmore. Types of clients: industrial, financial and corporate. Examples of recent projects: "The American Dream," GECAP (multi-image); CTT (multi-image); and Exide Electronics (print).
Needs: Works with 3 freelance photographers/month for audiovisual uses. Interested in reviewing stock photos.
Audiovisual Needs: Uses photos for multi-image slide presentation and multimedia.
First Contact & Terms: Interested in receiving work from newer, lesser-known photographers. Provide resume, business card, brochure, flyer or tearsheets to be kept on file for possible future assignments. Works with freelancers on assignment only. Cannot return material. Reports in 1 month. Pays $100 maximum/hour; $800 minimum/day; $50/color photo; $100/stock photo. Pays within 30 days of invoice. Buys all rights; negotiable. Model release, property release and photo captions required. Credit line given sometimes; negotiable.
Tips: "We have a greater need to be able to scan photos for multimedia computer programs."

North Dakota

KRANZLER, KINGSLEY COMMUNICATIONS LTD., P.O. Box 693, Bismarck ND 58502. (701)255-3067. Ad agency. Art Director: Scott Montgomery. Types of clients: industrial, financial, etc.
Needs: Works with 1 freelance photographer/month. Uses photographers for consumer and trade magazines, direct mail, P-O-P displays, catalogs, posters and newspapers. Subjects include local and regional.
Specs: Uses 8 × 10 glossy b&w/color prints; 35mm, 2¼ × 2¼ and 4 × 5 transparencies.
First Contact & Terms: Query with list of stock photo subjects. Provide resume, business card, brochure, flyer or tearsheets to be kept on file for possible future assignments. Works with freelance photographers on assignment basis only; local freelancers 90% of time. SASE. Reports in 2 weeks. Pays $50/b&w photo; $25-300/color photo; hour and day rates are negotiable depending on location and travel. Pays on publication. Buys all and one-time rights. Model release required; captions preferred. Credit line given.
Tips: In reviewing a photographer's portfolio or samples, prefers to see "people – working, playing – various views of each shot, including artistic angles, etc., creative expressions using emotions."

Ohio

∎BARON ADVERTISING, INC., Suite 645, 1422 Euclid Ave., Cleveland OH 44115-1901. (216)621-6800. Ad agency. President: Selma Baron. Types of clients: food, industrial and financial. In particular, serves various manufacturers of tabletop and food service equipment.
Needs: Uses 20-25 freelance photographers/month. Uses photos for direct mail, catalogs, newspapers, consumer magazines, P-O-P displays, posters, trade magazines, brochures and signage. Subject matter "diverse."
Audiovisual Needs: Works with freelance filmmakers for AV presentations.
First Contact & Terms: Arrange a personal interview to show portfolio. Query with list of stock photo subjects; provide resume, business card, brochure, flyer or tearsheets to be kept on file for possible future assignments. Works with freelancers on assignment only. Does not return unsolicited material. NPI. Payment "depends on the photographer." Pays on completion. Buys all rights. Model release required.

Tips: Prefers to see "food and equipment" photos in the photographer's samples. "Samples not to be returned other than regional photographers."

*■ELITE VIDEO, INC., P.O. Box 2789, Toledo OH 43606. Director: David Thompson. Types of clients: advertising agencies, audiovisual firms, cable companies, home video distributors, closed circuit television firms, both domestic and international.
Needs: Works with 6-7 freelance photographers/month. Uses photos for audiovisual. Needs glamour, erotic, nude, bikini and humorous videos from snippets to full blown and edited features.
Specs: Needs clear VHS tape for initial samples. "The master should be professional quality."
First Contact & Terms: Send sample footage via certified mail with a SASE. Keeps samples on file. Reports in 3 weeks. "Don't send a resume or listing of education. You can either produce this material, or you can't. If you can, we will call you quickly." Pays 50-67% commission for domestic sales and 50% for international sales. "We offer whatever rights the producer/videographer is willing to sell."
Tips: "This market is exploding. Don't sit on good material. Send it to us. If we return it, it will usually be with suggestions. If we like it, you will get a contract sent out and we will begin to aggressively market you and your work. In addition, we will happily make suggestions to help you improve the salability of your future work."

*■FUNK/LUETKE, INC., 12th Floor, 405 Madison Ave., Toledo OH 43604. (419)241-1244. FAX: (419)242-5210. PR firm. Project Manager: Kristin M. Paquette. Estab. 1985. Types of clients: corporate, industrial, finance, health/hospitals.
Needs: Works with 20 freelance photographers. Uses photographs for newspapers, audiovisual, employee newsletter. Subjects include: photojournalism (b&w), health-related-hospitals, corporate communications, industrial, location assignments and video newsletters.
Audiovisual Needs: Uses photos and/or film or video for broadcast quality videotape.
Specs: Uses 8×10, b&w prints; 35mm transparencies; BetaCam SP/broadcast quality.
First Contact & Terms: Provide resume, business card, brochure, flyer or tearsheets to be kept on file for possible future assignments. Works with freelancers on assignment only. Keeps samples on file. Reports in 1-2 weeks. Pays $50-100/hour; $500-1,000/day; $50-1,500/job; $100/color photo; $75/b&w photo. Pays 45 days after receipt of invoice. Model release required or preferred depending on project. Credit line sometimes given depending upon project.
Tips: In samples and queries, wants to see "photojournalism (b&w), ability to cover location assignments, ability to work independently and represent firm professionally, enthusiasm for work, service-oriented, deadline oriented, available on short notice and willing to travel." Sees trend toward "more use of freelancers because of the need to match the right person with the right job." To break in with this firm, "be enthusiastic, eager to work and flexible. Be willing to research the client. Be a part of the assignment. Make suggestions; go beyond the assignment given. Be a partner in the job."

GRISWOLD INC., 101 Prospect Ave. W., Cleveland OH 44115. (216)696-3400. Executive Art Director: Bob Clancy. Ad agency. Types of clients: Consumer and industrial firms; client list provided upon request. Provide brochure to be kept on file for possible future assignments.
Needs: Works with freelance photographers on assignment only basis. Uses photographers for billboards, consumer and trade magazines, direct mail, P-O-P displays, brochures, catalogs, posters, newspapers and AV presentations.
First Contact & Terms: Works primarily with local freelancers but occasionally uses others. Arrange interview to show portfolio. NPI. Payment is per day or project; negotiates according to client's budget. Pays on production.

■HARDING PRODUCTIONS, 4782 Unity Line Rd., New Waterford OH 44445. (216)457-7352. Owner: William R. Harding. Estab. Estab. 1983. Types of clients: industrial and corporate accounts, retail and television commercials.
Audiovisual Needs: Works with 5 freelancers/month for videotapes, audio and lighting, plus writing. Also looking for new ideas for the home VCR market, possibly 'how-to' data.
First Contact & Terms: Arrange a personal interview to show video demo reel. Provide resume, business card, self-promotion piece or tearsheets to be kept on file for possible future assignments. Works with freelancers on assignment only. SASE. Reports in 2 weeks. Payment "very dependent on needs and skills"; $5-10/hour and $50-300/day. Pay is "negotiated at time of hiring." Buys all rights. May negotiate for use on certain projects. Credit line given.

> ■ *The solid, black square before a listing indicates that the market uses various types of audiovisual materials, such as slides, film or videotape.*

Tips: "Call first and we will set up an appointment to see your work. We are interested only in self-starters who are motivated to get into this business and are willing to do what it takes to make it. Be prepared to show work you have actually done and not work of a crew you just happened to be on. If on a crew, tell us what you did yourself. Video is starting to dominate the industrial and corporate field. Clients are finding more and more ways to use it. We now do video exclusively."

■HAYES PUBLISHING CO., INC., 6304 Hamilton Ave., Cincinnati OH 45224. (513)681-7559. Office Manager: Marge Lammers. AV producer. Types of clients: school, civic and right-to-life groups. Produces filmstrips and slide/cassette sets.
Needs: Subjects include "miscellaneous baby, child and adult scenes." Needs photos of prenatal development of the human body and shots relating to abortion. Buys all rights. Contact by mail first. Reports in 2 weeks. SASE.
Specs: Contact by mail about specifications and needs for b&w first. For color, uses 35mm transparencies, or negatives with 5×7 glossy prints. Captions and model release required. Pays $50 minimum.
Tips: "We are always looking for excellent, thoroughly documented and authenticated photographs of early developing babies and of any and all types of abortions."

■HOLLAND ADVERTISING, 252 Ludlow Ave., Cincinnati OH 45220. (513)221-1252. Ad agency. Creative Director: Mark Holland. Types of clients: retail, industrial and finance. Examples of ad campaigns: Astromet (trade magazines ad for ceramic furnace filters); Hilton Davis (brochure and ads for food colorings); Cincinnati Time (brochure for time clock systems).
Needs: Uses 2 freelance photographers/month. Uses photographers for billboards, consumer magazines, trade magazines, direct mail, P-O-P displays, catalogs, posters and newspapers. Subjects vary. Reviews stock photos, film or video.
Specs: Vary according to clients needs.
First Contact & Terms: Query with list of stock photo subjects, query with samples; provide resume, business card, brochure, flyer or tearsheets to be kept on file for possible future assignments. Works with freelancers on an assignment basis only. SASE. Reports in 2 weeks. Pays $20-35/hour; $500-1,000/day, $75-150/color photo; and $50-100/b&w photo. Also pays on estimate basis. Pays on publication. Buys all rights. Model release preferred. Credit line given "depending on assignment and price."
Tips: Trend toward "more stock photography being solicited and used."

■THE JAYME ORGANIZATION, One Corporate Exchange, 25825 Science Park Dr., Cleveland OH 44122. (216)831-0110. FAX: (216)464-2308. Ad agency. Contact: Associate Creative Director or Senior Art Director. Estab. 1947. Clients include: industrial, financial, food and business-to-business. Examples of recent campaigns: Dow Chemical (new business direct mail); Sherwin Williams (new business direct mail); and Interbold (new company introduction).
Needs: Works with 5-10 freelancers/year. Uses photos for trade magazines, direct mail, P-O-P displays, catalogs and audiovisual uses. Subject matter varies. Reviews stock photos and videotape footage.
Audiovisual Needs: Uses slides and videotape as needed.
Specs: Uses 8×10 and 16×20 color and b&w prints; also uses 35mm, 2¼×2¼ and 4×5 transparencies. Occasionally uses videotape; formats not specified.
First Contact & Terms: Submit portfolio for review. Provide resume, business card, brochure, flyer or tearsheets to be kept on file for possible future assignments. Works on assignment only. Keeps samples on file. Cannot return materials. Reports as needed; "we'll only call if interested in using them." NPI; payment determined by project budget. Pays on receipt of invoice. Most rights negotiable; cases of buying all rights are negotiable, "depending upon client." Model and property release required. Credit lines sometimes given according to "project/client."
Tips: "We need to see a dynamite book."

■JONES, ANASTASI, BIRCHFIELD ADVERTISING INC., (formerly Jones, Anastasi, Lennon Advertising, Inc.), 6065 Frantz Rd., Dublin OH 43017. (614)764-1274. Creative Director/VP: Joe Anastasi. Ad agency. Types of clients: hospitals, insurance, colleges, food and restaurants and industrial.
Needs: Works on assignment basis only. Uses photographers for billboards, consumer and trade magazines, brochures, posters, newspapers and AV presentations.
First Contact & Terms: Arrange interview to show portfolio. NPI. Payment is per hour, per day, and per project; negotiates according to client's budget.

■LIGGETT STASHOWER ADVERTISING, INC., 1228 Euclid Ave., Cleveland OH 44115. (216)348-8500. FAX: (216)736-8113. Ad agency. Contact: Linda M. Barberic. Estab. 1932. Types of clients: full service agency. Examples of recent projects: Society Bank, Sears Optical, and Babcock and Wilcox.

Needs: Works with 50+ freelance photographers—filmmakers—videographers/month. Uses photographers for billboards, consumer magazines, trade magazines, direct mail, P-O-P displays, catalogs, posters, newspapers, signage and audiovisual. Interested in reviewing stock photos/film or video footage.
Audiovisual Needs: Uses photos/film/commercials.
Specs: Uses b&w/color prints (size and finish varies); 35mm, 2¼×2¼, 4×5, 8×10 (rarely) transparencies; 16mm film; ¼-¾″ videotape.
First Contact & Terms: Send unsolicited photos by mail for consideration; query with samples; provide resume, business card, brochure, flyer or tearsheets to be kept on file for possible future assignments. Works with local freelancers only. SASE. Reports in 1-2 weeks. Pays $100 minimum/b&w photo; $50-200/hour; $800-2,500/day. Pays within 45 days of acceptance. Rights purchased depends on jobs. Model release required. Credit line given sometimes, depending on usage.

LOHRE & ASSOCIATES INC., Suite 101, 2330 Victory Pkwy., Cincinnati OH 45206. (513)961-1174. Ad agency. President: Charles R. Lohre. Types of clients: industrial.
Needs: Works with 1 photographer/month. Uses photographers for trade magazines, direct mail, catalogs and prints. Subjects include: machine-industrial themes and various eye-catchers.
Specs: Uses 8×10 glossy b&w and color prints; 4×5 transparencies.
First Contact & Terms: Query with resume of credits; provide resume, business card, brochure, flyer or tearsheets to be kept on file for possible future assignments. Works with local freelancers only. SASE. Reports in 1 week. Pays $60/b&w photo; $250/color photo; $60/hour; $275/day. Pays on publication. Buys all rights.
Tips: Prefers to see eye-catching and thought-provoking images/non-human. Need someone to take 35mm photos on short notice in Cincinnati plants.

■**MIDWEST TALENT/CREATIVE TALENT**, 1102 Neil Ave., Columbus OH 43201. (614)294-7827. FAX: (614)294-3396. Talent Developer: Gary Aggas. Also 700 W. Pete Rose Way, Cincinnati OH 45203. (513)241-7827. Contact: Betty McCormick. Types of clients: talent and advertising agencies; production companies.
Needs: Works with 2-3 freelance photographers/month. Uses photographers for slide sets and videotapes. Subjects include portfolios and promotional shots of models and actors.
Specs: Uses 5×7 and 11×14 b&w prints; 35mm transparencies; and U-matic ¾″ videotape.
First Contact & Terms: Query with samples or resume. Works with freelancers by assignment only. SASE. Reports in 2-3 weeks. Pays $4-10/b&w photo, $4-25/color photo, $25-65/hour and $100-275/job. Pays on acceptance. Buys all rights. Credit line given.
Tips: "Be concise, to the point and have good promotional package. We like to see well lit subjects with good faces."

NATIONWIDE ADVERTISING, INC., The Halle Bldg., 1228 Euclid Ave./Sixth Floor, Cleveland OH 44115. (216)579-0300. Creative Director: Jim Herringshaw. Ad agency. "This is a recruitment agency which is utilized by a wide variety of clientele, really indiscriminate."
Needs: Works with "very few freelancers, but this could change." Uses freelancers for billboards, consumer and trade magazines, newspapers and TV.
First Contact & Terms: Send samples, but "does not want actual portfolio." Selects freelancers "by how easily accessible they are and the characteristics of their work." NPI. Negotiates payment based on client's budget. Does not return unsolicited material.

SMILEY/HANCHULAK, INC., 47 N. Cleveland-Massillon Rd., Akron OH 44313. (216)666-0868. Ad agency. Associate Creative Director: Dominick Sorrent, Jr. Clients: all types.
Needs: Works with 1-2 photographers/month. Uses freelance photographers for consumer magazines, trade magazines, direct mail, P-O-P displays, catalogs, posters and sales promotion.
Specs: Uses 11×14 b&w and color prints, finish depends on job; 35mm or 2¼×2¼ (location) or 4×5 or 8×10 (usually studio) transparencies, depends on job.
First Contact & Terms: Arrange a personal interview to show portfolio; query with resume of credits, list of stock photo subjects or samples; send unsolicited photos by mail for consideration; or submit portfolio for review. Provide resume, business card, brochure, flyer or tearsheets to be kept on file for possible future assignments. If a personal interview cannot be arranged, a letter would be acceptable. Works with freelance photographers on assignment basis only. SASE. Report depends on work schedule. NPI. Pays per day, or per job. Buys all rights unless requested otherwise. Model release required. Captions preferred.
Tips: Prefers to see studio product photos. "Jobs vary—we need to see all types with the exception of fashion. We would like to get more contemporary but photo should still do the job."

Close-up

Nancy Clendaniel
Nancy Clendaniel Photography
Renton, Washington

© Nancy Clendaniel

When Nancy Clendaniel photographed Paul McCartney, his daughter described her work as "painterly." Such a term works well for Clendaniel, an accomplished photojournalist who began her career as a portrait painter, but quickly moved to photography.

In 1978 she began working at The Beverly Theater in Los Angeles, shooting everyone from Count Basie to Bob Dylan. Her photos were viewed by performers and others who saw how she caught key moments. Because of her talent she has worked with Wolfman Jack, Ray Charles, Tina Turner, The Manhattan Transfer and comedian Gallagher.

Clendaniel finds work without using a rep. "Too often they find jobs not suited to me," she says. Instead, she may have an associate show prospects her portfolios—a corporate book for editorial jobs, an illustrative display for fine art jobs, one for portrait work, and another with strictly theatrical and performance photography.

"Pick jobs carefully," Clendaniel suggests. "Getting started, I took some that were over my head, like on-location album covers. Directing lighting, set-ups, make-up, costumes was not my thing."

Instead, Clendaniel prefers invisibility. "I try to capture the essence of a performer without breaking the mood," says Clendaniel, who finds strobes and motor drives to be distractions. "Working in 'sacred space,' I make every frame count. I learned to burn film, but I can't always do that. If it's a choice between getting a shot or trashing the magic, I hold back. This respect has opened doors for me."

In addition to respect and dependability, Clendaniel earns repeat jobs because she enjoys people. "I try to give something back. My corporate work is a big change from shooting celebrities." One public relations professional calls her "a role model for corporate photographers. When she works an event, people are happy to have her there."

"I blend in and build trust," says Clendaniel. "I meet everyone—security guards, camera crew, even the fire marshall, so I'm not a stranger." To help her blend into the background, she wears dark colors and avoids wearing squeaky shoes. "Don't show up loaded with clattering equipment." She travels light, normally carrying three camera bodies (OM-1's) and a variety of lenses, ranging from 24mm to 85mm, a 200mm telephoto or comparable zoom, and a 2x adapter. For events like the Grammy Awards, she uses two Vivitar 283s, powered by a Quantum battery pack.

She also suggests picking one film and staying with it. "Theatrical lights make it hard to get a correct reading, so know how your film performs," says Clendaniel. She uses a Kodak movie stock film from RGB lab in Los Angeles. "It's a negative film, ranging from ASA 50 to ASA 500, good for prints or slides. Using it I can send out slides and keep the negatives."

Clendaniel carefully defines projects and budgets at the outset and suggests newcomers do the same. "Nail down usage rights and include expenses in your quote." Her billing slip lists four categories of projects: editorial/journalism, advertising, promotion and miscellaneous, and corporate/industrial. Usage might include book jackets, catalogs or album covers. "Understand how your work will be used."

Clendaniel's mentor, Phil Douglis, taught her an important lesson in her early days. "Give them what they say they want, but don't forget to capture what you see," she recalls. "Lend your imagination and personal interpretation to any assignment and give more than is expected."

Although beginning photographers are anxious to find work, they should be wary of working for free. "Don't give your work away. I did my share of free jobs to get my lens in the door, but don't sell yourself short," she says.

In 1983 The Manhattan Transfer asked her to shoot recording sessions for their *Vocalese* album. Her rate was competitive, but management told her it was too much. Fed up with battling for appropriate payment, she told them to find someone else and at the same time wondered if she'd lost her mind. They called her back shortly to say the Transfer wanted her, no matter what the fee. "It built my confidence," remembers Clendaniel.

As director of the nonprofit educational organization Women in Photography (WIP), Clendaniel values communication and networking among photographers. "It's easy to be isolated. I talk to others whenever I can, learning about pitfalls, hourly and day rates, places to buy film." WIP has been a valuable resource, she says.

Clendaniel tells aspiring photographers to have confidence and cultivate innate skills. "Photography isn't more important than family and friends. It's not the cure for cancer. But I enjoy my work and look forward to each job. I'm very lucky to do what I love."

—Rick Pender

© Nancy Clendaniel

Whether she is shooting concert footage of a vibrant Tina Turner or snapping portraits like this one of musician John Mayall, Nancy Clendaniel wants to uncover the essence of her subjects. The bold silver jewelry Mayall wears tells a lot about his character and also adds to the impressive lighting and sharpness of the photo.

WATT, ROOP & CO., 1100 Superior Ave., Cleveland OH 44114. (216)566-7019. PR firm. Vice President/Manager of Design Operations: Thomas Federico. Estab. 1981. Types of clients: industrial, financial and medical. Examples of recent projects: Frances Payne Bolton School of Nursing and memorabilia shots for capabilities brochure; Cleveland Indians (marketing piece).
Needs: Works with 4 freelance photographers/month. Uses photos for trade magazines and corporate/capabilities brochures. Subjects include: corporate.
First Contact & Terms: Interested in receiving work from newer, lesser-known photographers. Provide resume, business card, brochure, flyer or tearsheets to be kept on file for possible future assignments. Works with local freelancers on assignment only. Reports "as needed." Pays $100-1,500/b&w photo; $400-2,000/color photo; $50-75/hour; $400-1,500/day. Pays on receipt of invoice. Buys all rights (work-for-hire); one-time rights; rights negotiable. Model release, property release and photo captions preferred. Credit line sometimes given.
Tips: Wants to see "variety, an eye for the unusual. Be professional." Sees a trend in the way photographers are cutting their prices.

■**WOLF, BLUMBERG, KRODY**, 19 Garfield Pl., Cincinnati OH 45202. (513)784-0066. Ad agency. Contact: Art Directors. Types of clients: industrial, retail, financial.
Needs: Works with 8 freelance photographers/month. Uses photographers for billboards, consumer and trade magazines, direct mail, P-O-P displays, catalogs, posters, signage, newspapers and videos. Subject matter varies.
Specs: Uses all sizes b&w and color prints; 35mm, 2¼ × 2¼, 4 × 5 and 8 × 10 transparencies.
First Contact & Terms: Arrange a personal interview to show portfolio. Works with freelance photographers on assignment basis only. Does not return unsolicited material. Reports in 1 week. Pays $200-1,000/day, other rates vary. Pays within 30 days. Buys all rights. Model release required.

Oklahoma

ADVERTISING IN THREE-DIMENSION, 8921 E. 49th Place, Tulsa OK 74145. (918)664-1339. President: James W. Wray II. Types of clients: real estate, product advertisers, industrial, tourism, archaeology studies and medical.
Specs: Uses 3-D pictures taken with 35mm or larger format cameras. Accepts both b&w and color, but "no collectible stereoscopic cards."
First Contact & Terms: Arrange interview to present work in person. Send list of 3-D photo subjects. NPI; payment negotiable according to usability.
Tips: "Our needs are very specialized and require very sharp, high-quality pictures in both standard and hyper-stereo."

■**JORDAN ASSOCIATES ADVERTISING & COMMUNICATIONS**, 1000 W. Wilshire, P.O. Box 14005, Oklahoma City OK 73113. (405)840-3201. Director of Photography: John Williamson. Ad agency. Uses photographers for billboards, consumer and trade magazines, direct mail, foreign media, newspapers, P-O-P displays, radio and TV, annual reports and public relations. Types of clients: banking, manufacturing, food, clothing.
Needs: Generally works with 2-3 freelance photographers/month on assignment only.
Specs: Uses b&w prints and transparencies. Works with freelance filmmakers in production of 16mm industrial and videotape, TV spots; short films in 35mm.
First Contact & Terms: Arrange a personal interview to show portfolio (prefers to see a complete assortment of work in a portfolio); provide flyer and business card to be kept on file for possible future assignments. SASE. Reports in 2 weeks. Pays $25-55 minimum/hour for b&w, $200-400 minimum/day for b&w or color (plus materials). Payment negotiable according to client's budget and where the work will appear. Buys all rights. Model release required.

Market conditions are constantly changing! If you're still using this book and it's 1994 or later, buy the newest edition of Photographer's Market *at your favorite bookstore or order directly from Writer's Digest Books.*

Oregon

*■ADFILIATION ADVERTISING, 323 W. 13th, Eugene OR 97401. (503)687-8262. FAX: (503)687-8576. Ad Agency. Creative Director: Gary Schubert. Types of clients: industrial, food, computer, medical and sports.
Needs: Works with 2 freelance photographers/filmmakers/videographers/month. Uses photos for billboards, consumer and trade magazines, P-O-P displays, catalogs and posters. Interested in reviewing stock photos/film or video footage.
Audiovisual Needs: Uses slides, film and videotape.
Specs: Uses color and b&w prints and 35mm transparencies.
First Contact & Terms: Submit portfolio for review. Query with resume of credits. Query with stock photo list. Provide resume, business card, brochure, flyer or tearsheets to be kept on file for possible future assignments. Works on assignment only. Keeps samples on file. SASE. Reports in 1-2 weeks. NPI; depends on job and location. Pays on receipt of invoice. Rights purchased depends on usage. Will negotiate with a photographer not willing to sell all rights. Model and/or property release and captions required. Credit line given sometimes, depending on project and client.

BEAR CREEK DIRECT , P.O. Box 906, Medford OR 97501. (503)776-2121, ext. 3404. FAX: (503)734-2901. In-house ad agency for mail order companies. Photo Coordinator: Dave Bjurstrom. Types of clients: mail order fruit, food, bakery, floral, gardening and gifts. Examples of recent projects: Harry & David and Jackson & Perkins Co. (catalogs, promotional literature and ads).
Needs: Works with 3 freelance photographers/month. Uses photos for direct mail, catalogs and brochures.
Specs: Uses 35mm, 120mm and 4×5 transparencies.
First Contact & Terms: Interested in receiving work from newer, lesser-known photographers. Provide resume, business card, brochure, flyer or tearsheets to be kept on file for possible future assignments. Does not return unsolicited material. Reports in 2 weeks. Pays $500-1,500/day; or $150-300/shot. Pays on receipt. Buys one-time and all rights; negotiable. Model/property release required for anything with identifiable people or locations.
Tips: "I want to see 'perfect' gardens with spectacular color, romantic feeling. Food shots must be warm and friendly—no blemishes or unsightly areas. Be able to provide large quantities of photography to choose from. We are very particular with all of the details of the shots. Look at our catalogs to see the kinds of feeling we present."

■CREATIVE COMPANY, 3276 Commercial St. SE, Salem OR 97302. (503)363-4433. FAX: (503)363-6817. Ad agency. President/Creative Director: Jennifer L. Morrow. Estab. 1978. Types of clients: food products, health care, tourism, miscellaneous. Examples of recent projects: Supra Products, Marquis Spas, Oregan fruit products and Cherriots.
Needs: Works with 1-2 freelancers/month. Uses photographers for direct mail, P-O-P displays, catalogs, posters, audiovisual and sales promotion packages.
Specs: Uses 5×7 and larger glossy color or b&w prints; 2¼×2¼, 4×5 transparencies.
First Contact & Terms: Arrange personal interivew to show portfolio; provide resume, business card, brochure, flyer or tearsheets to be kept on file for possible future assignments. Works with local freelancers only. SASE. Reports "when needed." Pays $50-300/b&w photo; $100-400/color photo; $20-75/hour; $400-1,200/day. Pays on publication or "when client pays." Buys all rights. Model release preferred. Credit line not given.
Tips: In freelancer's porfolio, looks for "product shots, lighting, creative approach, understanding of sales message and reproduction." Sees trend toward "more special effect photography, manipulation of photos in computers." To break in with this firm, "do good work, be responsive and understand what color separations and printing will do to photos."

Pennsylvania

HAWBAKER COMMUNICATIONS, INC., 1 Oliver Plaza, Pittsburgh PA 15222. (412)261-6519. Head Art Director: Ron Larson. Ad agency. Uses direct mail, newspapers, trade magazines, radio and TV. Serves primarily industrial clients. Commissions 10 photographers/year.
Specs: Uses b&w 8×10 glossy prints; contact sheet and negatives OK. Also uses 8×10 color glossy prints, and 35mm and 4×5 transparencies.
First Contact & Terms: Query with resume of credits. SASE. Reports in 2 weeks. Pays $100-500/b&w or color photo; $400-1,200/day. Buys all rights. Model release required.

■**JERRYEND COMMUNCATIONS INC.**, 6334 Daniel Boone Rd., Birdsboro PA 19508. (215)689-9118. PR firm. Vice President: Jerry End. Types of clients: industrial, automotive aftermarket, financial, heavy equipment, nonprofit and public service. Examples of projects: Ingersoll-Rand Co./Motorsports (The Real Winners); Willson Safety Products (VIP/Very Important Products); Goodwill Industries (Projects With Industry).

Needs: Works with 2 freelance photographers/month. Uses photographers for consumer and trade magazines, catalogs, newspapers and AV presentations. Subjects include case histories/product applications.

Audiovisual Needs: Works with freelance filmmakers to produce training films, etc.

Specs: Uses 8×10 b&w repro-quality prints and color negatives.

First Contact & Terms: Provide resume, business card, brochure, flyer or tearsheets to be kept on file for possible future assignments. "Specify charges and terms." Works with freelance photographers on assignment basis only. SASE. Reports in 1 week. Pays "by estimate for project, $350 maximum." Pays on receipt of photos. Buys all rights. Model release required; captions preferred.

Tips: "We look for technical expertise in photo technique; clear reproducible photos for publicity use; and product photos reflecting scale of product to an identifiable subject."

KEENAN-NAGLE ADVERTISING, (formerly Helriegel-Keenan Advertising), 1301 S. 12th St., Allentown PA 18103-3814. (215)797-7100. FAX: (215)797-8212. Ad agency. Art Director: Judith Nentwig. Types of clients: industrial, retail, fashion, finance, health care and high-tech.

Needs: Works with 7-8 freelance photographers/month. Uses photographers for billboards, consumer magazines, trade magazines, direct mail, posters, signage and newspapers.

Specs: Uses b&w and color prints; 35mm, 2¼×2¼, 4×5 and 8×10 transparencies.

First Contact & Terms: Query with samples. Provide resume, business card, brochure, flyer or tearsheets to be kept on file for possible future assignments. Does not return unsolicited material. NPI. Pays on receipt. Model release required. Credit line sometimes given.

*■**MUDERICK MEDIA,** 101 Earlington Rd., Havertown PA 19083. (215)449-6970. Owner: Michael Muderick. Estab. 1984. Types of clients: industrial and financial.

Needs: Works with 4 photographers and/or videographers/month. Uses photos for audiovisual.

Audiovisual Needs: Uses slides and videotape.

Specs: Uses Betacam/¾" videotape, VHS for demo.

First Contact & Terms: Provide resume, business card, brochure, flyer or tearsheets to be kept on file for possible future assignments. Works with local freelancers only. Keeps samples on file. Does not report on unsolicited material. NPI; "payment depends on budget." Pays on acceptance or receipt of invoice. Buys all rights; negotiable. Model/property release required. Credit line not given.

ROSEN-COREN AGENCY INC., 902 Fox Pavilion, Jenkintown PA 19046. (215)572-8131. PR firm. Office Administrator: Ellen R. Coren. Types of clients: industrial, retail, fashion, finance, entertainment.

Needs: Works with 4 freelance photographers/month. Uses photos for PR shots.

Specs: Uses b&w prints.

First Contact & Terms: "Follow up with phone call." Works with local freelancers onlys. Reports when in need of service. Pays $50-65/hour; or /b&w and color photo. Pays when "assignment completed and invoice sent—30 days."

ROSKA DIRECT MARKETING, 1364 Welsh Rd., North Wales PA 19454. (215)643-9100. FAX: (215)643-2562. Art Director: Earl W. Weldon. Estab. 1981. Types of clients: retail, resort, finance, industrial, service and publishers.

Needs: Works with 2 photographers/month. Uses photos for direct mail and print advertising. Subject matter includes mostly people, but also some product and scenes.

Specs: Uses 8×10 prints and 2¼×2¼, 4×5 and 8×10 transparencies.

First Contact & Terms: Arrange a personal interview to show portfolio. Provide resume, business card, brochure, flyer or tearsheets to be kept on file for possible future assignments. SASE. Works on assignment only. Reports in 2 weeks. Pays $50-800/b&w photo; $100-1,500/color photo; $50-200/hour; $300-2,000/day. Rights negotiable. Model release required; property release and captions preferred.

Tips: Looks for creativity, clarity/focus, lighting. "Be competitive with rates, experience, studio size and location." To break in with firm, be willing to try all aspects, angles and be flexible in pricing.

SCEPTER GROUP, INC., Box 265, Morgantown PA 19543. (215)286-6020. Ad agency. Art Director: Bruce Becker. Types of clients: industrial, retail, financial.
Needs: Works with 3-5 freelance photographers/month. Uses photographers for consumer and trade magazines, P-O-P displays, catalogs and newspapers. Subjects include people and products.
Specs: Uses 8×10 glossy prints; 2¼×2¼ and 4×5 transparencies.
First Contact & Terms: Arrange a personal interview to show portfolio. Send unsolicited photos by mail for consideration. Does not return unsolicited material. Pays $500-2,000/day. Pays on receipt of invoice. Rights negotiable. Model release required.
Tips: Looks for "creativity, good product, situation, flair. Send samples, contact by phone."

■**THE SLIDEING BOARD**, 216 Blvd. of Allies, Pittsburgh PA 15222. (412)261-6006. Production Manager: Bob Fleck. Estab. 1979. Types of clients: consumer, industrial, financial and business-to-business.
Needs: Works with 5-6 photographers/month. Uses freelance photographers for slide sets, multimedia productions and videotapes. Prefers to work with local freelancers; works with national freelancers for stock, location and some video work. Subjects vary by assignment.
Specs: Uses 35mm, 4×5, 8×10 transparencies; also Betacam SP videotape.
First Contact & Terms: Local freelancers call to arrange personal interview to show portfolio, slides or demo materials. All others provide resume, business card, self-promotion piece or tearsheets to be kept on file for possible future assignments. SASE. Reports in 2 weeks. NPI. Payment made upon acceptance. Buys one-time rights or all rights. Captions and model releases preferred. Credit line sometimes given.
Tips: Photographers must have knowledge of how to shoot for multi-image, be able to understand objectives of assignment and have ability to work unsupervised.

■**STEWART DIGITAL VIDEO**, (formerly E.J. Stewart Inc.), 525 Mildred Ave., Primos PA 19018. (215)626-6500. FAX: (215)626-2638. Studio and video facility. Director of Sales: David Bowers. Estab. 1970. Types of clients: corporate, commercial, industrial, retail.
Audiovisual Needs: Uses 15-25 freelancers/month for film and videotape productions.
Specs: Reviews film or video of industrial and commercial subjects. Uses various film and videotape (specs).
First Contact & Terms: Provide resume, business card, brochure, to be kept on file for possible future assignments. Works with freelancers on assignment basis only. Reports as needed. Pays $250-800/day; also pays "per job as market allows and per client specs." Photo captions preferred.
Tips: "The industry is really exploding with all types of new applications for film/video production." In freelancer's demos, "looks for a broad background with particular attention paid to strong lighting and technical ability." To break in with this firm, "be patient. We work with a lot of freelancers and have to establish a rapport with any new ones that we might be interested in before we will hire them." Also, "get involved on smaller productions as a 'grip' or assistant, learn the basics and meet the players."

*■**U-GRAPH INC.**, P.O. Box 105, Westtown PA 19395. (215)399-1521. Multimedia firm. President: Rob Morris. Estab. 1986. Types of clients: industrial, financial and retail. Examples of recent projects: Bell Atlantic, Adria Labs and DuPont (trade shows).
Needs: Works with a few freelancers/month. Uses photos for direct mail, posters, audiovisual and computer graphics.
Audiovisual Needs: Uses videotape and computer graphics/digitized images.
Specs: Uses color prints.
First Contact & Terms: Provide resume, business card, brochure, flyer or tearsheets to be kept on file for possible future assignments. Works with local freelancers only on assignment. Keeps samples on file. Cannot return material. Reports in 1 month. NPI; "rates determined by budget." Pays on receipt of invoice. Rights negotiable. Model/property release required. Credit line given sometimes, depending on the photographer.
Tips: Looks for "strength, imagination, skill. The use of photography is growing."

■**DUDLEY ZOETROPE PRODUCTIONS**, 19 E Central Ave., Paoli PA 19301. (215)644-4991. Producer: David Speace. Types of clients: corporate.
Needs: Works with 1-2 photographers/month. Uses freelance photographers for slide sets, multi-image productions, films and videotapes. Subject depends on client.
Specs: Uses 35mm transparencies; videotape; 16mm and 35mm film.
First Contact & Terms: Arrange a personal interview to show portfolio. Provide resume, business card, self-promotion piece or tearsheets to be kept on file for possible future assignments. Works with freelancers on assignment only. Does not return unsolicited material. Reports in 1 week. NPI. Pays per day. Payment made on acceptance. Buys all rights. Credit line sometimes given.

Tips: "Make your approach straight forward. Don't expect an assignment because someone looked at your portfolio. We are interested in photographers who can shoot for AV. They must be able to shoot from varied angles and present sequences that can tell a story."

Rhode Island

MARTIN THOMAS, INC., Advertising & Public Relations, 293 South Main St., Providence RI 02903. (401)331-8850. Ad agency and PR firm. President and Creative Director: Thomas R. Rankin. Estab. 1987. Types of clients: industrial and business-to-business. Examples of ad campaigns: include Gloucester Engineering (New England Craftsmanship); Inoex, Inc. (cost savings with materials reduction); Geo. Mann & Co. (reduced labor, maintenance).
Needs: Works with 3-5 freelance photographers/month. Uses photos for trade magazines. Subjects include: location shots of equipment in plants and some studio.
Specs: Uses 8×10 color and b&w prints; 35mm and 4×5 transparencies.
First Contact & Terms: Send stock photo list. Provide resume, business card, brochure, flyer or tearsheets to be kept on file for possible future assignments. Send materials on pricing, experience. Works with local freelancers on assignment only. Does not return unsolicited material. Pays $1,000/day. Pays 30 days following receipt of invoice. Buys all rights. Model release required; photo captions preferred.
Tips: To break in, demonstrate you "can be aggressive, innovative, realistic and can work within our parameters and budgets."

South Carolina

*■BROWER, LOWE & HALL ADVERTISING, INC., 215 W. Stone Ave., P.O. Box 3357, Greenville SC 29602. (803)242-5350. Art Director: Ken Howie. Estab. 1945. Ad agency. Uses billboards, consumer and trade magazines, direct mail, newspapers, P-O-P displays, radio and TV. Types of clients: consumer and business-to-business.
Needs: Commissions 6 freelancers/year; buys 50 photos/year.
Specs: Uses 8×10 b&w and color semigloss prints; also videotape.
First Contact & Terms: Interested in receiving work from newer, lesser-known photographers. Arrange personal interview to show portfolio or query with list of stock photo subjects; will review unsolicited material. SASE. Reports in 2 weeks. NPI. Buys all rights; negotiable. Model release required.

LESLIE ADVERTISING AGENCY, 874 S. Pleasantburg Dr., Greenville SC 29607. (803)271-8340. Ad agency. Creative Coordinator: Marilyn Neves. Types of clients: industrial, retail, finance, food, resort.
Needs: Works with 1-2 freelance photographers/month. Uses photographers for consumer and trade magazines and newspapers.
Specs: Varied.
First Contact & Terms: Query with resume of credits, list of stock photo subjects and samples. Submit portfolio for review "only on request." Provide resume, business card, brochure, flyer or tearsheets to be kept on file for possible future assignments. Occasionally works with freelance photographers on assignment basis only. SASE. Reports ASAP. Pays $150-3,000/b&w photo; $150-3,000/color photo; $500-3,000/day. Pays on receipt of invoice. Buys all rights or one-time rights. Model release preferred.
Tips: "We always want to see sensitive lighting and compositional skills, conceptual stengths, a demonstration of technical proficiency and proven performance. Send printed promotional samples for our files. Call or have rep call for appointment with creative coordinator. Ensure that samples are well-presented and that they demonstrate professional skills."

■SOUTH CAROLINA FILM OFFICE, State Development Board, Box 927, Columbia SC 29202. (803)737-0400. Director: Isabel Hill. Types of clients: motion picture and television producers.
Needs: Works with 8 freelance photographers/month. Uses photos to recruit feature films/TV productions. Subjects include: location photos for feature films, TV projects, and national commercials.
Specs: Uses 3×5 color prints; 35mm transparencies; 35mm film; VHS, U-matic ¾" videotape.
First Contact & Terms: Submit portfolio by mail. Provide resume, business card, self-promotion piece or tearsheets to be kept on file for possible future assignments. Works with local freelancers on assignment only. Does not return unsolicited material. NPI. Pays per yearly contract, upon completion of assignment. Buys all rights.

Tips: "Experience working in the film/video industry is essential. Ability needed to identify and photograph suitable structures or settings to work as a movie location."

Tennessee

■**CARDEN & CHERRY ADVERTISING AGENCY**, 1220 McGavock St., Nashville TN 37203. (615)255-6694. Ad agency. Art Director: David Thomas. Types of clients: TV stations, dairies, savings and loans, car dealers (40%), industrial (40%), all others (20%).
Needs: Works with 2 freelance photographers/month. Uses photographers for direct mail, trade magazines and brochures. Subject needs vary.
Specs: Uses 8×10 b&w prints; 35mm and 4×5 transparencies and 16mm film.
First Contact & Terms: Provide resume, business card, brochure, flyer or tearsheets to be kept on file for possible future assignments. Works with local freelancers. Does not return unsolicited material. Reports in 3 weeks. Pays $40-120/hour; $300-1,000/day. Pays on acceptance. Buys all rights. Model release preferred.

■**K.P. PRODUCTIONS**, 3369 Joslyn St., Memphis TN 38128. (901)726-1928. Audiovisual firm. Creative Director: Michael Porter. Estab. 1990. Types of clients: industrial. Examples of recent projects: "Powership," for Federal Express, (training video); Redwing Grain Nozzle, for Redwing Technical Systems, (sales video); and Big Bend Ranch, for Kossman/Klein Advertising, (sales video).
Needs: Occasionally works with freelance filmmaker or videographer.
Audiovisual Needs: Uses film and videotape.
Specs: Uses 35mm motion picture film and Betacam videotape.
First Contact & Terms: Arrange personal interview to present demo reels or cassettes. Works on assignment only. Keeps samples on file. SASE. Reports in 1-2 weeks. Pays $350-400/day. Pays on acceptance or receipt of invoice. Buys all rights; negotiable. Model/property release required. Credit line sometimes given.
Tips: Primarily looks for good composition and a "leading edge look." To break in with this firm, "have a good attitude and work within budget."

■**THOMPSON & COMPANY**, 8th Floor, 65 Union Ave., Memphis TN 38103. (901)527-8000. FAX: (901)527-3697. Full service ad agency. Art Director: Trace Hallowell. Estab. 1980.
Needs: Works with 2-3 freelance photographers/month. Uses photographs for billboards, consumer and trade magazines, direct mail, P-O-P displays, catalogs, posters and newspapers. Subjects include film for TV commercials. Reviews stock photos; subject matter depends on need.
Specs: Uses b&w prints; 35mm, 2 ¼×2¼, 4×5 or 8×10 transparencies; 35mm film.
First Contact & Terms: Query with samples. Works on assignment only. Returns unsolicited material if SASE is enclosed. NPI; payment "depends upon job, usage, photographer's experience." Rights negotiable. Model release required. Credit line not given.
Tips: In samples, looks for "ideas, not fads." To break in with this firm, "show you can think. Show that you can bring something to a concept."

Texas

DORSEY ADVERTISING/PR., % Streetpeople's Weekly News (Homeless Editorial), P.O. Box 270942, Dallas TX 75227-0942. Ad agency, newspaper publisher. Publisher: Lon G. Dorsey, Jr.. Estab. 1977. Types of clients: retail.

The First Markets Index preceding the General Index in the back of this book provides the names of those companies/ publications interested in receiving work from newer, lesser-known photographers.

Needs: Uses photos for newspapers. Subjects include: photojournalists on articles about homeless or street people.

First Contact & Terms: Interested in receiving work from newer, lesser-known photographers. Send unsolicited photos by mail for consideration with SASE for return of all materials. Reports promptly. Pays $5-10/b&w photo; $7-20/color photo; $20-500/job. Pays on acceptance or publication. Buys all rights; negotiable. Model/property release and photo captions required. Credit line sometimes given.

Tips: In freelancer's demos, wants to see "Professionalism, clarity of purpose, without sex or negative atmosphere which could harm purpose of paper." The trend is toward "kinder, gentler situations, the 'let's help our fellows' attitude." To break in, "find out what we're about so we don't waste time with exhausting explanations. The name of our publication in question is "Streetpeople's Weekly News." We're interested in all homeless situations. For a copy of the paper send $2 to cover immediate handling (same day as received) and postage."

*■DYKEMAN ASSOCIATES INC., 4115 Rawlins, Dallas TX 75219. (214)528-2991. FAX: (214)528-0241. PR and AV firm. Contact: Production Manager. Estab. 1974. Types of clients: industrial, financial, sports, varied. Examples of recent projects: "Save Battleship Texas," Alcoa (publicity/documentation); and "Data Marketing," Data Dallas (brochure).

Needs: Works with 4-5 photographers and/or videographers. Uses photos for publicity, billboards, consumer and trade magazines, direct mail, P-O-P displays, catalogs, posters, newspapers, signage, and audiovisual uses. Subjects include: photojournalism, brochures, PSAs. Reviews stock photos.

Audiovisual Needs: Uses photos for slides and videotape. "We produce and direct video. Just need crew with good equipment and people and ability to do part."

Specs: Uses 8½×11 and up glossy color prints; ½" VHS videotape.

First Contact & Terms: Arrange personal interview to show portfolio. Provide resume, business card, brochure, flyer or tearsheets to be kept on file for possible future assignments. Works on assignment only. Cannot return material. Pays $800-1,200/day; $250-400/1-2 hours. "Currently we work only with photographers who are willing to be part of our trade dollar network. Call if you don't understand this term." Pays 30 days after receipt of invoice. Buys exclusive product rights. "We handle model and/or property releases." Credit line sometimes given, "maybe for lifestyle publications—especially if photographer helps place."

Tips: Reviews portfolios with current needs in mind. "If PSA, we would want to see examples. If for news story, we would need to see photojournalism capabilities. Show portfolio, state pricing, remember that either we or our clients will keep negatives or slide originals."

■EDUCATIONAL FILMSTRIPS, 1401 19th St., Huntsville TX 77340. (409)295-5767. FAX: (409)294-0233. CEO: George H. Russell. Types of clients: Jr. high through college (education only).

Needs: Subjects include various educational topics.

Specs: Uses videotape.

First Contact & Terms: Submit videotape. SASE. Reports in 1 month. NPI. Pays per filmstrip or video, royalty or purchase. Pays on acceptance or December of each year. Buys exclusive product rights. Credit line given.

Tips: Visit local schools and ask to see most popular recent videos. Looks for "ability to produce a clear, concise curriculum-oriented educational product."

■EDUCATIONAL VIDEO NETWORK, 1401 19th St., Huntsville TX 77340. (409)295-5767. FAX: (409)294-0233. AV firm. Chief Executive Officer: George H. Russell. Estab. 1954. Types of Clients: educational.

Needs: Works with 2 freelancers/month. Reviews stock video footage of any secondary educational subjects.

Audiovisual Needs: Uses videotape for all projects.

Specs: Uses super VHS or ¾" videotape.

First Contact & Terms: Query with samples. Send copy of work on ½" VHS. SASE. Reports in 3 weeks. NPI. Pays in royalties or flat fee based on length, amount of post-production work, and marketability; royalties paid annually. Credit line given.

Tips: In freelancer's demos, looks for "compatibility with curriculum-oriented educational subjects." To break in with this firm, "review most popular curriculum-oriented subjects in your local high school media library. Shoot and review your work until you perfect your technique."

GROUP 400 ADVERTISING, Suite 301, 8480 Fredericksburg, San Antonio TX 78229. (512)697-8055. Ad agency. General Manager: Gary T. Young. Types of clients: industrial.

Needs: Works with 2-3 freelance photographers/month. Uses photos for trade magazines, direct mail and special projects (special effects photography). Subjects include auction activity/equipment.

Specs: Uses 3x5 color prints; 35mm, 2¼×2¼ and 4×5 transparencies.

First Contact & Terms: Query with resume of credits and list of stock photo subjects. Provide resume, business card, brochure, flyer or tearsheets to be kept on file for possible future assignments. Works with freelance photographers on assignment basis only. SASE. Reports in 3 weeks. NPI; payment negotiable. Pays on receipt of invoice, usually 30 days, net. Buys all rights. Model release required. Credit line sometimes given.

Tips: "Location is important for specific photo assignments. We use a substantial amount of photography for main auction company client—much internal production—freelance for special projects."

■**HANCOCK ADVERTISING AGENCY,** P.O. Box 630010, Nacogdoches TX 75963. (409)564-9559. FAX: (409)560-0845. Ad agency. Art Director: Judith Butler. Types of clients: Industrial, financial and retail. Example of recent campaign: "The Team" for Fredonia State Bank, (newspaper campaign).
Needs: Works with 6 freelance photographers/month. Uses photographs for billboards, trade magazines, direct mail, posters, newspapers, audiovisual, brochure/annual report/newsletter. Subjects include: people, product and still life.
Audiovisual Needs: Uses photos for slides, film and videotape.
Specs: Uses b&w prints; 35mm, 2¼×2¼, 4×5 transparencies; ¾" videotape.
First Contact & Terms: Submit portfolio for review. Query with resume of credits. Send stock photo list. Provide resume, business card, brochure, flyer or tearsheets to be kept on file for possible future assignments. Works on assignment only. Keeps samples on file. SASE. Reports in 1-2 weeks. Pays $40-100/hour; $350-1,000/day. Pays on receipt of invoice. Buys all rights; negotiable. Model release preferred. Credit line sometimes given depending upon usage.
Tips: Looks for "mood lighting and designer's eye." Also needs quick turn around. Sees trend toward "more use of photography in more markets, mainly Texas and South."

■**HEPWORTH ADVERTISING CO.,** 3403 McKinney Ave., Dallas TX 75204. (214)220-2415. President: S.W. Hepworth. Ad agency. Estab. 1952. Uses all media except P-O-P displays. Types of clients: industrial, consumer and financial. Examples of recent projects: Houston General Insurance, Holman Boiler, Hillcrest State Bank.
Needs: Uses photos for trade magazines, direct mail, P-O-P displays, newspapers and audiovisual.
Specs: Uses 8×10 glossy color prints, 35mm transparencies.
First Contact & Terms: Cannot return material. Reports in 1-2 weeks. Pays $350 minimum/job; negotiates payment based on client's budget and photographer's previous experience/reputation. Submit portoflio by mail. Works on assignment only. SASE. Pays on acceptance. Buys all rights. Model release preferred. Credit line sometimes given.
Tips: "For best relations with the supplier, we prefer to seek out a photographer in the area of the job location." Sees trend toward machinery shots. "Contact us by letter or phone."

LEVENSON & HILL, Box 619507, Dallas/Fort Worth Airport TX 75261. (214)556-0944. Ad agency. Creative Director: Jerry McPhail. Types of clients: retail products and service related.
Needs: Works with 2 photographers/month. Uses photographers for consumer and trade magazines, and newspapers.
Specs: Uses 35mm, 4×5 and 8×10 transparencies.
First Contact & Terms: Send unsolicited photos by mail for consideration. Provide resume, business card, brochure, flyer or tearsheets to be kept on file for possible future assignments. Works with freelance photographers on an assignment basis only. Does not return unsolicited material. Pays $500-3,500/day; rates depend on usage and budget. Pays on receipt of invoice. Rights purchased with photos vary. Model release preferred. Credit lines may be given.
Tips: Prefers to see "fashion, dramatic lighting and new clean looks in samples submitted. Send brochures and tearsheets, call in a few weeks. We tend to shoot a lot at one time then have a lot of dead time."

■**POLLARO MEDIA ADVERTISING & PRODUCTIONS,** 400 West Main, Denison TX 75020. (903)463-2294. FAX: (903)465-2372. Ad agency. Art Director: Greg Mack. Estab. 1972. Types of clients: retail. Examples of ad campaigns: country music video for Atlantic Records; "Bored with Ford," TV/print campaign for Regional Oldsmobile; and Jessie White Series, TV ads for Tri State Acura Dealers.
Needs: Works with 10 freelance photographers—videographers/month. Uses photographers for billboards, consumer magazines, trade magazines, direct mail, P-O-P displays, catalogs, posters, newspapers, signage and audiovisual uses. Subjects include: retail automotive and miscellaneous retail. Interested in reviewing stock photos/video footage of various retail subjects.
Audiovisual Needs: Uses film and videotape.
First Contact & Terms: Query with samples. Provide resume, business card, brochure, flyer or tearsheets to be kept on file for possible future assignments. Works on assignment only. Cannot return material. Reports as needed. NPI. Pays within 30 days. Buys one-time rights. Model release required; photo captions preferred. Credit line given sometimes, depending on project.

■**CARL RAGSDALE ASSOC., INC.**, 4725 Stillbrooke, Houston TX 77035. (713)729-6530. President: Carl Ragsdale. Types of clients: industrial and documentary film users.
Needs: Uses photographers for multimedia productions, films, still photography for brochures. Subjects include: industrial subjects—with live sound—interiors and exteriors.
Specs: Uses 35mm, 2¼×2¼, 4×5 transparencies; 16mm, 35mm film.
First Contact & Terms: Provide resume to be kept on file for possible future assignments. Works on assignment only. Does not return unsolicited material. Reports as needed. Pays $350-800/day; negotiable. Pays upon delivery of film. Buys all rights.
Tips: "Do not call. We refer to our freelance file of resumes when looking for personnel. Swing from film to video is major change—most companies are now hiring in-house personnel to operate video equipment. Resurgence of oil industry should improve the overall use of visuals down here." Photographer should have "ability to operate without supervision on location. Send samples of coverage of the same type of assignment for which they are being hired."

TED ROGGEN ADVERTISING AND PUBLIC RELATIONS, Suite 224, 1800 Augusta Dr. James Place, Houston TX 77057. (713)789-6216. Contact: Ted Roggen. Ad agency and PR firm. Handles clients in construction, entertainment, food, finance, publishing, and travel. Photos used in billboards, direct mail, radio, TV, P-O-P displays, brochures, annual reports, PR releases, sales literature and trade magazines.
Needs: Buys 25-50 photos/year; offers 50-75 assignments/year.
Specs: Uses 5×7 b&w glossy or matte prints; contact sheet OK. Also uses 4×5 transparencies and 5×7 color prints.
First Contact & Terms: Provide resume to be kept on file for possible future assignments. Pays $25-35/b&w photo; $50-275/color photo. Pays on acceptance. Model release required; captions preferred.

■**SANDERS, WINGO, GALVIN & MORTON ADVERTISING**, Suite 100, 4110 Rio Bravo, El Paso TX 79902. (915)533-9583. Creative Director: Roy Morton. Ad agency. Uses billboards, consumer and trade magazines, direct mail, foreign media, newspapers, P-O-P displays, radio and TV. Types of clients: retailing and apparel industries. Free client list.
Needs: Works with 5 photographers/year.
Specs: Uses b&w photos and color transparencies. Works with freelance filmmakers in production of slide presentations and TV commercials.
Payment & Terms: Pays $65-500/hour, $600-3,500/day, negotiates pay on photos. Buys all rights. Model release required.
Making Contact: Query with samples, list of stock photo subjects. Send material by mail for consideration. Submit portfolio for review. SASE. Reports in 1 week.

■**EVANS WYATT ADVERTISING & PUBLIC RELATIONS**, 346 Mediterranean Dr., Corpus Christi TX 78418. (512)854-1661. FAX: (512)854-7722. Ad agency, PR firm. Owner: E. Wyatt. Estab. 1975. Types of clients: industrial, financial, healthcare, automotive, educational and retail.
Needs: Works with 3-5 freelance photographers—videographers/month. Uses photos for consumer magazines, trade magazines, direct mail, catalogs, posters and newspapers. Subjects include people and industrial. Interested in reviewing stock photos/video footage of any subject matter.
Audiovisual Needs: Uses slide shows and videos.
Specs: Uses 5×7 glossy b&w/color prints; 35mm, 2¼×2¼ transparencies; ½" videotape.
First Contact & Terms: Query with resume of credits. Query with list of stock photo subjects. Query with samples. Submit portfolio for review. Provide resume, business card, brochure, flyer or tearsheets to be kept on file for possible future assignments. Works on assignment only. Reports in 1 month. Pays $400-1,000/day; $100-500/job; negotiated in advance of assignment. Pays on receipt of invoice. Buys all rights. Model release required; photo captions preferred. Credit line given sometimes, depending on client's wishes.
Tips: Resolution and contrast are expected. Wants to see "sharpness, clarity and reproduction possibilities." Also, creative imagery (mood, aspect, view and lighting). Advises freelancers to "do professional work with an eye to marketability. Pure art is used only rarely." Video demo tape should be ½" VHS format.

■**ZACHRY ASSOCIATES, INC.**, 709 North 2nd, Box 1739, Abilene TX 79604. (915)677-1342. Vice President/Production: Marvin Kirkham. Types of clients: industrial, institutional, religious service.
Needs: Works with 2 photographers/month. Uses photographers for slide sets, videotapes and print. Subjects include industrial location, product, model groups.
Specs: Uses 5×7, 8×10 b&w prints; 8×10 color prints; 35mm, 2¼×2¼ transparencies; VHS videotape.
First Contact & Terms: Query with samples and stock photo list. Provide resume, business card, self-promotion piece or tearsheets to be kept on file for possible future assignments. Works with freelancers by assignment only; interested in stock photos/footage. SASE. Reports as requested. NPI; payment

negotiable. Pays on acceptance. Buys one-time and all rights. Model release required. Credit line usually given.

Utah

EVANS/SALT LAKE, 110 Social Hall Ave., Salt Lake City UT 84111. (801)364-7452. Ad agency. Art Director: Michael Cullis. Types of clients: industrial, finance.
Needs: Works with 2-3 photographers/month. Uses photographers for billboards, consumer and trade magazines, direct mail, P-O-P displays, posters and newspapers. Subject matter includes scenic and people.
Specs: Uses color prints and 35mm, 2¼ × 2¼ and 4 × 5 transparencies.
First Contact & Terms: Query with list of stock photo subjects; submit portfolio for review; provide resume, business card, brochure, flyer or tearsheets to be kept on file for possible future assignments. Works with freelance photographers on assignment only. SASE. Reports in 1-2 weeks. NPI; payment negotiable. Pays on receipt of invoice. Buys one-time rights. Model release required; captions preferred. Credit live given when possible.

FOTHERINGHAM & ASSOCIATES, Suite 300, 215 S. State St., Salt Lake UT 84111. (801)521-2903. Ad agency. Art Director: Randy Stroman. Types of clients: industrial, financial, development, resort, retail, commercial, automotive, high-tech.
Needs: Works with 6 photographers/month. Uses photographers for trade magazines, direct mail, P-O-P displays, catalogs and newspapers. Purchases all subjects. "We're growing."
Specs: Uses 8 × 10 b&w and color prints; 35mm, 2¼ × 2¼ and 4 × 5 transparencies.
First Contact & Terms: Arrange a personal interview to show portfolio. Query with samples. Provide resume, business card, brochure, flyer or tearsheets to be kept on file for possible future assignments. Works with freelance photographers on assignment only. Does not return unsolicited material. Reports in 2 weeks. NPI; payment negotiable. Pays on receipt of invoice. Buys all rights or one-time rights. Model release required. Credit line sometimes given.

■**HARRIS & LOVE, INC.**, Suite 1800, 136 E. So. Temple, Salt Lake City UT 84111. (801)532-7333. FAX: (801)532-6029. Art Directors: Eric Bate and Preston Wood. Estab. 1938. Types of clients: industrial, retail, tourism, finance and winter sports.
Needs: Works with 4 freelance photographers—filmmakers—videographers/month. Uses photos for billboards, consumer magazines, trade magazines, newspapers and audiovisual. Needs mostly images of food and people. Interested in reviewing stock photos/film or video footage on people, science, health-care and industrial.
Audiovisual Needs: Contact Creative Director, Bob Wassom by phone or mail.
Specs: Uses 35mm, 2¼ × 2¼, 4 × 5 transparencies.
First Contact & Terms: Interested in receiving work from newer, lesser-known photographers. Send unsolicited photos by mail for consideration; submit portfolio for review; provide resume, business card, brochure, flyer or tearsheets to be kept on file for possible future assignments. Works with freelancers on assignment basis only. NPI. Buys all rights (work-for-hire); rights negotiable. Model and property releases required. Credit line given sometimes, depending on client, outlet or usage.
Tips: In freelancer's portfolio or demos, wants to see "craftsmanship, mood of photography and creativity." Sees trend toward "more abstract" images in advertising. "Most of our photography is a total buy out (work-for-hire). Photographer can only reuse images in his promotional material."

■**PAUL S. KARR PRODUCTIONS, UTAH DIVISION**, 1024 N. 250 East, Orem UT 84057. (801)226-8209. Vice President & Manager: Michael Karr. Types of clients: education, business, industry, TV-spot and theatrical spot advertising. Provides inhouse production services of sound recording, looping, printing and processing, high-speed photo instrumentation as well as production capabilities in 35mm and 16mm.
Needs: Same as Arizona office but additionally interested in motivational human interest material—film stories that would lead people to a better way of life, build better character, improve situations, strengthen families.
First Contact & Terms: Query with resume of credits and advise if sample reel is available. NPI. Pays per job, negotiates payment based on client's budget and ability to handle the work. Pays on production. Buys all rights. Model release required.

*■**SOTER ASSOCIATES INC.**, 209 N. 400 West, Provo UT 84601. (801)375-6200. FAX: (801)375-6280. Ad agency. President: N. Gregory Soter. Types of clients: industrial, financial and other. Examples of recent projects: Cat ad, Dynix, Inc. (cats and computers, magazine ad); "Ready to do this?" for

Deseret Bank (construction loans, multiple media print); and Journal Writer campaign, Eagle Marketing (software, multiple media print).
Needs: Uses photos for consumer and trade magazines, direct mail and newspapers. Subjects include: product, editorial or stock. Reviews stock photos/videotape.
Audiovisual Needs: Uses photos for slides and videotape.
Specs: Uses 8×10 b&w prints; 2¼×2¼, 4×5 transparencies; videotape.
First Contact & Terms: Arrange personal interview to show portfolio. Query with samples. Provide resume, business card, brochure, flyer or tearsheets to be kept on file for possible future assignments. Works on assignment only. Keeps samples on file. SASE. Reports in 1-2 weeks. NPI; payment negotiable. Pays on receipt of invoice. Buys all rights; negotiable. Model/property release required. Credit line not given.

Virginia

■**CARLTON COMMUNICATIONS INC.,** 300 W. Franklin St., Richmond VA 23220. (804)780-1701. FAX: (804)225-8036. Ad agency and PR firm. President: Dick Carlton. Types of clients: tourism, hi-tech, retirement, financial, and economic development. Examples of ad campaigns: safety belt campaign for State of Virginia; West Coast Campaign for Lawyers Title; and repeat work for Pioneer Federal Savings Bank.
Needs: Works with 2-3 freelancers/month. Uses photographers for billboards, consumer magazines, trade magazines, direct mail, P-O-P displays, catalogs, posters, newspapers, signage and audiovisual.
Audiovisual Needs: Uses film and videotape.
Specs: Uses b&w print; 35mm, 2¼×2¼, 4×5, 8×10 transparencies; 35mm or 16mm film; Betacam videotape.
First Contact & Terms: Provide resume, business card, brochure, flyer or tearsheets to be kept on file for possible future assignments. Works with freelancers on assignment basis only. SASE. Reports in 1 month. Pays $1,200/day; by project or day rate. Pays on receipt of invoice. Buys all rights. Model release required. Credit line sometimes given.
Tips: In freelancer's portfolio or demos, looks for "high level of quality." Sees trend back toward black-and-white work. "Persistence" is best for breaking in with this firm.

Washington

MATTHEWS ASSOC. INC., Suite 1018, 603 Stewart St., Seattle WA 98101. (206)340-0680. PR firm. President: Dean Matthews. Types of clients: industrial.
Needs: Works with 0-3 freelance photographers/month. Uses photographers for trade magazines, direct mail, P-O-P displays, catalogs and public relations. Frequently uses architectural photography; other subjects include building products.
Specs: Uses 8×10 b&w and color prints; 35mm, 2¼×2¼ and 4×5 transparencies.
First Contact & Terms: Arrange a personal interview to show portfolio if local. If not, provide resume, business card, brochure, flyer or tearsheets to be kept on file for possible future assignments. SASE. Works with freelance photographers on assignment only. NPI. Pays per hour, day or job. Pays on receipt of invoice. Buys all rights. Model release preferred.
Tips: Samples preferred depends on client or job needs. "Be good at industrial photography."

West Virginia

■**CAMBRIDGE CAREER PRODUCTS,** 90 MacCorkle Ave., S.W., South Charleston WV 25303. (800)468-4227. FAX: (304)744-9351. President: E.T. Gardner, Ph.D.. Managing Director: Amy Pauley. Estab. 1981.
Needs: Works with 2 still photographers and 3 videographers per month. Uses photographers for multimedia productions, videotapes and catalog still photography. "We buy b&w prints and color transparencies for use in our 9 catalogs."
Specs: 5×7 or 8×10 b&w prints; 35mm, 2¼×2¼, 4×5, and 8×10 transparencies and videotape.
First Contact & Terms: Video producers arrange a personal interview to show portfolio. Still photographers should submit portfolio by mail. Interested in stock photos/footage on sports, hi-tech, young people, parenting, general interest topics and other. SASE. Reports in 2 weeks. Pays $20-80/b&w

photo, $250-850/color photo and $8,000-45,000 per video production. Buys one-time and all rights (work-for-hire). Model release required. Credit line given. "Cover color transparencies used for catalog covers and video production, but not for b&w catalog shots."
Tips: Still photographers should call our customer service department and get a copy of *all* our educational catalogs. Review the covers and inside shots, then send us appropriate high-quality material. Video production firms should visit our headquarters with examples of work. For still color photographs we look for high-quality, colorful, eye-catching transparencies. B&w photographs should be on sports, home economics (cooking, sewing, child rearing, parenting, food, etc.), and guidance (dating, sex, drugs, alcohol, careers, etc.). We have stopped producing educational filmstrips and now produce only full-motion video. Always need good b&w or color still photography for catalogs."

Wisconsin

BIRDSALL-VOSS & KLOPPENBURG, INC., 1355 W. Towne Square Rd., Mequon WI 53209. (414)241-4890. Ad agency. Art Director: Scott Krahn. Estab. 1984. Types of clients: travel, healthcare, financial, industrial and fashion clients such as Musebeck Shoes, Piedmont Vacations, Continental Vacations, WFSI-Milwaukee and Lavelle Industries.
Needs: Uses 5 freelance photographers/month. Works with billboards, consumer magazines, trade magazines, direct mail, catalogs, posters and newspapers. Subjects include: travel and healthcare. Interested in reviewing stock photos of travel scenes in Carribean, California, Nevada, Mexico and Florida.
Specs: Uses 35mm, 2¼ × 2¼, 4 × 5, 8 × 10 transparencies.
First Contact & Terms: Arrange a personal interview to show portfolio or query with resume of credits or list of stock photo subjects. Provide resume, business card, brochure, flyer or tearsheets to be kept on file for possible future assignments. Cannot return material. NPI. Pays 30 days on receipt of invoice. Buys all rights. Model release required.
Tips: Looks for "primarily cover shots for travel brochures; ads selling Florida, the Caribbean, Mexico, California and Nevada destinations."

WALDBILLIG & BESTEMAN, INC., 6225 University Ave., Madison WI 53705. (608)238-4767. Vice President/Senior Art Director: Gary Hutchins. Creative Director: Tom Senatori. Types of clients: industrial, financial and health care.
Needs: Works with 4-8 freelance photographers/month. Uses photographers for consumer and trade magazines, direct mail, P-O-P displays, catalogs, posters, newspapers, brochures and annual reports. Subject matter varies.
Specs: Uses 8x9 glossy b&w and color prints; 35mm, 2¼ × 2¼, 4 × 5 transparencies.
First Contact & Terms: Provide resume, business card, brochure, flyer or tearsheets to be kept on file for possible future assignments. Works with freelance photographers on assignment basis only. Reports in 2 weeks. $100-200/b&w photo; $200-400/color photo. Pays on receipt of invoice. Buys all rights. Model release and captions required.
Tips: "Send unsolicited samples that do *not* have to be returned. Indicate willingness to do *any* type job. Indicate he/she has access to full line of equipment."

Canada

■✹**JACK CHISHOLM FILM PRODUCTIONS LTD.,** #50, 99 Atlantic Ave., Toronto, ON M6J 3J8 Canada. (416)588-5200. FAX: (416)588-5324. Production house and stock shot, film and video library. President: Mary Di Tursi. Chief Librarian: Susanne Donato. Estab. 1956. Types of clients: finance and industrial, government, corporate, advertising agencies and television networks.
Needs: Uses stock film and video footage.
First Contact & Terms: Works with freelancers on an assignment basis only.

■✹**WARNE MARKETING & COMMUNICATIONS,** Suite 810, 111 Avenue Rd., Toronto, ON M5R 3M1 Canada. (416)927-0881. FAX: (416)927-1676. Ad agency. President: Keith Warne. Estab. 1979. Types of clients: business-to-business.
Needs: Works with 5 photographers/month. Uses photos for trade magazines, direct mail, P-O-P displays, catalogs and posters. Subjects include: in-plant photography, studio set-ups and product shots. Special subject needs include in-plant shots for background use.

Audiovisual Needs: Uses both videotape and slides for product promotion.
Specs: Uses 8×10 glossy b&w and color prints; also 4×5 transparencies.
First Contact & Terms: Send letter citing related experience plus 2 or 3 samples. Works on assignment only. Does not return unsolicited material. Reports in 2 weeks. Pays $1,000-2,000/day. Pays within 30 days. Buys all rights. Model release required.
Tips: In portfolio/samples, prefers to see industrial subjects and creative styles. "We look for lighting knowledge, composition and imagination." Send letter and 3 samples, and wait for trial assignment.

Advertising, Public Relations and Audiovisual Firms/'92-93 changes

The following markets appeared in the 1992 edition of *Photographer's Market* but are not listed in the 1993 edition. They may have been omitted for failing to respond to our request for updates of information, they may have gone out of business or they may no longer wish to receive freelance work.

Ad Hoc Marketing Resources, Inc. (did not respond)
Alamo Ad Center, Inc. (did not respond)
Alwes & Ebber (did not respond)
Art Direction, Colorado (did not respond)
Ayer Tuttle (merger)
Bandy Carroll Hellige Advertising (did not respond)
Basinger Company, The (did not respond)
Beerger Productions, Norman (not reviewing work)
Bitton Advertising Agency (out of business)
Blate Associates, Samuel R. (not reviewing work)
Borgmeyer & Musen Advertising, Inc. (not reviewing work)
Bosustow Video (did not respond)
Bright Light Productions (did not respond)
Brown Advertising Agency, E.H. (not reviewing work)
Cameron Newell Advertising (did not respond)
Catalog Publishing Group (not reviewing work)
Cerrell Associates Inc. (not reviewing work)
Communicators, Inc., The (not reviewing work)
Cook Advertising, Wm. (did not respond)
Cramer-Krasselt Co. (did not respond)
Crawford/Fenton Associates, Inc. (did not respond)
De Palma & Hogan Advertising (did not respond)
Ditzel Productions, William (not reviewing work)
Donohue Associates, Inc., Jody (did not respond)
DPR Company (not reviewing work)
Duke Unlimited (did not re

spond)
Epstein & Walker Associates (not reviewing work)
Evans Advertising Agency Inc. (did not respond)
Falk Associates, Richard (did not respond)
Franson, Hagerty & Associates, Inc. (did not respond)
Fred/Alan, Inc. (out of business)
Froehlich-Producer, Paul (did not respond)
Gannon Communications (not reviewing work)
Goodwick Associates, Inc. (did not respond)
Hamilton Sweeney Advertising (did not respond)
Houlgate Enterprises, Deke (not reviewing work)
Jackson Productions Inc., David (did not respond)
Johnston Group, The (not reviewing work)
Kahn & Associates, Inc., Howard (did not respond)
Katz, Inc. (did not respond)
Klepper Associates, Michael (not reviewing work)
Kovach Marketing & Communications, Hubbert (not reviewing work)
Kroloff, Marshall & Associates, Ltd. (not reviewing work)
Krypton Corp. (did not respond)
Kunis & Company, Inc., S.R. (out of business)Inter-Image, Inc. (did not respond)
Lawrence & Schiller (did not respond)Lavidge and Associates (did not respond)
Le Duc Video, (not reviewing work)
Lewis & Associates, Richard Bond (did not respond)
McMullen Design & Marketing (did not respond)
Maler, Inc., Roger, (did not respond)

Manhattan Video Productions, Inc. (did not respond)
Marshfilm, Inc. (not reviewing work)
Martin Assoc. Inc., Peter (not reviewing work)
Martinez & Associates (did not respond)
Nelson Productions, Inc. (did not respond)
Neuger & Associates, Edwin (did not respond)
Norton-Wood PR Services (did not respond)
Parker's Gateways Inst., Jonathan (not reviewing work)
Richard-Lewis Corp. (did not respond)
Ruder Finn (did not respond)
Ryan, Barbara (did not respond)
Sanchez & Levitan, Inc. (did not respond)
Save the Children (did not respond)
Smiley Visual Productions, Inc., Ron (did not respond)
Smith & Associates, Inc. (not reviewing work)
Smith Company, Inc., Marc (did not respond)
Spottswood Video/Film Studio (not reviewing work)
Stephan Advertising Agency, Inc. (not reviewing work)
Stremmel & Co., David H. (out of business)
Tele-Press Associates, Inc. (did not respond)
Tracy-Locke (did not respond)
UNIMAR (did not respond)
Van Sant, Dugdale & Company, Inc. (not reviewing work)
Video Imagery (did not respond)
Videosmith, Inc. (did not respond)
White Advertising, Roger (did not respond)

Art/Design Studios

In the 1980s many photographers reaped the benefits of flourishing advertising and PR firms. Those agencies were cash cows to many artists and business was booming with large assignments and wide open budgets. But now that photo assignments are harder to come by in those two areas, some photographers are finding art/design studios much more appealing.

Because of competitive factors in the advertising marketplace, design firms are doing more of the work once handled by ad agencies. The variety of freelance opportunities that art/design studios offer matches the diversity of projects studios handle. Studios provide all forms of visual communication for various businesses—corporate identity, product/brand identity, publication design, direct marketing materials, catalogs, annual reports, brochures, exhibits, direct mail pieces and so on.

Photography has become an increasingly essential element in such communication. Photographers are called upon to capture the perfect product shot or possibly portray the happy-go-lucky CEO on a company's annual report. In annual reports, for example, following popular themes such as environmental awareness and economics can attract business for a photographer.

Studios range in size, scope and purpose. There are one-person studios that generally turn to freelance help when the workload becomes too heavy. Then there are large operations with account executives who turn to outside help for either a fresh approach or for mechanical skills.

This is the second year for the Art/Design Studios section in *Photographer's Market* and the number of listings has nearly doubled from last year. Study the listings in this section to find out what type of work they do, who the buyers are, what they have done in the past, who their clients are, and the size of the studios. Use your skills as a visual communicator to contact studios. Learn as much about prospects as you can before contacting them. Then send samples that match the prospect's needs along with a cover letter asking for a portfolio review unless otherwise instructed in a listing. If a studio shows interest, find out what type of work might be available for you, then select appropriate pieces to show in your portfolio.

Design your portfolio as carefully as you would compose images for another client's project. Present your work in a neat, organized fashion. Show that you know how to pinpoint a client's needs by focusing on the needs of your current prospect. For instance, if you are showing your work to a studio that specializes in collateral material, present samples of brochures which include your photography instead of tearsheets of trade ads. Identify what your involvement was in each project, how you worked with the art director and so on.

Since studios usually bill clients by the hour or by the project, freelancers are paid similarly. Variables in pricing are use of color, turnaround time, rights purchased, complexity of the project and the level of your ability. When you are first discussing a project, ask whether or not you will retain ownership of the copyright and receive credit. Some projects call for the company or client to retain all rights. Unless a photographer clarifies this, an art director may assume the photographer is selling the rights to his images. (See Copyright/rights in the Business of Photography on page 11.)

We have made the effort to get specific rates of payment from the listings. However, in cases where a specific dollar amount was not quoted we have inserted a code, NPI—for "no payment information given." Many studios will prefer to work with local photographers because of the need to meet tight deadlines and to make last-minute changes. When you query or submit work to a studio, the reporting time may vary somewhat from the time given under "Reports . . ." in its listing. Usually, the longer times are more realistic. For additional art and design studio listings, see the directory, *Artist's Market*, also published by Writer's Digest Books.

*ART ETC., 316 W. 4th St., Cincinnati OH 45202. (513)621-6225. FAX: (513)621-6316. Art Studio. Art Director: Doug Carpenter. Estab. 1971. Specializes in industrial, financial, food and OTC drugs.
Needs: Works with 1-2 freelance photographers/month. Uses photographs for consumer and trade magazines, direct mail, P-O-P displays, catalogs and posters. Subjects include: musical instruments, OTC drugs, pet food, people and skin products. Reviews stock photos.
Specs: Uses 4×5, 8×10 color and b&w prints; 35mm, 2¼×2¼, 4×5, 8×10 transparencies.
First Contact & Terms: Contact through rep. Arrange personal interview to show portfolio. Query with list of stock photo subjects. Provide resume, business card, brochure, flyer or tearsheets to be kept on file for possible future assignments. Works with local freelancers on assignment only. Keeps samples on file. SASE. Reports in 1-2 weeks. Pays $40-250/hour; $600-2,000/day; $150-3,500/job;$150/ color photo; $50/b&w photo. Pays on receipt of invoice. Buys all rights; negotiable. Model/property release required; photo captions preferred. Credit line sometimes given depending upon market.
Tips: Wants to see food, people and product shots.

*JACK BARNES & ASSOCIATES, 16 W. Erie, Chicago IL 60610. (312)943-2012. FAX: (312)943-2973. Design and sales promotion firm. Photo Director: Elizabeth A. Barnes. Estab. 1975. Specializes in display design, packaging, direct mail, signage, sales brochures, cookbooks and free standing inserts. Types of clients: retail, automotive after market, food retailers and toy companies. Examples of recent projects: Sales incentive signage, Sears, Roebuck & Co. (signage used in-house); Philly Christmas Cookbook, Kraft General Foods (holiday promotion); and Fido Dido Sell Sheet/Display, Western Publishing (consumers/retailers promotion).
Needs: Works with 2-3 freelance photographers/month. Uses photographs for P-O-P displays, cata-logs, posters, packaging, signage and free standing inserts. Subjects include: tabletop product, tabletop food, modeling shots, car photography. Reviews stock photos of people and locations.
Specs: Uses 2¼×2¼, 4×5, 8×10 transparencies.
First Contact & Terms: Arrange personal interview to show portfolio. Query with samples. Provide resume, business card, brochure, flyer or tearsheets to be kept on file for possible future assignments. Works with local freelancers only. Keeps samples on file. SASE. Reports in 1-2 weeks. Pays $900-1,500/day; $150-900/job. "Depends on a client's budget." Pays on 30-day terms. Buys all rights. Model/property release required. Credit line sometimes given, "depending on the client, usually no."
Tips: Trends include use of "a lot of artistic backgrounds, creative lighting/propping and filters. Be flexible with your hours. Work with my budgets and don't be pushy, call when asked to."

■AUGUSTUS BARNETT DESIGN & CREATIVE SERVICES, 632 St. Helens Ave. S., Tacoma WA 98402. (206)627-8508. FAX: (206)593-2116. Ad agency and design firm. President: Charlie Barnett. Estab. 1981. Specializes in industrial, financial, retail and food. Examples of recent projects: "Flavor of the Great Northwest," Nalley Potato Chips (sales meeting video); "Recipes With Vanilla," Cook Flavoring Co. (in-store video); and "Light Fantastic," Bernstein's Salad Dressing (sales meeting product intro).
Needs: Works with 1-2 freelance photographers/month. Uses photographs for consumer magazines, trade magazines, direct mail, P-O-P displays, newspapers and audiovisual. Subjects include: industrial, food-related, product photography.
Audiovisual Needs: Reviews stock photos, slides and videotape. Uses "combo of 35mm (either simple or complex up to 15 projectors) plus either ¾" or ½" video, large projection system and some other special effects on occasion."
Specs: Uses 5×7, 8×10, color and b&w glossy prints; 35mm, 2¼×2¼, 4×5 transparencies; VHS ½" videotape and some ¾" format.
First Contact & Terms: Call for interview or to drop off portfolio. Works on assignment only. Keeps samples on file. SASE. Reports in 1-2 weeks. Pays $600-1,200/day; negotiable. Pays on receipt of invoice. Buys one-time, exclusive product and all rights. Model/property release required for fine art,

The asterisk before a listing indicates that the market is new in this edition. New markets are often the most receptive to freelance submissions.

vintage cars, boats and documents. Credit line sometimes given "if the photography is partially donated for a nonprofit organization."
Tips: To break in "make appointment to leave portfolio and references/resumé or to meet face-to-face."

BOB BARRY ASSOCIATES, Box H, Newtown Square PA 19073. Phone: (215)353-7333. FAX: (215)356-5759. Design firm. Contact: Bob Barry. Estab. 1964. Specializes in annual reports, publication design, displays, packaging, direct mail, signage, interiors and audiovisual installations. Clients include: industrial, financial, commercial and government. Examples of recent projects: Corporate Profile brochure, Cornell & Co. (text illustration); Marketing program, Focht's Inc. (ads, brochures and direct mail); and ECC exhibit (large color transparencies in display installations).
Needs: Works with 2-3 freelancers per month. Uses photos for annual reports, consumer and trade magazines, direct mail, P-O-P displays, catalogs, posters, packaging and signage. Subject matter usually of products, on-site installations and people working. Reviews stock images of related subjects.
Specs: Uses b&w and color prints, "very small to cyclorama (mural) size;" matte finish. Also uses 35mm, 2¼ × 2¼, 4 × 5 and 8 × 10 transparencies.
First Contact & Terms: Provide resume, business card, brochure, flyer or tearsheets to be kept on file for possible future assignments. Works on assignment only. Keeps samples on file. SASE. Reports as needed; can be "days to months." Pays $50-150/hour; $600-1200/day; other payment negotiable. Pays on variable basis, according to project. Buys all rights; negotiable. Model release preferred for individual subjects. Credit lines sometimes given, depending upon "end use and client guidelines."
Tips: Wants to see "creative use of subjects, color and lighting. Also, simplicity and clarity. Style should not to be too arty." Points out that the objective of a photo should be readily identifiable. Sees trend toward more use of photos within the firm and in the design field in general. To break in, photographers should "understand the objective" they're trying to achieve. "Be creative within personal boundaries. Be my eyes and ears and help me to see things I've missed. Be available and prompt."

BOB BOEBERITZ DESIGN, 247 Charlotte St., Asheville NC 28801. (704)258-0316. Graphic design studio. Owner: Bob Boeberitz. Estab. 1984. Types of clients: realtors, developers, retail, recording artists, mail-order firms, industrial, restaurants, hotels and book publishers.
Needs: Works with 1 freelance photographer every 2 or 3 months. Uses photographers for consumer and trade magazines, direct mail, brochures, catalogs and posters. Subjects include studio product shots; some location; some stock photos.
Specs: Uses 8 × 10 b&w glossy prints; 35mm or 4 × 5 transparencies.
First Contact & Terms: Provide resume, business card, brochure, flyer or tearsheets to be kept on file for possible future assignments. Does not return unsolicited material. Reports "when there is a need." Pays $50-200/b&w photo; $100-500/color photo; $50-100/hour; $350-1,000/day. Pays on per-job basis. Buys one-time and all rights. Model release preferred.
Tips: "I usually look for a specific specialty. No photographer is good at everything. I also consider studio space and equipment. Show me something different, unusual, something that sets them apart from any average local photographer. If I'm going out of town for something it has to be for something I can't get done locally."

*CENTRO ARTE, 3rd Floor, 96 South St., Boston MA 02111. (617)422-0535. Design firm and art studio. Art Director: Marcos Carvajal. Estab. 1991. Specializes in direct mail, fine arts, public art, art workshops and graphic design. Types of clients: nonprofit and educational institutions. Examples of recent projects: CLAS, Cambridge College (brochure) and Portafolio Slides, Centro Arte (press releases).
Needs: Works with 1 freelance photographer/month. Uses photographs for direct mail, catalogs, posters and public relations. Subjects include: slides documentation, public relations. Reviews stock photos of advertising.
Specs: Uses 8 × 10 b&w prints; 35mm transparencies.
First Contact & Terms: Arrange personal interview to show portfolio. Provide resume, business card, brochure, flyer or tearsheets to be kept on file for possible future assignments; include personal references. Works with local freelancers on assignment only. Keeps samples on file. NPI; "pays per assignment." Pays on receipt of invoice. Buys all rights; negotiable. Credit line given depending on project.
Tips: In samples wants to see "group of people, sculpture, tailor-made for publications."

■ *The solid, black square before a listing indicates that the market uses various types of audiovisual materials, such as slides, film or videotape.*

THE COMARK GROUP INC., Suite 2080, 200 Renaissance Center, Detroit MI 48243. (313)259-2060. FAX: (313)567-4486. Design firm. Production Manager: Jim Atkin. Estab. 1986. Specializes in annual reports, publications, displays, packaging, direct mail, signage and corporate identity. Types of clients: industrial, financial, retail, publishers, nonprofit and general business. Examples of recent projects: Annual report, IBM Great Lakes Area, (IBM people); sales brochure, Hearst Publications, (product promotion); and annual report, Alexander Hamilton Life, (corporate identity).
Needs: Works with 1-2 freelancers/month. Uses photos "for practically anything that appears in print." Reviews stock photos occasionally, as needed.
Specs: Uses b&w and color prints; no format preference. Also uses 35mm, 2¼×2¼, 4×5 and 8×10 transparencies.
First Contact & Terms: Provide resume, business card, brochure, flyer or tearsheets to be kept on file for possible future assignments. Works mostly on assignment. Keeps samples on file. SASE. Reports upon client approval of project proposal. Pays $50-150/hour; $300-1,200/day; and $200-1,500/job. Pays in "30 days net." Buys all rights. Model release required. Credit line sometimes given, "depending upon circumstances."
Tips: Wants to see "creativity, technical expertise and credentials." Work is occasional, so patience is important in breaking in.

CONTOURS CONSULTING DESIGN GROUP, INC., 864 Stearns Rd., Bartlett IL 60103. Phone: (708)837-4100. Design firm. Art Director: June Maher. Estab. 1960. Specializes in packaging and industrial design. Types of clients: industrial. Examples of recent projects: Desk accessories, Sanford, (packaging); and cutlery, Revere, (packaging).
Needs: Works with 2-3 freelancers annually. Reviews stock photos as needed.
Specs: Uses color prints; no format preference. Also uses 4×5 and 8×10 transparencies.
First Contact & Terms: Contact through rep. Arrange personal interview to show portfolio. Send unsolicited photos by mail for consideration. Provide resume, business card, brochure, flyer or tearsheets to be kept on file for possible future assignments. Works on assignment only. Keeps samples on file. Cannot return material. Reports in 1-2 weeks. Pays $500-2,000/day; "quote for job is always required." Buys all rights. Model release required. Credit line sometimes given, depending upon project.
Tips: Wants to see "product photography, showing photographer's problem-solving abilities." Sees trend toward "continued use of photos in packaging field."

*JAMIE DAVISON DESIGN, INC., Suite 339, 2325 3rd St., San Francisco CA 94107. (415)864-5775. FAX: (415)864-1289. Design firm. Estab. 1985. Specializes in packaging brochures, ads, P-O-P. Types of clients: industrial, retail and nonprofit. Examples of recent projects: product photography for Microtrac Trackball, Microspeed; promotional materials, Oral-B; and cosmetics/personal care holiday collection, Shaklee.
Needs: Works with 2-3 photographers/month. Uses photographs for consumer and trade magazines, P-O-P displays, catalogs and packaging. Subjects include: product photography. Reviews stock photos on various subjects as needed.
Specs: Uses 35mm, 2¼×2¼, 4×5 transparencies.
First Contact & Terms: Submit portfolio for review. Provide resume, business card, brochure, flyer or tearsheets to be kept on file for possible future assignments. Has drop-off policy for submissions. Keeps samples on file. SASE. Pays $1,200-1,800/day; bid by day rate and materials or by project. Pays on receipt of invoice and P.O. within 30 days. Rights negotiable; "prefer buy-out, with photographer maintaining rights for self-promo." Model/property release required. Credit line sometimes given "depending on format. Can't credit on a package, usually."
Tips: In portfolio, looks for "excellent work experience, good client list and good product photography."

DESIGNWORKS, INC., 48 Grove St., Somerville MA 02144. Phone: (617)628-8600. FAX: (617)628-0622. Design firm. Estab. 1974. Specializes in publication design. Types of clients: publishers.
Needs: Works with freelancers on occasional basis. Uses photos for brochures and educational books. Subjects are usually people on location, with some set-up-type shots. Reviews stock photos.
Specs: Uses 8×10 b&w prints; 35mm transparencies.
First Contact & Terms: Query with resume credits. Send stock photo list. Provide resume, business card, brochure, flyer or tearsheets to be kept on file for possible assignments. Works with local freelancers only. Keeps samples on file. SASE. Reports in 1 month. NPI; pays on per-job basis; negotiable. Pays on receipt of invoice. Buys one-time rights. Model release required. Credit line sometimes given depending upon client.
Tips: Points out that "companies are increasingly interested in solving photo needs through stock photos."

*DINA DESIGNS, Moose Lake Outpost 697, Ely MN 55731. (218)365-6285. FAX: (218)365-6285. Design firm. Designer: Dina Villalpando. Estab. 1982. Specializes in annual reports, publication design, packaging and direct mail. Types of clients: industrial, retail, publishers and nonprofit. Examples of recent projects: viewbook, Vermilion (catalog/brochure); video covers, Razors Edge (video/instruction); and brochure, The Moose Bay Co. (direct mail).
Needs: Works with 2 freelance photographers/month. Uses photographs for annual reports, direct mail, catalogs, posters and packaging. Subjects include: beauty and on location catalog. Reviews stock photos of beauty, outdoors, people (old and young), fishing, canoeing and office.
Specs: Uses 5×7 color and b&w prints; 35mm transparencies.
First Contact & Terms: Submit portfolio for review. Query with list of stock photo subjects. Send unsolicited photos by mail for consideration. Provide resume, business card, brochure, flyer or tearsheets to be kept on file for possible future assignments. Works with local freelancers only. Keeps samples on file. SASE. Reports in 3 weeks. Pays $200-1,000/day; $300/color photo; $150/b&w photo; depends on assignment. Pays on receipt of invoice. Buys one-time and all rights; negotiable. Model/property release preferred. Photo captions preferred. Credit line given.
Tips: In samples, looks for "style and quality."

*THE DRAWING BOARD GRAPHIC DESIGN, 3rd Floor, 652 Broadway, New York NY 10012. (212)979-2610. FAX: (212)979-2731. Design firm. Art Directors: Cey Adams/Steven Carr. Estab. 1989. Specializes in packaging and album design. Types of clients: retail.
Needs: Works with 3 photographers/month. Uses photographs for consumer and trade magazines, catalogs, posters and packaging. Subjects include: albums. Reviews stock photos.
Specs: Uses 11×14 color and b&w prints.
First Contact & Terms: Submit portfolio for review. Reports in 1-2 weeks. NPI. Pays on acceptance or receipt of invoice. Buys all rights; negotiable. Model/property release required. Credit line given.

*MAUREEN ERBE DESIGN, 1948 S. La Cienega Blvd., Los Angeles CA 90034. (213)839-1954. Design firm. Estab. 1984. Specializes in annual reports, publication design and packaging. Types of clients: industrial, financial, retail, publishers and nonprofit. Examples of recent projects: marketing brochure, music center; marketing brochure, architect; and catalog, furniture company.
Needs: Works with 2 freelance photographers/month. Uses photographs for annual reports, trade magazines, catalogs, posters and packaging. Subject matter varies. Reviews stock photos.
Specs: Uses color and b&w prints; 35mm, 2¼×2¼, 4×5 transparencies.
First Contact & Terms: Arrange personal interview to show portfolio. Send unsolicited photos by mail for consideration. Works with local freelancers on assignment only. Keeps samples on file. Cannot return material. Reports "only if interested in hiring." NPI; "payment varies." Pays on acceptance. Model/property release required. Photo captions preferred. Credit line sometimes given depending on project.

*FRANZ-HATLEM DESIGN GROUP, INC., 111 3rd St. S., LaCrosse WI 54601. (608)791-1020. FAX: (608)791-1021. Design firm. Creative Director: Paul Hatlem. Estab. 1990. Specializes in publication design, display design and packaging. Types of clients: industrial, retail. Examples of recent projects: "In Line in Life" video, Rollerblade, Inc. (cover photo for video); Schmidt Loon Search, G. Heileman Brewing Co. (point of purchase display); and 1991 catalog, Burros Promotional Products (catalog).
Needs: Works with 2 freelance photographers/month. Uses photographs for trade magazines, P-O-P displays, catalogs and packaging. Subjects include: models, products and food. Reviews stock photos of studio-food and location-models.
Specs: Uses 2¼×2¼, 4×5 transparencies.
First Contact & Terms: Provide tearsheets to be kept on file for possible future assignments. Works with freelancers on assignment only. Keeps samples on file. SASE. Reports in 1-2 weeks. Pays $100-3,500/job. Pays on receipt of invoice. Buys all rights; negotiable. Model/property release preferred; usually need model shots. Captions preferred. Credit lines sometimes given depending on the project; "yes, if we can make the decision."
Tips: Interested in "general quality of portfolio and specifically the design and styling of each photo." Sees trend toward "more product with models interacting and less product only on some sci-fi setting. We like to work with photographers who can suggest solutions to lighting and styling problems—no 'yes' men/women!"

The code NPI (no payment information given) appears in listings that have not given specific payment amounts.

*FULLMOON CREATIONS INC., 74 S. Hamilton St., Doylestown PA 18901. (215)345-1233. FAX: (215)368-5378. Design firm. Art Director: Frederic Lelen. Estab. 1986. Specializes in annual reports, publication design, display design, packaging, direct mail and signage. Types of clients: industrial. Examples of recent projects: brochures, 4/Y (corporate) and mailers, Yves Rocher (retail mailorder). **Needs:** Works with 1 freelance photographer/month. Uses photographs for annual reports, direct mail, P-O-P displays, catalogs and packaging.
Specs: Uses color and b&w prints; 35mm, 4×5 transparencies.
First Contact & Terms: Submit portfolio for review. Provide resume, business card, brochure, flyer or tearsheets to be kept on file for possible future assignments. Works with local freelancers on assignment only. Keeps samples on file. Reports in 3 weeks. Pays $250-800/day; $250-4,000/job. Pays on receipt of invoice, 30 days. Rights negotiable. Sometimes gives credit line depending on clients.
Tips: In samples, considers "spontaneity, lighting and angles."

*FUSION INTERNATIONAL, 2371 Ridgewood Rd., Jacksonville FL 32207-3531. Design firm. Creative Director: Michael O'Connell. Estab. 1991. Specializes in annual reports, publication design, display design, direct mail and corporate communications/music industry. Types of clients: industrial, financial, retail, publishers, nonprofit and environmental/music. Examples of recent projects: quarterly health/fitness publication, *Jacksonville Medical Journal*; parenting publication, *First Coast Parent*; and video album packaging.
Needs: Works with 0-4 freelance photographers/month. Uses photographs for trade magazines, direct mail, catalogs, posters. Subjects include: editorial for publications. Reviews stock photos of entertainment and medical.
Specs: Uses 8×10 color and b&w prints; 35mm, 2¼×2¼ transparencies.
First Contact & Terms: Interested in receiving work from newer, lesser-known photographers. Provide resume, business card, brochure, flyer or tearsheets to be kept on file for possible future assignments. Works with freelancers on assignment only. Keeps samples on file. SASE. Reports in 2-4 weeks. NPI. Pays on publication. Rights negotiable. Model/property release required. Captions preferred. Credit line sometimes given depending on project/client specification.
Tips: In portfolio "looking for unique styles and subject matters. Photography and video/film in particular will become more important as the medium moves into the age of multi-media. My company is involved in the entertainment and publication industry with a great concern for the unique visual."

ERIC GLUCKMAN COMMUNICATIONS INC., 24 E. Parkway., Scarsdale NY 10583. (914)723-0088. FAX: (201)262-0481. Graphic design firm. President: Eric Gluckman. Estab. 1973. Types of clients: Industrial, finance and editorial work. Examples of recent projects: Group W Cable (sales presentation book); American Express (employee magazine); and GTE Telenet (sales brochures).
Needs: Works with 2 freelance photographers/month. Uses photographs for consumer magazines, trade magazines, direct mail, catalogs, posters and editorial. Subjects include: "now mostly location still life."
Specs: Uses 8×10 color and b&w prints; 35mm, 2¼×2¼, 4×5, 8×10 transparencies.
First Contact & Terms: Arrange personal interview to show portfolio. Send unsolicited photos by mail for consideration. Query with samples. Provide resume, business card, brochure, flyer or tearsheets to be kept on file for possible future assignments. Works with freelancers on assignment only. Does not return unsolicited material. Reports in 3 weeks. Pays $1,000/day; $1,000/job; page rate—magazine. Pays on receipt of invoice. Buys all rights; negotiable, but prefers all rights.
Tips: In portfolio or samples, wants to see "exciting different views of everyday objects (still life). Unfortunately, trends are not creative—still they're economic. There's a much tighter financial squeeze all around." To break in with this firm, "be patient, persevere."

THE GRAPHICS STUDIO, 811 N. Highland Ave., Los Angeles CA 90038. (213)466-2666. FAX: (213)466-5685. Creative Director: Gerry Rosentswieg. Estab. 1965. Specializes in publication design, display design and direct mail. Types of clients: financial, retail, publishers, nonprofit.
Needs: Works with 1-5 freelance photographers/month. Uses photographs for trade magazines, direct mail, catalogs, posters and brochures.
Specs: Uses 11×14, b&w prints; 35mm, 2¼×2¼, 4×5, 8×10 transparencies.
First Contact & Terms: Query with resume of credits. Provide resume, business card, brochure, flyer or tearsheets to be kept on file for possible future assignments. Works on assignment only. Keeps samples on file. SASE. Reporting time "varies as to project." NPI; "payment varies as to budget." Pays within 30 days of acceptance. Rights, including all rights, negotiable. Credit line sometimes given depending on usage.
Tips: Wants to see style, talent and organization.

*■JOHN HOFFMAN DESIGN, 27 St. Joseph Ave., Long Beach CA 90803. (213)433-3343. Ad agency, advertising design. Creative Director: John Hoffman. Estab. 1978. Types of clients: industrial, retail, fashion and finance.

Needs: Works with 2-3 freelance photographers/month. Uses photographs for billboards, consumer and trade magazines, direct mail, P-O-P displays, catalogs, posters, newspapers, signage and audiovisual. Subjects include: food, package goods and autos. Reviews stock photos.
Specs: Uses color and b&w prints; 35mm, 2¼×2¼, 4×5, 8×10 transparencies; film; videotape.
First Contact & Terms: Arrange personal interview to show portfolio. Query with resume of credits. Query with list of stock photo subjects. Send unsolicited photos by mail for consideration. Query with samples. Submit portfolio for review. Provide resume, business card, brochure, flyer or tearsheets to be kept on file for possible future assignments. Works with freelancers on assignment only. SASE. Reports in 3 weeks. NPI; "payment estimated only on job." Pays on receipt of invoice. Buys all rights. Model release preferred. Credit line sometimes given.

*HUTCHINSON ASSOCIATES, 2327 N. Southport Ave., Chicago IL 60614. (312)525-2594. FAX: (312)525-7282. Design firm. Contact: Jerry Hutchinson. Estab. 1985. Specializes in annual reports, marketing brochures, etc. Types of clients: financial, retail, nonprofit. Examples of recent projects: annual report (architectural) and fund-raiser (still life, memories).
Needs: Works with 1 freelance photographer/month. Uses photographs for annual reports, brochures. Subjects include: still life.
Specs: Uses 4×5, 8×10 color and b&w prints; 35mm, 4×5 transparencies.
First Contact & Terms: Arrange personal interview to show portfolio. Provide resume, business card, brochure, flyer or tearsheets to be kept on file for possible future assignments. Keeps samples on file. SASE. Reports in 1-2 weeks. NPI; payment rates depend on the client. Pays within 30 days. Rights negotiable. Credit line given.
Tips: In samples "quality and composition count." Sees a trend toward "more abstraction."

*INNOVATIVE DESIGN AND ADVERTISING, Suite 7, 1214 Idaho Ave., Santa Monica CA 90403. (310)395-4332. FAX: (310)394-6925. Design firm. Partners: Susan Nickey and Kim Crossett. Estab. 1991. Specializes in annual reports, publication design, corporate identity. Types of clients: industrial, financial, retail, nonprofit and corporate. Examples of recent projects: general brochure, Kasler Corp. (product/construction); and direct mail, Herbert Hawkins Realtors (studio/people/Polaroid transfer).
Needs: Works with 1 freelance photographer/month. Uses photographs for annual reports, trade magazines, direct mail and brochures. Subjects include: people, studio and outdoor construction. Reviews stock photos on a per-assignment basis.
Specs: Uses 35mm, 2¼×2¼, 4×5 transparencies.
First Contact & Terms: Provide resume, business card, brochure, flyer or tearsheets to be kept on file for possible future assignments. Works with freelancers on assignment only. Keeps samples on file. SASE. Reports in 1 month. "When we receive a job in-house we request photographers." NPI; payment "on a per-job basis as budget allows." Pays within 30 days. Rights negotiable. Model/property release required for models, any famous works. Credit lines sometimes given depending on client. "We like to give credit where credit is due!"
Tips: In samples or portfolio, looks for "uniqueness, capability." Sees a trend toward use of Polaroid transfers. "Be punctual and willing to work within our client's budget."

*INNOVATIVE DESIGN & GRAPHICS, Suite 214, 1234 Sherman Ave., Evanston IL 60202. Art Director: Tim Sonder. Photos used in magazines, brochures, newsletters and catalogs.
Needs: Product shots, people shots, and topical shots for magazines.
Specs: Uses 8×10 b&w glossy prints, 35mm, 2¼×2¼, and 4×5 transparencies, b&w contact sheets, and b&w negatives.
First Contact & Terms: Provide resume, business card, brochure, flyer or tearsheets to be kept on file for possible future assignments. Works on assignment only. Reviews stock photos. SASE. "Reports when applicable assignment is available." NPI; payment negotiable per job. Buys one-time rights or all rights. Model release required; captions preferred. Credit line given.
Tips: "We look for crisp photos to illustrate ideas, clear photos of products and products in use, and relaxed photos of business people at work. We prefer that freelancers submit work produced on larger-format equipment. Do not phone us to arrange to show your book. Send samples instead."

BRENT A. JONES DESIGN, 328 Hayes St., San Francisco CA 94102. Phone: (415)626-8337. Design firm. Contact: Brent A. Jones. Estab. 1983. Specializes in annual reports and publication design. Types of clients: industrial, financial, retail, publishers and nonprofit.
Needs: Works with one freelancer/month. Uses photos for annual reports, consumer magazines, catalogs and posters. Reviews stock photos as needed.
Specs: Uses color and b&w prints; no format preference. Also uses 35mm, 4×5 and 8×10 transparencies.
First Contact & Terms: Query with resume of credits. Query with samples. Provide resume, business card, brochure, flyer or tearsheets to be kept on file for possible future assignments. Works with local freelancers only. Keeps samples on file. Cannot return material. Reports in 1 month. NPI; pays on

per hour basis. Pays on receipt of invoice. Buys one-time rights; other rights negotiable. Model/property release required; photo captions preferred. Credit line given sometimes; conditions not specified.

*LAWRENCE DESIGN GROUP, INC., 126 Fifth Ave., New York NY 10011. (212)675-4838. Graphic design firm. Estab. 1990. Specializes in all industries. Examples of recent projects: 1990 Annual Report, Enzo Biochem (laboratory researches); 1989 Annual Report, Ultimate Corp. (capability); and Cannes Film Festival, *Variety* (promotion).
Needs: Uses photographs for corporate communications. Subjects include: industrial. Reviews stock photos; "varied subject matter."
Specs: Uses 35mm, 2¼×2¼, 4×5 transparencies.
First Contact & Terms: Query with resume of credits. Query with list of stock photo subjects. Send unsolicited photos by mail for consideration. Query with samples. Provide resume, business card, brochure, flyer or tearsheets to be kept on file for possible future assignments. Works with freelancers on assignment only. Keeps samples on file. Cannot return material. Reports in 3 weeks. Pays $700-1,500/day. Pays on receipt of invoice. Buys one-time rights. Model/property release required. Credit line given except for stock photos.
Tips: In samples, looks for "originality, style, good technique. Don't show run-of-the-mill work." Sees a trend toward "unusual vision."

*M. DESIGNS, Suite 104, 10 Avocet Dr., Redwood City CA 94065. (415)637-1560. Design firm. President: Marta Krampitz. Estab. 1990. Specializes in packaging. Types of clients: financial. Examples of recent projects: "Spacemaker," Konami Inc. and "Paperboy 2," Software Toolworks (both package/computer entertainment software); and MRP brochure, Marketing Resources Plus (corporate brochure).
Needs: Works with 2 freelance photographers/month. Uses photographs for trade magazines, catalogs, packaging. Subject matter "varies dramatically." Reviews stock photos.
Specs: Uses 35mm, 2¼×2¼, 4×5 transparencies.
First Contact & Terms: Submit portfolio for review. Send unsolicited photos by mail for consideration. Provide resume, business card, brochure, flyer or tearsheets to be kept on file for possible future assignments. Works with freelancers on assignment only. Keeps samples on file. SASE. Does not report; "photographers must call to follow-up." Pays $1,500-2,000/day; $2,000-6,000/job. Pays on receipt of invoice. Buys all rights; negotiable. Model/property release required. Captions preferred. Credit lines sometimes given depending on amount of space, applicability and client."
Tips: In samples or portfolio, wants to see "great lighting, interesting composition—whether stylist used or not, strong concept or idea must be apparent." To break in with this firm "send samples and follow up. Job will depend on personality and portfolio and willingness to be negotiable with pricing according to project budget."

MCKENZIE & COMPANY, 1599 Post Road West, Westport CT 06880. (203)254-8302. FAX: (203)454-0416. Design firm. Account Executive: Jennifer Pacelli. Estab. 1980. Specializes in annual reports, corporate identity, publication design and direct mail. Types of clients: industrial, financial, nonprofit, consumer goods and travel. Examples of recent clients: Tropicana, McNeil Specialty Products and Citicorp.
Needs: Works with 1 freelance photographer/month. Uses photographs for annual reports, direct mail and catalogs.
Specs: Uses 35mm, 4×5 transparencies.
First Contact & Terms: Provide resume, business card, brochure, flyer or tearsheets to be kept on file for possible future assignments. Works with local freelancers only. Keeps samples on file. SASE. Reports as needed. Pays $1,200-1,500/day. Pays within 30 days of completion. Buys first rights; negotiable. Model release required; photo captions preferred.
Tips: Wants to see "great technical skill, flexibility and ability to put people at ease." Points out that "less and less photography is being used because of recession."

MITCHELL STUDIOS DESIGN CONSULTANTS, 1111 Fordham Lane, Woodmere NY 11598. (516)374-5620. FAX: (516)374-6915. Design firm. Principal: Steven E. Mitchell. Estab. 1922. Types of clients: corporations with consumer products. Examples of recent clients: Lipton Cup-A-Soup, Thomas J.

Can't find a listing? Check at the end of each market section for the " '92-'93 Changes" lists. These lists include any market listings from the '92 edition which were either not verified or deleted in this edition.

Lipton, Inc.; Colgate Toothpaste, Colgate Palmolive Co.; Chef Boy-Ar-Dee, American Home Foods"—all three involved package design.
Needs: Works with variable number of photographers/month. Uses photographs for direct mail, P-O-P displays, catalogs, posters, signage and package design. Subjects include: still life/product. Reviews stock photos of still life/people.
Specs: Uses all sizes and finishes of color and b&w prints; 35mm, 2¼ × 2¼, 4 × 5 and 8 × 10 transparencies.
First Contact & Terms: Interested in receiving work from newer, lesser-known photographers. Submit portfolio for review, provide resume, business card, brochure, flyer or tearsheets to be kept on file for possible future assignments. Cannot return material. Reports as needed. Pays $35-75/hour; $350-1,500/day; $500 and up/job. Pays on receipt of invoice. Buys all rights. Model release required. Property release and photo captions preferred. Credit line sometimes given depending on client approval.
Tips: In portfolio, looks for "ability to complete assignment." Sees a trend toward "tighter budgets." To break in with this firm, keep in touch regularly.

MORRIS BEECHER, 1000 Potomac St. NW, Washington DC 20007. (202)337-5300. FAX: (202)333-2659. Ad agency. Contact: Diane Beecher. Estab. 1983. Specializes in publications, P-O-P, display design, direct mail, signage, collateral, ads and billboards. Types of clients: sports, health and nutrition, the environment, real estate, resorts and shopping centers.
Needs: Works with 3-4 freelance photographers/month. Uses photographs for billboards, direct mail, posters, signage, ads and collateral materials. Subjects include real estate, fashion and lifestyle. Reviews stock photos.
Specs: Uses any size or finish of color and b&w prints; 35mm transparencies.
First Contact & Terms: Arrange personal interview to show portfolio. Provide business card, brochure, flyer or tearsheets to be kept on file for possible future assignments. Works on assignment only. Keeps samples on file. SASE. Usually pays per job; "approx. $1,000-1,500 day rate." Buys all rights. Model release required; photo captions preferred. Credit line not given.
Tips: Wants to see "very high quality work." Uses a lot of stock.

*MTC DESIGN COMMUNICATIONS, 4111 71st Ave., Landover Hills MD 20784. (301)772-8471. Full service design firm. Principal/Art Director: Michael T. Chinn. Estab. 1991. Specializes in pubilcation design, display design, direct mail, signage, corporate identity and advertising design. Types of clients: industrial, financial, publishers, high-tech, associations and consultants. Examples of recent projects: *National Contract Management* magazine, NCMA (covers, articles); and Global Telecommunications (brochures, print advertising and promotional).
Needs: Works with 0-1 freelance photographer/month. Uses photographs for trade magazines, posters, print advertising, capability brochures etc. Subjects include: on site of employees, equipment, systems and architectural; studio set up using models, props, equipment, systems, etc. Reviews stock photos on high-tech, office and management subjects.
Specs: Uses 8 × 10 b&w prints; 35mm, 2¼ × 2¼, 4 × 5 transparencies.
First Contact & Terms: Arrange personal interview to show portfolio. Query with resume of credits. Query with list of stock photo subjects. Query with samples. Provide resume, business card, brochure, flyer or tearsheets to be kept on file for possible future assignments. Works with local freelancers only. Keeps samples on file. SASE. Reports in 1-2 weeks. Pays $30-50/hour; $200-500/day; varies depending on size, usage, client budget—able to work with photographer." Pays on acceptance or on receipt of invoice. Buys all rights; negotiable. Model/property release required. Credit line sometime given depending on size and usage.
Tips: Wants to see all kinds of subjects in portfolio and samples. Looks for "distinct creative style; ability to push the medium for various effects. To cross over to different styles; use of computer enhancement. "Photographer must be creative in use of design, color/b&w, lighting, etc." In high tech sees a need to "break away from traditional tech-looking subjects. Need a different edge. We see usage of industrial and vintage photo/subject matter and computer enhanced/montage etc." To break in with this firm "don't be afraid to experiment—push the medium to the limits. Be creative. Keep in continual contact by phone or mail. We're always interested in seeing new sample/work."

■LOUIS NELSON ASSOCIATES INC., 80 University Place, New York NY 10003. (212)620-9191. FAX: (212)620-9194. Design firm. Estab. 1980. Types of clients: corporate, retail.
Needs: Works with 3-4 freelance photographers/year. Uses photographs for consumer and trade magazines, catalogs and posters. Reviews stock photos only with a specific project in mind.
Audiovisual Needs: Occasionally needs visuals for interactive displays as part of exhibits.
First Contact & Terms: Submit portfolio for review. Provide resume, business card, brochure, flyer or tearsheets to be kept on file for possible future assignments. Works on assignment only. Cannot return material. Does not report; call for response. NPI. Pays on receipt of invoice. Credit line sometimes given depending upon client needs.

Tips: In portfolio, wants to see "the usual . . . skill, sense of aesthetics that doesn't take over and ability to work with art director's concept." One trend is that "interactive videos are always being requested."

ODEN & ASSOCIATES, 5140 Wheelis, Memphis TN 38817. (901)683-8055. FAX: (901)683-2070. Design firm. Senior Vice President and Creative Designer: Bert Terwilleder. Estab. 1970. Specializes in annual reports, packaging, direct mail, signage, capabilities brochures and identity systems. Types of clients: industrial, financial, retail, paper companies and nonprofit organizations.
Needs: Works with 3 photographers/month. Photos used in annual reports, direct mail, trade magazines, P-O-P displays and catalogs. Open to wide range of subject matter. Reviews stock photos of all kinds, as needed.
Specs: Uses 8×10 b&w and color prints; also 35mm, 2¼×2¼, 4×5 and 8×10 transparencies.
First Contact & Terms: Arrange personal interview to show portfolio. Provide resume, business card, brochure, flyer or tearsheets to be kept on file for possible future assignments. Works mostly on assignment. Solicits stock only as needed. Keeps samples on file. SASE. Reports in 1-2 weeks. NPI; "payment depends upon job—usually determined by photographer's day rate plus expenses." Pays in 30 days after completion of assignment. Rights negotiable. Model release required. Credit line sometimes given according to end usage.
Tips: In samples looks for "quality images that communicate a message, are technically good and translate well to printing." Also notes: "We typically try to stay away from trends—that's why we are always looking for new photographers." Accordingly, best strategy is to "show wide range of subjects and techniques."

*THE PRINT GROUP, Suite 200, 2735 N. Sheffield, Chicago IL 60657. (312)880-2200. FAX: (312)880-2409. Design firm. Executive Director: Monica Paxson. Estab. 1990. Specializes in publication design. Types of clients: financial, publishers and nonprofit. Examples of recent projects: Login Publishers Consortium (catalog cover); Dupage Senior Citizens Council (annual report illustration); and Hitec Group International Products (catalog).
Needs: Works with 1 freelance photographer/month. Uses photographs for annual reports, catalogs, cover art, book covers. Subjects include: people, products and fine art.
Specs: Uses color and b&w prints.
First Contact & Terms: Submit portfolio for review. Works with local freelancers only. Keeps samples on file. SASE. Pays $250-1,500/day; $250/color photo; $100/b&w photo. Pays on receipt of invoice. Buys first and one-time rights; negotiable. Model/property release required. Credit line given.
Tips: In reviewing portfolio looks for "warmth in people shots, ability to style own product shots. Fine art shots must be show stoppers—surreal or very interesting. We don't buy lots of photography, but we like to use the best people for a variety of jobs."

ARNOLD SAKS ASSOCIATES, 350 E. 81st St., New York NY 10028. (212)861-4300. FAX: (212)535-2590. Graphic design firm. Manager of Client Services & Production: Timothy Coppins. Estab. 1968. Types of clients: Industrial, financial, legal, pharmaceutical and utilities. Clients include: Bristol-Myers Squibb, Alcoa, Goldman Sachs and International Paper.
Needs: Works with approximately 15 photographers during busy season. Uses photographs for annual reports and corporate brochures. Subjects include: corporate situations and portraits. Reviews stock photos; subjects vary according to the nature of the annual report.
Specs: Uses b&w prints; 35mm, 2¼×2¼, 4×5, 8×10 transparencies.
First Contact & Terms: Interested in receiving work from newer, lesser-known photographers. "Appointments are set up during the spring for summer review on a first-come only basis. We have a limit of approximately 30 portfolios each season." Call Tim Coppins to arrange an appointment. Works on assignment only. Reports as needed. Payment negotiable, "based on project budgets. Generally we pay $1,250-2,250/day." Pays on receipt of invoice and payment by client; advances provided. Buys all rights; negotiable. Model release required; photo captions preferred. Credit line sometimes given depending upon client specifications.
Tips: "Ideally a photographer should show a corporate book indicating his success with difficult working conditions and establishing an attractive and vital final product." This "company is well known in the design community for doing classic graphic design. We look for solid, conservative, straightforward corporate photography that will enhance these ideals."

STEVEN SESSIONS, INC., Suite 500, 5177 Richmond Ave, Houston TX 77056. Phone: (713)850-8450. FAX: (713)850-9324. Design firm. President: Steven Sessions. Estab. 1982. Specializes in annual reports, packaging and publication design. Types of clients: industrial, financial, women's fashion, cosmetics, retail, publishers and nonprofit.

Needs: Always works with freelancers. Uses photos for annual reports, consumer and trade magazines, P-O-P displays, catalogs and packaging. Subject matter varies according to need. Reviews stock photos.
Specs: Uses b&w and color prints; no preference for format or finish. Also uses 35mm, 2¼×2¼, 4×5 and 8×10 transparencies.
First Contact & Terms: Submit portfolio for review. Send unsolicited photos by mail for consideration. Provide resume, business card, brochure, flyer or tearsheets to be kept on file for possible future assignments. Keeps samples on file. SASE. Reports in 1-2 weeks. Pays $1,800-5,000/day. Pays on receipt of invoice. Buys all rights; negotiable. Model/property release preferred. Credit line given.

DEBORAH SHAPIRO DESIGNS, 150 Bentley Ave., Jersey City NJ 07304. (201)432-5198. Design firm. Contact: Deborah Shapiro. Estab. 1979. Specializes in annual reports, publication design, direct mail and signage. Types of clients: industrial, financial, publishers and nonprofit organizations.
Needs: Occasionally works with freelance photographers. Typically needs still lifes and people shots. Reviews stock photos.
Specs: Uses color prints and 35mm transparencies.
First Contact & Terms: Send unsolicited photos by mail for consideration. Works with local freelancers only. Keeps samples on file. Cannot return material. Reports in 1 month. NPI; amount of payment "depends upon the photographer's ability and the client's budget." Pays on receipt of invoice. Buys one-time rights. Model release required. Credit line sometimes given depending upon client's usage.

*SHERIN & MATEJKA, INC., 404 Park Ave. South, New York NY 10016. (212)686-8410. Graphic Design Organization. President: Jack Sherin. Estab. 1973. Types of clients: industrial, financial. Examples of recent projects: Group Health Incorporated ("New York City Reopener" ads and annual report).
Needs: Works with 1 freelance photographer/month. Uses photographs for trade magazines, direct mail, posters, newspapers, brochures, ads and annual reports. Subjects include: people.
Specs: Uses 35mm, 2¼×2¼, 4×5, 8×10 transparencies.
First Contact & Terms: Interested in receiving work from newer, lesser-known photographers. Provide resume, business card, brochure, flyer or tearsheets to be kept on file for possible future assignments. Works with freelancers on assignment only. Keeps samples on file. SASE. Does not report unless interested. Pays $250 minimum/b&w photo; $250/color photo; $1,500-2,000/day; $350 and up/job; "all projects are negotiated prior to assignment." Pays on publication. Buys one-time and all rights; negotiable. Model/property release required for people and environments. Credit line sometimes given depending on client's preference.

*SMART ART, 1077 Celestial St., Cincinnati OH 45202. (513)241-9757. Design firm, advertising art. President: Fred Lieberman. Estab. 1979. Specializes in annual reports, display design, packaging, direct mail, signage and advertising art. Types of clients: industrial, retail, health. Examples of recent projects: catalogs, Tropic Formals Ltd. (wholesale/retail rentals); exhibit booth, brochure/trade, advertising campaign/consumer, Future Health Care Research Centers (to recruit test studies/trade and subjects/consumer); and package design, collateral material, Neyra Industries (in-store display material). Uses photographs for consumer and trade magazines, direct mail, P-O-P displays, catalogs, posters, packaging and signage for a wide diversity of clients. Reviews stock photos "on a wide variety of subjects; client list varies."
Specs: Uses 8×10 color and b&w prints; 2¼×2¼, 4×5, 8×10 transparencies.
First Contact & Terms: Query with list of stock photo subjects. Provide resume, business card, brochure, flyer or tearsheets to be kept on file for possible future assignments. Works with local freelancers only. Keeps samples on file. Cannot return material. Reporting time "depends entirely on kinds of projects planned." Pays $50-200/hour; $350-1,500/day. Pays on receipt of invoice. "Generally client pays directly upon receipt of invoice." Buys all rights; negotiable. Model/property release required; photo captions preferred. Credit lines sometimes given depending on what might be negotiated.

*SPIKER COMMUNICATIONS, INC., 229 E. Main, Box 8567, Missoula MT 59807. (406)721-0785. FAX: (406)728-8915. Ad agency, design house. Art Directors: Marlene Hutchins, Laura Blaker. Specializes in industrial, financial, tourism. Examples of recent projects: "Step into the New Frontier," Rocky Mountain Log Homes (ad campaign, image photography of custom homes); "Montana's Timeless Treasure," Glacier Country Tourism (ad campaign, stock photos of the region); and "Fables," Montana Bank Systems (ad campaign, print and TV ads using animals).
Needs: Uses photographs for consumer and trade magazines, direct mail, P-O-P displays, catalogs, posters and newspapers. Uses photographs of tourism-related images taken in the "Glacier Country" region, background textures for log home brochures. Reviews stock photos of "wildlife, native to our region, any photography of our region, textures or backgrounds for collateral projects."

Specs: Uses minimum 8 × 10 or larger, matte b&w prints; 35mm, 2¼ × 2¼, 4 × 5, 8 × 10 transparencies; ½" or ¾" videotape.

First Contact & Terms: Arrange personal interview to show portfolio. Can send in portfolio on "drop off" basis. Provide resume, business card, brochure, flyer or tearsheets to be kept on file for possible future assignments. Keeps samples on file. SASE. Reports as soon as possible. Payment "negotiated on a job-by-job basis. Prices reflect Montana cost of living." Pays on receipt of invoice during 30-day billing cycle. Buys first, one-time and all rights. Rights negotiable. Model/property release required for people with recognizable faces. Captions preferred; include place of image. Credit line sometimes given depending on use.

Tips: In samples, looks for "good lighting, sharpness, crisp detail (unless it is supposed to be moody)." Sees trend in "sharp, clean images with emotional impact."

SPOT DESIGN, 775 6th Ave., New York NY 10001. Phone: (212)645-8684. Design firm. Art Director: Drew Hodges. Estab. 1986. Types of clients: fashion and entertainment industry. Examples of recent projects: Rolling Stone Clothing, *Rolling Stone* magazine, (consumer ads).

Needs: Works with 1 freelancer/month. Uses photos for consumer and trade magazines and catalogs. Photos are usually fashion, table-top and related stock photos. Reviews "archival-type stock photos, like those used in *Spy* magazine."

Specs: Uses b&w prints; no preference for format or finish. Also uses 35mm, 2¼ × 2¼, 4 × 5 and 8 × 10.

First Contact & Terms: Submit portfolio for review. Query with samples. Provide resume, business card, brochure, flyer or tearsheets to be kept on file for possible future assignments. Works on assignment only. Keeps samples on file. Cannot return material. Reports only if interested. Pays $1,500-3,000/day; $400-1,500/job; $400-600/stock photo. Pays within 45 days from receipt of invoice. Rights negotiable. Credit line sometimes gven, depending upon client approval.

Tips: Wants to see "innovative, nontraditional work with energy or fun." Not interested in conservative, "annual report-type" images.

*STUDIO Q, 225 West 57th St., New York NY 10019. (212)645-0071. FAX: (212)645-0071. Design firm. Art Director: Carolyn Quan. Estab. 1991. Specializes in album covers and art. Types of clients: music and entertainment. Examples of recent projects: album covers and collateral (posters, flyers, etc.) for Arista Records.

Needs: Works with 1 freelance photographer/month. Uses photographs for trade magazine, direct mail, posters and packaging. Subjects include: portraiture. Reviews stock photos of backgrounds, textures and scenics.

Specs: Uses any size, color and b&w prints; 35mm, 2¼ × 2¼ transparencies.

First Contact & Terms: Arrange personal interview to show portfolio. Provide resume, business card, brochure, flyer or tearsheets to be kept on file for possible future assignments. Keeps samples on file. Cannot return material. NPI; payment depends on client's budget. Rights depend on project. Credit line given.

*SUISSA DESIGN, Suite 205, 924 Lincoln Rd., Miami Beach FL 33139. (305)672-4142. FAX: (305)672-4067. Design firm. Partner: Joel Suissa. Estab. 1990. Non-specialization. Types of clients: industrial, retail and nonprofit.

Needs: Works with 1 freelance photographer/month. Uses photographs for trade magazines, direct mail, catalogs, posters, packaging. Subject matter varies. Reviews stock photos.

Specs: Uses color and b&w prints; 4 × 5 transparencies.

First Contact & Terms: Provide resume, business card, brochure, flyer or tearsheets to be kept on file for possible future assignments. Works with freelancers on assignment only. Keeps samples on file. Cannot return material. Reports in 3 weeks. Pays $75-150/hour; $250-700/day; $500-2,000/job. Pays on receipt of invoice. Rights negotiable.

*THE TRAVER COMPANY, GRAPHIC DESIGNERS, Suite 615, 1601 2nd Ave., Seattle WA 98101. (206)441-0611. (206)728-6016. Design firm. Office Manager: Julia Fiset. Estab. 1976. Specializes in publication design, direct mail, brochures, catalogs, books. Types of clients: nonprofit, travel and hospitality, health care. Examples of recent projects: Capabilities Brochure, Swedish Hospital (innovation, symbolic imagery); "Front Door to the City" ad, Westin Hotel (studio, multiple exposure); and Canadian Rockies Brochure, Princess Tours (scenic).

Needs: Works with 1-2 freelance photographers/month. Uses photographs for annual reports, brochures, corporate magazines, ads. Subjects vary. Reviews stock photos on travel and tourism: Alaska, Southeast Alaska, Canadian Rockies.

Specs: Uses various sizes b&w prints; 35mm, 2¼ × 2¼, 4 × 5 transparencies.

First Contact & Terms: Query with samples. Provide resume, business card, brochure, flyer or tearsheets to be kept on file for possible future assignments. Keeps samples on file. SASE. Reports in 1-2 weeks. NPI; payment negotiated by job. Pays on receipt of invoice plus 30 days. Rights negotiated

© Jim Sims

Washington photographer Jim Sims began working with Steven Sessions Inc., 14 years ago and he continues to supply the design firm with interesting photos. This photo was used in a 1990 annual report for Southdown Corporation. Sims obviously had fun with the assignment, taking advantage of the surroundings and placing a worker inside this monstrous wheel.

by job. Model/property release preferred; usually needed for travel, health care. Credit lines sometimes given depending on scale of project, photo credits on larger projects.
Tips: In reviewing samples looks for "innovation, appropriateness of solution to marketing objective and visual qualities."

*WINTER GRAPHICS, 1310 Tradewinds Circle, Sacramento CA 95691. (916)372-6229. Design firm. Owner/Designer: Mary Winter. Estab. 1987. Specializes in annual reports, publication design. Types of clients: financial, publishers, associations. Examples of recents projects: Annual Report, CHFA (first-time home buyers/photos, testimonials); and brochure cover, Messersmith (progress of association).
Needs: Works with 1-2 freelance photographers/month. Uses photographs for annual reports, trade magazines and posters. Subjects include: location shots, people and housing. Reviews stock photos of people, industrial and housing.
Specs: Uses 3×5 color prints; 4×5 transparencies.
First Contact & Terms: Arrange personal interview to show portfolio. Works with freelancers on assignment only. Keeps samples on file. SASE. Reports in 1-2 weeks. Pays $100-400/hour; $400-800/day. Pays on receipt of invoice. Buys one-time rights; negotiable. Model/property release required; photo captions preferred. Credit line sometimes given depending on the client and their job requirements.
Tips: In portfolio wants to see "different angles, new viewing ideas, the blend of photography with the designed page. Integrating photography and design are ways to meet goals, and there is a trend to using photo in the computer." Freelancer should "show different subject matter in new ways and how one works with an art director."

CLARENCE ZIERHUT, INC., 2014 Platinum, Garland TX 75042. Phone: (214)276-1722. FAX: (214)272-5570. Design firm. President: Clarence Zierhut. Estab. 1973. Specializes in displays, packaging and product design. Types of clients: industrial, retail, publishers and nonpofit.
Needs: Uses photos for direct mail, catalogs and packaging. Subjects usually are "prototype models."
Specs: Uses 8×10 color prints, matte finish; 35mm transparencies.
First Contact & Terms: Provide resume, business card, brochure, flyer or tearsheets to be kept on file for possible future assignments. Works with local freelancers only. Keeps samples on file. Cannot return material. Reports in 1-2 weeks. NPI; payment negotiable on bid basis. Pays on receipt of invoice. Buys all rights. Model release required. Credit line sometimes given depending upon client.
Tips: Wants to see product photos showing "color, depth and detail."

Art/Design Studios/'92-93 changes

The following markets appeared in the 1992 edition of *Photographer's Market* but are not listed in the 1993 edition. They may have been omitted for failing to respond to our request for updates of information, they may have gone out of business or they may no longer wish to receive freelance work.

Allen Design Associates, Inc., Mark Andrew (did not respond)

Ligature, Inc. (did not respond)
Market Direct, Inc. (did not respond)

Read Ink./Illustration (did not respond)
Unit 1, Inc. (did not respond)

Book Publishers

The allure of photography, a desire to be the next Ansel Adams or to travel the world in search of exotic images, have created an era in which photographers are graduating en masse from institutions all over the United States. Christopher Bain, of the Michael Friedman Publishing Group in New York City, sees this phenomenon as one reason for the low photo prices in the book publishing field. "It's basic supply and demand," says Bain. The multitude of photographers is capturing so many images, book publishers are being inundated with photos and they are not interested in seeing the same old shots. On page 131, Bain discusses this trend and others as this year's book publishing Close-up subject in *Photographer's Market*.

Bain's observations bring out an obvious, yet interesting point for any photographer who wants to succeed. It is important for all artists to meet the demands of the buyers, particularly in book publishing where books are scheduled months or even years in advance. By supplying a book publisher with innovative and useful images a photographer can build an ongoing relationship with the publisher. He can become a regular supplier of images through his many stock photos and he can possibly develop a business relationship that can lead to the publishing of his own book.

Since many of the images purchased from freelancers are from the photographer's stock, it is often appropriate for the photographer to query the art director, photo editor or other photo buyer with a stock photo list — plus samples or tearsheets if requested — as the initial contact.

Aside from photos that are good- to top-quality and that are up-to-date in terms of styles and themes, book publishers look for various qualities when dealing with freelancers. Some publishers will want photos that speak to a very specific audience, such as a strong regional readership or one concerned with a shared special interest. Some publishers will have a need for a large quantity of photos from which to make selections or to develop an internal stock file, while others will specify only a few very select photos that will possibly meet their needs. Most place a great deal of importance on the overall professionalism of the freelancer, in everything from presentations or portfolios to pricing. In particular, one need quickly becoming common to all book publishers is to keep down their costs. Accordingly, they expect a photographer to "be flexible" on his pricing, or they turn to one who *is* flexible or to stock photo agencies.

Payment rates in the book publishing market vary a great deal, from the low end to above average. Publishers typically pay on either a per-image basis or by time, such as an hour or day rate. Many times the method of determining payment will depend upon whether it's for one or a few images, for a large bulk purchase of stock or for assigned work.

Remember that much of your success in this market can come from multiple sales. However, unless a market indicates an "OK" in regard to simultaneous submissions or previously published work, you may be limited in reselling an image, at least for the duration of the first usage. So, read the listings closely for related information and plan your marketing strategy carefully to maximize your sales.

A.D. BOOK CO., 6th Floor, 10 E. 39 St., New York NY 10016. (212)889-6500. FAX: (212)889-6504. Art Director: Van Aaron. Estab. 1949. Publishes trade books for advertising visual professionals. Photos used for text illustration, book covers and dust jackets. Buys 20 freelance photos and offers 5-10 assignments annually.

Subject Needs: Current advertising.
Specs: Uses 8×11 b&w prints; 35mm transparencies.
Payment & Terms: Pays $100-350/color photo; $50-100/b&w photo. Credit line given sometimes. Buys book rights. Model release and photo captions required.
Making Contact: Provide resume, business card, brochure, flyer or tearsheets to be kept on file for possible future use. SASE. Reports in 1 month. Photo guidelines free with SASE.

*ALLYN AND BACON PUBLISHERS, 160 Gould St., Needham MA 02194. (617)455-1265. FAX: (617)455-1294. Art Director: Linda Dickinson. Textbook publisher (college). Offers 4 assignments plus 80 stock projects/year. Photos used in textbook covers and interiors.
Subject Needs: Multiethnic photos in education, business, social sciences and good abstracts. Examples of recent uses: Teaching Children Science (cover, 35mm); Modern Management (cover, 8×10 transparency); Becoming A Teacher (cover, 4×5 transparency).
Specs: Uses 8×10 or larger, matte b&w prints; 35mm, 2¼×2¼, 4×5, 8×10 transparencies.
Payment & Terms: Pays $100-500/job; $300-500/color photo; $50-200/photo. Pays on usage. Credit line given on back cover. Buys one-time rights; negotiable. Model/property release required.
Making Contact: Provide resume, business card, self-promotion piece or tearsheets to be kept on file for possible future assignments. "Do not call." Reviews stock photos. Keeps samples on file. Cannot return material. Reports back in "24 hours to 4 months."
Tips: "Watch for our photo needs listing in photo bulletin. Send tearsheet and promotion pieces. Don't send stock lists. Need bright, strong, clean abstracts and unstaged, nicely lit people photos."

AMERICAN ARBITRATION ASSOCIATION, 140 West 51st St., New York NY 10020-1203. (212)484-4000. Editorial Director: Jack A. Smith. Publishes law-related materials on all facets of resolving disputes in the labor, commercial, construction and insurance areas. Photos used for text illustration. Buys 100 photos annually; assigns 15 freelance projects annually. Examples of recently published titles: *The Arbitration Journal*, cover and text; *Arbitration Times*, text; and *AAA Annual Report*, text.
Subject Needs: General business and industry-specific photos.
Specs: Uses 8×10 glossy b&w prints; 35mm transparencies.
Payment & Terms: Pays $250-400/color photo, $75-100/b&w photo, $75-100/hour. Credit lines given "depending on usage." Buys one-time rights. Also buys all rights "if we hire the photographer for a shoot." Model release and photo captions preferred. Simultaneous submissions and previously published work OK.
Making Contact: Provide resume, business card, brochure, flyer or tearsheets to be kept on file for possible future assignments. Interested in stock photos. SASE. Reports "as time permits."
Tips: In samples, looks especially for "good business and meeting photos." Over time, company is using less photography "because of scarcity of good photos in our area."

AMPHOTO BOOKS, 1515 Broadway, New York NY 10036. (212)764-7300. Senior Editor: Robin Simmen. Publishes instructional and how-to books on photography. Photos usually provided by the author of the book.
Payment & Terms: NPI. Pays on royalty basis. Buys one-time rights. Submit model release with photos. Photo captions explaining photo technique required. Reports in 1 month. SASE. Simultaneous submissions and previously published work OK.
Making Contact: Query with resume of credits and book idea, or submit material by mail for consideration.
Tips: "Submit focused, tight book ideas in form of a detailed outline, a sample chapter, and sample photos. Be able to tell a story in photos and be aware of the market."

AND BOOKS, 702 S. Michigan, South Bend IN 46618. (219)232-3134. Senior Editor/Visuals: Emil Krause. Publishes nonfiction, adult and general. Photos used for text illustration and book covers. Buys 5-10 photos annually.
Subject Needs: Variable. Very limited: Chicago blues musicians.
Payment & Terms: NPI; payment variable. Credit line given. Buys all rights. Simultaneous submissions and previously published work OK. Model release required; captions preferred.
Making Contact: Provide resume, business card, brochure, flyer or tearsheets to be kept on file for possible future assignments. Interested in stock photos. SASE. Reports in 1 month.

The asterisk before a listing indicates that the market is new in this edition. New markets are often the most receptive to freelance submissions.

APPLEZABA PRESS, P.O. Box 4134, Long Beach CA 90804. (213)591-0015. Publisher: D.H. Lloyd. Estab. 1977. Publishes adult trade books. Photos used for promotional materials and book covers. Buys 1-2 photos annually; offers 1-2 freelance assignments annually. Recently published *D.R. Poems*, *Horse Medicine* and *Gridlock*. For all three books, photos used for cover illustration.
Subject Needs: Photo needs depend on book.
Specs: Uses 8×10 b&w prints.
Payment & Terms: Pays $25-50/b&w photo. Credit line given. Buys all rights; negotiable. Model release required; photo captions preferred.
Making Contact: Submit portfolio for review. Provide resume, business card, brochure, flyer or tearsheets to be kept on file for possible future assignments. SASE. Reports in 1 month.
Tips: In portfolio, wants to see photocopies or prints of samples. One trend is that "we are tending to use a greater percentage for our book covers rather than straight graphic art. Photos must illustrate title or content of book."

ARJUNA LIBRARY PRESS, 1025 Garner St., D, Space 18, Colorado Springs CO 80905. Director: Joseph A. Uphoff, Jr. Estab. 1979. Publishes research monographs, theory, biography, commentary in fine arts, surrealism and visual poetics with associated developments in mathematics. Photos used for text illustration and book covers. Example of recently published titles: *Mythology And The Surrealist Family* (illustrative caricature), theoretical premise for a one-person exhibition by Joseph Uphoff at Regis University in Colorado Springs. Photos by Darlis Lamb, Elton Nesselrodt.
Subject Needs: Surrealist (static drama, cinematic expressionism) suitable for a general audience, including children.
Specs: Uses 5×7 glossy (maximum size) b&w and color prints.
Payment & Terms: Payment is one copy of published pamphlet. Credit line given. Rights dependent on additional use. Model release and photo captions preferred. Simultaneous submissions and previously published work OK.
Making Contact: Interested in receiving work from newer, lesser-known photographers. Query with samples. Send unsolicited photos by mail for consideration. Submit portfolio for review. Provide resume, business card, brochure, flyer or tearsheets to be kept on file for possible future assignments. Cannot return material. Reports in "one year."
Tips: "We are not soliciting the stock photography market. We are searching for examples that can be applied as illustrations to conceptual and performance art. These ideas can be research in the contemporary context, new media, unique perspectives, animate (poses and gestures), or inanimate (landscapes and abstracts). Our preference is for enigmatic, obscure or esoteric compositions. This material is presented in a forum for symbolic announcements, *The Journal of Regional Criticism*. We prefer conservative and general audience compositions." It's helpful "to translate color photographs in order to examine the way they will appear in black and white reproduction of various types. Make a photocopy. It is always a good idea to make a photocopy of a color work for analysis."

ART DIRECTION BOOK CO., 6th Floor, 10 E. 39th St., New York NY 10016. (212)889-6500. FAX: (212)889-6504. Art Director: William Brooks. Estab. 1939. Publishes advertising art, design, photography. Photos used for dust jackets. Buys 10 photos annually.
Subject Needs: Advertising.
Payment & Terms: Pays $200 minimum/b&w photo; $500 minimum/color photo. Buys one-time rights. Model release and photo captions required. Simultaneous submissions OK.
Making Contact: Submit portfolio for review. Uses photos by assignment only. SASE. Reports in 1 month.

***ASIAN HUMANITIES PRESS**, P.O. Box 3523, Fremont CA 94539. (415)659-8272. FAX: (415)659-8272. Publisher: M.K. Jain. Estab. 1976. Publishes adult trade and textbooks (Asian religions, literature, philosophy and spirituality). Photos used for text illustration, book covers and dust jackets. Buys 15 photos annually; offers 15 freelance assignments annually. Examples of recently published titles: *Toward a Superconsciousness* (text illustrations); *The Wind & the Waves: Four Modern Korean Poets* and *Journey of a Master* (book covers).
Subject Needs: Looking for photos specific to Asia.
Specs: Uses 3×5, 5×7 and 8×10 color and b&w glossy prints; 4×5 and 8×10 transparencies.
Payment & Terms: Pays $25-50/color photo; $10-25/b&w photo. Credit line sometimes given depending on the extent of use. Buys all rights; negotiable. Model/property release preferred. Simultaneous submissions OK.
Making Contact: Query with list of stock photo subjects. Works with local freelancers only. Does not keep samples on file. SASE. Reports in 1 month.

AUGSBURG FORTRESS, PUBLISHERS, Publication Services, P.O. Box 1209, Minneapolis MN 55440. (612)330-3300. FAX: (612)330-3455. Publishes Protestant/Lutheran books (mostly adult trade), religious education materials, audiovisual resources and periodicals. Photos used for text illustration, book covers, periodical covers and church bulletins. Buys 1,000 color photos and 250 b&w photos annually. No assignments.

Subject Needs: People of all ages, variety of races, activities, moods and unposed. In color, wants to see nature, seasonal, church year and mood.

Specs: Uses 8 × 10 glossy or semiglossy b&w prints, 35mm and 2¼ × 2¼ color transparencies.

Payment & Terms: Pays $25-75/b&w photo; $40-125/color photo. Credit line nearly always given. Buys one-time rights. Model release required. Simultaneous submissions and previously published work OK.

Making Contact: Send material by mail for consideration. "We are interested in stock photos." Provide tearsheets to be kept on file for possible future assignments. SASE. Reports in 6-8 weeks. Guidelines free with SASE. "Write for guidelines, then submit on a regular basis."

© William Hopkins

Photographer William Hopkins, of Granada Hills, California, routinely submits 20 slides to Augsburg Fortress Publishers for the company to review. The publisher has used Hopkins' work several times in the past and used this particular shot twice to illustrate topics regarding high school youths. Because he kept all rights to the photo, Hopkins was able to cash in on the shot both times, $75 for the first use and $50 the second time.

AVON BOOKS, 1350 Avenue of the Americas, New York NY 10019. (212)261-6800. Art Director: Tom Egner. Publishes adult and juvenile fiction and nonfiction in mass market and softcover trade. Photos used for book covers. Gives several assignments monthly.

Subject Needs: Hand-tinted photographs, "mood shots"; food still lifes and stock photography.

Specs: Uses 35mm, 4 × 5 and 8 × 10 transparencies.

Payment & Terms: Generally pays $600-1,200 for shots already taken; $1,000 and up for shoots, though seldom done; depends on job. Buys one time reproduction rights for the book, plus all advertising and promotional rights.

Making Contact: Drop off portfolio on Thursdays. Provide business card, flyer, brochure and tearsheets to be kept on file for possible future assignments. SASE. "Our photo needs vary with each assignment."

BEAUTIFUL AMERICA PUBLISHING COMPANY, 9725 SW Commerce Circle, P.O. Box 646, Wilsonville OR 97070. (503)682-0173. Librarian: Andrea Tronslin. Estab. 1986. Publishes nature, scenic, pictorial and history. Photos used for text illustration, pictorial. Assigns 10 freelance projects annually; buys small number of additional freelance photos. Examples of recently published titles: *Top Dog—Canines and Their Companions* (photos of celebrities and dogs); *The Rockies—Canada's Magnificent Wilderness* (scenic photos); and *The Victorian Express* (Victorian homes, details, interiors and exteriors).
Subject Needs: Nature and scenic.
Specs: Uses 35mm, 2¼×2¼, 4×5, and 8×10 transparencies.
Payment & Terms: Payment varies based on project; $100 minimum/color photo. Credit line given. Buys one-time rights. Model release and captions required; include location, correct spelling of topic in caption. Simultaneous submissions and previously published work OK.
Making Contact: Provide resume, business card, brochure, flyer or tearsheets to be kept on file for possible future assignments. "Do not send unsolicited photos!! Please do not ask for guidelines. We are using very little freelance, other than complete book or calendar projects."

*BEDFORD BOOKS OF ST. MARTIN'S PRESS, 29 Winchester St., Boston MA 02116. (617)426-7440. FAX: (617)426-8582. Advertising and Promotion Manager: George Scribner. Estab. 1981. Publishes college textbooks (freshman composition, literature and history). Photos used for text illustration, promotional materials and book covers. Buys 12 photos annually; offers 6 freelance assignments annually. Examples of recently published titles: *The Bedford Reader, Fourth Edition* (cover and brochure); *Our Times/2* (cover); and *Life Studies, Fourth Edition* (cover).
Subject Needs: Artistic, abstract, conceptual photos; nature or city; people—America or other cultures, multi-racial often preferred. Also uses product shots for promotional material.
Specs: Uses 8×10 b&w and color prints; 35mm, 2¼×2¼, 4×5 transparencies.
Payment & Terms: Pays $50-500/color photo; $50-200/b&w photo; $250-1,000/job; $500-1,500/day. Credit line sometimes given; "always covers, never promo." Buys one-time rights and all rights; depends on project; negotiable. Model/property release required. Simultaneous submissions and/or previously published work OK.
Making Contact: Interested in receiving work from newer, lesser-known photographers. Query with samples. Query with list of stock photo subjects. Provide resume, business card, brochure, flyer or tearsheets to be kept on file for possible future assignments. Works with local freelancers only for product shots. Reviews stock photos. Keeps samples on file. SASE. Reports in 3 weeks.

BEHRMAN HOUSE INC., 235 Watchung Ave., West Orange NJ 07052. (201)669-0447. Editor: Ms. Ruby G. Strauss. Estab. 1921. Publishes Judaica textbooks. Photos used for text illustration, promotional materials and book covers. Recently published title: *My Jewish World*.
Specs: No specific specifications for photography submitted/used.
Payment & Terms: Pays $50-500/color photo, $20-250/b&w photo. Credit line given. Model release preferred.
Making Contact: Query with resume of credits. Query with samples. Provide resume, business card, brochure, flyer or tearsheets to be kept on file for possible future assignments. Interested in stock photos. SASE. Reports in 3 weeks. No photo guidelines.
Tips: Company trend is increasing use of photography.

*BENFORD BOOKS, 27 W. 20th St., New York NY 10011. (212)206-9093. FAX: (212) 206-8978. Editorial Director: Elizabeth Loonan. Estab. 1991. Publishes books for all markets and subjects, nonfiction. Photos used for text illustration, book covers and dust jackets. Buys over 400 stock photos/year. Examples of recent titles: *California Indians, Indians of the Plains, Indians of the Southwest*.
Subject Needs: Looks for a variety of subjects. Model/property release preferred. Captions required.
Specs: Uses all sizes of b&w prints; 35mm, 2¼×2¼, 4×5, 8×10 transparencies. Pays $50-250/color photo; $25-100/b&w photo. Credit line given. Buys one-time and book rights; negotiable. Simultaneous submissions and previously published work OK.
Making Contact: Query with list of stock photo subjects. Reviews stock photos. "No unsolicited material accepted."
Tips: "We do not review portfolios."

Can't find a listing? Check at the end of each market section for the " '92-'93 Changes" lists. These lists include any market listings from the '92 edition which were either not verified or deleted in this edition.

*BONUS BOOK, INC., 160 E. Illinois St., Chicago IL 60611. (312)467-0580. Production Manager: Berry Gustafson. Estab.1980. Publishes adult trade: sports, consumer, self-help, how-to and biography. Photos used for text illustration and book covers. Buys 5 freelance photos annually; gives 1 assignment annually. Examples of recent projects: *Stuck in the 70s* (front cover), *Hank Stram's Pro football Scouting Report* (front cover) and *Hanging Out on Halsted*, (front cover).
Specs: Uses 8 × 10 matte b&w prints and 35mm transparencies. Pays in contributor's copies and $250 maximum for color transparency. Credit line given if requested. Buys one-time rights.
Payment & Terms: NPI. Model release and captions required. Property release preferred with identification of location and objects or people.
Making Contact: Interested in receiving work from newer, lesser-known photographers. Query with resume of credits, query with samples; provide resume, business card, brochure, flyer or tearsheets to be kept on file for possible future assignments. Solicits photos by assignment only. Does not return unsolicited material. Reports in 1 month.
Tips: "Don't call. Send written query. In reviewing a portfolio, we look for composition, detail, high quality prints, well-lit studio work. We are not interested in nature photography or greeting-card type photography."

*DON BOSCO MULTIMEDIA, P.O. Box T, New Rochelle NY 10802. (914)576-0122. FAX: (914)654-0443. Production Director: John A. Thomas. Estab. 1964. Publishes educational/religious books for teachers, children and parents. Photos used for text illustration, promotional materials and book covers. Buys 20 photos annually; offers 2 freelance assignments annually. Examples of recently published titles: *1992 Catalog* (cover), *Families Sharing Faith* (cover) and *Families Experienceing Faith*.
Subject Needs: Photos of youths, families and religiously symbolic.
Specs: Uses 5 × 7 b&w and color glossy prints, transparencies.
Payment & Terms: Pays $50/color photo; $75/hour; $500/day. Rights negotiable. Model/property release preferred. Simultaneous submissions and previously published work OK.
Making Contact: Query with resume of credits. Query with samples. Query with stock photo list. Interested in stock photos. Samples kept on file. SASE. Reports in 3 weeks. Photo guidelines free on request.
Tips: "Style tends to be realistic or religiously symbolic."

BROOKS/COLE PUBLISHING COMPANY, 511 Forest Lodge Rd., Pacific Grove CA 93950. (408)373-0728. Photo Coordinator: Larry Molmud. Publishes college textbooks only—political science, child development, social psychology, family, marriages, chemistry, computers, criminal justice, etc. Photos used for text illustration, book covers and dust jackets.
Subject Needs: Interested in stock photos.
Specs: Uses 8 × 10 glossy b&w prints; also transparencies, any format.
Payment & Terms: Pays $25-100/b&w photo; $250-850/color photo. Credit line given. Buys one-time rights. Model release preferred.
Making Contact: Query with list of stock photo subjects. Submit portfolio for review. Provide resume, business card, brochure, flyer or tearsheets to be kept on file for possible future assignments. "Also looking for photo researchers." SASE. Reports in 2-3 months.

WILLIAM C. BROWN COMMUNICATIONS INC., (formerly William C. Brown Co. Publishers), 2460 Kerper Blvd., Dubuque IA 52001. (319)588-1451. Vice President of Operations: Beverly Kolz. Manager of Design: Faye Schilling. Estab. 1944. Publishes college textbooks for most disciplines (music, computer and data processing, education, natural sciences, psychology, sociology, physical education, health, biology, art). In all cases, photos used for covers and/or interiors.
Payment & Terms: Pays up to $90/b&w interior photo; up to $135/color interior photo. Cover photos negotiable. Pays on acceptance. Buys one-time rights; also all editions and derivative works. Reports in 1-2 months. SASE. Previously published work OK.
Making Contact: Submit material by mail for consideration. Provide business card, brochure or stock list to be kept on file for possible future use. Direct material to photo research.
Specs: Uses 8 × 10 glossy or matte prints; also transparencies.
Tips: "We prefer to note your areas of specialties for future reference. We need *top quality* photography. To break in, be open to lower rates."

CAMBRIDGE UNIVERSITY PRESS, 40 W. 20th St., New York NY 10011. (212)924-3900. FAX: (212)691-3239. Associate Editor: Caroline Liou. Publishes textbooks for people learning English as a second language (ESL). Uses photos for text illustration and book covers. Buys 20 freelance photos annually; offers 2 freelance assignments annually.

Subject Needs: See "Tips."
Specs: Uses 5×7 or 8×10 b&w glossy prints; also transparencies.
Payment & Terms: Payment depends on job; pays $75-125/b&w photo; $100-150/color photo. Credit line given. Buys non-exclusive world English-language rights for first edition and reprints. Model release required. Simultaneous submissions and previously published work OK.
Making Contact: Interested in receiving work from newer, lesser-known photographers. Query with samples. Provide stock photo list, business card, brochure, flyer or tearsheets to be kept on file for future reference. "Since we cannot be responsible for loss and/or damage, we prefer you not send transparencies and/or slides. Black and white and color photographs only." Reviews stock photos. SASE. Reports as needed.
Tips: "Although our ESL textbooks span the entire gamut, some specialized subjects occur in almost every book: travel shots, especially big cities worldwide (overviews and famous landmarks), interesting people shots showing people from various nationalities and ethnic backgrounds in typical (but not stereotypical) communication situations, people on their jobs, famous people and celebrities. We can always use humorous situations. We use few historical subjects. Since our textbooks are geared toward the adult learner, we prefer photographs that feature adults."

*CAPSTONE PRESS, INC., P.O. Box 669, Mankato MN 56001. (507)387-4992. FAX: (507)625-2748. Contact: Photo Research Editor. Estab. 1991. Publishes educational library books. Photos used for text illustration and book covers. Buys 250 photos annually. Examples of recently published titles: *Sky Diving* (text illustration); *Monster Vehicles* (text illustration); and *The White House* (text illustration).
Specs: Uses 35mm, 2¼×2¼ transparencies. Pays $10-50/color photo. Credit line given. Buys one-time rights. Model/property release preferred; photo captions preferred. Previously published work OK.
Making Contact: Query with stock photo list. Interested in stock photos. SASE. Reports in 1 month.
Tips: "We like to use about 20 photos from same source for each book that requires photos. Send a listing of your subject areas so that we can review whenever we have a photo book."

CASCADE GEOGRAPHIC SOCIETY, P.O. Box 398, Rhododendron OR 97049. (503)622-4798. Curator: Michael P. Jones. Estab. 1979. Photos used for text illustration, interpretative exhibits.
Subject Needs: Native American, Oregon Trail, fur trade, wildlife, natural environment, fisheries, outdoor recreation, anti-pollution, etc. Need photos for one- or multi-person shows.
Specs: Uses 3×5, 8×10 b&w or color prints; 35mm transparencies.
Payment & Terms: Offers copies of published images in place of payment. Credit line given. Buys one-time rights. Model release and photo captions preferred. Simultaneous submissions and previously published work OK.
Making Contact: Query with resume of credits. Query with stock photo list. Submit portfolio for review. Provide resume, business card, brochure, flyer or tearsheets to be kept on file for possible future assignments. Reviews stock photos. SASE. Reports in 1 month. Photo guidelines free with SASE.
Tips: "We are new to the publishing field. Looking for photos for historical books *and* historical exhibits. Send us enough samples of your work so we can gauge your true ability. We are the perfect place for a photographer to break in the field. Black and white photos are still being used because they portray realism so appropriately. We need more photographers like the legendary Edward E. Curtis."

*CELO VALLEY BOOKS, 346 Seven Mile Ridge Rd., Burnsville NC 28714. Production Manager: D. Donovan. Estab. 1987. Publishes all types of books. Photos used for text illustration, book covers and dust jackets. Buys very few photos annually; offers 1-2 freelance assignments annually. Examples of recently published titles: *My Golden Tapestry* (text illustration); *Pieces of My Mind* (text and jacket); and *Crises in the Middle East* (text and cover).
Specs: Uses various sizes b&w prints.
Payment & Terms: NPI; negotiates with photographer. Credit line not given. Buys one-time rights and book rights. Simultaneous submissions OK.
Making Contact: Provide resume, business card, brochure, flyer or tearsheets to be kept on file for possible future assignments. Keeps samples on file. Reports only as needed.
Tips: "Send listing of what you have. We will contact you if we have a need."

CHATHAM PRESS, Box A, Old Greenwich CT 06870. (203)531-7807. Editor: Roger Corbin. Estab. 1971. Publishes New England and ocean-related topics. Photos used for text illustration, book covers, art and wall framing. Buys 25 photos annually; offers 5 freelance assignments annually.

Subject Needs: New England and ocean-related topics.
Specs: Uses b&w prints.
Payment & Terms: NPI. Credit line given. Buys all rights. Model release preferred; photo captions required.
Making Contact: Query with samples. SASE. Reports in 1 month.
Tips: To break in with this firm, "produce superb b&w photos. There must be an Ansel Adams-type of appeal—which is instantaneous to the viewer!"

*CHATSWORTH PRESS, Suite B, 9135 Alabama Ave., Chatsworth CA 91311. (818)341-3156. FAX: (818)341-3562. President: Scott Brastow. Estab. 1975. Publishes trade paper erotica and sexual information. Photos used for text illustration, promotional materials and book covers. Buys 50 photos annually; offers 1-2 freelance assignments annually. Examples of recently published titles: *Sappho Femme-a-Femme*, *Raffaelli's Passion* and *The Ultimate Kiss*.
Subject Needs: Erotic, sensual and subtle, couples and beautiful big-busted models.
Specs: Uses 8×10 and 11×14 b&w matte or glossy prints; 35mm, 2¼×2¼, 4×5, or 8×10 transparencies.
Payment & Terms: Pays $25-100/color photo; $10-25/b&w photo; depends on extent of photo use. Credit line given. Buys book rights; negotiable. Model/property release required. Simultaneous submissions and previously published work OK.
Making Contact: Query with resume of credits. Provide resume, business card, brochure, flyer or tearsheets to be kept on file for possible future assignments. Keeps samples on file. SASE. Reports in 1 month.
Tips: In sample photos looks for erotica with subtle style. "We need to appeal to women as well as men."

*CHINA BOOKS & PERIODICALS, 2929 24th St., San Francisco CA 94110. (415)282-2994. FAX: (415)282-0994. Art Director: Robbin Henderson. Estab. 1960. Publishes fiction, travel, health, language learning, art, history, culture and contemporary affairs. Photos used for text illustration, book covers and dust jackets. Examples of recently published titles: *SF Chinatown: A Walking Tour*, *Chinese Furniture* and *Chinese Rural Architecture*.
Subject Needs: Those photos with a China-related theme.
Specs: Uses b&w and color prints; 35mm, 2¼×2¼, 4×5, 8×10 transparencies.
Payment & Terms: Pays $50-100/color photo; $25-50/b&w photo; $15-25/hour; $100-500/job. Credit line given. Buys one-time rights; negotiable. Model/property release and captions preferred. Simultaneous submissions and previously published work OK.
Making Contact: Query with resume of credits. Query with samples. Reviews stock photos. Keeps samples on file. SASE. Reports in 1 month. Photo guidelines free with SASE.
Tips: Sample photos "must be related to China, Southeast Asia or Chinese-Americans." To break into the publishing field, "learn as much as you can about the specific needs of the publishers and what field each one concentrates in."

*CHRISTIAN BOARD OF PUBLICATION, Box 179, St. Louis MO 63166. (314)231-8500. FAX: (314)231-8524. Director of Product Development Design and Promotion: Nancy Dothage. Estab. 1910. Publishes religious curriculum, books and program materials. Photos used for text illustration and book covers. Buys 5-10 photos annually. Examples of recently published titles: "A Mini-history of the Christian Church (Disciples of Christ)" (inside); "Curriculum for all age levels" (inside) and "Camp and conference materials" (inside).
Subject Needs: Photos with people. Pays $25/inside; $50/cover. Model/property release required; photo captions preferred. Simultaneous submissions OK.
Making Contact: Send unsolicited photos by mail for consideration. Keeps samples on file. SASE. Reports in 1 month. Photo guidelines free with SASE.
Tips: "Prefer photos of people interacting with each other."

◑ CLEANING CONSULTANT SERVICES, 1512 Western Ave., P.O. Box 1273, Seattle WA 98111. (206)682-9748. Publisher: William R. Griffin. "We publish books on cleaning, maintenance and self-employment. Examples are related to janitorial, housekeeping, maid services, window washing, carpet cleaning, etc." Photos are used for text illustration, promotional materials, books covers and all uses related to production and marketing of our books. Buys 20-50 freelance photos annually; offers 5-15 freelance assignments annually.

Subject Needs: Photos of people doing cleaning work.

Specs: Uses 5×7 and 8×10 glossy b&w and color prints.

Payment & Terms: Pays $5-50/b&w photo; $5/color photo; $10-30/hour; $40-250/job; negotiable depending on specific project. Credit lines generally given. Buys all rights; depends on need and project; will negotiate rights purchased. Model release and captions preferred. Simultaneous submissions and previously published work OK.

Making Contact: Query with resume of credits, samples, list of stock photo subjects or send unsolicited photos by mail for consideration. Provide resume, business card, brochure, flyer or tearsheets to be kept on file for possible future assignments. Reviews stock photos. SASE. Reports in 3 weeks.

Tips: "Photos of specific cleaning situations, people doing the work, before and after shots, unique work sites. Be willing to work at reasonable rates. Selling two or three photos does not qualify you to earn top-of-the-line rates. We expect to use more photos, but they must be specific to our market, which is quite select. Don't send stock sample sheets. Send photos that fit our specific needs. Call if you need more information or would like specific guidance."

*CLEIS PRESS, P.O. Box 14684, San Francisco CA 94114. Production Editor: Frédérique Delacoste. Estab. 1980. Publishes adult trade, fiction. Photos used for book covers. Examples of recently published titles: *Boomer* (nonfiction); *Susie Sexpert Lesbian Sexworld* and *The Wall* (fiction).

Specs: Uses color/b&w prints and 8×10 transparencies.

Payment & Terms: Pays $100/color photo; $100/b&w photo. Credit line given on back cover. Buys books and promotional rights. Buys all rights; negotiable. Simultaneous submissions and previously published work OK.

Making Contact: Send unsolicited photos by mail for consideration. Reviews stock photos. Keeps samples on file. Cannot return material.

*CONSERVATORY OF AMERICAN LETTERS, P.O. Box 7, N. Waterford ME 04267. (207)583-4143. President: Robert Olmsted. Publishes "all types of books except porn and evangelical." Photos used for promotional materials, book covers, and dust jackets. Buys 2-3 photos annually.

Specs: Uses 3×5 to 8×10 b&w glossy prints, also 5×7 or 6×9 color prints.

Payment & Terms: Pays $5-40/b&w photo; $35-150/color photo; per job payment negotiable. Credit line given. Buys one-time or book rights. Model release required if people are identifiable.

Making Contact: Query with list of stock photo subjects. Send unsolicited photos by mail for consideration. SASE. Reports in 1 week.

CONTEMPORARY BOOKS, 180 N. Michigan, Chicago IL 60611. (312)782-9181. FAX: (312)782-2157. Art Director: Georgene Sainati. Estab. 1965. Publishes adult trade, adult education (how-to, cookbooks, general nonfiction). Photos used for book covers and dust jackets. Buys 10-15 photos annually; offers 5 freelance assignments annually.

Subject Needs: Largely needs color tabletop work with emphasis on food. Also, uses b&w location shots with models.

Specs: Uses 5×7 b&w prints; 35mm, 2¼×2¼, 4×5 and 8×10 transparencies.

Payment & Terms: Pays $750-1,000/color photo; $100-400/b&w photo. Credit line given. Buys book rights. Model release required; captions preferred. Simultaneous submissions and previously published work OK.

Making Contact: Query with samples. "Send samples (either prints, tearsheets or photocopies) that do not need to be returned and a cover letter including list of clients. Follow up with a phone call about two weeks later." Reviews stock photos. Keeps samples on file. Cannot return material. Reporting time varies, depending on time of year.

Tips: Looks for "technical competence combined with a sense of style and a sense of humor—not necessarily regarding the subject matter, but maybe an unusual juxtaposition of subjects." Sees trend in "more expository, storyboard-style b&w photography."

CPI GROUP, INC., 311 E. 51st St., New York NY 10022. (212)753-3800. Publishes science, English, math literature, adult education and children's books. Photos are used for text illustration and book covers. Buys 4,500 photos annually. Recently published *The Wonders of Science*, 6 science workbooks for remedial high school students, published by Steck-Vaughn, created by us. Used color photos for covers and b&w for ⅛ of page (text illustration).

Subject Needs: Uses earth science, people and scientific.

Specs: Uses b&w prints; 35mm transparencies.

Payment & Terms: Pays $65-120/color photo; $50-75/b&w photo. Credit line given. Buys one-time rights. Model release, photo captions preferred. Previously published work OK.

Making Contact: Provide resume, business card, brochure, flyer or tearsheets to be kept on file for possible future assignments. SASE. Reports in 1 month.

Tips: "Send samples for our files. In samples, doesn't want to see anything too slick and no advertising. Wants to see educational shots (scientific and/or technical) and people of all ages doing specific things."

CRAFTSMAN BOOK COMPANY, 6058 Corte Del Cedro, Carlsbad CA 92008. (619)438-7828. FAX: (619)438-0398. Art Director: Bill Grote. Estab. 1957. Publishes construction books. Photos used for text illustration, promotional materials, and book covers. Buys 60 freelance photos annually; offers 10 freelance assignments annually. Examples of recently published titles: *National Repair and Remodeling Estimator, National Construction Estimator* and *Electrical Construction Estimator*.

Subject Needs: Photos of construction contractors and carpenters at work.

Specs: Uses 5×7 b&w prints; 35mm transparencies.

Payment & Terms: Pays $35-45/b&w photo; $100-150/color photo. Buys one-time rights; negotiable. Model release required. Simultaneous submissions and previously published work OK.

Making Contact: Interested in receiving work from newer, lesser-known photographers. Query with samples/slides. Provide resume, business card, brochure, flyer or tearsheets to be kept on file for possible future assignments. Reviews stock photos. SASE. Reports in 2 weeks.

Tips: Wants to see "subjects interacting in residential construction. We look for unusual, brightly colored shots that are artistic and capture attention. We especially need shots of construction workers on rooftops with lots of sky visible."

© James Clifford

"This image is more than just a little slice of America," says photographer James Clifford, of Somerville, New Jersey. "It's what the American worker is all about." Clifford took this photo with Craftsman Book Company in mind and the publisher liked the image so much it paid Clifford $150 to use the shot on the cover of a 1992 construction catalog. Clifford says the catalog has served as a great promotional piece and opened other doors for him.

DELMAR PUBLISHERS INC., 2 Computer Drive W, Box 15-015, Albany NY 12212. (518)459-1150. Contact: Art/Design Department. Publishes vocational/technical and college textbooks.

Subject Needs: Agriculture, air conditioning/heating/refrigeration, automotive/power technology, blueprint reading, business, computer/data processing, construction, drafting/CAD, early childhood education, electrical trades, electronics technology, graphic arts, health occupations/nursing, hospitality/food/travel/tourism, machine trades, mathematics, metalworking, physics/mechanical technology, technical communication, technology/industrial arts and welding.

Specs: Uses 8×10 or 5×7 glossy b&w prints; also transparencies.
Payment & Terms: Buys one-time rights, all rights, and "rights for all editions of that particular book." Pays $25-50/b&w or color photo for internal use; $50-100/b&w cover and $50-350/color photo used for covers.
Making Contact: Provide flyer to be kept on file for future assignments. Works on assignment only. "We prefer to buy all rights to material used in interiors."
Tips: "When writing please mention areas of expertise." "Quality and deadlines are most important."

*DUTTON CHILDREN'S BOOKS, 375 Hudson St., New York NY 10014. (212)366-2600. FAX: (212)366-2011. Executive Editor: Donna Brooks. Associate Editor: Karen Lotz. Photos used for text illustration and book covers. Buys 0 photos annually; offers 2 freelance assignments annually. Examples of recently published titles: *Atlantic Salmon* and *WASPS at Home.*
Subject Needs: Nature material, events on subjects of interest to children. Uses very few stock photos.
Specs: Uses color/b&w prints; 35mm transparencies. Pays advance against royalties and expenses. Credit line given. Buys book rights. Buys all rights; negotiable. Simultaneous submissions and previously published work OK.
Making Contact: Query with samples. Query with stock photo list. Provide resume, business card, brochure, flyer or tearsheets to be kept on file for possible future assignments. Keeps samples on file. Reports in 3 months.
Tips: "We look for photos that portray a child's vision of the world, that capture a subject with the wonder and creativity that appeal to children. Photo essays are essential to the nonfiction market for children."

*EAST COAST PUBLISHING, P.O. Box 2829, Poughkeepsie NY 12603. (914)471-9577. Contact: Vice President. Publishes adult trade, nonfiction, textbooks involving law and business. Photos used for text illustration, promotional materials, book covers and dust jackets. Buys 6 photos annually. Examples of recently published titles: *Notary Public Handbook: A Guide for New York, Second Ed.* and *Notary Public Handbook: A Guide for New Jersey* (illustrations).
Subject Needs: Varies with assignment.
Specs: Uses $8 \times 10''$ glossy b&w and color prints; 35mm, 4×5 transparencies.
Payment & Terms: Pays $35-50/color or b&w photo. Credit line given. Buys all rights; negotiable. Model/property release required. Captions required. Simultaneous submissions and previously published work OK.
Making Contact: Query with list of stock photo subjects. Provide resume, business card, brochure, flyer or tearsheets to be kept on file for possible future assignments. Reviews stock photos. Keeps samples on file. SASE. Reports in 1 month.
Tips: "We utilize photographs in the editorial functions and in the marketing phase of book publishing."

ELYSIUM GROWTH PRESS, 700 Robinson Rd., Topanga CA 90290. (213)455-1000. FAX: (213)455-2007. Editor: Ed Lange. Estab. 1961. Publishes adult trade books on nudist/naturist/clothing-optional resorts, parks and camps. Photos used for text illustration, promotional, book covers and dust jackets. Buys 50 photos annually. Examples of recently published titles: *Nudist Nudes, Shameless Nude* and *Fun in the Sun Book III.* Photos used for cover and text in all three.
Specs: Uses 5×7 glossy b&w and color prints; 35mm and $2\frac{1}{4} \times 2\frac{1}{4}$ transparencies.
Payment & Terms: Pays $50-100/color photo, $35-50/b&w photo. Credit line given. Buys all rights; negotiable. Model release, photo captions required. Simultaneous submissions OK.
Making Contact: Provide resume, business card, brochure, flyer or tearsheets to be kept on file for possible future assignments. Interested in stock photos. SASE. Reports in 2 weeks. Photo guidelines free with SASE; catalog, with SASE, 45¢ postage.
Tips: In samples, looking for "nudist/naturist lifestyle photos only."

*EMC PUBLISHING, 300 York Ave., St. Paul MN 55101. (612)771-1555. Design and Production Manager: Eileen K. Slater. Publishes educational textbooks. Photos used for text illustration and book covers.
Subject Needs: Variable.
Specs: Uses 35 mm and 4×5 transparencies.
Payment & Terms: NPI; payment negotiable. Credit line given. Rights negotiable.
Making Contact: Query with resume of credits. Provide resume, business card, brochure, flyer or tearsheets to be kept on file. Reviews stock photos. Does not return unsolicited material. Reports only as needed.

ENTRY PUBLISHING, INC., 27 W. 96th St., New York NY 10025. (212)662-9703. President: Lynne Glasner. Publishes education/textbooks, secondary market. Photos used for text illustrations. Number of freelance photos bought and freelance assignments given vary.
Subject Needs: "Currently working on geography text, may need specific places. Often looks for 'shots of young teens in school settings.' "
Specs: Uses b&w prints.
Payment & Terms: NPI; payment depends on job requirements. Credit line given if requested. Buys book rights. Model release required. Captions preferred. Simultaneous submissions and previously published work OK.
Making Contact: Query with list of stock photo subjects. Provide resume, business card, brochure, flyer or tearsheets to be kept on file for possible future assignments. Reviews stock photos. SASE. Reports in 3 weeks.
Tips: "Have wide range of subject areas for review and use. Stock photos are most accessible and can be available quickly during production of book."

J.G. FERGUSON PUBLISHING CO., 200 West Monroe, Chicago IL 60606. Editorial: Carol Summerfield. Publishes vocational guidance works for high schools and college, subscriptions, reference books and corporate histories. Photos used for text illustration. Buys several hundred freelance photos biannually. Examples of recently published titles: *Career Discovery Encyclopedia*, elementary school 6 volume set with jobs explained and illustrated by b&w photos and *Encyclopedia of Career and Vocational Guidance*, high school/college level.
Subject Needs: Persons at work in various occupational settings only.
Specs: Uses 8×10 b&w glossy prints; 35 mm transparencies.
Payment & Terms: NPI; payment negotiable. Credit line given. Buys book rights. Model release and captions preferred. Simultaneous submissions and previously published work OK.
Making Contact: Reviews stock photos. Send stock list and resume.
Tips: Wants to see "encyclopedia style black and white photos of people in their jobs with good caption information. We search mainly for specific career images, so a list indicating what a photographer has that may fulfill our needs is the single best method of getting work with us."

J. FLORES PUBLICATIONS, P.O. Box 163001, Miami FL 33116. Editor: Eli Flores. Estab. 1982. Publishes adult trade, nonfiction only: military, firearms and current events. Uses photos for text illustration, promotional materials and book covers. Examples of recently published titles: *The Force Option* (cover); *Unlikely Assassins* and *Wings for the Valiant* (both cover/inside).
Subject Needs: Action oriented, on-the-spot photographs.
Specs: Uses any size glossy b&w prints, also color transparencies.
Payment & Terms: Pays $50-150/color photo; $30-100/b&w photo. Credit line given. Buys one-time rights; negotiable. Model release required; captions preferred. Simultaneous submissions and previously published work OK.
Making Contact: Interested in receiving work from newer, lesser-known photographers. Query with samples and list of stock photo subjects. Reviews stock photos. SASE. Reports in 1 month.
Tips: "We look for stock that matches our need for a particular book or ad. The photographer should study the subject matter of books published by a particular publisher and submit photos that match. Photos are being used more than ever by book publishers. There are many books in which photographs play a more important role than the text."

MICHAEL FRIEDMAN PUBLISHING GROUP, INC., 15 W. 26th St., New York NY 10010. (212)685-6610. Photography Editor: Christopher Bain. Estab. 1979. Publishes adult trade: science and nature series; sports; food and entertainment; design; and gardening. Photos used for text illustration, promotional materials, book covers and dust jackets. Buys 3,500 freelance photos annually; offers 20-30 freelance assignments annually.
Specs: Uses 35mm, 2¼×2¼, 4×5 and 8×10 transparencies.
Payment & Terms: Payment upon publication of book for stock photos; within 30-45 days for assignment. Pays $50-100/color stock photo; $350-500/day. Credit line given 95% of time, on page. Buys one-time rights (all editions of book). Captions preferred. Simultaneous submissions and previously published work OK.
Making Contact: Query with list of stock photo subjects. Reviews stock photos.

The code NPI (no payment information given) appears in listings that have not given specific payment amounts.

Close-up

Christopher Bain
Photography Editor
Michael Friedman Publishing Group Inc.
New York City

As a corporate and magazine photographer in the mid-1980s, Christopher Bain didn't see a bright future for free-lancers, so he got out. Now, after five years with the Michael Friedman Publishing Group, Inc., in New York City, the industry is even tougher to break into, says Bain.

"I think when I got out of school in 1977 there were about a dozen programs that offered a degree in photography. Recently I heard there are over 90 in the United States right now," he says. "It's very hard. The field is glutted with photographers. I get so many great pieces from people I've never heard of." Bain says he sorts through six to eight portfolios every day.

Traditionally a firm that packaged books on gardening, cooking, sports, architecture and crafts, Bain's company has begun to look at packaging books with compact disks. This additional endeavor and others, made possible because Michael Friedman Publishing was purchased by J.B. Fairfax USA (Int'l) Inc., will create more photo needs for the company in the future, he says. J.B. Fairfax is a subsidiary of Marinya Holding Pty Ltd.

Despite the tight photo market, there is room for new photographers who can offer fresh images, he says. When examining portfolios Bain keeps on file the names of photographers who have stock of very specific items. Photographers stand a good chance of having their work published if, for example, they have shots of 30 different species of birds in the Florida Everglades or over 100 images of Shaker furniture. The names of those photographers are stored in a data base. When the company wants to produce a book Bain searches the computer and finds who has the photographs he needs.

For his purposes, Bain likes shots that have razor sharp focus and great lighting. He does not like to see images spruced up by unnatural color which comes from some of today's film. "I tend not to look at the standard stock images," he says. "I won't name companies, but a lot of the catalogs that come out have the same happy-go-lucky couples, families having a picnic on a really green grass or two senior citizens running through a field flying a kite."

The book publishing industry as a whole is a solid market for someone wanting to gather tearsheets for their portfolio, he says. "I think there is a lot of room in books. There's a lot of room in magazines. Calendars are a little tougher. Greeting cards are a little tougher, but there is still room there. Those are both really tough markets because there is so much quality out there," says Bain.

Michael Friedman Publishing packages 60-75 books annually, more if the firm plans to produce several series of books. Of those produced, about 75 percent of the ideas are developed inhouse. The remainder come from outside sources, including photographers who may be interested in submitting a text-photo package, he says.

"There are ways to get in, you just have to be a little more aggressive sometimes than just mailing a letter," says Bain.

—Michael Willins

FRIENDSHIP PRESS, National Council of the Churches of Christ in the U.S.A., Room 552, 475 Riverside Dr., New York NY 10115. (212)870-2280. Art Director: E. Paul Lansdale. Publishes adult and juvenile textbooks on social consciousness, especially of US and Third World. Photos used for text illustration, promotional material, book covers, dust jackets and PR work. Buys 10+ freelance photos annually. Examples of recently published titles: *Breach Of Promise, South Africa's Moment Of Truth* and *A New View Of The World (Map Book)*." Photos used for covers and/or text.
Subject Needs: Social consciousness, people and places. Has yearly themes.
Specs: Uses 8×10 glossy b&w and color prints; 2¼×2¼, 4×5 and 8×10 transparencies.
Payment & Terms: Pays $25-300/b&w photo and $75-450/color photo. Credit line given. Buys one-time rights or all rights; negotiable. Model release required; captions preferred. Simultaneous submissions and previously published work OK.
Making Contact: Arrange personal interview to show portfolio. Query with resume of credits, samples or list of stock photo subjects. Submit portfolio for review. Provide resume, business card, brochure, flyer or tearsheets to be kept on file for possible future assignments. Works on assignment only. Reviews stock photos. Does not return unsolicited material.
Tips: "I like photocopies for my files with names, address and phone number."

GLENCOE PUBLISHING/MACMILLAN/MCGRAW HILL, 15319 Chatsworth St., Mission Hills CA 91345. Attention: Photo Editor. Publishes elementary and high school textbooks, religion, careers, business, office automation, social studies and fine arts. Photos used for text illustration and book covers. Buys 500 photos annually. Occasionally offers assignments. Recently published titles: *Art Talk, Career Skills* and *Marketing Essentials*.
Subject Needs: Children and teens at leisure, in school, in Catholic church; interacting with others: parents, siblings, friends, teachers; Catholic church rituals; young people (teens, early 20s) working, especially in jobs that go against sex-role stereotypes.
Specs: Uses 8×10 glossy b&w prints and 35mm slides.
Payment & Terms: Pays $50/b&w photo, $100/color photo (¼ page). Buys one-time rights, but prefers to buy all rights on assignment photography with some out takes available to photographer. Model release preferred. Simultaneous submissions and previously published work OK.
Making Contact: Send stock photo list. List kept on file for future assignments.
Tips: "A good ethnic mix for models is important. We look for a contemporary, unposed look."

GRAPEVINE PUBLICATIONS, INC., P.O. Box 2449, Corvallis OR 97339. (503)754-0583. Managing Editor: Chris Coffin. Estab. 1983. Publishes adult trade, textbooks and how-to books. Occasionally uses photos for promotional materials and book covers.
Payment & Terms: Pays $100-200/color photo; $50-100/b&w photo. Buys all rights. Model release required; photo captions preferred. Simultaneous submissions and previously published work OK.
Making Contact: Provide resume, business card, brochure, flyer or tearsheets to be kept on file for possible future assignments. Works on assignment only. "Cannot guarantee returns or replies to queries/submittals."
Tips: Just beginning to use photos.

GRAPHIC ARTS CENTER PUBLISHING COMPANY, P.O. Box 10306, Portland OR 97210. (503)226-2402. Editorial Director: Douglas A. Pfeiffer. Publishes adult trade photographic essay books. Photos used for photo essays. Offers 5 freelance assignments annually.
Subject Needs: Landscape, nature, people, historic architecture and other topics pertinent to the essay.
Specs: Uses 35mm, 2¼×2¼ and 4×5 transparencies (35mm as Kodachrome 25 or 64).
Payment & Terms: NPI; pays by royalty—amount varies based on project; minimum, but advances against royalty are given. Credit line given. Buys book rights. Captions preferred. Simultaneous submissions OK.
Making Contact: "Photographers must be previously published in book form, and have a minimum of five years full-time professional experience to be considered for assignment."
Tips: "Prepare an original idea as a book proposal. Full color essays are expensive to publish, so select topics with strong market potential. We see color essays as being popular compared to b&w in most cases."

GROLIER, INC., Sherman Turnpike, Danbury CT 06816. Chief Photo Researcher: Ann Eriksen. Estab. 1829. Publishes encyclopedias and yearbooks. Photos used for text illustration. Buys 2,000 freelance photos/year; offers 5 assignments/year. Examples of recently published titles: *The New Book of Knowledge Annual* (encyclopedia); *The Americana Annual* and *The New Book of Popular Science Annual*. All photo use is text illustration unless otherwise negotiated. (Other uses are very rare!)

Subject Needs: "Encyclopediac." Interested in photos that aren't posed, of the subject in its natural habitat that are current and clear.
Specs: Uses 8×10 glossy b&w/color prints; 35mm, 2¼×2¼, 4×5, 8×10 (originals preferred) transparencies.
Payment & Terms: Pays $50-100/b&w photo; $150-200/color photo; $700-1,000/day. Very infrequent freelance photography is negotiated by the job. Credit line given "either under photo or in back of book." Buys one-time rights; negotiable. Occasional foreign language rights. Model release preferred for any photos used in medical articles, education articles, etc. Photo captions required; natural history subjects should carry latin identifications. Simultaneous submissions and previously published work OK.
Making Contact: Interested in working with newer, lesser-known photographers. Query with list of stock photo subjects. Provide resume, business card, brochure, flyer or tearsheets to be kept on file for possible future assignments. Cannot return unsolicited material. "Will contact when needed."
Tips: "Send subject lists and small selection of samples for file photocopy or printed samples *only* please. We do not return unsolicited photographs. In reviewing samples we consider the quality of the photographs, range of subjects and editorial approach. Keep in touch but don't overdo it. We continue to use about 50% b&w photos but have an increasingly hard time finding good photos in our price range. Quality often looks like bad conversions from color instead of good b&w original. Color use will increase and we see a trend toward increasing use of computerized images."

HANCOCK HOUSE PUBLISHERS, 1431 Harrison Ave., Blaine WA 98230. (206)354-6953. FAX: (604)538-2262. President: David Hancock. Estab. 1968. Publishes trade books. Photos used for text illustration, promotional, book covers. Examples of recently published titles: *Working with Dr. Schweitzer*, *Border Bank Bandits* and *To Heal the Earth*. In all three, photos used for text illustration.
Subject Needs: Birds/nature.
Payment & Terms: NPI. Credit line given. Buys non-exclusive rights. Model release and photo captions preferred. Simultaneous submissions and previously published work OK.
Making Contact: Reviews stock photos. SASE. Reports in 1 month.

HARMONY HOUSE PUBLISHERS, 1008 Kent Rd., Goshen KY 40026. (502)228-4446. Owners: William Strode and William Butler. Estab. 1984. Publishes photographic books on specific subjects. Photos used for text illustration, promotion materials, book covers and dust jackets. Number of freelance photos purchased varies. Assigns 30 shoots each year. Recent book titles: *Country U.S.A.*, *Emblems of Southern Valor* and *Georgia Tech*.
Specs: Uses 35mm, 2¼×2¼, 4×5 or 8×10 transparencies.
Payment & Terms: NPI; payment negotiable. Credit line given. Buys one-time rights and book rights. Captions required. Simultaneous submissions and previously published work OK.
Making Contact: Query with resume of credits along with business card, brochure, flyer or tearsheets to be kept on file for possible future assignments. Query with samples or stock photo list. Submit portfolio for review. Works on assignment mostly.
Tips: To break in, "send in book ideas to William Strode, with a good tray of slides to show work."

*HARPERCOLLINS CHILDREN'S BOOKS, 10 East 53rd St., New York NY 10022. (212)207-7044. FAX: (212)207-7192. Editor: Marc Aronson. Estab. 1877. Publishes juvenile travel and reference books. Photos used for text illustration, book covers and dust jackets. Buys over 200 photos annually. Examples of recently published titles: *The Land and People of Canada*, *The Land and People of Malaysia and Brunei* and *The Land and People of Venezuela* (text illustrations and jackets).
Subject Needs: Interiors only black and white, contemporary-looking of daily life, political strife, geography; also archival illustrations for history; color covers.
Specs: Uses b&w prints.
Payment & Terms: Pays $400-700/color photo; $50-100/b&w photo. Credit line given. Buys book rights; negotiable. Model/property release preferred. Photo captions preferred; include "time, place, nature of activity so that author can write caption." Simultaneous submissions and previously published work OK.
Making Contact: Query with resume of credits. Reviews stock photos. Does not keep samples on file. SASE. "Final selection can take months."
Tips: For color cover shots, wants to see "lively, contemporary, not tourist-oriented. For black and white interiors, a sense of country as it is today, not institutional or staged; we do not use face-to-camera poses."

HERE'S LIFE PUBLISHERS, #F, 2700 Little Mountain Dr., San Bernardino CA 92405. (714)886-7981. (714)886-7985. Cover Development: Michelle Treiber. Photos used for promotional materials, book cover and dust jackets. Buys 20-30 photos annually; majority of photos shot on assignment. Examples of recently published titles: *When Your Dreams Die, Pathway Through Pain, Genesis, What Makes a Marriage Last* and *When Victims Marry*. All used as cover art.

Subject Needs: People, tabletop stills and landscape.

Specs: Uses 8×10 glossy color prints; 2¼×2¼ and 4×5 transparencies.

Payment & Terms: Pays $300-500/color photo. Credit lines "sometimes" given. Buys all rights. Model release required.

Making Contact: Query with resume of credits and samples. Provide resume, business card, brochure, flyer or tearsheets to be kept on file for possible future assignments. Reviews stock photos. SASE. Reports in 2 weeks.

*HOBBY HOUSE PRESS, INC., 900 Frederick St., Cumberland MD 21502. (301)759-3770. FAX: (301)759-4940. Art Editor: Danielle Brayer. Estab. 1942. "Our trade is mostly adult collectors of dolls, teddy bears and vintage clothing. We also have a doll making (how-to) magazine." Photos used for text illustration, promotional materials, book covers, dust jackets and magazine covers. Buys over 33 photos annually; offers over 27 freelance assignments annually. Examples of recently published titles: *Vintage Fashions, Doll Reader* and *Teddy Bear & Friends* (magazines, front covers).

Subject Needs: Dolls (antique, collectable, modern); teddy bears (antique, collectable, modern); and vintage clothing (clothing not newer than 1969).

Specs: Uses 35mm, 2¼×2¼, 4×5, 8×10 transparencies.

Payment & Terms: "We pay upon publication date and prices range depending on cover or inside magazine use: $65-225 per slide/transparency." Credit line given. Buys all rights. Model/property release required for people and items from collections. Captions required; details given in guidelines.

Making Contact: Send unsolicited photos by mail for consideration. Provide resume, business card, brochure, flyer or tearsheets to be kept on file for possible future assignments. Keeps samples on file. SASE. Reports in 3 weeks. Photo guidelines free with SASE.

Tips: In samples looks for "a good eye for subject matter; ability to bring the subject matter to life with lighting; good close-up shots with room for sellines; bright (colorwise) photos; authenticity of subject. Do not become impatient about work. Be published because schedules run almost one year ahead of time. Use bright backgrounds for subject matter for teddy bears and doll, but don't be afraid of a crisp white either. For vintage cloths think soft and romantic."

HOLT, RINEHART AND WINSTON, 1627 Woodland Ave., Austin TX 78741. (512)440-5700. FAX: (512)440-5737. Manager of Photo Research: Debra Saleny. Estab. 1866. "The Photo Research Department of the HRW School Division in Austin obtains photographs for our textbooks in all subject areas taught in secondary schools." Photos are used for text illustration, promotional materials and book covers. Buys 3,500 photos annually. Examples of recently published titles: *Elements of Writing, Science Plus, People and Nations, World Literature, Biology Today* and *Modern Chemistry*.

Subject Needs: Photos to illustrate mathematics, the sciences—life, earth and physical, chemistry, history, foreign languages, art, English, literature, speech and health.

Specs: Uses any size glossy b&w prints and transparencies.

Payment & Terms: Pays $125-180/b&w photo; $150-225/color photo; $75-125/hour and $700-1,000/day. Credit line given. Buys one-time rights. Model/property releases preferred; photo captions required that include scientific explanation, location and/or other detailed information.

Making Contact: Interested in receiving work from newer, lesser-known photographers. Query with resume of credits, stock photo list or samples. Reviews stock photos. Cannot return unsolicited material. Reports as needed.

Tips: "We use a wide variety of photos, from portraits to studio shots to scenics. We like to see slides displayed in sheets. We especially like photographers who have specialties . . . limit themselves to one/two subjects." Send a letter and printed flyer with a sample of work and a list of subjects in stock. Do not call! Looks for "natural looking, uncluttered photographs, labeled with exact descriptions, technically correct, and including no evidence of liquor, drugs, cigarettes or brand names." Photography should be specialized, with photographer showing competence in one or more areas.

HOME PLANNERS, INC., Suite 110, 3275 W. Ina Road, Tucson, AZ 85741. (602)297-8200. FAX: (602)297-6219. Art Director: Cindy J. Coatsworth. Estab. 1940. Publishes material on home building and planning and landscape design. Photos used for text illustration, promotional materials and book covers. Buys 50 freelance photos and offers 5 freelance assignments annually. Examples of recently published titles: *Deck Planner, The Home Landscaper* and *Colonial Houses*. In all three, photos used for cover and text illustrations.

Subject Needs: Homes/houses — "but for the most part, it must be a specified house built by one of our plans."

Specs: Uses 4×5 transparencies.

Payment & Terms: Pays $25-100/color photo; $500-750/day; maximum $500/4-color cover shots. Credit line given. Buys all rights. Property release preferred. Simultaneous submissions and previously published work OK.

Making Contact: Send unsolicited photos by mail for consideration. Provide resume, business card, brochure, flyer or tearsheets to be kept on file for possible assignments. Works on assignment only. SASE. Reports in 1 month.

Tips: Looks for "ability to shoot architectural settings and convey a mood. Looking for well-thought, professional project proposals."

HOMESTEAD PUBLISHING, Box 193, Moose WY 83012. Editor: Carl Schreier. Publishes 3-7 titles per year in adult and children's trade, natural history, Western American and art. Photos used for text illustration, promotional, book covers and dust jackets. Buys 100-200 photos annually; offers 3-4 freelance assignments annually. Examples of recently published titles: *Yellowstone: Selected Photographs, Field Guide to Yellowstone's Geysers, Hot Springs and Fumaroles* and *Field Guide to Wildflowers of the Rocky Mountains*.

Subject Needs: Natural history.

Specs: Uses 8×10 glossy b&w prints; 35mm, 2¼×2¼, 4×5 and 6×7 transparencies.

Payment & Terms: Pays $70-300/color photo, $50-300/b&w photo. Credit line given. Buys one-time and all rights; negotiable. Model release preferred. Photo captions required; accuracy very important. Simultaneous submissions and previously published work OK.

Making Contact: Query with samples. Provide resume, business card, brochure, flyer or tearsheets to be kept on file for possible future assignments. Reviews stock photos. SASE. Reports in 3-4 weeks.

Tips: In freelancer's samples, wants to see "top quality — must contain the basics of composition, clarity, sharp, in focus, etc. Looking for well-thought out, professional projects proposals."

*HOWELL PRESS, INC., Bay 2, 1147 River Road, Charlottesville VA 22901. (804)977-4006. FAX: (804)971-7204. President: Ross A. Howell, Jr. Estab. 1986. Publishes coffee table, illustrated books.

Subject Needs: Aviation, military history, gardening, maritime history, cookbooks only.

Specs: Uses b&w and color prints.

Payment & Terms: NPI; payment varies. Rights vary.

Making Contact: Query. Reviews stock photos. Keeps samples on file. SASE. Reports in 1-2 weeks. Simultaneous submissions and previously published work OK.

ILR PRESS, NY State School of Industrial and Labor Relations, Cornell University, Ithaca NY 14853-3901. (607)255-3061. Marketing and Promotion Manager: Andrea Fleck Clardy. Publishes books about all aspects of work and labor relations for academics, practitioners and the general public. Photos used for book covers and catalog of publications. Buys 5-10 freelance photos annually.

Subject Needs: People at work in a wide variety of contexts, with high human interest and excellence in photo design.

Specs: Uses b&w prints.

Payment & Terms: Pays $25-100/b&w photo. Credit line given. Buys one-time rights or book rights. Simultaneous submissions and previously published work OK.

Making Contact: Query with samples. Reviews stock photos. SASE. Reports in 1 month.

Tips: Prefers to see "b&w prints of high human interest images of people in the workforce. Particularly interested in photos that include women and people of color, high-tech professions and worker/manager groups."

*IMAGINE, INC., P.O. Box 9674, Pittsburgh PA 15226. (412)571-1430. President: R. Michelucci. Estab. 1982. Publishes trade paperback books: horror, sports, swimsuit and cheesecake; trading cards. Photos used for text illustration and book covers. Buys 100-150 photos annually; offers 1-2 freelance assignments annually. Examples of recently published titles: *Bruno Sammartino* (cover); and *Scream Queens* (card set).

Subject Needs: Bathing beauty starlett, Hollywood cheesecake.

Specs: Uses 35mm, 2¼×2¼ transparencies.

Payment & Terms: Pays $25-50/color photo. Credit line given. Buys one-time rights and all rights; negotiable. Model/property release required. Captions preferred; include model resume.

Making Contact: Query with samples. Reviews stock photos. Keeps samples on file. SASE. Reports in 1 month.

© Jim West

Specializing in labor photography, Jim West, of Detroit, Michigan, spotted the ILR Press listing in **Photographer's Market** *and thought the publisher would be a perfect market for his work. West says he wanted to create a positive image in which different racial groups worked together. The unusual angle used in this photo also creates an attractive scene for viewers.*

INTERNATIONAL MARINE PUBLISHING COMPANY, P.O. Box 220, Camden ME 04843. (207)236-6046. Production Director: Molly Mulhern. Publishes how-to books on nautical subjects. Photos used for text illustration, book covers and dust jackets. Buys 100 freelance photos and offers 5 freelance assignments annually. Examples of recently published titles: *A Cruising Guide to the Maine Coast*; *Water Shots* and *Fiberglass Boat Repair Manual* (photos used for cover and text in all three).
Subject Needs: Any nautically-related photos.
Specs: Uses transparencies, any size.
Payment & Terms: Pays $30-100/color photo, $10-50/b&w photo and $15-30/hour. Credit line given. Buys book rights. Model release preferred; captions required. Previously published work OK.
Making Contact: Query with samples. Sometimes reviews stock photos. Cannot guarantee return of unsolicited material. Reports in 1 month. No photo guidelines available.

JAMESTOWN PUBLISHERS, P.O. Box 9168, Providence RI 02940. Courier Delivery: 544 Douglas Ave., Providence RI 02908. (401)351-1915. Production Supervisor: Diane Varone. Estab. 1969. Publishes reading developmental textbooks. "We need photos to illustrate covers and text material, covering a wide range of photo matter." Buys 20-40 photographs annually, and assigns 3 projects annually. Examples of recently published titles: *Topics for the Restless*; all photos used for text illustrations.
Subject Needs: "We use a wide variety of photos: biographical subjects, illustrative photos for covers, historical photos, nature, science, people, etc."
Specs: Uses 8×10 glossy b&w prints; 35mm, 4×5 transparencies.
Payment & Terms: Pays $100-150/b&w photo; $135-350/color photo. Credit line given. Buys one-time rights. Previously published work OK.
Making Contact: Query with list of stock photo subjects. Provide resume, business card, brochure, flyer or tearsheets to be kept on file for possible future assignments. Reviews stock photos. Does not return unsolicited material. Reports in 1 month. Will work with U.S. photographers only.
Tips: Looks for "creativity, high contrast (for our b&w texts), plus diversity. Send stock lists. I keep all stock sources on a computer file. Keep sending updated lists."

JUST US BOOKS, INC., 301 Main Street, #22-24, Orange NJ 07050. (201)676-4345. FAX: (201)677-7570. Design Director: Cheryl Willis Hudson. Estab. 1987. Publishes juvenile and picture books for children. Photos used for text illustration and book covers. Buys 30-40 photos annually. Examples of recently published titles: *Afro-Bets First Book About Africa, Afro-Bets Book of Black Heroes,* and *Harambee,* a newspaper for young readers. All three titles are nonfiction.

Subject Needs: Needs photos of African-American children, their parents, their interests, and their communities both urban and suburban. Stock photos are often used.
Specs: Uses 8×10 b&w prints; 35mm and 4×5 transparencies.
Payment & Terms: Pays $25-150/color photo, $25-75/b&w photo. Pays on publication. Credit line given. Buys one-time rights and book rights. Model release and photo captions preferred. Simultaneous submissions and previously published work OK.
Making Contact: Arrange a personal interview to show portfolio. Query with list of stock photo subjects. Provide resume, business card, brochure, flyer or tearsheets to be kept on file for possible future assignments. SASE. No unsolicited photos accepted.
Tips: In photographer's portfolio, wants to see "fresh, positive, realistic depictions of African-American children in various situations." To break in, have "a positive, open attitude, a high degree of professionalism and a creative approach to illustrating children's materials with photos."

KALEIDOSCOPIX, INC., P.O. Box 389, Franklin MA 02038. (508)528-3242. Art Director: Jason Kruz. Estab. 1982. Publishes children's New Englandiana, historical, nautical, cooking. Photos used for text illustration, book covers and dust jackets.
Subject Needs: Subjects depend upon manuscript needs. For example, *ABC's of Covered Bridges* will require action-type photos of specific New England and Ohio covered bridges.
Specs: Uses 7×10, b&w prints; 11×14 color prints; 35mm transparencies.
Payment & Terms: Pays $50/color photo; $25/b&w photo. Credit line given. Buys all rights. Model release required; photo captions preferred. Previously published work OK.
Making Contact: Query with samples. Works on assignment only. SASE. Reports in 1 month. Photo guidelines free with SASE.
Tips: In samples, wants to see contact sheet of related subjects on 3×5 prints, not original slides or full size prints. Show some samples or brochure of style and techniques.

*KALMBACH PUBLISHING COMPANY, 21027 Crossroads Circle, Waukesha WI 53187. (414)796-8776. FAX: (414)796-0126. Editor: Bob Hayden. Estab. 1942. Publishes how-to, hobby books on radio control model line, model railroading and model building (planes, tanks). Photos used for text illustration. Examples of recently published titles: *The Spirit Of Railroading* and *Steel Rails Across America*.
Subject Needs: Needs photos of prototype locomotives, planes and tanks.
Specs: Uses 5×7 or 8×10 glossy b&w prints; and 4×5 transparencies.
Payment & Terms: Pays $20-25 minimum. Credit line given. Buys all rights. Photo captions preferred. Simultaneous submissions OK.
Making Contact: Query with samples. Works on assignment only. Keeps samples on file. SASE. Reports in 1 month.
Tips: "Since we deal with books and modeling magazine, we need photos of tanks, planes, etc. that include detail."

*KLUTZ PRESS, 2121 Staunton Ct., Palo Alto CA 94306. Art Director: Mary Ellen Podgorski. Publishes humorous how-to and juvenile books. Photos used for text illustration, book covers and catalog cover. Buys 200-300 photos (individuals and stock agency) annually; offers 6 freelance assignments annually. Examples of recently published titles: *Face Painting* (cover, text illustrations); *Explorabook* and *Time Book* (text illustrations).
Subject Needs: "Quirky, old-timey or kitsch flying stunts; studio table-top assignments; kids."
Specs: Uses 8×10 glossy b&w prints; 35mm, 2¼×2¼, 4×5 transparencies.
Payment & Terms: Pays $75-300/color photo; $40-100/b&w photo; $350 and up/day. Credit line given. Buys book rights; negotiable. Model/property release required. Captions required. Simultaneous submissions and previously published work OK.
Making Contact: Provide resume, business card, brochure, flyer or tearsheets to be kept on file for possible future assignments. Reviews stock photos. Keeps samples on file. SASE.
Tips: "We want to see good people shots, especially kids—natural, not arty or high-fashion. We're always looking for offbeat cover shot for our 'Flying Apparatus Catalog'—aviation stunt, juggling, kitsch, etc. Assignments are usually table-top product shots or location people/kid action shots. Agency photos used vary—all kinds of subjects."

■ *The solid, black square before a listing indicates that the market uses various types of audiovisual materials, such as slides, film or videotape.*

*■KNOWLEDGE UNLIMITED, INC., 2348 Pinehurst Dr., Middleton WI 53562. (608)836-6660. FAX: (608)831-1570. Associate Editor: Annette Czarnecki. Estab. 1983. Types of clients: schools, nursing homes and prisons. Publishes educational materials, teacher's guides, posters, filmstrips and videos on current events, history, science and geography. Photos used for text illustration, promotional materials, filmstrips and videos. Buys 50-100 photos annually. Examples of recently published titles: *The Press and the Presidency* and *Toxic Wastes* (filmstrips and teacher's guides); and *Journey Through the Solar System* (video and teacher's guide).
Subject Needs: All kinds—"emphasis on current events. Also need people, places, animals, industries, etc." Needs slides and video of current events, science, geography, education and senior citizens.
Specs: Uses color prints; 35mm transparencies.
Payment & Terms: Pays $10-50/color photo; $100-300/job. Credit line sometimes given, depending on where photo is used. Buys one-time rights; negotiable. Model/property release preferred. Captions preferred; include locations, names, description of action. Simultaneous submissions and previously published work OK.
Making Contact: Interested in receiving work from newer, lesser-known photographers. Query with samples. Query with list of stock photo subjects. Keeps samples on file. SASE. Reports in 3 weeks.
Tips: "We need all kinds of images (still and video). In general, we are looking for candid shots involving some action. We also use many landscape and environmental photos. Images depicting government, technology, youth issues and senior citizens are also needed. Be flexible on price. There is a trend toward more "volume" purchases at lower prices; more images of ethnic groups, urban strife, environmental problems."

KREGEL PUBLICATIONS, P.O. Box 2607, Grand Rapids MI 49501. (616)451-4775. FAX: (616)459-6049. Director of Publications: Al Bryant. Publishes textbooks for Christian and Bible colleges, reference works and commentaries, sermon helps and adult trade books. Photos used for book covers and dust jackets. Buys 12-40 photos annually.
Subject Needs: Scenic and/or biblical (i.e., Holy Land, etc.).
Specs: Uses 35mm 2¼×2¼ transparencies.
Payment & Terms: Pays $100-400/color photo. Credit line given. Buys book rights. Model release preferred. Previously published work OK.
Making Contact: Query with resume of credits. Query with samples. Send stock photo list. Reviews stock photos. Keeps samples on file. SASE. Reports in 1 month.
Tips: "We are tending to use more color photos on covers."

LAYLA PRODUCTION INC., 310 E. 44, New York NY 10017. (212)697-6285. Manager: Lori Stein. Estab. 1980. Publishes adult trade, how-to gardening and cooking books. Photos used for text illustration and book covers. Buys over 150 photos annually; offers 6 freelance assignments annually. Examples of recently published titles: *Golf's Magnificent Challenge*, used stock photos of courses as text; *That's All Folks*, assigned shooting of documents for illustration; and *Children of Bellevue Journal*, assigned shoot of kids in hospital.
Subject Needs: Gardening and cooking.
Specs: Specifications for submissions are very flexible.
Payment & Terms: Pays $20-200/color photo, $10-100/b&w photo, $25-100/hour. Other methods of pay depends on job, budget and quality needed. Buys all rights; negotiable. Simultaneous submissions and previously published work OK.
Making Contact: Provide resume, business card, brochure, flyer or tearsheets to be kept on file for possible future assignments. SASE. Reports in 1 month; prefers no unsolicited material.
Tips: "We're usually looking for a very specific subject. We *do* keep all resumes/brochures received on file—but our needs are small, and we don't often use unsolicited material. We will be working on a series of gardening books through 1995."

LEBHAR-FRIEDMAN, 425 Park Ave., New York NY 10022. (212)756-5000. Senior Art Director: Milton Berwin. Publishes trade books, magazines and advertising supplements for the entire retailing industry. Photos used for text illustration, book covers and ad supplements. Reports in 2 weeks.
Subject Needs: In-store location and related subject matter.
Specs: Uses 8×10 prints; also 2¼×2¼ transparencies.
Payment & Terms: Pays $250/day and on a per-photo basis. Buys all rights. Model release required. Send material by mail for consideration. SASE. Pays $50-100/b&w photo or less, according to size and use; $150-300/color photo and $50-300/cover photo.

LIBERTY PUBLISHING COMPANY, INC., Suite 202, 440 S. Federal Hwy., Deerfield Beach FL 33441. (305)360-9000. President: Jeffrey B. Little. Publishes adult trade paperbacks, software and videos. Subjects: how-to, cooking and general interest. Photos used for book covers. Buys 4-6 freelance photos annually.

Subject Needs: Still lifes, horse racing/gambling scenes, nature scenes.

Specs: Uses any size or finish color prints; 35mm and 2¼ × 2¼ transparencies. "Chance of our paying attention to a submitted print is greater than with transparencies."

Payment & Terms: Pays $350 maximum/color photo; and $350 maximum/job. Credit line given. Buys all rights. Model release required. Simultaneous submissions and previously published work OK.

Making Contact: Query with resume of credits and list of stock photo subjects. Provide resume, business card, brochure, flyer or tearsheets to be kept on file for possible future assignments. Reviews stock photos. SASE. Reports in 1 month.

Tips: "We only want to see samples if we have solicited photos for use as a book cover with a specific subject in mind. In that case, we evaluate balance of photo. Is there empty space in the proper place for book title and author's name to appear? Sharpness of image and pleasing combination of colors is also important. Subject matter would determine specifics. Availability and applicability of photo, as well as price, would determine whether we would go with the photo."

LITTLE, BROWN & CO., 41 Mt. Vernon St., Boston MA 02108. (617)227-0730. Jacket Art Coordinator: Janet Kimball. Publishes adult trade. Photos used for book covers and dust jackets.

Payment and Terms: NPI. Credit line given. Buys one-time rights. Model release required.

Making Contact: Provide resume, business card, brochure, flyer or tearsheets to be kept on file for possible future assignments. "Samples should be nonreturnable." SASE. Reviews stock photos. Reporting time varies.

LLEWELLYN PUBLICATIONS, P.O. Box 64383, St. Paul MN 55164. (612)291-1970. Art Director: Terry Buske. Publishes consumer books (mostly adult trade paperback) with astrology, psychology, mythology and New Age subjects, geared toward an educated audience. Also publishes book catalogs. Uses photos for book covers. Buys 5-10 freelance photos annually.

Subject Needs: Science/fantasy, sacred sites, gods and goddesses (statues, etc.), high-tech and special effects.

Specs: Uses 8 × 10 glossy color prints; 35mm or 4 × 5 transparencies.

Payment & Terms: Pays $125-600/color cover photo. Pays on publication. Credit line given. Buys one-time rights. Model release preferred.

Making Contact: Query with samples. Provide slides, brochure, flyer or tearsheets to be kept on file for possible future assignments. Reviews stock photos. SASE. Reports in 5 weeks.

Tips: "Send materials that can be kept on file."

LODESTAR BOOKS, (an affiliate of Dutton Children's Books) 375 Hudson St., New York NY 10014. (212)366-2626. Senior Editor: Rosemary Brosnan. Publishes photographic essays, picture books, non-fiction picture books and juvenile/young adult fiction and nonfiction. Photos used primarily for text illustration and occasionally dust jackets. Offers approximately 5 freelance assignments annually. All photos used as text illustration in nonfiction picture books. Examples of recently published titles: *Pioneer Settlers of New France*, photos by George Ancona; *Your Cat's Wild Cousins*, photos by Hope Ryden.

Subject Needs: Nature, animals, people — especially children — and history. "We don't usually use stock photos, except in historical nonfiction. Please don't send stock photo lists."

Payment & Terms: NPI. "For text illustration in a photo essay we pay advances and royalties. We don't usually buy individual photos." Credit line given. Buys book rights. Model release required; captions preferred.

Making Contact: Provide resume, brochure, flyer or tearsheets to be kept on file. Keeps queries and photos on file; reports as needed. Cannot return unsolicited material.

Tips: "We are doing more photographic essays in 48-page books for children ages 8-12. Also using more color photographs." Please do not contact by phone.

*LOOMPANICS UNLIMITED, P.O. Box 1197, Port Townsend WA 98368. Editorial Director: Steve O'Keefe. Estab. 1975. Publishes how-to and nonfiction for adult trade. Photos used for book covers. Buys 2-3 photos annually; offers 1-2 freelance assignments annually. Examples of recently published titles: *Serial Slaughter: What's Behind America's Murder Epidemic* (cover), *The Big House: How American Prisons Work* (cover) and *Techniques of Safecracking* (inside).

> ***** *The asterisk before a listing indicates that the market is new in this edition. New markets are often the most receptive to freelance submissions.*

Subject Needs: "We're always interested in photography documenting crime and criminals."
Specs: Uses b&w prints.
Payment & Terms: Pays$10-250 for cover photo; $5-20 interior photo. Credit lines given. Buys book rights; rights negotiable. Model/property release preferred. Captions preferred. Simultaneous submissions and previously published work OK.
Making Contact: Query with samples. Query with stock photo list. Provide tearsheets to be kept on file for possible future assignments. Reviews stock photos. Samples kept on file. SASE. Reports in 1 month.
Tips: "We look for clear, high contrast b&w shots that *clearly* illustrate a caption or product. Find out as much as you can about what we are publishing and tailor your pitch accordingly."

*LUCENT BOOKS, 10907 Technology Pl., San Diego CA 92127. (619)485-7424. FAX: (619)485-9549. Production Coordinator: Jill Campana. Estab. 1987. Publishes juvenile nonfiction—science, controversial topics and biographies. Photos used for text illustration and book covers. Buys hundreds of photos annually. Examples of recently published titles: *Telescopes: Encyclopedia of Discovery and Invention* (text illustration), *Rainforests* (text illustration) and *Ocean Pollution* (text illustration).
Subject Needs: Controversial topics such as eating disorders, abortion, garbage, pollution, gangs and science/medical oriented photos.
Specs: Uses 5×7, 8½×11 b&w prints.
Payment & Terms: Pays $75-100/color photo; pays $25-55/b&w photo. Credit lines sometimes given on request. Buys one-time rights. Model/property release preferred; photo captions preferred. Simultaneous submissions and previously published work OK.
Making Contact: Submit portfolio for review. Query with resume of credits. Query with samples. Provide resume, business card, brochure, flyer or tearsheets to be kept on file for possible future assignments. Reviews stock photos. Keeps samples on file. SASE. Reports in 1 month.
Tips: "Most photographers do landscape photos and advertising photos, which we can't use. We use photos to illustrate text in books. Take pictures resembling news photos—poor people, pregnant teens, alcohol treatment centers, homeless children, etc."

MCDOUGAL, LITTELL AND COMPANY, 1560 Sherman Ave., Evanston IL 60201. (708)869-2300. FAX: (708)869-0841. Picture Editor: Carmine Fantasia. Publishes textbooks for grades K-12. Photos used for text illustration and book covers. "We usually purchase from stock submissions of existing photos from freelance photographers or stock agencies."
Subject Needs: "We use photos to illustrate nonfiction literature selections and illustrate history books with historic sites—therefore we need nature scenes, news events, children age 4-18 and many different things based on which book is being prepared. We always need fine art photographers who shoot paintings."
Specs: Uses 35mm and 4×5 transparencies. "Prefer 4×5 but use a lot of 35mm. Black and whites normally accepted only for historic pictures shot when only b&w was available."
Payment & Terms: Pays $100-150/b&w photo; $135-210/color photo. Credit line given. Buys one-time rights. Model release preferred and captions required. Simultaneous submissions and previously published work OK.
Making Contact: Query with list of stock photo subjects. Provide resume, business card, brochure, flyer or tearsheets to be kept on file for possible future assignments. Reviews stock photos. SASE. Reports in 1 month.
Tips: "We are very open to seeing sophisticated computerized images or very new concepts combining art media. Please do not send unsolicited original work."

MCGRAW-HILL, College Division, 27 Floor, 1221 Avenue of the Americas, New York NY 10020. Manager: Safra Nimrod. Estab. 1889. Photos used for college textbooks. Examples of recently published titles: *Bovée/Thill: Principles of Marketing* Thill: (220 photos); *Carola: Human Anatomy* (260 photos); and *Gilbert: Living with Art* (640 photos); all photos used as illustrations.
Subject Needs: Subjects include editorial, reportage, news, sociology, psychology, special effects, natural history, science, micrography—all college subjects.
Specs: Uses 8×10 repro quality b&w prints; also transparencies or repro-quality dupes.
Payment & Terms: NPI; payment varies. Pays on acceptance after sizes are determined. Buys one-time rights. Captions and model releases preferred. Credit line given.
Making Contact: Provide resume, business card, self-promotion piece or tearsheets to be kept on file for possible future assignment. Do not send unsolicited photos. Reviews stock photos.
Tips: "We look for professionalism in presentation, well edited work, consistent high quality. If there's one bad shot, we question the photographer's judgment." Looks for "editorial approach, clean, sharp images, unposed people and an interesting angle on a familiar subject. Send tearsheets or xeroxes. Be willing to negotiate prices. There is continuing lack of good, new b&w photography."

*McKINZIE PUBLISHING COMPANY, P.O. Box 241-777, 11000 Wilshire Blvd., Los Angeles CA 90024. (213)934-7685. FAX: (213)931-7217. Personnel Manager: Robert Reed. Estab. 1969. Publishes adult trade, "how-to," description and travel, sports, adventure, fiction and poetry. Photos used for text illustration, promotional materials and book covers. Offers 4 or 5 freelance assignments annually.
Subjects Needs: Shots of sports figures and events.
Specs: Uses 3×5 glossy b&w/prints.
Payment & Terms: Pays $10-50/b&w photo; $50/hour. Credit line not given. Buys all rights; negotiable. Model/property release required. Previously published work OK.
Making Contact: Arrange personal interview to show portfolio. Query with samples. Reviews stock photos. SASE. Reports in 3 weeks.

MACMILLAN PUBLISHING COMPANY, 445 Hutchinson Ave., Columbus OH 43235. Publishes college textbooks. Photo editor: Anne Vega. (800)228-7854, ext. 3704. Photos for text illustration with emphasis in education, special education, physical education, counseling, management and personnel, health and nutrition, fashion merchandising, and clothing and textiles. Cover Design: Russ Maselli (800)228-7854, ext. 3688. Photos for book covers with emphasis in education, special education, physical education, counseling, management and personnel, health and nutrition, fashion merchandising, clothing and textiles, computer science, business marketing, criminal justice, geography and geology.
Subject Needs: Professionally lighted, cover quality, color and b&w photos of lively and unique general K-12 education activities with ethnic mix; special education students, mainstreamed students; computer usage in K-1, college, business and home; world geography with and without people; and oceanography, including surface and underwater shots.
Specs: 8×10 glossy b&w prints with minimum ¼" border, 35mm transparencies.
Payment & Terms: Competitive textbook prices paid on publication. In-text photos pays $65-100/b&w photo; $80-200/color photo; $70-90/hour; $800-1,000/day; $400-800/cover photo. Pay scale depends on rights and priority level of book. Credit line given. Buys one-time, North American, world and limited exclusive rights. All photos should be model-released. Previously published work in competing college textbooks not acceptable.
Making Contact: Inquire by sending a list of stock photo subjects, business card, brochure, flyer or tearsheets. Reviews stock photos only after inquiry and authorization to submit material with SASE and phone number. Averages 1-3 months return time for rejected or considered work, 3-9 months return time for published work. All photos for cover should be in color and addressed to Russ Maselli. Majority of photos used by Anne Vega are b&w and of education orientation.
Tips: "If you don't have a promo piece, we prefer to receive duplicate slides or extra prints to hold until needed. Will accept quality photocopies to keep on file upon approving the quality from submissions of actual glossy prints/slides."

MACMILLAN PUBLISHING COMPANY, 866 3rd Ave., New York NY 10022. (212)702-2000. Art Director: Susan Newman. Publishes adult trade and fiction; "almost any type of book, except pornography." Photos used for book covers.
Subject Needs: "A variety of photos are used with our books."
Payment & Terms: NPI; payment varies per project and print run. Credit line given. Buys one-time rights; negotiable, depending on use. Model release required.
Making Contact: Provide resume, business card, brochure, flyer or tearsheets to be kept on file for possible future assignments. "Do not send photos by Federal Express." Reviews stock photos. SASE.

METAMORPHOUS PRESS, Box 10616, Portland OR 97210. (503)228-4972. Editor: Lori Stephens. "We publish books and tapes in the subject areas of communication, health and fitness, education, business and sales, psychology, women and children. Photos used for text illustration, promotional materials, book covers and dust jackets. Examples of recently published titles: *The Challenge of Excellence*; *Re-Creating Your Self*; and *Power to the Dancers*. Photos used for cover and/or text illustration.
Payment & Terms: NPI; payment negotiable. Credit line given. Buys one-time and book rights. Also buys all rights, but willing to negotiate. Simultaneous submissions and previously published work OK.
Making Contact: Query with samples list of stock photo subjects. Provide resume, business card, brochure, flyer or tearsheets to be kept on file for possible future assignments. Works on assignment only. Reviews stock photos. Cannot return material. Reports as soon as possible.
Tips: "Let us have samples of specialties so we can match contents and styles to particular projects."

MILADY PUBLISHING CORPORATION, 4th Floor, 220 White Plains Rd., Tarrytown NY 10591. 1-800-836-5239. Contact: Editorial Director. Publishes textbooks for vocational education in areas of cosmetology, fashion and personal development. Photos used for text illustration and trade magazine illustration.

Subject Needs: Hair styling, manicuring, aesthetics and modeling.
Specs: Uses b&w glossy prints.
Payment & Terms: NPI; payment negotiable. Credit line given. Rights purchased vary per usage. Model release and captions preferred. Simultaneous submissions and previously published work OK.
Making Contact: Provide resume, business card, brochure, flyer or tearsheets to be kept on file for possible future assignments. Works on assignment only. SASE. Reports in 2 weeks.

MILKWEED EDITIONS, Box 3226, Minneapolis MN 55403. (612)332-3192. FAX: (612)332-6248. Art Director: R.W. Scholes. Estab. 1979. Publishes fiction, nonfiction and poetry. Photos used for text illustration, book covers and dust jackets. Examples of recently published titles: *Minnesota Gothic*, (counter poems throughout); *Twin Sons of Different Mirrors* (b&w photos used for text illustration) and *The Freedom of History* (color photo used for cover art).
Subject Needs: Interested in high-quality photos, able to stand on own; "should not be journalistic."
Specs: Uses 10×12 b&w glossy prints and 35mm transparencies.
Payment & Terms: Pays $10-100/b&w photo; $20-150/color photo; $10-650/job. "We buy piece work. We are a nonprofit organization. Credit line given. Buys one-time rights. Model release required; photo captions preferred. Simultaneous submissions and previously published work OK.
Making Contact: Arrange personal interview to show portfolio. Query with samples. Provide resume, business card, brochure, flyer or tearsheets to be kept on file. SASE. Reports in 1 month.
Tips: Would like to see series works, usually b&w. "Look at our books for use. Then send in a fairly good copy (or original) to keep on file, plus a slide sheet with address and SASE." Sees trend in company toward "an increased use (of photos) compared to past graphic works." The same is generally true among book publishers.

MOON PUBLICATIONS, INC., 722 Wall St., Chico CA 95928. (916)345-5473. Creative Director: David Hurst. Estab. 1974. Publishes trade paper, travel guides and pictorial travel guides. Photos used for text illustration, promotional materials and book covers. Buys "a few" photos annually. Examples of recently published titles: *Bali Handbook* (cover); *Nevada Handbook* (cover); and *New Mexico Handbook* (cover).
Subject Needs: Travel—all 50 states.
Specs: Uses 3×5, 5×7 b&w prints; 35mm, 2¼×2¼, 4×5, 8×10 transparencies.
Payment & Terms: Pays $50-300/color photo; $20-70/b&w photo. Credit line given. Buys one-time rights and rights for all editions (life of book). Photo captions preferred. Simultaneous submissions and previously published work OK.
Making Contact: Query with stock photo list. Provide resume, business card, brochure, flyer or tearsheets to be kept on file for possible future assignments. Reviews stock photos. SASE. Reports in 2 weeks.
Tips: Looks for unusual travel shots, people, places, things; entire US, the Pacific and Asia. "Be sure to query with list of stock photo subjects and tearsheets."

MOTORBOOKS INTERNATIONAL, 275 South Third St., Stillwater MN 55082. (612)439-6001. FAX: (612)439-5627. Publisher: Tim Parker. Estab. 1965. Publishes trade and specialist and how-to, automotive, aviation and military. Photos used for text illustration, book covers and dust jackets. Buys 30 freelance photos and offers 12 assignments annually. Examples of recently published titles: *How to Restore Your Musclecar*, *Desert Shield* and *How to Custom Paint*.
Subject Needs: Anything to do with transportation (not sailboats), tractors, cycles or airplane.
Specs: Any size prints or transparencies.
Payment & Terms: NPI; payment negotiable. Credit line given. Rights negotiable. Model release and captions preferred. Simultaneous submissions and previously published work OK.
Making Contact: Works mostly on assignment. Reviews stock photos. SASE. Reports in 2 weeks.
Tips: To break in, "present manuscript with photos."

*MOUNTAIN AUTOMATION CORPORATION, P.O. Box 6020, Woodland Park CO 80866. (719)687-6647. President: Claude Wiatrowski. Estab. 1976. Publishes souvenir books. Photos used for text illustration, promotional materials and book covers. Examples of recently published titles: *Colorado's Black Canyon* (throughout); *Pike's Peak By Rail* (extra illustrations in video) and *Georgetown Loop RR* (extra illustrations in video).
Subject Needs: Complete projects for illustrated souvenir books, not individual photos.
Specs: Uses 35mm, 2¼×2¼, 4×5 transparencies.
Payment & Terms: NPI; royalty on complete book projects. Credit lines given. Buys all rights. Model/property release preferred; photo captions required. Simultaneous submissions OK.
Making Contact: Query with book project. Keeps samples on file. SASE. Reports in 1 month.
Tips: "We *only* are interested in complete illustrated book projects for the souvenir market with very targeted markets."

*JOHN MUIR PUBLICATIONS, P.O. Box 613, Santa Fe NM 87504. (505)982-4078. FAX: (505)988-1680. Art Director: Ken Wilson. Estab. 1969. Publishes adult travel (trade), juvenile nonfiction (science, inter-cultural). Photos used for text illustration and book covers. Buys "hundreds" of photos annually. Examples of recently published titles: *Ranch Vacations, Extremely Weird Frogs* and *California Public Gardens*.
Specs: Uses 35mm, 4×5 transparencies.
Payment & Terms: NPI. Credit line given. Buys book rights, all rights and foreign. Rights negotiable. Model/property release preferred. Simultaneous submissions and previously published work OK.
Making Contact: Query with samples. Query with stock photo list. Provide resume, business card, brochure, flyer or tearsheets to be kept on file for possible future assignments. Reviews stock photos. Keep samples on file. SASE. Reports back "only if we wish to use material or photographer."
Tips: "After sending list or samples follow up regularly."

MUSEUM OF NORTHERN ARIZONA, Route 4, Box 720, Flagstaff AZ 86001. (602)774-5211. FAX: (602)779-1527. Graphic Designer: Libby Jennings. Estab. early 1900s. Publishes biology, geology, archaeology, anthropology and history. Photos used for book covers. Buys approx. 90 photos annually. Examples of recently published titles: *The Sinagha, Exploring the Colorado Plateau,* and *The San Juan River.* Forty b&w and color photos used for text in each.
Subjects Needs: Biology, geology, history, archaeology and anthropology — subjects on the Colorado Plateau.
Specs: Uses 8×10 glossy b&w prints; also 35mm, 2¼×2¼, 4×5 and 8×10 transparencies.
Payment & Terms: Pays $25-75/color photo; $25-75/b&w photo. Credit line given. Buys one-time and all rights; negotiable. Photo captions preferred. Simultaneous submissions and previously published work OK.
Making Contact: Interested in receiving work from newer, lesser-known photographers. Reviews stock photos. SASE. Reports in 1 month.
Tips: Wants to see top-quality, natural history work. To break in, send only pre-edited photos. Prefers 2¼×2¼ transparencies or larger. Include captions indicating location and definition.

MUSIC SALES CORP., 225 Park Ave. S., New York NY 10003. (212)254-2100. Contact: Daniel Earley. Publishes instructional music books, song collections and books on music. Recent titles include: *Judy Collins Anthology, Tom Waits* and *Rock Chord Guide*. Photos used for cover and/or interiors. Buys 200 photos annually.
Specs: Uses 8×10 glossy prints; 35mm, 2×2 or 5×7 transparencies.
Payment & Terms: Buys one-time rights. Present model release on acceptance of photo. Captions required. Pays $35-50/b&w photo, $100-500/color photo. Simultaneous submissions and previously published work OK.
Making Contact: Query first with resume of credits. Provide business card, brochure, flyer or tearsheet to be kept on file for possible future assignments. SASE. Reports in 2 months.
Tips: In samples, wants to see "the ability to capture the artist in motion with a sharp eye for framing the shot well. Portraits must reveal what makes the artist unique. We need rock, jazz, classical — on stage and impromptu shots. Please send us an inventory list of available stock photos of musicians. We rarely send photographers on assignment and buy mostly from material on hand." Send "business card and tear sheets or prints stamped 'proof' across them. Due to the nature of record releases and concert events, we never know exactly when we may need a photo. We keep photos on permanent file for possible future use."

*NEW SOCIETY PUBLISHERS, 4527 Springfield Ave., Philadelphia PA 19143. (215)382-6543. Production Manager: Annie Hanaway or Marketing Manager: T.L. Hill. Estab. 1980. Publishes nonfiction trade books that promote fundamental social change through nonviolent action. Photos used for text illustration and book covers. Buys 3-4 photos annually; offers 3-4 freelance assignments annually. Examples of recently published titles: *Colonialism on Trial; One World, One Earth* and *Living with the Land*.
Subject Needs: Needs photo/text packages. Photos should be vertical to fit 6×9 or 8½×11 covers, without dated images or figures.
Specs: Uses 6×9, 8½×11 glossy, color/b&w prints.
Payment & Terms: Pays $100 minimum/color photo; $50 minimum/b&w photo. Credit line given. Buys one-time, book rights and all rights; negotiable. Model/property release required. Captions required. Simultaneous submissions and previously published work OK.
Making Contact: Query with samples. Works on assignment only. Reviews stock photos. SASE. Reports only when interested.
Tips: "Be flexible. We're a small nonprofit collective; therefore, overworked and underpaid."

*NORDICPRESS, (division of NordicTrack, Inc.), 104 Peavey Rd., Chaska MN 55318. (612)368-2545. FAX: (612)368-2555. Senior Editor: Barbara Pribyl. Estab. 1976. Publishes how-to, self-help, fitness, health and nutrition. Photos used for catalog covers and magazine layouts. Buys 100 photos annually. Examples of recently published titles: *Self Health Catalog* (cover photo) and *Personal Fitness and Weight Loss Magazine.*
Subject Needs: Outdoor recreation (all seasons), active lifestyle and exercise (indoors and out).
Specs: Uses color prints and 2¼ × 2¼ transparencies.
Payment & Terms: Pays $20/color photo; negotiable. Credit line given. Buys one-time rights. Model and property release preferred. Captions preferred. Simultaneous submissions and previously published work OK.
Making Contact: Query with stock photo list. Send unsolicited photos by mail for consideration. Reviews stock photos. Keeps samples on file. SASE. Reports in 1 month.
Tips: Needs photos of people in action, "not posed," men, women, couples ages 35-49.

*NORTHWORD PRESS, INC., Box 1360, Minocqua WI 54548. (715)356-9800. FAX: (715)356-9762. Director of Photography: Robert Baldwin. Estab. 1983. Photos used for text illustration, promotional materials, book covers and dust jackets. Buys 500 photos annually. Examples of recently published titles: *Wild Wisconsin, Spirit of the North* and *Elk Country.*
Subject Needs: Wildlife, nature and outdoor activity.
Specs: Uses 35mm, 2½ × 2½, 4 × 5 and 8 × 10 transparencies.
Payment & Terms: Pays $50-500/color photo. Credit line given. Buys one-time rights and project rights. Model/property release required. Photo captions required. Simultaneous submissions and previously published work OK.
Making Contact: Query with stock photo list. Reviews stock photos. Keeps samples on file. Cannot return materials. Reports in 3 weeks. Photo guidelines free with SASE.
Tips: "Please submit only extremely high quality, well composed, 'razor sharp' focused images. Edit your submissions carefully. Do not include multiples of the same image. We look for creativity and imagination. Give your work that extra 'nudge' to make the shot unique."

C. OLSON & CO., P.O. Box 5100-PM, Santa Cruz CA 95063. (408)458-3365. Editor: C. L. Olson. Estab. 1977.
Subject Needs: Uses 5 photos/year – b&w or color; all supplied by freelance photographers. "Looking for color photos of glaciers – from land, sea and air. Photos of well-known natural hygienists. Also, photos of fruit and nut trees (in blossom with fruit) in public access locations like parks, schools, churches, streets, businesses, etc."
Making Contact: Interested in receiving work from newer, lesser-known photographers. Query with samples. SASE, plus #10 window envelope. Reports in 2 weeks.
Payment & Terms: NPI; "all rates negotiable." Pays on either acceptance or publication. Credit line given on request. Buys all rights. Model/property release required for posed people and private property; captions required. Simultaneous submissions and previously published work OK.
Tips: Open to both amateur and professional photographers. "To ensure that we buy your work, be open to payment based on a royalty for each copy of a book we sell."

OUTDOOR EMPIRE PUBLISHING, INC., Box C-19000, Seattle WA 98109. (206)624-3845. Human Resource Director: Margaret Durante. Publishes how-to, outdoor recreation and large-sized paperbacks. Photos used for text illustration, promotional materials, book covers and newspapers. Buys 6 photos annually; offers 2 freelance assignments annually.
Subject Needs: Wildlife, hunting, fishing, boating, outdoor recreation.
Specs: Uses 8 × 10 glossy b&w and color prints; 35mm, 2¼ × 2¼ and 4 × 5 transparencies.
Payment & Terms: NPI; payment "depends on situation/publication." Credit line given. Buys all rights. Model release and captions preferred. Simultaneous submissions and previously published work OK.
Making Contact: Query with samples or send unsolicited photos by mail for consideration. Provide resume, business card, brochure, flyer or tearsheets to be kept on file for possible future assignments. Works on assignment only. SASE. Reports in 3 weeks.
Tips: Prefers to see slides or contact sheets as samples. "Be persistent; submit good quality work. Since we publish how-to books, clear informative photos that tell a story are very important."

*PAPIER-MACHÉ PRESS, 795 Via Manzana, Watsonville CA 95076. (408)726-2933. FAX: (408)726-1255. Editor: Sandra Martz. Estab. 1984. Publishes adult trade paperbacks focusing on issues of interest to mid-life and older women. Photos used for text illustration and promotional materials. Buys 60-80 photos annually; offers 2-3 freelance assignments annually. Examples of recently published titles: *If I Had a Hammer* (25 photos); *Ric Masten Speaking* (20 photos); and *Flight of the Wild Goose* (18 photos).

Subject Needs: Human interest, usually women in "doing" role; sometimes couples, families, etc.
Specs: Uses 8 × 10 glossy b&w prints.
Payment & Terms: Pays $25-50/b&w photo; $300-500/job; photographers also receive "copies of books, generous discount on books." Credit line given. Buys one-time rights and rights to use photos in promo materials for books, e.g. flyers, ads, etc.; negotiable. Model/property release preferred. "Generally we do not caption photos except for photographer's name." Simultaneous submissions and previously published work OK.
Making Contact: Query with samples (including photocopies). Provide resume, business card, brochure, flyer or tearsheets to be kept on file for possible future assignments. Sometimes reviews stock photos. Keeps samples on file. SASE. Reports in 3-6 months. "Guidelines for current theme anthologies are available with #10 SASE."
Tips: "We are generally looking for photos to complement a specific theme anthology or poetry collection. It is essential for photographers to know what those current themes are."

PEANUT BUTTER PUBLISHING, 200 2nd West Ave., Seattle WA 98119. (206)281-5965. Publisher: Elliott Wolf. Estab. 1971. Publishes cookbooks (primarily gourmet); restaurant guides; assorted adult trade books. Photos used for promotional materials and book covers. Buys 24-36 photos/year; offers up 5 freelance assignments/year.
Subject Needs: "We are primarily interested in shots displaying a variety of foods in an appealing table or buffet setting. Good depth of field and harmonious color are important. We are also interested in cityscapes that capture one or another of a city's more pleasant aspects. No models."
Specs: Uses 2¼ × 2¼ or 4 × 5 slides.
Payment & Terms: Pays $50-300/color photo. Credit line given. Buys one-time, exclusive product and all rights. Simultaneous submissions and previously published work OK.
Making Contact: Arrange a personal interview to show portfolio. Query with samples or send unsolicited photos by mail for consideration. Reviews stock photos. SASE. Reports in 2 weeks.

THE PHOTOGRAPHIC ARTS CENTER, 163 Amsterdam Ave. #201, New York NY 10023. (212)838-8640. FAX: (212)873-7065. Publisher: Robert S. Persky. Estab. 1980. Publishes books on photography and art, emphasizing the business aspects of being a photographer, artist and/or dealer. Photos used for book covers. Examples of recently published titles: *Publishing Your Art As Cards & Posters* (stock photo deskbook—cover illustration); and *The Photographer's Complete Guide To Exhibition & Sales Spaces* (text illustration).
Subject Needs: Business of photography and art.
Specs: Uses 5 × 7 glossy b&w or color prints; 35mm transparencies.
Payment & Terms: Pays $25-100/color photo, $25-100/b&w photo. Credit line given. Buys one time rights. Model release required.
Making Contact: Query with samples and text. SASE. Reports in 3 weeks.
Tips: Sees trend in book publishing toward "books advising photographers how to maximize use of their images by finding business niches such as gallery sales, stock and cards and posters." In freelancer's submissions, looks for "manuscript or detailed outline of manuscript with submission."

PLAYERS PRESS INC., P.O. Box 1132, Studio City CA 91614. (818)789-4980. Vice President: David Cole. Estab. 1965. Publishes entertainment books including theater, film and television. Photos used for text illustration, promotional materials book covers and dust jackets. Buys 50-1,000 photos annually. Examples of recently published titles: *Playing the Game*, (cover/text illustration); *Period Costume* (Vols. 1&2, text illustration); and *The Bear* (production photos of play).
Subject Needs: Entertainers, actors, directors, theatres, productions, actors in period costumes, scenic designs and clowns.
Specs: Uses 8 × 10 glossy or matte b&w prints; 5 × 7 glossy color prints; 35mm, 2¼ × 2¼ transparencies.
Payment & Terms: Pays $5-500/color photo, $1-200/b&w photo. Credit line sometimes given, depending on book. Buys all rights; negotiable in "rare cases." Model release required for productions/personalities. Photo captions preferred for name of principals and project/production. Simultaneous submissions and previously published work OK.
Making Contact: Query with list of stock photo subjects, send unsolicited photos by mail for consideration. Reviews stock photos. SASE. Reports in 3 weeks.
Tips: Wants to see "photos relevant to the entertainment industry. Do not telephone; submit only what we ask for."

POCKET BOOKS, 1230 Avenue of the Americas, New York NY 10020. (212)698-7000. VP/Executive Art Director: Barbara Buck. Estab. 1939. Publishes hardcover, mass market and trade paperbacks. Photos used for book covers—uses mostly people and still life.

Payment & Terms: NPI; payment varies with each project, negotiable. Buys one-time rights. Model release required.
Making Contact: Submit portfolio for review any day but Friday. Provide tearsheets to be kept on file for possible future assignments. Reviews stock photos. SASE. Previously published work OK.
Tips: "I look for people who are conceptual as well as technically skilled. Please do not call. Drop off portfolio with us regularly with a variety of tearsheets to show us new work."

*PRAKKEN PUBLICATIONS, INC., 416 Longshore Dr., Ann Arbor MI 48107. (313)769-1211. FAX: (313)769-8383. Production & Design Mgr.: Sharon K. Miller. Estab. 1934. Publishes *The Education Digest* (magazine), *School Shop/Tech Directions* (magazine for technology and vocational/technical educators), text and reference books for technology and vocational/technical education and general education reference. Photos used for text illustration, promotional materials, book covers, magazine covers and text. Buys 6 photos annually. Examples of recently published titles: *Handbook II for Aerospace Education* (cover and text, marketing), *Oral Communication for Vo-Tech Students* (text) and *The Education Digest, School Shop/Tech Directions* (covers and marketing).
Subject Needs: Education "in action" and especially technology and vocational-technical education.
Specs: Uses up to 8 × 10 glossy color and b&w prints.
Payment & Terms: Pays $75/color photo; $50/b&w photo; other methods of payment to be arranged. Credit line sometimes given. Rights negotiable. Model/property release required. Photo captions preferred; scene location, activity. Simultaneous submissions and previously published work OK.
Making Contact: Query with resume of credits. Query with samples. Query with stock photo list. Send unsolicited photos by mail for consideration. Reviews stock photos. Keep sample on file. SASE. Reports in 1 month. No photo guidelines available.
Tips: Wants to see "experience in education and knowledge of high-tech equipment" when reviewing portfolios. Send inquiry with relevant samples to be kept on file.

*PRINCETON BOOK COMPANY, PUBLISHERS/DANCE HORIZONS, P.O. Box 57, Pennington NJ 08534. (609)737-8177. Managing Editor: Debi Elfenbein. Estab. 1975. Publishes dance books for college, trade and specialty markets. All aspects of dance – ballet, jazz, modern, folk, social, etc. Photos used for text illustration and book covers. Buys 40-50 photos annually. Examples of recently published titles: *Dance Film and Video Guide, Dance as a Theatre Art,* Second Edition and *Dance: Rituals of Experience.*
Subject Needs: Black and white photos of dance, sometimes specific performers, specific choreographers or companies.
Specs: Uses 8 × 10 b&w prints.
Payment & Terms: Pays $15-75/b&w photo. Credit line given. Buys book rights, all rights; negotiable. Model/property release required. Photo captions required; include names of performers, date of photo, date of copyright and holder of copyright. Simultaneous submissions and previously published work OK.
Making Contact: Provide resume, business card, brochure, flyer or tearsheets to be kept on file for possible future assignments. Works with freelancers on assignment only. Keeps samples on file. SASE. Reports in 3 months.
Tips: Looks for "exciting and realistic portraits of dancers performing, perhaps photos of demonstrations of ballet positions or exercises as needed. Always stamp name, phone and address on every sample photo, also copyright date and holder."

G.P. PUTNAM & SONS, 200 Madison Ave., New York NY 10016. (212)951-8400. Vice President/Art Director: Ann Spinelli. Publishes adult trade, how-to, cooking and fiction. Photos used for book covers and dust jackets.
Subject Needs: Sports, cookbook features, how-to.
Payment & Terms: NPI; payment rate "varies according to project." Credit line given. Buys one-time rights. Model release required. Simultaneous submissions and previously published work OK.
Making Contact: Query with samples. Works "mostly" with local freelancers. Reviews stock photos. Cannot return material.

*REDBIRD PRESS, INC., P.O. Box 11441, Memphis TN 38111. (901)323-2233. Editor: Virginia McLean. Estab. 1984. Publishes juvenile and travel books. Photos used for text illustration. "Have only bought 1 freelance photo; thinking of using freelance in future." Examples of recently published titles: *Chasing the Moon to China* and *Kenya, Jambo!* (text illustration).
Subject Needs: Children, lifestyles in India, Greece, Turkey, Peru, Saudi Arabia, Italy and England.
Specs: Uses 35mm and 4 × 5 transparencies.
Payment & Terms: "We have not used freelance work in past but are considering it." Pays $10-50/color photo. Credit line given. Buys all rights; negotiable. Model/property release preferred. Simultaneous submissions and previously published work OK.

Making Contact: Interested in receiving work from newer, lesser-known photographers. Query with list of stock photo subjects. Provide resume, business card, brochure, flyer or tearsheets to be kept on file for possible future assignments. Reviews stock photos. Keeps samples on file. Cannot return material. Reports in 3 weeks.

*❦**REIDMORE BOOKS INC.**, Suite 1200, 10109 106th St., Edmonton AB T5J 3L7. (403)424-4420. FAX: (403)441-9919. Contact: Visuals Editor. Estab. 1979. Publishes textbooks for K-12; textbooks published cover all subject areas. Photos used for text illustration and book covers. Buys 250 photos annually; offers 1-3 freelance assignments annually. Examples of recently published titles: *Global Forces of the 20th Century, A Changing World: Global Political & Economic System* and *Canadian Connections.*
Subject Needs: "Photo depends on the project, however, images should contain unposed action."
Specs: No specific requirements as long as image is good quality.
Payment & Terms: Pays $50-200/color photo; $50-200/b&w photo. Credit line given. Buys one-time rights and book rights; negotiable. Model/property release preferred; photo captions required. Simultaneous submissions and previously published work OK.
Making Contact: Arrange personal interview to show portfolio. Submit portfolio for review. Query with resume of credits. Query with samples. Query with stock photo list. Provide resume, business card, brochure, flyer or tearsheets to be kept on file for possible future assignments. Reviews stock photos. Keeps samples of tearsheets, etc. on file. Cannot return material. Reports in 1 month. No photo guidelines available.
Tips: "I look for unposed images which show lots of action. Please be patient when you submit images for a project. The editorial process can take a long time and it is in your favor if your images are at hand when last minute changes are made."

*RESOURCE PUBLICATIONS, INC.**, Suite 290, 160 E. Virginia St., San Jose CA 95112. Editorial Director: Kenneth Guentert. Publishes imaginative resources for professionals in ministry and education. Photos used for text illustration and promotional materials. Buys 6 photos/year.
Specs: Uses 8 × 10 b&w prints and color transparencies.
Payment & Terms: Pays $5-25/photo; $15-35/hour. Credit line given. Buys all rights, but may reassign rights to photographer after publication. Model release required.
Making Contact: Send query by mail for consideration. SASE. Reports in 6 weeks.
Tips: "Book authors tend to work with their own photographers. However, we will talk with anyone dedicated to taking photos of liturgical space or situations. We're building a consignment file."

○ **WILLIAM H. SADLIER, INC.**, 7 Pine St., New York NY 10005. (212)227-2120. Director of Photo Research: Jim Saylor. Publishes religious education materials for all ages; academic textbooks, kindergarten/adult. Photos used for text illustration, promotional materials, book covers and posters.
Subject Needs: Children interacting with families, friends, community service activities (all ethnic groups); nature; religious artwork.
Specs: Uses 35mm, 2¼ × 2¼ and 4 × 5 transparencies; also b&w prints.
Payment & Terms: Pays $25-100/b&w photo; $50-350/color photo. "Assignments are negotiated individually." Credit line given. Buys one-time rights, book rights or all rights. Model release required. Simultaneous submissions OK.
Making Contact: Query with stock photo list. Provide brochure, flyer or tearsheets to be kept on file for possible future assignments. Reviews stock photos. SASE.
Tips: Looks for colorful photos with good interaction and ethnic mix.

*❦**ST. REMY PRESS**, Suite 300, 417 St. Pierre, Montreal PQ H24 2M4 Canada. (514)288-9250. FAX: (514)288-2535. Picture Editor: Chris Jackson. Estab. 1984. Publishes adult trade. "We are a packager for Time-Life Books, Alexandria, VA." Photos used for text illustraton and book covers. Recently published titles include: *How Things Work* (series), *Woodworking Machines* (inside), *Oceans* (inside) and *Medicine* (inside).

❦ *The maple leaf before a listing indicates that the market is Canadian. The symbol is new this year in* **Photographer's Market.**

Subject Needs: Travel and technology.
Specs: Uses 35mm, 2¼×2¼, 4×5 transparencies.
Payment & Terms: NPI; payment negotiable. Credit line given. Buys one-time rights; negotiable. Model release preferred; photo captions required. Previously published work OK.
Making Contact: Interested in receiving work from newer, lesser-known photographers. Arrange personal interview to show portfolio. Provide resume, business card, brochure, flyer or tearsheets to be kept on file for possible future assignments. Reviews stock photos. SASE. Reports in 1 month. No photo guidelines available.
Tips: "We are now starting a travel series for Reader's Digest Books called 'Explore America': first title is *National Parks*, second is *Historic Places*. Looking for fresh material on both."

SANDHILL CRANE PRESS, INC., P.O. Box 147050, Gainesville FL 32614. (904)375-6610. Acquisitions Editor: Ross H. Arnett. Publishes nature books (natural history, conservation, etc.). Photos used for text illustration, book covers and dust jackets. Examples of recently published titles: *Florida Butterflies*; *In Search of Reptiles and Amphibians* and *Biogeography of the West Indies*.
Subject Needs: "We use only author-supplied illustrations."
Specs: Uses 8×10 glossy b&w prints; 35mm transparencies.
Payment & Terms: NPI.
Making Contact: Query with book proposal only. SASE. Reports in 2 weeks.
Tips: "Fill frame with subject."

***☀SELF-COUNSEL PRESS**, 1481 Charlotte Rd., Vancouver BC V7J 1H1 Canada. (604)986-3366. FAX: (604)986-3947. Designer: Rod Poland. Estab. 1971. Publishes adult trade, self-help books, legal, business, reference, financial, retirement, psychology and travel series. Photos used for promotional materials (book dummies, blurbs, posters) and book covers. Buys 6 photos and offers 6 freelance assignments annually. Examples of recently published titles: *The Body Image Trap, The Minute Takers Handbook* and *Assertiveness for Managers*. All photography used as cover art.
Subject Needs: Needs photos of business and people (business, seniors), architectural (interior and exterior).
Specs: Uses color prints; 35mm and 2¼×2¼ transparencies.
Payment & Terms: Pays $100-200/b&w photo; $100-400/color photo; $400/day. Credit line sometimes given depending on agreed price, other circumstances. Buys all rights; negotiable. Model/property releases required. Simultaneous submissions and previously published work OK, depending on circumstances.
Making Contact: Interested in receiving work from newer, lesser-known photographers. Arrange a personal interview to show portfolio if possible. Query with samples or with stock photo lists. Provide resume, business card, brochure, flyer or tearsheets to be kept on file for possible future assignments. Reviews stock photos. Cannot return material.
Tips: "Send samples but not originals. Generally unsolicited phone calls are not well-received since product is visual."

M. E. SHARPE, INC., 80 Business Park Dr., Armonk NY 10504. (914)273-1800. FAX: (914)273-2106. Director of Marketing: Thomas Grant. Estab. 1958. Publishes adult trade, supplementary textbooks, academic and professional books. Photos used for text illustration, promotional materials, book covers and dust jackets. Occasionally buys freelance photos.
Subject Needs: Journalistic-type photos of former Soviet Union, China, Eastern Europe; political subjects.
Specs: Uses 5×7 glossy b&w prints; 35mm transparencies.
Payment & Terms: Pays $200-500/color photo; $150-450/b&w photo. Credit line given. Buys one-time rights. Photo captions required; include name of owner/photographer. Simultaneous submissions and previously published work OK.
Making Contact: Query with samples. Send stock photo list. Provide resume, business card, brochure, flyer or tearsheets to be kept on file for possible future assignments. Reviews stock photos. Samples kept on file. Reports in 3 weeks.
Tips: Prefers human interest (people shots) to landscapes. "Touristy" foreign photos are not used. Sees trend toward more usage of photos in their books.

SIERRA PRESS, INC., P.O. Box 430, El Portal CA 95318. (209)379-2330. General Manager: Jim Wilson. Estab. 1984. Publishes color gift books, postcard books, postcards, posters and prints of national parks and monuments. Photos used for text illustration and book covers. Uses 300 photos annually; offers 4-5 freelance assignments annually. Examples of published titles: *Wildflowers of Yosemite,* wildflower field guide; *Wish You Were Here®*, Yellowstone gift book (landscapes); and *Wish You Were Here® Postcard Books*, Grand Canyon postcards.

Subject Needs: Brilliant and colorful landscapes utilizing dramatic lighting and intimate details of nature.
Specs: Uses 35mm, 2¼ × 2¼, 4 × 5, 8 × 10 transparencies; they must be sharp, clear and concise.
Payment & Terms: Pays $50-250/color photo. Credit line given. Buys one-time rights. Photo captions required. Simultaneous submissions and previously published work OK.
Making Contact: Query with stock photo list. SASE.

THE SPEECH BIN INC., 1766 Twentieth Avenue, Vero Beach FL 32960. (407)770-0007. FAX: (407)770-0006. Senior Editor: Jan J. Binney. Estab. 1984. Publishes textbooks and instructional materials for speech-language pathologists, audiologists and special educators. Photos used for book covers, instructional materials and catalogs. Examples of recently published titles: *Talking Time* (cover); also catalogs.
Subject Needs: Children; children with adults; school scenes; elderly adults; handicapped persons of all ages.
Specs: Uses 8 × 10 glossy b&w prints. Full color for catalog.
Payment & Terms: NPI; negotiable. Buys all rights; negotiable. Model release required. Credit line "sometimes" given. Previously published work OK.
Making Contact: Interested in receiving work from newer, lesser-known photographers. Provide resume, business card, brochure, flyer or tearsheets to be kept on file for possible future assignments. Works on assignment plus purchases stock photos from time to time. SASE. Reports in 3 weeks.

*ST PUBLICATIONS, 407 Gilbert Ave., Cincinnati OH 45202. (531)421-2050. FAX: (531)421-5144. Manager: George B. Harper. Estab. 1906. Publishes professional books for the sign, screen printing and visual merchandising and store design industries. "Mostly how-to books." Photos used for text illustration and book covers. Buys 3 or 4 photos annually; offers 3 or 4 freelance assignments annually. Examples of recently published titles: *Practical Sign Shop Operation* and *Gold Leaf Techniques.*
Specs: Uses 5 × 9 color/b&w prints; 35mm, 2¼ × 2¼ transparencies.
Payment & Terms: NPI; payment negotiable according to job. Credit line given. Buys book rights; negotiable. Photos are used in advertisements. Model/property release required. Simultaneous submissions and previously published work OK.
Making Contact: Query with resume of credits. Query with samples. Works on assignment only. Reports in 3 months.
Tips: Judges the "quality of the photo, as well as the care given to capture the subject in a communicative way. Most of our work is with book authors. We need photos for illustrations. We will need to use more freelance photography in the future."

STANDARD EDUCATIONAL CORP., 200 W. Monroe St., Chicago IL 60606. (312)346-7440. FAX: (312)580-7215. Picture Editor: Irene L. Ferguson. Publishes the New Standard Encyclopedia. Photos used for text illustration. Buys stock photos only; about 300 photos/year. To see style/themes used, look at encyclopedias in library, especially New Standard Encyclopedia.
Subject Needs: Major cities and countries, points of interest, agricultural and industrial scenes, plants and animals. Photos are used to illustrate specific articles in encyclopedia — the subject range is from A-Z.
Specs: Uses 8 × 10 glossy b&w prints; contact sheet OK; uses transparencies.
Payment & Terms: Pays $75-125/b&w photo; $135-300/color photo. Credit line given. Buys one-time rights. Model release preferred; captions required.
Making Contact: Query with stock photo list. SASE. Do not send unsolicited photos. Simultaneous submissions and previously published work OK. Reports in 1 month.

STANDARD PUBLISHING, 8121 Hamilton Ave., Cincinnati OH 45231. (513)931-4050. Editor: Richard Briggs. Estab. 1866. Publishes adult trade books, journals, religious curriculum for all ages and children's books. Photos used for text illustration and book covers. Buys 300 freelance photos annually.
Subject Needs: Pictures of human interest — people of all ages, individuals and small groups involved in activities and family situations. People should have a natural appearance, not an artificial, posed, "too perfect" look. Pictures with a definite Christian connotation, such as a church, cross, a still life composed of a Bible, communion cup and bread, grapes, wheat, candle, lamp, etc., and other inspira-

---

The double dagger before a listing indicates that the market is located outside the United States and Canada. The symbol is new this year in Photographer's Market.

tional scenes and symbols. Pictures of landscapes, seascapes and natural forms or elements.
Specs: Use 8×10 b&w and color prints and also b&w and color transparencies.
Payment & Terms: Pays $25-50/b&w photo; $50-135/color inside; $120-200/color cover. Credit line usually given. Buys one-time and book rights. Model release required. Simultaneous submissions and previously published work OK "if known where."
Making Contact: Interested in receiving work from newer, lesser-known photographers. Query with samples/I.D. list. Reviews stock photos. SASE. Reports in 6-8 weeks.

STAR PUBLISHING COMPANY, 940 Emmett Ave., Belmont CA 94002. (415)591-3505. Managing Editor: Stuart Hoffman. Estab. 1978. Publishes textbooks, regional history, professional reference books. Photos used for text illustration, promotional materials and book covers. Recently published *Microbiology Techniques*, (cover and text illustration); *Keyboarding with Computer Applications*, (text illustration); and *Principles and Practices of Anaerobic Bacteriology*, (text illlustration).
Subject Needs: Biological illustrations, photomicrographs, business, industry and commerce.
Specs: Uses 5×7 minimum b&w and color prints, 35mm transparencies.
Payment & Terms: Pays $50/b&w photo; $100 up/color photo. Payment variable "depending on publication, placement and exclusivity." Credit line given. Buys one-time rights; negotiable. Model release and captions required. Previously published submissions OK.
Making Contact: Query with samples and list of stock photo subjects. Provide resume, business card, brochure, flyer or tearsheets to be kept on file for possible future assignments. Reviews stock photos. SASE. Reports within 90 days when a response is appropriate.
Tips: Wants to see photos that are technically (according to book's subject) correct, showing photographic excellence.

STONE WALL PRESS, INC., 1241 30th St. NW, Washington DC 20007. President: Henry Wheelwright. Estab. 1972. Publishes national outdoor/conservation books and nonfiction. Photos used for text illustration, book covers and dust jackets. Example of recently published title: *The Trout Unlimited Book of Basic Trout Fishing* (cover and text).
Subject Needs: Dramatic color cover shots; very occasionally representative text illustrations.
Specs: Uses 7×9 glossy color prints.
Payment & Terms: NPI. Credit line given. Buys one-time rights. Model release required; captions preferred. Simultaneous submissions and previously published work OK.
Making Contact: Provide resume, business card, brochure, flyer or tearsheets to be kept on file for possible future assignments. Reviews stock photos. Cannot return material.

THEOSOPHICAL PUBLISHING HOUSE, 306 W. Geneva Rd., P.O. Box 270, Wheaton IL 60189-0270. (708)665-0130. Production Manager: John White. Estab. 1875. Publishes adult trade books on metaphysics, comparative religions, oriental philosophies, theosophy, astrology, transpersonal psychology, and New Age topics. Photos used for text illustration, promotional materials, book covers and dust jackets. Buys 5-10 photos annually. Examples of recently published titles: *The Wholeness Principle* (cover), *Intelligence Came First* (cover) and *Goddess Re-Awakening*, (cover & text).
Subject Needs: Subjects that might evoke a spiritual experience. Top quality nature scenes.
Specs: Uses 5×7 glossy or matte b&w prints; 2¼×2¼ transparencies.
Payment & Terms: Pays $50-275/color photo, $25-150/b&w photo, pays in copies of books. Buys all rights; negotiable. Previously published work OK.
Making Contact: Query with samples. Provide resume, business card, brochure, flyer or tearsheets to be kept on file for possible future assignments. Reviews stock photos. SASE. Reports in 1 month.
Tips: "Send for our book catalog. Our text photo needs are limited. However, we are always seeking good color photos (transparencies) for covers. Ten to twelve new titles are published yearly." To break into publishing in general "examine closely each houses' catalogs to determine if their needs might be met by your specialty."

THORNDIKE PRESS, Box 159, Thorndike ME 04986. (207)948-2962. Art Director: Michael Anderson. Publishes adult trade in large print. Photos used for book covers and dust jackets. Buys 20 photos annually.
Subject Needs: "Types of photos depend on the particular project."
Specs: Uses 5×7 or larger b&w matte prints; 35mm, 2¼×2¼ and 4×5 transparencies.
Payment & Terms: Pays $20-300/b&w photo and $20-300/color photo. Credit line given. Buys one-time rights. Model release required; captions preferred. Simultaneous submissions and previously published work OK.
Making Contact: Query with non-returnable samples of work; interested in New England locales. SASE. Reports in 1 month.

TRANSPORTATION TRAILS, 9698 W. Judson Rd., Polo IL 61064. (815)946-2343. Editor: Larry Plachmo. Estab. 1977. Publishes historical transportation titles. Photos used for text illustration, promotional materials, book covers, dust jackets and condensed articles in magazines. Buys over 500 photos annually. Examples of recently published titles: *The Longest Interurban Charter* (text and cover); *Sunset Lines – The Story of The Chicago Aurora & Elgin Railroad* (text); *The Steam Locomotive Directory of North America* (text).
Subject Needs: Transportation, mainly bus or interurban, mainly historical.
Specs: Uses glossy b&w prints; 35mm transparencies.
Payment & Terms: Rates vary depending on needs; $2.50-150/b&w photo. Credit line given. Buys one-time, book and all rights; negotiable. Model release preferred. "Company name, date and location are expected on photo or slides." Simultaneous submissions and previously published work OK.
Making Contact: Query with samples of historical transportation photos. Reviews stock photos. SASE. Reports in 1 week.
Tips: In photographer's samples, "quality is not as important as location and date." Looks for "historical photos of buses and interurbans. Don't bother us with photos less than 30 years old."

*THE TRINITY FOUNDATION, Box 700, Jefferson MD 21755. (301)371-7155. President: John Robbins. Estab. 1978. Publishes religion and philosophy and adult trade paperbacks. Photos used for book covers.
Specs: Uses any size color transparencies.
Payment & Terms: NPI. Credit line given. Buys book rights. Model release, photo captions preferred. Simultaneous submissions and previously published work OK.
Making Contact: Query with samples. Reviews stock photos. SASE. Reports in 1 month.
Tips: Looks for "sharp, clear pictures related to Christianity and philosophy."

2M COMMUNICATIONS LTD., 121 W. 27 St., New York NY 10001. (212)741-1509. FAX: (212)691-4460. President: Madeleine Morel. Estab. 1982. Publishes adult trade biographies. Photos used for text illustration. Buys approximately 200 photos annually. Examples of previously published titles: *Diane Keaton, Magic and the Bird* and *The Princess and the Duchess;* all for text illustration.
Subject Needs: Candids and publicity.
Specs: Uses b&w prints; 35mm transparencies.
Payment & Terms: Pays $100-200/color photo, $50-100/b&w photo. Credit line given. Buys one-time book and world English language rights. Model release required; photo captions preferred. Simultaneous submissions OK.
Making Contact: Query with stock photo list. Reviews stock photos. Reports in 1 month.

TYNDALE HOUSE PUBLISHERS, 351 Executive Dr., Wheaton IL 60189. (708)668-8300. Photo Editor: Marlene Muddell. Estab. 1960. Publishes books "on a wide variety of subjects from a Christian perspective." Photos used for book jackets and text illustration. Buys 125 photos annually. Examples of recently published titles: *Bible Discovery Collection: Bible Animals* (inside editorial); *Life Application Bible Study Guides Series* (covers); and *Great Christmas Ideas* (cover).
Subject Needs: Nature, conservation and people, especially families of mixed ages and backgrounds. Especially needed are color photos of various ethnics working together.
Specs: Uses 8 × 10 glossy b&w prints, for text and cover; transparencies for cover.
Payment & Terms: Pays $75-150/b&w inside photo and $200-1,000/cover photo. The upper-end figures are offered for high-quality work. Buys one-time, nonexclusive world rights for the life of the product; negotiable. Model/property release required; all photos using people regardless of situation or event require release. Previously published work OK "if in non-competitive books."
Making Contact: Call before sending photos. Cannot return submissions.
Tips: "The best photos for our use usually tell a story. We want to see only your best work. We are looking only for unique, fresh images. We do not publish portraitures. Keep in mind that book covers require titles when shooting. Photos should be clean from background and landscape clutter. We need high quality transparenecies of various ethnic groups or people working together for a common goal. We need family shots that tell a story – especially families of different races. We also need intergenerational photos and photos that tell about America's elderly, but in a positive way."

UNIVELT, INC., P.O. Box 28130, San Diego CA 92198. (619)746-4005. Manager: H. Jacobs. Estab. 1970. Publishes technical books on astronautics. Photos used for text illustration and dust jackets. Examples of recently published titles: *Men & Woman of Space* and *History of Rocketry and Astronautics*. Photos used for front cover.

Subject Needs: Uses astronautics; most interested in photographer's concept of space, and photos depicting space flight and related areas.
Specs: Uses 6×9 or 4½×6 b&w photos.
Payment & Terms: Pays $25-100/b&w photo. Credit line given, if desired. Buys one-time rights. Captions required. Simultaneous submissions and previously published work OK.
Making Contact: Interested in receiving work from newer, lesser-known photographers. Query with resume of credits. Provide business card and letter of inquiry to be kept on file for possible future assignments. Reviews stock photos: space related only. SASE. Reports in 1 month.
Tips: "Photos should be suitable for front cover or frontispiece of space books."

UNIVERSITY PUBLICATIONS OF AMERICA, Suite 800, 4520 East-West Hwy., Bethesda MD 20814-3389. (301)657-3200, ext. 625. Print Production Manager: Doris Brown. Publishes mostly foreign intelligence and history-type books—some subjects include *The Secret War in Central America*—current history; also Indian Documents; some books on Apartheid are upcoming. Uses photos for promotional materials and dust jackets. Buys no photos at present.
Subject Needs: Portraits, actual scenes of the important events.
Specs: Uses 5×7 or 8×10 matte b&w prints.
Payment & Terms: NPI. "Since we have not yet used services like these we have no information; we are 'shopping' to see how cost effective it would be for us to use freelance photography." Buys one-time rights or book rights. Model release and captions preferred. Simultaneous submissions and previously published work OK.
Making Contact: Query with list of stock photo subjects. Send unsolicited photos by mail for consideration. Provide resume, business card, brochure, flyer or tearsheets to be kept on file for possible future assignments. SASE. Reporting time depends on project.

*VAN PATTEN PUBLISHING, 4204 S.E. Ogden St., Portland OR 97206. (503)775-3815. FAX: (503)775-3815. Owner: George Van Patten. Estab. 1990. Publishes garden books. Photos used for book covers. Buys 2-10 photos annually. Examples of recently published titles: *Organic Garden Vegetables* (cover), *Gardening Indoors* (cover) and *Gardening: The Rockwood Book* (cover).
Specs: Uses 35mm, 2¼×2¼, 4×5, 8×10 transparencies.
Payment & Terms: Pays $100-300/color photo. Credit line given. Buys one-time, book and all rights; negotiable. Model/property release preferred. Captions required; include variety of plant, city, state and climate zone. Simultaneous submissions and previously published work OK.
Making Contact: Query with stock photo list. Reviews stock photos. Keeps samples on file. SASE. Reports in 1 month.
Tips: Wants photos with vertical format, strong composition and clarity of focus. "Show me your best work. We use color photos for covers only."

VICTIMOLOGY, INC., 2333 N. Vernon St., Arlington VA 22207. (703)528-3387. Photography Director: Sherry Icenhower. Publishes books about victimology focusing on the victims not only of crime but also of occupational and environmental hazards. Examples of recently published titles: *Spouse Abuse, Child Abuse, Fear of Crime* and *Self-defense*. Photos used for text illustration. Buys 20-30 photos/year.
Specs: Send b&w contact sheet or 8×10 glossy prints; color contact sheet or 5×7 or 8×10 glossy prints; 35mm transparencies.
Payment & Terms: Pays $30-150/color photos. Buys all rights, but may reassign to photographer after publication. Submit model release with photo. Captions required.
Making Contact: "We will look at color photos only if part of an essay with text." Reports in 6 weeks. SASE. Simultaneous submissions and previously published work OK.

J. WESTON WALCH, PUBLISHER, 321 Valley St., P.O. Box 658, Portland ME 04104-0658. (207)772-2846. FAX: (207)772-3105. Contact: Acquisitions. Estab. 1927. Publishes supplementary educational materials for grades 6-12 and adult education. All subject areas. Photos used for text illustration, promotional materials and book covers. Buys 5-10 or more photos/year; varies widely. Offers up to 5 freelance assignments annually. Examples of recently published titles: *True Adventure Readers* (3 Art series) (cover photos); *Steps to Good Grammar* (cover photo) and *Science and Social Issues* (text illustration).
Subject Needs: Black and white and color photos of middle school and high school students, ethnically diverse, in-school, library or real-life situations; historical photos, current events photos, special needs students and chemistry, ecology and biology.
Specs: Uses 8×10 glossy b&w prints; also 35mm, 2¼×2¼, 4×5 and 8×10 transparencies.
Payment & Terms: Pays $35-100/b&w; $200-400/color photo. Credit line sometimes given depending on photographer's request. Buys one-time rights. Model release required; photo captions preferred.
Making Contact: Interested in receiving work from newer, lesser-known photographers. Provide resume, business card, brochure, flyer or tearsheets to be kept on file for possible future assignments. Reviews stock photos. SASE.

Tips: One trend with this company is a "growing use of b&w and color photos for book covers." Especially wants to see "subjects/styles suitable for use in secondary schools."

WARNER BOOKS, 9th Floor, 1271 Avenue of the Americas, New York NY 10020. (212)522-7200. Creative Director: Jackie Merri Meyer. Publishes "everything but text books." Photos used for book covers and dust jackets. Buys approximately 20 freelance photos and offers approximately 30 assignments annually.
Subject Needs: People, food still life, glamourous women and couples.
Specs: Uses color prints/transparencies; also some b&w and hand-tinting.
Payment & Terms: Pays $800/color photo; $650-1,200/job. Credit line given. Buys one-time rights. Model release required; captions preferred. Simultaneous submissions and previously published work OK.
Making Contact: Submit portfolio for review. Send brochure, flyer or tearsheets to be kept on file for possible future assignments. Reviews stock photos. Cannot return unsolicited material.
Tips: "Printed and published work (color copies are OK, too) are very helpful. Do not call, we do not remember names—we remember samples—be persistent. Drop book off as often as possible and leave samples."

WASATCH PUBLISHERS, 4460 Ashford Dr., Salt Lake City UT 84124. (801)278-5826. Publisher: John Veranth. Estab. 1973. Publishes books on outdoor recreation. Photos used for text illustration and book covers. Buys 50 photos annually. Examples of recently published titles: *Wasatch Winter Trails*, (cover, text illustration); and *Canyon Country Camping* (cover, text illustration).
Subject Needs: Hiking and other muscle-powered sports. Emphasis on Utah and Wyoming.
Specs: Uses b&w prints; 35mm transparencies.
Payment & Terms: Pays $5-25/b&w photo. Credit line given. Buys book rights. Model release preferred. Photo captions required; include location. Simultaneous submissions and previously published work OK.
Making Contact: Query with list of stock photo subjects. Provide resume, business card, brochure, flyer or tearsheets to be kept on file for possible future assignments. SASE. Reports in 2 weeks.

*●WEIGL EDUCATIONAL PUBLISHERS LIMITED, 2114 College Ave., Regina SK S4T 7V9 Canada. (306)569-0766. FAX: (306)757-4721. Senior Editor: Iain MacDonald. Estab. 1979. Publishes textbooks and educational resources: social studies, life skills, environment/science studies, multicultural, language arts and geography. Photos used for text illustration and book covers. Buys 15-25 photos annually; offers 2-3 freelance assignments annually. Examples of recently published titles: *Alberta Our Province*, *The Living Soil: A Renewable Resource* and *The Living Soil: Land Use and Society*.
Subject Needs: Social issues and events, politics, education, technology, people gatherings, multicultural, environment, science, agriculture, life skills, landscape, wildlife and people doing daily activities.
Specs: Uses 5×7, 3×5, 4×6, 8×10 color/b&w prints; 35mm, 2¼×2¼ transparencies.
Payment & Terms: Pays $15 or more for images used in publication, including publication fee. Price is negotiable. Credit line given (photo credits as appendix). Buys one-time, book and all rights; negotiable. Model/property release required. Captions required. Simultaneous submissions and previously published work OK.
Making Contact: Query with samples. Query with stock photo list. Provide tearsheets to be kept on file for possible future assignments. Tearsheets or samples that don't have to be returned are best. Reviews stock photos. Keeps samples on file. SASE. "We generally get in touch when we actually need photos."
Tips: Need "clear, well-framed shots that don't look posed. Action, expression, multicultural representation are important, but above all, education value is sought. People must know what they are looking at. Please keep notes on what is taking place, where and when. As an educational publisher, our books use specific examples as well as general illustrations."

*SAMUEL WEISER INC., P.O. Box 612, York Beach ME 03910. (207)363-4393. Art Director: Phillip Augusta. Estab. 1956. Publishes books on esoterica, oriental philosophy, alternative health and mystery traditions. Photos used for book covers. Buys 2-6 photos annually. Examples of recently published titles: *Heisler: Path to Power* (cover), *Durkheim: Japanese Cult of Tranquility* (cover) and *Bennett: Idiots in Pan's* (cover).
Subjects Needs: Photos of flowers, abstracts (such as sky, paths, roads, sunsets) and inspirational themes.
Specs: Uses color prints, 2¼×2¼ and 4×5 transparencies.
Payment & Terms: Pays $100-200/color photo. Credit line given. Buys book rights; negotiable. "We pay once for life of book because we do small runs." Simultaneous submissions and previously published work OK.

Making Contact: Query with samples. Send unsolicited photos by mail for consideration. Provide resume, business card, brochure, flyer or tearsheets to be kept on file for possible future assignments. "We'll take color snapshots to keep on file, or color copies." Reviews stock photos. Keeps samples on file. SASE. Reports in 1 month. Photo guidelines free with SASE.

Tips: "We like to keep inexpensive proofs because we may see a nice photo and not have anything to use it on now. We search our files for covers, usually on tight deadline. We don't want to see goblins and halloween costumes."

THE WHEETLEY COMPANY, INC., Suite 1100, 4709 Golf Rd., Skokie IL 60076. (708)675-4443. General Manager: Julie Kuppenheimer. Estab. 1986. Produces elementary and high school textbooks in all subjects. Photos used for text illustration and book covers. Examples of recently produced books: *World Geography* (photos used for text and cover illustration, Scholastic); *Mathematics of Money* (photos used for text and cover illustration, South-Western).

Subject Needs: Subject matter depends upon the book being produced. Most photos used are "unposed." Photos frequently call for pictures of children and young people, including minorities.

Specs: Uses glossy b&w prints; 35mm, 2¼ × 2¼, 4 × 5 transparencies.

Payment & Terms: Pays $135-165/quarter page of color photos; $60-120/quarter page of b&w photos. Credit line sometimes given depending on the "style established for the book." Buys one-time, North American or world rights. Model releases/photo captions preferred. Simultaneous submissions and previously published work OK.

Making Contact: Query with list of stock photo subjects. Provide resume, business card, brochure, flyer or tearsheets to be kept on file for possible future assignments. Reviews stock photos. Cannot return unsolicited material. Reports in 1 month.

Tips: Send all information attention: Linda Rogers, Human Resources Manager.

WIESER & WIESER, INC., 118 E. 25th St., New York NY 10010. (212)260-0860. FAX: (212) 505-7186. Editor: George J. Wieser. Estab. 1975. Publishes adult trade—how-to, cooking, travel and history. Photos used for text illustration and book covers. Serves industrial clients. Buys 1,000 photos and offers 12 freelance assignments annually.

Specs: Uses 35mm and 4 × 5 transparencies.

Payment & Terms: Pays $20-100/color photo, $15-50/b&w photo; $2,500-4,000/job. Buys all rights; negotiable. Model release required; photo captions preferred.

Making Contact: Query with resume of credits and samples. Works on assignment only. SASE. Reports in 3 weeks.

JOHN WILEY & SONS, INC., 605 3rd Ave., New York NY 10158. (212)850-6731. Photo Research Director: Stella Kupferberg. Estab. 1807. Publishes college texts in all fields. Photos used for text illustration. Buys 4,000 photos/year. Examples of recently published titles: *Geography* by deBlij; *Physics* by Cutnell; and *Psychology* by Huffman. In all three titles, 200+ photos used for text and cover illustration.

Subject Needs: Uses b&w and color photos for textbooks in psychology, business, computer science, biology, chemistry, geography, geology and foreign languages.

Specs: Uses 8 × 10 glossy and semigloss b&w prints; also 35mm and large format transparencies.

Payment & Terms: Pays $75-125/b&w print and $100-175/color transparency. Credit line given. Captions required. Simultaneous submissions and previously published work OK.

Making Contact: Query with list of stock photo subjects. SASE. "We return all photos securely wrapped between double cardboard by UPS."

Tips: "Initial contact should spell out the material photographer specializes in, rather than a general inquiry about our photo needs. Tearsheets and flyers welcome."

WISCONSIN TRAILS BOOKS, P.O. Box 5650, Madison WI 53705. (608)231-2444. Production Manager: Nancy Mead. Estab. 1960. Publishes adult nonfiction, guide books and photo essays. Photos used for text illustration and book covers. Buys many photos and gives large number of freelance assignments annually. Recently published: *Oh Wisconsin*, all photographs and *Best Wisconsin Bike Trips*, cover and ⅓ inside-photos.

Subject Needs: Wisconsin nature and historic scenes and activities.

Specs: Uses 5 × 7 or 8 × 10 b&w prints and any size transparencies.

Payment & Terms: Pays $25-75/b&w photo; $50-175/color photo. Credit line given. Buys one-time rights. Location information for captions preferred. Simultaneous submissions and previously published work OK.

Making Contact: Query with samples or stock photo list. Send unsolicited photos by mail for consideration. Provide resume to be kept on file for possible assignments. SASE. Reports in 1 month. Photo guidelines free on request with SASE.

If there ever was a photo that fit perfectly with a topic this may be it. This very captivating image of a winding dirt path inside a face was created by German photographer Stephen King and serves as a perfect illustration for a book on mental strength. Phillip Augusta, art director for book publisher Samuel Weiser, Inc., learned of King's work at a book fair in Frankfurt.

WORD PUBLISHING, 5221 N. O'Connor, Irving TX 75239. (214)556-1900. Design Director: Tom Williams. Estab. 1951. Publishes Christian books. Photos used for book covers, publicity, brochures, posters, product advertising and stock photos. Examples of recently published titles: *The New World Order* by Pat Robertson; *Why America Doesn't Work* by Chuck Colson and Jack Eckerd; and *Miracle Man: Nolan Ryan Autobiography*. Photos used for covers.
Subject Needs: Nature, portraits, studio shots and special effects.
Payment & Terms: Assignment prices determined by job. Pays for stock $350-550. Credit line given. Buys all rights "for the life of the product." Model release required; property release preferred.
Making Contact: Provide business card, brochure, flyer or tearsheets to be kept on file for possible future assignments. SASE. Reports in 1 month. Please don't call.
Tips: In portfolio or samples, looking for people, nature, strikingly lighted shots of symbolic elements in nature, good composition, clarity of subject. Something unique and unpredictable. "We use the same kinds of photos as the secular market. I don't need crosses, church windows, steeples, or wheat waving in the sunset. We are very busy with internal schedules. Don't phone. Don't send just a letter. Send your best work only. Give me something to look at, not to read about." Opportunity is quite limited: "We have hundreds of photographers on file, and we use about 3% of them."

WRITERS PUBLISHING SERVICE CO., 1512 Western Ave., Seattle WA 98101. (206)284-9954. Publisher: William R. Griffin. "We publish all types of books for independent authors, plus 10 to 15 books under our own imprint." Photos used for text illustration, promotional materials, book covers and dust jackets. Uses 80-100 freelance photos and offers 50 freelance assignments annually.
Subject Needs: Open to all types of material. Separate division of company especially interested in photos of cleaning- and maintenance-related duties.
Specs: Uses 5×7 and 8×10 glossy b&w and color prints.
Payment & Terms: Pays $5-50 per b&w photo. Credit line given. Buys one-time, book or all rights; negotiable. Model release preferred; captions required. Simultaneous submissions and previously published work OK.
Making Contact: Query with samples, or stock photo list. Submit portfolio for review. Contact regarding ideas. Works with local freelancers on assignment only. SASE. Reports within 30 days.
Tips: Prefers "original, creative, clear shots. Contact publishers to find out what they want, then shoot to fill that need. Be willing to pay your dues. Don't give up, but be realistic about income potential in early phases of career. There is more use of photos and illustrations by book publishers. Don't just send us standard sample shots. Send items that relate specifically to our market and needs."

Book Publishers/'92-93 changes

The following markets appeared in the 1992 edition of *Photographer's Market* but are not listed in the 1993 edition.

Abbey Press (not reviewing work)
APA Publications (did not respond)
ARCsoft Publishers (did not respond)
Ashley Books, Inc. (did not respond)
Berkley Books (did not respond)
Blue Bird Publishing (did not respond)
Bowker, R.R. (not reviewing work)
Broadman Press (not reviewing work)
Capra Press (did not respond)
Catholic Press Association of the United States (did not respond)
Congressional Information Service (not reviewing work)
Cook Publishing Co., David C. (did not respond)
Dillon Press, Inc. (sold to Macmillan and Co.)
Fell Publishers, Inc. (not re

viewing work)
Fulcrum Publishing (did not respond)
Gallaudet University Press (not reviewing work)
Grand Canyon Natural History Association (not reviewing work)
Harrison House Publishers (did not respond)
Lion Publishing (did not respond)
Liturgy Training Publications (did not respond)
New Leaf Press, Inc. (did not respond)
Newbury House Publishers Inc. (did not respond)
Nitech Research Corporation (did not respond)
Northland Publishing (not reviewing work)
Norton and Company, W.W. (did not respond)
Praxis Publications Inc. (not reviewing work)
St. Anthony Messenger Press

(not reviewing work)
St. Martin's Press Inc. (did not respond)
Smithsonian (Books) Institution (not reviewing work)
South-Western Publishing Company (did not respond)
Stewart, Tabori & Chang (not reviewing work)
T.F.H. Publications, Inc. (did not respond)
Trumpet Club, The/Bantam/Doubleday/Dell, The (did not respond)
Waterfront Books (did not respond)
Western Producer Prairie Books (no longer publishing books)
White Cliffs Media Company (did not respond)
Windsor Publications, Inc. (did not respond)
Workman Publishing Co. Inc. (did not respond)
Wyrick & Company (not reviewing work)

Businesses and Organizations

The field of commercial photography covers a lot of ground, from shooting food and health care products to sports cars and portraits. It is an area in which photographers can use their *own* artistic visions to make a company or its products look good because there are fewer restraints imposed by artistic directors. Another bonus in this market is that photographers who become well-known for innovative and technically excellent images can make a healthy profit.

Working with prestigious companies, or even respected nonprofit organizations, lends credibility and prestige to an artist's work. Such assignments serve as important promotional tools for the photographer and can draw in even more clients through referrals. (For more on self-promotion please see Maria Piscopo's article beginning on page 5).

With more than 3 million businesses and many more organizations of various types in this country, freelance photographers interested in working directly with clients have many potential prospects. This section in *Photographer's Market* offers just a sampling of many different types of for-profit businesses as well as nonprofit associations or institutions. While many companies and organizations may already be working with advertising or public relations firms for promoting their products and activities, the listings in this section also welcome direct contact from freelancers.

You will find a wide range of markets, from major corporations such as insurance companies to public interest and trade associations to universities and arts organizations. The types of photography which these listings usually require overlap somewhat with advertising markets. However, unlike that work which is largely directed toward external media or audiences, the photography for listings in this section tends to be more for specialized applications. Among these are employee or membership commmunications, annual reports, and documentary purposes such as recording meetings and other group functions or theatrical presentations.

A fair number of these listings are receptive to stock images, while many have rather specific needs for which they assign photographers. These projects will sometimes require studio-type skills (again similar to the advertising/PR market), particularly in shooting corporate interiors and portraits of executives for annual reports. However, much of the coverage of meetings, events and performances calls for a different set of skills involving use of available light and fill flash. In particular, coverage of sporting events or theatrical performances may require agility with extreme or rapidly changing light conditions.

Unless these businesses and organizations are active at the national level, they typically prefer to work with local freelancers. Rates will vary widely depending upon the individual client's budget. We have tried to list current rates of payment where possible, but some listings have still only indicated "negotiable terms," or a per-shot, per-hour or per-day basis. Listings which have not provided a specific dollar amount now include the code NPI, for "no payment information given." When quoting a price, especially for assigned work, remember to start with a basic day rate plus expenses and negotiate for final number of images, types of usage and time period for usage.

In particular, many of these clients wish to buy all rights to the images since they are often assigned for specific needs. In such cases, be sure to negotiate your terms in such a way that these clients get all the rights they need but that you also ultimately retain the copyrights. (For more on this, see Copyright/rights, in the Business of Photography on page 11).

Another tendency which this market has in common with advertising and PR is the occasional to regular need for audiovisual materials. Listings in this section with any kind of audiovisual, film or video needs have been marked with special AV symbol—a solid, black square—before the listing's name for easier recognition. Some of the listings also include more detailed descriptions under the subheading, Audiovisual Needs.

On page 172, Kathy Getsey of Whittle Communications in Knoxville, Tennessee, outlines her likes and dislikes when it comes to dealing with photographers and she provides insight into the field.

*ALFRED PUBLISHING CO., INC., P.O. Box 10003, Van Nuys CA 91410-0003. Art Director: Ted Engelbart. Estab. 1922.
Needs: Photos of musical instruments. Examples of recent uses: Educational music book covers (4×5); Yamaha Band Student ad campaign (2¼×2¼) and brochures for sales promotions (35mm and 2¼×2¼).
Specs: Uses 35mm, 2¼×2¼, 4×5, 8×10 transparencies.
Payment & Terms: Pays $150-600/job. Buys all rights (unless stock); negotiable. Model/property release required for people and music halls.
Making Contact: Provide resume, self-promotion piece or tearsheets to be kept on file for possible future assignments. Works on assignment only. Reviews stock photos/footage of musical instruments. Does not report back, keeps on file.
Tips: "Send requested profile. Do not call. Provide any price or release requirements." Looks for "graphic or mood presentation of musical instruments; general interest such as fireworks, Americana, landscapes."

ALLRIGHT CORPORATION, Suite 1300, 1111 Fannin St., Houston TX 77002. (713)222-2505. FAX: (713)222-6833. National Director of Public Relations: H. M. Sinclair. Estab. 1926. Company operates in 87 cities in the US and Canada. Uses photos of parking facilities, openings, before and after shots, unusual parking situations, and Allright facilities.
Needs: Photos used in brochures, newsletters, newspapers, audiovisual presentations and catalogs.
Specs: Uses 8×10 glossy b&w or color prints; also 35mm transparencies.
Payment & Terms: Pays $25 minimum/hour or on a per-photo basis. Buys all rights. Model release preferred.
Making Contact: Arrange a personal interview to show portfolio. Provide resume, brochure, flyer and tearsheets to be kept on file for future assignments. Does not notify photographer if future assignments can be expected. SASE. Reports in 2 weeks.
Tips: "We hire local photographers in our individual operating cities through the local manager, or directly by phone with photographers listed at national headquarters, or by prints, etc. sent in with prices from local cities to national headquarters or through local city headquarters."

AMATEUR SOFTBALL ASSOCIATION, 2801 NE 50th St., Oklahoma City OK 73111. (405)424-5266. Director of Fund Raising, Publications and Communications: Ronald A. Babb. Media/PR Director: Bill Plummer III. Promotion of amateur softball. Buys 3-4 photos/year; offers 2-3 assignments annually. Photos used in newsletter, newspapers.
Needs: Subjects include action sports shots.
Specs: Uses 8½×11 prints.
Payment & Terms: Pays $20/b&w photo; $50/color photo. Credit line given. Buys all rights. Model release preferred; captions required. SASE. Reports in 2 weeks.
Making Contact: Contact ASA National office first before doing any work.

*AMERICAN ALLIANCE FOR HEALTH, PHYSICAL EDUCATION RECREATION AND DANCE, 1900 Association Dr., Reston VA 22091. (703)476-3400. FAX: (703)476-9527. Director of Publications: Debra H. Lewin. Estab. 1885. Buys 50 photos/year; offers 2-3 assignments/year. Photos used in brochures, newsletters, magazines and catalogs.
Needs: Wants photos of sports, recreation, outdoor activities, health practices, physical education and other education specific settings, handicapped and special populations are also interested.
Audiovisual Needs: Uses slides.
Specs: Uses all sizes and finishes of b&w and color prints; 35mm transparencies; 35mm film.
Payment & Terms: Pays $100/color photo; $25/b&w photo. Pays upon usage. Credit line given. Buys one-time rights; negotiable. Model/property release preferred, especially for children and handicapped.

Making Contact: Query with stock photo list. Provide resume, business card, self-promotion piece or tearsheets to be kept on file for possible future assignments. Call. Reviews stock photos. Keeps samples on file. SASE. Reports in 1-2 weeks.
Tips: "We are always looking for strong action or emotion. We usually need vertical formats for magazine covers with color work."

AMERICAN ASSOCIATION FOR VOCATIONAL INSTRUCTIONAL MATERIALS (AAVIM), 745 Gaines School Rd., Athens GA 30605. (404)543-7557. Production Coordinator: Jim Wren. Estab. 1949. Photos used in catalogs and textbooks.
Needs: Freelancers are used to shoot covers and illustrations depending upon subjects. Examples of recent uses: "GMAW/GTAW Welding" (cover, 2¼ × 2¼); "Roof Framing" (cover, 2¼ × 2¼) and "Diesel Engines" (cover, 2¼ × 2¼).
Specs: Uses 5 × 7 glossy b&w prints; 35mm, 2¼ × 2¼ transparencies.
Payment & Terms: NPI; "prefer to work from quoted price of photographer." Pays on acceptance. Credit line sometimes given depending on requests and difference in price. Buys all rights. Model and/ or property release preferred. Usually needed for photos of businesses, schools or personal release.
Making Contact: Provide resume, business card, self-promotion piece or tearsheets to be kept on file for possible future assignments. Interested in stock photos. Does not keep samples on file. SASE.
Tips: "Cover shots need to be clear and interesting in either composition or lighting. Text illustrations must be very clear and emphasize subject of illustrations or activity."

AMERICAN DENTAL HYGIENISTS' ASSOCIATION, 444 N. Michigan Ave., Chicago IL 60611. (312)440-8900. Contact: Jean Majesky. Publishes journal 9 times/year. Buys 4 photos/year; gives 6 assignments/year. Photos used in posters and magazines.
Needs: Photos of dental hygienists; young, professional women; children with good smiles; older citizens. Special subject needs include hazards in the workplace, sexual harassment, AIDS.
Specs: Uses 35mm, 2¼ × 2¼, 4 × 5 transparencies; b&w and color contact sheets.
Payment & Terms: Pays $35-200/b&w photo; $300-500/color photo. Credit line given. Buys one-time rights. Model release required.
Making Contact: Query with resume of credits and with samples. Solicits photos by assignment only. Does not return unsolicited material. Reports in 1 week.
Tips: Prefers to see clarity, quality, good graphic potential and creativity—the ability to illustrate a subject in a fresh way. "Work closely with a dental professional when shooting a technical shot. Members of our association are extremely particular about the popular depiction of dental hygienists."

AMERICAN FUND FOR ALTERNATIVES TO ANIMAL RESEARCH, Suite 16-G, 175 W. 12th St., New York NY 10011. (212)989-8073. Contact: Dr. E. Thurston. Finances research to develop research methods which will not need live animals. Also informs the public of this and about current methods of experimentation.
Needs: Needs b&w or color photos of laboratory animal experimentation and animal use connected with fashions (trapping) and cosmetics (tests on animals). Uses photography for reports, advertising and publications. Buys 10+ freelance photos/year; gives 5+ freelance assignments/year.
Specs: Uses 5 × 7 b&w prints. Also uses 16mm film for educational films.
Payment & Terms: Pays $5 minimum/b&w photo, $5 or more/color photo; $30 minimum/job. Credit line given. Buys one-time rights and exclusive product rights; arranged with photographer. Model release preferred.
Making Contact: Arrange a personal interview to show portfolio; query with samples and list of stock photo subjects. Provide brochure and flyer to be kept on file for possible future assignments. Notifies photographer if future assignments can be expected. SASE. Reports in 2 weeks.
Tips: In portfolios or samples wants to "see clear pictures of animals in cosmetic tests or testing labs, or fur ranches, and in the wilds."

*AMERICAN MUSEUM OF NATURAL HISTORY LIBRARY, PHOTOGRAPHIC COLLECTION, Library Services Department, Central Park West, 79th St., New York NY 10024. (212)769-5419. FAX: (212) 769-5233. Manager, Special Collections: Andrea LaSala. Estab. 1869. Provides services for advertisers, authors, film and TV producers, general public, government agencies, picture researchers, publishers, scholars, students and teachers who use photos for brochures, newsletters, posters, newspapers, annual reports, catalogs, magazines, books and exhibits.

The asterisk before a listing indicates that the market is new in this edition. New markets are often the most receptive to freelance submissions.

Payment & Terms: "We accept only donations with full rights (non-exclusive) to use; we offer visibility through credits. Buys all rights. Credit line given. Model release and captions required.
Making Contact: Interested in receiving work from newer, lesser-known photographers.
Tips: "We do not review portfolios. Unless the photographer is willing to give up rights and provide images for donation with full rights (credit lines are given), the museum is not willing to accept work."

■AMERICAN POWER BOAT ASSOCIATION, 17640 E. Nine Mile Rd., Box 377, East Detroit MI 48021. (313)773-9700. Executive and Publications Editor: Renee Mahn Olejnik. Managing Editor: Marie Masters. Estab. 1903. Sanctioning body for US power boat racing; monthly magazine. Majority of assignments made on annual basis. Photos used in monthly magazine, brochures, audiovisual presentations, press releases and programs.
Needs: Power boat racing—action and candid.
Specs: Uses 5×7 and up, b&w prints and b&w contact sheets; 35mm slides for cover.
Payment & Terms: Payment varies. Standard is $50 for cover; $15 for inside. Credit line given. Buys one-time rights; negotiable. Captions required. Photo usage must be invoiced by photographer within the month incurred.
Making Contact: Interested in receiving work from newer, lesser-known photographers. Initial personal contact preferred. Send unsolicited photos by mail for consideration; provide resume, business card, brochure, flyer or tearsheets to be kept on file for possible future assignments. SASE. Reports in 2 weeks when needed. "Suggests initial contact by phone possibly to be followed by evaluating samples."
Tips: Prefers to see selection of shots of power boats in action or pit shots, candids, etc., (all identified). Must show ability to produce clear b&w action shots of racing events.

AMERICAN RED CROSS, Photographic Services, 431 18th St. NW, Washington DC 20006. (202)639-3560. Photographic Manager: Joseph Matthews.
Needs: Photos used to illustrate annual reports, articles, slide shows, ads and brochures. Model release must accompany photo. "We need pictures of Red Cross volunteers working to provide the range of service to the public that the organization does, especially dramatic scenes at disasters. The ability to capture a 'moment' or the interaction between people is important. Never present yourself as shooting for the Red Cross unless you are currently under contract to do so." "Needs" list not available. "We use people pictures and do not want to see scenic, art, portraits or generic photographs. Quality should be very high."
Specs: Send b&w contact sheet or 8×10 glossy prints. For color, send 35mm or larger transparencies.
Payment & Terms: Assignment varies according to type and length of assignment and rights purchased; payment depends on applications to Red Cross and rights purchased. "We distribute photographs to all chapters nationally and cannot control use. We normally buy unlimited, nonexclusive rights."
Making Contact: Query by mail to describe material available. *Do not send unsolicited photographs.* Because of small staff size we can only respond to specific queries. No general mailings will be answered."
Tips: "We have photographers on staff, so we use freelancers infrequently. We are interested in knowing photojournalists in other areas of the U.S. who could provide coverage there if the need should arise. If in the Washington, D.C. area, call for an interview; if in other areas, send an introductory letter stating the type of work you do best and some samples of your published work. Take the time to research the type of work the Red Cross does; if you have the skill and the interest to help us support the goals of the Red Cross, contact me. Please also contact your local chapter. Many need newsletter and annual report photography, although this is best for 'new' photographers since many chapters have little or no budget for pictures. Volunteering time and work can sometimes get you published. Edit yourself more critically. Also, get opinion of someone whom you trust about your portfolio *before* you show it around."

AMERICAN SOCIETY FOR THE PREVENTION OF CRUELTY TO ANIMALS (ASPCA), 424 E. 92nd St., New York NY 10128. (212)876-7700 Ext. 3249. FAX: (212) 348-3031. Photo Editor: Dave McMichael. Estab. 1866. Publishes quarterly newsletter, pamphlets, booklets. Examples: *Traveling With Your Pet* and *ASPCA Magazine.*
Needs: Photos of animals (domestic and wildlife): farm, domestic, lab, stray and homeless animals, endangered, trapped, injured, fur animals, marine and wildlife. Also, rain forest scenes and wildlife.
Payment & Terms: Pays $30/b&w photo (inside use); $35/color photo (inside use); $100 for cover use. Buys one-time rights; negotiable. Credit line given. Model and property releases preferred.
Making Contact: Interested in receiving work from newer, lesser-known photographers. Provide brochure and resume to be kept on file for possible future assignments. SASE. Reports when needed. Please send a detailed, alphabetized stock list that can be kept on file for future reference.

Tips: "I'm looking for good clear slides and sharp black and white prints. Of course, I look for mainly animal-related photos. It's nice to see unique work with a different look to it. Photos that tell the story. A description of each photo is helpful." Freelancers should "realize that the ASPCA is a nonprofit organization, so it has a small budget for photos."

AMERICAN SOUVENIR & NOVELTY COMPANY, P.O. Box 9, Lebanon OR 97355. (503)259-1471. President: Edward Black. Manufactures souvenirs. Buys about 100 freelance photos annually. Uses photos for souvenir photo products.
Needs: Scenics, wildlife, sports and attractions.
Specs: Uses 35mm color prints, negatives or transparencies.
Payment & Terms: Pays $10-50/color photo, depending on subject and our manufacturing requirements. Buys "rights in our products only." Model releases and captions preferred.
Making Contact: Query with stock photo list. Reviews stock photos. Does not return unsolicited material. Reports in 1 month.
Tips: "Query with list of stock photo subjects first. We have strict format guidelines that must fit our products. We like to review many shots of one subject to find one or two that may be suitable for our needs since we add graphics to some products."

*AMERICAN YOUTH SOCCER ORGANIZATION, 5403 W. 138th St., Hawthorne CA 90250. (800)USA-AYSO. FAX: (310)643-5310. Publications Mgr.: Sean T. Hilferty. Estab. 1964. Coordinates youth soccer programs. Offers 1-4 assignments/year. Photos used in brochures, newsletters, posters, annual reports and magazines.
Needs: AYSO soccer action; looking for sideline, atmosphere, practice and coaching shots, also limited professional soccer (specific to story).
Specs: Uses b&w/color prints and transparencies.
Payment & Terms: Pays $30/color photo; $30/b&w photo. Pays on usage. Credit line given. Rights negotiable. Model/property release preferred. Captions preferred.
Making Contact: Query with samples. Provide resume, business card, self-promotion piece or tearsheets to be kept on file for possible future assignments. Keeps samples on file. SASE. Reports in 2 months.
Tips: "We're looking for photos that reflect AYSO's philosophies/attitudes. AYSO isn't just kids; it's parents too. And it isn't just soccer; it's having fun with soccer."

*ASBO INTERNATIONAL, 11401 N. Shore Dr., Reston VA 22090. (703)478-0405. FAX: (703)478-0205. Production Coordinator: Kristen L. Flessate. Estab. 1924. Professional association. Buys 12 photos/year; offers 12 assignments/year. Photos used in newspapers, magazines, press releases and catalogs.
Needs: School or business-related photos.
Specs: Uses 5×7 glossy b&w prints; 2¼×2¼ and 4×5 transparencies.
Payment & Terms: NPI. Pays on acceptance depending upon usage. Buys one-time or all rights; negotiable.
Making Contact: Query with samples. Works with local freelancers only. Reviews stock photos. Keeps samples on file. SASE. Reports in 3 weeks.

■BANKERS LIFE & CASUALTY CO., 1000 Sunset Ridge Rd., Northbrook IL 60062. (708)498-1500. FAX: (708)205-1742. Graphics Manager: Chuck Pusateri. Estab. 1879. Buys freelance photos occasionally; offers about 2-3 freelance assignments annually. Photos used in brochures, newsletters, posters and audiovisual.
Specs: Uses 35mm, 4×5, 8×10 transparencies; "some 1-inch videotape."
Payment & Terms: NPI. Pays on acceptance. Buys one-time rights; sometimes buys other rights; negotiable. Model/property release preferred.
Making Contact: Provide resume, business card, self-promotion piece or tearsheets to be kept on file for possible future assignments. Reviews stock photos. Reports in 1-2 weeks.
Tips: After initial query, "follow up a week or so later with a call or letter." In freelancer's samples looks mostly for good composition. Sees trend toward "increased use of staff members for shoots."

■ *The solid, black square before a listing indicates that the market uses various types of audiovisual materials, such as slides, film or videotape.*

CALIFORNIA REDWOOD ASSOCIATION, Suite 200, 405 Enfrente Dr., Novato CA 94949. (415)382-0662. FAX: (415)382-8531. Contact: Pamela Allsebrook. Estab. 1916. "We publish a variety of literature, a small black and white periodical, run color advertisements and constantly use photos for magazine and newspaper publicity. We use new, well-designed redwood applications—residential, commercial, exteriors, interiors and especially good remodels and outdoor decks, fences, shelters." Gives 40 assignments/year.
Needs: Prefers photographers with architectural specialization.
Specs: Uses b&w prints. For color, uses 2¼×2¼ and 4×5 transparencies; contact sheet OK.
Payment & Terms: NPI; payment based on previous use and other factors." Credit line given whenever possible. Usually buys all but national advertising rights. Model release required.
Making Contact: Send query material by mail for consideration for assignment or send finished speculation shots for possible purchase. Reports in 1 month. Simultaneous submissions and previously published work OK if other uses are made very clear.
Tips: "We like to see any new redwood projects showing outstanding design and use of redwood. We don't have a staff photographer and work only with freelancers. We do, however, tend to use people who are specialized in architectural photography. We generally look for justified lines, true color quality, projects with style and architectural design, and tasteful props. Find and take 'scout' shots or finished pictures of good redwood projects and send them to us."

CHICAGO COMPUTER & LIGHT, INC., 5001 N. Lowell Ave., Chicago IL 60630. (312)283-2749. President: Larry Feit. Estab. 1976. Buys 24 photos annually; offers 4 freelance assignments annually. Photos used in newsletters, magazines, catalogs, press releases.
Needs: New computer products for special sections and ads in trade journals.
Specs: Uses 35mm transparencies.
Payment & Terms: Pays $2,000/job. Pays on acceptance. Credit line sometimes given. Buys all rights; negotiable. Model release required; photo captions preferred.
Making Contact: Provide resume, business card, self-promotion piece or tearsheets to be kept on file for possible future assignments. SASE. Reports in 1-2 weeks.
Tips: In freelancer's samples, looks for "nice quality."

CHILD AND FAMILY SERVICES OF NEW HAMPSHIRE, 99 Hanover St., P.O. Box 448, Manchester NH 03105. (603)668-1920. FAX: (603)668-1937. Public Relations Coordinator: Renée Robertie. Estab. 1840. Statewide social service agency providing counseling to children and families.
Needs: Uses photos of children, teenagers and families; "pictures depicting our services, such as an unwed mother, teenager on drugs or emotionally upset, couples and/or families—possibly indicating stress or conflict. Also looking for photos depicting healthy, happy children and families." Photos used in brochures, newspapers, posters, annual reports, news releases, and displays and exhibits. Buys 3-4 photos/year; gives 1-2 assignments/year.
Specs: Uses 5×7 glossy b&w and color prints.
Payment & Terms: Pays $10-50/b&w or color photo; $10 minimum/hour and on a per-photo basis. Credit line given on request. Buys one time rights; negotiable. Model release required.
Making Contact: Interested in receiving work from newer, lesser-known photographers. Send material by mail for consideration. Stock photos OK. Provide business card and tearsheets to be kept on file for future assignments. Notifies photographer if future assignments can be expected. SASE. Reports in 1 month.
Tips: "Submit a few copies of applicable photos in which we might be interested rather than just a letter or form telling us what you have done or can do." Looks for "someone who can compose a photo that achieves an expression of feeling, emotion. Because we are primarily a service agency we want our artwork to reflect the clients we serve—people working on problems or solving them. We are looking for a range of emotions."

CUSTOM STUDIOS, INC., 1333-37 W. Devon, Chicago IL 60660. (312)761-1150. FAX: (312)761-7477. President: Gary Wing. Estab. 1966. Manufactures custom imprinted products such as T-shirts, jackets, caps, custom printed cups, key tags, ashtrays. Buys 10 freelance photos/year; offers 10 freelance assignments/year. Photos used in brochures, posters, newspapers, catalogs and magazines.
Needs: Product shots and models wearing custom imprinted products.
Specs: Uses 4×5 to 8×10 matte or glossy b&w and color prints; b&w and color contact sheets.
Payment & Terms: Pays $35-80/b&w photo; $40-90/color photo; $40-60/hour; $120-200/day; $30-80/job. Credit line given. Buys one-time rights. Model release required.
Making Contact: Interested in receiving work from newer, lesser-known photographers. Send unsolicited photos, preferably with models, by mail for consideration. Provide resume, business card, brochure, flyer or tearsheets to be kept on file for possible future assignments. Cannot return material. Reports in 3 weeks.

Tips: "Looking for models that have very attractive and sexy looks. Mostly fashion-type photos, female models wearing T-shirts, shorts, some lingerie and underwear, some sweatshirts and other tops."

*DAYTON BALLET, 140 N. Main St., Dayton OH 45402. (513)449-5060. FAX: (513)461-8353. Public Relations/Marketing Director: Dana Maybee. Estab. 1937. Schedules performances yearly. Offers 2-3 freelance assignments/year. Photos used in publicity materials and newspapers.
Needs: "We're looking for photographers in our region who can capture fast movement in a low-light theater situation."
Specs: Uses b&w and color contact sheets; also transparencies.
Payment & Terms: Pays $3-6/b&w photo; $5-10/color photo. "We do not pay hourly fees—basically photographers can receive exposure if they are good and their photos are used for publication. We will negotiate if someone is exceptional and we want them to continue shooting for us." Credit line given. Buys all rights.
Making Contact: Interested in receiving work from newer, lesser-known photographers. Send resume, business card, brochure, flyer or tearsheets to be kept on file for possible future assignments. SASE. "Also, make an appointment to come and shoot a dress rehearsal (no fee) and submit your contact sheets. If you're good, we'll order from the sheet and we'll invite you to shoot in the future and negotiate a fee."
Tips: To be successful for this type of market, have "a background in dance and a knowledge of shooting dance. Be quick and able to anticipate fast movement. Send samples of past dance photography work. Specifically ballet. Pictures should show dance movement captured with good lighting effects. Also they should be clear and sharp and show expression. Great opportunity for someone just starting out."

■**E&B MARINE INC.,** 201 Meadow Rd., Edison NJ 08818. (908)819-7400. FAX: (908)819-4771. Manager of Creative Services: Gail Engel. Estab. 1950. Mail order catalog of boating equipment. Buys 650 freelance photos annually; offers 30 freelance assignments annually.
Needs: Photos used for newsletters, newspapers, annual reports, catalogs, PR releases and store signage.
Audiovisual Needs: Works with freelance filmmakers on educational/promotional films.
Specs: Uses 4×5+ b&w prints; 35mm, 2¼×2¼ and 4×5 transparencies; b&w contact sheets.
Payment & Terms: Pays $50-250/color photo; $600-800/day. Buys one-time or all rights. Model release required. Captions preferred.
Making Contact: Query with resume of credits, samples or list of stock photo subjects. Provide resume, business card, brochure, flyer or tearsheets to be kept on file for possible future assignments. SASE. Reports as needed.
Tips: Always looking for lifestyle and mood shots of boaters. "Be flexible, familiar with boating. Understand layouts and how to 'shoot-to-size' for assembled separations."

■**SCOTT EVANS PRODUCTIONS, MUSIC & ENTERTAINMENT,** 660 NE 139th St., N. Miami FL 33161. (305)891-4449 or 891-0158. General Manager: Ted Jones. Estab. 1979. Entertainment services, party planning, producing and directing. Buys 25-50 photos/year. Photos used in brochures, newsletters, newspapers, magazines, press releases, audiovisual, catalogs, model shoots, production shots and location shoots.
Needs: Interview shots for promotional publications.
Audiovisual Needs: "We frequently videotape shows and performances for promotional purposes (demos) as well as for rehearsal purposes or selling products not readily available for quick viewing."
Specs: Uses 35mm, b&w prints; 3×5, 8×10, color prints; ½" and ¾", videotape.
Payment & Terms: NPI. Pays on acceptance, usage. Credit line given. Buys all rights; negotiable. Model release required; photo captions required.
Making Contact: Provide resume, business card, self-promotion piece or tearsheets to be kept on file for possible future assignments; each circumstance is unique. Works with local freelancers on assignment only. Reviews stock photos; variety, entertainment related. Cannot return material. Reports as needed.
Tips: "Put together a simple, concise, sample resume demo as needed to project artists skills to buyers in a manner/format that can be kept on file for quick reference." In samples or demos wants to see versatility, composition, sharpness, creativity, easy interpretation.

GARY PLASTIC PACKAGING CORP., 530 Old Post Rd., No. 3, Greenwich CT 06830. (203)629-1480. Marketing Director: Marilyn Hellinger. Estab. 1963. Manufacturers of custom injection molding; thermoforming; and stock rigid plastic packaging. Buys 10 freelance photos/year; offers 10 assignments/year. Photos used in brochures, catalogs and flyers.

Needs: Product photography.
Specs: Uses 8×10 b&w and color prints; 2¼×2¼ slides; and b&w or color negatives.
Payment & Terms: Pays up to $150/color photo; up to $900/day. Pays by the job and the number of photographs required. Buys exclusive product rights. Model release required.
Making Contact: Query with resume of credits or with samples. Follow up with a call to set up an appointment to show portfolio. Prefers to see b&w and color product photography. Works with local freelancers only. Solicits photos by assignment only. Provide resume to be kept on file for possible future assignments. Notifies photographer if future assignments can be expected. Does not return unsolicited material. Reports in 2 weeks.
Tips: The photographer "has to be willing to work with our designers."

GREEN MOUNTAIN POWER, P.O. Box 850, Burlington VT 05402. (802)864-5731. FAX: (802)865-9129. Communications Manager: Dorothy Schnure. Estab. 1928. Provides electric utility.
Needs: Buys 5 photos/year; offers 20 freelance assignments/year. Photos used in brochures and annual reports. Wants to see Vermont scenics, company events, portraits, dramatic use of electricity or electrical equipment.
Specs: Uses transparencies, all formats.
Payment & Terms: NPI; payment negotiable according to project. Pays on acceptance. Credit line not given. Buys one-time rights and all rights; negotiable. Model release and photo captions required.
Making Contact: Provide resume, business card, self-promotion piece or tearsheets to be kept on file for possible future assignments. Reviews stock photos of Vermont scenics, dramatic electrical equipment. SASE. Reports in 1-2 weeks.
Tips: "Most photos must be of Vermont subjects, if showing a recognizable location." In freelancers' portfolios and samples, looks for "sense of drama, personal connection with subject."

HILLSDALE COLLEGE, 33 College St., Hillsdale MI 49242. (517)437-7341. FAX: (517)437-3923. Director of Public Affairs: Bill Koshelnyk. Publishes alumni magazine, political/social action newsletter, brochures, books, etc. Photos used for text illustration, promotional materials, book covers and dust jackets. Buys 20-30 photos annually; assigns 5-10 shoots per year. Recently published *Hillsdale Magazine* and assorted brochures.
Needs: Looking for photos "that deal with the college's national outreach programs, athletics or alumni." Model release preferred; photo captions required.
Specs: Uses 5×7 glossy b&w prints; 35mm, 2¼×2¼ transparencies.
Payment & Terms: Pays $50-100/color or b&w photo. Additional rates vary according to assignment. Credit lines given where possible. Buys all rights; negotiable. Simultaneous submissions and previously published work OK.
Making Contact: Send unsolicited photos by mail for consideration. Reviews stock photos. SASE. Reports in 2 weeks.
Tips: "Photos must have something to do with the activities of Hillsdale College or prominent figures who participate in our programs. Our needs are rapidly growing."

*■HORIZONS MAGAZINE, P.O. Box 2467, Fargo ND 58108. (701)237-9461. FAX: (701)237-9463. Editor: Sheldon Green. Estab. 1971. Quality regional magazine. Buys 50 photos/year; offers 25 assignments/year. Photos used in magazines, audiovisual and calendars.
Needs: Scenics of North Dakota events, places and people. Examples of recent uses: "Scenic North Dakota" calendar, *Horizons Magazine* (winter edition) and "North Dakota Bad Lands."
Audiovisual Needs: Uses slides and videotape.
Specs: Uses 8×10 glossy b&w prints; 35mm, 2¼×2¼, 4×5 transparencies.
Payment & Terms: Pays $150-250/day; $200-300/job. Pays on usage. Credit line given. Buys one-time rights; negotiable. Model/property release preferred. Captions preferred.
Making Contact: Query with samples. Query with stock photo list. Works on assignment only. Does not keep samples on file. SASE. Reports in 1-2 weeks.
Tips: "Know North Dakota events, places. Have strong quality of composition and light." Sees trend developing in scanning of photos on disc. "Multiple use of original image."

■HUBBARD MILLING COMPANY, 424 N. Riverfront Dr., P.O. Box 8500, Mankato MN 56002. (507)388-9528. Supervisor, Marketing Communications: Scott W. Roemhildt. Estab. 1878. The Hubbard Feed Division manufactures animal feeds, pet foods and animal health products. Buys 20 freelance photos annually; offers 10 freelance assignments annually. Photos used in brochures, newsletters, posters and audiovisual presentations.

Needs: Livestock—beef cattle, dairy cattle, pigs, horses, sheep, dogs, cats.
Specs: Uses 3×5 and 5×7 matte b&w and color prints; 2¼×2¼ and 4×5 transparencies; and b&w and color negatives.
Payment & Terms: Pays $50-100/b&w photo; $200/color photo; $50-300/job. Buys one-time and all rights; negotiable. Model release required.
Making Contact: Query with samples. Query with list of stock photo subjects. Submit portfolio for review. Provide resume, business card, brochure, flyer or tearsheets to be kept on file for possible future assignments. Works on assignment only. SASE. Reports in 2 weeks.
Tips: Prefers "to see the types of work the photographer does and what types of subjects done. We look for lots of agricultural photos in a more serious setting. Keep up with modern farming methods and use confinement shots when deemed necessary. Stay away from 'cutesy' shots."

*INSTITUTE OF REAL ESTATE MANAGEMENT, 430 N. Michigan Ave,. Chicago IL 60611. (312)329-6066. FAX: (312)661-0217. Art and Production Manager: Gail Thompson. Estab. 1933. Professional trade association. Buys 20 photos/year; offers 5 or 6 assignments/year. Photos used in brochures, magazines and catalogs.
Needs: Photos of people in office situations, maintenance and building photos. Examples of recent uses: *Journal of Property Management* (photos of buildings and employees in office situations) and *"Institute of Real Estate Management"* (cover shot, tabletop product).
Specs: Uses 4×5, 5×7, 8×10 matte b&w prints; 5×7, 8×10 matte color prints; 35mm, 2¼×2¼, 4×5 transparencies.
Payment & Terms: Pays $150-1,200/job. Pays in 30 days. Credit line given. Buys first and one-time rights. Model/property release preferred. Captions preferred.
Making Contact: Provide resume, business card, self-promotion piece or tearsheets to be kept on file for possible future assignments. "No calls." Reviews stock photos of buildings. Keeps samples on file. Cannot return material. Reports in 2 months.
Tips: Need photos with "good color that will print well in magazine" and "a personal viewpoint, original approach to making shot."

*INTERNATIONAL PHOTO CORPORATION. 1035 Wesley Ave., Evanston IL 60202. (708)475-6400. FAX: (708)475-6418. President: Gerald W. Hoos. Estab. 1965. Print media/advertising. Offers 65-70 assignments/year.
Specs: Uses 35mm, 2¼×2¼, 4×5 and 8×10 transparencies.
Payment & Terms: Pays $50-500/job. Buys one-time, all and exclusive product rights. Captions required.
Making Contact: Provide resume, business card, self-promotion piece or tearsheets to be kept on file for possible future assignments. Keeps samples on file. SASE. Reports in 2 weeks.

■INTERNATIONAL RESEARCH & EDUCATION (IRE), 21098 IRE Control Center, Eagan MN 55121. (612)888-9635. IP Director: George Franklin, Jr. IRE conducts in-depth research probes, surveys, and studies to improve the decision support process. Company conducts market research, taste testing, brand image/usage studies, premium testing, and design and development of product/service marketing campaigns. Buys 75-110 photos/year; gives 50-60 assignments/year. Photos used in brochures, newsletters, posters, audiovisual presentations, annual reports, catalogs, press releases, and as support material for specific project/survey/reports.
Needs: "Subjects and topics cover a vast spectrum of possibilities and needs."
Audiovisual Needs: Uses freelance filmmakers to produce promotional pieces for 16mm or videotape.
Specs: Uses prints (15% b&w, 85% color), transparencies and negatives.
Payment & Terms: NPI; pays on a bid, per job basis. Credit line given. Buys all rights. Model release required.
Making Contact: Provide resume, business card, brochure, flyer or tearsheets to be kept on file for possible future assignments; "materials sent are put on optic disk for options to pursue by project managers responsible for a program or job." Works on assignment only. Does not return unsolicited material. Reports when a job is available.
Tips: "We look for creativity, innovation, and ability to relate to the given job and carry out the mission accordingly."

JUVENILE DIABETES FOUNDATION INTERNATIONAL, 432 Park Ave. S., New York NY 10016. (212) 889-7575. Publications Manager: Sandy Dylak. Estab. 1970. Produces 4-color, 32-page quarterly magazine to deliver research information to a lay audience; also produces brochures, pamphlets, annual report and audiovisual presentations. Buys 30 photos/year; offers 20 freelance assignments/year.

Needs: Needs "mostly portraits of people, but always with some environmental aspect."
Specs: Uses 2¼×2¼ transparencies.
Payment & Terms: Pays $500/color photo; $500-700/day. Also pays by the job—payment "depends on how many days, shots, cities, etc." Credit line given. Buys one-time rights. Model release and captions preferred.
Making Contact: Query with samples. Provide resume, business card, brochure, flyer or tearsheets to be kept on file for possible future assignments. Reviews stock photos. Cannot return unsolicited material. Reports as needed.
Tips: Looks for "a style consistent with commercial magazine photography—upbeat, warm, personal, but with a sophisticated edge. Call and ask for samples of our publications before submitting any of your own samples so you will have an idea what we are looking for in photography. Nonprofit groups have seemingly come to depend more and more on photography to get their message across. The business seems to be using a variety of freelancers, as opposed to a single inhouse photographer."

***■HELEN KELLER INTERNATIONAL,** 15 W. 16th St., New York NY 10011. (212)807-5800. FAX: (212)463-9341. Communications Consultant: Malcolm Carter. Deals with blindness prevention, education and rehabilitation in the developing world. Buys varying number of photos/year; offers 3-4 assignments/year. Photos used in newsletters and annual reports.
Needs: Examples of blindness prevention work in the field. Examples of recent uses: annual report (b&w) and award special event (b&w, slides).
Audiovisual Needs: Uses b&w slides.
Specs: Uses 8×10 glossy b&w prints; 35mm transparencies.
Payment & Terms: Pays $200/day. Pays on acceptance. Credit line depends on space requirements. Buys all rights; negotiable. Captions preferred; include description of activity.
Making Contact: Provide resume, business card, self-promotion piece or tearsheets to be kept on file for possible future assignments; query when already planning to travel to developing world. Does not keep samples on file. SASE. Reports in 1-2 weeks.

***METAL FORMING MAGAZINE/PMA SERVICES, INC.,** 27027 Chardon Rd., Richmond Heights OH 44143. (216)585-8800. FAX: (216)585-3126. Art Director: Beth Vosmik. Estab. 1942. Publishes trade magazine serving those who give utility to sheet metal by shaping it using tooling in machines. Buys 10 photos/year; offers 4 assignments/year. Photos used in brochures and magazine.
Needs: Photos of stamping presses, press brakes, roll formers, washers, turret presses and items produced by this machinery, product shots and location shots.
Specs: Uses 2¼×2¼, 4×5 transparencies.
Payment & Terms: Pays $125/editorial photo; $750/editorial cover photo. Pays on acceptance. Credit line given. Buys all rights. Model/property release required. Captions required; include details about manufacturers and location.
Making Contact: Provide resume, business card, self-promotion piece or tearsheets to be kept on file for possible future assignments. Works on assignment only. Reviews stock photos of metal formings—stampings, presses, etc. Keeps samples on file. Cannot return material. Reports in 6 months.

MID AMERICA DESIGNS, INC., P.O. Box 1368, Effingham IL 62401. (217)347-5591. FAX: (217)347-2952. Operations Manager: Jeff Bloemker. Estab. 1975. Provides mail order catalog for Corvette parts & accessories. Buys 300 freelance photos and offers 6 freelance assignments annually.
Needs: Apparel and automotive parts.
Specs: Uses 2¼×2¼, 4×5 and 8×10 transparencies.
Payment & Terms: Pays $65/b&w or color photo. Buys all rights; negotiable. Model release required; property release preferred.
Making Contact: Provide resume, business card, brochure, flyer or tearsheets to be kept on file for possible future assignments. Works on assignment. Reviews stock photos. Does not return unsolicited material. Reports in 2 weeks.

MIRACLE OF ALOE, 521 Riverside Ave., Westport CT 06880. (203)454-1919. FAX: (203)226-7333. Vice President: Jess F. Clarke, Jr. Estab. 1980. Manufacturers for mail order buyers of healthcare products. Works with 2 freelancers per month. Photos used in newsletters, catalogs, direct mail and consumer magazines.

The asterisk before a listing indicates that the market is new in this edition. New markets are often the most receptive to freelance submissions.

Needs: Uses testimonial photos and aloe vera plants.
Specs: Uses 4×5 b&w or color prints and 35mm transparencies.
Payment & Terms: Pays $30-45/photo. Pays on receipt of invoice. Credit line given. Buys one-time rights. Model release preferred.
Making Contact: Provide resume, business card, self-promotion piece or tearsheets to be kept on file for possible future assignments. Works on assignment only. SASE. Reports in 1 month.
Tips: In freelancer's samples, looks for "older folks, head shots and nice white hair ladies. Also show Aloe Vera plants in fields or pots; shoot scenes of Southern Texas aloe farms."

*■NATIONAL ASSOCIATION OF DISPLAY INDUSTRIES (NADI), 470 Park Ave. S., New York NY 10016. (212)213-2662. FAX: (212)889-0727. Marketing Communications Director: Patricia Vitsky. Estab. 1943. Offers 2 assignments/year. Photos used for NADI trade shows. "Our 300 exhibitors use them as well."
Needs: Freelancers are used to photograph exhibitors' booths at trade show. Examples of recent uses: videotape for promo at trade show and videotape for awards dinner.
Audiovisual Needs: Uses slides and videotape.
Specs: Uses 5×7 b&w prints.
Payment & Terms: NPI. Rights negotiable.
Making Contact: Provide resume, business card, self-promotion piece or tearsheets to be kept on file for possible future assignments. Works with local freelancers on assignment only. Does not keep samples on file. SASE.

NATIONAL BLACK CHILD DEVELOPMENT INSTITUTE, 1463 Rhode Island Ave. NW, Washington DC 20005. (202)387-1281. Deputy Director: Vicki D. Pinkston. Estab. 1970. Photos used in brochures, newsletters, newspapers, annual reports and annual calendar.
Needs: Subjects include: candid, action photos of black children and youth.
Specs: Uses 5×7 or 8×10 glossy b&w prints and b&w contact sheets.
Payment & Terms: Pays $25/cover photo and $15/inside b&w photo. Credit line given. Buys one-time rights. Model release required.
Making Contact: Query with samples. Send unsolicited photos by mail for consideration. Reviews stock photos. SASE. Reports in 1 month.
Tips: "Candid, action photographs of one black child or youth or a small group of children or youths. Most photographs selected are used in annual calendar and are placed beside an appropriate poem selected by organization. Therefore, photograph should communicate a message in an indirect way. Other photographs are used in quarterly newsletter and reports. Obtain sample of publications published by organization to see the type of photographs selected."

*NATIONAL GLASS ASSOCIATION, #302, 8200 Greensboro Dr., McLean VA 22102. (703)442-4890. FAX: (703)442-0630. Graphic Designer: A. Jill Wagner. Trade association. Buys 3 photos/year; offers 3 assignments/year. Photos used in magazines.
Needs: Photos of cars and buildings—glass. Examples of recent uses: building shot for magazine cover (transparency).
Specs: 8×10 transparencies.
Payment & Terms: Pays $10-15/hour; $150/color photo. Pays on usage. Credit line given. Buys one-time rights.
Making Contact: Provide resume, business card, self-promotion piece or tearsheets to be kept on file for possible future assignments. Works on assignment only. Reviews stock photos of buildings and cars. Keeps samples on file. Cannot return material. Reports in 1 month.

NEW EXPOSURE—A Catalog of Fine Art Photography, 8150 E. Smokehouse Tr., Scottsdale AZ 85262. (602)488-2831. Executive Director: Susan Brachocki. Estab. 1987. Specializes in marketing original fine art photographic prints. Consigns approximately 80 freelance photos annually. Does not want stock photos.
Needs: Specializes in "a wide variety of black and white and color photographs, including landscapes, urban scenes, portraits and abstracts. We are interested in photographers who have exhibited a long-term commitment to their craft and produce *unique* images." No "commercial work, depressing or violent images."
Specs: Reviews color or b&w prints and contact sheets; also slides.
Payment & Terms: Pays 50% royalty on retail print sales. Pays on completion of sale.
Making Contact: Query with samples. SASE. Reports in 1 month. Simultaneous submissions and previously published work OK.
Tips: "We are interested in fine-art black and white and color photography, not commercial stock work. Unique perspectives, superior print quality, experience are all important. Ability to provide prints of an image on a timely basis is key as well. Prints are reproduced in a high-quality mail-order catalog; and displayed in gallery exhibitions at various locations."

*OVERSEAS DEVELOPMENT COUNCIL, 10th Floor, 1875 Connecticut Ave. NW, Washington DC 20009. (202)234-8701. FAX: (202)745-0067. Assistant Director of Public Affairs: Marguerite Turner Day. Estab. 1969. Think tank on US/Third World issues. Offers 3-6 assignments/year. Photos used in annual report.
Needs: Freelancers are used to take both posed and candid pictures of Overseas Development Council conferences. Examples of recent uses: "1989/1990 Annual Report," "1987/89 Annual Report" and "1985/86 Annual Report" (all b&w).
Specs: Uses 5×7 b&w prints.
Payment & Terms: Pays $75-125/hour. Pays on receipt of contact sheets. Credit lines given.
Making Contact: Arrange a personal interview to show portfolio. Provide resume, business card, self-promotion piece or tearsheets to be kept on file for possible future assignments. Works on assignment only. Keeps samples on file. SASE, "but would like to keep 1 sample." Reports in 1-2 weeks.
Tips: "Must be experienced with conference photography. Need clarity, composition. Look for most people in a composite picture to look good."

PALM SPRINGS DESERT RESORT CONVENTION AND VISITORS BUREAU, 69-930 Highway 111, Rancho Mirage CA 92270. (619)770-9000. FAX: (619)770-9001. Director of Publicity: Laurie Smith. "We are the tourism promotion entity of Palm Springs and the entire Coachella Valley." Buys 50 freelance photos/year; gives 20 assignments/year. Photos used in brochures, posters, newspapers, audiovisual presentations, magazines and PR releases.
Needs: "Those of tourism interest . . . specifically in Coachella Valley."
Specs: Uses 8×10 b&w prints; 35mm slides; b&w contact sheet and negatives OK. "We buy only 35 mm transparencies."
Payment & Terms: Pays $25/b&w photo; $40-75/hour. Buys all rights—"all exposures from the job. On assignment, we provide film and processing. We own all exposures." Model release and captions required.
Making Contact: Query with resume of credits or stock photo list. Provide resume, business card, brochure, flyer, and tearsheets to be kept on file for possible future assignments. Notifies photographer if future assignments can be expected. SASE. Reports in 2 weeks.
Tips: "We will discuss only photographs of the Coachella Valley, California. No generic materials will be considered."

PGA OF AMERICA, Suite 200, 2155 Butterfield, Troy MI 48084. (313)649-1110. Contact: Heidi Russell. Services 15,500 golf club professionals and apprentices nationwide. Photos used for brochures, posters, annual reports and monthly feature magazine.
Needs: Special needs include golf scenery, good color action of amateurs as well as tour stars. Buys 50 freelance photos and offers 15 freelance assignments annually.
Payment & Terms: Pays $25 minimum/b&w photo; $50-200/color photo. Credit line given. Buys one-time and all rights. Model release preferred.
Making Contact: Arrange personal interview to show portfolio and query with list of stock photo subjects. Prefers to see 35mm slides in the portfolio. Provide tearsheets to be kept on file for possible future assignments. SASE.

PHI DELTA KAPPA, 8th & Union Sts., P.O. Box 789, Bloomington IN 47402. Design Director: Carol Bucheri. Estab. 1915. Produces Kappan magazine and supporting materials. Buys 10 photos/year; offers 1 assignment/year. Photos used in magazine, flyers, and subscription cards.
Needs: Teachers, classrooms and high school students.
Specs: Uses 8×10 b&w prints, b&w contact sheets.
Payment & Terms: Pays $20-100/b&w photo; $30-400/color photo; $30-500/job. Credit line and tearsheets given. Buys one-time rights. Model release required. Photo captions required; include who, what, when where.
Making Contact: Query with list of stock photo subjects. Provide photocopies, brochure or flyer to be kept on file for possible future assignments. Reviews stock photos. SASE. Reports in 3 weeks.
Tips: "Don't send photos that you wouldn't want to hang in a gallery. Just because you do a photo for publications does not mean you should lower your standards. Spots should be touched up (not with a ball point pen), the print should be good and carefully done, subject matter should be in focus. Send me photocopies of your black-and-white prints that we can look at. We don't convert slides and rarely use color."

*■PHOTO MARKETING ASSOCIATION, 3000 Picture Place, Jackson MI 49201. (517)788-8100. FAX: (517)788-8371. Publications Director: Margaret Hooks. Estab. 1924. Buys 20 photos/year; offers 5 assignments/year. Photos used in brochures and magazines.

Needs: Photo industry related images.
Audiovisual Needs: Uses slides and film.
Specs: Uses 4×6 glossy b&w and color prints; 35mm, 2¼×2¼, 4×5 transparencies; 35mm film.
Payment & Terms: Pays $300-500/day. Pays on usage. Credit lines given. Buys one-time rights. Model/property release preferred. Captions preferred.
Making Contact: Query with samples. Query with stock photo list. Provide resume, business card, self-promotion piece or tearsheets to be kept on file for possible future assignments. Reviews stock photos related to photo industry. Keeps samples on file. SASE. Reports in 1 month.
Tips: Interested in "lifestyle" shots of men and women using cameras, also photo lab workers.

RECREATION WORLD SERVICES, INC., Drawer 17148, Pensacola FL 32522. (904)477-2123. Executive Vice President: K.W. Stephens. Estab. 1983. Serves publishers and membership service organizations including recreation, leisure and travel industries. Buys 5-10 photos/year; gives 2-5 assignments/year. Photos used in brochures, newsletters, newspapers, magazines and press releases.
Needs: Recreation type.
Specs: Uses 3×4 prints. Model release required; property release preferred.
Payment & Terms: NPI. "We request photographers to state their price." Buys all rights; negotiable.
Making Contact: Send unsolicited photos by mail for consideration; provide resume, business card, brochure, flyer or tearsheets to be kept on file for possible future assignments. SASE. Reports in 2 weeks.

REPERTORY DANCE THEATRE, P.O. Box 8088, Salt Lake City UT 84108. (801)581-6702. General Manager: Kathy Johnson. Uses photos of dance company for promotion. Photos used in brochures, newspapers, posters, news releases and magazines.
Needs: Prefers to see dance or movement photos.
Specs: Uses 8×10 b&w glossy prints; contact sheet OK.
Payment & Terms: NPI; payment negotiable. Buys all rights.
Making Contact: Arrange a personal interview to show portfolio. Queries by mail OK; SASE. Reports in 2 weeks.

■RIPON COLLEGE, P.O. Box 248, Ripon WI 54971. (414)748-8115. Contact: Director of College Relations. Estab. 1851. Photos used in brochures, newsletters, posters, newspapers, audiovisual presentations, annual reports, magazines and press releases. Offers 3-5 assignments/year.
Needs: Formal and informal portraits of Ripon alumni, on-location shots, architecture.
Payment & Terms: Pays $10-25/b&w photo; $10-50/color photo; $30-40/hour; $300-500/day; $300-500/job; negotiable. Buys one-time and all rights; negotiable. Model release, property release and captions preferred.
Making Contact: Interested in receiving work from newer, lesser-known photographers. Provide resume, business card, brochure, flyer or tearsheets to be kept on file for possible future assignments. Works on assignment only. SASE. Reports in 1 month.

RSVP MARKETING, INC., Suite 5, 450 Plain St., Marshfield MA 02050. President: Edward C. Hicks. Direct marketing consultant/agency. Buys 50-100 photos/year; gives 5-10 assignments/year. Photos used in brochures, catalogs and magazines.
Needs: Industrial equipment, travel/tourism topics and modeled, i.e., clothing, sports events.
Specs: Uses 2×2 and 4×6 b&w and color prints, and transparencies.
Payment & Terms: NPI; payment negotiable per photo and per job. Buys all rights. Model release preferred.
Making Contact: Query with list of stock photo subjects. Provide resume, business card, brochure, flyer or tearsheets to be kept on file for possible future assignments. Works on assignment only. Reviews stock photos. Reports as needed.
Tips: "We look for photos of industrial and office products, high-tech formats and fashion."

SAN FRANCISCO CONSERVATORY OF MUSIC, 1201 Ortega St., San Francisco CA 94122. (415)564-8086. Publications Editor: Daphne Powell. Estab. 1917. Provides publications about the conservatory programs, concerts and musicians. Buys 25 photos/year; offers 10-15 assignments/year. Photos used in brochures, posters, annual reports, catalogs and news releases.
Needs: Musical photos—musicians.
Specs: Uses 5×7 b&w prints and color slides; color slides for publication only.
Payment & Terms: Payment varies by photographer; "credit line" to $25/b&w photo; $200-700/job. Credit line given "most of the time." Buys one-time rights and all rights; negotiable. Works with local freelancers only.

© Ripon College

Oshkosh, Wisconsin, photographer James Koepnick has worked with Ripon College for the past four or five years and often tends to assignments for the school. This photo of a student working in a lab was used by the office of college relations to kick off a $40 million campaign at Ripon. The shot appeared on the cover of Ripon Magazine.

Making Contact: Interested in receiving work from newer, lesser-known photographers. Prefers to see in-performance shots, and studio shots of musicians. "Contact us only if you are experienced in photographing performing musicians."

■**SAN FRANCISCO OPERA CENTER,** War Memorial Opera House, San Francisco CA 94102. (415)565-6491. FAX: (415)255-6774. Business Manager: Russ Walton. Estab. 1982. Produces live performances of opera productions of both local San Francisco area performances and national touring companies. Estab. 1982. Buys 2-3 photos/year; offers a minimum 1 assignment/year. Photos used in brochures, newspapers, annual reports, PR releases and production file reference/singer resume photos.
Needs: Production and performance shots, and artist/performer shots.
Audiovisual Needs: "We produce some video documentaries of our cultural exchanges, opera productions and training programs. Slides and film may also be used to cover these events."
Specs: Uses 8×10 standard finish b&w prints, and b&w negatives.
Payment & Terms: Pays $8/b&w photo, $8/color photo, and $50-500/complete job. Credit line given. Buys all rights; negotiable.
Making Contact: Query with resume of credits. Provide resume, business card, brochure, flyer or tearsheets to be kept on file for possible future assignments. SASE. Reports in 2 weeks.
Tips: "In portfolio or samples wants to see live action shots in a wide variety of lighting—including stage and outdoor—and performance settings. We need live performance shots and action shots of individuals; scenery also. Photographers should have extensive experience in shooting live performances and be familiar with the opera product. Once good photographers are located, we contract them regularly for various production/social/public events."

■**SCHWINN BICYCLE COMPANY,** 217 N. Jefferson St., Chicago IL 60661. Manager/Marketing Communications: Paul Chess. Products include bicycles. Photos used in brochures, newsletters, posters, audiovisual presentations, catalogs, magazines, and press releases.
Needs: Subjects include "identifiable" Schwinn bicycles in use.
Specs: "Depends on final use."
Payment & Terms: NPI; payment negotiable. Credit line given if requested. Buys all rights. Model release and captions required.
Making Contact: Send unsolicited photos by mail for consideration. Not interested in stock photos. Reports ASAP.

■**THE SOCIETY OF AMERICAN FLORISTS,** 1601 Duke St., Alexandria VA 22314. (703)836-8700. Editor: Kate Foster. Estab. 1894. National trade association representing growers, wholesalers and retailers of flowers and plants. Offers 3-5 assignments/year. Photos used in magazines and promotional materials.
Needs: Needs photos of personalities, greenhouses, inside wholesalers, flower shops and conventions, as well as studio photography.
Audiovisual Needs: Uses slides (with graphics) for convention slide shows.
Specs: Uses b&w prints, or transparencies.
Payment & Terms: Pays $600-800/cover shot; $25-150/b&w photo; $50-75/color photo; $75-150/hour; $125-250/job. Credit line given. Model release required; captions preferred. Buys one-time rights.
Making Contact: Query with samples. Provide resume, business card, brochure, flyer or tearsheets to be kept on file for possible future assignments. Reviews stock photos. SASE. Reports in 1 week.
Tips: "We shoot a lot of tightly composed, dramatic shots, so we look for these skills. We also welcome input from the photographer on the concept of the shot."

*■**SPECIAL OLYMPICS INTERNATIONAL,** Suite 500, 1350 New York Ave. NW, Washington DC 20005. (202)628-3630. FAX: (202)737-1937. Media Production Coordinator: Jill Dixon. Estab. 1968. Provides sports training/competition to people with mental retardation. Buys 300 photos/year; offers 5 assignments/year. Photos used in brochures, newsletters, posters, annual reports and audiovisual.
Needs: Sports action and special events.
Audiovisual Needs: Uses slides and videotape.
Specs: Uses 3×5, 5×7 and 8×10, glossy color prints; 35mm transparencies; VHS, U-matic, Betacam, 1-inch videotape.
Payment & Terms: Pays $50/hour minimum; $150/job. "Many volunteer time and processing because we're a not-for-profit organization." Pays on acceptance. Credit line depends on the material it is used on (no credit on brochure/credit in magazines). Buys one-time and all rights; negotiable. Model/ property release preferred for athletes and celebrities. Captions preferred.
Making Contact: Provide resume, business card, self-promotion piece or tearsheets to be kept on file for possible future assignments. Keeps samples on file. SASE. Reports in 2-4 weeks.
Tips: Specific guidelines can be given upon request. Looking for "good action shots. We use primarily video instead of film."

*■**SPECIAL REPORT,** (published by Whittle Communications), 333 Main Ave., Knoxville TN 37902. (615)595-5429. FAX: (615)595-5877. Photo Editor: Kathy Getsey. Estab. 1988. Buys 200 photos/year; offers 125 assignments/year. Photos used in posters, magazines and press releases.
Needs: There is an emphasis on portraiture, environmental portraits, concepts or photo illustration.
Audiovisual Needs: Uses slides.
Specs: Uses all sizes of b&w prints; 35mm, $2\frac{1}{4}\times2\frac{1}{4}$, 4×5 transparencies.
Payment & Terms: Pays $350-500/day; $1,000/color cover photo; $750-1,000/b&w cover photo; $200-250/color or b&w inside photo. Pays on acceptance. Credit line given. Buys one-time rights; negotiable. Model/property release preferred; photo captions required.
Making Contact: Submit portfolio for review. Provide resume, business card, brochure, flyer or tearsheets to be kept on file for possible assignments. Reviews photos with or without accompanying ms. Keeps samples on file. Cannot return material.
Tips: "I look for photos that tell a story in a single image, or at least show the person or place in a unique way. If you can make anything ordinary look fresh or interesting, I'll look at your portfolio. Know what's happening in your own backyard. I find photographers always want to go to New York or Los Angeles, but rarely do they know their own city. We look for interesting people and places all over the country to profile."

■**THIEL COLLEGE,** 75 College Ave., Greenville PA 16125. (412)589-2187. FAX: (412)589-2021. Director of Communications: Ian Scott Forbes. Estab. 1866. Provides education; undergraduate and community programs. Buys 20-25 photos/year; offers 3-5 assignments/year. Photos used in brochures, newsletters, newspapers, audiovisual presentations, annual reports, catalogs, magazines and news releases.
Needs: "Basically we have an occasional need for photography depending on the job we want done."
Specs: Uses 35mm transparencies.
Payment & Terms: NPI; payment negotiable. Credit line given depending on usage. Buys all rights; negotiable.
Making Contact: Interested in receiving work from newer, lesser-known photographers. Query with resume of credits. Works on assignment only. Reports as needed.

Close-up

Kathy Getsey
Health Division Picture Editor
Whittle Communications
Knoxville, Tennessee

© Katie Musgrave

With a Rolodex on her desk housing over 4,000 names, Kathy Getsey says it's not easy for her to remember every photographer who submits work to her company. But it's not impossible either.

As picture editor for a firm that has been on the move since it was founded in 1970, Getsey says she receives stacks of portfolios on a weekly basis. With the multitude of images that constantly passes before her eyes, she must sift through the work to find useable images for Whittle Communication's many ventures. The firm produces the health magazine *Special Reports*; college publications, such as *Campus Voice* and *Connections*; and has begun to move into book publishing and video, she says. The company also operates an educational network which produces a daily news program for students, called Channel One.

With such a diverse group of needs, ranging from travel and health photos to animals and portraiture, the company is always looking for interesting photographs. "We're very open with what we want to do," says Getsey, who has been with the company for around 10 years. "I try not to put too many boundaries on photographers."

A photographer who considers selling to Whittle should strive to create striking images. By turning mundane subjects into eye-catching photos, freelancers will find themselves receiving assignments from Getsey, who maintains a nationwide network of photographers. "I'm much more likely to go back to photographers if I talk to them and find they can bring something into the project—and they don't mind doing a little bit of the homework themselves because it'll create a better project for them," she says.

Nothing aggravates Getsey more than when she supplies a freelancer with materials concerning an upcoming shoot and that photographer doesn't review the information. "I see people who find a niche and stay there," says Getsey, referring to the more lackluster images. "If you reach a level of acceptance and recognition, maybe you're not as hungry."

Rather than review the work and start imagining the potential shots that can be created, some photographers begin to shoot without much preparation, or they rely on Getsey to come up with photo ideas. "In this recessionary age, I don't think it's too much to ask for them to get involved with my project," she says. Involvement for a photographer also should include getting to know the people who are participating in the project. This type of interest can do nothing but enhance the photos.

Getsey, whose company has around 1,700 employees, searches for freelancers who take interest in the firm's work. Once she becomes familiar with a photographer's style, she often calls upon him to shoot assignments at a wage of $350 or more per day. "I try very hard to match the photographer with the (subject)," she says.

Because there are so many submissions, Getsey advises photographers who are submitting material to place identification on all their images. Freelancers also should send a memo sheet detailing what has been submitted so that nothing gets lost. Most of all they should not be afraid to show their eagerness to work. "Be persistent," says Getsey. "Send me a portfolio and update me on what you're doing. Send tearsheets. I don't really toss anybody out."

— *Michael Willins*

© Frank Ockenfels

The apparent camaraderie between this boy and beautiful raptor make this a perfect shot for a story on the relationships between humans and animals. Kathy Getsey assigned photographer Frank Ockenfels to do the shot for the October 1991 issue of *Special Report*, a bimonthly magazine published by Whittle Communications.

T-SHIRT GALLERY LTD., 154 E. 64, New York NY 10021. (212)838-1212. President: Finn. Estab. 1976. Manufactures clothing and printed fashions.
Needs: Buys 30 photos/year; gives 20 assignments/year. Photos used in brochures, newspapers, magazines and PR releases. Retail and fashion clients; previous/current clients include *Elle, Seventeen* and *Vogue.* Wants to see models in T-shirts.
Specs: Uses b&w and color prints; 8×10 transparencies.
Payment & Terms: Pays $50-200/b&w photo and $100-400/color photo. Buys exclusive product and all rights; negotiable. Model release required.
Making Contact: Interested in receiving work from newer, lesser-known photographers. Query with samples or send unsolicited photos by mail for consideration. SASE. Reports in 3 weeks.

*UNITED STATES CHESS FEDERATION, 186 Route 9W, New Winsor NY 12553. (914)562-8350. FAX: (914)561-2437. Art Director: Jami Anson. Estab. 1939. Buys 150-250 photos/year; offers 10-20 assignments/year. Photos used in brochures, newsletters, posters, newspapers, annual reports, magazines, press releases, catalogs and for audiovisual uses.
Needs: "We use any photography that has to do with chess, people playing, kids playing, tournaments. We put out monthly publication called *Chess Life.*"
Specs: Uses 5×7 or 8×10 matte b&w prints; 4×6 or 8×10 matte color prints; 35mm, 2¼×2¼, 4×5 original transparencies.
Payment & Terms: Pays $25/b&w photo; $200-300/color photo. Payment depends on job. Pays on usage. Credit line given unless used in ad or catalog. Buys one-time and all rights; negotiable. Model release and captions preferred.
Making Contact: Query with samples. Query with stock photo list. Provide resume, business card, self promotion piece or tearsheets to be kept on file for possible future assignments. Works on assignment only. Reviews stock photos. Reports in 3 weeks.
Tips: "Shoot anything that has to do with chess." Wants to see quality photos.

■**UNITED STATES PROFESSIONAL TENNIS ASSOCIATION**, One USPTA Centre, 3535 Briarpark Dr., Houston TX 77042. (713)97-USPTA. Contact: Public Relations Coordinator. Estab. 1927. Professional trade association for tennis instructors. "We produce a monthly member magazine in which we use tennis-related photographs." Photos used in brochures, books, audiovisual presentations and magazines. Examples: "How To Hire a Tennis Professional," "USPTA Sports Science and Sports Medicine Guide," and "How To Prepare for USPTA Certification." In all cases, photos used for text illustration.
Needs: Tennis-related photos.
Specs: Uses b&w and color prints, b&w and color negatives.
Payment & Terms: Pays $15-40/b&w photo; $15-50/color photo; $20-40/hour, and $40-100/day. Convention and tournament coverage negotiable. Credit line given. Buys all rights; negotiable. Model and property release preferred.
Making Contact: Query with samples. Does not return unsolicited material. Reports in 2-3 weeks.
Tips: Prefers to see "good tennis cover shots (vertical), clear image, good expression certain, type of player and racquet, USPTA member or *Pro*. Send photos to us with a cover letter (include phone number), a price list and a description of what you can do."

*■UNITED STATES SAILING ASSOCIATION, P.O. Box 209, Newport RI 02840. (401)849-5200. FAX: (401)849-5208. Communications Director: Allison Peter. Estab. 1897. *American Sailor Magazine* provided to members of United States Sailing Association. Buys 30-50 photos/year. Photos used in brochures, posters and magazines.
Needs: Examples of recent uses: *AMERICAN SAILOR* cover, color slide; "US Sailing Directory" cover; and membership brochure, b&w and color.
Audiovisual Needs: Slides.
Specs: Uses 5×7 matte b&w prints; 8×10 glossy color prints; 35mm transparencies.
Payment & Terms: Pays $300-400/cover photo; $100-200/inside photo; $50-75 research fee if photo is not used. Pays on usage. Credit line given. Buys one-time rights. Captions preferred; include boat type/name, regatta name.
Making Contact: Query with stock photo list. Reviews stock photos, action sailing/racing shots; close-up face shots. SASE. Reports in 2-3 weeks.

UNIVERSITY OF NEW HAVEN, 300 Orange Ave., West Haven CT 06516. (203)932-7243. Public Relations Director: Toni Blood.
Needs: Uses University of New Haven campus photos. Photos used in brochures, newsletters, newspapers, annual reports, catalogs and news releases.
Specs: Uses b&w 5×7 glossy prints and 35mm transparencies; contact sheet OK.
Payment & Terms: Pays $2-9/b&w photo; $10-25/color photo; $10-20/hour; $100-200 and up/day; payment negotiable on a per-photo basis. Buys all rights.
Making Contact: Query with resume "and non-returnable samples for our files. We'll contact to arrange a personal interview to show portfolio." Local freelancers preferred. SASE. "Can't be responsible for lost materials." Reports in 1 week.

Tips: Looks for good people portraits, candids, interaction, news quality. Overall good versatility in mixed situations. "Call first to see if we need additional photographers. If yes, send samples and rates. Make appointment to show portfolio. Be reasonable on costs (we're a nonprofit institution). Be a resident in local area available for assignment." Sees a "need for better and better quality photo reproduction."

■**VAC-U-MAX**, 37 Rutgers St., Belleville NJ 07109. (201)759-4600. FAX: (201)759-6449. Director of Marketing: John Andrew. Provides pneumatic conveying systems for dry powders, pellets, granules etc. in pharmaceutical, chemical, food processing, plastics plants, etc. Also, pneumatically- and electrically-operated industrial vacuum cleaners. Offers 10-12 freelance assignments/year. Photos used for brochures, audiovisual presentations, catalogs, magazines and press releases.
Needs: "We will be looking for photos of installations of our products."
Audiovisual Needs: Sees possible trend toward using freelancers for video. "Most video is now done inhouse, although we are interested in video coverage of operation of equipment in the field and testimonials of users."
Specs: Uses b&w prints; 35mm, 2¼ × 2¼ transparencies; b&w negatives.
Payment & Terms: Payment negotiable; typically pays $50-100/b&w photo; $100-250/color photo; $50-100/hour. "We have engaged several photographers for on-site photography, and we have paid up to $1,000/day plus film, processing and travel." Buys all rights. Model release and captions preferred.
Making Contact: Query with resume of credits. Send unsolicited photos by mail for consideration. SASE. Reports in 2 weeks.
Tips: "We are interested in photographer's capability in photographing industrial equipment in an operating environment. We prefer that he bring installations to our attention which he knows he will be permitted to photograph. Since our venues are strictly industrial, we look for his ability to handle adverse lighting and proper use of lenses in restricted areas."

■**WALTER VAN ENCK DESIGN LIMITED**, 3830 N. Marshfield, Chicago IL 60613. President: Walter Van Enck. Estab. 1978. Produces corporate communications materials (primarily print). Buys 25 photos/year; gives 10 assignments/year. Photos used in brochures, newsletters, posters, audiovisual presentations, annual reports and catalogs.
Needs: Corporate service related activities and product and architectural shots.
Audiovisual Needs: Uses transparencies in audiovisual presentations.
Specs: Uses 8 × 10 glossy and matte b&w prints, 2¼ × 2¼ and 4 × 5 transparencies, and b&w contact sheets.
Payment & Terms: Pays $600-2,000/day. Credit line seldom given. Model release required.
Making Contact: Arrange a personal interview to show portfolio or query with samples. Provide resume, business card, brochure, flyer or tearsheets to be kept on file for possible future assignments. Works with local freelancers only. Reviews stock photos. SASE. Reports as needed.
Tips: "We look for straight corporate (conservative) shots with a little twist of color or light, and ultra high quality b&w printing. Try to keep your name and personality on the tip of our minds."

*■**WORCESTER POLYTECHNIC INSTITUTE**, 100 Institute Rd., Worcester MA 01609. (508)831-5000. FAX: (508)831-5604. University Editor: Michael Dorsey. Estab. 1865. Publishes periodicals and promotional, recruiting and fund-raising printed materials. Gives "4 each" assignments/year. Photos used in brochures, newsletters, posters, audiovisual presentations, annual reports, catalogs, magazines and press releases.
Needs: On-campus, comprehensive and specific views of all elements of the WPI experience. Relations with industry, alumni.
Specs: Uses 5 × 7 (minimum) glossy b&w prints; 35mm, 2¼ × 2¼, 4 × 5 transparencies; b&w contact sheets.
Payment & Terms: Pays maximum $500/day. Credit line given in some publications. Buys one-time rights or all rights; negotiable. Captions preferred.
Making Contact: Interested in receiving work from newer, lesser-known photographers. Arrange a personal interview to show portfolio or query with stock photo list. Provide resume, business card, brochure, flyer or tearsheets to be kept on file for possible future assignments. "No phone calls." Reviews stock photos. SASE. Reports in 2 weeks.

YEARBOOK ASSOCIATES, Box 91, Millers Falls MA 01349. (413)863-8093. Contact: Richard C. Baker, Jr. Estab. 1977. Provides portraits and candids for yearbooks. Gives 5,000 assignments/year. Photos used in yearbooks.
Payment & Terms: Pays $35-160/day. Credit line sometimes given. Buys exclusive product rights and all rights.
Making Contact: Interested in receiving work from newer, lesser-known photographers. Provide resume with current address and phone number. Note: Although most assignments are on a national basis, YBA has local needs in San Francisco, Washington DC and the New England area. Works on

assignment only. Does not return unsolicited material. Scheduling is set up during June, July and August. Shooting starts in September.

Tips: "In addition to portrait photographers we need people with school group and environmental portrait experience. Photographer should like to work with people and be willing to follow our directions. Candid photographer should bring or send a roll of 35mm b&w undeveloped with group shots, action shots of sports, general candids of people."

Businesses and Organizations/'92-93 changes

The following markets appeared in the 1992 edition of *Photographer's Market* but are not listed in the 1993 edition. They may have been omitted for failing to respond to our request for updates of information, they may have gone out of business or they may no longer wish to receive freelance work.

Air-Conditioning & Refrigeration Wholesalers (did not respond)

American Stage Festival (not reviewing work)

Blount, Inc. (did not respond)

Drexel University (not reviewing work)

Hampden-Sydney College (not reviewing work)

La Crosse Area Convention & Visitor Bureau (did not respond)

McGuire Associates (did not respond)

MacIntosh Communications, Inc., Rob (did not respond)

Minnesota Opera, The (did not respond)

Missouri Repertory Theatre (did not respond)

MSD Agvet (not reviewing work)

National Association of Evangelicals (not buying freelance work)

National Association of Legal Secretaries (did not respond)

Posey School of Dance, Inc. (did not respond)

The Quarasan Group, Inc. (did not respond)

Recreational Equipment, Inc. (did not respond)

Salinger Academy of Fashion, Louise (did not respond)

San Jose Repertory Theatre (not reviewing work)

Syracuse Stage (did not respond)

Toledo Area Chamber of Commerce (did not respond)

Union Institute (did not respond)

United Auto Workers (UAW) (did not respond)

Universal Underwriters Group (did not respond)

Woolly Mammoth Theatre Company (did not respond)

World Wildlife Fund/The Conservation Founation (not reviewing work)

Galleries

Making it big in the fine art field is not easy. Most photographers don't have the name recognition of an Annie Lebovitz, Edward Weston or Herb Ritts. It is very likely that, while trying to get your foot in the door, you will have it stepped on more than once. But it's important to remember that at one time in their careers these three photographic wizards weren't well-known either. It took years before they were recognized for their talents.

For those photographers willing to persevere, the fine art field can be rewarding. It takes a lot of dedication and skill, but most importantly it takes thick skin. Not all galleries are going to be receptive to photographers who are eager to gain exposure for their images. In such cases, alternative spaces, such as lobbies, restaurants and corporate offices, may be perfect for someone eager to show off their work and gain recognition. After all, a person waiting in a corporate office for an afternoon appointment may just be the person who can make you famous. He may purchase your work outright or might have the contacts to get you that hard to find publicity.

One photographer who has found some success in the fine art field is Mark Chester, of San Francisco. As our Close-up subject on page 190, Chester discusses the industry and his work.

There was a time, not too long ago, when galleries weren't interested in photography as an art form. Those attitudes have changed in recent years, however, as more collectors have begun to realize that they can acquire original photos from outstanding artists at a lower price than some paintings. Such a trend has created more opportunities in the fine art field and now it is up to photographers to take advantage of the improving marketplace.

Surprisingly, photographers may find it easier to show their work in galleries because of the recent recession. During a recession curators and directors may not have the money to build up gallery inventories because work is selling at a slow rate. Rather than tie up all their income in inventory that is not selling, a director may be willing to accept works on consignment. Such an agreement gives photographers much needed exposure and it provides stock for galleries. By selling on consignment a photographer receives payment from a gallery after a photo is sold.

Quite often, because of their own motivations and concerns, galleries are looking for photographers whose work is outstanding in some important way. It may be the medium or the format or the subject matter. It may also involve such factors as the photographer's proximity to the gallery, his reputation in the region and his overall track record. On the other hand, it will often have less to do with such things and more with just the photographer's having an unusual point of view and ability to excite viewers.

With the varied types of exhibit spaces listed in this section, photographers at all levels have avenues open to them in finding their niche in the gallery market. Some galleries deal only with more experienced, serious photographers, but the gallery market in general remains quite open to discovering and cultivating new talent. More than 120 galleries and museums appear this year in *Photographer's Market*. These listings include both local and regional outlets for photographic art, as well as the needs and requirements of making contact and arranging for an exhibit of your work.

Within the last couple of years, interest in film, video and other audiovisual media has been increasing among galleries and their patrons. Accordingly, we have included more information about a gallery's interest in such media in this edition. In particular, listings which are interested in seeing and exhibiting work in these various media have been marked with a special AV symbol—a solid, black square—before the listing's name for easier recognition.

THE AFTERIMAGE PHOTOGRAPH GALLERY, The Quandrangle 115, 2828 Routh St., Dallas TX 75201. (214)871-9140. Owner: Ben Breard. Estab. 1971. Interested in any subject matter. Frequently sells landscapes.
Exhibits: Examples of recent exhibitions: "New York City in the 1930s" by Berenice Abbott; landscapes by John Sexton; and portraits by Nicholas Nixon. Sponsors openings; "an opening usually lasts 2 hours, and we have several a year." Photographer should "have many years of experience and a history of publications and museum and gallery display; although if one's work is strong enough, these requirements may be negated." Open to exhibiting work of newer photographers, "but that work is usually difficult to sell." Prefers Cibachrome "or other fade-resistant process" for color and "archival quality" for b&w.
Terms & Making Contact: Charges 50% sales commission on most pictures handled directly (photographer sets price). Price range: $40-10,000. Query first with resume of credits and biographical data or call to arrange an appointment. SASE. Reports in 2 days-2 months. Unframed work only.
Tips: Currently landscapes sell the best. "Work enough years to build up a sufficient inventory of, say, 20-30 superb prints, and make a quality presentation. Sees trend toward more color, bigger sizes, and more hand-painted prints."

AKRON ART MUSEUM, 70 E. Market St., Akron OH 44308. (216)376-9185. Curator: Barbara Tannenbaum. Interested in innovative works by contemporary photographers; any subject matter.
Exhibits: Requirements: To exhibit, photographers must possess "a notable record of exhibitions, inclusion in publications, and/or a role in the historical development of photography. We also feature local photographers (Akron area)." Examples of recent exhibitions: "Ralph Eugene Meatyard: An American Visionary," "The Cuyahoga Valley: Photographs by Robert Glenn Ketchum," Cibachrome color photographs; and "Czech Modernism: Photography," a historical survey of Czechoslovakian photography. Presents 3-5 exhibits/year. Shows last 2 months. Sponsors openings; provides light food, beverages and sometimes entertainment. Photographer's presence at opening preferred. Presence during show is not required, but willingness to give a gallery talk is appreciated.
Terms & Making Contact: NPI; buys photography outright. Annually awards Knight Purchase Award to living artist working with photographic media. Will review transparencies. Send material by mail for consideration. SASE. Reports in 1-2 months "depending on our workload."
Tips: "Prepare a professional looking packet of materials including high-quality slides, and always send a SASE. Never send original prints."

*ALAN GALLERY, 61 W. Bridge St., Berea OH 44017. (216)243-7794. President: Alan Boesger. Estab. 1984.
Exhibits: Examples of recent exhibitions: Works by Robert Pabst and Ken McCarthy. Presents 1 show/year. Sponsors openings. Photographer's presence at opening preferred.
Terms & Making Contact: Charges 40% commission. Buys photography outright. General price range: $200-600. Reviews transparencies. Interested in unframed work only. Send material by mail for consideration. SASE. Reports in 3 weeks.

*ALBER GALLERIES, #5111, 3300 Darby Rd., Haverford PA 19041. (215)896-9297. Director: Howard Alber. Estab. 1977.
Exhibits: Requirements: Professional presentation, well priced for sales, good back up of images, consistent quality and willingness to deliver promptly. Interested in fine landscapes, artful treatments of creative presentation. Has shown work by Michael Hogan, Harry Auspitz and Barry Slavin. Photographer's presence at opening is not required. "Cooperative show space only."
Terms & Making Contact: Charges 40% commission. General price range: $75-1,000. Reviews transparencies. Slides only on first presentation. Query with samples. Send material by mail for consideration. SASE. Reports in 3 weeks.
Tips: "Give us copies of all reproduced photos, calendars etc."

The asterisk before a listing indicates that the market is new in this edition. New markets are often the most receptive to freelance submissions.

*THE ALBUQUERQUE MUSEUM, 2000 Mountain Road NW, Albuquerque NM 87104. (505)243-7255. FAX: (505)764-6546. Curator of Art: Ellen Landis. Estab. 1967.
Exhibits: Requirements: Send photos, resume and artist's statement. Interested in all subjects. Examples of recent exhibitions: "Gus Foster," by Gus Foster (panaramic photographs); "Santiago," by Joan Myers (b&w 16×20) and "Frida Kahlo," by Lola Alvaraz Bravo (b&w various sizes). Presents 3-6 shows/year. Shows last 8-12 weeks. Photographer's presence at opening preferred, presence during show preferred.
Terms & Making Contact: Buys photos outright. Reviews transparencies. Interested in framed or unframed work, mounted or unmounted work, matted or unmatted work. Arrange a personal interview to show portfolio. Submit portfolio for review. Send material by mail for consideration. "Sometimes we return material; sometimes we keep works on file." Reports in 1 month.

a.k.a. SKYLIGHT GALLERY OF BEACON HILL, 43 Charles St., Boston MA 02114. (617)720-2855. Director: John Chittick. Open to all types of photography.
Exhibits: Requirements: All images framed or matted; rent of gallery space; produce a postcard. Examples of recent exhibitions: Personal photographs from the father of American documentary film, Richard Leacock; large architectural street scenes, by Roger Kingston; manipulated polaroids/pinhole photography, by Fay Breed. Shows last 1 month. Sponsors openings. Photographer's presence at opening preferred.
Terms & Making Contact: Photographer pays $1,650 for 4-week show. This includes all fees. No gallery commission. "We strive to publicize the photographers and their works in the most marketable way so that the reception brings in many buyers. Our gallery offers a complete gallery exhibition and marketing plan to the photographer." Rental package includes: 3,200 postcards of one of photographer's images on exhibit. Gallery mails out 1,700 to selected Boston list, photographer gets 1,500. Gallery handles all publicity and press kits to 80 local media (TV, radio and newspapers); Gallery plans and pays for opening reception for 200 people with wine and cheese and live music; paid advertising in *Art New England* and *Gallery Guide* (national issue); $5,000 insurance. Will review transparencies. Interested in mounted work. Arrange a personal interview to show portfolio. SASE. Reports in 1 month.
Tips: "If the photographer is interested in a Boston exhibit, this is a good idea. Sales prospects are rather good. The public is looking for 'original' photos to fit in home or office."

AMERICAN SOCIETY OF ARTISTS, INC., Box 1326, Palatine IL 60078. (708)991-4748 or (312)751-2500. Membership Chairman: Helen Del Valle. "Our members range from internationally known artists to unknown artists—quality of work is the important factor. We have about 25 shows throughout the year which accept photographic art."
Terms & Making Contact: Members and non-members may exhibit. NPI; price range varies. Send SASE for membership information and application (state media). Reports in 2 weeks. Framed, mounted or matted work only. Accepted members may participate in lecture and demonstration service. Member publication: *ASA Artisan.*

ART MUSEUM OF SOUTHEAST TEXAS, Box 3703, Beaumont TX 77704. (409)832-3432. Curator of Exhibitions: Lynn Castle. Interested in 19th and 20th century American photography.
Exhibits: Requirements: Framed works only. Examples of recent exhibitions: "Uncertain to Blue," b&w prints of Texas communities, people, by Keith Carter; Manipulated Poloroids by Debbie Fleming Caffery (New Orleans); 36×72″ Cibachrome prints - sets a stage and photographs by Nic Nicosia (Dallas). Presents "at least 1" exhibit/year. Shows last 10-16 weeks. Sponsors openings; includes invitations, reception with hors d'oeurves, occasional live music or performance. Photographer's presence at opening preferred.
Terms & Making Contact: "Photography can be sold in the gallery, but we do not solicit - we are nonprofit." Museum charges 20% commission on sales. Buys photography outright. General price range: $400-800. Will review transparencies. "We request that artists not schedule any other major exhibitions in the Beaumont area at least one year prior to their museum exhibition." Send slides and resumé by mail for consideration. SASE. "Sorry to say we are slow in returning material though due to volume sent." Reports in 1 month "hopefully."
Tips: "Send slides and resume, prints should be mounted on white mats-simple frames. Sometimes black mats are OK."

*ARTISTS FOUNDATION GALLERY AT CITYPLACE, 8 Park Plaza, Boston MA 02116. (617)227-2787. FAX:(617)523-1764. Director: Mark Booth. Estab. 1988.
Exhibits: "All work for review must be submitted in the form of 35mm plastic slide examples of the artworks, sent to the attention of the gallery director. All decisions for exhibits are made by the gallery director, and all decisions are final." Interested in works that strive to push beyond the limits of traditional definitions of the media. Examples of recent exhibitions: "Seven By Seven," by Margaret

Tuitt (silver prints); "Attraction/Repulsion," by Joel-Peter Witkin (photo collage) and "Images of the Midtown Cultural District," by A. Samuel Laundon (color prints). Presents 8-10 shows/year. Shows last 6 weeks. Sponsors openings. Photographer's presence at opening preferred, photographer's presence during show preferred.
Terms & Making Contact: Charges 30% commission. General price range: $250-2,500. Interested in framed, mounted and matted work only. Requires exclusive representation within metropolitan area. Send material by mail for consideration. Send 10-20 35mm plastic slide examples of the artworks, submitted in a clear-plastic slide page. "Each slide must be labeled with the artist's name, the year the artwork was completed, and an arrow or dot to indicate the top of the image. Please send copies of slides; do not send the one and only original set of slides. We cannot be held responsible if slides are lost or damaged in the mail." Send a brief cover letter addressed to the gallery director, a resume, or list of current and past exhibits, and an artist's statement. SASE. Reports in 1-2 weeks.

ASCHERMAN GALLERY/CLEVELAND PHOTOGRAPHIC WORKSHOP, Suite 4, 1846 Coventry Village, Cleveland Heights OH 44118. (216)321-0054. FAX: (216)321-4372. Director: Herbert Ascherman, Jr. Estab. 1977. Sponsored by Cleveland Photographic Workshop. Subject matter: all forms of photographic art and production. "Membership is not necessary. A prospective photographer must show a portfolio of 40-60 slides or prints for consideration. We prefer to see distinctive work—a signature in the print, work that could only be done by one person, not repetitive or replicative of others."
Exhibits: Presents 6 shows/year. Shows last about 8 weeks. Openings are held for some shows. Photographers are expected to contribute toward expenses of publicity. Photographer's presence at show "always good to publicize, but not necessary." Recent photography exhibits include: annual group open show with five national photographers; "Gum Arabics," by Jacques Goddard, France.
Terms & Making Contact: Interested in receiving work from newer, lesser-known photographers. Charges 25-40% commission, depending on the artist. Sometimes buys photography outright. Price range: $100-1,500. "Photos in the $100-300 range sell best." Will review transparencies. Matted work only for show.
Tips: "Be as professional in your presentation as possible; identify slides with name, title, etc.; matte, mount, box prints. We are a Midwest gallery and for the most part, people here respond to competent, conservative images more so than experimental or trendy work, though we are always looking for innovative work that best represents the artist (all subject matter)."

*A-SPACE GALLERY, 544 State St., Madison WI 53703. (608)255-4813. Director: Julie Shoner. Estab. 1984.
Exhibits: Requirements: framed, in glass or plexi. Interested in "regional emerging and experimental artists—cutting edger." Examples of recent exhibitions: Jean Langer, b&w photos, framed and matted, experimental; Chris Foos, b&w photos, framed and matted, representational; and Mark Aumann, b&w photos, framed, realistic/Third World studies. Presents 5 shows/year. Shows last 5 weeks. Sponsors openings; provides wine, coffee, crackers, cheese, artist provides an additional beverage or food.
Terms & Making Contact: Charges 25% commission. Reviews transparencies. Interested in framed or unframed work, mounted or unmounted work, matted work only. Arrange a personal interview to show portfolio. Query with resume of credits. Query with samples. Send material by mail for consideration. Submit portfolio for review. SASE. Reports in 2 weeks.

THE BALTIMORE MUSEUM OF ART, Art Museum Dr., Baltimore MD 21218. (410)396-6345. FAX: (410)396-6562. Contact: Department of Prints, Drawings and Photographs. Interested in work of quality and originality; no student work.
Terms & Making Contact: Arrange a personal interview to show portfolio or query with resume of credits. SASE. Reports in 2 weeks-1 month. Unframed and matted work only. NPI.

BARRON ARTS CENTER, Dept. PM, 582 Rahway Ave., Woodbridge NJ 07095. (908)634-0413. Director: Stephen J. Kager. Estab. 1975.
Exhibits: Examples of recent exhibitions: "Silver Prints" by Victor Macarol (urban street scenes); "Faces of Maya" by Joseph Macko (color portraits and photo documentary of Mayan tribe); and "Portraits of Artists" by Michael Bergman (black and white portraits). Presents 1-2 shows/year. Shows last 4-5 weeks. Sponsors openings; refreshments (excluding wine). Photographer's presence at opening required.
Terms & Making Contact: Photography sold in gallery. Charges 20% commission. General price range: $150-400. Reviews transparencies but prefers portfolio. Submit portfolio for review. Cannot return material. Reports "depending upon date of review, but in general within a month of receiving materials."
Tips: "Make a professional presentation of work in all pieces matted or treated in a like manner." In terms of the market, we tend to hear that there are not enough galleries existing that will exhibit photography." One trend is that there is a fair amount of "both representational and art and photography."

*HANK BAUM GALLERY, P.O. Box 26689, San Francisco CA 94126. (415)752-4336. Director/Owner: Hank Baum. Estab. 1968.
Exhibits: Examples of recent exhibits: Works by Jacques-Henri Lartigue (photographs); William Henry Jackson (photochromes) and "Photos of China," by Hank Baum (Cibachromes). Shows last 2 months.
Terms & Making Contact: Charges 50% commission. General price range: $100-1,000. Arrange a personal interview to show portfolio. SASE. Reports in 1-2 weeks.

BERKSHIRE ARTISANS GALLERY, 28 Renne Ave., Pittsfield MA 01201. (413)499-9348. Commissioner: Daniel M. O'Connell. Estab. 1975. "Photographer should send SASE with slides and resume by mail only to gallery."
Exhibits: Examples of recent exhibitions: "Helen Rose Has Alzheimer's Disease" by Nicholas Decandia (b&w); "Between Assignments" by Joel Librizzi (newspaper photojournalism); and "The Other Side of Florida" by Woody Walters (b&w). Presents 10 shows/year. Exhibits last 6 months. Sponsors openings; "we provide publicity announcements, artist provides refreshments." Artists presence at opening and during shows preferred.
Terms & Making Contact: Interested in receiving work from newer, lesser-known photographers. Charges 20% commission. General price range: $50-1,500. Will review transparencies of photographic work. Interested in seeing framed, mounted, matted work only. Send material by mail for consideration with SASE.
Tips: To break in, "Send portfolio and SASE. We accept all art photography. Work must be professionally presented. We have a professional juror look at slide entries once a year (usually January-April). Expect that work to be tied up for 6-8 months in jury." Sees trend toward "black and white and Cibachrome architectural photography."

BIRD-IN-HAND GALLERY, 323 7th St. SE, P.O. Box 15258, Washington DC 20003-0258. (202)543-0744. Owner: Christopher Ackerman. Estab. 1987. Interested in interpretive b&w, architectural, landscape and special technique; quite receptive to newer photographers.
Exhibits: Requirements: professionalism. Examples of exhibitions: "Saguaro Cactus, Images of a Threatened Species," photographs by Madge Matteo; "Cape Cod," (b&w palladium and platinum prints) by Alan Scherr; b&w prints by Ester Espejo; and aerial photography by Robert Perron, (color and b&w prints of environmentally sensitive regions of the world and Amazonia). Presents 4-6 shows/year. Shows last 2½ weeks. Sponsors openings. Photographer's presence at opening preferred.
Terms & Making Contact: Exhibitors are represented throughout the year. Charges 40% commission. General price range $75-375. Reviews transparencies. Interested in framed or unframed work, matted or unmatted work. Size and quantity of photos considered on individual basis. Query with samples. SASE. Reports in 2 weeks.
Tips: "Photography is like any other business—be prepared to start at the bottom and work hard. Remain original. We have good experience with lower priced work. We receive many submissions that are obtuse and impossible to interpret without being able to read a photographer's mind. Remember form as well as content makes great art. Human subjects, landscape and special technique currently sells best at our gallery."

*BLANDEN MEMORIAL ART MUSEUM, 920 Third Ave. S., Ford Dodge IA 50501. (515)573-2316. FAX: (515)573-2317. "Telephone before faxing." Director: Philip La Douceur. Estab. 1930.
Exhibits: Requirements: slides, resume and artist's statement. Presents 3 or more shows/year. Shows last 2 months. Sponsors openings; receptions and lectures. Photographer's presence at opening preferred, photographer's presence during show preferred.
Terms & Making Contact: Charges 35% commission. Buys photos outright. Open price range. Reviews transparencies. Interested in exhibiting framed work only. Send material by mail for consideration. SASE. Reports in 1 month.
Tips: "Send quality slides. Take time to prepare your work for exhibition. Use white or off-white mat."

*BRENT GALLERY, P.O. Box 66034, Houston TX 77266. (713)522-5013. Director: Kevin Mercier. Estab. 1984. Interested in something previously not seen.
Exhibits: Examples of recent exhibitions: Francisco Barragán (color prints of surrealistic imagery); "Feet First," by María Inés Roqué (b&w prints of feet in various contexts); "Contracurtis: Early American Coverups, Series #4," by Warren Neidich (platinum prints simulations of antique photos taken from B-grade TV westerns, a la Edward S. Curtis). Presents 1 show/year. Shows last 12 weeks. Sponsors openings; gallery pays invitations and reception. Photographer's presence at opening preferred.
Terms & Making Contact: Charges 50% commission. General price range: $200-950. Will review transparencies. Interested in framed or unframed, mounted or unmounted, and matted or unmatted work. Requires exclusive representation within metropolitan area. Send material by mail for consideration. SASE. Reports in 1 month.

Tips: This is a "progressive gallery looking for unique, historically important work. Landscapes/romanticized subjects seem to be leading the way for other media." The buying public is "still wrapped up in post-modernism (Sherman, et al)."

THE BROKEN DIAMOND, 201 Grand Ave., Billings MT 59101. Owner: Frederick R. Longan. Estab. 1978.
Exhibits: "Since we moved exhibiting is minimal. We are working more as a private dealer and less as a gallery."
Terms & Making Contact: Charges 50% commission; buys photography outright. General price range: $350-5,000+. Arrange a personal interview to show portfolio.

J.J. BROOKINGS GALLERY, P.O. Box 1237, San Jose CA 95108. (408)287-3311. Director: Timothy C. Duran. Interested in photography created with a painterly eye.
Exhibits: Requirements: Professional presentation, realistic pricing, numerous quality images. Examples of recent exhibitions: Ansel Adams, James Crable, Linda Gray, Duane Michals, Edward Curtis, Ben Schonzeit, Sandy Skoglund and Todd Watts. Presents 3+ shows (not including group shows)/year. Sponsors openings. Photographers presence at opening preferred.
Terms & Making Contact: Charges 50% commission. Buys some photography outright. General price range: $500-10,000+. Reviews transparencies. Send material by mail for consideration. Reports in 3 weeks; "if not acceptable, reports immediately."
Tips: Interested in "whatever the artist thinks will impress me the most. 'Painterly' work is best. No documentary, landscape or politically-oriented work."

CALIFORNIA MUSEUM OF PHOTOGRAPHY, University of California, Riverside CA 92521. (714)787-4787. Director: Jonathan Green. The photographer must have the "highest quality work."
Exhibits: Presents 12-18 shows/year. Shows last 6-8 weeks. Sponsors openings; inclusion in museum calendar, reception.
Terms & Making Contact: Curatorial committee reviews transparencies and/or matted or unmatted work. Query with resume of credits. SASE. Reports in 90 days.
Tips: "This museum attempts to balance exhibitions among historical, technology, contemporary, etc. We do not sell photos but provide photographers with exposure. The museum is always interested in newer, lesser-known photographers who are producing interesting work. We can show only a small percent of what we see in a year. The CMP has moved into a renovated 23,000 sq. ft. building. It is the largest exhibition space devoted to photography in the west."

THE CAMERA OBSCURA GALLERY, 1309 Bannock St., Denver CO 80204. (303)623-4059. Director: Hal Gould. Estab. 1963.
Exhibits: Examples of recent exhibitions: Sebastiao Salgado, Jock Sturges, O. Winston Link and Jay Dunitz. Shows last 6 weeks. Sponsors openings. Photographer's presence at opening preferred.
Terms & Making Contact: Receptive to exhibiting work of newer, lesser-known photographers "if it is good enough." Charges 40-50% commission. Buys photography outright. General price range: $200-25,000. Will review transparencies. Interested in mounted or unmounted work, matted or unmatted work. Requires exclusive representation within metropolitan area. Arrange a personal interview to show portfolio. SASE. Reports in 2 weeks.
Tips: Sees trend toward "more traditional principles of photography."

WILLIAM CAMPBELL CONTEMPORARY ART, Dept. PM, 4935 Byers Ave., Ft. Worth TX 76107. (817)737-9566. Owner/Director: William Campbell. Estab. 1974. "Primarily interested in photography which has been altered or manipulated in some form."
Exhibits: Requirements: An established record of exhibitions. Examples of recent exhibitions: A group show, "The Figure In Photography: An Alternative Approach," by Patrick Faulhaber, Francis Merritt-Thompson, Steven Sellars, Dottie Allen and Glenys Quick. Presents 8-10 shows/year. Shows last 5 weeks. Sponsors openings; provides announcements, press releases, installation of work, insurance, cost of exhibition. Photographer's presence during show preferred.
Terms & Making Contact: Charges 50% commission. General price range: $75-500. Reviews transparencies. Interested in framed or unframed work; mounted work only. Requires exclusive representation within metropolitan area. Send slides and resume by mail. SASE. Reports in 1 month.

THE CANTON ART INSTITUTE, 1001 Market Ave., Canton OH 44702. (216)453-7666. Executive Director: M.J. Albacete. "We are interested in exhibiting all types of quality photography, preferably using photography as an art medium, but we will also examine portfolios of other types of photography work as well: architecture, etc."

Exhibits: Requirements: "The photographer must send preliminary letter explaining desire to exhibit; send samples of work (upon our request); have enough work to form an exhibition; complete *Artist's Form* detailing professional and academic background, and provide photographs for press usage." Presents 2-5 shows/year. Shows last 6 weeks. Sponsors openings. Major exhibits (in galleries), postcard or other type mailer, public reception.

Terms & Making Contact: Charges commission. General price range: $50-500. Interested in exhibition-ready work. No size limits. Query with samples. Submit letters of inquiry first, with samples of photos. SASE. Reports in 2 weeks.

Tips: "We look for photo exhibitions which are unique, not necessarily by 'top' names. Anyone inquiring should have some exhibition experience, and have sufficient materials; also, price lists, insurance lists, description of work, artist's background, etc. Most photographers and artists do little to aid galleries and museums in promoting their works—no good publicity photos, confusing explanations about their work, etc. We attempt to give photographers—new and old—a good gallery exhibit when we feel their work merits such. While sales are not our main concern, the exhibition experience and the publicity can help promote new talents. If the photographer is really serious about his profession, he should design a press-kit type of package so that people like me can study his work, learn about his background, and get a pretty good concept of his work. This is generally the first knowledge we have of any particular artist, and if a bad impression is made, even for the best photographer, he gets no exhibition. How else are we to know? We have a basic form which we send to potential exhibitors requesting all the information needed for an exhibition. My article, 'Artists, Get Your Act Together If You Plan to Take it on the Road,' shows artists how to prepare self-promoting kits for potential sponsors, gallery exhibitors, etc. Copy of article and form sent for $2 and SASE."

CASSAZA GRAPHICS GALLERY, % Nevada Museum of Art, 160 W. Liberty St., Reno NV 89501. (702)329-3333. Curator of Art: Howard Spencer. Estab. 1931.

Exhibits: Requirements: Nationally emerging photographers with art photography, 19th-20th century historic development, new trends. Presents 6-8 shows/year. Shows last 6-8 weeks. Sponsors openings; provides catered reception for up to 400 people, book signings, etc. Photographer's presence at opening and during show preferred.

Terms & Making Contact: Charges 40% commission—not first priority. General price range: $75-2,000. Reviews transparencies. Interested in framed or unframed work. Does not require exclusive representation, but doesn't work with people who have already had recent exposure in the area. Query with samples; send material by mail for consideration. SASE. Reports in 1 month.

Tips: "Be mature in style with consistent body of work." Opportunities are fair "if photographer prepares his work." Sees trend toward more "multi-media installations and electronically (computer) generated images."

*CENTER FOR EXPLORATORY AND PERCEPTUAL ART, Fourth Floor, 700 Main St., Buffalo NY 14202. (716)856-2717. FAX: (716)855-3959. Executive Director: Gail Nicholson. Estab. 1974.

Exhibits: Requirements: Work must be photographically related (film, digital, installation, non-silver, etc.). Artist should have enough work to fill at least half of the space. The total space is approximately 225 working feet. Interested in political, culturally diverse, contemporary and conceptual works. Examples of recent exhibitions: Lorna Simpson (conceptual/assemblage/image and text pieces), "Photographs of Widely-Known Non-Existent Beings," a solo show by Kathleen Campbell (hand-painted, gelatin silver prints) and "Vestigial Remains," by Sigrid Casey (digital electrostatic collage/color copy). Presents 5-6 shows/year. Shows last 6 weeks. Sponsors openings; reception with lecture. Photographer's presence at opening required, presence during show preferred.

Terms & Making Contact: NPI. Interested in framed or unframed work, mounted or unmounted. Arrange a personal interview to show portfolio. Submit portfolio for review. Send material by mail for consideration. SASE. Reports in 1 month.

CENTER FOR PHOTOGRAPHY AT WOODSTOCK, Dept. PM, 59 Tinker St., Woodstock NY 12498. (914)679-9957. Exhibitions Director: Kathleen Kenyon. Interested in all creative photography.

Exhibits: Presents 10 shows/year. Shows last 4 weeks. Sponsors openings.

Terms & Making Contact: Charges 25% sales commission. Price range: $75-1,000. Send 20 slides plus resume by mail for consideration. SASE. Reports in 4 months.

Tips: "Visit us first—set up an appointment, or write us a brief letter. Enclose resume, statement on the work, 20 slides, SASE. We are closed Wednesdays and Thursdays. We show contemporary photography."

CITY OF LOS ANGELES PHOTOGRAPHY CENTERS, Dept. PM, 412 S. Park View St., Los Angeles CA 90057. (213)383-7342. Contact: Director. Estab. 1960. Interested in all types of photography.
Exhibits: Examples of recent exhibits: "Selected Photographs 1975-1990," by Peter Reiss, (documentary); "Power of Site: Landscape Photography," group exhibit with 16 photographers (landscape); and "Los Angeles Photography Biennial 1990," group exhibit with 10 emerging photographers (mixed media with photos). Presents 8 shows/year. Exhibits last 4-6 weeks.
Terms & Making Contact: Very receptive to exhibiting work of newer, lesser-known photographers. Offers rental darkrooms, studio space, outings, lectures, classes, bi-monthly newsletter, juried annual photography contest, a photo library and photographer's slide registry. "Send up to 20 slides with resume for us to keep on file. Send SASE if you want them returned." Reports in 1 month. Matted work only. Charges 20% commission.
Tips: "We are interested in seeing professional photography which explores a multitude of techniques and styles, while expanding the notion of the art of photography. We are interested in seeing series of works that are unique, that hold together with a theme, that explore a particular subject matter, that have extremely high print quality and excellent presentation (mats). Notes that "Both contemporary avant-garde and more traditional photographs are currently selling equally well." Sees trend toward "Use of other media in combination with photographs (such as paint, collage, metal, sculpture)." To break in, "Present a strong series of works that hold together thematically (explore a particular issue or technique)."

WILSON W. CLARK MEMORIAL LIBRARY GALLERY, 5000 N. Willamette Blvd., Portland OR 97203-5798. (503)283-7111. FAX: (503)283-7491. Director: Rev. Joseph P. Browne. Estab. 1959.
Exhibits: General, excluding nudes. Can be color or b&w. Examples of exhibitions: "Faces of Ireland" by Donald Gedman (color prints). Presents 1 or 2 shows/year. Shows last 1 month.
Terms & Making Contact: Interested in exhibiting work of newer, lesser-known photographers. Charges 10% commission. General price range: $100-200. Reviews transparencies. Interested in mounted work only; matted or unmatted work. Query with samples. SASE. Reports in 1 month.

*DAVID CLAY GALLERY, 1600 Hartford, Austin TX 78703. Owner: David Clay. Estab. 1989.
Exhibits: Interested in figurative images. Presents 4 shows/year. Shows last 6 weeks. Sponsors openings. Photographer's presence at opening preferred.
Terms & Making Contact: Charges 50% commission. Buys photos outright. General price range: $40-500. Reviews transparencies only. Requires exclusive representation within metropolitan area. Send slides by mail for consideration. SASE. Reports in 1 month.
Tips: "Send your best work not all your work. Knock my socks off."

*CONCEPT ART GALLERY, 1031 S. Braddock, Pittsburgh PA 15218. (412)242-9200. FAX: (412)242-7443. Director: Sam Berkovitz. Estab. 1972.
Exhibits: Desires "interesting, mature work." Work that stretches the bounds of what is percieved as typical photography. Examples of recent exhibitions: "Home Earth Sky," by Seth Dickerman and "Eliza," by Mark Perrott. Presents 1-2 shows/year. Shows last 30-45 days. Sponsors openings; color mailer and installation services. Photographer's presence at opening preferred.
Terms & Making Contact: Charges 30-50% commission. Buys photos outright. General price range: $250-8,500. Reviews transparencies. Interested in unmounted work only. Requires exclusive representation within metropolitan area. Send material by mail for consideration. SASE. Reports in 1-2 weeks.
Tips: "Mail portfolio with SASE for best results. Will arrange appointment with artists if interested."

THE CONTEMPORARY ARTS CENTER, Dept. PM, 115 E. Fifth St., Cincinnati OH 45202. (513)721-0390. Curator: Stacy Sims. Nonprofit arts center. Interested in avant garde, innovative photography. Photographer must be selected by the curator and approved by the board.
Exhibits: Examples of recent exhibits: "Warhol/Makos," the work of New York photographer Christopher Makos; "Images of Desire," contemporary advertising photography; "The Perfect Moment: Robert Mapplethorpe." Presents 1-3 shows/year. Exhibits last 6 weeks. Sponsors openings; provides printed invitations, music, refreshments, cash bar. Photographer's presence at opening preferred.
Terms & Making Contact: Photography sometimes sold in gallery. Charges 10% commission. General price range: $200-500. Will review transparencies. Send query with resume and slides of work. SASE. Reports in 2 months.

*CONVERSE COLLEGE MILLIKEN GALLERY, 580 E. Main St., Spartanburg SC 29302. (803)596-9177. FAX: (803)596-9158. Director: Mac Boggs. Estab. 1971.
Exhibits: Must have 24 to 30 pieces ready to hang. All artists require slide preview before show. Interested in creative and experimental. Presents 1 or 2 shows/year. Shows last 30 days. Sponsors openings. Provides food and drink. Photographer's presence at opening preferred.

Terms & Making Contact: General price range: $30-250. Reviews transparencies. Interested in framed work only. No size limit. Send material by mail for consideration. SASE. Reports in 1 month.
Tips: "We are a college gallery and, although we send 1,200 invitations to the community, the gallery primarily serves as an extension of the classroom."

*CROSSMAN GALLERY, University of Wisconsin-Whitewater, 800 W. Main St., Whitewater WI 53190. (414)472-5708. Dierctor: Susan Walsh. Estab. 1971.
Exhibits: Requirements: Resume, artist's statement, list insurance information, 10-20 slides, work framed and ready to mount and have 4×5 transparencies available. Interested in all types, especially cibachrome as large format and controversial subjects. Examples of recent exhibitions: "Color Photography Invitational," by Regina Flanagan, "Color Photography Invitational," by Leigh Kane and "Color Photography Invitational," by Janica Yoder. Presents 1 show/biannually. Shows last 3-4 weeks. Sponsors openings; food, beverage and possible visiting artist lecture/demo. Photographer's presence at opening preferred, presence during show preferred.
Term & Making Contact: Buys photos outright. General price range: $250-2,800. Reviews transparencies. Interested in framed and mounted work only. Send material by mail for consideration. SASE. Reports in 1 month.

ELEVEN EAST ASHLAND (Independent Art Space), 11 E. Ashland, Phoenix AZ 85004. (602)271-0831. Director: David Cook. Estab. 1986.
Exhibits: Requirements: Contemporary only; (portrait, landscape, genre, mixed media in b&w, color, non-silver, etc.), photographers must represent themselves, complete exhibition proposal form and be responsible for own announcements. Example of recent exhibitions: Color city scapes by Tom Coaker; "China Series" color images by Mark Abrahamson; and "Post Earthquake S.F." by David Cook. Presents 13 shows/year. Shows last 1 month. Sponsors openings; two inhouse juried/invitational exhibits/year. Photographer's presence during show preferred.
Terms & Making Contact: Very receptive to exhibiting work of newer, lesser-known photographers. Charges 25% commission. General price range: $100-500. Reviews transparencies. Interested in framed or unframed work, mounted or unmounted work, matted or unmatted work. Shows are limited to material able to fit through the front door and in the space (4' × 8' max.). Query with resume of credits; query with samples. SASE. Reports in 2 weeks.
Tips: To break in, "be sincerely interested in exhibiting your work and representing yourself." Opportunities in this market are fair. General public is especially interested in color, manipulated work city scapes and landscapes. Sees trend toward straight photographs, documentation.

ETHERTON/STERN GALLERY, 135 S. 6th Ave., Tucson AZ 85701. (602)624-7370. Director: Terry Etherton. Estab. 1981. Interested in contemporary photography with emphasis on artists in Western and Southwestern US. Photographer must "have a high-quality, consistent body of work—be a working artist/photographer—no 'hobbyists' or weekend photographers."
Exhibits: Examples of recent exhibitions: "Sign Language," Cibachrome prints by Skeet McAuley; gelatin silver prints by Joel-Peter Witkin; and Cibachrome prints by William Lesch. Presents 8-9 shows/year. Shows last 5 weeks. Sponsors openings; provides wine and refreshments, publicity, etc. Photographer's presence at opening and during show preferred.
Terms & Making Contact: Charges 50% commission. Occasionally buys photography outright. General price range: $200-20,000. Reviews transparencies. Interested in matted or unmatted, unframed work. Arrange a personal interview to show portfolio or send material by mail for consideration. SASE. Reports in 3 weeks.
Tips: "You must be fully committed to photography as a way of life. You should be familiar with the photo art world and with my gallery and the work I show. Do not show more than 20 prints for consideration. Show only the best of your work—no fillers. Have work sent or delivered so that it is presentable and professional." Wants to see "cutting edge, issue-oriented photos. Not interested in classical or traditional work." Figurative and expressive styles currently popular with visitors. To break in, "be aware of current trends and issues."

FILM IN THE CITIES, 2388 University Ave., St. Paul MN 55114. (612)646-6104. Gallery Director: James Dozier. Estab. 1977. "Film in the Cities shows a wide variety of contemporary photographic styles from documentary to experimental to mixed media."
Exhibits: "The main criterion for exhibiting work at Film in the Cities is a cohesive, mature body of work." Examples of recent exhibitions: "Convergence" by African-American Photographers; "Barrage" by Unda Swartz, Sunil Gupta, Youngsoon Min, Cadi Gofbarg; and "Cuba-USA" by 12 Cuban-American photographers. Presents 9-10 shows/year. Shows last 4-5 weeks. Sponsors openings. "*We* host the opening receptions for gallery shows and the only requirement is the photographer's presence if possible." Photographer's presence at opening is preferred.

Terms & Making Contact: Charges 10% commission. General price range: $75 and up. Reviews transparencies. Interested in framed or unframed, mounted or unmounted, matted or unmatted work. Send material by mail for consideration or submit portfolio for review. SASE. Reports in 1 month.

●**FLEISHER ART MEMORIAL, DENE M LOUCHHEIM GALLERIES,** 709-721 Catharine St., Philadelphia PA 19147. (215)922-3456. Gallery Coordinator: Lanny Bergner.
Exhibits: Interested in contemporary, avant-garde and experimental. Applicant must enter the juried Challenge Competition. Categories include photography. February deadline. Call for entry form. Also, photographers must live within 50 mile radius of Philadelphia. Presents 2-4 shows/year. Shows last 1 month. Sponsors openings. Photographer's presence during show preferred.
Terms & Making Contact: Charges 20% commission. General price range: $200-2,000. Enter challenge competition only. SASE. Returns material submitted for "Challenge" exhibit approximately 6 weeks following February deadline.
Tips: To be exhibited, "abide by the guidelines of the Challenge Competition." Photographers should be aware that "there is limited representation in Philadelphia."

○ **FOCAL POINT GALLERY,** 321 City Island Ave., New York NY 10464. (212)885-1403. Photographer/ Director: Ron Terner. Estab. 1974.
Exhibits: Subject matter open. Examples of recent exhibitions: Thomas Tulis, winner and Jose Arquimides Guzman, Amy Heller and Viviann Rose, finalists, in 3rd annual juried exhibition. Presents 9 shows/year. Shows last 1 month. Photographer's presence at opening preferred.
Terms & Making Contact: Very receptive to exhibiting work of newer, lesser-known photographers. Charges 30% sales commission.General price range: $175-700. Artist should call for information about exhibition policies. Open to all subjects, styles and capabilities. Nudes and landscapes sell best.
Tips: Sees trend toward more use of alternative processes. "The gallery is geared toward exposure— letting the public know what contemporary artists are doing—and is not concerned with whether it will sell. If the photographer is only interested in selling, this is not the gallery for him/her, but if the artist is concerned with people seeing the work and gaining feedback, this is the place. Most of the work shown at Focal Point Gallery is of lesser-known artists. Don't be discouraged if not accepted the first time. But continue to come back with new work when ready."

FREEPORT ART MUSEUM, 121 N. Harlem Ave., Freeport IL 61032. (815)235-9755. Director: Becky Hewitt. Estab. 1976.
Exhibits: Interested in general, especially landscapes, portraits, senior citizens and country life. Examples of recent exhibitions: "Photographs" by Michael Johnson (large b&w landscapes); "The Many Faces of Hull-House" by Wallace Kirkland (b&w). Presents 1 or 2 shows/year. Shows last 6 weeks. Sponsors openings, "usually on Friday evenings." Pays mileage. Photographer's presence at opening required.
Terms & Making Contact: Charges 10% commission. Reviews transparencies. Interested in framed work only. Send material by mail for consideration. SASE. Reports in 2 months.

*GALERIA MESA, P.O. Box 1466, 155 N. Center, Mesa AZ 85211-1466. (602)644-2242. Contact: curator. Estab. 1980.
Exhibits: Interested in contemporary photography as part of its national juried exhibitions in any and all media. Presents 7-9 national juried exhibits/year. Shows last 4-6 weeks. Sponsors openings; refreshments and sometimes slide lectures (all free).
Terms & Making Contact: Charges 25% commission. General price range: $300-800. Interested in seeing only slides of work to start. Must fit through a standard size door and be ready for hanging. Enter national juried shows. SASE. Reports in 1 month.
Tips: "We do invitational or national juried exhibits only. Only submit professional quality work."

GALESBURG CIVIC ART CENTER, 114 E. Main St., Galesburg IL 61401. (309)342-7415. Director: Paulette Thenhaus. Estab. 1965.
Exhibits: Interested in landscapes, still lifes, abstract color and b&w. "Do not send actual work." Examples of recent exhibitions: "Gale XXV," and "Members and Friends Show." Presents one show every other year, but also features photography in general shows. Sponsors openings. Provides advertising, receptions, space, insurance, etc. Photographer's presence during show is preferred.
Terms & Making Contact: Interested in exhibiting work of newer, lesser-known photographers. Charges 40% commission. General price range: $100-300. Reviews transparencies. Interested in framed, matted work only. Requires exclusive representation within metropolitan area. Query with resume of credits. Send material by mail for consideration. Submit slides to exhibition committee to consider along with resume. Requirements are forwarded upon receipt. SASE. Reports according to specified deadlines.

Tips: This space is "primarily an art center." Opportunities in this market are improving gradually. Sees trend toward more photographers participating in shows. "Unsolicited work will not be accepted."

*THE GALLERY AT CENTRAL BANK, Box 1360, Lexington KY 40590. (800)637-6884. FAX: (606)253-6244. Curator: John G. Irvin. Estab. 1987.
Exhibits: Requirements: No nudes and only Kentucky photographers. Interested in all types of photos. Examples of recent exhibitions: "Covered Bridges of Kentucky," by Jeff Rogers, "Portraits of Children in Black and White," by Jeanne Walter Garvey and "The Desert Storm Series," by Brother Paul of the Abbey of Gethsemane. Presents 2-4 shows/year. Shows last 3 weeks. Sponsors openings; "We pay for everything, invitations, receptions and hanging. We give the photographer 100 percent of the proceeds."
Terms & Making Contact: Charges no commission. General price range $75-1,500. Mounted, matted or unmatted work only. "If you can get it in the door we can hang it." Query with telephone call. Reports back probably same day.

*THE GALLERY AT CORNERSTONE, 62 First Ave., Waltham MA 02154. (617)890-3773. FAX: (617)890-8049. Gallery Coordinator: Robert Zinck. Estab. 1983.
Exhibits: Requirements: Work must be of good quality, clean and cohesive. Hanging work is the responsibility of the photographer. Interested in any style or subject matter. Examples of recent exhibitions: "Prossopographies," by George Totskas (large mixed media portraits); "Situations: Incongruous" by Peter Eberlin (large color diptychs) and "Rocks and Trees" by Jeremy Barnard (b&w landscapes). Presents 8 shows/year. Shows last 6 weeks. Sponsors openings; provides food and beverages. Photographer's presence at opening required.
Terms & Making Contact: General price range: $100-1,000. Reviews transparencies. Interested in unframed, mounted or matted work only. "No size limits, but mural prints are discouraged. Artist is urged to see exhibition space." Arrange a personal interview to show portfolio; provide slides, letter of intent and resume. SASE. Reports in 1 month.
Tips: "Prefer to see finished work intended for the exhibition before a show date is set. Put some thought into your show. Don't be afraid to ask questions. Have the necessary materials ready when requested. There are a lot of 'controversial' shows after the Mapplethorpe and N.E.A. flap. It seems to be a freer market now, not as many restrictions, perhaps as a result of the controversy."

GALLERY ONE, % New England School of Photography, 537 Commonwealth Ave., Boston MA 02215. (617)437-1868. Gallery Director: Samantha McCarthy. Estab. 1972.
Exhibits: Interested in commercial, art, photojournalism, documentary and mixed media. Examples of recent exhibitions: "Collotypes" by Kent Kirby. Sponsors openings. Supplies food and shares cost of postcard invitations to 500 names. "There is no opening if artist is not present."
Terms & Making Contact: Charges 20% commission. Reviews at least 20 transparencies. Work must be matted consistently, preference for framed work, but will accept unframed. Send slides, resume artist statement by mail during June, July and August for consideration. SASE. Reports ASAP.
Tips: Gallery is very receptive to new photographers, as well as, experimental photography."

GALLERY 614, 0350 County Rd. #20, Corunna IN 46730. (219)281-2752. Contact: Robert Green. Interested only in carbro and carbon prints (nonsilver processes).
Exhibits: Examples of recent exhibitions: carbro/carbon prints by Margaret Viles; and a tri-color/carbro print by Robert Green. "The only limitations are the imagination." Sponsors openings.
Terms & Making Contact: Charges 30% commission. Buys photos outright. Price range: $750-3,000. Call to arrange an appointment. No unsolicited material. SASE. Mounted or matted work only. Also, teaches monochrome, tri-chrome carbro/carbon printing.
Tips: Open to the work of newer, lesser-known photographers, especially in nonsilver work. Sees "a return to style—classicism and b&w." Portraits and pictorials sell most frequently.

Can't find a listing? Check at the end of each market section for the " '92-'93 Changes" lists. These lists include any market listings from the '92 edition which were either not verified or deleted in this edition.

*GALLERY TEN, 514 E. State St., Rockford IL 61104. (815)964-1743. Partner: Jean Apgar. Estab. 1985.
Exhibits: "We are in a conservative Midwest location, therefore, we have the best chance of selling and showing work of a somewhat conservative nature, but we will consider all work." Interested in fine art. Examples of recent exhibitions: Works of Joe Sarff, (b&w, figurative, landscape); Tom Ferguson, (b&w, color, floral, landscape); and Judy Mandwolf, (hand-tinted b&w, various subjects). Number of exhibits varies. Shows last 6 weeks. Sponsors openings; gallery provides publicity, mailer and opening refreshments. Photographer's presence at opening preferred.
Terms & Making Contact: Charges 40% commission. General price range: $50-300. Reviews transparencies. Interested in mounted or unmounted work, matted or unmatted work. "We prefer 20 × 24 or smaller." Send material by mail for consideration. SASE. Reports in 1 month.
Tips: "We can only judge by the materials (we receive). Sloppy presentation prejudices us before we even look at the work . . . . It is essential that the photographer present the work as fine art if it is to be considered as such. We have a harder time selling the public on photography as fine art that is as valuable as a painting."

STEPHEN GILL GALLERY, 135 E. 55th St., New York NY 10022. (212)832-0800. Vice President: Anne Gill. Estab. 1986.
Exhibits: Requirements: "Must be photography or photography used with mixed media (one of a kind)." Conceptual work only. Shows last 120 days.
Terms & Making Contact: Very receptive to exhibiting work of newer, lesser-known photographers. Charges 50% commission. General price range: $250-2,500. Reviews transparencies. Send material by mail for consideration. SASE with slides only. Reports in 1-3 months.
Tips: Photographer must have an original vision. "Make me think, laugh or feel something. No copycats allowed." Opportunities for photographers with galleries are "excellent."

FAY GOLD GALLERY, Dept. PM, 247 Buckhead Ave., Atlanta GA 30305. (404)233-3843. FAX: (404)365-8633. Owner/Director: Fay Gold. Hours: Monday-Saturday 9:30 a.m. to 5:30 p.m. Interested in surreal, nudes, allegorical, landscape (20th century); strong interest in contemporary color photography. The photographer must be inventive, speak a new language, and present something not seen before of quality, historical importance or corporate-oriented material.
Exhibits: Presents 12 shows/year. Shows last 4 weeks. Sponsors openings. Provides invitation, mailing, press releases to all media, serves wine, contacts all private and corporate collectors. Photographer's presence at opening preferred. Photography sold in gallery.
Terms & Making Contact: Charges 50% commission. Buys photography outright. General price range: $350-15,000. Will review transparencies. Interested in unframed work, mounted work and matted work only. Generally requires exclusive representation within metropolitan area. Send slides and resume. SASE.
Tips: Trends are toward more surreal, figurative work for collectors; contemporary color for corporate collections.

HILLWOOD ART MUSEUM, Dept. PM, Long Island University, C.W. Post Campus, Brookville NY 11548. (516)299-2788. Director: Dr. Judy Collischan Van Wagner. Estab. 1974.
Exhibits: Interested in unconventional (not standard 8 × 10″ format), three-dimensional, collage/montage and experimental. Examples of recent exhibitions: "Montage," by John Heartfield, Barbara Morgan and The Starn Twins; "Futurism and Photography," by Bragaglia; and "Photojournalism in the 80s," by Claudia Andujar. Presents exhibit "every few years." Shows last 6 weeks. Sponsors openings; supplies announcement card, refreshments. Photographer's presence at opening and at show preferred.
Terms & Making Contact: Charges 10% commission. Reviews transparencies. No preferences as to matting, mounting, or framing. Send material by mail for consideration; include slides or black and white prints and resume. SASE. Reports at earliest opportunity.
Tips: Sees trend toward "theme shows."

*THE HOPKINS GALLERY, Main Street, Wellfleet MA 02667. (508)349-7246. Director: River Karmen. Estab. 1981.
Exhibits: "We accept varied work, seeking high quality and uniqueness." Examples of recent exhibitions: Works by Kristine Hopkins (hand colored), Karin Rosenthal (b&w nudes/landscapes) and Dan Larkin. Presents 2 shows/year. Shows last 3 weeks. Sponsors openings; reception, invitations and press release. Photographer's presence at opening is preferred.
Terms & Making Contact: Charges 45% commission. General price range: $300-1,000. Reviews transparencies. Interested in framed work only. Send material by mail for consideration. SASE. Reports in 2 months.

Tips: Submit portfolio by March 1. "We have a very successful photography show each year and have cultivated a following with collectors."

HUGHES FINE ARTS CENTER, Dept. of Visual Arts, Box 8134, Grand Forks ND 58202-8134. (701)777-2257. Director: Brian Paulsen. Estab. 1979.
Exhibits: Interested in any subjects. Examples of recent exhibitions: Dana Sherman, Roger Sopher and Harley Strauss. All three exhibited b&w 35mm and 4×5 formats. Presents 1-3 shows/year. Shows last 2-3 weeks.
Terms & Making Contact: Interested in receiving work of newer, lesser-known photographers. Does not charge commission; sales are between artist-buyer. Reviews transparencies. "Works should be framed and matted." No size limits or restrictions. Send transparencies only. SASE. Reports in 2 weeks.
Tips: "Send slides of work . . . we will dupe originals and return ASAP and contact you later." Needs "less photos imitating other art movements. Photographers should show their own inherent qualities."

HYDE PARK ART CENTER, Dept. PM, 1701 East 53rd, Chicago IL 60615. (312)324-5520. Contact: Exhibition Committee. Estab. 1939.
Exhibits: Receptive but selective with new work. "The gallery has a history of showing work on the cutting edge—and from emerging artists. Usually works with Chicago—area photographers who do not have gallery representation. Examples of recent exhibitions: "Ectoplasmic Desires," group show curated by Lynda Barekert; "Ink and Silver," by the photography faculty from the Art Institute (curated by Fred Ensley, Karen Savage). Shows last 5 weeks. Sponsors openings. "The Art Center prints and mails the show announcements. A cash bar and chips are provided."
Terms & Making Contact: Charges 25% commission. Interested in framed or unframed work, matted or unmatted work; "whatever best fits the photographer's vision." Send slides and resume to exhibition committee. SASE. Reports quarterly. "Exhibition committee meets 4 times each year, artists will be notified of next meeting when slides are received and then contacted after the meeting."
Tips: "Don't make solicitations by phone; the exhibition committee does not have office hours."

*IMAGES, Images, Images, 328 West Fourth St., Cincinnati OH 45202. (513)241-8124. Administrative Director: Stephen Johnston. Estab. 1981.
Exhibits: Interested in fine quality photographs in all mediums. No commercial work or travel photography. Documentary photographs which speak to social issues will be considered. Must have a portfolio of work which contains a strong thematic series dealing with a subject. Presents lectures and workshops by photographers. Publishes photography magazine. Examples of recent exhibitions: "Desert Cantos VI: The Pit," by Richard Misrach (documentary), "Suspended Animation," by Lois Greenfield (photos of dancers) and "Spirit Level," by Arno Rafael Minkkinen (self-portraits). Presents 6 shows/year. Shows last 6 weeks. Sponsors openings, by invitation (no food or beverage). Photographer's presence at opening preferred.
Terms & Making Contact: Charges 40% commission. Rarely buys photographs. General price range: $150-800. Reviews transparencies. Interested in mounted and matted work only. Arrange a personal interview to show portfolio or send material for consideration. SASE. Reports in 3 months.
Tips: "We are a nonprofit organization whose purpose is to educate the residents of the region in regards to contemporary fine art photography. Photographers selected for exhibition have strong compositions in a unique personal style."

JANAPA PHOTOGRAPHY GALLERY LTD., Dept. PM, 402-A E. 12th St., New York NY 10009-4020. Stanley Simon. Estab. 1980. Interested in contemporary, fine-art, avant-garde photography.
Exhibits: Photographers must be professional. Sponsors openings; provides press and public relations, mailing list, local newspaper listings and advertising, with all costs at photographer's expense. "We charge a fee of $250 for one-person show, or proportionate amount for more than one." Photographer's presence preferred at openings and during show. Photographer should be aggressive and willing to participate in own marketing.
Terms & Making Contact: Commission 25-50%, depending on artist. General price range: $150-250/ b&w; $250-500/color, (16×20), archival work, matted and normally sold in portfolio groups. "We request exclusive area representation, if possible." Interviews are arranged by appointment for portfolio reviews. Mail queries including workprints, slides, resume and credits (incl. SASE). Reports ASAP.
Tips: "JANAPA has changed its concept toward becoming a consulting and resource organization, in which gallery viewing is arranged by appointment (except for openings). We are also seeking staff to work in sales, administrative and managerial career positions for expansion nationally. We look for exceptional work in composition, originality and technical concepts. We lean toward innovative styles, multi-imaging, abstracts, hand coloring, infrared toning. Fine art and contemporary photos sell most frequently. Submit good quality portfolio with cohesive body of work or a theme; could be style, technique or many things but must work together as a whole."

Close-up

Mark Chester
Freelance Photographer
San Francisco, California

© Tom McAfee

Twenty years after Mark Chester's first photo exhibition in a New Jersey playhouse, he still considers himself a new-comer in the fine art field. As with many photographers who strive for notoriety as artists, Chester realizes the journey is long and difficult. "You almost have to be dead," he says, joking about making it on the fine art circuit.

A self-taught photographer who learned his trade while working with the Peace Corps, Chester is a former director of photography and staff photographer for the American Society of Composers, Authors and Publishers. Also a freelance writer, he has had work published in the *New York Times*, *Los Angeles Times*, *Washington Post* and the *Christian Science Monitor*.

He has fought to market his work since the early 1970s and his resilience has helped him garner dozens of exhibitions throughout the country. Chester, whose first show took place in 1972, realizes that a determined attitude is a must for any photographer who wants to share his work with others. He remembers a time early in his career when he took some photographs to a New York gallery to have them reviewed for a possible exhibition. The gallery director took "ten seconds" to flip through the stack of photos like a deck of cards and then walked out of the room. "It was rude," says Chester recalling the incident. "I just remember thinking, 'This is not a happy person.' But you can't let that bother you.

"Photographers ought to be encouraged and not take themselves so seriously . . . but they should be serious about what they do. And photographers should be very thick-skinned because there are a lot of people out there who might think their work is terrible."

Chester says he spends a large amount of his time marketing his work and coming up with diverse topics for self-assigned projects. His ambitious nature led to the publication of the book *No in America*, in which he takes a "tongue-in-cheek" look at "no" signs in the U.S. One photo from the book depicts a cemetery with a gate in the foreground. A sign on the gate reads "No Permanent Plantings Allowed."

"I don't go out and try to shoot things that are funny. But I see things that kind of make me chuckle and I try to capture that," says Chester, a 1967 graduate of the University of Arizona.

When Chester begins a project his main purpose is to create and tell a story in the best way possible. He spends hours editing, researching and devising ways to capture the appropriate images. Through his yearning to tell a story, Chester managed to raise over $20,000 in funds to sponsor a trip to Shanghai, China, San Francisco's sister city. He wanted to put together a portfolio of photographs to commemorate the relationship between the two cities. After numerous failed attempts to gain support, the project was eventually funded and exhibited at the San Francisco Main Library. "The process was a real eye-opener," he says.

He also has realized that photographers wanting to display and sell their work should not restrict themselves to galleries and museums. Many alternative spaces, such as lobbies and restaurants, prove to be extremely useful while gaining recognition. "I think what photographers have to realize is that a gallery is a business," says Chester, whose first San Francisco exhibit was inside a stock brokerage firm. "If the person who runs the gallery is not concerned about losing revenue, then they can show what they want . . . . They don't have to earn an income from selling work that's on their walls."

One downside to alternative locations is that photographers may not make much money off those kinds of exhibits. But Chester does not see monetary gains as the only advantages a photographer should pursue. "I don't think they should be motivated to make money. They should be dedicated to creating a good image that's interesting," he says.

"It takes a long time to establish yourself as collectible and I don't aim for that. I just aim for being able to share my new work, show it, get the exposure and get feedback."

— Michael Willins

© Mark Chester

Mark Chester says he doesn't go looking for comical photos, but when he spots a humorous situation, like this one in San Francisco's Julius Kahn Park, he likes to share it with viewers. Chester has spent years developing his photographic eye and he genuinely enjoys seeing his work on display in galleries or alternative spaces.

JEB GALLERY, INC., 295 Albany St., Fall River MA 02720. (508)673-8010. Contact: Ronald Caplain or Claire Caplain. Estab. 1978. All contemporary photographers are represented. Color is accepted.
Terms & Making Contact: Interested in exhibiting work of newer, lesser-known photographers. Charges 40% commission. General price range: $300-5,000. No slides. "Portfolios of photographers are reviewed by appointment."

*KENDALL CAMPUS ART GALLERY – MIAMI-DADE COMMUNITY COLLEGE, (formerly South Campus Art Gallery), 11011 SW 104 St., Miami FL 33176-3393. (305)237-2322. FAX: (305)237-2658. Director: Robert J. Sindelir. Estab. 1970.
Exhibits: Requirements: Must be professional, creative and have an identifiable point of view. Interested in all types, styles and subjects. Examples of recent exhibitions: "Water Mythologies," by J. Tomas Lopez. Presents 1-2 shows/year. Shows last 1 month. Sponsors openings; printing and sending of mailers and refreshments. Photographer's presence at opening preferred.
Terms & Making Contact: Sales have been made. We put buyer in touch with artist. Buys photos outright. Reviews transparencies. Interested in framed or unframed, mounted or unmounted, matted or unmatted work. Submit portfolio for review. Send material by mail for consideration. SASE. Reports in 1-2 weeks.

KENT STATE UNIVERSITY SCHOOL OF ART GALLERY, Dept. PM, KSU, 201 Art Building, Kent OH 44242. (216)672-7853. Director: Fred T. Smith. Interested in all types, styles and subject matter of photography. Photographer must present quality work.
Exhibits: Presents 1 show/year. Exhibits last 3 weeks. Sponsors openings; provides hors d'oevres, wine and non-alcoholic punch. Photographer's presence at opening preferred.
Terms & Making Contact: Photography can be sold in gallery. Charges 20% commission. Buys photography outright. Will review transparencies. Write a proposal and send with slides. Send material by mail for consideration. SASE. Reports usually in 1 month, but it depends on time submitted.

KIRKLAND ART CENTER, P.O. Box 213, East Park Row, Clinton NY 13323. (315)853-8871. Activities Coordinator: Elizabeth Hunt. Estab. 1960.
Exhibits: Interested in "all types/styles/subjects which are suitable for a community arts center. Only serious art, not work aimed at a commercial market, will be considered." Work "must be approved by the exhibition committee." Examples of recent exhibitions: "Photograms" by Judith Mohns; "Remembering: Women and Their Relationships" by Susan Landgraf; and "KAC Photography Annual." Presents 2-3 shows/year. Shows last 3½ weeks. Sponsors openings; "We send out and print black & white announcement cards, provide a wine and cheese reception, and encourage a talk by the artist." Photographer's presence at opening preferred.
Terms & Making Contact: Charges 25% commission. No size limits or restrictions on photography. Send material by mail for consideration. SASE. Reports within 2 months, "after review by exhibition committee."
Tips: The opportunities for photographers in galleries are "less than with other media such as painting/sculpture, but all artists are considered by the KAC. The quality of the work, not the resume, is the major consideration." Sees trend toward "more experimental works – combining photography with other media." Interest of public in buying photography "seems to remain stable . . . not great and yet not indifferent. People here are unwilling to pay high prices for any artwork."

ROBERT KLEIN GALLERY, Dept. PM, 207 South St., Boston MA 02116. (617)482-8188. Contact: Robert Klein or Erin Wright. Interested in museum quality, fine 19th and 20th century art photos.
Exhibits: Presents 8 shows/year. Shows last 6 weeks. Sponsors openings; provides book signing, reception, radio, TV, newspaper coverage. Photographer's presence at opening preferred. Photographer's presence during show is preferred.
Terms & Making Contact: Photography sold in gallery. Charges 50% commission. Buys photography outright. General price range: $500-50,000. Will review transparencies. Interested in matted or unmatted work. Arrange a personal interview to show portfolio. Submit portfolio for review. SASE. Reports in 1 week.
Tips: "Be aware of what is happening in world of revolutionary trends. Be flexible and able to accept criticism. Be organized, dependable."

JOHN MICHAEL KOHLER ARTS CENTER, 608 New York Ave., P.O. Box 489, Sheboygan WI 53082-0489. (414)458-6144. Exhibitions Department: Nancy Bless. Estab. 1967.
Exhibits: Examples of recent exhibitions: "Dreams, Lies and Exaggerations: Photomontage in America" and "Notes from the Material World: Contemporary Photomontage" by multiple artists. Shows last 10-12 weeks. Sponsors openings. Generally only main gallery openings (four per year). Food, drink and entertainment are provided. Photographer's presence at opening preferred. Photography sold in gallery by artist's request.

Terms & Making Contact: Very receptive to exhibiting work of newer, lesser-known photographers. NPI. Reviews transparencies. Interested in framed or unframed work, mounted or unmounted work and matted or unmatted work. Send material by mail for consideration. SASE if requested, "but we prefer to keep artists' materials on file permanently. Reporting time varies depending upon scheduling. We will acknowledge receipt of materials."
Tips: Focuses on emerging artists. "We do not exhibit work of commercial photographers. We are interested in all strong work in any style, non-traditional photographic practice."

�‌ **LA MAMA LA GALLERIA,** 6 East First Street, New York NY 10003. (212)505-2476. Director/Curator: Lawry Smith. Estab. 1982.
Exhibits: Interested in all types of works. Examples of recent exhibitions: "Sacred Monsters," by Shayla Baykal (theater portraits); "Tatoo," by Seth Guritz (tatooed nudes); and "Illustion," by Charles Gustina (men in drag). Presents 2 shows/year. Shows last 3 weeks. Sponsors openings. Photographer's presence at opening required.
Terms & Making Contact: Very receptive to exhibiting work of newer, lesser-known photographers. Charges 20% commission. General price range: $500-2,000. Reviews transparencies. Interested in framed or unframed, mounted, matted or unmatted work. Requires exclusive representation within metropolitan area. Arrange a personal interview to show portfolio. Send material by mail for consideration. SASE. Reports in 1 month.

LEEDY-VOULKOS GALLERY, 1919 Wyandotte, Kansas City MO 64108. (816)474-1919. Director: Sherry Leedy. Estab. 1985.
Exhibits: Requirements: Photographer must have "an established exhibition record." Open to all styles and subject matter. Examples of recent exhibitions: Linda Robbennolt (Polaroids and Cibach-romes); Peter Feldstein (cliches verre) and Michael Eastman. Shows last 6 weeks. Sponsors openings. Photographer's presence at opening preferred.
Terms & Making Contact: Charges 50% commission. Does not buy photography outright. General price range: $200-900. Reviews transparencies. Interested in framed or unframed work. Requires exclusive representation within metropolitan area. Send slides by mail for consideration. SASE. Reports in 1 month.
Tips: "Visit the gallery to get the general 'feel' of work exhibited."

LEHIGH UNIVERSITY ART GALLERIES, Chandler-Ulmann, #17, Bethlehem PA 18015. (215)758-3615. Director/Curator: Ricardo Viera.
Exhibits: Interested in all types of works. The photographer should "preferably be an established professional." Presents 5-8 shows/year. Shows last 4-6 weeks. Sponsors openings. Photographer's presence at opening and during the show preferred.
Terms & Making Contact: NPI. Reviews transparencies. Arrange a personal interview to show portfolio. SASE. Reports in 1 month.
Tips: Don't send more than 20 (top) slides.

◌ **LEWIS LEHR INC.,** Box 1008, Gracie Station, New York NY 10028. (212)288-6765. Director: Lewis Lehr. Estab. 1984. Private dealer.
Terms & Making Contact: Photography sold in gallery. Charges 50% commission. Buys photography outright. General price range: $500 plus. Reviews transparencies. Interested in mounted or unmounted work. Requires exclusive representation within metropolitan area. Query with resume of credits. SASE. Member AIPAD.
Tips: Vintage American color sells best. Sees trend toward "more color and larger" print sizes. To break in, "knock on doors." Do not send work.

■**THE LIGHT FACTORY PHOTOGRAPHIC ARTS CENTER,** P.O. Box 32815, Charlotte NC 28232. (704)333-9755. Contact: Gallery Manager. Nonprofit. Estab. 1972.
Exhibits: Requirements: Photographer must have a professional exhibition record for main gallery. Interested in contemporary and vintage art photography, documentary photography, any subject matter. Presents 8-10 shows/year. Examples of recent exhibitions: "Another Side of Progress," "Personal Scenarios" and "Double Vision." Presents 8-10 shows/year. Shows last 1-2 months. Sponsors openings; reception (3 hours) with food and beverages, artist lecture following reception. Photographer's presence at opening preferred.
Terms & Making Contact: Photography sold in the shop. "Artists price their work." Charges 33% commission. Rarely buys photography outright. General price range: $100-3,000. Reviews transparencies. Write for gallery guidelines. Query with resume of credits and slides. SASE. Reports in 2 months.
Tips: Among various trends such as fine art prints and documentary work, "we are seeing more mixed media using photography, painting, sculpture and videos. We have several smaller galleries to show work from up and coming photographers." Currently, documentary and landscape subjects are selling

best through this gallery. "In general we are interested in the work as a whole and how the ideas have been expressed in the work. The photographs should also be a cohesive body of work which reflect the artist intent and purpose."

LIGHT IMPRESSIONS SPECTRUM GALLERY, 439 Monroe Ave., Rochester NY 14607. Gallery Director: Lance Speer. Estab. 1985. "Shows 19th and 20th century silver and non-silver photography by photographers of national reputation."
Exhibits: Requirements: To be considered to show work in the Light Impressions Spectrum Gallery, an artist must have a national reputation. Examples of exhibits: "Aaron Siskind: Photogravures & Platinum Prints," (large format gravures); "Duane Michals: The Nature of Desire," (silver photographic prints); "Italy by Armchair: Stereographs and Their Antecedents," (large format etchings, albumen prints, and stereographs, by multiple artists and photographers). Presents 8 shows/year. Shows last 4-6 weeks. Sponsors openings; provides invitations, press releases and food and beverage for the opening. Photographer's presence at opening preferred.
Terms & Making Contacts: Charges 40% commission. General price range: $300-3,500.
Tips: Sees continued trend toward individual expressive directions, eclecticism and a rejection of some of the ideas of the Postmodern Aesthetic. Currently selling best are traditional high-focus landscapes as well as the untraditional and emerging technology based imagery.

*MARBLE HOUSE GALLERY, 44 Exchange Place, Salt Lake City UT 84111. (801)532-7332. Owner: Dolores Kohler. Estab. 1988.
Exhibits: Requirements: Professional presentation, realistic pricing and munerous quality images. Interested in painterly, abstract and landscapes. No documentary or politically-oriented work. No nudes. Examples of recent exhibitions: Include the works of John Stevens, Dolores Kohler and Kent Ethington. Presents 2 shows/year. Shows last 1 month. As a member of the Salt Lake Gallery Association, there are monthly downtown gallery strolls. Also provide public relations, etc. Photographer's presence at opening preferred.
Terms & Making Contact: Charges 50% commission. Buys photos outright. General price range: $50-1,000. Reviews transparencies. Interested in framed or unframed work, mounted or unmounted work, matted or unmatted work. Requires exclusive representation within metropolitan area. No size limits. Arrange a personal interview to show a portfolio. Submit portfolio for review. Query with resume of credits. Query with samples. Send material by mail for consideration. SASE. Reports in 1 month.

*MARI GALLERIES OF WESTCHESTER, LTD., 133 E. Prospect Ave., Mamaroneck NY 10543. (914)698-0008. Director: Carla Reuben. Estab. 1966.
Exhibits: Requirements: "Must review work, a few originals to exhibition size and smaller photos or slides of body of work. Price list required." Interested in b&w and color exhibitions. "The works must have a cohesive theme or idea." Examples of recent exhibitions: Lange Mozian (colorized antique photographs); Arthur Goldenberg (color photography landscapes); and Gary Strausberg (nature photography). Presents 8 shows/year. Shows last 4-5 weeks. "We do a direct mailing to our customers and send a press release describing each artist to our press list. Beverage and food at opening reception for artists." Photographer's presence at opening required.
Terms & Making Contact: Charges 50% commission. General price range: $100-800. Reviews transparencies. Interested in framed or unframed work. Requires exclusive representation within metropolitan area. Arrange a personal interview to show a portfolio. SASE. Reports in 1-2 weeks.

*MARLBORO GALLERY, Prince George's Community College, 301 Largo Road, Largo MD 20772-2199. (301)322-0967. Gallery Curator: John Krumrein. Estab. 1976.
Exhibits: Not interested in commercial work. Examples of recent exhibitions: "Faces of China" by David Orbock and Fran Statina (framed, b&w and color photos) and "Mainscapes" (framed, b&w and color photos). Shows last 3-4 weeks. Sponsors openings. Photographer's presence at opening required.
Terms & Making Contact: General price range: $200-16,000. Reviews transparencies. Interested in framed work only. Query with samples. Send material by mail for consideration. SASE. Reports in 3-4 weeks.
Tips: "Send examples of what you wish to display and explanations if photos do not meet normal standards (i.e. in focus, experimental subject matter)."

*MARSH GALLERY, University of Richmond, Richmond VA 23173. (804)289-8276. FAX: (804)287-6006. Director: Richard Waller. Estab. 1966.
Exhibits: Interested in all subjects. Examples of recent exhibitions: documentary works by Builder Levy, Walker Evans and Dorothea Lange. Presents 2-3 shows/year. Shows last 4 weeks. Photographer's presence at opening preferred.

Terms & Making Contact: Reviews transparencies. Interested in framed or unframed, mounted or unmounted, matted or unmatted work. Charges 10% commission. Work must be framed for exhibition. Query with resume of credits. Query with samples. Send material by mail for consideration. Reports in 1 month.
Tips: If possible, submit material which can be left on file and fits standard letter file. "We are a nonprofit university gallery interested in presenting contemporary art."

*ERNESTO MAYANS GALLERIES, 601 Canyon Rd., Santa Fe NM 87501. (505)983-8068 or (505)983-8008. FAX: (505)982-1999. Owner: Ernesto Mayans. Estab. 1977.
Exhibits: Requirements: Photographer must work with gallery to sell the work. Examples of recent exhibitions: "Cholos/East L.A.," by Graciela Iturbide (b&w); "Fressòn Images," by Doug Keats (Fressòn) and "Selected Works," by Andrè Kertész (b&w). Sponsors openings. Photographer's presence at opening preferred.
Terms & Making Contact: Charges 50% commission. Buys photos outright. General price range: $200-8,500. Reviews transparencies. Interested in framed or unframed, mounted or unmounted work. Requires exclusive representation within metropolitan area. Shows are limited to up to 16×20. Arrange a personal interview to show portfolio. Send material by mail for consideration. SASE. Reports back in 1-2 weeks. "Please call before submitting."
Tips: "Despite small exhibition space and large stable, we have theme invitationals."

MINOT ART GALLERY, P.O. Box 325, Minot ND 58701. (701)838-4445. Director: Judith Allen. Estab. 1970.
Exhibits: Examples of recent exhibitions: wildlife photos by Pat Gerlach; "Landscapes of Scotland," by Martin Guppy; and "The Color of Ireland," by Susan Hayden. Presents 3 shows/year. Shows last about 1 month. Sponsors openings; "the first Sunday of each month is usually when we have each exhibit's grand opening."
Terms & Making Contact: Very receptive to work of newer photographers. Charges 30% sales commission. General price range: $25-150. Submit portfolio or at least six examples of work for review. Prefer transparencies. SASE. Reports in 1 month.
Tips: "Wildlife, landscapes and floral pieces seem to be the trend in North Dakota. We get many slides to review for our 3 photography shows a year. Do something unusual, creative, artistic. Do not send postcard photos."

MONTEREY PENINSULA MUSEUM OF ART, 559 Pacific St., Monterey CA 93940. (408)372-5477. Director: Jo Farb Hernandez. Estab. 1959.
Exhibits: Interested in all subjects. Examples of recent exhibitions: "Morley Baer: 40 Years of Photographs," by Morley Baer; "People/Landscapes 1940s-1960s," by William Heick; and "Photographic views of Maiji: a Portrait of Old Japan," by Leonard Loeb. Presents 4-6 shows/year. Shows last approximately 6-12 weeks. Sponsors openings.
Terms & Making Contact: Buys photography outright. NPI. Reviews transparencies. Work must be framed to be displayed; review can be by slides, transparencies, unframed or unmatted. Send material by mail for consideration. SASE. Reports in 1 month.
Tips: "Very receptive" to working with newer, lesser-known photographers. Send 20 slides and resume at any time to the attention of the museum director.

*MOREAU GALLERIES, Department of Saint Mary's College, Notre Dame IN 46556-5001. (219)284-4655. Director: William Tourt Illotte. Estab. 1968.
Exhibits: Requirements: Send slides, resume and SASE for application. Interested in contemporary and experimental works in b&w, color, video, film or computer generated. Presents 1-2 shows/year. Shows last 1 month. Sponsors openings; includes reception, lecture stipend and housing. Photographer's presence at opening preferred, presence during show preferred.
Terms & Making Contact: Charges no commission. Buys photography outright. General price range: $100-1,000. Reviews transparencies. Interested in framed or unframed work, mounted or unmounted work, matted or unmatted work. Submit portfolio for review. Query with samples. Send material by mail for consideration. Reports in 1 month; normal screening occurs each year between October and November for the following academic year.

THE MUSEUM OF CONTEMPORARY PHOTOGRAPHY, COLUMBIA COLLEGE CHICAGO, 600 S. Michigan Ave., Chicago IL 60605-1996. (312)663-5554. FAX: (312)663-1707. Director: Denise Miller-Clark. Assistant Director: Ellen Ushioka. Estab. 1984.
Exhibits: Interested in fine art, documentary, photojournalism, commercial, technical/scientific. "All high quality work considered." Examples of recent exhibitions: "Open Spain/Espana Abierta" contemporary documentary Spanish photography/group show; "The Duane Michals Show," by Duane Michals (b&w narrative sequences, surreal, directorial); "Irving Penn: Master Images," by Irving Penn

(b&w fashion, still life, portraiture). Presents 5 main shows and 8-10 smaller shows/year. Shows last 8 weeks. Sponsors openings, announcements.
Terms & Making Contact: "We do exhibit the work of newer and lesser known photographers if their work is of high professional quality." Charges 30% commission. Buys photos outright. General price range: $300-2,000. Reviews transparencies. Interested in reviewing unframed work only, matted or unmatted. Submit portfolio for review. SASE. Reports in 2 weeks. No critical review offered.
Tips: "Professional standards apply; only very high quality work considered."

MUSEUM OF PHOTOGRAPHIC ARTS, 1649 El Prado, Balboa Park, San Diego CA 92101. (619)239-5262. Assistant to the Director: Cathy Boemer. Estab. 1983.
Exhibits: "The criteria is simply that the photography be the finest and most interesting in the world, relative to other fine art activity." Examples of recent exhibitions: *Night Light: A Survey of 20th Century Night Photography* (approximately 70 photographers represented, b&w and color); *An Uncertain Grace: The Photographs of Sebastião Salgado* (b&w photojournalism); *Persona,* eight contemporary artists whose work explores issues of personal identity and maleness (photographers: Lucas Samaras, Chuck Close, William Parker, John Coplans, Todd Gray, Neil Winokur, Jeffrey Wolin and Albert Chong; b&w, color and mixed media). Presents 6-8 exhibitions annually from 19th century to contemporary. Each exhibition last approximately 2 months. Exhibition schedules planned 2-3 years in advance. The Museum holds a private Members' Opening Reception for each exhibition.
Terms & Making Contact: For space, time and curatorial reasons, there are few opportunities to present the work of newer, lesser-known photographers. Send resume of credits with a portfolio (unframed photographs) or slides. Send return address and postage. Response in 3 weeks. Portfolios may be submitted for review with advance notification. However, the Museum's mandate is to exhibit the finest photography available and files are kept on contemporary artists for future reference.
Tips: "Exhibitions presented by the museum represent the full range of artistic and journalistic photographic works." There are no specific requirements."The executive director/curator makes all decisions on works that will be included in exhibitions. There is an enormous stylistic diversity in the photographic arts. The Museum does not place an emphasis on one style or technique over another."

○ **NEIKRUG PHOTOGRAPHICA LTD.,** 224 E. 68th St., New York NY 10021. (212)288-7741. FAX: (212)737-3208. Owner/Director: Marjorie Neikrug. Estab. 1970.
Exhibits: Interested in "photography which has a unique way of showing the contemporary world. Special needs include photographic art for our annual Rated X exhibit." Examples of recent exhibitions: "A Guerrilla of Photography," by Stephan Lufino; "Intimate Impressions," by Marie-Claire Montanari. Sponsors openings "in cooperation with the photographer." Photographer's presence preferred.
Terms & Making Contact: Interested in receiving work from newer, lesser-known photographers. Charges 50% sales commission. Price range: $100-5,000. Requires exclusive representation in metropolitan area. Call to arrange an appointment or submit portfolio in person. "We view portfolios twice a month. They should be left on Friday between 1-5 p.m. and picked up Saturday between 1-5 p.m." SASE. Size: 11×14, 16×20 or 20×30.
Tips: "We are looking for meaningful and beautiful images — images with substance and feeling! Show us themes, organization of work, print interpretation and originality. Edit work carefully and make it easy for the viewer. Have neat presentation." Nudes and color landscapes currently sell best at this gallery.

NEW ORLEANS MUSEUM OF ART, Box 19123, City Park, New Orleans LA 70179. (504)488-2631. Curator of Photography: Nancy Barrett.
Exhibits: Interested in all types of photography. Presents shows continuously. Shows last 1-3 months.
Terms & Making Contact: Buys photography outright; NPI. Present budget for purchasing contemporary photography is very small. Query with resume of credits only. SASE. Reports in 1-3 months.

NORTHERN ILLINOIS UNIVERSITY ART GALLERY IN CHICAGO, Suite 306, 212 W. Superior, Chicago IL 60610. (312)642-6010. Director: Peggy Doherty. Estab. 1985.
Exhibits: Requirements: Must be producing high-quality work in a series or within a theme. Interested in fine art, documentary and experimental. Examples of recent exhibitions: "Chicago Blues" by Marc Pokempner; "Summer Portraits" by Dan Cochrane; and "City Still" by James ISKA. Presents 2-4 shows/year. Shows last 6 weeks. Photographer's presence at opening preferred.
Terms & Making Contact: Interested in reviewing work of newer, lesser-known photographers. Photographers may arrange sales with buyers, but gallery does not do the selling. General price range: $100-700. Reviews transparencies. Interested in matted or unmatted work. Send material by mail for consideration. SASE. Reports in 1 month.
Tips: "Submit a body of cohesive work, at least 10-15 images on a theme."

*NORTHPORT/B.J. SPOKE GALLERY, 299 Main Street, Huntington NY 11743. (516)549-5106. Director: Carol L.Davis.
Exhibits: Requirements: juried shows; send for prospectus or deadline. Interested in "all styles and genres, photography as essay as well as 'beyond' photography." Examples of recent exhibitions: Works by Abbey Rust (sea/landscape) and Norman Seider (gel-silver print). Shows last 1 month. Sponsors openings. Photographer's presence at opening preferred.
Terms & Making Contact: Charges 25% commission. General price range: $250-800. Reviews transparencies. Interested in framed or unframed, matted or unmatted work. Arrange a personal interview to show portfolio. Query with resume of credits. Send material by mail for consideration. SASE. Reports back in 2 months.
Tips: "Send challenging, cohesive body of work. May include photography and mixed media."

*O.K. HARRIS WORKS OF ART, 383 West Broadway, New York NY 10012. (212)431-3600. Director: Ivan C. Karp. Estab. 1969.
Exhibits: Requirements: "The images should be startling or profoundly evocative." No rock, dunes, weeds or nudes reclining on any of the above or seascapes." Interested in urban and industrial subjects and cogent photojournalism. Examples of recent exhibitions: Works by Jay Wolke (chromogenic color prints of Atlantic City), Vaughn Sills (b&w toned silver prints) and Eduardo Del Valle and Mirta Gomez (ektacolor type C photos). Presents 5-8 shows/year. Shows last 3 weeks.
Terms & Making Contact: Charges 40% commission. General price range: $350-1,200. Interested in matted or unmatted work. Appear in person, no appointment: Tuesday-Saturday 10-6. SASE. Reports back immediately.
Tips: "Do not provide a descriptive text."

*OLIN FINE ARTS GALLERY, Washington & Jefferson College, Washington PA 15301. (412)222-4400. Contact: Paul Edwards. Estab. 1982.
Exhibits: Requirements: Photographer must be at least 18 years old, American citizen and artists assume most show costs. Interested in large format, experimental traditional photos. Examples of recent exhibitions: One-person show by William Wellman; "The Eighties" by Mark Perrott. Presents 1 show/year. Shows last 3 weeks. Sponsors openings; pays for non-alcoholic reception if artist attends. Photographer's presence at opening preferred.
Terms & Making Contact: Charges 20% commission. General price range: $50-1,500. Reviews transparencies. Interested in framed work only. Shows are limited to works that are no bigger than 6 feet; subject matter that is not for publication. Send material by mail for consideration. SASE. Reports in 1 month.

♣OPEN SPACE ARTS SOCIETY, 510 Fort St., Victoria BC V8W 1E6 Canada. (604)383-8833. Director: Sue Donaldson. Estab. 1972.
Exhibits: Interested in photographs as fine art in an experimental context, as well as interdisciplinary works involving the photograph. No traditional documentary, scenics, sunsets or the like. Examples of recent exhibitions: "Bed of Roses," (sexual imagery); "Companēras de Mexico," (Mexican women) and "Carnet Photographique," by Joanne Tremblay (female model). Sponsors openings. Presents 5 shows/year. Shows last 3-4 weeks.
Terms & Making Contact: Interested in receiving work from newer, lesser-known photographers. General price range: $100-1,000. Pays the C.A.R.F.A.C. fees; no commission. Query with transparencies of work. SASE. Reports 2 times a year.
Tips: "Submit 10-20 slides and artist statement of what the work is about or how you feel about it. Send for information about Open Space to give you an idea of how large the space is." Sees trend in multi-media installation work where photography is used as part of a larger artwork.

ORLANDO GALLERY, Dept. PM, 14553 Ventura Blvd., Sherman Oaks CA 91403. (818)789-6012. Director: Philip Orlando. Interested in photography demonstrating "inventiveness" on any subject.
Exhibits: Examples of recent exhibitions: mixed media photos by Joan Weber; prints by Roger Camp. Sponsors openings. Open to work of newer photographers. Shows last 4 weeks.
Terms & Making Contact: Charges 50% sales commission. Price range: $550-10,000. Submit portfolio. SASE. Framed work only. Requires exclusive representation in area.

♣ *The maple leaf before a listing indicates that the market is Canadian. The symbol is new this year in* Photographer's Market.

PACE/MACGILL GALLERY, Dept. PM, 9th Floor, 32 E. 57th St., New York NY 10022. (212)759-7999. Assistant to the Director: Chris Ruggieri. Estab. 1983.
Exhibits: "We like to show original work that changes the direction of the medium." Presents 18 shows/year. Shows last 3-5 weeks. Sponsors openings. Photographer's presence at opening preferred.
Terms & Making Contact: Photography sold in gallery. Commission varies. On occasion, buys photos outright. General price range: $1,000-200,000. Reviews transparencies with a letter of recommendation. Interested in unframed, unmatted work only. Requires exclusive representation. No size limits. Have established, reputable third party recommend them. SASE. Reports in 3 weeks.
Tips: "Look at our exhibitions. Then ask, 'Does my work make a similar type of contribution to photography?' If so, seek third party to recommend your work."

PALO ALTO CULTURAL CENTER, 1313 Newell Rd., Palo Alto CA 94303. (415)329-2179. Contact: Exhibitions Dept. Estab. 1971.
Exhibits: "Exhibit needs vary according to curatorial context." Seeks "imagery unique to individual artist." Examples of recent exhibitions: "Light, Time, & Place" by Sharmon Goff, Stephen C. Johnson, Paul Klein, Joel Meyerowitz, Arthur Ollman, Len Jenshel. Number of shows per year varies. "No standard policy. Photography may be integrated in group exhibits." Shows last 1-3 months. Sponsors openings. Photographer's presence at opening preferred.
Terms & Making Contact: Charges 30% commission. Reviews transparencies. Interested in framed work only. Send material by mail for consideration; include transparencies, slides, bio and artistic statement. SASE. Reports following periodic review.

THE PHOTO GALLERY AT PORTLAND SCHOOL OF ART, 619 Congress St., Portland ME 04101. (207)775-3052. Head, Photo Department: John Eide. Estab. 1972.
Exhibits: Examples of recent exhibitions: "Boxers & Brokers," by Larry Fink (b&w photos of boxers and stock brokers); "Recent Photographs," by Paul D'Amato (color images of street gangs); "New Landscapes," by Mark Klett (b&w large format images of western landscape). Presents 6 shows/year. Shows last 5 weeks.
Terms & Making Contact: Very receptive to newer, lesser-known photographers. General price range: $100-500. Will review transparencies. Interested in unmounted work only. Requires work that has been matted and ready to hang. Submit portfolio for review. SASE. Reporting time varies.

*PHOTO GRAPHIA GALLERY, 248 North Trade St., Tryon NC 28782. (704)859-2212. FAX: (704)894-2718. Owner: Michael McCue. Estab. 1991.
Exhibits: Requirements: strong composition, mastering both complexity and subtlety. Interested in photos with timeless quality, not topical or faddish. Examples of recent exhibitions: Works by Stephania Serena (cibachrome); William Lemke (gelatin silver print); David Haas (gelatin silver print) and Edward Weston (gelatin silver print). Presents numerous shows/year. Shows last one month. Sponsors openings, all at gallery's expense. Photographer's presence at opening preferred; photographer's presence during show preferred.
Terms & Making Contact: Charges 50% commission. General price range: $200-2,000. Reviews transparencies. Interested in framed or unframed, mounted, matted or unmatted work only. Shows are limited to images no smaller than 11 × 14. Submit portfolio for review. Send material by mail for consideration. SASE. Reports in 2 weeks.
Tips: "Large formats are best."

PHOTOGRAPHIC IMAGE GALLERY, 208 SW First, Portland OR 97204. (503)224-3543. Director: Guy Swanson. Estab. 1984.
Exhibits: Interested in primarily mid-career to contemporary Master-Traditional Landscape in color and b&w. Examples of recent exhibitions: "Trains" by O. Winston Link; and "My Tibet" by Galen Rowell. Presents 12 shows/year. Shows last 1 month. Sponsors openings. Photographer's presence at opening preferred.
Terms & Making Contact: Charges 50% commission. General price range: $300-1,500. Reviews transparencies. Requires exclusive representation within metropolitan area. Query with resume of credits. SASE. Reports in 1 month.
Tips: Current opportunities through this gallery are fair. Sees trend toward "more specializing in imagery rather than trying to cover all areas."

*■PHOTOGRAPHIC RESOURCE CENTER, 602 Commonwealth Ave., Boston MA 02215. (617)353-0700. Curator: Anita Douthat.
Exhibits: Interested in contemporary and historical photography and mixed-media work incorporating photography. "The photographer must meet our high quality requirements." Examples of recent exhibitions: "El Salvador In the Eye of the Beholder," documentary photos from Salvadoran archive; "Future Gardens," by Betsy Connors (holography installation) and "Spiral Journey," by Linda Connor

(retrospective). Presents 5-6 group thematic exhibitions in the David and Sandra Bakalar Gallery and 8-10 one- and two-person shows in the Natalie G. Klebenov Gallery/year. Shows last 6-8 weeks. Sponsors openings; receptions with refreshments for the Bakalar Gallery shows.
Terms & Making Contact: Interested in receiving work from newer, lesser-known photographers. Will review transparencies. Interested in matted or unmatted work. Query with samples or send material by mail for consideration. SASE. Reports in 2-3 months "depending upon frequency of programming committee meetings."

PHOTOGRAPHY GALLERY, Dept. PM, % Park School of Communications, Ithaca College, Ithaca NY 14850. (607)274-3242. Director and Associate Professor: Danny Guthrie. Estab. 1980.
Exhibitions: "Open to all photo-based work; recent and contemporary work by known and emerging artists. No requirements, but most exhibitions are semi-established artists or artists/academics. Presents 10 shows/years. Shows last 1 month. "We do a national mailing of the annual calendar with one image from a selected photographer."
Terms & Making Contact: Photography is occasionally sold. Does not charge commission. General price range: $300-1,500. "We review slides during the month of September for the next year." Interested in matted work only. No frames. Large unmatted work is OK. 4 × 8 maximum size. Send material by mail for consideration only in month of September. SASE. Reports in 1 month.
Tips: Send work in September. Submit good quality, labeled slides with statement, vitae and support material.

*PHOTO-SPACE AT ROCKLAND CENTER FOR THE ARTS, 27 S. Greenbush Rd., West Nyack NY 10994. (914)358-0877. Executive Director: Julianne Ramos. Estab. 1947.
Exhibits: Requirements: Geographic Limits: Rockland, Westchester and Orange counties in New York and Bergen County in New Jersey. Interested in all types of photos. Examples of recent exhibitions: "Second Thoughts" by Ned Harris and "Photo Structures" by Gordon Rapp. Presents 4-5 shows/year. Shows last 2 months. Photographer's presence at opening preferred.
Terms & Making Contact: Charges 33% commission. General price range: $250-2,500. Reviews transparencies. Interested in matted or unmatted work. Shows are limited to 32 × 40. Query with samples. Send material by mail for consideration. SASE. Reports in 3 months.

PRAKAPAS GALLERY, 800 Prospect St., #3C, La Jolla CA 92037-4204. (619)454-1622. FAX: (619)454-9686. Director: Eugene J. Prakapas. Estab. 1976.
Exhibits: "Primary interest is Modernism of the 20s and 30s. But, we are interested in any work that is not just good or accomplished but remarkable – genuinely outstanding." Examples of recent exhibitors: Ralph Steiner, Lazlo Moholy-Nagy and Man Ray. "Our specialty is historical work and at the moment we are doing no exhibitions."
Terms & Making Contact: Commission received "depends entirely upon the situation." Buys photography outright. General price range: $500-100,000. Reviews transparencies, "but only if we request them – i.e., if prior arrangements are made." Requires exclusive representation within metropolitan area. Query with resume of credits. "We are not interested in seeing unsolicited material."
Tips: Opportunities offered photographers by galleries in general are "excellent, better than ever before. But in exhibiting a photographer's work, a gallery makes a substantial commitment in terms of reputation and money. If a photographer hopes for/expects such commitment, he should ensure that his submission reflects at least equal commitment on his part. All too often, submissions are sloppy, haphazard and unprofessional – an immediate turnoff."

QUEEN EMMA GALLERY, 1301 Punchbowl St., Honolulu HI 96813. (808)538-7696 (808)547-4397. Director: Masa Morioka Taira. Estab. 1977.
Exhibits: Interested in all types, especially original, experimental, etc. in fine arts category. Presents 1-2 shows/year. Sponsors openings. Photographer's presence at opening preferred.
Terms & Making Contact: Charges 30% commission. Buys photos outright. General price range: $50-500. Interested in slides for review committee, mounted work only. Request proposal forms from gallery and submit along with 20 or fewer slides in plastic sheet. SASE. Reports in 2 months or less.
Tips: "Present work ready for hanging. For portfolio viewing, have works matted or dry mounted with borders." Opportunities generally are "not very good in Honolulu." Sees more galleries making effort "to inform the art buying public that photography is a fine art form also."

QUEENS COLLEGE ART CENTER, Benjamin S. Rosenthal Library, Queens College, Flushing NY 11367-6701. (718)997-3770. FAX: (718)997-3753. Director: Suzanna Simor. Curator: Alexandra de Luise. Estab. 1952.
Exhibits: Requirements: Open to all types, styles, subject matter; decisive factor is quality. Photographer must be ready to deliver all the work in ready-to-be-exhibited condition and is responsible for installation, removal, transportation. Examples of recent exhibitions: "Romauldo Garcia: Portraitist

..." (Mexican portraits); "Marta Povo: Photographs from Spain ..." (sculptural pieces and dancers); and "Bruno Forel: Photographs" (travelogue through US in '30s). Presents 4 shows/year. Shows last 1 month. Sponsors openings. Photographer is responsible for providing, arranging, refreshments and cleanup. Photographer's presence at opening required; presence during show preferred.
Terms & Making Contact: Charges 33⅓% commission. General price range: $10-500. Interested in framed or unframed, mounted or unmounted, matted or unmatted work. Arrange a personal interview to show portfolio. Query with resume of credits. Query with samples. Send material by mail for consideration. Submit portfolio for review. SASE. Reports in 2-4 weeks.

QUINCY COLLEGE/GRAY GALLERY, 1800 College, Quincy IL 62301. (217)228-5371. Curator of Art: Robert Lee Mejer. Estab. 1968.
Exhibits: Requirements: Interested in all types, styles and subject matter. Requirements: Must be professionally presentable for hanging and display. Examples of recent exhibitions: "Photo Constructions" by Les Barta; "500 Miles," by William Sladcik (color photographs); and hand-colored photos by Nancy Hutchinson. Presents 1-2 shows/year. Shows last 3-4 weeks.
Terms & Making Contact: Very receptive to exhibiting work of newer, lesser-known photographers. Charges 20% commission. General price range: $50-400. Reviews transparencies. Interested in framed or unframed, mounted and matted work only. Shows limited to standard sizes. Query with resume of credits. Send material by mail for consideration. SASE. Reports in 1 month.
Tips: "Be consistent with work/quality. Have a point of view." Looks for "well crafted, direct, honest, straight photography and unique, inventive, creative photography. Have a body of work ready to exhibit; be professional in presentation and personal in your vision. Sees a trend toward hand color; personal and surreal."

© Nancy Hutchinson

In capturing this image called "Simulated Wood: Bedroom," Indiana photographer Nancy Hutchinson worked to express a sense of "home" for viewers. The photo was part of a two-person show put on by Quincy College Art Gallery in 1988 and several of her images were kept in gallery exhibit records. Curator Robert Lee Mejer says the gallery's selection committee was impressed by Hutchinson's approach to photography through which she investigated wood forms and simulated materials.

*RANDOLPH STREET GALLERY, 756 N. Milwaukee Ave., Chicago IL 60622. (312)666-7737. Exhibitions Director: Paul Brenner. Estab. 1979.
Exhibits: Exhibits work in all media, mostly in group exhibitions dealing with a specific topic, theme, social issue or asthetic concept. Examples of recent exhibitions: "Embodiment" by Jo Spence, "Speak" by Lorna Simpson and "Backtalk" by Esther Paradd. Presents 7 shows/year. Shows last 5 weeks. Sponsors openings; publicity brochure for exhibition. Photographer's presence at opening preferred.
Terms & Making Contact: NPI. Reviews slides. Interested in framed or unframed, mounted or unmounted and matted or unmatted work. Send material by mail for consideration. SASE. Reports in 1-4 months depending on when the slides are received.
Tips: "We review quarterly and view slides only. We are a nonprofit exhibition space, therefore we do not represent artists, but can facilitate sales through the artist's gallery or directly through artist."

REAL ART WAYS, Dept. PM, 56 Arbor St., Hartford CT 06106. (203)232-1006. Curator: Jackie McAllister.
Exhibits: Interested in avant-garde/experimental styles. Examples of recent exhibitors: Coreen Simpson, Hunter Reynolds. Presents 6 shows/year. Shows last 4 weeks. Sponsors openings; provides refreshments from 6-8 p.m.
Terms & Making Contact: Will review slides. Interested in framed or unframed work, matted or unmatted work. Send material by mail for consideration — slides/resume/clippings. SASE. Reports in 2 months.
Tips: "Looks for work that is on the cutting edge of artistic experimentation. As a nonprofit arts organization we seek only to present the best and freshest work around. For proposals send about 20 of your best slides, along with resume, and any reviews or articles which you feel represent your work."

*ROBINSON GALLERIES, 3514 Lake St., Houston TX 77098. (713)526-0761. FAX: (713)526-0763. Director: Thomas J. Robinson. Estab. 1969.
Exhibits: Requirements: Archivally framed and ready for presentation. Limited editions only. Work must be professional. Not interested in pure abstractions. Examples of recent exhibitions: Works by Pablo Corral (cibachrome) and Ron English (b&w). Presents 1 show every other year. Shows last 4-6 weeks. Sponsors openings; invitations, reception and traditional promotion.
Terms & Making Contact: Charges 50% commission. General price range $100-400. Reviews transparencies. Interested in framed or unframed, matted or unmatted work. Requires exclusive representation within metropolitan area. Arrange a personal interview to show portfolio. Submit portfolio for review. Query with resume of credits. SASE. Reports in 1-2 weeks.
Tips: "Robinson Galleries is a fine arts gallery first, the medium is second."

*HOLLY ROSS ASSOC., 516 "C" St. NE, Washington DC 20002. (202)544-0400. Art Consultant: Sheryl Ameen.
Exhibits: Interested in contemporary color photos of all types. Subjects include landscape, architectural, whimsical, abstract and Deco-50s. Photographers must pass a quality review by the gallery. Sponsors openings; provides 50/50 split on invitations, advertising and refreshments. Photographer's presence at opening preferred.
Terms & Making Contact: Charges 50% commission. General price range: $150 and up. Reviews transparencies. Send slides by mail for consideration. SASE. Reports in 1 month or as soon as possible.
Tips: "We are constantly reviewing new artists and would be happy to see new work. Opportunities offered by galleries are "getting much better." Trend is toward showing more moderately priced photos regularly.

*THE ROTUNDA GALLERY, Suite 1400W, 16 Court St., Brooklyn NY 11241. (718)855-7882. FAX: (718)802-9095. Director: Janet Riker.
Exhibits: Requirements: Must live in, work in or have studio in Brooklyn. Interested in contemporary works. Examples of recent exhibitions: "This is Historic Brooklyn," by Tony Velez (photographs, framed); "Photo Alternatives," by E.E. Smith, D. Carlton Broght, Joyce Weiner, Andrew Roberts Grey (Serigraphs, stereo viewers, cyanotypes, xerox); and "The Enigmatic Object," by Bill Jones (unique photographic print cliche verre). Presents 1 show/year. Shows last 5 weeks. Sponsors openings; wine and seltzer. Photographer's presence at opening preferred.
Terms & Making Contact: Charges 20% commission. Reviews transparencies. Interested in framed or unframed, mounted or unmounted, matted or unmatted work. Shows are limited by walls that are 12 feet high. Arrange a personal interview to show portfolio. Send material by mail for consideration. Join artists slide registry, call for form. SASE.

*SANTA BARBARA CONTEMPORARY ARTS FORUM, 2nd Floor, 653 Paseo Nuevo, Santa Barbara CA 93101. (805)966-5373. FAX: (805)962-1421. Director: Nancy Doll. Estab. 1976.

Exhibits: Requirements: Non-commercial photographers, although photojournalists are considered. Interested in works that deal with contemporary, aesthetic, critical and social issues. Examples of recent exhibitions: "Fire on Film," a group exhibition of the 1990 Santa Barbara Fire; "The Guiding Light," by Marta Peluso (b&w documentary); "Homeland," by Kathryn Clark (color installation-related work). Presents 1 or 2 shows/year, "but interested in more." Shows last 6-8 weeks. Sponsors openings; artist asked to give gallery talk. Photographer's presence at opening preferred.

Terms & Making Contact: NPI. Submit slides and resume for review. Send material by mail for consideration. Appointments *must* be arranged in advance. SASE. Reports in 4-6 weeks.

*MARTIN SCHWEIG STUDIO AND GALLERY, 4658 Maryland Ave., St. Louis MO 63108. (314)361-3000. Gallery Director: Cena Pohl.

Exhibits: Requirements: Photographs must be matted to standard frame sizes. Interested in all types, expecially interested in seeing work that pushes the boundaries of photography, in technique and subject. Examples of recent exhibitions: "Surfaces" by Yvette Drury Dubinsky and "Florence and Abroad" by Stan Strembicki. Presents 8 shows/year. Shows last 1 month. Sponsors openings. Photographer's presence at opening preferred.

Terms & Making Contact: Charges 40% commission. General price range: $100-700. Reviews transparencies. Interested in mounted or unmounted work, matted or unmatted work. Submit portfolio for review. Query with samples. SASE. Reports in 1 month.

Tips: "Our show schedule is decided by a panel of jurors. Usually a portfolio must be submitted twice."

*SECOND STREET GALLERY, 201 Second St. NW, Charlottesville VA 22902. (804)977-7284. Executive Director: Mary Scrupe. Estab. 1973.

Exhibits: Requirements: Request exhibition guidelines. Presents 2-3 shows/year. Shows last 1 month. Sponsors openings. Photographer's presence at opening required.

Terms & Making Contact: Charges 30% commission. General price range: $250-2,000. Reviews transparencies. Interested in unmatted work only. Submit portfolio for review. SASE. Reports in 6-8 weeks.

THE SILVER IMAGE GALLERY, 318 Occidental Ave. S., Seattle WA 98104. (206)623-8116. Director: Dan Fear. Estab. 1973.

Exhibits: Interested in masters, traditional landscapes, nudes and contemporary photography.

Terms & Making Contact: General price range: $250 and up. Send SASE for additional information.

Tips: "The Silver Image Gallery is interested in working with photographers who are committed and have been working seriously in fine art photography for at least five years."

SOMERSTOWN GALLERY, Box 379, Somers NY 10589. (914)277-3461. FAX: (914)234-7522. Photography Curator: Leandra Pope. Estab. 1979.

Exhibits: Interested in straight, unmanipulated and antique processes; photojournalism too. Examples of recent exhibitions: "Photos of Middle East," by Milbrey Polk; "A Look at Apartheid," by Marylyn Herbert and "Endangered Species," by Jeanne Baubion Mecker. Present 8 shows/year. Shows last 4 weeks. Photographer's presence at opening preferred.

Terms & Making Contacat: Interested in receiving work from newer, lesser-know photographers. Charges 30-50% commission. Interested in mounted or unmounted work, matted or unmatted work. All work must be archivally processed and presented. Submit portfolio for review. SASE. Reports in 3 weeks.

Tips: "Edit. Edit. Edit. Bring works which you feel very good about." New gallery space available at The Schoolhouse as of January 1991.

*STATE OF ILLINOIS ART GALLERY, Suite 2-100, 100 W. Randolph, Chicago IL 60601. (312)814-5322. Director: Kent Smith. Assistant Director: Jane Stevens.

Exhibits: Requirements: Must be a resident of Illinois or have had a strong connection with Illinois. Interested in historic and contemporary art. Examples of recent exhibitions: "Life's Lessons," by Bea Nettles (b&w Polaroid); "Spirited Visions," by Patty Carroll (color portraits) and "A New Vision for Chicago," by Moholy-Nagy (b&w photograms). Presents 2 shows/year. Shows last 2 months. Sponsors openings; provides refreshments. Photographer's presence at opening and during show preferred.

Terms & Making Contact: NPI. "We do not sell photos, only exhibit work." Reviews transparencies. Send slides, "if we are interested we will arrange appointment." SASE. Work juried twice a year.

SUNPRINT CAFE & GALLERY, 638 State St., Madison WI 53703. (608)255-1555. Director: Rena Gelman. Estab. 1976.
Exhibits: Interested in all types of photography; 2-3 of 7-8 shows a year feature photography. "We get far more 'nature-photo' submissions than we could ever use. We look for a well-developed eye and a unique voice or statement. Professional quality—but not interested in slick comercially oriented work. Style and subjects can vary. We are interested in non silver, color and/or b&w work. Examples of recent exhibitions: "Natural Extracts," by Erik Moshen (cibachrome); handpainted archival and other photos by Dianne Francis and Andy Kraushaar; and "Poland," by Wendy Mukluk (b&w photos).
Terms & Making Contact: Very receptive to exhibiting the work of newer, lesser-known photographers. General price range: $100-400. Call for more information. Framed work only. "We need 1 month to view each portfolio, expect a follow-up letter from us. Include a SASE for return of slides."
Tips: "We have a restaurant and gallery business which encourages work to be viewed in a relaxed atmosphere. Lots of natrual light and track lighting. We schedule 6-week shows. Artists usually sell 0-3 pieces during show. Low-cost work sells more."

*THE TAMPA MUSEUM OF ART, 601 Doyle Carlton Dr., Tampa FL 33602. (813)223-8130. FAX: (813)223-8732. Director: Andrew Maass. Estab. 1979.
Exhibits: Requirements: Be willing to be included in group exhibitions. Interested in manipulated images, subjects relating to the Greek and Roman antique culture, innovations in technique, style and subject. Examples of recent exhibitions: "Aaron Siskind" by Aaron Siskind, "Larry Silver" by Larry Silver and "Carl Chirenza: Landscapes of the Mind," by Carl Chiarenza all (silver print, mounted murals). Presents 6 shows/year. Shows last 6-8 weeks. Sponsors openings in conjunction with other exhibits opening simultaneously, prints invitations and announcements other regional publicity. Photographer's presence at opening preferred.
Terms & Making Contact: Charges 35% commission. Buys photos outright. General price range: $200-20,000. Reviews transparencies. Interested in unframed work only, mounted or unmounted work, matted or unmatted work. Query with resume of credits. Query with samples. Send material by mail for consideration. SASE. Reports in 1-2 weeks.
Tips: "The museum is an educational institution where strong exhibitions are the goal. Sale of works not strongly promoted."

UNION SQUARE GALLERY/ERNST HAAS VIEWING ROOM, 118 E. 17th St., New York NY 10003. (212)777-8393. FAX: (212)614-0688. Director: Todd Weinstein. Estab. 1980.
Exhibits: Interested in all types. "We show a lot of emerging artists." Examples of recent exhibitors: Ed Grazda (b&w photography); Maggie Steber (color photography); and Arlene Gottfried (color photography). Presents 6-7 shows/year. Shows last 6 weeks. Photographer's presence at opening required.
Terms & Making Contact: General price range: $250-1,200. Call. SASE.
Tips: "Get to know the gallery and follow shows."

*UNIVERSITY OF MASSACHUSETTS MEDICAL CENTER GALLERY, 55 Lake Ave. N., Worcester MA 01655. (508)856-2558. Coordinator: Margaret G. Cope. Estab. 1979.
Exhibits: Requirements: Portfolio review by a jury. Write for additional information. Examples of recent exhibitions: "Every Color Has Its Song," by Lou Jones. Presents 3-4 shows/year. Shows last 1 month. Sponsors opening for 50-100 people, if desired. Provides refreshment; also publicity and announcement for opening and show. Photographer's presence at opening is required.
Terms & Making Contact: Interested in receiving work from newer, lesser-known photographers. Photography rarely sold in gallery. Asks 15% donation. General price range: $75 and up. "We notify when jury meets (usually once a year)." SASE. Reports in 1 week.

VIRIDIAN GALLERY, 24 West 57 St., New York NY 10019. (212)245-2882. Director: Paul Cohen. Estab. 1968.
Exhibits: Interested in eclectic. Member of Cooperative Gallery. Examples of recent exhibitions: "Curtain Time & Coast to Coast," by Robert Smith (abstract & figurative images); "Re-Visioned," by Glenn Rothman (computer-enhanced works, ink jet and monitor-shot work); "Ties that Bind, " by Yoland Skeete (exploration of self and mores in sequenced sets, predominantly b&w). Presents 3 shows/year. Shows last 3 weeks. Photographer's presence at opening preferred.
Terms & Making Contact: Is receptive to exhibiting work of newer photographers "if members are cooperative." Charges 20% commission. Will review transparencies only if submitted as membership application. Interested in framed or unframed, mounted, and matted or unmatted work. Request membership application details. SASE. Reports in 2 weeks.
Tips: Opportunities for photographers in galleries are "improving." Sees trend toward "a broad range of styles" being shown in galleries. "Cibachromes seem a 'given.' There are fewer hand-painted and altered types of work. More abstracts. The buying public seems open to this, too. The less 'complicated'

© Todd Weinstein

This photo taken by New York City photographer Todd Weinstein leaves the viewer wondering about the subjects. "Are they waiting for someone?" or "Are they sitting in the car because they have nowhere else to go?" The lighting and the car work well together to create the photo's mood. Images that get the viewer to think work well in galleries. This shot has sold twice to publications and was on display at the Union Square Gallery in New York City.

and explicit pieces sell best. Presentation is vital! Initially, at least, offer less 'explicit' work. Be persistent!!"

■VISUAL STUDIES WORKSHOP GALLERY, 31 Prince St., Rochester NY 14607. (716)442-8676. Exhibitions Coordinator: James B. Wyman.
Exhibits: Interested in contemporary mid-career and emerging artists working in photography, video, and artists' books; new approaches to the interpretation of historical photographs. Presents 15-20 shows/year. Shows last 8-10 weeks. Sponsors openings; provides lectures, refreshments. Photographer's presence at opening preferred.
Terms & Making Contacts: Charges 40% commission. Rarely buys photography outright. General price range: $350-3,000. Reviews transparencies. Send material by mail for consideration. SASE. Submissions are reviewed twice yearly—spring and fall. "We prefer slides which we can keep and refer to as needed."
Tips: "It is important that the photographer be familiar with the overall programs of the Visual Studies Workshop. We respond to what imagemakers are producing. We represent mostly younger, emerging photographers whose work we see as being significant in our time. Therefore, I feel that most of our clients buy the work they do because they are responding to the qualities of the image itself."

*WESTCHESTER GALLERY, County Center, White Plains NY 10606. (914)684-0094. FAX: (914)684-0608. Gallery Coordinator: Jonathan G. Vazquez-Haight.
Exhibits: Requirements: submit 10 slides or actual work to be juried by panel of artists. Examples of recent exhibitions: works by Susi Dugaw, Cosmo Prete and Robin Schwartz. Presents usually 2 photo shows/year. Shows last 1 month. Sponsors openings. Gallery covers cost of space, light, insurance,

mailers (printing and small mailing list) and modest refreshments. Photographer's presence at opening preferred.
Terms & Making Contact: Charges 33⅓% commission. General price range $150-5,000. Reviews transparencies. Interested in any presentable format ready to hang. Arrange a personal interview to show portfolio. Submit portfolio for review. Query with resume of credits. Send material by mail for consideration. SASE. Reports in 1 month.
Tips: "Most sales are at low end, $150. Gallery space is flexible and artists are encouraged to do their own installation."

*EDWARD WESTON FINE ART, 19355 Business Center Dr., Northridge CA 91324. (818)885-1044. FAX: (818)885-1021. Vice President: Ann Weston. Estab. 1960.
Exhibits: Requirements: Submit presentation for review. "Do not send originals as we're not insured or responsible for loss." Interested in unique and unusual techniques, imagery to broaden "our look and stigma of just having Hollywood glamour and Marilyn Monroe." Examples of recent exhibitions: "Hollywood Glamour," by Hurrell, Bull and Willinger (glamour portraits 1920s, 30s, 40s); "Marilyn Monroe," by Stern, Greene, Barris and DeDienes (candid and staged shoots) and "Norma Jean and Marilyn," (complete body of work covering 16 years). Shows last 1 month. Photographer's presence at opening required.
Terms & Making Contact: Charges 40-60% commission. Buys photos outright. General price range: $50-5,000. Reviews transparencies. Interested in mounted or unmounted, matted or unmatted. Requires exclusive representation within metropolitan area. Submit portfolio for review. Send material by mail for consideration. SASE. Reports in 1 month.
Tips: "We are publishers and artists and estates' representatives. We also do posters as well as original photography."

WHITE GALLERY-PORTLAND STATE UNIVERSITY, Box 751, Portland OR 97207. (503)725-4452. Contact: Art Exhibition Committee.
Exhibits: Presents 8 shows/year. Exhibits last 3 weeks. Sponsors openings. Photographer's presence at opening and during show is preferred.
Terms & Making Contact: Charges 20% commission. General price range: $100-300. Interested in framed or unframed, mounted, matted work. Send material by mail for consideration. SASE. Reports in 1 month.
Tips: "Best time to submit is September-October of the year prior to the year show will be held. We only go by what we see, not the name. We see it all and refrain from the trendy. Send slides. Do something different . . . view life upside down."

*WIESNER GALLERY, LTD., 425 W. 13th St., New York NY 10014. (212)675-8722. Director: Nikola Vizner.
Exhibits: Requirements: Must have high quality works. Interested in all types of work. Examples of recent exhibitions: "Pictures From Here to There," by George Zimmermann (silver prints); and "Eye of a Camera," by Fred R. Tannery (silver prints). Presents 3-4 shows/year. Shows last 3-4 weeks. Sponsors openings; invitations and opening reception. Photographer's presence at opening and presence during show preferred.
Terms & Making Contact: Charges 50% commission. General price range: $200-10,000. Reviews transparencies. Interested in matted work only. Arrange a personal interview to show portfolio. Send material by mail for consideration. SASE. Reports in 1 month.
Tips: "Only serious photographers need to apply."

WOODSTOCK GALLERY OF ART, Dept. PM, Gallery Place, Rt. 4 East, Woodstock VT 05091. (802)457-1900. Gallery Owner: Charles Fenton. Estab. 1972. Represents professional artists of Vermont and New England.
Exhibits: Interested in experimental and new forms. Presents 2 photography-only exhibits/year. Shows last 1 month. Sponsors openings; shares expenses. Photographer's presence at opening is preferred.
Terms & Making Contact: "Very receptive" to exhibiting the work of newer, lesser-known photographers. Charges 40% commission. Occasionally buys outright. General price range: $300-2,500. Generally requires exclusive representation in area. Unless labeled and priced accordingly, color photographs should be cibachrome or dye transfer prints. Submit portfolio and resume for consideration. All work should be archivally mounted and matted, preferably framed. Arrange a personal interview

The asterisk before a listing indicates that the market is new in this edition. New markets are often the most receptive to freelance submissions.

to show portfolio. Query with samples. Send material by mail for consideration. Slides reviewed 4 times/year.
Tips: Sees trend toward painting with light. "Best sellers are innovative works with strong use of imagery and technique. Non-traditional work is coming on fast." Photographs carried and displayed in gallery at all times.

CHARLES A. WUSTUM MUSEUM OF FINE ARTS, Dept. PM, 2519 Northwestern Ave., Racine WI 53404. (414)636-9177. Director: Bruce W. Pepich. "Interested in all fine art photography. It's regularly displayed in our Art Sales and Rental Gallery and the Main Exhibition Galleries. Many of our exhibitors are emerging artists. We sponsor a biennial exhibit of Wisconsin photographers."
Exhibits: The biennial show is limited to residents of Wisconsin; the sales and rental gallery is limited to residents of the Midwest. Many new and lesser-known photographers are featured. There is no limit to applicants for solo or group exhibitions, but they must apply in November of each year. Presents an average of 3 shows/year. Shows last 4-6 weeks. Sponsors openings. "We provide refreshments and 50 copies of the reception invitation to the exhibitor." Photographer's presence at opening preferred.
Terms & Making Contact: Charges 30% commission from exhibitions, 40% from sales and rental gallery. General price range: $125-350. Will review transparencies. Interested in framed or unframed work. "Must be framed unless it's a 3-D piece. Sale prices for sales and rental gallery have a $1,000 ceiling." Query with resume of credits or send material by mail for consideration. SASE.
Tips: "Photography seems to fare very well in our area. Both the exhibitors and the buying public are trying more experimental works. The public is very interested in presentation and becoming increasingly aware of the advantage of archival mounting. They are beginning to look for this additional service. Our clients are more interested in work of newer (and more affordable) photographers. Landscapes currently sell best at our gallery. Sees trend toward increasing uses of combinations of drawing and painting media with photography. We always look for the best quality in the photographs we exhibit. The technical process involved is not as important to us as the idea or message in the work."

Galleries/'92-93 changes

The following markets appeared in the 1992 edition of *Photographer's Market* but are not listed in the 1993 edition. They may have been omitted for failing to respond to our request for updates of information, they may have gone out of business or they may no longer wish to receive freelance work.

Alias Gallery (late verification)
Art Atelier Kafka (not reviewing work)
Art Center of Battle Creek (did not respond)
Artemisia Gallery (did not respond)
Arts for Living Center (did not respond)
Artspace (did not respond)
BC Space (did not respond)
Besser Museum, Jesse (did not respond)
Brown Contemporary Art, Robert (not reviewing work)
Bush Exhibit Room, Steve (did not respond)
Creative Photography Gallery (did not respond)
Edelman Gallery, Catherine (did not respond)
Edelstein Gallery, Paul (did not respond)
Engle Gallery, William (did not respond)
Fine Arts Museum of the South (did not respond)
Gallery of Art, University of Northern Iowa (did not

respond)
Graham Gallery, W.A. (did not respond)
Halsted Gallery Inc., The (did not respond)
International Center of Photography (did not respond)
International Museum of Photography at George Eastman House (did not respond)
Kresge Art Museum (not reviewing work)
Labor Gallery (did not respond)
Louisville Visual Art Association (did not respond)
Northern Illinois University Art Museum (did not respond)
Photo Gallery, The (did not respond)
Photographic Center of Monterey Peninsula, The (did not respond)
Plains Indians & Pioneer Museum and Art Gallery (did not respond)
Reflections (did not respond)
Rockridge Cafe (did not

respond)
Schomburg Center for Research in Black Culture (did not respond)
Schweinfurth Memorial Art Center (did not respond)
Sea Cliff Gallery Ltd. (did not respond)
Shapiro Gallery, Michael (did not respond)
South Shore Art Center, Inc. (did not respond)
Southern Light (did not respond)
Spiritus Gallery, Susan (did not respond)
SUNY Plattsburgh Art Museum (did not respond)
Three Galleries: Steve Bush Exhibit Room; Outer Space; The Wall (did not respond)
Ward Gallery, A. Montgomery (did not respond)
Washington Project for the Arts (did not respond)
Worcester Center for Crafts (not reviewing work)
Yeshiva University Museum (did not respond)

Paper Products

In any area of photography, freelancers must remember for whom they are working and they must respond to the needs of the clients. A photographer who captures stunning images may be an outstanding talent, but if nobody is buying the work he creates he will not last long in the industry.

In order to succeed a photographer must know what the market demands, capture those photos and then find buyers for the work. Quoting a survey by Western Publishing Company, *Greetings Magazine* pointed out in its April 1992 issue that preteens spent around $75 billion on merchandise in 1990. The magazine, which caters to the greeting card industry, suggested that retailers make a note of this figure and find ways to reach buyers in that age group. Photographers should do the same. A photographer who reacts to such trends in the marketplace can carve a niche for himself when it comes to companies in the paper products field. That way, when he knocks on the doors of potential buyers, or better, when they knock on his, he will have the images they want to buy.

Within the paper products field there is a variety of potential buyers, including companies which produce greeting cards, posters and calendars. It is a field that uses a multitude of different images, from playful pets and children to nudes and boudoir. However, unlike other segments of publishing, this industry is relatively narrow in the total number of companies.

It is quite prosperous, with annual sales in the range of several billion dollars. Some larger companies have staff photographers for routine assignments, but also look to freelancers to supply images. Usually, this is in the form of stock images, and images are especially desirable if they are of unusual subject matter or remote scenic areas for which assignments—even to staff shooters—would be too costly. Freelancers are usually offered assignments once they have established a track record with a company and demonstrate a flair for certain techniques, subject matters or locations. Also, smaller companies are more receptive to working with freelancers, though they are less likely to assign work because of smaller budgets for photography.

The pay in this market can be quite lucrative if you can provide the right image at the right time for a client desperately in need of it, or if you develop a working relationship with one or a few of the better paying markets. You should be aware, though, that one reason for higher rates of payment in this market is that these companies may want to buy all rights to images. With changes in the copyright law (see Copyright/rights, in the Business of Photography, on page 11), many companies are more willing to negotiate sales which specify all rights for limited time periods or exclusive product rights rather than complete surrender of copyright.

Another key consideration is that an image with good market value can effectively be taken out of the market during the selection process. Many paper products companies work on lead times of up to two years before products are ready to market. It can be weeks, months or as much as a year before they report to photographers on their interest in using their images. In addition, some companies will pay only on publication or on a royalty basis after publication. For these reasons as well as the question of rights, you may want to reconsider selling images with high multiple resale potential in this market. Certainly, you will want to pursue selling to companies which do not present serious obstacles in these ways or which offer exceptionally good compensation when they do.

Long-time photographer Laurance Aiuppy (see Close-up, page 218) believes photographers can take advantage of opportunities in the paper products field. Although the majority of his work is in stock photography, Aiuppy has used his talents to garner several sales for calendars. He suggests that photographers research buyers' needs before attempting to sell their work. After your initial research, query to the companies you are interested in working with and send a stock photo list. Since these companies receive large volumes of submissions, they often appreciate knowing what is available rather than actually receiving it. This kind of query can lead to future sales even if your stock inventory doesn't meet their needs at the time because they know they can request a submission as their needs change. Some listings in this section advise sending quality samples along with your query while others specifically request only the list. As you plan your queries, it's important that you follow their instructions. It will help you establish a better rapport with the companies from the start.

One tendency within this market which photographers should also keep in mind is varying degrees of professionalism among the companies. For instance, some smaller companies can be a source of headaches in a number of ways, including failing to report in a timely manner on submissions, delaying return of submissions or using images without authorization. This sometimes happens with the seemingly more established companies, too, though it's less common. Typically, many smaller companies have started as one- or two-person operations, and not all have acquired adequate knowledge of industry practices which are standard among the more established firms.

Since smaller firms usually offer the freelancer more opportunity in terms of breaking in and learning the industry, it's best not to write them off entirely but study them sufficiently before doing business with them.

One final note on the greeting card industry. In the past the Greeting Card Creative Network (GCCN) helped writers and artists in the greeting card field by providing access to a network of industry professionals, including publishers and licensing agents. It also acted as a clearinghouse for information on design and marketing trends, and legal and financial concerns within the industry. Those same services are still offered, but the organization now also helps photographers. Annual membership fees in GCCN range from $40 (student) to $70 (professional artist). For more information contact the GCCN, Suite 615, 1350 New York Ave. NW, Washington DC 20005. (202)393-1780.

ACME GRAPHICS, INC., Box 1348, Cedar Rapids IA 52406. (319)364-0233. President: Stan Richardson. Estab. 1913. Specializes in printed merchandise for funeral directors.
Subject Needs: Religious, nature.
Specs: Uses 35mm transparencies; color contact sheets; and color negatives.
Payment & Terms: Pays $50/b&w photo; $50/color photo. Also, pays according to price set by photographer. Pays on acceptance. Buys all rights.
Making Contact: Query with samples. Send unsolicited photos by mail for consideration. Reviews stock photos. SASE. Reports in 2 weeks.

ADVANCED GRAPHICS, (see Angel Graphics).

*AFRICA CARD CO., INC., Box 91, New York NY 10108. (718)672-5759. President: Vince Jordan. Specializes in all occasion cards. Buys 25 photos annually.
Specs: Uses 5×7 color glossy prints; 35mm, 2¼×2¼ transparencies.
Payment & Terms: Pays $15 minimum/color photo. Buys all rights. Submit model release with photo.
Making Contact: Call to arrange an appointment. Query with resume of credits. Submit material by mail for consideration. Submit seasonal material 2 months in advance. Reports in 6-10 weeks. SASE.
Tips: "Do an assortment of work and try to be as original as possible."

ALASKA WILD IMAGES, P.O. Box 13149, Trapper Creek AK 99683. (907)733-2467. Editorial Director: Rollie Ostermick. Estab. 1976. Specializes in greeting cards, postcards and posters. Minimum of five freelance photos assigned annually.

Subject Needs: Alaskan and Canadian wildlife and wilderness. Does not want non-Alaska/Canadian material.
Specs: Uses 35mm, 2¼×2¼, or 4×5 transparencies.
Payment & Terms: Pays $75 and up/color photo. Pays on publication. Credit line given. Buys exclusive product rights; negotiable. Model release preferred. Seldom uses people in photos; if they are recognizable must have release. Captions preferred.
Making Contact: Interested in receiving work from newer, lesser-known photographers. Reviews stock photos. Query with stock photo list. SASE. Reports in 1 month. Simultaneous submissions and previously published work OK. Photo guidelines free with SASE.
Tips: Looking for "dramatic close-ups of wildlife, wildflowers and awesome scenics, especially with pleasant mood lighting. We print primarily once a year and contact photographers to request submissions and to discuss actual needs prior to this time."

AMERICAN ARTS & GRAPHICS, INC., 10915 47th Ave. W., Everett WA 98117. (206)353-8200. FAX: (206)348-6296. Estab. 1948. Licensing Director: Shelley Pedersen. Estab. 1948. Specializes in posters. Works with 3-4 freelance photographers per month.
Subject Needs: Humorous, cute animals, exotic sports cars, male and female models (no nudes), some scenic. Images that would be appealing to our 12-20-year-old poster market.
Specs: Uses 2¼×2¼, 4×5, 8×10 transparencies.
Payment & Terms: Pays $500 or more/color photo. Pays on acceptance. Credit line given. Buys poster rights only. Model release required. Captions are helpful
Making Contact: Contact by phone to request guidelines. Reviews stock photos. Submit seasonal material 5 months in advance. SASE. Reports in 2 weeks. Simultaneous submissions and previously published work OK (if not posters). Photo guidelines free with SASE.
Tips: "Subject and style must appeal to our young, teenage market. A good way to get a feel for what we do is to look at our poster rack in your area."

*ANGEL GRAPHICS, division of Angel Gifts Inc., P.O. Box 530, Fairfield IA 52556. (515)472-5481. FAX: (515)472-7353. Photo Editor: Jay Kreider. Estab. 1982. Specializes in posters, framing prints and wall decor. Buys 100-200 photos annually. Assigns 10-15 photos/year.
Subject Needs: Seeks photos of wildlife, including endangered species, humerous, religious and inspirational, cute cats, dogs, scenics, celebrities, American Indians, black ethnic, florals and still life. Does not want risque photos.
Specs: Uses 35mm, 2¼×2¼, 4×5, 8×10 transparencies. "Bigger is better."
Payment & Terms: Pays $100-600/color photo; $100-500/b&w photo; negotiable. Pays upon usage. Credit line "depends on artist's needs." Buys exclusive product rights; negotiable. Model/property release preferred. Captions preferred.
Making Contact: Submit portfolio for review. Query with samples with SASE. Samples kept on file. Reports in 1 month. Simultaneous submission and previously published work OK.
Tips: "Must have sharp focus. We like colorful pieces. We need pieces that appeal to the general public (mall-type shoppers). Any piece that is well done, that all your friends would love to put on their walls is what we want to put in our catalog. We see a trend toward earth awareness."

ANGLER'S SPORT CALENDARS, 4955 E. 2900 N, Murtaugh ID 83344. (208)432-6625. FAX: (208)432-6625. Editor: Barbara Wolverton. Estab. 1976. Specializes in calendars. Buys stock images from freelancers. Buys 40 photos/year. Examples of recently published calendars: "Angler's Calendar," "Decoy Calendar" and "Saltwater Fishing Calendar" (monthly photos).
Subject Needs: Fly fishing, decoys, saltwater fishing, wildlife, waterfowl and bass fishing.
Specs: Uses 35mm, 2¼×2¼ and 4×5 transparencies.
Payment & Terms: Pays $60-200/color photo. Pays on publication. Credit line given. Buys one-time rights. Model release preferred. Photo captions required—include location and species of fish or animal.
Making Contact: Interested in receiving work from newer, lesser-known photographers. Query with stock photo list. SASE. Reports in 1-2 weeks. Previously published work OK if advised of previous publication and date.

The First Markets Index preceding the General Index in the back of this book provides the names of those companies/publications interested in receiving work from newer, lesser-known photographers.

Tips: Interested in action shots; no dead fish or animals. "Look at past calendars to see style and format."

ART RESOURCE INTERNATIONAL LTD., Fields Lane, Brewster NY 10509. (914)277-8888. Vice President: Robin Bonnist. Estab. 1980. Specializes in posters and fine art prints. Buys 500 photos/year.
Subject Needs: All types but does not wish to see regional.
Specs: Uses 35mm, 4×5 and 8×10 transparencies.
Payments & Terms: Pays $50-250/photo. Pays on publication. Credit line given if required. Buys all rights; exclusive product rights. Model release required; photo captions preferred.
Making Contact: Send unsolicited photos by mail for consideration. Submit portfolio for review. Must send SASE for return. Works on assignment only. Accepts seasonal material anytime. SASE. Reports in 1 month. Simultaneous submissions and previously published work OK. Photo guidelines free with SASE.
Tips: Looks for "new and exciting material; subject matter with universal appeal."

CAROLYN BEAN PUBLISHING, LTD., 1129 N. McDowell Blvd., Petaluma CA 94954. President/Creative Director: Bruce Wilson. Specializes in greeting cards and stationery. Buys 50-100 photos/year for the Sierra Club Note card and Christmas card series and new line of ASPCA cards.
Subject Needs: Sierra Club—wilderness and wildlife; ASPCA—cats, dogs, puppies, kittens.
Specs: Uses 35mm, 2¼×2¼, 4×5, etc., transparencies.
Payment & Terms: Pays $200/color photo. Credit line given. Buys exclusive product rights. Anticipates marketing broader product lines for Sierra Club and may want to option other limited rights. Model release required.
Making Contact: Submit by mail. Reviews stock photos. Prefers to see dramatic wilderness and wildlife photographs "of customary Sierra Club quality." Provide business card and tearsheets to be kept on file for possible future assignments. Submit seasonal material 1 year in advance; all-year-round review "include return postage." Publishes Christmas series December; everyday series January and May. SASE. Reports in 1 month. Simultaneous submissions and previously published work OK.
Tips: "Send only your best—don't use fillers."

BEAUTYWAY, Box 340, Flagstaff AZ 86002. (602)779-3651. President: Kenneth Schneider. Specializes in postcards, note cards and posters. Estab. 1979. Uses 300-400 freelance photos/year (fee pay and joint venture). "Joint Venture is emphasized and is a program within Beautyway in which the photographer invests in his own images and works more closely in overall development. Through Joint Venture, photographers may initiate new lines or subjects with Beautyway which emanate from the photographer's strongest images."
Subject Needs: (1)Nationwide landscapes, emphasizes subjects of traveler interest and generic scenes of sea, lake and river. (2) Animals, birds and sealife, with particular interest in young animals, eyes and interaction. (3) Air, water and winter sports, as well as hiking, fishing and hunting. (4) The most important attractions and vistas of major cities, emphasizing sunset, storm, cloud and night settings.
Specs: All transparency formats OK. Ship in protective sleeves with photographer name, title and location on frame.
Payment & Terms: Pays $30 per each 2400 units printed. Usual minimum is $120 after publication. Model release required.
Making Contact: Interested in receiving work from newer, lesser-known photographers. Query with samples, stock list and statement of interests or objectives. SASE. Previously published work OK if not potentially competitive. First report averages two weeks, others vary.
Tips: Looks for "very sharp photos with bright colors and good contrast. Subject matter should be easily identified at first glance. We seek straightforward, basic scenic or subject shots. Obvious camera manipulation such as juxtaposing shots or unnatural filter use is almost always rejected. When submitting transparencies, the person's name, address and name and location of subject should be upon each transparency sleeve."

BOKMON DONG COMMUNICATIONS, P.O. Box 75358, Seattle WA 98125. Photo Editor: Jean Haner. Estab. 1983. Specializes in greeting cards.
Subject Needs: "The subject matter is not as important as the treatment. We are looking for a strong, original image that creates a mood and evokes positive feelings. It is essential that the photograph be unusual and innovative in style. A good balance of foreground and background interest, strong color, composition and lighting are important. Avoid cliches; no pictures of people. Special needs for 1993 include animals or flowers in uncommon situations."
Specs: Uses any size transparencies.
Payment & Terms: Payment negotiable; depends on purchase, $150 minimum. Pays on publication. Credit line given. Buys one-time and exclusive product rights. Model/property release and captions required. In captions include information about name of flower, animal, location of landscape.

Making Contact: Interested in receiving work from newer, lesser-known photographers. Send SASE for photographer's guidelines. For a sample card, send a 5×7 or larger SASE and include $1 in loose postage stamps (don't send cash or checks). Reviews stock photos. Submit seasonal material 8-12 months in advance. Reports in 2 weeks on queries; 2 months on photos. Simultaneous and previously published submissions OK "but not if submitted, published or sold to another card publisher."
Tips: "Read guidelines carefully! The photographer must remember the function of a greeting card — to communicate positive feelings from one person to another. The image must create a mood and have strong visual impact. The kinds of photographs we are looking for are ones that: you can recall without having to look through your files, people remember you by, are hanging on your walls." To break in, "be persistent. Study market to see what is selling. Keep submitting with our needs in mind. Avoid copying previously published material."

CATCH AMERICA, INC., 32 South Lansdowne Ave., Lansdowne PA 19050. (215)626-7770. President: Michael Markowicz. Estab. 1988. Specializes in postcards and posters.
Subject Needs: Contemporary.
Specs: Uses 8×10 b&w prints and 35mm transparencies.
Payment & Terms: NPI. Pays quarterly or monthly on sales. Credit line given. Rights purchased vary, but usually exclusive. Model release required; captions preferred.
Making Contact: Query with samples or send unsolicited photos by mail for consideration. SASE.

*CHILDREN'S DEFENSE FUND, 25 E St. NW, Washington DC 20001. (202)628-8787. FAX: (202)737-5007. Production Manager: Janis Johnston. Specializes in calendars and books. Buys stock and assigns work. Buys 20 photos/year.
Subject Needs: Children of all ages and ethnicity, serious, playful, poor, middle class, school setting, home setting and health setting. Does not want to see studio portraits.
Specs: Uses b&w prints; 35mm, 2¼×2¼, 4×5, 8×10 transparencies.
Payment & Terms: Pays $50-75/hour; $125-200/day; $50-150/b&w photo. Pays on usage. Credit line given. Buys one-time rights. Model/property release required.
Making Contact: Provide resume, business card, self-promotion piece or tearsheets to be kept on file for possible future assignments. Keeps samples on file. SASE. Reports in 1-2 weeks. Previously published work OK.
Tips: Looks for "good, clear focus, nice composition, variety of settings and good expressions on faces."

CLASS PUBLICATIONS, INC., 71 Bartholomew Ave., Hartford CT 06106. (203)951-9200. Contact: Scott Moynihan. Specializes in posters. Buys 50 photos/year.
Subject Needs: Creative photography, especially humorous, cars, semi-nudes, guys, girls, etc.
Specs: Uses b&w and color prints, contact sheets, negatives; 35mm, 2¼×2¼, 4×5 and 8×10 transparencies.
Payment & Terms: NPI. Pays per photo or royalties on sales. Pays on acceptance or publication. Credit line sometimes given. Buys one-time and exclusive poster rights. Model release and captions preferred.
Making Contact: Query with samples. Submit portfolio for review. Interested in stock photos. SASE. Reports in 2 weeks. Simultaneous submissions and previously published work OK.
Tips: Looks for "creativity that would be widely recognized and easily understood."

COMSTOCK CARDS, 600 S. Rock Blvd., #15, Reno NV 89502. (702)333-9400. Production Manager: Gene Romaine. Estab. 1986. Specializes in greeting cards, invitations, notepads, magnets. Buys/assigns 100+ photos/year.
Needs: Outrageous humor, seasonal, boudoir, swimsuit, semi-nudes. Does not want to see traditional, sweet, cute, animals, or scenics.
Specs: Uses 5×7 color prints, 35mm or 2¼×2¼ transparencies.
Payment & Terms: Pays $50-150/color photo. Pays on acceptance. Credit line given "if they request it." Buys all rights; negotiable. Model/property release required; captions preferred.
Making Contact: Interested in receiving work from newer, lesser-known photogaphers. Query with samples. Reviews stock photos. Submit seasonal material 9-10 months in advance. SASE. Reports in 2 weeks. Simultaneous submissions OK. Photo guidelines free with SASE.

DAYRUNNER, INC., 2750 Moore Ave., Fullerton CA 92633. (714)680-3500. Art Director: Diana Dearin. Estab. 1980. Specializes in calendars and stationery. Assigns 30+ freelance photos/year.
Subject Needs: Environment/product.
Specs: Uses 8½×11 b&w or color prints, 4×5 transparencies, b&w contact sheets and b&w negatives.
Payment & Terms: NPI. Pays on acceptance. Buys all rights. Model release required.
Making Contact: Query with samples. Send unsolicited photos by mail for consideration. Works with local freelancers only. Reviews stock photos. Submit seasonal material 6 months in advance. SASE. Reports in 1 month. Simultaneous submissions OK.

*DESIGN DESIGN, INC., P.O. Box 2266, Grand Rapids MI 49501. (616)774-2448. FAX: (616)774-4020. Art Director: Don Kallil. Estab. 1986. Specializes in greeting cards, calendars and gift wrap. Buy stock images from freelancers and assigns work.
Subject Needs: Specializes in humorous, seasonal and traditional topics.
Specs: Uses color prints.
Payment & Terms: NPI. Pays royalties. Pays upon sales. Credit line given. Buys exclusive product rights; negotiable. Model/property release required; captions preferred.
Making Contact: Submit portfolio for review. Provide resume, business card, self-promotion piece or tearsheets to be kept on file for possible future assignments. Submit seasonal material one year in advance. Samples kept on file. SASE. Reports in 3 weeks.

*DIEBOLD DESIGNS, P.O. Box 236, High Bridge Rd., Lyme NH 03768. (603)795-4592. FAX: (603)795-4222. Owner: Peter D. Diebold. Estab. 1978. Specializes in greeting cards (Christmas greeting cards). Buys stock and assigns work.
Subject Needs: Nautical scenes which make appropriate Christmas card illustrations.
Specs: Uses color prints; 35mm, 4×5, 8×10 transparencies.
Payment & Terms: Pays $100+/color photo. Pays on acceptance. Credit lines negotiable. Buys exclusive product rights.
Making Contact: Provide self-promotion piece to be kept on file for possible future assignments. Keeps samples on file. SASE. Reports in 3 weeks. Simultaneous submissions and previously published work OK.
Tips: "We are seeking photos primarily for our nautical Christmas card line but would also be interested in any which might have potential for business to business Christmas greeting cards."

*THE DUCK PRESS, 216 Country Garden Lane, San Marcos CA 92069. (619)471-1115. FAX: (619)591-0990. Owner: Don Malm. Estab. 1982. Specializes in greeting cards, calendars, posters and framing prints. Buys stock and assigns work. Buys 25-50 images/year. Offers 4-6 assignments/year.
Subject Needs: Humorous photos related to golf.
Specs: Color prints; 35mm, 2¼×2¼ transparencies.
Payment & Terms: Pays 7% commission. Pays on usage. Credit line given. Rights negotiable. Model/property release required.
Making Contact: Query with samples. Query with stock photo list. Submit seasonal material 6 months in advance. Keeps samples on file. SASE. Reports in 1-2 weeks. Considers simultaneous submissions.
Tips: Needs "true-to-life, but humorous photos of golfers, also, scenic shots of golf courses. We generally look for 12-24 related images as basis for golf greeting card lines."

*ENCORE STUDIOS, INC., 150 River Rd., Edgewater NJ 07020. (201)943-0824. FAX: (201)943-1299. Art Director: Ceil Benjamin. Estab. 1977. Specializes in greeting cards, stationery and personalized invitations. Works on assignment only.
Specs: Uses 35mm, 4×5 tranaparencies.
Payment & Terms: NPI; pay open depending on job. Pays on acceptance. Buys all rights.
Making Contact: Provide resume, business card, self-promotion piece or tearsheets to be kept on file for possible future assignments. Keeps samples on file. SASE. Reports in 1-2 weeks.
Tips: "Our photos are taken of our invitations, stationery, etc. when specifically needed for an ad in a trade magazine, editorial or for a brochure for our company. Send samples of creative photography. Must be creative not the look of any old retail brochure."

 The asterisk before a listing indicates that the market is new in this edition. New markets are often the most receptive to freelance submissions.

EPCONCEPTS, P.O. Box 363, Piermont NY 10968. (914)359-7137. President: Steve Epstein. Estab. 1983. Specializes in greeting cards, calendars, postcards, posters, stationery, gift wrap. Buys 20-30 photos/year.
Subject Needs: Humorous, nature, children, romantic, sexy women, sports and cars. No religious.
Specs: Uses any size glossy or matte b&w or color prints; 35mm, 2¼×2¼ and 4×5 transparencies; b&w or color contact sheets; b&w or color negatives.
Payment & Terms: Pays $50/b&w or color photo. Pays on acceptance. Credit line given. Buys exclusive product rights. Model release required.
Making Contact: Query with samples. Query with list of stock photo subjects. Send unsolicited photos by mail for consideration. Reviews stock photos. Submit seasonal material 3-6 months in advance. SASE. Reports in 2 weeks. Previously published work OK.
Tips: In photographer's samples, wants to see humorous treatments. Children in innocent yet loving poses; adults in less innocent, lightly risque loving poses. No 'hard core' please."

FERN-WOOD DESIGNS AND PHOTO MARKETING AGENCY (a division of Fern-Wood Enterprises, Inc.), P.O. Box 948, Wrightsville Beach NC 28480. (919)256-2897. FAX: (919)256-3299. Vice President/Secretary: Carol G. Wood. President/Treasurer: Mary C. Fernandez de Castro. Estab. 1990. Specializes in greeting cards, calendars, postcards, gift wrap and playing cards. Buys stock and assigns work. Buys 50-75 photos/year. Represents photographers worldwide.
Subject Needs: Variety especially. Flowers, beach areas, humorous and "the true-to-life with a uniqueness about it." Prefers natural settings to staged sets.
Specs: Uses 5×7 glossy color prints; 35 mm, 2¼×2¼ and 4×5 transparencies.
Payment & Terms: Pays $100-250/job; $50-100/color photo. Pays upon usage. Credit line given when possible. Buys one-time and other negotiated rights. Model/property releases required for photos of full face, recognizable people and personal property. Caption sheet required including location and file number.
Making Contact: Interested in receiving work from newer, lesser-known photographers. Query with samples. Send stock photo list. Provide resume, business card, self-promotion piece or tearsheets to be kept on file for possible future assignments. Submit seasonal material 6-12 months in advance. Keeps samples on file. SASE. Reports in 3 weeks. Simultaneous submissions OK.

FLASHCARDS, INC., 1136 NE Flagler Dr., Fort Lauderdale FL 33304. (305)467-1141. Photo Researcher: Micklos Huggins. Estab. 1980. Specializes in postcards, greeting cards, notecards and posters. Buys 500 photos/year.
Subject Needs: Humorous, human interest, animals in humorous situations, nostalgic looks, Christmas material, valentines, children in interesting and humorous situations. No traditional postcard material; no florals or scenic. "If the photo needs explaining, it's probably not for us."
Specs: Uses any size color or b&w prints, transparencies and color or b&w contact sheets.
Payment & Terms: Pays $100 for exclusive product rights. Pays on publication. Credit line given. Buys exclusive product rights. Model release required.
Making Contact: Query with sample. Send photos by mail for consideration. Provide resume, business card, brochure, flyer or tearsheets to be kept on file for possible future assignments. SASE. Reviews stock photos. Submit seasonal material 8 months in advance. Reports in 3 weeks. Simultaneous and previously published submissions OK. Photo guidelines free with SASE.

FREEDOM GREETINGS, 1619 Hanford St., Levittown PA 19057. (215)945-3300. FAX: (215)547-0248. President: Jay Levitt. Estab. 1969. Specializes in greeting cards. Buys 200 freelance photos/year.
Subject Needs: General greeting card type photography of scenics and stills, etc., and black ethnic people.
Specs: Uses larger than 5×7 color prints; 35mm and 2¼×2¼ transparencies.
Payment & Terms: Payment negotiable. Typically pays $100-225/color photos. Pays on acceptance. Model release required. "Looking for exclusive rights only."
Making Contact: Query with samples. Submit seasonal material 1½ years in advance. SASE. Reports in 1 month. Simultaneous submissions OK. Photo guidelines free on request.
Tips: "Keep pictures bright—no 'soft touch' approaches. Having difficult time finding black ethnic photos. Willing to pay premium for fine quality greeting card photos."

*GALISON BOOKS, 36 West 44th St., New York NY 10036. (212)354-8840. FAX: (212)391-4037. Editorial Department: Mia Galison. Estab. 1980. Specializes in greeting cards, posters, framing prints. Buys stock images from freelancers. Buys 50 photos/year.

© Jann Nance

The intricate designs of this stained glass window make for an interesting image that works well on a greeting card. Getting in close to the subject and showing detail were keys to the photo's success. Fern-Wood Designs and Photo Marketing Agency in Wrightsville Beach, North Carolina, purchased the image from photographer Jann Nance.

Subject Needs: Sierra Club-like images, nature, animals, wild flowers, gardening.
Specs: Uses 2¼ × 2¼, 4 × 5 transparencies.
Payment & Terms: Pays $200/color or b&w photo. Pays upon usage. Credit line given. Buys one-time rights.
Making Contact: Query with samples. Query with stock photo list. SASE. Previously published work OK.
Tips: In samples wants to see brightly colored work; no man-made objects. "Paper product companies are using more recycled papers so need more saturated images."

GLENN ELLEN PRESS, 2 Seton Rd., Irvine CA 92715. (714)552-4295. FAX: (714)552-4170. Art Director: Robert Hutchinson. Estab. 1988. Specializes in greeting cards, calendars, framing prints. Buys/ assigns 50-150 photos/year.
Subject Needs: Transparencies of religious art works, churches and cathedrals, archaeology, Israel, ancient Greece (ruins), monks, nature and religious subjects.
Specs: Uses 35mm, 2¼ × 2¼, 4 × 5, 8 × 10 transparencies and b&w contact sheets.
Payment & Terms: Pays $25/b&w photo; $50-100/color photo; $25-50/hour; $100-1,500/job. Royalties negotiable. Pays on acceptance and publication. Credit line given. Buys one-time rights. Model release and photo captions preferred.
Making Contact: Query with samples. Query with list of stock photo subjects. Reviews stock photos. Submit seasonal 6 months to 1 year in advance. SASE. Reports in 1 month. Simultaneous submissions and previously published work OK. Photo guidelines free with SASE.
Tips: Wants to see "one sheet of the photographer's best work in 35mm format." Sees trend toward "better color saturation and computer graphics."

GOES LITHOGRAPHING CO., 42 W. 61st St., Chicago IL 60621. (312)684-6700. FAX: (312)684-2065. Art Buyer: Barbara Habich. Estab. 1879. Specializes in calendars.
Subject Needs: Western and Eastern seaboard harbors, such as Camden Bay; fall scenes, covered bridges, period churches, Western scenes (mountains, scenics, rodeos), coastal scenes, historic sights, country, Americana; forests, streams, lakes, festivals—cultural costumes, activities and family gatherings. Does not wish to see people in any scenes submitted.
Specs: Uses 2¼×2¼, 4×5 and 8×10 transparencies only; primarily 4×5's. No photographs.
Payment & Terms: Pays $50-200/transparency. Buys all rights for certain lines and usage rights. "We purchase rights to republish in future years with original purchase."
Making Contact: Send unsolicited transparencies by mail for consideration. SASE. Photo guidelines sheet available. Always enclose envelope and return postage/insurance. Reports in 2 weeks.
Tips: "Send horizontal work. A vertical can usually be taken out of horizontal work. We seldom use veriticals. Be sure the transparencies you send have good lighting. This enhances all colors throughout the slide. Many submissions that we receive have colors which are washed out. If the subject is a desirable subject for our calendar line and the colors are flat and washed out, it will be rejected. Deep shadows are definitely discouraged for our use."

GRAND RAPIDS CALENDAR CO., 906 S. Division Ave., Grand Rapids MI 49507. Photo Buyer: Rob Van Sledright. Specializes in retail druggist calendars.
Subject Needs: Buys 10-12 photos/year. Used for drug store calendars. Baby shots, family health, medical/dental (doctor/patient situations), pharmacist/customer situations, vacationing shots, family holiday scenes, winter play activities, senior citizen, beauty aids and cosmetics. No brand name of any drug or product may show.
Specs: Uses 5×7 and 8×10 b&w glossy prints.
Payment & Terms: Pays $10-20/photo. Pays on acceptance. Model release required.
Making Contact: Submit material January through June. SASE. Simultaneous submissions and previously published work OK. Free photo guidelines for SASE.

‡GREETWELL, D-24, M.I.D.C., Satpur., Nasik 422 007 India. Phone: 30181. Chief Executive: Ms. V.H. Sanghavi. Estab. 1974. Specializes in greeting cards and calendars. Buys approx. 100 photos/year.
Subject Needs: Landscapes, wildlife, nudes. No graphic illustrations.
Specs: Uses any size color prints.
Payment & Terms: Pays $25/color photo. Pays on publication. Credit line given. Model release preferred.
Making Contact: Query with samples. Reviews stock photos. Submit seasonal material anytime throughout the year. SASE. Reports in 1 month. Previously published work OK.
Tips: In photographer's samples, "quality of photo is important; would prefer nonreturnable copies. No originals please."

HALLMARK CARDS, INC., 2501 McGee, Drop #152, Kansas City MO 64108. (Not reviewing freelance work.)

*IMPACT, 4961 Windplay Dr., El Dorado Hills CA 95630. (916)933-4700. FAX: (916)933-4717. Estab. 1975. Specializes in calendars, postcards, posters and books for the tourist industry. Buys stock and assigns work. Buys 3,000 photos/year. Offers 10-15 assignments/year.
Subject Needs: Wildlife, scenics, US travel destinations, national parks, theme parks and animals.
Specs: Uses 35mm, 2¼×2¼, 4×5, 8×10 transparencies.
Payment & Terms: Pays $75/color photo. Pays on usage. Credit line given. Buys exclusive product rights; negotiable. Model/property release required.
Making Contact: Query with samples. Query with stock photo list. Provide resume, business card, self-promotion piece or tearsheets to be kept on file for possible future assignments. Submit seasonal material 4-5 months in advance. Keeps samples on file. SASE. Reports in 1 month. Simultaneous submissions and previously published work OK. Photo guidelines free with SASE.

 The double dagger before a listing indicates that the market is located outside the United States and Canada. The symbol is new this year in Photographer's Market.

INTERCONTINENTAL GREETINGS, 176 Madison Ave., New York NY 10016. (212)683-5830. FAX: (212)779-8564. Art Director: Robin Lipner. Estab. 1967. Specializes in greeting cards, calendars, post cards, posters, framing prints, stationery, gift wrap and playing cards. Buys 20-50 photos/year.
Subject Needs: Graphics, sports, occasions (i.e. baby, birthday, wedding), "soft-touch" romantic themes, graphic studio photography. No nature, landscape or cute children.
Specs: Uses glossy color prints; 35mm, 2¼×2¼, 4×5 and 8×10 transparencies.
Payment & Terms: Pays 20% royalties on sales. Pays on publication. No credit line given. Buys one-time rights and exclusive product rights. Model release preferred.
Making Contact: Interested in receiving work from newer, lesser-known photogaphers. Query with samples. Send unsolicited photos by mail for consideration. Submit portfolio for review. Provide resume, business card, brochure, flyer or tearsheets to be kept on file for possible future assignments. Works with freelancers only. Accepts seasonal material any time. SASE. Reports in 3 weeks. Simultaneous submissions and previously published work OK. Photo guidelines free with SASE.
Tips: In photographer's portfolio samples, wants to see "a neat presentation, perhaps thematic in arrangement." The trend is toward "modern, graphic studio photography."

ARTHUR A. KAPLAN CO., INC., 460 West 34th St., New York NY 10001. (212)947-8989. President: Reid Fader. Art Director: Elizabeth Randazzo. Estab. 1956. Specializes in posters, wall decor, and fine prints and posters for framing. Buys 50-100 freelance photos/year.
Subject Needs: Flowers, scenes, animals, ballet, still life, oriental motif, musical instruments, abstracts, Americana, hand-colored and unique imagery.
Specs: Uses any size color prints; 35mm, 2¼×2¼, 4×5 and 8×10 transparencies.
Payment & Terms: Royalty 5-10% on sales. Offers advances. Pays on publication. Buys all rights, exclusive product rights. Model release required.
Making Contact: Send unsolicited photos or transparencies by mail to Elizabeth Randazzo for consideration. Reviews stock photos. Reports in 1-2 weeks. Simultaneous submissions OK.
Tips: "Our needs constantly change, so we need diversity of imagery. We are especially interested in images with international appeal."

KOGLE CARDS, INC., #212, 5575 S. Sycamore St., Littleton CO 80120. (303)795-3090. President: Patricia Koller. Estab. 1982. Specializes in greeting cards and postcards. Buys about 12 photos/year.
Subject Needs: Thanksgiving and Christmas holiday; also humorous.
Specs: Will work with color only.
Payment & Terms: NPI; works under royalty with no advance. "The photographer makes more that way." Monthly royalty check. Buys all rights; negotiable. Model release required.
Making Contact: Query with samples. Reviews stock photos. Submit seasonal material 9 months in advance. SASE. Reports in 4 weeks.

LANDMARK CALENDARS, P.O. Box 6105, 51 Digital Drive, Novato CA 94948-6105. (415)883-1600. Contact: Photo Editor. Estab. 1979. Specializes in calendars. Buys/assigns 3,000 photos/year.
Subject Needs: Scenic, nature, travel, sports, automobiles, collectibles, animals, food, people, miscellaneous. Does not want to see unfocused, grainy, under- and over-exposed photos; no nudes.
Specs: Uses 8×10 to 11×14 b&w and color glossy prints; 35mm, 2¼×2¼, 4×5 and 8×10 transparencies.
Payment & Terms: Generally pays $100/photo. Pays in April of each year. Credit line given. Buys one-time and exclusive product rights, plus rights to use photo in sales material and catalogs. Model release and captions required.
Making Contact: Send SASE for free submission guidelines. Unsolicited submissions are not accepted. Reviews stock photos. "We accept all photos from November through February two years prior to the calendar product year. Send photos only within the terms of our guidelines." Previously published work OK.
Tips: Looks for "tack-sharp focus, good use of color, interesting compositions, correct exposures. Most of our calendars are square or horizontal, so work should allow cropping to these formats. Our customers are demanding higher quality photos, and so are we."

Market conditions are constantly changing! If you're still using this book and it's 1994 or later, buy the newest edition of Photographer's Market *at your favorite bookstore or order directly from* Writer's Digest Books.

LASERCRAFT, 3300 Coffey Lane, Santa Rosa CA 95403. (707)528-1060. Specializes in wall decor, picture frames. Buys 15 photos/year. Assigns work.
Subject Needs: Seeks photos of happy kids in primary colors, fashion, love and romance, florals all for frame insert labels.
Specs: Uses 35mm, 4x5 transparencies
Payment & Terms: Pays $200/color photo; $150/b&w photo. Pays upon usage. Buys exclusive product rights; negotiable. Model/property release required.
Making Contact: Provide resume, business card, self-promotion piece or tearsheets to be kept on file for possible future assignments. Submit seasonal material 6 months in advance. Samples kept on file. SASE. Material will not be returned without postage. Previously published work OK.
Tips: "Do not send unsolicited original material. Visual representation is most important. We want to see professionalism. Spell words correctly. Make sure submission is clean and easily viewed."

LOVE GREETING CARDS, INC., 1717 Opa Locka Blvd., Opa Locka FL 33054. (305)685-LOVE. Vice President: Norman Drittel. Specializes in greeting cards, postcards and posters. Buys 75-100 photos/year.
Subject Needs: Nature, flowers, boy/girl (contemporary looks).
Specs: Uses 5 × 7 or 8 × 10 color prints; 35mm, 2¼ × 2¼ and 4 × 5 transparencies; color contact sheets, color negatives.
Payment & Terms: Pays $75-150/color photo. Pays on publication. Credit line given. Buys exclusive product rights. Model release preferred.
Making Contact: Query with samples or stock photo list. Send unsolicited photos by mail for consideration. Provide resume, business card, brochure, flyer or tearsheets to be kept on file for possible future assignments. Reviews stock photos. Submit seasonal material 6 months in advance. SASE. Reports in 1 month. Previously published work OK.
Tips: "We are looking for outstanding photos for greeting cards and new age posters." There is a "larger use of photos in posters for commercial sale."

*MCCLEERY-CUMMING COMPANY, INC., 915 East Tyler St., Washington IA 52353. (319)653-2185. FAX: (319)653-4424. Art Director: Sandy Burns. Estab. 1903. Specializes in calendars. Buys stock images from freelancers. Buys 150 photos/year.
Subject Needs: Kittens and puppies (posed); hunting dogs (adult or pups, posed situation with hunting equipment); cheesecake (girls no younger than 17, in negligee or swimsuit); juvenile (4-8 years old, with or without pets); Afro-Americans (children doing something interesting, family, glamor); Spanish/Mexican (dancers in colorful costumes); home interior (prefer living room or family room); cars (collectibles); and black & white glossies (typical Americana; 1940s, 1950s, 1960s). Does not want to see medical, business, abstract, technology or babies.
Specs: Uses 8 × 10 glossy b&w American Album prints; 35mm, 2¼ × 2¼, 4 × 5, 8 × 10 sharp, bright transparencies.
Payment & Terms: NPI; negotiable. Buys one year exclusive, four year non-exclusive rights; negotiable. Model release required for people. Captions preferred.
Making Contact: Interested in receiving work from newer, lesser-known photogaphers. Submit resume, stock photo list, credits, and tearsheets by mail. Submit seasonal material beginning in October of each year. Samples kept on file. SASE. Reports in 1-2 weeks. Photo guidelines free with SASE.

THE NATURE COMPANY, Dept. PM, 750 Hearst Ave., Berkeley CA 94710. (510)644-1337. Assistant Director of Fine Arts: Will Hooper. Estab. 1973. Specializes in greeting cards, posters, framing prints, stationery, gift wrap, and package design (books and videotapes). Buys/assigns up to 300 photos/year.
Subject Needs: Wildlife photos and images — "but only realistically depicted with no obvious presence of man; and other natural images like landscapes or plant life. No dead or stuffed animals. No seashells unless they're 'alive' with the animal intact. No domestic animals."
Specs: Uses 35mm, 2¼ × 2¼, 4 × 5 and 8 × 10 transparencies.
Payment & Terms: NPI; sometimes pays per photo and most often pays 2-3% royalties on sales. Payment interval varies. Buys exclusive product rights. Model release preferred; photo captions required.
Making Contact: Call first, then send unsolicited photos by mail for consideration. "Please do not send original work." Submit seasonal material 6 months to 1 year in advance. SASE. Reports in 1 month. Simultaneous submissions and previously published work OK. Photo guidelines free with SASE.
Tips: Wants to see "realistically depicted wildlife in its natural setting, landscapes with no visible people, and nature close-ups of patterns and textures like leaves, rocks, feathers, etc." Observes that "companies are getting more particular as more and more nature photographers surface."

Close-up

Laurance Aiuppy
Freelance Photographer
Livingston, Montana

For Laurance Aiuppy, selling photos for a living was never one of his goals growing up and to this day he has never taken photos as a hobby. Even though he was an honor student in philosophy at Mt. Union College in Ohio, Aiuppy dropped out of college one quarter shy of graduation. His interest in the great outdoors led him west in the late 1960s and eventually to a position as a wilderness ranger.

As a ranger he was given a camera and some lenses to record back-country wilderness trails and campsite conditions. "That was the extent of my photography background at the time," says Aiuppy, whose clients today include paper companies, businesses and publications worldwide.

It was not until the early 1970s, when he met world-renowned photographer Jay Maisel, that Aiuppy realized his own potential as a photographer. Aiuppy was hired to be a "Sherpa," or guide, for Maisel who was working on a wilderness book for a Time-Life Books series. The shoots lasted several weeks and in that time Aiuppy watched Maisel work and saw the types of subjects he was shooting.

"I started helping him find pictures," recalls Aiuppy. "While he was shooting on one side of a meadow, for instance, I would be off on the other side looking for shots that he might be interested in." After Aiuppy pointed out a subject, Maisel almost always photographed it. Aiuppy did not realize that he had "the photographic eye" and his suggestions to Maisel over a couple weeks were made without understanding his special talent.

"One day he just stopped me in my tracks and he said, 'You really don't know what you're doing, do you?' " recounts Aiuppy. "I said, 'What do you mean?' and he said 'You don't realize this, but there are probably only one or two other people in the whole world whose advice I would take on a shot. You have a gift. You have an eye. You shouldn't be a mountain guide. You're wasting your life. You should be shooting pictures.' "

Maisel later gave Aiuppy a camera and some lenses to get started and since then he has acquired a list of impressive clients, including LL Bean, *Audubon*, *Field & Stream* and *National Geographic*. He and his wife, Janis, operate their business for both domestic and international markets and he holds two workshops a year at the 63 Ranch in Livingston, Montana. The workshops are limited to only 10 participants to allow Aiuppy individual time with those attending.

Calling himself a "generalist," Aiuppy shoots everything from landscapes and wildlife to cowboys and industry. He has found a viable market in paper product companies predominantly with photos of fly-fishing, one of his many passions.

"I try to find the niches in paper products," says Aiuppy, whose work has been published in several calendars, catalogs and on greeting cards. "I think many people can be the most competitive in an area that they know really well . . . . What they should do is find those niche markets within the overall paper products market."

As an avid fisherman, Aiuppy sets up many shots dealing with the sport. But because he considers himself an expert, and has most of the equipment, he can prop shots without spending a lot of money. He also knows exactly what pieces of equipment should be in the photos and this helps add authenticity, he says. Those principles can work for other freelancers interested in various hobbies, he says.

Although most of his sales are through stock photos, Aiuppy sees paper products as a worthwhile market for photographers. A typical shot for a calendar can be worth $250-450 depending on the image, he says. One of his fly-fishing stills has sold fives times for the front of a calendar printed by Silver Creek. The photo has made him around $1,500, he says. "If I wanted to concentrate on paper products what I probably would shoot are kids and pets, dogs and cats. I think there's a lot of money to be made," he says, adding that holiday shots also can be profitable.

While most paper companies buy only one or two photos from a photographer for one calendar, freelancers can create their own opportunities. In 1984 Aiuppy hooked up with several firms to put together a calendar. Each contributed different aspects of expertise, such as design, printing and binding, and they all used the calendar as a promotional piece.

Aiuppy also suggests that freelancers go to stores where paper goods are sold and research the types of images companies are buying. "Greeting cards are very involved with concepts, moods, symbols and I think if you want to be competitive in greeting cards you really have to think very symbolically and very conceptually as to what you shoot," he says.

— *Michael Willins*

© Laurance Aiuppy

Early in Laurance Aiuppy's career he was taught by Jay Maisel to study light and the way it affects subjects. He also is very interested in geometric shapes, such as those seen in this photo of a house in Seneca, South Carolina. The image was used in a promotional calendar for a Japanese company and, at the time, Aiuppy was only the second American to have images in the calendar.

*NATURE'S DESIGN, P.O. Box 255, Davenport CA 95017. (408)426-8205. Publisher: Frank S. Balthis. Estab. 1982. Specializes in postcards, notecards, books and posters. Buys stock images from freelancers. Buys 10-25 images/year. Offers 0-5 assignments/year.
Subject Needs: Natural history, wildlife and scenics from parks and forests.
Specs: Uses 35mm, 120 film, 4×5 transparencies.
Payment & Terms: Pays $100-200/color photo. Pays on publication. Credit line given. Buys one-time rights and exclusive card rights. Model/property release preferred; captions required.
Making Contact: "Do not send unsolicited submissions." Query with resume of credits. Query with stock photo list. Provide resume, business card, self-promotion piece or tearsheets to be kept on file for possible future assignments. Keeps samples on file. SASE. Reports in 6 months.
Tips: "Looking for strong images that stand on their own. Buyers must want to pick them up in a rack of many other cards. Excellent color and sharpness are a necessity. We are especially looking for photographers who wish to assist with marketing in their area. We pay a 20% sales commission on card sales."

NEW HEIGHTS, a division of Museum Graphics, Dept. PM, 703 Sandoval Way, Hayward CA 94544. (510)429-1452. President: Alison Jaques. Estab. 1988. Specializes in greeting cards, postcards and framing prints. Buys 40 photos/year.
Subject Needs: Needs humorous, seasonal, colorful, contemporary or cute photos. No scenic shots.
Specs: Uses 8×10 b&w and color prints.
Payment & Terms: Pays 10% royalties on sales. Credit line given. Buys 10-year exclusive product rights for stationery usage. Model release and photo captions required.
Making Contact: Send unsolicited photos by mail for consideration. Submit portfolio for review. Provide resume, business card, brochure, flyer or tearsheets to be kept on file for possible future assignments. Reviews stock photos. Submit seasonal material 6-8 months in advance for printing. SASE. Reports in 1 month. Simultaneous submissions and previously published work OK. Photo guidelines free with SASE.
Tips: "New Heights is now looking for contemporary photographers to contribute to our card line. We are interested in fine art photography that is technically excellent and embodies a fresh, creative and humorous approach."

🍁NORMAILY MARKETING SYSTEMS, 2467 Newport St., Burlington ON L7M3X8 Canada. (416)332-1455. Contact: John Mignardi. Estab. 1988. Specializes in brochures, posters, magazines and other paper products, advertisments, retail and fashion.
Subject Needs: Exotic cars, jets, people, "cheesecake and beefcake," nudes and humorous.
Specs: Uses 4×6 glossy b&w/color prints; 35mm and 2¼×2¼ transparencies. Slides preferred.
Payment & Terms: Pays $25/b&w photo; $50/color photo; $40/hour; $200/day; $200/complete job. Royalties on sales. Pays on usage. Credit line given. Buys one-time rights; negotiable. Model release required on sale. Property release required. Captions preferred.
Making Contact: Interested in receiving work from newer, lesser-known photographers. Query with samples which can be kept on file. Provide resume, business card, brochure, flyer or tearsheets to be kept on file for possible future assignments. Send IRC's for returned samples. Reports in 4-8 weeks.
Tips: "We place a high degree of emphasis on colors, sending a message and promoting healthy body/lifestyle."

■NORTHWORD PRESS INC., P.O. Box 1360, Minocqua WI 54548. (715)356-9800. FAX: (715)356-9762. Director of Photography: Robert W. Baldwin. Estab. 1984. Specializes in calendars, books, audio and videotapes. Buys/assigns 500 photos/year.
Subject Needs: North American nature and wildlife, hunting and fishing, hunting dogs, outdoor related sports such as canoeing, camping, etc. and northern scenics. "Do not submit anything that is even slightly soft focus. Submit only top quality originals. Do not send a lot of similars."
Specs: Uses 35mm, 2¼×2¼, 4×5, 8×10 transparencies.
Payment & Terms: Pays $50-500/color photo. Pays on publication. Credit line given. Buys one-time rights. Model/property release and captions required.
Making Contact: Interested in receiving work from newer, lesser-known photographers. Query with stock photo list. Provide resume, business card, brochure, flyer or tearsheets to be kept on file for possible future assignments. SASE. Does not return unsolicited material. Reports in 1 month. Simultaneous submissions and previously published work OK. Photo guidelines free with SASE.

🍁 *The maple leaf before a listing indicates that the market is Canadian. The symbol is new this year in* Photographer's Market.

Tips: Always looking for a different angle or point of view. Edit slides carefully. Prefer large format and Kodachrome slides. "We notify photographers by mail or phone of upcoming projects. I want to see a professional, well-presented submission that is well packaged, properly researched, and is pertinent to our product line. Be very critical, because we are."

*THE NOSTALGIA COMPANY, 16176 Westwoods Business Park, St. Louis MO 63021. (314)230-0333. FAX: (314)230-0334. President: Marc Bluestone. Estab. 1986. Buys stock images from freelancers. Buys 1,000 images/year.
Subject Needs: Photographs of nostalgic, historic or sentimental value in subject areas including sports, politics, entertainment, humor, American cities, military, transportation and places of interest.
Specs: Uses color and b&w prints; 35mm, 2¼×2¼, 4×5 transparencies.
Payment & Terms: NPI; "Pays by photo, also willing to purchase larger collections. Sometimes willing to pay royalty." Buys exclusive product rights. Model/property release preferred for photos with a primary subject who is not a "public figure." Captions required.
Making Contact: Query with samples. Include photo list. Samples kept on file. SASE. Reports in 1 month. Simultaneous submissions and previously published work OK. Photo guideline free with SASE.
Tips: Wants "unique photographs which will promote an emotional or intellectual response by the viewer. We sell these photographs in our own retail stores and therefore require work which will be of interest to the general public."

*ONE SUN COMMUNICATIONS, P.O. Box 2252, Kirkland WA 98083. (206)821-9361. Photo Editor: Robert Heckerl. Estab. 1991. Specializes in calendars. Buys stock images from freelancers. Buys 50-60 photos/year.
Subject Needs: Any annual event, festival, parade or happening from around the world. All nations and specifically the east and west coasts of the U.S. Must be an annual event! Does not want to see "average tourist snapshots."
Specs: Uses 35mm, 2¼×2¼, 4×5 transparencies; horizontal compositions only.
Payment & Terms: Pays $125+/color photo. Pays upon publication. Credit line given. Buys one-time rights. Model/property release preferred. Captions required; include specific name of event, location and month of event.
Making Contact: Interested in receiving work from newer, lesser-known photographers. Query with list of events on file or make direct submission. Submissions accepted between May 1st and August 1st of any given year. Samples not kept on file. Reports in 2 weeks on queries; 3 months on photo submissions. Simultaneous submissions and previously published work OK. Photo guidelines free with SASE.
Tips: "Horizontal compositions only. Please send for guidelines first. We need to see artistry, extraordinary angles, uncommon perspectives."

*OUTREACH PUBLICATIONS: DAY SPRING & JOYFULLY YOURS CARDS, P.O. Box 1010, Siloam Springs AR 72761. (501)524-9381. Line Designer/Photo Editor: Sandy Kelley. Estab. 1971. Specializes in greeting cards, calendars, postcards and stationery. Works on assignment only. Approximately 6 out of 12 images on calendars are photographs; cards and stationery, 100-200.
Subject Needs: Nature, seasonal, atmosphere, Bible still lifes (warm, not "high church") good Victorian still lifes. Does not want people in photos.
Specs: Uses 35mm, 2¼×2¼ transparencies.
Payment & Terms: Pays $200-600/job. Credit line given.
Making Contact: Submit portfolio for review. Provide resume, business card, self-promotion piece or tearsheets to be kept on file for possible future assignments. Submit seasonal material one year in advance. Samples kept on file. SASE. Reports in 3 weeks. Photo guidelines free with SASE.
Tips: "If the photo is to be used as a full bleed on a card make sure there is an area for copy."

*PALM PRESS, INC., 1442A Walnut St., Berkeley CA 94709. (510)486-0502. FAX: (510)486-1158. Assistant Photo Editor: Courtney Murphee. Estab. 1980. Specializes in greeting cards. Buys stock images from freelancers. Buys 100 photos/year.
Subject Needs: Wildlife, humor, nostalgia, unusual and interesting b&w and color, Christmas. Does not want abstracts or portraits.
Specs: Uses b&w and color prints; 35mm transparencies.
Payment & Terms: NPI; pays royalty on sales. Pays on usage. Credit line given. Buys exclusive product rights. Model/property release required.
Making Contact: Query with resume of credits. Query with samples. Submit seasonal material 1 year in advance. Samples kept on file. SASE. Reports in 1-2 weeks. Photo guidelines free with SASE.
Tips: Sees trend in increased use of "occasion" photos.

PEMBERTON & OAKES, Dept. PM, 133 E. Carrillo St., Santa Barbara CA 93101. (805)963-1371. Photo Editor: Marian Groff. Specializes in limited edition lithographs and collector's porcelain plates. Buys 20-25 photos/year.
Subject Needs: "Interested only in photos of children between the ages of two and four using specific guidelines; photos capturing that moment in a million in a child's world."
Specs: Uses any size or finish color or b&w prints; any size transparencies.
Payments & Terms: Pays $1,000 minimum/color or b&w photo. Payment on acceptance. Buys all rights. No model release necessary. Photos used for artist inspiration for paintings.
Making Contact: Send for free photo guidelines.
Tips: "Submit a good selection, carefully following guidelines. Keep us in mind when shooting new material. We're always interested in new photos. USA kids only. No adults. Child must be actively involved in an activity, not just looking at the camera. No man-made toys. Showing interaction with pet, something from nature or one other child is best."

PORTAL PUBLICATIONS, Dept. PM, Suite 400, 770 Tamalpais Dr., Corte Madera CA 94925. (415)924-5652. FAX: (415)924-7439. Photo Editor: Scott Graham. Estab. 1954. Specializes in greeting cards, calendars, posters, wall decor and note cards. Gives up to 400 or more assignments annually.
Subject Needs: Contemporary photography (florals, landscapes, black & white and hand-tinted black & white). Nostalgia, nature and wildlife, endangered species. Sports, travel, food and youth-oriented popular icons such as celebrities, movie posters and cars. Nothing too risque.
Specs: Uses 35mm, 2¼×2¼, 4×5 and 8×10 transparencies. No originals; dupes only.
Payment & Terms: NPI. Payment determined by the product format. Pays on acceptance or publication. Credit line given. Buys one-time and exclusive product rights. Model release required; captions preferred.
Making Contact: Query with samples. Submit portfolio for review. "Please limit submission to a maximum of 40 images showing the range and variety of work. All slides and transparencies should be clearly labeled and marked." Works with local freelancers on assignment only. Interested in stock photos. SASE. Reports in 1 month (within 6-8 weeks during busy seasons). Simultaneous submissions and previously published work OK. Photo guidelines free with SASE.
Tips: "Ours is an increasingly competitive business, so we look for the highest quality and most unique imagery that will appeal to our diverse market of customers."

PRODUCT CENTRE-S.W. INC., THE TEXAS POSTCARD CO., P.O. Box 860708, Plano TX 75086. (214)423-0411. Art Director: Susan Hudson. Specializes in postcards, melamine trays and coasters. Buys approximately 100 freelance photos/year.
Subject Needs: Texas towns, Texas scenics, Oklahoma towns/scenics, regional (Southwest only) scenics, humorous, inspirational, nature (including animals), staged studio shots — model and/or products. No nudity.
Specs: Uses "C" print 8×10; 35mm, 2¼×2¼, 4×5 transparencies.
Payment & Terms: Pays up to $100/photo. Pays on publication. Buys all rights. Model release required.
Making Contact: Send insured samples with return postage/insurance. Include Social Security number and telephone number. Submit seasonal material 1 year in advance. SASE. No material returned without postage. Reports usually 3-4 months, depending on season.
Tips: "Submit slides only for viewing. Must be in plastic slide sleeves and each labeled with photographer's name and address. Include descriptive material detailing where and when photo was taken."

QUADRIGA ART, INC., 11 E. 26th St., New York NY 10010. (212)685-0751. Creative Director: Ira Kramer. Specializes in greeting cards, calendars, postcards, posters and stationery. Buys 400-500 photos/year; all supplied by freelance photographers.
Subject Needs: Religious, all-occasion, Christmas, Easter, seasonal, florals, sunsets. No buildings or sports.
Specs: Uses 4×5 or 8×10 transparencies. Transparencies only submitted in sets of 4 to 6. Does not use color prints.
Payment & Terms: Pays $50-200/color shot; payment varies. Pays on acceptance.
Making Contact: Arrange a personal interview to show portfolio. Query with samples. Send photos by mail for consideration, or submit portfolio for review. Reviews stock photos. Submit seasonal material 1 year in advance. SASE. Reports in 1 week. Simultaneous submissions OK.
Tips: "We prefer shots that focus on a singular subject, rather than a subject hidden in a busy backdrop."

RECYCLED PAPER PRODUCTS, INC., Dept. PM, 3636 N. Broadway, Chicago IL 60613. (312)348-6410. Art Director: Melinda Gordon. Specializes in greeting cards and postcards. Buys 30-50 photos/year.

Subject Needs: "Primarily humorous photos for postcards and greeting cards. Photos must have wit and a definite point of view. Unlikely subjects and offbeat themes have the best chance, but will consider all types."
Specs: Uses 4×5 b&w and color prints; b&w or color contact sheets. Please do not submit slides.
Payment & Terms: Pays $250 per b&w or color photo. Pays on acceptance. Credit line given. Buys all rights; negotiable. Model release required.
Making Contact: Send for artists' guidelines. SASE. Reports in 1 month. Simultaneous submissions OK.
Tips: Prefers to see "up to 10 samples of photographer's best work." Cards are printed 5×7 vertical format. Please include messages. "The key word for submissions is wit."

RENAISSANCE GREETING CARDS, P.O. Box 845, Springvale ME 04083. (207)324-4153. Art Director: Janice Keefe. Estab. 1977. Buys/assigns 20-30 photos/year.
Subject Needs: "We're interested in nature photographs as well as images that are artsy, nostalgic, dramatic, innovative and humorous. Special treatment such as hand tinted b&w images are also of interest." No animals in clothing, risqué or religious.
Specs: Uses b&w, color prints; 35mm, 2¼×2¼, 4×5 transparencies; b&w, color contact sheets.
Payment & Terms: NPI; negotiates advance against royalties or flat fee. Pays 50% on acceptance, 50% on publication. Credit line given. Buys all rights or exclusive product rights; negotiable. Model release preferred.
Making Contact: Query for our guidelines with SASE. Reviews stock photos. Submit seasonal material 1 year in advance. SASE. Reports in 1 month. Simultaneous submissions and previously published work OK. Photo guidelines free with SASE.
Tips: "It helps to start with our guidelines, which indicate what we're looking for at various times during the year."

ROCKSHOTS, INC., 632 Broadway, New York NY 10012. FAX: (212)353-8756. Art Director: Bob Vesce. Estab. 1978. Specializes in greeting cards. Buys 20 photos/year.
Subject Needs: Sexy (including nudes and semi-nudes), outrageous, satirical, ironic, humorous photos. Buys all rights; may settle for greeting card and postcard rights.
Specs: Uses b&w and color prints; 35mm, 2¼×2¼ and 4×5 slides. "Do not send originals!"
Payment & Terms: Pays $50-125/b&w, $125-300/color photo; other payment negotiable. Pays on acceptance. Model release required.
Making Contact: Send SASE requesting photo guidelines. Provide flyer and tearsheets to be kept on file for possible future assignments. Submit seasonal material at least 6 months in advance. SASE. Reports in 8-10 weeks. Simultaneous submissions and previously published work OK.
Tips: Prefers to see "greeting card themes, especially birthday, Christmas, Valentine's Day. We like to look at life with a very zany slant, not holding back because of society's imposed standards."

THE RYTEX CO., Dept. PM, 5850 West 80th, Indianapolis IN 46278. (317)872-8553. Vice President of Sales: Gretchen Beasley. Specializes in stationery and wedding invitations. Buys 80-120 photos/year.
Subject Needs: Shots of personalized stationery.
Specs: Uses 4×5 or 8×10 transparencies.
Payment & Terms: Pays $100-250/color photo, "open"/hour or job. Pays on acceptance. Buys all rights. Model release required.
Making Contact: Query with samples. Provide resume, business card, brochure, flyer or tearsheets to be kept on file for possible future assignments. Works with local freelancers only. Submit seasonal material 8 months in advance. SASE. Reports in 1 week.

SACRED MOUNTAIN ASHRAM, 10668 Gold Hill Rd., Boulder CO 80302-9716. (303)447-8581. Editor: Bob Comrow. Estab. 1974. Specializes in books and calendars. Buys/assigns 30-35 photos/year.
Subject Needs: Religious (universal); prayer/meditation. "Devotional and reverential mood plus spontaneity are important."
Specs: Uses b&w, color prints; 35mm, 2¼×2¼, 4×5, 8×10 transparencies; color contact sheets; color negatives.
Payment & Terms: Pays $25-100/b&w; $50-200/color photo. "Rates are negotiable, depending on photograph and specific publication." Pays on acceptance. Credit line given. Buys one-time rights. Model release preferred. Photo captions preferred.

The code NPI (no payment information given) appears in listings that have not given specific payment amounts.

Making Contact: Query with stock photo list. Reviews stock photos. Submit seasonal 3 months in advance. SASE. Reports in 3 weeks. Simultaneous submissions and previously published work OK.
Tips: Wants to see shots of "people in prayer or meditation."

SCAFA-TORNABENE PUBLISHING CO., 100 Snake Hill Rd., West Nyack NY 10994. (914)358-7600. Contact: Jim Nicoletti. Specializes in inspirationals, religious, contemporary florals, dramatic wildlife, nostalgia and children of yesteryear.
Specs: Uses camera ready prints; 35mm, 2¼×2¼, 4×5 and 8×10 transparencies.
Payment & Terms: Pays $150-250/b&w or color photo. Also pays royalty; negotiable. Pays on acceptance. Credit line sometimes given. Buys one-time, exclusive product and all rights; sometimes negotiable. Model release required.
Making Contact: Query with samples. Works with local freelancers only. SASE. Reports in 2-3 weeks.
Tips: "Send a good cross section of your work. Prefer prints of hand-colored work." In samples wants to see "florals, still life, animals (cats, teddy bears), autos, trucks, musical instruments. Black and white, hand-colored, sepia. Dramatic unique imagery."

*SCANDECOR INC., 430 Pike Rd., Southampton PA 18966. (215)355-2410. FAX: (215)368-8737. Vice President of Operations: Dan Griffin. Estab. 1972. Specializes in calendars, posters, framing prints and wall decor. Buys stock and assign work. Buys 300-500 photos/year.
Subject Needs: Needs underwater photos, nature, humorous, seasonal, animals, guys and girls.
Specs: Uses color prints; 35mm, 2¼×2¼, 4×5, 8×10 transparencies.
Payment & Terms: Pays at least 3% royalties on sales, $100 sales minimum. Pays upon usage. Credit line given. Buys all rights; exclusive product rights; negotiable. Model/property release required.
Making Contact: Query with samples. Submit seasonal material 1 year in advance. Samples not kept on file. SASE. Reports in 1 month. Simultaneous submissions and previously published work OK.

*SEABRIGHT PRESS, P.O. Box 7285, Santa Cruz CA 95061. (408)457-1568. Photo Editor: Jim Thompson. Estab. 1990. Specializes in greeting cards. Buys stock images from freelancers. Buys 25-35 photos/year.
Subject Needs: Nature, landscapes, seasonal and any California images.
Specs: Uses 4×6 glossy color prints; 35mm transparencies.
Payment & Terms: Pays $35-100/color photo; royalties on sales may be negotiated. Pays on acceptance. Buys exclusive product rights; negotiable. Model/property release preferred. Captions preferred.
Making Contact: Query with samples. Submit seasonal material 6 months in advance. Samples kept on file. SASE. Reports in 3 weeks. Simultaneous submissions and previously published work OK.
Tips: "Submit only your best photos; photos with exceptional lighting are most likely to be of interest to us."

SIERRA CLUB BOOKS, Dept. PM, 100 Bush St., San Francisco CA 94104-7813. Photo Editor: Geoffrey Hiller. Calendar Editor: Frances Spear. Specializes in nature calendars. Request guidelines by postcard only. Buys more than 140 photos annually. Send for free photo guidelines (mailed in February of every year), then submit material by mail for consideration. "We accept submissions *only* March 1 to April 30 of each year for calendars covering the year after the following" (i.e., photos for the 1995 calendar will be reviewed in the spring of 1993).
Subject Needs: Needs photos of wildlife, natural history, scenery, hiking, etc. Captions required. Calendars: nature/scenic; wildlife; "Trail" (people in the outdoors); engagement (nature and wildlife). No animals in zoos; no people engaged in outdoor recreation with machines.
Specs: Uses transparencies.
Payment & Terms: Pays $225-450. Pays on publication. Buys exclusive calendar rights for the year covered by each calendar. Reports in 6-10 weeks. Simultaneous submissions OK.
Tips: "We're using international, as opposed to strictly North American, subjects in some of the calendars. We get lots of good scenics but not as many good wildlife shots or shots appropriate for the 'Trail' calendar (can include human subjects in activities such as climbing, canoeing, hiking, cross country skiing, etc.). *Be selective.* Don't submit more than 100 transparencies. Follow the guidelines in the spec sheet. We're looking for strong images and seasonal appropriateness."

SOUNDYCARDS, Box 420007, Naples FL 33942. (813)566-8343. President: William Leverick. Specializes in greeting cards. Buys 50+ photos/year.
Subject Needs: Nature photos only, featuring water (lakes, rivers, streams, waterfalls, rain, oceans, beaches etc.; winter and summer scenes OK). Animals and people OK in photos as long as they are not primary subjects. Example: a couple in a canoe on a beautiful mountain lake with breathtaking scenery but the couple is secondary interest . . . silhouetted against sky.

Specs: Uses 8×10 color prints; 35mm, 2¼×2¼, 4×5 and 8×10 transparencies.
Payment & Terms: Pays $150/color photo. Pays on acceptance. Buys exclusive and non-exclusive product rights. Model release preferred.
Making Contact: Send SASE to be placed on mailing list. Does not accept unsolicited submissions. Company will notify by mail with exact guidelines and shipping information as material is needed. Interested in stock photos. Previously published work OK.

*STARMAKERS PUBLISHING CORP., 47-51 33rd St., Long Island City NY 11101. (718)767-8377. FAX: (718)482-7708. President: Eileen Miller. Estab. 1980. Specializes in posters and wall decor. Buys stock and assigns work. Buys 50 photos/year. Assigns 100 photos/year.
Subject Needs: Pin-ups, male and female, humorous. Does not want to see religious subjects.
Specs: Uses color prints; 2¼×2¼, 4×5, 8×10 transparencies.
Payment & Terms: Pays $1,000-3,000/assignment. $500-1,500/color photo. Pays upon usage. Credit line given. Buys exclusive product rights; negotiable. Model release required.
Making Contact: Query with samples. Query with stock photo list. Samples kept on file. SASE. Reports in 1-2 weeks. Simultaneous submissions OK.
Tips: "Male and female pin-up models must be extremely beautiful, with healthy-looking bodies. No nudity." Sees a trend toward b&w and sepia posters.

SYRACUSE CULTURAL WORKERS, Box 6367, Syracuse NY 13217. (315)474-1132. Research/Development Director: Dik Cool. Posters, cards and calendars. Buys 15-25 freelance photos/year. Uses photos for posters, cards and calendars.
Subject Needs: Images of social content, reflecting a consciousness of peace/social justice, environment, liberation, etc..
Specs: Uses any size b&w; 35mm, 2¼×2¼, 4×5 or 8×10 color transparencies.
Payment & Terms: Pays $50-100/b&w or color photo. Credit line given. Buys one-time rights. Model release and captions preferred.
Making Contact: Send unsolicited photos by mail for consideration. SASE. Reports in 2-4 months.
Tips: "We are interested in photos that reflect a consciousness of peace and social justice, that portray the experience of people of color, disabled, elderly, gay/lesbian—must be progressive, feminist, non-sexist. Look at our catalog (available for $1)—understand our philosophy and politics. Send only what is appropriate and socially relevant. We are looking for positive, upbeat and visionary work."

TIDE MARK PRESS, Box 280311, East Hartford CT 06128-0311. Editor: Scott Kaeser. Art Director: C. Cote. Specializes in calendars. Buys 300-400 photos/year; few individual photos.
Subject Needs: Complete calendar concepts which are unique, but also have identifiable markets; groups of photos which could work as on entire calendar; ideas and approach must be visually appealing and innovative but also have a definable audience. No general nature or varied subjects without a single theme.
Specs: Uses 35mm, 2¼×2¼, 4×5 and 8×10 transparencies.
Payment & Terms: Pays $150-250/color photo; royalties on sales if entire calendar supplied. Pays on publication or per agreement. Credit line given. Buys one-time rights. Model release preferred; captions required.
Making Contact: "Contact us to offer specific topic suggestion which reflect specific strengths of your stock." Reviews stock photos. Submit seasonal material March-September for next calendar year. SASE. Reports as soon as possible.

VAGABOND CREATIONS, INC., 2560 Lance Dr., Dayton OH 45409. (513)298-1124. President: George F. Stanley, Jr. Specializes in greeting cards. Buys 2 photos/year.
Subject Needs: General Christmas scene . . . non-religious.
Specs: Uses 35mm transparencies.
Payment & Terms: Pays $100/color photo. Pays on acceptance. Buys all rights.
Making Contact: Query with stock photo list. Reviews stock photos. Submit seasonal material 9 months in advance. SASE. Reports in 1 week. Simultaneous submissions OK.

*VITAL IMAGES, INC., Suite A 211, 5846 Ridgeway Rd., Jackson MS 39211. (601)978-3693. FAX: (601)978-3695. President: Thomas Howard. Estab. 1991. Specializes in framing prints and fine art photography. Buys stock images from freelancers. Buys 50-100 photos/year.

Subject needs: Any subject. "We are interested in seeing a photographer's best artistic work. Originality is paramount."
Specs: Uses color (cibachrome) b&w, zone system original prints; 35mm, 2¼ × 2¼ transparencies.
Payment & Terms: NPI; pays royalties. Pays on usage. Buys one-time rights. Model/property release preferred. Captions preferred.
Making Contact: Arrange personal interview to show portfolio. Submit portfolio for review. Query with resume of credits. Provide resume, business card, self-promotion piece or tearsheets to be kept on file for possible future assignments. Samples kept on file. SASE. Reports in 1 month. Simultaneous submissions and previously published work OK.
Tips: "We are interested in images which elicit a strong emotional response while remaining an artistic expression suitable for upscale decor or special interest groups. People who buy from us are interested in the photographer and the photograph. Tell us who you are, why you shot the image; what emotion did you want to capture? Is there a story behind it? We see the small production run based on a precisely defined theme, marketed to a narrowly defined niche as the venue of a blooming industry."

WEST GRAPHICS, 238 Capp St., San Francisco CA 94110. (415)621-4641. FAX: (415)621-8613. Art Director: Tom Drew. Specializes in greeting cards, calendars, gift bags and humorous note pads. Buys 24-48 freelance photos/year.
Subject Needs: Humorous, animals, people in humorous situations or anything of an unusual nature; prefer color. Does not want to see scenics.
Specs: Uses 8 × 10 b&w glossy prints; 35mm, 2¼ × 2¼ and 4 × 5 transparencies.
Payment & Terms: Pays $200/color or b&w photo and/or 5% royalty on sales. Pays 30 days after publication. Credit line given. Buys 5-year greeting card rights. Model release required.
Making Contact: Interested in receiving work from newer, lesser-known photographers. Query with samples. Send unsolicited photos by mail for consideration. Submit portfolio for review. Submit seasonal material 1 year in advance. SASE. Reports in 1 month. Simultaneous submissions and previously published work OK. Photo guidelines free with SASE.
Tips: "Humor is our primary concern."

© 1989 West Graphics

Who doesn't love a strong comedic photo, especially when the subject matter is a lovable pooch named Czonka? This photo, taken by photographer Mala Mahlebashian, was used for the front of a get well card, produced by West Graphics, of San Francisco, California.

*WISCONSIN TRAILS, Box 5650, Madison WI 53705. (608)231-2444. Production Manager: Nancy Mead. Estab. 1960. Bimonthly magazine. Calendar portraying seasonal scenics, some books and activities from Wisconsin.
Subject Needs: Needs photos of nature, landscapes, wildlife and Wisconsin activities. Buys 35 photos/issue.
Making Contact: Submit material by mail for consideration or submit portfolio. Makes selections in January for calendar-6 months ahead for issues; "we should have photos by December." Simultaneous submissions OK "if we are informed, and if there's not a competitive market among them." Previously published work OK.
Specs: Send 35mm, 2¼×2¼ and 4×5 transparencies.
Payment & Terms: Pays $25-100/b&w photo; $50-175/color photo. Captions required. Buys one-time rights. Reports in 4 weeks.
Tips: "Be sure to inform us how you want materials returned and include proper postage. Calendar scenes must be horizontal to fit 8½×11 format. See our magazine and books and be aware of our type of photography. Submit only Wisconsin scenes."

Paper Products/'92-93 changes

The following markets appeared in the 1992 edition of *Photographer's Market* but are not listed in the 1993 edition. They may have been omitted for failing to respond to our request for updates of information, they may have gone out of business or they may no longer wish to receive freelance work.

A&A Creations (did not respond)
Berlin Publications, Inc. (not reviewing work)
Brazen Images Inc. (did not respond)
Bright of America (did not respond)
Cedco Publishing Co. (did not respond)

JII Sales Promotion Associates, Inc. (did not respond)
Like It Is (did not respond)
Maid in the Shade (not reviewing work)
P.S. Greetings, Inc., d/b/a Fantus Paper Products (did not respond)
Photo/Chronicles, Ltd. (did not respond)

Plymouth, Inc. (did not respond)
Reedproductions (did not respond)
Sandpiper Publishing (did not respond)
Sormani Calendars (did not respond)
Zephyr Press (not reviewing work)

Publications

The wide assortment and multitude of listings in the Publications section of *Photographer's Market* make it an obvious starting point for many photographers. Some of these markets can serve as a training ground for newcomers wanting to hone their skills as professionals but there are also many listings that provide substantial income for the proven artist.

There are four main categories in the Publications section—Consumer Publications, Newspapers & Newsletters, Special Interest Publications and Trade Publications. While most of the listings are magazines, there are also journals, catalogs, newspapers and newsletters. In recent years many of the listings in these categories lost revenue from advertising. Those losses cut into the space available for copy and photos and, in turn, decreased the profits of photographers and writers. In some cases the financial setbacks for publishers were so severe that the publications were discontinued. Those publications which appeared in last year's edition of *Photographer's Market* but do not appear in this year's book are contained in the '92-'93 Changes at the end of each category. Reasons for their absence also are given.

If you have little experience in marketing your photography, this market does still represent one of the better avenues for entering the field. However, it's important to realize that with the increased competition, setting your work apart from that of other photographers with a creative approach to the subject and overall professionalism is more vital than ever to your success.

You can benefit a great deal from studying the markets and doing some self-assignment work before actually querying a specific publication. Aside from reading the listing carefully, request a publication's guidelines or a sample copy. With the insights you gather, you can then set up a few self-assignments. Then, when you do query or send samples, your work will be much closer to meeting the unique needs and problems of the publication. Remember: Your work must be more than just pretty pictures or technically perfect images; they must also relate to the interests of the publication's readers.

Once you have arrived at a clear understanding of the publication and its audience, your next step is actually to submit work or solicit assignments. Some publications are flexible and advise contacting them in various ways—querying, sending unsolicited materials or calling—while others are more particular and will not tolerate deviations. In any case, it's important that you follow their directions as specified to make the best first impression and promote your working relationship with them.

The standards of professional freelancing practiced in other markets are recognized too in the publications market. Such practices as providing clear, accurate captions and signed model releases are nearly universal needs. Enclosing a self-addressed, stamped envelope (SASE) facilitates a response from the publication, and is also an often-stated requirement. Providing adequate packaging and postage is also important if you are mailing your submissions and expect to have them returned safely. In particular, when a listing indicates it cannot return material you must take this direction seriously or risk loss of your images. When you query or submit images to a publication, the response or reporting time may actually take longer than indicated under the phrase, "Reports . . . ," in the listing. Keep in mind that because of deadlines and other factors there may be delays and that the longer "reporting" times are usually more reliable.

One special note for photographers who are also skilled as writers is to look for publications that indicate text as well as photo needs. This is usually indicated by a "ms" or "mss"—manuscript(s)—in the listing. Some publications will purchase photos only in a photo/text package for a flat fee while others will purchase photos from existing stock, on assignment or as part of a package. Publications which purchase packages only will often recommend that photographers team up with a writer with expertise in that particular subject as a way of working for them. Generally, shooting for packages tends to pay better and can give you an advantage over other photographers. On page 238, Tom Hamilton, publisher of *Balloon Life* in Sacramento, California, discusses the concept of text-photo packages and explains why he finds the combination so appealing.

If you are just breaking into photography or have not worked in this market previously, you may find it helpful to start with some smaller publications. Perhaps you will want to try those that feature subjects in which you have a personal interest or expertise. The smaller markets are generally less lucrative than higher-circulation national markets. However, working for them first is an excellent way to learn about the publications market, to you will then be able to build upon your success by selling to larger publications.

Another guide to help you locate markets which cater to newer, lesser-known photographers is the First Markets Index. This reference, located in the back of this book, has been expanded and contains over 600 markets.

Currently, more magazines are buying stock images—from both stock photo agencies and photographers' stock—because it's more economical to pay for existing photos than to assign special shoots. However, story outlines are occasionally specific enough to justify the extra expense of assigning new photos. It's much more likely that as a newcomer you will be successful in selling stock initially. As you develop a working relationship with an editor or photo editor, though, you may be offered assignments. Building a reputation as someone who understands a publication's needs and deadlines takes time and persistence, but it's worth the effort.

Consumer Publications

The consumer publications market is the most extensive section in *Photographer's Market*. Traditionally, this market has offered photographers the most variety in terms of subject matter, professional challenge and income. For these reasons, it remains the most popular among beginning and veteran photographers alike.

Many magazines in this category are household names, well-known regional publications and highly specialized, topic-oriented magazines. Nearly every kind of interest is represented—from nature to sports, from economics to religion, from home to health and beauty. Regardless of subject, however, these publications all have a great need in common—to communicate visually to their readers the excitement, intricacies or special values of the particular subjects.

In general, many listings in this section include substantial changes. For instance, some publications have provided new descriptions of their photo needs, or have revised their payment rates and terms concerning rights. Also, the listings reflect the usual changing of the guard on editorial and art staffs, as well as relocation of offices. In particular, listings which have not provided specific dollar amounts in their payment details now include the code NPI, for "no payment information given."

As the second Close-up subject in this section, Lisl Dennis of Sante Fe, New Mexico discusses on page 304 her views of editorial assignments. Dennis is a highly recognized travel photographer who understands the foibles of the photography industry and what it takes to be a success.

ABOARD MAGAZINE, Suite 220, 100 Almeria Ave., Coral Gables FL 33134. (305)441-9744. FAX: (305)441-9744. Editor: Pedro Gonzaléz Munné. Photo Editor: Alex Sanchez. Estab. 1976. Inflight magazine for 10 separate Latin American national airlines. Bilingual; bimonthly. Emphasizes travel through Central and South America. Readers are mainly Latin American businessmen, and American

tourists and businessmen. Circ. 110,000. Sample copy free with SASE. Photo guidelines free with SASE.
Needs: Uses 50 photos/issue; 30 supplied by freelance photographers. Needs photos of travel, scenic, fashion, sports and art. Special needs include good quality pix of Latin American countries, particularly Chile, Guatemala, Ecuador, Bolivia, Rep. Dominicana, El Salvador, Peru, Nicaragua, Honduras. Model/property release and captions preferred.
Making Contact & Terms: Interested in receiving work from newer, lesser-known photogaphers. Query with samples; provide business card, brochure, flyer or tearsheets to be kept on file for possible future assignments. SASE. Reports in 1 month. Payment varies; pays $20/color photo; $150 for photo/text package. Pays on publication. Credit line given. Buys one-time rights. Previously published work OK.
Tips: If photos are accompanied by an article, chances are much better of them being accepted.

ACCENT ON LIVING, P.O. Box 700, Bloomington IL 61702. (309)378-2961. Editor: Betty Garee. Quarterly magazine. Emphasizes successful disabled people who are getting the most out of life in every way and *how* they are accomplishing this. Readers are physically disabled individuals of all ages and socioeconomic levels and professionals. Circ. 19,500. Sample copy $2.50 with 5×7 SAE and 90¢ postage. Free photo guidelines; enclose SASE.
Needs: Buys 20-50 photos annually. Uses glossy prints. Manuscript required. 90% supplied by freelancers. Photos dealing with coping with the problems and situations peculiar to handicapped persons: how-to, new aids and assistive devices, news, documentary, human interest, photo essay/photo feature, humorous and travel. "All must be tied in with physical disability. We want essentially action shots of disabled individuals doing something interesting/unique or with a new device they have developed. Not photos of disabled people shown with a good citizen 'helping' them."
Making Contact & Terms: Query first with ideas, get an OK, and send contact sheet for consideration. Provide letter of inquiry and samples to be kept on file for possible future assignments. SASE. Reports in 2 weeks. Cover is usually tied in with the main feature inside. Also use color photos, transparencies preferred. Pays $50-up/cover. Pays on publication. Simultaneous submissions and previously published work OK "if we're notified and we OK it."
Tips: Needs photos for Accent on People department, "a human interest photo column on disabled individuals who are gainfully employed or doing unusual things." Also uses occasional photo features on disabled persons in specific occupations: art, health, etc. Pays $25-200 for text/photo package; and $10 min. color photo. Send for guidelines. "Concentrate on improving photographic skills. Join a local camera club, go to photo seminars, etc. We find that most articles are helped a great deal with *good* photographs—in fact, good photographs will often mean buying a story and passing up another one with very poor or no photographs at all." Looking for *good* quality photos depicting what article is about. Query first. We almost always work on speculation."

ADIRONDACK LIFE, Dept. PM, Rt. 86, Box 97, Jay NY 12941. (518)946-2191. Art Director: Ann Eastman. Bimonthly. Emphasizes the people and landscape of the north country of New York State. Circ. 50,000. Sample copy $4 with 9×12 SASE and $1.10 postage. Photo guidelines free with SASE.
Needs: "We use about 40 photos/issue, most supplied by freelance photographers. All photos must be taken in the Adirondacks and all shots must be identified as to location and photographer."
Making Contact & Terms: Send one sleeve (20 slides) of samples. Send b&w prints (preferably 8×10) or 35mm color transparencies. SASE. Reports in 1 month. Pays $300/cover photo; $50-200/color or b&w photo; $125/day + expenses. Pays on publication. Credit line given. Buys first N.A. serial rights. Simultaneous submissions OK.
Tips: "Send quality work pertaining specifically to the Adirondacks. In addition to technical proficiency, we look for originality and imagination. We avoid using typical shots of sunsets, lakes, reflections, mountains, etc. We are using more pictures of people and action."

AFRICA REPORT, Dept. PM, 833 UN Plaza, New York NY 10017. (212)949-5666. Editor: Margaret A. Novicki. Bimonthly magazine. Emphasizes African political and economic affairs, especially those significant for US. Readers are Americans with professional or personal interest in Africa. Circ. 12,000. Free sample copy.
Needs: Uses 20 photos/issue. Personality, documentary, photo feature, scenic, spot news, human interest, travel, socioeconomic and political. Photos must relate to African affairs. "We will not reply to 'How I Saw My First Lion' or 'Look How Quaint the Natives Are' proposals." Wants, on a regular

 The asterisk before a listing indicates that the market is new in this edition. New markets are often the most receptive to freelance submissions.

basis, photos of economics, African international affairs, development, conflict and daily life. Captions required.
Making Contact & Terms: Provide samples and list of countries/subjects to be kept on file for future assignments. Query on accompanying ms. SASE. Pays $25-35/inside photo; $25-75/cover photo; $150-250/ms. Pays on publication. Credit line given. Buys one-time rights. Reports in 1 month. Simultaneous submissions and previously published work OK. Uses 8 × 10 glossy prints; vertical format preferred for cover.
Tips: "Live and travel in Africa; and make political, economic and social events humanly interesting."

AFTER FIVE MAGAZINE, P.O. Box 492905, Redding CA 96049. (800)637-3540 only from northern California. Otherwise (916)335-4533. Publisher: Katie Harrington. Monthly tabloid. Emphasizes news, arts and entertainment. Circ. 24,207. Estab. 1986. Sample copy $1.
Needs: Uses 8-12 photos/issue; 25% supplied by freelance photographers. Needs photos of animal/ wildlife shots, travel and scenics of Northern California. Model release and photo captions preferred.
Making Contact & Terms: Provide resume, business card, brochure, flyer or tearsheets to be kept on file for possible assignments. SASE. Reports in 1-2 weeks. Pays $50/color cover photo; $50/b&w cover photo; $20/b&w inside photo; $60/b&w page rate. Pays on publication. Credit line given. Buys one-time rights. Previously published work OK.
Tips: "Need photographs of subjects north of Sacramento to Oregon-California border, plus southern Oregon."

AIM MAGAZINE, P.O. Box 20554, Chicago IL 60620. (312)874-6184. Editor: Ruth Apilado. Quarterly magazine. Magazine dedicated to promoting racial harmony and peace. Readers are high school and college students, as well as those interested in social change. Circ. 7,000. Estab. 1974. Sample copy for $3.50 with 9 × 12 SASE and 4 first-class stamps.
Needs: Uses 10 photos/issue. Needs "ghetto pictures, pictures of people deserving recognition, etc." Needs photos of "integrated schools with high achievement." Model release required.
Making Contact & Terms: Send unsolicited photos by mail for consideration. Send b&w prints. SASE. Reports in 1 month. Pays $25/color cover photo; $10/b&w cover photo. Pays on acceptance. Credit line given. Buys one-time rights. Simultaneous submissions OK.
Tips: Looks for "positive contributions."

ALABAMA LITERARY REVIEW, 253 Smith Hall, Troy State University, Troy AL 36082. (205)566-3000, ext. 3286. Editor: Theron Montgomery. Semi-annual journal. Emphasizes short stories, poetry, essays, short drama, art and photography. Readers are anyone interested in literature and art of all ages. Circ. 800 +. Estab. 1987. Sample copy for $4.50/issue and 9 × 12 SASE.
Needs: Uses 5-6 photos/issue; 100% supplied by freelance photographers, 10% on assignment, 90% from stock. Will consider all kinds of photos. Special needs include anything artistic or thought-provoking. Model release required; property release preferred.
Making Contact & Terms: Interested in receiving work from newer, lesser-known photogaphers. Send 8 × 10 b&w glossy prints by mail for consideration. SASE. Reports in 1-2 months. Pays in copies. Pays on publication. Credit line given. Buys first rights; returned upon publication. Simultaneous submissions OK.
Tips: "We take pride in discovering amateur photographers and presenting their work to a serious audience across the U.S. *ALR* is a good place for a new photographer to break in." Looks for "Playoff on b&w, people and forms. Also, something that tells a story." The trend is towards b&w art forms. "Think of the completeness, proportion and metaphoric implications of the pictures."

ALASKA, Suite 200, 808 E St., Anchorage AK 99501. Editor: Tobin Morrison. Managing Editor: Nolan Hester. Photo Editor: Roy Corral. Monthly magazine. Readers are people interested in Alaska. Circ. 260,000. Estab. 1963. Sample copy $4; free photo guidelines.
Making Contact & Terms: Buys 400 photos annually, supplied mainly by freelancers. Send carefully edited, captioned submission of 35mm, 2¼ × 2¼ or 4 × 5 transparencies. Reports in 4 weeks. SASE. Pays $300/full page, $500/cover.
Tips: "Each issue of *Alaska* features 6- to 10-page photo feature. We're looking for themes and photos to show the best of Alaska. We want sharp, artistically composed pictures. Cover photo always relates to stories inside the issue.

ALASKA GEOGRAPHIC, P.O. Box 93370, Anchorage AK 99509. (907)258-2515. Editor: Penny Rennick. Quarterly magazine. Covers Alaska and Northwestern Canada only. Readers are professional men and women, ages 30 and up. Circ. 9,000. Estab. 1972. Guidelines free with SASE.
Needs: Uses about 70 photos/issue; most supplied by freelancers. Needs photos of scenics, animals, natural history and people. Each issue covers a special theme. Model release preferred; photo captions required.

Making Contact & Terms: Interested in receiving work from newer, lesser-known photogaphers. Query with list of stock photo subjects. SASE. Usually reports in 1 month. "We don't have time to deal with inappropriate submissions, so know the area and subjects very well to avoid wasting time." Pays $200/color cover photo; $100/inside full-page color; $50/inside half-page color. Pays on publication. Credit line given. Buys one-time rights. Simultaneous submissions and previously published work OK.

Tips: Do not send mss, "just photos. Our freelance writing is done by assignment only."

alive now! MAGAZINE, Dept. PM, 1908 Grand Ave., Box 189, Nashville TN 37202. (615)340-7218. Assistant Editor: Beth A. Richardson. Bimonthly magazine published by The Upper Room. "*alive now!* uses poetry, short prose, photography and contemporary design to present material for personal devotion and reflection. It reflects on a chosen Christian concern in each issue. The readership is composed of primarily college-educated adults." Circ. 80,000. Sample copy free with 6 × 9 SASE and 85¢ postage; themes list free with SASE; photo guidelines available.

Needs: Uses about 25-30 b&w prints/issue; 90% supplied by freelancers. Needs b&w photos of "family, friends, people in positive and negative situations; scenery; celebrations; disappointments; ethnic minority subjects in everyday situations – Native Americans, Hispanics, Asians and blacks." Model release preferred.

Making Contact & Terms: Query with samples. Send 8 × 10 glossy b&w prints by mail for consideration. Submit portfolio for review. SASE. Reports in 2 months; "longer to consider photos for more than one issue." Pays $20-30/b&w inside photo; no color photos. Pays on publication. Credit line given. Buys one-time rights. Simultaneous and previously published submissions OK.

Tips: Prefers to see "a variety of photos of people in life situations, presenting positive and negative slants, happy/sad, celebrations/disappointments, etc. Use of racially inclusive photos is preferred."

ALOHA, THE MAGAZINE OF HAWAII, Suite 309, 49 S. Hotel St., Honolulu HI 96813. (808)523-9871. FAX: (808)533-2055. Editor: Cheryl Tsutsumi. Art Director: Sanford Mock. Emphasizes Hawaii. Readers are "affluent, college-educated people from all over the world who have an interest in Hawaii." Bimonthly. Circ. 65,000. Sample copy $2.95 with 9 × 11 SAE and $2.40 postage; photo guidelines with SASE.

Needs: Uses about 50 photos/issue; 40 of which are supplied by freelance photographers. Needs "scenics, travel, people, florals, strictly about Hawaii. We buy primarily from stock. Assignments are rarely given and when they are it is to one of our regular local contributors. Subject matter must be Hawaiian in some way. A regular feature is the photo essay, 'Beautiful Hawaii,' which is a 6-page collection of images illustrating that theme." Model release required if the shot is to be used for a cover; captions required.

Making Contact & Terms: Send by mail for consideration actual 35mm or 2¼ × 2¼ color transparencies; or arrange personal interview to show portfolio. SASE. Reports in 6-8 weeks. Pays $25/b&w photo; $60/color transparency; $125 for photo running across a two-page spread; $175 for cover shots. Pays on publication. Credit line given. Buys one-time rights.

Tips: Prefers to see "a unique way of looking at things, and of course, well-composed images. Generally, we are looking for outstanding photos of Hawaii scenery that are not standard sunset shots printed in every Hawaii publication. We need to see that the photographer can use lighting techniques skillfully, and we want to see pictures that are sharp and crisp. Many photographers break in to being published by submitting transparencies for Beautiful Hawaii, a photo essay section that is run in every issue. Competition is fierce, and it helps if a photographer can first bring in his portfolio to show to our art director. Then the art director can give him ideas regarding our needs."

AMELIA MAGAZINE, 329 "E" St., Bakersfield CA 93304. (805)323-4064. Editor: Frederick A. Raborg, Jr. Quarterly magazine. Emphasizes literary: fiction, non-fiction, poetry, reviews, fine illustrations and photography etc. "We span all age groups, the three genders and all occupations. We are also international in scope. Average reader has college education." Circ. 1,250. Sample copy $7.95 and SASE. Photo guidelines free with SASE.

Needs: Uses up to 4 photos/issue depending on availability; 100% supplied by freelance photographers. "We look for photos in all areas and try to match them to appropriate editorial content. Sometimes use photos alone; color photos on cover. We use the best we receive; the photos usually convince us." Model release required; photo captions preferred.

Making Contact & Terms: Send unsolicited photos by mail for consideration. Send b&w or color, 5 × 7 and up, glossy or matte prints, or 35mm or 2¼ × 2¼ transparencies. SASE. Reports in 2 weeks. Pays $100/color cover photo, $50/b&w cover photo and $5-25/b&w inside photo. Pays on acceptance. Credit line given. Buys one-time rights or first N.A. serial rights. "We prefer first N.A., but one-time is fine." Simultaneous submissions OK.

Tips: In portfolio or samples, looks for "a strong cross-section. We assume that photos submitted are available at time of submission. Do your homework. Examine a copy of the magazine, certainly. Study the 'masters of contemporary' photography, i.e. Adams, Avedon, etc. Experiment. Remember we are looking for photos to be married to editorial copy usually."

AMERICA WEST AIRLINES MAGAZINE, Dept. PM, Suite 240, 7500 N. Dreamy Draw Dr., Phoenix AZ 85020. (602)997-7200. Art Director: Elaine Rettger. America West Airlines inflight magazine. Monthly. Emphasizes general interest—including: travel, interviews, business trends, food, etc. Readers are primarily business people and business travelers; substantial vacation travel audience. Circ. 125,000. Photo guidelines free with SASE. Sample copy $3.
Needs: Uses about 60-100 photos/issue; all supplied by freelance photographers. "Each issue varies immensely, we primarily look for stock photography of places, people, subjects such as animals, plants, scenics—we assign some location and portrait shots. We publish a series of photo essays with brief, but interesting accompanying text." Model release and captions required.
Making Contact & Terms: Provide resume, business card, brochure, tearsheets or color samples to be kept on file for possible future assignments. Pays $100-225/color inside photo, depends on size of photo and importance of story; $75-100/hour; $350/day+ film and expenses. Pays on publication. Credit line given. Buys one-time rights. Previously published work OK.
Tips: "We judge portfolios on technical quality, consistency, ability to show us that you can give us what we ask for with a certain uniqueness in style or design, versatility and creativity. Photographers we work with most often are those who are both technically and creatively adept, and who can take the initiative conceptually by providing new approaches or ideas."

AMERICAN CAGE-BIRD MAGAZINE, One Glamore Court, Smithtown NY 11787. (516)979-7962. Editor: Arthur Freud. Photo Editor: Anne Frizzell. Monthly. Emphasizes care, breeding and maintenance of pet cage birds. Readers include bird fanciers scattered throughout the United States, Canada and other countries. Circ. 50,000. Estab. 1928. Sample copy $3.
Needs: Uses about 15 photos/issue; 6 supplied by freelance photographers, 70% on assignment, 30% from stock. Needs sharp, clear black & white and color photos of budgies, cockatiels, canaries, parrots, toucans and people with such birds. Clever seasonal shots also good (Christmas, etc.). "We choose photos which inform and/or entertain. Identification of the bird type or species is crucial." Special needs include Christmas theme, Fourth of July theme, etc. Model/property release preferred; captions required.
Making Contact & Terms: Interested in receiving work from newer, lesser-known photogaphers. Send 5×7 glossy b&w prints, 35mm color slides or 2¼×2¼ transparencies by mail for consideration. SASE. Reports in 2 weeks. Pays $25/b&w photo; $25-100/color photo. "Vertical format color slides with dead space at top of slide are considered for cover with a higher payment." Pays on publication. Credit line given. Buys one-time rights. Previously published work OK.

***AMERICAN DANE MAGAZINE,** 3717 Harney St., Omaha NE 68131. (402)341-5049. FAX: (402)341-0830. Editor-in-Chief: Jennifer Denning-Kock. Monthly magazine. For an audience of "primarily Danish origin, interested in Danish traditions, customs, etc." Send contact sheet or prints for consideration. Circ. 10,000. Estab. 1916. Sample copy $1 with 8½×11 SAE and 75¢ postage.
Needs: Wants no scenic photos "unless they are identifiably Danish in origin." Avoid general material. Buys approximately 6 photos annually. Photo captions preferred.
Making Contact & Terms: Interested in receiving work from newer, lesser-known photographers. Send b&w contact sheet or 5×7 glossy or semigloss prints. Send cover contact sheet or glossy or semigloss prints for b&w. SASE. Reports in 1-2 weeks. Pays $10-20/color photo; $20-40/photo/text package. Pays on publication. Buys first rights. Previously published work OK.
Tips: "Photos must be identifiably Danish in content and have the ability to capture Danish culture." Contact by mail.

AMERICAN HORTICULTURIST, 7931 East Boulevard Dr., Alexandria VA 22308. (703)768-5700. FAX: (703)768-7533. Editor: Kathleen Fisher. Monthly. "Alternate 4-color magazine with 2-color newsletter." Emphasizes horticulture. Readers are advanced amateur gardeners. Circ. 25,000. Estab. 1927. Sample copy $2.50. Photo guidelines free with SASE.
Needs: Uses 20-25 (color/magazine), 5 (b&w/news edition) photos/issue; all supplied by freelancers. "Assignments are rare. 2-3/year need portraits to accompany profiles." Needs shots of people gardening, people engaged in horticulture research, public gardens, close-ups of particular plant species showing detail. "We only review photos to illustrate a particular ms which has already been accepted." Sometimes uses seasonal cover shots. Model release preferred; captions and botanical names required.
Making Contact & Terms: Query with list of stock photo subjects, photo samples; provide resume, business card, brochure, flyer or tearsheets to be kept on file for possible future assignments. SASE. Reports in 3 weeks. Pays $50/color inside photo; $80/color cover photo; $25-50 for b&w photo. Pays on publication. Buys one-time rights.

Tips: Wants to see "ability to identify precise names of plants, clarity and vibrant color."

*AMERICAN SKATING WORLD, 1816 Brownsville Rd., Pittsburgh PA 15210-3908. (412)885-7600. FAX: (412)885-7617. Managing Editor: H. Kermit Jackson. Monthly tabloid. Emphasizes ice skating and figure skating primarily, speed skating secondary. Readers are figure skating participants and fans of all ages. Circ. 15,000. Estab. 1981. Sample copy $2.95 with 8×12 SASE and 3 first class stamps. Photo guidelines free with SASE.
Needs: Uses 20-25 photos/issue; 40% supplied by freelancers. Needs performance and candid shots of skaters and "industry heavyweights." Reviews photos with or without manuscript. Model/property release preferred; children and recreational skaters. Photo captions required; include name, locale, date and move being executed (if relevant).
Making Contact & Terms: Query with resume of credits. Keeps samples on file. SASE. Report on unsolicited submissions could take 3 months. Pays $25/color cover photo; $5/b&w inside photo. Pays 30 days after publication. Buys one-time rights color; all rights b&w; negotiable. Simultaneous submissions and/or previously published work OK.
Tips: "Pay attention to what's new, the newly emerging competitors, the newly developed events. In general, be flexible!"

AMERICAN SURVIVAL GUIDE, 2145 W. La Palma Ave., Anaheim CA 92801. (714)778-5773. FAX: (714)533-9979. Editor: Jim Benson. Monthly magazine. Emphasizes firearms, military gear, food storage and self-defense products. Average reader is male, mid-30s, all occupations and with conservative views. Circ. 72,000. Estab. 1980. Sample copy $3.25. Photo guidelines free with SASE.
Needs: Uses 125 photos/issue; 30% supplied by freelance photographers. Photos purchased with accompanying manuscript only. Model release and photo captions required.
Making Contact & Terms: Interested in receiving work from newer, lesser-known photogaphers. Send written query detailing article and photos. Note: Will not accept text without photos or other illustrations. Pays $70/color and b&w page rate. Pays on publication. Credit line given. Buys all rights; negotiable.
Tips: Wants to see "Professional looking photographs—in focus, correct exposure, good lighting, interesting subject and people in action. Look at sample copies to get an idea of what we feature. We only accept photos with an accompanying manuscript. The better the photos, the better chance you have of being published."

AMERICANA MAGAZINE, Dept. PM, 29 W. 38 St., New York NY 10018. (212)398-1550. Editor: Sandra Wilmot. Bimonthly magazine. Emphasizes an interest in American history and how it relates to contemporary living. Circ. 200,000. Estab. 1973. Sample copy $3 and free photo guidelines.
Needs: Freelancers supply 95% of the photos; 50% stock, 50% assigned. Photos purchased with or without accompanying mss. Celebrity/personality (outstanding in the field of Americana—curator of White House, head of National Trust, famous painter, etc.); fine art; scenic (US—must relate to specific article); human interest; humorous; photo essay/photo feature (majority of stories); US travel; museum collections and old photography. "*Americana*'s stories should open the door on the past by giving the reader the opportunity to participate in the activity we are covering, be it crafts, collecting, travel or whatever. Travel, preservation, collecting and history are only a few of the subjects we cover. We often rely on contributors to point out new areas that are suitable for *Americana*. Many of the articles are very service-oriented, including practical advice and how-to information." Model release preferred. Photo captions required; include name, place, subject matter, date.
Making Contact & Terms: Send query with resume of credits. "Look at several issues of the magazine and then have story ideas before talking to us." SASE. "Make envelope large enough to hold material sent." Uses 8×10 b&w matte prints; color 35mm, 2¼×2¼, 4×5 and 8×10 transparencies; color covers only with vertical format. Reports in 3 months. Previously published work OK. Pays $25 minimum/b&w photo; $25-300/color photo; $350 maximum/day. Pays by assignment or on a per-photo basis. All payments negotiable. Pays on publication. Credit line given. Buys one-time rights and first N.A. serial rights.
Tips: Wants to see "technical competence; artistic abilities; aptitude to shoot for an editorial assignment. Rarely accepts freelance work that does not relate to a specific story."

Can't find a listing? Check at the end of each market section for the " '92-'93 Changes" lists. These lists include any market listings from the '92 edition which were either not verified or deleted in this edition.

AMERICA'S EQUESTRIAN, (formerly *Horse World USA*), P.O. Box 249, Huntington Station NY 11746. (516)549-0620. FAX: (516)423-0567. Publisher: Bill Bohn. Publishes 7 issues/year: 6 bimonthly and 1 special calendar issue. Emphasizes horses. Circ. 17,000. Estab. 1978. Sample copy $2 and 9×12 SAE with $1.50 postage. Photo guidelines free with SASE.
Needs: Uses 25-50 photos/issue; 2 supplied by freelance photographers. Needs photos of horse shots from specific events, and horse-related photos for special features. Reviews photos with or without accompanying ms. Special needs include "photos taken at major national and international equine events. We sometimes do photo essays tied in with our editorial themes." Model release preferred; captions required; name/address/phone on back of photo, no name on front of photo. No Polaroids.
Making Contact & Terms: Query with samples; send unsolicited photos by mail for consideration. Must include cover letter. Provide resume, business card, brochure, flyer or tearsheets to be kept on file for possible future assignments. Uses b&w prints and color. SASE. Reports in 2 months. Pays $20/ inside photo; $100 for photo essays of 10-20 photos. Pays on publication. Credit line given. Buys first N.A. serial rights. "We keep photos published. No payment for unassigned photos, but will consider publishing for credit line."
Tips: Looks for people "who understand horse photography. Clear, crisp, good contrast and cropped so the subject fills the photo, a knowledge of how to shoot horses. We like to work with new people who want and need the exposure and would supply us with complimentary photos in exchange for a credit line."

ANYTIME TRAVEL GUIDE, Dept. PM, Box G3, Aspen CO 81612. (303)920-4040. FAX: (303)920-4044. Art Director: Bob Maraziti. Bimonthly magazine. Emphasizes Aspen—lifestyle, sports, local issues. Readers are "Aspenites, both locals, part-time residents and lovers of the town wherever they live." Circ. 15,000. Estab. 1974. Sample copy free with 10×12 SASE and 6 first class stamps.
Needs: Uses "35 photos/issue; most supplied by freelancers, usually on assignment." Needs scenics, sports—skiing in winter and other mountain sports in summer—profiles, travel shots, etc. Model release preferred. "We're eager to see work of shooters who are in our area for work or pleasure."
Making Contact & Terms: Provide resume, business card, brochure, flyer or tearsheets. Does not keep samples on file. Cannot return material. Reports in 1 month. Pays $200, 30 days of publication. Credit line given. Buys exclusive rights in our market, one-time rights; negotiable.
Tips: Wants to see "technical proficiency, appropriate subject matter, vision and creative sensibility. We strive for the highest level of photography in all areas and design. Do *not* send inappropriate submissions that are unrelated to Aspen, CO. All our photography (and editorial text) are geared to our role as a 'city' magazine. When we do use stock shots they are usually from photographers who have worked extensively in our town, but we still like to see the work of others as long as they have shots *from our area. No general submissions please.*"

AQUARIUM FISH MAGAZINE, P.O. Box 6050, Mission Viejo CA 92690. (714)855-8822. Editor: Edward Bauman. Monthly magazine. Emphasizes aquarium fish. Readers are both genders, all ages. Circ. 75,000. Estab. 1988. Sample copy $3.50. Photo guidelines free with SASE.
Needs: Uses 30 photos/issue; 100% supplied by freelance photographers. Needs photos of aquariums and fish, freshwater and saltwater; ponds.
Making Contact & Terms: Query with list of stock photo subjects. Submit portfolio for review. Send 35mm, 2¼×2¼ transparencies by mail for consideration. SASE. Reports in 1 month. Pays $150/color cover photo; $50-75/color inside photo; $25/b&w inside photo; $75/color page rate; $25/b&w page rate. Pays on publication. Credit line given. Buys one-time rights. Previously published work OK.

ARIZONA HIGHWAYS, 2039 W. Lewis Ave., Phoenix AZ 85009. (Not reviewing freelance work.)

***A.IZONA LITERARY REVIEW,** (formerly *Northern Arizona Mandala*), P.O. Box 2426, Prescott AZ 86302. (602)776-7960. Editor: Stephen Bruno. Monthly magazine. Literary magazine emphasizing art, photography, and environment. Readers are 21-80 with creative occupations and interests. Circ. 15,000. Estab. 1991. Sample copy free with 11½×14½ SASE and $3 postage. Photo guidelines free with SASE.
Needs: Uses 25-40 photos/issue; minimum 50% supplied by freelancers. Needs photos in all categories. Special photo needs include "avant garde, very creative." Model release preferred for shots of individuals. Captions preferred.
Making Contact & Terms: Interested in receiving work from newer, lesser-known photographers. Arrange personal interview to show portfolio. Submit portfolio for review. Query with resume of credits. Query with list of stock photo subjects. Send unsolicited photos by mail for consideration. Provide resume, business card, brochure, flyer or tearsheets to be kept on file for possible assignments. Send 3×5 b&w and color, Poly Contrast, Hi-Gloss prints and contact sheets; 35mm transparencies. Keeps samples on file. Reports in 1 month. Pays $100/color cover photo; $75/b&w cover; $50/color inside photo; $35/b&w inside photo; $25/color page rate; $50-100/photo/text package. Pays on publica-

tion. Credit line given. Buys first N.A. serial rights; negotiable. Previously published work OK.
Tips: "Photos have to make an emotional impact. Stretch your creativity to the maximum, then go further."

ASIA PACIFIC TRAVEL AND HEALTH WORLD, 1540 Gilbreth Rd., Burlingame CA 94010. (415)697-8038. Managing Editor: Jeff Kravitz. Bimonthly magazine. Emphasizes Asia and Pacific Rim travel. Circ. 50,000. Estab. 1990. Sample copy $2.50. Free photo guidelines.
Needs: Uses 25 photos/issue. Needs wildlife, travel and scenic photos. Model release required.
Making Contact & Terms: Arrange a personal interview to show portfolio; query with list of stock photo subjects; submit portfolio for review. Cannot return material. Pays $15/color cover photo. Pays on publication. Buys one-time rights. Simultaneous submissions OK.

ASPEN MAGAZINE, Dept. PM, Box G3, Aspen CO 81612. (303)920-4040. FAX: (303)920-4044. Art Director: Bob Maraziti. Bimonthly magazine. Emphasizes Aspen—lifestyle, sports, local issues. Readers are "Aspenites, both locals, part-time residents and lovers of the town wherever they live." Circ. 15,000. Estab. 1974. Sample copy free with 10×12 SASE and 6 first class stamps.
Needs: Uses "35 photos/issue; most supplied by freelancers, usually on assignment." Needs scenics, sports—skiing in winter and other mountain sports in summer—profiles, travel shots, etc. Model release preferred. "We're eager to see work of shooters who are in our area for work or pleasure."
Making Contact & Terms: Provide resume, business card, brochure, flyer or tearsheets. Does not keep samples on file. Cannot return material. Reports in 1 month. Pays $200, 30 days of publication. Credit line given. Buys exclusive rights in our market, one-time rights; negotiable.
Tips: Wants to see "technical proficiency, appropriate subject matter, vision and creative sensibility. We strive for the highest level of photography in all areas and design. Do *not* send inappropriate submissions that are unrelated to Aspen, Colorado. All our photography (and editorial text) are geared to our role as a 'city' magazine. When we do use stock shots they are usually from photographers who have worked extensively in our town, but we still like to see the work of others as long as they have shots *from our area. No general submissions please.*"

ATLANTA JEWISH TIMES, Suite 470, 1575 Northside Dr., Atlanta GA 30318. (404)352-2400. Managing Editor: Fran Rothbard. Weekly tabloid. Emphasizes news of interest to Jewish community. Readers are well educated, upscale and knowledgeable. Circ. 10,000+. Estab. 1925. Sample copy free with 9×13 SAE and 4 first-class stamps.
Needs: Uses approximately 15 photos/issue; 15% supplied by freelance photographers. Needs photos of Jewish holidays, personalities and events of interest (like rallies against the Klan, for example). Photo captions required.
Making Contact & Terms: Provide resume, business card, brochure, flyer or tearsheets to be kept on file for possible assignments. SASE. Reports in 1 month. Pays $75/color cover photo; $50/b&w cover photo; $25/b&w inside photo. Photo/text package negotiable. Pays on publication. Credit line given. Buys with rights for use with 2 sister publications. Simultaneous and previously published work OK.
Tips: "Call us first if you have an idea so we can discuss options."

ATLANTIC CITY MAGAZINE, Dept. PM, Box 2100, Pleasantville NJ 08232. (609)272-7900. Editor: Ken Weatherford. Art Director: Michael Lacy. Monthly. Circ. 50,000. Sample copy $2 plus $1 postage.
Needs: Uses 50 photos/issue; all are supplied by freelance photographers. Model release and captions required. Prefers to see b&w and color fashion, product and portraits, sports, theatrical.
Making Contact & Terms: Query with portfolio/samples. Does not return unsolicited material. Reports in 3 weeks. Provide resume and tearsheets to be kept on file for possible future assignments. Payment negotiable; usually $35-50/b&w photo; $50-100/color; $250-450/day; $175-300 for text/photo package. Pays on publication. Credit line given. Buys one-time rights.
Tips: "We promise only exposure, not great fees. We're looking for imagination, composition, sense of design, creative freedom and trust."

AUDUBON MAGAZINE, 950 3rd Ave., New York NY 10022. Picture Editor: Peter Howe. Bimonthly magazine. Circ. 475,000. Emphasizes wildlife. Sample copy $4. First-class $5.
Needs: Freelancers supply 100% of the photos. Photo essays of nature subjects, especially wildlife, showing animal behavior, unusual portraits with good lighting and artistic composition. Nature photos should be artistic and dramatic, not the calendar or post card scenic. Uses color covers only; horizontal wraparound format requires subject off-center. Also uses journalistic and human interest photos. Captions are required. Also seeks articles with accompanying photos on environmental topics, natural areas or wildlife, predominantly North America.

Making Contact & Terms: Important: Query first before sending material; include tearsheets or list previously published credits. Portfolios should be geared to the magazine's subject matter. Must see original transparencies as samples. Uses 8×10 glossy b&w prints; 35mm, 2¼×2¼ and 4×5, transparencies. Plastic sheets only; no prints, no dupes. SASE. Reports in 1 month. Pays $125-300/b&w and color inside; $700/color cover; $450/table of contents. Pays on publication. Credit line given. Buys one-time rights. No simultaneous submissions.

Tips: "Query first. Study recent issues (last 6 months). Do not send unsolicited material. If you do submit unsolicited material, it should be accompanied by return postage. We cannot assume the cost of sending back unsolicited material. All photos submitted must be accompanied by adequate captions or they will not be considered for publication."

AUTOGRAPH COLLECTORS MAGAZINE, (formerly *The Autograph Collector's Magazine*), Suite 104-283, 541 N. Main St., Corona CA 91720. (714)734-9636. Editors: Bill Miller and Darrell Talbert. Magazine published 12 times/year. Emphasizes autograph collecting. Readers are all ages and occupations. Circ. 5,000. Estab. 1986. Sample copy $4.25.

Needs: Uses 30-40 photos/issue; all supplied by freelancers. Needs photos of "autograph collectors with collections, autographs and VIPs giving autographs, historical documents in museums, etc." Model release preferred. Photo captions preferred.

Making Contact & Terms: Send unsolicited photos by mail for consideration. Provide resume, business card, brochure, flyer or tearsheets to be kept on file for possible assignments. Send 4×5, 8×10 glossy b&w or color prints. SASE. Reports in 3 weeks. NPI. Pays on publication. Credit line given. Buys first N.A. serial rights. Simultaneous submissions OK.

AUTOMOBILE MAGAZINE, 120 E. Liberty, Ann Arbor MI 48104. (313)994-3500. Art Director: Larry Crane. Monthly magazine. Emphasizes automobiles. Readers are 97% male, $35,000-85,000/year income. Circ. 500,000. Estab. 1986. Sample copy $5.

Needs: Uses more than 100 photos/issue; all supplied by freelancers. Model release preferred. Photo captions required.

Making Contact & Terms: Query with resume. SASE. Reports in 1-2 weeks. Pays $900/color cover photo; $50-250/color inside photo; $750/day. Pays on acceptance. Credit line given. Buys one-time rights.

Tips: Looks for "car photos with an interesting twist—great compositions, super action, great ideas. Our photographers shoot on their own with little direction. Great ideas are *vital.*"

AUTOWEEK MAGAZINE, A Crain Publication, Dept. PM, 1400 Woodbridge, Detroit MI 48207-3187. (313)446-0344. FAX: (313)446-0347. Executive Art Director: Charles Krasner. Weekly magazine. Emphasizes automotive news, sheetmetal and motorsports. Readers are primarily male executives, ages 25-54, $83,900 average income. Circ. 265,000. Free sample copy with SASE.

Needs: Uses 60-80 photos/issue; 85% supplied by freelancers. Needs photos focusing on automotive news and industry—new cars, motorsports, travel. Also, spy photos. Special photo needs include shots of motorsports and production cars. Model release required. Photo captions preferred. Include who, what, where, when, why, how.

Making Contact & Terms: Arrange personal interview to show portfolio; provide resume, business card, brochure, flyer or tearsheets to be kept on file for possible assignments; call first for permission to submit. Keeps samples on file. SASE. Reports in 1 month. Pays $250-500/day. Pays on acceptance. Credit line given. Buys one-time rights; negotiable as needed. Simultaneous submissions and previously published work OK.

Tips: "We are primarily interested in genuine automotive/motorsport enthusiasts who are dependable and reliable. Have a willingness to experiment but always be able to deliver the basics. Don't take up our time seeking assignments. There's nothing worse than a telephone nuisance; they are least likely to get assignments."

BACK HOME IN KENTUCKY, P.O. Box 681629, Franklin TN 37068-1629. (615)794-4338. Editor: Nanci Gregg. Estab. 1977. Bimonthly magazine. Emphasizes the state of Kentucky. Readers are interested in the heritage and future of Kentucky. Circ. 13,000. Sample copy $2 with 9×12 SAE and $1.25 postage (first class).

Needs: Uses 25 photos/issue; all supplied by freelance photographers, less than 10% on assignment. Needs photos of scenic, specific places, events, people. Reviews photos with accompanying ms. Also seeking vertical cover (color) photos. Special needs include holidays in Kentucky; Christmas; the Kentucky Derby sights and sounds. Model release and captions required.

Making Contact & Terms: Interested in receiving work from newer, lesser-known photographers. Send any size, glossy b&w and color prints, 35mm transparencies by mail for consideration. Reports in 2 weeks. Pays $15/b&w photo; $20/color photo; $50+/cover photo; $15-100/text/photo package.

Close-up

Tom Hamilton
Publisher
Balloon Life
Sacramento, California

"Stunning photographs of colorful hot air balloons may not be enough to land your work on the pages of *Balloon Life*," says Tom Hamilton, publisher. Although this magazine for sport-balloon enthusiasts uses plenty of photos, it also features stories that are just as colorful as its photography. For this reason, photographers should consider submitting story-photo packages to make their work more attractive to the editors and increase the likelihood that the materials will be published, says Hamilton.

With a growing circulation of around 4,000, a smaller magazine like *Balloon Life* has found packaging to be a very successful way to satisfy their needs and those of their readers, he says. It is simply easier to have a "ready-to-use" package. "It works for us and I would think particularly for other smaller magazines it would work well," says Hamilton. But before any package is assembled, photographers should make sure the story they are writing is a good one. "The story needs to be there first, then the illustration," he says.

Given that this highly photographed sport yields many beautiful shots, Hamilton emphasizes that something written to accompany photos might set the material apart from the many images the magazine receives each month. "We see lots of great photographs, but they don't do much without an accompanying story to satisfy our balloon-enthusiast readership," he says. *Balloon Life* features news of ballooning ventures around the country, from the premier hot air balloon fiesta in Albuquerque, New Mexico, to profiles of interesting balloonists and significant feats that would not normally be covered by the staff. "These are the stories we've always wanted to run, but no one has wanted to write them," says Hamilton. One problem *Balloon Life* and other small specialty publications have is that they don't maintain large staffs to cover every event.

A photographer does not necessarily have to be an expert writer to consider submitting a story as part of a package, he says. Basically, he must be able to communicate clearly and concisely. "Tell us about an event and illustrate what makes it unique," says Hamilton. If editors see potential in the work, they can help polish it. Along with correcting grammatical errors, they will help the writer/photographer develop a story idea.

Of the nearly 150 stories they run each month, about 90 percent are unsolicited material with photographs sent to them by freelancers, he says. Freelancers have a good chance to have their work published, especially in the "logbook" section of the magazine which summarizes balloon events. Those stories usually run 400-500 words and are accompanied by an illustration. A longer feature piece also may deal with people, commercial ballooning operations or unique aspects of ballooning, but would generally run about 1,500 words with the possibility for several photos, says Hamilton.

One option for photographers who don't want to play the word game is teamwork. Hamilton sees a lot of packages that are created by writer/photographer combinations. This works particularly well for friends or co-workers who turn a leisurely balloon outing into a profitable venture, he says.

For those who may have an interest in ballooning, this could be the perfect way to check out an event and do some work while they are there. The important thing is to "capture the flavor" of what is happening, the people, the preparation and the behind-the-scenes shots, he says. "What makes this event neat?" Like many publications, *Balloon Life* is interested in diversity. It does not want photographers to limit their photos to balloons. What is going on around the balloons may actually provide the true color of the sport, he says.

—Susan Liller

Tom Hamilton's shot of the National Balloon Museum in Indianola, Iowa, is the type of photograph his magazine likes to publish. Balloon Life contains photos of colorful hot air balloons, but that's not all. With this shot Hamilton wanted to show the building's entrance and, in particular, the inverted balloon and basket design.

Pays on publication. Credit line given. Usually buys one-time rights. Simultaneous submissions and previously published work OK.

Tips: "We look for someone who can capture the flavor of Kentucky—history, events, people, homes, etc. Have a great story to go with the photo—by self or another."

An interesting angle can change an otherwise average scene into something wonderful. In this case, getting close to the flowers was the key to success for Owensboro, Kentucky, photographer Bonnie Nance. The antique plow set in the field of flowers helps depict springtime in the Bluegrass state, a subject sought by Back Home in Kentucky.

© Bonnie Nance

BACKPACKER MAGAZINE, 135 N. 6th St., Emmaus PA 18098. (Not reviewing freelance work).

BALLOON LIFE, 2145 Dale Ave., Sacramento CA 95678. (916)922-9648. Editor: Glen Moyer. Monthly. Emphasizes sport ballooning. Readers are sport balloon enthusiasts. Circ. 3,500. Estab. 1986. Sample copy free with 9 × 12 SAE and $2 postage; photo guidelines free with SASE.
Needs: Uses about 15-20 photos/issue; 90% supplied by freelance photographers, 5% on assignment. Needs how-to photos for technical articles, scenic for events. Model release and captions preferred.
Making Contact & Terms: Interested in receiving work from newer, lesser-known photographers. Send b&w or color prints; 35mm transparencies by mail for consideration. "We are now scanning our own color and doing color separations in house. As such we prefer 35mm transparencies above all other photos." SASE. Reports in 2 weeks. Pays $50/color cover photo; $15/b&w or color inside photo. Pays on publication. Credit line given. Buys first N.A. serial rights. Simultaneous submissions and previously published work OK.
Tips: "Photographs, generally, should be accompanied by a story. Cover the basics first. Good exposure, sharp focus, color saturation, etc. Then get creative with framing and content. Often we look for one single photograph that tells readers all they need to know about a specific flight or event. We're evolving our coverage of balloon events into more than just 'pretty balloons in the sky.' I'm looking for photographers who can go the next step and capture the people, moments in time, unusual happenings, etc. that make an event unique. Query first with interest in sport, access to people and events, experience shooting balloons or other outdoor special events."

*BALLSTREET JOURNAL, Suite 356, 7200 Montgomery NE, Albuquerque NM 87109. (505)888-1515. FAX: (505)888-0717. Editor: Marybeth Connelly. Monthly magazine. Emphasizes sports card collections. Readers are male and female card collectors, ages 25-60. Circ. 60,000. Estab. 1991. Sample copy $6.95. Photo guidelines free with SASE.

Needs: Uses 11 photos/issue; 100% supplied by freelancers. Needs photos of professional athletes in action. Reviews photos with or without ms. Model/property release preferred. Photo captions preferred; include where and when photo was taken and what was happening.
Making Contact & Terms: Query with resume of credits. Provide resume, business card, brochure, flyer or tearsheets to be kept on file for possible assignments. Keeps samples on file. SASE. Reports in 1-2 weeks. Pays $200/color cover photo; $100/color inside photo. Pays on publication. Credit line given. Buys one-time rights; negotiable. Simultaneous submissions and/or previously published work OK.
Tips: "We are looking for action photos with plenty of border on all sides. In each issue there are shots of offensive and defensive plays, and a limited number of headshots. For the action photos, we look for a good angle on the player's face and evidence of action, like sprays of dirt from a player's shoes or a moving baseball. Often we look at 10-12 photos of the same player before choosing the best shot. Take as many shots of an interesting scene as possible so you have several submissions to compare with others."

BASEBALL CARDS, 700 E. State St., Iola WI 54990. (715)445-2214. FAX: (715)445-4087. Editor: Kit Kiefer. Monthly. Emphasizes sports memorabilia collecting. Readers are 12-45, male collectors. Circ. 310,000. Estab. 1981. Sample copy for 9×12 SAE with 5 first class stamps.
Needs: Uses about 10 photos/issue; all supplied by freelance photographers. Needs photos of baseball players, portrait and action. Model release and captions preferred.
Making Contact & Terms: Send color prints and 35mm and 2¼×2¼ transparencies. SASE. Reports in 2 weeks. Pays $25-50/b&w photo, $50-100/color photo. Pays on publication. Credit line given. Buys first and one-time reprint rights. Previously published work OK.
Tips: Seeing trend toward "more use of photographs. Since introducing a line of baseball cards bound in the publication, our photo needs are now 8-10 an issue." In portfolio or samples, "I'm looking for candid-portrait and action shots of baseball players, shots that capture a player's personality." To break in, "look at the magazine. See what we use. Then go out and shoot that sort of photo. And please don't ask us to credential you until you send us something we can use."

BASKETBALL DIGEST, Dept. PM, 990 Grove St., Evanston IL 60201-4370. (708)491-6440. Editor: Vince Aversano. Monthly. Emphasizes pro-basketball. Circ. 85,000.
Needs: Uses about 40 photos/issue; 100% supplied by freelance photographers. Needs sports action and portraits.
Making Contact & Terms: Provide resume, business card, brochure, flyer or tearsheets to be kept on file for possible future assignments. Uses 5×7 glossy b&w prints and 35mm transparencies. NPI. Pays on publication. Buys one-time rights.

BASSIN', Dept. PM, 15115 S. 76th East Ave., Bixby OK 74008. (918)366-4441. Managing Editor: Gordon Sprouse. Published 8 times/year. Emphasizes bass fishing. Readers are predominantly male, adult; nationwide circulation with heavier concentrations in South and Midwest. Circ. 275,000 subscribers, 100,000 newsstand sales. Sample copy $2.50. Photo guidelines free.
Needs: Uses about 50-75 photos/issue; "almost all of them" are supplied by freelance photographers. "We need both b&w and Kodachrome action shots of freshwater fishing; close-ups of fish with lures, tackle, etc., and scenics featuring lakes, streams and fishing activity." Captions required.
Making Contact & Terms: Query with samples. SASE. Reports in 6 weeks. Pays $250-300/color cover photo; $25/b&w inside photo; $35-150/color inside photo. Pays on publication. Credit line given. Buys first N.A. serial rights.
Tips: "Send lots of photos and give me a specific deadline in which to send them back. Don't send lists—I can't pick a photo from a grocery list. In the past, we used only photos sent in with stories from freelance writers. However, we would like higher quality stuff. I urge freelance photographers to participate."

BC OUTDOORS, 202-1132 Hamilton St., Vancouver, BC V6B 2S2 Canada. (604)687-1581. FAX: (604)687-1925. Editor: George Will. Estab. 1943. Emphasizes fishing, both fresh water and salt; hunting; RV camping; wildlife and management issues. Published 8 times/year (January/February, March, April, May, June, July/August, September/October, November/December). Circ. 42,000. Free sample copy with $2 postage.
Needs: Uses about 30-35 photos/issue; 99% of which are supplied by freelance photographers on assignment. "Fishing (in our territory) is a big need—people in the act of catching, or releasing fish. Hunting, canoeing and camping. Family oriented. By far most photos accompany mss. We are always on lookout for good covers—fishing, wildlife, recreational activities, people in the outdoors—horizontal and square format, primarily of B.C. and Yukon. Photos with mss must, of course, illustrate the story. There should, as far as possible, be something happening. Photos generally dominate lead spread of each story. They are used in everything from double-page bleeds to thumbnails. Column needs

basically supplied inhouse." Model/property release preferred; captions or at least full identification required.
Making Contact & Terms: Send by mail for consideration actual 5×7 or 8×10 b&w prints; 35mm, 2¼×2¼, 4×5 or 8×10 color transparencies; color contact sheet; if color negative, send jumbo prints and negatives only on request; or query with list of stock photo subjects. SASE, Canadian stamps. Reports in 1-2 weeks normally. Pays $40-75/b&w photo; $50-300/color photo; and $150 up/cover photo. "Payment for photos when layout finalized so we know what we're using. We try to give 'photos-only' contributors an approximate publication date at time of acceptance. We reach an arrangement with the contributor in such cases (usually involving dupes)." Credit line given. Buys one-time rights inside; with covers "we retain the right for subsequent promotional use." Simultaneous submissions not acceptable if competitor; previously published work OK.
Tips: "We see a trend toward more environmental/conservation issues."

🍁**BEST WISHES,** Dept. PM, Unit 1, 37 Hanna Ave., Toronto, ON M6K 1X1 Canada. (416)537-2604. Editor: Betty Bradley. Biannual magazine. Emphasizes concerns of expectant women and new families. Readers are mothers and/or new families. Circ. 200,000.
Needs: Needs photos of mothers, babies, expectant woman, young family shots. Written release preferred.
Making Contact & Terms: Send unsolicited photos by mail for consideration. SASE. Reports in 1 month. Pays $200-400/color cover photo. Pays on publication. Credit line given. Buys one-time rights (for covers); all rights (for everything else). Simultaneous submissions and previously published work OK.

BETTER NUTRITION FOR TODAY'S LIVING, Dept. PM, 6255 Barfield Rd., Atlanta GA 30328. (404)256-9800. Contact: Art Director. Monthly magazine. Emphasizes "health food, healthy people." Readers are 30-40. Circ. 470,000. Sample copy free with 9×12 SASE and 2 first-class stamps. Free guideline sheet with SASE.
Needs: Uses 8-10 photos/issue; 6 supplied by freelancers. Needs photos of "healthy people exercising (skiing, running, etc.) food shots, botanical shots." Model release preferred.
Making Contact & Terms: Send unsolicited photos by mail for consideration. Send 35mm transparencies. SASE. Reports in 1 month. Pays $300/color cover photo; $150/color inside photo. Pays on publication. Credit line given. Buys one-time rights. Simultaneous submissions and previously published work OK.
Tips: "We are looking for photos of healthy people (all ages) in outdoor settings, innovative shots of healthy foods and shots of herbs. We work on a limited budget, so do not send submissions if you cannot work within it. Review past issues for photo style."

*****BICYCLING PLUS MT BIKE,** 135 N. 6th St., Emmaus PA 18098. (215)967-5171. Editor and Publisher: James C. McCullagh. Photography Director: Mike Shaw. Publishes 10 monthly issues, 2 bimonthly issues. Circ. 300,000. Emphasizes touring, commuting, health, fitness and nutritional information, recreational riding and technical gearing for the beginning to advanced bicyclist. Credit line given. Pays on publication. Buys one-time rights. Sample copy $2; writer's/photo guidelines free with SASE.
Needs: Buys 10-20 photos/issue. Prefers photos with accompanying ms. Celebrity/personality, documentary, how-to, human interest, photo essay/photo feature, product shot, scenic, special effects and experimental, sport, spot news and travel. Seeks mss on any aspects of bicycling (nonmotorized); commuting, health, fitness and nutritional information, touring or recreational riding. Captions for destination, travel, race photography are required. Captioning on slide mounts is acceptable.
Making Contact & Terms: Send material by mail for consideration or query with resume of credits. SASE a must. Reports in 1 month. Uses b&w negatives; all formats of transparencies; vertical format required for *Mt Bike* cover. Pays $35-70/b&w photo; $75-300/color photo; $300/cover photo. Credit line given. Pays on publication. Buys one-time rights. Pays $25-300/ms.
Tips: "Major bicycling events (those that attract 500 or more) are good possibilities for feature coverage in the magazine. Use some racing photos. The freelance photographer should contact us and show examples of his/her work; then, talk directly to the editor for guidance on a particular shoot. For Mt Bike covers: Shoot vertical. The logo and blurbs run on every cover. These are constant; be aware of their location and what that means while shooting. A large single image that creates a simple cover often works best. Riding: While shooting people riding, be aware of the background. Watch out for wires, shadows, or other major distractions. Make sure people are riding in proper positions; must be

---

🍁 *The maple leaf before a listing indicates that the market is Canadian. The symbol is new this year in* Photographer's Market.

wearing a helmet, dressed properly and on the correct side of the road. Models must be attractive, competent riders. A little color in their clothing helps lift them off the page. We are interested in receiving good, off-road, Mt Biking pictures. Singletrack riding through great landscapes are desirable, however, we do not want to see riders off the trail. Our photos comply with NORBA guidelines for off-road riding. Stay on trails, stay off delicate, living environments."

BILLIARDS DIGEST, Dept. PM, Suite 1430, 200 S. Michigan Ave., Chicago IL 60604. (312)341-1110. FAX: (312)341-1469. Editor: Michael Panozzo. Bimonthly magazine. Circ. 10,000. Emphasizes billiards and pool for tournament players, room owners, tournament operators, dealers, enthusiasts and beginning players, distributors, etc.
Needs: Buys 5-10 photos/issue "unusual, unique photos of billiards players, particularly at major tournaments. Should also stress human emotions, their homelife and outside interests." No stock hunched-over-the-table shots. "We want photos that convey emotion, either actively or passively. Show pool people as human beings." Captions required.
Making Contact & Terms: Send material by mail for consideration. Works with freelance photographers on assignment only basis. Provide resume, tearsheet and samples (photostats of 6 are adequate) to be kept on file for possible future assignments. Uses b&w prints and transparencies. Reports in 2 weeks. SASE. Pays $5-50/b&w photo; $10-50/color and cover photo. Pays on publication. Credit line given. Not copyrighted.

BIRD TALK, P.O. Box 6050, Mission Viejo CA 92690. (714)855-8822. Photo Editor: Kathleen Etchepare. Monthly magazine. Emphasizes "better care of pet birds through informative and entertaining articles. Some birds of interest are: canaries, finches, parrots, parakeets, toucans, macaws, conures, lovebirds, cockatiels, cockatoos, mynahs." Readers are "owners of one pet bird or breeders of many." Sample copy $4.50. Photo guidelines free with SASE.
Needs: Uses 50-75 photos/issue; all by freelance photographers. Needs photos of "any and all pet birds either in portraits or in action—doing anything a bird is able to do." Model release and captions preferred.
Making Contact & Terms: Send 35mm, 5×7, 8×10 b&w prints; 35mm, 2¼×2¼, 4×5, 8×10 transparencies by mail for consideration. SASE. Reports in 4 weeks. Pays inside partial page: $15/b&w photo, $50/color photo; full page: $25/b&w, $75/color; $150/cover and centerfold. Color prints acceptable but will often be used b&w. Pays on publication. Credit line given. Buys one-time rights.
Tips: Prefers to see "sharp feather focus. Cage bars acceptable, cages and perches must be clean. More b&w photos are used per issue than color. Send us clear shots of any pet birds with cover letter specifying *species* of bird. We also need a variety of shots of people interacting with their birds."

BIRD WATCHER'S DIGEST, Dept. PM, Box 110, Marietta OH 45750. (614)373-5285. Managing Editor/ Photography and Art: Bill Thompson III. Bimonthly. Circ. 80,000. Emphasizes birds and bird watchers. Readers are bird watchers/birders (backyard and field, veterans and novices). Digest size. Sample copy $3.50.
Needs: Uses 25-35 photos/issue; all supplied by freelance photographers. Needs photos of North American species. For the most part, photos are purchased with accompanying ms. Model release preferred.
Making Contact & Terms: Query with list of stock photo subjects and samples. SASE. Reports in 2 months. Pays $25 up/color inside. Pays on publication. Credit line given. Buys one-time rights. Previously published work OK.

BLADE MAGAZINE, Dept. PM, P.O. Box 22007, Chattanooga TN 37422. (615)894-0354. FAX: (615)892-7254. Managing Editor: Steve Shackleford. Bimonthly magazine. Specializes in handmade and factory knives. Readers are aged 30-70, blue collar, outdoors types, collectors. Circ. 100,000. Estab. 1973. Sample copy free with 9×12 SASE and $2 postage. Photo guidelines free with SASE.
Needs: Uses 130 photos/issue; freelancer photography/issue—10% assignment and 60% freelance stock. Needs photos of how-tos on knifemaking, knife shots with artsy backgrounds, knives being used, knives on display, etc. Special needs include shots of the latest factory and handmade knives; any kind of colorful knife shot. Model release required; captions required.
Making Contact & Terms: Send unsolicited photos by mail for consideration. Uses 4×5 or 5×7 color prints or 35mm transparencies. SASE. Reports in 1 month. Pays $50 up/b&w or color cover photo; $7/color or b&w inside photo. Pays on acceptance. Credit line given. Buys all rights; will negotiate with photographers unwilling to sell all rights. Also publishes *Edges*, a pocketknife collector's tabloid. Black and white photos only used; read *Blade Magazine* listing for *Edges* information. Also publishes *Blade Trade*, b&w only; same rates and rules apply as for *Blade Magazine*.
Tips: Looks for "a true appreciation for the subtleties of knife design. Closeups of individual knife parts that tell more about the knife than any editorial can are also telling. Appreciation of appropriate props, ability to keep glare off blades (or to keep it on in an artistic manner). Make the shot as animate

as possible, even though knives are inanimate objects. Provide a variety of shots at reasonable prices and in plenty of time for each deadline."

THE BLOOMSBURY REVIEW, Dept. PM, 1028 Bannock St., Denver CO 80204. (303)892-0620. Art Director: Chuck McCoy. Editor: Tom Auer. Published 8 times a year. Circ. 50,000. Emphasizes book reviews, articles and stories of interest to book readers. Sample copy $3.50.
Needs: Uses 2-3 photos/issue; all supplied by freelance photographers. Needs photos of people who are featured in articles. Photos purchased with or without accompanying ms. Model release and captions preferred.
Making Contact & Terms: Provide brochure, tearsheets and sample print to be kept on file for possible future assignments. SASE. Reports in 1 month. NPI. Payment by the job varies. Pays on publication. Credit line and one-line bio given. Buys one-time rights.
Tips: "Send good photocopies of work to Art Director."

BLUE RIDGE COUNTRY, P.O. Box 21535, Roanoke VA 24018. (703)989-6138. Art Director: Rob Agee. Bimonthly magazine. Emphasizes outdoor scenics of Blue Ridge Mountain region. Readers are upscale couples, ages 30-70. Circ. 70,000. Estab. 1988. Sample copy for 9×12 SAE and $1.65. Photo guidelines free with SASE.
Needs: Uses up to 20 photos/issue; 100% supplied by freelance photographers; 10% assignment and 90% freelance stock. Needs photos of travel, scenics and wildlife. Future photo needs include themes of the Blue Ridge region. Model release preferred; photo captions required.
Making Contact & Terms: Query with list of stock photo subjects; send unsolicited photos by mail for consideration. Uses 35mm, 2¼×2¼, 4×5 transparencies. SASE. Reports in 1-2 months. Pays $100/color cover photo; $25-75/b&w photo; $25-100/color photo. Pays on publication. Credit line given. Buys one-time rights.
Tips: In photographer's samples looks for "Photos of Blue Ridge region, color saturated, focus required and photo abilities. Freelance should present him/herself neatly and organized."

THE B'NAI B'RITH INTERNATIONAL JEWISH MONTHLY, 1640 Rhode Island Ave. NW, Washington DC 20036. (202)857-6645. Editor: Jeff Rubin. Monthly magazine. Circ. 200,000. Estab. 1886.
Needs: Emphasizes Jewish religious, cultural and political concerns worldwide. Buys 100 photos annually, stock and on assignment. Occasional photo essays.
Making Contact & Terms: Present samples and text (if available). Buys first serial rights. Pays on publication. Reports in 6 weeks. SASE. Pays $25-300/b&w or color photo (cover); $300/day; $100-500/ photo/text package.
Tips: Be familiar with our format and offer suggestions or experience relevant to our needs. Looks for "technical expertise, ability to tell a story within the frame."

BOAT PENNSYLVANIA, Dept. PM, Box 1673, Harrisburg PA 17105-1673. (717)657-4518. Editor: Art Michaels. Quarterly magazine. Emphasizes "non-angling boating in Pennsylvania: powerboating, canoeing, kayaking, sailing, personal watercraft and water skiing." Published by the Pennsylvania Fish Commission. Sample copy and guidelines free with 9×12 SASE and 4 first-class stamps.
Needs: Uses about 30 photos/issue; 80% supplied by freelance photographers. Model release and complete identifying captions required.
Making Contact & Terms: Query with resume of credits. Send 35mm, 2¼×2¼ transparencies by mail for consideration. SASE. Reports in 1 week on queries; 3 months on submissions. NPI. Pays on acceptance. Credit line given. Buys variable rights, most often first rights.
Tips: "We are hungry for top-quality materials, but no matter how good a picture is, we insist on a few items. We feature subjects appropriate to Pennsylvania, so we can't use pictures with obviously non-Pennsylvania backgrounds. We prefer to show boats registered in Pennsylvania. If this is a problem, try to hide the boat registration completely. Finally, *Boat Pennsylvania* stresses safety, so pictures must show boaters accordingly. For instance, we would not publish a picture of a powerboat under way with people lying on the gunwale or leaning over the side. Submit a selection of cover possibilities. We look for verticals mostly, but we'd love to see horizontals for possible wraparounds."

BODYBOARDING MAGAZINE, Suite C, 950 Calle Amanecer, San Clemente CA 92672. (714)492-7873. Photo Editor: Peter Brouillet. Annual magazine. Emphasizes hardcore bodyboarding action and bodyboarding beach lifestyle photos and personalities. Readers are 15-16 years old, mostly males (96%). Circ. 40,000. Photo guidelines free with SASE.
Needs: Uses roughly 70 photos/issue; 30-50% supplied by freelancers. Needs photos of hardcore bodyboarding action, surf lineups, beach scenics, lifestyles and bodyboarding personalities. Special needs include bodyboarding around the world; foreign bodyboarders in home waves, local beach scenics.

סטיק · טישקאבב · שיואתו

Shaya Mizrachi and his mother Sarah in front of their Brooklyn restaurant. Sarah, an Ashkenazic Jew, met her Sephardic husband in Israel. Photo by David Hoffman.

© David Hoffman

Snapping at the correct moment helped make photographer David Hoffman's photo a fun and salable piece of art. Hoffman, based in San Francisco, California, shot the image during an assignment for the B'Nai B'Rith International Jewish Monthly Magazine. Editor Jeff Rubin says he was attracted by Hoffman's clear style and perseverance which make him ideal as a photojournalist. Hoffman also has "an artistic eye that lifts his work above the merely documentary," says Rubin.

Making Contact & Terms: Send unsolicited photos by mail for consideration. Uses 35mm and 2¼ × 2¼ transparencies; b&w contact sheets & negatives. SASE. Reports in 2 weeks. Pays $500/color cover photo; $40/b&w page rate; $75/color page rate. Pays on publication. Credit line given. Buys one-time rights.

Tips: "We look for clear, sharp, high action bodyboarding photos preferably on Kodachrome 64. We like to see a balance of land and water shots. Be persistent and set high standards."

BOSTON MAGAZINE, Dept. PM, 300 Massachusetts Ave., Boston MA 02115. (617)262-9700. Art Director: Greg Klee. Associate Art Director: Lisa Puccio. Monthly magazine. Emphasizes a wide variety of subjects with Boston/New England focus. Readers are primarily residents of greater Boston metro area, and most of eastern Massachusetts, Cape Cod, southern New England; largely college-educated professionals who regard Boston as focal point of their lives. Circ. 140,000. Sample copy free with 9 × 12 SASE and $2.40 postage.

Needs: Uses about 70 photos/issue; 50 supplied by freelance photographers. Needs portraits, drama-tized, journalistic or documentary, food, design, interiors, sports, fashion, travel, slice-of-life, photo essays. All city (Boston)-oriented. Model release and captions required.

Making Contact & Terms: Query with samples. Submit portfolio for review. Does not return unsolic-ited material. Photographers should follow up for report. Pays $600/color cover photo; $75-300/b&w inside photo; $100-400/color inside photo; $300/b&w page; $400/color page; $800-1,500/text/photo package. Pays on publication. Credit line given. Buys one-time rights.

Tips: Prefers to see "editorial work, preferably portraits in portfolio or samples. Examine the magazine carefully before the interview and edit your portfolio to suit it."

BOSTONIA MAGAZINE, 10 Lenox St., Brookline MA 02146. (617)353-9711. Editor: Keith Botsford. Art Director: Douglas Parker. Estab. 1900. Bimonthly. Circ. 150,000. Sample copy $3.50.

Needs: Uses 100 photos/issue; many photos are supplied by freelance photographers. Works with freelance photographers on assignment only basis. Provide resume, brochure and samples to be kept on file for possible future assignments. Needs include documentary photos and international travel photos; photo essay/photo features and human interest; and possibly art photos presented in long portfolio sections. Also seeks feature articles on people and the New England area accompanied by photos. Model releases and captions required.

Making Contact & Terms: Call for appointment or send photos by mail for consideration; send actual 5 × 7 b&w glossies for inside. SASE. Reports in 2 weeks. Pays on acceptance $50-400 for b&w photo; $300-600/color photo. 10¢/word or flat fee (depending on amount of preparation) for feature articles. Credit line given. Buys all rights, but may reassign to photographer after publication. No simultaneous submissions or previously published work.

BOW & ARROW, Dept. PM, Box HH, Capistrano Beach CA 92624. (714)493-2101. Editor: Jack Lewis. Bimonthly magazine. Circ. 106,000. For archers and bowhunters. "We emphasize bowhunting—with technical pieces, how-tos, techniques, bowhunting tips, personality profiles and equipment tests."

Needs: Photos purchased with accompanying ms; rarely without. "We buy approximately 4 text/photo packages per issue: Technical pieces, personality profiles, humor, tournament coverage, how-to stories, bowhunting stories (with tips), equipment tests and target technique articles. Writer's guide-lines included with photo guidelines. Most cover shots are freelance." Needs photos of animal (for bowhunting stories); celebrity/personality (if the celebrity is involved in archery); head shot (occasion-ally used with personality profiles, but we prefer a full-length shot with the person shooting the bow, etc.); how-to (must be step-by-step); human interest; humorous; nature, travel and wildlife (related to bowhunting); photo essay/photo feature; product shot (with equipment tests); scenic (only if related to a story); sport (of tournaments); and sport news. "No snapshots (particularly color snapshots), and no photos of animals that were not hunted by the rules of fair chase. We occasionally use photos for Bow Pourri, which is a roundup of archery-related events, humor, laws and happenings." Captions required.

Making Contact & Terms: Query with samples OK, but prefers to see completed material by mail on speculation. Uses 5 × 7 or 8 × 10 glossy b&w prints. Also uses 35mm or 2¼ × 2¼ transparencies. SASE. Reports in 2-3 weeks. Pays $50-300 for text/photo package or on a per-photo basis for photos without accompanying ms. Pays on acceptance. Credit line given. Buys first rights.

Tips: "We rarely buy photos without an accompanying manuscript, so send us a good, clean manuscript with good-quality b&w glossies (our use of color is limited)."

✦BOWBENDER, Suite 200, 807 Manning Rd. NE, Calgary, AB T2E 7M8 Canada. (403)335-9445. FAX: (403)569-9590. Editor: Mrs. Kathleen Windsor. Five times/year. Emphasizes archery in Canada, especially bowhunting. Readership consists of married, professional males, 25-40 years of age with $20-40,000 annual income. Circ. 45,000. Estab. 1984. Sample copy for $2.50 and 9 × 12 SAE. Photo

guidelines free with SASE; postage from U.S. must be submitted through Canadian mail order; postage from Canada, 39¢ stamp.
Needs: Uses 30 photos/issue; 100% supplied by freelance photographers; 99% comes from freelance stock and rest freelance photography from assignment. Uses big game animal shots only. Written release and captions preferred.
Making Contact & Terms: Query with list of stock photos or send unsolicited photos by mail for consideration. Send color and b&w, all sizes, all formats. SASE. Reports in 3 weeks maximum. Pays $200/color cover photo; $60/color inside photo; $30/b&w inside photo; 8-10¢ word/photo/text package (Canadian currency). Pays on publication. Credit line given. Buys first N.A. serial rights. Does not consider simultaneous submissions or previously published work.
Tips: Looking for shots of "any huntable big game for front cover: vertical shots clear, especially eyes. Close-up shots are best. Trend is mostly b&w inside shots. Submit samples first along with stock file. Label slides somehow. If photos are not catalogued by some code, at least label them. Slides especially are irreplaceable. We use as many photos as we can each issue. Look at a past issue before submitting."

BOWHUNTER, 6405 Flank Dr., P.O. Box 8200, Harrisburg PA 17105. (717)657-9555. Editor/Publisher: M.R. James. Editorial Director: Dave Canfield. Estab. 1971. Published 8 times/year. Circ. 250,000. Emphasizes bow and arrow hunting. Sample copy $2.
Needs: Buys 50-75 photos/year. Scenic (showing bowhunting) and wildlife (big and small game of North America). No cute animal shots or poses."We want informative, entertaining bowhunting adventure, how-to and where-to-go articles." Writer's guidelines free with SASE.
Making Contact & Terms: Send material by mail for consideration or query with samples. SASE. Reports on queries in 1-2 weeks; on material in 4-6 weeks. Photos purchased with or without accompanying ms. Uses 5×7 or 8×10 glossy b&w and color prints; both vertical and horizontal format; 35mm and 2¼×2¼ transparencies; vertical format; vertical format preferred for cover. Pays $35-100/b&w photo; $50-250/color photo; $300/cover photo, "more if photo warrants it"; occasionally more. Pays on acceptance. Credit line given. Pays on acceptance. Buys one-time publication rights.
Tips: "Know bowhunting and/or wildlife and study several copies of our magazine before submitting any material. We're looking for better quality and we're using more color on inside pages. Most purchased photos are of big game animals. Hunting scenes are second. In b&w we look for sharp, realistic light, good contrast. Color must be sharp; early, late light is best. We avoid anything that looks staged; we want natural settings, quality animals. Send only your best, and if at all possible let us hold those we indicate interest in. Very little is taken on assignment; most comes from our files or is part of the manuscript package. If your work is in our files it will probably be used."

BOWHUNTING WORLD, Dept. PM, Suite 101, 319 Barry Ave. South, Wayzata MN 55391. (612)476-2200. Editor: Tim Dehn. Published 11 times/year. *"Bowhunting World* is the oldest and most respected magazine in print for the hunting archer." It focuses editorially on all aspects of hunting with a bow and arrow in North America. Readers are primarily male, college-educated, avid bowhunters who participate in their sport year-round and who make an above-average income. Circ. 250,000. Estab. 1952. Free sample copy and photo guidelines.
Needs: Uses 10-25 photos/issue; most from freelancer stock. "We want to see wildlife subjects commonly hunted as big game and small game species in North America." Special needs include "big game species for cover selections."
Making Contact & Terms: Send 35mm by mail for consideration. SASE. Reports in 2-4 weeks. Pays $250/color cover photo; $40/b&w inside photo; $75-125 color/inside photo; and $200-500/text/photo package. Pays on publication. Credit line given. Buys one-time rights. Simultaneous submissions and previously published work OK "but please so state in cover letter."
Tips: "We look for technically excellent photos with trophy-class animals and/or unusual and beautiful settings. We're using more color than ever before, far less freelance b&w. And our covers are no longer limited to deer—we're using elk, bear and are open to moose, caribou and antelope as well. Send small, carefully screened submissions—not more than 60 slides. 20 excellent ones will get a far better reception than 20 excellent mixed with 40 average. Be prepared for us to hold your slides on file up to a year, and if there's a limit to the number we should hold, say so."

BOWLERS JOURNAL, Dept. PM, 200 S. Michigan Ave., Chicago IL 60604. (312)341-1110. Editor: Mort Luby. Managing Editor: Jim Dressel. Monthly magazine. Circ. 22,000. Emphasizes bowling. For people interested in bowling: tournament players, professionals, dealers, etc.
Needs: Needs "unusual, unique photos of bowlers." Buys 20-30 annually.
Making Contact & Terms: Pays $5-50/b&w photo; $10-75/color photo. Pays on publication. Not copyrighted. Send contact sheet or photos for consideration; captions required. Reports in 3 weeks. SASE. Simultaneous submissions OK.
Tips: "Bowling is one of the most challenging areas for photography, so try it at your own risk ... poor lighting, action, etc."

*BOWLING DIGEST, 990 Grove St., Evanston IL 60201-4370. (708)491-6440. Editor: Vince Aversano. Bimonthly. Emphasizes pro and amateur bowling. Circ: 150,000.
Needs: Uses 50 photos/issue; 100% provided by freelance photographers. Needs sports action and portraits.
Making Contact & Terms: Provide resume, business card, brochure, flyer or tearsheets to be kept on file for possible future assignments. NPI. Pays on publication. Buys one-time rights.

*BRIDE'S & YOUR NEW HOME, Condé Nast Publications. 350 Madison Ave., New York NY 10017. (212)880-8829. FAX: (212)880-8331. Assistant to the Art Director: Ashley Thompson. Bimonthly magazine. Emphasizes weddings, marriage, honeymoon and setting up "your new home." Readers are engaged couples and their families reading for marriage advice and ideas at any age. Circ. 350,000-400,000. Estab. 1934. Sample copy free with SASE.
Needs: Uses photos of fashion, beauty, home interiors and stills, lifestyle, travel and scenics. Reviews photos with or without a ms. Model/property release required.
Making Contact & Terms: Contact through rep. Submit portfolio for review. Query with stock photo list. Provide resume, business card, brochure, flyer or tearsheets to be kept on file for possible assignments. Keeps samples on file. Reporting time depends on work and prospect of job. Pays $1,500/color cover photo; $250/color page rate; $200/b&w page rate; $200 & up/day. Pays day rate upon completion and page rate upon publication. Credit line given. Buys one-time rights and all rights (travel only); negotiable.
Tips: "Don't send us only examples of bridal fashion."

BRIGADE LEADER, P.O. Box 150, Wheaton IL 60189. (708)665-0630. FAX: (708)665-0372. Associate Editor: Deborah Christensen. Art Director: Robert Fine. Quarterly magazine. Circ. 9,000. Estab. 1959. For Christian men, age 20 and up. Seeks "to make men aware of their leadership responsibilities toward boys in their families, churches and communities." Sample copy $1.50 with 9×12 SASE and 98¢ postage. Photo guidelines free with SASE.
Needs: Buys 2-7 photos/issue; 50% freelance photography/issue comes from assignment and 50% from freelance stock. Needs photos of men in varied situations (alone, with their sons, with groups of boys or with one boy, with their families or at work), head shot, photo essay/photo feature and scenic.
Making Contact & Terms: Interested in receiving work from newer, lesser-known photographers. Arrange a personal interview to show portfolio or send photos for consideration. Reports in 6 weeks. Pays $35/inside b&w photo; $75-100/b&w cover photo. Pays on publication. Buys first and second serial rights. Simultaneous submissions and previously published work OK. Send 8×10 glossy prints.
Tips: "Do not send pornography or nudes. Study the magazine before submitting. Submit sharp and clear photos. We receive too much second-rate work."

BRITISH CAR, Dept. PM, P.O. Box 9099, Canoga Park CA 91309. (818)710-1234. FAX: (818)710-1877. Editor: Dave Destler. Bimonthly magazine. Publication for owners and enthusiasts of British motor cars. Readers are U.S. citizens, male, 40 years old and owners of multiple cars. Circ. 30,000. Estab. 1985. Sample copy $3.50. Photo guidelines free for SASE.
Needs: Uses 100 photos/issue; 50-75% (75% are b&w) supplied by freelancers. "Photos with accompanied manuscripts preferred. However, sharp uncluttered photos of different British marques may be submitted for file photos to be drawn on as needed." Photo captions required that include description of vehicles, owner's name and phone number, interesting facts, etc.
Making Contact & Terms: Send unsolicited photos by mail for consideration. Send 5×7 and larger, b&w prints. Does not keep samples on file unless there is a good chance of publication. SASE. "Publisher takes all reasonable precautions with materials, however cannot be held liable for damaged or lost photos." Reports in 6-8 weeks. Pays $25-100/color inside photo; $10-35/b&w inside photo. Payment negotiable, however standard rates will be paid unless otherwise agreed in writing prior to publication." Pays on publication. Buys world rights; negotiable.
Tips: "Find a journalist to work in cooperation with. Good photos submitted with a manuscript have a better chance of publication."

BRITISH HERITAGE, Cowles Magazines, Inc., P.O. Box 8200, Harrisburg PA 17105. (717)657-9555. FAX: (717)657-9552. Editor: Mrs. Gail Huganir. Bimonthly magazine. Emphasizes British history and travel. Readers are professional, middle-aged. Circ. 110,000. Estab. 1974. Sample copy $4.85, photographic guidelines available with SASE.
Needs: Uses about 50 photos/issue; 95% supplied by freelance photographers; 99% freelance stock and 1% assignment. Needs travel, scenic and historical photos. Captions required.
Making Contact & Terms: Provide resume, business card, brochure, flyer or tearsheets to be kept on file for possible future assignments. SASE. Reports in 4-6 weeks. Negotiates pay for cover photos. Pays $50-100/b&w inside photo; $75-250/color inside photo. Pays on publication. Credit line given. Buys one-time rights.

Tips: Looks for "Good focal point, bright colors and sharp image. We prefer 2″ × 2″ or 2½″ square color transparencies. Call before submitting and for photographic guidelines."

*BUSINESS IN BROWARD, P.O. Box 7375, Ft. Lauderdale FL 33338-7375. (305)563-8805. Publisher: Sherry Friedlander. Bi-monthly magazine. Emphasizes business. Readers are male and female executives, ages 30-65. Circ. 20,000. Estab. 1986. Sample copy $4.
Needs: Uses 30-40 photos/issue; 75% supplied by freelancers. Needs photos of local sports, local people, ports, activities and festivals. Model/property release required. Photo captions required.
Making Contact & Terms: Contact through rep. Submit portfolio for review. Reports in 1-2 weeks. Pays $150/color cover photo; pays $75/color inside photo. Pays on publication. Buys one-time rights; negotiable. Previously published work OK.
Tips: "Know the area we service." Also publishes *Business in Palm Beach County.*

*BUXOM, 10th Floor, 801 Second Ave., New York NY 11217. (212)661-7878. FAX: (212)692-9297. Editor: Marc Medoff. Quarterly magazine. Emphasis on large-breasted women. Readers are young males, blue collar workers, over 18 years old. Circ. 81,000. Estab. 1989. Sample copies free with 8½ × 11 SASE and 10 first class stamps. Photo guidelines free with SASE.
Needs: Uses 100-200 photos/issue; 100% supplied by freelancers. Needs photos of nude women with large breasts. Reviews photos with or without accompanying ms. Model/property release required, include copies of photo identification with date of birth over 18 years old.
Making Contact & Terms: Submit portfolio for review. Send unsolicited photos by mail for consideration. Provide resume, business card, brochure, flyer or tearsheets to be kept on file for possible future assignments. Send 35mm transparencies. Keeps samples on file. SASE. Reports in 1 month. Payment varies from $10/shot to $3,000/full set. Pays on acceptance. Credit line given. Buys one-time rights; negotiable. Simultaneous submissions and previously published work OK.
Tips: "We require technical perfection. Focus, lighting, composition, etc. must be 100% perfect. Look at our magazine and competing titles."

BUZZWORM: The Environmental Journal, Suite 206, 2305 Canyon Blvd., Boulder CO 80302. (303)442-1969. Photo Editor: Ann Carey. Bimonthly magazine. Emphasizes environmental issues and worldwide conservation. Readers are affluent, educated, active, both sexes and a median age of 37. Circ. 100,000. Estab. 1988. Sample copy $5. Photo guidelines free with SASE.
Needs: Uses 50 photos/issue. Most are supplied by freelance photographers. Photo needs are specific to articles in issue, mostly wildlife and environment. Model release and photo captions information preferred.
Making Contact & Terms: Query with resume of credits and list of stock photo subjects. Provide resume, business card, brochure, flyer or tearsheets to be kept on file. No unsolicited calls or photos. SASE. Reports in 1 month. Pays $400/color cover photo; $200/color page rate. Pays 60-90 days after publication. Credit line given. Buys one-time rights.
Tips: Wants to see photographer's tearsheets, stock lists, resume, specialties and future travel plans. "Send information requested and update us by mail as to your most recent photography, travels, etc."

CALIFORNIA ANGLER, Dept. PM, 1921 E. Carnegie St. N., Santa Ana CA 92705. (714)261-9779. Editor: Tim Matthews. Monthly magazine. Emphasizes fresh and saltwater fishing in California and travel destinations. Readers are dedicated California sport fishermen. Circ. 30,000. Sample copy free.
Needs: Uses 40-50 photos/issue; all supplied by freelance photographers. Needs shots depicting angling action rather than dead fish, and pictures illustrating angling how-to, technical skills. Special needs include underwater pictures of game fish, especially saltwater species. Model release preferred; captions required.
Making Contact & Terms: Query with samples. Send 35mm or 2¼ × 2¼ transparencies by mail for consideration. SASE. Reports in 2 weeks. Pays $300/color cover photo; $25/b&w inside photo; $25-100/color inside photo; $300 for text/photo package. Pays on publication. Credit line given. Buys one-time rights or first N.A. serial rights. Simultaneous submissions and previously published work sometimes OK.
Tips: Looks for "someone who has good action, scenic, supplemental, and people photos of fishing. Send samples. We get so little honestly good material, we hug the good stuff."

The First Markets Index preceding the General Index in the back of this book provides the names of those companies/publications interested in receiving work from newer, lesser-known photographers.

*CALLIOPE, World History for Young People, 7 School St., Peterborough NH 03458. (603)924-7209. FAX: (603)924-7380. Picture Editor: Francelle Carapetyan. Magazine published 5 times/year. Emphasis on Non-United States history. Readers are children, ages 8-14. Circ. 7,000. Estab. 1990. Sample copies $3.95 with 7½×10½ or larger SASE and 5 first-class stamps. Photo guidelines free with SASE.

Needs: Uses 40-45 photos/issue; 15% supplied by freelancers. Needs contemporary shots of historical locations, buildings, artifacts, historical reenactments and costumes. Reviews photos with or without accompanying ms. Model/property release preferred. Captions preferred.

Making Contact & Terms: Query with stock photo list. Send unsolicited photos by mail for consideration. Provide resume, business card, brochure, flyer or tearsheets to be kept on file for possible future assignments. Send b&w or color prints; 35mm transparencies. Samples kept on file. SASE. Reports in 3 weeks. Pays on individual basis/color cover photo; $15-50/b&w inside photo. Pays on publication. Credit line given. Buys one-time rights; negotiable. Simultaneous submissions and previously published work OK.

Tips: "Given our young audience we like to have pictures which include people, both young and old. Pictures must be dynamic to make history appealing. Submissions must relate to themes in each issue."

✗ **CAMERA & DARKROOM,** (formerly *Darkroom Photography Magazine*), Suite 300, 9171 Wilshire Blvd., Beverly Hills CA 90210. (310)858-7155. Editor-in-Chief: Ana Jones. Executive Editor: Dave Howard. Monthly publication. Circ. 80,000. Emphasizes darkroom-related and general photographic subjects.

Needs: Any subject if photography related. Model release preferred; captions required.

Making Contact & Terms: Query with samples. SASE. Send 8×10 or 11×14 glossy b&w prints and 35mm, 2¼×2¼, 4×5 or 8×10 color transparencies or 8×10 glossy color prints. Don't submit mounted prints. Uses color covers; vertical format required. Reports in 1 month-6 weeks. Free editorial guide. Pays $75-750/text/photo package, $30-75/b&w photo; $50 minimum/color photo and $200-350/cover; $500-750/portfolio. Credit line given. Pays on publication. Buys one-time rights.

CAMPUS LIFE, 465 Gundersen Dr., Carol Stream IL 60188. (708)260-6200. FAX: (708)260-0114. Editor: Jim Long. Photo Coordinator: Doug Johnson. Estab. 1944. Monthly magazine except May/June and July/August. Circ. 130,000. "*Campus Life* is a magazine for high school and college-age youth. We emphasize balanced living—emotionally, spiritually, physically and mentally." Sample copy $2; photo guidelines for SASE.

Needs: Buys 15 photos/issue. Head shots (of teenagers in a variety of moods); humorous, sport and candid shots of teenagers/college students in a variety of settings. "We want to see multiracial teenagers in different situations, and in every imaginable mood and expression, at work, play, home and school. No travel, how-to, still life, travel scenics, news or product shots. We stay away from anything that looks posed. Shoot for a target audience of 18-year-olds." Model release required. Uses 8×10 glossy b&w prints and 35mm or larger transparencies. SASE. Simultaneous submissions and previously published work OK. Reports in 4-6 weeks.

Making Contact & Terms: Photos purchased with or without accompanying ms. Credit line given. Pay rates start at $70/b&w photo; $125/color photo. Pays on publication. Buys one-time rights.

Tips: "We choose photos that express the contemporary teen experience. We look for unusual lighting and color. Our guiding philosophy: that readers will 'see themselves' in the pages of our magazine." Looks for ability to catch teenagers in real-life situations that are well-composed but not posed. Technical quality; communication of an overall mood or emotion or action. "Look at a few issues to get a feel for what we choose. We're not interested in posed shots."

♣**CANADIAN BIKER MAGAZINE,** P.O. Box 4122, Station A, Victoria BC V8X 3X4 Canada. (604)384-0333. Editor: Len Creed. Monthly magazine, published 8 times/year. Emphasizes motorcycle riding, off-road, street, touring and toys for tots. Readers are motorcycle enthusiasts of all ages. Circ. 15,000. Estab. 1980. "Canada's largest motorcycle editorial publication." Sample copy free with 9×12 SASE. Photo guidelines free with SASE.

Needs: Uses 55 photos/issue; 90% supplied by freelance photographers. Needs photos of motorcycles; people involved in related activities. Model release and photo captions required.

Making Contact & Terms: Query with list of stock photo subjects or send unsolicited photos by mail for consideration. Send b&w or color, any size, format or finish. SASE. Reports "according to situation." Pays $30-50/cover photo ($40 is standard). Pays on publication. Credit line given.

Tips: "Most photographs published in the magazine should be accompanied by articles. The most helpful contributors to the magazine are photo-journalists (with good writing ability as well)."

CANOE, Dept. PM, P.O. Box 3146, Kirkland WA 98083. (206)827-6363. Editor: Les Johnson. Bimonthly magazine. Circ. 63,000+. Emphasizes a variety of paddle sports as well as how-to material and articles about equipment. For upscale canoe and kayak enthusiasts at all levels of ability. Also publishes special projects/posters. Simultaneous submissions and previously published work OK, in

noncompeting publications. Reports in 1 month. Free sample copy with 9 × 12 SASE and postage only.
Needs: Photos only occasionally purchased without accompanying mss. Uses 30 photos/issue: 90% supplied by freelancers. Canoeing, kayaking, ocean touring, canoe sailing, fishing when compatible to the main activity, canoe camping but not rafting. No photos showing disregard for the environment, be it river or land; no photos showing gasoline-powered, multi hp engines; no photos showing unskilled persons taking extraordinary risks to life, etc. Model release required "when potential for litigation." Captions are required, unless impractical. Accompanying mss for "Editorial coverage strives for balanced representation of all interests in today's paddling activity. Those interests include paddling adventures, both close to home and far away; camping; fishing; flatwater; whitewater; ocean kayaking; poling; sailing; outdoor photography; how-to projects; instruction and historical perspective. Regular columns feature paddling techniques, conservation topics, safety, interviews, equipment reviews, book/movie reviews, new products and letters from readers."
Making Contact & Terms Query or send material. "Let me know those areas in which you have particularly strong expertise and/or photofile material. Send best samples only and make sure they relate to the magazine's emphasis and/or focus. (If you don't know what that is, pick up a recent issue first, before sending me unusable material.) We will review dupes for consideration only. Originals required for publication. Also, if you have something in the works or extraordinary photo subject matter of interest to our audience, let me know! It would be helpful to me if those with substantial reserves would supply indexes by subject matter." SASE. Uses 5 × 7 and 8 × 10 glossy b&w prints; 35mm, 2¼ × 2¼ and 4 × 5 transparencies; for cover uses color transparencies; vertical format preferred. Pays $250/cover color photo; $150/full page b&w or color photos: $100/half to full page photos; $75/quarter to half page photos; $50/quarter or less. NPI for accompanying ms. Credit line given. Pays on publication. Buys one-time rights, first serial rights and exclusive rights.
Tips: "We have a highly specialized subject and readers don't want just any photo of the activity. We're particularly interested in photos showing paddlers' *faces*; the faces of people having a good time. We're after anything that highlights the paddling activity as a lifestyle and the urge to be outdoors." All photos should be "as natural as possible with authentic subjects. We receive a lot of submissions from photographers to whom canoeing and kayaking are quite novel activities. These photos are often clichéd and uninteresting. So consider the quality of your work carefully before submission if you are not familiar with the sport. We are always in search of fresh ways of looking at our sport."

THE CAPE ROCK, Southeast Missouri State University, Cape Girardeau MO 63701. (314)651-2156. Editor-in-Chief: Harvey Hecht. Emphasizes poetry and poets for libraries and interested persons. Semiannual. Circ. 1,000. Free photo guidelines.
Needs: Uses about 13 photos/issue; all supplied by freelance photographers. "We like to feature a single photographer each issue. Submit 25-30 thematically organized b&w glossies (at least 5 × 7), or send 5 pictures with plan for complete issue. We favor most a series that conveys a sense of place. Seasons are a consideration too: we have spring and fall issues. Photos must have a sense of place: e.g., an issue featuring Chicago might show buildings or other landmarks, people of the city (no nudes), travel or scenic. No how-to or products. Sample issues and guidelines provide all information a photographer needs to decide whether to submit to us." Model release not required "but photographer is liable"; captions not required "but photographer should indicate where series was shot."
Making Contact & Terms: Send by mail for consideration actual b&w photos, query with list of stock photo subjects, or submit portfolio by mail for review. SASE. Reporting time varies. Pays $100 and 10 copies on publication. Credit line given. Buys "all rights, but will release rights to photographer on request." No simultaneous submissions or previously published work.
Tips: "We don't make assignments, but we look for a unified package put together by the photographer. We may request additional or alternative photos when accepting a package."

CAR COLLECTOR & CAR CLASSICS, P.O. Box 28571, Atlanta GA 30328. (404)998-4603. Editor: Westley D. Peterson. Monthly. Emphasizes collector automobiles. Readers are 98% male, average age 41. Circ. 54,000. Estab. 1977. Sample copy $2 postpaid. Photo and writers guidelines free with SASE.
Needs: Uses about 50-75 photos/issue; "nearly all" supplied by freelance photographers; 30% of photos on assignment per issue. Needs photos of "automobiles of the 1925-1965 era." Photos purchased with accompanying manuscript only. Model release and captions required.
Making Contact & Terms: Telephone first; send b&w prints; 35mm, 2¼ × 2¼, 4 × 5 and/or 8 × 10 transparencies by mail for consideration. SASE. Reports ASAP, but no schedule. Pays $5/b&w inside photo; $10/color inside photo; $50-400/text/photo package. Pays on publication. Credit line always given. Buys all rights, but will negotiate with photographer.
Tips: "Do not submit photos to us without accompanying story and captions. Get connected with a writer so that a complete package can be offered. We are looking for cars shot from pleasing angles with good backgrounds. No 'fish-eye' or other 'trick lens' photos purchased."

Photographer Timothy Bernsau, of Los Angeles, California, says he wanted to capture the motion and excitement of funny-car driver John Force in action at the Pomona Raceway in Pomona, California. The sharpness of the car coupled with the smoke rising from the tires made this an appealing photograph for **Car Craft Magazine.** *The magazine paid Bernsau, $250 for a photo-text package.*

CAR CRAFT MAGAZINE, 8490 Sunset Blvd., Los Angeles CA 90069. (310)854-2250. FAX: (310)854-2263. Editor: John Baechtel. Monthly magazine. Emphasizes street machines, muscle cars and modern, high-tech performance cars. Readership is mostly males ages 18-34. Circ. 500,000. Estab. 1953. Sample copy free with SASE. Model release required.

Needs: Uses 100+ photos/issue. Uses freelancers occasionally; all on assignment. Model release required.

Making Contact & Terms: Interested in receiving work from newer, lesser-known photographers. Query with resume of credits. Provide resume, business card, brochure, flyer or tearsheets to be kept on file for possible assignments. Send 35mm and 8×10 b&w prints; 35mm and 2¼×2¼ transparencies by mail for consideration. SASE. Reports in 1 month. Pays $35-75/b&w photo; $75-250/color photo, cover or text; $60 minimum/hour; $250 minimum/day; $500 minimum/job. Payment for b&w varies according to subject and needs. Pays on publication. Credit line given. Buys all rights. Model/property release required; photo captions preferred.

Tips: "We use primarily b&w shots. When we need something special in color or see an interesting color shot, we'll pay more for that. Review a current issue for our style and taste."

CAREER FOCUS, Dept. PM, 250 Mark Twain Tower, 106 W. 11th St., Kansas City MO 64105. (816)221-4404. FAX: (816)221-1112. Assistant Editor: Molly Christiansen. Bimonthly magazine. Emphasizes career development. Readers are male and female professionals, ages 18-35 (black and Hispanic). Circ. 250,000. Estab. 1985. Sample copy free with 9×12 SASE and 4 first class stamps. Photo guidelines free with SASE.

Needs: Uses approximately 10-20 photos/issue. Needs technology photos and shots of personalities. Model release preferred. Photo captions that include name, date, place, why required.

Making Contact & Terms: Query with resume of credits and list of stock photo subjects. Keeps samples on file. SASE. Reports in 3 weeks. Pays $25/color cover photo; $20/b&w cover photo. Pays on publication. Credit line given. Buys one-time rights. Simultaneous submissions and previously published work OK.

Tips: "Freelancer must be familiar with our magazine to be able to submit appropriate manuscripts and photos."

CAREER WOMAN, Equal Opportunity Publications, Inc., 44 Broadway, Greenlawn NY 11740. (516)261-8917. FAX: (516)261-8935. Editor: Eileen Nester. Estab. 1972. Published 3 times a year. Emphasizes career guidance and career opportunities for women at the college and professional level. Readers are college-age and entry-level professional women. Circ. 10,500. Sample copy free with 9×12 SAE and 5 first-class stamps.
Needs: Uses at least one photo per issue (cover); planning to use freelance work for covers and possibly editorial; many photos come from freelance writers who submit photos with their articles. Contact for needs. Model release preferred. Photo captions required; include person's name and title.
Making Contact & Terms: Interested in receiving work from newer, lesser-known photographers. Query with list of stock photo subjects; send unsolicited prints or 35mm transparencies by mail for consideration. SASE. Reports in 2 weeks. Pays $15/color and b&w photo; $100/cover shot. Pays on publication. Credit line given. Buys one-time rights. Simultaneous submissions and previously published work OK, "but not in competitive career-guidance publications."
Tips: "We are looking for clear color slides of women in a variety of professions and work environments. We are looking primarily for women (ages 25-35) who represent role models for our readers. They should be dressed and groomed in a professional manner. We've decided to use more cover photos than we have in the past. We are also open to using inside photos, but freelancers should contact us and discuss upcoming stories before sending photos. Read our magazine to get an idea of the editorial content. Contact us with ideas for cover shots. Cover photos do not have to tie in to any particular story in the magazine, but they have to be representative of the magazine's editorial content as a whole."

CAREERS & THE DISABLED, EQUAL OPPORTUNITY PUBLICATIONS, INC., Dept. PM, Suite 420, 150 Motor Parkway, Hauppauge NY 11788-5145. (516)273-0066. Art Director: Jamie Stroud. Magazine published three times a year. Emphasizes career guidance for people with disabilities at the college and professional levels. Readers are disabled college students and young working professionals of all occupations that require a college degree. Circ. 10,000. Sample copy free with 9×12 SASE and 6 first-class stamps.
Needs: Uses at least one photo per issue (cover); planning to use freelance work for covers and possibly editorial. Contact for needs. Model release preferred; photo captions required.
Making Contact & Terms: Query with list of stock photo subjects. Send unsolicited prints or 35mm transparencies by mail for consideration. SASE. Reports in 2 weeks. Pays $25/color cover photo. Pays on publication. Credit line given. Buys one-time rights. Simultaneous submissions and previously published work OK, "but not in competitive career-guidance publications."
Tips: "We are looking for clear color shots of disabled students and young professionals who are involved in activities related to their academic studies or professions. We've decided to use more cover photos than we have in the past. We are also open to using inside photos, but freelancers should contact us and discuss upcoming stories before sending photos. Read our magazine to get an idea of editorial content. Cover photos do not have to tie in with any particular story in the issue, but they have to be representative of magazine's editorial content as a whole."

CARIBBEAN SPORTS & TRAVEL, (formerly *Pleasure Boating*), 1995 NE 150th St., North Miami FL 33181. (305)945-7403. FAX: (305)947-6410. Associate Publisher Packages: Vic Hanna Guantally. Circ. 30,000. Estab. 1971. Emphasizes fishing, diving, golf, in the Bahamas and the Caribbean. Readers are "recreational boaters interested in these areas, regardless of where they live." Sample copy $2.50 and $1 for mailing and handling.
Needs: Uses about 35-40 photos/issue; most freelance photography comes from assignment. Needs photos of "people in, on, around boats and water." Model release and captions preferred.
Making Contact & Terms: Query with samples. Provide brochure to be kept on file for possible future assignments. SASE. Reports in 4 weeks. Pays $15-75/b&w photo; $25-200/color photo; $100-300/color photo/feature illustrations; $250-375/day and per photo/text package. Pays 30 days after publication. Credit line given. Buys one-time rights and full rights. Simultaneous submissions OK.
Tips: Prefers 35mm slides, good quality. Prefers verticals, strong colors; people involved in water and/or boating activity. Interested in boating related and watersports related that have composition originality, etc. "Contact editorial department on telephone regarding photos available. Submit in envelope with stiffener for protection. Most freelance photography comes from assignment. Include SASE."

CARIBBEAN TRAVEL AND LIFE MAGAZINE, 8403 Colesville Rd., Silver Spring MD 20910. (301)588-2300. FAX: (301)588-2256. Editorial Assistant: Stacy Small. Published 6 times a year. Emphasizes travel, culture and recreation in islands of Caribbean, Bahamas and Bermuda. Circ. 100,000. Estab. 1985. Sample copy free with 9×12 SAE with $1.30 postage. Photo guidelines free with SASE.

Needs: Uses about 87 photos/issue; 75% supplied by freelance photographers: 10% assignment and 90% freelance stock. "We combine scenics with people shots. Where applicable, we show interiors, food shots, resorts, water sports, cultural events, shopping and wildlife/underwater shots." Special needs include "cover shots—attractive people on beach; striking images of the region, etc." Captions required. "Provide thorough caption information. Don't submit stock that is mediocre."

Making Contact & Terms: Arrange a personal interview to show portfolio; query with samples and list of stock photo subjects. Provide stock list, business card, brochure, flyer or tearsheets to be kept on file for possible future assignments. Uses 4-color photography. SASE. Reports in 2 weeks. Pays $400/color cover photo; $150/color full page; $125/color ¾ page; $100/color ½ page and $75/color ¼ page; $75-400/color photo; $1,200-1,500 per photo/text package. Pays 30 days after publication. Buys one-time rights. Does not pay research or holding fees.

Tips: Seeing trend toward "fewer but larger photos with more impact and drama. We are looking for particularly strong images of color and style, beautiful island scenics and people shots—images that are powerful enough to make the reader want to travel to the region; photos that show people doing things in the destinations we cover; originality in approach, composition, subject matter. Good composition, lighting and creative flair. Images that are evocative of a place, creating story mood. Good use of people. Submit stock photography for specific story needs, if good enough can lead to possible assignments. Let us know exactly what coverage you have on a stock list so we can contact you when certain photo needs arise."

CAROLINA QUARTERLY, Greenlaw Hall, CB#3520, University of North Carolina, Chapel Hill NC 27599-3520. (919)962-0244. Editor: Will Phillips. Circ. 1,200. Estab. 1948. Emphasizes "current poetry, short fiction." Readers are "literary, artistic—primarily, though not exclusively, writers and serious readers." Sample copy $5.

Needs: Uses 1-8 photos/issue; all supplied by freelance photographers from stock. "No set subject matter. Artistic outdoor as well as interior scenes. Attention to form. No photojournalism, please." Model release and captions preferred.

Making Contact & Terms: Interested in receiving work from newer, lesser-known photographers. Send b&w prints by mail for consideration. SASE. Reports in 1-3 months, depending on deadline. Pays $25/photo. Pays on publication. Credit line given. Buys one-time rights.

Tips: Prefers to see "high-quality artistic photography. Attention to form, design. Look at a few high-quality small literary magazines that use photos. Subject matter is up for grabs."

CAT FANCY, Fancy Publications, Inc., P.O. Box 6050, Mission Viejo CA 92690. (714)855-8822. Editor-in-Chief: K.E. Segnar. Readers are "men and women of all ages interested in all phases of cat ownership." Monthly. Circ. 332,000. Estab. 1965. Sample copy $4.50; photo guidelines for SASE.

Needs: Uses 20-30 photos/issue; 100% freelance supplied. "For purebred photos, we prefer shots that show the various physical and mental attributes of the breed. Include both environmental and portrait-type photographs. We also need good-quality, interesting b&w and color photos of mixed-breed cats for use with feature articles and departments." Model release required.

Making Contact & Terms: Send by mail for consideration actual 8×10 b&w photos, 35mm or 2¼×2¼ color transparencies. No duplicates. SASE. Reports in 6 weeks. Pays $15-25/b&w photo; $50-250/color photo; and $50-450 for text/photo package. Credit line given. Buys first N.A. serial rights.

Tips: "Nothing but sharp, high contrast shots, please. Send SASE for list of specific photo needs. We are using more color photos and prefer more action shots, fewer portrait shots. We look for photos of all kinds and numbers of cats doing predictable feline activities—eating, drinking, grooming, being groomed, playing, scratching, taking care of kittens, fighting, being judged at cat shows and accompanied by people of all ages."

CATHOLIC DIGEST, St. Paul's Square, P.O. Box 64090, St. Paul MN 55164. (612)647-5323. Editor: Henry Lexau. Photo Editor: Susan Schaefer. Monthly magazine. Emphasizes religion, family life. Readers are mostly Catholic, mature with teenagers or grown children. Circ. 600,000. Sample copy free with SASE (6½×9½ envelope, $1.05 postage).

Needs: Uses 6-9 photos/issue; 1 supplied by freelance photographer. Needs photos of religious symbols and scenes, family life, senior citizens, middle-age, young adults, health, medical. Special needs include Catholic photos of all kinds, holiday/religious feasts. Model release required; captions preferred.

Making Contact & Terms: Send b&w and color prints, contact sheets, negatives or color slides by mail for consideration. SASE. Reports in 3 weeks. NPI. Pays on publication. Credit line given. Buys one-time rights. Previously published work OK.

Tips: "More of a demand for pictures which tell the thoughts and emotions of the people in them—pictures which draw the viewer into the 'private moment' of the shot." Looks for "candid, natural expressions of people in photos—limited use of (appropriate) props—classic, simple clothing—high contrast in b&w photos; rich harmony in 4/color. Seasonal photos should be received 4 to 5 months in advance of month of issue. Avoid clichés."

CATHOLIC NEAR EAST MAGAZINE, 1011 First Ave., New York NY 10022-4195. FAX: (212)838-1344. Editor: Michael LaCività. Quarterly magazine. Circ. 100,000. Estab. 1974. Emphasizes "the living faith of native peoples in the Near East; charitable work conducted among poor and refugees in Near East; religious history and contemporary culture of Near East; Eastern Rites of the Church (both Catholic and Orthodox)." General readership, mainly Catholic; wide educational range. Sample copy and photo guidelines free with 6½ × 9½ SAE with 60¢ postage.
Needs: Buys 40 photos/year; 80% supplied by freelancers. "Evocative photos of people, places and activity in the Middle East and India. Mainly, though, we require people pictures, especially those which show current and historical Christian influences in the Near East. We are also interested in good shots of artistic and cultural objects/painting, crafts and of the Eastern Rite Churches, etc." No posed shots, or "purely political pictures of the area." Uses 8 × 10 b&w glossy prints, also 35mm or larger transparencies or color negatives. Captions required.
Making Contact & Terms: Interested in receiving work from newer, lesser-known photographers. Query first. "Please do not send an inventory, rather, send a letter that explains the ideas." SASE. Reports in 3 weeks; acknowledges receipt of material immediately. Credit line given. "Credits appear on page 3 with masthead and table of contents." Pays $50-150/b&w photo; $75-300/color photo; $20 maximum/hour; $60 maximum/day. Pays on publication. Buys first N.A. serial rights. Simultaneous submissions and previously published work OK, "but neither one is preferred. If previously published please tell us when and where."
Tips: "We want to see contemporary photographs that reveal the ancient heritage of the people, but do not appear to be museum societies. Generally, we use shots which show our readers what the people and places of the Middle East really look like. In other words, the shot should have a distinctly Eastern look. We always need *people* pictures. Finally, we do a 'day in the life' story on the people of different places and cultures of the Middle East and India in almost every issue. If the pictures were good enough, we would consider doing a photo story in any of the above categories." Also, "try to put the photos you send into some kind of specific context of a family, community or religious heritage. We welcome a ms accompanying photos, especially when the freelancer has a detailed knowledge about the area and its people."

THE CATHOLIC WORLD, Dept. PM, 997 Macarthur Blvd., Mahwah NJ 07430. (201)825-7300. Managing Editor: Laurie Felknor. Bimonthly magazine. Circ. 9,000. Estab. 1865.
Needs: Human interest, nature, religious (Roman Catholic). Buys 5-10 photos/issue.
Making Contact & Terms: Send material by mail for consideration. Uses 8 × 10 b&w glossy prints. SASE. Credit line given. Pays $20-35/photo. Pays on publication. Buys one-time rights. Simultaneous submissions and previously published work OK. Reports in 1 month.
Tips: Photos of people must reflect current hairstyles, clothing, etc. Each issue of *The Catholic World* is on a specific theme. Send query as to themes for the 6 issues per year.

CATS MAGAZINE, P.O. Box 290037, Port Orange FL 32029. (904)788-2770. FAX: (904)788-2710. Editor: Linda J. Walton. Monthly magazine. Circ. 150,000. For cat owners and breeders. Free sample copy (must include 9 × 12 SAE with 6 first class stamps) and photo guidelines. Provide tearsheets to be kept on file for possible future assignments.
Needs: Buys 30-50 photos/year. Felines of all types; celebrity/personality (with their cats); fine art (featuring cats); head shot (of cats); how-to (cat-oriented activities); human interest (on cats); humorous (cats); photo essay/photo feature (cats); sport (cat shows); travel (with cats); and wildlife (wild cats). No shots of clothed cats or cats doing tricks.
Making Contact & Terms: Buys first serial rights. Send contact sheet or photos for consideration. Pays on publication. Reports in 8-12 weeks. SASE. Send b&w contact sheet or 5 × 7 or 8 × 10 glossy prints. No silk finish. Pays $15-50. Send 2¼ × 2¼ color transparencies for covers. Prefers "shots showing cats in interesting situations." Pays $150; $50/photo/text package.
Tips: "We are always receptive to seasonal themes." If purebred cats are used as subjects, they must be representative specimens of their breed. Should be clear, sharp photographs of cats. "Our most frequent causes for rejection: cat image too small; backgrounds cluttered; uninteresting; poor quality

purebred cats; dirty pet-type cats; shot wrong shape for cover; colors untrue; exposure incorrect. Cats should be protrayed in a realistic manner—no clothed cats. Just submit your best work."

CHANGING MEN: Issues in Gender, Sex & Politics, P.O. Box 306, 305 N. Brooks St., Madison WI 53715. Editor: Michael Biernbaum. Estab. 1978. Biannual. Emphasizes men's issues, feminist, male politics, gay and heterosexual personal and political issues. Readers are anti-sexist men, feminists, gay and political activists. Circ. 6,000. Sample copy $6 (4-issue subscriptions $24).
Needs: Uses 6-8 photos/issue; 100% supplied by freelance photographers. Needs art photography; male body shots (not standard "nudes" or explicit sexual poses); images of men at work, play, in social and emotional relationships, etc.; journalism on gay and male feminist gatherings. Special needs include features on men's issues, AIDS, relationships with women, special issues of men of color, men's health, gay issues, antiporn, third world masculinities, etc. Model release preferred.
Making Contact & Terms: Interested in receiving work from newer, lesser-known photographers. Query with list of sample relevant stock photo subjects. Send b&w prints (photocopies acceptable) and contact sheets. SASE. Reports in 2 months. Pays $10-25/b&w inside photo; $25-50/covers; plus 2 sample copies. Pays on publication. Credit line given. Buys one-time rights.
Tips: "Display sensitivity to subject matter; provide political photos showing conscience, strong journalism on feminist and gay issues." In samples, wants to see "emotional content of image; or strong statement about a man's situation; or humor/irony in 'changing' situations." To break in, shoot "well-composed images that stand on their own, by showing emotional feeling or mood or by making a statement."

CHARISMA MAGAZINE, Dept. PM, 600 Rinehart Rd., Lake Mary FL 32746. (407)333-0600. Art Director: Eric T. Jessen. Monthly magazine. Emphasizes Christians. General readership. Circ. 200,000. Sample copy $2.50.
Needs: Uses approximately 20 photos/issue; 100% supplied by freelance photographers. Needs editorial photos—appropriate for each article. Model release required; photo captions preferred.
Making Contact & Terms: Send unsolicited photos by mail for consideration. Provide resume, business card, brochure, flyer or tearsheets to be kept on file for possible assignments. Send color 35mm, 2¼ × 2¼, 4 × 5 or 8 × 10 transparencies. Cannot return unsolicited material. Reports ASAP. Pays $300/color cover photo, $150/b&w inside photo, $50-150/hour or $400-600/day. Pays on publication. Credit line given. Buys all rights, but willing to negotiate. Simultaneous submissions and previously published work OK.
Tips: In portfolio or samples, looking for "good color and composition with great technical ability. To break in, specialize; sell the sizzle rather than the steak!"

*CHERI, 801 Second Ave., New York NY 10017. (212)661-7878. FAX: (212)692-9297. Editor-in-Chief: Ken Kimmel. Magazine published 13 times/year. Emphasis on adult entertainment, gentlemen's clubs, etc. Readers are males, various occupations and ages. Estab. 1976. Photo guidelines free with SASE.
Needs: Uses 250 photos/issue; 100% supplied by freelancers. Needs photos of nude women, erotic in soft focus. Reviews photos with or without accompanying ms. Model/property release required.
Making Contact & Terms: Submit portfolio for review. Send 35mm, 2¼ × 2¼ transparencies. Does not keep samples on file. SASE. Reports in 1-2 weeks. Pays $1,000-2,000/ photo set. Pays on acceptance. Credit line given. Buys one-time rights; negotiable. Simultaneous submissions and previously published work OK.
Tips: Work must be technically excellent. Concentrate on the "beauty and erotic depiction of the model."

THE CHESAPEAKE BAY MAGAZINE, 1819 Bay Ridge Ave., Annapolis MD 21403. (410)263-2662, (DC)261-1323. Art Director: Christine Gill. Monthly. Circ. 35,000. Estab. 1972. Emphasizes boating—Chesapeake Bay only. Readers are "people who use Bay for recreation." Sample copy available.
Needs: Uses "approximately" 21 photos/issue; 60% supplied by freelancers; 20% by freelance assignment. Needs photos that are "Chesapeake Bay related (must); vertical powerboat shots are badly needed (color)." Special needs include "vertical 4-color slides showing boats and people on Bay."
Making Contact & Terms: Query with samples or list of stock photo subjects; send 35mm, 2¼ × 2¼, 4 × 5 or 8 × 10 transparencies by mail for consideration. SASE. Reports in 3 weeks. Pays $200/color cover photo; $25-75/b&w photo; $25-250/color photo; $150-1,000/photo/text package. Pays on publication. Credit line given. Buys one-time rights. Simultaneous submissions OK.
Tips: "We prefer Kodachrome over Ektachrome. Vertical shots of the Chesapeake bay with power boats badly needed. Looking for: boating, bay and water-oriented subject matter. Qualities and abilities include: fresh ideas, clarity, exciting angles and true color. We're using larger photos—more double-page spreads. Photos should be able to hold up to that degree of enlargement. When photographing boats on the Bay—keep the 'safety' issue in mind. (People hanging off the boat, drinking, women 'perched' on the bow are a no-no!)"

CHICAGO LIFE MAGAZINE, P.O. Box 11311, Chicago IL 60611. Publisher: Pam Berns. Bimonthly magazine. Emphasizes self-improvement. Readers are upscale men and women, ages 35-50, college-educated professionals, interested in improving their lifestyles through health, fitness, travel and business. Circ. 60,000. Estab. 1986.
Needs: Uses 15 photos/issue; 80% supplied by freelancers. Uses photos for travel, health, food, cover and celebrity. Reviews photos with or without a manuscript. Model release and photo captions required.
Making Contact & Terms: Provide resume, business card, brochure, flyer or tearsheets to be kept on file for possible assignments. Does not return material. Reports in 1 week on queries. Pays $30/color cover and color inside photos, $30/b&w inside photo. Pays on acceptance. Credit line given. Buys one-time rights. Simultaneous submissions and previously published work OK.

CHICAGO PARENT NEWS MAGAZINE, Dept. PM, 141 South Oak Park Ave., Oak Park IL 60302. Managing Editor: Mary Haley. News magazine published 12 times/year. Emphasizes parenting. Readers are parents. Circ. 70,000. Sample copy $1.
Needs: Uses about 10 photos/issue; 2-5 supplied by freelance photographers. Needs photos of children. Model release required; photo captions preferred.
Making Contact & Terms: Query with samples. Query with list of stock photo subjects. Send b&w prints or contact sheets by mail for consideration. SASE. Reports in 3 weeks. Pays $25/b&w photo. Pays on publication. Credit line given. Simultaneous submissions and previously published work OK.
Tips: "Send us great photos of children. We will use them."

🍁**CHICKADEE MAGAZINE,** Suite 306, 56 The Esplanade, Toronto ON M5E 1A7 Canada. (416)868-6001. FAX: (416)868-6009. Photo Researcher: Robin Wilner. Published 10 times/year, 1 summer issue. Circ. 110,000. Estab. 1979. A natural science magazine for children 3-9 years. Sample copy for $4.28 with 9×12 SAE and $1.50 money order to cover postage. Photo guidelines free.
Needs: Uses about 3-6 photos/issue; 2-4 supplied by freelance photographers. Needs "crisp, bright, close-up shots of animals in their natural habitat." Model/property release required. Captions required.
Making Contact & Terms: Request photo package before sending photos for review; send 35mm transparencies. SAE with $1.50 money order to cover postage. Reports in 6-8 weeks. Pays $325 Canadian/color cover; $200 Canadian/color page; text/photo package negotiated separately. Pays on acceptance. Credit line given. Buys one-time rights, nonexclusive, to reproduce in *Owl* and *Chickadee* in Canada and affiliated children's publications in remaining world countries. Previously published work OK.

CHILDREN'S DIGEST, P.O. Box 567, Indianapolis IN 46206. (317)636-8881. Editor: Elizabeth Rinck. Magazine published 8 times/year. Emphasizes health and fitness. Readers are preteens—kids 10-13. Circ. 125,000. Estab. 1950. Sample copy $1.25. Photo guidelines free with SASE.
Needs: "We have featured photos of wildlife, children in other countries, adults in different jobs, how-to projects." Reviews photos with accompanying ms only. "We would like to include more photo features." Model release preferred.
Making Contact & Terms: Send complete manuscript and photos on speculation. 35mm transparencies. SASE. Reports in 8-10 weeks. Pays $50-100/color cover photo; $20/color inside photo; $10/b&w inside photo. Pays on publication. Buys one-time rights.

CHILDREN'S MINISTRY MAGAZINE, % Group Publishing, Inc. Dept. PM, P.O. Box 481, 2890 N. Monroe Ave., Loveland CO 80539. (303)669-3836. Art Director: Lisa Rhode. Bimonthly magazine. Provides ideas and support to adult workers (professional and volunteer) with children in Christian churches. Circ. 10,000. Estab. 1991. Sample copy $1 with 9×12 SAE. Photo guidelines free with SASE.
Needs: Uses 20-25 photos/issue; 3-6 supplied by freelancers. Needs photos of children (preschool—6th grade) involved in school, church, recreational activities; with or without adults; generally upbeat and happy. Reviews photos with or without a manuscript. Especially needs good portrait-type shots of individual children, suitable for cover use; colorful, happy. Model release required in some cases. Photo captions not needed.
Making Contact & Terms: Query with list of stock photo subjects; send unsolicited photos by mail for consideration. Send 8×10 b&w glossy prints; 35mm, 2¼×2¼ transparencies. SASE. Reports in 1 month. Pays minimum $150/color cover photo; minimum $75/color inside photo; $35-50/b&w inside

---

🍁 **The maple leaf before a listing indicates that the market is Canadian. The symbol is new this year in Photographer's Market.**

photo. Pays on publication. Credit line given. Buys one-time rights. Simultaneous submissions and previously published work OK.

Tips: Wants to see "sharp, well-composed and well-exposed shots of young children with an active, upbeat, colorful feel; ethnic mix is highly desirable." To be considered, "photos must appear current and contemporary. Professionalism must be evident in photos and their presentation. No under- or overexposed 'snapshot'-style photos, please."

CHILDREN'S PLAYMATE, Dept. PM, P.O. Box 567, Indianapolis IN 46206. (317)636-8881. Editor: Elizabeth A. Rinck. Published 8 times/year. Emphasizes better health for children. Readers are children between the ages of 6-8. Circ. 115,000. Sample copy 75¢ with 5×7 SASE. Photo guidelines free with SASE.

Needs: Number of photos/issue varies; 100% supplied by freelancers. Reviews photos with accompanying ms only. Model release required; captions preferred.

Making Contact & Terms: Send unsolicited photos, accompanied by ms. Uses b&w prints and 35mm transparencies. SASE. Reports in 8-10 weeks. Pays $10/b&w inside photo; $20/color inside photo. Pays on publication. Credit line given. Buys one-time rights.

*CHILE PEPPER, P.O. Box 4278, Albuquerque NM 87196. (505)266-8322. FAX: (505)266-0141. Art Director: Lois Bergthold. Bimonthly magazine. Emphasizes world cuisine, emphasis on hot, spicy foods and chile peppers. Readers are male and female consumers of spicy food, age 35-55. Circ. 70,000. Estab. 1986. Sample copy $2.95. Photo guidelines not available.

Needs: Uses 8-12 photos/issue; 10-20% supplied by freelancers. Needs photos of still life ingredients, location shots specifically of locales which are known for spicy cuisine, shots of chiles. Reviews photos with or without a manuscript. "We will be doing features on the cuisine of Louisiana, Mexico, Arizona and the Caribbean." Model/property preferred. Photo captions required; include location and species of chile (if applicable).

Making Contact & Terms: Query with stock photo list. Send unsolicited photos by mail for consideration. Provide resume, business card, brochure, flyer or tearsheets to be kept on file for possible assignments. Send b&w/color prints; 35mm, 4×5, 8×10 transparencies. Keeps samples on file. SASE. Reports in 3 weeks. Pays $150/color cover photo; $50/color inside photo; $25/b&w inside photo. Pays on publication. Credit line given. Buys one-time rights. Simultaneous submissions and/or previously published work OK.

Tips: "Looking for shots that capture the energy and exotica of locations, and still-life food shots that are not too classical, with a "fresh eye" and interesting juxtapositions."

THE CHRISTIAN CENTURY, 407 S. Dearborn St., Chicago IL 60605. (312)427-5380. FAX: (708)427-1302. Editor: James M. Wall. Photo Editor: Matt Giunti. Magazine published 36 times/year. Circ. 37,000. Estab. 1884. Emphasizes "concerns that arise at the juncture between church and society, or church and culture." Deals with social problems, ethical dilemmas, political issues, international affairs, the arts, and theological and ecclesiastical matters. For college-educated, ecumenically minded, progressive church clergy and laypersons. Free sample copy and writer's/photo guidelines for SASE.

Needs: Photos with or without accompanying ms. Buys 50 photos/year; all supplied by freelancers. People of various races and nationalities; celebrity/personality (primarily political and religious figures in the news); documentary (conflict and controversy, also constructive projects and cooperative endeavors); scenic (occasional use of seasonal scenes and scenes from foreign countries); spot news; and human interest (children, human rights issues, people "in trouble," and people interacting). For accompanying mss seeks articles dealing with ecclesiastical concerns, social problems, political issues and international affairs. Model release and captions preferred.

Making Contact & Terms: Credit line given. Pays $20-70/photo; $35-100/accompanying ms. Pays on publication. Buys one-time rights. Send material by mail for consideration. SASE. Simultaneous submissions OK. Reports in 1 month. Uses 5×7 or 8×10 glossy b&w prints. Alternates among vertical, square and horizontal formats for cover.

Tips: Needs sharp, clear photos. "We use photos sparingly. Since we use photos primarily to illustrate articles, it is difficult to determine very far in advance or with much specificity just what our needs will be. Therefore, we prefer to keep photos in our files for extended periods of time."

THE CHRONICLE OF THE HORSE, P.O. Box 46, Middleburg VA 22117. (703)687-6341. FAX: (703)687-3937. Editor: John Strassburger. Estab. 1937. Weekly magazine. Emphasizes English horse sports. Readers range from young to old. "Average reader is a college-educated female, middle-aged, well off financially." Circ. 23,000. Sample copy for $2. Photo guidelines free with SASE.

Needs: Uses 10-25 photos/issue; 90% supplied by freelance photographers. Needs photos from competitive events (horse shows, dressage, steeplechase, etc.) to go with news story or to accompany personality profile. "A few stand alone. Must be cute, beautiful or news-worthy. Reproduced in b&w." Prefer purchasing photos with accompanying ms. Special photo needs include good photos to accom-

pany our news stories, especially horse shows. Photo caption required with every subject identified.
Making Contact & Terms: Interested in receiving work from newer, lesser-known photographers. Query with what photographer has in mind. Send b&w and color prints (reproduced b&w). SASE. Reports in 3 weeks. Pays $15-30/photo/text package. Pays on publication. Credit line given. Buys one-time rights. Prefer first N.A. rights. Simultaneous and previously published work OK.
Tips: "We do not want to see portfolio or samples. Contact us first, preferably by letter. Know horse sports."

THE CHURCH HERALD, 6157 28th St. SE, Grand Rapids MI 49546-6999. (616)957-1351. Editor: Jeffrey Japinga. Photo Editor: Christina Van Eyl. Published 11 times annually. Circ. 40,000. Emphasizes current events, family living, evangelism and spiritual growth, from a Christian viewpoint. For members and clergy of the Reformed Church in America. Sample copy $2 with 9×12 SASE.
Needs: Needs photos of life situations—families, couples, vacations, school; religious, moral and philosophical symbolism; seasonal and holiday themes; nature scenes—all seasons. Buys 1-2 photos/issue; 50% freelance photography/issue comes from assignment and 50% from freelance stock.
Making Contact & Terms: Buys first serial rights, second serial (reprint) rights, first N.A. serial rights or simultaneous rights. Send photos for consideration. Pays $25-35/b&w inside photo; $50/color inside photo; $50-100/color cover photo. Pays on acceptance. Reports in 4 weeks. SASE. Simultaneous submissions and previously published work OK. Sample copy $2 with 9×12 SAE.
Tips: Looks for "good photo quality—photos that our readers will relate to in a positive way—a lot of what we get is junk photos we can't use. Have an understanding of the kinds of articles we run. I want to see interesting photos of good quality that depict real-life situations. We're using more color and commissioning more. Don't send me a list of what you have unless it's accompanied by a selection of photos. I'm happy to look at someone's work, but I'm frustrated by resumes and checklists."

CIRCLE K MAGAZINE, 3636 Woodview Trace, Indianapolis IN 46268. (317)875-8755. Executive Editor: Nicholas K. Drake. Published 5 times/year. Circ. 15,000. For community service-oriented college leaders "interested in the concept of voluntary service, societal problems, leadership abilities and college life. They are politically and socially aware and have a wide range of interests." Free sample copy.
Needs: Assigns 0-5 photos/issue. Needs general interest photos, "though we rarely use a nonorganization shot without text. Also, the annual convention requires a large number of photos from that area." Prefers ms with photos. Seeks general interest features aimed at the better-than-average college student. "Not specific places, people topics." Captions required, "or include enough information for us to write a caption."
Making Contact & Terms: Works with freelance photographers on assignment only basis. Provide calling card, letter of inquiry, resume and samples to be kept on file for possible future assignments. Send query with resume of credits. SASE. Reports in 3 weeks. Uses 8×10 glossy b&w prints or color transparencies. Uses b&w and color covers; vertical format required for cover. Pays up to $225-350 for text/photo package, or on a per-photo basis—$15 minimum/b&w print and $50 minimum/cover. Pays on acceptance. Credit line given. Previously published work OK if necessary to text.

CIRCLE TRACK MAGAZINE, 8490 Sunset Blvd., Los Angeles CA 90069. (213)854-2350. Editor: Robert Carpenter. Monthly magazine. Emphasizes American oval track racing. Readers are male, age 32, income $37,000, some college, car racing hobby. Circ. 110,000. Photo guidelines free with SASE.
Needs: Uses about 70-100 photos/issue; 80% supplied by freelance photographers. Needs photos of race cars, racing personalities, parts. Special needs include continuing coverage of major events. Model release and captions required. Uses 35mm or larger color transparencies (no prints), b&w prints (5×7 or larger).
Making Contact & Terms: Query with samples. SASE. Reports in 3 weeks. Pays $150-250/color cover photo; $10-100/b&w inside photo; $10-150/color inside photo; $100/b&w page; $150/color page; $100-500/text/photo package. Pays on publication. Credit line given. Buys all rights, but will negotiate.
Tips: Prefers to see "action shots, slides, unique race car shots."

*CLIMAX, 10th Floor, 801 Second Ave., New York NY 11217. (212)661-7878. FAX: (212)692-9297. Editor: Marc Medoff. Quarterly magazine. Emphasis on male and female relations between couples. Readers are young males, blue collar workers, over 18 years old. Circ. 83,000. Estab. 1990. Sample copies free with 8½×11 SASE and 10 first class stamps. Photo guidelines free with SASE.
Needs: Uses 100-200 photos/issue; 100% supplied by freelancers. Needs photos of explicit sexuality involving couples only, "male-female, female-female." Reviews photos with or without accompanying ms. Model/property release required, include copies of photo identification with date of birth over 18 years old.

Making Contact & Terms: Submit portfolio for review. Send unsolicited photos by mail for consideration. Provide resume, business card, brochure, flyer or tearsheets to be kept on file for possible future assignments. Send 35mm transparencies. Keeps samples on file. SASE. Reports in 1 month. Payment varies from $10/shot to $3,000/full set. Pays on acceptance. Credit line given. Buys one-time rights; negotiable. Simultaneous submissions and previously published work OK.
Tips: "We require technical perfection. Focus, lighting, composition, etc., must be 100% perfect. Look at our magazine and competing titles."

*THE CLIMBING ART, 5620 S. 49th, Lincoln NE 68516. (402)421-2591. FAX: (402)421-1268. Editor: Pat Ament. Quarterly magazine. Emphasizes climbing. Readers are climbers of all types. Circ. 2,000. Estab. 1986. Sample copy free with 9 × 12 SASE and 5 first class stamps. Photo guidelines not available.
Needs: Uses 20 photos/issue; 50% supplied by freelancers. Reviews photos with or without a manuscript. Model/property release preferred. Photo captions preferred.
Making Contact & Terms: Query with stock photo list. Send unsolicited photos by mail for consideration. Call. Send b&w prints. Keeps samples on file. SASE. Reports in 1 month. Pays $10/b&w cover photo; $10/b&w inside photo; $10/b&w page rate; pays $20-25/photo/text package. Pays on publication. Credit line given. Buys one-time rights and first N.A. serial rights (preferred). Simultaneous submissions and/or previously published work OK. Wants to know status of other submissions.
Tips: "TCA is not a news or how-to magazine. It is an art magazine. We look at the artistic quality of pictures. Give a fresh look to new and old subjects. We're not interested in clichés, although we do like artfully humorous pictures."

COBBLESTONE: THE HISTORY MAGAZINE FOR YOUNG PEOPLE, Cobblestone Publishing, Inc., 7 School St., Peterborough NH 03458. (603)924-7209. Photo Editor: Sarah E. Hale. 10 issues/year. Emphasizes American history; each issue covers a specific theme. Readers are children 8-14, parents, teachers. Circ. 37,000. Sample copy for $3.95 and 7½ × 9½ SAE with $1.25 postage. Photo guidelines free with SASE.
Needs: Uses about 30 photos/issue; 3-5 supplied by freelance photographers. "We need photographs related to our specific themes (each issue is theme-related) and urge photographers to request our themes list." Model release required; captions preferred.
Making Contact & Terms: Query with samples or list of stock photo subjects; send 8 × 10 glossy b&w prints, or 35mm or 2¼ × 2¼ transparencies. SASE. "Photos must pertain to themes, and reporting dates depend on how far ahead of the issue the photographer submits photos; we work on issues 6 months ahead of publication. Pays $50-75/cover photo; $10-15/inside photo. Pays on publication. Credit line given. Buys one-time rights. Simultaneous submissions and previously published work OK.
Tips: "In general, we use few contemporary images; most photos are of historical subjects. However, the amount varies with each monthly theme."

*COLLAGES & BRICOLAGES, P.O. Box 86, Clarion PA 16212. (814)226-5799. Editor: Marie-José Fortis. Annual magazine. Emphasizes literary works, avant-garde, poetry, fiction, plays and nonfiction. Readers are educated people, writers, college professors in the U.S. and abroad. Estab. 1986. Sample copy $6.
Needs: Uses 5-10 photos/issue; 100% supplied by freelancers. Needs photos that make a social statement, surrealist photos and photo collages. Reviews photos with or without a manuscript. Special photo needs include photos on China, if sent before 1993. Photo captions preferred; include title of photo and short biography of artist/photographer.
Making Contact & Terms: Send unsolicited photos by mail for consideration. Send matte b&w prints. SASE. Reports in 2 weeks to 3 months. Pays in copies. Buys one-time rights. Rights negotiable. Simultaneous submissions and/or previously published work OK.
Tips: "*C&B* is primarily meant for writers. It will include photos if: a) they accompany or illustrate a story, a poem or an essay; b) they constitute the cover of a particular issue; or c) they make a statement (political, social, spiritual)."

*COLLECTOR EDITIONS, 170 5th Ave., New York NY 10010. (212)989-8700. Editor: Joan Pursley. Bimonthly magazine. Emphasizes limited edition ceramic and glass collectibles. Circ. 75,000. Sample copy $2.
Needs: Uses about 60 photos/issue; 5-10 supplied by freelance photographers. Photos purchased with accompanying ms only. Captions preferred.
Making Contact & Terms: "Ideally, suggest an article idea and send sample photos with it—transparencies (any size) and/or b&w prints, no color prints." Provide resume, business card, brochure, flyer or tearsheets to be kept on file for possible future assignments. SASE. Reports in 6 weeks. Pays $200-400/day. Pays within 30 days of acceptance. Credit line given. Buys first North American rights only.

Tips: "We don't purchase stock photos. About 25% of our photos are by assignment. The majority of our photos are product-type shots, so we're looking for someone who excels in close-up work of porcelain and glass objects, often under one foot in height. Good lighting is essential."

COLONIAL HOMES MAGAZINE, Dept. PM, 1790 Broadway, New York NY 10019. (212)830-2950 or 830-2956. Editor: Jason Kontos. Bimonthly. Circ. 600,000. Emphasizes traditional architecture and interior design. Sample copy available.
Needs: All photos supplied by freelance photographers. Needs photos of "American architecture of 18th century or 18th century style—4-color chromes—no people in any shots; some food shots." Special needs include "American food and drink; private homes in Colonial style; historic towns in America." Captions required.
Making Contact & Terms: Submit portfolio for review. Send 4×5 or 8×10 transparencies by mail for consideration. Provide resume, business card, brochure, flyer or tearsheets to be kept on file for possible future assignments. SASE. Reports in 1 month. Pays $500/day. Pays on acceptance. Credit line given. Buys all rights. Previously published work OK.

COLUMBUS MONTHLY, P.O. Box 29913, 5255 Sinclair Rd., Columbus OH 43229-7513. (614)888-4567. Editor: Lenore Brown. Assistant Editor: Laura Messerly. Art Director: Sharon Hunley. Monthly magazine. Circ. 38,000. Estab. 1975. Emphasizes local and regional events, including feature articles; personality profiles; investigative reporting; calendar of events; and departments on politics, sports, education, restaurants, movies, books, media, food and drink, shelter and architecture and art. "The magazine is very visual. People read it to be informed and entertained." Sample copy $3.57.
Needs: Buys 150 photos/year. Celebrity/personality (of local or regional residents, or former residents now living elsewhere); fashion/beauty (local only); fine art (of photography, fine arts or crafts with a regional or local angle); head shot (by assignment); photo essay/photo feature on local topics only; product shot; and scenic (local or regional Ohio setting usually necessary, although once or twice a year a travel story, on spots far from Ohio, is featured). No special effects or "form art photography." Model and property releases required; captions required.
Making Contact & Terms: Interested in receiving work from newer, lesser-known photographers. Photos purchased on assignment. Pays $20/b&w photo; $40/color photo; $45-80/assigned photo. Covers negotiated. Credit line given. Pays on acceptance. Buys one-time rights. Arrange personal interview with art director to show portfolio or query with resume of credits. Works with freelance photographers on assignment only basis. Provide calling card, samples and tearsheet to be kept on file for possible future assignments. SASE. Previously published work OK. Uses 8×10 glossy b&w prints, contact proofsheet requested; 35mm, 2¼×2¼ or 4×5 transparencies, contact proof sheet requested for negative color; 2¼×2¼ or 4×5 color transparencies, vertical format required for cover. "Send mailer first with tearsheets or nonreturnable samples; follow up with phone call."
Tips: "Live in the Columbus area. Prior publication experience is not necessary. Call for an appointment. Need consistency, ability to make something as dull as a headshot a little more interesting. Should have ability to take 'news' type photos."

COMPLETE WOMAN, 1165 N. Clark, Chicago IL 60610. (312)266-8680. Art Director: Evelyn Lui-Shafts. Bimonthly magazine. General interest magazine for women. Readers are "females, 21-40, from all walks of life." Estab. 1980.
Needs: Uses 50-60 photos/issue. Needs "how-to beauty shots, women with men, etc." Model release required. Photo captions preferred.
Making Contact & Terms: Query with list of stock photo subjects; send unsolicited photos by mail for consideration; provide resume, business card, brochure, flyer or tearsheets to be kept on file for possible assignments. Send b&w, color prints; 35mm transparencies. SASE. Reports in 1 month. Pays $75/color inside photo; $50/b&w inside photo. Pays on publication. Credit line given. Buys one-time rights. Simultaneous and previously published work OK.

*CONFRONTATION: A LITERARY JOURNAL, English Dept., C.W. Post of L.I.U., Brookville NY 11548. (516)299-2391. Editor: Martin Tucker. Semiannual magazine. Emphasizes literature. Readers are college-educated lay people interested in literature. Circ. 2,000. Estab. 1968. Sample copy $3.
Needs: Reviews photos with or without a manuscript.
Making Contact & Terms: Query with resume of credits. Query with stock photo list. Reports in 1 month. Pays $50-100/color cover photo; $20-40/b&w page rate. Pays on publication. Credit line given. Buys first N.A. serial rights. Rights negotiable. Simultaneous submissions OK.

CONSERVATIONIST MAGAZINE, Dept. PM, NYSDEC, 50 Wolf Rd., Albany NY 12233. (518)457-5547. Contact: Photo Editor. Bimonthly. Emphasizes natural history and environmental interests. Readers are people interested in nature and environmental quality issues. Circ. 200,000. Sample copy $3 and 8½×11 SASE. Photo guidelines free with SASE.

Needs: Uses 40 photos/issue; 80% supplied by freelance photographers. Needs wildlife shots, forest and land management, fisheries and fisheries management, environmental subjects (pollution shots, a few), effects of pollution on plants, buildings, etc. Model release and captions required.
Making Contact & Terms: Arrange personal interview to show portfolio. Query with samples. Send 35mm, 2¼ × 2¼, 4 × 5 or 8 × 10 transparencies by mail for consideration. Submit portfolio for review. Provide resume, business card, brochure, flyer or tearsheets to be kept on file for possible future assignments. SASE. Reports in 3 weeks. Pays $15/b&w or color inside photo. Pays on publication. Buys one-time rights. Simultaneous submissions and previously published work OK.
Tips: Looks for "artistic interpretation of nature and the environment," unusual ways of picturing environmental subjects (even pollution, oil spills, trash, air pollution, etc.); wildlife and fishing subjects from above and underwater at all seasons. "Try to have the camera see the subject differently."

DAVID C. COOK PUBLISHING CO., Dept. PM, 850 N. Grove, Elgin IL 60120. (708)741-2400. Director of Design Services: Randy Maid. Photo Acquisition Coordinator: Ruth Corcorean. Publishes books and Sunday school material for pre-school through adult readers. Photos used primarily in Sunday school material for text illustration and covers, particularly in *Sunday Digest* (for adults), *Christian Living* (for senior highs) and *Sprint* (for junior highs). Younger age groups used, but not as much.
Needs: Buys 200 photos minimum/year; gives 20 assignments/year. Uses more b&w than color photos. Model release preferred. Prefers to see Sunday school, church activities, social activities, family shots, people, action, sports. SASE. Previously published work OK. Mostly photos of junior and senior high age youth of all races and ethnic backgrounds, also adults and children under junior high age, and some preschool.
Making Contact & Terms: "Send material to the attention of Brenda Fox, Photo Acquisitions Coordinator. We use black and white people shots almost daily. Submissions can be sent 1-2 times per month." Uses glossy b&w and semigloss prints; 8 × 10 prints are copied or kept on file for ordering at a later date. 35mm and larger transparencies; contact sheet OK; glossy b&w prints and 35mm and larger color transparencies for cover. Pays $50-250/job or on per-photo basis: $30-50/b&w photo; $75-200/color photo; $50-250/cover photo. Credit line given. Usually buys one-time rights.
Tips: "Make sure your material is identified as yours. We are always looking for new photos. Send only high quality shots in good condition."

COSMOPOLITAN, Dept. PM, 8th Floor, 224 W. 57th St., New York NY 10019. Art Director: Linda Cox. Photo Editor: Larry Mitchell. Monthly magazine.
Needs: Fashion, beauty, and still lifes of food and decorating. Model release required.
Making Contact & Terms: Arrange personal interview to show portfolio. "It's best to make appointment by phone for Tuesday or Thursday drop-off." Also, query with stock photo list. Provide resume, business card, brochure, flyer or tearsheets to be kept on file for possible future assignments. Keeps samples on file. SASE. Does not always report. "Feel free to call to check on status of material." Pays $250/inside color photo or b&w page. Also covers expenses and any agent fees that apply. Credit line given. Buys one-time and all rights; negotiable.

*COUNTRY, 5925 Country Lane, Greendale WI 53129. (414)423-0100. FAX: (414)423-1143. Editorial Assistant: Trudi Bellin. Estab. 1987. Bimonthly magazine. "For those who live in or long for the country." Readers are rural-oriented, male and female, ages 50-plus. "*Country* is supported entirely by subscriptions and accepts no outside advertising." Sample copy $2. Photo guidelines free with SASE.
Needs: Uses 150 photos/issue; 20% supplied by freelancers. Needs photos of scenics—country only. Model/property release required. Captions preferred; include season, location.
Making Contact & Terms: Interested in receiving work from newer, lesser-known photographers. Query with list of stock photo subjects. Send unsolicited photos by mail for consideration. Send 35mm, 2¼ × 2¼, 4 × 5 and 8 × 10 transparencies. Tearsheets kept on file but not dupes. SASE. Reports "as soon as possible; sometimes days, other times months." Pays $200/color cover photo; $50-125/color inside photo; $150/color page (full page bleed); $10-25/b&w photo. Pays on publication. Credit line given. Buys one-time rights. Previously published work OK.
Tips: "Technical quality is extremely important: focus must be sharp, no soft focus; colors must be vivid so they 'pop off the page.' Study our magazine thoroughly—we have a continuing need for sharp, colorful images, and those who can supply what we need can expect to be regular contributors."

■ *The solid, black square before a listing indicates that the market uses various types of audiovisual materials, such as slides, film or videotape.*

COUNTRY JOURNAL, Dept. PM, P.O. Box 8200, 6405 Flank Dr., Harrisburg PA 17105. (717)657-9555. Art Editor: Sheryl O'Connell. Bimonthly magazine. Emphasizes practical concerns and rewards of life in the country. Readers are mostly male, ages 35-55, occupations varied—most have good disposable income. Circ. 200,000. Estab. 1974. Sample copy for $4. Photo guidelines free with SASE.
Needs: Uses 40 photos/issue; 95% supplied by freelance photographers. Needs photos of animal/wildlife, country scenics, vegetable and flower gardening, home improvements, personality profiles, environmental issues and other subjects relating to rural life. Model release and photo captions required.
Making Contact & Terms: Provide resume, business card, brochure, flyer or tearsheets to be kept on file for possible assignments. Send b&w prints and 35mm, 2¼×2¼, 4×5 and 8×10 prints with SASE by return mail for consideration. Reports in 1 month. Pays $500/color and b&w cover photo; $135/¼ page color and b&w page inside photo; $235/color and b&w page rate; $275-325/day. Pays on publication. Credit line given. Buys one-time rights. Simultaneous submissions OK.
Tips: "Know who you are submitting to. You can waste time, money and a possible opportunity by sending inappropriate samples and queries. If you can't find samples of the publication, call or send for them."

COUNTRY WOMAN, Dept. PM, P.O. Box 643, Milwaukee WI 53201. Managing Editor: Kathy Pohl. Circ. 700,000. Emphasizes rural life and a special quality of living to which country women can relate; at work or play in sharing problems, etc. Sample copy $2. Free photo guidelines with SASE.
Needs: Photos purchased with or without accompanying ms. Uses 75-100 photos/issue. Good quality photo/text packages featuring interesting country women are much more likely to be accepted than photos only. "We're always interested in seeing good shots of farm, ranch and country women (in particular) and rural families (in general) at work and at play." Uses photos of farm animals, children with farm animals, farm and country scenes (both with and without people) and nature. Want on a regular basis scenic (rural), seasonal, photos of rural women and their family. "We're always happy to consider cover ideas. Covers are often seasonal in nature and *always* feature a country woman. Additional information on cover needs available." Captions are required. Work 6 months in advance. "No poor quality color prints, posed photos, etc."
Making Contact & Terms: Pays $100-225 for text/photo package depending on quality of photos and number used. Pays on acceptance. Buys one-time rights. Send material by mail for consideration. Provide brochure, calling card, letter of inquiry, price list, resume and samples to be kept on file for possible future assignments. SASE. Previously published work OK. Reports in 2-3 months. Uses transparencies. Pays $35-225 (cover only), depending on size used. Many photos are used at ¼ page size or less, and payment for those is at the low end of the scale. (No b&w photos used).
Tips: Prefers to see "rural scenics, in various seasons; emphasis on farm women, ranch women, country women and their families. Slides appropriately simple for use with poems or as accents to inspirational, reflective essays, etc."

THE COVENANT COMPANION, 5101 N. Francisco Ave., Chicago IL 60625. (312)784-3000. Editor: James R. Hawkinson. Managing Editor: Jane K. Swanson-Nystrom. Art Director: David Westerfield. Monthly denominational magazine of The Evangelical Covenant Church. Circ. 23,500. Emphasizes "gathering, enlightening and stimulating the people of our church and keeping them in touch with their mission and that of the wider Christian church in the world."
Needs: Mood shots of nature, commerce and industry, home life, church life, church buildings and people. Also uses fine art, scenes, city life, etc.
Making Contact & Terms: Credit line given. Pays within one month following publication. Buys one-time rights. Send photos. SASE. Simultaneous submissions OK. "We need to keep a rotating file of photos for consideration." Send 5×7 and 8×10 glossy prints; color slides for cover only. Pays $15/b&w photo; $50-75/color cover.
Tips: "Give us photos that illustrate life situations and moods. We use b&w photos which reflect a mood or an aspect of society—wealthy/poor, strong/weak, happiness/sadness, conflict/peace. These photos or illustrations can be of nature, people, buildings, designs, and so on. Give us a file from which we can draw—rotating all the time—and we will pay per use in month after publication."

*THE CREAM CITY REVIEW, University of Wisconsin-Milwaukee, English Department, Box 413, Milwaukee WI 53201. (414)229-4708. Art Director: Laurie Buman. Biyearly magazine. Emphasizes literature. Readers are mostly males and females with PH. D's in English, ages 18-over 70. Circ. 2,000. Estab. 1975. Sample copy $1.50-5. Photo guidelines free with SASE.
Needs: Uses 6-20 photos/issue; 100% supplied by freelancers. Needs photos of fine art and other works of art.
Making Contact & Terms: Send unsolicited photos by mail for consideration. Send all sizes b&w and color prints; 35mm, 2¼×2¼, 4×5, 8×10 transparencies. SASE. Reports in 2 months. Pays $25/color cover photo; $25/b&w cover photo; $5/b&w inside photo; $5/b&w page rate. Pays on publication.

Credit line given. Buys one-time rights. Simultaneous submissions and/or previously published work OK.

Tips: "The artistic merit of submitted work is important. We have been known to change our look based on exciting work submitted. Take a look at *Cream City Review* and see how we like to look. If you have things that fit, send them."

CROSSCURRENTS, Dept. PM, 2200 Glastonbury Rd., Westlake Village CA 91361. (818)991-1694. Editor-in-Chief: Linda Brown Michelson. Photo Editor: Michael Hughes. "This is a literary quarterly that uses a number of photos as accompaniment to our fiction. We are aimed at an educated audience interested in reviewing a selection of fiction and graphic arts." Circ. 3,000. Sample copy $6. Free photo guidelines with SASE.

Needs: Uses about 8-11 photos/issue; half supplied by freelance photographers. Needs "work that is technically good: sharp focus, high b&w contrast. We are also eager to see arty, experimental b&w shots." Photos purchased with or without accompanying ms.

Making Contact & Terms: "Send us a sampling. Include SASE with all submissions." Reports in 1 month. Pays $15/b&w photo; $50-75/color photo. Pays on acceptance. Credit line given. Buys first one-time use.

Tips: "We are seeing higher quality submissions; therefore, the situation here has become more competitive. We want the following: b&w submissions – 5 × 7 vertical print, publication quality, glossy, no matte; color submissions – slide plus 5 × 7 vertical print. Almost all work we use is purchased from stock. Study our publication. We are in greatest need of b&w material."

CRUISE TRAVEL, 990 Grove St., Evanston IL 60201. (708)491-6440. Managing Editor: Charles Doherty. Bimonthly magazine. Emphasizes cruise ships, ports, vacation destinations, travel tips, ship history. Readers are "those who have taken a cruise, plan to take a cruise, or dream of taking a cruise." Circ. 160,000. Estab. 1979. Sample copy $3 with 9 × 12 SAE with $1.44 postage. Photo guidelines free with SASE.

Needs: Uses about 50 photos/issue; 75% supplied by freelance photographers. Needs ship shots, interior/exterior; scenic shots of ports; shopping shots; native sights, etc. Photos purchased with or without accompanying ms, but manuscript strongly preferred. Model release preferred; captions required.

Making Contact & Terms: Query with samples. Uses color prints; 35mm (preferred), 2¼ × 2¼, 4 × 5, 8 × 10 transparencies. SASE. Reports in 2 weeks. Pays variable rate for color cover; $25-150/color inside photo; $200-500/text/photo package for original work. Pays on acceptance or publication; depends on package. Credit line usually given, depends on arrangement with photographer. Buys one-time rights. Simultaneous submissions and previously published work OK.

Tips: "We look for bright colorful travel slides with good captions. Nearly every purchase is a photo/ms package, but good photos are key. We prefer 35mm originals for publication, all color."

CRUISING WORLD MAGAZINE, 5 John Clark Rd., Newport RI 02840. (401)847-1588. Photo Editor: Paul F. Mirto. Circ. 130,000. Estab. 1974. Emphasizes sailboat maintenance, sailing instruction and personal experience. For people interested in cruising under sail. Sample copy free for 9 × 12 SAE.

Needs: Buys 25 photos/year. Needs "shots of cruising sailboats and their crews anywhere in the world. Shots of ideal cruising scenes. No identifiable racing shots, please." For covers photos "must be of a cruising sailboat with strong human interest, and can be located anywhere in the world." Prefers vertical format. Allow space at top of photo for insertion of logo. Model release preferred; captions required.

Making Contact & Terms: Send 35mm color transparencies. "We rarely accept miscellaneous b&w shots and would rather they not be submitted unless accompanied by a manuscript." For cover, "submit original 35mm Kodachrome slides. *No* duplicates, no Ektachrome. Most of our editorial is supplied by author. We look for good color balance, very sharp focus, the ability to capture sailing, good composition and action. Always looking for *cover shots*." Reports in 2 months. Pays $50-500/inside photo; $500/cover photo. Pays on publication. Credit line given. Buys all rights, but may reassign to photographer after publication; first N.A. serial rights; or one-time rights.

Tips: "For 1994 calendar. Horizontal only. Leisure sailing (no racing). Any locale around the world. Sailboats of all sizes. *Boat can be under sail or at anchor,* with emphasis on the boat, not the people on it. Depiction of sailing as tranquility, serenity and beauty. Unusually sharp focus, outstanding color balance, required. Pays $200-300."

*CUPIDO, % Red Alder Books, P.O. Box 2992, Santa Cruz CA 95063. (408)426-7082. Photo Representative: David Steinberg. Monthly magazine. Emphasizes quality erotica. Circ. 100,000. Estab. 1984. Sample copy $10.

Needs: Uses 50 photos/issue. Needs quality erotic photography, visually interesting, imaginative, showing human emotion, tenderness, warmth, humor OK, sensuality emphasized. Reviews photos with or without a manuscript.
Making Contact & Terms: Contact through rep. Arrange personal interview to show portfolio or submit portfolio for review. Query with stock photo list. Send unsolicited photos by mail for consideration. Send 8 × 10 or 11 × 14 b&w, color prints; 35mm, 2¼ × 2¼, 4 × 5, 8 × 10 transparencies. Keeps samples on file. SASE. Reports in 2-4 weeks. Pays $1,000-1,600/color cover photo; $60-120/color inside photo; $60-120/b&w inside photo. Pays on publication. Credit line given. Buys one-time rights. Simultaneous submissions and/or previously published work OK.
Tips: "Not interested in standard, porn-style photos. Imagination, freshness, emotion emphasized. Glamor OK, but not necessary."

CYCLE WORLD MAGAZINE, Dept. PM, 1499 Monrovia Ave., Newport Beach CA 92663. (714)720-5300. Editorial Director: Paul Dean. Monthly magazine. Circ. 350,000. For active motorcyclists who are "young, affluent, educated and very perceptive." For motorcycle enthusiasts.
Needs: "Outstanding" photos relating to motorcycling. Buys 10 photos/issue. Prefers to buy photos with mss. For Slipstream column see instructions in a recent issue.
Making Contact & Terms: Buys all rights. Send photos for consideration. Pays on publication. Reports in 6 weeks. SASE. Send 8 × 10 glossy prints. "Cover shots are generally done by the staff or on assignment." Uses 35 mm color transparencies. Pays $50-100/b&w photo; $150-225/color photo.
Tips: Prefers to buy photos with mss. "Read the magazine. Send us something good. Expect instant harsh rejection. If you don't know our magazine, don't bother us."

D MAGAZINE, Dept. PM, Suite 1200, 3988 North Central Expwy., Dallas TX 75204. (214)827-5000. FAX: (214)827-8844. Art Department: Liz Tindall, Jim Darilek. Consumer publication. Monthly magazine. Emphasizes Dallas issues and lifestyles. Circ. 120,000. Estab. 1975. Sample copy available for $2.50.
Needs: Uses 45 photos/issue; 95% supplied by freelancers. All photos are assigned. Subjects vary according to nature of story. Occasionally needs photo essay material. Model/property release required; photo captions preferred.
Making Contact & Terms: Submit portfolio for review. Provide business card, brochure, flyer or tearsheets to be kept on file for possible future assignments. Keeps samples on file. SASE. Reports in 1 month. Pays $650/color cover photo; $200/color inside photo. Credit line given. Buys one-time rights. Simultaneous submissions OK.
Tips: Expects to see "very creative work," but "it's very hard to find."

DAKOTA OUTDOORS, P.O. Box 669, Pierre SD 57501. (605)224-7301. Contact: Editor. Monthly magazine. Emphasizes outdoor life in the Dakotas. Readers are "outdoor-oriented." Circ. 7,000. Estab. 1978. Sample copy free for 9 × 12 SAE. Photo guidelines free with SASE.
Needs: Uses 15-20 photos/issue; 10% supplied by freelancers. Needs photos of animal/wildlife, fish, outdoor pursuits, scenics. Model/property release and photo captions preferred.
Making Contact & Terms: Interested in receiving work from newer, lesser-known photographers. Send unsolicited photos by mail for consideration. Send 5 × 7, glossy, b&w and color prints. SASE. Reports in 1 month. Pays $10-50 depending upon photo, subject and use; have paid up to $200 for specialty items.. Pays on publication. Credit line given. Usually buys one-time rights but negotiable. Simultaneous submissions and previously published work OK.
Tips: "We want good quality outdoor shots, good lighting, identifiable faces, etc. – photos shot in the Dakotas. Use some imagination and make your photo help tell a story. Photos with accompanying story are accepted."

DALLAS LIFE MAGAZINE, DALLAS MORNING NEWS, Communications Center, P.O. Box 655237, Dallas TX 75265. (214)977-8433. Managing Editor: Mike Maza. Art Director: Lesley Becker. Weekly magazine. Emphasizes Dallas. Circ. 850,000. Sample copy free with SASE.
Needs: "We buy only Dallas-pegged material – this is a very locally-focused publication." Uses 20 photos/issue; 5% supplied by freelance photographers. Reviews photos with accompanying ms only. Captions required.
Making Contact & Terms: Query with resume of credits; provide resume, business card, brochure, flyer or tearsheets to be kept on file for possible future assignments. SASE. Reports in 1 month. Pays $50-200/color inside photo. Pays on acceptance. Credit line given. Buys one-time rights.

DANCE MAGAZINE, 33 W. 60th St., New York NY 10023. (212)245-9050. FAX: (212)956-6487. Photo Editor: Jane Buchanan. Monthly magazine. Estab. 1927. Emphasizes "all facets of the dance world." Readers are 85% female, age 18-40. Circ. 50,000.

Needs: Uses about 60 photos/issue; almost all supplied by freelance photographers. Needs photos of all types of dancers—from ballroom to ballet. Dance, dancer, company and date of photo must accompany all submissions. Occasionally buys stock images; 95% of photos are assigned.
Making Contact & Terms: Send query letter describing photos, slides, transparencies and how the work would suit the magazine's needs. Pays up to $285/color cover photo; $25-150/b&w inside photo; $60-200/color inside photo. Pays on publication. Credit line given. Buys one-time rights. Previously published work OK.
Tips: "We look for a photojournalistic approach to the medium—photos that catch the height of a particular performance or reveal the nature of a particular dancer. We occasionally will print a photo that is strikingly revealing of life backstage, or in rehearsal."

DEER AND DEER HUNTING, P.O. Box 1117, Appleton WI 54912. (414)734-0009. FAX: (414)734-2919. Managing Editor: Al Hofacker. 8 issues/year. Distribution 200,000. Emphasizes whitetail deer and deer hunting. Readers are "a cross-section of American deer hunters—bow, gun, camera." Estab. 1977. Sample copy and photo guidelines free with 9 × 12 SAE with $2 postage.
Needs: Uses about 25 photos/issue; 20 supplied by freelance photographers. Needs photos of deer in natural settings. Model release and captions preferred.
Making Contact & Terms: Query with resume of credits and samples. "If we judge your photos as being usable, we like to hold them in our file. It is best to send us duplicates because we may hold the photo for a lengthy period." SASE. Reports in 2 weeks. Pays $500/color cover; $40/b&w inside; $75-250/color inside. Pays within 10 days of publication. Credit line given. Buys one-time rights. Simultaneous submissions and previously published work OK.
Tips: Prefers to see "adequate selection of b&w 8 × 10 glossy prints and 35mm color transparencies, action shots of whitetail deer only as opposed to portraits. We also need photos of deer hunters in action. We are currently using almost all color—very little b&w. Submit a limited number of quality photos rather than a multitude of marginal photos. Have your name on all entries. Cover shots must have room for masthead."

*DIRT WHEELS, (formerly *3 & 4 Wheel Action*), 10600 Sepulveda, Mission Hills CA 91345. (818)365-6831. FAX: (818)361-4512. Editor: Steve Casper. Monthly magazine. Emphasizes ATVs (all-terrain vehicles), also known as 3&4 wheelers. Readers are young adult males. Circ. 50,000. Sample copy free on request.
Needs: Uses 75-100 photos/issue; 25 supplied by freelance photographers. Needs photos of travel and scenic shots from different parts of the country; hunting and fishing (all with ATVs in the photos). Special photo needs include "unique spots to ride off-road vehicles." Photo captions preferred.
Making Contact & Terms: Interested in receiving work from newer, lesser-known photographers. Call and leave message. Reports in 1 month. Pays $50/color cover photo; $40/color inside photo; $20/b&w inside photo; $100-300/photo/text package. Pays on publication. Credit line given. Buys one-time rights. Simultaneous submissions and previously published work OK.
Tips: "Go on a trip with a local ATV club—they'll probably be glad to put you up and show you a good time. Take great photos."

THE DIVER, Dept. PM, Box 313, Portland CT 06480. (203)342-4730. Publisher/Editor: Bob Taylor. 6 issues/year. Emphasizes springboard and platform diving. Readers are divers, coaches, officials and fans. Circ. 1,500. Sample copy $2 with SASE and 75¢ postage.
Needs: Uses about 10 photos/issue; 30% supplied by freelance photographers. Needs action shots, portraits of divers, team shots and anything associated with the sport of diving. Special needs include photo spreads on outstanding divers and tournament coverage. Captions required.
Making Contact & Terms: Send 4 × 5 or 8 × 10 b&w glossy prints by mail for consideration; "simply query about prospective projects." SASE. Reports in 4 weeks. Pays $25-50/b&w cover photo; $10-25/b&w inside photo; $35-100 for text/photo package; $15-100/day. Pays on publication. Credit line given. Buys one-time rights. Simultaneous submissions and previously published work OK.
Tips: "Study the field, stay busy."

✿DIVER MAGAZINE, 295-10991 Shellbridge Way, Richmond BC V6X 3C6 Canada. (604)273-4333. FAX: (604)273-0813. Publisher: Peter Vassilopoulos. Estab. 1975. Magazine published 9 times/year. Emphasizes sport scuba diving, ocean science, technology and all activities related to the marine environment.
Making Contact & Terms: Interested in receiving work from newer, lesser-known photographers. Credit line given. Pays $7-50/b&w photo; $15-100/color photo. Pays within 6 weeks of publication. Buys one-time rights. Send material by mail for consideration. SAE and IRC must be enclosed. Reports in 4 weeks. Guidelines available for SAE and IRC.

Needs: Limited photo/text packages on dive sites around the world; diving travel features—prefer Canadian material; marine life—habits, habitats, etc.; personal experiences, ocean science/technology; commercial, military and scientific diving; written in laymen's terms. Photos purchased with accompanying ms only. Model release preferred; captions required.
Tips: Prefers to see "a variety of work: close-ups, wide angle—some imagination!"

DOG FANCY, P.O. Box 6050, Mission Viejo CA 92690. (714)855-8822. Editor: Kim Thornton. Readers are "men and women of all ages interested in all phases of dog ownership." Monthly. Circ. 150,000. Estab. 1970. Sample copy $4.50; photo guidelines available with SASE.
Needs: Uses 20-30 photos/issue, 90% supplied from freelance stock. Specific breed featured in each issue. Prefers "photographs that show the various physical and mental attributes of the breed. Include both environmental and portrait-type photographs. We also have a major need for good-quality, interesting b&w photographs of any breed or mixed breed in any and all canine situations (dogs with veterinarians; dogs eating, drinking, playing, swimming, etc.) for use with feature articles." Model release required. Captions preferred (include dog's name and breed and owner's name and address).
Making Contact & Terms: Send by mail for consideration actual 8×10 b&w photos, 35mm or 2¼×2¼ color transparencies. Reports in 6 weeks. Pays $15-35/b&w photo; $50-150/color photo; $100-300 per text/photo package. Credit line given. Buys first N.A. serial rights; buys one-time rights.
Tips: "Nothing but sharp, high contrast shots. Send SASE for list of photography needs. We're looking more and more for good quality photo/text packages that present an interesting subject both editorially and visually. Bad writing can be fixed, but we can't do a thing with bad photos. Subjects should be in interesting poses or settings with good lighting, good backgrounds and foregrounds, etc. We are very concerned with sharpness and reproducibility; the best shot in the world won't work if it's fuzzy, and it's amazing how many are. Submit a variety of subjects—there's always a chance we'll find something special we like."

DOLLS—The Collector's Magazine, 170 5th Ave., New York NY 10010. (212)989-8700. Editor: Joan Muyskens-Pursley. 9 times a year. Circ. 110,000. Emphasizes dolls—antique and contemporary. Readers are doll collectors nationwide. Sample copy $2.
Needs: Uses about 75-80 photos/issue; 12 supplied by freelance photographers. Needs photos of dolls to illustrate articles. Photos purchased with accompanying ms only. "We're looking for writers/photographers around the country to be available for assignments and/or submit queries on doll collections, artists, etc."
Making Contact & Terms: Query with samples; provide resume, business card, brochure, flyer or tearsheets to be kept on file for possible future assignments. SASE. Reports in 6-8 weeks. Pays $100-300/job; $150-350 for text/photo package. Pays within 30 days of acceptance. Credit line given. Buys one-time or first N.A. serial rights ("usually"). Previously published work "sometimes" OK.
Tips: Prefers to see "relevant (i.e., dolls) color transparencies or black and white prints; clear, precise—not 'artsy'—but well-lit, show off doll."

DOWN BEAT MAGAZINE, Jazz Blues & Beyond, 180 West Park Ave., Elmhurst IL 60126. (708)941-2030. Editorial Director: Frank Alkyer. Monthly. Emphasizes jazz musicians. Circ. 90,000. Estab. 1934. Sample copy available.
Needs: Uses about 30 photos/issue; 95% supplied by freelancers. Needs photos of live music performers/posed musicians/equipment, "primarily jazz and blues." Captions preferred.
Making Contact & Terms: Query with list of stock photo subjects; send 8×10 b&w prints; 35mm, 2¼×2¼, 4×5, 8×10 transparencies; b&w or color contact sheets by mail. Unsolicited samples for consideration will not be returned unless accompanied by SASE. Provide resume, business card, brochure, flyer or tearsheets to be kept on file for possible future assignments. "Send us two samples of your best work and a list of artists photographed." Reports only when needed. Pays $35/b&w photo; $75/color photo; $175/complete job. Credit line given. Buys one-time rights. Simultaneous submissions and previously published work OK.
Tips: "We prefer live shots and interesting candids to studio work."

DOWN EAST MAGAZINE, Dept. PM, Camden ME 04843. (207)594-9544. Managing Editor: Dale Kuhnert. Monthly magazine. Circ. 80,000. Emphasizes Maine contemporary events, outdoor activities, vacations, travel, history and nostalgia. For residents and lovers of the Pine Tree State.
Needs: Buys 25-40 photos/issue. Needs vary widely according to individual story needs, but heavy emphasis is on landscape and "photo-illustration." Photos must relate to Maine people, places and events.
Making Contact & Terms: Buys first N.A. serial rights. Virtually all photographs used are shot on assignment. Very few individual stock photos purchased. Query with portfolio and/or story ideas. SASE. Reports in 6 weeks. Send 8×10 or larger prints; 35mm or larger transparencies. Brief captions

required. Transparencies must be in sleeves and stamped with photographer's name. Do *not* submit color prints. Pays $25 minimum.

Tips: Prefers to see landscapes, people. In portfolios, on-location lighting. Submit seasonal material 6 months in advance.

*DULUTH NEWS-TRIBUNE, 424 W. First St., P.O. Box 169000, Duluth MN 55816-9000. (218)723-5233. FAX: (218)723-5295. Contact: Cindy Nelson. Publications vary to include tourism, consumer products, homes and more. Markets to all readers with certain publication targeting various groups. Circ. 65,000-150,000. Sample copy free with SASE.

Needs: Uses 60 photos/issue; 30% supplied by freelancers. Needs photos of winter and summer tourists: camping, fishing, skating, skiing, snowmobiling, etc. Other publications use home decorating, office and flowers. Model/property release required. Photo captions preferred.

Making Contact & Terms: Query with stock photo list. Reports in 3 weeks. Pays $125/color cover photo; $30/b&w inside photo. Credit line given. Buys one-time rights. Rights negotiable. Simultaneous and/or previously published work OK.

Tips: "If interested in submitting work to newspaper, ask for a copy of special projects for the year, and any other questions, too."

E MAGAZINE, Dept. PM, 28 Knight St., Norwalk CT 06851. (203)854-5559. FAX: (203)866-0602. Photo Editor: Christina Vaamonde. Nonprofit consumer magazine. Emphasizes environmental issues. Readers are environmental activists; people concerned about the environment. Circ. 75,000. Estab. 1990. Sample copy for 9 × 12 SASE and $2 postage. Photo guidelines free with SASE.

Needs: Uses 42 photos/issue; 55% supplied by freelancers. Needs photos of threatened landscapes, environmental leaders, people and the environment and coverage of when environmental problem figures into background of other news. Model and/or property release preferred. Photo captions required: location, identities of people in photograph, date, action in photograph.

Making Contact & Terms: Query with resume of credits and list of stock photo subjects. Keeps samples on file. Reports in 1-6 weeks. Pays $75/color photo; negotiable. Pays several weeks after publication. Credit line given. Buys one-time rights. Simultaneous submissions and previously published work OK.

Tips: Wants to see "straightforward, journalistic images. Abstract or art photography or landscape photography is not used." In addition, "please do not send manuscripts with photographs. These can be addressed as queries to the managing editor."

EAST WEST MAGAZINE, Suite 209, 3660 Waialai Ave., Honolulu HI 96816. (808)733-3333. Publisher: Chris Pearce. Quarterly magazine. Emphasizes "all aspects of countries in Asia and the Pacific Rim." Readers are male and female, 18-65, various occupations." Circ. 13,500. Estab. 1980. Sample copy $3 with 9 × 12 SASE and $2.40 postage.

Needs: Uses 30 photos/issue; 90% supplied by freelancers. Needs "travel, scenics, personalities, depending on editorial content." Model release and photo captions required.

Making Contact & Terms: Query with list of stock photo subjects; send unsolicited photos by mail for consideration. Send 35mm, 2¼ × 2¼, 4 × 5 transparencies. SASE. Reports in 1 month. Pays $200/color cover photo; $75/color and b&w inside photo; $200/day; $300-600/photo/text package (depending on word count for feature articles). Credit line given. Buys one-time rights. Previously published work OK.

Tips: "We use only sharp, true-color images. We rarely publish all-photo features, preferring features with *both* uncompromising photos and editorial content."

EASYRIDERS MAGAZINE, Dept. PM, P.O. Box 3000, Agoura Hills CA 91301. (818)889-8740. FAX: (818)889-4726. Editor: Keith R. Ball. Estab. 1971. Monthly. Emphasizes "motorcycles (Harley-Davidsons in particular), motorcycle women, bikers having fun." Readers are "adult men—men who own, or desire to own, custom motorcycles. The individualist—a rugged guy who enjoys riding a custom motorcycle and all the good times derived from it." Free sample copy. Photo guidelines free with SASE.

Needs: Uses about 60 photos/issue; "the majority" supplied by freelance photographers; 70% assigned. Needs photos of "motorcycle riding (rugged chopper riders), motorcycle women, good times had by bikers, etc." Model release required. Also interested in technical articles relating to Harley-Davidson.

Making Contact & Terms: Send b&w prints, 35mm transparencies by mail for consideration. SASE. Reports in 1 month. Pays $30-100/b&w photo; $40-250/color photo; $30-2,500/complete package. Other terms for bike features with models to satisfaction of editors. For usage on cover, gatefold and feature. Pays 30 days after publication. Credit line given. Buys all rights. All material must be exclusive.

Tips: Trend is toward "more action photos, bikes being photographed by photographers on bikes to create a feeling of motion." In samples, wants photos "clear, in-focus, eye-catching and showing some emotion. Read magazine before making submissions. Be critical of your own work. Check for sharpness. Also, label photos/slides clearly with name and address."

*ELLERY QUEEN'S MYSTERY MAGAZINE, 380 Lexington Ave., New York NY 10168-0035. (212)856-6300. FAX: (212)697-1567. Art Director: Terri Czeczko. Monthly magazine. Readers are female and male, ages 40 and over. Circ. 250,000. Estab. 1941. Photo guidelines free with SASE.
Needs: Uses 1 cover shot/issue. Needs photos of famous authors and personalities. Model/property release required.
Making Contact & Terms: Submit portfolio for review. Keeps samples on file. NPI. Pays on publication. Credit line given. Buys all rights. Rights negotiable.

ENTREPRENEUR, Dept. PM, 2392 Morse Ave., Irvine CA 92714. (714)261-2325. Publisher: Jim Fitzpatrick. Editor: Rieva Lesonsky. Design Director: Richard R. Olson. Photo Editor: Chrissy Borgatta. Monthly. Circ. 340,000. Emphasizes business. Readers are existing and aspiring small business owners.
Needs: Uses about 30 photos/issue; many supplied by freelance photographers. Needs "editorially specific, conceptual and how-to, and industrial" photos. Model release required.
Making Contact & Terms: Arrange a personal interview to show portfolio. Query with sample or list of stock photo subjects. Provide resume, business card, brochure, flyer or tearsheets to be kept on file for possible future assignment; "follow-up for response." Pays $75-200/b&w photo; $125-225/color photo; $350-400 day. Pays on publication. Credit line given. Rights individually negotiated.

ENVIRONMENT, Dept. PM, 1319 18th St. NW, Washington DC 20036. (202)296-6267. Editor: Barbara T. Richman. Photo Editor: Amie Freling. Magazine published 10 times/year. Covers science and science policy from a national, international and global perspective. "We cover a wide range of environmental topics—acid rain, tropical deforestation, nuclear winter, hazardous waste disposal, worker safety, energy topics and environmental legislation." Readers include libraries, colleges and universities and professionals in the field of environmental science and policy. Circ. 12,500. Sample copy $4.50.
Needs: Uses 15 photos/issue; varying number supplied by freelance photographers. "Our needs vary greatly from issue to issue—but we are always looking for good photos showing human impacts on the environment worldwide—industrial sites, cities, alternative energy sources, pesticide use, disasters, third world growth, hazardous wastes, sustainable agriculture and pollution. Interesting and unusual landscapes are also needed." Model release preferred; captions required.
Making Contact & Terms: Query with list of stock photo subjects. Send unsolicited photos by mail for consideration. Provide business card, brochure, flyer or tearsheets to be kept on file for possible future assignments. Send any size b&w print by mail for consideration. SASE. Reports in 2 months. Pays $35-100/b&w inside photo; $50-300/color photo. Pays on publication. Credit line given. Buys one-time rights. Simultaneous submissions and previously published work OK.
Tips: "We are looking for international subject matter—especially environmental conditions in developing countries."

EQUAL OPPORTUNITY, Equal Opportunity Publications, Inc., Dept. PM, 44 Broadway, Greenlawn NY 11740. (516)261-8917. Art Director: Jamie Ctroud. Magazine published 3 times/year. Emphasizes career guidance for members of minority groups at the college and professional levels. Readers are college-age, minority students and young working professionals of all occupations that require a college degree. Circ. 15,000. Sample copy with 9 × 12 SASE and 5 first class stamps.
Needs: Uses at least one photo per issue (cover); planning to use freelancers for cover and possibly editorial. Contact for needs. Model release preferred; photo captions required.
Making Contact & Terms: Query with list of stock photo subjects or send unsolicited photos by mail for consideration. Send color 35mm transparencies. SASE. Reports in 2 weeks. Pays $25/color cover photo. Pays on publication. Credit line given. Buys one-time rights. Simultaneous submissions and previously published work OK, "but not in competitive career-guidance publications."
Tips: "We are looking for clear color shots of minority students and young professionals who are involved in activities related to their academic studies or professions. We've decided to use more cover photos than we have in the past. We are also open to using inside photos, but freelancers should contact us and discuss upcoming stories before sending photos. Read our magazine to get an idea of the editorial content. Cover photos do not have to tie in to any one particular story in the issue, but they have to be representative of the magazine's editorial content as a whole."

The code NPI (no payment information given) appears in listings that have not given specific payment amounts.

❀EQUINOX MAGAZINE, 7 Queen Victoria Rd., Camden East ON K0K 1J0 Canada. (613)378-6661. Editor: Bart Robinson. Bimonthly. Circ. 175,000. Emphasizes "Canadian subjects of a general 'geographic' and scientific nature." Sample copy $5 with 8½×14 SAE; photo guidelines free with SAE and IRC.
Needs: Uses 80-100 photos/issue; all supplied by freelance photographers. Needs "photo stories of interest to a Canadian readership as well as occasional stock photos required to supplement assignments. Story categories include wildlife, international travel and adventure, science, Canadian arts and architecture and Canadian people and places." Captions required.
Making Contact & Terms: Query with samples; submit portfolio for review. SASE. Reports in 6 weeks. "Most stories are shot on assignment basis—average $2,000 price. We also pay expenses for people on assignment. We also buy packages at negotiable prices and stock photography at about $250 a page if only one or two shots used." Pays on publication. Credit line given. Buys first N.A. serial rights.
Tips: We look for "excellence and in-depth coverage of a subject, technical mastery and an ability to work intimately with people. Many of the photographs we use are of people, so any portfolio should emphasize people involved in some activity. Stick to Kodachrome/Ektachrome transparencies."

EVANGELIZING TODAY'S CHILD, Child Evangelism Fellowship Inc., P.O. Box 348, Warrentown MO 63383. (314)456-4321. Editor: Mrs. Elsie Lippy. Bimonthly magazine. Circ. 23,000. Estab. 1942. Written for people who work with children, ages 5-12, in Sunday schools, Bible clubs and camps. Sample copy for $1; free photo guidelines with SASE.
Needs: Buys 1-4 photos/issue. Buys 50% from freelance asssignment, 50% from freelance stock. Children, ages 6-11; unique, up-to-date. Candid shots of various moods and activities. If full color needs to include good color combination. "We use quite a few shots with more than one child and some with an adult, mostly closeups. The content emphasis is upon believability and appeal. Religious themes may be especially valuable." No nudes, scenery, fashion/beauty, glamour or still lifes.
Making Contact & Terms: Interested in receiving work from newer, lesser-known photographers. Pays on a per-photo basis. Pays $30 minimum/b&w photo; $40 minimum/color inside photo; $100/color cover shot. Credit line given. Buys one-time rights. Prefers to retain good-quality photocopies of selected glossy prints and duplicate slides in files for future use. Send material by mail with SASE for consideration; 8×10 b&w glossy prints or 35mm and larger transparencies. Publication is under no obligation to return materials sent without SASE. Simultaneous submissions and previously published work OK. Sample copy for $1; free photo guidelines with SASE.

*EXECUTIVE REPORT MAGAZINE, 3 Gateway Center, Pittsburgh PA 15222. (412)471-4585. Art/Production Director: Steve Karlovich. Monthly magazine. Emphasizes business reporting. Readers are primarily male, average age 45-50, mid to upper management. Circ. 26,000. Estab. 1981. Sample copy free with SASE. Photo guidelines not available.
Needs: Uses 4-15 photos/issue; 100% supplied by freelancers. Needs photos relating to business and business issues. Photo captions preferred.
Making Contact & Terms: Query with stock photo list. Provide resume, business card, brochure, flyer or tearsheets to be kept on file for possible assignments. Keeps samples on file. Cannot return material. "We will contact if interested." Pays $400/color cover photo; $50-"and up"/color and b&w inside photo and color and b&w page rate. Pays on acceptance. Credit line given.

EXPECTING MAGAZINE, 685 3rd Ave., New York NY 10017. (212)878-8700. Art Director: Claudia Waters. Quarterly. Circ. 1,200,000. Emphasizes pregnancy and birth. Readers are pregnant women 18-40.
Needs: Uses about 12 photos/issue. Works with freelance photographers on assignment basis only for fashion, pregnant women and mothers with newborns; more than 50% of the issue comes from assignment. Provide card to be kept on file for future assignments. Occasionally uses stock color transparencies of women during labor and birth, and newborn babies, hospital or doctor visits. Model release required.
Making Contact & Terms: Arrange for drop-off to show portfolio. SASE. Do not send originals. No b&w photos used. Payment varies; $150-300/color photo. Pays on publication. Credit line given. Buys one-time rights. Previously published work OK.
Tips: In photographer's portfolio looks for "nice lighting, warm, friendly people, babies and candid lifestyle shots. Should not look too 'cataloguey.' Present a portfolio of transparencies and tearsheets of published work. I hire experienced professionals only."

FACES: The Magazine About People, 7 School St., Peterborough NH 03458. (603)924-7209. FAX: (603)924-7380. Picture Editor: Francelle Carapetyan. Monthly (except June, July and August) magazine. Emphasizes cultural anthropology for young people ages 8-15. Circ. 13,000. Estab. 1984. Sample copy $3.95 with 7½×10½ SASE and $1.25 postage.

Needs: Uses about 30-35 photos/issue; about 75% supplied by freelancers. "Photos (b&w use) for text must relate to themes; cover photos (color) should also relate to themes." Send SASE for themes. Photos purchased with or without accompanying ms. Model release and captions preferred.

Making Contact & Terms: Query with stock photo list and/or samples. SASE. Reports in 2 weeks. Pays $15-50/text photos; cover photos negotiated. Pays on publication. Credit line given. Buys one-time rights. Simultaneous submissions and previously published work OK.

Tips: "Photographers should request our theme list. Most of the photographs we use are of people from other cultures. We look for an ability to capture people in action—at work or play. We primarily need photos showing people, young and old, taking part in ceremonies, rituals, customs and with artifacts and architecture particular to a given culture. Appropriate scenics and animal pictures are also needed. All submissions must relate to a specific future theme."

*FANTASY BASEBALL, 700 E. State St., Iola WI 54990. (715)445-2214. FAX: (715)445-4087. Editor: Greg Ambrosius. Bimonthly magazine. Emphasizes baseball. Readers are 99% male, ages 25-40, college-educated, professionals. Circ. 150,000. Estab. 1990. Sample copy free with 9×12 SASE. Photo guidelines free with SASE.

Needs: Uses 30 photos/issue; 90% supplied by freelancers. Needs photos of action game shots of major-league baseball. Reviews photos with accompanying ms only. Special needs include NFL and NBA photos.

Making Contact & Terms: Query with list of stock photo subjects. Send color slides. Does not keep samples on file. SASE. Reports in 1-2 weeks. Pays $100/color cover photo; $50/color inside photo; $25/b&w inside photo. Pays on publication. Buys one-time rights.

Tips: Wants "clear, precise action shots of top players. Have some great photos to show me."

FARM & RANCH LIVING, 5400 S. 60th St., Greendale WI 53129. (414)423-0100. FAX: (414)423-1143. Editorial Assistant: Trudi Bellin. Bimonthly magazine. Estab. 1978. "Concentrates on farming and ranching as a way of life." Readers are full-time farmers and ranchers. Sample copy for $2; photo guidelines free with SASE.

Needs: Uses about 130 photos/issue; about 30 from freelance photographers, 25% from stock. Needs agricultural and scenic photos. Photo caption preferred with season and location.

Making Contact & Terms: Interested in receiving work from newer, lesser-known photographers. Query with samples or list of stock photo subjects; send 35mm, 2¼×2¼, 4×5, 8×10 transparencies by mail for consideration. SASE. "We only want to see one season at a time; we work one season in advance." Reporting time varies; "ASAP: can be a few days, may be a few months." Pays $200/color cover photo; $50-125/color inside photo; $150/color page (full page bleed); $10-25/b/w photo. Pays on publication. Buys one-time rights. Previously published work OK. "We assume you have secured releases. If in question, don't send the photos." Captions should include season, location.

Tips: "Technical quality extremely important. Colors must be vivid so they pop off the page. Study our magazines thoroughly. We have a continuing need for sharp, colorful images. Those who supply what we need can expect to be regular contributors."

FIELD & STREAM, 2 Park Ave., New York NY 10016. (212)779-5364. Photo Editor: Scott William Hanrahan. This is a broad-based service magazine. The editorial content ranges from very basic "how it's done" filler stories that tell in pictures and words how an outdoor technique is accomplished or device is made, to feature articles of penetrating depth about national conservation, game management, and resource management issues; and recreational hunting, fishing, travel, nature and outdoor equipment. Writer's/photographer's guidelines available.

Needs: Photos using action and a variety of subjects and angles in both b&w and color. "We are always looking for cover photographs, in color, which may be vertical or horizontal. Remember: a cover picture must have room at the left for cover lines." Needs photo information regarding subjects, the area, the nature of the activity and the point the picture makes. Don't attach caption information to color photos.

Making Contact & Terms: Send 8×10 b&w photos; 35mm and 2¼×2¼ transparencies. Will also consider 4×5 or 8×10 transparencies, but "majority of color illustrations are made from 35mm or 2¼ film." Submit photos by registered mail. Send slides in 8½×11 plastic sheets, and pack slides and/or prints between cardboard. SASE. Pays $75+/per b&w photo, $450/color photo depending on size used on single page; $700/partial color spread; $900/full color spread; $1,000+/color cover. Buys first North American serial rights returned after publication.

FIFTY SOMETHING MAGAZINE, Unit #E, 8250 Tyler Blvd., Mentor OH 44060. (216)974-9594. Editor: Linda L. Lindeman. Bimonthly magazine. Emphasizes lifestyles for the fifty-and-better-reader. Readers are men and women 50+. Circ. 25,000. Estab. 1990. Sample copy free with 9×12 SAE and 4 first-class stamps. Photo guidelines free with SASE.

Needs: Uses 25-40 photos/issue; 30+ supplied by freelancers. Needs "anything pertaining to mature living—travel, education, health, fitness, money, etc." Model release and photo captions preferred.
Making Contact & Terms: Interested in receiving work from newer, lesser-known photographers. Query with list of stock photo subjects; send unsolicited photos by mail for consideration;.submit portfolio for review; provide resume, business card, brochure, flyer or tearsheets to be kept on file for possible assignments. Send b&w, color prints; 35mm, 2¼×2¼, 4×5, 8×10 transparencies. SASE. Reports in 6 months. Pays $100/color cover photo; $10/color inside photo; $5/b&w inside photo; $25-75/hour; $100-400/day; $25-125/photo/text package. Pays on publication. Credit line given. Buys one-time rights. Simultaneous submissions and previously published work OK.
Tips: "We are an upbeat publication with the philosophy that life begins at 50. Looking for stories/pictures that show this lifestyle. Also, use a lot of travel/photo essays."

*FIGHTING WOMAN NEWS, 6741 Tung Ave. W., Theodore AL 36582. Editor: Debra Pettis. Quarterly. Circ. 5,000. Estab. 1975. Covers women's martial arts. Readers are "adult females actively practicing the martial arts or combative sports." Sample copy $3.50 postpaid; photo guidelines free with SASE.
Needs: Uses several photos/issue; most supplied by freelance photographers. Needs powerful images of female martial artists; "action photos from tournaments and classes/demonstrations; studio sequences illustrating specific techniques and artistic constructions illustrating spiritual values. Obviously, photos illustrating text have a better chance of being used. We have little space for fillers. We are always short of photos suitable to our magazine." Model release preferred; captions and identification required.
Making Contact & Terms: Query with resume of credits or with samples or send 8×10 glossy b&w prints or b&w contact sheet by mail for consideration; provide resume, business card, brochure, flyer or tearsheets to be kept on file for possible future assignments. SASE. Reports "as soon as possible." Payment for text/photo package to be negotiated." Pays on publication. Credit line given. Buys one-time rights. Simultaneous submissions and previously published work OK; "however, we insist that we are *told* concerning these matters; we don't want to publish a photo that is in the current issue of another martial arts magazine."
Tips: Prefers to see "technically competent b&w photos of female martial artists in action; good solid images of powerful female martial artists. We don't print color. No glamour, no models; no cute little kids unless they are also skilled. Get someone knowledgeable to caption your photos or at least tell you what you have—or don't have if you are not experienced in the art you are photographing. We are a poor alternative publication chronically short of material, yet we reject 90% of what is sent because the sender obviously never saw the magazine and has no idea what it's about. Five of our last seven covers were live action photos and we are using fewer "enhancements" than previously. Best to present yourself and your work with samples and a query letter indicating that you have *seen* our publication. The cost of buying sample copies is a lot less than postage these days."

FINE HOMEBUILDING, 63 S. Main St., P.O. Box 5506, Newtown CT 06470. (203)426-8171. FAX: (203)426-3434. Editor: Mark Feirer. Estab. 1981. Bimonthly plus 7th issue each spring. Emphasizes residential architecture and construction. Readers are architects, builders, owner/builders, contractors and craftsmen. Circ. 230,000. Sample copy for 9×12 SAE with $2.40 postage.
Needs: Uses 120 photos/issue; 20 supplied by freelancers. Needs photos of unusual houses; photos of carefully crafted architectural details; wood, stained glass, wrought iron, etc. Special needs include unusual windows, doors, stairs, chimneys, fences and gates. Model release required.
Making Contact & Terms: Interested in receiving work from newer, lesser-known photographers. Send unsolicited photos by mail for consideration or call. Uses 35mm, 2¼×2¼, 4×5 or 8×10 transparencies. SASE. Reports in 1 month. Negotiated payments. Credit line given.
Tips: Prefers to see "good, clear compositions with lots of detail, not 'art' shots."

FINESCALE MODELER, 21027 Crossroads Circle, P.O. Box 1612, Waukesha WI 53187. (414)796-8776. Editor: Bob Hayden. Photo Editor: Paul Boyer. Published 8 times/year. Circ. 82,000. Emphasizes "how-to-do-it information for hobbyists who build nonoperating scale models." Readers are "adult and juvenile hobbyists who build nonoperating model aircraft, ships, tanks and military vehicles, cars and figures." Sample copy $2.95; photo guidelines free with SASE.
Needs: Uses more than 50 photos/issue; "anticipates using" 10 supplied by freelance photographers. Needs "in-progress how-to photos illustrating a specific modeling technique; photos of full-size aircraft, cars, trucks, tanks and ships." Model release and captions required.
Making Contact & Terms: Provide resume, business card, brochure, flyer or tearsheets to be kept on file for possible future assignments. "Phone calls are OK." Reports in 8 weeks. Pays $25 minimum/color cover photo; $5 minimum/b&w inside photo; $7.50 minimum/color inside photo; $30/b&w page; $45/color page; $50-500 for text/photo package. Pays for photos on publication, for text/photo package

on acceptance. Credit line given. Buys one-time rights. "Will sometimes accept previously published work if copyright is clear."

Tips: Looking for "clear b&w glossy 5 × 7 or 8 × 10 prints of aircraft, ships, cars, trucks, tanks and sharp color positive transparencies of the same. In addition to photographic talent, must have comprehensive knowledge of objects photographed and provide copious caption material. Freelance photographers should provide a catalog stating subject, date, place, format, conditions of sale and desired credit line before attempting to sell us photos. We're most likely to purchase color photos of outstanding models of all types for our regular feature, FSM Showcase."

FINGER LAKES MAGAZINE, Box 0, 108 S. Albany St., Ithaca NY 14851. (607)272-3470. Editor: Linda McCandless. Bimonthly magazine. Emphasizes life in the Finger Lakes of New York. Circ. 20,000. Sample copy $1.95 with 9½ × 11 SAE and $1 postage.

Needs: Uses about 20-30 photos/issue; all supplied by freelance photographers. Needs photos on Finger Lake scenics, people, animals, photo essays. Model release preferred; captions required.

Making Contact & Terms: Arrange a personal interview to show portfolio; query with samples; query with list of stock photo subjects; send 35mm transparencies and b&w contact sheets by mail for consideration. Provide resume, business card, brochure, flyer or tearsheets to be kept on file for possible future assignments. SASE. Reports in 1 month or longer. Stock: Pays $150/color cover; $40-150/inside color; $25-100 inside b&w. Assignments: $125/day plus 20¢/mile plus film not processing (also negotiable). Pays 1 month after publication. Buys first N.A. serial rights. Simultaneous submissions OK.

Tips: "Keep trying. Sell us on a story idea as well as the pictures."

FISHING WORLD, 51 Atlantic Ave., Floral Park NY 11001. (516)352-9700. FAX: (516)437-6841. Editor: Keith Gardner. Bimonthly magazine. Circ. 300,000. Emphasizes techniques, locations and products of both freshwater and saltwater fishing. For men interested in sport fishing.

Needs: Photos of "worldwide angling action." Buys 18-30/annually; all freelance photography comes from freelance stock. Buys first N.A. serial rights. Send photos for consideration. Photos purchased with accompanying ms; cover photos purchased separately. Pays on publication. Reports in 3 weeks. SASE. Free sample copy and photo guidelines. Captions required.

Making Contact & Terms: Send transparencies. Requires originals. Pay rates for color: $300/cover; $50/¼ page; $75/½ page; $100/¾ page; $125/full page; $150/1½ page; $200/2-page spread. Black and white flat rate of $50.

Tips: "First, look at the magazine. In general, queries are preferred, though we're very receptive to unsolicited submissions accompanied by smashing photography." Inside photos are color. Trend is more boats. "Drama is desired rather than tranquility. Good-looking women are a plus."

*FLORIDA LEADER MAGAZINE, P.O. Box 14081, Gainesville FL 32604-2081. (904)373-6907. FAX: (904)373-8120. Art Director: Jeff Riemersma. Quarterly magazine. Emphasizes college living. Readers are male and female college students, ages 18-40. Circ. 27,000. Estab. 1983. Sample copy free with 8½ × 11 SASE and 3 first class stamps.

Needs: Uses 4-8 photos/issue; 100% supplied by freelancers. Assignment only. Model/property release required. Photo captions required.

Making Contact & Terms: Provide resume, business card, brochure, flyer or tearsheets to be kept on file for possible assignments. Reports in 3 weeks. Pays $100/color cover photo; $50/color inside photo. Pays on publication. Credit line given. Buys one-time rights. Rights negotiable. Simultaneous submissions and/or previously published work OK.

Tips: "We are looking for contacts around the state of Florida to do assignments for us as they come up."

FLOWER AND GARDEN MAGAZINE, 4251 Pennsylvania Ave., Kansas City MO 64111. (816)531-5730. FAX: (816)531-3873. Editor: Kay Melchisedech Olson. Estab. 1957.

Needs: Uses 50-75% freelance stock. "We purchase a variety of subjects relating to home lawn and garden activities. Specific horticultural subjects must be accurately identified. We return photos by certified mail—other means of return must be specified and paid for by the individual submitting them. We publish 6 times a year and require several months of lead time. It is not our policy to pay holding fees for photographs."

Making Contact & Terms: Interested in receiving work from newer, lesser-known photographers. To make initial contact, "Do not send great numbers of photographs, but rather a good selection of 1 or 2 specific subjects. We do not want photographers to call." Pays $25-100/b&w photo; $50-250/color photo. Pays on publication. Buys one-time rights. Model and property releases and photo captions preferred.

Tips: Wants to see "clear shots with crisp focus. Also, appealing subject matter—good lighting."

*FLY FISHERMAN, Cowles Magazines, Inc., Editorial Offices, 6405 Flank Dr., P.O. Box 8200, Harrisburg PA 17112. (717)657-9555. Editor and Publisher: John Randolph. Managing Editor: Philip Hanyok. Emphasizes all types of fly fishing for readers who are "99% male, 79% college educated, 79% married. Average household income is $62,590 and 55% are managers or professionals. 85% keep their copies for future reference and spend 35 days a year fishing." Bimonthly. Circ. 140,000. Sample copy $3 with 9×12 SAE and $1 postage; photo/writer guidelines for SASE.
Needs: Uses about 45 photos/issue, 70% of which are supplied by freelance photographers. Needs shots of "fly fishing and all related areas—scenics, fish, insects, how-to." Column needs are: Fly Tier's Bench (fly tying sequences). Captions required.
Making Contact & Terms: Send by mail for consideration 35mm, 2¼×2¼, 4×5 or 8×10 color transparencies. SASE. Reports in 4-6 weeks. NPI. Pays on publication. Credit line given. Buys one-time rights. No simultaneous submissions; no previously published work.

FLY ROD & REEL: THE MAGAZINE OF AMERICAN FLY-FISHING, Dept. PM, P.O. Box 370, Camden ME 04843. (207)594-9544. FAX: (207)594-7215. Managing Editor: Jim Butler. Magazine published 6 times/year, irregular intervals. Emphasizes fly-fishing. Readers are primarily fly fishermen ages 30-60. Circ. 44,000. Estab. 1979. Free sample copy with SASE. Photo guidelines free with SASE.
Needs: Uses 25-30 photos/issue; 15-20 supplied by freelancers. Needs "photos of fish, scenics (preferrably with anglers in shot), equipment." Photo captions preferred that include location, name of model (if applicable).
Making Contact & Terms: Query with list of stock photo subjects. Send unsolicited photos by mail for consideration. Provide resume, business card, brochure, flyer or tearsheets to be kept on file for possible assignments. Send glossy b&w, color prints; 35mm, 2¼×2¼, 4×5 transparencies. Keeps samples on file. SASE. Reports in 1 month. Pays $500/color cover photo; $75/color inside photo; $75/b&w inside photo; $125/color page rate; $100/b&w page rate. Pays on publication. Credit line given. Buys one-time rights.
Tips: "Photos should avoid appearance of being too 'staged.' We look for bright color (especially on covers), and unusual, visually appealing settings. Trout and salmon are preferred for covers."

FLYING, Dept. PM, 1633 Broadway, New York NY 10019. (212)767-6950. FAX: (212)767-5620. Art Director: Nancy Bink. Monthly magazine. Emphasizes airplanes. Readers are male pilots. Circ. 325,000. Estab. 1928.
Needs: 90% of photos supplied by freelance photographers. Needs photos of airplanes and related scenes and settings.
Making Contact & Terms: Provide resume, business card, brochure, flyer or tearsheets to be kept on file for possible assignments. Reports when interested. Pays $400-500/day. Credit line given. Buys one-time rights.
Tips: Send cover letter; "be brief and straightforward."

FOOD & WINE, Dept. PM, 1120 Avenue of the Americas, New York NY 10036. (212)382-5600. Art Director: Elizabeth Woodson. Monthly. Emphasizes food and wine. Readers are an "upscale audience who cook, entertain, dine out and travel stylishly." Circ. 850,000. Estab. 1978.
Needs: Uses about 25-30 photos/issue; freelance photography on assignment basis 85%, 15% freelance stock. "We look for editorial reportage specialists who do restaurants, food on location and travel photography." Model release and captions required.
Making Contact & Terms: Drop-off portfolio by appointment. Submission of flyers, tearsheets, etc. to be kept on file for possible future assignments and stock usage. Pays $450/color page; $100-450 color photo. Pays on acceptance. Credit line given. Buys one-time world rights.

*FOOTBALL DIGEST, 990 Grove St., Evanston IL 60201-4370. (312)491-6440. Editor: Vince Aversano. Monthly. Emphasizes pro football. Circ. 170,000.
Needs: Uses about 40 photos/issue; 100% supplied by freelance photographers. Needs photos of sports action and portraits.
Making Contact & Terms: Provide resume, business card, brochure, flyer or tearsheets to be kept on file for possible assignments. Uses 5×7 glossy b&w prints and 35mm transparencies. NPI. Pays on publication. Buys one-time rights.

FORTUNE, Time-Life Bldg., Dept. PM, New York NY 10020. (212)522-3803. Managing Editor: Marshall Loeb. Picture Editor: Michele F. McNally. Picture Editor reviews photographers' portfolios on an overnight drop-off basis. Emphasizes analysis of news in the business world for management personnel. Photos purchased on assignment only. Day rate on assignment (against space rate): $350; page rate for space: $400; minimum for b&w or color usage: $150.

FOUR WHEELER MAGAZINE, 6728 Eton Ave., Canoga Park CA 91303. (818)992-4777. Editor: John Stewart. Monthly magazine. Emphasizes four-wheel drive vehicles and enthusiasts. Circ. 325,000. Photo guidelines free with SASE.
Needs: Uses 100 color/100 b&w photos/issue; 2% supplied by freelance photographers. Needs how-to, travel/scenic/action (off-road 4×4s only) photos. Travel pieces also encouraged. Reviews photos with accompanying ms only. Model release and captions required.
Making Contact & Terms: Provide resume, business card, brochure, flyer or tearsheets to be kept on file for possible future assignments. Does not return unsolicited material. Reports in 1 month. Pays $10-50/inside b&w photo; $20-100/inside color photo; $100/b&w and color page; $200-600/text/photo package. Pays on publication. Credit line given. Buys all rights.

FREEDOM MAGAZINE, #1200, 6331 Hollywood Blvd., Hollywood CA 90028. (213)960-3500. Editor: Tom Whittle. Production Manager: Geoff Brown. Bimonthly magazine. News magazine: Emphasizes investigative reporting, news and current events. Estab. 1968. Sample copy $2 with 9×12 SAE.
Needs: Uses 30-40 photos/issue; 70% supplied by freelance photographers. Needs photos of famous people, current politicians, legislators and public figures. Special photo needs include new current news stories—particular current issues in alignment with stories. Model release preferred. Photo captions required.
Making Contact & Terms: Query with list of stock photo subjects. Send nonreturnable photos or promotion. Unsolicited material sent will not be returned. Provide resume, business card, brochure, flyer or tearsheets to be kept on file for possible assignments. No specifications for samples. SASE. Reports in 1 month. Pays up to $150/b&w photo; up to $500/color photo; $100-1,500/complete job. Payment varies depending on photo. Pays on publication. Credit line given. Buys one-time rights.

*FRONT PAGE DETECTIVE, Official Detective Group, 20th Floor, 460 W. 34th St., New York NY 10001. (212)947-6500. Editor-in-chief: Rose Mandelsberg-Weiss. Managing Editor: Christofer Pierson. Emphasizes factual articles and fact-based stories about crime. Readers are "police buffs, detective story buffs, law and order advocates." Magazine published 9 times/year. Circ. 100,000. Sample copy $3.50; photo guidelines for SASE.
Needs: "Only color covers are bought from freelance photographers. Situations must be crime, police, detective oriented; man and woman; action must portray impending disaster of a crime about to happen; *No bodies*. Modest amount of sensuality, but no blatant sex." Model release required; captions not required. "Interesting weapons a plus."
Making Contact & Terms: Send by mail for consideration actual color photos, or 35mm, 2¼×2¼, 4×5 color transparencies. SASE. Reports in 1 month, after monthly cover meetings. Pays on acceptance $200/color photo. No credit line given. Buys all rights. No simultaneous or previously published submissions. Send chromes to: Editor-in-chief: Rose Mandelsberg-Weiss.

FUN IN THE SUN, Dept. PM, 5436 Fernwood Ave., Los Angeles CA 90027. (213)465-7121. Publisher: Ed Lange. Quarterly. Emphasizes nudism/naturism/alternative lifestyles. Circ. 10,000. Photo guidelines free with SASE.
Needs: Uses about 50 photos/issue; 20 supplied by freelance photographers. Needs photos of "nudity; fun in sun (nonsexist)." Nudist, naturist, body self acceptance. Model release and captions required.
Making Contact & Terms: Query with samples. SASE. Reports in 3 weeks. Pays $50/b&w cover photo; $100/color cover photo; $25/b&w or color inside photo. Pays on acceptance. Credit line given. Buys one-time or all rights. Previously published work OK.

FUN/WEST, P.O. Box 2026, North Hollywood CA 91610-0026. Editor: John D. Adlai. Managing Editor: Ms. Tracey. Quarterly magazine. Emphasizes living on the West Coast for young, single people; resorts in the US and jet set activities. Monthly features on best wines of France, Germany, Italy and California. Photo and text.
Needs: Travel, fashion/beauty, glamour, ("good taste only"), product shots, wine and gourmet food. Captions preferred; model release required. Uses 8×10 b&w and color prints and covers.
Making Contact & Terms: Query only with list of stock photo subjects. Unsolicited materials will be discarded. SASE. Reports in 1 month or more. NPI; payment negotiable. Credit line given. Pays on publication. Buys all rights. Simultaneous submissions and previously published work OK.
Tips: Articles dealing with Hollywood and stars are encouraged, especially those with photos. "Exercise good taste at all times. Concentrate on showing the same subjects under different light or style."

The asterisk before a listing indicates that the market is new in this edition. New markets are often the most receptive to freelance submissions.

FUTURIFIC MAGAZINE, The Foundation for Optimism, Suite 1210, 280 Madison Ave., New York NY 10016. Editor-in-Chief: Mr. Balint Szent-Miklosy. Monthly. Circ. 10,000. Emphasizes future-related subjects. Readers range from corporate, government and religious leaders. Sample copy with $5 – for postage and handling.
Needs: Uses up to 10 photos/issue; all supplied by freelance photographers. Needs photos of subjects relating to the future. Photos purchased with or without accompanying ms. Captions preferred.
Making Contact & Terms: Send by mail for consideration b&w prints or contact sheets. Reports in 1 month. NPI; payment negotiable. Pays on publication. Buys one-time rights. Simultaneous submissions and/or previously published work OK.
Tips: "Photographs should illustrate what directions society and the world are heading. Optimistic only."

GALLERY MAGAZINE, FOX MAGAZINE, POCKETFOX MAGAZINE, 401 Park Ave. S., New York NY 10016-8802. Photo Editor: Judy Linden. Emphasizes men's interests. Readers are male, collegiate, middle class. Estab. 1972. Free photo guidelines with SASE.
Needs: Uses 80 photos/issue; 10% supplied from freelancers (no assignments). Needs photos of nude women and celebrities, plus sports, adventure pieces. Model release required.
Making Contact & Terms: Send by mail for consideration at least 100 35mm transparencies. SASE. Reports in 4 weeks. Girl sets: pays $800-1,800; cover extra. Buys first N.A. serial rights plus nonexclusive international rights. Girl Next Door contest: $250 entry photo; $2,500 monthly winner; $25,000 yearly winner. Photographer: entry photo/receives 1-year free subscription, monthly winner $500; yearly winner $2,500. Send by mail for contest information.
Tips: In photographer's samples, wants to see "beautiful models and good composition. Trend in our publication is outdoor settings – avoid soft focus! Send complete layout."

GAME & FISH PUBLICATIONS, Suite 110, 2250 Newmarket Pkwy., Marietta GA 30067. (404)953-9222. FAX: (404)933-9510. Photo Editor: Tom Evans. Editorial Director: Ken Dunwoody. Publishes 31 different monthly outdoors magazines: *Alabama Game & Fish, Arkansas Sportsman, California Game & Fish, Florida Game & Fish, Georgia Sportsman, Great Plains Game & Fish, Illinois Game & Fish, Indiana Game & Fish, Iowa Game & Fish, Kentucky Game & Fish, Louisiana Game & Fish, Michigan Sportsman, Mid-Atlantic Game & Fish, Minnesota Sportsman, Mississippi Game & Fish, Missouri Game & Fish, New England Game & Fish, New York Game & Fish, North Carolina Game & Fish, Ohio Game & Fish, Oklahoma Game & Fish, Pennsylvania Game & Fish, Rocky Mountain Game & Fish, South Carolina Game & Fish, Tennessee Sportsman, Texas Sportsman, Virginia Game & Fish, Washington-Oregon Game & Fish, West Virginia Game & Fish, Wisconsin Sportsman,* and *North American Whitetail.* Combined circulation 525,000. Estab. 1975. All magazines (except *Whitetail*) are for experienced fishermen and hunters and provide information about where, when and how to enjoy the best hunting and fishing in their particular state or region, as well as articles about game and fish management, conservation and environmental issues. Sample copy $2.50 with 10×12 SAE; photo guidelines free with SASE.
Needs: 50% of photos supplied by freelance photographers; 5% assigned. Needs photos of live game animals/birds in natural environment and hunting scenes; also underwater game fish photos and fishing scenes. Model release preferred. Captions and numbering of slides/prints required. In captions, identify species and location.
Making Contact & Terms: Query with samples. Send 8×10 glossy b&w prints or 35mm transparencies (preferably Kodachrome) with SASE for consideration. Reports in 1 month. Pays $250/color cover photo; $75/color inside photo; $25/b&w inside photo. Pays 75 days prior to publication. Credit line given. Buys one-time rights. Simultaneous submissions not accepted. Tearsheet provided.
Tips: "Study the photos that we are publishing before sending submission. We'll return photos we don't expect to use and hold remainder in-house so they're available for monthly photo selections. Please do not send dupes. Photos will be returned upon publication or at photographer's request."

GAMUT, Cleveland State University, FT1218, 1983 E. 24th St., Cleveland OH 44115-2440. (216)687-4679. Editor: Louis T. Milic. Triannual journal. General interest. Circ. 1,500. Sample copy $3.
Needs: Uses about 25-50 photos/issue; "several" supplied by freelance photographers. Subject needs "depend on the sort of articles we print. But we also print groups of interesting photographs (portfolios) on any subject." Model release preferred; captions required.
Making Contact & Terms: Query with b&w samples. SASE. Reports in 2 months. Pays in cash and contributor's copies. Range is $25 for a single full-page photo to $125 for a group (portfolio). Pays on publication. Credit line given. Buys first N.A. serial rights.

GARDEN DESIGN, Dept. PM, 4401 Connecticut Ave. NW, Washington DC 20008. (202)686-2752. FAX: (202)686-1001. Senior Editor: Cheryl Weber. Bimonthly. Emphasizes residential landscape architecture and garden design. Readers are gardeners, home owners, architects, landscape architects, garden designers and garden connoisseurs. Estab. 1982. Sample copy $5; photo guidelines free with SASE.

Needs: Uses about 80 photos/issue; nearly all supplied by freelance photographers; 80% from assignment and 20% from freelance stock. Needs photos of "public and private gardens that exemplify professional quality design." Needs to see both the design intent and how garden subspaces work together. Model release and captions required.

Making Contact & Terms: Submit proposal with resume and samples. Reports in 2 months or sooner if requested. Publishes color only, and uses original transparencies only for separation—do not send dupes. Pays $300/color cover photo; $150/inside photo over ⅓ page; $200/double page special; $75/⅓ page or smaller. Credit line given. Buys one-time first N.A. magazine publication rights. Previously published work may be acceptable but is not preferred.

Tips: "Show both detailed and comprehensive views that reveal the design intent and content of a garden, as well as subjective, interpretive views of the garden. A letter and resume are not enough— must see evidence of the quality of your work, in samples or tearsheets. Need excellent depth of field and superior focus throughout. Our trend is away from the large estate and/or public gardens, to smaller scale, well-conceived and executed residential ones."

GENERAL LEARNING CORP., 60 Revere Dr., Northbrook IL 60062-1563. (708)205-3000. Photo Editor: Larry Glickman. Photo/Graphics Coordinator: Sheryl Mersfelder. Estab. 1969. Publishes four monthly school magazines running September through May. *Current Health I* is for children aged 9-12. *Current Health II, Writing!, Career World* are for high school teens. An article topics list and photo guidelines will be provided free with 9×12 SAE.

Needs: B&w and color photos of children aged 9-12 and teens geared to our topic themes for inside use. Color: 35mm or larger transparencies geared to our monthly focus article for cover use. Model release preferred. Photo captions preferred.

Making Contact & Terms: Interested in receiving work from newer, lesser-known photographers. Send 8×10 b&w prints or Xerox copies of photos. Label all photos with name and address for easy return. Simultaneous submissions and previously published work OK. Pays $35/b&w, $75/color inside photo; $200/color cover photo. Pays on publication. Credit line given. Buys one-time rights; negotiable.

Tips: "We are looking for contemporary photos of children and teens. Do not send outdated looking photos. Clothing and hairstyles should be current. We are always looking for ethnic children/teens. When sending photos for a specific article or magazine please specify which one and specify which month."

*GENESIS MAGAZINE, 1776 Broadway, New York NY 10019. (212)265-3500. FAX: (212)265-8087. Art Director: Don Lewis. Monthly magazine. Emphasizes nude women. Readers are male, ages 25-45. Circ. 500,000. Estab. 1973. Photo guidelines free with SASE.

Needs: Uses 100 photos/issue. Needs photos of nudes. Special photo needs include surreal photojournalism and artistic nudes. Model release required (2 pieces of identification).

Making Contact & Terms: Send unsolicited photos by mail for consideration. Send color prints, 35mm, 2¼×2¼ transparencies. SASE. Reports in 1 month. Pays $1,000-3,000 per set. Pays 60 days after acceptance. Credit line given.

Tips: Needs "beautiful photos of beautiful women, no styled sets in historic costumes, or photos in poor taste."

GENT, Suite 600, 2600 Douglas Rd., Coral Gables FL 33134. (305)443-2378. Editor: Steve Dorfman. Monthly magazine. Circ. 150,000. Showcases full-figured, D-cup nude models. Sample copy $5 (postpaid). Photo guidelines free with SASE.

Needs: "Nude models must be extremely large breasted (minimum 38" bust line). Sequence of photos should start with woman clothed, then stripped to brassiere and then on to completely nude. Bikini sequences also recommended. Cover shots must have nipples covered. Chubby models also considered if they are reasonably attractive and measure up to our 'D-Cup' image." Model release and photocopy or photograph of picture ID required. Buys in sets, not by individual photos. "We publish mss on sex, travel, adventure, cars, racing, sports, gambling, grooming, fashion and other topics that traditionally interest males."

Making Contact & Terms: Credit line given. Pays on publication. Buys one-time rights or second serial (reprint) rights. Send material by mail for consideration. SASE. Previously published work OK. Reports in 4-6 weeks. Send transparencies. Prefer Kodachrome or large format; vertical format required for cover. Pays 1st rights, $150/page; 2nd rights, $80/page; $300/cover photo; $250-400 for text and photo package.

❀GEORGIA STRAIGHT, 2nd Floor, 1235 W. Pender St., Vancouver, BC V6E 2V6 Canada. (604)681-2000. FAX: (604)681-0272. Managing Editor: Charles Campbell. Weekly tabloid. Emphasizes entertainment. Readers are generally well-educated people between 20 and 45 years old. Circ. 80,000. Estab. 1967. Sample copy free with 10×12 SAE.

Needs: Uses 20 photos/issue; 35% supplied by freelance photographers on assignment. Needs photos of entertainment events and personalities. In particular looking for "portraits of high-profile movie stars." Photo captions preferred.
Making Contact & Terms: Query with list of stock photo subjects. Include resume, business card, brochure, flyer or tearsheets to be kept on file for possible assignments. Reports in 1 month. Pays $125/b&w cover photo and $75/b&w inside photo. Pays on publication. Credit line given. Buys one-time rights. Simultaneous submissions and previously published work OK.
Tips: In portfolio or samples, wants to see "portraits and concert photos. Almost all needs are for in-Vancouver assigned photos, except for high-quality portraits of film stars."

GOLF DIGEST, Dept. PM, 5520 Park Ave., Box 0395, Trumbull CT 06611. (203)373-7000. Art Director/Graphic Administrator: Nick DiDio. Monthly magazine. Circ. 1,350,000. Emphasizes golf instruction and features on golf personalities and events. Free sample copy. Free photo guidelines with SASE.
Needs: Buys 10-15 photos/issue from freelance photographers. Needs celebrity/personality (nationally known golfers, both men and women, pros and amateurs); fashion/beauty (on assignment); head shot (golfing personalities); photo essay/photo feature (on assignment); product shot (on assignment); scenics (shots of golf resorts and interesting and/or unusual shots of golf courses or holes); and sport (golfing). Model release preferred; captions required. "The captions will not necessarily be used in print, but are required for identification."
Making Contact & Terms: Send 8×10 glossy b&w prints, no contact sheet; 35mm transparencies, no duplicates. Uses 35mm color transparencies for cover; vertical format required. Pays $100 minimum/job and also on a per-photo or per-assignment basis. Pays $75-200/b&w photo; $100-600/color photo; $500 minimum/cover photo. Credit line given. Pays on publication. Send material by mail for consideration. "The name and address of the photographer must appear on every slide and print submitted." SASE. Simultaneous submissions OK. Reports in 1 month.
Tips: "We are a very favorable market for a freelance photographer who is familiar with the subject. Most of the photos we use are done on specific assignment, but we do encourage photographers to cover golf tournaments on their own with an eye for unusual shots, and to let the magazine select shots to keep on file for future use. We are always interested in seeing good quality color and b&w work." Prefers Kodachrome-64 film; no Ektachrome.

*GOLF JOURNAL, Golf House, Far Hills NJ 07931. (201)234-2300. Editor: David Earl. Staff Writer: Marty Parkes. Art Director: Diane Chrenko-Becker. Emphasizes golf for golfers of all ages and both sexes. Readers are "literate, professional, knowledgeable on the subject of golf." Eight issues per year. Circ. 285,000. Free sample copy.
Needs: Uses 20-25 photos/issue, 5-20 supplied by freelance photographers. "We use color photos extensively, but usually on an assignment basis. Our photo coverage includes amateur and professional golfers involved in national or international golf events, and shots of outstanding golf courses and picturesque golf holes. We also use some b&w, often mugshots, to accompany a specific story about an outstanding golfing individual. Much of our freelance photo use revolves around USGA events, many of which we cover. As photo needs arise, we assign photographers to supply specific photo needs. Selection of photographers is based on our experience with them, knowledge of their work and abilities, and, to an extent, their geographical location. An exceptional golf photo would be considered for use if accompanied by supportive information." Column needs are: Great Golf Holes, a regular feature of the magazine, calls for high quality color scenics of outstanding golf holes from courses around the country and abroad. Model release not required; captions required.
Making Contact & Terms: Query Editor David Earl with resume of photo credits; or call (do not call collect). Works with freelance photographers on assignment only basis. Provide calling card, resume and samples to be kept on file for possible future assignments. SASE. Reports in 2 weeks. Pays on acceptance. Negotiates payment based on quality, reputation of past work with the magazine, color or b&w and numbers of photos. Pays $25 minimum. Credit line given. Rights purchased on a work-for-hire basis. No simultaneous or previously published work.

GOLF MAGAZINE, Dept. PM, 2 Park Ave., New York NY 10016. (212)779-5000. Editor-in-Chief: George Peper. Art Director: Ron Ramsey. Monthly magazine. Emphasizes golf. Readers are male, ages 15-80, college educated, professional. Circ. 1,000,000. Free sample copy; photo and writer's guidelines free with SASE.
Needs: Celebrity/personality, head shot, golf travel photos, scenic, special effects and experimental, spot news, human interest, humorous and travel. Photos purchased with accompanying ms—golf related articles. Photos must be golf-related. Model release preferred; captions required. No cartoons.
Making Contact & Terms: Pays $50 minimum/job and on a per-photo basis. Pays $50 minimum/b&w photo; $50-600/color photo; $25-750/ms. Pays on acceptance. Buys first serial rights. Query with samples. SASE. Simultaneous submissions OK. Reports in 3 weeks. Send 8×10 glossy prints and transparencies. Uses 2¼×2¼ transparencies for cover; vertical format preferred.

GOLF TRAVELER, Dept. PM, 1137 East 2100 South, Salt Lake City UT 84106. (801)486-9391. FAX: (800)453-4260, ext. 40. Managing Editor: Larry Jaramillo. Bimonthly magazine. Emphasizes golf; senior golfers. Readers are "avid golfers who have played an average of 24 years." Circ. 72,500. Estab. 1976. Free sample copy with SASE.
Needs: Uses 15-35 photos/issue; all supplied by freelancers. Needs photos of "affiliated golf courses associated with Golf Card; personality photos of Senior Tour golfers. Model release required. Photo captions preferred that include who and where.
Making Contact & Terms: Send unsolicited photos by mail for consideration. Send 35mm transparencies. Does not keep samples on file. SASE. Reports in 1-2 weeks. Pays $150/color cover photo; $50/color inside photo. Pays on publication. Credit line given. Buys one-time rights. Previously published work OK.
Tips: Looks for "clarity of golf hole or property being featured. Good color-realistic greens and blues. Something out of the ordinary is good. All golf courses are green. Capture something not seen by everyone, but still found at the property."

＊✹GOSPEL HERALD, 4904 King St., Beamsville ON L0R 1B6 Canada. (416)563-7503. Editor: Roy D. Merritt or Managing Editor: Eugene Perry. Estab. 1936. Consumer publication. Monthly magazine. Emphasizes Christianity. Readers are primarily members of the Churches of Christ. Circ. 1,600. Sample copy free with SASE.
Needs: Uses 2-3 photos/issue; percentage supplied by freelancers varies. Needs scenics, shots, especially those relating to readership—moral, religious and nature themes.
Making Contact & Terms: Send unsolicited photos by mail for consideration. Send b&w, any size and any format. Payment not given, but photographer receives credit line.
Tips: "We have never paid for photos. Because of the purpose of our magazine, both photos and stories are accepted on a volunteer basis."

GRAND RAPIDS MAGAZINE, 549 Ottawa Ave. NW, Grand Rapids MI 49503-1444. (616)459-4545. FAX: (616)459-4800. Publisher: John H. Zwarensteyn. Editor: Carole Valade Smith. Monthly magazine. Estab. 1963. Emphasizes community-related material of Western Michigan; local action and local people.
Needs: Animal, nature, scenic, travel, sport, fashion/beauty, photo essay/photo feature, fine art, documentary, human interest, celebrity/personality, humorous, wildlife, vibrant people shots and special effects/experimental. Wants on a regular basis western Michigan photo essays and travel-photo essays of any area in Michigan. Model release and captions required.
Making Contact & Terms: Freelance photos assigned and accepted. Provide business card to be kept on file for possible future assignments; "only people on file are those we have met and personally reviewed." Buys one-time rights. Arrange a personal interview to show portfolio, query with resume of credits, send material by mail for consideration, or submit portfolio for review. SASE. Reports in 3 weeks. Send 8×10 or 5×7 glossy b&w prints; contact sheet OK; 35mm, 120mm or 4×5 transparencies or 8×10 glossy color prints; Uses 2¼×2¼ and 4×5 color transparencies for cover, vertical format required. Pays $25-35/b&w photo; $35-50/color photo; $100-150/cover photo.
Tips: "Most photography is by our local freelance photographers, so freelancers should sell us on the unique nature of what they have to offer."

GREAT LAKES FISHERMAN, 1432 Parsons Ave., Columbus OH 43201. (614)445-7507. Editor: Dan Armitage. Monthly. Circ. 41,000. Estab. 1976. Emphasizes fishing for anglers in the 8 states bordering the Great Lakes. Sample copy and photo guidelines free with SASE.
Needs: 12 covers/year supplied by freelance photographers; 100% from freelance stock. Needs transparencies for covers; 99% used are verticals. No full frame subjects; need free space top and left side for masthead and titles. Fish and fishermen (species common to Great Lakes Region) action preferred. Photos purchased with or without accompanying ms. "All b&w is purchased as part of ms package. Covers are not assigned but purchased as suitable material comes in." Model release required for covers; captions preferred.
Making Contact & Terms: Query with tearsheets or send unsolicited photos by mail for consideration. Prefers 35mm transparencies. SASE. Reports in 1 month. Provide tearsheets to be kept on file for possible future assignments. Pays $200/color photo; covers only. Pays on 15th of month preceding issue date. Credit line given. Buys one-time rights.
Tips: Sees trend toward: "More closeups of *live* fish." To break in, freelancer should "look at 1992 covers" for insight.

GUIDEPOSTS ASSOCIATES, INC., Dept. PM, 21st Floor, 16 E. 34th St., New York NY 10016. (212)754-2225. FAX: (212)832-4870. Photo Editor: Courtney Reid-Eaton. Monthly magazine. Circ. 4,000,000. Estab. 1945. Emphasizes tested methods for developing courage, strength and positive attitudes through faith in God. Free sample copy and photo guidelines with 6×9 SASE and 65¢ postage.

Needs: 85% assignment, 15% stock (variable). "Photos mostly used are of an editorial reportage nature or stock photos, i.e., scenic landscape, agriculture, people, animals, sports. We work four months in advance. It's helpful to send stock pertaining to upcoming seasons/holidays. No lovers, suggestive situations or violence."

Making Contact & Terms: Pays by job or on a per-photo basis; pays $150-400/color photo; $400-750/cover photo; $300-500/day. Credit line given. Pays on acceptance. Buys one-time rights. Send photos or arrange a personal interview. SASE. Simultaneous submissions OK. Reports in 1 month. Send 35mm transparencies; vertical format required for cover. Usually shot on assignment.

Tips: "I'm looking for photographs that show people in their environment well. I like warm, saturated color for portraits and scenics. We're trying to appear more contemporary. We want to stimulate a younger audience and yet maintain a homey feel. For stock—scenics; graphic images with intense color. *Guideposts* is an 'inspirational' magazine. NO violence, nudity, sex. No more than 60 images at a time. Write first and ask for a photo guidelines/sample issue; this will give you a better idea of what we're looking for. I will review transparencies on a light box or in a carousel. I am interested in the experience as well as the photograph. I am also interested in the photographer's sensibilities—Do you love the city? Mountain climbing? Farm life?"

*GULF MARINER, P.O. Box 1220, Venice FL 34284. (813)488-9307. Editor: Thomas Kahler. Biweekly tabloid. Readers are recreational boaters, both power and sail. Circ. 15,000+. Estab. 1984. Sample copy free with 9×12 SASE and $1 postage.

Needs: Uses cover photo each issue—24 a year; 100% supplied by freelance photographers. Needs photos of boating related fishing, water skiing, racing and shows. Use of swimsuit-clad model or fisherman with boat preferred. All photos must have *vertical* orientation to match our format. Model release required. Photo captions preferred.

Making Contact & Terms: Interested in receiving work from newer, lesser-known photographers. Send 35mm transparencies by mail for consideration. SASE. Reports in 1-2 weeks. Pays $50/color cover photo. Pays on acceptance. Credit lines optional. Rights negotiable. May use photo more than once for cover. Simultaneous and previously published work acceptable.

Tips: "We are willing to accept outtakes from other assignments which is why we pay only $50. We figure that is better than letting an unused shot go to waste or collect dust in the drawer."

GUN WORLD, Box HH, 34249 Camino Capistrano, Capistrano Beach CA 92624. (714)493-2101. Editor: Jack Lewis. Monthly. Emphasizes firearms, all phases. Readers are middle to upper class, aged 25-60. Circ. 136,000. Sample copy $3 postpaid; photo guidelines free with SASE.

Needs: Uses 70-80 photos/issue; about 50% (with mss) supplied by freelance photographers. Needs hunting and shooting scenes. Reviews photos with accompanying ms only. Model release preferred; captions required.

Making Contact & Terms: Query with samples; send unsolicited photos by mail for consideration at your own risk. Send 5×7 minimum glossy b&w prints and 35mm, 2¼×2¼ and 4×5 transparencies. SASE. Reports in 1 month. Pays $100/color cover photo; $10-100/inside b&w photo; $40/color inside photo; $100-350/text/photo package. Pays on acceptance. Credit line given if requested. Buys all rights, will release to author on request.

*GUNS & AMMO MAGAZINE, 8490 Sunset Blvd., Los Angeles CA 90069. (213)854-2160. Editor: E.G. "Red" Bell, Jr. Art Director: Carol Winet. Monthly. "Technical to semi-technical firearms journal." Readers are shooters, gun collectors, do-it-yourselfers. Circ. 500,000+. "Writer's guide with brief tips on photo packages free with SASE."

Needs: Uses about 450 photos/issue. Needs photos of generally top-quality, still shots of firearms, action shots of guns being fired, sometimes wildlife shots and how-tos. Photos purchased with accompanying ms only. Model release preferred; captions required.

Making Contact & Terms: Submit photos with mss on speculation. SASE. NPI. Pays on acceptance. Credit line given. Buys one-time rights and all rights; will negotiate. Simultaneous submissions OK.

Tips: Prefers to see "sharp, well-lit photos with uncluttered backgrounds. In our case, photos are most likely accepted with an article. It would be easier to 'break into' *G&A* for the writer/photographer, rather than the photographer."

✸HARROWSMITH, 7 Queen Victoria Rd., Camden East ON K0K 1J0 Canada. (613)378-6661. Editor-in-chief: Michael Webster. Estab. 1976. Magazine published 6 times/year. Circ. 154,000. Emphasizes alternative lifestyles, self-reliance, energy conservation, gardening, solar energy and homesteading. Sample copy $5 with 8½×14 SASE; free photo and writer's guidelines.

Needs: Buys 400 photos/year, 50 photos/issue; 40% assigned. Animal (domestic goats, sheep, horses, etc., on the farm); how-to; nature (plants, trees, mushrooms, etc.); photo essay/photo feature (rural life); horticulture and gardening; scenic (North American rural); and wildlife (Canadian, nothing exotic). "Nothing cute. We get too many unspecific, pretty sunsets, farm scenes and landscapes." Captions preferred. Photos purchased with or without accompanying ms and on assignment.
Making Contact & Terms: Interested in receiving work from newer, lesser-known photographers. Provide calling card, samples and tearsheet to be kept on file for possible future assignments. Uses 8×10 b&w glossy prints, contact sheet and negatives OK; 35mm and 2¼×2¼ transparencies and 8×10 glossy color prints. Query with samples and list of subjects. SAE. Reports in 4 weeks. Pays $50-500/job; $200-1,000 for text/photo package; $100-250/b&w photo; $100-300/color photo. Pays on acceptance. Credit line given. Buys first N.A. rights. Previously published work OK.
Tips: Prefers to see portfolio with credits and tearsheets of published material. Samples should be "preferably subject oriented. In portfolio or samples, wants to see "clarity, ability to shoot people, nature and horticulture photo essays. Since there's a trend toward strong photo essays, success is more likely if a submission is made in a photo essay type package."

HAWAI'I REVIEW, % University of Hawai'i, 1733 Donaghho Rd., Dept. of English, Honolulu HI 96822. (808)956-8548. Editor-in-Chief: Jeanne K. Tsutsui. Triannual journal. Literary and arts readership. Circ. 2,000. Estab. 1973. Sample copy $5 with 9×12 SASE with 95¢ postage.
Needs: Freelance photography is all from stock. Prefers b&w experimental or "art" photos. No scenic or postcard-type shots. Special photo needs include cover photos. Model release required; captions should include artistic explanation and title.
Making Contact & Terms: Interested in receiving work from newer, lesser-known photographers. Send unsolicited photos by mail for consideration. Reports in 4 months. Pays $25-75/b&w photo. Pays on publication. Credit line given. Buys one-time rights; copyright reverts to artist upon publication. Simultaneous submissions OK if so noted in cover letter. *Must* include self-addressed stamped envelope..
Tips: "Photographs should make some kind of statement or be so stunning that they speak for 'Beauty's Sake.' We use either 2-color or monochrome, so high-contrast b&w photos are best." To break in, "send a lot and often."

HEALTH WORLD, 1540 Gilbreth Rd., Burlingame CA 94010. (415)697-8038. Managing Editor: Jeff Kravitz. Bimonthly magazine. Emphasizes health and nutrition. Circ. 50,000. Estab. 1985. Sample copy $2.50. Photo guidelines free with SASE.
Needs: Uses 25 photos/issue. Model release required.
Making Contact & Terms: Arrange personal interview to show portfolio; submit portfolio for review; query with list of stock photo subjects. Cannot return material. Pays $15/color cover photo. Pays on publication. Credit line given. Buys one-time rights. Simultaneous submissions OK.

THE HERB QUARTERLY, P.O. Box 548, Boiling Springs PA 17007. (717)245-2764. Contact: Linda Sparrowe. Readers are "herb enthusiasts interested in herbal aspects of gardening, cooking or crafts." Quarterly. Circ. 25,000. Sample copy $6.
Needs: Needs photo essays related to some aspect of herbs. Captions required.
Making Contact & Terms: Query with resume of credits. SASE. Reports in 1 month. Pays on publication $50/essay. Credit line given. Buys first N.A. serial rights or reprint rights.

*HIGH SOCIETY MAGAZINE, 801 Second Ave., New York NY 10017. (212)661-7878. FAX: (212)692-9297. Photo editor: Jennifer Rothstein. Monthly magazine. Emphasis on "everything of sexual interest to the American male." Readers are young males, ages 21-40. Circ. 400,000. Estab. 1976. Sample copies free with SASE. Photo guidelines available.
Needs: Uses 300 photos/issue; 50% supplied by freelancers. Needs sexually stimulating, nude photos of gorgeous women, ages 21-35. Reviews photos with or without accompanying ms. Special needs include outdoor and indoor scenes of nude women. Model/property release required. Captions preferred.
Making Contact & Terms: Arrange personal interview to show portfolio. Send color prints; 35mm, 2¼×2¼ transparencies by mail for consideration. Does not keep samples on file. SASE. Reports in 1-2 weeks. Pays $300/color cover photo; $150/color inside photo; $100/b&w inside photo; $800/color page rate; $400/b&w page rate; $1,500/photo-text package. Pays on acceptance. Credit line given. Buys one-time rights; negotiable. Simultaneous submissions and previously published work OK.
Tips: Looks for "clear, concise color, interesting set preparation and props, strong contrast, backgrounds and settings, and knock-'em-out models."

HIGHLIGHTS FOR CHILDREN, Dept. PM, 803 Church St., Honesdale PA 18431. Photo Essay Editor: Kent L. Brown, Jr. Art Director: Rosanne Guararra. Monthly magazine. Circ. 3,000,000+. For children, age 2-12.

Needs: "We will consider outstanding photo essays on subjects of high interest to children." Buys 20 annually. Photos purchased with accompanying ms. Wants no single photos without captions or accompanying ms. Free sample copy.

Making Contact & Terms: Buys all rights. Send photo essays for consideration. Reports in 3-7 weeks. SASE. Send 8×10 b&w glossy or matte prints; 5×7 or 8×10 color glossy or matte prints, prefer transparencies. Captions required. Pays $30 minimum/b&w photo; $55 minimum/color photo; NPI on ms.

Tips: "Tell a story which is exciting to children. We are glad to keep on file names of those who maintain a stock of photos, particularly of current sports personalities and wildlife subjects. We also need mystery photos, puzzles that use photography/collage, special effects, anything unusual that will visually and mentally challenge children."

*ALFRED HITCHCOCK'S MYSTERY MAGAZINE, 380 Lexington Ave., New York NY 10168-0035. (212)557-9100. Editor: Cathleen Jordan. Published every four weeks. Emphasizes short mystery fiction. Readers are mystery readers, all ages, both sexes. Circ. 225,000. Sample copy $3. Photo guidelines free with SASE.

Needs: Uses 1 photo/issue; all supplied by freelance photographers. Needs mysterious photographs that contain a narrative element, should allow for a variety of possible interpretations. No gore; no accidents; no crime scenes. Black and white photos only. Model release required.

Making Contact & Terms: Query with samples, "nonreturnable photocopies only." Does not return unsolicited material. Reports in 2 months. NPI; negotiated. Pays on acceptance. Credit line given. Buys one-time rights.

*HOCKEY DIGEST, 990 Grove St., Evanston IL 60201-4370. (708)491-6440. Editor: Vince Aversano. Monthly. Emphasizes pro hockey for sports fans. Circ. 90,000.

Needs: Uses about 40 photos/issue; 100% supplied by freelance photographers. Needs photos of sports action and portraits.

Making Contact & Terms: Provide resume, business card, brochure, flyer or tearsheets to be kept on file for possible assignments. Uses 5×7 glossy b&w prints and 35mm transparencies. NPI. Pays on publication. Buys one-time rights.

HOCKEY ILLUSTRATED, 355 Lexington Ave., New York NY 10017. (212)391-1400. FAX: (212)986-5926. Editor: Stephen Ciacciarelli. Published 3 times/year, in season. Emphasizes hockey superstars. Readers are hockey fans. Circ. 50,000. Sample copy $2.50 with 9×12 SASE.

Needs: Uses about 60 photos/issue; all supplied by freelance photographers. Needs color slides of top hockey players in action. Captions preferred.

Making Contact & Terms: Query with action color slides. SASE. Pays $150/color cover photo; $75/color inside photo. Pays on acceptance. Credit line given. Buys one-time rights.

HOME EDUCATION MAGAZINE, P.O. Box 1083, Tonasket WA 98855. (509)486-1351. Managing Editor: Helen Hegener. Bimonthly magazine. Emphasizes home schooling. Readers are parents of children, ages 2-18. Circ. 4,700. Estab. 1983. Sample copy for $4.50. Photo guidelines free with SASE.

Needs: Number of photos used/issue varies based on availability; 50% supplied by freelance photographers. Needs photos of parent/child or children. Special photo needs include home school personalities and leaders. Model and property releases and photo captions preferred.

Making Contact & Terms: Interested in receiving work from newer, lesser-known photographers. Send unsolicited b&w prints by mail for consideration. SASE. Reports in 1 month. Pays $25-50/b&w cover photo; $5-20/b&w inside photo; $20/b&w page rate; $10-50/photo/text package. Pays on publication. Credit line given. Buys first N.A. serial rights. Simultaneous submissions and previously published work OK.

Tips: In photographer's samples, wants to see "sharp clear photos of children doing things alone, in groups or with parents. Know what we're about! We get too many submissions that are simply irrelevant to our publication."

THE HOME SHOP MACHINIST, P.O. Box 1810, Traverse City MI 49685. (616)946-3712. Editor: Joe D. Rice. Bimonthly. Circ. 25,000. Emphasizes "machining and metal working." Readers are "amateur machinists, small commercial machine shop operators and school machine shops." Sample copy free with 9×12 SAE and 90¢ postage; photo guidelines free with SASE.

Needs: Uses about 30-40 photos/issue; "most are accompanied by text." Needs photos of "machining operations, how-to-build metal projects." Special needs include "good quality machining operations in b&w."

Making Contact & Terms: Send 4×5 or larger b&w glossy prints by mail for consideration. SASE. Reports in 3 weeks. Pays $40/b&w cover photo; $9/b&w inside photo; $30 minimum for text/photo package ("depends on length"). Pays on publication. Credit line given. Buys one-time rights. Simultaneous submissions OK.

Tips: "Photographer should know about machining techniques or work with a machinist. Subject should be strongly lit for maximum detail clarity."

HORSE & RIDER MAGAZINE, #103, 1060 Calle Cordillera, San Clemente CA 92672. (714)361-1955. Photo Editor: Lisa Wrigley. Monthly consumer magazine. Emphasizes training and care of horses. Circ. 100,000. Sample copy $2; free photo guidelines with SASE.
Needs: Uses 45 photos/issue; 40 supplied by freelance photographers or photojournalists; 10% assigned. Needs photos of horses, prefer action, verticals, slides or 8×10 prints. Riders must be wearing Western hats and boots. The horse should be the emphasis of the photo; the horse's expression is also important. If horse is wearing bit, bridle, saddle, etc., all gear must be Western. Reviews photos with or without accompanying ms. Captions a must. Little use for pretty scenery or pasture shots.
Making Contact & Terms: Send 8×10 matte b&w or color prints; 35mm, 2¼×2¼ transparencies; b&w contact sheets with ms, b&w negatives with ms by mail for consideration. SASE. Reports in 1 month unless used in magazines. Pays $100/color cover photo; $5-20/inside b&w photo; $5-25/color photo; $25/page. Pays upon publication. Credit line given. "Be patient if your material is not published right away."
Tips: "We use predominantly 1 page/1 photo, however 2-4 shot series are also used. Shots being considered should be simple and get the feeling of Western training or riding across quickly. Contrast and sharpness are crucial. Good solid areas in background are preferred over busy or areas of contrasting lights and darks. *A horse photographer must know his subject.* Go vertical format as much as possible. Concentrate on the subject not the scenery. Be double sure subjects are in full Western gear. Leave room for cropping, logo, bleed, etc."

HORSE ILLUSTRATED, Dept. PM, P.O. Box 6050, Mission Viejo CA 92690. (714)855-8822. FAX: (714)855-3045. Editor: Susan Wells. Associate Editor: Kathryn Shayman. Readers are "primarily adult horsewomen between 18-40 who ride and show mostly for pleasure and who are very concerned about the well being of their horses." Circ. 120,000. Sample copy $3.50; photo guidelines free with SASE.
Needs: Uses 20-30 photos/issue, all supplied by freelance photographers; 50% from assignment and 50% from freelance stock. Specific breed featured every issue. Prefers "photos that show various physical and mental aspects of horses. Include environmental, action and portrait-type photos. Prefer people to be shown only in action shots (riding, grooming, treating, etc.). We like riders—especially those jumping—to be wearing protective headgear. We also need good-quality, interesting b&w photos of horses for use in feature articles."
Making Contact & Terms: Send by mail for consideration actual 8×10 b&w photos or 35mm and 2¼×2¼ color transparencies. Reports in 8 weeks. Pays $15-25/b&w photo; $50-150/color photo and $100-350 per text/photo package. Credit line given. Buys one-time rights.
Tips: "Nothing but sharp, high-contrast shots. Looks for clear, sharp color & b&w shots of horse care and training. Healthy horses, safe riding and care atmosphere is the current trend in our publication. Send SASE for a list of photography needs and for photoguidelines and submit work (pref. color trans.) on spec."

HORSEPLAY MAGAZINE, Dept. PM, P.O. Box 130, 11 Park Ave., Gaithersburg MD 20884. (301)840-1866. FAX: (301)840-5722. Art Director: Lisa Kiser. Monthly magazine. Emphasizes English riding (show jumping, fox hunting, dressage, eventing). Readers are ages 15-35, female, middle to upper middle class. Circ. 50,000. Estab. 1972. Sample copy $2.95. Photo guidelines free with SASE.
Needs: Uses 45 photos/issue; 95% supplied by freelance photographers. Needs photos of horse shows, training photos and general horses being ridden. Special photo needs include world championship events, major grand prix, major 3-day, major dressage competitions. Photo captions required and must identify horse and rider.
Making Contact & Terms: Send b&w prints and 35mm transparencies by mail for consideration. Pays $200/color cover photo; $45/color inside photo; $22.50/b&w inside photo; $75 assignment fee. SASE. Buys first N.A. serial rights. Previously published work OK.
Tips: Wants to see "good quality photo for reproduction, knowledge of subject matter with an artistic flair."

HORSES MAGAZINE, Dept. PM, 21 Greenview, Carlsbad CA 92009. (619)931-9958. FAX: (619)931-0650. Managing Editor: Terry Reim. Magazine published 6 times per year. Emphasizes show jumping and dressage. Readers are from teens to active seniors, primarily female with substantial number of males. Circ. 6,500. Estab. 1961. Sample copy $5. Call for specs (619)931-9958.
Needs: Uses approximately 134 photos/issue; 35% supplied by freelance photographers. Needs photos of people, ring, jumps and performance. "Send action photos or class winners for major international events." Special needs include "photos to accompany show reports of 'A'-rated horse shows to which we do not send staff photographers." Captions required.

Making Contact & Terms: Send 4×5 and 8×10 glossy b&w and color prints and 35mm and 2¼×2¼ transparencies by mail for consideration. SASE. Reports in 1-2 weeks. Pays $10-25/color inside photo; $10-25/b&w inside photo. Pays 30 days after publication. Credit line given. Buys first N.A. serial rights.
Tips: "Prefer action photos to presentation photos." In photographer's samples "no proof sheets; 3×5, 5×7 and 8×10 b&w or color prints of action, people and win photos. Know the subject, do good work and look at what kinds of photos we publish."

HORTICULTURE MAGAZINE, Suite 1220, Statler Office Bldg., 20 Park Plaza, Boston MA 02116. (617)482-5600. Photo Editor: Tina Schwinder. Monthly magazine. Emphasizes gardening. Readers are all ages. Circ. 250,000. Estab. 1904. Sample copy $2.50 with 9×12 SAE with $2 postage. Photo guidelines free with SASE.
Needs: Uses 25-30 photos/issue; 20-25 supplied by freelance photographers. Needs photos of gardening, individual plants. Model release preferred; captions required.
Making Contact & Terms: Arrange a personal interview to show portfolio; query with samples; send color prints, 35mm transparencies by mail for consideration; submit portfolio for review; provide resume, business card, brochure, flyer or tearsheets to be kept on file for possible future assignments. SASE. Reports in 1 month. Pays $500/color cover photo; $50-200/color page. Pays on publication. Credit line given. Buys one-time rights. Simultaneous submissions OK.
Tips: Wants to see gardening images, i.e., plants and gardens.

HOT ROD MAGAZINE, Dept. PM, 8490 Sunset Blvd., Los Angeles CA 90069. (213)854-2280. Editor: Jeff Smith. Monthly magazine. Circ. 850,000. For enthusiasts of high performance and personalized automobiles.
Needs: Typical subject areas include drag racing, street rods, customs, modified pickups, off-road racing, circle track racing. Will consider b&w and color photo features on individual vehicles; of race or event coverage with information; or b&w photos of technical or how-to subjects accompanied by text. However, best market is for "Roddin' at Random" section, which uses single photo and/or short copy on any "newsy" related subject, and "Finish Line," which runs short pieces on a wide variety of vehicular racing or other competition. These sections pay $50-150 per photo or item used.
Making Contact & Terms: Model release necessary. Buys all rights. Credit line given. Pays on acceptance. Reports in 2 weeks. Send 8×10 glossy prints or contact sheets with negs. Pays $50-250. Send transparencies. Pays $100-500.
Tips: "Look at the magazine before submitting material. Use imagination, bracket shots, allow for cropping, keep backgrounds clean. We generally need very sharp, crisp photos with good detail and plenty of depth of field. Majority of material is staff generated; best sell is out-of-area (non-Southern California) coverage or items for news/human interest/vertical interest/curiosity columns (i.e., 'Roddin' at Random' and 'Finish Line'). Again, study the magazine to see what we want."

*HOUSE OF WHITE BIRCHES, 306 East Parr Rd., Berne IN 46711. (219)589-8741. Editor: Rebekah Montgomery. Bimonthly magazine. Emphasizes doll collecting. Readers are doll lovers—any type doll. Circ. 60,000. Sample copy $2.
Needs: Uses 60 photos/issue; 25% supplied by freelance photographers on assignment. "We need romance and product shots of dolls with identification." Model release required; captions preferred.
Making Contact & Terms: Send b&w, color prints; 35mm, 2¼×2¼, 4×5, 8×10 transparencies by mail for consideration. Provide resume, business card, brochure, flyer or tearsheets to be kept on file for possible future assignments. SASE. Reports in 2 weeks. Pays $60/color cover photo; $15/color inside photo; $40/color page. Pays on publication. Credit line given. Buys one-time rights, all rights, but will negotiate. Previously published work OK.
Tips: In portfolio or samples wants to see "clear photos without sharp shadows."

HUDSON VALLEY MAGAZINE, Dept. PM, 297 Main Mall, Poughkeepsie NY 12601. (914)485-7844. FAX: (914)485-5975. Art Director: Lynn Hazelwood. Emphasizes contemporary living in the Hudson Valley. Readers are upscale, average age 45, average combined income $81,000. Circ. 26,000. Estab. 1986. Sample copy for 9×12 SASE.
Needs: Uses 30-40 photos/issue; 50% supplied by freelancers. Needs photos of scenic portraiture, architecture (all pertinent to the Hudson Valley). Model release and captions required.
Making Contact & Terms: Uses 8×10 glossy b&w and color prints; 35mm, 2¼×2¼, 4×5 and 8×10 transparencies. SASE. Reports in 1 month. Pays $50-250/b&w photo; $75-350/color photo; $350/day. Pays on publication. Credit line given. Previously published work OK.
Tips: Prefers to see "clear, sharp imagery capable of summing up the story at a glance; impact with subtlety and excellence! Initial contact should be an excellent quality color or b&w promotion piece with printed example of their work on it."

HUMM'S GUIDE TO THE FLORIDA KEYS, P.O.Box 2921, Key Largo FL 33037. (305)451-4429. Publisher: Gibbons Cline. Quarterly consumer magazine; digest size. Emphasizes Florida Keys travel and leisure-oriented subjects. Readers are visitors and seasonal residents. Circ. 55,000. Estab. 1972. Photo guidelines sheet free with SASE.
Needs: Uses 25-30 photos/issue; 100% supplied by freelancers. Needs photos of animal/wildlife, travel and scenics. Especially needs cover photos in vertical composition. Model release and captions preferred.
Making Contact & Terms: Query with list of stock photo subjects. Send unsolicited photos by mail for consideration; send 35mm and 2¼ × 2¼transparencies. SASE. Reports in 1 month. Pays $100/color cover photo; $50/color inside photo. Pays on publication. Buys one-time rights. Simultaneous submissions outside of Keys area and previously published work OK.

IDAHO WILDLIFE, P.O. Box 25, Boise ID 83707. (208)334-3748. FAX: (208)334-2114. Editor: Diane Ronayne. Bimonthly magazine. Emphasizes wildlife, hunting, fishing. Readers are aged 25-70, 80% male, purchase Idaho hunting or fishing licenses; ⅔ nonresident, ⅓ resident. Circ. 27,000. Estab. 1978. Sample copy $1. Photo guidelines free with SASE.
Needs: Uses 20-40 photos/issue; 30-60% supplied by freelancers. Needs shots of "wildlife, hunting, fishing in Idaho; habitat management." Photos of wildlife/people should be "real," not too "pretty" or obviously set up. Model release preferred. Photo captions required.
Making Contact & Terms: Interested in receiving work from newer, lesser-known photographers. Query with list of stock photo subjects. SASE. Reports in 1 month. Pays $70/color cover photo; $40/color or b&w inside photo; $40/color or b&w page rate. Pays on publication. Credit line given. Buys one-time rights. Simultaneous submissions and previously published work OK.
Tips: "Write first for want list. 99% of photos published are taken in Idaho. Seldom use scenics. Love action hunting or fishing images but must look 'real' (i.e., natural light). Only send you *best* work. We don't pay as much as commercial magazines but our quality is as high or higher and we value photography and design as much as text."

IDEALS MAGAZINE, Ideals Publishing Corp., Suite 800, 565 Marriott Dr., Nashville TN 37210. (615)885-8270. FAX: (615)885-9578. Editor: D. Fran Morley. Magazine published 8 times/year. Emphasizes an idealized, nostalgic look at America through poetry and short prose, using "seasonal themes — bright flowers and scenics for Thanksgiving, Christmas, Valentine, Easter, Mother's Day, Friendship, Country and Home — all thematically related material. Issues are seasonal in appearance." Readers are "mostly college-educated women who live in rural areas, aged 50 +." Circ. 200,000. Estab. 1944. Sample copy $3. Photo guidelines free with SASE.
Needs: Uses 20-25 photos/issue; all supplied by freelancers. Needs photos of "bright, colorful flower close-ups, scenics, still life, children, pets, home interiors; subject-related shots depending on issue. We regularly send out a letter listing the photo needs for our upcoming issue." Model/property release required. No research fees.
Making Contact & Terms: Submit portfolio for review. Send unsolicited photos by mail for consideration. Provide resume, business card, brochure, flyer or tearsheets to be kept on file. Send b&w prints and 2¼ × 2¼, 4 × 5, 8 × 10 transparencies by insured mail. Does not keep samples on file. SASE. Reports in 1 month. NPI; rates negotiable. Pays on publication. Credit line given. Buys one-time rights. Simultaneous and previously published work OK.
Tips: "We want to see *sharp* shots. No moody or artsy photos, please. Would suggest the photographer purchase several recent issues of *Ideals* magazine and study photos for our requirements. *Ideals'* reputation is based on quality of its color reproduction of photos."

ILLINOIS ENTERTAINER, #150, 2250 E. Devon, Des Plaines IL 60018. (708)298-9333. FAX: (708)298-7973. Editor: Michael C. Harris. Monthly magazine. Emphasizes music, video, theater, entertainment. Readers are male and female, 16-40, music/clubgoers. Circ. 80,000. Estab. 1975. Sample copy $5.
Needs: Uses 20+ photos/issue; approximately 5 supplied by freelancers on assignment or from stock. Needs "live concert photos; personality head shots — crisp, clean, high-contrast b&ws." Model/property release required; "releases required for any non-approved publicity photos or pics with models." Photo captions required.
Making Contact & Terms: Interested in receiving work from newer, lesser-known photographers. Query with resume of credits and list of stock photo subjects; send unsolicited photos by mail for consideration. Send 8 × 10 or 5 × 7, b&w prints. Does not keep samples on file. SASE. Reports in 1 month. Pays $100-125/color cover photo; $20-30/b&w inside photo. Pays no sooner than 60 days after publication. Buys one-time rights. Simultaneous submissions and previously published work OK.

Tips: Send high-contrast b&w photos. "We print on newsprint paper. We are seeing some more engaging publicity photos, though still fairly straightforward stuff abounds."

ILLINOIS MAGAZINE, P.O. Box 40, Litchfield IL 62056. (217)324-3425. Creative Director: Joyce Talley. Editor: Peggy Kuethe. Bimonthly. Emphasizes travel, history, current events, points of interest, people—all in Illinois. Readers are people primarily interested in Illinois history, (e.g., genealogists, teachers, students, historians), mostly rural. Circ. 12,000. Estab. 1964. Sample copy $1.50 with 9×12 SAE. Photo guidelines free with SASE.
Needs: Uses about 35-40 photos/issue; 50% supplied by freelance stock. Needs "cover photos: 35mm vertical photos of Illinois scenes, natural attractions, points of interest, botanical subjects." Model release preferred; photo captions required.
Making Contact & Terms: Query with list of stock photo subjects; send 35mm transparencies by mail for consideration. SASE. Reports in 2 months. Pays $50/color cover photo; $10-50/color photo; $5-15/b&w inside photo; $40-150/photo/text package. Pays on publication. Credit line given. Buys one-time rights. Previously published work OK.
Tips: "Obtain a sample copy to see what we've published in the past—and stick to the standards *already* set—we do *not* deviate." In photographer's samples looks for "composition, clarity, subject and we're not impressed by special effects. Uses fewer wildflowers and more scenics. Look at several back issues and then talk to us." Prefers 35mm or medium-format, slow-speed film.

IN THE WIND, P.O. Box 3000, Agoura Hills CA 91301. (818)889-8740. FAX: (818)889-1252. Photo Editor: Kim Peterson. Art Director: Rowan Johnson. Bimonthly magazine. Emphasizes riding Harley-Davidson motorcycles and the enjoyment derived therein. Readers are 18, male/female working people. Circ. 263,529. Estab. 1979. Sample copy for $2 with 8×10 SASE. Photo guidelines free with SASE.
Needs: Uses hundreds of photos/issue; 75% supplied by freelance photographers, approximately 10% on assignment. Needs b&w or color prints and transparencies of riding and lifestyle situations. Always in need of action photos, bikes being ridden, no helmets if possible and people having fun with motorcycles worldwide. Model release required for nudes, posed photos; property release preferred. Photo captions preferred including location.
Making Contact & Terms: Interested in receiving work from newer, lesser-known photographers. Send 35mm b&w and color glossy prints and 35mm and 2¼×2¼ transparencies by mail for consideration. Provide resume, business card, brochure, flyer or tearsheets to be kept on file for possible assignments. Reports in 3 months. Pays $200/color cover photo, $35/color inside photo; $35/b&w inside photo; $50-500/photo/text package; and $35-1,500/job, for feature including cover, poster. Pays on publication. Buys all rights; will negotiate.
Tips: "Read the magazine, be sure to include name and address on photos in Sharpie Permanent Marker ink. Not ball-point as it shows through. We want to see clarity, sharpness, feeling in work submitted. We are seeing more submissions of color prints—they are often converted to b&w. Include model releases with submissions of nudity or posed photos."

INCOME PLUS, Dept. PM, 73 Spring St., New York NY 10012. (212)925-3180. Art Director: Michele Cooper. Monthly magazine. Emphasizes small and new businesses. Readers are male and female independent entrepreneurs, ages 25-50. Circ. 250,000. Estab. 1988. Sample copy $2. Photo guidelines free with SASE.
Needs: Uses 2-10 photos/issue; 75% supplied by freelancers. Needs travel, business-oriented and how-to photos. Special needs include automobile, food and outdoor recreation photos. Model release preferred for businesses. Photo captions preferred that include names and pertinent information.
Making Contact & Terms: Arrange personal interview to show portfolio. Query with list of stock photo subjects. Send unsolicited photos by mail for consideration. Send 8×10 color prints; 35mm, 2¼×2¼ transparencies. Does not keep samples on file. SASE. Reports in 1 month. Pays $200-400/color cover photo; $100/b&w cover photo; $75/color or b&w inside photo. Pays on publication. Credit line given. Buys one-time rights. Simultaneous submissions OK.

INDEPENDENT LIVING, Dept. PM, Suite 420, 150 Motor Parkway, Hauppauge NY 11788-5145. (516)273-8743. Art Director: Jamie Stroud. Quarterly magazine. Emphasizes lifestyles for people with disabilities. Readers are ages 18 and up, male and female with disabilities. Circ. 25,000. Estab. 1988. Sample copy free with 9×12 SASE and 5 first-class stamps.

 The double dagger before a listing indicates that the market is located outside the United States and Canada. The symbol is new this year in **Photographer's Market.**

Needs: Uses 25 photos/issue; trend is toward using more freelancers. Needs photos of lifestyle (work, recreation, etc.) for people with disabilities. Model release and photo captions preferred.
Making Contact & Terms: Query with list of stock photo subjects. Send unsolicited prints or transparencies by mail for consideration. Provide resume, business card, brochure, flyer or tearsheets to be kept on file for possible assignments. SASE. Reports in 1-2 months. Pays $25/color cover photo; $15/color or b&w inside photo. Pays on publication. Buys one-time rights. Simultaneous submissions and previously published work OK.

●**THE INDEPENDENT SENIOR**, Dept. PM, 1268 W. Pender St., Vancouver, BC V6E 2S8 Canada. (604)688-2271. Editor: Brenda Radies. Monthly tabloid. Emphasizes primarily senior activities. Other features include Canadian personalities, travel, health, finance, sports, news and veterans. Readers are male and female, working or retired. Circ. 45,000. Sample copy free with 10 × 12 SASE.
Needs: Uses 20-30 photos/issue; 50-75% supplied by freelance photographers. Needs photos of active, interesting seniors. Photo captions required.
Making Contact & Terms: Query with list of stock photo subjects or send unsolicited photos by mail for consideration. Send b&w or color 5 × 7 prints. SASE. Reports in 1-4 weeks. Pays $20-50/photo depending on how used. Pays on publication. Credit line given. Buys one-time rights.
Tips: "We will buy killer stand-alone photos with cutlines. We prefer graphically strong photos."

INDIANAPOLIS MONTHLY, Dept. PM, Suite 1200, 950 N. Meridian, Indianapolis IN 46204. (317)237-9288. Art Director: David Rellich. Monthly. Emphasizes regional/Indianapolis. Readers are upscale, well-educated. Circ. 50,000. Sample copy for $3.05 and 9 × 12 SASE.
Needs: Uses 50-60 photos/issue; 10-12 supplied by freelance photographers. Needs seasonal, human interest, humorous, regional. Model release and captions preferred.
Making Contact & Terms: Query with samples; send 5 × 7 or 8 × 10 glossy b&w prints or 35mm or 2¼ × 2¼ transparencies by mail for consideration. SASE. Reports in 1 month. Pays $25/b&w inside photo; $35/color inside photo. Pays on publication. Credit line given. Buys first N.A. serial rights. Previously published work on occasion OK, if different market.
Tips: "Read publication. Send photo similar to those you see published. If we do nothing like what you are considering, we probably don't want to."

*****INSIDE DETECTIVE**, Official Detective Group, 20th Floor, 460 W. 34th St., New York NY 10001. (212)947-6500. Editor-in-chief: Rose Mandelsberg-Weiss. Managing Editor: Christofer Pierson. Readers are "police buffs, detective story buffs, law and order advocates." Magazine published 9 times/year. Circ. 400,000. Sample copy $2.50; photo guidelines for SASE.
Needs: "Only color covers are bought from freelance photographers. Subjects must be crime, police, detective oriented, man and woman. Action must portray impending disaster of a crime about to happen. *No women in subservient position.* Covert sensuality but no blatant sex." Model release required. "Interesting weapons a plus."
Making Contact & Terms: Send by mail for consideration color photos or 35mm, 2¼ × 2¼ or 4 × 5 color transparencies. SASE. Reports in 1 month after monthly cover meetings. Pays on publication $200/color photo. No credit line given. Buys all rights. No simultaneous or previously published submissions. Send all chromes to Editor-in-Chief: Rose Mandelsberg-Weiss.

INSIDE SPORTS, 990 Grove St., Evanston IL 60201-4370. (312)491-6440. Editor: Vince Aversano. Monthly. Emphasizes pro and college sports. Readers are median age: 31, median income $35,116; men. Circ. 450,000.
Needs: Uses about 50 photos/issue; 100% supplied by freelance photographers. Needs photos of sports action and portraits.
Making Contact & Terms: Provide resume, business card, brochure, flyer or tearsheets to be kept on file for possible assignments. Uses 35mm and 2¼ × 2¼ transparencies. NPI. Pays on publication. Buys one-time rights.

INSIGHT, Dept. PM, 3600 New York Ave. NE, Washington DC 20002. (202)636-8800. Photo Director: Brig Cabe. Photo Editor: Lee Van Grack. Weekly full-color news magazine. Readers are highly educated (66% are college graduates), affluent ($51,000+ median family income), largely professional, managerial and VIP. Sample copy $3.
Needs: Uses about 80 photos/issue; 1-5 supplied by freelance photographers on *Insight* assignments; one-third by stock photo agencies. Needs photos of personalities and places figuring in stories. Photos reviewed with or without accompanying ms. "We don't buy freelance writing." Special needs include historic persons and events; names in the news, especially government officials, authors and thinkers around the world; some news events; many stock 'generic' images. Model release preferred; captions required.

Making Contact & Terms: Send for "Freelance Photography Terms" pamphlet, contract. Call before sending samples or portfolio; 35mm transparencies in sheets preferred. Provide resume, business card, brochure, flyer or tearsheets to be kept on file for future assignments. SASE. Reports in 2 weeks. Pays $200-400/job. Pays on publication. Credit line given. Buys all rights to a small select edit; buys first-use rights when assignment is made through a stock photography agency. Simultaneous submissions and previously published work OK.
Tips: Prefers to see a mixture of people, places, things and events. Looks for both field and studio expertise; reproducible quality; a variety of poses, backgrounds, etc.; the ability to create photographs that communicate issues and concepts, generic situations.

INTERNATIONAL PHOTOGRAPHER, P.O. Box 18205, Washington DC 20036. (919)945-9867. Photography Editor: Vonda H. Blackburn. Bi-monthly magazine. Emphasizes making money with photography. Readers are 90% male photographers. Circ. 131,000. Estab. 1986. For sample copy, send 9×12 SAE. Photo guidelines free with SASE.
Needs: Uses 100 photos/issue; all supplied by freelance photographers. Model release required. Photo captions preferred.
Making Contact & Terms: Send 35mm, 2¼×2¼, 4×5, 8×10 b&w and color prints or transparencies by mail for consideration. SASE. Reports at end of the quarter. NPI; payment negotiable. Credit line given. Buys one-time rights, per contract. Simultaneous submissions and previously published work OK.
Tips: Wants to see "consistently fine quality photographs and good captions or other associated information. Present a portfolio which is easy to evaluate—keep it simple and informative. Be aware of deadlines. Submit early."

INTERNATIONAL WILDLIFE, 8925 Leesburg Pike, Vienna VA 22184. (703)790-4419. FAX: (703)442-7332. Photo Editor: John Nuhn. Senior Photo Editor: Steve Freligh. Bimonthly magazine. Emphasizes world's wildlife, nature, environment, conservation. Readers are people who enjoy viewing high-quality wildlife and nature images, and who are interested in knowing more about the natural world and man's inter-relationship with animals and environment on all parts of the globe. Circ. 650,000. Estab. 1970. Sample copy $3 from National Wildlife Federation Membership Services (same address); do not include order with guidelines request. Photo guidelines free with SASE.
Needs: Uses about 45 photos/issue; all supplied by freelance photographers; 30% on assignment, 70% from stock. Needs photos of world's wildlife, wild plants, nature-related how-to, conservation practices, conservation-minded people (tribal and individual), environmental damage, environmental research, outdoor recreation. Special needs include single photos for cover possibility (primarily wildlife but also plants, scenics, people); story ideas (with photos) from Canada, Europe, former Soviet republics, Pacific, China; b&w accompanying unique story ideas that should not be in color. Model release preferred; captions required.
Making Contact & Terms: Send 8×10 glossy b&w prints; 35mm, 2¼×2¼, 4×5, 8×10 transparencies by mail for consideration. Query with samples, credits and stock listings. SASE. Reports in 3 weeks. Pays $800/color cover photo; $300-750/color inside photo; $100-400/day; $750-2,500/complete package. Pays on acceptance. Credit line given. Buys one-time rights with limited magazine promotion rights. Previously published work OK.
Tips: Looking for a variety of images that show photographer's scope and specialization, organized in slide sheets, along with tearsheets of previously published work. "Study our magazine; note the type of images we use and send photos equal or better; think editorially when submitting story queries or photos; assure that package is complete—sufficient return postage (no checks), proper size return envelope, address inside and do not submit photos in glass slides, trays or small boxes."

THE IOWAN MAGAZINE, Suite 350, 108 Third St., Des Moines IA 50309. (515)282-8220. FAX: (515)282-0125. Editor: Karen Massetti-Miller. Quarterly magazine. Emphasizes "Iowa—its people, placcs, events and history." Readers are over 30, college-educated, middle to upper income. Circ. 25,000. Estab. 1952. Sample copy $4.50 with 9×12 SAE and $2.25 postage. Photo guidelines free with SASE.
Needs: Uses about 50 photos/issue; 95% by freelance photographers on assignment and 5% freelance stock. Needs "Iowa scenics—all seasons." Model and property releases preferred. Photo captions required.
Making Contact & Terms: Interested in receiving work from newer, lesser-known photographers. Send b&w prints; 35mm, 2¼×2¼ or 4×5 transparencies; or b&w contact sheet by mail for consideration. SASE. Reports in 1 month. Pays $25-50/b&w photo; $50-100/color photo; $200-500/day. Pays on publication. Credit line given. Buys one-time rights; negotiable.

ISLANDS, Dept. PM, 3886 State St., Santa Barbara CA 93105. (805)682-7177. Photo Editor: Zorah Krueger. Art Director: Albert Chiang. Bimonthly magazine. Emphasizes travel/islands. Readers are male, 40-60, affluent. Circ. 160,000. Sample copy $3.95. Photo guidelines free with SASE.

Needs: Uses 100 photos/issue; all supplied by freelancers. Needs travel shots and island photos. Model release preferred. Photo captions required.

Making Contact & Terms: Arrange a personal interview to show portfolio; query with resume of credits and list of stock photo subjects; submit portfolio for review; provide resume, business card, brochure, flyer or tearsheets to be kept on file for possible assignments. SASE. Reports in 1 month. Pays $500-1,000/color cover photo; $50-350/color inside photo. Pays on acceptance. Credit line given. Buys one-time rights. Simultaneous submissions OK.

*JOTS (Journal of the Senses), 814 Robinson Rd., Topanga CA 90290. (310)455-1000. FAX: (310)455-2007. Photo Editor: Iris Bancroft. Bimonthly journal. Emphasizes nudism: clothing optional lifestyle. Readers are families, couples and singles. Circ. 12,000. Estab. 1961. Sample copy for $1. Photo guidelines sheet available.

Needs: Uses 16 photos/issue; 10% supplied by freelancers. Needs photos of nudists recreational activities. Model/property release required for all people. Captions required.

Making Contact & Terms: Query with stock photo list. Does not keep samples on file. SASE. Reports in 1-2 weeks. Pays $100/color cover photo; $50/b&w cover photo; $50/color inside photo; $25/b&w inside photo. Pays on publication. Credit line given. Buys one-time rights; negotiable. Simultaneous submissions OK.

*JOURNEYMEN, 513 Chester Turnpike, Candia NH 03034. (603)483-8029. Editor: Paul S. Boynton. Quarterly magazine. Emphasizes male-oriented issues. Readers are male, ages 20-70. Sample copy $6. Photo guidelines available.

Needs: Uses 10-12 photos/issue; almost 100% supplied by freelancers. Needs photos of men: at work, at play, with children, friends and spouses. Model/property release preferred. Captions preferred.

Making Contact & Terms: Interested in receiving work from newer, lesser-known photographers. Submit portfolio for review. Send unsolicited photos by mail for consideration. Send 5×7 b&w prints. Keeps samples on file. SASE. Reports in 3 weeks. Pays $25-100/b&w cover photo. Pays on publication. Credit line given. Buys first N.A. serial rights. Rights negotiable. Simultaneous submissions and/or previously published works OK.

Tips: "Almost all photos used are by freelancers. Guidelines and upcoming needs are available. Great opportunity for beginners. Happy to look at all submissions. We're interested in photos of men portrayed in positive images. We're interested in developing long term relationships with freelancers from all over the U.S. to work on assignments."

JUNIOR SCHOLASTIC, 730 Broadway, New York NY 10003. (212)505-3071. Editor: Lee Baier. Senior Photo Researcher: Deborah Thompson. Biweekly educational school magazine. Emphasizes junior high social studies (grades 6-8): world and national news, US history, geography, how people live around the world. Circ. 600,000. Sample copy $1.75 with 9×12 SAE.

Needs: Uses 20 photos/issue. Needs photos of young people ages 11-14; non-travel photos of life in other countries; US news events. Reviews photos with accompanying ms only. Model release (under 18) and captions required.

Making Contact & Terms: Arrange a personal interview to show portfolio. "Please do not send samples—only stock list or photocopies of photos. Nonreturnable." Reports in 1 month. Pays $200/color cover photo; $75/b&w inside photo; $100/color inside photo. Pays on acceptance. Credit line given. Buys one-time rights. Simultaneous submissions OK.

Tips: Prefers to see young teenagers; in US and foreign countries. "Personal interviews with teenagers worldwide with photos."

KALLIOPE, A Journal of Women's Art, 3939 Roosevelt Blvd., Jacksonville FL 32205. (904)381-3511. Contact: Art Editor. Journal published 3 times/year. Emphasizes art by women. Readers are interested in women's issues. Circ. 1,000. Estab. 1978. Sample copy $7. Photo guidelines free with SASE.

Needs: Uses 18 photos/issue; all supplied by freelancers. Needs art and fine art that will reproduce well in b&w. Model release required. Photo captions preferred. Artwork should be titled.

Making Contact & Terms: Interested in receiving work from newer, lesser-known photographers. Send unsolicited photos by mail for consideration. Send 5×7 b&w prints. SASE. Reports in 1 month. Pays contributor 3 free issues or 1 year subscription free. Buys one-time rights. Credit line given.

Tips: "Send excellent quality photos with an artist's statement (50 words) and resume."

KANSAS, 5th Floor, 400 W. 8th St., Topeka KS 66603. (913)296-3479. Editor: Andrea Glenn. Estab. 1945. Quarterly magazine. Circ. 54,000. Emphasizes Kansas scenery, arts, recreation and people. Photos are purchased with or without accompanying ms or on assignment.

Needs: Animal, human interest, nature, photo essay/photo feature, scenic, sport, travel and wildlife, all from Kansas. No nudes, still life or fashion photos. Transparencies must be identified by location and photographer's name on the mount. Uses 35mm, 2¼×2¼ or 4×5 transparencies. Model/property release preferred; photo captions required.

Making Contact & Terms: Interested in receiving work from newer, lesser-known photographers. Buys 60-80 photos/year; buys 75% from freelance assignment, 25% from freelance stock. Pays $50 minimum/color photo; pays $100 minimum/cover photo. Credit line given. Pays on acceptance. Not copyrighted. Buys one-time rights. Send material by mail for consideration. No b&w. SASE. Previously published work OK. Reports in 1 month. Free sample copy and photo guidelines. Photos are returned after use.

Tips: Kansas-oriented material only. Prefers Kansas photographers. "Follow guidelines, submission dates specficially. Shoot a lot of seasonal scenics."

KARATE/KUNG FU ILLUSTRATED, P.O. Box 918, Santa Clarita CA 91380-0918. Executive Editor: William K. Beaver. Bimonthly magazine. Readers are enthusiasts of martial arts and fighting styles. Circ. 45,000. Photo guidelines free with SASE.

Needs: Uses 50-75 photos/issue; at least 50% supplied by freelance photographers. Needs photos on how to maintain arts; some how-to fitness and exercise shots. Model release required; captions preferred.

Making Contact & Terms: Query with samples; send 3½×5 or larger glossy or matte b&w and color prints; 35mm, 2¼×2¼ transparencies; b&w and color contact sheets; b&w negatives or color slides by mail for consideration. Phone query. SASE. Reports in 1 week. Pays $150-175/color cover photo. Pays on publication. Credit line given. Buys all rights. Previously published work OK.

Tips: Wants crisp, clean, captivating shots. "Rarely, if ever, buys photos without accompanying manuscript."

KASHRUS MAGAZINE – The Guide for the Kosher Consumer, P.O. Box 204, Parkville Station, Brooklyn NY 11204. (718)336-8544. Editor: Rabbi Yosef Wikler. Bimonthly. Emphasizes kosher food and food technology. Readers are kosher food consumers, vegetarians and producers. Circ. 10,000. Sample copy for 9×12 SAE with $1.21 postage.

Needs: Uses 3-5 photos/issue; all supplied by freelance photographers. Needs photos of travel, food, food technology, seasonal nature photos and Jewish holidays. Model release and captions preferred.

Making Contact & Terms: Send unsolicited photos by mail for consideration; provide resume, business card, brochure, flyer or tearsheets to be kept on file for possible future assignments. Uses 2¼×2¼, 3½×3½ or 7½×7½ matte b&w prints. SASE. Reports in 1 week. Pays $50-100/b&w cover photo; $25-50/b&w inside photo; $75-200/job; $50-200/text/photo package. Pays part on acceptance; part on publication. Buys one-time rights, first N.A. serial rights, all rights. Rights negotiable. Simultaneous submissions and previously published work OK.

KEYBOARD, 20085 Stevens Creek Blvd., Cupertino CA 95014. (408)446-1105. Editor: Dominic Milano. Art Director: Richard Leeds. Monthly magazine. Circ. 82,000. Emphasizes "biographies and how-to feature articles on keyboard players (pianists, organists, synthesizer players, etc.) and keyboard-related material. It is read primarily by musicians to get background information on their favorite artists, new developments in the world of keyboard instruments, etc." Free sample copy and photographer's and writer's guidelines.

Needs: Buys 10-15 photos/issue. Celebrity/personality (photos of keyboard players at their instruments). Prefers shots of musicians with their instruments. Photos purchased with or without accompanying ms and infrequently on assignment. Captions required for historical shots only.

Making Contact & Terms: Query with list of stock photo subjects. Send first class to Richard Leeds. Uses 8×10 b&w glossy prints; 35mm color, 120mm, 4×5, transparencies for cover shots. Leave space on left-hand side of transparencies for cover shots. SASE. Reports in 2-4 weeks. Pays on a per-photo basis. Pays expenses on assignment only. Pays $35-150/b&w inside photo; $300-500/photo for cover; $75-250/ color inside photo. Pays on publication. Credit line given. Buys rights to one-time use with option to reprint. Simultaneous submissions OK.

Tips: "Send along a list of artist shots on file. Photos submitted for our files would also be helpful – we'd prefer keeping them on hand, but will return prints if requested. Prefer live shots at concerts or in clubs. Keep us up to date on artists that will be photographed in the near future. Freelancers are vital to us."

KIDSPORTS MAGAZINE, 1101 Wilson Blvd., Arlington VA 22209. (703)276-3030. Art Director: John Herne. Magazine published 6 times/year. Professional athletes write articles about themselves and the sports they play. Readers are children ages 7-14. Circ. 100,000. Estab. 1989.

Needs: Uses 20 photos/issue. Needs shots of professional athletes and shots of kids (ages 9-15) playing sports. Model release required. Photo captions preferred.

Making Contact & Terms: Send unsolicited photos by mail for consideration; provide resume, business card, brochure, flyer or tearsheets to be kept on file for possible assignments. Send 8×10, b&w, color prints; 35mm, 2¼×2¼, 4×5 transparencies. SASE. Reports in 3 weeks. NPI. Pays on publication. Credit line given. Rights negotiable. Simultaneous submissions and previously published work OK.

KIPLINGER'S PERSONAL FINANCE MAGAZINE, (formerly *Changing Times Magazine*), 1729 H St., NW, Washington DC 20006. (202)887-6492. FAX: (202)331-1206. Picture Editor: Douglas J. Vann. Monthly magazine. Emphasizes personal finance. Circ. 1,000,000. Estab. 1935.
Needs: Uses 15-25 photos/issue; 90% supplied by freelancers. Needs "business portraits and photo illustration dealing with personal finance issues (i.e. investing, retirement, real estate). Model release and photo captions required.
Making Contact & Terms: Contact through rep; arrange personal interview to show portfolio; query with list of stock photo subjects; provide resume, business card, brochure, flyer or tearsheets to be kept on file for possible assignments. Keeps samples on file. SASE. Reports in 1-2 weeks. Pays $1,200/color and b&w cover photo; $350/day against space rate per page. Pays on acceptance. Credit line given. Buys one-time rights.

KITE LINES, P.O. Box 466, Randallstown MD 21133-0466. (410)922-1212. FAX: (410)922-4262. Publisher-Editor: Valerie Govig. Quarterly. Circ. 13,000. Estab. 1977. Emphasizes kites and kite flying exclusively. Readers are international adult kiters. Sample copy $5; photo guidelines free with SASE.
Needs: Uses about 35-50 photos/issue; "up to about 50% are unassigned or over-the-transom—but nearly all are from *kiter*-photographers." Needs photos of "unusual kites in action (no dimestore plastic kites), preferably with people in the scene (not easy with kites). Needs to relate closely to *information* (article or long caption)." Special needs include major kite festivals; important kites and kiters. Captions required. "Identify *kites* as well as people."
Making Contact & Terms: Query with samples or send 2-3 b&w 8×10 uncropped prints or 35mm or larger transparencies by mail for consideration. Provide relevant background information, i.e., knowledge of kites or kite happenings. SASE. Reports in "2 weeks to 2 months (varies with work load, but any obviously unsuitable stuff is returned quickly—in 2 weeks." Pays $0-30 per inside photo; $0-50 for color photo; special jobs on assignment negotiable; generally on basis of expenses paid only. We provide extra copies to contributors. Our limitations arise from our small size. However, *Kite Lines* is a quality showcase for good work. Pays on publication. Buys one-time rights; usually buys first world serial rights. Previously published work OK.
Tips: In portfolio or samples wants to see "ability to select important, *noncommercial* kites. Just take a great kite picture, and be patient with our tiny staff. Considers good selection of subject matter; good composition—angles, light, background; and sharpness. But we don't want to look at "portfolios"—just *kite* pictures, please."

LADIES HOME JOURNAL, Dept. PM, 100 Park Ave, New York NY 10017. (212)351-3563. Contact: Photo Editor. Monthly magazine. Features women's issues. Readership consists of women with children and working women in 30's age group. Circ. 6 million.
Needs: Uses 90 photos per issue; 100% supplied by freelancers. Needs photos of children, celebrities and women's lifestyles/situations. Reviews photos only without ms. Model release and captions preferred. No photo guidelines available.
Making Contact & Terms: Provide resume, business card, brochure, flyer or tearsheet to be kept on file for possible assignment. Reports in 3 weeks. Pays $185/b&w inside photo; $185/color page rate. Pays on acceptance. Credit line given. Buys one-time rights.

LAKE SUPERIOR MAGAZINE, Lake Superior Port Cities, Inc., P.O. Box 16417, Duluth MN 55816-0417. (218)722-5002. FAX: (218)722-4096. Editor: Paul L. Hayden. Bimonthly magazine. "Beautiful picture magazine about Lake Superior." Readers are ages 35-55, male and female, highly educated, upper middle and upper management level through working. Circ. 20,000. Estab. 1979. Sample copy for $3.95, 9×12 SAE and 5 first-class stamps. Photo guidelines free with SASE.
Needs: Uses 30 photos/issue; 70% supplied by freelance photographers. Needs photos of scenic, travel, wildlife, personalities, underwater, all photos Lake Superior-related. Photo captions preferred.
Making Contact & Terms: Interested in receiving work from newer, lesser-known photographers. Send unsolicited photos by mail for consideration; provide resume, business card, brochure, flyer or tearsheets to be kept on file for possible assignments. Uses b&w prints; 35mm, 2¼×2¼, 4×5 transparencies. SASE. Reports in 3 weeks. Pays $75/color cover photo; $35/color inside photo; $20/b&w inside photo. Pays on publication. Credit line given. Buys first N.A. serial rights; reserves second rights for future use. Simultaneous submissions OK.
Tips: "Be aware of the focus of our publication—Lake Superior. Photo features concern only that. Features with text can be related. We are known for our fine color photography and reproduction. It has to be 'tops.' We try to use image large, therefore detail quality and resolution must be good. We look for unique outlook on subject, not just snapshots. Must communicate emotionally."

LAKELAND BOATING MAGAZINE, Suite 1220, 1560 Sherman Ave., Evanston IL 60201. (708)869-5400. Editor: Sarah D. Wortham. Monthly magazine. Emphasizes powerboating in the Great Lakes. Readers are affluent professionals, predominantly men over 35. Circ. 45,000. Estab. 1945. Sample copy for $6 with 9×12 SASE and $2.80 postage.
Needs: Needs shots of particular Great Lakes ports and waterfront communities. Model release and photo captions preferred.
Making Contact & Terms: Query with list of stock photo subjects. Provide resume, business card, brochure, flyer or tearsheets to be kept on file for possible assignments. SASE. Will give photo credit. Pays $20-100/b&w photo; $25-100/color photo. Pays on acceptance. Credit line given. Buys one-time rights.

◆LEISURE WORLD, 1215 Ouellette Ave., Windsor, ON N9A 6N3 Canada. (519)971-3207. FAX: (519)977-1197. Editor-in-Chief: Doug O'Neil. Bimonthly magazine. Emphasizes travel and leisure. Readers are auto club members, 50% male, 50% female, middle to upper middle class. Circ. 280,000. Estab. 1988. Sample copy $2.
Needs: Uses 9-10 photos/issue; 25-30% supplied by freelance photographers. Needs photos of travel, scenics. Special needs include exotic travel locales. Model release preferred; photo captions required.
Making Contact & Terms: Interested in receiving work from newer, lesser-known photographers. Send unsolicited photos by mail for consideration. Provide business card, brochure, flyer or tearsheets to be kept on file for possible assignments. Send b&w or color 35mm, 2¼×2¼, 4×5, or 8×10 transparencies. SASE. Reports in 2 weeks. Pays $100/color cover photo, $80/b&w cover photo, $40/color inside photo, $25/b&w inside photo, or $100-300/photo/text package. Pays on publication. Credit line given. Buys one-time rights. Mail to Doug O'Neil, Editor-in-Chief.
Tips: "We expect that the technical considerations are all perfect—frames, focus, exposure, etc. Beyond that we look for a photograph that can convey a mood or tell a story by itself. We would like to see more subjective and impressionistic photographs. Don't be afraid to submit material. If your first submissions are not accepted, try again. We encourage talented and creative photographers who are trying to establish themselves."

LETTERS, Dept. PM, 310 Cedar Lane, Teaneck NJ 07666. Associate Editor: Lisa Rosen. Monthly. Emphasizes "sexual relations between people, male/female; male/male; female/female." Readers are "primarily male, older; some younger women." Sample copy $3.
Needs: Uses 1 photo/issue; all supplied by freelance photographers. Needs photos of scantily attired females; special emphasis on shots of semi- or completely nude buttocks. Model release required.
Making Contact & Terms: Query with samples. Send 2¼×2¼ slides by mail for consideration. Provide brochure, flyer and tearsheets to be kept on file for possible future assignments. SASE. Reports in 2-3 weeks. Pays $150/color photo. Pays on publication. Buys first N.A. serial rights.
Tips: Would like to see "material germane to our publication's needs. See a few issues of the publication before you send in photos. Please send slides that are numbered and keep a copy of the list, so if we do decide to purchase we can let you know by the number on the slide. All of our covers are purchased from freelance photographers."

LIFE, Dept. PM, Time-Life Bldg., Rockefeller Center, New York NY 10020. (212)522-1212. Photo Editor: Barbara Baker Burrows. Monthly magazine. Emphasizes current events, cultural trends, human behavior, nature and the arts, mainly through photojournalism. Readers are of all ages, backgrounds and interests. Circ. 1,400,000.
Needs: Uses about 100 photos/issue. Prefers to see topical and unusual photos. Must be up-to-the minute and newsworthy. Send photos that could not be duplicated by anyone or anywhere else. Especially needs humorous photos for last page article "Just One More."
Making Contact & Terms: Send material by mail for consideration. SASE. Uses 35mm, 2¼×2¼, 4×5 and 8×10 slides. Pays $500/page; $600/page in color news section; $1,000/cover. Credit line given. Buys one-time rights.
Tips: "Familiarize yourself with the topical nature and format of the magazine before submitting photos and/or proposals."

LIVE STEAM MAGAZINE, Dept. PM, P.O. Box 629, Traverse City MI 49685. (616)941-7160. Editor-in-Chief: Joe D. Rice. Monthly. Emphasizes "steam-powered models and full-size equipment (i.e., locomotives, cars, boats, stationary engines, etc.)." Readers are "hobbyists—many are building scale models." Circ. 13,000. Sample copy free with 9×12 SASE and $1 postage; photo guidelines free with SASE.
Needs: Uses about 80 photos/issue; "most are supplied by the authors of published articles." Needs "how-to-build (steam models), historical locomotives, steamboats, reportage of hobby model steam meets. Unless it's a cover shot (color), we only use photos with ms." Special needs include "strong transparencies of steam locomotives, steamboats or stationary steam engines."

Making Contact & Terms: Query with samples. Send 3×5 b&w glossy prints by mail for consideration. SASE. Reports in 3 weeks. Pays $40/color cover photo; $8/b&w inside photo; $30/page plus $8/photo; $25 minimum for text/photo package (maximum payment "depends on article length"). Pays on publication—"we pay quarterly." Credit line given. Buys one-time rights. Simultaneous submissions OK.

Tips: "Be sure that mechanical detail can be seen clearly. Try for maximum depth of field."

LONG ISLAND POWER & SAIL, Dept. PM, 403 Main St., Port Washington NY 11050. (516)944-8654. FAX: (516)944-8663. Art Director: Amy Berger. Bimonthly magazine. Emphasizes boating. Readers are male boat owners, 25+. Circ. 35,000. Estab. 1989. Sample copy $5.
Needs: Uses 50 photos/issue; 30 supplied by freelancers. Needs boating photos. Model release preferred. Photo captions preferred.
Making Contact & Terms: Query with list of stock photo subjects; provide resume, business card, brochure, flyer or tearsheets to be kept on file for possible assignments. Does not keep samples on file. Reports in 1 month. Pays $100/color cover photo; $50/color inside photo; $25/b&w inside photo. Pays on publication. Credit line given. Buys one-time rights. Previously published work OK.

LOS ANGELES MAGAZINE, Dept. PM, 1888 Century Park E., Los Angeles CA 90067. (213)557-7569. Editor: Lew Harris. Design Director: William Delorme. Executive Art Director: James Griglak. Assistant Art Director: Pamela Thornberg. Monthly magazine. Circ. 170,000. Emphasizes sophisticated southern California personalities and lifestyle, particularly Los Angeles area.
Needs: Buys 45-50 photos/issue. Celebrity/personality, fashion/beauty, human interest, head shot, photo illustration/photo journalism, photo essay/photo feature (occasional), sport (occasional), food/restaurant and travel. Most photos are assigned; occasionally purchased with accompanying ms. Free writer's guidelines.
Making Contact & Terms: Provide brochure, calling card, flyer, resume and tearsheets to be kept on file for possible future assignments. Submit portfolio for review. Send b&w contact sheet or contact sheet and negatives; 4×5, 2¼×2¼ or 35mm transparencies. All covers are assigned. Uses 2¼×2¼ color transparencies; vertical format required. SASE. Reports in 2 weeks. Pays $100 minimum/job; $100-300/b&w photo; $100-500/color photo; $450/cover photo. Pays 10¢/word minimum for accompanying ms. Pays on publication. Credit line given. Buys first serial rights. Simultaneous submissions and previously published work OK.
Tips: To break in, "bring portfolio showing type of material we assign. Leave it for review during a business day (a.m. or p.m.) to be picked up later. Photographers should mainly be active in L.A. area and be sensitive to different magazine styles and formats."

LOUISIANA LIFE MAGAZINE, P.O. Box 308, Metairie LA 70004. (504)456-2220. FAX: (504)887-8003. Managing Editor: Nick Marinello. Bimonthly magazine. Emphasizes topics of special interest to Louisianians; a people-oriented magazine. Readers are statewide; upper middle class; college educated; urban and rural. Circ. 46,000. Estab. 1981. Sample copy $4 including postage. Photo guidelines free with SASE.
Needs: Uses 45 photos/issue; all supplied by freelance photographers, 80% on assignment. Photos are assigned according to stories planned for each issue. Color transparencies are used for features, b&w for columns. Special needs include people, places, events in Louisiana. Photo captions required.
Making Contact & Terms: Interested in receiving work from newer, lesser-known photographers. Arrange a personal interview to show portfolio; query with resume of credits and with samples; provide resume, business card, brochure, flyer or tearsheets to be kept on file for possible future assignments. "Follow up on the interview. Continue to send samples. Send story queries along with slides." Send 8×10 glossy b&w prints; 35mm, 2¼×2¼, 4×5, 8×10 transparencies; b&w contact sheet by mail for consideration. SASE. Reports in 3 weeks. Pays $75-200/color and b&w photo; $225 for cover. Pays on publication. Credit line given. Buys one-time rights.
Tips: In portfolio or samples, wants to see "technical excellence. Portraits, interiors, landscapes, *industrial* shots with a creative style." Seeks quality, not quantity. Can send duplicates for review. "Study *Louisiana Life* to become familiar with our needs."

*LUTHERAN FORUM, P.O. Box 327, Delhi NY 13753. (607)746-7511. Editor: Paul Hinlicky. Emphasizes "Lutheran concerns, both within the church and in relation to the wider society, for the leadership of Lutheran churches in North America." Quarterly. Circ. 4,500.
Needs: Uses cover photo occasionally. "While subject matter varies, we are generally looking for photos that include people, and that have a symbolic dimension. We use *few* purely 'scenic' photos. Photos of religious activities, such as worship, are often useful, but should not be 'cliches'—types of photos that are seen again and again." Model release not required; captions not required but "may be helpful."

Making Contact & Terms: Query with list of stock photo subjects. SASE. Reports in 1-2 months. Pays on publication $15-25/b&w photo. Credit line given. Buys one-time rights. Simultaneous or previously published submissions OK.

*MAGICAL BLEND, P.O. Box 11303, San Francisco CA 94101. (415)673-1001. Art Directors: Matthew Courtway and Yuka Hirota. Quarterly magazine. Emphasizes New Age consciousness, visionary painting, collage and photography. Readers include people of "all ages interested in an alternative approach to spirituality." Circ. 45,000. Sample copy $4.
Needs: Uses 1-12 photos/issue; 100% supplied by freelance photographers. Looks for creative, visionary and surreal work. Model release preferred if needed. Send without captions.
Making Contact & Terms: Send unsolicited photos by mail for consideration. Send b&w, color prints; 35mm, 2¼ × 2¼, 4 × 5, and 8 × 10 transparencies. SASE. Reports in 3 weeks. Payment not given; credit line only. Buys one-time rights. If desired, print photographer's address with photo so readers can contact for purchases.
Tips: In portfolio or samples, looking for "images that are inspiring to look at that show people in celebration of life. Try to include positive images. The best way to see what we're interested in printing is by sending for a sample copy."

*MAINSTREAM,Magazine of the Able-Disabled, 2973 Beech St., San Diego CA 92102. (619)234-3138. Managing Editor: William G. Stothers. 10 times per year magazine. Emphasizes disability rights. Readers are upscale, active men and women who are disabled. Circ. 15,500. Estab. 1975. Sample copy $3 with 9 × 12 SASE with 6 first class stamps.
Needs: Uses 3-4 photos/issue. Needs photos of disabled people doing things, sports, travel, working, etc. Reviews photos with accompanying ms only. Model/property release preferred. Photo captions required.
Making Contact & Terms: Provide resume, business card, brochure, flyer or tearsheets to be kept on file for possible assignments. Keeps samples on file. SASE. Reports in 2 months. Pays $75/color cover photo; $35/b&w inside photo. Pays onpublication. Credit line given. Buys all rights. Rights negotiable. Previously published work OK "if not in one of our major competitors' publications."
Tips: "We definitely look for signs the photographer empathizes with and understands the perspective of the disability rights movement."

MARLIN MAGAZINE, P.O. Box 12902, Pensacola FL 32576. (904)434-5571. Editor: Dave Lear. Bimonthly magazine. Emphasizes offshore big game fishing for billfish, sharks and tuna. Readers are 99% male, 75% married, average age 43, businessmen. Circ. 30,000. Estab. 1981. Free sample copy with 8 × 10 SAE. Photo guidelines free with SASE.
Needs: Uses 40-50 photos/issue; 98% supplied by freelancers. Needs photos of fish/action shots, some scenics and how-to. Special photo needs include big game fishing action photos. Model release preferred. Photo captions required.
Making Contact & Terms: Send unsolicited photos by mail for consideration. Send b&w, color prints; 35mm transparencies. SASE. Reports in 1 month. Pays $300/color cover photo; $50/color inside photo; $35/b&w inside photo; $125/color page rate; $200-450/photo/text package. Pays on acceptance. Buys first N.A. rights. Simultaneous submissions OK.

MARRIAGE PARTNERSHIP, Christianity Today, Inc. 465 Gundersen Dr., Carol Stream IL 60188. (312)260-6200. Contact: Art Director, Gary Gnidovic. Quarterly magazine. Emphasizes all issues of marriage and family life. Readers are 24-44 years old, middle to upper-middle class and are 60% women. Circ. 80,000. Estab. 1988. Sample copy for 9 × 12 SAE, upon assignment.
Needs: Uses 15 photos/issue; 100% supplied by freelance photographers. Model release required.
Making Contact & Terms: Provide resume, business card, brochure, flyer or tearsheets to be kept on file for possible assignments. SASE. Reports in 2 weeks. Pays $800/b&w and color cover photo; $400/b&w and color page rate for assigned work. Pays $400-800/day. Approximately $200-300 page rate for stock b&w or color. Simultaneous submissions and previously published work OK.
Tips: Looks for "a strong sense of individual approach to problem solving."

MARTIAL ARTS TRAINING, P.O. Box 918, Santa Clarita CA 91380-9018. (805)257-4066. FAX: (805)257-3028. Editor: Marian K. Castinado. Bimonthly. Emphasizes martial arts training. Readers are martial artists of all skill levels. Circ. 40,000. Sample copy free. Photo guidelines free with SASE.
Needs: Uses about 100 photos/issue; 90 supplied by freelance photographers. Needs "photos that pertain to fitness/conditioning drills for martial artists. Photos purchased with accompanying ms only. Model release and captions required.
Making Contact & Terms: Send 5 × 7 or 8 × 10 b&w prints; 35mm transparencies; b&w contact sheet or negatives by mail for consideration. SASE. Reports in 1 month. Pays $50-150 for text/photo package. Pays on publication. Credit line given. Buys all rights.

Tips: Photos "must be razor-sharp, b&w. Technique shots should be against neutral background. Concentrate on training-related articles and photos."

MASTER OF LIFE, P.O. Box 38, Malibu CA 90265. (818)889-1575. Editor: Dick Sutphen. Quarterly magazine. Estab. 1976. Emphasizes metaphysical, psychic development, reincarnation, self-help with tapes. Everyone receiving the magazine has attended a Sutphen Seminar or purchased Valley of the Sun Publishing books or tapes from a line of over 300 titles: video and audio tapes, subliminal/hypnosis/meditation/New Age music/seminars on tape, etc. Circ. 120,000. Sample copy free with 12×15 SAE and 5 first-class stamps.
Needs: "We purchase about 50 photos per year for the magazine and also for cassette album covers. We are especially interested in surrealistic photography which would be used as covers, to illustrate stories and for New Age music cassettes. Even seminar ads often use photos that we purchase from freelancers." Model release required.
Making Contact & Terms: Interested in receiving work from newer, lesser-known photographers. Send b&w and color prints; 35mm, 2¼×2¼ transparencies by mail for consideration. SASE. Reports in 2 weeks. Pays $100/color photo; $50/b&w photo. Pays on publication. Credit line given if desired. Buys one-time rights, negotiable. Simultaneous submissions and previously published work OK.

MENNONITE PUBLISHING HOUSE, 616 Walnut Ave., Scottdale PA 15683. (412)887-8500. Photo Secretary: Debbie Cameron. Publishes *Story Friends* (ages 4-9), *On The Line* (ages 10-14), *Christian Living, Gospel Herald, Purpose* (adults).
Needs: Buys 10-20 photos/year. Needs photos of children engaged in all kinds of legitimate childhood activities (at school, at play, with parents, in church and Sunday School, at work, with hobbies, relating to peers and significant elders, interacting with the world); photos of youth in all aspects of their lives (school, work, recreation, sports, family, dating, peers); adults in a variety of settings (family life, church, work, and recreation); abstract and scenic photos. Model release preferred.
Making Contact & Terms: Send 8½×11 b&w photos by mail for consideration; provide resume, business card, brochure, flyer or tearsheets to be kept on file for possible assignments. SASE. Reports in 1 month. Pays $20-50/b&w photo. Credit line given. Buys one-time rights. Simultaneous submissions and previously published work OK.

The rustic look of this wooden mallet and nails makes for an interesting display. Mount Joy, Pennsylvania, photographer Dale Gehman set up the shot while attending an Amish barnraising. At lunch time he found the tools sitting on the hayloft floor and he spent time arranging the tools for the photo. Attention to detail may have helped him sell the image three times, twice to Magazine *and once to the Mennonite Publishing House as a cover photo for* Builder Magazine.

© Dale Gehman

METAL EDGE, Dept. PM, 355 Lexington Ave., New York NY 10017. (212)949-6850. FAX: (212)986-5926. Editor: Gerri Miller. Monthly magazine. Emphasizes heavy metal music. Readers are young fans. Circ. 250,000. Estab. 1985. Sample copy free with large manila SASE.
Needs: Uses 125 photos/issue; 100 supplied by freelance photographers. Needs studio b&w and color, concert shots and behind-the-scenes (b&w) photos of heavy metal artists.
Making Contact & Terms: Arrange a personal interview to show portfolio. Query with samples and list of stock photo subjects. Reports ASAP. Pays $25-35/b&w inside photo; $75 + /color; job. Pays on publication. Buys one-time rights for individual shots. Buys all rights for assigned sessions or coverage. Previously published work OK.
Tips: Prefers to see very clear, exciting concert photos; studio color with vibrancy and life that capture subject's personality.

MICHIGAN NATURAL RESOURCES MAGAZINE, P.O. Box 30034, Lansing MI 48909. (517)373-9267. Managing Editor: Richard Morscheck. Photo Editor: Gijsbert van Frankenhuyzen. Bimonthly. Circ. 100,000. Estab. 1931. Emphasizes natural resources in the Great Lakes region. Readers are "appreciators of the out-of-doors; 15% readership is out of state." Sample copy $4; photo guidelines free with SASE.
Needs: Uses about 40 photos/issue; freelance photography in given issue—50% from assignment and 50% from freelance stock. Needs photos of Michigan wildlife, Michigan flora, how-to, travel in Michigan, outdoor recreation. Also, photos of people, especially minorities and handicapped, enjoying outdoor pursuits. Captions preferred.
Making Contact & Terms: Query with samples or list of stock photo subjects; send original 35mm color transparencies by mail for consideration. SAE. Reports in 1 month. Pays $75-250/color page; $500/job; $800 maximum for text/photo package. Pays on acceptance. Credit line given. Buys one-time rights.
Tips: Prefers "Kodachrome 64 or 25 or Fuji 50 or 100, 35mm, *razor sharp in focus!* Send about 20 slides with a list of stock photo topics. Be sure slides are sharp, labeled clearly with subject and photographer's name and address. Send them in plastic slide filing sheets. Looks for unusual outdoor photos. Flora, fauna of Michigan and Great Lakes region. Strongly recommend that photographer look at past issues of the magazine to become familiar with the quality of the photography and the overall content."

MICHIGAN OUT-OF-DOORS, P.O. Box 30235, Lansing MI 48909. (517)371-1041. FAX: (517)371-1505. Editor: Kenneth S. Lowe. Monthly magazine. Circ. 130,000. Estab. 1947. For people interested in "outdoor recreation, especially hunting and fishing; conservation; environmental affairs." Sample copy $2; free editorial guidelines.
Needs: Use 1-6 freelance photos/issue. Animal; nature; scenic; sport (hunting, fishing and other forms of noncompetitive recreation); and wildlife. Materials must have a Michigan slant. Photo captions preferred.
Making Contact & Terms: Send any size b&w glossy prints; 35mm or 2¼ × 2¼ transparencies. SASE. Reports in 1 month. Credit line given. Pays $15 minimum/b&w photo; $100/cover photo; $25/inside color photo. Buys first N.A. serial rights. Previously published work OK "if so indicated."
Tips: Submit seasonal material 6 months in advance. Wants to see "new approaches to subject matter."

MINORITY ENGINEER, Equal Opportunity Publications, Inc., Dept. PM, 44 Broadway, Greenlawn NY 11740. (516)261-8917. Art Director: Jamie Ctroud. Quarterly. Emphasizes career guidance for minority engineers at the college and professional levels. Readers are college-age minority engineering students and young working minority engineers. Circ. 16,000. Sample copy free with 9 × 12 SASE and 6 first-class stamps.
Needs: Uses at least one photo per issue (cover); planning to use freelance work for covers and possibly editorial. Contact for needs. Model release preferred; photo captions required.
Making Contact & Terms: Query with list of stock photo subjects. Send by mail for consideration unsolicited prints or 35mm color transparencies. SASE. Reports in 2 weeks. Pays $25/color cover photo. Pays on publication; provide resume, business card, brochure flyer or tearsheets to be kept on file for possible assignments. Credit line given. Buys one-time rights. Simultaneous submissions and

Can't find a listing? Check at the end of each market section for the " '92-'93 Changes" lists. These lists include any market listings from the '92 edition which were either not verified or deleted in this edition.

previously published work OK, "but not in competitive career-guidance publications."
Tips: "We are looking for clear color shots of minority students and young professionals who are involved in activities related to their academic studies or professions. Most of the photography we use is submitted by the freelance writer with his or her manuscript. Also looking for more stock photos. We've decided to use more cover photos than we have in the past. We are also open to using inside photos, but freelancers should contact us and discuss upcoming stories before sending photos. Cover photos do not have to tie in to any one particular story in the magazine, but they have to be representative of the magazine's editorial content as a whole."

MODERN BRIDE, Dept. PM, 249 W. 17th St., New York NY 10011. (212)337-7063. Art Director: Debra Gill. Monthly magazine.
Needs: Uses photos of travel, fashion and housewares. Model release required.
Making Contact & Terms: Query with resume of credits. Send stock photo list. Also, "drop off portfolios on Wednesday only and pick up on Thursday." Keeps samples on file. SASE. Reports as needed. NPI; payment rates variable. Credit line given. Buys all rights.

MODERN DRUMMER MAGAZINE, 870 Pompton Ave., Cedar Grove NJ 07009. (201)239-4140. FAX: (201)239-7139. Editor: Ron Spagnardi. Photo Editor: Scott Bienstock. Magazine published 12 times/year. Circ. 100,000. For drummers at all levels of ability: students, semiprofessionals and professionals. Sample copy with 9×12 SAE and $1.50 postage.
Needs: Buys 100-150 photos annually. Needs celebrity/personality, product shots, action photos of professional drummers and photos dealing with "all aspects of the art and the instrument."
Making Contact & Terms: Submit freelance photos with letter. Send for consideration b&w contact sheet, b&w negatives, or 5×7 or 8×10 glossy b&w prints; 35mm, 2¼×2¼, 8×10 color transparencies. Uses color covers. SASE. Pays $150/cover, $50-100/color, $25-50/b&w photos. Pays on publication. Credit line given. Buys one-time international usage rights per country. Previously published work OK.

MOMENT, Suite 300, 3000 Connecticut Ave. NW, Washington DC 20008. (202)387-8888. FAX: (202)483-3423. Managing Editor: Suzanne Singer. Bimonthly magazine. Emphasizes Jewish issues—social, political, religious, historical, cultural, literary, artistic and Israel. Readers are English-speaking Jews in U.S. and elsewhere. Circ. 30,000. Sample copy free with 9×12 SAE.
Needs: Uses 10-20 photos/issue; 50% supplied by freelance photographers. Needs photos of people events, scenic and art.
Making Contact & Terms: Query with resume of credits and samples or list of stock photo subjects. Provide resume, business card, brochure, flyer or tearsheets to be kept on file for possible future assignments. Pays $100-150/b&w cover photo; $50/¼ b&w or color page; $75/½ b&w or $100/¾ b&w or color page. Pays on publication. Credit line given. Buys first N.A. serial rights. Previously published work OK.

MONITORING TIMES, P.O. Box 98, Brasstown NC 28902. (704)837-9200. FAX: (704) 837-2216. Photo Editor: Beverly Berrong. Monthly. Emphasizes radio communications, scanners and shortwave. Circ. 30,000. Estab. 1982. Sample copy for $2.50 (postpaid) and 9×12 SAE.
Needs: Uses about 40 photos/issue; 20 supplied by freelance photographers. Needs photos of radio equipment, action scenes involving communications, individuals connected with story line. Special needs include b&w and color (cover) concerning radio, antennas, equipment, boats, planes, military exercises, anything dealing in radio communications. Model release and captions preferred.
Making Contact & Terms: Interested in receiving work from newer, lesser-known photographers. Query with samples or list of stock photo subjects. SASE. Reports in 2 weeks. Pays $35-75/color cover photo; $10-50/b&w inside photo; $50-200/text/photo package. Pays on acceptance. Credit line given if requested. Buys one-time rights.
Tips: "First, acquaint yourself with the publication and anticipate its reader profile. Product shots must be contrasty and sharp, suitable for camera-ready application. Action shots must revolve around story lines dealing with radio broadcasting (international), news events, scanner excitement: air shows, emergencies. We would prefer the photographer to submit samples for us to keep on file, to be paid as used. A photocopy or contact print to be kept on file is also acceptable."

MOTHERING MAGAZINE, P.O. Box 1690, Santa Fe NM 87504. (505)984-8116. FAX: (505)986-8335. Photo Editor: John Inserra. Quarterly magazine. Emphasizes parenting. Readers are progressive parents, primarily aged 25-40, with children of all ages, racially mixed. Estab. 1976. Free sample copy, photo guidelines and current photo needs.

Needs: Uses about 40-50 photos/issue; nearly all supplied by freelance photographers. Needs photos of children of all ages, mothers, fathers, breastfeeding, birthing, education. Model release required.
Making Contact & Terms: Interested in receiving work from newer, lesser-known photographers. Send 5×7 or 8×10 (preferred) b&w prints by mail for consideration. SASE. Reports in 3 months. Pays $500/color cover photo; $50 for full page, $35 for less than full page/b&w inside photo. Pays on publication. Credit line given. Buys one-time rights.
Tips: "For cover: we want technically superior, sharply focused image evoking a strong feeling or mood, spontaneous and unposed; unique and compelling; eye contact with subject will often draw in viewer; color slide only. For inside: b&w prints, sharply focused, action or unposed shots; 'doing' pictures—family, breastfeeding, fathering, midwifery, birth, reading, drawing, crawling, climbing, etc. No disposable diapers, no bottles, no pacifiers. We are being flooded with submissions from photographers acting as their own small stock agency—when the reality is that they are just individual freelancers selling their own work. As a result, we are using fewer photos from just one photographer, giving exposure to more photographers."

MOTORHOME, Dept. PM, 29901 Agoura Rd., Agoura CA 91301. (818)991-4980. Managing Editor: Gail Harrington. Monthly. Circ. 150,000. Emphasizes motorhomes and travel. Readers are "motorhome owners with above-average incomes and a strong desire for adventurous travel." Sample copy free; photo guidelines for SASE.
Needs: Uses 25 photos/issue; at least 12 from freelancers. Needs "travel-related stories pertaining to motorhome owners with accompanying photos and how-to articles with descriptive photos. We usually buy a strong set of motorhome-related photos with a story. Also we are in the market for cover photos. Scenes should have maximum visual impact, with a motorhome included but not necessarily a dominant element. Following a freelancer's query and subsequent first submission, the quality of his work is then evaluated by our editorial board. If it is accepted and the freelancer indicates a willingness to accept future assignments, we generally contact him/her when the need arises." Captions required.
Making Contact & Terms: Send by mail for consideration 8×10 (5×7 OK) b&w prints or 35mm or 2¼×2¼ (4×5 or 8×10 OK) slides. Also send standard query letter. SASE. Reports as soon as possible, "but that sometimes means up to one month." Pays on acceptance $300-500 for text/photo package; up to $600 for cover photos. Credit line given. Buys first rights. No simultaneous submissions or previously published work.

🌸**MUSCLE/MAG INTERNATIONAL,** Unit 7, 2 Melanie Dr., Brampton ON L6T 4K8 Canada. (416)457-3030. FAX: (416)796-3563. Editor: Johnny Fitness. Monthly magazine. Circ. 260,000. Estab. 1974. Emphasizes male and female physical development and fitness. Sample copy $5.
Needs: Buys 2,000 photos/year; 50% assigned; 50% stock. Needs celebrity/personality, fashion/beauty, glamour, how-to, human interest, humorous, special effects/experimental and spot news. "We require action exercise photos of bodybuilders and fitness enthusiasts training with sweat and strain." Wants on a regular basis "different" pics of top names, bodybuilders or film stars famous for their physique (i.e., Schwarzenegger, The Hulk, etc.). No photos of mediocre bodybuilders. "They have to be among the top 20 in the world or top film stars exercising." Photos purchased with accompanying ms. Captions preferred.
Making Contact & Terms: Send material by mail for consideration; send $3 for return postage. Uses 8×10 b&w glossy prints. Query with contact sheet. Send 35mm, 2¼×2¼ or 4×5 transparencies; vertical format preferred for cover. Reports in 2-4 weeks. Pays $85-100/hour and $1,000-3,000 per complete package. Pays $15-35/b&w photo; $25-500/color photo; $300-500/cover photo; $85-300/accompanying ms. Pays on acceptance. Credit line given. Buys all rights.
Tips: Hulk image. "We would like to see photographers take up the challenge of making exercise photos look like exercise motion." In samples wants to see "sharp, color balanced, attractive subjects, no grain, artistic eye. Someone who can glamorize bodybuilding on film." To break in, "get serious: read, ask questions, learn, experiment and try, try again. Keep trying for improvement—don't kid yourself that you are a good photographer when you don't even understand half the attachments on your camera. Immerse yourself in photography."

NATIONAL GEOGRAPHIC, (Not reviewing freelance work).

NATIONAL GEOGRAPHIC TRAVELER, 1145 17th St. NW, Washington DC 20036. Senior Illustrations Editor: Winthrop Scudder. Bimonthly. Stories focus primarily on the U.S. and Canada with two foreign articles per issue on high interest, readily accessible areas. Minimal emphasis on rugged sporting themes. Occasional photographic essay with no text. Approximately 104 editorial pages, 8½×11, 6-7 articles per issue." Circ. 850,000+. Photo guidelines free with SASE. Sample copy available for $5.60 from Robert Dove, National Geographic Society, Gaithersburg MD 20760.

Needs: Uses approximately 80 photos per issue. 95% assigned to freelance photographers. Occasional needs for travel-related stock. Captions required. "Most main features are live assignments. 'Front & Back of the Book' features are using more stock. Ratios are probably 80% live; 20% stock."

Making Contact & Terms: Send only top quality portfolio of not more than 100 images. SASE. Reports in 1 month. Pays $100 minimum/b&w and color inside photo; $250-300/color or b&w page; $500/cover. Pays on publication. Credit line given. Buys one-time world rights. Does not piggyback on other assignments or accept articles previously published or commissioned by other magazines.

Tips: "The best approach is with a good story idea well presented in writing after submitting convincing sample of work. Do *not* telephone. Do not ask for appointment unless your work has been seen and you have a good idea to present. Do not send form letters. We are looking for impact, atmosphere, human interest and involvement. We want pictures that will appeal to and motivate readers to visit the places profiled. *Study the magazine!* Be patient but realistic. Don't underestimate the difficulty or the competition. I'm looking for images that suggest technical ability and a strong aesthetic vision: photos should reflect strong visual architecture (a sense of how to use light and composition along with strong color palette sensibility). Photographs should also show an ability to work well with people."

NATIONAL GEOGRAPHIC WORLD, (Not reviewing freelance work.)

NATIONAL PARKS MAGAZINE, 1776 Massachusetts Ave. NW, Washington DC 20036. (202)223-6722. Editor: Sue Dodge. Bimonthly magazine. Circ. 285,000. Estab. 1919. Emphasizes the preservation of national parks and wildlife. Sample copy $3; free photo guidelines with SASE.

Needs: Photos of wildlife and people in national parks, scenics, national monuments, national recreation areas, national seashores, threats to park resources and wildlife. Also seeks mss on national parks, wildlife with accompanying photos.

Making Contact & Terms: Send stock list with example of work if possible. Uses 4×5 or 35mm transparencies. SASE. Reports in 1 month. Pays $75-150/color photos; $200 full-bleed color covers. Pays on publication. Buys one-time rights.

Tips: "Photographers should be more specific about areas they have covered. We are a specialized publication and are not interested in extensive lists on topics we do not cover. Trends include 'more dramatic pictures.' "

NATIONAL WILDLIFE, 8925 Leesburg Pike, Vienna VA 22184. (703)790-4419. FAX: (703)442-7332. Photo Editor: John Nuhn. Senior Photo Editor: Steve Freligh. Bimonthly magazine. Estab. 1962. Emphasizes wildlife, nature, environment and conservation. Readers are people who enjoy viewing high-quality wildlife and nature images, and who are interested in knowing more about the natural world and man's interrelationship with animals and environment. Circ. 850,000. Sample copy $3; send to National Wildlife Federation Membership Services (same address). Photo guidelines free with SASE. Please keep sample copy and guidelines requests separate.

Needs: Uses 45 photos/issue; all supplied by freelance photographers; 80% stock vs. 20% assigned. Needs photos of wildlife, wild plants, nature-related how-to, conservation practices, environmental damage, environmental research, outdoor recreation. Subject needs include single photos for cover possibility (primarily wildlife but also plants, scenics, people); b&w accompanying unique story ideas that should not be in color. Model release preferred; captions required.

Making Contact & Terms: Interested in receiving work from newer, lesser-known photographers. Send 8×10 glossy b&w prints; 35mm, 2¼×2¼, 4×5, 8×10 transparencies (magazine is 95% color) by mail for consideration. Query with samples, credits and stock listings. SASE. Reports in 3 weeks. Pays $300-750/b&w inside photo; $800/color cover photo; $300-750/color inside photo; text/photo negotiable. Pays on acceptance. Credit line given. Buys one-time rights with limited magazine promotion rights. Previously published work OK.

Tips: Interested in a variety of images that show photographer's scope and specialization, organized in slide sheets, along with tearsheets of previously published work. "Study our magazine; note the types of images we use and send photos equal or better. We look for imagination (common subjects done creatively, different views of animals and plants); technical expertise (proper exposure, focusing, lighting); and the ability to go that one step further and make the shot unique. Think editorially when submitting story, queries or photos; assure that package is complete—sufficient return postage (no checks), proper size return envelope, address inside, and do not submit photos in glass slides, trays or small boxes."

NATURAL HISTORY MAGAZINE, Dept. PM, Central Park W. at 79th St., New York NY 10024. (212)769-5500. Editor: Alan Ternes. Picture Editor: Kay Zakariasen. Monthly magazine. Circ. 520,000. Buys 400-450 annually. For primarily well-educated people with interests in the sciences. Free photo guidelines.

Needs: Animal behavior, photo essay, documentary, plant and landscape. Photos used must relate to the social or natural sciences with an ecological framework. Accurate, detailed captions required.
Making Contact & Terms: Query with resume of credits. Uses 8×10 glossy, matte and semigloss b&w prints; and 35mm, 2¼×2¼, 4×5, 6×7 and 8×10 color transparencies. Covers are always related to an article in the issue. SASE. Reports in 2 weeks. Pays $75-250/b&w print, $75-400/color transparency and $500 minimum/cover. Pays on publication. Credit line given. Buys one-time rights. Previously published work OK but must be indicated on delivery memo.
Tips: "Study the magazine—we are more interested in ideas than individual photos. We do not have the time to review portfolios without a specific theme in the social or natural sciences."

NATURAL LIFE MAGAZINE, Dept. PM, 4728 Byrne Rd., Burnaby, BC V5H 3X7 Canada. (604)438-1919. Photo Editor: Siegfried Gursche. Bimonthly magazine. Readers are health and nutrition, lifestyle and fitness oriented. Circ. 110,000. Sample copy $2.50 (Canadian) and 9½×11 SASE. Photo guidelines free with SASE.
Needs: Uses 12 photos/issue; 50% supplied by freelance photographers. Looking for photos of healthy people doing healthy things. Subjects include environment, ecology, organic farming and gardening, herbal therapies, vitamins, mineral supplements and good vegetarian food, all with a family orientation. Model release required; photo captions preferred.
Making Contact & Terms: Send unsolicited photos by mail for consideration with resume, business card, brochure, flyer or tearsheets to be kept on file for possible assignments. Send color 4×5 prints and 35mm, 2¼×2¼, or 4×5 transparencies. SASE. Reports in 2 weeks. Pays $125/color cover photo; $60/color inside photo. Pays on publication. Credit line given. Buys all rights; will negotiate. Simultaneous submissions and previously published work OK.
Tips: "Get in touch with the 'Natural Foods' and 'Alternative Therapies' scene. Observe and shoot healthy people doing healthy things."

NATURE PHOTOGRAPHER, P.O. Box 2037, West Palm Beach FL 33402. (407)586-7332. Photo Editor: Helen Longest-Slaughter. Bimonthly 4-color and b&w high quality magazine. Emphasizes "conservation-oriented, low-impact nature photography" with strong how-to focus. Readers are male and female nature photographers of all ages. Circ. 8,000. Estab. 1990. Sample copies available; free with 10×13 SAE with $1.80 postage.
Needs: Uses 25-35 photos/issue; 90% supplied by freelancers. Needs nature shots of "all types—abstracts, animal/wildlife shots, flowers, plants, scenics, etc." Shots must be in natural settings; no setups, zoo or captive animal shots accepted. Reviews photos with or without ms. Especially wants to see "excellent quality photos (35mm slides) that can be converted to b&w without losing impact of photo." Photo captions required. Essential details: description of subject, location, type of equipment, how photographed. "This information published with photos."
Making Contact & Terms: Interested in receiving work from newer, lesser-known photographers. Query with resume of credits. Send stock photo list. Provide resume, business card, brochure, flyer or tearsheet to be kept on file for possible assignments. Does not keep samples on file. SASE. Reports within 2 months, according to deadline. Pays $100/color cover photo; $50/b&w cover photo; $40/color inside photo; $25/b&w inside photo; $75-150/photo/text package. Pays on publication. Credit line given. Buys one-time rights. Simultaneous submissions and previously published work OK.
Tips: Prefers to see 35mm, 2¼×2¼ and 4×5 transparencies. Recommends working with "the best lens you can afford and slow speed slide film." Suggests editing with a 4× or 8× lupe (magnifier) on a light board to check for sharpness, color saturation, etc.

NEVADA MAGAZINE, Capitol Complex, Carson City NV 89710. (702)687-5416. FAX: (702)687-6159. Art Director: Jim Crandall. Estab. 1936. Bimonthly. Circ. 130,000. State tourism magazine devoted to promoting tourism in Nevada, particularly for people interested in travel, people, history, events and recreation; age 30-70. Sample copy $1.50.
Needs: Buys 40-50 photos/issue; 30-35 supplied by freelance photographers; Buys 10% freelance on assignment, 20% from freelance stock. (Nevada stock photos only—not generic). Towns and cities, scenics, outdoor recreation with people, events, state parks, tourist attractions, travel, wildlife, ranching, mining and general Nevada life. Must be Nevada subjects. Captions required; include place, date, names if available.
Making Contact & Terms: Interested in receiving work from newer, lesser-known photographers. Send samples of *Nevada* photos. Send 8×10 glossy prints; 35mm, 2¼×2¼, 4×5, 8×10 transparencies; prefers vertical format for cover. Must be labeled with name, address and captions on each. SASE. Reports in 2-4 months. Pays $20-100/inside photo; $150/cover photo; $50 minimum/job. Pays on publication. Credit line given. Buys first N.A. serial rights.

Tips: "Send variety of good-quality Nevada photos, well-labeled. Self-edit work to 20-40 slides maximum. Increasing use of events photos from prior years events. Real need for current casino shots. Label each slide or print properly with name, address and caption on each, not on a separate sheet. Send 35mm slides in 8×10 see-through slide sleeves."

*NEW AGE JOURNAL, 342 Western Ave., Brighton MA 02135. (617)787-2005. FAX: (617)787-2879. Art Director: Dan Mishkind. Bimonthly magazine. Emphasizes holistic health, spirituality, psychology, environment. Readers are 60% female, 40% male. Circ. 150,000. Estab. 1975. Sample copy for $5.
Photo Needs: Uses 10-15 photos/issue. Needs personality/environmental portraits.
Making Contact & Terms: Provide resume, business card, brochure, flyer or tearsheets to be kept on file for possible assignments. Keeps samples on file. SASE. Pays $750/color cover photo; $250/color inside photo; $200-300/day. Pays on publication. Credit line given. Buys one-time rights.
Tips: In samples wants to see dramatic environmental portraits. "Send promo pieces that can be kept on file."

NEW CLEVELAND WOMAN JOURNAL, Dept. PM, 104 E. Bridge St., Berea OH 44107. (216)243-3740. Editorial Director: June Vereeke-Hutt. Monthly magazine. Emphasizes "news and features pertaining to working women in the Cleveland/Akron area." Readers are working women, 50% married, average age 35. Circ. 34,000.
Needs: Uses about 6 photos/issue; half supplied by freelance photographers. Needs "photo illustrations of subject-careers, travel, finance, etc." Model release and captions required.
Making Contact & Terms: Query with samples. Provide business card and brochure to be kept on file for possible future assignments. SASE. Reports in 1 month. Pays $25/b&w inside photo. Pays on publication. Credit line given. Buys first N.A. serial rights. Simultaneous submissions OK.

NEW DOMINION MAGAZINE, Dept. PM, 210 Reinekers, Alexandria VA 22314. (703)683-7336. Editor: Phil Hayward. Monthly magazine. Emphasizes business and lifestyle for northern Virginia. Readers are 65% male, 35% female, affluent, median age early 40's. Circ. 50,000. Estab. 1987. Sample copy for $2.95 with 9×12 SASE.
Needs: Uses 40 photos/issue; 60% supplied by freelance photographers. Needs photos of stock landscape, tourism, assignment people, studio (still lifes, concept shots). *No* newspaper photo journalism, no fashion. Model release and photo captions preferred.
Making Contact & Terms: Provide resume, business card, brochure, flyer or tearsheets to be kept on file for possible assignments. SASE. Reports in 1 month. Pays $250/day; $125/half day plus expenses. Buys one-time rights. Previously published work OK.
Tips: Wants to see "a brief selection of the photographer's work that demonstrates his/her style and capabilities. For samples, we prefer tearsheets, printed samples or copies."

NEW MEXICO MAGAZINE, Dept. PM, Joseph Montoya State Building, 1100 St. Francis Dr., Santa Fe NM 87503. (505)827-0220. FAX: (505)827-0346. Editor: Emily Drabanski. Art Director: John Vaughan. Monthly magazine. Circ. 110,000. For people interested in the Southwest or who have lived in or visited New Mexico. Sample copy $2.75 with 9×12 SASE and 75¢ postage; free photo guidelines with SASE.
Needs: Needs New Mexico photos only—landscapes, people, events, architecture, etc. "Most work is done on assignment in relation to a story, but we welcome photo essay suggestions from photographers." Cover photos usually relate to the main feature in the magazine. Captions required. Buys 40 photos/issue; 70% on assignment, 30% on stock.
Making Contact & Terms: Submit portfolio to John Vaughan; uses transparencies. SASE. Pays $50-100/color photo; $150/cover photo. Pays on publication. Credit line given. Buys one-time rights.
Tips: Prefers transparencies submitted in plastic pocketed sheets. Interested in different viewpoints, styles not necessarily obligated to straight scenic. "All material must be taken in New Mexico. Representative work suggested. If photographers have a preference about what they want to do or where they're going, we would like to see that in their work. Transparencies or dupes are best for review and handling purposes."

NEW MEXICO PHOTOGRAPHER, Dept. PM, Box 2582—ENMU, Portales NM 88130. (505)562-2253. Publisher: Wendel Sloan. Biennial magazine. Emphasizes high-quality b&w photography taken anywhere in the world. Readers are photographers and patrons of high-quality photography. Circ. 2,000. Estab. 1989. Sample copy for $3. Photo guidelines free with SASE.

Needs: Uses 50 photos/issue; 100% supplied by freelancers. "We are devoted to all subject matters from b&w photographers everywhere." Likes to see seasonal photos for summer and winter issues; deadlines—April 15, October 15. Model release and photo captions preferred.

Making Contact & Terms: Send unsolicited b&w prints by mail for consideration. "Photos need not be mounted. However, the technical quality needs to be faultless. We've rejected great photos because of dust, water spots, etc." SASE. Reports after selections made, prior to publication. Photos selected on basis of semi-annual contest; photos are published and cash prizes also offered. Credit line given. Buys one-time rights. Simultaneous submissions and previously published work OK.

Tips: "Since we run very little advertising, we sponsor a contest for each issue to help pay for publication of the magazine. A $5 entry is charged for each entry, and all entrants in photo contest receive a copy of the magazine. Don't be fooled by our name. Although we do publish a lot of photography with a 'Southwestern' feel, *original* photography from anywhere excites us."

N.Y. HABITAT, 928 Broadway, New York NY 10010. (212)505-2030. Managing Editor: Lloyd Chrein. Magazine published 8 times/year. Emphasizes real estate, co-op/condo management. Readers are board members and owners at co-ops, condos and are all ages, occupations (mid- or upper-middle class). Circ. 10,000. Estab. 1982. Sample copy $5. Photo guidelines free with SASE.

Needs: Uses 11 photos/issue. Half freelance photography in a given issue comes from assignment and half from freelance stock. Needs photos of people, candid, action—photojournalism.

Making Contact & Terms: Provide resume, business card, brochure, flyer or tearsheets to be kept on file for possible assignments. Reports in 1 month. Pays $50/b&w inside photo. Pays on publication. Credit line given. Buys one-time rights. Previously published work OK.

Tips: Looks for "photojournalism with depth, action and expression." The trend is "people. Show me people in situations. Give me b&w photos with depth and contrast."

NEW YORK MAGAZINE, 755 Second Ave., New York NY 10017. (212)880-0829. Editor: Edward Kosner. Photography Director: Jordan Schaps. Picture Editor: Susan Vermazen. Weekly magazine. Full service city magazine: national and local news, fashion, food, entertaining, lifestyle, design, profiles, etc. Readers are 28-55 years average with $90,000+ average family income. Professional people, family people, concerned with quality of life and social issues affecting them, their families and the community. Circ. 430,000. Estab. 1968. Sample copy free with SASE.

Needs: Uses about 50 photos/issue; 85% assigned; 15% stock. Needs full range: photojournalism, fashion, food, product still lifes, conceptual and stock (occasionally). Always need great product still life, and studio work. "Model release and captions preferred for professional models; require model release for 'real' people." Photo captions required.

Making Contact & Terms: Arrange a personal interview to show portfolio, submit portfolio for review, "as this is a *fast* paced weekly, phone appointments are *essential*, time permitting." Drop-offs, every Thursday. *Does not return unsolicited material.* Reports as soon as possible. Pays $1,000/color cover photo; $300/page of color; $125-200/photo spot; $150-300/b&w and color photo; $300/day. Pays on publication and receipt of original invoices. Credit line given. Buys one-time rights. We reserve the right to reuse photography in context for house ads and self-promotion at no additional charge.

Tips: "We look for strong high-quality images that work with the text but tell their own story as well. We want the kind of photographer who can deliver images whether on his own or with spirited art direction. You need to really get to know the magazine and its various departments ("Intelligencer," "Fast Track," "Hot Line," "Best Bets," etc.) as well as the way we do fashion, entertaining, lifestyle, etc. *New York* is a great showcase for the talented newcomer looking for prestige exposure, the solid working photojournalist and the well-established advertising specialist looking for the creative freedom to do our kind of work. We lean toward traditional high-quality photographic solutions to our visual needs, but are ever mindful of and sensitive to the trends and directions in which photography is moving. Of course, the photographs must be strong, accessible, well lit and in focus. Freelancers interested in working with us should: 1. make an appointment; 2. be prompt; 3. have materials geared to what we need and what you'd like to do in our pages; 4. leave a photo image with phone number; 5. not call frequently asking for work; 6. remember that this is a fast-paced weekly magazine. We're courteous, but on constant deadline."

*NEW YORK OUTDOORS, 51 Atlantic Ave., Floral Park NY 11001. (516)352-9700. FAX: (516)437-6841. Editor: Keith Gardner. Associate Editor: Gary P. Joyce. Published 10 times a year. Covers the entire gamut of outdoor participatory recreation.

Needs: Quality "adventure" sports photography. Buys first N.A. serial rights. Photos purchased with accompanying ms.; cover and other purchased separately. Pays on publication. Reports in 3 weeks. SASE. Captions required.
Making Contact & Terms: Queries preferred. Send transparencies. Requires originals. Pay rates for color: $250/cover; $100/full page; $75/¾ page; $50/½ page; $25/¼ page. B&w flat rate $25.
Tips: "We're a regional with emphasis on New York action. Cover New Jersey, Connecticut, Rhode Island and Pennsylvania as well. Well stocked on fishing/hunting, interested in everything else relating to active outdoor sports."

NORTHEAST OUTDOORS, P.O. Box 2180, Waterbury CT 06722. (203)755-0158. Editorial Director: John Florian. Monthly tabloid. Emphasizes camping in the Northeast. Circ. 14,000. Estab. 1968. Sample copy free with SASE.
Needs: Reviews photos with accompanying manuscript *only*. Model release required. Photo captions preferred.
Making Contact & Terms: Query with story ideas and resume. SASE. Reports in approximately 1 month. Pays $40-80/photo text package. Pays on publication. Credit line given. Buys one-time rights, first N.A. serial rights. Previously published work OK if not in competing publication.

NORTHERN OHIO LIVE, Dept. PM, 11320 Juniper Rd., Cleveland OH 44106. (216)721-1800. Art Director: Michael Wainey. Monthly magazine. Emphasizes arts, entertainment, lifestyle and fashion. Readers are upper income, ages 25-60, professionals. Circ. 38,000. Estab. 1980. Sample copy for $2 with 9×12 SAE.
Needs: Uses 30 photos/issue; 20-100% supplied by freelance photographers. Needs photos of people in different locations, fashion and locale. Model release preferred. Photo captions preferred (names only is usually OK).
Making Contact & Terms: Arrange a personal interview to show portfolio. Send 35mm, 2¼×2¼, b&w and color prints by mail for consideration. Provide resume, business card, brochure, flyer or tearsheet to be kept on file for possible assignments. Follow up phone call OK. SASE. Reports in 3 weeks. Pays $250/color cover photo; $250/b&w cover photo; $100/color inside photo; $50/b&w inside photo; $30-50/hour; $250-500/day. Pays on publication. Credit line given. Buys one-time rights. Previously published work OK.
Tips: In photographer's portfolio wants to see "good portraits, people on location, photojournalism strengths, quick turn-around and willingness to work on *low* budget. Mail sample of work, follow up with phone call. Portfolio review should be short—only *best quality* work!"

NORTHWEST TRAVEL, P.O. Box 18000, 1870 Hwy. 126, Florence OR 97439. (800)727-8401. Photo Coordinator: Barbara Grano. Bimonthly magazine. Emphasizes Pacific Northwest travel—Oregon, Washington, Idaho and British Columbia (southern). Readers are middle-age male and female, upper income/middle income. Circ. 40,000. Estab. 1991. Sample copy $3.50. Photo guidelines free with SASE.
Needs: Uses 8-12 (full page) photos/issue; all supplied by freelancers. Needs photos of travel, scenics. Model release preferred. Photo captions required.
Making Contact & Terms: Send unsolicited photos by mail for consideration. Send 35mm, 2¼×2¼, 4×5 transparencies. SASE. Reports in 1 month. Pays $250/color cover photo; $50/color inside photo; $50/b&w inside photo; $100-250/photo/text package. Pays on publication. Credit line given. Buys one-time rights.
Tips: "Mainly interested in scenics. Avoid colored filters. Use only film that can enlarge without graininess."

NUGGET, Dept. PM, Suite 600, 2600 Douglas Rd., Coral Gables FL 33134. (305)443-2378. Editor: Christopher James. Bimonthly magazine. Emphasizes sex and fetishism for men and women of all ages. Circ. 100,000. Sample copy $5 postpaid; photo guidelines free with SASE.
Needs: Uses 100 photos/issue. Interested only in nude sets; single woman, female/female or male/female. All photo sequences should have a fetish theme (sadomasochism, leather, bondage, transvestism, transsexuals, lingerie, infantilism, wrestling—female/female or male/female—women fighting women or women fighting men, amputee models, etc.). Model release required. Buys in sets, not by individual photos. No Polaroids or amateur photography. Also seeks accompanying mss on sex, fetishism and sex-oriented products.
Making Contact & Terms: Submit material (in sets only) for consideration. Send 8×10 b&w glossy prints, contact sheet OK; transparencies, prefers Kodachrome or large format; vertical format required for cover. SASE. Reports in 2 weeks. Pays $250 minimum/b&w set; $250-400/color set; $150/cover photo; $250-350/ms. Pays on publication. Credit line given. Buys one-time rights or second serial (reprint) rights. Previously published work OK.

Close-up

Lisl Dennis
Freelance Photographer
Santa Fe, New Mexico

© Nancy Brown

After 30 years as a freelancer, Lisl Dennis is realistic when it comes to discussing the life of a travel photographer. The perks that go along with visiting exotic locales worldwide tend to keep wages low for such work. And there is always the battle between photographer and editor in which photographers practically never have a say over which images work best in a publication, she says.

"I think the travel editors and the art directors are really very conservative about the kind of images they run in magazines," says Dennis, who began shooting foreign destinations at 18 while studying sculpting in Florence, Italy. Typically, travel editors will choose the "safe" photos for publication even though they may like the more intriguing shots a photographer has captured, she says. "I think that's true despite the looser interpretation of travel photography that, say, *Condé Nast Traveler* has brought to the editorial side."

However, her vision of photography's future portrays a greater need for more stock images and Dennis believes travel photography can be a great opportunity to acquire photos for agencies. Dennis, who would like to devote more time to shooting stock, says she often takes time to harvest images for her portfolio while on assignment shooting other

© Lisl Dennis

Whether Lisl Dennis is shooting photos of the pyramids in Egypt, above, or the Taj Mahal in India, right, she always captures her subject with a unique vision. By photographing from diverse angles in both cases, and including more than just the landmarks, Dennis gives the viewer something extraordinary to look at. The silhouetted figures in the foreground of the pyramids add mystery to the photo, while the man's face on the right of the Taj Mahal portrays the mystery and wisdom of the tomb behind him.

projects. She also believes professional photographers must step into electronic imaging and stock photography in order to be successful in the future.

A one-time *Boston Globe* photographer, Dennis has authored several books on travel photography, including *Travel Photography: Developing a Personal Style* and *How to Take Better Travel Photos*, which sold over 90,000 copies. In 1979, she and her husband, Landt, developed the Travel Photography Workshop in Santa Fe, New Mexico, which caters to the serious amateurs or professionals who are interested in advancing their skills. The workshop serves as one of the nation's best, but very few photographers sign up with the idea of starting a travel photography career. "Out of the entire season's participants we may have three or four people who write to us saying they got calendars published or photos in a magazine."

When Dennis began shooting travel photos in the 1960s it was much "groovier" for college kids to see themselves as artists, writers or photographers, rather than follow their parents' footsteps into traditional professions. "It's a good field assuming a newcomer can get in the door," she says of travel photography. "When I started 30 years ago there were fewer photographers spewing out of institutions."

Although her parents did not want to send her to art school, Dennis does credit them for paving the way toward her present love, shooting architectural interiors. Her father worked as an architect and her mother was an interior designer in New Jersey. Even though she maintains a travel photography schedule, Dennis has become an expert at shooting architectural interiors. The switch to interiors was a decision made in the early 1980s primarily to help her make a comfortable living, something editorial travel assignments were not doing. Too much of her time and income were eaten up by the cost of writing proposals, equipment and travel expenses.

She, however, concedes that newcomers entering the professional arena may find travel photography wages satisfactory. "The pay scale seems to be high for the average amateur who thinks that it's very glamorous to get paid to travel and shoot pictures."

A profession on the go has led Dennis to some fascinating locations, including India and Morocco which are two of her favorite countries for shooting photographs. "The people are marvelous photographically in both countries," she says "I love the 'mystery' that surrounds their cultures.'"

— *Michael Willins*

© Lisl Dennis

OCEAN NAVIGATOR, 18 Danforth St., Portland ME 04101. (207)772-2466. Art Director: Denny Ryus. Magazine publishing 8 times/year. Emphasizes marine navigation and ocean voyaging. Readers are primarily male, 40 and up, inboard auxiliary sailboat owners. Circ. 35,000. Estab. 1985. Sample copy $3.50.
Needs: Uses 20 photos/issue; 100% supplied by freelance photographers. Needs photos of boats and related machinery, marine hardware, marine situations, marine technology and events—commercial and recreational. Model release and photo captions required.
Making Contact & Terms: Send 35mm, 2¼×2¼, 4×5 b&w and color prints; 35mm, 2¼×2¼, 4×5 transparencies by mail for consideration. SASE. Reports in 1 month. Pays $400/color cover photo; $50/color inside photo. Pays on publication. Credit line given. Buys one-time rights. Simultaneous submissions and previously published work OK.
Tips: Looks for "almost anything that has to do with marine navigation or ocean voyaging."

*ODYSSEY, Science That's Out of This World, 7 School St., Peterborough NH 03458. (603)924-7209. FAX: (603)924-7380. Picture Editor: Francelle Carapetyan. Monthly magazine. Emphasis on astronomy and space exploration. Readers are children, ages 8-15. Circ. 60,000. Estab. 1979. Sample copy $3.95 with 7½×10½ or larger SASE and 5 first-class stamps. Photo guidelines available.
Needs: Uses 30-35 photos/issue. Needs photos of astronomy and space exploration from NASA and observatories, museum shots and others illustrating activities from various organizations. Reviews photos with or without ms. Model/property release required. Captions preferred.
Making Contact & Terms: Query with stock photo list. Send unsolicited photos by mail for consideration. Provide resume, business card, brochure, flyer or tearsheets to be kept on file for possible future assignments. Send color prints or transparencies. Samples kept on file. SASE. Reports in 1 month. Pays on individual basis/color cover photo; $160-210/color page rate. Pays on publication. Credit line given. Buys one-time and all rights; negotiable.
Tips: "We like photos that include kids in reader-age range and plenty of action. Each issue is devoted to a single theme. Photos should relate to those themes."

OHIO FISHERMAN, 1432 Parsons Ave., Columbus OH 43207. (614)445-7506. Editor: Dan Armitage. Monthly. Circ. 41,000. Estab. 1974. Emphasizes fishing. Readers are the Buckeye State anglers. Sample copy and photo guidelines free with SASE.
Needs: Uses 10 covers/year supplied by freelance photographers. Needs transparencies for cover; 99% used are verticals with as much free space on top and left side of frame as possible. Fish and fishermen (species should be common to coverage area) action preferred. Photos purchased with or without accompanying ms. Model and property releases preferred; required for covers. Captions preferred.
Making Contact & Terms: Query with tearsheets or send unsolicited photos by mail for consideration. Requires 35mm transparencies. SASE. Reports in 1 month. Provide tearsheets to be kept on file for possible future assignments. Pays $200/color cover. Pays 15th of month prior to issue date. Credit line given. Buys one-time rights.
Tips: In reviewing photographs looks for clarity, action, color and suitability of format. Study our covers to know where we need space for logos and cover blurbs. Don't give up easily, it sometimes takes a number of tries before you hit the right photo for us, as our needs are very specific."

OHIO MAGAZINE, 62 E. Broad St., Columbus OH 43215. (614)461-5083. Contact: Brooke Wenstrup. Estab. 1979. Monthly magazine. Emphasizes features throughout Ohio for an educated, urban and urbane readership. Sample copy $3 postpaid.
Needs: Travel, photo essay/photo feature, b&w scenics, personality, sports and spot news. Photojournalism and concept-oriented studio photography. Model/property releases preferred. Photo captions required.
Making Contact & Terms: Interested in receiving work from newer, lesser-known photographers. Send material by mail for consideration. Query with samples. Arrange a personal interview to show a portfolio. Send 8×10 b&w glossy prints; contact sheet requested. Also uses 35mm, 2¼×2¼ or 4×5 transparencies; square format preferred for covers. SASE. Reports in 1 month. Pays $30-250/b&w photo; $30-250/color photo; $350/day; and $150-350/job. Pays within 90 days after acceptance. Credit line given. Buys one-time rights; negotiable.
Tips: "Please look at magazine before submitting to get an idea what type of photographs we use." Send sheets of slides and/or prints with return postage and they will be reviewed. Dupes for our files are always appreciated—and reviewed on a regular basis. We are leaning more toward well-done documentary photography and less toward studio photography. Trends in our use of editorial photography include scenics, single photos that can support an essay, photo essays on cities/towns, more use of 180° shots. In reviewing a photographer's portfolio or samples we look for humor, insight, multi-level photos, quirkiness, thoughtfulness; stock photos of Ohio; ability to work with subjects (i.e., an obvious indication that the photographer was able to make subject relax and forget the camera—even

difficult subjects); ability to work with givens, bad natural light, etc.; creativity on the spot—as we can't always tell what a situation will be on location."

OLD WEST, P.O. Box 2107, Stillwater OK 74076. Editor: John Joerschke. Quarterly. Circ. 30,000. Estab. 1963. Emphasizes history of the Old West (1830 to 1910). Readers are people who like to read the history of the West. Sample copy free with 9 × 12 SAE and $2.
Needs: Uses 100 or more photos/issue; "almost all" supplied by freelance photographers. Needs "mostly Old West historical subjects, some travel, some scenic (ghost towns, old mining camps, historical sites). Prefers to have accompanying ms. Special needs include western wear, cowboys, rodeos, western events. Captions required.
Making Contact & Terms: Interested in receiving work from newer, lesser-known photographers. Query with samples, b&w only for inside, color covers. SASE. Reports in 1 month. Pays $75-150/color cover photos; $10/b&w inside photos. Payment on publication. Credit line given. Buys one-time rights.
Tips: "Looking for transparencies of existing artwork as well as scenics for covers, pictures that tell stories associated with Old West for the inside. Most of our photos are used to illustrate stories and come with manuscripts; however, we will consider other work (scenics, historical sites, old houses)."

*OMNI MAGAZINE, 1965 Broadway, New York NY 10023. (212)496-6100. Art Director: Dwayne Flinchum. Monthly magazine. Emphasizes science. Circ. 850,000. Estab. 1978. Sample copy for contributors only (free). Photo guidelines free with SASE.
Needs: Uses 20-30 photos/issue; 100% supplied by freelancers. Needs photos of technology and portraiture. Mostly scientific or special-effect, "surreal" photography. Model/property release required. Photo captions preferred.
Making Contact & Terms: Send unsolicited photos by mail for consideration. Provide resume, business card, brochure, flyer or tearsheets to be kept on file for possible assignments. Send any format. Keeps samples on file. SASE. Reports in 1-2 weeks. Pays $800/color cover photo; $500/b&w cover photo; pays $300/color inside photo; $225/b&w inside photo; $450/color page rate; $350/b&w page rate; $500/day; $500-2,000/photo/text package. Pays on publication. Credit line given on opening spreads only. Buys one-time rights. Rights negotiable. Previously published work OK.
Tips: "We are always seeking surreal, graphic images for our cover, which are upbeat and will function well commercially on the newsstand. Have an understanding of our needs. Research our past 3 issues for an idea of what we commission. We assign a great deal of portraiture of leading scientists."

ON THE LINE, 616 Walnut Ave., Scottdale PA 15683. (412)887-8500. Contact: Editor. Weekly magazine. Circ. 10,000. Estab. 1875. For children, ages 10-14. Free sample copy and editorial guidelines.
Needs: Very little photography from assignment and 95%+ from freelance stock. "We need quality b&w photos only. Prefers vertical shots, use some horizontal. We need photos of children, age 10-14 representing a balance of male/female, white/minority/international, urban/country. Clothing and hair styles must be contemporary, but not faddish. Wants to see children interacting with each other, with adults and with animals. Some nature scenes as well (especially with kids)."
Making Contact & Terms: Buys one-time rights. Send 8 × 10 b&w prints for consideration. SASE. Reports in 1 month. Pays $20-50/b&w (cover). Pays on acceptance. Simultaneous submissions and previously published work OK.

*ON-DIRT MAGAZINE, P.O. Box 6246, Woodland Hills CA 91365. (818)340-5750. FAX: (818)348-4648. Photo Editor: Lonnie Peralta. Monthly magazine. Emphasizes all forms of off-roading and racing. Readers are male and female off-road enthusiasts, ages 15-65. Circ. 120,000. Estab. 1984. Sample copy $2.50.
Needs: Uses 100-135 photos/issue; 50% supplied by freelancers. Needs photos of off-road action from events, races or fun. Reviews photos with or without a manuscript. Special needs are "fun" drives, "jomborees" and how-to articles w/photos. Model/property release preferred. Photo captions required.
Making Contact & Terms: Send unsolicited photos by mail for consideration. Send 5 × 7, 8 × 10 glossy w/border b&w, color prints; 35mm transparencies. Keeps samples on file. SASE. Reports in 1-2 weeks. Pays $50/cover photo; $7/b&w inside photo; $7/color page rate; $7/b&w page rate; $7/hour. Pays on publication. Credit line given. Buys all rights. Rights negotiable.

*ONTARIO OUT OF DOORS MAGAZINE, 227 Front St. E., Toronto ON M5A 1E8 Canada. (416)368-0185. FAX: (416)941-9113. Art Director: Yukio Yamada. Monthly magazine. Emphasizes hunting and fishing in Ontario. Readers are male ages 20-65. Circ. 56,000. Estab. 1968. Sample copies free with SAE, IRC. Photo guidelines free with SAE, IRC.
Needs: Uses 30 photos/issue; 50% supplied by freelancers, half on assignment, half from stock. Needs photos of game and fish species sought in Ontario; also scenics with anglers or hunters. Releases required for photos used in advertising. Captions preferred.

Making Contact & Terms: Interested in receiving work from newer, lesser-known photographers. Query with list of stock photo subjects. Send b&w prints; 35mm transparencies. Keeps samples on file. Reports in 1 month. Pays $300-500/color cover photo; $100-200/color inside photo; $35-75/b&w inside photo. Pays on acceptance. Credit line given. Buys one-time rights. Previously published work OK.

OPEN WHEEL MAGAZINE, P.O. Box 715, 27 S. Main St., Ipswich MA 01938. (508)356-7030. FAX: (508)356-2492. Editor: Dick Berggren. Monthly. Circ. 100,000. Estab. 1981. Emphasizes sprint car, supermodified, Indy and midget racing. Readers are fans, owners and drivers of race cars and those with business in racing. Photo guidelines free for SASE.
Needs: Uses 100-125 photos/issue supplied by freelance photographers; almost all come from freelance stock. Needs documentary, portraits, dramatic racing pictures, product photography, special effects, crash. Photos purchased with or without accompanying ms. Model release required for photos not shot in pit, garage or on track; captions required.
Making Contact & Terms: Send by mail for consideration 8 × 10 b&w or color glossy prints and any size slides. Kodachrome 64 preferred. SASE. Reports in 6 weeks. Pays $20/b&w inside; $35-250/color inside. Pays on publication. Buys all rights.
Tips: "Send the photos. We get dozens of inquiries but not enough pictures. We file everything that comes in and pull 80% of the pictures used each issue from those files. If it's on file, the photographer has a good shot."

OPERA NEWS, Dept. PM, 70 Lincoln Center, New York NY 10023-6593. (212)769-7080. FAX: (212)769-7007. Senior Editor: Jane L. Poole. Published by the Metropolitan Opera Guild. Biweekly (December-April) and monthly (May-November) magazine. Emphasizes opera performances and personalities for opera-goers, members of opera and music professionals. Circ. 120,000. Sample copy $2.50.
Needs: Uses about 45 photos/issue; 15 supplied by freelance photographers. Needs photos of "opera performances, both historical and current; opera singers, conductors and stage directors." Captions preferred.
Making Contact & Terms: Query with samples. Provide resume, business card, brochure, flyer or tearsheets to be kept on file for possible future assignments. SASE. Reporting time varies. NPI. Payment negotiated. Pays on publication. Credit line given. Buys one-time rights. Simultaneous submissions OK.

ORANGE COAST MAGAZINE, Suite D, 245 D Fischer Ave., Costa Mesa CA 92626. (714)545-1900. FAX: (714)545-1932. Editor: Palmer Jones. Photo Editor: Sarah McNeill. Monthly. Circ. 38,000. Emphasizes general interest—all subjects. Sample copy $3.
Needs: Uses 20-25 photos/issue; 50% supplied by freelance photographers. Needs graphic studio shots, food shots and some travel shots; mostly 35mm, 4 × 5 format. Model release preferred; captions required.
Making Contact & Terms: Interested in receiving work from newer, lesser-known photographers. Query with samples. SASE. Reports in 1-2 months. Pays $50/color photo for features only. Credit line given. Buys one-time rights; negotiable. Simultaneous submissions and previously published work OK.
Tips: "Studio and location work, graphic still life and travel shots."

OREGON COAST MAGAZINE, P.O. Box 18000, Florence OR 97439. (800)727-8401. Photo Coordinator: Barbara Grano. Estab. 1982. Bimonthly magazine. Emphasizes Oregon coast life. Readers are middle class, middle age. Circ. 62,000+. Sample copy $2.95 and $1.50 postage; photo guidelines available for SASE with 52¢.
Needs: Uses 6-10 photos/issue; 100% supplied by freelancers. Needs scenics. Especially needs photos of typical subjects—waves, beaches, lighthouses—but from a different angle. Model release required. Photo captions required; include specific location and description. "Label all slides and transparencies with captions and photographer's name."
Making Contact & Terms: Interested in receiving work from newer, lesser-known photographers. Send unsolicited 35mm, 2¼ × 2¼, 4 × 5 transparencies by mail for consideration. SASE. Reports in 1 month. Pays $250/color cover photo; pays $100 for calendar usage; pays $50/color inside photo; $50/b&w inside photo; $100-250/photo/text package. Credit line given. Buys one-time rights. "Send only the very best. Mainly interested in scenics. Use only slide film that can be enlarged without graininess. An appropriate submission would be 20-60 slides."
Tips: "Don't use color filters. Protect slides with sleeves-put in plastic holders. Don't send in little boxes."

*ORLANDO MAGAZINE, 341 N. Maitland Ave., Maitland FL 32751. (407)539-3939. FAX: (407)539-0533. Art Director: Mike Havekotte. Monthly magazine. Emphasizes business, real estate, arts, medical, local topics, golf. Readers are male, businessmen around age 40. Circ. 35,000. Estab. 1945.

Needs: Uses 36 photos/issue average; 2-3 supplied by freelancers. "Many photos include local people in local places." Special photo needs include: medical, real estate, small business. Model release preferred. Captions preferred.
Making Contact & Terms: Provide flyer or tearsheets to be kept on file. Cannot return material. Reports in 1 month to 1 year. Pays $400/color cover photo; $100/color inside photo; $75/b&w inside photo. Pays on publication. Credit line given. Buys one-time rights. Rights negotiable; "some repeat usage." Simultaneous submissions and previously published work OK.
Tips: In samples looks for style and design and clarity of idea or "story."

THE OTHER SIDE, 300 W. Apsley St., Philadelphia PA 19144. (215)849-2178. Art Director: Cathleen Benberg. Bimonthly magazine. Circ. 12,000. Estab. 1965. Emphasizes social justice issues from a Christian perspective. Sample copy $2.
Needs: Buys 6 photos/issue; 95-100% from stock, 0-5% on assignment. Documentary, human interest and photo essay/photo feature. "We're interested in human-interest photos and photos that relate to current social, economic or political issues, both here and in the Third World." Model/property release and captions preferred.
Making Contact & Terms: Interested in receiving work from newer, lesser-known photographers. Send samples of work to be photocopied for our files and/or photos; a list of subjects is difficult to judge quality of work by. Send 8×10 b&w glossy prints; transparencies for cover, vertical format required. Materials will be returned on request. SASE. Pays $20-30/b&w photo; $50-100/cover photo. Credit line given. Buys one-time rights. Simultaneous submissions and previously published work OK.
Tips: In reviewing photographs/samples, looks for "sensitivity to subject and good quality darkroom work."

♦OUR FAMILY, P.O. Box 249, Battleford SK S0M 0E0 Canada. FAX: (306)937-7644. Editor: Nestor Gregoire. Monthly magazine. Circ. 14,265. Estab. 1949. Emphasizes Christian faith as a part of daily living for Roman Catholic families. Sample copy $2.50 with 9×12 SAE and $1.08 Canadian postage. Free photo and writer's guidelines with SAE and 48¢ Canadian postage.
Needs: Photos are purchased with or without accompanying ms. Buys 5 photos/issue; cover by assignment, contents all freelance. Head shot (to convey mood); human interest ("people engaged in the various experiences of living"); humorous ("anything that strikes a responsive chord in the viewer"); photo essay/photo feature (human/religious themes); and special effects/experimental (dramatic—to help convey a specific mood). "We are always in need of the following: family (aspects of family life); couples (husband and wife interacting and interrelating or involved in various activities); teenagers (in all aspects of their lives and especially in a school situation); babies and children; any age person involved in service to others; individuals in various moods (depicting the whole gamut of human emotions); religious symbolism; and humor. We especially want people photos, but we do not want the posed photos that make people appear 'plastic', snobbish or elite. In all photos, the simple, common touch is preferred. We are especially in search of humorous photos (human and animal subjects). Stick to the naturally comic, whether it's subtle or obvious." Model release required if editorial topic might embarrass subject; captions required when photos accompany ms.
Making Contact & Terms: Send material by mail for consideration or query with samples after consulting photo spec sheet. Provide letter of inquiry, samples and tearsheets to be kept on file for possible future assignments. Send 8×10 b&w glossy prints; transparencies or 8×10 color glossy prints are used on inside pages, but are converted to b&w. SAE and IRC. (Personal check or money order OK instead or IRC.) Reports in 4 weeks. Pays $35/b&w photo. Pays 7-10¢/word for original mss; 5¢/word for nonoriginal mss. Pays on acceptance. Credit line given. Buys one-time rights and simultaneous rights. Simultaneous submissions or previously published work OK.
Tips: "Send us a sample (20-50 photos) of your work after reviewing our Photo Spec Sheet. Looks for "photos that center around family life—but in the broad sense — i.e., our elderly parents, teenagers, young adults, family activities. Our covers (full color) are a specific assignment. We do not use freelance submissions for our cover."

♦OUTDOOR CANADA, Suite 202, 703 Evans Ave., Toronto, ON M9C 5E9 Canada. (416)695-0311. Editor: Teddi Brown. Estab. 1972. Magazine published 9 times/year. Circ. 125,000. Free writers' and photographers' guidelines "with SASE or SAE and IRC only." No phone calls, please.
Needs: Buys 70-80 photos annually. Needs Canadian photos of people fishing, hunting, hiking, wildlife, cross-country skiing. Action shots. Photo captions required including identification of fish, bird or animal.
Making Contact & Terms: Send transparencies for consideration. For cover allow undetailed space along left side of photo for cover lines. SAE and IRC for American contributors, SASE for Canadians *must* be sent for return of materials. Reports in 3 weeks; "acknowledgement of receipt is sent the same day material is received." Pays $400 maximum/cover photo; $30-225/inside color photo depending on size used. Pays on publication. Buys first serial rights.

Tips: "Study the magazine and see the type of articles we use and the types of illustration used" and send a number of pictures to facilitate selection. "We are using more photos. We are looking for pictures that tell a story. We also need photos of people in the outdoors. A photo that captures the outdoor experience and shows the human delight in it. Take more fishing photos. It's the fastest-growing outdoor pastime in North America."

OUTDOOR LIFE MAGAZINE, Dept. PM, 2 Park Ave., New York NY 10016. (212)779-5000. Art Director: Jim Eckes. Monthly. Circ. 1,500,000. Emphasizes hunting, fishing, shooting, camping and boating. Readers are "outdoorsmen of all ages." Sample copy "not for individual requests." Photo guidelines free with SASE.
Needs: Uses about 50-60 photos/issue; 75% supplied by freelance photographers. Needs photos of "all species of wildlife and fish, especially in action and in natural habitat; how-to and where-to. No color prints—preferably Kodachrome 35mm slides." Captions preferred. No duplicates.
Making Contact & Terms: Send 5×7 or 8×10 b&w glossy prints; 35mm or 2¼×2¼ transparencies; b&w contact sheet by mail for consideration. Pays $35-275/b&w photo, $50-700/color photo depending on size of photos; $800-1,000/cover photo. SASE. Reports in 1 month. Rates are negotiable. Pays on publication. Credit line given. Buys one-time rights. "Multi subjects encouraged."
Tips: "Have name and address clearly printed on each photo to insure return, send in 8×10 plastic sleeves."

*OUTDOOR PHOTOGRAPHER, Suite 1220, 12121 Wilshire Blvd., Los Angeles CA 90025. (310)820-1500. Art Director: Kurt R. Smith. Magazine published 10 times per year. Emphasizes professional and semi-professional scenic, travel, wildlife and sports photography. Readers are photographers of all ages and interests. Circ. 200,000+. Photo guidelines free with SASE.
Needs: Uses about 50-60 photos/issue; 90% supplied by freelance photographers. Model release and captions preferred.
Making Contact & Terms: Query with samples; send b&w prints or color transparencies by mail for consideration. SASE. Reports in 60 days. NPI. Payment for cover photos, inside photos and text/photo package to be arranged. Pays on publication. Credit line given. Buys one-time rights but will negotiate. Previously published work OK.

*OUTLOOK, 602 El Portal Center, San Pablo CA 94806. (510)215-1565. Senior Editor: Jeanne Ewing. Bimonthly magazine. Emphasizes ethical concerns. Circ. 10,000. Estab. 1991. Sample copy free with 9×12 SASE and 2 first-class stamps. Photo guidelines free with SASE.
Needs: Uses 2-3 photos/issue; all supplied by freelancers. Needs photos of current events, families, multi-ethnic and health. Model/property release required. Photo captions required.
Making Contact & Terms: Query with stock photo list. Send unsolicited photos by mail for consideration. Provide resume, business card, brochure, flyer or tearsheets to be kept on file for possible assignments. SASE. Reports in 3 weeks. Pays $50/color cover photo; $25/b&w inside photo. Pays on publication. Credit line given. Buys one-time rights. Simultaneous submissions OK.

‡OVERSEAS!, Kolpingstr. 1, 6906 Leimen, West Germany (06 224) 7060. Editor: Greg Ballinger. Monthly magazine. Circ. 83,000. Emphasizes entertainment and European travel information of interest to military personnel and their families in Europe. Read by American and Canadian military personnel stationed in Europe, mostly males ages 20-35. Sample copy free with 9×12 SAE and 4 IRC. Photo guidelines available.
Needs: Needs cover photos of unusual or dramatic travel scenes in Europe. Don't want the standard "Leaning Tower of Pisa" or "Eifel Tower" photo, but something with a little more energy and excitement.
Making Contact & Terms: Query with samples; send b&w or color prints; 35mm, 2¼×2¼ transparencies; color contact sheets by mail for consideration. Please send 5 IRCs for return. Reports in 3 weeks. Pays $250-400. Pays on publication. Credit line given. Buys first European serial rights. Previously published work OK.
Tips: Send 15-50 slides. "The more color and action in the photo the better chance of being selected."

*❋OWL MAGAZINE, Suite 306, 56 The Esplanade, Toronto ON M5E 1A7 Canada. (416)868-6001. FAX: (416)868-6009. Photo Researcher: Robin Wilner. Published 10 times/year; 1 summer issue. A science and nature magazine for children ages 8-13. Circ. 110,000. Estab. 1976. Sample copy $4.28 (incl. GST) and 9×12 SAE and IRC. Photo guideline sheet free with SAE and IRC.
Needs: Uses approximately 15 photos/issue; 4% supplied by freelancers. Needs photos of animals/wildlife. Model/property release preferred; captions required.
Making Contact & Terms: Request photo package before sending photos for review. Send 35mm transparencies. Keeps samples on file. SAE and IRCs. Reports in 6-8 weeks. Pays $325 Canadian/color cover photo; $100 Canadian/color inside photo; $200 Canadian/color page rate. Pays on accep-

tance. Credit line given. Buys one-time rights. Previously published work OK.

Tips: "Photos should be sharply focused with good lighting showing animals in their natural environment. It is important that you present your work as professionally as possible. Become familiar with the magazine—look at back issues."

PAINT HORSE JOURNAL, P.O. Box 961023, Fort Worth TX 76161. (817)439-3400. Editor: Darrell Dodds. Emphasizes horse subjects—horse owners, trainers and show people. Readers are "people who own, show or simply enjoy knowing about registered Paint horses." Monthly. Circ. 13,000. Sample copy $1 postpaid; photo guidelines for SASE.

Needs: Uses about 50 photos/issue; 3 of which are supplied by freelance photographers. "Most photos will show Paint (spotted) horses. Other photos used include prominent Paint horse showmen, owners and breeders; notable Paint horse shows or other events; overall views of well-known Paint horse farms. Most freelance photos used are submitted with freelance articles to illustrate a particular subject. The magazine occasionally buys a cover photo, although most covers are paintings. Freelance photographers need to query before sending photos, because we rarely use photos just for their artistic appeal—they must relate to some article or news item." Wants on a regular basis Paint horses as related to news events, shows and persons. No "posed, handshake and award-winner photos." Model release and captions required.

Making Contact & Terms: Query with resume of photo credits or state specific idea for using photos. Provide resume, business card, brochure, flyer and tearsheets to be kept on file for possible future assignments. SASE. Reports in 3-6 weeks. Pays on acceptance $7.50 minimum/b&w photo; $10 minimum/color transparency; $50 minimum/color cover photo; $50-200 for text/photo package. Credit line given. Buys first NA serial rights or per individual negotiation.

Tips: "Send us a variety of Paint horse photos. We buy action, unusual situations, humor, but rarely buy halter shots."

*PALM BEACH ILLUSTRATED MAGAZINE, 1016 N. Dixie Hwy., W. Palm Beach FL 33401. (407)659-0210. FAX: (407)659-1736. Editor: Judy Di Edwardo. Monthly magazine. Emphasizes upscale, first-class living. Readers are highly influential, established people, ages 35-54. Circ. 15,000. Estab. 1950s. Sample copy free with SASE. Photo guidelines free.

Needs: Needs photos of travel. Reviews photos with or without a manuscript. Model/property release preferred. Photo captions preferred.

Making Contact & Terms: Send color prints; 35mm, 2¼×2¼ transparencies. SASE. Reports in 1 month. NPI; payment made on individual basis. Pays on publication. Credit line given. Buys one-time rights. Simultaneous submissions OK.

Tips: Looks for "travel and related topics such as resorts, spas, yacht charters, trend and lifestyle topics. Materials should appeal to affluent readers: budget travel is not of interest, for example. Editorial material on the latest best investments in the arts would be appropriate; editorial material on investing in a mobile home would not."

PALM BEACH LIFE, 265 Royal Poinciana Way, Palm Beach FL 33480. (407)837-4762. Design Director: Anne Wholf. Monthly magazine. Circ. 30,000. Emphasizes entertainment, affluent lifestyle, travel, environment, personalities, decorating and the arts. For regional and general audiences. Sample copy $4.18.

Needs: Freelance photographers supply 50% of the photos. Fine art, scenic, human interest and nature. Captions are required.

Making Contact & Terms: Query or make appointment. Uses any size b&w glossy prints; 35mm, 2¼×2¼ and 4×5 transparencies; vertical or square format for cover. SASE. "*Palm Beach Life* cannot be responsible for unsolicited material." Reports in 4-6 weeks. Pays $200-600/job, or on a per-photo basis. Pays $25-50/b&w photo; $50-100/color photo; cover photo negotiable. Pays on acceptance. Credit line given. Simultaneous submissions OK.

Tips: "Don't send slides—make an appointment to show work. We have staff photographers, are really only interested in something really exceptional or material from a location that we would find difficult to cover."

PALM SPRINGS LIFE MAGAZINE, 303 N. Indian Canyon Ave., P.O. Box 2724, Palm Springs CA 92263. (619)325-2333. FAX: (619)325-7008. Editor: Jamie Pricer. Monthly. Emphasizes Palm Springs/California desert area. Readers are extremely affluent, 45+ years old. Primarily for our readers, Palm Springs is their second/vacation home. Circ. 20,000. Estab. 1957. Sample copy $5. Photo guidelines free with SASE.

Needs: Uses 50+ photos/issue; 50% supplied by freelance photographers; 80% from assignment. Needs desert photos, scenic wildlife, gardening, fashion, beauty, travel and people. Special needs include photo essays, art photography. Model release required; captions preferred.

Making Contact & Terms: Interested in receiving work from newer, lesser-known photographers. Arrange a personal interview to show portfolio; query with list of stock photo subjects; or send unsolicited photos by mail for consideration. Uses 35mm, 2¼ × 2¼, 4 × 5 or 8 × 10 transparencies. SASE. Reports in 1 month. Pays $325/color cover photo; $75-200/color inside photo; $125/color page; $25-100/b&w photo; $50-325/color photo; payment/job, negotiable. Pays on publication. Credit line given. Buys all rights. Will negotiate with photographer unwilling to sell all rights. Simultaneous submissions and previously published work OK.

Tips: In photographer's portfolio looks for published photographs, the "unusual" bend to the "usual" subject. "We will try anything new photographically as long as it's gorgeous! Must present professional-looking portfolio."

*PARENTS MAGAZINE, 685 3rd Ave., New York NY 10017. (212)878-8700. FAX: (212)867-4583. Photo Editor: Meryl Levy. Emphasizes family relations and the care and raising of children. Readers are families with young children. Monthly. Circ. 1,800,000. Free photo guidelines.

Needs: Uses about 100 photos/issue; all supplied by freelance photographers. Needs family and/or children's photos. No landscape or architecture photos. Model release required. Pays for b&w; color: standard rates change yearly.

Making Contact & Terms: Interested in receiving work from newer, lesser-known photographers. Some work with freelance photographers on assignment only basis. Arrange for drop off to show portfolio. "Clifford Gardener, Art Director, and Meryl Levy, Photo Editor. By looking at portfolios of photographers in whom we are interested we may assign a job." Report time depends on shooting schedule, usually 2-6 weeks. NPI. Payment depends on space usage and expenses. SASE. Credit line given. Buys one-time rights. No simultaneous submissions; previously published work OK.

Tips: Interested in seeing consistency within the work of photographers. "Don't be a jack of all trades, master of none. Send work that applies to parents' needs. Don't send samples of studio portraits."

PENNSYLVANIA, P.O. Box 576, Camp Hill PA 17011. (717)761-6620. Editor: Albert E. Holliday. Bimonthly. Emphasizes history, travel and contemporary issues and topics. Readers are 40-60 years old, professional and retired; average income is $46,000. Circ. 40,000. Sample copy $2.95; photo guidelines free with SASE.

Needs: Uses about 40 photos/issue; most supplied by freelance photographers. Needs include travel and scenic. Reviews photos with or without accompanying ms. Captions required. All photos must be in Pennsylvania.

Making Contact & Terms: Query with samples and list of stock photo subjects; send 5 × 7 and up b&w prints and 35mm and 2¼ × 2¼ transparencies (duplicates only, no originals) by mail for consideration (4 × 5 or 4 × 6 color prints also OK). SASE. Reports in 2 weeks. Pays $100-150/color cover photo, $15-25/inside photo, $50-400/text/photo package. Credit line given. Buys one-time rights. Simultaneous submissions and previously published work OK.

PENNSYLVANIA GAME NEWS, Dept. PM, 2001 Elmerton Ave., Harrisburg PA 17110-9797. (717)787-3745. Editor: Bob Mitchell. Monthly magazine. Published by the Pennsylvania Game Commission. For people interested in hunting, wildlife management and conservation in Pennsylvania. Circ.150,000. Free sample copy with 9 × 12 SASE; free editorial guidelines.

Needs: Considers photos of "any outdoor subject (Pennsylvania locale), except fishing and boating." Photos purchased with accompanying ms.

Making Contact & Terms: Submit seasonal material 6 months in advance. Send 8 × 10 b&w glossy prints. SASE. Reports in 2 months. Pays $5-20/photo. Pays on acceptance. Buys all rights, but may reassign after publication.

PENNSYLVANIA SPORTSMAN, P.O. Box 90, Lemayne PA 17043. (717)761-1400. Publisher: Lou Hoffman. Regional magazine, published 8 times/year. Features fiction, nonfiction, how-to's, where-to's, various game and wildlife in Pennsylvania. Readers are men and women of all ages and occupations.Circ. 68,000. Estab. 1971. Sample copy for $2. Photo guidelines free with SASE.

Needs: Uses 40 photos/issue; 5 supplied by freelancers. Primarily needs animal/wildlife shots. Especially interested in shots of deer, bear, turkeys and game fish such as trout and bass. Photo captions preferred.

Making Contact & Terms: Query with list of stock photo subjects. SASE. Reports in 1 month. NPI. negotiable. Pays on acceptance. Credit line given. Buys one-time rights. Simultaneous submissions OK.

Tips: "Read the magazine to determine needs."

PETERSEN'S 4 WHEEL, Dept. PM, 8490 Sunset Blvd., Los Angeles CA 90069. (213)854-2360. Art Director: Karen Hawley. Monthly magazine. Emphasizes 4 wheel drive vehicles. Readers are male, 18-35. Circ. 400,000. Estab. 1978. Call for samples.

Needs: "We use our own photographers except on rare occasions, but we do review photos on spec." Needs action photos of vehicles. Model release and photo captions preferred.
Making Contact & Terms: Submit portfolio for review. Does not keep samples on file. SASE. Reports in 1-2 weeks. NPI. Pays on publication. Credit line given. Buys all rights.

PETERSEN'S HUNTING MAGAZINE, Dept. PM, 8490 Sunset Blvd., Los Angeles CA 90069. (213)854-2222. Editor: Craig Boddington. Monthly magazine. Readers are sport hunters who "hunt everything from big game to birds to varmints." Circ. 300,000. Free photo guidelines.
Needs: "Good sharp wildlife shots and hunting scenes. No scenic views or unhuntable species." Buys 4-8 color and 10-30 b&w photos/issue. Present model release on acceptance of photo. Identify subject of each photo.
Making Contact & Terms: Send photos for consideration. Send 8 × 10 b&w glossy prints; transparencies. SASE. Reports in 3-4 weeks. Pays $25/b&w photo; $75-250/color photo; $500/color cover. Pays on publication. Buys one-time rights.
Tips: Prefers to see "photos that demonstrate a knowledge of the outdoors, heavy emphasis on game animal shots, hunters and action. Try to strive for realistic photos that reflect nature, the sportsman and the flavor of the hunting environment. Not just simply 'hero' shots where the hunter is perched over the game. Action—such as running animals, flying birds, also unusual, dramatic photos of same animals in natural setting. Submit a small selection of varied subjects for review—20-40 slides. Majority of photographs used are author-supplied; approx. 20% from outside photographers."

PETERSEN'S PHOTOGRAPHIC MAGAZINE, Dept. PM, 8490 Sunset Blvd., Los Angeles CA 90069. (213)854-2200. FAX: (213)854-6823. Editor: Bill Hurter. Monthly magazine. For the beginner, advanced amateur and professional in all phases of still photography. Circ. 225,000. Estab. 1972. Sample copy $3. Photo guidelines free with SASE.
Needs: Uses about 100 photos/issue; 50 supplied by freelance photographers. Needs imaginative photos on all subjects. Model release and captions required.
Making Contact & Terms: Query with samples. Uses 8 × 10 b&w and color glossy or matte prints or transparencies. Send article outline with sample photos. SASE. Reports in approximately 1 month. Pays $35/b&w or color inside photo; $60/b&w or color page. Pays on publication. Credit line given. Buys one-time rights or all rights, but will negotiate.
Tips: Prints should have wide margins; "the margin is used to mark instructions to the printer." Photos accompanying how-to articles should demonstrate every step, including a shot of materials required and at least one shot of the completed product. "We can edit our pictures if we don't have the space to accommodate them. However, we cannot add pictures if we don't have them on hand. Hit as many markets as frequently as possible. Seek feedback. "We look for the ability to apply photographic techniques to successfully solve creative and practical challenges. The work should be exemplary of the technique(s) employed, and be appealing visually as well. We do not look for specific trends, per se, but rather photographic techniques that will be of interest to our readers. A freelancer should have a good working knowledge of photographic techniques, and be able to discuss and communicate them clearly, both in his/her imagery as well as editorially. Even if not a writer, the freelancer should be able to supply some form of an outline to accompany his/her work, whether this be verbal or written. We welcome submissions from freelancers."

✽PETS MAGAZINE, Dept. PM, 10th Floor, 797 Don Mills Rd., Don Mills ON M3C 355 Canada. (416)696-5488. Editor: Janet Piotrowski. Estab. 1983. Bimonthly magazine. Emphasizes pets (mainly cats and dogs). Readers are about 85% female, 30 yrs.+, middle income and better. Circ. 67,000. Sample copy for 9 × 12 SASE. "Please use IRC or *Canadian* stamps."
Needs: Uses 10-15 photos/issue; 3-5 supplied by freelance photographers. Needs animal shots. Model release and photo captions preferred.
Making Contact & Terms: Provide resume, business card, brochure, flyer or tearsheets to be kept on file for possible assignments. SASE. Reports in 1-5 weeks (or more). Pays $25/color cover photo or b&w inside photo. Pays on publication. Credit line given. Buys all rights; will negotiate. Previously published work OK.
Tips: "To be frank, we rarely buy just photos—our writers (all freelance) send any photos needed for specific articles, or we use "generic" photos from our (large) collection of photos (gathered through four photo contests)."

PHOENIX MAGAZINE, Dept. PM, 4707 N. 12th St., Phoenix AZ 85014. (602)248-8900. Executive Editor/Publisher: Dick Vonier. Art Director: James Forsmo. Monthly magazine. Circ. 50,000. Emphasizes "subjects that are unique to Phoenix: its culture, urban and social achievements and problems, its people and the Arizona way of life. We reach a professional and general audience of well-educated, affluent visitors and long-term residents." Buys 10-35 photos/issue.

Needs: Wide range, all dealing with life in metro Phoenix. Generally related to editorial subject matter. Wants on a regular basis photos to illustrate features, as well as for regular columns on arts. No "random shots of Arizona scenery, etc. that can't be linked to specific stories in the magazine." Photos purchased with or without an accompanying ms.
Payment & Terms: B&w: $25-75; color: $50-200; cover: $400-1,000. Pays within two weeks of publication. Payment for manuscripts includes photos in most cases. Payment negotiable for covers and other photos purchased separately.
Making Contact: Query. Works with freelance photographers on assignment only basis. Provide resume, samples, business card, brochure, flyer and tearsheets to be kept on file for possible future assignments. SASE. Reports in 3-4 weeks.
Tips: "Study the magazine, then show us an impressive portfolio."

🍁**PHOTO LIFE**, 130 Spy Court, Markham ON L3R 5H6 Canada. (416)475-8440. FAX: (416)475-9246 ext. 285. Editor: Jerry Kobalenko. Consumer publication. Magazine published 8 times/year. Readers are advanced amateur and professional photographers. Circ. 55,000. Sample copy or photo guidelines free with SASE.
Needs: Uses 50 photos/issue; 80% supplied by freelance photographers. Needs animal/wildlife shots, travel, scenics and so on. Usually only by Canadian photographers or on Canadian subjects.
Making Contact & Terms: Query with resume of credits. SASE. Reports in 1 month. Pays $60/b&w photo; $60-100/color photo; $400 maximum/complete job; $700 maximum/photo/text package. Pays on publication. Buys first N.A. serial rights and one-time rights.
Tips: "Looking for good writers to cover any subject interesting to the advanced photographer. Fine art photos should be striking, innovative. General stock, outdoor and travel photos should be presented with a strong theme."

PHOTOGRAPHER'S MARKET, 1507 Dana Ave., Cincinnati OH 45207. (513)531-2222. Editor: Michael Willins. Annual hardbound directory for freelance photographers. Circ. 40,000.
Needs: Publishes 30-35 photos per year. Uses general subject matter. Photos must be work sold to listings in *Photographer's Market*, and photographer must own rights to the photos. Photos are used to illustrate to readers the various types of images being sold to photo buyers listed in the book. Will also consider photos for cover usage. Captions should explain how the photo was used by the buyer, why it was selected, how the photographer sold the photo or got the assignment, how much the buyer paid the photographer, what rights were sold to the buyer and any self-marketing advice the photographer can share with readers. Look at book for examples.
Making Contact & Terms: Submit photos for inside text usage in fall and winter to ensure sufficient time to review them by spring deadline (late February to early March). Submit photos for cover usage by end of December. All photos are judged according to subject uniqueness in a given edition, as well as technical quality and composition within the market section in the book. Photos are held and reviewed at close of deadline. Reports are immediate if a photo is selected; photos not chosen are returned within 6-8 weeks of selection deadline. Buys second reprint rights and occasionally buys additional rights for promotional use. Pays $50 plus complimentary copy of book. Promotional rights negotiable. Pays upon acceptance. Book forwarded in September upon arrival from printer. Credit line given in descriptive caption. Uses b&w glossy prints, any size and format; 5 × 7 or 8 × 10 preferred. Also uses tearsheets and 35mm transparencies. Simultaneous submissions and previously published work OK.
Tips: "Send photos with brief cover letter describing the background of the sale. If sending more than one photo, make sure that photos are clearly identified with name and a code that corresponds to a comprehensive list. Slides should be enclosed in plastic slide sleeves, and original prints should be reinforced with cardboard. Cannot return material if SASE is not included. Tearsheets will be considered disposable unless SASE is provided and return is requested. Because photos are printed in black and white on newsprint stock, some photos, especially color shots, may not reproduce well. Photos should have strong contrast and not too much fine detail that will fill in when photo is reduced to fit our small page format. Usual reprint sizes are 2 × 3 and 3 × 4½. We prefer original photos whenever possible, but we will use tearsheets if photos are used in an interesting collage or striking cover layout."

PLANE & PILOT, Dept. PM, 12121 Wilshire Blvd., Los Angeles CA 90025. (310)820-1500. Art Director: Steve Curtis. Monthly magazine. Emphasizes personal, business and homebuilt aircraft. Readers are private, business and hobbyist pilots. Circ. 70,000-100,000.

🍁 *The maple leaf before a listing indicates that the market is Canadian. The symbol is new this year in* Photographer's Market.

Needs: Uses about 50 photos/issue; 90% supplied by freelance photographers. Needs photos of "production aircraft and homebuilt experimentals." Special needs include "air-to-air, technical, general aviation and special interest" photos. Written release and captions preferred.
Making Contact & Terms: Query with samples. Send 5×7 or 8×10 b&w glossy prints; 35mm transparencies; b&w contact sheets. SASE. Reports in 1 month. Pays $150-200 color cover photo; $25-50/inside photo; $100-150/color inside photo; $500/job; $250-500/text/photo package. Pays on acceptance. Credit line given. Buys one-time rights. Simultaneous submissions and previously published work OK.
Tips: Prefers to see "a variety of well-shot and composed color transparencies and b&w prints dealing with mechanical subjects (aircraft, auto, etc.)" in samples. "Use good technique, a variety of subjects and learn to write well."

POLO MAGAZINE, Dept. PM, 656 Quince Orchard Rd., Gaithersburg MD 20878. (301)977-0200. FAX: (301)990-9015. Editor: Martha LeGrand. Publishes monthly magazine 10 times/year with combined issues for January/February and June/July. Emphasizes the sport of polo and its lifestyle. Readers are primarily male; average age is 40. Some 90% of readers are professional/managerial levels, including CEO's and presidents. Circ. 7,000. Estab. 1975. Sample copy free with 10×13 SASE. Photo guidelines free with SASE.
Needs: Uses 50 photos/issue; 70% supplied by freelance photographers; 20% of this by assignment. Needs photos of polo action, portraits, travel, party/social and scenics. Most polo action is assigned, but freelance needs range from dynamic action photos to spectator fashion to social events. Photographers may write and obtain an editorial calendar for the year, listing planned features/photo needs. Model release and photo captions preferred, where necessary. In captions, include subjects and names.
Making Contact & Terms: Query with list of stock photo subjects. Provide resume, business card, brochure, flyer or tearsheets to be kept on file for possible assignments. SASE. Reports in 2 weeks. Pays $25-150/b&w photo, $30-300/color photo, $150/½ day, $300/full day, $200-500/complete package. Pays on publication. Credit line given. Buys one-time or all rights; negotiable. Simultaneous submissions and previously published work OK "in some instances."
Tips: Wants to see tight focus on subject matter and ability to capture drama of polo. "In assigning action photography, we look for close-ups that show the dramatic interaction of two or more players rather than a single player. On the sidelines, we encourage photographers to capture emotions of game, pony picket lines, etc." Sees trend toward "more use of quality b&w images." To break in, "send samples of work, preferably polo action photography."

❦POOL & SPA MAGAZINE, 46 Crockford Blvd., Scarborough, ON M1R 3C3 Canada. (416)752-2500. Editor: David Barnsley. Quarterly. Emphasizes swimming pools, spas, hot tubs, outdoor entertaining, landscaping (patios, decks, gardens, lawns, fencing). Readers are homeowners and professionals 30-55 years old. Equally read by men and women. Circ. 40,000.
Needs: Uses 20-30 photos/issue; 30% supplied by freelance photographers. Looking for shots of models dressed in bathing suits, people swimming in pools/spas, patios. Plans annual bathing suit issue late in year. Model release required.
Making Contact & Terms: Send unsolicited photos by mail for consideration. Send color, glossy, 35mm or 8×10 prints. SASE. Reports in 2 weeks. NPI; will negotiate payment. Pays on publication. Credit line given. Buys all rights; will negotiate. Simultaneous submissions and previously published work OK.
Tips: Looking for "photos of families relaxing outdoors around a pool, spa or patio. We are always in need of visual material, so send in whatever you feel is appropriate for the magazine. Photos will be returned."

POPULAR ELECTRONICS, Dept. PM, 500-B Bi-County Blvd., Farmingdale NY 11735. (516)293-3000. Editor: Carl Laron. Monthly magazine. Emphasizes hobby electronics. Readers are hobbyists in electronics, amateur radio, CB, audio, TV, etc.—"Mostly male, ages 13-59." Circ. 100,000. Sample copy free with 9×12 SASE and 90¢ postage.
Needs: Uses about 20 photos/issue; 20% supplied by freelance photographers. Photos purchased with accompanying ms only. Special needs include regional photo stories on electronics. Model release and captions preferred.
Making Contact & Terms: Arrange a personal interview to show portfolio; query with samples. SASE. Reports in 2 weeks. Pays $250-400/color cover photo; $200-350 for text/photo package. Pays on acceptance. Credit line given. Buys all rights but will negotiate. Simultaneous submissions and previously published work OK.

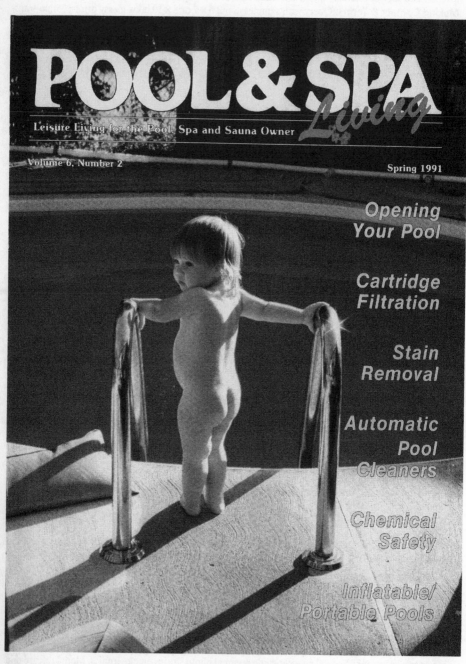

The light and the subject matter create a perfect setting for this photo published on the cover of Pool & Spa Magazine. Photographer Lorna White didn't have to search high and low for the shot either. The child in the photo is White's daughter Chelsea. David Barnsley, editor of the magazine, said the photo depicts a family atmosphere, a perfect theme for the publication.

PORTLAND-THE UNIVERSITY OF PORTLAND MAGAZINE, 5000 N. Willamette Blvd., Portland OR 97203. (503)283-7202. Editor: Brian Doyle. Publishes quarterly, 40-page magazine.
Needs: Buys 20 photos/year; offers 5 assignments/year. Photos used in magazines. Subjects include people. Model release preferred.
Making Contact & Terms: Query with resume of credits; query with list of stock photo subjects. Solicits photos by assignment only; interested in stock photos. Uses 8×10 glossy b&w prints; b&w contact sheets; 35mm and 2½×2½ transparencies. SASE. Reports in 2 weeks. Pays $100-300/b&w photo; $100-500/color photo. Credit line given. Buys one-time rights.
Tips: "Our needs are fairly specific. Tell me how you can help me. We want strong, creative photos. Fewer mugs and 'grip and grins.'" In portfolio of samples wants to see "interpretive ability more so than photojournalistic work. Also show work with other magazines. Strong composition and color is important. Often buy already completed work/stock photos. University magazines are a growing market for first rate photography. Our needs are not extensive. A good promotional brochure gives me someone to contact in various areas on various subjects."

Many times a photographer's ability to shoot strong portraits is overlooked, but not in this case. Brian Doyle, editor of Portland—The University of Portland Magazine, hired photographer Jerome Hart, of Portland, Oregon, to shoot this photo for a profile story in the magazine. "It's a damn good photo," exclaims Doyle. We agree.

© Jerome Hart

POWDER MAGAZINE, Dept. PM, Box 1028, Dana Point CA 92629. (714)496-5922. Managing Editor: Steve Casimiro. Published September through March. Emphasizes skiing. Circ. 150,000 plus. Sample copy $1; photo guidelines free with SASE.
Needs: Uses 70-80 photos/issue; 90% supplied by freelance photographers. Needs "ski action, ski action, ski action! Also scenics, personalities and humorous ski photos."
Making Contact & Terms: Query with samples or call to discuss requirements, deadlines, etc. SASE. Reports in 2 weeks. Pays $500/color cover photo; $200/color page, $50/color minimum. Pays on publication. Credit line given. Buys first N.A. serial rights. Simultaneous submissions OK.
Tips: "Our readers are advanced and expert skiers. Your submissions should reflect that. Be bold and exciting—lots of action. Avoid static, staged photos. Be creative (and weird). We *are* a market for experimental photos as well as 'traditional' action shots. We look for photographers who break the standards of ski photography."

*PRACTICAL HORSEMAN, Gumtree Corner, Unionville PA 19375. (215)857-1101. FAX: (215)857-3832. Art Director: Steven Zerby. Monthly magazine. Emphasizes English horse riding and training and horse care. Circ. 60,000. Estab. 1969. Sample copy $2.95.

Needs: Uses 30-50 photos/issue; 15-25 supplied by freelancers. Needs photos of English horse riding, training, care. "About half of our freelance needs are stock purchases, about half on assignment." Captions required.
Making Contact & Terms: Arrange personal interview to show portfolio; submit portfolio for review; provide resume, business card, brochure, flyer or tearsheets to be kept on file for possible assignments. Keeps samples on file. Cannot return material. Reporting time depends on if interested. Pays $150/color cover photo; $100/color page rate; $20/b&w page rate; $150/day. Credit line given. Rights negotiated. Simultaneous submissions and previously published work OK.
Tips: "We need to see horse subject matter, riding/training/showmanship, as well as scenic horse photos. Above all, we need to see striking photographs."

PRAYING, P.O. Box 419335, Kansas City MO 64141. (800)821-7926. Editor: Art Winter. Photo Editor: Rich Heffern. Bimonthly. Emphasizes spirituality for everyday living. Readers include mostly Catholic laypeople. Circ. 20,000. Estab. 1986. Sample copy and photo guidelines free with SASE.
Needs: Uses 3 photos/issue; 100% supplied by freelance photographers. Needs quality photographs which stand on their own as celebrations of people, relationships, ordinary events, work, nature, etc. Reviews photos with or without accompanying ms.
Making Contact & Terms: Query with samples; send 8 × 10 b&w prints by mail for consideration. SASE. Reports in 2 weeks. Pays $50/b&w photo. Pays on publication. Credit line given. Buys one-time rights. Simultaneous submissions and previously published work OK.
Tips: Looking for "good *printing* composition. We get a lot of really *poor* stuff! Know how to take and print a quality photograph. Don't try to add holy element or reflective moment. Natural, to us, is holy. We have one rule: never to run a picture of someone praying."

PREVENTION MAGAZINE, 33 E. Minor St., Emmaus PA 18098. (215)967-5171. Executive Art Director: Wendy Ronga. Monthly magazine. Emphasizes health. Readers are mostly female, 35-50, upscale. Circ. 2,500,000.
Needs: Uses 12-15 photos/issue; 60% on assignment, 40% from stock, but seeing trend toward "more assignment work than usual." Photo needs very specific to editorial, health, beauty, food. Model release and captions required.
Making Contact & Terms: Provide resume, business card, brochure, flyer or tearsheets to be kept on file for possible future assignments; tearsheets and/or dupes very important. Does not return unsolicited material. Reports in 1 month. Pays $100-300/b&w photo; $150-600/color photo; $250-1,000/day. Pays on publication. Credit line given. Buys one-time rights.
Tips: Prefers to see ability to do one thing very well. "Good lighting technique is a must." Wants to see "something different, taking an unusual twist to an ordinary subject."

*PRIMAL VOICES, P.O. Box 3179, Poughkeepsie NY 12603. Editors: Carol Lambert and Susan McIntosh. Quarterly magazine. Emphasizes endangered species and "voiceless" people. Readers are male and female, adolescents to adults. Circ. 100. Estab. 1990. Sample copy $4.75
Needs: Uses 2 or 3 photos/issue. Needs photos of wildlife and aboriginal peoples (Native Americans, etc.). Reviews photos with accompanying manuscript only. Special needs are bats, whales, primates, birds and native peoples. Model/property release required. Photo captions required.
Making Contact & Terms: Submit portfolio for review. Query with resume of credits. Send unsolicited photos by mail for consideration. Send 5 × 7, 8 × 10 b&w prints. Keeps samples on file. SASE. Reports in 1 month. Pays in copies. Credit line given. Buys one-time rights. Previously published work OK "if stated where published and if not used as cover photo before."
Tips: Needs "clear b&w photo to be used for magazine cover, portrait photo of people or wildlife. Obtain a sample copy of the magazine or submit *National Geographic* type cover material."

PRIME TIME SPORTS & FITNESS, Dept. PM, P.O. Box 6097, Evanston IL 60204. (708)864-8113. Contact: Editor. Magazine publishes 8 times/year. Emphasizes sports, recreation and fitness. Readers are professional males (60%) and females (40%), 19-45. Circ. 29,000. Estab. 1977. Sample copy free with SASE. Photo guidelines free with 10 × 12 SASE.
Needs: Uses about 70 photos/issue; 60 supplied by freelancers. Needs photos concerning women's fitness and fashion, swimwear and aerobic routines. Special photo needs include women's workout and swimwear photos. Model release required. Photo captions preferred.
Making Contact & Terms: Send unsolicited photos by mail for consideration. SASE. Reports in 6 weeks. Pays $200/color and b&w cover photo; $20/color and b&w inside photo; $20/color page rate; $50/b&w page rate; $30-60/hour. Time of payment negotiable. Credit line given. Buys all rights; negotiable. Simultaneous submissions and previously published work OK.

PROBLEMS OF COMMUNISM, U.S. Information Agency, Room 402, 301 4th St. SW, Washington DC 20547. (202)619-4230. FAX: (202)619-4173. Editor: Wayne Hall. Bimonthly magazine. Circ. 24,000. Estab. 1952. Emphasizes scholarly, documented articles on the politics, economics and sociology of Communist states and related movements on transition from communism to democracy and on efforts to create market economies in postcommunist societies.. For all scholars, government officials, journalists, business people, opinion-makers—with higher education.

Needs: Needs current photography of Communist and "post-Communist" societies, and of other societies in transition to democracy and the market. Not interested in nature shots or travelogues, but in good incisive photos capturing economic and social life and political events. Although the magazine is not copyrighted, it does bear the following statement on the index page: "Graphics and pictures which carry a credit line are not necessarily owned by *Problems of Communism*, and users bear responsibility for obtaining appropriate permissions." Uses 8×10 glossy b&w prints. Also uses 35mm color transparencies, but will be converted to b&w. "The stress is on sharp recent personalities in Communist and post-Communist leaderships, although historical and mood shots are occasionally used. Captions with accurate information are essential." Free sample copy and photo guidelines.

Making Contact & Terms: Query first with resume of credits, summary of areas visited, dates and types of pix taken. Pays $100-150; $200-300 for cover. Pays on publication. Reports in 1 month. SASE. Simultaneous submissions and previously published work OK.

Tips: "Photos are used basically to illustrate scholarly articles on current Communist affairs and societies in transition to democracy and the market.. Hence, the best way to sell is to let us know what countries you have visited and what events you have covered." In samples, wants to see "clear, factual documentation with good contrast."

PROFITABLE GAMES, (formerly *Tavern Sports International*), Suite 1430, 2005 Michigan Ave., Chicago IL 60604. (312)341-1110. FAX: (312)341-1469. Managing Editor: Jocelyn Hathaway. Bimonthly magazine. Emphasizes the coin-operated game industry and recreational entertainment offered via organized tavern-based sports. Readers are ages 21-45; male and female; vendor/operators, manufacturers and location owners. Circ. 20,500. Estab. 1988. Sample copy free with 9×12 SAE and $1.40 postage.

Needs: Uses 20 photos/issue; 25% supplied by freelance photographers. Needs photos of personalties, creative visuals and location design. Model/property release preferred; photo captions required.

Making Contact & Terms: Interested in receiving work from newer, lesser-known photographers. Provide resume, business card, brochure, flyer or tearsheets to be kept on file for possible assignments. Reports in 1 month. Pays $150/color cover photo; $50/color inside photo; $125-175/photo/text package. Credit line given. Buys all rights. Simultaneous submissions OK.

Tips: "We look for an eye for architecture and interior design and ability to conceptualize industry issues and trends in creative visuals." Keep in mind this publication "is on a tight budget; therefore, the more reasonably photographers can work, the more assignments *Profitable Games* can offer to freelancers." Also, there is a growing demand and expectation of participatory entertainment.

THE PROGRESSIVE, 409 E. Main St., Madison WI 53703. Art Director: Patrick JB Flynn. Monthly. Circ. 40,000. Estab. 1909. Emphasizes "political and social affairs—international and domestic." Free sample copy and photo guidelines upon request.

Needs: Uses 5 or more b&w photos/issue; all supplied by freelance photographers and photo agencies. Looking for images documenting the human condition and the social/political structures of contemporary society (Central America, Middle East, Africa, etc.). Special photo needs include "Third World societies, labor activities, environmental issues and war resistance." Captions and credit information required.

Making Contact & Terms: Query with photocopies to be kept on file for possible future assignments. SASE. Reports in 1 month. Pays $200/b&w cover photo; $30-150/b&w inside photo; $150/b&w full-page. Pays on publication. Credit line given. Buys one-time rights. Simultaneous submissions and previously published work OK.

Tips: "Interested in photo essays and in images that make a visual statement."

THE QUARTER HORSE JOURNAL, P.O. Box 32470, Amarillo TX 79120. (806)376-4811. FAX: (806)376-8364. Executive Editor: Audie Rackley. Monthly magazine. Circ. 65,000. Estab. 1948. Emphasizes breeding and training of quarter horses. Free sample copy and editorial guidelines.

Needs: Photos purchased with accompanying ms only. "Materials should be current and appeal or be helpful to both children and adults." No photos of other breeds. "The only freelance photos we use are for our covers."

Making Contact & Terms: Write for details. Uses 5×7 or 8×10 b&w glossy prints; 2¼×2¼, 35mm or 4×5 transparencies and 8×10 color glossy prints; "we don't accept color prints on matte paper." Captions required. SASE. Reports in 2-3 weeks. Pays $50-250 for text/photo package; $150 for first publication rights for cover. Pays on acceptance. Buys first N.A. serial rights and occasionally buys all rights.

Not only does this photo convey a sense of motion, but it also keeps the viewer's eyes moving and interested in the pool balls. Photographer Art Noel, of Grayslake, Illinois, has twice sold the photo. He received $75 for the shot which appeared on the cover of Tavern Sports International, *now known as* Profitable Games.

© Art Noel

QUILT WORLD, QUICK & EASY QUILTING, STITCH 'N SEW QUILTS, Dept. PM, 306 E. Parr Rd., Berne IN 46711. (219)589-8741. Editor: Sandra L. Hatch. Bimonthly. Quarterly (*Quilting Omnibook*). Emphasizes quilts. Readers are quilters, traditionally oriented, not contemporary. Circ. 120,000-140,000. Sample copy $2.50.

Needs: Uses 30-50 photos/issue 75% supplied by freelancers. Needs photos of quilts—close-ups and set-ups with 1 over-all photo of quilt. Special needs include coverage of shows all over country and the world. Model release preferred; captions required.

Making Contact & Terms: Send unsolicited photos by mail for consideration. Provide resume, business card, brochure, flyer or tearsheets to be kept on file for possible future assignments. Uses 35mm and 2¼×2¼ transparencies. SASE. Reports in 4 weeks. Pays $50/color cover photo; $15/b&w and color inside photo. Pays on publication usually. Credit line given. Buys all rights; negotiable. Previously published work OK.

Tips: "Quilts are difficult to photograph, especially at shows. You should know something about the patterns. We have printed most common ones. I prefer the convenience of having photographers in many locations."

RADIANCE, The Magazine for Large Women, P.O. Box 30246, Oakland CA 94604. (510)482-0680. Publisher/Editor: Alice Ansfield. Quarterly magazine. "We're a positive/self-esteem magazine for women all sizes of large. We have diverse readership, 90% women, ages 25-70 from all ethnic groups, lifestyles and interests." Circ. 25,000. Estab. 1984. Sample copy for $3.50, writer's guidelines for SASE. Photo guidelines not available.

Needs: Uses 20+ photos/issue; 100% supplied by freelance photographer. Needs portraits, cover shots, fashion photos. Model release and photo captions preferred.

Making Contact & Terms: Arrange a personal interview to show portfolio; send unsolicited photos by mail for consideration; provide resume, business card, brochure, flyer or tearsheets to be kept on file for possible assignments. SASE. Reports in 1-2 months. Pays $50-200/color cover photo; $15-25/b&w inside photo; $8-20/hour; $400/day. Pays on publication. Credit line given. Buys one-time rights. Simultaneous submissions considered.

Tips: In photographer's portfolio or samples wants to see "clear, crisp photos, creativity, setting, etc." Recommends freelancers "get to know the magazine they're talking with. Work with the publisher (or photo editor) and get to know" her requirements. "Try to help the magazine with its goals."

*RAG MAG, Box 12, Goodhue MN 55027. (612)923-4590. Editor: Beverly Voldseth. Magazine. Emphasizes poetry and fiction. Circ. 200. Estab. 1982. Sample copy $6 with 6¼×9¼ SASE and $1.05 postage.
Needs: Uses 3-4 photos/issue; 100% supplied by freelancers. Needs photos that work well in a literary magazine; faces, bodies, stones, trees, water, etc. Reviews photos without a manuscript. Uses photos on covers.
Making Contact & Terms: Send unsolicited photos by mail for consideration. Send b&w, color prints. Does not keep samples on file. SASE. Reports in 2 weeks-2 months. Pays in copies. Pays on publication. Buys one-time rights. Simultaneous submissions and previously published work OK.
Tips: "I do not want anything abusive, sadistic or violent. Could send copies of photos and then if they are something I want I'll request photos."

RAILROAD MODEL CRAFTSMAN, P.O. Box 700, Newton NJ 07860. (201)383-3355. Editor: W. Schaumburg. Monthly. Emphasizes scale model railroading. Readers are adults interested in the hobby of model railroading. Circ. 75,000. Sample copy $2.50. Photo guidelines free with SASE.
Needs: Uses 100+ photos/issue; 95% supplied by freelance photographers. Needs photos of creative and good railroad modeling, as well as photos accompanying "how-to" articles. Reviews photos with accompanying ms only. Model release preferred; captions required.
Making Contact & Terms: SASE. Reports in 1 month. Pays $200/color cover photo. Pays on publication. Credit line given. Buys all rights; negotiable.

‡R&R SHOPPERS NEWS, Kolpingstrasse 1, 6906, Leimen West Germany. (0049)6224 7060. FAX: 0049-6224-70616. Editor: Margo W.R. Steiner. Monthly magazine. Emphasizes entertainment including travel, music/concerts and movies/TV. Readers are military personnel and families living in Europe. Circ. 100,000. Sample copy available for 6 International Reply Coupons.
Needs: Uses 20 photos/issue. Uses primarily European travel photos with people. Photo captions preferred. Freelancers used only seldomly.
Making Contact & Terms: Send 35mm transparencies by mail for consideration; provide resume, business card, brochure, flyer or tearsheets to be kept on file for possible assignments. Reports in 2 months, but slides are *only* returned if accompanied by 6 International Reply Coupons. Pays $100/color cover photo; $55-60/color inside photo. Pays on publication. Credit line given. Buys one-time rights. Simultaneous submissions and previously published work OK.

RANGER RICK, 8925 Leesburg Pike, Vienna VA 22184-0001. Photo Editor: Robert L. Dunne. Monthly magazine. Readers are children, ages 6-12, interested in the natural world, wildlife, conservation and ecology. Circ. 850,000. Estab. 1967. Sample copy $2. Photo guidelines free with SASE.
Needs: Buys 400 photos annually; 90% supplied by freelancers. 0-10% on assignment. Needs photos of wild animals (U.S. and foreign birds, mammals, insects, reptiles, etc.); humorous (wild animals in funny poses or situations); photo essay/photo feature (with captions); celebrity/personality; and children (especially girls or racial minorities) doing things involving wild animals, outdoor activities, crafts, recycling and helping the environment. No plants, weather or scenics. No soft focus, grainy, or weak color shots. Reviews photos with or without accompanying ms, but query first on articles.
Making Contact & Terms: Interested in receiving work from newer, lesser-known photographers. Submit portfolio of 20-40 photos for review and a list of available material. Uses original color transparencies; vertical format on cover. "Allow space in upper left corner or across the top for insertion of masthead." SASE. Reports in 2 weeks. Pays $225/half page or less; $660/2-page spread; $500/color cover photo. Pays 3 months before publication. Buys first serial rights and right to reuse for promotional purposes at half the original price. Previously published work OK.
Tips: "Come in close on subjects." Wants no "obvious flash." Mail transparencies inside 20-pocket plastic viewing sheets, backed by cardboard, in a manila envelope. "Do your own editing. We don't want to see 20 shots of almost the same pose. We pay by reproduction size. Check printed issues to see our standards of quality, which are high. Looking for fresh, colorful, clean images. New approaches to traditional subject matter welcome."

The double dagger before a listing indicates that the market is located outside the United States and Canada. The symbol is new this year in Photographer's Market.

By acquiring written guidelines from **Ranger Rick,** *photographer* **Robert A. Rives, Jr.,** *of Cashmere, Washington, was able to tailor his submissions to fit the needs of the magazine. Rives caught this little guy napping on the beaches of Australia. The humorous scene was perfect for the magazine's young audience and it ran on the Letters to the Editor page. Rives received $160 for the image's use and, after it was published, the* **National Enquirer** *contacted him. The tabloid also ran the photo and paid Rives $150.*

REAL PEOPLE, 950 Third Ave., 16th Floor, New York NY 10022. (212)371-4932. Editor: Alex Polner. Bimonthly magazine. Emphasizes celebrities. Readers are women 35 and up. Circ. 170,000. Estab. 1988. Sample copy for $3.50 with 6×9 SAE.
Needs: Uses 30-40 photo/issue; 10% supplied by freelancers. Needs celebrity photos. Reviews photos with accompanying ms only. Model release preferred. Photo captions required.
Making Contact & Terms: Query with resume of credits and list of stock photo subjects; provide resume, business card, brochure, flyer or tearsheets to be kept on file for possible assignments. SASE. Reports only when interested. Pays $100-200/day. Pays on publication. Credit line given. Buys one-time rights.

REDBOOK, Dept. PM, 224 W. 57th St., New York NY 10019. (212)649-3330. FAX: (212)581-7605. Promotional Art Director: David Chase. Monthly magazine.
Needs: Typically uses photos of mothers/children; children; teens; and families. Photos should "not be commercial or artsy." Model release required.
Making Contact & Terms: Send unsolicited photos by mail for consideration. Keeps samples on file. Cannot return material. Reports in 1 month. NPI; payment rates variable per photo. Credit line given. Buys one-time rights, with one-year exclusivity.

*RELIX MAGAZINE, P.O. Box 94, Brooklyn NY 11229. (718)258-0009. FAX: (718)692-4345. Editor: Toni A. Brown. Bimonthly. Circ. 100,000. Estab. 1974. Emphasizes rock and roll music. Readers are music fans, ages 13-50. Sample copy $3.

Needs: Uses about 50 photos/issue; "about 30%" supplied by freelance photographers; assignment — 20%; stock — 80%. Needs photos of "music artists — in concert and candid, backstage, etc." Special needs: "Photos of rock groups, especially the Grateful Dead, San Francisco-oriented groups and sixties related bands." Photo captions preferred.

Making Contact & Terms: Interested in receiving work from newer, lesser-known photographers. Send 5×7 or larger b&w and color prints by mail for consideration. SASE. Reports in 1 month. "We try to report immediately; occasionally we cannot be sure of use." Pays $15-75/b&w photo; $25-300/color. Pays on publication. Credit line given. Buys all rights, negotiable. Simultaneous submissions and previously published material OK.

Tips: "B&w photos should be printed on grade 4 or higher for best contrast."

*REMINISCE, 5400 S. 60th St., Greendale WI 53129. (414)423-0100. FAX: (414)423-1143. Editorial Assistant: Trudi Bellin. Estab. 1990. Bimonthly magazine. "For people who love reliving the good times." Readers are male and female, interested in nostalgia, ages 55+. "*Reminisce* is supported entirely by subscriptions and accepts no outside advertising." Sample copy $2. Photo guidelines free with SASE.

Needs: Uses 100 photos/issue; 35 supplied by freelancers. Needs photos with people interest — "we need high-quality color shots with nostalgic appeal." Model/property release required. Captions preferred; season, location.

Making Contact & Terms: Interested in receiving work from newer, lesser-known photographers. Query with list of stock photo subjects. Send unsolicited photos by mail for consideration. Send 35mm, 2¼×2¼, 4×5, 8×10 transparencies. Submit seasonally. Tearsheets filed but not dupes. SASE. Reports as soon as possible; "anywhere from a few days to a couple of months." Pays $200/color cover photo; $50-125/color inside photo; $150/color page rate; $10-50/b&w photo. Pays on publication. Credit line given. Buys one-time rights. Previously published work OK.

Tips: "Technical quality is extremely important; focus must be sharp, no soft focus; colors must be vivid so they 'pop off the page.' Color photos of nostalgic subjects stand the best chance of making our covers. Study our magazine thoroughly — we have a continuing need for sharp, colorful images, and those who can supply what we need can expect to be regular contributors."

REPTILE & AMPHIBIAN MAGAZINE, RD3, Box 3709-A, Pottsville PA 17901. (717)622-6050. FAX: (717)622-5858. Editor: Dr. Norman Frank. Bimonthly magazine. Specializing in reptiles and amphibians only. Readers are college-educated, interested in nature and animals, familiar with basics of herpetology, many are breeders and conservation oriented. Circ. 9,000. Estab. 1989. Sample copy $4. Photo guidelines with SASE.

Needs: Uses 20-30 photos/issue; 80% supplied by freelance photographers. Needs photos of related subjects. Model and property releases preferred. Captions required; clearly identify species with common and/or scientific name on slide mount. Photos purchased with or without ms.

Making Contact & Terms: Interested in receiving work from newer, lesser-known photographers. Send cover letter describing qualifications with representative samples. Must identify species pictured. Provide resume, business card, brochure, flyer or tearsheets to be kept on file for possible assignments. Send b&w and glossy prints; 35mm transparencies. SASE. Reports in 2-4 weeks. Pays $25-50/color cover photo; $25/color inside photo; and $10/b&w inside photo. Pays on acceptance if needed immediately, or publication if the photo is to be filed for future use. Originals returned in 60-90 days. Credit line given. Buys one-time rights. Previously published work OK.

Tips: In photographer's samples, looks for quality — eyes in-focus; action shots — animals eating, interacting, in motion. "Avoid field-guide type photos — try to get shots with action and/or which have 'personality.' " All animals should be clearly identified with common and/or scientific name.

*REVIEW OF OPTOMETRY, Chilton Way, Radnor PA 19380. (215)964-4376. Editor: Rick Kirkner. Monthly. Emphasizes optometry. Readers include 25,000 practicing optometrists nationwide; academicians, students. Circ. 30,000. Estab. 1891.

Needs: Uses 40 photos/issue; 3-8 supplied by freelance photographers. "Most photos illustrate news stories or features. Ninety-nine percent are solicited. We rarely need unsolicited photos. We will need top-notch freelance news photographers in all parts of the country for specific assignments." Model and property releases preferred; captions required.

Making Contact & Terms: Provide resume, business card, brochure, flyer or tearsheets to be kept on file for possible assignments; tearsheets and business cards or resumes preferred. Pay varies. Credit line given. Rights negotiable. Simultaneous submissions and previously published work OK.

RICHMOND SURROUNDINGS MAGAZINE, Dept. PM, Suite 110, 7814 Carousel Ln., Richmond VA 23294. (804)346-4130. Managing Editor: Frances Helms. Art Director: John Hoar. Bimonthly magazine; "includes special newcomer annual edition." Emphasizes lifestyle, including business, health, education, leisure. Readers are upper income, college-educated, 30 and up. Circ. 20,000. Estab. 1979. Sample copy free with 8½×11 SASE and $1.50 postage.

Needs: Special photo needs, creative cover, editorial humor, advertising. 90% freelance photography in given issue from assignment and 10% from freelance stock. Model release and photo captions required.

Making Contact & Terms: Query with samples, send unsolicited photos by mail for consideration. Provide resume, business card, brochure, flyer or tearsheets to be kept on file for possible future assignments. Send 5×7 glossy, 35mm transparencies, b&w contact sheet, color negatives. SASE. Reports in 4-6 weeks. Pays $150/b&w cover photo and $30-400/color cover photo, $25-150/b&w photo; $25-100/color photo; $10-100/hour; $100-500/day. Pays on publication. Credit line given. Buys all rights; willing to negotiate.

Tips: Looks for "creativity, photographs conveying emotion, as well as good technical quality. Be flexible. Be willing to accept lower fees for exposure and portfolio. Show versatility."

ROAD KING MAGAZINE, 23060 S. Cicero, Richton Park IL 60471. (708)481-9240. Editor: Rich Vurva. Photo Editor: Mary Beth Burns. Bimonthly magazine. Emphasizes trucks, truckers and trucking. Readers are over-the-road, long-haul truckers. Circ. 224,000. Sample copy free with 6×9 SAE and 85¢ postage.

Needs: Uses 20-25 photos/issue; 10-15 supplied by freelance photographers. Needs photos of trucks, truckstops and facilities, truckers. "We will need and use freelancers to accompany our reporters gathering stories. Our reporters also take back-up pictures simultaneously." Model release required.

Making Contact & Terms: Interested in receiving work from newer, lesser-known photographers. "Let us know who you are, where you are, if you are available for story assignments and your day rate." SASE. Pays $150-250/text/photo package. Buys all rights.

THE ROANOKER, P.O. Box 21535, Roanoke VA 24018. (703)989-6138. FAX: (703)989-7603. Editor: Kurt Rheinheimer. Monthly. Circ. 14,000. Estab. 1974. Emphasizes Roanoke and western Virginia. Readers are upper income, educated people interested in their community. Sample copy $2.

Needs: Uses about 40 photos/issue; most are supplied on assignment by freelance photographers. Needs "travel and scenic photos in western Virginia; color photo essays on life in western Virginia." Model and property releases preferred; captions required.

Making Contact & Terms: Interested in receiving work from newer, lesser-known photographers. Send any size b&w or color glossy prints and transparencies by mail for consideration. SASE. Reports in 1 month. Pays $15-25/b&w photo; $20-35/color photo; $100/day. Pays on publication. Credit line given. Rights purchased vary; negotiable. Simultaneous submissions and previously published work OK.

*ROBB REPORT For The Affluent Lifestyle, One Acton Place, Acton MA 01720. (508)263-7749. Design Director: Christine Koch. Monthly. Emphasizes "the good life, e.g., yachting, exotic autos, investments, art, travel, lifestyle and collectibles." The magazine is aimed at the connoisseur who can afford an affluent lifestyle. Circ. 50,000. Photo guidelines free with SASE.

Needs: Uses 30-50 photos/issue. Generally uses existing photography; freelance work is assigned once story manuscripts have been reviewed for design treatment.

Making Contact & Terms: Arrange a personal interview to show portfolio or send promotional mailers to be kept on file for possible future assignments. Uses 35mm (Kodachrome preferred), 2¼×2¼, 4×5, 8×10 color transparencies. Reports within 1 month. Pay is individually negotiated prior to assignment. Rates vary depending on whether photography purchased is stock or assigned. Pays on publication. Prefers to buy all rights, but will negotiate. Credit lines given. Captions preferred.

ROCK & ICE, P.O. Box 3595, Boulder CO 80307. (303)499-8410. Editor: George Bracksieck. Bimonthly magazine. Emphasizes rock and ice climbing and mountaineering. Readers are predominantly professional, ages 17-50. Circ. 19,000. Estab. 1984. Sample copy for $5. Photo guidelines free with SASE.

Needs: Uses 90 photos/issue; 100% supplied by freelance photographers, 20% on assignment, 80% from stock. Needs photos of climbing action shots, personalities and scenics. Buys photos with or without ms. Model release not required; photo captions required.

Making Contact & Terms: Interested in receiving work from newer, lesser-known photographers. Query with list of stock photo subjects. Send unsolicited photos by mail for consideration. Send b&w prints; 35mm, 2¼×2¼ and 4×5 transparencies. SASE. Pays $250/color cover photo; $100/color and b&w page rate. Pays on publication. Credit line given. Buys one-time rights and first N.A. serial rights. Previously published work OK.

Tips: "Samples must show some aspect of technical rock climbing, ice climbing, mountain climbing or indoor climbing. Climbing is one of North America's fastest growing sports."

ROLLING STONE, Dept. PM, 1290 Avenue of the Americas, New York NY 10104. (212)484-1616. Photo Editor: Laurie Kratochvil. Associate Photo Editor: Jodi Peckman. Emphasizes all forms of entertainment (music, movies, politics, news events).
Needs: "All our photographers are freelance." Provide brochure, calling card, flyer, samples and tearsheet to be kept on file for future assignments. Needs famous personalities and rock groups in b&w and color. No editorial repertoire. SASE. Reports immediately. Pays $150-350/day.
Tips: "Drop off portfolio at front desk any Wednesday between 10 am and noon. Pickup same day between 4 pm and 6 pm or next day. Leave a card with sample of work to keep on file so we'll have it to remember."

RUNNER'S WORLD, Dept. PM, 135 N. 6th St., Emmaus PA 18049. (215)967-5171. FAX: (215)965-5670. Executive Editor: Amby Burfoot. Photo Editor: Chuck Johnson. Monthly magazine. Emphasizes running. Readers are median aged: 37, 65% male; median income $40,000, college-educated. Circ. 450,000. Photo guidelines free with SASE.
Needs: Uses 100 photos/issue; 55 supplied by freelance photographers; features are generally assigned; columns and departments often come from stock. Needs photos of action, features, photojournalism. Model release and captions preferred.
Making Contact & Terms: Query with samples. Send b&w and color prints, and 35mm transparencies by mail for consideration. Submit portfolio for review. Provide resume, business card, brochure, flyer or tearsheets to be kept on file for possible future assignments. SASE. Pays as follows: color—$200/full page, $125/half page, $75/quarter page, $300/spread; b&w—$100/full page, $60/half page, $35/quarter page, $150/spread. Cover shots are assigned. Pays on publication. Credit line given. Photographic rights vary with assignment. Simultaneous submissions and previously published work OK.
Tips: "Become familiar with the publication and send photos in on spec. Also send samples that can be kept in our source file. Show full range of expertise; lighting abilities—quality of light—whether strobe sensitivity for people—portraits, sports, etc.. Both action and studio work if applicable, should be shown." Current trend is non-traditional treatment of sports coverage and portraits. Call prior to submitting work. Be familiar with running as well as the magazine.

SACRAMENTO MAGAZINE, Dept. PM, 1021 Second St., Sacramento CA 95814. (916)446-7548. Managing Editor: Karen Coe. Design Director: Chuck Donald. Emphasizes business, government, culture, food, outdoor recreation and personalities for middle to upper middle class, urban-oriented Sacramento residents. Monthly magazine. Circ. 30,000.
Needs: Uses about 40-50 photos/issue; mostly supplied by freelance photographers. "Photographers are selected on the basis of experience and portfolio strength. No work assigned on speculation or before a portfolio showing. Photographers are used on an assignment only basis. Stock photos used only occasionally. Most assignments are to area photographers and handled by phone. Photographers with studios, mobile lighting and other equipment have an advantage in gaining assignments. Darkroom equipment desirable but not necessary." Needs news photos, essay, avant-garde, still life, landscape, architecture, human interest and sports. All photography must pertain to Sacramento and environs. Captions required.
Making Contact & Terms: Send slides, contact sheets (no negatives) by mail or arrange a personal interview to show portfolio. Also query with resume of photo credits or mail portfolio. SASE. Reports up to 4 weeks. Pays $5-45/hour; pays on acceptance. Average payment is $15-20/hour; all assignments are negotiated to fall within that range. Credit line given on publication. Buys one-time rights. Will consider simultaneous submissions and previously published work, providing they are not in the northern California area.

SAIL MAGAZINE, 275 Washington St., Newton MA 02158-1630. (617)630-3726. FAX: (617)964-8948. Photo Editor: Erik Nelson. Monthly magazine. Emphasizes all aspects sailing. Readers are managers and professionals, average age 44. Circ. 175,000. Estab. 1970. Sample copy $2.50, 9×12 or larger SAE and $2.90 postage. Photo guidelines free with SASE.
Needs: Uses 40 photos/issue; 100% supplied by freelancers. "We are particularly interested in photos for 'Under Sail' section. Photos for this section should be original 35mm transparencies only and should humorously depict some aspect of sailing." Model release required. Photo captions preferred.
Making Contact & Terms: Interested in receiving work from newer, lesser-known photographers. Send unsolicited 35mm and 2¼×2¼ transparencies by mail for consideration. SASE. Pays $600/cover photo; $75 minimum/color inside photo; $50 minimum/b&w inside photo. Pays on publication. Credit line given. Buys one-time rights. Simultaneous submissions and previously published work OK.

© Jacob Valdez

Photographers who take advantage of their own hobbies sometimes can put them-selves in positions to snap incredible images. In this case, photographer Jacob Val-dez, of Lander, Wyoming, shares the experience of mountain climbing in Thailand. The photo earned him $250 from Rock & Ice Magazine, *which used the image on its cover, and he plans to use the shot as part of an Asian climbing calendar.*

SAILING, Dept. PM, 125 E. Main St., Box 248, Port Washington WI 53074. (414)284-3494. Editor: Micca L. Hutchins. Monthly magazine. Emphasizes sailing. Our theme is "the beauty of sail." Readers are sailors with great sailing experience—racing and cruising. Circ. 40,000. Sample copy free with 11×15 SASE and $2.40 postage. Photo guidelines free with SASE.
Needs: "We are a photo journal-type publication so about 50% of issue is photos. "Needs photos of exciting sailing action, onboard deck shots; sailor-type boat portraits seldom used. Special needs include largely b&w, some inside color—mainly good *sailing* (not simply sailboats) shots. "We must have area sailed, etc. identification."
Making Contact & Terms: Query with samples. Send 8×10 glossy b&w prints, 35mm transparencies by mail for consideration. "Request guidelines first—a big help." SASE. Reports in 1 month. Pays $100/color cover photo; $15-50/b&w inside photo; $50-100/color inside photo (depends on size used); text/photo package by arrangement. Pays 30 days after publication. Credit line given. Buys one-time rights. Simultaneous submissions and previously published work OK "if not with other sailing publications who compete with us."
Tips: "We are looking for good, clean, sharp photos of sailing action—exciting shots are for us. No 'fly-spec' sails against the horizon—we use close work from a sailor's perspective. Please request a sample copy to become familiar with format. Knowledge of the sport of sailing a requisite for good photos for us."

SAILING WORLD, 5 John Clarke Rd., Newport RI 02840. (401)847-1588. FAX: (401)848-5048. Editor: John Burnham. Art Director: Rachel Cocroft. Monthly magazine. Circ. 62,000. Estab. 1962. Emphasizes sailboat racing and performance cruising for sailors, upper income. Sample copy $5; free photo guidelines with SASE.
Needs: "We will send an updated photo letter listing our needs on request. Freelance photography in a given issue: 20% assignment and 80% freelance stock. "We are using more 4-color photos and need high-quality work." Covers most sailing races.
Making Contact & Terms: Uses 35mm and 2¼×2¼ transparencies for covers. Vertical and square (slightly horizontal) formats. Reports in 1 month. Pays $500 for cover shot; regular color $50-300 (varies with use). Pays on publication. Credit line given. Buys first N.A. serial rights.
Tips: We look for photos that are unusual in composition, lighting and/or color that feature performance sailing at its most exciting. We would like to emphasize speed, skill, fun and action. Photos must be of high quality. We prefer Kodachrome 64 or Fuji Velvia film. We have a format that allows us to feature work of exceptional quality. A knowledge of sailing and experience with on-the-water photography is really a requirement." Please call with specific questions or interests. "We cover current events and generally only use photos take in the past 30-60 days."

ST. LOUIS MAGAZINE, Dept. PM, Suite 2120, 1 Metropolitan Square, St. Louis MO 63102. (314)231-7200. Art Director: Deanna Lowe. Paid circ. 38,330. Emphasizes life in St. Louis for "those interested in the St. Louis area, recreation issues, lifestyles, etc." Sample copy $1.95 and free photo guidelines.
Needs: Celebrity/personality, documentary, fine art, scenic, local color, sport, human interest, travel, fashion/beauty and political. Photos purchased with or without accompanying mss. Freelancers supply 90% of the photos. Pays by assignment or on a per-photo basis.
Making Contact & Terms: Provide business card, resume and samples to be kept on file for possible future assignments. Uses 8×10 b&w glossy prints; 35mm, 2¼×2¼ and 4×5 transparencies. Uses color covers only; vertical format required. Arrange a personal interview to submit portfolio for review. SASE. Reports in 1 month. Pays $50-250/b&w photo; $100-300/color photo; $200-350/cover photo. Pays on publication. Credit line given.
Tips: Prefers to see "b&w prints, color photos or transparencies of St. Louis people, events and places, fashion and history. Any printed samples, especially from magazines. Don't be a jack-of-all-trades. Any photographer who has an 'I can do it all' portfolio is not as likely to get a general assignment as a specialty photographer."

SALT WATER SPORTSMAN, 280 Summer St., Boston MA 02111. (617)439-9977. FAX: (617)439-9357. Editor: Barry Gibson. Monthly magazine. Circ. 135,000. Estab. 1939. Emphasizes all phases of salt water sport fishing for the avid beginner-to-professional salt water angler. "Only strictly marine sport fishing magazine in the world." Sample copy free with 9×12 SAE and $2 postage. Free photo guidelines.
Needs: Buys 1-6 photos/issue (including covers) without ms; 20-30 photos/issue with ms. Needs salt water fishing photos. "Think scenery with human interest, mood, fishing action, storytelling close-ups of anglers in action. Make it come alive—and don't bother us with the obviously posed 'dead fish and stupid fisherman' back at the dock. Wants, on a regular basis, cover shots, vertical Kodachrome (or equivalent) original slides depicting salt water fishing action or 'mood.'" For accompanying ms needs fact/feature articles dealing with marine sportfishing in the US, Canada, Caribbean, Central and South America. Emphasis on how-to. Free writer's guidelines.

Making Contact & Terms: Send material by mail for consideration or query with samples. Provide resume and tearsheets to be kept on file for possible future assignments. Accepting slides and holding them for 1 year and will pay as used. Uses 8 × 10 b&w and color glossy prints and 35mm or 2¼ × 2¼ transparencies; cover transparency vertical format required. SASE. Reports in 1 month. Pay included in total purchase price with ms, or pays $20-200/b&w photo; $50-400/color photo; $600 minimum/cover photo; $250-up/text photo package. Pays on acceptance. Buys one-time rights.

Tips: "Prefers to see a selection of fishing action or mood — no scenics, lighthouses, birds, etc. — must be sport fishing oriented. Be familiar with the magazine and send us the type of things we're looking for. Example: no horizontal cover slides with suggestions it can be cropped etc. Don't send Ektachrome. We're using more 'outside' photography — that is, photos not submitted with ms package. Take lots of verticals and experiment with lighting. Most shots we get are too dark."

SANTA BARBARA MAGAZINE, Dept. PM, Suite H, 226 East Canon Perdido, Santa Barbara CA 93101. (805)965-5999. FAX: (805)965-7627. Editor: Daniel Denton. Photo Editor: Kimberly Kavish. Bimonthly magazine. Emphasizes Santa Barbara community and culture. Circ. 11,000. Estab. 1975. Sample copy $2.95 with 9 × 12 SASE.

Needs: Uses 50-60 photos/issue; 40% supplied by freelance photographers. Needs portrait, environmental, architectural, travel, celebrity, et al. Reviews photos with accompanying ms only. Model release required; captions preferred.

Making Contact & Terms: Provide resume, business card, brochure, flyer or tearsheets to be kept on file for possible future assignments; "portfolio drop off Thursdays, pick up Fridays." Does not return unsolicited material. Reports in 4-6 weeks. Pays $75-250/b&w or color photo. Pays on publication. Credit line given. Buys first N.A. serial rights.

Tips: Prefers to see strong personal style and excellent technical ability. "Work needs to be oriented to our market. Know our magazine and its orientation before contacting me."

THE SATURDAY EVENING POST SOCIETY, Dept. PM, Benjamin Franklin Literary & Medical Society, 1100 Waterway Blvd., Indianapolis IN 46202. (317)634-1100. Editor: Cory SerVaas, M.D. Photo Editor: Patrick Perry. Magazine published 9 times annually. For family readers interested in travel, food, fiction, personalities, human interest and medical topics — emphasis on health topics. Circ. 600,000. Sample copy $4; free photo guidelines with SASE.

Needs: Prefers the photo essay over single submission. Model release required.

Making Contact & Terms: Send photos for consideration; 8 × 10 b&w glossy prints; 35mm or larger transparencies. Provide business card to be kept on file for possible future assignments. SASE. Reports in 1 month. Pays $50 minimum/b&w photo or by the hour; pays $150 minimum for text/photo package; $75 minimum/color photo; $300/color cover photo. Pays on publication. Prefers all rights. Simultaneous submissions and previously published work OK.

SCIENCE OF MIND MAGAZINE, Dept. PM, 3251 West Sixth St., Los Angeles CA 90020. (213)388-2181. FAX: (213)388-1926. Editor: Kathy Juline. Photo Coordinator: Randall Friesen. Monthly. Emphasizes Science of Mind philosophy. Readers include positive thinkers, holistic healing, psychological thinkers. Circ. 100,000. Estab. 1927. Sample copy and photo guidelines free with 6 × 9 SASE.

Needs: Uses 7-10 photos/issue; 4-8 supplied by freelance photographers. Needs scenic nature, sensitive (e.g., baby, baby animals, people situations, ethnic). Reviews with or without accompanying ms. Model and property release required; captions preferred.

Making Contact & Terms: Send 5 × 7, 8 × 10 b&w prints; high-quality duplicate 35mm transparencies by mail for consideration. Include 6 × 9 SASE. Reports in 4 weeks. Pays $100/color cover photo, $25/inside b&w photo; $50/inside color photo. Pays 30 days after masthead date. Credit line given. Buys one-time rights unless otherwise specified. Simultaneous submissions and previously published work OK.

Tips: Wants to see "abstract, artsy, unusual theme and ethnic references and people. On first contact, do not send more than 24 slides. Send duplicates only."

✴SCORE, Canada's Golf Magazine, 287 MacPherson Ave., Toronto, ON M4V 1A4 Canada. (416)928-2909. FAX: (416)928-1357. Managing Editor: Bob Weeks. Magazine published 7 times/year. Emphasizes golf. "The foundation of the magazine is Canadian golf and golfers." Readers are affluent, well-educated, 80% male, 20% female. Circ. 110,000. Estab. 1980. Sample copy $2 (Canadian). Photo guidelines free with SAE with IRC.

Needs: Uses between 10 and 15 photos/issue; approximately 95% supplied by freelance photographers. Needs "professional-quality, golf-oriented color and b&w material on prominent Canadian male and female pro golfers on the US PGA and LPGA tours, as well as the European and other international circuits, scenics, travel, closeups and full-figure." Model releases (if necessary) and captions required.

Making Contact & Terms: Query with samples and with list of stock photo subjects. Send 8 × 10 or 5 × 7 glossy b&w prints and 35mm or 2¼ × 2¼ transparencies by mail for consideration. Provide resume, business card, brochure, flyer or tearsheets to be kept on file for possible future assignments. SASE with IRC. Reports in 3 weeks. Pays $75-100/color cover photo; $30/b&w inside photo; $50/color inside photo; $40-65/hour; $320-520/day; and $80-2,000/job. Pays on acceptance. Credit line given. Buys all rights. Simultaneous submissions OK.

Tips: "When approaching *Score* with visual material, it is best to illustrate photographic versatility with a variety of lenses, exposures, subjects and light conditions. Golf is not a high-speed sport, but invariably presents a spectrum of location puzzles: rapidly changing light conditions, weather, positioning, etc. Capabilities should be demonstrated in query photos. Scenic material follows the same rule. Specific golf hole shots are certainly encouraged for travel features, but wide-angle shots are just as important, to 'place' the golf hole or course, especially if it is located close to notable landmarks or particularly stunning scenery. Approaching *Score* is best done with a clear, concise presentation. A picture is absolutely worth a thousand words, and knowing your market and your particular strengths will prevent a mutual waste of time and effort. Sample copies of the magazine are available and any photographer seeking to work with *Score* is encouraged to investigate it prior to querying."

*SCRIPTS AND SCRIBBLES, University Arts Resources, 141 Wooster, New York NY 10012. (212)473-6695. Contact: Larry Qualls. Journal. Emphasizes theater, dance, contemporary art and architecture. Readers are university professors. Estab. 1988. Sample copy available.

Needs: Reviews photos with or without a manuscript. Model/property release required. Photo captions required.

Making Contact & Terms: Query with resume of credits. Reports in 3 weeks. NPI. Pays on publication. Credit line given. Rights negotiable. Previously published work OK.

SCUBA TIMES MAGAZINE, Suite 16, 14110 Perdido Key Dr., Pensacola FL 32507. (904)492-7805. FAX: (904)492-7807. Copy Editor: Gwen Roland. Bimonthly magazine. Emphasizes scuba diving. Circ. 30,000. Estab. 1972. Sample copy $3. Photo guidelines free with SASE.

Needs: Uses 50-60 photos/issue; 100% supplied by freelance photographers. Needs animal/wildlife shots, travel, scenics, how-to, all with an underwater focus. Provides an editorial schedule with SASE. Model release and photo captions preferred.

Making Contact & Terms: Interested in receiving work from newer, lesser-known photographers. "Send a sample (40-60 dupes) for our stock file with each slide labelled according to location rather than creature. Send a complete list of destinations you have photographed. We will build a file from which we can make assignments and order originals." Send 35mm transparencies. SASE. Reports in 1 to 2 months. Pays $150/color cover photo, $75/color page rate and $75/b&w page rate. Pays 30 days after publication. Credit line given. Buys one-time rights. Previously published work OK "under certain circumstances."

Tips: Looks for underwater and "topside" shots of dive destinations around the world, close-ups of marine creatures, divers underwater with creatures or coral. "We look for photographers who can capture the details that, when combined, create not only a physical description, but also capture the spirit of a dive destination. In portfolio or samples, likes to see "broad range of samples, majority underwater."

SEA, The Magazine of Western Boating, Suite C, 17782 Cowan, 2nd Floor, Irvine CA 92714. (714)660-6150. FAX: (714)660-6172. Executive Editor: Linda Yuskaitis. Art Director: Jeffrey Fleming. Monthly magazine. Circ. 60,000. Emphasizes "recreational boating in 13 western states (including some coverage of Mexico and British Columbia) for owners of recreational power boats." Sample copy and photo guidelines free with 9½ × 13 SAE.

Needs: Uses about 50-75 photos/issue; most supplied by freelance photographers; 10% assignment; 70% requested from freelancers existing photo files or submitted unsolicited. Needs people enjoying boating activity and scenics shots; shots which include parts or all of a boat are preferred." Special needs include "vertical-format shots involving power boats for cover consideration." Photos should have West Coast angle. Model release and captions required.

Making Contact & Terms: Query with samples. SASE. Reports in 1 month. Pays $250/color cover photo; inside photo rate varies according to size published. Range is from $25 for b&w and $50-150 for color. Pays on publication. Credit line given. Buys one-time N.A. rights.

Tips: "We are looking for sharp color transparencies with good composition showing pleasureboats in action, and people having fun aboard boats in a West Coast location. We also use studio shots of marine products and do personality profiles. B&w also accepted, for a limited number of stories. Color preferred. Send samples of work with a query letter and a resume or clips of previously published photos."

*SEEK, 8121 Hamilton Ave., Cincinnati OH 45231. (513)931-4050, ext. 365. Publisher: Eugene Wigginton. Editor: Eileen H. Wilmoth. Emphasizes religion/faith. Readers are church people—young and middle-aged adults. Quarterly, in weekly issues; 8 pages per issue; bulletin size. Circ. 60,000.
Needs: Uses about 3 photos/issue; supplied by freelance photographers. Needs photos of people, scenes and objects to illustrate stories and articles on a variety of themes. Must be appropriate to illustrate Christian themes. Model release required.
Making Contact & Terms: Send for consideration 8×10 b&w photos or query with list of stock photo subjects. SASE. "Freelance photographers submit assortments of b&w 8×10 photos that are circulated among all our editors who use photos." Reports in 4 weeks. Pays on acceptance $15-25/ b&w photo. Credit line given. Buys first North American serial rights. Simultaneous submissions and previously published work OK if so indicated. Free sample copy with 6×9 SAE and 39¢ postage.
Tips: "Make sure photos have sharp contrast. We like to receive photos of young or middle-aged adults in a variety of settings."

SELF, Dept. PM, 350 Madison Ave., New York NY 10017. (212)880-8864. Editor-in-Chief: Alexandra Penney. Monthly magazine. Emphasizes self-improvement and physical and mental well being for women of all ages. Circ. 1,091,000.
Needs: Needs photos emphasizing health, beauty, medicine, relationships and psychology relating to women. Uses up to 200 photos/issue; all supplied by freelancers.
Making Contact & Terms: Works with photographers on assignment basis only. Provide tearsheets to be kept on file for possible future assignments. Pays $200/b&w and color photos; $350/day.

SENIOR MAGAZINE, 3565 South Higuera, San Luis Obispo CA 93401. (805)544-8711. Publisher: Gary Suggs. Monthly magazine, tabloid. Emphasizes "the wonderful life over 40." Readers are male and female, ages 40 and older. Circ. 500,000. Estab. 1981. Sample copies for 9×12 SAE and $1.25 postage.
Needs: Uses 5-15 photos/issue; most supplied by freelance photographers. Needs mainly personality shots. Special photo needs include WWII photos—people, planes and famous wartime people. Buys photos with or without ms. Model release required.
Making Contact & Terms: Query with list of stock photo subjects. SASE. Reports in 1-2 weeks. Pays $100/b&w cover photo; $50-75/b&w inside photo. Pays on acceptance. Credit lines given. Buys one-time rights, also second reprint rights. Previously published work OK if not from competitive 'senior' publications.
Tips: "We really need photos of the famous; photos of unknowns and people over 50 with ms, only."

*SHEET MUSIC MAGAZINE, 223 Katonah Ave., Katonah NY 10536. (914)232-8108. Editor-in-Chief: E. Shanaphy. Photo Editor: Josephine Sblendorio. Emphasizes keyboard music (piano, organ and guitar) for amateur musicians. Monthly. Circ. 262,000.
Needs: Uses about 3 photos/issue, mostly for covers. Needs musical still lifes in 4-color and b&w. Photos accompanying articles usually supplied by writers. Model release required.
Making Contact & Terms: Send by mail for consideration actual 5×7 or 8×10 b&w or color prints; 35mm or 2¼×2¼ color transparencies. SASE. Reports in 2 weeks. Pays on publication $25-50/b&w photo; $200-300/color transparency; $75-200 for text/photo (b&w) package. Credit line given. Buys one-time rights. Simultaneous submissions and previously published work OK. Sample copy $2; photo guidelines for SASE.
Tips: "Our freelance material is used mostly for covers. We are interested in musical theme photos in 4-color and black and white. Because of our specific subject matter, for cover photos we look for originality, creativity in design and clear identification of the subject matter—popular sheet music— within the issue."

*SHOWBOATS INTERNATIONAL, Suite 200, 1600 SE 17th St., Ft. Lauderdale FL 33316. (305)525-8626. FAX: (305)525-7954. Executive Editor: Marilyn Mower. Bimonthly magazine. Emphasizes exclusively large yachts (100 feet or over). Readers are mostly male, 40 plus, incomes above $1 million, international. Circ. 60,000. Estab. 1981. Sample copy $5.
Needs: Uses 100-200 photos/issue; 65% supplied by freelancers. Needs photos of very large yachts and exotic destinations. "Almost all shots are commissioned by us." Model/property releases required.
Making Contact & Terms: Arrange personal interview to show portfolio. Submit portfolio for review. Query with resume of credits. Provide resume, business card, brochure, flyer or tearsheets to be kept on file for possible assignments. Does not keep samples on file. SASE. Reports in 3 weeks. Pays $350-

The asterisk before a listing indicates that the market is new in this edition. New markets are often the most receptive to freelance submissions.

500/color cover photo; $300/color page rate; $350-750/day. Pays on publication. Credit line given. Buys first N.A. serial rights, all rights, negotiated rights. Previously published work OK, however, exclusivity is important.
Tips: "Don't send pictures that need any excuses. The larger the format, the better."

SIMPLY SEAFOOD, Dept. PM, 454 N. 34th St., Seattle WA 98103. (206)547-6030. FAX: (206)548-9346. Managing Editor: Courtney Schrieve. Quarterly magazine. Emphasizes seafood recipes, step-by-step cooking of seafood, profiles of chefs. Estab. 1991. Sample copy $1.95. Photo guidelines free with SASE.
Needs: Uses 40 photos/issue; 25% are supplied by freelancers. Needs "mainly food shots, a few travel, historic and fishing shots, chefs in different locations." Model and property release and photo captions preferred.
Making Contact & Terms: Query with list of stock photo subjects. Provide resume, business card, brochure, flyer or tearsheets to be kept on file for possible assignments. Keeps samples on file. SASE. Reports as needed. Pays $100/color cover photo; $50/color inside photo. Pays on publication. Credit line given. Buys one-time rights. Simultaneous submissions and previously published work OK.
Tips: "Looking for two types of photographers: food photographers to shoot our recipes, and photographers who can go and shoot a chef or scene in different locales."

*SINGLE PROFILE MAGAZINE, P.O. Box 6098, Delray Beach FL 33484. (305)974-6453. Editor: Darin Bosse. Quarterly magazine. Readers are male and female business and professional single people, ages 18-65. Circ. 60,000. Estab. 1989. Brochure free with SASE. Photo guidelines free with SASE.
Needs: Uses 120-450 photos/issue; 50% supplied by freelancers. Needs photos of attractive, interesting, single, eligible men and women, 18-65, showing them at work or at play. There should be a relaxed atmosphere with clear view of face. Photo should say something about the subject. Reviews photos with or without a manuscript. Model/property release required. Photo captions required; include first name, marital status, age, profession and interests.
Making Contact & Terms: Query with stock photo list. Send unsolicited photos by mail for consideration. Provide resume, business card, brochure, flyer or tearsheets to be kept on file for possible assignments. Send 4×5, 5×7, 8×10 b&w, color glossy prints; 35mm, 4×5, 8×10 transparencies. Keeps samples on file. SASE. Reports in 4-6 weeks. Pays $250-750/color cover photo; $25-250/color inside photo; $25-250/b&w inside photo; $150-400/day. Pays on publication. Credit line given. Buys first N.A. serial rights. Simultaneous submissions and previously published work OK within 1 year.
Tips: "Pick attractive, interesting subjects and locations that tell something about the subject."

SINGLELIFE MILWAUKEE, Dept. PM, 606 W. Wisconsin Ave., Milwaukee WI 53203. (414)271-9700. Art Director: Paul Rosanski. Bimonthly. Emphasizes recreation and special interests for single adults. Readers are single adults 18-70. Circ. 24,000. Sample copy $2.50.
Needs: Uses about 20 photos/issue; all supplied by freelance photographers. Need photos of skiing, biking, dining, dancing, picnics, sailing—single people, couples or groups of people in recreational settings. Model release and captions required.
Making Contact & Terms: Send b&w or color glossy prints, 2¼×2¼ transparencies, b&w contact sheet by mail for consideration. SASE. Pays $30-100/b&w photo; $40-300/color photo; $50-300/job. Pays on publication. Credit line given. Buys all rights. Previously published work OK.
Tips: "We look for recreational scenes (active and passive) of couples or individuals in a portfolio. We also are getting very active in fashion photography."

*SINISTER WISDOM, P.O. Box 3252, Berkeley CA 94703. Contact: Editor. Published 3 times/year. Emphasizes lesbian/feminist themes. Readers are lesbians/women, ages 20-90. Circ. 3,000. Estab. 1976. Sample copy $6.50. Photo guidelines sheet free with SASE.
Needs: Uses 3-6 photos/issue. Needs photos relevant to specific theme, by lesbians only. Reviews photos with or without a ms. Model/property release required. Captions preferred.
Making Contact & Terms: Send unsolicited photos by mail for consideration. Provide resume, business card, brochure, flyer or tearsheets to be kept on file for possible assignments. Send all sizes or finishes. Reports in 2-9 months. Pays in copies. Pays on publication. Credit line given. Buys one-time rights. Rights negotiable.
Tips: "Read at least one issue of *Sinister Wisdom*."

SKI, Dept. PM, 2 Park Ave, New York NY 10016. (212)779-5000. (212)779-5469. Editor: Dick Needham. Art Director: Doug Rosensweig. Monthly. Circ. 440,000. Estab. 1936. Emphasizes skiing for skiers.

Needs: All photos supplied by freelance photographers, 20% assigned; 80% freelance stock. Model release and captions required.
Making Contact & Terms: Send 35mm, 2¼×2¼ or 4×5 transparencies by mail (dupes OK) for consideration. SASE. Reports in 1 week. Pays $750 color cover photo; $50-250/b&w inside photo, $50-350/color inside photo; $75-100/b&w half page; $150 b&w page, $250/color page; $200-600/job; $75-750/b&w or color photo; by the day, $350; $500-850 for text/photo package. Pays on acceptance. Credit line given. Buys one-time rights.
Tips: "I look for a particular style or point of view that the photographer may have. We are getting more involved with the 'ski-lifestyle' in an effort to show our readers what the *total* ski experience will be like—food, lodging, local color."

❧**SKI CANADA**, Dept. PM, 10 Pote Ave., Toronto, ON 2S7 M4N Canada. (416)322-9606. FAX: (416)941-9113. Editor: Cathy Carl. Monthly magazine published 6 times/year, fall and winter only. Readership is 75% male, ages 19-40, with high income. Circ. 60,000. Sample copy free with SASE.
Needs: Uses 80 photos/issue; 100% supplied by freelance photographers. Needs photos of skiing—competition, equipment, travel (within Canada and abroad), instruction, news and trends. Model release required; photo captions preferred.
Making Contact & Terms: Send unsolicited photos by mail for consideration. Provide resume, business card, brochure, flyer or tearsheets to be kept on file for possible assignments. Send color and 35mm transparencies. SASE. Reports in 1 month. Pays $100/photo/page or smaller; $200/ photo larger than 1 page; cover $400; rates are for b&w or color. Pays on publication. Credit line given. Buys first N.A. serial rights. Simultaneous submissions OK.
Tips: In samples, wants to see "sharp, good action shots. Also, shots that depict ski areas accurately, in good variety. In addition to payment receives 1 issue of our summer magazine *SunSports*—on newsstands first week of May each year—all summer sports: tennis, golf, windsurfing, waterskiing, cycling, footwear, fashion, beach activities, triathlon, etc."

SKIES AMERICA, Dept. PM, 7730 S.W. Mohawk St., Tualatrin OR 97069. (503)691-1955. Photo Editor: Terri J. Wallo. Owner: James Rullo. Monthly magazine. "We publish 5 inflight magazines for regional airlines on topics ranging from business to leisure and travel." Readers are affluent; frequent fliers; business owners/executives. Circ. 132,000. Sample copy $3.
Needs: Uses 20 photos/issue; 5 supplied by freelance photographers. Needs photos of cityscapes, travel. Captions preferred.
Making Contact & Terms: Query with resume of credits and list of stock photo subjects. SASE. Reports in 1 month. Pays $300/text/photo package; separate photo payments negotiable. Pays on publication. Credit line given. Buys one-time rights. Simultaneous submissions and previously published work OK.

SKIING MAGAZINE, Two Park Ave., New York NY 10016. (212)779-5000. FAX:(212)779-5537. Art Director: Diane Steinmetz. Published monthly (September through March). Circ. 454,266. Emphasizes skiing for Alpine skiers. Photo guidelines free with SASE.
Needs: Uses 75-120 photos/issue; 75% supplied by freelance photographers; 60% from assignment and 10% freelance stock. Needs photos of ski action, people, resorts and competitions. Name on slides; captions required including skier, location, trail and year shot.
Making Contact & Terms: Interested in receiving work from newer, lesser-known photographers. Query with dupes, not original samples or with list of stock photo subjects; send 8×10 b&w prints, 35mm transparencies or b&w contact sheet by mail for consideration; submit portfolio for review; or provide resume, business card, brochure, flyer or tearsheets to be kept on file for possible assignments. SASE. Reports in 1 month. Pays $700/color cover photo; $350/color full page photo; $100 minimum color inside photo; $250/b&w full page photo; $75 minimum/b&w inside photo. Pays on acceptance. Buys one-time rights.
Tips: "Show work *specifically* suited to *Skiing*—and be familiar with the magazine before submitting We look for skiing experience—ski action, ski people and ski resorts. High quality a must, unique lighting and a sense of drama. Freeze those moments that express skiing's many moods. We want you to create new images of our favorite sport, capture the joy, the beauty, the excitement, the challenge of skiing. Trend is fashionable clothing, bright colors and people skiing. Study the publication. Variety is always good (action, people, scenics)."

SKIN DIVER, Dept. PM, Suite 503, 8490 Sunset Blvd., Los Angeles CA 90069. (213)854-2222. Editor/Publisher: Bill Gleason. Executive Editor: Bonnie J. Cardone. Monthly magazine. Circ. 219,035. Emphasizes scuba diving in general, dive travel and equipment. "The majority of our contributors are divers-turned-writers." Free writer's/photographer's guidelines.

Needs: Photos purchased with accompanying ms only. Buys 60 photos/year; 85% supplied by freelance photographers. Adventure; how-to; human interest; humorous (cartoons); wreck diving, game diving, local diving. All photos must be related to underwater subjects. Model release required; captions preferred.

Making Contact & Terms: Send material by mail for consideration. Uses 5×7 and 8×10 b&w glossy prints; 35mm and 2¼×2¼ transparencies; 35mm color transparencies for cover, vertical format preferred. SASE. Pays $50/published page. Pays on publication. Credit line given. Buys one-time rights.

Tips: "Read the magazine; submit only those photos that compare in quality to the ones you see in *Skin Diver*."

SKY (Inflight Magazine of Delta Air Lines), Suite 300, 600 Corporate Dr., Ft. Lauderdale FL 33334. (305)776-0066. (800)523-6809. FAX: (305)493-8969. Photo Editor: Coni Kaufman. Monthly magazine. Emphasizes general interest and business/finance topics. Circ. 480,000 (print run). Sample copy $3 and 9×12 SAE.

Needs: Uses about 70 photos/issue; 35% supplied by freelance photographers. Needs photos of travel, consumer, entertainment, business, lifestyle, sports, technology, collectibles. Reviews photos with accompanying ms only unless submitting for "Places" department. "We are actively seeking materials for 'Places' department, our photo end page that features interesting perspectives on Delta destination cities (vertical format only)." Model release and captions required.

Making Contact & Terms: Interested in receiving work from newer, lesser-known photographers. Send 35mm and 2¼×2¼ transparencies by mail for consideration; provide resume, buisness card, brochure, flyer or tearsheets to be kept on file for possible future assignments. SASE. Reports in 1 month. Pays $450/color cover photo; $100-175/color inside photo; $500/text/photo package. Pays on publication. Credit line given. Buys one-time rights. Simultaneous submissions and previously published work OK.

SNOW WEEK, Dept. PM, Suite 101, 319 Barry Ave., Wayzata MN 55391. (612)476-2200. Editor: Dick Hendricks. Tabloid published 16 times from July through March. Emphasizes snowmobile racing. Circ. 30,000. Photo guidelines free with SASE.

Needs: Uses 30-40 photos/issue; 30% supplied by freelance photographers. Needs race photos. Purchases photos with accompanying ms only. Model release preferred; photo captions required.

Making Contact & Terms: Query with resume of credits. SASE. Reports in 3 weeks. Pays $75/b&w cover photo; $25/b&w inside photo; $50-250/photo/text package. Pays on publication. Credit line given. Buys first N.A. serial rights.

SNOWMOBILE MAGAZINE, Dept. PM, Suite 101, 319 Barry Ave., Wayzata MN 55391. (612)476-2200. Editor/Associate Publisher: Dick Hendricks. Published 3 times/year. Emphasizes "snowmobiles and snowmobiling, people, industry, places." Readers are 500,000 owners of two or more registered snowmobiles. Sample copy $2. Photo guidelines free with SASE.

Needs: Uses about 70 photos/issue; 5 or more supplied by freelance photographers. Needs "scenic photography of winter, primarily with snowmobiles as primary subject interest – travel slant is needed – people." Special needs include "scenics, great snowmobiling tour places, snowmobiling families and family activities, snowmobiles together with other winter activities." Written release preferred.

Making Contact & Terms: Query with samples. SASE. Reports in 1 month. Pays $25 and up/b&w inside photo; $40 and up/color inside photo. Pays on publication. Credit line negotiable. Buys one-time rights. Simultaneous submissions and previously published work OK.

Tips: "Snowmobiling is a beautiful and scenic sport that most often happens in places and under conditions that make good pictures difficult; capture one of these rare moments for us and we'll buy."

SNOWMOBILE WEST, Dept. PM, 520 Park Ave., Idaho Falls ID 83402. (208)524-7000. Editor: Steve Janes. Magazine published 4 times/year. Emphasizes where to go snowmobiling, new machine previews and tips on modifying. Circ. 135,000. Sample copy $1; free photo guidelines.

Needs: Buys 6-8 photos/issue. Needs celebrity/personality, photo essay/photo feature, special effects/experimental, sport, how-to, human interest, nature and travel. Captions preferred. Also seeks accompanying ms on snowmobiling. Free writer's guidelines.

Making Contact & Terms: Send material by mail for consideration or phone. Uses 8×10 b&w glossy prints; 35mm transparencies, square format preferred for cover. Provide business card and tearsheets to be kept on file for possible future assignments. SASE. Reports in 1 month. Pays $5-15/b&w photo; $10-35/color photo; $25-50/cover photo. Pays on publication. Credit line given. Buys one-time rights.

Tips: "We want photos that focus on people having fun, not so much on speed of machines. The photos of people should be with helmets off. We want family-oriented, fun-oriented pix. Send query. Let us know who you are. Then send a follow-up letter to remind us every now and then. Once we use a photographer, we tend to go back to him time and time again."

SOLDIER OF FORTUNE MAGAZINE, P.O. Box 693, Boulder CO 80306. (303)449-3750. Editor: John Coleman. Monthly magazine. Emphasizes adventure, combat, military units and events. Readers are mostly male—interested in adventure and military related subjects. Circ. 175,000. Estab. 1975. Sample copy $5.

Needs: Uses about 60 photos/issue; 33% on assignment, 33% from stock. Needs photos of combat—under fire, or military units, military—war related. "We always need front-line combat photography." Not interested in studio or still life shots. Model/property release preferred. Captions required, include as much tech information as possible.

Making Contact & Terms: Contact Tom Slizewski, photo editor, by phone with queries; send 8×10 glossy b&w, color prints, 35mm transparencies, b&w contact sheets by mail for consideration. SASE. Reports in 3 weeks. Pays $50-150/b&w photo; $50-500/color cover; $150-2,000/complete job. Will negotiate a space-rate payment schedule for photos alone. Pays on acceptance. Credit line given. Buys one-time rights.

Tips: "Combat action photography gets first consideration for full-page and cover layouts. Photo spreads on military units from around the world also get a serious look, but stay away from 'man with gun' shots. *Give us horizontals and verticals!* The horizontal-shot syndrome handcuffs our art director. *Get close!* Otherwise, use telephoto. Too many photographers send us long distance shots that just don't work for our audience. *Give us action!* People sitting, or staring into the lens, mean nothing. *Consider using b&w* along with color. It gives us options in regard to layout; often, b&w better expresses the combat/military dynamic."

SOUNDINGS, Dept. PM, 35 Pratt St., Essex CT 06441. (203)767-3200. Editor-in-Chief: Narleah Ross. Monthly tabloid. Emphasizes recreational boating. Readers are men, ages 40-60, with approximately $70,000 annual income. Circ. 105,000. Sample copy free with 12×18 SASE and $2.50 postage. Photo guidelines free with SASE.

Needs: Uses 50 photos/issue; 40% supplied by freelance photographers. Needs photos for story illustrations, plus a few pictures of boating enterprises. Editorial calendar available. Model release preferred; photo captions required.

Making Contact & Terms: Send unsolicited photos by mail for consideration. Provide resume, business card, brochure, flyer or tearsheets to be kept on file for possible assignments. Send b&w prints, any size and format, or 35mm transparencies. SASE. Reports in 1 month. Pays $200-400/color cover photo, $35 and up/b&w inside photo and $400/day. Pays on publication. Credit line given. Buys one-time rights. Previously published work OK.

Tips: In portfolios, looking for a range of skills: action, fill flash, portrait, etc."

SOUTHERN ACCENTS, 2100 Lakeshore Dr., Birmingham AL 35209. (205)877-6000. FAX: (205)877-6600. Art Director: Lane Gregory. Estab. 1977. 6 issues/year. Emphasizes interiors, gardens. Readers are "upper class." Circ. 500,000. Sample copy available for 9×12 SAE and $2.50 postage.

Needs: Uses 200 photos/issue, 75% supplied by freelancers. Needs interior and garden photos exclusively; our choice of locations. Model release required.

Making Contact & Terms: Interested in receiving work from newer, lesser-known photographers. Provide resume, business card, brochure, flyer or tearsheets to be kept on file for possible future assignments. SASE. Reports in 1 month. Pays $500-1,000/job (day rate). Pays on publication. Credit line given. Buys rights for one year; will negotiate with photographer unwilling to sell all rights.

Tips: "Send only samples of interiors, table scapes and gardens—no food or fashion."

SOUTHERN BOATING, 1766 Bay Rd., Miami Beach FL 33139. (305)538-0700. Editorial Director: Andree Conrad. Monthly magazine. Emphasizes "boating (mostly power, but also sail) in the Southeastern US and the Caribbean." Readers are "concentrated in 30-50 age group; male and female; affluent—executives mostly." Circ. 26,000. Estab. 1972. Sample copy $4.

Needs: Number of photos/issue varies; 100% supplied by freelancers. Needs "photos to accompany articles about cruising destinations, the latest in boats and boat technology, boating activities (races, rendezvous); cover photos of a boat in a square format (a must) in the context of that issue's focus (see editorial calendar)." Model release preferred. Photo captions required.

Making Contact & Terms: Query with list of stock photo subjects. SASE. Reporting time varies. Pays $50 up/color cover photo; $25 up/color inside photo; $10 up/b&w inside photo; $75-150/photo/text package. Pays on publication. Credit line given. Buys one-time rights. Simultaneous submissions and previously published work OK.

Tips: "Photography on the water is very tricky. We are looking for first-rate work, preferably Kodachrome or Fujichrome, and prefer to have story *and* photos together, except in the case of cover material."

SPECTACULAR SF RESCUE IN IRAQ

SOLDIER OF FORTUNE

APRIL 1992
$ 48493

INTERNATIONAL
BRIGADE WANTS
VOLUNTEERS

STEALTH:
SOUND-SUPPRESSED
.22 FOR UNDER $600

POW/MIA:
KGB CONNECTION?

CONGRESSIONAL SELLOUT

BLUEPRINT FOR A
BREAKTHROUGH

CAN. $4.75 • UK £2.60 • U.S. $3.95

© Eric Micheletti

While covering the fighting in what was once Yugoslavia, French photographer Eric Micheletti snapped this striking cover shot for Soldier of Fortune Magazine. Editorial Director Tom Slizewski says the shot, which earned Micheletti $500, fits in well with the magazine's theme. "Obviously only a small percentage of photographers are willing to undergo the risks involved in shooting a Soldier of Fortune feature, but that's what makes finding an image such as this all the more rewarding," says Slizewski.

SOUTHERN EXPOSURE, Dept. PM, P.O. Box 531, Durham NC 27702. (919)419-8311. Managing Editor: Eric Bates. Quarterly. Emphasizes the politics and culture of the South, with special interest in women's issues, black affairs and labor. Estab. 1972. Photo guidelines free with SASE. Sample copy $4 with 9 × 12 SASE.
Needs: Uses 30 photos/issue; most supplied by freelance photographers. Needs news and historical photos; photo essays. Model release and captions preferred.
Making Contact & Terms: Query with samples. Send b&w glossy prints by mail for consideration. SASE. Reports in 3-6 weeks. Pays $50/b&w cover photo; $75/color cover photo; $15-30/b&w inside photo. Credit line given. Buys all rights "unless the photographer requests otherwise." Simultaneous submissions and previously published work OK.

*SPEEDWAY LIMITED EDITION, Ste. 356, 7200 Montgomery NE, Albuquerque NM 87109. (505)888-1515. FAX: (505)888-0717. Editor: Marybeth Connelly. Bimonthly magazine. Emphasizes NASCAR racing card and memorabilia collections. Readers are male and female NASCAR fans and collectors, ages 25-65. Circ. 50,000. Estab. 1991. Sample copy $9.95. Photo guidelines free with SASE.
Photo Needs: Uses 13 photos/issue; 100% supplied by freelancers. Needs photos of NASCAR drivers and pit crews in action and awards ceremonies. Model/property release preferred. Photo captions preferred; include where and when photo was taken; description of scene.
Making Contact & Terms: Query with resume of credits. Provide resume, business card, brochure, flyer or tearsheets to be kept on file for possible assignments. Keeps samples on file. SASE. Reports in 1-2 weeks. Pays $200/color cover photo; $100/color inside photo. Pays on publication. Credit line given. Buys one-time rights; negotiable. Simultaneous submissions and previously published work OK.
Tips: "We are looking for centered action photos that also show the drivers' faces. Bright lighting, crisp subject lines and interesting angles are ideal. We print a limited number of close-up portraits, as well. Take as many shots of an interesting scene as you can so we have several of your submissions to compare with others."

SPORT FISHING, P.O. Box 2456, Winter Park FL 32790. (407)628-4802. FAX: (407)628-7061. Managing Editor: Connie White. Estab. 1986. Publishes 8 issues/year. Emphasizes off-shore fishing. Readers are upscale boat owners and off-shore fishermen. Circ. 85,000. Sample copy $2.50 with 9 × 12 SAE and $1.58 postage. Photo guidelines free with SASE.
Needs: Uses 50 photos/issue; 75% supplied by freelance photographers. Needs photos of off-shore fishing—big boats/big fish, travel destinations. "We are working more from stock—good opportunities for extra sales on any given assignment." Model release preferred; releases needed for subjects (under "unusual" circumstances) in photo. Photo captions preferred.
Making Contact & Terms: Interested in receiving work from newer, lesser-known photographers. Query with samples; send unsolicited photos by mail for consideration; provide resume, business card, brochure, flyer or tearsheets to be kept on file for possible future assignments. Send 35mm, 2¼ × 2¼ and 4 × 5 transparencies by mail for consideration. "Kodachrome and slow Fuji are preferred." Reports in 3 weeks. Pays $20-100/b&w page; $50-500/color page. Buys one-time rights unless otherwise agreed upon. Simultaneous submissions OK.
Tips: "We need razor sharp images. The best guideline is the magazine itself. Get used to shooting on, in or under water. Most of our needs are found there."

SPORT MAGAZINE, Dept. PM, 8490 Sunset Blvd., Los Angeles CA 90069. (213)854-2268. Picture Editor: Ira Gabriel. Monthly magazine. Emphasizes sports, both professional and collegiate. Readers are ages "9-99, male and female." Circ. 1 million. Photo guidelines free with SASE.
Needs: Uses 80+ photos/issue; 20% supplied by freelance photographers. Needs photos of sports action, strobed basketball, hockey, football, baseball.
Making Contact & Terms: Query with resume of credits or stock photo subjects. "No unsolicited work accepted." Reports in 1 month. Pays $600/color cover photo or $350/day. Pays on publication. Credit line given. Buys one-time rights.
Tips: In portfolio or samples looking for "tight, sharp, action—hockey and basketball must be strobed, color transparencies preferred, well-lighted portraits of athletes. No prints. Shoot as much as you can on your own. Continue to call upon publications. Don't get let down; be patient. Freelance photographers have a good opportunity to do a lot of work for our magazine on an assignment basis. More assignments are being given to those who continue to excel and are creative."

SPUR, 13 W. Federal, P.O. Box 85, Middleburg VA 22117. (703)687-6314. FAX: (703)687-3925. Editor: Cathy Laws. Bimonthly magazine. Emphasizes Thoroughbred horses. Readers are "owners, breeders, trainers and enthusiasts in the sports of racing, steeplechasing, polo, fox hunting, horse showing and three-day eventing." Circ. 15,000+. Sample copy $5. Photo guidelines free with SASE.

Needs: Uses about 45-55 photos/issue; all supplied by freelance photographers. Buys 40% on freelance assignment, 60% from freelance stock. Needs photos of "horses and action (racing, steeplechasing, polo), scenic shots, people involved in Thoroughbred sports." Special needs include "covers—colorful, original approaches." All photos must be identified including names of people and horses.
Making Contact & Terms: Interested in receiving work from newer, lesser-known photographers. Query with samples. Send transparencies, slides or prints by mail for consideration. Provide resume, business card, brochure, flyer or tearsheets to be kept on file for possible future assignments. SASE. Reports in 3 weeks. Pays $250-500/day; $300 up/color cover photo; $20-100/b&w inside photo; $50-250/color inside photo. Pays on publication. Buys one-time rights. Credit line given.
Tips: "We want good action shots, great color—not too dark—we sometimes have problems on press with darkness. There is a trend toward increased use of Fuji Velvia film—colors print rich. Send samples—it doesn't matter if subjects are not horse-related. We want to see good examples of outdoor action as well as well-lit interiors."

*STAR, 660 White Plains Rd., Tarrytown NY 10591. (914)332-5000. Editor: Richard Kaplan. Photo Director: Alistair Duncan. Weekly. Emphasizes news, human interest and celebrity stories. Circ. 3,102,000. Sample copy and photo guidelines free with SASE.
Needs: Uses 100-125 photos/issue; 75% supplied by freelancers. Reviews photos with or without accompanying ms. Model release preferred; captions required.
Making Contact & Terms: Query with samples and with list of stock photo subjects, send 8 × 10 b&w prints; 35mm, 2¼ × 2¼ transparencies by mail for consideration. SASE. Reports in 2 weeks. NPI. Pays on publication. Credit line sometimes given. Simultaneous submissions and previously published work OK.

THE STATE: Down Home in North Carolina, Suite 2200, 128 S. Tryon St., Charlotte NC 28202. (704)371-3265. Editor: Scott Smith. Monthly magazine. Circ. 21,000. Estab. 1933. Regional publication, privately owned, emphasizing travel, history, nostalgia, folklore, humor, all subjects regional to North Carolina for residents of, and others interested in, North Carolina. "Send for our photography guidelines." Sample copy $3.
Needs: Photos on travel, history and human interest in North Carolina. Freelance photography used; 5% assignment and 5% stock. Captions required.
Making Contact & Terms: Send material by mail for consideration. Uses 5 × 7 and 8 × 10 glossy b&w prints; also glossy color prints and slides. Uses b&w and color cover photos, vertical preferred. SASE. Pays $25/b&w photo; $25-125/color photo; $125-150/complete job. Credit line given. Pays on publication.
Tips: Looks for "North Carolina material; solid cutline information."

STOCK CAR RACING MAGAZINE, 27 S. Main St., P.O. Box 715, Ipswich MA 01938. (508)356-7030. FAX: (508)356-2492. Editor: Dick Berggren. Monthly magazine. Circ. 400,000. Estab. 1966. Emphasizes all forms of stock car competition. Read by fans, owners and drivers of race cars and those with racing businesses. Free photo guidelines for SASE.
Needs: Buys 50-70 photos/issue. Photos purchased with or without accompany ms and on assignment. Documentary, head shot, photo essay/photo feature, product shot, personality, crash pictures, special effects/experimental, technical and sport. No photos unrelated to stock car racing. Model release required unless subject is a racer who has signed a release at the track; captions required.
Making Contact & Terms: Send material by mail for consideration. Uses 8 × 10 b&w glossy prints; 35mm or 2¼ × 2¼ transparencies. Kodachrome 64 or Fuji 100 preferred. Pays $20/b&w photo; $35-250/color photo; $250/cover photo. Pays on publication. Credit line given. Buys one-time rights.
Tips: "Send the pictures. We will buy anything that relates to racing if it's interesting, if we have the first shot at it, and it's well printed and exposed. Eighty percent of our rejections are for technical reasons—poorly focused, badly printed, too much dust, picture cracked, etc. We get far fewer cover submissions than we would like. We look for full bleed cover verticals where we can drop type into the picture and position our logo."

STRAIGHT, 8121 Hamilton Ave., Cincinnati OH 45231. (513)931-4050. FAX: (513)931-0904. Editor: Carla J. Crane. Estab. 1950. Readers are ages 13-19, mostly Christian; a conservative audience. Weekly. Circ. 60,000.
Needs: Uses about 4 photos/issue; all supplied by freelance photographers. Needs color and b&w photos of teenagers involved in various activities such as sports, study, church, part-time jobs, school activities, classroom situations. Outside nature shots, groups of teens having good times together are also needed. "Try to avoid the sullen, apathetic look—vital, fresh, thoughtful, outgoing teens are what we need. Any photographer who submits a set of quality b&w glossies or color transparencies for our consideration, whose subjects are teens in various activities and poses, has a good chance of selling to us. This is a difficult age group to photograph without looking stilted or unnatural. We want to

purport a clean, healthy, happy look. No smoking, drinking or immodest clothing. We especially need masculine-looking guys and minority subjects. Submit photos coinciding with the seasons (i.e., winter scenes in December through February, spring scenes in March through May, etc.). Model release required. Photo captions preferred.

Making Contact & Terms: Interested in receiving work from newer, lesser-known photographers. Send 5×7 or 8×10 b&w photos and color transparencies by mail for consideration. Enclose sufficient packing and postage for return of photos. Reports in 4-6 weeks. Pays on acceptance. Pays $30-50/b&w photo; $75-125/color photo. Credit line given. Buys one-time rights. Simultaneous submissions and previously published work OK. Sample copy free with SASE and 39¢ postage. Photo guidelines for SASE.

Tips: "Our publication is almost square in shape. Therefore, 5×7 or 8×10 prints that are cropped closely will not fit our proportions. Any photo should have enough 'margin' around the subject that it may be cropped square. This is a simple point, but absolutely necessary. Look for active, contemporary teenagers with light backgrounds for photos. For our publication, keep up with what teens are interested in. Due to design changes, we will be purchasing more photographs. Subjects should include teens in school, church, sports and other activities. Although our rates may be lower than the average, we try to purchase several photos from the same photographer to help absorb mailing costs. Review our publication and get a feel for our subjects."

THE STRAIN, P.O. Box 330507, Houston TX 77233-0507. (713)733-6042. For articles contact: Alicia Adler; for columns, Charlie Mainze. Monthly magazine. Emphasizes interactive arts and 'The Arts'. Readers are mostly artists and performers. Circ. 1,000. Estab. 1987. Sample copy $5 with 9×12 SASE and 7 first class stamps. Photo guidelines free with SASE.

Needs: Uses 5-100 photos/issue; 95% supplied by freelance photographers. Needs photos of scenics, personalities, portraits. "During the upcoming year we will be concentrating on portraiture." Model release required. Photo captions preferred.

Making Contact & Terms: Send any format b&w and color prints or transparencies by mail for consideration. SASE. The longer it is held, the more likely it will be published. Reports in 1 year, however. Pays $50/color cover photo; $100/b&w cover photo; $5 minimum/color inside photo; $5 minimum/b&w inside photo; $5/b&w page rate; $50-500/photo/text package. Pays on publication. Credit line given. Buys one-time rights or first North American serial rights. Simultaneous submissions and previously published work OK.

SUMMIT, The Mountain Journal, 1221 May St., Hood River OR 97031. Art Director: Adele Hammond. Quarterly magazine. Features news related to the world of mountains. Readers are mostly male professionals, ages 35-45. Circ. 25,000. Estab. 1990. Sample copy for $6 with 10×13 SAE and $2 postage.

Needs: Uses up to 40 photos/issue; 100% supplied by freelancers. Needs "landscape shots of mountains, flowers, mountain people, animals and mountain environments from all over the world. All imagery must have strong interpretative element as well as being graphically powerful. Both abstract and figurative photos welcome." Photos must be high-quality b&w or color only. Model release preferred (when applicable); photo captions required.

Making Contact & Terms: Interested in receiving work from newer, lesser-known photographers. Query with list of stock photo subjects. Provide resume, business card, brochure, flyer or tearsheets to be kept on file for possible assignment. Reports in 3 weeks. Pays $250-300/color cover photo; $50-170/various page rates. Pays on publication. Credit line given. Buys one-time rights.

THE SUN, 107 N. Roberson, Chapel Hill NC 27516. (919)942-5282. Editor: Sy Safransky. Monthly magazine. Circ. 12,000. Sample copy $3 and 9×12 SAE with $1 postage. Photo guidelines free with SASE.

Needs: Uses about 6 photos/issue; all supplied by freelance photographers. Model release preferred.

Making Contact & Terms: Send b&w prints by mail for consideration. SASE. Reports in 2 months. Pays $25-50/b&w cover and inside photo. Pays on publication. Credit line given. Buys one-time rights. Previously published work OK.

Tips: Looks for "artful and sensitive photographs that are not overly sentimental. We use many photos of people. All the photographs we publish come to us as unsolicited submissions."

SUNDAY SCHOOL COUNSELOR, 1445 Boonville Ave., Springfield MO 65802. (417)862-2781. Editor: Sylvia Lee. Readers are local church school teachers and administrators. Monthly. Circ. 35,000.

Needs: Uses about 5 photos/issue; 3-4 supplied by freelance photographers. Needs photos of people, "babies to senior adults." Model release required.

Making Contact & Terms: Submit portfolio by mail for review (5×7 or 8×10 b&w and color photos; 35mm, 2¼×2¼ or 4×5 color transparencies). SASE. Reports in 2 weeks. Pays on acceptance $25-35/b&w photo; $35-100/color transparency. Credit line given. Buys one-time rights. Simultaneous submissions and previously published work OK. Free sample copy and photo guidelines.

SURFING MAGAZINE, P.O. Box 3010, San Clemente CA 92672. (714)492-7873. Editor: Nick Carroll. Photo Editor: Larry Moore. Monthly. Circ. 120,000. Emphasizes "surfing and bodyboarding action and related aspects of beach lifestyle. Travel to new surfing areas covered as well. Average age of readers is 18 with 92% being male. Nearly all drawn to publication due to high quality, action packed photographs." Free photo guidelines with SASE. Sample copy free with legal size SAE and $2.25 postage.
Needs: Uses about 80 photos/issue; 35%+ supplied by freelance photographers. Needs "in-tight front-lit surfing and bodyboarding action photos as well as travel-related scenics. Beach lifestyle photos always in demand."
Making Contact & Terms: Send by mail for consideration 35mm or 2¼ × 2¼ transparencies; b&w contact sheet and negatives. SASE. Reports in 2-4 weeks. Pays $500/color cover photo; $30-125/color inside photo; $20-70/b&w inside photo; $500/color poster photo. Pays on publication. Credit line given. Buys one-time rights.
Tips: Prefers to see "well-exposed, sharp images showing both the ability to capture peak action as well as beach scenes depicting the surfing and bodyboarding lifestyle. Color, lighting, composition and proper film usage are important. Ask for our photo guidelines prior to making any film/camera/lens choices."

*SWANK, 1700 Broadway, New York NY 10019. (212)541-7100. FAX: (212)245-1241. Editor: Brian J. English. 13 times a year magazine. Emphasizes adult entertainment. Readers are mostly male of all backgrounds, ages 22 to 55. Circ. 250,000. Estab. 1954. Sample copy $5.95.Photo guidelines free with SASE.
Needs: Needs photos of new models for explicit, all nude photo shoots. Reviews photos with or without a manuscript. Model/property release required.
Making Contact & Terms: Send unsolicited photos by mail for consideration. Send color prints, 35mm transparencies. SASE. Reports in 1-2 weeks. Average pay for one set $1,100. Rates vary. Pays on publication. Buys all rights.
Tips: "We mostly work with established erotic photographers, but always looking for new talent. Make sure there are enough photos submitted for us to have a good idea of your ability."

*TAMPA REVIEW, P.O. Box 19F, The University of Tampa, Tampa FL 33606-1490. Editor: Richard B. Mathews. Literary magazine. Semiannual magazine. Emphasizes literature and art. Readers are intelligent, college level. Circ. 500. Estab. 1988. Sample copy $6.95. Photo guidelines free with SASE.
Needs: Uses 6 photos/issue; 100% supplied by freelancers. Needs photos of artistic, museum quality images. "We will not be accepting material before February 1993." Photographer must hold right, or release. Photo captions required.
Making Contact & Terms: Provide resume, business card, brochure, flyer or tearsheets to be kept on file for possible assignments. Send b&w, color prints "suitable for verticle 6 × 8 or 6 × 9 reproduction." SASE. Reports in 12 weeks. Pays $10/printed page. Pays on publication. Credit line given. Buys first N.A. serial rights.
Tips: "We are looking for artistic photography, not for illustration, but to generally enhance our magazine. We will consider paintings, prints, drawings, photographs, or other media suitable for printed production. Submissions should be made in February and March for publication the following year."

TEENS TODAY, Dept. PM, 6401 The Paseo, Kansas City MO 64131. (816)333-7000, ext. 209. Editorial Accountant: Rosemary Postel. Editor: Karen DeSollar. Weekly magazine. Circ. 60,000. Readers are by junior and senior high school age. Photo guidelines free with SASE.
Needs: Buys 60 photos/year. Needs shots of high school age kids. Junior and senior highs (grades 7-12) must be the subjects. Shots of driving, talking, eating, walking, sports, singles, couples, groups, etc. Also needs accompanying ms. Free writer's guidelines with SASE.
Making Contact & Terms: Send material by mail for consideration. "Send photo submissions with SASE to our central distribution center to Rosemary Postel and they will be circulated through other editorial offices." Uses 8 × 10 b&w glossy prints. SASE. Reports in 6-8 weeks. Pays $15-25/b&w photo; 3½¢ minimum/word first rights, 3¢/word for second rights for ms. Pays on acceptance. Credit line given. Buys one-time rights. Simultaneous submissions and previously published work OK.
Tips: "Make sure your work has good contrast and is dealing with the teenage group."

TENNIS WEEK, 124 E. 40th St., New York NY 10016. (212)808-4750. Publisher: Eugene L. Scott. Managing Editors: Steven Sheer, Julie Tupper and Merrill Chapman. Readers are "tennis fanatics." Biweekly. Circ. 62,000. Sample copy $3.

Needs: Uses about 16 photos/issue. Needs photos of "off-court color, beach scenes with pros, social scenes with players, etc." Emphasizes originality. No captions required; subject identification required.
Making Contact & Terms: Send by mail for consideration actual 8 × 10 or 5 × 7 b&w photos. SASE. Reports in 2 weeks. Pays on publication, $25/b&w photo; $50/cover; $100/color cover. Credit line given. Rights purchased on a work-for-hire basis.

TEXAS FISH & GAME, P.O. Box 701250, San Antonio TX 78270-1250. (512)545-4288. FAX: (512)545-4058. Editor: Marvin Spivey. Estab. 1983. Magazine published monthly, 10 times per year. Features all types of hunting and fishing. Must be Texas only. Circ. 120,000. Photo guidelines free with SASE.
Needs: Uses 20-30 photos/issue; 95% supplied by freelance photographers. Needs photos of fish: action, close up of fish found in Texas; hunting: Texas hunting and game of Texas. Model release preferred; photo captions required.
Making Contact & Terms: Interested in receiving work from newer, lesser-known photographers. Query with list of stock photo subjects. SASE. Reports in 1 month. Pays $200-300/color cover photo and $50-100/color inside photos. Pays on publication. Credit line given. Buys one-time rights.
Tips: "Query first. Ask for guidelines. No b&w used. For that 'great' shot, prices will go up. Send best shots and only of subjects the publication you're trying to sell to uses."

TEXAS GARDENER, P.O. Box 9005, Waco TX 76714. (817)772-1270. Editor/Publisher: Chris S. Corby. Bimonthly. Circ. 35,000. Emphasizes gardening. Readers are "65% male, home gardeners, 98% Texas residents." Sample copy $1.
Needs: Uses 20-30 photos/issue; 90% supplied by freelance photographers. Needs "color photos of gardening activities in Texas." Special needs include "photo essays on specific gardening topics such as 'Weeds in the Garden.' Must be taken in Texas." Model release and captions required.
Making Contact & Terms: Query with samples. SASE. Reports in 3 weeks. Pays $100-200/color cover photo; $5-15/b&w inside photo; $10-200/color inside photo. Pays on acceptance. Credit line given. Buys all rights.
Tips: "Provide complete information on photos. For example, if you submit a photo of watermelons growing in a garden, we need to know what variety they are and when and where the picture was taken."

TEXAS HIGHWAYS, P.O. Box 141009, Austin TX 78714. (512)483-3675. Editor-in-Chief: Ms. Tommie Pinkard. Photo Editor: Bill Reaves. Monthly. Circ. 430,000. *"Texas Highways* interprets scenic, recreational, historical, cultural and ethnic treasures of the state and preserves the best of Texas heritage. Its purpose is to educate and entertain, to encourage recreational travel to and within the state, and to tell the Texas story to readers around the world." Readers are "45 and over (majority); $24,000 to $60,000/year salary bracket with a college education." Sample copy and photo guidelines free.
Needs: Uses about 50 photos/issue; 50% supplied by freelance photographers. Needs "travel and scenic photos in Texas only." Special needs include "fall, winter, spring and summer scenic shots and wildflower shots (Texas only)." Captions required.
Making Contact & Terms: Query with samples. Provide business card and tearsheets to be kept on file for possible future assignments. SASE. Reports in 1 month. Pays $120/½ page color inside photo; $170/full-page color photo; $400/front cover photo. Pays on acceptance. Credit line given. Buys one-time rights. Simultaneous submissions OK.
Tips: "Know our magazine and format. We take only color originals, 35mm Kodachrome or Fujichrome, 2¼ × 2¼ or 4 × 5 transparencies. No negatives. Don't forget to caption and name names. We publish only photographs of Texas. We accept only high-quality, professional level work—no snapshots."

THANATOS, P.O. Box 6009, Tallahassee FL 32314. (904)224-1969. FAX: (904)224-7965. Associate Editor: Alana Schwermer. Quarterly magazine. Covers death, dying and bereavement. Readers include healthcare professionals, thanatologists, clergy, funeral directors, counselors, support groups, volunteers, bereaved family members, students, et al. Circ. 6,000. Estab. 1975. Photo guidelines free with SASE.
Needs: Uses 8 photos/issue; 100% supplied by freelancers. Needs many b&w scenic and people shots to accompany articles. Also, full-color scenics to illustrate seasons for each quarterly edition. Model release required; photo captions preferred.
Making Contact & Terms: Query with list of stock photo subjects. Provide resume, business card, brochure, flyer or tearsheets to be kept on file for possible assignment. Cannot return unsolicited material. Reports in 4 weeks. Pays $100/color cover photo; $50/b&w inside photo. Pays on acceptance. Buys all rights; negotiable. Simultaneous submissions OK.

*****THIGH HIGH,** 10th Floor, 801 Second Ave., New York NY 11217. (212)661-7878. FAX: (212)692-9297. Editor: Marc Medoff. Quarterly magazine. Emphasis on leg and foot fetishism. Readers are young males, blue collar workers, over 18 years old. Circ. 89,000. Estab. 1991. Sample copies free with

8½×11 SASE and 10 first class stamps. Photo guidelines free with SASE.
Needs: Uses 100-200 photos/issue; 100% supplied by freelancers. Needs photos of nude women with emphasis on legs and feet. Reviews photos with or without accompanying ms. Model/property release required, include copies of photo identification with date of birth over 18 years old.
Making Contact & Terms: Submit portfolio for review. Send unsolicited photos by mail for consideration. Provide resume, business card, brochure, flyer or tearsheets to be kept on file for possible future assignments. Send 35mm transparencies. Keeps samples on file. SASE. Reports in 1 month. Payment varies from $10/shot to $3,000/full set. Pays on acceptance. Credit line given. Buys one-time rights; negotiable. Simultaneous submissions and previously published work OK.
Tips: "We require technical perfection. Focus, lighting, composition, etc., must be 100% perfect. Look at our magazine and competing titles."

*THRASHER MAGAZINE, P.O. Box 884570, San Francisco CA 94188-4570. (415)822-3083. FAX: (415)822-8359. Photo Editor: Bryce Kanights. Monthly magazine. Emphasizes skateboarding, snowboarding and alternative music. Readers are primarily male between ages 12-24. Circ. 250,000. Estab. 1981. Sample copy $3.25. Photo guidelines free with SASE.
Needs: Uses 55 photos/issue; 20 supplied by freelancers. Needs photos of skateboarding, snowboarding and alternative music. Reviews photos with or without a manuscript. Special needs are b&w action sequences. Model/property release preferred; release needed for minors. Photo captions preferred; include name of subject, location and date of shoot.
Making Contact & Terms: Send unsolicited photos by mail for consideration. Send 5×7, 8×10 b&w prints; 35mm, 2¼×2¼ transparencies. Keeps samples on file. SASE. Reports in 1-2 weeks. Pays $250/color cover photo; $200/b&w cover photo; $65/color inside photo; $50/b&w inside photo; $110/color page rate; $85/b&w page rate. Pays on publication. Credit line given. Buys all rights.
Tips: "Get to know the sports of skateboarding and snowboarding, the lifestyles and current trends."

*TOURING AMERICA, P.O. Box 6050, Mission Viejo CA 92690. (714)855-8822, ext. 410. FAX: (714)855-1850. Editor: Gene Booth. Bimonthly magazine. Emphasizes travel in US, Canada and Mexico. Readers are male and female, 30-55 primarily. Circ. 75,000. Estab. 1991. Photo guidelines free with SASE.
Needs: Uses 100-150 photos/issue; 99% supplied by freelancers. Needs travel photos, scenics with people in frame. Reviews photos with or without a manuscript—only by pre-arrangement. "Our covers seem to be difficult to find." Model/property release preferred. Captions required; include "location, what's going on."
Making Contact & Terms: Query with list of stock photo subjects; "explain story idea." Keeps samples on file. SASE, "but do not send unsolicited material." Reports in 3 weeks. Pays $250 minimum/color cover photo; $50-150/color inside photo; $250-750/photo/text package, "preferred." Credit line given. Buys one-time rights; first N.A. serial rights for text; and anthology rights for text. Previously published work OK for photos only.
Tips: "We prefer story/photo packages. Writing must be excellent, with a lead that grabs the reader. Photos must have people in them, no Sierra Club scenics. Request our Authors' Guide, then do what it says."

TOURS!, 546 E. Main St., Lexington KY 40508. (606)253-1036. Editor: Kim Finley. Quarterly magazine. Emphasizes escorted travel. Readers are 75% female and over age 50. Circ. 100,000. Estab. 1988. Sample copy free with 9×12 SAE.
Needs: Uses 35-40 photos/issue; 1 supplied by freelancer. Send travel photos. Special photo needs include escorted vacationers at popular destinations. Model release required. Photo captions required.
Making Contact & Terms: Query with list of stock photo subjects; send unsolicited photos by mail for consideration; submit portfolio for review; provide resume, business card, brochure, flyer or tearsheets to be kept on file for possible assignments. Send 35mm, 2¼×2¼, 4×5 transparencies. SASE. Reports in 1 month. Pays $200/color cover photo. Pays on acceptance. Credit line given. Buys one-time rights. Simultaneous submissions and previously published work OK.

TQ, Dept. PM, P.O. Box 82808, Lincoln NE 68501. (402)474-4567. Managing Editor: Lisa Thompson. Monthly magazine. Circ. 70,000. Emphasizes Christian living for Christian young people, ages 14-17. Free sample copy (with 9×12 SASE) and photographer's guidelines.
Needs: Buys 5-10 photos/issue. Photos of young people 14-17 years old in unposed, everyday activities. Scenic, sport, photo essay/photo feature, human interest, head shot, still life, humorous and special effects/experimental. Interested in photos of minorities. Current fashion.
Making Contact & Terms: Send photos for consideration, or send contact sheet. Send contact sheet or 8×10 b&w glossy prints; color transparencies. Address to Photo Coordinator. SASE. Reports in 2-4 weeks. Pays $35 for most b&w photos; $60 for most color photos. Pays on acceptance. Buys one-time-use rights. Simultaneous submissions and previously published work OK.

Tips: "Close-up shots featuring moody, excited or unusual expressions needed. Would like to see more shots featuring unusual and striking camera and darkroom techniques. Looks for "wholesome youth 14-17 in fun situations, school, family: good-quality technical and creative work. We have a limited budget but high standards. Take care in printing your b&w photos. Also review your work and send only those pictures that have a shot at being printed. Limit your submissions."

TRACK AND FIELD NEWS, Suite 606, 2570 El Camino Real., Mountain View CA 94040. (415)948-8417. FAX: (415)948-9445. Associate Editor (Features/Photography): Jon Hendershott. Estab. 1948. Monthly magazine. Circ. 35,000. Emphasizes national and world-class track and field competition and participants at those levels for athletes, coaches, administrators and fans. Sample copy free with 9×12 SAE. Free photo guidelines.
Needs: Buys 10-15 photos/issue; 75% of freelance photos on assignment, 25% from stock. Wants on a regular basis photos of national-class athletes, men and women, preferably in action. "We are always looking for quality pictures of track and field action as well as offbeat and different feature photos. We always prefer to hear from a photographer before he/she covers a specific meet. We also welcome shots from road and cross-country races for both men and women. Any photos may eventually be used to illustrate news stories in *T&FN*, feature stories in *T&FN* or may be used in our other publications (books, technical journals, etc.). Any such editorial use will be paid for, regardless of whether or not material is used directly in *T&FN*. About all we don't want to see are pictures taken with someone's Instamatic or Polaroid. No shots of someone's child or grandparent running. Professional work only."
Making Contact & Terms: Interested in receiving work from newer, lesser-known photographers. Query with samples or send material by mail for consideration. Uses 8×10 glossy prints; contact sheet preferred; 35mm transparencies. Captions required: subject name, meet date/name. SASE. Reports in 1 week. Pays $20/b&w photo inside; $50 color photo inside; $150/color cover photo. Payment is made bimonthly. Credit line given. Buys one-time rights.
Tips: "No photographer is going to get rich via *T&FN*. We can offer a credit line, nominal payment and, in some cases, credentials to major track and field meets to enable on-the-field shooting. Also we can offer the chance for competent photographers to shoot major competitions and competitors up close as well as the most highly regarded publication in the track world as a forum to display a photographer's talents."

TRAILER BOATS MAGAZINE, Poole Publications Inc., 20700 Belshaw Ave., Carson CA 90746. (310)537-6322. FAX: (310)537-8735. Editor: Wiley Poole. Monthly magazine. Circ. 85,000. Estab. 1971. "Only magazine devoted exclusively to legally trailerable boats and related activities" for owners and prospective owners. Sample copy $1.25.
Needs: Uses 15 photos/issue with ms. 95-100% of freelance photography comes from assignment; 0-5% from stock. Scenic (with ms), how-to, humorous (monthly "Over-the-Transom" funny or weird shots in the boating world), travel (with ms). Photos must relate to trailer boat activities. Captions preferred; include location of travel pictures. No long list of stock photos or subject matter not related to editorial content. Photos purchased with or without accompanying ms. Captions required. For accompanying ms, articles related to trailer boat activities. Free writer's guidelines
Making Contact & Terms: Query or send photos or contact sheet by mail for consideration. Uses 5×7 glossy b&w prints; transparencies. SASE. Reports in 1 month. Pays per text/photo package or on a per-photo basis. Pays $7.50-50/b&w photo; $15-100/color photo; 7-10¢/word/ms and $7.50-50/photo; $150-300/cover photo. Pays on publication. Credit line given. Buys one-time rights and all rights; negotiable.
Tips: "Shoot with imagination and a variety of angles. Don't be afraid to 'set-up' a photo that looks natural. Think in terms of complete feature stories; photos and mss. It is rare any more that we publish freelance photos only, without accompanying ms; with one exception, 'Over the Transom'—a comical, weird or unusual boating shot."

TRAILER LIFE, Dept. PM, 29901 Agoura Rd., Agoura CA 91301. (818)991-4980. Editor: Bill Estes. Monthly magazine. Emphasizes the why, how and how-to of owning, using and maintaining a recreational vehicle for personal vacation or full-time travel. Circ. 315,000. Send for editorial guidelines.
Needs: Human interest, how-to, travel and personal experience. The editors are particularly interested in photos for the cover; an RV must be included. Also accompanying ms related to recreational vehicles and ancillary activities.
Making Contact & Terms: Send material by mail for consideration or query with samples. Uses 8×10 b&w glossy prints; 35mm and 2¼×2¼ transparencies. SASE. Reports in 3 weeks. Pays $50-150/b&w photo; $75-300+/color photo. Pays on acceptance. Credit line given. Buys first N.A. rights.

*TRAJECTORIES, P.O. Box 49249, Austin TX 78765. (512)441-5610. Publisher: Richard Shannon. Quarterly magazine. Emphasizes science fiction culture, lifestyle and arts. Readers cross boundries of sex, age, race, employment and cultures. Circ. 3,000. Estab. 1987. Sample copy $3. Photo guidelines free with SASE.

Needs: Uses over 12 photos/issue. Needs photos of space/technology and computer/robotics shows, science fiction/fantasy conventions, famous science fiction people and scientists with interviews. Reviews photos with or without a manuscript. Special needs are covention coverage, interviews and photo-illustrated fiction. Model/property release required. Photo captions required.

Making Contact & Terms: Submit portfolio for review. Query with stock photo list. Provide resume, business card, brochure, flyer or tearsheets to be kept on file for possible assignments. Keeps samples on file. SASE. Reports in 30-90 days. Pays $50 and up/color cover photo; $50/b&w cover photo; $10/color inside photo; $10/b&w inside photo; $5-15/photo/text package. Pays on publication. Credit line given. Buys first N.A. serial rights; negotiable. Simultaneous submissions and previously published work OK.

Tips: Looks for "photojournalistic credits, good artistic use of b&w when shooting, staging ability, availability and flexibility in scheduling and meeting deadlines." Photographers should "develop interest in subjects, look for unusual angles and odd moments."

TRANSITIONS ABROAD, 18 Hulst Rd., P.O. Box 344, Amherst MA 01004. (413)256-0373. Assistant Publisher: Lisa Aciukewicz. Bimonthly magazine. Emphasizes travel. Readers are people interested in traveling, learning, living, or working abroad, all ages, both sexes. Circ. 15,000. Estab. 1977. Sample copy for $3.50. Photo guidelines free with SASE.

Needs: Uses 15 photos/issue; all photographers are freelancers. Needs photos of travelers in international settings or the people of other countries. Each issue has an area focus: Jan/Feb.—Asia and the Pacific Rim; Mar./Apr.—Europe and the former Soviet Union; May/June—The Mediterranean Basin and the Near East; Nov./Dec.—The Americas and Africa (South of the Sahara).

Making Contact & Terms: Query with list of stock photo subjects; send unsolicited 8×10 b&w prints by mail for consideration. SASE. Reports in 1 month. Pays $10-125/b&w cover photo. Pays on publication. Credit line given. Buys one-time rights. Simultaneous submissions and previously published work OK.

Tips: In freelance photographer's samples, wants to see "mostly people shots—travelers and people of other countries. We use very few landscapes or abstract shots and use only vertical shots on cover."

TRAVEL & LEISURE, Dept. PM, 1120 Avenue of the Americas, New York NY 10036. (212)382-5600. Editor: Ila Stanger. Art Director: Bob Ciano. Picture Editor: Hazel Hammond. Monthly magazine. Emphasizes travel destinations, resorts, dining and entertainment. Circ. 1,200,000. Free photo guidelines. SASE.

Needs: Nature, still life, scenic, sport and travel. Model release and captions required.

Making Contact & Terms: Uses 8×10 b&w semigloss prints; 35mm, 2¼×2¼, 4×5 and 8×10 transparencies, vertical format required for cover. Pays $200-500/b&w photo; $200-500/color photo; $1,000/cover photo or negotiated. Sometimes pays $450-1,200/day; $1,200 minimum/complete package. Pays on publication. Credit line given. Buys first world serial rights, plus promotional use. Previously published work OK.

Tips: Seeing trend toward "more editorial/journalistic images, more use of b&w with color, use of photographers in proximity to destination, larger formats and 35mm." Demonstrate prior experience or show published travel-oriented work. Have a sense of "place" in travel photos. "Allow me to become familiar with your work, perhaps with stock requests, and then grow from there with smaller stories leading up to more comprehensive stories. We are proximity oriented when we can and are not likely to fly people great distances at great expense."

TRIATHLETE MAGAZINE, Dept. PM, #303, 1415 Third St., Santa Monica CA 90401. (213)394-1321. Contact: Timothy Downs. Monthly magazine. Covers multi-sport events: biathlon, triathlon, etc. Circ. 60,000.

Needs: Uses 50-80 photos/issue; 30% supplied by freelances. Needs action photos of athletes. "Photos should be dramatic, exciting coverage of events." Model release and photo captions preferred.

Making Contact & Terms: Query with resume of credits. Send unsolicited 35mm transparencies by mail for consideration. SASE required. Reports in 1 month. Pays $350/color cover photo. Pays on publication. Credit line given. Buys one-time rights.

Tips: "Know triathlon; know the stars."

*TROPICAL FISH HOBBYIST MAGAZINE, One T.F.H. Plaza, Neptune NJ 07753. (908)988-8400. Contact: Editor. Monthly magazine. Emphasizes tropical and marine fishes. General readership. Circ. 60,000. Sample copy $3, 9×12 SASE and 4 first-class stamps.

Needs: Needs photos of fresh and saltwater fishes, garden ponds and other marine hobby related photos. Uses approx. 100 photos/issue; 100% supplied by freelance photographers. Model release and photo captions preferred.

Making Contact & Terms: Send unsolicited photos by mail for consideration. Send color 35mm transparencies. SASE. Reports in 1 month. Pays $10/color inside photo. Pays on acceptance. Credit line given. Buys all rights, but "photographer may sell elsewhere after *TFH* publication." Previously published work OK.

Tips: In porfolio or samples, looking especially for shots of endangered and rare species.

TRUE WEST, P.O. Box 2107, Stillwater OK 74076. (405)743-3370. Editor: John Joerschke. Monthly. Circ. 30,000. Emphasizes "history of the Old West (1830 to about 1910)." Readers are "people who like to read the history of the West." Estab. 1953. Sample copy $2 with 9 × 12 SAE.

Needs: Uses about 100 or more photos/issue; almost all are supplied by freelance photographers. Needs "mostly Old West historical subjects, some travel, some scenic, (ghost towns, old mining camps, historical sites). We prefer photos with ms." Special needs include western wear; cowboys, rodeos, western events. Captions required.

Making Contact & Terms: Interested in receiving work from newer, lesser-known photographers. Query with samples—b&w only for inside; color for covers. SASE. Reports in 1 month. Pays $75-150/color cover photo; $10/b&w inside photo; "minimum of 3¢/word for copy." Pays on acceptance. Credit line given. Buys one-time rights.

Tips: Prefers to see "transparencies of existing artwork as well as scenics for cover photos. Inside photos need to tell story associated with the Old West. Most of our photos are used to illustrate stories and come with manuscripts; however, we will consider other work, scenics, historical sites, old houses. Even though we are Old West history, we do need current photos, both inside and for covers—so don't hesitate to contact us."

TURN-ONS, TURN-ON LETTERS, OPTIONS, BEAU, Box 470, Port Chester NY 10573. Photo Editor: Wayne Shuster. Periodical magazines. Emphasizes "sexually oriented situations. We emphasize good, clean sexual fun among liberal-minded adults." Readers are mostly male; ages 18-65. Circ. 75,000. Sample copy $2.95 with 6 × 9 SAE and $1 postage.

Needs: Uses approximately 20-30 b&w photos/issue, all stock. Black and white preferred, but will accept color sets for conversion to b&w. Pays $200/set. Needs a "variety of b&w photos depicting sexual situations of boy-girl, girl-girl, boy-boy, girl-boy-girl scenes. Also need color transparencies of single girls, girl-girl, and single boys for cover; present in a way suitable for newsstand display." Model release required.

Making Contact & Terms: Query with samples. Send 8 × 10 glossy b&w prints or 35mm, 2¼ × 2¼, 4 × 5 transparencies by mail for consideration. SASE. Reports in 2 weeks. Pays $250/color cover photo and $20/b&w inside photo. Pays on publication. Buys one-time rights on covers, second rights OK for b&w.

Tips: "Please examine copies of our publications before submitting work. In reviewing samples we consider composition of color photos for newsstand display and look for recently photographed b&ws for inside."

TV GUIDE, Radnor PA 19088. (Not reviewing freelance work).

TWINS MAGAZINE, P.O. Box 12045, Overland Park KS 66212. (913)722-1090. FAX: (913)722-1767. Editor: Barbara Unell. Bimonthly. Emphasizes parenting twins, triplets, quadruplets, or more and being a twin, triplet, quadruplet or more. Readers include the parents of multiples. Circ. 50,000. Estab. 1984. Sample copy free with SASE. Free photo guidelines with SASE.

Needs: Uses about 10 photos/issue; all supplied by freelance photographers. Needs family related—children, adults, family life. Usually needs to have twins, triplets or more included as well. Reviews photos with or without accompanying ms. Model release and captions required.

Making Contact & Terms: Interested in receiving work from newer, lesser-known photographers. Query with resume of credits and samples. Provide resume, business card, brochure, flyer or tearsheets to be kept on file for possible assignments. SASE. Reports in 4-6 weeks. Pays $100 minimum/cover photo. Pays on publication. Credit line given. Buys all rights. Simultaneous submissions OK.

UNITY, Unity Village MO 64065. Editor: Philip White. Associate Editor: Janet McNamara. Monthly magazine. Circ. 150,000. Emphasizes spiritual, metaphysical, self-help, poetry and inspirational articles. Free sample copy and photo guidelines.

Needs: Uses 20-25 photos/issue. Buys 280 photos/year, 90% from freelancers. Wants on a regular basis people and nature scenics for covers and 10-20 b&w scenics. Also human interest, nature, still life and wildlife. Animal photos used sparingly. Model release, captions and stock numbers required.

Making Contact & Terms: Send insured material by mail for consideration; no calls in person or by phone. Uses 5 × 7 or 8 × 10 b&w semigloss prints; 4 × 5 or 2 × 2 color transparencies. Vertical format required for cover, occasional horizontal wraparound used. Send self-addressed envelope and check or money order for return postage. Do not send stamps or stamped envelopes. 7-8 month lead time

for seasonal material. Reports in 4-8 weeks. Pays $35/b&w photo; $200/cover, $65-125 inside color photo. Pays on acceptance. Credit line given. Buys first N.A. serial rights.
Tips: "Don't overwhelm us with hundreds of submissions at a time. We look for nature scenics, human interest, some still life and wildlife, photos of active people (although the primary interest of the photo is not on the person or persons). We are looking for photos with a lot of color and contrast."

❦**UP HERE,** P.O. Box 1350, Yellowknife, NT X1A 2N9 Canada. (403)920-4652. FAX: (403)873-2844. Editor: R. Allerston. Bimonthly magazine. Estab. 1984. Emphasizes Canada's north. Readers are white collar men and women ages 30 to 60. Circ. 25,000. Sample copy $3 and 9×12 SAE. Photo guidelines free with SASE.
Needs: Uses 20-30 photos/issue; 90% supplied by freelance photographers. Purchases photos with accompanying ms only. Photo captions required.
Making Contact & Terms: Provide resume, business card, brochure, flyer or tearsheets to be kept on file for possible assignments. SASE. Reports in 1-2 months. Pays $35-100/b&w photo; $50-500/color photo; $150-500/cover. Pays on publication. Credit line given. Buys one-time rights.
Tips: "We are a *people* magazine. We need northern subjects—lots of faces. We're moving more into "outdoor adventure"—soft type, as they say in the industry—and wildlife. Few scenics as such. We approach local freelancers for given subjects, but are building a library. We can't always make use of photos alone, but a photographer could profit by sending sheets of dupes for our stock files." Wants to see "Sharp, clear photos, good color and composition—We always need verticals to consider for the cover, but they usually tie in with an article inside."

UTAH HOLIDAY MAGAZINE, Dept. PM, Suite 200, 807 E. South Temple, Salt Lake City UT 84102. (801)532-3737. Art Director: Jeff Ray. Monthly magazine. Emphasizes Salt Lake City and Utah in general. Readers are professional, business or self-employed people, 30-49 years of age. Circ. 18,000. Sample copy free with 9×12 SASE and 5 first-class stamps.
Needs: Uses 30-40 photos/issue; 100% supplied by freelance photographers. Needs photos of travel, scenics, people. Purchases photos with accompanying ms only. Model release and photo captions required.
Making Contact & Terms: Query with resume of credits and list of stock photo subjects. SASE. Reports in 1 month. Pays $300/color cover photo; $200/color inside photo; $100-150/b&w inside photo. Pays on publication. Credit line given. Buys one-time rights. Simultaneous submissions and previously published work OK.

VEGETARIAN TIMES, Dept. PM, P.O. Box 570, Oak Park IL 60303. (708)848-8100. Art Director: Dawn Fend. Published 12 times annually. Circ. 100,000. Sample copy $2.
Needs: Buys 80 photos/year; 90% specific, 10% stock. Primary: food (with styling) to accompany articles. Celebrity/personality (if vegetarians), sport, spot news, how-to (cooking and building), humorous. Model release and captions preferred.
Making Contact & Terms: Send material by mail for consideration. SASE. Reports in 6 weeks. Uses 8×10 glossy prints. Pays $40 minimum b&w/photos. Pays $300 up/(color slide) cover. Pays 30 days after acceptance. Rights vary. Credit line given. Simultaneous submissions OK.
Tips: "We consider composition, color usage, flair with food when reviewing photographer's samples."

VENTURE, P.O. Box 150, Wheaton IL 60189. (708)665-0630. FAX: (708)665-0372. Editor: Deborah Christensen. Art Director: Robert Fine. Magazine published 6 times/year. Circ. 20,000. Estab. 1959. Sample copy $1.85 with 9×12 SAE and 98¢ postage. "We seek to provide entertaining, challenging, Christian reading for boys 10-15." Photo guidelines available (SASE).
Needs: Photos of boys involved in sports, hobbies, camping, family life and just having fun. Also need photos of interest to boys: ecology, nature, adventure, occupations, etc. Buys 2-3 photos/issue. Buys 100% from freelance stock.
Making Contact & Terms: Arrange a personal interview to show portfolio or send photos for consideration. Send 8×10 b&w glossy prints. SASE. Reports in 6 weeks. Pays $35/inside photo; $75-100/cover photo. Pays on publication. Buys first serial rights. Simultaneous submissions and previously published work OK.

VERMONT LIFE, 61 Elm St., Montpelier VT 05602. (802)828-3241. Editor: Tom Slayton. Quarterly magazine. Circ. 90,000. Estab. 1946. Emphasizes life in Vermont: its people, traditions, way of life, farming, industry and the physical beauty of the landscape for "Vermonters, ex-Vermonters and would-be Vermonters." Sample copy $4 with 9×12 SAE; free photo guidelines.
Needs: Buys 30 photos/issue; 90-95% supplied by freelance photographers, 5-10% from stock. Wants on a regular basis scenic views of Vermont, seasonal (winter, spring, summer, autumn), submitted 6 months prior to the actual season; animal; documentary; human interest; humorous; nature; photo essay/photo feature; still life; travel; and wildlife. "We are using fewer, larger photos and are especially

interested in good shots of wildlife, birds." No photos in poor taste, nature close-ups, cliches or photos of places other than Vermont. Model and property releases preferred. Captions required.

Making Contact & Terms: Interested in receiving work from newer, lesser-known photographers. Query first. Send 35mm or 2¼×2¼ color transparencies. SASE. Reports in 3 weeks. Pays $75-200/b&w photo; $75-200/color photo; $100-200/day; $700-800 job. Pays on publication. Credit line given. Buys one-time rights; negotiable. Simultaneous submissions OK.

Tips: "We look for clarity of focus; use of low-grain, true film (Kodachrome is best); unusual composition or subject."

VERMONT MAGAZINE, P.O. Box 288, 14 School St., Bristol VT 05443. (802)453-3200. Picture Editor: Julie Nordmeyer. Bimonthly magazine. Emphasizes all facets of Vermont and nature, politics, business, sports, restaurants, real estate, people, crafts, art, architecture, etc. Readers are all people interested in state of Vermont, including residents, tourists and summer home owners. Circ. 50,000. Estab. 1989. Sample copy for $3, 9×12 SAE and 5 first-class stamps. Photo guidelines free with SASE.

Needs: Uses 30-40 photos/issue; 75% supplied by freelance photographers. Needs animal/wildlife shots, travel, Vermont scenics, how-to, portraits, products and architecture. Special photo needs include Vermont activities such as skiing, ice skating, biking, hiking, etc. Model release preferred; photo captions required.

Making Contact & Terms: Query with resume of credits and samples of work. Send 8×10 b&w prints or 35mm or larger transparencies by mail for consideration; submit portfolio for review; provide tearsheets to be kept on file for possible assignments. SASE. Reports in 1 month. Pays $450/color cover photo; $200/color page rate. Pays on publication. Photo credit given. Buys one-time rights and first N.A. serial rights. Previously published work OK, depending on "how it was previously published."

Tips: In portfolio or samples, wants to see tearsheets of published work, and at least 40 35mm transparencies. Looking for creative solutions to illustrate regional activities, profiles and lifestyles.

VIDEOMAKER MAGAZINE, P.O. Box 4591, Chico CA 95927. (916)891-8410. Editor: Stephen Muratore. Art Director: Sarah Ellis. Monthly magazine. Emphasizes video production from hobbyist to low-end professional level. Readers are mostly male, ages 25-40. Circ. 60,000. Estab. 1986. Sample copy free with 9×12 SAE.

Needs: Uses 50-60 photos/issue; 10-15% supplied by freelancers. Subjects include videomakers in action and video/film production settings. Reviews photos with or without ms. Model/property release and photo captions preferred.

Making Contact & Terms: Send unsolicited photos by mail for consideration; any size or format, color or b&w. SASE. Reports in 1 month. NPI. Pays on publication. Credit line given. Rights negotiable. Simultaneous submissions and previously published work OK.

*VISTA, Suite 600, 999 Ponce, Coral Gables FL 33134. (305)442-2462. FAX: (305)443-7650. Editor: Renato Perez. Monthly newspaper insert. Emphasizes Hispanic life in the U.S.A. Readers are Hispanic Americans of all ages. Circ. 1.2 million. Estab. 1985. Sample copy available.

Needs: Uses 10-50 photos/issue; all supplied by freelancers. Needs photos mostly of personalities with story only. No "stand-alone" photos. Reviews photos with accompanying ms only. Special photo needs include events in the Hispanic American communities. Model/property release preferred. Photo captions required.

Making Contact & Terms: Provide resume, business card, brochure, flyer or tearsheets to be kept on file for possible assignments. Keeps samples on file. SASE. Reports in 3 weeks. Pays $300/color cover photo; $150/color inside photo; $75/b&w inside photo; day assignments are negotiated. Pays on publication. Credit line given. Buys one-time rights. Previously published work OK.

Tips: "Build a file of personalities and events. Hispanics are America's fastest-growing minority."

VOLLEYBALL MONTHLY, Dept. PM, P.O. Box 3137, San Luis Obispo CA 93401. (805)541-2294. FAX: (805)541-2438. Co-Publishers/Editors: Jon Hastings, Dennis Steers. Monthly. Emphasizes volleyball. Readers are volleyball enthusiasts. Circ. 60,000. Estab. 1982. Sample copy free with 9×12 SASE and $2 postage.

Needs: Model release preferred; captions required.

Making Contact & Terms: Query with samples. Send b&w prints or transparencies by mail for consideration. SASE. Reports in 2 weeks. Pays $150/color cover photo; $25-50/b&w photo; $50-150/color photo; $150-300/day. Pays on publication. Credit line given. Buys one-time rights.

WASHINGTONIAN, Ste. 200, 1828 L St. NW, Washington DC 20036. (202)296-3600. FAX: (202)785-1822. Photo Editor: Kathleen Hennessy. Monthly city/regional magazine emphasizing Washington metro area. Readers are 40-50, 54% female, 46% male and middle to upper middle professionals. Circ. 160,000. Estab. 1965.

Needs: Uses 75-150 photos/issue; 100% supplied by freelance photographers. Needs photos for illustration, portraits, reportage; tabletop of products, food; restaurants; nightlife; house and garden; fashion; and local and regional travel. Model release preferred; photo captions required.
Making Contact & Terms: Submit portfolio for review; provide resume, business card, brochure, flyer or tearsheets to be kept on file for possible assignments. Pays $125-250/b&w photo; $150-300/color photo; $175-$350/day. Credit line given. Buys one-time rights ("on exclusive shoots we share resale").
Tips: "Read the magazine you want to work for. Show work that relates to their needs. Offer photostory ideas. Send samples occasionally of new work."

WATERWAY GUIDE, 6255 Barfield Rd., Atlanta GA 30328. FAX: (404)256-3116. Editor: Judith Powers. Quarterly cruising guide. Emphasizes recreational boating. Readers are men and women ages 25-65, management or professional, with average income $95,000 a year. Circ. 70,000. Estab. 1947. Sample copy $27.95 and $3 shipping. Photo guidelines free with SASE.
Needs: Uses 25-50 photos/issue; 100% supplied by freelance photographers. Needs photos of boats, Intracoastal Waterway, bridges, landmarks, famous sights and scenic waterfronts. Expects to use more coastal shots from Maine to the Bahamas; also, more Great Lakes and Gulf of Mexico. Model release and photo captions required.
Making Contact & Terms: Send unsolicited photos by mail for consideration. Send b&w and color prints or 35mm transparencies. SASE. Reports in 2 months. Pays $600/color cover photo or $25/b&w inside photo; $50-500/color photo. Pays on publication. Credit line given. Buys first N.A. serial rights.

*WEEKLY READER, US KIDS, READ, CURRENT SCIENCE, 245 Long Hill Rd., Middletown CT 06457. (203)638-2657. FAX: (203)638-2609. Graphics Director: Vickey Bolling. Weekly, biweekly and monthly magazines; 8½ × 11 newspaper. Emphasizes news and education for children. Readers are male and female children, ages 4 thru 15. Combined circ. 10,000,000. Estab. 1928. Sample copy free with 8½ × 11 SASE.
Needs: Uses 5 photos/issue; yearly over 10,000 photos; all supplied by stock houses. Needs photos of animal/wildlife, travel, scenics, technology, personalities, how-to, etc. Special photo needs include more children in photos; regular events, e.g. Memorial Day Parades, Martin Luther King Day. Model release required for children. Captions required; include name of people, ages, date, location, etc.
Making Contact & Terms: Query with resume of credits. Query with list of stock photo subjects. Send unsolicited 11 × 14 (maximum) b&w and color prints; 35mm, 2¼ × 2¼, 4 × 5, 8 × 10 transparencies by mail for consideration. Provide business card, brochure, flyer or tearsheets to be kept on file for possible assignments. Keeps samples on file. SASE. Reports in 1 month. Pays $250/color and b&w cover or inside photo; $250/color or b&w page rate; $10-100/hour; $400-800/day. Pays on publication. Credit line given. Buys one-time rights; all rights at times; negotiable. Simultaneous submissions and previously published work OK.
Tips: In samples looks for "juvenile news photos. Be as professional and organized as possible."

WEIGHT WATCHERS, Dept. PM, 360 Lexington Ave., New York NY 10017. (212)370-0644. Editor: Lee Haiken. Art Director: Shelly Stansfield. Monthly magazine. For those interested in weight control, fitness, nutrition, inspiration and self-improvement. Circ. 1,000,000.
Needs: All on assignment: food and tabletop still life, beauty, health and fitness subjects, fashion, personality portraiture. All photos contingent upon editorial needs.
Making Contact & Terms: Photos purchased on assignment only. Portfolio—drop-off policy only. Buys approximately 12 photos/issue. Pays $300/single page; $500/spread; $700/cover. Credit line given. Pays on acceptance. Buys first rights.

WESTERN HORSEMAN, 3850 N. Nevada Ave., P.O. Box 7980, Colorado Springs CO 80933. (719)633-5524. FAX: (719)633-1392. Editor: Pat Close. Monthly magazine. Circ. 198,000. Estab. 1936. For active participants in horse activities, including pleasure riders, ranchers, breeders and riding club members. Model release required. Captions required (include name of subject, date, location).
Needs: Articles and photos must have a strong horse angle, slanted towards the western rider—rodeos, shows, ranching, stable plans, training. We also buy 35mm color slides for our annual cowboy calendar. Slides must depict ranch cowboys/cowgirls."
Making Contact & Terms: Submit material by mail for consideration. Pays $10-25/b&w photo; $50-150/color photo. "We buy mss and photos as a package. Payment for 1,500 words with b&w photos ranges from $100-400. Buys first rights.

The code NPI (no payment information given) appears in listings that have not given specific payment amounts.

WESTERN OUTDOORS, 3197-E Airport Loop, Costa Mesa CA 92626. Editor-in-Chief: Burt Twilegar. Magazine published 9 times/year. Circ. 138,000. Estab. 1961. Emphasizes hunting, fishing for 11 western states, Alaska, Western Mexico and Canada. Sample copy $1.50 with SASE. Free editorial guidelines; with SASE.

Needs: Cover photos of hunting and fishing in the Western states. "We are moving toward 100% four-color books, meaning we will be buying only color photography in the near future. A special subject need will be photos of boat-related fishing, particularly small and trailerable boats." Most photos purchased with accompanying ms. Model/property release preferred; captions required.

Making Contact & Terms: Interested in receiving work from newer, lesser-known photographers. Query or send photos for consideration. Send 35mm Kodachrome II transparencies. Captions required. SASE. Reports in 4 weeks. Pays $25-100/b&w photo; $25-150/color photo; $200-250/cover photo; $400-500 for text/photo package. Pays on acceptance for covers. Buys one-time rights "but will negotiate."

Tips: "Submissions should be of interest to western fishermen or hunters, and should include a 1,120-1,500 word ms; a Trip Facts Box (where to stay, costs, special information); photos; captions; and a map of the area. Emphasis is on fishing and hunting how-to, somewhere-to-go. Submit seasonal material 6 months in advance. Make your photos tell the story and don't depend on captions to explain what is pictured. Avoid 'photographic cliches' such as 'dead fish with man,' dead pheasants draped over a shotgun, etc. Get action shots, live fish and game. We avoid the 'tame' animals of Yellowstone and other national parks. In fishing, we seek individual action or underwater shots. For cover photos, use vertical format composed with action entering picture from right; leave enough left-hand margin for cover blurbs, space at top of frame for magazine logo. Add human element to scenics to lend scale. Get to know the magazine and its editors. Ask for the year's editorial schedule (available through advertising department) and offer cover photos to match the theme of an issue. In samples, looks for color saturation, pleasing use of color components; originality, creativity; attractiveness of human subjects as well as fish or game; above all—sharp, sharp, sharp focus! Send duplicated transparencies as samples, but be prepared to provide originals." Sees trend toward electronic imagery, computer enhancement and electronic transmission of images.

♦**WESTERN SPORTSMAN,** P.O. Box 737, Regina, Saskatchewan S4P 3A8 Canada. (306)352-2773. FAX: (306)565-2440. Editor: Roger Francis. Bimonthly magazine. Audited Circ. 26,000. Estab. 1967. Emphasizes fishing, hunting and outdoors activities in Alberta, Saskatchewan and Manitoba. Sample copy $4; free photo/writer's guidelines with SASE.

Needs: Sport (fishing, hunting, camping); nature; and wildlife. Captions required. Buys 100 freelance photos/year; 90% freelancers "who send stuff on a whim" and 10% stock. Photos purchased with or without accompanying ms. Accompanying mss on fishing, hunting and camping.

Making Contact & Terms: Interested in receiving work from newer, lesser-known photographers. Send material by mail for consideration or query with a list of stock photo subjects. Uses 35mm and 2¼ × 2¼ transparencies, vertical format for cover preferred. SASE. Reports in 3 weeks. Pays $75-200/ color photo; $250-350/cover photo; $75-325/ms; $350/photo/text package. Pays on acceptance. Buys one-time rights.

Tips: Looks for "covers—strong vertical components that work well within our established masthead layout; interiors—crisp, clear definition of main figure. Animal *action* rather than animal portraiture. Close up shots or still shots of animals and fish often look posed. Reality comes through with movement and dimension. Don't let the main subject look like a stuffed museum piece! Send a small selection for the photo editor to review. We keep notes on many photographers, their strengths and weaknesses—and often call back for specific items."

WESTWAYS, Dept. PM, P.O. Box 2890, Los Angeles CA 90051. (213)741-4760. FAX: (213)741-3033. Art Director: Don Letta. Emphasizes Western US and world travel, leisure time activities, people, history, culture and western events. Estab. 1909.

Making Contact & Terms: Query first with sample of photography enclosed. Pays $50-200/b&w photo; $50-450/color transparency; $300-350 plus $50 per photo published for text/photo package.

Tips: "We like to get photos with every submitted manuscript. We take some photo essays (with brief text), but they must be unusual and of interest to our readers. All photos should be tack sharp originals for final reproduction and well captioned. Trends in our use of editorial photography include high drama and high photographic art."

WHEELINGS, P.O. Box 389, Franklin MA 02038. (508)528-6211. Editor: J.A. Kruza. Published 6 times/year, tabloid magazine. Emphasizes auto body shops, auto paint shops, auto dealers, auto paint manufacturers. Readers are auto industries with 8 or more employees. Circ. 14,000. Photo guidelines free.

Needs: Uses 25 photos/issue; usually 10-15 supplied by freelance photographers. "We need news-type photos relating to the industry." Captions required.
Making Contact & Terms: Query with samples. SASE. Reports in 2 weeks. Pays $25 first photo, $10 for each additional photo; buys 3-5 photos in a series. Pays on acceptance. Credit line given. Prefers all rights; reassigns to photographer after use. Simultaneous submissions and previously published work OK.

*WHERE CHICAGO MAGAZINE, 1165 N. Clark St., Chicago IL 60610. (312)642-1896. FAX: (312)642-5467. Editor: Margaret Doyle. Monthly magazine. Emphasizes shopping, dining, nightlife and entertainment available in Chicago and its suburbs. Readers are male and female traveling executives and tourists, ages 25-55. Circ. 100,000/month. Estab. 1985. Sample copy $3.
Needs: Uses 1 photo/issue; 90% supplied by freelancers. Needs scenic, seasonal shots of Chicago, must include architecture or landmarks that identify a photo as being shot in Chicago. Reviews photos with or without a manuscript. "We look for seasonal shots on a monthly basis." Model/property release required. Photo captions required.
Making Contact & Terms: Send unsolicited photos by mail for consideration. Provide resume, business card, brochure, flyer or tearsheets to be kept on file for possible assignments. Send 35mm, 2¼×2¼, 4×5, 8×10 transparencies. SASE. Reports in 1 month. Pays $300/color cover photo. Pays on acceptance. Credit line given. Buys one-time rights. Rights negotiable. Simultaneous submissions and previously published work OK.
Tips: "We only consider photos of downtown Chicago, without people in them. Shots should be colorful and current, in a vertical format. Keep our deadlines in mind. We look for covers two months in advance of issue publication."

WHERE MAGAZINE, 15th Floor, 600 Third Ave., New York NY 10016. (212)687-4646. FAX: (212)687-4661. Editor-in-Chief: Michael Kelly Tucker. Estab. 1936. Monthly. Emphasizes points of interest, shopping, restaurants, theater, museums, etc., in New York City (specifically Manhattan). Readers are visitors to New York staying in the city's leading hotels. Circ. 119,000/month. Sample copy available in hotels.
Needs: Buys cover photos only. Covers showing New York scenes; color photos only. Vertical compositions preferred. No mss. Model release and captions preferred.
Making Contact & Terms: Interested in receiving work from newer, lesser-known photographers. Arrange a personal interview to show portfolio. Does not return unsolicited material. Pays $300/color photo. Pays on publication. Credit line given. Rights purchased vary. Simultaneous submissions and previously published work OK.

*THE JAMES WHITE REVIEW, P.O. Box 3356, Traffic Station, Minneapolis MN 55403. (612)339-8317. Art Editor: Terry Carlson. A gay men's literary quarterly. Emphasizes gay men's writing, poetry and artwork. Readers are mostly gay men. Estab. 1983. Sample copy $3.
Needs: Uses 8-10 photos/issue; 100% supplied by freelancers. Reviews photos with or without a manuscript. Photo captions preferred; include title of work and media used.
Making Contact & Terms: Send unsolicited photos by mail for consideration. Send 5×7 or 8×10 glossy b&w prints. Keeps samples on file. SASE. Reports in 1 month. Pays $25/b&w cover photo; $25-50/photo package. Pays on publication. Credit line given. Buys one-time rights. Simultaneous submissions and previously published work OK.
Tips: "We are seeking work by emerging and established gay male artists, any style and theme. Please include biographical information."

WILDLIFE CONSERVATION MAGAZINE, Dept. PM, New York Zoological Park, Bronx NY 10460. (212)220-5121. FAX: (212)584-2625. Editor: Joan Downs. Picture Consultant: Niki Barrie. Photo Researcher: Miriam Helbok. Bimonthly. Emphasizes wildlife conservation and natural history, especially of endangered species. Readers include mature people (over 12), interested in wildlife and nature. Circ. 140,000. Sample copy available for $2.95; photo guidelines free with SASE.
Needs: Uses 60 photos/issue; supplied by freelance photographers, researchers and agencies. Needs wildlife photos. Captions required.
Making Contact & Terms: Query with list of stock photo subjects. Send ideas for photo essays but do not send unsolicited photos. Reports in 1 month. Pays $50-200/b&w photo; $75-400/color photo. Other page sizes and rates available; request rate sheet. Pays on publication. Credit line given. Buys one-time rights. Simultaneous submissions OK.
Tips: "We're looking for very striking images that can be blown up large and still be very clear." In portfolio or samples, wants to see "brilliant color, unusual views and wildlife in action." To break in, "compile a fairly specific list of species and geographic areas; concentrate on specific species; get series of behavioral shots."

WIN MAGAZINE, #213, 16760 Stagg St., Van Nuys CA 91406. Editor: Cecil Suzuki. Monthly magazine. Circ. 50,000. Emphasizes gambling.
Needs: Buys 6-12 photos/issue. Celebrity/personality (in a gambling scene, e.g., at the track); sport (of football, basketball, jai alai and all types of racing); and gambling scenes. Model release not required if photo is of a general scene; photo captions preferred. Uses 5×7 or 8×10 b&w prints; contact sheet OK. Also uses transparencies or color prints. Vertical format preferred.
Making Contact & Terms: Send material by mail for consideration. SASE. Reports in 4 weeks. Credit line given. Pays on publication. Buys all rights. Pays $5-25/b&w photo; $75/color cover.

*WINDSURFING, P.O. Box 2456, Winter Park FL 32790. (407)628-4802. Photo Editor: Lisa Damerst. Monthly magazine. Emphasizes boardsailing. Readers are all ages and all income groups. Circ. 70,000. Sample copy free with SASE. Photo guidelines free with SASE.
Needs: Uses 80 photos/issue; 60% supplied by freelance photographers. Needs photos of boardsailing, flat water, recreational travel destinations to sail. Model release and captions preferred.
Making Contact & Terms: Query with samples; send unsolicited photos by mail for consideration; provide resume, business card, brochure, flyer or tearsheets to be kept on file for possible future assignments. Send 35mm, 2¼×2¼ and 4×5 transparencies by mail for consideration. Kodachrome and slow Fuji preferred. SASE. Reports in 3 weeks. Pays $20-100/b&w page; $30-350/color page. Credit line given. Buys one-time rights unless otherwise agreed on. Simultaneous submissions OK.
Tips: Prefers to see razor sharp, colorful images. The best guideline is the magazine itself. "Get used to shooting on, in or under water. Most of our needs are found there."

WISCONSIN TRAILS, Dept. PM, P.O. Box 5650, Madison WI 53705. (608)231-2444. Photo Editor: Nancy Mead. Bimonthly magazine. For people interested in history, travel, recreation, personalities, the arts, nature and Wisconsin in general. Circ. 30,000. Photo guidelines with SASE; sample copy $3.
Needs: Seasonal scenics and photos relating to Wisconsin. Annual Calendar: uses horizontal format; scenic photographs. Wants no color or b&w snapshots, color negatives, cheesecake, shots of posed people, b&w negatives ("proofs or prints, please") or "photos of things clearly not found in Wisconsin." Buys 200 photos annually.
Making Contact & Terms: Query with resume of credits, arrange a personal interview to show portfolio, submit portfolio or submit contact sheet or photos for consideration. Provide calling card and flyer to be kept on file for possible future assignments. Send contact sheet or 5×7 or 8×10 b&w glossy prints. "We greatly appreciate caption info." Most done on assignment. Send transparencies; "We use all sizes." Locations needed. Send 35mm, 2¼×2¼ or 4×5 transparencies for cover; "should be strong seasonal scenics or people in action." Uses vertical format; top of photo should lend itself to insertion of logo; or a square to be boxed. Locations preferred. SASE. Reports in 3 weeks. Pays $200/calendar and cover photos; $50/b&w photo. Pays on publication. Buys first serial rights or second serial (reprint) rights. Simultaneous submissions OK "only if we are informed in advance." Previously published work OK.
Tips: "Because we cover only Wisconsin and because most photos illustrate articles (and are done by freelancers on assignment), it's difficult to break into *Wisconsin Trails* unless you live or travel in Wisconsin." Also, "be sure you specify how you want materials returned. Include postage for any special handling (insurance, certified, registered, etc.) you request."

WITH, P.O. Box 347, Newton KS 67114. (316)283-5100. Co-editors: Eddy Hall, Carol Duerksen. Magazine published eight times a year. Circ. 5,600. Estab. 1968. Emphasizes "Christian values in lifestyle, vocational decision making, conflict resolution for US and Canadian high school students." Sample copy for 9×12 SAE and 98¢ postage; photo guidelines free with SASE.
Needs: Documentary (related to concerns of high school youth "interacting with each other, with family and in school environment; intergenerational"); fine art; head shot; photo essay/photo feature; scenic; special effects & experimental; how-to; human interest; humorous; still life; and travel. Particularly interested in action shots of teens, especially of ethnic minorities. We use some mood shots and a few nature photos. Prefers candids over posed model photos. Few religious shots, e.g., crosses, steeples, etc. Photos purchased with or without accompanying ms and on assignment. Buys 75 photos/year; 8-10 photos/issue. Buys 35% of freelance photography from assignment; 65% from stock. For accompanying mss wants issues involving youth—school, peers, family, hobbies, sports, community involvement, sex, dating, drugs, self-identity, values, religion, etc. Model release preferred. Writer's guidelines and theme list free with SASE.
Making Contact & Terms: Interested in receiving work from newer, lesser-known photographers. Send material by mail for consideration. Uses 8×10 b&w glossy prints. SASE. Reports in 6 weeks. Pays $20-35/b&w photo inside; $30-50/b&w cover photo; 4¢/word for text/photo packages, or on a per-photo basis. Pays on acceptance. Credit line given. Buys one-time rights. Simultaneous submissions and previously published work OK.

Tips: "Freelancers are our lifeblood. We're interested in photo essays, but good ones are scarce. Candid shots of youth doing ordinary daily activities and mood shots are what we generally use. Photos dealing with social problems are also often needed. We rely greatly on freelancers, so we're interested in seeing work from a number of photographers. *With* is one of several periodicals published at this office, and we also publish Sunday school curriculum for all ages here, so there are many opportunities for photographers. Needs to relate to teenagers—either include them in photos or subjects they relate to; using a lot of 'nontraditional' roles, also more ethnic and cultural diversity, more emphasis on current global events. Use models who are average-looking, not obvious model-types. Teenagers have enough self-esteem problems without seeing 'perfect' teens in photos."

WOMAN ENGINEER, Equal Opportunity Publications, Inc., 44 Broadway, Greenlawn NY 11740. (516)261-8917. FAX: (516)261-8935. Editor: Anne Kelly. Quarterly magazine. Emphasizes career guidance for women engineers, at the college and professional levels. Readers are college-age and professional women in engineering. Circ. 16,000. Estab. 1979. Sample copy free with 9 × 12 SAE and 6 first-class stamps.
Needs: Uses at least one photo per issue (cover); planning to use freelance work for covers and possibly editorial; most of the photos are submitted by freelance writers with their articles. Contact for needs. Model release preferred; photo captions required.
Making Contact & Terms: Query with list of stock photo subjects or call to discuss our needs. SASE. Reports in 2 weeks. Pays $25/color cover photo; $15/b&w photo; $15/color photo. Pays on publication. Credit line given. Buys one-time rights. Simultaneous submissions and previously published work OK, "but not in competitive career-guidance publications."
Tips: "'We are looking for strong, sharply focused photos or slides of women engineers. The photo should show a woman engineer at work, but the background should be uncluttered. The photo subject should be dressed and groomed in a professional manner. Cover photo should represent a professional woman engineer at work, convey a positive and professional image. Read our magazine, and find actual women engineers to photograph. We're not against using cover models, but we prefer cover subjects to be women engineers working in the field."

WOMAN'S WORLD, Dept. PM, 270 Sylvan Ave., Englewood Cliffs NJ 07632. (201)569-0006, Ext. 400. Editor-in-Chief: Dena Vane. Photo Editor: Melinda Patelli. Weekly. Emphasizes women's issues. Readers are women 25-60 nationwide of low to middle income. Circ. 1,200,000. Sample copies available.
Needs: Uses up to 100 photos/issue; all supplied by freelancers and stock houses. Needs travel, fashion, crafts and celebrity shots. "For editorial pages we look for informative straightforward photos of women's careers, travel, people in everyday personal situations—couples arguing, etc., and medicine. Photographers should be sympathetic to the subject, and our straightforward approach to it." Photos purchased with or without accompanying ms. Model release and captions required. "Not responsible for any materials sent on spec. Please talk with someone at the magazine before sending anything."
Making Contact & Terms: Query with 8 × 10 b&w glossy prints or 35mm transparencies or provide basic background and how to contact. Prefers to see tearsheets of published work, or prints or slides of unpublished work, as samples. SASE. Reports in 1 month. Provide resume and tearsheets to be kept on file for possible future assignments. Pays $250/day plus expenses; $300/page for color and fashion; $150-200/day for b&w. Pays on acceptance. Credit line given. Buys one-time rights.

WOMEN'S SPORTS AND FITNESS MAGAZINE, Dept. PM, Suite 421, 1919 14th St., Boulder CO 80302. (303)440-5111. Photo Editor/Art Director: Janis Llewelyn. Monthly. Readers are active women who are vitally interested in health and fitness. Recreational interests include participation in two or more sports, particularly cycling, running and swimming. Circ. 250,000. Sample copy and photo guidelines free with SASE.
Needs: 80% of photos supplied by freelance photographers. Call to receive photo schedule. Model release and captions preferred.
Making Contact & Terms: Call before submitting material. Provide resume, business card, brochure, flyer or tearsheets to be kept on file for possible future assignments. SASE. Reports in 1 month. Pays $400/color cover; $50-300/color inside; $200/color page. Pays on publication. Credit line given. Buys one-time rights.
Tips: Looks for "razor sharp images and nice light. Check magazine before submitting query. We look especially for photos of women who are genuinely athletic in active situations that actually represent a particular sport or activity."

WOODENBOAT MAGAZINE, Dept. PM, Naskeag Rd., P.O. Box 78, Brooklin ME 04616. (207)359-4651. Art Director: Lindy Gifford. Bimonthly magazine. Emphasizes wooden boats. Readers are builders, designers, owners and lovers of wooden boats. Circ. 120,000. Estab. 1974. Sample copy $3.50 with 9 × 12 SASE and $1.50 postage. Photo guidelines free with SASE.

Needs: Uses 100-150 photos/issue; 20-50% supplied by freelance stock; 0-10% assigned. Needs photos relating to articles. "Much better chance of purchase with ms." Model release required only for advertising purposes; captions preferred (indicate boat name and location).
Making Contact & Terms: Query with samples. SASE. Reports in 3 weeks. Pays $350/color cover photo; $15-75/b&w photo; $25-350/color photo; $100-300/day and complete job. Pays on publication. Credit line given. Buys first N.A. serial rights. Simultaneous submissions and previously published work OK with notification.
Tips: "Please become familiar with our publication before contacting us."

*WORDSMITH, P.O. Box 891, Ft. Collins CO 80522-0891. (303)224-5218. Editor: Brian Kaufman. Annual magazine. Readers interested in poetry and fiction. Estab. 1991. Sample copy $3. Photo guidelines free with SASE.
Needs: Uses 1 photo/issue. "This is a literary magazine. We look at many different styles and subjects. We will consider submissions from all areas." Reviews photos with or without a manuscript. Model/property release required.
Making Contact & Terms: Send unsolicited photos by mail for consideration. Send 5×7 b&w, color prints. Keeps samples on file. SASE. Pays $25/color cover photo; $25/b&w cover photo; $10/b&w inside photo. Pays on publication. Credit line given. Buys one-time rights.
Tips: "We look for visual art that will help to sell our magazine."

WORKBENCH MAGAZINE, 4251 Pennsylvania Ave., Kansas City MO 64111. FAX: (816)531-3873. Editor: Robert N. Hoffman. Managing Editor: A. Robert Gould. Bimonthly magazine. Circ. 860,000. Estab. 1957. Emphasizes do-it-yourself projects for the woodworker and home remodeler. Free sample copy and photo guidelines.
Needs: Looks for residential architecture (interiors and exteriors of homes), wood crafts, furniture, wood toys and folk art. How-to; needs step-by-step shots. Model and property releases required for product shots, homeowner's or craftspeople's projects and profile shots. Captions required, include people's names and what action is shown in photo. Photos are purchased with accompanying ms. "We also purchase photos to illustrate articles, including 'beauty' lead photographs." Free writer's guidelines.
Making Contact & Terms: Ask for writer's guidelines, then send material by mail for consideration. Uses 5×7 or 8×10 b&w glossy prints; 2¼×2¼ or 4×5 transparencies and 8×10 color glossy prints; 4×5 color transparencies for cover, vertical format required. SASE. Reports in 4 weeks. Pay for b&w photos included in purchase price of ms.; $125 minimum/color photo; $450 minimum/cover photo; $150-300/published page. Pays on acceptance. Credit line given with ms. Buys all rights; negotiable.
Tips: Prefers to see "sharp, clear photos; they must be accompanied by story with necessary working drawings. See copy of the magazine. We are happy to work with photographers in developing story ideas."

WRESTLING WORLD, Lexington Library, Inc., 355 Lexington Ave., New York NY 10017. FAX: (212)986-5926. Editor: Stephen Ciacciarelli. Magazine published bimonthly. Emphasizes professional wrestling superstars. Readers are wrestling fans. Circ. 50,000. Sample copy $2.95 with 9×12 SAE and 75¢ postage.
Needs: Uses about 60 photos/issue; all supplied by freelance photographers. Needs photos of wrestling superstars, action and posed, color slides and b&w prints.
Making Contact & Terms: Query with representative samples, preferably action. SASE. Reports ASAP. Pays $150/color cover photo; $75/color inside photo; $50-125/text/photo package. Pays on acceptance. Credit line given on color photos. Buys one-time rights.

YELLOW JERSEY PUBLICATIONS: TEXAS BICYCLIST, FLORIDA BICYCLIST AND CALIFORNIA BICYCLIST, Dept. PM, 490 Second St., #304, San Francisco CA 94107. (415)546-7291. Contact: Editor. Monthly tabloid. Emphasizes bicycling. Readers are 80% male-20% female professionals, ages 18 and older. Circ. 300,000. Estab. 1983. Sample copy for 10×14 SASE with $1 postage.
Needs: Uses 15-20 photos/issue; most supplied by freelance photographers. Needs photos of bicycling—all aspects. Model release preferred.
Making Contact & Terms: Query with list of stock photo subjects. SASE. Reports "when we can get to it." Pays $300/color cover photo; $50/color inside photo; $50/b&w inside photo. Pays on publication. Credit line given.

YELLOW SILK: Journal of Erotic Arts, P.O. Box 6374, Albany CA 94706. (510)644-4188. Editor: Lily Pond. Quarterly magazine. Circ. 16,000. Emphasizes literature, arts and erotica. Readers are well educated, creative, liberal. Sample copy $7.50

Needs: Uses about 15-20 photos "by one artist" per issue. Have published the work of Judy Dater, Tee Corinne, Sandra Russell Clark, Stephen John Phillips and Jan Saudek. "All photos are erotic; none are cheesecake or sexist. No porn. We define 'erotic' in its widest sense; trees and flowers can be as erotic as humans making love. They are fine arts." Model release required.
Making Contact & Terms: Query with samples; submit prints, transparencies, contact sheets or photocopies by mail for consideration; submit portfolio for review. SASE. Reports in 3 months. NPI. Payment to be arranged. Pays on publication. Credit line given. Buys one-time rights; "use for promotional and/or other rights arranged."
Tips: "Get to know the publication you are submitting work to and enclose SASE in all correspondence. Interested in color work at this time."

YM, Dept. PM, 685 Third Ave., New York NY 10017. (212)878-8636. Photo Editor: Chantal Belsheim. Monthly magazine. Readers are girls from ages 17-21. Magazine emphasizes fashion/beauty. Circ. 1 million and growing. Sample copy free upon request. Photo guidelines available.
Needs: Needs "street photos of fashion, fashion, beauty and celebrities. Model release and photo captions preferred; "depending on subject."
Making Contact & Terms: Submit portfolio for review. Reports in 2 weeks, sometimes longer. Pays $300/color page rate or $200-250/b&w page rate. Buys all rights; non-negotiable. Simultaneous submissions and previously published work OK.
Tips: In portfolio or samples, looking for "good sense of color, light and composition." Also, photos that are "natural, fun, hip, well-styled and fairly unique." To break in, "send only your best and favorite work. Look at our magazine before contacting us."

YOUR HEALTH, 5401 NW Broken Sound Blvd., Boca Raton FL 33487. (800)233-7733, (407)997-7733. Editor: Susan Gregg. Photo Editor: Judy Browne. Biweekly magazine. Emphasizes healthy lifestyles: aerobics, sports, eating, celebrity fitness plans, plus medical advances and the latest technology. Readers are consumer audience; males and females 20-70. Circ. 40,000. Estab. 1963. Sample copy free with 9×12 SASE. Call for photo guidelines.
Needs: Uses 40-45 photos/issue; all supplied by freelance photographers. Needs photos depicting nutrition and diet, sports (runners, tennis, hiking, swimming, etc.), food, celebrity workout, pain and suffering, arthritis and bone disease, skin care and problems. Also any photos illustrating exciting technological or scientific breakthroughs. Model release required.
Making Contact & Terms: Interested in receiving work from newer, lesser-known photographers. Provide resume, business card, brochure, flyer or tearsheets to be kept on file for possible future assignments, and call to query interest on a specific subject. SASE. Reports in 2 weeks. Pay depends on photo size and color. Pays on publication. Pays $25-75/b&w photo; $75-200/color photo; $75-150/photo/text package. Buys one-time rights. Simultaneous submissions and previously published work OK.
Tips: "Pictures and subjects should be interesting; bright and consumer-health oriented. We are using both magazine-type mood photos, and hard medical pictures. We are looking for different, interesting, unusual ways of illustrating the typical fitness, health nutrition story; e.g. an interesting concept for fatigue, insomnia, vitamins. Send prints or dupes to keep on file. Our first inclination is to use what's on hand."

*YOUR HOME, Meridian Publishing, P.O. Box 10010, Ogden UT 84409. Editor/Publisher: Caroll Shreeve. Distributed to businesses to be used, with their inserts, as their house magazine. "A monthly pictorial magazine with emphasis on home decor, buying, home construction, financing, landscaping and working with realtors. Send SASE for guidelines. Sample copy $1 plus 9×12 envelope.
Needs: We prefer manuscripts (800 to 1,200 words) with color transparencies." No do-it-yourself pieces, emphasize using professionals. Model release required. Photo captions preferred.
Making Contact & Terms: Interested in receiving work from newer, lesser-known photographers. Pays 15¢/word; $35 for color transparencies. Also needed are vertical transparencies for covers. $50/cover, negotiable for outstanding work. "These should have dramatic composition with sharp, contrasting colors." Six-month lead time. Buys first North American rights. Credit line given. Payment on acceptance.
Tips: Prefers to see "interior and exterior views of homes; good interior decor ideas; packages (photos with text) on home, garden, decorating and improvement ideas." Photos and text are commonly purchased as a package. About 95% of work is assigned. Send clear sharp pictures with contrasting colors for our review. The photo department is very strict about the quality of pictures chosen for the articles."

YOUR MONEY MAGAZINE, (formerly *Money Maker Magazine*), 5705 N. Lincoln Ave., Chicago IL 60659. (312)275-3590. Editor: Dennis Fertig. Art Director: Beth Ceisel. Bimonthly personal finance, consumer magazine. Circ. 165,000. Estab. 1979.

Needs: Uses 18-25 photos/issue, 130-150 photos/year; all supplied by freelance photographers who work on assignment only. Considers all styles depending on needs. "Always looking for quality location photography, especially environmental portraiture." Model and property releases required.
Making Contact & Terms: Interested in receiving work from newer, lesser-known photographers. Arrange a personal interview to show portfolio and provide a business card, flyer or tearsheets to be kept on file. Transparencies, slides, proofs or prints returned after publication. Samples not filed are returned with SASE. Reports in 1 month. Pays up to $1,200/color cover photo; $450/b&w page; $650/color page. Pays on acceptance. Credit line given.
Tips: "Show your best work. Include tearsheets in portfolio."

*ZUZU'S PETALS QUARTERLY, P.O. Box 4476, Allentown PA 18105. (215)821-1324. Editor: T. Dunn. Quarterly magazine. Emphasis on literature. Readers are male and female literary afficianados. Circ. 150. Estab. 1992. Sample copies $5.
Needs: Uses 20 photos/issue; 50% supplied by freelancers. Needs photos of scenics (technological and natural), people and "artsy" shots. Reviews photos with or without accompanying ms. Model/property release preferred. Captions preferred, including location of subject.
Making Contact & Terms: Interested in receiving work from newer, lesser-known photographers. Send 8x10 or smaller glossy b&w prints by mail for consideration. Does not keep samples on file. SASE. Reports in 3 weeks. Pays in copies. Pays on publication. Credit line given. Buys one-time rights; negotiable. Simultaneous submissions and previously published work OK.
Tips: "We're looking for freshness, a different perspective on the everyday and the commonplace."

Newspapers & Newsletters

While many publications have seen advertising drop off in recent years, there were some signs in 1992 that the newspaper industry was improving economically. The cost of newsprint dropped and some publishers saw increases in advertising for the first time in years which is essential, since advertising makes up almost 80 percent of the revenue for many newspapers. If these trends continue it could mean good things for photographers who are trying to sell photos to weekly and daily newspapers.

While most of the newspapers in this section are interested in images that hold a regional appeal for readers, there are a number of publications interested in spot news and feature shots from all over the world. As for newsletters, many serve as information vehicles for associations with special interests and very specific audiences. Photographers should closely study the needs of each market so as not to waste time and money sending inappropriate photos.

Some photographers prefer to shoot spot news, and so they keep alert to any situations or locations that may present photo opportunities. Such photographers take their cameras with them everywhere they go. Other photographers, especially those aiming for the special interest audiences, cultivate news leads by taking part in community activities or by keeping in touch with particular fields of interest, such as politics, business, sports or entertainment. Both types of photographers watch for scheduled events and monitor other news sources such as TV and radio for tips on upcoming meetings, performances, games and other potentially newsworthy events.

One area in which photographers must be especially careful is attempting to gain entry to limited-access events. Press credentials for major sporting events, visits by political figures or appearances by celebrities are usually limited and available only to qualified, legitimate news photographers. It is very difficult to get press credentials if you do not have an assignment to cover such an event. Some photographers, unable to get the necessary identification, attempt to bluff, sneak or forge papers to get themselves into events. In some cases, some people even resort to fake IDs and certificates which certain unethical companies are marketing. Such "scams" are frowned upon by all news professionals, and using them will only do irreparable damage to your reputation.

The best method of access is still to win a photo editor's respect and assignments with good work and consistent professionalism. Many of the photos that appear in metropolitan dailies are shot by staff photographers, but some opportunities exist for freelancers to work on a "stringer," or as-needed, basis. One photographer who has almost 20 years of experience in the field of photojournalism is Melvin Grier of the *Cincinnati Post*. Grier discusses his profession on page 362 as this year's Close-up in the Newspapers & Newsletters category.

Though weekly papers are generally not represented in the listings in this section, many freelancers find that working with them first is an ideal way to gain experience and news insight, to build a portfolio of clips, and to establish a pricing structure before approaching some of the regional and national markets listed in this section. Newsletters, like newspapers, provide current news for readers. However, because of a tendency among newsletters toward monthly, bimonthly and quarterly publication cycles, the news in these markets will often be less time-bound. Like weekly newspapers, newsletters can also provide beginning photographers with excellent opportunities to break in and gain experience.

Since both of these market areas are businesses, they usually pay as little as possible. Accordingly, try to retain resale rights to shots of major news events. High news value means high resale value, and strong news photos can be resold repeatedly to the right newspapers or newsletters. Another option in making up for low payment is syndicating images to newspapers around the country. However, most photographers break into syndication from fulltime newspaper work, and usually not until they have track records which show they're capable of producing newsworthy images on a consistent basis.

If you find yourself on the scene of a breaking news event, cover it from a variety of news angles and rush it to editors of publications which may already be covering the story. Explain the story angles to each editor. If they are already planning coverage of the event which takes similar angles but they do not have photos lined up, chances are that they will want to use your photos. From there, they will negotiate a price and terms for using the photos, and you will have proved both your news sense and photojournalistic skills.

With newsletters in particular, payment often varies widely according to the publisher's budget. Corporations generally will have higher budgets for photos than will nonprofit organizations. Whether or not you decide to work with a particular newsletter will depend largely upon your interest in the type of business or activity the newsletter covers, your existing inventory of relevant images that might be purchased, or your potential to break in or receive steady work and income.

*AGRI-TIMES NORTHWEST, 206 SE Court, Box 189, Pendleton OR 97801. (503)276-7845. Editor: Virgil Rupp. Weekly newspaper. Emphasizes agriculture of eastern Oregon, eastern Washington and northern Idaho. Readers are agribusiness people and farmers, both men and women, of all ages. Circ. 5,500. Estab. 1983. Sample copy free with 9×12 SASE and 4 first-class stamps. Photo guidelines free with SASE.
Needs: Uses 15-20 photos/issue; 70% supplied by freelance photographers. Uses all agriculturally related photos including crop production and animals such as cattle, hogs, horses and sheep. Request editorial calendar for special subject needs. Model release preferred; photo captions required.
Making Contact & Terms: Query with list of stock photo subjects. Send unsolicited photos by mail for consideration. Send 5×7 or 8×10 glossy b&w prints. SASE. Reports in 1 month. "All b&w $10 per photo except 1 column photo, which is $5." Pays on publication. Credit line given. Buys one-time rights. Simultaneous submissions OK.
Tips: Especially looking for "photos of farmers and farming in our circulation area."

AMERICAN METAL MARKET, 825 7th Ave., New York NY 10019. (212)887-8550. FAX: (212)887-8520. Capital Cities/ABC, Inc. Diversified Publishing Group. Editor: Michael G. Botta. Daily newspaper. Emphasizes metals production and trade. Readers are top level management (CEO's, chairmen, and presidents) in metals and metals related industries. Circ. 13,000. Estab. 1882. Sample copies free with 10×13 SASE.
Needs: 90% of photos supplied by freelancers. Needs photos of press conferences, executive interviews, industry action shots and industry receptions. Photo captions required.
Making Contact & Terms: Provide resume, business card, brochure, flyer or tearsheets to be kept on file for possible assignments. Cannot return material. Credit line given. NPI. Buys all rights; negotiable. Simultaneous submissions OK.
Tips: "We tend to avoid photographers who are unwilling to release all rights. We produce a daily newspaper and maintain a complete photo file. We cover events worldwide and often need to hire freelance photographers. Best bet is to supply business card, phone number and any samples for us

to keep on file. Keep in mind action photos are difficult to come by. Much of the metals industry is automated and it has become a challenge to find good 'people' shots."

AMERICAN SPORTS NETWORK, Box 6100, Rosemead CA 91770. (818)572-4727. President: Louis Zwick. Publishes four newspapers covering "general collegiate, amateur and professional sports; i.e., football, baseball, basketball, track and field, wrestling, boxing, hockey, powerlifting and bodybuilding, etc." Circ. 50,000-755,000.
Needs: Uses about 10-85 photos/issue in various publications; 90% supplied by freelancers. Needs "sport action, hard-hitting contact, emotion-filled photos. Have special bodybuilder annual calendar, collegiate and professional football pre- and post-season editions." Model release and captions preferred.
Making Contact & Terms: Send 8×10 glossy b&w prints and 4×5 transparencies by mail for consideration. Provide resume, business card, brochure, flyer or tearsheets to be kept on file for possible future assignments. SASE. Reports in 1 week. Pays $1,000/color cover photo; $250/inside b&w photo; negotiates rates by the job and hour. Pays on publication. Buys first N.A. serial rights. Simultaneous and previously published submissions OK.

ANCHORAGE DAILY NEWS, Dept. PM, 1001 Northway Dr., Anchorage AK 99508. (907)257-4347. Editor: Howard Weaver. Photo Editor: Richard Murphy. Daily newspaper. Emphasizes all Alaskan subjects. Readers are Alaskans. Circ. 60,000. Estab. 1946. Sample copy free with 11×14 SASE and $2 postage.
Needs: Uses 10-50 photos/issue; 5% supplied by freelance photographers; most from assignment. Needs photos of all subjects, primarily Alaskan subjects. In particular, looking for freelance images for travel section; wants photos of all areas, especially Hawaii. Model release and captions required.
Making Contact & Terms: Contact photo editor with specific ideas. SASE. Reports in 1-3 weeks. Pays $25 minimum/b&w photo; $35 minimum/color photo: photo/text package negotiable. Pays on publication. Credit line given. Buys one-time rights. Simultaneous submissions OK.
Tips: "We, like most daily newspapers, are primarily interested in timely topics, but at times will use dated material." In portfolio or samples, wants to see "eye-catching images, good use of light and active photographs. More color is being used on a daily basis."

*AUDITIONING, Suite 220, 115 W. Allegan St., Lansing MI 48933. (517)485-7800. Publisher: Ben Campbell. Quarterly newsletter. Emphasizes acting in T.V. commercials, screenplays. Readers are actors, actresses, producers and directors of all ages. Circ. 5,000. Estab. 1991. Sample copy $20. Photo guidelines $5.
Needs: Buys 20-30 photos/issue; 10-20 supplied by freelancers. Photographs of celebrities, movie stars, producers, travel, personalities, how-to. Reviews photos of movie producers. Model release and captions preferred.
Making Contact & Terms: Arrange a personal interview to show portfolio. Query with resume of credits. Query with list of stock photo subjects. Send unsolicited b&w or color prints; 35mm, 2¼×2¼, 4×5 or 8×10 transparencies by mail for consideration. Submit portfolio for review. Provide resume, business card, brochure, flyer or tearsheets to be kept on file for possible assignments. SASE. Reports in 3 weeks. Pays $100/color cover photo; $50/b&w cover photo; $50/color inside photo; $35/b&w inside photo; $50/color page rate; $35/b&w page rate. Pays on publication. Credit line given. Buys one-time rights and first N.A. serial rights. Simultaneous submissions and previously published work OK.
Tips: "Be patient. Look for the ideal time to enhance your career. Don't take no for an answer. Always be on time. Be persuasive. Use graphics when designing your resume. Write and use a biography or a personal history in addition to your resume."

AVSC NEWS, 79 Madison Ave., New York NY 10016. (212)561-8000. FAX: (212)779-9439. Editor: Robert Goldberg. Publications Manager: Pam Harper. Publication of the Association for Voluntary Surgical Contraception. Quarterly newsletter. Emphasizes health care, contraception. Readers are health care professionals in the US and abroad. Circ. 4,500. Estab. 1962. Sample copies for 4×9 SASE.
Needs: Uses 2-3 photos/issue; 1 supplied by freelancer. Needs photos of mothers and fathers with children in US and developing worlds. Photos only; does not accept mss. Special needs include annual report 15-20 photos; brochures throughout the year. Model release required; captions preferred.

The asterisk before a listing indicates that the market is new in this edition. New markets are often the most receptive to freelance submissions.

Making Contact & Terms: Interested in receiving work from a newer, lesser-known photographer. Query with list of stock photo subjects. Reports in 2 weeks. Pays $100-200/b&w cover photo; $50-150/b&w inside photo. Pays on publication. Buys one-time rights. Previously published work OK.
Tips: Prefers to see a "sharp, good range of tones from white through all greys to black, and appealing pictures of people."

BAJA TIMES, P.O. Box 5577, Chula Vista CA 91912. General Manager: Carlos Chabert. Editor: John W. Utley. Emphasizes Baja California and Mexico travel and history. Readers are travelers to Baja California, Mexico and Baja aficianados from all over US and Canada. Monthly Circ. 65,000. Estab. 1978. Free sample copy and writer/photographer guidelines with SASE (9×12) and $1 postage.
Needs: Uses about 12 photos/issue; most supplied by freelance photographers. Needs current travel, scenic, wildlife, historic, women, children, fishing, Baja fashions and beach photos. Photos purchsed with or without accompanying ms. Special needs include: History of cities in Baja California and resorts, Baja shopping, sports and general recreation. Model release preferred. Captions required; include who, what, when, where and why.
Making Contact & Terms: Interested in receiving work from a newer, lesser-known photographer. Send by mail for consideration b&w prints, or query with list of stock photo subjects. Now using full color photos for front cover. Avidly seeking outstanding Baja California, Mexico subjects. Will review color prints, but prefer transparencies for publication. Reports in 6 weeks. Pays $5-10/b&w photos; $45/color cover photo. Buys one-time rights.
Tips: "We need sharp photography with good definition. Photo essays are welcome but please remember the basic subject matter is Baja California, Mexico."

BANJO NEWSLETTER INC., Box 364, Greensboro MD 21639. (301)482-6278. Editor: Hub Nitchie. Monthly. Emphasizes 5-string banjo information. Readers include musicians, teachers. Circ. 8,000.
Needs: Uses 3-8 photos/issue; very few supplied by freelance photographers. Needs musical instruments, cases, well known banjo players, bands, PR shots; could include technical instruction. Model release preferred.
Making Contact & Terms: Query with samples; usually writers provide photos from banjo manufacturers or musicians. Reports in 1 month. Pays $40-50/b&w cover photo, $10-15/b&w inside photo. Pays on publication. Credit line given. Buys one-time rights. Simultaneous submissions and previously published work OK with permission from publisher.

BEAR ESSENTIAL NEWS FOR KIDS, Dept. PM, P.O. Box 26908, Tempe AZ 85285. (602)345-READ. Executive Editor: Bob Henschen. Monthly newspaper. Circ. 500,000. Estab. 1979.
Needs: Uses 5-10 photos/issue; 1-2 supplied by freelancers. Model release preferred. Photo captions preferred.
Making Contact & Terms: Arrange a personal interview to show portfolio. Send b&w, color prints. SASE. Reports in 2 months. Pays $100/color cover photo; $25/any inside photo. Pays on publication. Credit line given. Buys all rights; negotiable. Simultaneous submissions OK. Would appreciate stock list.

CALIFORNIA SCHOOL EMPLOYEE, P.O. Box 640, San Jose CA 95106. (408)263-8000, ext. 298. FAX: (408)954-0948. Senior Designer: Lisa Yordy. Publication labor union, California School Employees Association (CSEA). Monthly (October-July) newspaper. Circ. 100,000+. Estab. 1932. Sample copy free upon request.
Needs: Uses freelance photos on assignment (70%) and from stock (30%). Needs photos of people. Special photo needs include school work sites, crowds, school and college related; wants to see facial emotion, action. Model release required; photo captions required including subject names.
Making Contact & Terms: Interested in receiving work from newer, lesser-known photographers. Provide resume, business card, brochure, flyer or tearsheets to be kept on file for possible assignments. SASE. NPI; payment negotiable. Pays on publication. Credit line given. Rights purchased are negotiable. Simultaneous submissions and previously published work OK.
Tips: "Know publisher's subject matter."

THE CAPITAL, 2000 Capital Dr., Annapolis MD 21401. (301)268-5000. Graphics Editor: Brian Henley. Daily newspaper. Circ. 45,000. Estab. 1877.
Needs: Uses 25 photos/issue; 1 supplied daily by freelancer; one monthly from freelance stock. Needs stock slides on boating, football, aging (senior citizens). Model release/captions preferred.
Making Contact & Terms: Query with list of stock photo subjects. Send unsolicited photos by mail for consideration. Submit portfolio for review. Uses b&w and color prints; 35mm transparencies. Reports in 1 week. Pays $50/color cover photo; $30/b&w cover photo; $20/color inside photo; $15/b&w inside photo. Pays on publication. Credit line given. Buys one-time rights.
Tips: "We use mostly spot news from freelancers."

CAPPER'S, 616 Jefferson, Topeka KS 66607. (913)295-1108. Editor: Nancy Peavler. Estab. 1879. Bi-weekly tabloid. Emphasizes human-interest subjects. Readers are "mostly Midwesterners in small towns and on rural routes." Circ. 370,000. Sample copy 85¢.

Needs: Uses about 20-25 photos/issue, "one or two" supplied by freelance photographers. "We make no photo assignments. We select freelance photos with specific issues in mind." Needs "35mm color slides of human-interest activities, nature (scenic), etc., in bright primary colors. We often use photos tied to the season, a holiday or an upcoming event of general interest." Captions preferred.

Making Contact & Terms: Interested in receiving work from newer, lesser-known photographers. "Send for guidelines and a sample copy (SASE, 85¢ postage). Study the types of photos in the publication, then send a sheet of 10-20 samples with caption material for our consideration. Although we do most of our business by mail, a phone number is helpful in case we need more caption information. Phone calls to try to sell us on your photos don't really help." Reporting time varies. Pays $10-15/b&w photo; $15-25/color photo; only cover photos receive maximum payment. Pays on publication. Credit line given. Buys one-time rights.

Tips: "Generally, we're looking for photos of everyday people doing everyday activities. If the photographer can present this in a pleasing manner, these are the photos we're most likely to use. Season shots are appropriate for Capper's, but they should be natural, not posed. We steer clear of dark, mood shots; they don't reproduce well on newsprint. Most of our readers are small town or rural Midwesterners, so we're looking for photos with which they can identify. Although our format is tabloid, we don't use celebrity shots and won't devote an area much larger than 5×6 to one photo."

CATHOLIC HEALTH WORLD, Dept. PM, 4455 Woodson Rd., St. Louis MO 63134. (314)427-2500. FAX: (314)427-0029. Editor: Suzy Farren. Publication of Catholic Health Association. Biweekly newspaper emphasizing healthcare—primary subjects dealing with our member facilities. Readers are hospital and long-term care facility administrators, public relations staff people. Circ. 7,000. Estab. 1985. Sample copy free with 9×12 SASE.

Needs: Uses 4-15 photos/issue; 1-2 supplied by freelancers. Any photos that would help illustrate health concerns (i.e., pregnant teens, elderly). Model release required.

Making Contact & Terms: Send unsolicited photos by mail for consideration. Uses 5×7 or 8×10 b&w glossy prints. SASE. Reports in 2 weeks. Pays $40-60/photo. Pays on publication. Credit line given. Buys one-time rights. Simultaneous submissions OK.

THE CHICAGO TRIBUNE MAGAZINE, Dept. PM, Room 532, 435 N. Michigan Ave., Chicago IL 60611. (312)222-3232. Editor: Denis Gosselin. Managing Editor: Jack Wade. Weekly. Profiles, in-depth stories, photo essays, book excerpts. Readers are basically the Tribune's audience (general), with slightly higher demographics. Circ. 1.1 million. Sample copy free with 11×14 SASE.

Needs: Uses 25 photos/issue; number supplied by freelancers varies. Needs photos of various kinds of stock and occasional out-of-town assignments. Model release preferred; captions required.

Making Contact & Terms: Query with list of stock photo subjects. Provide resume, business card, brochure, flyer or tearsheets to be kept on file for possible future assignments. SASE. Reports in 2 weeks. NPI. Payment negotiable; different areas of magazine pay on their own scale. Pays on publication. Credit line given. Buys one-time rights, first N.A. serial rights or all rights for assignment photography. Will negotiate with photographer unwilling to sell all rights. Simultaneous submissions and previously published work OK.

Tips: "We're looking for photos that tell a story, not just random samples of photographers' works. The Tribune has a staff of almost 50 photographers, so make sure that what you're offering is something that we can't get ourselves. Prefers regional subjects."

CMD PROFILES, (formerly *Construction Today*), 7625 Ora Glen Dr., Green Belt MD 20770. Editor: Jim Neeham. Weekly tabloid. Emphasizes construction. Readers are construction company executives and estimators, especially in Washington and Baltimore metropolitan areas. Circ. 4,000. Sample copy free with SASE.

Needs: Uses 2-10 photos/issue; 1 supplied by freelance. Needs photos of construction. Model release, photo captions preferred.

Making Contact & Terms: Provide resume, business card, brochure, flyer or tearsheets to be kept on file for possible assignments. SASE. Reports in 1 month. Payment negotiable. Pays on publication. Credit line given. Buys all rights; negotiable. Simultaneous submissions and previously published work OK.

THE COLUMBUS TIMES NEWSPAPER, Dept. PM, 2230 Buena Vista Rd., Columbus GA 31906. (404)324-2404. Managing Editor: Helmut Gertjegerdes. Weekly newspaper. Emphasizes minority news (African-American and Spanish). Readers are teenagers to senior citizens, professionals, men and women. Circ. 10,000. Estab. 1959. Free sample copy. No photo guidelines.

Needs: Uses 10 photo/issue; 1-2 supplied by freelancers. Needs photos of events and news stories. Especially wants to see "minority news from third world nations." Model release and photo captions preferred.
Making Contact & Terms: Provide resume, business card, brochure, flyer or tearsheets to be kept on file for possible assignments. Send 4×5 b&w prints. SASE. Reports in 3 weeks. Pays $10/b&w cover photo. Pays on publication. Credit line given. Buys all rights; negotiable. Simultaneous submissions OK.

COMMERCIAL PROPERTY NEWS, Dept. PM, 1515 Broadway, New York NY 10036. (212)869-1300. Editor-in-chief: Mark A. Klionsky. Biweekly tabloid emphasizing commercial real estate. Readers are commercial real estate developers, brokers, property managers and financial institutions. Circ. 37,000. Sample copy available.
Needs: Uses 60 photos/issue; 5% supplied by freelancers. Needs photos of people and buildings. Model release required; captions preferred.
Making Contact & Terms: Query with samples or list of stock photo subjects. Reports in 2 weeks. Pays $250/b&w cover; $300/color cover; $50/b&w inside photo; $125/hour; $100/job. Pays on publication. Credit line sometimes given. Simultaneous and previously published work OK.

CRAIN'S DETROIT BUSINESS, 1400 Woodbridge, Detroit MI 48207. (313)446-6000. Graphics Editor: Nancy Kassen. Weekly tabloid. Emphasizes business. Estab. 1985. Sample copy for 11×14 SASE and 2 first-class stamps.
Needs: Uses 30 photos/issue; 9-10 supplied by freelancers. Needs environmental portraits of business executives illustrating product and/or specialty. Model release preferred; photo captions required.
Making Contact & Terms: Arrange a personal interview to show a portfolio. Submit portfolio for review. Provide resume, business card, brochure, flyer or tearsheets to be kept on file for possible assignments. SASE. Reports in 2 weeks. NPI; pays on acceptance. Credit line given. Buys one-time rights.

CYCLE NEWS, Dept. PM, P.O. Box 498, Long Beach CA 90801. (310)427-7433. Publisher: Michael Klinger. Editor: Jack Mangus. Art Director: Ree Johnson. Weekly tabloid. Emphasizes motorcycle news for enthusiasts and covers nationwide races. Circ. 45,000. Estab. 1964.
Needs: Needs photos of motorcycle racing accompanied by written race reports; prefers more than one bike to appear in photo. Wants current material. Buys 1,000 photos/year. Buys all rights, but may revert to photographer after publication.
Making Contact & Terms: Send photos or contact sheet for consideration or call for appointment. "Payment on 15th of the month for issues cover-dated the previous month." Reports in 3 weeks. SASE. For b&w: send contact sheet, negatives (preferred for best reproduction) or prints (5×7 or 8×10, glossy or matte), captions required, pays $10 minimum. For color: send transparencies. captions required, pays $50 minimum. For cover shots: send contact sheet, prints or negatives for b&w; transparencies for color, captions required, payment negotiable.
Tips: Prefers sharp action photos utilizing good contrast. Study publication before submitting "to see what it's all about." Primary coverage area is nationwide.

*THE DAILY NEWS, P.O. Box 189, Longview WA 98632. (206)577-2522. FAX: (206)577-2538. Photo Editor: Roger Werth. Company publication. Newspaper. Circ. 24,000.
Needs: Needs lifestyle shots, "newsy photos of people and sports." Reviews photos with accompanying ms only. Model/property release preferred. Captions required.
Making Contact & Terms: Provide resume, business card, brochure, flyer or tearsheets to be kept on file for possible assignments. Send b&w, color prints; 35mm transparencies. Reports in 1-2 weeks. Pays $35/all photos. Pays on publication. Buys one-time rights. Simultaneous submissions OK.

EAST BAY EXPRESS, Dept. PM, 3234 Adeline St., Berkeley CA 94703. (510)652-4610. Photo Editor: Steve Aibel. Weekly newspaper. Readers are students and professionals ages 18-45. Circ. 100,000. Estab. 1979.

Can't find a listing? Check at the end of each market section for the " '92-'93 Changes" lists. These lists include any market listings from the '92 edition which were either not verified or deleted in this edition.

Needs: Uses 10 photos/issue; 100% supplied by freelancers. Needs environmental portraits. Model release required.
Making Contact & Terms: Arrange a personal interview to show portfolio. SASE. Reports in 2 weeks. Pays $200/color cover photo; $150/b&w cover photo; $50/b&w inside photo. Pays on publication. Credit line given. Buys one-time rights.
Tips: Wants to see "b&w images where the photographer controls the subject. No 'street shooters.' "

EYECARE BUSINESS, 50 Washington St., Norwalk CT 06854. (203)838-9100. FAX: (203)838-2550. Art Director: Marianne Gjersvik. Monthly tabloid. Emphasis on the eyecare industry—frames, contact lenses, service and fashion. Readers are opticians and optometrists. Circ. 35,000.
Needs: Uses 60 photos/issue; 12 supplied by freelancers. Needs photos of people in eyeglasses; eyeglasses. Model release and captions required.
Making Contact & Terms: Query with samples. Provide resume, business card, brochure, flyer or tearsheets to be kept on file for possible future assignments. Does not return unsolicited material. Pays $400/color cover photo; $200/color inside photo. Pays on publication. Credit line given. Buys all rights; negotiable.

FISHING AND HUNTING NEWS, Dept. PM, 511 Eastlake Ave. E., Box C-19000, Seattle WA 98109. (206)624-3845. Managing Editor: Vence Malernee. Photo Editor: Dave Ellithorpe. Biweekly tabloid. Emphasizes how-to material, fishing and hunting locations and new products for hunters and fishermen. Circ. 133,000. Free sample copy and photo guidelines.
Needs: Buys 300 or more photos/year. Wildlife—fish/game with successful fishermen and hunters. Captions required.
Making Contact & Terms: Send samples of work for consideration. Uses 5×7 or 8×10 glossy b&w prints or negatives for inside photos. Uses color covers and some inside color photos—glossy 5×7 or 8×10 color prints, 35mm, 2¼×2¼ or 4×5 color transparencies. When submitting 8×10 color prints, negative must also be sent. SASE. Reports in 2 weeks. Pays $5-15 minimum/b&w print, $50-100 minimum/cover and $10-20 editorial color photos. Credit line given. Pays on acceptance. Buys all rights, but may reassign to photographer after publication. Submit model release with photo.
Tips: Looking for fresh, timely approaches to fishing and hunting subjects. Query for details of special issues and topics. "We need newsy photos with a fresh approach. Looking for near-deadline photos from Oregon, California, Utah, Idaho, Wyoming, Montana, Colorado, Texas, Alaska and Washington (sportsmen with fish or game)."

FLORIDA GROWER AND RANCHER, Dept. PM, 1331 N. Mills, Orlando FL 32803. (407)894-6522. Editor: Frank Garner. Monthly. Emphasizes commercial agriculture in Florida. Readers are "professional farmers, growers and ranchers in the state of Florida." Sample copy and photo guidelines free with 9×12 SASE and $1 postage.
Needs: Uses about 20-25 photos/issue; "presently few" supplied by freelance photographers. Needs photos of "Florida growers and ranchers in action in their day-to-day jobs. Prefers modern farm scenes, action of specific farm which can be identified." Model release preferred; captions required.
Making Contact & Terms: Query with stock photo list. Provide resume, business card, brochure, flyer or tearsheets to be kept on file for possible future assignments. SASE. Reports in 3 weeks. Pays $10/b&w; $50/color cover. Pays by the line plus photo for text/photo package. Pays on publication. Credit line given if required. Buys one-time rights.
Tips: "Query first—photography usually tied in with writing assignment."

FULTON COUNTY DAILY REPORT, Dept. PM, 190 Pryor St. SW, Atlanta GA 30303. (404)521-1227. Art Director: Andrea Kock. Daily newspaper, 5 times/week. Emphasizes legal news and business. Readers are male and female professionals age 25 up, involved in legal field, court system, legislature, etc. Sample copy 75¢, 9½×12½ SASE and $1.50 postage.
Needs: Uses 5-10 photos/issue; 30% supplied freelancers. Needs informal environmental photographs of lawyers, judges and others involved in legal news and business. Some real estate, etc. Especially wants to be able to get "a good freelancer in Georgia when I need one." Photo captions preferred; complete name of subject and date shot, along with other pertinent information. Two or more people should be identified from left to right.
Making Contact & Terms: Submit portfolio for review—call first. Query with list of stock photo subjects. Keeps samples on file. SASE. Reports in 1 month. "Freelance work generally done on an assignment-only basis." Pays $75/assignment (this covers first publication of photo). Then $25 is paid for subsequent publication. Pays on publication. Credit line given. Simultaneous submissions and previously published work OK.
Tips: Wants to see ability with "casual, environmental portraiture, people—especially in office settings, urban environment, courtrooms, etc.; and photojournalistic coverage of people in law or courtroom settings." In general, needs "competent, fast freelancers from time to time around the state of

Georgia who can be called in at the last minute. We keep a list of them for reference. Good work keeps you on the list." Recommends that "when shooting for FCDR, it's best to avoid law-book-type photos if possible, along with other overused legal cliches."

GENERAL AVIATION NEWS & FLYER, P.O. Box 98786, Tacoma WA 98498-0786. (206)588-1743. FAX: (206)588-4005. Editor: Dave Sclair. Biweekly tabloid. General aviation newspaper for private pilots, homebuilders and owner-flown business aviation. Readers are pilots, experimental aircraft builders. Circ. 40,000. Estab. 1949. Sample copy $3.50; photo guidelines free with SASE ($1 postage).
Needs: Uses about 25-30 photos/issue; 40-50% supplied by freelancers. Needs photos of aircraft, destinations, aviation equipment. Photos purchased with accompanying ms only. Complete captions required for each photo.
Making Contact & Terms: Query with samples; "news photos may be sent unsolicited." Send b&w or color prints, contact sheets, negatives by mail for consideration. "Query first on slides." SASE. Reports in 2 weeks. Pays $10-25/b&w inside photo; $15-50/color photo; up to $3/column inch plus $10/ photo used for text/photo package. Credit line given. Buys one-time rights.
Tips: "Learn something about aviation subjects—we don't need or use pictures of air show teams flying maneuvers, airplanes flying overhead, people patting their airplanes affectionately, etc."

GIFT AND STATIONERY BUSINESS, Dept. PM, 1515 Broadway, New York NY 10036. (212)869-1300. Editor: Katherine Krassner. Monthly tabloid. Emphasizes trend and merchandising information of interest to gift and stationery retailers. Readers are gift retailers. Circ. 40,000. Sample copy free with SASE.
Needs: "Cover shot and 5 inside shots by assignment only" supplied by freelance photographers. Needs environmental portraits, plus store shots or showroom shots. Special needs include 1 cover shot per month in various geographic locations.
Making Contact & Terms: Provide resume, business card, brochure, flyer or tearsheets to be kept on file for possible future assignments. Does not return unsolicited material. Reports in 1 month. Pays $350-500/job. Pays on acceptance. Credit line given on cover. Buys all rights; negotiable.
Tips: Wants "imaginative and insightful portraits of retailers and manufacturers in their work environment."

GLOBE, Dept. PM, 5401 NW Broken Sound Blvd., Boca Raton FL 33487. (407)997-7733. Photo Editor: Ron Haines. Weekly tabloid. Circ. 2,000,000. "For everyone in the family. *Globe* readers are the same people you meet on the street, and in supermarket lines—average, hard-working Americans."
Needs: Needs human interest photos, celebrity photos, humorous animal photos, anything unusual or offbeat. Captions required. Buys all photos from freelancers.
Making Contact & Terms: Pays $75/b&w photo (negotiable); $125/color photo (negotiable); day and package rates negotiable. Buys first serial rights. Send 8×10 b&w glossy transparencies or color prints for consideration. Pays on publication unless otherwise arranged. Reports in 1 week. SASE. Previously published work OK.
Tips: Advises beginners to look for the unusual, offbeat shots. "Do not write for photo guidelines. Study the publication instead. Tailor your submission to my market." Use of color is increasing.

🖋GRAIN MATTERS, Dept. PM, Box 816, 423 Main St., Winnipeg MB, R3C 2P5 Canada. (204)983-3423. Information Officer: Brian Stacey. Bimonthly newsletter. Emphasizes grain industry, transportation (rail and water). Readers are farmers (ages 18 and over). Circ. 150,000. Sample copy free with SASE.
Needs: Uses 2 photos/issue; 1 supplied by freelance photographer. Needs photos of farm scenes, grain deliveries, country elevators, terminal elevators, railcars, lake vessels and farm meetings. Photo captions required.
Making Contact & Terms: Provide resume, business card, brochure, flyer or tearsheets to be kept on file for possible assignments. Cannot return material. Pays $100 (Canadian)/inside photo. Pays on acceptance. Buys one-time rights. Previously published work OK.

GRIT, 208 W. 3rd St., Williamsport PA 17701. (717)326-1771. Contact: Assignment Editor. Weekly tabloid. Emphasizes "people-oriented material which is helpful, inspiring and uplifting. When presenting articles about places and things, it does so through the experiences of people. Readership is small-town and rural America." Circ. 600,000.
Needs: Photos purchased with or without accompanying ms. Buys "hundreds" of photos/year. Needs on a regular basis "photos of all subjects, provided they have up-beat themes that are so good they surprise us. Human interest, sports, animals, celebrities. Get action into shot, implied or otherwise, whenever possible. Be certain pictures are well composed, properly exposed and pin sharp. All color transparencies for the cover are square in format. We use 35mm and up." Captions required. "Single b&w photos that stand alone must be accompanied by 50-100 words of meaningful caption informa-

Close-up

Melvin Grier
Staff Photographer
Cincinnati Post
Cincinnati, Ohio

"Newspaper work can be the most rewarding, the most exciting career you can imagine," says Melvin Grier, a former "Ohio News Photographer of the Year." "There are moments that are so great, it makes the job all worth it. However, those days are rare, and the average day as a photojournalist is very routine."

Grier's photographs are anything but routine and have been shown in many exhibits throughout Ohio. In 1982, he was nominated for a Pulitzer Prize for his photos of El Salvador. He also is active with galleries and community arts programs in Cincinnati.

His interest in photography began in the military service. "As luck would have it, I entered a contest open to military persons and won a first and second place prize," says Grier. When his career as a medic ended, he returned to Cincinnati, to learn photography.

For Grier, this meant finding work in a commercial studio. "I took out the Yellow Pages, made some phone calls and put on a suit. The first few studios didn't show any interest, but I kept on looking," he says. Persistence paid off when he landed a job doing catalog work. He stayed with it for about a year, but wasn't satisfied.

Always interested in what he now calls "street photography," Grier pursued photography in a more photojournalistic approach. After working eight years shooting half-tones for a printing company Grier finally got the break he needed in 1974 when a position opened up at the *Cincinnati Post*.

"Basically, newspaper photographers have to do a lot of things," says Grier. "We have to cover the news, handle sports photography and are required to do work for sections like the Living department." Grier is a firm believer that newspaper photographers make the best photographers. "We have to do so many things, and sometimes that clouds the issue of whether or not I'm the right photographer for the job. One day I'm shooting a fire and an hour later I'm shooting interiors." Grier finds this to be an advantage because it creates many challenges and provides great diversity in his shooting.

"Newspapers have changed from a vocation to more of a business," says Grier. "They don't have the same mix of people, the same passions I used to see. When I started, I worked with some real characters, people with real defined personalities who were in the business because they loved journalism."

He remembers the feeling of being a crusader, of trying to go out and right society's wrongs. "I don't see that as much anymore, partly because of ownership changes and also due to economic realities," says Grier. "Television has taken a lot away from us, it has become more a part of a person's mental image of the news than reading the paper. Newspapers don't have the immediacy that television offers."

Grier also attributes the change to "the media-representative types." "These are the people who make sure I take the picture they want to show," explains Grier. It used to be that he could walk into a situation, look around, and decide where he wanted to take pictures. Now somebody manages that aspect of his job.

"I started learning how to photograph for a newspaper. This means coming in a little tighter on the shot and keeping all the information right there. I also learned the pace of newspaper photography. It's get it in and get it out . . . bang!" says Grier.

After 18 years with the *Post*, he still aims to find something positive in every story. "We are in the business of exploiting people," says Grier. "We need to be able to use them in order to produce our product. Newspaper photographers always show up at the worst possible moment. There are feelings of guilt and invasions, and sometimes you have to back off." Sometimes this means walking away from a scene and from a photograph. One of his finest moments in photojournalism occurred when he walked away from a shot. It was a rare occasion, but the tragedy was too great to misuse. A mother was grieving over her lost son, and Grier was there to see it all.

But he also has learned the fine art of persistence. "You never ask them if you can do it, you just do it," declares Grier. "Make them tell you to stop; make them kick you out!"

With all his experience, Grier is asked weekly, if not daily, for his advice on how to get into the business. "My perspective is different from the kid who comes down and 'hangs out' for the day. To someone new, what I do can be pretty exciting." He doesn't try to talk them out of anything, he just tries to make them understand that the business has changed. "There is still a lot of work to be done and many opportunities," he says. "However, some of the things that used to be a given, just aren't there, and the work has gotten harder."

— Gretchen Wukasch

In both of these photos, Melvin Grier does exactly what a photojournalist should do — he tells stories. Whenever a photographer enters a child's world, whether it's in a school or on a Cincinnati playground, left, children always mug for the camera. In this case, Grier had the children line up for the shot, but they kept waving their hands to get in the photo. After he ordered them to quit waving, they had these surprised looks. On the right, the natural lighting, the man's grizzled face and the card game show the loneliness that exists in a home for disadvantaged men in Cincinnati.

tion." Model release preferred. "No cheesecake. No pictures that cannot be shown to any member of the family. No pictures that are out of focus or grossly over/or under-exposed. No ribbon-cutting, check-passing or hand-shaking pictures."

Making Contact & Terms: Send material by mail for consideration. Uses transparencies for cover only. SASE. Previously published work OK. Pays on acceptance. Reports in 2-3 weeks. Sample copy $1, photo guidelines free with SASE. Pays $35/b&w photo; $15/b&w photo for second rights. Pays $25/photo for pix accompanying mss, $10 for reprints rights on pix accompanying mss. Pays 12¢/word, first rights; 6¢/word for second or reprint rights. Free writer's guidelines for SASE. Buys one-time, first serial or second serial (reprint) rights.

Tips: "Good major-holiday subjects seldom come to us from freelancers. For example, Easter, Fourth of July, Christmas or New Year. "Remember that *Grit* publishes on newsprint and therefore requires sharp, bright, contrasting colors for best reproduction. Avoid sending shots of people whose faces are in shadows; no soft focus. When photo requires action make sure action is *in* photo."

GUARDIAN NEWSWEEKLY, Dept. PM, 33 W. 17th St., New York NY 10011. (212)691-0404. Photo Editor: Greg Jocz. Weekly newspaper. Emphasizes "progressive politics and national and international news; focuses on Third World and on women's movement, disarmament, labor, economy, environment, grassroots community groups." Readers are "activists, students, workers; we have subscribers around the world." Circ. 20,000. Sample copy for SASE and $1 postage.

Needs: Uses about 25 photos/issue; "at least 50%" supplied by freelance photographers. Needs "news photos—local, international and national. Includes mugs of figures in the news, local rallies and features, most to accompany stories." Captions preferred.

Making Contact & Terms: Prefers query with 2 samples or list of stock photo subjects. Send any size b&w glossy prints by mail for consideration. SASE. Reports in 1 month "or sooner." Pays $15/b&w inside photo. Pays on publication. Credit line given. Buys one-time rights. Simultaneous and previously published submissions OK.

Tips: Prefers to see "good quality, good sense of political side of subject *and* human interest aspect" in samples. "We pay low rates, but our photos are often requested by other publications for reprinting and they will pay photographer, too. We feature photos on cover and in centerfold." In portfolio or samples, wants to see "flexibility, good news sense, full compositions which make a statement, boldness. Get up close to subjects, avoid posed shots." Needs "more coverage from geographical areas other than Northeast US."

*GULF COAST GOLFER, Suite 212, 9182 Old Katy Rd., Houston TX 77055. (713)464-0308. Editor: Bob Gray. Monthly tabloid. Emphasizes golf in the gulf coast area of Texas. Readers average 48.5 years old, $72,406 income, upscale lifestyle and play golf 2-5 times weekly. Circ. 30,000. Sample copy free with SASE and $2 postage.

Needs: Uses about 20 photos/issue; none supplied by freelance photographers. "Photos are bought only in conjunction with purchase of articles." Photos purchased with accompanying ms only. Model release and captions preferred.

Making Contact & Terms: "Use the telephone." SASE. Reports in 2 weeks. NPI. Pays on publication. Credit line given. Buys one-time rights or all rights, if specified.

INSIDE TEXAS RUNNING, Dept. PM, 9514 Bristlebrook, Houston TX 77083. (713)498-3208. Publisher/Editor: Joanne Schmidt. Monthly tabloid. Emphasizes running and jogging with biking insert. Readers are Texas runners and joggers of all abilities. Circ. 10,000. Estab. 1977. Sample copy $2.50

Needs: Uses about 20 photos/issue; 10 supplied by freelancers. 80% percent of freelance photography in issue comes from assignment from freelance stock. Needs photos of "races, especially outside of Houston area; scenic places to run; how-to (accompanying articles by coaches); also triathlon and bike tours and races." Special needs include "top race coverage; running camps (summer); variety of Texas running terrain." Captions preferred.

Making Contact & Terms: Send b&w or color glossy prints by mail for consideration. SASE. Reports in 1 month. Pays $10-15/b&w or color photo; $25 per photo/text package. Pays on publication. Credit line given. Buys one-time rights. Simultaneous submissions outside Texas and previously published work OK.

Tips: Prefers to see "human interest, contrast and good composition" in photos. Transparencies are now used for covers. "Look for the unusual. Race photos tend to look the same." Wants "clear photos with people near front; too often photographers are too far away when they shoot and subjects are a dot on the landscape." Wants to see road races in Texas outside of Houston area.

INTENSIVE CARING UNLIMITED, Dept. PM, 910 Bent Lane, Philadelphia PA 19118. (215)233-4723. Editor: Lenette S. Moses. Bimonthly newsletter. Covers children with medical or developmental problems. Readers are families—all ages. Circ. 3,000. Estab. 1983. Samples copy free with 65¢ postage. Photo guidelines free with SASE.

Needs: Uses 2-3 photos/year; all supplied by freelancers. Needs photos of parents with babies or children, parents or children alone, medical professionals with babies. Special photo needs include premature babies, high-risk pregnant mothers, grieving parents, families. Model release required; photo captions preferred.
Making Contact & Terms: Query with list of stock photo subjects. Send unsolicited 2¼×2¼ or 4×5 glossy or matte b&w photos by mail for consideration. SASE. Reports 1 month. Credit line given. NPI. Buys one-time rights. Simultaneous submissions and previously published work OK.
Tips: "Ours is a nonprofit organization. We offer no pay, but photographers get nationwide exposure."

JAZZ TIMES, 7961 Eastern Ave., Silver Spring MD 20910. (800)866-7664. FAX: (301)588-2009. Assignment Editor: Mike Joyce. Monthly tabloid. Emphasizes jazz. Readers are jazz fans, record consumers, music industry. Circ. 57,000. Estab. 1969. Sample copy $3.50
Needs: Uses about 35 photos/issue; all supplied by freelance photographers. Needs performance shots, portrait shots of jazz musicians. Captions preferred.
Making Contact & Terms: Interested in receiving work from a newer, lesser-known photographer. Send 5×7 b&w prints by mail for consideration. SASE. "If possible, we keep photos on file till we can use them." Pays $50/b&w cover slide; $10/b&w inside photo. Pays $50/color photo. Pays on publication. Credit line given. Buys one-time or reprint rights; negotiable.
Tips: "Send whatever photos you can spare. We keep them on file until we can use them. Name and address should be on back."

JEWISH EXPONENT, Dept. PM, 226 S. 16th St., Philadelphia PA 19102. (215)893-5740. Managing Editor: Al Erlick. Weekly newspaper. Emphasizes news of impact to the Jewish community. Circ. 70,000.
Needs: Buys 15 photos/issue. On a regular basis, wants news and feature photos of a cultural, heritage, historic, news and human interest nature involving Jews and Jewish issues. Query as to photographic needs for upcoming year. No art photos. Photos purchased with or without accompanying mss. Captions required. Uses 8×10 glossy prints; 35mm or 4×5 transparencies.
Making Contact & Terms: Pays $15-50/hour; $10-100/job. Also pays $10-35/b&w print; $10-75/color print or transparency; $10-75/cover photo. Credit line given. Pays on publication. Buys one-time, all, first serial, first North American serial and all rights. Rights are negotiable. Query with resume of credits or arrange a personal interview. "Telephone or mail inquiries first are essential. Do not send original material on speculation." Provide resume, business card, letter of inquiry, samples, brochure, flyer and tearsheets to be kept on file. SASE. Model release required "where the event covered is not in the public domain." Reports in 1 week. Free sample copy.
Tips: "Photographers should keep in mind the special requirements of high-speed newspaper presses. High contrast photographs probably provide better reproduction under newsprint and ink conditions."

THE JOURNAL OF LIGHT CONSTRUCTION, Box 146, RR2, Richmond VT 05477. (802)864-5495. Art Director: Theresa Emerson. Monthly tabloid. Emphasizes light construction. Readers are architects, remodelers. Circ. 70,000. Sample copy free; photo guidelines free with SASE.
Needs: Uses 20 photos/issue; 5 supplied by freelancers. Needs photos of contruction work in progress. Model release preferred; captions required.
Making Contact & Terms: Query with samples. Send unsolicited photos by mail for consideration. Provide resume, business card, brochure, flyer or tearsheets to be kept on file for possible future assignments. Uses 35mm, 2¼×2¼, 4×5 and 8×10 transparencies. SASE. Reports in 1 month. Pays $250/color cover photo; $20/color inside photo. Pays on acceptance. Credit line given. Buys first N.A. serial rights. Previously published work OK.
Tips: "*The Journal of Light Construction* has 12 themes for its issues. Covers reflect these themes. An editorial calendar is available by request."

*KANE COUNTY CHRONICLE, 1000 Randall Rd., Geneva IL 60134. (708)232-9255 Ext. 336. Chief Photographer: Robert Gerrard. Daily newspaper (5 days/week). General readership in Kane County, Illinois. Circ. 20,000. Estab. 1881. Sample copy 50¢.
Needs: Uses 5-10 photos/issue; number of freelance photographers varies. Needs photos mostly of sports action, but also news/feature and food/fashion. "No unsolicited work is considered for publication." Photo captions required.
Making Contact & Terms: Interested in receiving work from a newer, lesser-known photographer. Arrange a personal interview to show portfolio. Provide resume, business card, brochure, flyer or tearsheets to be kept on file for possible assignments. Reports in 1-2 weeks. Pays $25-50/b&w photo; $35-60/color photo; all assignments pay a minimum of $25, even if a picture is not published. Pays on publication. Buys one-time rights.

Tips: In photographer's portfolio, wants to see "strictly photojournalism/newsphotography work, with an emphasis on clean, strong images, especially news and sports. No art/scenic or travel. Primary interest is b&w, but transparencies are also needed. This publication is a goldmine for a person who has the talent to make high-quality news and sports pictures in our area. Freelance and stringer work may also lead to full-time employment. Needs both b&w and color negatives."

MEDICAL TRIBUNE, Dept. PM, 257 Park Ave. South, New York NY 10010. (212)674-8500. FAX: (212)982-4398. Photo Editor: Mike Tamborrino. Tri-monthly broadsheet. Emphasizes medical news. Readers are physicians. Circ. 150,000. Estab. 1960. Sample copy free with 8 × 11 SASE and $1 postage.
Needs: Uses 40 photos/issue; 5 supplied by freelancers. Needs photos of doctors, medical devices to illustrate a specific story. Runs 6-8 color assignments/issue. Reviews photos with accompanying ms only. Model release preferred; captions required.
Making Contact & Terms: Provide resume, business card, brochure, flyer or tearsheets to be kept on file for possible future assignments. SASE. Reports in 1 week. Pays $200/b&w photo; $350/assignment. Pays on publication. Credit line given. Buys one-time rights; one-time rights include right to use in our foreign edition. Simultaneous submissions and previously published work OK.
Tips: Wants "versatility (close-up shots as well as over-all shots), good use of lighting, ability to shoot color. To contribute he/she should not be from NYC area. We do not hire photographers from here. Should be from areas in which we need photos."

THE MERCURY, Dept. PM, Hanover & King Sts., Pottstown PA 19464. (215)323-3000. Photo Editor: John Strickler. Daily and Sunday newspaper. Emphasizes daily news, features and sports, food and human interest. Circ. 31,000. Sample copy $1 (current issue) with 9 × 12 SASE and $1 postage.
Needs: Uses about 20 photos/issue; 2 supplied by freelance photographers. Needs photos of animal or wildlife shots, how-to, travel, scenic, sports; and especially news and human interest. Captions required.
Making Contact & Terms: Submit portfolio for review. Provide resume, business card, brochure, flyer or tearsheets to be kept on file for possible future assignments. SASE. Reports in 2 weeks. Pays $25-35/cover photo and $20/b&w inside photo. Pays on publication. Credit line given. Buys one-time and all rights, but will negotiate.
Tips: "Best chance for publication in our newspaper is photos from immediate circulation area (west of Philadelphia) or dramatic news photos from anywhere."

METRO, 550 S. First St., San Jose CA 95113. (408)298-8000. Managing Editor: Sharan Street. Alternative newspaper, weekly tabloid format. Emphasis on news, arts and entertainment. Readers are adults ages 25-44, in Silicon Valley. Circ. 70,000. Sample copy free with SASE and 3 first-class stamps.
Needs: Uses 15 photos/issue; 25% supplied by freelance photographers. Model release required for model shots; photo captions preferred.
Making Contact & Terms: Query with resume of credits, list of stock photos subjects. Provide resume, business card, brochure, flyer or tearsheets to be kept on file for possible assignments. Does not return unsolicited material. Pays $75-100/color cover photo, $50-75/b&w cover photo, $25/b&w inside photo. Pays on publication. Credit line given. Buys one-time rights. Simultaneous submissions and previously published work OK "if outside of San Francisco Bay area."

MISSISSIPPI PUBLISHERS, INC., Dept. PM, 311 E. Pearl St., Jackson MS 39201. (601)961-7073. Photo Editors: Chris Todd and Scott Boyd. Daily newspaper. Emphasizes photojournalism: news, sports, features, fashion, food and portraits. Readers are very broad age range of 18-70 years; male and female. Circ. 100,000. Sample copy for 11 × 14 SASE and 54¢.
Needs: Uses 10-15 photos/issue; 1-5 supplied by freelance photographers. Needs news, sports, features, portraits, fashion and food photos. Special photo needs include food and fashion. Model release, photo captions required.
Making Contact & Terms: Provide resume, business card, brochure, flyer or tearsheets to be kept on file for possible assignments. Uses 8 × 10 matte b&w and color prints; 35mm, 2¼ × 2¼, 4 × 5, 8 × 10 transparencies. SASE. Reports 1 week. Pays $50-100/color cover photo; $25-50/b&w cover photo; $25/b&w inside photo; $20-50/hour; $150-400/day. Pays on publication. Credit line given. Buys one-time or all rights; negotiable.

MOM GUESS WHAT NEWSPAPER, 1725 L St., Sacramento CA 95814. (916)441-6397. Editor: Linda Birner. Every two weeks tabloid. Gay newspaper that emphasizes political, entertainment, etc. Readers are gay and straight people. Circ. 21,000. Estab. 1978. Sample copy $1. Photo guidelines free with SASE.

Needs: Uses about 8-10 photos/issue; all supplied by freelancers, 80% from assignment and 20% from stock. Model release and captions required.
Making Contact & Terms: Arrange a personal interview to show portfolio. Send 8 × 10 glossy b&w prints by mail for consideration. SASE. Pays $5-200/b&w photo; $10-15/hour; $25-50/day; $5-200 per photo/text package. Pays on publication. Credit line given. Buys one-time rights. Previously published work OK.
Tips: Prefers to see gay related stories/human rights/civil rights and some artsy stuff, photos in portfolio; *no* nudes or sexually explicit photos.

NATIONAL EXAMINER, 5401 NW Broken Sound Blvd., Boca Raton FL 33487. (407)997-7733. Editor: Lee Harrison. Photo Editor: Linda McKune. Weekly tabloid. General interest. Circ. 1,000,000.
Needs: Uses 80-100 photos/issue. Needs color and b&w: human interest, humorous animal/children pictures, action sequences, celebrities. Model release preferred. Captions required.
Making Contact & Terms: Query with samples or send photos for consideration. SASE. Pays $125/color and $50/b&w; some fees are negotiable. Pays on publication; assignments paid upon completion of work. Previously published work OK.

NATIONAL MASTERS NEWS, Box 2372, Van Nuys CA 91404. (818)785-1895. FAX: (818)782-1135. Editor: Al Sheahen. Monthly tabloid. Official world and US publication for Masters (age 35 and over) track and field, long distance running and race walking. Circ. 5,200. Estab. 1977. Sample copy free with 8 × 12 SASE and $1.05 postage.
Needs: Uses 25 photos/issue; 20% assigned and 80% from freelance stock. Needs photos of Masters athletes (men and women over age 35) competing in T&F events, LDR races or racewalking competitions. Captions preferred.
Making Contact & Terms: Send any size matte or glossy b&w print by mail for consideration, "may write for sample issue." SASE. Reports in 1 month. Pays $20/b&w cover photo; $7.50-10/inside b&w photo. Pays on publication. Credit line given. Buys one-time rights. Simultaneous submissions and previously published work OK.

NATIONAL NEWS BUREAU, P.O. Box 5628, Philadelphia PA 19129. (215)546-8088. Editor: Andrea Diehl. Weekly syndication packet. Emphasizes entertainment. Readers are leisure/entertainment-oriented, 17-55 years old. Circ. 400.
Needs: "Always looking for new female models for our syndicated fashion/beauty columns." Uses about 20 photos/issue; 15 supplied by freelance photographers. Captions required.
Making Contact & Terms: Arrange a personal interview to show portfolio. Query with sample, submit portfolio for review. Send 8 × 10 b&w prints, b&w contact sheet by mail for consideration. SASE. Reports in 1 week. Pays $50 minimum/job. Pays on publication. Credit line given. Buys all rights.

NEW YORK TIMES MAGAZINE, 229 W. 43 St., New York NY 10036. (212)556-3026. Photo Editor: Kathy Ryan. Weekly. Circ. 1,650,000.
Needs: The number of freelance photos varies. Model release and photo captions required.
Making Contact & Terms: Drop off portfolio for review. SASE. Reports in 1 week. Pays $250/b&w page rate; $300/color page rate; $225/half page; $350/job (day rates); $650/color cover photo. Pays on acceptance. Credit line given. Buys one-time rights.

NEWS-GAZETTE, Dept. PM, P.O. Drawer 2068, Kissimmee FL 32741. (407)846-7600. Photography Editor: Scott Fisher. Triweekly newspaper. Emphasizes local interests. Readers are all ages, sexes and occupations. Circ. 26,000. Sample copy for 25¢ with legal SASE and $2 postage.
Needs: Uses 20 photos/issue; approx. one supplied by freelancers. Needs photos of local interest only for Osceola County. Model release preferred. Photo captions required.
Making Contact & Terms: Send 35mm and 8 × 10 b&w prints by mail for consideration. Cannot return unsolicited material. Reports in 3 weeks. NPI. Pays on publication. Buys one-time rights.

🍁NORTH ISLAND NEWS, P.O. Box 3013, Courtenay BC V9N 5N3 Canada. (604)334-4446. FAX: (604)334-4983. Editor: Jamie Bowman. Weekly newspaper. Emphasizes social issues, entertainment. Circ. 30,000. Estab. 1965. Sample copy free with SASE and $1 postage

---

🍁 *The maple leaf before a listing indicates that the market is Canadian. The symbol is new this year in* **Photographer's Market.**

Needs: Uses 4-5 photos/issue; 1-2 supplied by freelancers. Needs variety of photos especially of animal, action and illustrations for articles. Model release required. Photo captions preferred that include who, what, when, where and why.

Making Contact & Terms: Interested in receiving work from newer, lesser-known photographers. Send unsolicited photos by mail for consideration. Send any size b&w, color prints; 35mm, 2¼ × 2¼ tranparencies. Keeps samples on file. SASE. Pays $15/color cover photo; $10/color or b&w inside photo; $10/color page rate. Pays on publication. Credit line given. Buys one-time rights. Simultaneous submissions and previously published work OK.

Tips: "Call with idea, then for sample. Wants to see "action, local application or relevance. Clearly defined images with strong color."

*NORTH TEXAS GOLFER, Suite 212, 9182 Old Katy Rd., Houston TX 77055. (713)464-0308. Editor: Bob Gray. Monthly tabloid. Emphasizes golf in the gulf coast area of Texas. Readers average 48.5 years old, $72,406 income, upscale lifestyle and play golf 2-5 times weekly. Circ. 28,000. Sample copy free with SASE and $2 postage.

Needs: Uses about 20 photos/issue; none supplied by freelance photographers. "Photos are bought only in conjunction with purchase of articles." Photos purchased with accompanying ms only. Model release and captions preferred.

Making Contact & Terms: "Use the telephone." SASE. Reports in 2 weeks. NPI. Pays on publication. Credit line given. Buys one-time rights or all rights, if specified.

ON TRACK, Unit M, 17165 Newhope St., Fountain Valley CA 92708. (714)966-1131. FAX: (714)556-9776. Photo Coordinator: Pat Oxman. Bimonthly magazine. Emphasizes auto racing. Readers are auto racing enthusiasts. Estab. 1981. Sample copy $1.50. Photo guidelines free with SASE.

Needs: Uses about 120 photos/issue; all supplied by freelance photographers (50% on assignment, 50% from stock). Needs photos of auto racing action and drivers. Special needs filled by assignment. Captions, dates, locality required.

Making Contact & Terms: Send 5 × 7 or 8 × 10 glossy b&w prints with borders; 35mm transparencies by mail for consideration. SASE. Reports in 1 month. Pays $12.50/b&w photo, $25-100/color photo. Pays on publication. Credit line given. Buys first North American serial rights. "Address photo submissions to the attention of Photo Coordinator."

Tips: In samples, wants to see that the photographer can "catch the news and story of a car race on film. Stay away from autofocus cameras, the cars move too fast. Our photos are moving toward action rather than static car shots. We're also seeing more creative photographs." Looks for "photos that complement our writers' styles; photos that add a human element to a mechanical subject. Get to know the subject. One needs to understand the sport in order to photograph it well. Try to shoot important events during a race—not just race cars going by. Look for relationships between drivers and cars and try to find excitement—it's harder than it seems."

THE PATRIOT LEDGER, 400 Crown Colony Dr., Quincy MA 02169. (617)786-7084. FAX: (617)786-7025. Photo Editor: Joe Lippincott. Estab. 1837. "Daily except Sunday" newspaper. General readership. Circ. 100,000. Photo guidelines free with SASE.

Needs: Uses 15-25 photos/issue; most photos used come from staff; some freelance assigned. Needs general newspaper coverage photos—especially spot news and "grabbed" features from circulation area. Model release preferred; photo captions required.

Making Contact & Terms: Query with resume of credits. SASE. Reports as needed. Pays $15-75/b&w inside photo or more if material is outstanding and especially newsworthy, $10-15/hour. Pays on publication. Credit line given. Rights negotiable. Simultaneous submissions and previously published work OK "depending on time and place."

Tips: Looks for "diversity in photojournalism: use NPPA pictures of the year categories as guidelines. Dynamite grabber qualities: unique, poignant images properly and accurately identified and captioned which concisely tell what happened. We want images we're unable to get with staff due to immediacy of events, shot well and in our hands quickly for evaluation and possible publication. To break in to our publication call and explain what you can contribute to our newspaper that is unique. We'll take it from there, depending on the results of the initial conversation."

THE PRODUCE NEWS, Dept. PM, 2185 Lemoine Ave., Fort Lee NJ 07024. (201)592-9100. Editor: Gordan Hochberg. Weekly tabloid. For people involved with the fresh fruit and vegetable industry: growers, shippers, packagers, brokers, wholesalers and retailers. Circ. 10,000. Estab. 1987.

Needs: Needs feature photos of fresh fruit and vegetable shipping, packaging, growing, display, etc. Buys 5-10 photos annually, usually with articles only.

Making Contact & Terms: Majority of photos submitted on assignment. Pays $8-10/b&w photo. Pays on publication. Reports in 2 weeks. SASE. Sample copy free with 10 × 13 SASE; $1.25 postage. Free photo guidelines.

© Bert Lane

In order to shoot outstanding photos for newspapers it's important to fill the frame with your subject and snap the shutter at the perfect moment to show the emotion of the scene. Photographer Bert Lane, of Marshfield, Massachusetts, manages to do both in this picture shot on assignment for The Patriot Ledger. *Lane captured the warmth of the situation by exposing the joy of a father meeting his daughter for the first time as family members look on from behind.*

Tips: "Nothing fancy—just good quality."

REVIEW NEWSPAPERS, Dept. PM, 100 N.E. 7th St., Miami FL 33132. (305)347-6638. Chief Photographer: Barbaraellen Koch. Art Director: Michael Cole. Daily newspaper. Emphasizes law, business and real estate. Readers are 25-55 yrs., average net worth of $750,000, male and female. Circ. 18,000. Estab. 1926. Sample copy for $1 with 9×11 SASE.
Needs: Uses 8-15 photos/issue; 20-40% supplied by freelance photographers. Needs mostly portraits, however we use live news events, sports and building mugs. Photo captions "an absolute must."
Making Contact & Terms: Arrange a personal interview to show portfolio. Submit portfolio for review. Send 35mm, 8×10 b&w and color prints. Accepts all types of finishes. Cannot return unsolicited material. If used, reports immediately. Pays $85 for most photos; pays more if part of photo/text package. Credit line given. Buys all rights. Rights negotiable. Previously published work OK.
Tips: In photographer's portfolio, looks for "a good grasp of lighting and composition; the ability to take an ordinary situation and make an extraordinary photograph. We work on daily deadlines so promptness is a must and extensive cutline information is needed."

ROLL CALL NEWSPAPER, Suite 107, 900 2nd St. NE, Washington DC 20002. (202)289-4900. FAX: (202)289-2205. Photo Editor: Laura Patterson. Semi-weekly newspaper. Emphasizes U.S. Congress and politics. Readers are politicians, lobbyists and congressional staff. Circ. 18,000. Estab. 1955. Sample copy free with 9×12 SASE with $1 postage.
Needs: Uses 20-30 photos/issue; up to 5 supplied by freelancers. Needs photos of anything involving current congressional issues, good or unusual shots of congressmen. Captions required.
Making Contact & Terms: Query with samples or list of stock photo subjects. Send unsolicited photos by mail for consideration. Uses 8×10 glossy b&w prints; 35mm transparencies. Does not return unsolicited material. Reports in 1 month. Pays $25-85/b&w; $30-300/color (if cover); $50-75/hour or

job. Pays on publication. Credit line given. Buys one-time rights. Simultaneous submissions OK.
Tips: "We're always looking for unique candids of congressmen; or political events. In reviewing photographer's samples, we want to see good composition, pictures that tell a story and good use of light for newsprint."

RUBBER AND PLASTICS NEWS, 1725 Merriman Rd., Akron OH 44313. (216)836-9180. Editor: Edward Noga. Weekly tabloid. Emphasizes rubber industry. Readers are rubber product makers. Circ. 17,000. Sample copy free.
Needs: Uses 5-10 photos/issue. Needs photos of company officials, in-plant scenes, etc. to go with stories staff produces.
Making Contact & Terms: Query with samples. SASE. Reports in 2 weeks. Pays $50-200/b&w or color cover photo; $50-100/b&w or color inside photo. Pays on publication. Credit line given. Buys all rights; negotiable. Simultaneous submissions OK.
Tips: Prefers to see "news photos; mood shots suitable for cover; business-related photos. Call us. We'd like to use more freelance photographers throughout the US and internationally to produce photographs that we'd use in stories generated by our staff."

*SENIOR VOICE OF FLORIDA, Suite E, 6281 39th St. North., Pinellas Park FL 34665. (813)521-3837. Managing Editor: Nancy Yost. Monthly newspaper. Emphasizes lifestyles of senior citizens. Readers are Florida residents and tourists, 50 years old and older. Circ. 50,000. Estab. 1981. Sample copy $1. Photo guidelines free with SASE.
Needs: Uses 6 photos/issue; 1-2 supplied by freelancers. Needs photos of recreational activities, travel, seasonal, famous persons (only with story). Reviews photos purchased with accompanying ms only. Model/property release required. Captions required.
Making Contact & Terms: Send photos with manuscript. Samples kept on file. SASE. Reports in 1-2 months. Pays $10/color cover photo; $5/color inside photo; $5/b&w inside photo. Pays on publication. Credit line given. Buys one-time rights; negotiable. Simultaneous submissions and previously published work OK.
Tips: "We look for crisp, clean, clear prints. Photos that speak to us rate special attention. We use photos only to illustrate manuscripts. So we look at manuscript packages only."

*THE SENTINEL, P.O. Box 1309, Seaside CA 93955. (408)899-2305. FAX: (408)659-4170. Contact: Norman Spaulding. Weekly newspaper. Emphasizes community news. Circ. 10,000. Estab. 1946. Sample copy free with 9×12 SASE.
Needs: Uses 8-12 photos/issue; 4-8 supplied by freelancers. Needs photos of local events, places and people. Reviews photos with or without a manuscript. Model/property release required. Captions required.
Making Contact & Terms: Send unsolicited photos by mail for consideration. Send 4×6 or larger glossy b&w prints. SASE. Reports in 1-2 weeks. Pays $25/b&w cover photo; $10/b&w inside photo; $20/b&w page rage; $20/hour. Pays on publication. Credit line given. Buys one-time rights; negotiable. Simultaneous submissions and previously published work OK.

THE SENTINEL, Dept. PM, 1200 Gulf Breeze Pkwy., Gulf Breeze FL 32561. (904)934-1200. Publisher: Marlin Osborn. Weekly newspaper. Emphasizes local people. Readers are middle age and older, upper income. Circ. 10,000. Estab. 1960. Sample copy free with 9×12 SASE and 6 first-class stamps.
Needs: Uses 30-50 photos/issue; 50% supplied by freelancers. Needs photos of local people—scrapbook material.
Making Contact & Terms: Send b&w prints by mail for consideration. SASE. Reports in 1-2 weeks. Pays $5/b&w cover photo; $5/color inside photo. Pays on publication. Credit line given. Buys all rights; negotiable. Simultaneous and previously published work OK.
Tips: "Catch a local person doing something they would be proud to see in the local paper!"

SINGER MEDIA CORP., INC., Seaview Business Park, Unit #106, 1030 Calle Cordillera, San Clemente CA 92672. (714)498-7227. FAX: (714)498-2162. President: Kurt Singer. Newspaper syndicate (magazine, journal, newspaper, newsletter, tabloid). Emphasizes books and interviews. Circ. worldwide. Estab. 1940.
Needs: Needs photos for book covers, celebrities, text features with transparencies (35mm, 2¼×2¼, 4×5). Reviews photos with accompanying ms only. Will use dupes only, cannot guarantee returns. No models. Usually requires releases on interview photos. Photo captions required.
Making Contact & Terms: Interested in receiving work from newer, lesser-known photographers, depending on subject. Query with list of stock photo subjects. Reports in 3 weeks. Pays 50/50% of all syndication sales. Pays after collection. Credit line given. Buys one-time rights, foreign rights; negotiable. Previously published work OK.

Tips: "Worldwide, mass market, text essential. Trend is toward international interest. Survey the market for ideas."

SKIING TRADE NEWS, Dept. PM, 2 Park Ave., New York NY 10016. (212)779-5000. Editor: Isevlt Devlin. Tabloid published 8 times/year. Emphasizes news, retailing and service articles for ski retailers. Circ. 16,000. Free sample copy with 12 × 24 SASE.
Needs: Uses 2-6 photos/issue. Celebrity/personality; photo essay/photo feature ("if it has to do with ski and skiwear retailing"); spot news; and humorous. Photos must be ski related. Model release and captions preferred.
Making Contact & Terms: Photos purchased with accompanying ms or caption. Uses 5 × 7 glossy prints; transparencies. Pays $25-35/b&w photo. Pays on publication. Buys one-time rights. Credit line given. Send material by mail for consideration. SASE. Reports in 1 month.

SKYDIVING, P.O. Box 1520, DeLand FL 32721. (904)736-9779. Editor: Michael Truffer. Readers are "sport parachutists worldwide, dealers and equipment manufacturers." Monthly newspaper. Circ. 8,600. Sample copy $2; photo guidelines for SASE.
Needs: Uses 12-15 photos/issue; 8-10 supplied by freelancers. Selects photos from wire service, photographers who are skydivers and freelancers. Interested in anything related to skydiving — news or any dramatic illustration of an aspect of parachuting.
Making Contact & Terms: Send by mail for consideration actual 5 × 7 or 8 × 10 b&w photos. SASE. Reports in 2 weeks. Pays on publication minimum $25/b&w photo. Credit line given. Buys one-time rights. Simultaneous submissions (if so indicated) and previously published work (indicate where and when) OK.

SOUTHERN MOTORACING, P.O. Box 500, Winston-Salem NC 27102. (919)723-5227. Associates: Greer Smith, Randy Pettitt. Editor/Publisher: Hank Schoolfield. Biweekly tabloid. Emphasizes autoracing. Readers are fans of auto racing. Circ. 18,000-19,000. Sample copy 75¢ postpaid.
Needs: Uses about 10-15 photos/issue; some supplied by freelance photographers. Needs "news photos on the subject of Southeastern auto racing." Captions required.
Making Contact & Terms: Query with samples; send 5 × 7 or larger matte or glossy b&w prints; b&w negatives by mail for consideration. SASE. Reports in 1 month. Pays $25-50/b&w cover photo; $5-25/b&w inside photo; $50-100/page. Pays on publication. Credit line given. Buys first North American serial rights. Simultaneous submissions OK.
Tips: "We're looking primarily for *news* pictures, and staff produces many of them — with about 25% coming from freelancers through long-standing relationships. However, we're receptive to good photos from new sources, and we do use some of those. Good quality professional pictures only, please!"

THE SPORTING NEWS, 1212 N. Lindberg Blvd., St. Louis MO 63132. (Not reviewing freelance work.)

THE STAR NEWSPAPERS, Dept PM, 1526 Otto, Chicago Heights IL 60411. (708)755-6161. FAX: (708)755-0095. Photo Director: Todd Panagopolous. Publishes 19 weekly newspapers in south suburban Chicago. Circ. 100,000. Estab. 1920.
Needs: Buys 100 stock photos and offers 1,000 assignments annually. Uses photos for features, news, spot news and sports coverage. Photo captions required; include description of subject, especially of towns or events.
Making Contact & Terms: Arrange personal interview to show portfolio. Prefers b&w prints, any size over 5 × 7. Also uses 35mm and 2¼ × 2¼ transparencies. Works with local freelancers on assignment only. Does not keep samples on file. SASE. Pays $19-25/assignment. Credit line given. Buys one-time and all rights; negotiable.
Tips: Wants to see "variety of photojournalism categories." Also, show "ability both to utilize and supplement available light." To break in, "be ready to hustle and work lousy hours." Sees a trend toward more use of "a documentary style."

SUN, 5401 NW Broken Sound Blvd., Boca Raton FL 33487. (407)997-7733, ext. 286. Photo Editor: Maureen Scozzaro. Weekly tabloid. Readers are housewives, college students, middle Americans. Sample copy free with extra large SASE and 55¢ postage.
Needs: Uses about 60 photos/issue; 50% supplied by freelance photographers. Wants varied subjects: action, unusual pets, offbeat medical, human interest, inventions, spectacular sports action; black and white human interest and offbeat pix and stories; and b&w celebrity photos. "Also — we are always in need of interesting, offbeat color photos for the center spread." Model release and captions preferred.
Making Contact & Terms: Query with stock photo list. Send 8 × 10 b&w prints, 35mm transparencies, b&w contact sheet or b&w negatives by mail for consideration. Send through mail with SASE. Reports in 2 weeks. Pays $100/b&w cover photo; $200/color cover photo; $75/b&w inside photo; $125/color

inside photo. Pays on publication. Buys one-time rights. Simultaneous submissions and previously published work OK.

Tips: "We are specifically looking for the unusual, offbeat, freakish true stories and photos. *Nothing is too far out for consideration.* We would suggest you send for a sample copy and take it from there."

SUNSHINE: THE MAGAZINE OF SOUTH FLORIDA, 200 East Las Olas Blvd., Ft. Lauderdale FL 33301-2293. (305)356-4685. Editor: John Parkyn. Art Director: Kent H. Barton. "*Sunshine* is a Sunday newspaper magazine emphasizing articles of interest to readers in the Broward and Palm Beach counties region of South Florida." Readers are "the 800,000 readers of the Sunday edition of the *Sun-Sentinel.*" Sample copy and photo guidelines free with SASE.

Needs: Uses about 12-20 photos/issue; 30% supplied by freelancers. Needs "all kinds of photos relevant to the interests of a South Florida readership." Photos purchased with accompanying ms. Model release sometimes required. Captions preferred.

Making Contact & Terms: Query with samples. Provide resume, business card, brochure, flyer or tearsheets to be kept on file for possible future assignments. SASE. Reports in 1 month. "All rates negotiable; the following are as a guide only." Pays $150-200/color cover photo; $50-100/b&w photo; $75-100/color inside photo; $100-150/color page; $500-1,000 for text/photo package. Pays within 1 month of acceptance. Credit line given. Buys one-time rights. Simultaneous and previously published submissions OK.

TALENT MANAGEMENT, Suite 220, 115 W. Allegan St., Lansing MI 48933. (517)485-7800. Publisher: Ben Campbell. Quarterly newsletter. Emphasizes talent management, motion pictures. Readers are 18-24 and 25-65 years old, male and female, employed in motion pictures and talent management. Circ. 3-5,000. Estab. 1986. Sample copy $25.

Needs: Uses 6-18 photos/issue; 3-9 supplied by freelancers. Needs photos of talent management, celebrities, rich and famous individuals, talent agents, film producers, personalities, life shots, scenics and how-to. Model release and captions preferred.

Making Contact & Terms: Query with resume of credits. Query with list of stock photo subjects. Send unsolicited b&w and color prints or 35mm, 2¼ × 2¼, 4 × 5 or 8 × 10 transparencies by mail for consideration. Submit portfolio for review. Provide resume, business card, brochure, flyer or tearsheets to be kept on file for possible assignments. SASE. Reports in 3 weeks. Pays $15/b&w cover photo; $15/color or b&w inside photo. Pays on publication. Credit line given. Buys one-time rights. Simultaneous submissions and previously published work OK.

Tips: Wants to see "any photos of yet-to-be produced films, ad campaigns, actors and actresses, celebrities, rich and famous individuals."

*TRAVEL NEWS, 111 2nd Ave. NE, 15th Floor, St. Petersburg FL 33701. (813)895-8241. FAX: (813)894-6318. Editor: Matthew Wiseman. Monthly newspaper. Emphasizes travel. Readers are heads of households with middle- or upper-level income, ages 35 and up. Circ. 250,000. Estab. 1982. Sample copy for 9 × 12 SASE. Photo guidelines available.

Needs: Uses 16 photos/issue; 6 supplied by freelancers. Needs photos of travel. Reviews photos with or without manuscript. Model/property release preferred. Captions required.

Making Contact & Terms: Query with stock photo list. Reports in 1-2 months. Pays $50/color cover photo; $10/b&w inside photo; $25/color page rate; $10/b&w page rate; $60-175/photo/text package. Pay on publication. Credit line given. Buys one-time rights; negotiable. Simultaneous submissions and previously published work OK.

Tips: Wants photos of "travelers enjoying themselves, nice destination shots."

TRAVERSE CITY RECORD-EAGLE, P.O. Box 632, Traverse City MI 49685. (616)946-2000. FAX: (616)946-8273. Photo Coordinator: Greg Johnstone. Daily newspaper. Emphasizes concerns and interests of residents of northwest lower Michigan. Readers are general public of northwest lower Michigan. Circ. 27,000 daily. Estab. 1858.

Needs: Uses 6-8 photos/issue; occasionally uses freelancers. Especially needs photos of news events: fires, accidents, major news events or other news that involves residents of northwest lower Michigan. Photo captions required; include who, what, when, where, why, how.

Making Contact & Terms: Interested in receiving work from newer, lesser-known photographers. Call immediately after shooting news event. Does not keep samples on file. Cannot return material. Reports in 1-2 weeks. NPI; payment negotiable. Pays on publication. Credit line given. Buys one-time rights.

Tips: "Don't send unsolicited photos. As a daily newspaper, we find that immediacy is of utmost importance. We're only looking for major news events that aren't covered by the Associated Press or by our in-house photo staff, which supplies most of our photos."

U—THE NATIONAL COLLEGE NEWSPAPER, Suite 820, 1800 Century Park East, Los Angeles CA 90067. (310)551-1381. FAX: (310)551-1659. Managing Editor: Jacki Hampton. Monthly newspaper. Emphasizes college. Readers are college students at 400 schools nationwide. Circ. 1,425,000. Estab. 1987. Sample copy free for 9×12 SASE with 3 first-class stamps.
Needs: Uses 15 photos/issue; all supplied by freelancers; 80% from freelance stock. *Photographers must be college students who work for their college newspapers.* Needs b&w or color feature shots of students, college life and student-related shots. Model release preferred. Photo captions required that include name of subject, school.
Making Contact & Terms: Interested in receiving work from newer, lesser known photographers. Send unsolicited photos by mail for consideration. Provide resume, business card, brochure, flyer or tearsheets to be kept on file for possible assignments. Send any size b&w, color prints; 35mm, 2¼×2¼, 4×5, 8×10 transparencies. Keeps sample on file. Reports in 3 weeks. Pays $50/color cover photo; $50/b&w cover photo; $50/color inside photo; $50/b&w inside photo. Pays on publication. Credit line given. Buys one-time rights; negotiable. Simultaneous submissions and previously published work OK.
Tips: Wants to see "any photos that would be of interest to a national college interest, particularly color stand-alone feature shots."

VELONEWS, 1830 N. 55th, Boulder CO 80301-2700. (303)440-0601. FAX: (303)444-6788. Managing Editor: Tim Johnson. The journal of competitive cycling. Covers road racing and mountain bike events on a national and international basis. Paid circ. 35,000. Sample copy free with 9×12 SASE and $1.05 postage.
Needs: Bicycle racing and nationally important races. Looking for action shots, not just finish-line photos with the winner's arms in the air. Captions and identification of subjects required. No bicycle touring. Photos purchased with or without accompanying ms. Uses news, features, profiles.
Making Contact & Terms: Send samples of work or tearsheets with assignment proposal. Query first on mss. Send glossy b&w prints and transparencies. SASE. Reports in 3 weeks. Pays $16.50-50/b&w inside photo; $33-100/color inside photo; $75/b&w cover; $150/color cover; $15-100/ms. Credit line given, payment on publication for one-time rights.
Tips: "We're a newspaper; photos must be timely. Use fill flash to compensate for harsh summer light."

VENTURA COUNTY & COAST REPORTER, Dept. PM, 1583 Spinnaker Dr., #213, Ventura CA 93001. (805)658-2244. Editor: Nancy S. Cloutier. Weekly tabloid newspaper. Circ. 35,000. Estab. 1977.
Needs: Uses 12-14 photos/issue; 40-45% supplied by freelancers. Photos purchased with accompanying ms only. Model release required.
Making Contact & Terms: Send sample b&w original photos. SASE. Reports in 1-2 weeks. Pays $10/ b&w cover photo; $10/b&w inside photo. Pays on publication. Credit line given. Buys one-time rights. Simultaneous submissions OK.
Tips: "We prefer locally (Ventura County, CA) slanted photos."

VOYAGER INTERNATIONAL, Box 2773, 7 Northgate, Westport CT 06880. (203)226-1647. Feature Editor: Lois Anderson. Consumer publication. Monthly newsletter. Emphasizes travel. Readers are middle age, upscale. Circ. 20,000. Estab. 1986. Samples copy for $6. Photo guidelines not available.
Needs: Uses 10 b&w photos/issue; 20% supplied by freelancers. Needs photos of travel. Model release required; photo captions preferred.
Making Contact & Terms: Provide resume, business card, brochure, flyer or tearsheets to be kept on file for possible assignments. Send b&w prints. SASE. Reports in 3 weeks. Pays $25/b&w cover photo; $10/b&w inside photo. Pays on publication. Buys first North American serial rights. Does not consider simultaneous submissions or previously published work.

THE WASHINGTON BLADE, 8th Floor, 724 9th St. NW, Washington DC 20001. (202)347-2038. FAX: (202)393-6510. Senior Editor: Lisa M. Keen. Weekly tabloid. For and about the gay community. Readers are gay men and lesbians; moderate- to upper-level income; primarily Washington, DC metropolitan area. Circ. 34,000. Estab. 1969. Sample copy free with 9×12 SASE plus $1 postage.
Needs: Uses about 6-7 photos/issue; only out-of-town photos are supplied by freelance photographers. Needs "gay-related news, sports, entertainment events, profiles of gay people in news, sports, entertainment, other fields." Photos purchased with or without accompanying ms. Model release and captions preferred.
Making Contact & Terms: Interested in receiving work from newer, lesser-known photographers. Query with resume of credits. SASE. Reports in 1 month. Provide resume, business card and tearsheets to be kept on file for possible future assignments. Pays $25/inside photo. Pays within 45 days of publication. Credit line given. Buys all rights when on assignment, otherwise one-time rights. Simultaneous submissions and previously published work OK.

374 *Photographer's Market '93*

Tips: "Be timely! Stay up-to-date on what we're covering in the news and call us up if you know of a story about to happen in your city that you can cover. Also, be able to provide some basic details for a caption (*tell* us what's happening, too)." Especially important to "avoid stereotypes."

WATERTOWN PUBLIC OPINION, Dept. PM, Box 10, Watertown SD 57201. (605)886-6903. FAX: (605)886-4280. Editor: Gordon Garnos. Daily newspaper. Emphasizes general news of this area or former area people. Circ. 17,500. Estab. 1887. Sample copy 25¢.
Needs: Uses up to 8 photos/issue. Reviews photos with or without ms. model release. Photo captions required.
Making Contact & Terms: Send unsolicited photos by mail for consideration. Send b&w, color prints; 35mm, 2¼×2¼, 4×5, 8×10 transparencies. Does not keep samples on file. SASE. Reports in 1-2 weeks. Pays $5/color cover photo; $5/b&w cover photo; $5/color inside photo; $5/b&w inside photo; $5/color page rate. Pays on publication. Credit line given. Buys one-time rights; negotiable. Simultaneous submissions OK.

WESTART, Box 6868, Auburn CA 95604. (916)885-0969. Editor-in-Chief: Martha Garcia. Emphasizes art for practicing artists, artists/craftsmen, students of art and art patrons, collectors and teachers. Circ. 5,000. Free sample copy and photo guidelines.
Needs: Uses 20 photos/issue, 10 supplied by freelancers. "We will publish photos if they are in a current exhibition, where the public may view the exhibition. The photos must be b&w. We treat them as an art medium. Therefore, we purchase freelance articles accompanied by photos." Wants mss on exhibitions and artists in the western states. Model release not required; captions required.
Making Contact & Terms: Send by mail for consideration 5×7 or 8×10 b&w prints. SASE. Reports in 2 weeks. Payment is included with total purchase price of ms. Pays $25 on publication. Buys one-time rights. Simultaneous and previously published submissions OK.

★THE WESTERN PRODUCER, PO Box 2300, Saskatoon SK S7K 2C4 Canada. (306)665-3500. FAX: (306)653-1255. Editor: Garry Fairbairn. Weekly newspaper. Emphasizes agriculture and rural living in western Canada. Circ. 120,000. Estab. 1923. Photo guidelines free with SASE.
Needs: Buys up to 10 photos/issue; about 50-80% of photos supplied by freelancers. Livestock, nature, human interest, scenic, rural, agriculture, day-to-day rural life and small communities. Model release preferred for recognizable people. Captions required; include person's name and description of activity.
Making Contact & Terms: Send material by mail for consideration. SASE. Pays $20-40/photo; $35-100/color photo; $50-250 for text/photo package. Credit line given. Pays on acceptance. Buys one-time rights. SASE. Previously published work OK. Reports in 2 weeks.
Tips: Needs current photos of farm and agricultural news. "Don't waste postage on abandoned, derelict farm buildings or sunset photos. We want modern scenes with life in them—people or animals, preferably both. Farm kids are always a good bet." Also seeks mss on agriculture, rural Western Canada, history, fiction and contemporary life in rural western Canada.

THE WICHITA EAGLE, Dept. PM, 825 E. Douglas, Wichita KS 67201. (316)268-6468. Director of Photography: Brian Corn. Daily newspaper. Emphasizes news. General readership. Circ. 190,000. Estab. 1900.
Needs: Occasionally needs freelance submissions. "We have our own staff, so we don't require much freelance work. What little we do want, however, has to do with Kansas people." Model release preferred. Photo captions required.
Making Contact & Terms: Query with list of stock photo subjects. Submit portfolio for review. Provide resume, business card, brochure, flyer or tearsheets to be kept on file for possible assignments. Send 35mm b&w and color prints, or transparencies by mail for consideration. SASE. Reports in 3 weeks. Pays $50/color cover photo; $30/b&w cover photo. Pays on publication. Credit line given. Buys one-time rights. Simultaneous and previously published work OK.
Tips: In photographer's portfolio or samples, wants to see "20 or so images that show off what the shooter does best, i.e., news spots, fashion." To break in with newspapers, "work hard, shoot as much as possible, and *never* give up!"

Market conditions are constantly changing! If you're still using this book and it's 1994 or later, buy the newest edition of Photographer's Market at your favorite bookstore or order directly from Writer's Digest Books.

WISCONSIN, The Milwaukee Journal Magazine, P.O. Box 661, Milwaukee WI 53201. (414)224-2341. FAX: (414)224-2047. Editor: Alan Borsuk. Weekly magazine. General-interest Sunday magazine focusing on the places and people of Wisconsin or of interest to Wisconsinites. Circ. 510,000. Estab. 1969. Free sample copy with SASE.
Needs: Uses about 12 photos/issue; 1 supplied by freelancer. Needs "human-interest, wildlife, adventure, still life and scenic photos, etc." About 90% of photos are on assignment; very little stock. Model release and captions required.
Making Contact & Terms: Query with samples. SASE. Reports in 3 months. Pays $125/color cover photo; $50-100/b&w inside photo, $50-125/color inside photo. Pays on publication. Buys one-time rights, "preferably first-time rights."
Tips: "We're primarily interested in people and, to a lesser extent, nature. Our emphasis is strongly on Wisconsin themes."

WRITER'S FORUM, 1507 Dana Ave., Cincinnati OH 45207. (513)531-2222. Editor: Tom Clark. Quarterly newsletter. For students of Writer's Digest School. Emphasizes novel, short story and article writing techniques and marketing, student and faculty activities and interviews with freelance writers. Circ. 13,000. Free sample copy.
Needs: Buys photos occasionally. Celebrity/personality of well-known writers. Photos purchased with accompanying ms. No photos without related text of interest/help to writing students. Model release preferred; captions required.
Making Contacts & Terms: Uses 8×10 glossy prints for inside or cover photos. Pays $15/photo. SASE. Reports in 3 weeks. Pays on acceptance. Credit line given. Buys one-time rights. Send material by mail for consideration. Simultaneous submissions and previously published work OK. Accompanying mss include interviews with well-known writers on how they write and market their work; technical problems they overcame; people, places and events that inspired them, etc. 500-1,000 words. Pays $10-25/ms.
Tips: "Get a sample if you are interested in working with our publication."

YACHTSMAN, Dept. PM, 2019 Clement Ave., Alameda CA 94501. (510)865-7500. Editor: Bill Parks. Monthly tabloid. Emphasizes recreational boating for boat owners of northern California. Circ. 25,000. Sample copy $3.
Needs: Photos purchased with or without accompanying ms. Buys 5-10 photos/issue. Sport; power and sail (boating and recreation in northern California); spot news (about boating); travel (of interest to boaters); and product shots. Model release and captions preferred. Seeks mss about power boats and sailboats, boating personalities, locales, piers, harbors, and flora and fauna in northern California. Writer's guidelines free with SASE.
Making Contact & Terms: Send material by mail for consideration. Uses 5×7 or 8×10 b&w glossy prints or screen directly from negatives. Uses color slides for cover. Vertical (preferred) or horizontal format. SASE. Reports in 1 month. Pays $5 minimum/b&w photo; $150 minimum/cover photo; $1 minimum/inch for ms. Pays on publication. Credit line given. Buys all rights. Simultaneous submissions or previously published work OK but must be exclusive in Bay Area (nonduplicated).
Tips: Prefers to see action b&w, color slides, water scenes. "We do not use photos as stand-alones; they must illustrate a story. The exception is cover photos, which must have a Bay Area application—power, sail or combination; vertical format with uncluttered upper area especially welcome."

Special Interest Publications

Ron Austing, of Dillsboro, Indiana, is not your typical photographer. His photos of birds are requested from editors all over the United States and, surprisingly, he doesn't care if they like his work or not. Our Close-up subject on page 406, Austing has carved a niche for himself in the publications market.

Whether it's birds, cars, legal work or medical shots, a photographer can find a special interest publication that publishes the images he produces. Obviously the shots must have good composition, sharp focus and proper exposures, but many of the special interest markets are ready and waiting for newer, lesser-known photographers. Those publications interested in newer artists can be quickly found in the First Markets Index in the back of this book.

Most special interest publications are for clearly defined readerships, which are indicated in the beginning of the listing. For instance, association publications will generally be described with the phrase, "Publication of the (Name) Association." For company publications, the identifying phrase is, "Company publication for the (Name) Co. or Corp."

Some publications which are published by associations or companies but are generally intended for consumer or trade audiences may be found accordingly in the appropriate market sections.

Though the subject matter, readerships and circulation sizes of these publications vary, their photo editors do share a need for top-notch photos. Also, an ability to write can often make your work more desirable to photo editors with publications that look primarily for photo/text packages. These publications include a description of their subject and manuscript needs in the listing. When you query such a publication, be sure to point out your knowledge or expertise with their particular subject, activities or business.

As with most publications, breaking in will probably happen in stages. You may be assigned smaller projects at first, but once you supply quality material—on time and within budget—you may quickly find yourself a regular contributor to the publication. In addition to shooting editorial work, you may also be offered additional noneditorial opportunities as you become known within the parent company or organization. Among these would be shooting publicity materials, executive portraits, product advertising and documentation of company or organization events.

AAA MICHIGAN LIVING, 1 Auto Club Dr., Dearborn MI 48126. (313)336-1211. FAX: (313)336-1897. Editor-in-Chief: Len Barnes. Executive Editor: Ron Garbinski. Monthly magazine. Emphasizes auto use, as well as travel in Michigan, US, Canada and foreign countries. Circ. 1,023,000. Estab. 1918. Free sample copy and photo guidelines.
Needs: Scenic and travel. "We rarely buy photos without accompanying ms. Seeks mss about travel in Michigan, US and Canada. We maintain a file on stock photos and subjects photographers have available." Captions required.
Making Contact & Terms: Query with list of stock photo subjects. Uses 8×10 glossy b&w prints; 35mm, 2¼×2¼ or 4×5 transparencies. For covers in particular, uses 35mm, 4×5 or 8×10 color transparencies. Vertical format preferred. SASE. Reports in 6 weeks. Pays $25-35/b&w photo; up to $200/color photo depending on quality and size; $350/cover photo; $150-300/ms. Pays on publication for photos, on acceptance for mss. Credit line given. Buys one-time rights. Simultaneous submissions and previously published work OK.

AAA WORLD, Dept. PM, 1000 AAA Dr., Heathrow, FL 32746-5063. (407)444-8544. Editor/Associate Publisher: Doug Damerst. Association publication of AAA (ABC member). Bimonthly magazine emphasizing how to drive, car care, how to travel and travel destinations. Readers are above average income and age. Circ. 2,553,000. Estab. 1981. Sample copy free.
Needs: Uses 60 photos/issue; 20 supplied by freelancers. Needs photos of people enjoying domestic and international vacation settings. Model release required; captions preferred.
Making Contact & Terms: Provide resume, business card, brochure, flyer or tearsheets to be kept on file for possible future assignments. Does not return unsolicited material. Reports in 3 weeks. Pays $75/color inside photo. Pays on acceptance. Credit line given. Buys one-time rights. Simultaneous and previously published submissions OK.
Tips: "Our need is for travel photos, but not of places as much as of people enjoying travel."

ACADEME: BULLETIN OF THE AAUP, Dept. PM, Suite 500, 1012 14th St. NW, Washington DC 20005. (202)737-5900. Managing Editor: Julia Ridgely. Publication of the American Association of University Professors. Bimonthly. Emphasizes higher education. Readers are college and university professors, all disciplines. Circ. 43,000.
Needs: Uses about 4 photos/issue. Needs photos of classroom shots, campus scenes, general faculty photos. Model release preferred.
Making Contact & Terms: Query with samples; query with list of stock photo subjects; send 8×10 glossy b&w prints or b&w contact sheets by mail for consideration; or submit portfolio for review. Provide resume, business card, brochure, flyer or tearsheets to be kept on file for possible future assignments. SASE. Reports in 2 weeks. Pays approximately $250/b&w cover; $400/color cover; $50-100/b&w inside photo. Pays on publication. Credit line given. Buys one-time rights. Simultaneous submissions and previously published work OK.
Tips: "In reviewing a photographer's portfolio or samples, we look for ability to capture environment of college/university campus and the people who inhabit that environment."

ADVENTURE ROAD, Dept. PM, 200 E. Randolph Dr., Chicago IL 60601. (312)856-2583. Editor: Marilyn Holstein. Publication of Amaco Motor Club. Bimonthly magazine. Emphasizes vacation travel. Readers are 60% male and 40% female, typically ages 48 and up. Circ. 1,500,000. Estab. 1965. Sample copy free for SASE.
Needs: Uses 30-50 photos/issue; 100% supplied by freelance photographers. Model release and photo captions required.
Making Contact & Terms: Query with resume of credits. Pays $1,000/color cover photo; $200/color inside photo. Pays on publication. Credit line given. Buys one-time rights.

AG ALERT, Dept. PM, 1601 Exposition Blvd., Sacramento CA 95815. (916)924-4140. Editor: Steve Adler. Publication of the California Farm Bureau. Weekly tabloid. Covers agriculture for farmers of all ages. Circ. 50,000. Estab. 1978. Sample copy free with SASE.
Needs: Uses approx. 5 photos/issue; occasionally uses freelancers. Needs photos that cover agriculture in California. Especially wants to see transparencies of cotton production in California. Model release preferred; photo captions required.
Making Contact & Terms: Query with suggestions of photo possibilities. If sending samples, include SASE. Reports in 3 weeks. Pays $50-150/color cover photo; $50-100/b&w inside photo. Pays on acceptance. Credit line given. Buys first N.A. serial rights. Does not accept simultaneous submissions and previously published work.
Tips: Call editor and discuss publication's needs personally.

AI MAGAZINE, 445 Burgess Dr., Menlo Park CA 94025. (415)328-3123. FAX: (415)321-4457. Publishing Consultant: David Hamilton. Publication of American Association of Artificial Intelligence (AAAI). Quarterly. Emphasizes artificial intelligence. Readers are research scientists, engineers, high-technology managers, professors of computer science. Circ. 13,000. Estab. 1980. Sample copy $4 with 9 × 12 SASE and $2.40 postage.
Needs: Uses about 3-5 photos/issue; 100% supplied by freelancers. Needs photo of specialized computer applications. Model release required; captions preferred.
Making Contact & Terms: Interested in receiving work from newer, lesser-known photographers. Arrange a personal interview to show portfolio. Query with list of stock photo subjects. Provide resume, business card, brochure, flyer or tearsheets to be kept on file for possible future assignments. SASE. Reports in 3 weeks. Pays $100-1,000/color cover photo; $25-250/color inside photo. Pays on publication. Credit line given. Buys one-time and first N.A. serial rights. Simultaneous submissions and previously published work OK.
Tips: Looks for "editorial content of photos, not artistic merit."

AIR LINE PILOT, 535 Herndon Parkway, Box 1169, Herndon VA 22070. (703)689-4172. Photography Editor: Bob Moeser. Publication of Air Line Pilots Association. Monthly. Emphasizes news and feature stories for commercial airline pilots. Circ. 40,000. Estab. 1933. Photo guidelines for SASE.
Needs: Uses 12-15 photos/issue; 25% comes from freelance stock. Needs dramatic 35mm Kodachrome transparencies of commercial aircraft, pilots and co-pilots performing work-related activities in or near their aircraft. Special needs include dramatic 35mm Kodachromes technically and aesthetically suitable for full-page magazine covers. Especially needs vertical composition scenes. Model release and captions required.
Making Contact & Terms: Query with samples. Send unsolicited photos by mail for consideration. Uses 35mm transparencies. SASE. Pays $35/b&w photo; $35-250/color photo. Pays on acceptance. Buys one-time or all rights; negotiable. Simultaneous submissions and previously published work OK.
Tips: In photographer's samples, wants to see "strong composition, poster-like quality and high technical quality. Photos compete with text for space so they need to be very interesting to be published. Be sure to provide brief but accurate caption information and send in only top, professional quality work. For our publication, cover shots do not need to tie in with current articles. This means that the greatest opportunity for publication exists on our cover."

*ALABAMA MUNICIPAL JOURNAL, 535 Adams Ave., P.O. Box 1270, Montgomery AL 36102. (205)262-2566. Publications Manager: Anne Roquemore. Association publication of Alabama League of Municipalities. Monthly magazine. Emphasizes municipal government and its responsibilities. Readers are municipal officials—mayors, council members, judges, clerks, attorneys, male and female;

The asterisk before a listing indicates that the market is new in this edition. New markets are often the most receptive to freelance submissions.

ages 20-80; black and white, varied occupations besides municipal offices. Circ. 4,200. Estab. 1945. Sample copy and guidelines free with 8½×11 SASE.
Needs: Uses 2-3 photos/issue (more depending on availability and appropriateness of subjects). Needs photos of daily operations of municipal government—police, fire, courts, sanitation, etc. Model release required; photo captions preferred.
Making Contact & Terms: Interested in receiving work from a newer, lesser-known photographer. Query with resume of credits and list of stock photo subjects. Provide resume, business card, brochure, flyer or tearsheets to be kept on file for possible assignments. Returns unsolicited material if SASE is enclosed. Reports in 1 month. Does offer photo credit and pays in copies (usually 3). Credit line given. Previously published work OK.
Tips: "Photos which grab the reader's attention and contribute to the story we are telling are most welcome. Don't strive for fanciness yet maintain some artistry in the photos."

ALFA OWNER, Suite E, 1371 E. Warner Ave., Tustin CA 92680. (714)259-8240. Editor: Elyse Barrett. Publication of the Alfa Romeo Owners Club association. Monthly magazine. Emphasizes Alfa Romeo automobiles. Audience is upscale with median household income of $70,180. Majority hold executive, technical or professional positions. Average age is 35, with 75% male readership. Circ. 5,500. Sample copy free with 9×12 SASE and 4 first-class stamps.
Needs: Uses 12 photos/issue; 50% supplied by freelancers. Needs shots of Alfa Romeos on the road, under-the-hood tech shots, photos of historical figures related to Alfa and "glamour" shots of Alfas. Written release and captions preferred.
Making Contact & Terms: Submit portfolio for review. SASE. Reports in 2 weeks. Pays $75-100/ color cover photo; $10/b&w inside photo. Negotiates hour and day rate. Pays on publication. Credit line given. Simultaneous submissions and previously published work OK.
Tips: "We would like to see the photographer's background in automotive photography. Experience in automotive photography is preferable, though such a background isn't crucial if the person's work is good enough. Photographers should send a combination of color slides and/or 5×7 prints (if possible), plus some b&w prints. For *Alfa Owner*, knowledge of the tech aspects of automobiles is very valuable, as we need technical shots almost as much as we need glamour and "on-the-road" photos. Focus and, for the cover, a vertical format are crucial."

*AMERICAN BAR ASSOCIATION JOURNAL, 750 N. Lake Shore Drive, Chicago IL 60611. (312)988-6002. Photo Editor: Beverly Lane. Publication of the American Bar Association. Monthly magazine. Emphasizes law and the legal profession. Readers are lawyers of all ages. Circ. 400,000. Estab. 1915. Photo guidelines available.
Needs: Uses 50-100 photos per month; 80% supplied by freelance photographers. Needs vary; mainly shots of lawyers and clients.
Making Contact & Terms: Send non-returnable printed samples with resume and two business cards with rates written on back. "If samples are good, portfolio will be requested. ABA Journal keeps film. However, if another publication requests photos, we will release and send the photos. Then, that publication pays the photographer." NPI. Cannot return unsolicited material. Credit line given.
Tips: "NO PHONE CALLS. The ABA does not hire beginners."

AMERICAN BIRDS, Dept. PM, 950 3rd Ave., New York NY 10022. (212)546-9191. Editor-in-chief: Susan Roney Drennan. Publication of National Audubon Society. Published 5 times/year. Circ. 13,000. "Our major areas of interest are the changing distribution, population, migration and rare occurrence of the avifauna of North and South America, including Middle America and the West Indies. Readers are 'bird people only.' Of our 29,000 readers, 11% are professional ornithologists or zoologists, 79% serious amateurs, the rest novices." Sample copy $5; photo guidelines free with SASE.
Needs: Uses one cover-quality shot, vertical format, color/issue. This most often supplied by free-lancer. Also very interested in excellent color and b&w photos for inside use. Birds can be flying or perched, singly or in flocks, in any wild American habitat; picture essays on bird behavior. Avoid zoo or backyard shots. "Since we never know our needs too far in advance, best to send representative sampling."
Making Contact & Terms: Query with samples; send transparencies by mail for consideration; provide resume, business card, brochure, flyer or tearsheets to be kept on file for possible future assignments. SASE. Reports in 4 months. Pays up to $100/color cover photo. Pays on publication. Credit line given.
Tips: "We will probably be able to publish more photos this year than we have in the past. We look for very clear, easily identifiable birds. Diagnostic marks should be clearly visible, eyes open."

AMERICAN CRAFT, 72 Spring St., New York NY 10012. (212)274-0630. Editor: Lois Moran. Senior Editor: Pat Dandignac. Bimonthly magazine of the American Craft Council. Emphasizes contemporary creative work in clay, fiber, metal, glass, wood, etc. and discusses the technology, materials and ideas of the artists who do the work. Circ. 45,000. Estab. 1941. Free sample copy with 9×12 SASE and 64¢ postage.

Needs: Visual art. Shots of crafts: clay, metal, fiber, etc. Captions required.

Making Contact & Terms: Arrange a personal interview to show portfolio. Uses 8×10 glossy b&w prints; 4×5 transparencies and 35mm film; 4×5 color transparencies for cover, vertical format preferred. SASE. Reports in 1 month. Pays according to size of reproduction; $40 minimum/b&w and color photos; $175-350/cover photos. Pays on publication. Buys one-time rights. Previously published work OK.

AMERICAN FITNESS, Dept. PM, Suite 310, 15250 Ventura Blvd., Sherman Oaks CA 91403. (818)905-0040. Managing Editor: Rhonda J. Wilson. 6 issues/year. Estab. 1983. Publication of the Aerobics and Fitness Association of America. Emphasizes exercise, fitness, health, sports nutrition, aerobic sports. Readers are fitness enthusiasts and professionals, 75% college educated, 66% female, majority between 20-45. Circ. 25,100. Sample copy $2.50.

Needs: Uses about 20-40 photos/issue; most supplied by freelancers. Assigns 90% of work. Needs action photography of runners, aerobic classes, especially high drama for cover: swimmers, bicyclists, aerobic dancers, runners, etc. Special needs include food choices, male and female exercises, people enjoying recreation, dos and don'ts. Model release required.

Making Contact & Terms: Query with samples or with list of stock photo subjects. Send b&w prints; 35mm, 2¼×2¼ transparencies; b&w contact sheets by mail for consideration. SASE. Reports in 2 weeks. Pays $10-35/b&w or color photo; $50-100 for text/photo package. Pays 4-6 weeks after publication. Credit line given. Buys first N.A. serial rights. Simultaneous submissions and previously published work OK.

Tips: Looks for "firsthand fitness experiences—we frequently publish personal photo essays." Fitness-oriented outdoor sports are the current trend (i.e. mountain bicycling, hiking, rock climbing). Over-40 sports leagues and senior fitness are also hot trends. Wants high-quality, professional photos of people participating in high-energy activities—anything that conveys the essence of a fabulous fitness lifestyle. "Since we don't have a big art budget, freelancers usually submit piggyback pictures from their larger assignments."

AMERICAN FORESTS MAGAZINE, Dept. PM, 1516 P St. NW, Washington DC 20005. (202)667-3300. Editor: Bill Rooney. Publication for the American Forestry Association. Emphasizes use, enjoyment and management of forests and other natural resources. Readers are "people from all walks of life, from rural to urban settings, whose main common denominator is an abiding love for trees, forests or forestry." Monthly. Circ. 30,000. Sample copy and free photo guidelines with magazine-size envelope and $1.25 postage.

Needs: Uses about 40 photos/issue, 35 of which are supplied by freelance photographers (most supplied by article authors). Needs woods scenics, wildlife, woods use/management and forestry shots. Model release and captions preferred.

Making Contact & Terms: Query with resume of credits. SASE. Reports in 6-8 weeks. Pays on acceptance $300/color cover photo; $25-40/b&w inside; $50-100/color inside; $350-800 for text/photo package. Credit line given. Buys one-time rights.

Tips: Seeing trend away from "static woods scenics, toward more people and action shots." In samples wants to see "overall sharpness, unusual conformation, shots that accurately portray the highlights and 'outsideness' of outdoor scenes."

AMERICAN HUNTER, Suite 1000, 470 Spring Park Place, Herndon VA 22070. (703)481-3360. Editor: Tom Fulgham. Monthly magazine. Circ. 1,300,000. Sample copy and photo guidelines free with 9×12 SAE.

Needs: Uses wildlife shots and hunting action scenes. Photos purchased with or without accompanying mss. Seeks general hunting stories on North American game. Captions preferred. Free writer's guidelines with SASE.

Making Contact & Terms: Send material by mail for consideration. Uses 8×10 glossy b&w prints and 35mm color transparencies. (Uses 35mm color transparencies for cover). Vertical format required for cover. SASE. Reports in 1 month. Pays $25-75/b&w print; $40-275/color transparency; $300/color cover photo; $200-450 for text/photo package. Pays on publication for photos. Credit line given. Buys one-time rights.

AMERICAN LIBRARIES, 50 E. Huron St., Chicago IL 60611. (312)280-4216. Senior Production Editor: Edith McCormick. Publication of the American Library Association. Magazine published 11 times/year. Emphasizes libraries and librarians. Readers are "chiefly the members of the American Library Association but also subscribing institutions who are not members." Circ. 53,000. Sample copy free with SASE. General guidelines free with SASE.

Needs: Uses about 5-20 photos/issue; 1-3 supplied by freelance photographers. "Prefer vertical shots. Need sparkling, well-lit color prints or transparencies of beautiful library exteriors. Dramatic views; can be charming old-fashioned structure with character and grace or striking modern building. Library should be *inviting*. Added color enrichment helpful: colorful foliage, flowers, people engaged in some activity natural to the photo are examples." Special needs include "*color* photos of upbeat library happenings and events—must be unusual or of interest to sophisticated group of librarian-readers. Special need for school and academic library shots." All inside shots must be in color.
Making Contact & Terms: "Supply possible cover photos of library exterior—as many views as possible of same subject." Send transparencies or contact sheet by mail for consideration. SASE. Reports in 2-8 weeks. Pays $200-400/color cover photo; $75-150/color inside photo; and $100-450/text/photo package. Credit line always given. Buys first North American serial rights.
Tips: "Read or scan at least two issues thoroughly. We look for excellent, focused, well-lit shots, especially in color, of interesting events strongly related to library context—off-beat and upbeat occurrences in libraries of interest to sophisticated librarian audience. Also looking for rich color photos of beautiful library exteriors, both old-fashioned and charming and modern structures . . . people should be included in photos (e.g., one or two entering library building)."

AMERICAN MOTORCYCLIST, Dept. PM, P.O. Box 6114, Westerville OH 43081-6114. (614)891-2425. Vice President of Communication: Greg Harrison. Managing Editor: Bill Wood. Monthly magazine. Circ. 165,000. For "enthusiastic motorcyclists, investing considerable time in road riding or competition sides of the sport." Publication of the American Motorcyclist Association. "We are interested in people involved in, and events dealing with, all aspects of motorcycling."
Needs: Buys 10-20 photos/issue. Subjects include: travel, technical, sports, humorous, photo essay/feature and celebrity/personality.
Making Contact & Terms: Query with samples to be kept on file for possible future assignments. Sample copy and photo guidelines available for $1.50. Reports in 3 weeks. SASE. Send 5×7 or 8×10 semigloss prints; pays $20-50/photo. Also uses transparencies; pays $30-100/slide. Also buys photos in photo/text packages according to same rate; pays $6/column inch minimum for story. Captions preferred for all photos. Buys all rights. Pays on publication.
Tips: Uses transparencies for covers. "The cover shot is tied in with the main story or theme of that issue and generally needs to be with accompanying ms." Pays minimum $100/cover photo. "Show us experience in motorcycling photography and suggest your ability to meet our editorial needs and complement our philosophy."

THE AMERICAN MUSIC TEACHER, Suite 1432, 617 Vine St., Cincinnati OH 45202-2982. (513)421-1420. Director of Marketing: Diane M. Devillez. Publication of Music Teachers National Association. Bimonthly magazine. Emphasizes music teaching. Readers are music teachers operating independently from conservatories, studios and homes. Circ. 26,000.
Needs: Uses about 4 photos/issue; 3 supplied by freelancers. Needs photos of musical subject matter. Model release and captions preferred.
Making Contact & Terms: Query with resume of credits. Query with samples. Query with list of stock photo subjects. Send unsolicited photos by mail for consideration. Provide resume, business card, brochure, flyer or tearsheets to be kept on file for possible future assignments. Uses 3×5 to 8×10 glossy b&w prints; 35mm, 2¼×2¼, 4×5 and 8×10 transparencies; b&w contact sheets. SASE. Pays $150 maximum/b&w photo; $250 maximum/color photo. Pays on acceptance. Credit line given. Buys one-time rights. Simultaneous and previously published work OK.
Tips: In portfolio or samples, wants to see "teaching subjects, musical subject matter from classical to traditional, to computers and electronics, children and adults."

ANCHOR NEWS, 75 Maritime Dr., Manitowoc WI 54220. (414)684-0218. Editor: Bonnie J. Spencer. Publication of the Manitowoc Maritime Museum. Bimonthly magazine. Emphasizes Great Lakes maritime history. Readers include learned and lay readers interested in Great Lakes history. Circ. 1,900. Sample copy free with 9×12 SASE and $1 postage. Guidelines free with SASE.
Needs: Uses 8-10 photos/issue; infrequently supplied by freelance photographers. Needs historic/nostalgic, personal experience and general interest articles on Great Lakes maritime topics. How-to and technical pieces and model ships and shipbuilding are OK. Special needs include historic photography or photos that show current historic trends of the Great Lakes. Photos of waterfront development, bulk carriers, sailors, recreational boating, etc. Model release and captions required.
Making Contact & Terms: Query with samples. Send 4×5 or 8×10 glossy b&w prints by mail for consideration. SASE. Reports in 1 month. Pays in copies only on publication. Credit line given. Buys first N.A. serial rights. Simultaneous submissions and previously published work OK.
Tips: "Besides historic photographs I see a growing interest in underwater archaeology, especially on the Great Lakes, and underwater exploration—also on the Great Lakes. Sharp, clear photographs are a must. Our publication deals with a wide variety of subjects; however, we take an historical slant with

our publication. Therefore photos should be related to a historical topic in some respect. Also current trends in Great Lakes shipping. A query is most helpful. This will let the photographer know exactly what we are looking for and will help save a lot of time and wasted effort."

ANGUS JOURNAL, Dept. PM, 3201 Frederick Blvd., St. Joseph MO 64506. (816)233-0508. FAX: (816)233-0563. Editor: Jerilyn Johnson. Publication of the American Angus Association. Monthly. Circ. 17,000. Estab. 1979. Emphasizes purebred Angus cattle. Readers are Angus cattle breeders. Sample copy and photo guidelines free with 10×14 SAE and $2 postage.
Needs: "Only cover shots" are supplied by freelancers; 10% assigned and 10% from freelance stock. Needs scenic color shots of Angus cattle. Special needs include "cover shots, especially those depicting the four seasons. Winter scenes especially needed—vertical shots only." Identify as to farm's location.
Making Contact & Terms: Send slides and 8×10 color prints; 35mm, color contact sheet; and color negatives (all vertical shots). Provide resume, business card, brochure, flyer or tearsheets to be kept on file for possible future assignments. SASE. Pays $25-50/b&w photo; $150-225 color photo (cover); $150-200 photo/text package (photo story). Pays on acceptance. Credit line given. Buys all rights; rights purchased are negotiable.
Tips: "For covers: looks for creativity, pleasing-to-the eye scenery and compositions. Professional work *only*; perfect lighting, sharpness and composition. Would like to see more people (Angus farmers—kids, grandpa or grandma shots). Angus cattle shots should be purebred animals (black only) and quality animals preferred. Send us letter, sample of work and photo you would like to submit. Follow-up with a phone call or letter. We are often busy and may put letter aside. Be patient—allow us at least 2 months to reply."

ANIMALS, Dept. PM, 350 S. Huntington Ave., Boston MA 02130. (617)522-7400. FAX: (617)522-4885. Publication of the Massachusetts Society for the Prevention of Cruelty to Animals. Bimonthly. Emphasizes animals, both wild and domestic. Readers are people interested in animals, conservation, animal welfare issues, pet care and wildlife. Circ. 60,000. Estab. 1868. Sample copy $2.50 with 9×12 SAE. Photo guidelines free with SASE.
Needs: Uses about 45 photos/issue; approx. 95% supplied by freelance photographers. "All of our pictures portray animals, usually in their natural settings, however some in specific situations such as pets being treated by veterinarians or captive breeding programs." Special needs include clear, crisp shots of animals, wild and domestic, both close-up and distance shots with spectacular backgrounds, or in the case of domestic animals, a comfortable home or backyard. Model release and captions required.
Making Contact & Terms: Query with resume of credits; query with list of stock photo subjects. Provide resume, business card, brochure, flyer or tearsheets to be kept on file for possible future assignments. SASE. Reports in 1 month. Fees are usually negotiable; pays $50-150/b&w photo; $75-300/color photo. Pays on publication. Credit line given. Buys one-time rights.
Tips: Photos should be sent to Dietrich Gehring, P.O. Box 740, Altamont NY 12009. Gehring does first screening. "Offer original ideas combined with extremely high-quality technical ability. Suggest article ideas to accompany your photos, but only propose yourself as author if you are qualified. We have a never-ending need for sharp, high-quality portraits of mixed-breed dogs and cats for both inside and cover use. Keep in mind we seldom use domestic cats outdoors; we often need indoor cat shots."

APA MONITOR, American Psychological Association, Dept. PM, 750 First St. NE, Washington DC 20002. (202)336-5500. Editor: Laurie Denton. Managing Editor: John Bales. Monthly newspaper. Circ. 80,000. Emphasizes "news and features of interest to psychologists and other behavioral scientists and professionals, including legislation and agency action affecting science and health, and major issues facing psychology both as a science and a mental health profession." Sample copy with $3 and 9×12 envelope.
Needs: Buys 60-90 photos/year. Photos purchased on assignment. Needs portraits; feature illustrations; and spot news.
Making Contact & Terms: Arrange a personal interview to show portfolio or query with samples. Uses 5×7 and 8×10 b&w glossy prints; contact sheet OK. SASE. Pays by the job; $75/hour; $300-400/day. Pays on receipt. Credit line given. Buys first serial rights.
Tips: "Become good at developing ideas for illustrating abstract concepts and innovative approaches to cliches such as meetings and speeches. We look for quality in technical reproduction and innovative approaches to subjects."

APERTURE, Dept. PM, 20 E. 23rd St., New York NY 10010. (212)505-5555. Managing Editor: Michael Sand. Publication of Aperture. Quarterly. Emphasizes fine art and contemporary photography. Readers include photographers, artists, collectors. Circ. 16,000.

Needs: Uses about 60 photos/issue; all supplied by freelance photographers. Model release and captions required.
Making Contact & Terms: Submit portfolio for review. SASE. Reports in one month. Pay varies. Pays on publication. Credit line given.
Tips: "We are a nonprofit foundation and do not pay for photos." Also does not assign work.

APPALACHIAN TRAILWAY NEWS, Box 807, Harpers Ferry WV 25425. (304)535-6331. Editor: Judith Jenner. Publication of the Appalachian Trail Conference. Bimonthly. Emphasizes the Appalachian Trail. Readers are conservationists, hikers. Circ. 24,500. Guidelines free with SASE; sample copy $3 (includes postage and guidelines).
Needs: Uses about 20-30 b&w photos/issue; 4-5 supplied by freelance photographers (plus 13 color slides each year for calendar). Needs scenes from/on the Appalachian Trail; specifically of people using or maintaining the trail. Special needs include candids—people/wildlife/trail scenes. Photo information required.
Making Contact & Terms: Query samples. Send glossy 5×7 or larger b&w prints; b&w contact sheet; or 35mm transparencies by mail for consideration. SASE. Reports in 3 weeks. Pays on acceptance. Pays $100/b&w cover photo; $200 minimum/color slide calendar photo; $10-50/b&w inside photo. Credit line given. Rights negotiable. Simultaneous submissions and previously published work OK.

APPALOOSA JOURNAL, P.O. Box 8403, Moscow ID 83843. (208)882-5578. Editor: Debbie Moors. Association publication of Appaloosa Horse Club. Monthly magazine. Emphasizes Appaloosa horses. Readers are Appaloosa owners, breeders and trainers, child through adult. Circ. 17,000. Estab. 1946. Sample copy for $3. Photo guidelines sheet free with SASE.
Needs: Uses 30 photos/issue; 20% supplied by freelance photographers. Needs photos (color and b&w) to accompany features and articles. Special photo needs include photographs of Appaloosas (high quality horses) in winter scenes. Model release and photo captions required.
Making Contact & Terms: Send unsolicited 8×10 b&w and color prints or 35mm and 2¼×2¼ transparencies by mail for consideration. Reports in 3 weeks. Pays $100-300/color cover photo; $50-100/color inside photo; $25-50/b&w inside photo. Pays on acceptance. Credit line given. Buys first N.A. serial rights. Will consider previously published work.
Tips: In photographer's samples, wants to see "high quality color photos of high quality Appaloosa horses with people in outdoor environment. We often need a freelancer to illustrate a manuscript we have purchased. We need specific photos and usually very quickly."

ARCHAEOLOGY MAGAZINE, 135 William St., New York NY 10038. (212)732-5154. FAX: (212)732-5707. Photo Editor: Angela Schuster. Publication of the Archaeological Institute of America. Bimonthly. Emphasizes popular accounts of archaeological work, worldwide. Readers are upscale, highly educated, with avocational interest in archaeology. Circ. 150,000. Sample copy free with SASE.
Needs: Uses about 40 photos/issue; 5 supplied by freelancers. Needs photos of archaeological sites that are the subject of editorial features. Special needs include recent photos; sites change as excavations progress. Model and property release preferred. Photo captions required.
Making Contact & Terms: Query with list of stock photo subjects. Uses 35mm or larger transparencies. SASE. Reports in 3 weeks. NPI. Pays on publication. Buys one-time rights. Simultaneous submissions OK.
Tips: Wants to see "archaeological subject matter, with good technical ability. Read the magazine carefully."

ARMY RESERVE MAGAZINE, 1815 N. Fort Myer Dr., Room 501, Arlington VA 22209-1805. (703)696-3962. FAX: (703)696-5300/3745. Editor: Lt. Col. B.R. Devlin. Publication for U.S. Army Reserve. Quarterly magazine. Emphasizes training and employment of Army Reservists. Readers are ages 17-60, 60% male, 40% female, all occupations. No particular focus on civilian employment. Circ. 640,000. Estab. 1955. Sample copy free with 9×12 SASE and 2 first-class stamps. No photo guidelines.
Needs: Uses 35-45 photos/issue; 85% supplied by freelancers. Needs photos related to the mission or function of the U.S. Army Reserve. Uses 5×7 b&w prints; 35mm or 2¼×2¼ transparencies. Model release preferred (if of a civilian or non-affiliated person); photo captions required.
Making Contact & Terms: Interested in receiving work from newer, lesser-known photographers. "Contact editor to discuss potential job before execution." SASE. Reports in 1 month. "No pay for material; credit only since we are a nonprofit operation." Unable to purchase rights, but consider as "one-time usage." Simultaneous and previously published work OK.
Tips: "Make contact with the Public Affairs Officer of a local Army Reserve unit, preferably a major unit, to determine if you can photograph unit events or training which may be usable."

ASTA AGENCY MANAGEMENT MAGAZINE, Dept. PM, 1301 Carolina St., Greensboro NC 27401. (919)378-6065. FAX: (919)275-2864. Director of Art and Photography: Michael Robbins. Publication of the American Society of Travel Agents (ASTA). Monthly magazine. Emphasizes the business of travel. Readers are male and female travel agents, owners and managers, ages 35-60. Circ. 25,000. Estab. 1987. Sample copy free with 9×12 SAE and $3 postage. Free photo guidelines.

Needs: Uses 20-25 photos/issue; 50% supplied by freelancers. Needs executive portraits, hotel properties, cruise ships, ports, airports, aircraft, business environment and equipment. Especially wants to see photos of South Pacific destinations, Caribbean and Mexican resorts and domestic travel. Model release preferred for collateral subjects that include "who, what, when, where."

Making Contact & Terms: Query with list of stock photo subjects; provide resume, business card, brochure, flyer or tearsheets to be kept on file for possible assignments. Keeps samples on file. SASE. Reports in 1 month. Pays $350/color cover photo; $300/color inside photo; $200/b&w page rate; $300-350/day. Credit line given. Buys one-time rights, first N.A. serial rights. No submissions that other travel trade publications previously published.

Tips: Wants to see "everyday subject covered with imagination; use of light and color, variety of focal lengths, overalls, middle and long shots; portraits that show personality and dignity." Points out that "stock images must be current! I do not want 3 year old pictures of hotels and resorts. The travel industry is everchanging. Know the trade and the issues."

AUTO TRIM NEWS, Suite 300, North Bldg., 180 Allen Rd., Atlanta GA 30328. (404)252-8831. FAX: (404)252-4436. Editor: Gary Fong. Publication of National Association of Auto Trim Shops. Monthly. Emphasizes automobile restoration and restyling. Readers are upholsterers for auto/marine trim shops; body shops handling cosmetic soft goods for vehicles. Circ. 8,000. Estab. 1951.

Needs: Uses about 15 photos/issue; 6-10 supplied by freelance photographers, all on assignment. Needs "how-to photos; photos of new store openings; restyling showcase photos of unusual completed work." Special needs include "restyling ideas for new cars in the aftermarket area; soft goods and chrome add-ons to update Detroit." Captions required.

Making Contact & Terms: Interested in receiving work from newer, lesser-known photographers. Provide resume, business card, brochure, flyer or tearsheets to be kept on file for possible future assignments. Submit ideas for photo assignments in local area. Photographer should be in touch with a cooperative shop locally. SASE. Reports in 1 week. Pays $35/b&w cover photo; $75-95/job. Pays on acceptance. Credit line given if desired. Buys all rights; negotiable. Simultaneous submissions and previously published work OK.

Tips: "First learn the needs of a market or segment of an industry. Then translate it into photographic action so that readers can improve their business. In samples we look for experience in shop photography, ability to photograph technical subject matter within automotive and marine industries."

❋THE B.C. PROFESSIONAL ENGINEER, 210-6400 Roberts St., Burnaby, BC V5G 4C9 Canada. (604)299-7100. FAX: (604)299-8006. Editor: Colleen Chen. Publication of the Professional Engineers and Geoscientists Association. Monthly magazine. Emphasizes engineering. Readers are professional engineers and geoscientists of all ages. Circ. 14,000. Estab. 1950. Sample copy and photo guidelines free with 9×12 SAE with IRC.

Needs: Uses approximately 6 photos/issue; 50% supplied by freelancers. Needs photos including anything relating to any of the many engineering disciplines: biomedical, chemical, mining, forestry, civil and so on. Each year, needs a scenic winter photo for December issue. Model release preferred. Captions required.

Making Contact & Terms: Send unsolicited photos by mail for consideration. Uses 5×7 glossy color prints. SAE with IRC. Reports in 1 week. Unable to offer payment, but gives full credit. Simultaneous submissions and previously published work OK.

Tips: In portfolio or samples, wants to see "unique perspectives, sharp images, good print contrast, suitability. Prefers photos taken in B.C."

THE BIBLE ADVOCATE, P.O. Box 33677, Denver CO 80233. (303)452-7973. FAX: (303)452-0657. Editor: Roy A Marrs. Publication of the Church of God (Seventh Day). Monthly magazine; 11 issues/year. Emphasizes Christian and denominational subjects. Circ. 16,000. Estab. 1863. Sample copy free with 9×12 SAE and 87¢ postage.

Needs: Needs scenics and some religious shots (Jerusalem, etc.). Photo captions preferred, include name, place.

Making Contact & Terms: Interested in receiving work from newer, lesser-known photographers. Submit portfolio for review. SASE. Reports as needed. No payment offered. Rights negotiable. Simultaneous submissions and previously published work OK.

🍁 *The maple leaf before a listing indicates that the market is Canadian. The symbol is new this year in* Photographer's Market.

Tips: Wants to see "b&w prints for inside and 35mm color transparencies for front cover—religious, nature, people." To break in, "be patient—right now we use material on an as-needed basis. We will look at all work, but realize we don't pay for photos or cover art. Send samples and we'll review them."

*BICYCLE USA, Suite 120, 190 W. Ostend St., Baltimore MD 21230. (410)539-3399. FAX: (410)539-3496. Editor: John W. Duvall. Publications of the League of American Wheelmen Association. Magazine published 8 times a year. Emphasizes bicycling. Audience consists of avid, well-educated bicyclists of all ages, occupations and sexes. Circ. 22,000. Photo guidelines free with SASE.
Needs: Uses 15-20 photos/issue; 100% supplied by freelance photographers. Needs photos of travel, scenics and how-to. Cyclists must be shown with helmets. Prefers photos with accompanying manuscript, but will also consider without. Model release preferred; captions required.
Making Contact & Terms: Interested in receiving work from a newer, lesser-known photographer. Send unsolicited photos by mail for consideration. Uses b&w prints and 35mm transparencies. SASE. Reports in 1 month. Offers membership in the organization and sample copies as payment. Credit line given. Buys one-time rights. Previously published work OK.
Tips: "As an advocacy organization, we need photos of bicycle commuting, education and government relations in addition to general interest and travel photos."

BIKEREPORT, Box 8308, Missoula MT 59807. (406)721-1776. Editor: Dan D'Ambrosio. Publication of Bikecentennial Association. Magazine published 9 times/year. Emphasizes bicycle touring. Readers are mid-30s, mostly male, professionals. Circ. 20,000. Estab. 1974. Samples copy free with 9 × 12 SASE and $1 postage. No photo guidelines available.
Needs: Uses 8 photos/issue; 50% supplied by freelancers. Needs scenics with bicycles. Photos purchased with accompanying ms only. Model release preferred; photo captions required.
Making Contact & Terms: Submit portfolio for review. SASE. Reports in 3 weeks. Pays $100/color cover photo; $50/color page rate; $35/b&w page rate. Pays on publication. Credit line given. Buys one-time rights. Simultaneous submissions and previously published work OK.

THE BLACK WRITER, P.O. Box 1030, Chicago IL 60690. (312)995-5195. Editor: Mable Terrell. Publication of International Black Writers Association. Quarterly magazine. Emphasizes current African-American writers. Readers are ages 15-75 and of various occupations. Circ. 500. Estab. 1970. Sample copy free for 9½ × 12 SAE and 90¢ postage.
Needs: Uses 20 photos/issue; 100% supplied by freelancers. Needs photos of travel and personalities. Model release preferred; photo captions required.
Making Contact & Terms: Provide resume, business card, brochure, flyer or tearsheets to be kept on file for possible assignments. SASE. Reports in 1 month. Pays $25/b&w cover photo; $20/b&w inside photo. Pays on acceptance. Credit line given. Buys one-time rights. Previously published work OK.
Tips: Looking for "quality of the photography."

BOWLING MAGAZINE, 5301 S. 76th St., Greendale WI 53129. (414)421-6400. Editor: Bill Vint. Published by the American Bowling Congress. Emphasizes bowling for readers who are bowlers, bowling fans or media. Published bimonthly. Circ. 120,000. Free sample copy; photo guidelines for SASE.
Needs: Uses about 20 photos/issue, 1 of which, on the average, is supplied by a freelancer. Provide calling card and letter of inquiry to be kept on file for possible future assignments. "In some cases we like to keep photos. Our staff takes almost all photos as they deal mainly with editorial copy published. Rarely do we have a photo page or need freelance photos. No posed action." Model release and captions required.
Making Contact & Terms: Send 5 × 7 or 8 × 10 b&w or color photos by mail for consideration. SASE. Reports in 2 weeks. Pays on publication $20-25/b&w photo; $25-50/color photo. Credit line given. Buys one-time rights, but photos are kept on file after use. No simultaneous submissions or previously published work.

BULLETIN OF THE ATOMIC SCIENTISTS, Dept. PM, 6042 S. Kimbark, Chicago IL 60637. (312)702-2555. Art Director: Paula Lang. Monthly (except bimonthly in January-February, July-August, 10 issues/year). Circ. 25,000. Emphasizes science and world affairs. "Our specialty is nuclear politics; we regularly present disarmament proposals and analysis of international defense policies. However, the magazine prints more articles on politics and the effects of technology than it does on bombs. The *Bulletin* is *not* a technical physics journal." Readers are "educated, interested in foreign policy, moderate-to-left politically; high income levels; employed in government, academe or research facilities; about 50% are scientists." Sample copy $3.
Needs: Uses about 7-10 photos/issue; "few if any" supplied by freelance photographers. "Our publication is so specialized that we usually must get photos from the insiders in government agencies. However, we are looking for freelance photographers in the Washington DC area."

Making Contact & Terms: Provide resume, business card, brochure, flyer or tearsheets to be kept on file for possible future assignments. "Don't send a manuscript or photos without a preliminary query." SASE. Reports in 2-4 weeks. Photographers are paid by the job; amount of payment is negotiable—pay range is $25-100/b&w photo; $50-200/color photo. Pays on publication. Credit line given. Buys one-time rights. Previously published work OK "on occasion."
Tips: "Make sure you examine several issues of any magazine you consider soliciting. This will save you time and money. Editors weary of reviewing photos and art from contributors with no knowledge of the publication. You'll make a better impression if you know what the magazine's about."

CALIFORNIA LAWYER, Dept. PM, Suite 1210, 1390 Market St., San Francisco CA 94102. (415)558-9888. Editor and Publisher: Ray Reynolds. Art Director: Gordon Smith. Monthly. Emphasizes law/lawyers. Readers are lawyers and judges; some other subscribers. Circ. 115,000.
Needs: Innovative photos to illustrate stories on topical legal issues. Uses 12-18 photos/issue. Needs artistic interpretations of lawyers/courts/related issues. Model release required; captions preferred.
Making Contact & Terms: Query with samples; send 8×10 b&w glossy prints or 35mm and 2¼×2¼ transparencies by mail for consideration. SASE. Reports in 2 weeks. Pays $650/color cover photo; $100-350 color inside; $75/b&w inside photo. Pays on acceptance. Credit line given. Buys one-time rights. Simultaneous submissions OK.
Tips: "We look for an artistic eye; dramatic lighting. Offer new and innovative ways to illustrate legal stories, not simply variations on the scales of justice."

CALIFORNIA NURSE, Suite 670, 1855 Folsom St., San Francisco CA 94103. Managing Editor: Catherine Direen. Publication of California Nurses Association. Monthly tabloid. Emphasizes nursing. Readers are adults, mixed male and female nurses. Circ. 26,000. Estab. 1904. Sample copy free with SASE.
Needs: Uses 15-20 photos/issue; 10% supplied by freelancers. Needs photos of nurses, medical technology and populations served by health professionals, (e.g. elderly, infants, uninsured). Model release and photo descriptions required.
Making Contact & Terms: Send unsolicited 4×5 or 5×7 glossy b&w prints by mail for consideration. Provide resume, business card, brochure, flyer or tearsheets to be kept on file for possible assignments. Phone calls acceptable. SASE. Reports in 3 weeks. Pays $10-50/b&w cover photo; $10/b&w inside photo. Pays on publication. Buys one-time rights. Simultaneous submissions OK.
Tips: "Best choices are sensitive shots of people needing or receiving health care or RNs at work. Send sample photos, well-tailored to individual publication."

CALYPSO LOG, 8440 Santa Monica Blvd., Los Angeles CA 90069. (213)656-4422. FAX: (213)656-4891. Editor: Mary Batten. Publication of The Cousteau Society. Bimonthly. Emphasizes expedition activities of The Cousteau Society; educational/science articles; environmental activities. Readers are members of The Cousteau Society. Circ. 260,000. Sample copy $2 with 9×12 SASE and 65¢ postage. Photo guidelines with SASE.
Needs: Uses 10-14 photos/issue; 1-2 supplied by freelancers; 2-3 photos per issue come from freelance stock. Preference for underwater creature shots in natural habitats. We review duplicates only. Captions preferred.
Making Contact & Terms: Query with samples; and list of stock photo subjects. Send unsolicited photos (duplicates) by mail for consideration. Uses color prints; 35mm and 2¼×2¼ transparencies (duplicates only). SASE. Reports in 5 weeks. Pays $50-200/color photo. Pays on publication. Buys one-time rights and translation rights for our French publication. Previously published work OK.
Tips: Send "sharp, clear images of underwater life/creatures in duplicate form only." In samples, wants to see "photos that tell a story of animals interacting with each other and/or the environment." Also sharp, clear, good composition and color; unusual animals or views of environmental features. Prefers transparencies over prints. "We look for ecological stories, food chain, prey-predator interaction and impact of people on environment. Please request a copy of our publication to familiarize yourself with our style, content and tone and then send samples that best represent underwater and environmental photography."

✦CANADA LUTHERAN, 1512 St. James St., Winnipeg MB R3H 0L2 Canada. (204)786-6707. FAX: (204)783-7548. Art Director: Darrell Dyck. Editor: Ferdy Baglo. Publication of Evangelical Lutheran Church in Canada. Monthly. Emphasizes faith/religious content; Lutheran denomination. Readers are members of the Evangelical Lutheran Church in Canada. Circ. 32,000. Estab. 1986. Sample copy for $1.50/copy, 9×12 SAE and $1 postage (Canadian).
Needs: Uses 4-10 photos/issue; most supplied though article contributors; 1 or 2 supplied by freelancers. Needs photos of people (in worship/work/play etc.); scenics. Model release and captions preferred.
Making Contact & Terms: Interested in receiving work from newer, lesser-known photographers. Send 5×7 glossy prints or 35mm transparencies by mail for consideration. SASE. Pays $15-50/b&w photo; $40-75/color photo. Pays on publication. Credit line given. Buys one-time rights.

Tips: "Trend toward more men and women in non-stereotypical roles. Do not restrict photo submissions to just the categories you believe the client needs. Give us a pile of shots that show your range. Let us keep them on file—then we will turn to that file each month when we need to illustrate something on short notice."

CEA ADVISOR, Dept. PM, Connecticut Education Association, 21 Oak St., Hartford CT 06106. (203)525-5641. Managing Editor: Michael Lydick. Monthly tabloid. Circ. 30,000. Emphasizes education. Readers are public school teachers. Sample copy free for $1.50 postage.
Needs: Uses about 20 photos/issue; 1 or 2 supplied by freelancers. Needs "classroom scenes, students, school buildings." Model release and captions preferred.
Making Contact & Terms: Send b&w contact sheet by mail for consideration. Provide resume, business card, brochure, flyer or tearsheets to be kept on file for possible future assignments. Does not return unsolicited material. Reports in 1 month. Pays $50/b&w cover photo; $25/b&w inside photo. Pays on publication. Credit line given. Buys all rights. Simultaneous submissions and previously published work OK.

CHESS LIFE, 186 Route 9W, New Windsor NY 12553. (914)562-8350. FAX: (914)561-CHES. Editor-in-Chief: Glenn Petersen. Art Director: Jami Anson. Publication of the U.S. Chess Federation. Monthly. Circ. 60,000. *Chess Life* covers news of all major national and international tournaments; historical articles, personality profiles, columns of instruction, occasional fiction, humor . . . for the devoted fan of chess. Sample copy and photo guidelines free with SASE and 75¢ postage.
Needs: Uses about 10 photos/issue; 7-8 supplied by freelancers. Needs "news photos from events around the country; shots for personality profiles." Special needs include "Chess Review" section. Model release and captions preferred.
Making Contact & Terms: Query with samples. Provide business card and tearsheets to be kept on file for possible future assignments. SASE. Reports in "2-4 weeks, depending on when the deadline crunch occurs." Pays $100-200/b&w or color cover photo; $15-25/b&w inside photo; $15-30/hour; $150-250/day. Pays on publication. Credit line given. Buys one-time rights; "we occasionally purchase all rights for stock mug shots." Simultaneous submissions and previously published work OK.
Tips: Using "more color, and more illustrative photography. The photographer's name and date should appear on the back of all photos. 35mm color transparencies are preferred for cover shots. Looks for 'clear images, good composition and contrast—with a fresh approach to interest the viewer. Increasing emphasis on strong portraits of chess personalities, especially Americans. Tournament photographs of winning players and key games are in high demand."

*CHEVY OUTDOORS, 30400 Van Dyke Ave., Warren MI 48093. (313)574-9100. Art Director: Ken Cendrowski. Publication of the Chevrolet company. Quarterly magazine. Emphasizes outdoor life and travel, recreational vehicles and fishing. Readership consists of men and women of all occupations, ages 20 to 70. Circ. 1,080,000. Sample copy free with 9×12 SASE and $1.50 postage. Photo guidelines free with SASE.
Needs: Uses 80 photos/issue; 70% supplied by freelance photographers. Needs photos of animal/wildlife shots, travel, scenics. Model release and photo captions required.
Making Contact & Terms: Query with list of stock photo subjects. SASE. Reports in 2-6 weeks. Pays $350-600/b&w page. Pays on acceptance. Credit line given. Buys one-time rights. Simultaneous submissions and previously published work OK.
Tips: "Looking for intelligent, well-exposed and insightful outdoor photography. Photographers should have a genuine interest in subject."

CHILDHOOD EDUCATION, Suite 315, 11501 Georgia Ave., Wheaton MD 20902. (301)942-2443. Director of Publications/Editor: Lucy Prete Martin. Assistant Editor: Joan Saidel. Publication for the Association for Childhood Education International. Bimonthly journal. Emphasizes the education of children from infancy through early adolescence. Readers include teachers, administrators, day-care workers, parents, psychologists, student teachers, etc. Circ. 15,000. Sample copy free with 9×12 SAE and $1.44 postage; photo guidelines free with SASE.
Needs: Uses 5-10 photos/issue; 2-3 supplied by freelance photographers. Subject matter includes children infancy-14 years in groups or alone, in or out of the classroom, at play, in study groups; boys and girls of all races and in all cities and countries. Reviews photos with or without accompanying ms. Special needs include photos of minority children; photos of children from different ethnic groups together in one shot; boys and girls together. Model release required.
Making Contact & Terms: Send unsolicited photos by mail for consideration. Uses 8×10 glossy b&w and color prints and colored transparencies. SASE. Reports in 1 month. Pays $50-75/color cover photo; $25-50/b&w inside photo. Pays on publication. Credit line given. Buys one-time rights. Simultaneous submissions and previously published work are discouraged but negotiable.
Tips: "Send pictures of unposed children, please."

CHOSEN PEOPLE MAGAZINE, Dept. PM, 1300 Crossbeam Dr., Charlotte NC 28217. (704)357-9000. Communications Director: Andy Stebbins. Publication of the Chosen People Ministries. Monthly. Emphasizes Jewish subjects, Israel. Readers are Christians interested in Israel and the Jewish people. Circ. 85,000. Estab. 1906. Sample copy free with SASE.
Needs: Uses about 3-4 photos/issue; 3 supplied by freelancers. Needs "scenics of Israel, preferably b&w; photos of Jewish customs and traditions." Model release required. Photo captions preferred.
Making Contact & Terms: Query with samples or with list of stock photo subjects; send 8×10 glossy b&w photos by mail for consideration; provide resume, business card, brochure, flyer or tearsheets to be kept on file for possible future assignments. SASE. Reports in 3 weeks. Pays $50-100/b&w and color photo. Pays on acceptance. Credit line given. Buys one-time rights. Simultaneous submissions OK.
Tips: Wants to see photos of "Israel scenery, Jewish holidays and Jewish culture."

CHRISTIAN HOME & SCHOOL, 3350 E. Paris Ave. SE, Grand Rapids MI 49512. (616)957-1070. Associate Editor: Judy Zylstra. Publication of Christian Schools International. Published 6 times a year. Emphasizes Christian family issues. Readers are parents who support Christian education. Circ. 50,000. Estab. 1922. Sample copy free with 9×12 SASE with 4 first-class stamps; photo guidelines free with SASE.
Photos Needs: Uses 10-15 photos/issue; 7-10 supplied by freelancers. Needs photos of children, family activities, school scenes. Model release preferred.
Making Contact & Terms: Query with samples. Query with list of stock photo subjects. Send b&w prints or contact sheets by mail for consideration. SASE. Reports in 3 weeks. Pays $100/color cover photo; $30/b&w inside photo. Pays on publication. Credit line given. Buys one-time rights. Simultaneous submissions and previously published work OK.
Tips: Assignment work is becoming rare. Freelance stock most often used. "Photographers who allow us to hold duplicate photos for an extended period of time stand more chance of having their photos selected for publication than those who require speedy return of submitted photos."

CIVITAN MAGAZINE, P. O. Box 130744, Birmingham AL 35213-0744. (205)591-8910. Editor: Dorothy Wellborn. Publication of Civitan International. Bimonthly magazine. Emphasizes work with mental retardation/developmental disabilities. Readers are men and women, college age to retirement and usually managers or owners of businesses. Circ. 36,000. Estab. 1920. Sample copy free with 9×12 SASE and 2 first-class stamps. No photo guidelines.
Needs: Uses 8-10 photos/issue; 50% supplied by freelancers. Always looking for good cover shots (travel, scenic and how-to's). Model release and photo captions preferred.
Making Contact & Terms: Send unsolicited 2¼×2¼ or 4×5 transparencies or b&w prints by mail for consideration. Provide resume, business card, brochure, flyer or tearsheets to be kept on file for possible assignments. Reports in 1 month. Pays $50/color cover photo; $10 b&w inside photo. Pays on acceptance. Buys one-time rights. Simultaneous submissions and previously published work OK.

COAL VOICE, % National Coal Association, 1130 17th St. NW, Washington DC 20036. (202)463-2640. Editor: Aundrea Cika. Publication of the National Coal Association. Bimonthly magazine. Covers coal and energy issues. Readers are coal producers, major coal consumers, industry representatives and allies, and state and local regulatory/legislature members. Circ. 14,600. Estab. 1978. Sample copies free upon request.
Needs: Uses 15 photos/issue; 25% supplied by freelancers. Needs photos of technology, people and scenics.
Making Contact & Terms: Arrange personal interview to show portfolio. Query with list of stock photo subjects. Provide resume, business card, brochure, flyer or tearsheets to be kept on file for possible future assignment. Reports in 2 weeks. NPI; payment varies according to use. Pays on publication. Credit line given. Rights purchased vary. Simultaneous submissions and previously published work OK.
Tips: "Looking for someone who can break through stereotypes and help enhance a misunderstood industry."

Can't find a listing? Check at the end of each market section for the " '92-'93 Changes" lists. These lists include any market listings from the '92 edition which were either not verified or deleted in this edition.

COMMERCIAL INVESTMENT REAL ESTATE JOURNAL, Dept. PM, Suite 600, 430 N. Michigan Ave., Chicago IL 60611. (312)321-4464. Editor: Lorene Norton Palm. Publication of Commercial-Investment Real Estate Institute. Quarterly journal. Emphasizes commercial real estate brokerage and consulting. Readers are commercial real estate brokers, consultants, developers, mortgage bankers, attorneys. Circ. 12,000. Estab. 1983. Sample copy free with 9 × 12 SAE and $1.45 postage.
Needs: Uses 3-6 photos/issue; 100% supplied by freelance photographers. Photo needs vary; may be office scenes, buildings, high-resolution close-ups for special effects, etc.
Making Contact & Terms: Provide resume, business card, brochure, flyer or tearsheets to be kept on file for possible assignments. Pays $800-900/b&w cover photo; $150-250/b&w inside photo. Pays on acceptance. Credit line given. Buys first North American serial rights. Will consider previously published work.

COMMUNICATION WORLD, Suite 600, One Hallidie Plaza, San Francisco CA 94102. (415)433-3400. Editor: Gloria Gordon. Publication of International Association of Business Communicators. Monthly magazine. Emphasizes public relations, business and organizational communications. Readers are members in corporate communication, consultants, ages 30+. Circ. 15,000. Estab. 1969.
Needs: Uses 2-3 photos/issue; all supplied by freelancers. Needs photos that reflect communication in corporate atmosphere. Model release preferred; photo captions required.
Making Contact & Terms: Arrange a personal interview to show portfolio. Query with resume of credits. Submit portfolio for review. Provide resume, business card, brochure, flyer or tearsheets to be kept on file for possible assignments. SASE. Pays $350/color cover photo; $250/b&w cover photo; $275+/color inside photo; $100/b&w inside photo; $250/color page rate. Pays on publication. Credit line given. Buys one-time rights. Simultaneous submissions and previously published work OK.

COMPANY: A MAGAZINE OF THE AMERICAN JESUITS, Dept. PM, 3441 N. Ashland Ave., Chicago IL 60657. (312)281-1534. FAX: (312)281-0555. Editor: E.J. Mattimoe. Published by the Jesuits (Society of Jesus). Quarterly magazine. Emphasizes people; "a human interest magazine about people helping people." Circ. 156,000. Estab. 1983. Sample copy free with 9 × 12 SAE with 95¢ postage. Photo guidelines free with SASE.
Needs: All photos supplied by freelancers. Needs photo-stories of Jesuit and allied ministries and projects, only photos related to Jesuit works. Photos purchased with or without accompanying ms. Model release and captions required.
Making Contact & Terms: Query with samples. Provide resume, business card, brochure, flyer or tearsheets to be kept on file for possible future assignments. SASE. Reports in 1 month. Pays $300/color cover photo; $100-400/job. Pays on publication. Credit line given. Buys one-time rights.
Tips: "Avoid large-group 'smile at camera' photos. We are interested in people photographs that tell a story in a sensitive way—the eye-catching look that something is happening."

*COMPUTER MAGAZINE, 10662 Los Vaqueros Circle, P.O. Box 3014, Los Alamitos CA 90720-1264. (714)821-8380. FAX: (714)821-4010. Editor: Marilyn Potes. Association publication of IEEE Computer Society. Monthly magazine. Emphasizes computer industry and research. Readers are electrical engineers, technical managers, computer designers, value-added resellers and system integrators. Circ. 90,000. Estab. 1968. Sample copy free with 8½ × 11 SASE and $2 postage.
Needs: Uses 1 cover photo/issue; usually supplied by freelance photographers or stock photo house. Needs high-technology-oriented images or analogous images from other fields or nature.
Making Contact & Terms: Interested in receiving work from a newer, lesser-known photographer. Query with samples. Query with list of stock photo subjects. Send 8 × 10½ color prints, 35mm transparencies by mail for consideration. SASE. Reports in 1-4 weeks. Pays $300-450/color cover photo (8⅛ × 10⅞ full-bleed). Pays on publication. Credit line given. Buys one-time rights. Previously published work OK "depends on where published."

CONFIDENT LIVING, Box 82808, Lincoln NE 68501. (402)474-4567. Managing Editor: Jan Reeser. Publication of Back to the Bible. Monthly (July-Aug. combined) magazine. Emphasizes religious subjects (Protestant, conservative). Readers are adults, primarily ages 50 and up, conservative, middle class. Circ. 85,000. Estab. 1944. Sample copy for $1.95. Photo guidelines free with SASE.
Needs: Uses 25 photos/issue; 70% supplied by freelancers. Assigns 65%. Most photos are used to illustrate specific article topics, but interested in seeing seniors of all ages in numerous activities. Model release preferred.
Making Contact & Terms: Send unsolicited photos by mail for consideration. Uses 35mm, 2¼ × 2¼ transparencies; duplicates preferred. SASE. Reports in 1 month. Pays up to $85/color cover photo; up to $25/b&w inside photo. Pays on acceptance or publication (if accompanying article ms). Credit line given. Buys one-time rights. Simultaneous submissions and previously published work OK.
Tips: "Be familiar with the magazine!"

THE CONSTRUCTION SPECIFIER, Dept. PM, 601 Madison St., Alexandria VA 22314. (703)684-0300. FAX: (703)684-0465. Associate Editor: Kristine Kessler. Publication of the Construction Specifications Institute. Monthly magazine. Emphasizes construction. Readers are architects and engineers in commercial construction. Circ. 20,000. Estab. 1949. Sample copy free with 8½ × 11 SASE and 1 first-class stamp. Photo guidelines not available.
Needs: Uses 40 photos/issue; 15% supplied by freelance photographers; 85% from freelance stock. Needs architectural and construction shots. Model release and photo captions required.
Making Contact & Terms: Provide resume, business card, brochure, flyer or tearsheets to be kept on file for possible assignments. SASE. Pays $25-200/b&w photo; $50-400/color photo. Pays on publication. Credit line given. Buys one-time rights. Simultaneous submissions OK if in unrelated field. Previously published work OK.
Tips: Wants to see "photos depicting commercial construction: jobsite shots."

CONTACT MAGAZINE, IDS Financial Services, IDS Tower 10, T21/745, Minneapolis MN 55440. (612)671-8513. Photo Editor: Ron Lee. Publication of IDS Financial Services, Inc. Bimonthly. Emphasizes financial services. Readers are home office employees, registered representatives throughout the country, retirees and others. Circ. 10,000.
Needs: Uses about 35 photos/issue; some are supplied by freelancers. Needs photojournalistic coverage of IDS people at work.
Making Contact & Terms: Query with samples. SASE. Reports in 1 month. Pays $50-75/hour. Pays on acceptance. Credit line given. Buys all rights.
Tips: Prefers to see "b&w photojournalism" in samples, "bringing the human element into any type of story." Offers pleasant client/photographer working arrangements. Photo editor is involved in the whole project, from concept through completion.

CURRENTS, Voice of the National Organization for River Sports, Suite 200, 314 N. 20th St., Colorado Springs CO 80904. (719)473-2466. FAX: (719)475-1752. Editor: Greg Moore. Quarterly magazine. Membership publication of National Organization for River Sports, for canoeists, kayakers and rafters. Emphasizes river conservation and river access, also techniques of river running. Circ. 10,000. Estab. 1979. Free writer's and photographer's guidelines with #10 SASE; sample copy $1.
Needs: Photo essay/photo feature (on rivers of interest to river runners). Need features on rivers that are in the news because of public works projects, use regulations, wild and scenic consideration or access prohibitions. Sport newsphotos of canoeing, kayaking, rafting and other forms of (whitewater) river paddling, especially photos of national canoe and kayak races; nature/river subjects, conservation-oriented; travel (river runs of interest to a nationwide membership). Wants on a regular basis close-up action shots of whitewater river running and shots of dams in progress, signs prohibiting access. Especially needs for next year shots of whitewater rivers that are threatened by dams showing specific stretch to be flooded and dam-builders at work. No "panoramas of river runners taken from up on the bank or the edge of a highway. We must be able to see their faces, front-on shots. We always need photos of the twenty (most) popular whitewater river runs around the U.S." Photos purchased with or without accompanying ms. "We are looking for articles on whitewater rivers that are in the news regionally and nationally—for example, rivers endangered by damming; access is limited by government decree; rivers being considered for wild and scenic status; rivers offering a setting for unusual expeditions and runs; and rivers having an interest beyond the mere fact that they can be paddled. Also articles interviewing experts in the field about river techniques, equipment and history." Buys 10 photos/issue; 25% assigned and 75% unsolicited. Captions required.
Making Contact & Terms: Interested in receiving work from a newer, lesser-known photographer. Send material or photocopies of work by mail for consideration. "We need to know of photographers in various parts of the country." Provide tearsheets or photocopies of work to be kept on file for possible future assignments. Uses 5 × 7 and 8 × 10 glossy b&w prints. Occasional color prints. Query before submitting color transparencies. SASE. Reports in 2 weeks. Pays $20-60/b&w print or color prints or transparencies; $50-150 for text/photo package; $35 minimum/interview article. Credit line given. Buys one-time rights. Simultaneous submissions and previously published work OK if labeled clearly as such.
Tips: "Need more squirt boating photos; photos of women; and opening canoeing photos. Looks for close-up action shots of whitewater river runners in kayaks, rafts, canoes or dories. Little or no red. Show faces of paddlers. Photos must be clear and sharp. Tell us where the photo was taken—name of river, state, and name of rapid, if possible."

✻ CYCLING: BC, Dept. PM, 332-1367 W. Broadway, Vancouver BC V6H 4A9 Canada. (604)737-3034. FAX: (604)738-7175. Office Manager: Betty Third. Estab. 1974. Monthly newsletter. Publication of Bicycling Association of British Columbia. Emphasizes bicycling. Readers are 14-75 years old, male and female. Circ. 2,600. Sample copy with #10 SAE and IRC.

© Richard Jacobs

By coming in close on the subject and shooting a crystal clear photo which "froze" the action of a raging river, Richard Jacobs, of Wilmette, Illinois, gives the viewer a feel for the chaos involved in kayaking through rapids. Jacobs received $50 from Currents Magazine, which used the photo on one of its covers.

Needs: Uses 1 photo/issue, supplied by 1 freelancer. Needs action photos of bicycling. Special photo needs include all photos for newsletters, promo materials.
Making Contact & Terms: Send b&w and color prints by mail for consideration. SAE and IRC. No payment. Reports in 2 weeks. Credit line given. Previously published work OK.
Tips: Bicycling Association of British Columbia asks for donations of photos. Will give photographer credit and send sample copy of publication.

DEALER PROGRESS MAGAZINE, Dept. PM, 314 At the Barn, 15444 Clayton Rd., Ballwin MO 63011. (314)527-4001. Editor: K. Elliott Nowels. Publication of The Fertilizer Institute. Bimonthly. "We focus on managers of retail fertilizer and agricultural chemical dealerships. Our aim is to be the business magazine for agribusiness managers." Readers are retail business people dealing directly with farmers. Most readers are in small, rural communities and many are in the Midwest. Circ. 28,000. Sample copy free with 9×12 SAE.
Needs: Uses 3-4 photos/issue; all covers are assigned and 1-2 editorial photos are bought each year. Cover: studio shot based on *Dealer Progress* concept. Editorial photos should be illustrative of the topic. Scenes of actual retail facilities and activities are sought. No brand/chain affiliations visible if possible. Special needs include artistic photos suitable to accompany broad discussions of industry trends. Model release required; captions preferred.
Making Contact & Terms: Arrange a personal interview to show portfolio; provide resume, business card, brochure, flyer or tearsheets to be kept on file for possible future assignments. Uses 8×10 glossy b&w prints; 35mm transparencies. SASE. NPI; pay varies by the job. Pays on publication. Credit line given. Buys one-time rights. Simultaneous submissions OK.
Tips: Prefers to see "familiarity with our industry; variety of subjects and techniques; originality of approach; quality workmanship. Capitalize on your strengths. Be ambitious and persistent. Create opportunities."

DEFENDERS, 1244 19th St. NW, Washington DC 20036. (202)659-9510. FAX: (202)659-0680. Editor: James G. Deane. Membership publication of Defenders of Wildlife. Bimonthly. Emphasizes wildlife and wildlife habitat. Circ. 73,000. Sample copy free with 9×12½ SASE and $1.44 postage; photo guidelines free with SASE.
Needs: Uses 35 or more photos/issue; "almost all" from freelancers. Caption information required.
Making Contact & Terms: Query with list of stock photo subjects. SASE. Reports ASAP. In portfolio or samples, wants to see "wildlife group action and behaviorial shots in preference to static portraits. High technical quality." Pays $50-100/b&w photo; $75-450/color photo. Pays on publication. Credit line given. Buys one-time rights.
Tips: "*Defenders* focuses heavily on endangered species and destruction of their habitats, wildlife refuges and wildlife management issues, primarily North American, but also some foreign. Images must be sharp. Cover images usually must be vertical, able to take the logo up top, and be arresting and *simple*. Think twice before submitting anything but low speed (preferably Kodachrome) transparencies."

DISCOVERY MAGAZINE, Suite 1700, One Illinois Center, 111 E. Wacker Dr., Chicago IL 60601. (312)565-1200. FAX: (312)565-5923. Art Director: Deborah Clark. Publication of Allstate Motor Club. Quarterly. Emphasizes U.S. travel, especially by car and destinations—particular places or regions. Readers are middle-aged, average income, who travel by car. Circ. 1.7 million. Sample copy for 9×12 SASE and $1 postage. Photo guidelines free with SASE.
Needs: Uses 35 photos/issue; all supplied by freelance photographers. Needs photos of U.S. travel destinations—both urban and rural scenes, with people. Model release preferred; captions required.
Making Contact & Terms: Interested in receiving work from a newer, lesser-known photographer. Query with list of stock photo subjects. Provide resume, business card, brochure, flyer or tearsheets to be kept on file for possible future assignments. Reports in 1 month. Pays $225/color photo; 450 maximum/day. Pays on acceptance. Credit line given. Buys first North American serial rights. Simultaneous submissions and previously published work OK.
Tips: "Write for photo guidelines and a sample issue, sending us a SASE."

*DIVERSION MAGAZINE, 60 East 42nd St., New York NY 10165. (212)297-9600. FAX: (212)808-9079. Photo Researcher: Michele Hadlow. Monthly magazine. Emphasizes travel. Readers are doctors/physicians. Circ. 176,000. Sample copy free with SASE.
Needs: Uses varying number of photos/issue; all supplied by freelancers. Needs a variety of subjects, "mostly worldwide travel. Hotels, restaurants and people. Model/property release preferred. Captions preferred; include precise locations.
Making Contact & Terms: Query with list of stock photo subjects. Keeps samples on file. SASE. Reports in 3 weeks. Pays $350/color cover photo; $135/¼ color page inside photo; $125/¼ page b&w inside; $225/color full page rate; $200/b&w full page; $200-250/day. Pays on publication. Credit line

given. Buys one-time rights. Simultaneous submissions and previously published work OK.
Tips: "Send updated stock list and photo samples regularly."

THE DOLPHIN LOG, 8440 Santa Monica Blvd., Los Angeles CA 90069. (213)656-4422. Editor: Beth Kneeland. Publication of The Cousteau Society, Inc., a nonprofit organization. Bimonthly magazine. Emphasizes "ocean and water-related subject matter for children ages 7 to 15." Circ. 105,000. Estab. 1981. Sample copy $2 with 9×12 SASE and 75¢ postage. Photo guidelines free with SASE.
Needs: Uses about 20 photos/issue; 10 supplied by freelancers; 10% stock. Needs "selections of images of individual creatures or subjects, such as architects and builders of the sea, how sea animals eat, the smallest and largest things in the sea, the different forms of tails in sea animals, resemblances of sea creatures to other things. Also excellent potential cover shots or images which elicit curiosity, humor or interest." Please request photographer's guidelines. Model release required if person is recognizable. Captions preferred.
Making Contact & Terms: Query with samples, list of stock photos or send duplicate 35mm transparencies or b&w contact sheets by mail for consideration. Send duplicates only. SASE. Reports in 2 months. Pays $50/b&w photo; $50-200/color photo. Pays on publication. Credit line given. Buys one-time rights and worldwide translation rights. Simultaneous and previously published submissions OK.
Tips: Prefers to see "rich color, sharp focus and interesting action of water-related subjects" in samples. "No assignments are made. A large amount is staff-shot. However, we use a fair amount of freelance photography, usually pulled from our files, approx. 45-50%. Stock photos purchased only when an author's sources are insufficient or we have need for a shot not in file. These are most often hard-to-find creatures of the sea." To break in, "send a good submission of dupes which are in keeping with our magazine's tone/content; be flexible in allowing us to hold slides for consideration."

DUCKS UNLIMITED, Dept. PM, One Waterfowl Way, Long Grove IL 60047. (708)438-4300. Contact: Chris Stone, Production Assistant. Association publication of Ducks Unlimited. Bimonthly magazine. Emphasizes waterfowl conservation. Readers are professional males, ages 40-50. Circ. 550,000. Estab. 1937. Sample copy $2.50. Guidelines free with SASE.
Needs: Uses 20-30 photos/issue; 70% supplied by freelance photographers. Needs wildlife shots (waterfowl/waterfowling), scenics and personalities. Special photo needs: "I like to see photos with ideas on how to use them in photo stories."
Making Contact & Terms: To contact: Sample 20 to 40 or so 35mm or larger transparencies with ideas. SASE. Reports in 1 month. Pays $250/color cover photo; $50-150/color inside photo; $150-300/day plus expenses for assignments; $500/photo essay. Pays on acceptance. Credit line given. Buys one-time rights plus permission to reprint in our Mexican and Canadian publications. Previously published work OK.

*THE ELKS MAGAZINE, 425 W. Diversey, Chicago IL 60614. (312)528-4500. Editor: Fred D. Oakes. Publication of the B.P.O. Elks of the U.S. Publishes 10 times per year. Emphasizes general interest including travel, history, nostalgia, sports, business and self-improvement. Readers are 50+, 54% male, 46% female, broad occupational spectrum. Circ. 1.5 million. Estab. 1922. Sample copy for 9×12 SASE and 85¢ postage.
Needs: "We frequently use scenics for cover." Model release and photo captions preferred.
Making Contact & Terms: Interested in receiving work from a newer, lesser-known photographer. SASE. Reports in 3 weeks. Pays $350-450/color cover photo. Pays on acceptance. Credit line given. Buys first North American serial rights. Will consider simultaneous submissions.

ENVIRONMENTAL ACTION, Suite 600, 6930 Carroll Ave., Takoma Park MD 20910. (301)891-1106. FAX: (301)891-2218. Editor: Barbara Ruben. Association publication of Environmental Action, Inc. Quarterly magazine. Emphasizes environmental subjects for activists of all ages. Circ. 14,000. Estab. 1970. Sample copies available for $2.50.
Needs: Uses up to 10 photos/issue; 40% supplied by freelancers. Needs photos that "illustrate environmental problems and issues, including solid waste, toxic waste and energy." Model/property release and photo captions preferred.
Making Contact & Terms: Query with resume of credits. Send stock photo list. Provide resume, business card, brochure, flyer or tearsheet to be kept on file for possible assignments. Does not keep samples on file. Cannot return material. Reports in 1 month. Pays $40-150/b&w cover photo; $25-75/b&w inside photo. Pays on publication. Credit line given. Buys one-time rights. Simultaneous submissions and previously published work OK.
Tips: "We only publish in b&w, but we will consider both color and b&w original photos."

EXECUTIVE FEMALE, Dept. PM, 4th Floor, 127 W 24th St., New York NY 10011. (212)645-0770. Editor-in-Chief: Basia Hellwig. Art Director: Maxine Davidowitz. Publication of National Association for Female Executives. Bimonthly. Emphasizes career advancement, problems/solutions in work place.

Readers are "middle to upper level managers looking to move up in career. Also entrepreneurs and women starting or expanding small businesses." Circ. 250,000. Sample copy free with 10 × 13 SAE and $1.07 postage.

Needs: Uses about 20 photos/issue; 5 supplied by freelancers. Needs portraits of professional women, informal and formal. Model release required; captions and storyline preferred.

Making Contact & Terms: Query with resume of credits; provide resume, business card, brochure, flyer or tearsheets to be kept on file for possible future assignments. SASE. Reports in 4-6 weeks. Pays $600/color cover photo; $100/quarter page; $200/half page. Pays on publication. Credit line given. Buys one-time and all rights. Simultaneous submissions and previously published work OK.

Tips: Looks for "interesting portraits of women; professional but not boring business photos." Send transparencies only for best color.

FAMILY MOTOR COACHING, Dept. PM, 8291 Clough Pike, Cincinnati OH 45244. (513)474-3622. Editor: Pamela Wisby Kay. Publication of Family Motor Coach Association. Monthly. Emphasizes motor homes. Readers are members of national association of motor home owners. Circ. 90,000. Estab. 1963. Sample copy $2.50. Photo guidelines free with SASE.

Needs: Uses about 45-50 photos/issue; 40-45 supplied by freelance photographers. Each issue includes varied subject matter—primarily needs travel and scenic shots and how-to material. Photos purchased with accompanying ms only. Model release preferred; captions required.

Making Contact & Terms: Query with resume of credits. SASE. Reports in 1 month. Pays $100-500/ text/photo package. Pays on acceptance. Credit line given if requested. Prefers first N.A. rights, but will consider one-time rights on photos *only*.

FELLOWSHIP, Box 271, Nyack NY 10960. (914)358-4601. FAX: (914)358-4924. Editor: Robin Washington. Publication of the Fellowship of Reconciliation. Publishes 32-page b&w magazine 8 times/ year. Emphasizes peace-making/social justice/nonviolent social change. Readers are religious peace fellowships—interfaith pacifists. Circ. 8,500. Estab. 1935. Sample copy free with SASE on request.

Needs: Uses 8-10 photos/issue; 90% supplied by freelancers. Needs stock photos of monuments/civil disobedience/demonstrations—Middle East; South Africa; prisons; anti-nuclear; children; farm crisis; USSR. Captions required. Also natural beauty and scenic; b&w only.

Making Contact & Terms: Provide resume, business card, brochure, flyer or tearsheets to be kept on file for possible future assignments. "Call on specs." SASE. Reports in 3 weeks. Pays $25/b&w cover photo; $13.50/b&w inside photo. Pays on publication. Credit line given. Buys one-time rights. Simultaneous submissions and previously published work OK.

Tips: "You must want to make a contribution to peace movements. Money is simply token; (our authors contribute without tokens)."

FFA NEW HORIZONS, 5632 Mount Vernon Memorial Hwy., Alexandria VA 22309-0160. (703)360-3600. FAX: (703)360-5524. Associate Editor: Lawinna McGary. Publication of the National Future Farmers of America organization. Bimonthly magazine. Emphasizes agriculture and youth interest. Readers are agriculture students, ages 14-21. Circ. 396,000. Estab. 1953. Sample copy free. Photo guidelines free with SASE.

Needs: Uses 45 photos/issue; 18 supplied by freelancers. "We need exciting shots of our FFA members in action." Has continuing need for national coverage. Model and property release preferred. Photo captions required; names, hometowns.

Making Contact & Terms: Provide resume, business card, brochure, flyer or tearsheets to be kept on file for possible assignments. Keeps samples on file. SASE. Reports in 1 month. Pays $100/color cover photo; $35/color inside photo; $20/b&w inside photo. Pays on acceptance. Credit line given. Buys one-time rights.

Tips: "We want to see energy and a sense that the photographer knows how to work with teenagers." Contact editor before doing any work. "We have specific needs and need good shooters."

*FLORIDA FOLIAGE MAGAZINE, P.O. Box 2507, Apopka FL 32704. (407)886-1036. Contact: Editor. Publication of Florida Foliage Association. Monthly magazine. Emphasizes foliage. Readers are growers, nurserymen, retail outlets and grocery stores. Circ. 3,000. Estab. 1977. Sample copy free with SASE.

Needs: Usage of photos/issue varies. Needs cover photos of plants, nurseries and people. Needs monthly cover photos. Model release required; photo captions preferred.

Making Contact & Terms: Provide resume, business card, brochure, flyer or tearsheets to be kept on file for possible assignments. Report time varies depending on deadlines. NPI; payment varies. Pays within 10 days of acceptance. Buys "mainly the right to keep photo at our convenience." Simultaneous submissions and previously published work OK.

FLORIDA WILDLIFE, 620 S. Meridian St., Tallahassee FL 32399-1600. (904)488-5563. FAX: (904)488-6988. Editor: Andrea Blount. Publication of the Florida Game & Fresh Water Fish Commission. Bimonthly magazine. Emphasizes wildlife, hunting, fishing, conservation. Readers are wildlife lovers, hunters and fishermen. Circ. 29,000. Estab. 1947. Sample copy $1.25. Photo guidelines free with SASE.
Needs: Uses about 20-40 photos/issue; 75% supplied by freelance photojournalists. Needs 35mm color transparencies and b&w glossies of southern fishing and hunting, all flora and fauna of southeastern USA; how-to; covers and inside illustration. Do not feature products in photographs. No alcohol or tobacco. Special needs include hunting and fishing activities in southern scenes; showing ethical and enjoyable use of outdoor resources. Model release preferred.
Making Contact & Terms: Query with samples, or send "mostly 35mm transparencies, but we use some b&w enlarged prints" by mail for consideration. "Do not send negatives." SASE. Reports in 1 month or longer. Pays $50/color back cover; $100/color front cover; $20-50/b&w or color inside photo. Pays on publication. Credit line given. Buys one-time rights; "other rights are sometimes negotiated." Simultaneous submissions OK "but we prefer originals over duplicates." Previously published work OK but must be mentioned when submitted.
Tips: "Use flat slide mounting pages or individual sleeves. Show us your best. Annual photography contest often introduces us to good freelancers. Rules printed in March-April or May-June issue. Contest form must accompany entry; available in magazine or by writing/calling. Winners receive honorarium and are printed in Sept.-Oct. and Nov.-Dec. issues."

FOCUS, Dept. PM, Owens-Corning Fiberglas, Toledo OH 43659. (419)248-8000. FAX: (419)241-5210. Editor: Bill Hamilton. Monthly tabloid. Circ. 23,000. Estab. 1987. For employees of Owens-Corning Fiberglas. "We assign photo jobs based on our needs. We do not use unsolicited material. We use photojournalism; photography that tells a story. We do not use contrived, posed shots."
Needs: Works with 12 photographers annually; assigns 100%.
Making Contact & Terms: Query first with resume of credits. "Send photocopies of shots you think show your talent as a visual communicator." Free sample copy. Uses 8×10 b&w glossy prints; must send negatives. Captions required; make sure names are spelled correctly. NPI. Buys all rights.

FORD TIMES, Suite 1700, One Illinois Center, 111 E. Wacker Dr., Chicago IL 60601. (312)565-1200. FAX: (312)565-5923. Art Director: Debora Clark. Monthly. Circ. 1,200,000. General interest; current upbeat lifestyle subjects with a magazine featuring slant. Free sample copy and photo guidelines with 9×12 SASE and 56¢ postage.
Needs: Photos purchased with accompanying ms or by assignment. Model release and caption information required.
Making Contact & Terms: Interested in receiving work from newer, lesser-known photographers. Prefers to see published works in a printed form and original photography as samples. SASE. Reports in 1 month. Pays $350-500/b&w or color inside photo, full page or more; $150/b&w or color inside photo, less than page size; $500/cover photo; payment on complete package negotiable. Pays on publication. Credit line given. Buys (first time when applicable) one-time rights.
Tips: In portfolio or samples, wants to see "ability to take the mundane and creatively produce a variety of interesting images." To break in, "continually mail in printed samples which parallel type used in our magazines—general interest and travel." Go beyond the obvious requirements of an assignment, and come up with the unexpected." Sees trend toward more use of people shots.

THE FUTURIST, 4916 St. Elmo Ave., Bethesda MD 20814. (301)656-8274. Managing Editor: Cynthia Wagner. Publication of the World Future Society, general readership. Bimonthly magazine. Emphasizes the future. Circ. 30,000. Estab. 1967.
Needs: Uses variable number of photos/issue. Model release required; captions preferred.
Making Contact & Terms: Query with stock photo list. SASE. Reports within 6 weeks. Pays $25-100/b&w photo; $25-250/color photo. Pays on acceptance. Credit line given. Buys one-time rights.

GOLF COURSE MANAGEMENT, Dept. PM, 1421 Research Park Dr., Lawrence KS 66049-3859. (913)841-2240. FAX: (913)832-4490. Editor: Clay Loyd. Estab. 1926. Publication of the Golf Course Superintendents Association of America. Monthly. Circ. 22,000. Emphasizes "golf course maintenance/management." Readers are "golf course superintendents and managers." Sample copy free with 9×12 SAE plus $4 postage; photo guidelines free with SASE.
Needs: Uses about 25 photos/issue; 1-5 supplied by freelance photographers. Needs "scenic shots of famous golf courses, good composition, unusual holes dramatically portrayed." Also, golf course construction, maintenance, and renovation photos. Model release required; captions preferred.
Making Contact & Terms: Query with samples. Provide business card, brochure, flyer or tearsheets to be kept on file for possible future assignments. SASE. Reports in 3 weeks. Pays $125-250/color cover photo. Pays on acceptance. Credit line given. Buys one-time rights.
Tips: Prefers to see "good color, unusual angles/composition for vertical format cover."

GREEN BAY PACKER YEARBOOK, P.O. Box 1773, Green Bay WI 54305. (414)435-5100. Publisher: John Wemple. Sample copy free with 9×12 SASE.
Needs: Needs photos of Green Bay Packer football action shots in NFL cities other than Green Bay.
Making Contact & Terms: Query with resume of credits. Query with samples. Provide resume, business card, brochure, flyer or tearsheets to be kept on file for possible future assignments. Works with freelance photographers on assignment basis only. SASE. Reports in 2 weeks. Pays $50 maximum/ color photo. Pays on acceptance or receipt of invoice. Buys all rights. Captions preferred. Credit line given on table of contents page.
Tips: "We are looking for Green Bay Packer pictures when they play in other NFL cities—action photos. Contact me direct." Looks for "the ability to capture action in addition to the unusual" in photos.

THE GREYHOUND REVIEW, P.O. Box 543, Abilene KS 67410. (913)263-4660. Contact: Gary Guccione or Tim Horan. Publication of the National Greyhound Association. Monthly. Emphasizes greyhound racing and breeding. Readers are greyhound owners and breeders. Circ. 7,000. Sample copy with SASE and $2.50 postage.
Needs: Uses about 10 photos/issue; 2 supplied by freelance photographers. Needs "anything pertinent to the greyhound that would be of interest to greyhound owners." Captions required.
Making Contact & Terms: Query first. After response, send b&w or color prints and contact sheets by mail for consideration. Submit portfolio for review. Provide resume, business card, brochure, flyer or tearsheets to be kept on file for possible future assignments. Can return unsolicited material if requested. Reports within 1 month. Pays $75/color cover photo; $10-50/b&w; and $25-100/color inside photo. Pays on acceptance. Credit line given. Buys one-time and North American rights. Simultaneous and previously published submissions OK.
Tips: "We look for human-interest or action photos involving greyhounds. No muzzles, please, unless the greyhound is actually racing. When submitting photos for our cover, make sure there's plenty of cropping space on all margins around your photo's subject; full bleeds on our cover are preferred."

GUERNSEY BREEDERS' JOURNAL, Dept. PM, P.O. Box 666, Reynoldsburg OH 43068-0666. (614)864-2409. Co-editors: J. Mark Ligon and Sharyn W. Abbott. Publication of American Guernsey Association. Magazine published 10 times a year. Emphasizes Guernsey dairy cattle, dairy cattle management. Readership consists of male and female dairymen, 20-70 years of age. Circ. 2,200. Sample copy free with 8½×11 SASE.
Needs: Uses 40-100 photos/issue; uses less than 5% of freelance photos. Needs scenic photos featuring Guernsey cattle. Model release and captions preferred.
Making Contact & Terms: Query with resume of credits, business card, brochure, flyer or tearsheets to be kept on file for possible assignments. SASE. Reports in 1 month. Pays $100/color cover photo and $50/b&w cover photo. Pays on publication. Credit line given. Buys all rights; will negotiate. Simultaneous submissions and previously published work OK.

HICALL, Church School Literature Department, 1445 Boonville Ave., Springfield MO 65802. (417)862-2781. Editor: Deanna S. Harris. Publication of The General Council of the Assemblies of God. Thirteen weekly, 8-page issues published quarterly. Readers are primarily high school students (but also junior high). Circ. 80,000. Estab. 1936. Sample copy free for 6×9 SASE and 50¢ postage; photo guidelines free with SASE.
Needs: Uses 10-20 photos/quarter. "We use in-town photographers only." Buys 95% from freelance stock. Doesn't assign. Needs photos of teens in various moods (joy, loneliness, prayer, surprise). Some scenics used, including teens in the photo, nature close-ups; high school settings and activities. Reviews photos with or without accompanying ms. Model release preferred.
Making Contact & Terms: Interested in receiving work from newer, lesser-known photographers. Query with list of stock photo subjects. Send 8×10 glossy b&w prints; 35mm, 2¼×2¼ and 4×5 transparencies by mail for consideration. SASE. Pays $35-50/b&w photo; $50-100/color photo. Pays on acceptance. Credit line given. Buys one-time rights; all rights if assigned, negotiable. Simultaneous submissions and previously published work OK.
Tips: Wants to see "sharp, clear, colorful, usually close-up shots of teens involved in various activities and with other people." For submission, wants good "composition and contrast of teens working, playing eating, partying, relaxing, at school, home, church, etc. Also, mood shots, closeups." Be able to show emotion in subjects.

HISTORIC PRESERVATION, 1785 Massachusetts Ave. NW, Washington DC 20036. (202)673-4042. Art Director: Jeff Roth. Publication of National Trust for Historic Preservation. Bimonthly. Emphasizes historic homes, towns, neighborhoods, restoration. Readers are upper income. Average age fifties. Also restoration professionals, architects, etc. Circ. 224,000. Sample copy $2.50 and 9×12 SASE. Photo guidelines with SASE.

Needs: Uses about 80 photos/issue; almost all supplied by freelancers. Assigns photos of historic homes, restoration in progress, exteriors and interiors. Needs strong photo portfolio ideas, black & white or color, relating to the preservation of buildings, craftspeople, interiors, furniture, etc. Model release, captions required. Using an increasing number of environmental portraits. "Last page department, 'Observed,' in each issue features a single, artful photo (color or b&w) of any subject that has something to do with historic preservation. Examples: a building that has since been razed; a special building saved from wrecking ball; a beautiful restoration; photographic record of some preservation controversy. The overriding requirement is that the photo be artful/stunning/thought-provoking."

Making Contact & Terms: Arrange a personal interview to show portfolio. Query with samples. SASE. Reports in 1 month. Pays $50-200/b&w or color photo; $300-500/day. Other terms negotiable. Pays on acceptance. Credit line given. Buys first N.A. serial rights.

Tips: Prefers to see "interestingly or naturally lit architectural interiors and exteriors. Environmental portraits, artfully done. Become familiar with our magazine. Suggest suitable story ideas. Will use stock when applicable."

HOOF BEATS, Dept. PM, 750 Michigan Ave., Columbus OH 43215. (614)224-2291. FAX: (614)228-1385. Executive Editor: Dean Hoffman. Design/Production Manager: Jenny Gilbert. Publication of the US Trotting Association. Monthly. Circ. 24,000. Estab. 1933. Emphasizes harness racing. Readers are participants in the sport of harness racing. Sample copy free.

Needs: Uses about 30 photos/issue; about 20% supplied by freelancers. Needs "artistic or striking photos that feature harness horses for covers; other photos on specific horses and drivers by assignment only."

Making Contact & Terms: Query with samples. SASE. Reports in 3 weeks. Pays $25-150/b&w photo; $50-200/color photo; $150+/color cover photo; freelance assignments negotiable. Pays on publication. Credit line given if requested. Buys one-time rights. Simultaneous submissions OK.

Tips: "We look for photos with unique perspective and that display unusual techniques or use of light. Send query letter first. Know the publication and its needs before submitting. Be sure to shoot pictures of harness horses only, not Thoroughbred or riding horses." There is "more artistic use of b&w photography instead of color. More use of fill-flash in personality photos. We always need good night racing action or creative photography."

HORSE SHOW MAGAZINE, % AHSA, 220 E. 42nd St., New York NY 10017-5876. (212)972-2472, ext. 250. FAX: (212)983-7286. Editor: Kathleen Fallon. Publication of National Equestrian Federation of US. Monthly magazine. Emphasizes horses and show trade. Majority of readers are upscale women, median age 31. Circ. 57,000. Estab. 1937.

Needs: Uses up to 25 photos/issue; most are supplied by equine photographers; freelance 100% on assignment. Needs shots of competitions; works on assignment only. Reviews photos with or without accompanying ms. Especially looking for "excellent color cover shots" in the coming year. Model release required; property release preferred. Photo captions required; include name of owner, rider, name of event, date held, horse and summary of accomplishments.

Making Contact & Terms: Interested in receiving work from newer, lesser-known photographers. Arrange personal interview to show portfolio. Cannot return material. Reports in 1-2 weeks. Pays $200/color or b&w cover photo; $20/color and b&w inside photo. Pays on acceptance. Credit line given. Buys one-time rights; negotiable. Previously published work OK.

Tips: "Get best possible action shots. Call to set up interview. Call to see if we need coverage of an event."

HR MAGAZINE, Dept. PM, 606 N. Washington St., Alexandria VA 22314. (703)548-3440. Publisher/Editor: John T. Adams III. Art Director: Caroline Foster. Association publication of SHRM. Monthly magazine. Estab. 1956. Emphasizes human resource management. Readers are human resource professionals. Circ. 45,000. Sample copy $7.50.

Needs: Uses 10-25 photos/issue; 90% supplied by freelance photographers on assignment. Needs photos of worklife situations—software use, technology, work environments, human resource or personal situations/issues. Model release and captions preferred.

Making Contact & Terms: Query with samples and list of stock photo subjects; provide resume, business card, brochure, flyer or tearsheets to be kept on file for possible future assignments. Does not return unsolicited material. Reports in 2 weeks. Pays $600/color cover photo. Also pays $300-800/day. Pays on acceptance. Credit line given. Buys one-time reproduction world rights. Previously published work OK.

Tips: SHRM also publishes a monthly newspaper that uses b&w photos, HRNews. Editor: Ceel Pasternak. Art Director: Caroline Foster. In samples, looks for corporate portraits on location.

HSUS NEWS, 5430 Grovenor Ln., Bethesda MD 20814. Art Director: T. Tilton. Publication of The Humane Society of the US association. Quarterly magazine. Emphasizes animals. Circ. 500,000. Estab. 1954. Sample copy for 10×14 SASE.

Needs: Uses 60 photos/issue. Needs photos of animal/wildlife shots. Model release required.
Making Contact & Terms: Query with list of stock photo subjects. Send unsolicited transparencies by mail for consideration. Provide resume, business card, brochure, flyer or tearsheets to be kept on file for possible assignments. Reports in 3 weeks. Pays $300/color cover photo; $225/color inside photo; $150/b&w inside photo. Pays on acceptance. Credit line given. Buys one-time rights. Previously published work OK.
Tips: To break in, "don't pester us. Be professional with your submissions."

"IN THE FAST LANE", ICC National Headquarters, 2001 Pittston Ave., Scranton PA 18505. (717)347-5839. Editor: D.M. Crispino. Publication of the International Camaro Club. Bimonthly, 20-page newsletter. Emphasizes camaro car shows, events, cars, stories, etc. Readers are auto enthusiasts/Camaro exclusively. Circ. 2,000+. Sample copy $1.
Needs: Uses 20-24 photos/issue; 90% assigned. Needs Camaro-oriented photos only. "At this time we are looking for photographs and stories on the Camaro Pace cars 1967, 1969, 1982 and the Camaro 228's, 1967-1972." Reviews photos with accompanying ms only. Model release and captions required.
Making Contact & Terms: Send 3½×5 and larger b&w or color prints by mail for consideration. SASE. Reports in 2 weeks. Pays $5-20 for text/photo package. Pays on publication. Credit line given. Buys one-time rights. Previously published work OK.
Tips: "We need quality photos that put you at the track, in the race or in the midst of the show. Magazine is bimonthly; timeliness is even more important than with monthly."

*INTERNATIONAL OLYMPIC LIFTER, Box 65855, 3602 Eagle Rock, Los Angeles CA 90065. (213)257-8762. Editor: Bob Hise II. An international publication. Bimonthly magazine. Emphasizes Olympic-style weightlifting. Readers are athletes, coaches administrators enthusiasts of all ages. Circ. 1,000. Estab. 1973. Sample copy $4.50 and 5 first-class stamps. Reviews photos with or without ms. Photo captions preferred.
Needs: Uses 20 or more photos/issue; all supplied by freelancers. Needs photos of weightlifting action. Reviews photos with or without ms. Photo captions preferred.
Making Contact & Terms: Send unsolicited photos by mail for consideration. Send 5×7, 8×10 b&w prints. Does not keep samples on file. SASE. Reports in 1-2 weeks. Pays $25/b&w cover photo; $2-10/b&w inside photo. Pays on acceptance. Credit line given. Rights negotiable.
Tips: "Good, clear, b&w still and action photos of (preferably outstanding) olympic-style (overhead/lifting) weightlifters. Must know sport of weightlifting, not bodybuilding or powerlifting."

ITE JOURNAL, #410, 525 School St. SW, Washington DC 20024. (202)554-8050. Communications Director: Kathryn Harrington-Hughes. Publication of Institute of Transportation Engineers. Monthly journal. Emphasizes surface transportation, including streets, highways and transit. Readers are transportation engineers. Circ. 11,000. Estab. 1930.
Needs: One photo used for cover illustration per issue. Needs "strikingly scenic shots of streets, highways, bridges, transit systems." Model release required. Photo captions preferred, include location, name or number of road or highway and details.
Making Contact & Terms: Interested in receiving work from a newer, lesser-known photographer. Query with list of stock photo subjects. Send 35mm or 2¼×2¼ transparencies by mail for consideration. Provide resume, business card, brochure, flyer or tearsheets to be kept on file for possible assignments. Send originals; no dupes please. Pays $250/color cover photo; $50/b&w inside photo. Pays on publication. Credit line given. Buys one-time rights. Simultaneous submissions and previously published work OK.

JET SPORTS, (formerly *Jet Skier*), Suite E, 1371 E. Warner Ave., Tustin CA 92680. (714)259-8240. FAX: (714)259-9377. Editor: Elyse Barrett. Publication of the International Jet Sports Boating Association. Quarterly magazine. Emphasizes personal watercraft. Readers are male, aged 21-32. Circ. 41,000. Estab. 1983. Sample copy free with 9×12 SASE. Photo guidelines free with SASE.
Needs: Uses 30-50 photos/issue; 70% supplied by freelancers, 50% on assignment, 20% from stock. Needs photos of personalities, race action, engines, girls, some scenics. Model/property release preferred. Photo captions preferred; date, event, names, class.
Making Contact & Terms: Interested in receiving work from newer, lesser-known photographers. Send unsolicited 5×7 glossy b&w prints; 35mm or 2¼×2¼ transparencies by mail for consideration. Provide resume, business card, brochure, flyer or tearsheets to be kept on file for possible assignments. Does not keep samples on file. SASE. Reports in 2 months. Pays $250/color cover photo; $35-200/color inside photo; $10-20/b&w inside photo; $100/color page rate; $200-400/day. Pays on publication, or 30 days after mail date. Credit line given. Buys first N.A. serial rights or all rights; negotiable.
Tips: "As a quarterly, we need some guarantee of exclusivity, at least on some material." Looks for "different angles on race action and pan shots; reasonably tasteful girl pictures. More black & white will be needed: people pictures as well as action. More travel photography will be used: waterfront scenics (preferably with personal watercraft featured)."

JOURNAL OF PHYSICAL EDUCATION, RECREATION & DANCE, American Alliance for Health, Physical Education, Recreation & Dance, Reston VA 22091. (703)476-3400. Managing Editor: Frances Rowan. Monthly magazine. Emphasizes "teaching and learning in public school physical education, youth sports, youth fitness, dance on elementary, secondary or college levels (not performances; classes only), recreation for youth, children, families, girls and women's athletics and *physical* education and fitness." Circ. 35,000. Estab. 1896. Sample copy free with 9×12 SASE and $1.80 postage. Photo guidelines free with SASE.
Needs: Freelancers supply cover photos only; 80% from assignment. Written release and captions preferred. Buys b&w by contract. Model release required.
Making Contact & Terms: Interested in receiving work from newer, lesser-known photographers. Query with list of stock photo subjects. Buys 5×7 or 8×10 color prints; 35mm transparencies. Pays $30/b&w photo; $250/color photo. Returns unsolicited photos with SASE. Reports in 2 weeks. Credit line given. Buys one-time rights. Previously published work OK.
Tips: "Innovative transparencies relating to physical education, recreation and sport are considered for publication on the cover—vertical format." Looks for "action shots, cooperative games, no competitive sports and classroom scenes. Send samples of *relevant* photos."

JOURNAL OF SOIL AND WATER CONSERVATION, 7515 NE Ankeny Rd., Ankeny IA 50021. (515)289-2331. FAX: (515)289-1227. Editor: Max Schnepf. Publication for the Soil and Water Conservation Society. Bimonthly journal. Estab. 1946. Emphasizes land and water conservation. Readers include a multidisciplinary group of professionals and laymen interested in the wise use of land and water resources. Circ. 13,500. Free sample copy with 9×12 SASE and $1 postage.
Needs: Uses 25-40 photos/issue; 0-2 supplied by freelancers. Needs photos illustrating land and water conservation problems and practices used to solve those problems; including items related to agriculture, wildlife, recreation, reclamation and scenic views. Reviews photos with or without accompanying ms. Model release and captions preferred.
Making Contact & Terms: Send unsolicited photos by mail for consideration. Uses 5×7, 8×10 b&w prints; 35mm, 2¼×2¼, 4×5 and 8×10 color transparencies; b&w contact sheet. SASE. Reports in 2 weeks. Pays $50-100/color cover; $10 up/inside b&w. Pays on acceptance. Credit line given. Buys one-time rights.
Tips: In samples wants to see "good quality photos of people involved in conservation-related activities."

JOURNAL OF THE NATIONAL TECHNICAL ASSOCIATION, Dept. PM, 1240 S. Broad St., New Orleans LA 70125. (504)821-5694. FAX: (504)821-5713. Production Manager: K. Kazi Ferrouillet. Publication of National Technical Association. Quarterly journal. Emphasizes engineering/science. Readers are experienced African-American technical professionals. Circ. 10,000. Estab. 1970. Sample copy for $5 and $1.50 postage.
Needs: Uses 12 photos/issue; 4 supplied by local freelance photographers; assigns—10-15%, buys 85% stock. Needs photos of engineering, science and computers. Model release and captions preferred.
Making Contact & Terms: Arrange a personal interview to show a portfolio; query with resume or credits, samples or list of stock photo subjects. Reports in 1 month. Pays $25-50/b&w photo; $50-200/color photo. Pays on publication. Credit line given. Buys one-time rights.
Tips: Wants to see "African-American college students and young professionals in campus/work settings. Show sensitivity to the African-American experience. The trend is towards more action and more social/political activism. Examine our publication thoroughly before making proposal."

JUDICATURE, Suite 1600, 25 E. Washington, Chicago IL 60602. (312)558-6900. Editor: David Richert. Publication of the American Judicature Society. Bimonthly. Emphasizes courts, administration of justice. Readers are judges, lawyers, professors, citizens interested in improving the administration of justice. Circ. 20,000. Estab. 1917. Sample copy free with 9×12 SASE with $1.45 postage.
Needs: Uses 2-3 photos/issue; 1-2 supplied by freelancers. Needs photos relating to courts, the law. "Actual or posed courtroom shots are always needed." Model and property releases and captions preferred.
Making Contact & Terms: Interested in receiving work from a newer, lesser-known photographer. Send 5×7 glossy b&w prints by mail for consideration. Provide resume, business card, brochure, flyer or tearsheets to be kept on file for possible future assignments. SASE. Reports in 2 weeks. Pays $200/

The code NPI (no payment information given) appears in listings that have not given specific payment amounts.

b&w cover photo; $125/b&w inside photo. Pays on publication. Credit line given. Buys one-time rights. Simultaneous submissions and previously published work OK.

KEYNOTER, Dept. PM, 3636 Woodview Trace, Indianapolis IN 46268. (317)875-8755. Art Director: Jim Patterson. Publication of the Key Club International. Monthly magazine. Emphasizes teenagers, above average students and members of Key Club International. Readers are teenagers, ages 14-18, male and female, high GPA, college bound, leaders. Circ. 133,000. Sample copy free with 9×12 SAE and 65¢ postage. Photo guidelines free with SASE.
Needs: Uses varying number of photos/issue; varying percentage supplied by freelancers. Needs vary with subject of the feature article. Reviews photos purchased with accompanying ms only. Model release required. Photo captions preferred.
Making Contact & Terms: Query with resume of credits. Pays $500/color cover photo; $350/b&w cover photo; $200/color inside photo; $100/b&w inside photo. Pays on acceptance. Credit line given. Buys first N.A. serial rights and first international serial rights.

KIWANIS MAGAZINE, 3636 Woodview Trace, Indianapolis IN 46268. (317)875-8755. FAX: (317)879-0204. Executive Editor: Chuck Jonak. Art Director: Jim Patterson. Published 10 times/year. Emphasizes organizational news, plus major features of interest to business and professional men and women involved in community service. Circ. 285,000. Estab. 1915. Free sample copy and writer's guidelines with SASE and five first-class stamps.
Needs: Uses photos with or without ms.
Making Contact & Terms: Send resume of stock photos. Provide brochure, business card and flyer to be kept on file for future assignments. Assigns 95% of work. Uses 5×7 or 8×10 glossy b&w prints; 35mm but would rather use 2¼×2¼ and 4×5 transparencies. Pays $50-700/b&w photo; $75-1,000/color photo; $400-1,000/ms with photos. Buys one-time rights.
Tips: "We can offer the photographer a lot of freedom to work *and* worldwide exposure. And perhaps an award or two if the work is good. We are now using more conceptual photos. We also use studio set-up shots. When we assign work, we want to know if a photographer can follow a concept into finished photo without on-site direction." In portfolio or samples, wants to see "studio work with flash and natural light."

LACMA PHYSICIAN, P.O. Box 3465, Los Angeles CA 90051-1465. (213)483-1581. Managing Editor: Janice M. Nagano. Published 20 times/year—twice a month except January, July, August and December. Emphasizes Los Angeles County Medical Association news and medical issues. Readers are physicians and members of LACMA. Circ. 10,000. Estab. 1875.
Needs: Uses about 1-20 photos/issue; from both freelance assignment and freelance stock. Needs photos of association meetings, physician members, association events—mostly internal coverage. Photos purchased with or without accompanying ms. Model release required.
Making Contact & Terms: Arrange a personal interview to show portfolio. Does not return unsolicited material. Pays by hour, day or half day; negotiable. Pays $10/b&w photo; $15/color photo; $50-75/hour. Pays on publication with submission of invoice. Credit line given. Buys one-time rights or first North American serial rights "depending on what is agreed upon."
Tips: "We want photographers who blend in well, and can get an extraordinary photo from what may be an ordinary situation. We need to see work that demonstrates an ability to get it right the first time without a lot of set-up on most shoots."

LANDSCAPE ARCHITECTURE, Dept. PM, Fifth Floor, 4401 Conn. Ave. NW, Washington DC 20008. (202)686-2752. Managing Editor: Susan Waterman. Publication of the American Society of Landscape Architects. Monthly magazine. Emphasizes "landscape architecture, urban design, parks and recreation, architecture, sculpture" for professional planners and designers. Circ. 35,000. Sample copy $7; photo guidelines free with SASE.
Needs: Uses about 50-75 photos/issue; 50% supplied by freelance photographers. Needs photos of landscape- and architecture-related subjects as described above. Special needs include aerial photography. Model release required, captions preferred. "We also need American and international landscape photographs for our international sections of the magazine."
Making Contact & Terms: Query with samples or list of stock photo subjects; provide resume, business card, brochure, flyer or tearsheets to be kept on file for possible future assignments. SASE. Reporting time varies. Pays $500/color cover photo; $50-300/color inside. Pays on publication. Credit line given. Buys two-time rights. Previously published work OK.

LAW PRACTICE MANAGEMENT, (formerly Legal Economics), Box 11418, Columbia SC 29211-1418. (803)754-3563. Editor/Art Director: Delmar L. Roberts. Published 8 times/year. Publication of the Section of Law Practice Management, American Bar Association. For practicing attorneys and law students. Circ. 23,657. Sample copy $7 (make check payable to American Bar Association).

Needs: Uses 2-3 photos/issue; all supplied by freelance photographers. Needs photos of some stock subjects such as group at a conference table, someone being interviewed, scenes showing staffed office-reception areas; *imaginative* photos illustrating such topics as time management, employee relations, automatic typewriters, computers and word processing equipment, computer graphics of interest, record keeping, filing, malpractice insurance protection; abstract shots or special effects illustrating almost anything concerning management of a law practice. "We'll exceed our usual rates for exceptional photos of this latter type." No snapshots or Polaroid photos.

Making Contact & Terms: Uses 5×7 glossy b&w prints; 35mm, 2¼×2¼, 4×5 transparencies. Reports in 1-3 months. Pays $150-200/color cover photo (vertical format); $50-60/b&w inside photo; $100-200/job. Pays on publication. Credit line given. Usually buys all rights, and rarely reassigns to photographer after publication. Model releases and captions required. Send unsolicited photos by mail for consideration. They are accompanied by an article pertaining to the lapida "if requested." SASE. Simultaneous submissions OK.

THE LION, 300 22nd St., Oak Brook IL 60521-8842. (708)571-5466. Editor: Robert Kleinfelder. Monthly magazine. For members of the Lions Club and their families. Emphasizes Lions Club service projects. Circ. 650,000. Estab. 1918. Free sample copy and photo guidelines available.

Needs: Uses 10 photos/issue. Needs photos of Lions Club service or fundraising projects. "All photos must be as candid as possible, showing an activity in progress. Please, no award presentations, meetings, speeches, etc. Generally photos purchased with ms (300-1,500 words) and used as a photo story. We seldom purchase photos separately." Model release required; captions required.

Making Contact & Terms: Works with freelancers on assignment only. Provide resume to be kept on file for possible future assignments. Query first with resume of credits or story idea. Send 5×7, 8×10 glossy b&w and color prints; 35mm transparencies. SASE. Reports in 2 weeks. Pays $10-25/photo; $50-500/text/photo package. Pays on acceptance.

LOYOLA MAGAZINE, 820 N. Michigan, Chicago IL 60611. (312)915-6157. FAX: (312)915-6215. Editor: William S. Bike. Loyola University Alumni Publication. Magazine published 3 times/year. Emphasizes issues related to Loyola University of Chicago. Readers are Loyola University of Chicago alumni—professionals, ages 22 and up. Circ. 90,000. Estab. 1971. Sample copy free with 9×12 SASE and 3 first-class stamps.

Needs: Uses 50 photos/issue; 40% supplied by freelancers. Needs Loyola-related or Loyola alumni-related photos only. Model release and photo captions preferred.

Making Contact & Terms: Send unsolicited photos by mail for consideration. Provide resume, business card, brochure, flyer or tearsheets to be kept on file for possible assignments. Send 8×10 b&w/color prints; 35mm and 2¼×2¼ transparencies. SASE. Reports in 3 months. Pays $300/b&w and color cover photo; $85/b&w and color inside photo; $50-150/hour; $400-1,200/day. Pays on acceptance. Credit line given. Buys one-time rights. Simultaneous submissions and previously published work OK.

Tips: "Send us information, but don't call."

THE LUTHERAN, 8765 West Higgins Rd., Chicago IL 60631. (312)380-2546. Art Director: Jack Lund. Publication of Evangelical Lutheran Church in America. Monthly magazine. Circ. 1,000,000+. Estab. 1988. Sample copy 75¢ and 9×12 SASE.

Needs: Assigns 35-40 photos/issue; 4-5 supplied by freelancers. Needs current news, mood shots. Model release required; captions preferred.

Making Contact & Terms: Interested in receiving work from newer, lesser-known photographers. Query with list of stock photo subjects. Provide resume, brochure, flyer or tearsheets to be kept on file for possible future assignments. SASE. Reports in 3 weeks. Pays $35-100/b&w photo; $50-175/color photo; $175-300/day. Pays on publication. Credit line given. Buys one-time rights.

Tips: Trend toward "more dramatic lighting. Careful composition." In portfolio or samples, wants to see "candid shots of people active in church life, preferably Lutheran. Just churches have little chance of publication. Submit sharp well-composed photos with borders for cropping."

THE MAGAZINE FOR CHRISTIAN YOUTH!, Box 801, Nashville TN 37202. (615)749-6463. FAX: (615)749-6079. Editor. Publication of The United Methodist Church. Monthly. Emphasizes what it means to be a Christian teenager in the '90s—developing a Christian identity and being faithful. Readers are junior and senior high teenagers (Christian). Circ. estimated 40,000. Estab. 1985.

Needs: Uses about 25 photos/issue; 20 supplied by freelancers. Needs photos of teenagers. Special needs include "up-to-date pictures of teens in different situations—at school, at home, with parents, friends, doing activities, etc. Need photos of both white and ethnics." Model release required especially for "touchy social issues—AIDS, pregnancy, divorce, etc."

Making Contact & Terms: Interested in receiving work from a newer, lesser-known photographer. Query with samples and list of stock photo subjects. Send 8×10 b&w prints; 35mm, 2¼×2¼ and 4×5 transparencies; b&w contact sheet by mail for consideration. SASE. Reports in 1 month. Pays $10-

150/b&w photo and $35-250/color photo. Pays on acceptance. Credit line given. Buys one-time rights. Simultaneous submissions OK.

Tips: Prefers to see "quality photographs of teenagers in various situations, settings. Should appear realistic, not posed, and should be up-to-date in terms of clothing, trends, issues and fads. Photos of single teens plus some of teens with others. Don't give us photos that are blurry and/or have bad compositions. Give us pictures of *today's* teens." Interested in more color submissions. "We seldom assign photographers. We use approximately 90% stock and freelance. Submit work on speculation."

MAINSTREAM—ANIMAL PROTECTION INSTITUTE, P.O. Box 22505, Sacramento CA 95822, or 2831 Fruitridge Rd., Sacramento CA 95820. (916)731-5521. FAX: (916)731-4467. Contact: Art Department. Official Publication of the Animal Protection Institute. Quarterly. Emphasizes "humane education toward and about animal issues and events concerning animal welfare." Readers are "all ages; people most concerned with animals." Circ. 65,000. Estab. 1970. Sample copy and photo guidelines available with 9×12 SASE ($1.44 first-class mail).

Needs: Uses approximately 30 photos/issue; 15 supplied by freelancers. Needs images of animals in natural habitats. Especially interested in "one of a kind" situational animal slides. All species, wild and domestic: marine mammals, wild horses, primates, companion animals (pets), farm animals, wildlife from all parts of the world, and endangered species. Animals in specific situations: factory farming, product testing, animal experimentation and their alternatives; people and animals working together; trapping and fur ranching; animal rescue and rehabilitation; animals in abusive situations (used/abused) by humans; entertainment (rodeos, circuses, amusement parks, zoos); etc. *API* also uses high quality images of animals in various publications besides its magazine. Submissions should be excellent quality—sharp with effective lighting. Prefer tight to medium shots with good eye contact. Vertical format required for *Mainstream* covers. Model release required for vertical shots and any recognizable faces.

Making Contact & Terms: Interested in receiving work from newer, lesser-known photographers. Query with resume, credits, stock list and sample submission of no more than 20 of best slides; originals are preferred unless dupes are *high quality*. Provide business card, brochure, flyer or tearsheets for *API* files for future reference. We welcome all "excellent quality" contacts with SASE. B&w rarely used. However, will accept b&w images of outstanding quality of hard-to-get issue-oriented situations: experimentation, product testing, factory farming etc. Original transparencies or high-quality dupes only; 35mm Kodachrome 64 preferred; larger formats accepted. Reports in 2-4 weeks. Pays $150/color cover; $35-50/b&w (from slide or photo) inside; $50-150/color inside. Pays on publication. Credit line given; please specify. Buys one-time rights. Simultaneous submissions and previously published work OK.

Tips: "The images used in *Mainstream* touch the heart. We see a trend toward strong subject, eye contact, emotional scenes, inspirational close-ups and natural habitat shots."

MANAGEMENT ACCOUNTING, 10 Paragon Dr., Montvale NJ 07645. (201)573-9000. FAX: (201)573-0639. Editor: Robert Randall. Publication of Instititue of Management Accountants. Monthly. Emphasizes management accounting. Readers are financial executives. Circ. 95,000. Estab. 1919.

Needs: Uses about 25 photos/issue; 40% from stock houses. Needs stock photos of business, high-tech, production and factory. Model release required for identifiable people. Photo captions required.

Making Contact & Terms: Query with samples. Provide resume, business card, brochure, flyer or tearsheets to be kept on file for possible future assignments. Uses prints and transparencies. SASE. Reports in 2 weeks. Pays $100-200/b&w photo; $150-250/color photo. Pays on acceptance. Credit line given. Buys one-time rights. Simultaneous submissions and previously published work OK.

Tips: Prefers to see "ingenuity, creativity, dramatics (business photos are often dry), clarity, close-ups, simple but striking. Aim for a different slant."

✷THE MANITOBA TEACHER, 191 Harcourt St., Winnipeg MB R3J 3H2 Canada. (204)888-7961. Editor: Mrs. Miep van Raalte. Publication of The Manitoba Teachers' Society. Quarterly magazine. Emphasizes education in Manitoba—emphasis on teachers' interest. Readers are teachers and others in education. Circ. 17,000. Sample copy free with 10×14 SAE and Canadian stamps.

The First Markets Index preceding the General Index in the back of this book provides the names of those companies/publications interested in receiving work from newer, lesser-known photographers.

Photographer Ron Sanford, of Gridley, California, got in close on this young spotted owl to augment feelings of helplessness and trust that the endangered bird displays. Sanford hopes the shot, which appeared in the winter 1992 issue of Mainstream, will improve protection of endangered species. The magazine, which is published by the Animal Protection Institute of America, sent Sanford a 4-page "want" list filled with subjects it was seeking.

Needs: Uses approx. 4 photos/issue; 80% supplied by freelancers. Needs action shots of students and teachers in education-related settings. "Good cover shots always needed." Model release and captions required.

Making Contact & Terms: Send 8 × 10 glossy b&w prints by mail for consideration. Submit portfolio for review. Provide resume, business card, brochure, flyer or tearsheets to be kept on file for possible assignments. SASE. Reports in 1 month. Does not pay; only gives credit line.

Tips: "Always submit action shots directly related to major subject matter of publication and interests of readership of that publication."

MAP INTERNATIONAL, Dept. PM, P.O. Box 50, Brunswick GA 31520. (912)265-6010 or (800)-225-8550 (interstate toll free). Art Director: Michael Wilson. Publication of MAP International. Bimonthly. Reports on the organization's annual distribution of $35 million in donated medicines and supplies to relief agencies in 75 countries in the developing world, as well as work in community health development projects. Sample copy and photo guidelines free with SASE.

Needs: "Specifically, we need photos depicting the health needs of people in the developing countries of Africa, Asia and Latin America, and the work being done to meet those needs. Also use photos of disaster situations like the war in Kuwait, *while situation is current.*" Captions required.

Making Contact & Terms: Query with resume of credits; query with samples; query with list of stock photo subjects. Uses b&w 5 × 7 glossy prints; 35mm transparencies. SASE. Reports in 1 month. Pays $75/b&w cover photo; $25 + /b&w inside photo; payment for color photos individually negotiated. Pays on acceptance. Credit line given. Buys one-time rights. Simultaneous submissions and previously published work OK, "depending on where they had been submitted or used."

Tips: "Photos should center on people: children, patients receiving medical treatment, doctors, community health workers with the people they are helping, hospitals, health development projects and informal health education settings. Our interest is much broader than crisis situations and emergency aid alone, and we try to show the hopeful side of what is being done. Care about people. We are a people-developing agency and if a photographer cares about the problems of people in developing nations it will come through in the work."

MATURE YEARS, 201 Eighth Ave. S., Nashville TN 37203. (615)749-6292. FAX: (615)749-6512. Editor: Marvin W. Cropsey. Publication of the United Methodist Church. Quarterly magazine. "*Mature Years* is a leisure-time resource for older adults in The United Methodist Church. It contains fiction, articles dealing with health, faith and fun matters related to aging, poetry and lesson material." Readers are "adults over 55. The magazine may be used in Sunday school class, at home or in nursing and retirement homes." Circ. 80,000. Sample copy available for $2 and 9×12 SASE.
Needs: Uses about 15 photos/issue; many supplied by freelance photographers. Needs "mainly photos showing older adults in various forms of activities. We have problems finding older adults pictured as healthy and happy. We *desperately* need pictures of older adults who represent ethnic minorities."
Making Contact & Terms: Query with list of stock photo subjects to Dave Dawson, photo and art requisition. Send 8×10 glossy b&w prints and any transparencies by mail for consideration. SASE. Reports in 3-6 weeks. Pays $65-175/cover photo; $10-45/inside photo. Pays on acceptance. Credit line given on copyright page. Buys one-time rights. Simultaneous submissions and previously published work OK. Include social security number with submissions.
Tips: Prefers to see "ethnic minority older adults, older adults who are healthy and happy—pictures portraying the beauty and wonder of God's creation. Remember that not all older adults are sick, destitute or senile."

THE MEETING MANAGER, 1950 Stemmons Freeway, Infomart, Dallas TX 75207. (214)746-5262. Art Director: Robin Gailey. Publication of Meeting Planners International. Monthly magazine. Emphasizes planning meetings. Readers are ages 30-60, male and female. Circ. 10,500. Estab. 1972. Sample copy available.
Needs: Uses 10-20 photos/issue; 100% supplied by freelancers. Needs varies subjects for cover shots, other photos are specific events, some promotional material requiring photography. Special photo needs include cover photos and feature photos, some stock. Model release required; photo captions preferred.
Making Contact & Terms: Provide resume, business card, brochure, flyer or tearsheets to be kept on file for possible assignments. Reports as needed. NPI. Pays on publication. Credit line given. Rights negotiable. Will consider previously published work.
Tips: Wants to see photographers "slicks or printed samples. Send samples of photography to be kept on file until matched with a specific job."

✷**MENNONITE BRETHREN HERALD**, 3-169 Riverton Ave., Winnipeg MB R2L 2E5 Canada. (204)669-6575. FAX: (204)654-1865. Art Director: Fred Koop. Publication of the Canadian Mennonite Brethren Church. Biweekly magazine. Publication emphasizes "issues of spiritual and social concern." Readers are primarily adult church members. Circ. 14,000. Sample copy free with letter-size SAE (Canadian funds).
Needs: Uses 5-10 photos/issue; most are supplied by freelancers. Approximately 85% purchased from stock; 15% on assignment. Looking for people-oriented shots. Some religious, some scenics, some abstract, but mostly people of all ages in activity of all sorts. Model release required; captions preferred.
Making Contact & Terms: Send 5×7 or 8×10 glossy or matte b&w prints by mail for consideration. Letter-size SASE (Canadian funds). Reports in 3 months. Pays $20-25 (Cdn.)/b&w cover; $15-20 (Cdn.)/b&w inside photo. Pays on publication. Credit line given. Buys one-time rights and first N.A. serial rights. Simultaneous submissions and previously published work OK.

THE MIDWEST MOTORIST, Dept. PM, Auto Club of Missouri, 12901 N. Forty Dr., St. Louis MO 63141. (314)523-7350. Editor: Michael Right. Emphasizes travel and driving safety. Readers are "members of the Auto Club of Missouri, ranging in age from 25-65 and older." Bimonthly. Circ. 385,000. Free sample copy and photo guidelines when request is accompanied by SASE; use large manila envelope.
Needs: Uses 8-10 photos/issue, most supplied by freelancers. "We use four-color photos inside to accompany specific articles. Our magazine covers topics of general interest, historical (of Midwest regional interest), humor (motoring slant), interview, profile, travel, car care and driving tips. Our covers are full color photos mainly corresponding to an article inside. Except for cover shots, we use freelance photos only to accompany specific articles." Model release not required; captions required.

Making Contact & Terms: Send by mail for consideration 5 × 7 or 8 × 10 b&w photos; 35mm, 2¼ × 2¼ or 4 × 5 color transparencies. Query with resume of credits or query with list of stock photo subjects. SASE. Reports in 3-6 weeks. Pays $100-250/cover; $10-25/photo with accompanying ms; $10-50/b&w photo; $50-200/color photo; $75-200 for text/photo package. Pays on publication. Credit line given. Rights negotiable. Simultaneous submissions and previously published work OK.
Tips: "Send an 8½ × 11 SASE for sample copies and study the type of covers and inside work we use."

MODERN MATURITY, 3200 E. Carson St., Lakewood CA 90712. (310)496-2277. Photo Editor: M.J. Wadolny. Bimonthly. Readers are 50 years old and over. Circ. 20 million. Sample copy free with 9 × 12 SASE; guidelines sheet free with SASE.
Needs: Uses about 50 photos/issue; 5 supplied by freelancers; 75% from assignment and 25% from stock. Needs nature, scenic, personality and travel photos. Model release and captions preferred.
Making Contact & Terms: Arrange a personal interview to show portfolio. SASE. Pays $50-200/b&w photo; $150-1,000/color photo; $350/day. Pays on acceptance. Credit line given. Buys one-time and first North American serial rights.
Tips: Prefers to see clean, crisp images on a variety of subjects of interest to people 50 or over. "Present yourself and your work in a professional manner. Be familiar with *Modern Maturity*. Wants to see creativity, ingenuity and perserverance."

THE MORGAN HORSE, P.O. Box 960, Shelburne VT 05482. (802)985-4944. Editor: Suzy Lucine. Publication of official breed journal of The American Morgan Horse Association Inc. Monthly magazine. Emphasizes Morgan horses. Readers are all ages. Circ. 10,000. Estab. 1941. Sample copy for $4.
Needs: Uses 25 photos/issue; 50% supplied by freelancers. Needs photos of Morgan horses—farm scenes, "showing," trail riding, how-to and photos with owners. Special photo needs include covers and calendars. Model release and photo captions preferred.
Making Contact & Terms: Send unsolicited glossy b&w/color prints; 35mm, 2¼ × 2¼,4 × 5, 8 × 10 transparencies by mail for consideration. Will return unsolicited material if a SASE is enclosed. Reports in 3 weeks. Pays $150/color cover photo; $25/color inside photo; $5/b&w inside photo. Pays on publication. Credit line given. Buys either one-time or all rights; negotiable.
Tips: "Artistic color photographs of Morgan horses in natural settings, with owners, etc., are needed for calendars and covers."

MOTORLAND MAGAZINE, Dept. PM, 150 Van Ness Ave., San Francisco CA 94102. (415)565-2464. Editor: Lynn Ferrin. Art Director: Al Davidson. Membership publication for the California State Auto Association (AAA). Bimonthly. Emphasizes travel. Readers include RVH travelers 40-45 median age. Circ. 2,200,000. Free sample copy and photo guidelines with SASE.
Needs: Uses 35 photos/issue; 30 supplied by freelancers. Needs include travel, scenic. Model release and captions required.
Making Contact & Terms: Arrange a personal interview to show portfolio. SASE. Reports in 3 weeks. Pays $500/cover photo, $175/inside color photo, $400-600/text/photo package. Pays on acceptance. Credit line given. Buys one-time rights. Previously published (photos only) work OK.

NACLA REPORT ON THE AMERICAS, Dept. PM, Rm 454, 475 Riverside Dr., New York NY 10115. (212)870-3146. Photo Editor: Deidre McFadyen. Association publication of North American Congress on Latin America. Bimonthly journal. Emphasizes Latin American political economy, US foreign policy toward Latin America and the Caribbean and domestic development in the region. Readers are academic, church, human rights, political activists, foreign policy interested. Circ. 11,500. Sample copy for $5 (includes postage).
Needs: Uses about 25 photos/issue; all supplied by freelancers. Model release and captions preferred.
Making Contact & Terms: Arrange a personal interview to show portfolio; query with samples; or send b&w prints or contact sheets by mail for consideration. SASE. Reports in 2 weeks. Pays $25/b&w photo. Pays on publication. Credit line given. Buys one-time rights. Simultaneous submissions and previously published work OK.

NATIONAL GARDENING, Dept. PM, 180 Flynn Ave., Burlington VT 05401. (802)863-1308. Editor: Warren Schultz. Publication of the National Gardening Association. Monthly. Circ. 200,000. Covers fruits, vegetables and ornamentals. Readers are home and community gardeners. Sample copy free with 9 × 12 SAE and $1 postage. Photo guidelines free with SASE.
Needs: Uses about 50 photos/issue; 90% supplied by freelancers. "Most of our photographers are also gardeners or have an avid interest in gardening or gardening research." Needs photos of "people gardening; special techniques; how to; specific varieties (please label); unusual gardens and food gardens in different parts of the country. We often need someone to photograph a garden or gardener in various parts of the country for a specific story." Model release required; captions preferred.

Making Contact & Terms: Query with samples or list of stock photo subjects. SASE. Reports in 3 weeks. Pays $350/color cover photo; $30/b&w and $50/color inside photo. Also negotiates day rate against number of photos used. Pays on acceptance. Credit line given. Buys one-time rights.
Tips: "We're becoming more selective all the time, need top-quality work. Most photos used are color. We look for general qualities like clarity, good color balance, good sense of lighting and composition. Also interesting viewpoint, one that makes the photos more than just a record (getting down to ground level in the garden, for instance, instead of shooting everything from a standing position). Look at the magazine carefully and at the photos used. We work at making the stories friendly, casual and personal. When we write a story on growing broccoli, we love to have photos of people planting, harvesting or eating broccoli, not a formal shot of broccoli on a black background. We like to show process, step-by-step."

THE NATIONAL NOTARY, 8236 Remmet Ave., Box 7184, Canoga Park CA 91309-7184. (818)713-4000. Editor: Charles N. Faerber. Bimonthly. Circ. 80,000. Emphasizes "Notaries Public and notarization—goal is to impart knowledge, understanding and unity among notaries nationwide and internationally. Readers are employed primarily in the following areas: law, government, finance and real estate." Sample copy $5.
Needs: Uses about 20-25 photos/issue; 10 supplied by non-staff photographers. "Photo subject depends on accompanying story/theme; some product shots used." Unsolicited photos purchased with accompanying ms only. "Since photos are used to accompany stories or house ads, they cannot be too abstract or artsy. Notaries, as a group, are conservative, so photos should not tend toward an ultramodern look." Model release required.
Making Contact & Terms: Query with samples. Provide business card, tearsheets, resume or samples to be kept on file for possible future assignments. Prefers to see prints as samples. Does not return unsolicited material. Reports in 4-6 weeks. Pays $25-300 depending on job. Pays on publication. Credit line given "with editor's approval of quality." Buys all rights. Previously published work OK.
Tips: "Since photography is often the art of a story, the photographer must understand the story to be able to produce the most useful photographs."

THE NATIONAL RURAL LETTER CARRIER, Dept. PM, 1630 Duke St., Alexandria VA 22314-3465. Managing Editor: RuthAnn Saenger. Weekly magazine. Circ. 70,000. Emphasizes Federal legislation and issues affecting rural letter carriers and the activities of the membership for rural carriers and their spouses and postal management. Sample copy 34¢; photo guidelines free with SASE.
Needs: Photos purchased with accompanying ms. Buys 52 photos/year. Animal; wildlife; sport; celebrity/personality; documentary; fine art; human interest; humorous; nature; scenics; photo essay/photo feature; special effects and experimental; still life; spot news; and travel. Needs scenes that combine subjects of the Postal Service and rural America; "submit photos of rural carriers on the route." Model release and captions required.
Making Contact & Terms: Send material by mail for consideration or query with list of stock photo subjects. Uses 8×10 b&w or color glossy prints, vertical format preferred for cover. SASE. Reports in 4 weeks. Pays $60/photo. Pays on publication. Credit line given. Buys first serial rights. Previously published work OK.
Tips: "Please submit sharp and clear photos with interesting and pertinent subject matter. Study the publication to get a feel for the types of rural and postal subject matter that would be of interest to the membership. We receive more photos than we can publish, but we accept beginners' work if it is good."

*NATIONAL TRUST FOR HISTORIC PRESERVATION, 1785 Massachusetts Ave. NW, Washington DC 20036. (202)673-4042. FAX: (202)673-4172. Art Director: Jeff Roth. Bimonthly magazine. Emphasizes historic preservation. Readers are male and female with average income of $99,000, average age 50. Circ. 225,000. Estab. 1950. Sample copy $2.50 and 9×12 SASE. Photo guidelines free with SASE.
Needs: Uses 75-100 photos/year; 90% supplied by freelancers. Needs photos of architecture, environmental portraits and travel. Reviews photos with or without a manuscript. Model/property release preferred. Captions preferred.
Making Contact & Terms: Arrange personal interview to show portfolio. Submit portfolio for review. Provide brochure, flyer or tearsheets to be kept on file for possible assignments. Query with samples. Samples kept on file. SASE. Reports when interested. Pays up to $200/color stock inside photo; up to $200/b&w stock inside photo; $350-500/day. Pays on acceptance. Credit line given. Buys one-time rights.
Tips: "We want photographers who can shoot in natural, editorial style, producing artful and dramatic images."

THE NATURE CONSERVANCY MAGAZINE, 1815 N. Lynn St., Arlington VA 22209. (703)841-8742. Photo Editor: Susan Bournique. Publication of The Nature Conservancy. Bimonthly. Emphasizes "nature, rare and endangered flora and fauna, ecosystems in North and South America." Readers

Close-up

Ron Austing
Freelance Photographer
Dillsboro, Indiana

©Michael Willins

With bird photographer Ron Austing, selling his work is a take it or leave it proposition. He doesn't spend countless hours labeling slides or photos, packaging up award-winning shots and then sending them off to editors or ad agencies in a grand marketing scheme. "I don't like publicity. I don't belong to any groups. I just want to be left alone to do my work," says Austing, whose home is surrounded by woods where he practices his craft.

Despite Austing's minimal marketing interest, top editors know where to go when they are searching for stunning bird photos. His work has been published by *National Geographic*, *Audubon*, *Ranger Rick* and the *Saturday Evening Post*, to name a few, and he constantly receives requests for his photos.

One reason Austing's images are so in demand is that he constantly strives for top quality and he won't settle for anything less. "If the bird's not in prime condition I won't shoot it," he says. "A lot of professionals shoot captive birds that have scuffed up noses and broken feathers. I can spot those so fast. I wouldn't use a photo like that if I was starving to death."

Indeed, Austing can flip through a book and instantly spot photos that were taken of birds in captivity. He knows when an owl's talons are too long, or a bird's nest is not in proper order. He is not opposed to shooting captive animals and often finds viable markets for zoo shots of endangered species. However, he does become irate with photographers who use captions to misrepresent what is taking place in a photo. "It doesn't matter to the layman, but why should somebody have to lie about something like that. It's just a matter of principle," he says.

When talking about the work of someone Austing admires, he points to his friend and fellow nature photographer Larry West. "I know what he goes through to get the photos and he doesn't mind freezing his toes off," says Austing. "He knows what he's shooting; he's not going out there on speculation. He's not hip-shooting like so many aspiring nature photographers." By researching animals, knowing their lifestyles and habits, a photographer can put himself in place to take quality photos.

For Austing, studying and understanding birds were the easiest parts of his photography training. He spent 30 years as a park ranger and wildlife manager for the Hamilton County Parks District in Cincinnati, Ohio. He has taught ornithology classes at the University of Cincinnati and in 1966 he co-founded the Raptor Research Foundation. He also serves as staff photographer for the Cincinnati Zoo.

Austing decided to become a bird photographer when he was very young, raising and releasing hawks and owls. One day someone took a picture of him with a red shoulder hawk and gave him the photo. "It was an enlargement and I was fascinated with it. That's when I decided to be a photographer," he recalls.

To this day much of his photography revolves around birds of prey. "Most of the fun of all this is going out and locating a nesting pair of (birds), finding the nest, putting up your blind and living with that family for a week or whatever it takes to get the photos you want. In the case of a raptor, you may be with them for a month or six weeks until the young leave the nest," says Austing.

In recent years, he has seen an influx of newcomers to the nature photography field. "It's like having a gas station on every corner," says Austing of the added competition. In order for a photographer to succeed he must capture the best possible images. "They must be sharp. There's no room for bad composition," he says.

Newcomers also must "be prepared not to succeed financially and seek some other means of subsistence. Allow nature photography to be a sideline, a hobby," says Austing.

—*Michael Willins*

© Ron Austing

This photo of a Saw-whet owl's attack on a white-footed mouse almost makes you want to turn your head away from the action. Everyone, except the mouse, knows what will happen in the blink of an eye. The photo has become Ron Austing's trademark and has sold over 400 times.

are the membership of The Nature Conservancy. Circ. 640,000. Estab. 1951. Sample copy for 9×12 SASE and $1.21 postage.
Needs: Uses about 20-25 photos/issue; 70% comes from freelance stock. The Nature Conservancy welcomes permission to make duplicates of slides submitted to the *Magazine* for use in slide shows only and internegs for proposals. Model release required; property release preferred. Captions required (location and names of flora and fauna). Proper credit should appear on slides.
Making Contact & Terms: Write for guidelines. Many photographers contribute the use of their slides. Uses color transparencies. Pays $200/color cover photo; $75-150/color inside photo; $50/b&w photo; $300/day. Pays on publication. Credit line given. Buys one-time rights; starting to consider all rights for public relations purposes; negotiable.
Tips: "Membership in the Nature Conservancy is only $25/year and the *Magazine* will keep photographers up to date on what the Conservancy is doing in your state. Many of the preserves are open to the public. We look for rare and endangered species, wetlands and flyways, including Latin America, South Pacific, Caribbean and Canada."

NETWORK, for Public Schools, 900 2nd St. NE, Washington DC 20002. (202)408-0447. FAX: (202)408-0452. Editor: Susan Hlesciak Hall. Publication of the National Committee for Citizens in Education. Published 6 times/year. Emphasizes "parent/citizen participation in public school." Readers are "parents, citizens, educators." Circ. 8,000. Estab. 1975. Sample copy available.
Needs: Uses various number photos/issue; 90% from freelance stock and 10% from assignment. Needs photos of "children (elementary and high school) in school settings or with adults (parents, teachers) shown in helping role; meetings of small groups of adults." Model release required; captions preferred.
Making Contact & Terms: Interested in receiving work from a newer, lesser-known photographer. Query with samples. Send glossy prints, contact sheets or good quality duplicator facsimiles by mail for consideration. SASE. Reports in 2 weeks. Pays $50/b&w cover photo; $35/b&w inside photo. Pays on acceptance. Credit line given. Rights negotiable. Simultaneous submissions and previously published work OK.
Tips: "Photos of school buildings and equipment are more appealing when they include children. In reviewing samples we look for appropriate subject matter—school age children, often with helping adults (parents or teachers); good resolution, sharp focus of print; a picture conveying a mood and capturing expressions, telling a story with a message; picture must have focal point, good composition. Need to represent ethnic diversity among teachers and school children. Send b&w prints, not contacts. Include full name, address and phone number on back of every print. Enclose return postage."

NEVADA FARM BUREAU AGRICULTURE AND LIVESTOCK JOURNAL, 1300 Marietta Way, Sparks NV 89431. (702)358-7737. Contact: Norman Cardoza. Monthly tabloid. Emphasizes Nevada agriculture. Readers are primarily Nevada Farm Bureau members and their families; men, women and youth of various ages. Members are farmers and ranchers. Circ. 2,800. Sample copy free with 10×13 SASE with 3 first-class stamps.
Needs: Uses 5 photos/issue; 30% occasionally supplied by freelancers. Needs photos of Nevada agriculture people, scenes and events. Model release preferred; captions required.
Making Contact & Terms: Send b&w 3×5 and larger prints, any format and finish by mail for consideration. SASE. Reports in 1 week. Pays $10/b&w cover photo; $5/b&w inside photo. Pays on acceptance. Credit line given. Buys one-time rights.
Tips: "In portfolio or samples, wants to see newsworthiness, 50%; good composition, 20%; interesting action, 20%; photo contrast, resolution, 10%. Try for new angles on stock shots: awards, speakers, etc., We like 'Great Basin' agricultural scenery such as cows on the rangelands and high desert cropping. We pay little, but we offer credits for your resume."

*NEW ERA MAGAZINE, 50 E. North Temple St., Salt Lake City UT 84150. (801)240-2951. FAX: (801)240-1727. Art Director: Lee Shaw. Association publication of The Church Of Jesus Christ of Latter-day Saints. Monthly magazine. Emphasizes teenagers who are members of the Mormon Church. Readers are male and female teenagers, who are members of the Latter Day Saints Church. Circ. 200,000. Estab. 1971. Sample $1 with 9×12 SASE and 2 first-class stamps. Photo guidelines free with SASE.
Needs: Uses 60-70 photos/issue; 35-40 supplied by freelancers. Anything can be considered for "Photo of the Month," most photos of teenage Mormons and their activities. Model/property release preferred. Photo captions preferred.
Making Contact & Terms: Arrange personal interview to show portfolio. Submit portfolio for review. Query with stock photo list. Send unsolicited photos by mail for consideration. Send any b&w or color print; 35mm, 2¼×2¼, 4×5 transparencies. Keeps samples on file. SASE. Reports in 6-8 weeks. Pays $150-300/day; "rates are individually negotiated, since we deal with many teenagers, non-professionals, etc." Credit line given. Buys all rights; negotiable.

Tips: "Most work consists of assignments given to photographers we know and trust or of single item purchases for photo of the month."

*THE NEW PHYSICIAN, 1890 Preston White Dr., Reston VA 22091. (703)620-6600. Editor: Richard Camer. Publication of American Medical Student Association. Magazine published 9 times/year. Emphasizes medicine/health. Readers are medical students, interns, residents, medical educators. Circ. 30,000. Sample copy free with SASE.
Needs: Needs freelance photos for about 6 stories per year. Needs photos usually on health, medical, medical training. Special needs include commission photos to go with story or photo essay on above topics only. Model release and captions required.
Making Contact & Terms: Provide resume, business card, brochure, flyer or tearsheets to be kept on file for possible future assignments. NPI; pay negotiated. Pays 2-4 weeks after acceptance. Buys first North American serial rights.

NEW WORLD OUTLOOK, Rm. 1351, 475 Riverside Dr., New York NY 10115. (212)870-3758/3765. FAX: (212)870-3940. Editor: Alma Graham. Four-color magazine published 6 times/year. Circ. 33,000. Estab. 1910. Features United Methodist mission and Christian involvement in evangelism, social concerns and problems around the world. Sample copy available for $2 with 9 × 12 SAE.
Needs: Interested in photographers who are planning trips to countries and regions in which there are United Methodist mission projects. Query first for interest and needs. Model release required for closeups and for "people in difficult situations." Photo captions required; include who, what, where, when, why.
Making Contact & Terms: Query first, by phone or letter. Not responsible for return of unsolicited material. If an appointment is made, bring samples of published photos, slides and b&w prints. Color preferred. Most photos used are by in-house or United Methodist-related photographers. Previously published work OK. Credit line given. Pays $25-75/b&w photo; $50-100/color photo; $150-250/color cover. Pays on publication. Buys one-time rights.
Tips: Wants to see strong images, good composition, human interest, geographic setting, religious themes. Follow current world events and religious trends for spotting photo opportunities.

NEWS PHOTOGRAPHER, Dept. PM, 1446 Conneaut Ave., Bowling Green OH 43402. (419)352-8175. FAX: (419)354-5435. Editor: James R. Gordon. Publication of National Press Photographers Association, Inc. Monthly magazine. Emphasizes photojournalism and news photography. Readers are newspaper, magazine, television freelancers and photojournalists. Circ. 11,000, Estab. 1946. Sample copy free with 9 × 12 SAE and 9 first-class stamps.
Needs: Uses 50 photos/issue. Needs photos of photojournalists at work; photos which illustrate problems of photojournalists. Special photo needs include photojournalists at work, assaulted, arrested; groups of news photographers at work, problems and accomplishments of news photographers. Photo captions required.
Making Contact & Terms: Send glossy b&w/color prints; 35mm, 2¼ × 2¼ transparencies by mail for consideration. Provide resume, business card, brochure, flyer or tearsheets to be kept on file for possible assignments; make contact by telephone. Reports in 3 weeks. Pays $75/color page rate; $50/ b&w page rate; $50-150/photo/text package. Pays on acceptance. Credit line given. Buys one-time rights. Simultaneous submissions and previously published work OK.

NFPA JOURNAL, Dept. PM, 1 Batterymarch Park, Quincy MA 02169. (617)984-7566. Art Director: Jane Dashfield. Publication of National Fire Protection Association. Bimonthly magazine. Emphasizes fire protection issues. Readers are fire professionals, engineers, architects, building code officials, ages 20-65. Circ. 56,000. Sample copy for 9 × 12 SAE.
Needs: Uses 25-30 photos/issue; 50% supplied by freelance photographers. Needs photos of fires and fire-related incidents. Especially wants to use more photos for Fire Fighter Injury Report and Fire Fighter Fatality Report. Model release and photo captions preferred.
Making Contact & Terms: Query with list of stock photo subjects, send unsolicited photos by mail for consideration or provide resume, business card, brochure, flyer or tearsheets to be kept on file for possible assignments. Send color prints and 35mm transparencies in 3-ring slide sleeve with date. SASE. Reports in 3 weeks or "as soon as I can." NPI; payment negotiated. Pays on publication. Credit line given. Buys rights depending "on article and sensitivity of subject."
Tips: "Send cover letter, 35mm color slides preferably with manuscripts and photo captions.

NORTH AMERICAN WHITETAIL MAGAZINE, P.O. Box 741, Marietta GA 30061. (404)953-9222. FAX: (404)933-9510. Photo Editor: Gordon Whittington. Published 8 times/year (July-Feb.) by Game & Fish Publications, Inc. emphasizing trophy whitetail deer hunting. Circ. 150,000. Estab. 1982. Sample copy for $3. Photo guidelines free with SASE.

Needs: Uses 20 photos/issue; 40% from freelancers. Needs photos of large, live whitetail deer, hunter posing with or approaching downed trophy deer, or hunter posing with mounted head. Also use photos of deer habitat and sign. Model release preferred; capitons preferred including where scene was photographed and when.

Making Contact & Terms: Interested in receiving work from newer, lesser-known photographers. Query with resume of credits and list of stock photo subjects. Send unsolicited 8 × 10 b&w prints; 35mm transparencies (Kodachrome preferred). Will return unsolicited material in 1 month if accompanied by SASE. Pays $250/color cover photo; $75/inside color photo; $25/b&w photo. Pays 75 days prior to publication. Credit line given. Buys one-time rights. Simultaneous submissions not accepted. Tearsheets provided.

Tips: In samples we look for extremely sharp, well composed photos of whitetailed deer in natural settings. We also use photos depicting deer hunting scenes. "Please study the photos we are using before making submission. We'll return photos we don't expect to use and hold the remainder. Please do not send dupes. Use an 8 × loupe to ensure sharpness of images and put name and identifying number on all slides and prints. Photos returned at time of publication or at photographer's request."

OAK RIDGE BOYS "TOUR BOOK" AND FAN CLUB NEWSLETTER, 329 Rockland Rd., Hendersonville TN 37075. (615)824-4924. Art Director: Kathy Harris. Publication of The Oak Ridge Boys, Inc. Semiannual tour book and quarterly newsletter. Tour book: 24 pages, full color. Emphasizes The Oak Ridge Boys (music group) exclusively. Readers are fans of Oak Ridge Boys and country music. Circ. newsletter: 15,000; tour book: 50,000. Free sample copies available of newsletter; tourbook for $10.

Needs: Uses 2-4 photos/issue of newsletter, 2 supplied by freelance photographers; 20-150/tour book, 1-50 supplied by freelance photographers. Needs photos of Oak Ridge Boys. Will review photos with or without accompanying ms; subject to change without notice. "We need *good* live shots or candid shots—won't accept just average shots." Model release required; captions preferred.

Making Contact & Terms: Arrange a personal interview to show portfolio. Query with samples. SASE. Reports vary, 1-6 weeks. Pays $250/pg b&w inside; $500/pg color inside; $500/pg b&w or color cover; $50/b&w or color cover photo, $35/b&w or color inside photo for newsletter; rates can vary and subject to change without notice. Pays on publication. Credit line usually given. Buys one-time rights. Simultaneous submissions and previously published work OK.

Tips: "We are interested in Oak Ridge Boys photos only!!! Send only a few good shots at one time—send prints only. No original slides or negatives please."

OKLAHOMA TODAY, Box 53384, Oklahoma City OK 73152. (405)521-2496. FAX: (405)521-3992. Managing Editor: Jeanne M. Devlin. Bimonthly magazine. "We cover all aspects of Oklahoma, from history to people profiles, but we emphasize travel." Readers are "Oklahomans, whether they live in-state or are exiles; studies show them to be above average in education and income." Circ. 45,000. Estab. 1956. Sample copy $2.50; photo guidelines free with SASE.

Needs: Uses about 50 photos/issue; 90-95% supplied by freelancers. Needs photos of "Oklahoma subjects only; the greatest number are used to illustrate a specific story on a person, place or thing in the state. We are also interested in stock scenics of the state." Model release and photo captions required.

Making Contact & Terms: Interested in receiving work from a newer, lesser-known photographer. Query with samples or send 8 × 10 b&w glossy prints; 35mm, 2¼ × 2¼, 4 × 5, 8 × 10 transparencies or b&w contact sheets by mail for consideration. No color prints. SASE. Reports in 6-8 weeks. Pays $50-200/b&w photo; $50-200/color photo; $50-750/job. Payment for text material on acceptance; payment for photos on publication. Buys one-time rights with a six-month from publication exclusive, plus right to reproduce photo in promotions for magazine, without additional payment with credit line. Simultaneous submissions and previously published work OK (on occasion).

Tips: To break in, "read the magazine. Subjects are normally activities or scenics (mostly the latter). I want good composition and very good lighting. I look for photographs that evoke a sense of place, look extraordinary and say something only a good photographer could say about the image. Look at what Ansel Adams and Eliot Porter did and what Muench and others are producing and send me that kind of quality. We want the best photographs available and we give them the space and play such quality warrants."

♣**THE ONTARIO TECHNOLOGIST,** Suite 404, 10 Four Seasons Place, Etobicoke, ON M9B 6H7 Canada. (416)621-9621. FAX: (416)621-8694. Editor-in-Chief: Ruth M. Klein. Publication of the Ontario Association of Certified Engineering Technicians and Technologists. Bimonthly. Emphasizes engineering technology. Circ. 19,200. Sample copy free with SAE and IRC.

Needs: Uses 10-12 photos/issue. Needs how-to photos—"building and installation of equipment; similar technical subjects." Model release and captions preferred.
Making Contact & Terms: Prefers business card and brochure for files. Send 5×7 glossy b&w or color prints for consideration. SASE. Reports in 1 month. Pays $25/b&w photo; $50/color photo. Pays on publication. Credit line given. Buys one-time rights. Previously published work OK.

OPASTCO ROUNDTABLE, Suite 205, 2000 K St. NW, Washington DC 20006. (202)659-5990. FAX: (202)659-4619. Public Relations Director: Linda M. Buckley. Association publication of the Organization for the Protection and Advancement of Small Telephone Companies. Quarterly magazine. Covers news of small, rural, independent telephone companies. Readers are male and female owners and employees in small telephone companies. Circ. 3,200. Estab. 1988. Sample copies free with 9×12 SASE and 8 first-class stamps.
Needs: Uses 20-30 photos/issue. Needs photos of small telephone company operators/business ventures and other general telecommunications subjects. Reviews photos with or without ms. "We would like to work with more photographers in rural areas where our members are located. Often we need a good photo to go with an article and have to rely on our member's own photography." Model/property release preferred. Photo captions required; include names and titles of subjects in photos.
Making Contact & Terms: Provide resume, business card, brochure, flyer or tearsheets to be kept on file for possible assignments. Send stock photo list. Send unsolicited photos by mail for consideration. Accepts both b&w and color photos; "we're very flexible." Keeps samples on file. SASE. Reports in 1 month. Pays $125-250/color cover photo; $45-85 b&w inside or color page photo. Pays on acceptance. Credit line given. Buys all rights; negotiable. Simultaneous submissions and previously published work OK.

OUTDOOR AMERICA, Level B, 1401 Wilson Blvd., Arlington VA 22209. (703)528-1818. FAX: (703)528-1836. Editor: Kristin Clarke. Published quarterly. Emphasizes natural resource conservation and activities for outdoor enthusiasts, including hunters, anglers, hikers and campers. Readers are members of the Izaak Walton League of America and all members of Congress. Circ. 59,000. Estab. 1922. Sample copy $1.50 with 9×12 envelope; guidelines free with SASE.
Needs: Needs vertical wildlife or shots of anglers or hunters for cover. Buys pictures to accompany articles on conservation and outdoor recreation for inside. Model release preferred. Photo captions required; include date taken, model info, location and species.
Making Contact & Terms: Query with resume of photo credits. Send stock photo list. Tearsheets and non-returnable samples only. Not responsible for return of unsolicited material. Uses 35mm and 2¼×2¼ slides. SASE. Pays $200-250/color cover; $50-75/inside photo. Credit line given. Pays on publication. Buys one-time rights. Simultaneous and previously published work OK.
Tips: "*Outdoor America* seeks vertical photos of wildlife (particular game species); outdoor recreation subjects (fishing, hunting, camping or boating) and occasional scenics (especially of the Chesapeake Bay and Upper Mississippi river). We also like the unusual shot—new perspectives on familiar objects or subjects—for use on inside covers. We do not assign work. Approximately one half of the magazine's photos are from freelance sources." Points out that cover has moved from using a square photo format to full bleed.

PACIFIC DISCOVERY, Dept. PM, California Academy of Sciences, Golden Gate Park, San Francisco CA 94118. (415)750-7116. Art Director: Susan Schneider. Publication of California Academy of Sciences. Quarterly magazine. Emphasizes natural history and culture of California, the western U.S., the Pacific, and Pacific Rim countries. Circ. 26,000. Estab. 1948. Sample copy for $1.25, 9×12 SASE. Photo guidelines free with SASE.
Needs: Uses 60 photos/issue; most supplied by freelance photographers. Scenics of habitat as well as detailed photos of individual species that convey biological information. "Scientific accuracy in identifying species is essential. We do extensive photo searches for every story." Current needs listed in Guilfoyle Reports, natural history photographers' newsletter published by AG Editions. "Photo captions preferred, but captions are generally staff written."
Making Contact & Terms: Query with list of stock photo subjects and file stock lists, but recommend consulting Guilfoyle Report and calling first. Uses color prints; 35mm, 2¼×2¼, or 4×5 transparencies. SASE. Reports in 1 month. Pays $200/color cover photo; $75-90/color inside photo; $100/color page rate; $125 color 1 ⅓ pages. Also buys photo/text packages, but payment varies according to length of text and number of photos. Pays on publication. Credit line given. Buys one-time rights and first

---

■ *The solid, black square before a listing indicates that the market uses various types of audiovisual materials, such as slides, film or videotape.*

N.A. serial rights. Previously published work (for individual images) OK.
Tips: *"Pacific Discovery* has a reputation for high-quality photo reproduction and favorable layouts, but photographers must be meticulous about identifying what they shoot."

PENNSYLVANIA ANGLER, Dept. PM, P.O. Box 1673, Harrisburg PA 17105-1673. (717)657-4518. Editor: Art Michaels. Monthly. Circ. 53,000. *"Pennsylvania Angler* is the Keystone State's official fishing magazine, published by the Pennsylvania Fish Commission." Readers are "anglers who fish in Pennsylvania." Sample copy and photo guidelines free with 9×12 SAE and 4 first-class stamps.
Needs: Uses about 25 photos/issue; 80% supplied by freelancers. Needs "action fishing and boating shots." Model release preferred; captions required.
Making Contact & Terms: Query with resume of credits. Send 8×10 glossy b&w prints; 35mm or larger transparencies by mail for consideration. SASE. Reports in 2 weeks. Pays up to $200/color cover photo; $25-100/b&w inside photo; $25 up/color inside photo; $50-250 for text/photo package. Pays on acceptance. Credit line given. Buys variable rights.
Tips: "Crisp, well-focused action shots get prompt attention."

PENNSYLVANIA HERITAGE, Dept PM, P.O. Box 1026, Harrisburg PA 17108-1026. (717)787-7522. Editor: Michael J. O'Malley, III. Published by the Pennsylvania Historical & Museum Commission. Quarterly magazine. Emphasizes Pennsylvania history, culture and art. Readers are "varied—generally well-educated with an interest in history, museums, travel, etc." Circ. 10,000. Sample copy free with SASE and 65¢ postage. Photo guidelines free with SASE.
Needs: Uses approximately 75 photos/issue; supplied by freelance photographers. Uses about "60% on specific assignment; 40% from stock." Needs photos of "historic sites, artifacts, travel, scenic views, objects of material culture, etc." Photos purchased with accompanying ms only. "We are generally seeking illustrations for specific manuscripts." Captions required.
Making Contact & Terms: Query with samples and list of stock photo subjects. Provide resume, business card, brochure, flyer or tearsheets to be kept on file for possible future assignments. SASE. Reports in 1 month. Pays $5-50/b&w photo and $25-100/color photo. Pays on acceptance. Credit line given. Buys all rights. Simultaneous submissions OK.
Tips: "Send query *first* with sample and ideally, a list of Pennsylvania subjects that are available. Quality is everything. Don't bombard an editor or photo buyer with everything—be selective."

PENNSYLVANIAN MAGAZINE, Dept. PM, 2941 N. Front St., Harrisburg PA 17110. (717)236-9526. FAX: (717)236-8164. Editor: Patricia Hazur. Monthly magazine of Pennsylvania State Association of Boroughs (and other local governments). Emphasizes local government in Pennsylvania. "Readers are officials in small municipalities in Pennsylvania." Circ. 7,000. Estab. 1962. Sample copy for 9×12 SAE and 5 first-class stamps.
Needs: Number of photos/issues varies with inside copy. Needs "color photos of scenics (Pennsylvania), local government activities, Pennsylvania landmarks, ecology—for cover photos only; authors of articles supply their own photos." Special photo needs include photos of street and road maintenance work; wetlands scenic. Model release preferred. Photo captions preferred that include identification of place and/or subject.
Making Contact & Terms: Query with resume of credits; query with list of stock photo subjects; send unsolicited photos by mail for consideration; provide resume, business card, brochure, flyer or tearsheets to be kept on file for possible assignments. Send color prints and 35mm transparencies. Does not keep samples on file. SASE. Reports in 1 month. Pays $25-50/color cover photo. Pays on publication. Buys one-time rights.

PENTECOSTAL EVANGEL, 1445 Boonville, Springfield MO 65802. (417)862-2781. FAX: (417)862-8558. Editor: Richard G. Champion. Managing Editor: John T. Maempa. Weekly magazine. Official voice of the Assemblies of God, a conservative Pentecostal denomination. Emphasizes denomination's activities and inspirational articles for membership. Circ. 280,000. Free sample copy and photographer's/writer's guidelines.
Needs: Uses 25 photos/issue; 5 supplied by freelance photographers. Human interest (very few children and animals). Also needs seasonal and religious shots. "We are interested in photos that can be used to illustrate articles or concepts developed in articles. We are not interested in merely pretty pictures (flowers and sunsets) or in technically unusual effects or photos. We use a lot of people and mood shots." Model release and captions preferred.
Making Contact & Terms: Send material by mail for consideration. Uses 8×10 b&w and color prints; 35mm or larger transparencies; color 2¼×2¼ to 4×5 transparencies for cover; vertical format preferred. SASE. Reports in 1 month. Pays $20/photo (minimum). Pays on acceptance. Credit line given. Buys one-time rights; all rights, but may reassign to photographer after publication; simultaneous rights; or second serial (reprint) rights. Simultaneous submissions and previously published work OK if indicated.

Tips: "Writers and photographers must be familiar with the doctrinal views of the Assemblies of God and standards for membership in churches of the denomination. Send seasonal material 6 months to a year in advance—especially color."

THE PENTECOSTAL MESSENGER, P.O. Box 850, Joplin MO 64802. (417)624-7050. FAX: (417)624-7102. Editor: Don Allen. Monthly magazine. Official publication of the Pentecostal Church of God. Circ. 10,000. Estab. 1919. Free sample copy with 9 × 12 SASE; free photo guidelines with SASE.
Needs: Buys 20-30 photos/year; all supplied from freelance stock. Scenic; nature; still life; human interest; Christmas; Thanksgiving; Bible and other religious groupings (Protestant). No photos of women or girls in shorts, pantsuits or sleeveless dresses. No men with cigarettes, liquor or shorts.
Making Contact & Terms: Send samples of work for consideration. Uses 3½×5 and 8×10 color prints and 2¼ transparencies. Vertical format required for cover. SASE. Reports in 4 weeks. Pays $2-5/inside; $10-25/outside cover (front). Pays on publication. Credit line given. Buys second serial rights. Simultaneous submissions and previously published work OK.
Tips: "We must see the actual print or slides (120 or larger). Do not write on back of picture; tape on name and address. Enclose proper size envelope and adequate postage. We need open or solid space at top of photo for name of magazine. We also print in the foreground often. Several seasonal photos are purchased each year. In selecting photos, we look for good composition, good color, sharp focus, interesting subject and detail. We anticipate the use of *more* photography (and less art) on covers. Most of our cover material comes from stock material purchased from freelance photographers. We are needing more photos of people related to issues of our day, e.g. abortion, AIDS, suicide, etc. Keep in mind our holiness requirements and look for subjects that would lend themselves to proclaiming the gospel and speaking out on the issues by which we are confronted in today's world."

PERSIMMON HILL, 1700 NE 63rd, Oklahoma City OK 73111. FAX: (405)478-4714. Editor: M. J. Van Deventer. Publication of the National Cowboy Hall of Fame museum. Quarterly magazine. Emphasizes the West, both historical and contemporary views. Has diverse international audience with an interest in preservation of the west. Circ. 15,000. Estab. 1970. Sample copy $7 with 9 × 12 SAE and 6 first-class stamps. Photo guidelines free with SASE.
Needs: Uses 60 photos/issue; 95% supplied by freelancers. "Photos must pertain to specific articles unless it is a photo essay on the west." Model release required for children's photos. "Doesn't really apply in general since photos are usually done with a story." Photo captions required including location, names of people. Proper credit is required if photos are of an historical nature.
Making Contact & Terms: Interested in receiving work from newer, lesser-known photographers. Submit portfolio for review. SASE. Reports in 6 weeks. Pays $100/color cover photo; $50/color inside photo; $25/b&w inside photo; $200/photo/text package. Credit line given. Buys first N.A. serial rights.
Tips: Wants to see "photographs that have a strong focal point and have a direct relationship to our interest in preserving all facets of the American West. Make certain your photographs are high quality and have a story to tell. We are using more contemporary portraits of things that are currently happening in the West and using fewer historical photographs. Work must be high quality, original, innovative. Photograher can best present their work in a portfolio format and should keep in mind that we like to feature photo essays on the West in each issue."

PLANNING, American Planning Association, 1313 E. 60th St., Chicago IL 60637. (312)955-9100. Monthly magazine. Editor: Sylvia Lewis. Photo Editor: Richard Sessions. "We focus on urban and regional planning, reaching most of the nation's professional planners and others interested in the topic." Circ. 30,000. Estab. 1972. Free sample copy with 9½ × 12½ SASE ($1.10 first class, 70¢ fourth class) and photo guidelines.
Needs: Buys 50 photos/year, 95% from stock. Photos purchased with accompanying ms and on assignment. Photo essay/photo feature (architecture, neighborhoods, historic preservation, agriculture); scenic (mountains, wilderness, rivers, oceans, lakes); housing; and transportation (cars, railroads, trolleys, highways). "No cheesecake; no sentimental shots of dogs, children, etc.; no trick shots with special filters or lenses. High artistic quality is very important. "We publish high-quality nonfiction stories on city planning and land use. Ours is an association magazine but not a house organ, and we use the standard journalistic techniques: interviews, anecdotes, quotes. Topics include energy, the environment, housing, transportation, land use, agriculture, neighborhoods and urban affairs." Writer's guidelines included on photo guidelines sheet. Captions required.
Making Contact & Terms: Query with samples. Uses 8 × 10 glossy and semigloss b&w prints; contact sheet OK; 4-color prints; 35mm or 4 × 5 transparencies. SASE. Reports in 1 month. Pays $25-100/b&w photo; $25-200/color photo; up to $250/cover photo; $200-600/ms. Pays on publication. Credit line given. Buys all rights. Previously published work OK.
Tips: "Just let us know you exist. Eventually, we may be able to use your services. Send tearsheets or photocopies of your work, or a little self-promo piece. Subject lists are only minimally useful. How the work looks is of paramount importance."

POPULATION BULLETIN, Suite 520, 1875 Connecticut Ave., Washington D.C. 20009. (202)483-1100. FAX: (202)328-3937. Production Coordinator: Aichin Jones. Publication of the Population Reference Bureau. Quarterly journal. Publishes other population-related publications, including a monthly newsletter. Emphasizes demography. Readers are educators (both high school and college) of sociology, demography and public policy. Circ. 15,000. Estab. 1929.
Needs: Uses 8-10 photos/issue; 70% supplied by freelancers. Needs vary widely with topic of each edition—people, families, young, old, all ethnic backgrounds—everyday scenes, world labor force, working people, minorities. Special photo needs include environmental related scenes with or without people in it. Everyday scenes, closeup pictures of locals in developing countries in S. America., Asia, Africa and Europe. Model release and captions preferred.
Making Contact & Terms: Interested in receiving work from a newer, lesser-known photographer. Query with list of stock photo subjects. Send unsolicited photos by mail for consideration. Send b&w prints or photocopies. SASE. Reports in 1-2 weeks. Pays $25-75/b&w photo; $25-125/color photo. Pays on acceptance. Buys one-time rights. Simultaneous submissions and previously published work OK.

✸**THE PRESBYTERIAN RECORD,** Dept. PM, 50 Wynford Dr., Don Mills ON M3C 1J7 Canada. (416)441-1111. FAX: (416)441-2825. Editor: Rev. John Congram. Monthly magazine. Circ. 68,000. Emphasizes subjects related to The Presbyterian Church in Canada, ecumenical themes and theological perspectives for church-oriented family audience. Photos purchased with or without accompanying mss. Free sample copy and photo guidelines with 9×12 SAE and $1 Canadian postage minimum.
Needs: Religious themes related to features published. No formal poses, food, nude studies, alcoholic beverages, church buildings, empty churches or sports. Captions are required.
Making Contact & Terms: Send photos. Uses prints only for reproduction; 8×10, 4×5 glossy b&w prints and 35mm and 2¼×2¼ color transparencies. Usually uses 35mm color transparency for cover or ideally, 8×10 transparency. Vertical format used on cover. SAE, IRCs for return of work. Reports in 1 month. Pays $5-25/b&w print; $50 up/cover photo; $20-50 for text/photo package. Pays on publication. Credit line given. Simultaneous submissions and previously published work OK.
Tips: "Unusual photographs related to subject needs are welcome."

PRESERVATION NEWS, Dept. PM, 1785 Massachusetts Ave. NW, Washington DC 20036. (202)673-4075. Executive Editor: Arnold Berke. Publication of the National Trust for Historic Preservation. Monthly tabloid. Emphasizes historic preservation and building restoration. Readers are professional men and women, 20 years of age and older. Circ. 210,000. Estab. 1969. Sample copy free with 9×12 SASE.
Needs: Uses 20 photos/issue; 15% supplied by freelancers. Needs photos of buildings, people with buildings, "event" shots (ceremonies, parties, openings, etc.) and scenics. Model release and captions preferred.
Making Contact & Terms: Query with list of stock photos. Provide resume, business card, brochure, flyer or tearsheets to be kept on file for possible assignments. SASE. Reports in 3 weeks. Pays $25-100/b&w cover or inside photo; $300-400/day. Pays on publication. Credit line given. Buys one-time rights. Previously published work OK.

PRINCETON ALUMNI WEEKLY, Dept. PM, 194 Nassau St., Princeton NJ 08542. (609)258-4885. Editor-in-Chief: J.I. Merritt. Photo Editor: Stacey Wszola. Biweekly. Circ. 52,000. Emphasizes Princeton University and higher education. Readers are alumni, faculty, students, staff and friends of Princeton University. Sample copy $1.50 with 8½×11 SAE and 37¢ postage.
Needs: Uses about 15 photos/issue; 10 supplied by freelance photographers. Needs b&w photos of "people, campus scenes; subjects vary greatly with content of each issue. Show us photos of Princeton." Captions required.
Making Contact & Terms: Arrange a personal interview to show portfolio. Provide brochure to be kept on file for possible future assignments. SASE. Reports in 1 month. Pays $100/b&w and $200/color cover photos; $25/b&w inside photo; $50/color inside photo; $45/hour. Pays on publication. Buys one-time rights. Simultaneous submissions and previously published work OK.

PRINCIPAL MAGAZINE, Dept. PM, 1615 Duke St., Alexandria VA 22314-3483. (703)684-3345. Editor: Lee Greene. Publication of the National Association of Elementary School Principals. Bimonthly. Emphasizes public education—Kindergarten to 8th grade. Readers are mostly principals of elementary and middle schools. Circ. 25,000. Sample copy free with SASE.
Needs: Uses 5-10 b&w photos/issue; all supplied by freelancers. Needs photos of school scenes (classrooms, playgrounds, etc.); teaching situations; school principals at work; computer use and technology and science activities. The magazine sometimes has theme issues, such as back to school, technology and early childhood education. *No posed groups.* Close-ups preferred. Reviews photos with or without accompanying ms. Model release preferred; captions required.

Making Contact & Terms: Query with samples and list of stock photo subjects; send b&w prints, b&w contact sheet by mail for consideration. SASE. Reports in 1 month. Pays $50/b&w photo. Pays on publication. Credit line given. Buys one-time rights. Simultaneous submissions and previously published work OK.

PROCEEDINGS/NAVAL HISTORY, U.S. Naval Institute, Annapolis MD 21402. (301)268-6110. Photo Editor: Linda Cullen. Association publication. *Proceedings* is a monthly magazine and *Naval History* is a quarterly publication. Emphasizes Navy, Marine Corps, Coast Guard. Readers are age 18+, male and female, naval officers, enlisted, retirees, civilians. Circ. 110,000. Estab. 1873. Sample copy free with 9×12 SAE and 1 first-class stamp. Photo guidelines free with SASE.
Needs: Uses 25 photos/issue; 40% supplied by freelancers. Needs photos of foreign and US Naval, Coast Guard and Marine Corps vessels, personnel and aircraft. Photo captions required.
Making Contact & Terms: Send unsolicited photos by mail for consideration: 35mm or 8×10, glossy or matte, b&w or color prints; 35mm transparencies. SASE. Reports in 1 month. Pays $200/color or b&w cover photo; $25/color inside photo; $25/b&w page rate; $250-500/photo/text package; pays $50 opener/inside. Pays on publication. Credit line given. Buys one-time rights. Simultaneous submissions and previously published work OK.

PRORODEO SPORTS NEWS, Dept. PM, 101 Pro Rodeo Dr., Colorado Springs CO 80919. (719)593-8840. Editor: Kendra Santos. Publication of Professional Rodeo Cowboys Association. Biweekly tabloid. Emphasizes professional rodeo. Circ. 30,000. Sample copy $1.
Needs: Uses about 18 photos/issue; 5-6 supplied by freelancers. Needs action rodeo photos. Also uses behind-the-scenes photos, cowboys preparing to ride, talking behind the chutes—something other than action. Special needs include quality color prints from outdoor and indoor rodeos; also use b&w. Captions required.
Making Contact & Terms: Send 5×7, 8×10 glossy b&w and color prints by mail for consideration. SASE. Pays $50/color cover photo; $10/b&w and color inside photo. Other payment negotiable. Pays end of month. Credit line given. Buys all rights but will negotiate.
Tips: In portfolio or samples, wants to see "the ability to capture a cowboy's character outside the competition arena, as well as inside. In reviewing samples we look for clean, sharp reproduction—no grain. Photographer should respond quickly to photo requests. I see more PRCA sponsor-related photos being printed."

PTA TODAY, 700 N. Rush St., Chicago IL 60611-2571. (312)787-0977. Photo Editor: Moosi Raza Rizvi. Published 7 times/year. Emphasizes parent education. Readers are parents living in the US—rural, urban, suburban and exurban. Circ. 40,000. Sample copy $2.50 with 9×12 SASE.
Needs: Uses about 20-25 photos/issue; all supplied by freelancers; uses 100% stock. Needs "candid, not cutesy, shots of kids of all ages who live in the 1990s—their parents and teachers; anything to do with infancy through adolescence." Model release required "allowing photo to be used at the editor's discretion in *PTA Today* and other PTA publications."
Making Contact & Terms: Send b&w prints only (any size) by mail for consideration. SASE. Reports within 2 weeks. Pays $35/b&w inside photo; $75/b&w cover each time used. Pays on publication. Credit line given on contents page. Simultaneous submissions and previously published work OK. Every photo should have the name and address of photographer.
Tips: "Our preference is for the dramatic, uncluttered, strong contrast, crisp and clean photo. Desperately need minority children with parents, talking, discussing—all ages. Should be recent shots. Send SASE for schedule of topics to be covered in upcoming issues."

PUBLIC CITIZEN, 2000 P St. NW, Washington DC 20036. (202)833-3000. Production Manager: Laren Marshall. Bimonthly. "*Public Citizen* is the magazine of the membership organization of the same name, founded by Ralph Nader in 1971. The magazine addresses topics of concern to today's socially aware and politically active consumers on issues in consumer rights, safe products and workplaces, a clean environment, safe and efficient energy, and corporate and government accountability." Circ. 45,000. Sample copy free with 9×12 SAE and 2 first-class stamps.
Needs: Uses 7-10 photos/issue; 2 supplied by freelancers. Needs photos to go along with articles on various consumer issues—assigns for press conference coverage or portrait shot of interview; buys stock for other purposes.
Making Contact & Terms: Provide resume, business card, brochure, flyer or tearsheets to be kept on file for possible future assignments. Does not return unsolicited material. Pays $50-75/b&w inside photo. Pays on publication. Credit line given. Buys first North American serial rights. Simultaneous submissions and previously published work OK.
Tips: Prefers to see "good photocopies of photos and list of stock to keep on file. Common subjects: nuclear power, presidential administrations, health and safety issues, citizen empowerment, union democracy, etc."

© Charles Weber

Finding the perfect scene for a photograph often happens by accident. The trick is to be prepared for those situations. Charles Weber, of Beloit, Wisconsin, says he carries his camera everywhere and this practice allowed him to capture the above photo for PTA Today Magazine. He was driving down the road when he saw these children. The publication used the photo twice, both times to illustrate text on safety.

THE PUBLIC EMPLOYEE MAGAZINE, AFSCME, 1625 L St. NW, Washington DC 20036. (202)429-1150. Production Supervisor: Judy Sugar. Union publication of American Federation of State, County and Municipal Employees, AFL-CIO, 8 times/year color magazine. Emphasizes public employees, AFSCME members. Readers are "our members." Circ. 1,200,000.
Needs: Uses 35 photos/issue; majority supplied by freelancers. Assignment only.
Making Contact & Terms: Provide resume, business card, brochure, flyer or tearsheets to be kept on file for possible assignments. Will try to return unsolicited material if a SASE is enclosed, but no guarantee. Reports back as needed. NPI; depends on assignment, usually negotiate price. Pays on acceptance. Credit line usually given. Buys all rights; negotiable.
Tips: "Color transparencies, no fast film. Well lighted; use flash when needed. Show strong photojournalism skills and be skilled in use of flash."

PUBLIC POWER, Third Floor, 2301 M. St. NW, Washington DC 20037. (202)467-2948. Editor: Jeanne LaBella. Publication of the American Public Power Association. Bimonthly. Emphasizes electric power provided by cities, towns and utility districts. Circ. 12,000. Sample copy and photo guidelines free.
Needs: "We buy photos on assignment only."
Making Contact & Terms: Query with samples. Provide resume, business card, brochure, flyer or tearsheets to be kept on file for possible future assignments. SASE. Reports in 1-2 weeks. Pay varies—$25-75 each—more for covers. Pays on acceptance. Credit line given. Buys one-time rights. Simultaneous and previously published work OK.

THE PULLER, Dept. PM, Suite L, 6969 Worthington-Galena Rd., Worthington OH 43085. (614)436-1761. FAX: (614)436-0964. Editor: Rhdawnda Bliss. Publication of the National Tractor Pullers Association. Monthly magazine. Emphasizes tractor and truck pulling. Readers are mostly working class

men and women, ages 18-36. Circ. 10,000. Estab. 1970. Sample copies available for $2.50.
Needs: Uses up to 75 photos/issue; 60% supplied by freelancers. Needs photos of motorsport action and personalities in field. Reviews photos with or without ms. Especially wants to see coverage of NTPA's national pulling circuit in the coming year. Model release preferred. Photo captions required; include description of location, date, year and subject.
Making Contact & Terms: Send unsolicited 4 × 5 glossy b&w or color prints by mail for consideration. Also considers 35mm and 2¼ × 2¼ transparencies. Provide resume, business card, brochure, flyer or tearsheets to be kept on file for possible assignments. Keeps samples on file. SASE. Reports in 1 month. Pays $50/color cover; $15-50 inside photo. Pays on publication. Credit line given. Buys all rights; negotiable. Simultaneous submissions OK.

PURE–BRED DOGS/AMERICAN KENNEL GAZETTE, Dept. PM, 51 Madison Ave., New York NY 10010. (212)696-8333. Photo Editor: Lori Pepe. Publication of the American Kennel Club. Monthly. Emphasizes AKC pure-bred dogs. Readers are pure-bred dog fanciers and owners. Circ. 58,000. Estab. 1889. Photo guidelines free with SASE.
Needs: Uses about 50 photos/issue; 50% supplied by freelancers. Needs photos of AKC pure-bred dogs (outdoor candids, excellent breed representatives). Model release and captions preferred. About "50% of covers are on assignment; most other work is submitted by professional and freelance 'dog' photographers."
Making Contact & Terms: Query with samples; send 5 × 7 b&w and color prints; 35mm, 2¼ × 2¼ transparencies by mail for consideration (dupes only, no originals). SASE. Reports in 3 weeks. Pays $250/color cover photo; $25-100/color or b&w inside photo. Pays on publication. Buys first N.A. serial rights.
Tips: Prefers to see candids with attractive backgrounds. No show poses. Excellent show-quality representatives of AKC breeds, naturally posed or in action, "extremely sharp, with good contrast and lots of detail." Prefers duplicate transparencies. "Read the magazine and attend dog shows where quality dogs can be found as subjects." Trend is "more elegant rather than cute. No props or costumes. Simple backgrounds. Dog should be primary focus. Casual, not overly posed."

REAL ESTATE FINANCE TODAY, Dept. PM, 6th Floor, 1125 15th St. NW, Washington DC 20005. (202)861-1927. FAX: (202)861-0736. Deputy Editor: Lusien Salvant. Publication of the Mortgage Bankers Association. Weekly tabloid. Emphasizes housing, commercial buildings, banking, finance. Readership consists of predominantly male mortgage banking professionals, 30-65 years of age. Circ. 11,000. Estab. 1983. Sample copy free with 9 × 12 SASE and 2 first-class stamps.
Needs: Uses 1-2 photos/issue; 50% supplied by freelance photographers. Needs photos of some legislative work. Also, scenes of cities in which conferences are held. "We often use photos of housing or housing construction as backgrounds for graphs." Model release and captions preferred.
Making Contact & Terms: Query with list of stock photo subjects. Send b&w prints (any size of format) by mail for consideration. Provide resume, business card, brochure, flyer or tearsheets to be kept on file for possible assignments. SASE. Reports in 2 weeks. Pays $100/color cover photo, $75/b&w cover photo, $50/color or b&w inside photo. Pays on publication. Credit line given. Buys one-time rights. Simultaneous submissions and previously published work OK.

*RELAY MAGAZINE, P.O. Box 10114, Tallahassee FL 32302-2114. (904)224-3314. Editor: Stephanie Wolanski. Association publication of Florida Municipal Electric. Monthly magazine. Emphasizes municipally owned electric utilities. Readers are city officials, legislators, public power officials and employees. Circ. 1,800. Estab. 1957. Sample copy free for 9 × 12 SASE and 3 first-class stamps.
Needs: Uses various photos/issue; various number supplied by freelancers. Needs b&w photos of electric utilities in Florida (hurricane/storm damage to lines, utility workers, etc.). Special photo needs include hurricane/storm photos. Model/property release preferred. Photo captions required.
Making Contact & Terms: Send unsolicited photos by mail for consideration. Query with letter, description of photo. Send 5 × 7 or 8 × 10 b&w prints. Keeps samples on file. SASE. Reports in 1 month. Pays $20 and up/b&w cover photo; $10 and up/b&w inside photo. Pays on acceptance. Credit line given. Buys one-time rights, repeated use (stock); negotiable. Simultaneous submissions and/or previously published work OK.
Tips: "Must relate to our industry. Clarity and contrast important. Query first if possible."

THE RETIRED OFFICER MAGAZINE, 201 N. Washington St., Alexandria VA 22314. (800)245-8762. FAX: (703)838-8179. Contact: Associate Editor. Monthly. Publication represents the interests of retired military officers from the seven uniformed services: recent military history (particularly Vietnam and Korea), travel, health, second-career job opportunities, military family lifestyle and current military/political affairs. Readers are officers or warrant officers from the Army, Navy, Air Force, Marine Corps, Coast Guard, Public Health Service and NOAA. Circ. 380,000. Estab. 1945. Free sample copy and photo guidelines with 9 × 12 SASE and $1.25 postage.

Needs: Uses about 24 photos/issue; 8 (the cover and some inside shots) usually supplied by freelancers. "We're always looking for good color slides of active duty military people and healthy, active mature adults with a young 50s look—our readers are 55-65."

Making Contact & Terms: Interested in receiving work from newer, lesser-known photographers. Query with list of stock photo subjects. Provide resume, brochure, flyer to be kept on file. Do *not* send original photos unless requested to do so. Uses original 35mm, 2¼ × 2¼ or 4 × 5 transparencies. Pays $200/color cover photo; $20/b&w inside photo; $50-125 transparencies for inside use (in color). Other payment negotiable. Pays on acceptance. Credit line and complimentary copies given. Buys one-time rights.

Tips: "A photographer who can also write and submit a complete package of story and photos is valuable to us. Much of our photography is supplied by our authors as part of their manuscript package. We periodically select a cover photo from these submissions—our covers relate to a particular feature in each issue." In samples, wants to see "good color saturation, well-focused, excellent composition."

*ROCKFORD REVIEW & TRIBUTARY, P.O. Box 858, Rockford IL 61105. Editor: David Ross. Association publication of Rockford Writers' Guild. Review is annual, Tributary quarterly magazines. Emphasizes poetry and prose of all types. Readers are of all stages and ages who share an interest in quality writing and art. Circ. 1,000. Estab. 1982. Sample copy $6 Review, $2.50 Tributary.

Need: Uses 1-5 photos/issue; all supplied by freelancers. Needs photos of scenics and personalities. Model/property release preferred. Photo captions preferred; include when and where of the photos and biography.

Making Contact & Terms: Send unsolicited photos by mail for consideration. Send 8 × 10 or 5 × 7 glossy b&w prints. Does not keep samples on file. SASE. Reports in 4-6 weeks. Pays in one copy of magazine, but work is eligible for Review's $50 Editor's Choice prize and Tributary's $25 Readers' Poll prize. Pays on publication. Credit line given. Buys first N.A. serial rights. Simultaneous submissions OK.

Tips: "Experimental work with a literary magazine in mind will be carefully considered. Avoid the 'news' approach."

THE ROTARIAN, 1560 Sherman Ave., Evanston IL 60201. (312)866-3000. FAX: (312)328-8554. Editor: Willmon L. White. Photo Editor: Judy Lee. Monthly magazine. For Rotarian business and professional men and women and their families in 175 countries and geographic regions. Circ. 538,300. Estab. 1911. Free sample copy and photo guidelines with SASE.

Needs: "Our greatest need is for the identifying face or landscape, one that says unmistakably, 'This is Japan, or Minnesota, or Brazil, or France or Sierra Leone,' or any of the other countries and geographic regions this magazine reaches."

Making Contact & Terms: Interested in receiving work from newer, lesser-known photographers. Query with resume of credits or send photos for consideration. Uses 8 × 10 b&w glossy prints; contact sheet OK; 8 × 10 color glossy prints or transparencies; for cover uses transparencies "generally related to the contents of that month's issue." SASE. Reports in 1-2 weeks. Pays on acceptance. NPI; payment varies. Buys one-time rights; occasionally all rights, negotiable.

Tips: "We prefer vertical shots in most cases. The key words for the freelance photographer to keep in mind are *internationality* and *variety*. Study the magazine. Read the kinds of articles we publish. Think how your photographs could illustrate such articles in a dramatic, story-telling way. Key submissions to general interest, art-of-living material." Plans special pre-convention promotion coverage of June 1993 Rotary International convention in Melbourne, Australia.

SCIENCE AND CHILDREN, 3140 N. Washington Blvd., Arlington VA 22201. (703)243-7100. Publication of the National Science Teachers Association. Monthly (September to May) journal. Emphasizes teaching science to elementary school children. Readers are male and female elementary science teachers and other education professionals. Circ. 24,000.

Needs: Uses 40 photos/issue; 10 supplied by freelancers. Needs photos of "a variety of science-related topics, though seasonals, nature scenes and animals are often published. Also children." Special photo needs include children doing science in all settings, especially classroom. Model/property release and photo captions required.

Making Contact & Terms: Arrange personal interview to show portfolio. Send unsolicited b&w prints by mail for consideration. Pays $200/color cover photo; $50/color inside; $35 b&w inside. Pays on publication. Credit line given. Simultaneous submissions and previously published work OK.
Tips: "We can always use photographs of children and teachers working together."

THE SCIENCE TEACHER, NSTA, 3140 North Washington Blvd., Arlington VA 22201. (703)243-7100. FAX: (703)243-7100. Managing Editor: Shelley Carey. Publication of the National Science Teachers Association. Publishes 9 monthly issues per year. Emphasizes high school science education. Readers are adult science teachers. Circ. 27,000. Estab. 1950s. Sample copy and photo guidelines free upon request.
Needs: Uses 5-10 photos/issue; assigns 35% of photos; uses less than 5% from stock. Needs color and b&w shots of high school students and teachers; no nature/scenics needed. Model release "required only if run with article on special education." Property release preferred. "No photo captions, please."
Making Contact & Terms: Interested in receiving work from a newer, lesser-known photographer. Arrange personal interview to show portfolio. Query with stock photo list, or send 8×10 glossy b&w prints or 8×10 transparencies by mail for consideration. Provide resume, business card, brochure, flyer or tearsheets to be kept on file for possible assignments. SASE. "Often reports in 6 months for prints; sooner for queries." Pays $150/color cover; $50/b&w or color full page; or $35/b&w smaller page rate. Pays on publication. Credit line given. Buys one-time rights; rights negotiable. Simultaneous submissions and previously published work OK.
Tips: "Looking for a solid, basic style. We need photos of students and teachers in classroom and laboratory environments. The activities they are doing should not be too specific so we can use the photo in any article. We need more photos of women and minorities. Don't get too 'artsy.' "

SCOUTING MAGAZINE, Boy Scouts of America, 1325 Walnut Hill Lane, Irving TX 75062. Photo Editor: Brian Payne. Bimonthly magazine. For adults within the Scouting movement. Circ. 1,000,000. Free photo guidelines.
Needs: Needs photos dealing with success and/or personal interest of leaders in Scouting. Wants no "single photos or ideas from individuals unfamiliar with our magazine." Assigns 90% of photos; uses 10% from stock. Photo captions required.
Making Contact & Terms: "No assignments will be considered without a portfolio review by mail or in person." Call to arrange a personal appointment, or query with ideas. "SASE. Reports in 10 working days. NPI. Pays on acceptance Buys one-time rights."
Tips: Study the magazine carefully. In portfolio or samples, wants to see "diversity and ability to light difficult situations."

SCRAP PROCESSING AND RECYCLING, Suite 1000, 1325 G St. N.W., Washington DC 20005. (202)466-4050. FAX: (202)775-9109. Editor: Elise Browne. Publication of the Institute of Scrap Recycling Industries. Bimonthly magazine. Covers scrap recycling for owners and managers of private recycling operations worldwide. Circ. 6,000. Estab. 1988. Sample copy for $7.50.
Needs: Uses approx. 100 photos/issue; 15% supplied by freelancers. Needs operation shots of companies being profiled and studio concept shots. Model release and photo captions required.
Making Contact & Terms: Arrange personal interview to show portfolio. Query with list of stock photo subjects. Provide resume, business card, brochure, flyer or tearsheets to be kept on file for possible assignment. Reports in 1 month. Pays $500-800/day. Pays on publication. Credit line given. Rights negotiable. Previously published work OK.
Tips: Photographers must possess "ability to photograph people in corporate atmosphere as well as industrial operations; ability to work well with executives as well as laborers. We are always looking for good color photographers to accompany our staff writers on visits to companies being profiled. We try to keep travel costs to a minimum by hiring photographers located in the general vicinity of the profiled company. Other photography (primarily studio work) is usually assigned through freelance art director."

SEA FRONTIERS INC., Dept. PM, 4th Floor, UM Knight Theater, 400 SE Second Ave., Miami FL 33131. (305)375-8498. Executive Editor: Bonnie Gordon. Editor: Faith Schaefer. Bimonthly magazine. Circ. 55,000. For anyone with an interest in any aspect of the sea, the life it contains and its conservation. Sample copy $5 postpaid; photo guidelines.
Needs: Buys 80 photos annually. Animal, nature, photo feature, scenic, wildlife, industry, vessels, structures and geological features. Ocean-related subjects only. Captions required.
Making Contact & Terms: Send photos for consideration. Send 35mm or 2¼×2¼ transparencies. Uses vertical format for cover. Allow space for insertion of logo. SASE. Reports in 10 weeks. Pays $30-50/color photo; $200/front cover; $75/back cover. Pays on publication. Credit line given. Buys one-time rights.

THE SECRETARY, Suite 706, 2800 Shirlington Rd., Arlington VA 22206. (703)998-2534. Publisher: Debra J. Stratton. Association publication of the Professional Secretaries International. Published 9 times/year. Emphasizes secretarial profession – proficiency, continuing education, new products/ methods and equipment related to office administration/communications. Readers include career secretaries, 98% women, in myriad offices, with wide ranging responsibilities. Circ. 50,000. Estab. 1942. Free sample copy with SASE.

Needs: Uses 6 photos/issue; freelance photos 100% from stock. Needs secretaries (predominately women, but occasionally men) in appropriate and contemporary office settings using varied office equipment or performing varied office tasks. Must be in good taste and portray professionalism of secretaries. Reviews photos with or without accompanying ms. Model release preferred.

Making Contact & Terms: Interested in receiving work from newer, lesser-known photographers. Query with samples or send unsolicited photos by mail for consideration. Uses 3½ × 4½, 8 × 10 glossy prints; 35mm, 2¼ × 2¼, 4 × 5 and 8 × 10 transparencies. SASE. Reports in 1 month. Pays $150 maximum/b&w photo; $500 maximum/color photo. Pays on publication. Credit line given. Buys first N.A. serial rights. Simultaneous submissions and previously published work OK.

THE SENTINEL, Industrial Risk Insurers, Dept. PM, 85 Woodland St., Hartford CT 06102. (203)520-7300. Editor: Anson Smith. Quarterly magazine. Circ. 59,000. Emphasizes industrial loss prevention for "insureds and all individuals interested in fire protection." Free sample copy and photo guidelines.

Needs: Uses 4-8 photos/issue; 2-3 supplied by freelance photographers. Needs photos of fires, explosions, windstorm damage and other losses at industrial sites. Prefers to see good industrial fires and industrial process shots, industrial and commercial fire protection equipment. No photos that do not pertain to industrial loss prevention (no house fires) but can use generic shots of natural disaster damage, e.g., floods, hurricanes, tornadoes. Model release preferred.

Making Contact & Terms: Send material by mail for consideration. Uses b&w or color glossy prints. Horizontal or vertical format for cover. Reports in 2 weeks. Pays $35/b&w photo; $100/color photo; $100/cover photo. Pays on acceptance. Credit line given. Buys one-time rights. Previously published work OK.

SERVICES, Dept. PM, Suite 225, 10201 Lee Highway, Fairfax VA 22030. (703)359-7090 or (800)368-3414. Editor: Patrick G. Johnstone. Publication of the Building Service Contractors Association International. Monthly. Emphasizes building service contracting (janitorial mostly). Readers largely consist of building service contractors, manufacturers and distributors of sanitary supplies, building owners and managers, and hospitals. Circ. 15,000. Sample copy free with 9 × 12 SAE and $1.50 postage.

Needs: Needs photos of building maintenance services performed by outside contractors – office cleaning, floor and carpet care, window washing, lighting maintenance, exterior maintenance. Always needs good material on janitorial cleaning, floor and carpet care, upholstery and drapery care, water and fire damage restoration, window washing. Also needs photos for managerial articles – financial management, staff training, etc. Model release and captions required.

Making Contact & Terms: Arrange a personal interview to show portfolio. Send 8 × 10 matte b&w prints; 35mm transparencies; b&w contact sheets by mail for consideration. SASE. Reports in 1 week. Pays $350/color cover photo; $400-600/day. Pays on acceptance. Credit line given. Buys one-time rights. Simultaneous submissions and previously published work OK.

Tips: Prefers to see "strong communication values – photos that *tell me* something about the subject. Don't want something that looks like a set-up stock photo."

SHARING THE VICTORY, Publication of the Fellowship of Christian Athletes, Dept. PM, 8701 Leeds Rd., Kansas City MO 64129. Contact: John Dodderidge. Provides year-round outreach to athletes and coaches.

Needs: Buys 12-15 photos/year. Photos used in magazines. Close-up and thoughtful or dramatic sports-related shots: "lots of high quality 35mm transparencies and color prints depicting the gamut of action and emotion in high-school-age team and individual sports; shots depicting camaraderie, sportsmanship, loyalty, humor etc., among both male and female athletes will be favorably considered."

Making Contact: Query with samples. SASE. Reports in 1 week. "Best to study sample copy first. Send $1 plus 9 × 12 SASE." Uses b&w and color prints, 35mm transparencies, b&w contact sheets. Pays $50-100/b&w photo and $100-200/color photo. Credit line given on contents page. Buys one-time rights. Model release preferred with close-ups but not necessary. Payment upon publication.

Tips: In reviewing samples looks for "technical excellence (clarity, density, etc.); creativity (freshness of angle, mood, etc); and applications to magazine's target audience (in this case high school male/ female athletes)." Wants to see "35mm color slides of *Sports Illustrated* quality" in samples.

SHOOTING SPORTS USA, Dept. PM, 1600 Rhode Island Ave. NW, Washington DC 20036. (202)828-6000. Editor: Karen Elsner. Publication of the National Rifle Association of America. Monthly. Emphasizes competitive shooting sports (rifle, pistol and shotgun). Readers are mostly NRA-classified

competitive shooters including Olympic-level shooters. Circ. 125,000. Sample copy free with 9×12 SAE with $1 postage. Editorial guidelines for SASE.
Needs: Uses 1-10 photos/issue; about half or less supplied by freelance photographers. Needs photos of how-to, shooting positions, specific shooters. Model release required; captions preferred. Photos preferred with ms, but will accept quality photos for covers.
Making Contact & Terms: Query with photo and editorial ideas by mail. Uses 8×10 glossy b&w prints. SASE. Reports in 2 weeks. Pays $150-250 for photo/text package; amount varies for photos alone. Pays on publication. Credit line given. Buys first North American serial rights. Previously published work OK when cleared with editor.
Tips: Looks for "generic photos of shooters shooting—obeying all safety rules—proper eye protection and hearing protection. If text concerns certain how-to advice, photos are needed to illuminate this. Always query first. We are in search of quality photos to interest both beginning and experienced shooters."

SIGNPOST MAGAZINE, Dept. PM, #512, 1305 Fourth Ave., Seattle WA 98101. (206)625-1367. Editor: Dan Nelson. Publication of the Washington Trails Association. Monthly. Emphasizes "backpacking, hiking, cross-country skiing, all nonmotorized trail use, outdoor equipment and minimum-impact camping techniques." Readers are "people active in outdoor activities, primarily backpacking; residents of the Pacific Northwest, mostly Washington. Age group: 9-90, family-oriented, interested in wilderness preservation, trail maintenance." Circ. 3,800. Estab. 1966. Free sample copy. Photo guidelines free with SASE.
Needs: Uses about 10-15 photos/issue; 30% supplied by freelancers. Needs "wilderness/scenic; people involved in hiking, backpacking, canoeing, skiing; wildlife; outdoor equipment photos, all with Pacific Northwest emphasis." Captions required.
Making Contact & Terms: Send 5×7 or 8×10 glossy b&w prints by mail for consideration. SASE. Reports in 1 month. No payment for inside photos. Pays $25/b&w cover photo. Pays on publication. Credit line given. Buys one-time rights. Simultaneous submissions and previously published work OK.
Tips: "We are a b&w publication and prefer using b&w originals for the best reproduction. Photos must have a Pacific Northwest slant. Photos that meet our cover specifications are always of interest to us. Familiarity with our magazine would greatly aid the photographer in submitting material to us; a sample copy is free. Contributing to *Signpost* won't help pay your bills, but sharing your photos with other backpackers and skiers has its own rewards."

THE SINGLE PARENT, 8807 Colesville Rd., Silver Spring MD 20910. (301)588-9354. FAX: (301)588-9216. Contact: Editor. Publication of Parents Without Partners, Inc. Published 6 times/year. Emphasizes "issues of concern to single parents: widowed, divorced, separated or never-married, and their children, from legal, financial, emotional, how-to, legislative or first-person experience." Readers are "parents mainly between 30-55, US and Canada." Circ. 110,000. Estab. 1957. Sample copy free with SASE plus postage at 3 oz. rate.
Needs: Uses 4-7 photos/issue; all supplied by freelancers; 5-10% from assignment and 90-95% from stock. "We usually make assignments for a particular story. All photos relate to and illustrate articles in the magazine." Model release and captions required. Property release preferred.
Making Contact & Terms: Interested in receiving work from newer, lesser-known photographers. Query with samples. Send 8×10 b&w prints, b&w contact sheets and color slides/photos by mail for consideration. Provide resume, business card, brochure, flyer or tearsheets to be kept on file for possible future assignments. "35mm slides should be presented in multi-pocket, plastic slide pages, not jumbled loosely in an envelope. We're not interested in snapshots sent in by proud parents." SASE. Reports in 2 months. Pays $75-150/color cover photo; $35-50/b&w inside photo. Pays on publication. Credit line given. Buys one-time rights. Simultaneous submissions OK.
Tips: "We have received photo selections on long-term hold from several freelancers. Our first search for each issue is within these selections, and up to 6 photos in each issue are from these selections. We also have contact sheets and tearsheets from freelancers we query periodically for specific subjects and situations. Subjects we look for in samples are: children—happy, unhappy, angry, interacting; and children with one parent in all kinds of settings—reading, playing, working, especially dads/kids. Styles: abstract OK; sensitivity to mood, aesthetics. We occasionally need, and never find, children who are not on their best behavior. We usually look for a photo that easily relates to some aspect of the article to be illustrated. Often, this will establish a mood; sometimes it is symbolic of the theme of the article. Once in a great while, one will exactly match some situation portrayed in the article."

SOARING, Box E, Hobbs NM 88241-1308. (505)392-1177. FAX: (505)392-8154. Art Director: Steve Hines. Monthly magazine. Emphasizes the sport of soaring in sailplanes and motorgliders. Readership consists of white collar and professional males and females, ages 14 and up. Circ. 15,600. Estab. 1937. Sample copy and photo guidelines free with SASE.

© Donna Jernigan

By getting the subjects in this setup photo to interact, Charlotte, North Carolina, photographer Donna Jernigan was able to turn what could have been a stiff photo into a believable image. The shot worked so well it was bought by The Single Parent *for $50 to accompany a story on how to make a second marriage work.*

Needs: Uses 25+ photos/issue; 95% supplied by freelancers. "We hold freelance work for a period of usually 6 months, then it is returned. If we have to keep work longer, we notify the photographer. The photographer is always updated on the status of his or her material." Needs sharply focused transparencies, any format. Especially needs aerial photography. "We need a good supply of sailplane transparencies for our yearly calendar." Model release preferred; captions required.

Making Contact & Terms: Send unsolicited photos by mail for consideration. Uses b&w prints, any size and format. Also uses transparencies, any format. SASE. Reports in 2 weeks. Pays $50/color cover photo. Pays $100 for calendar photos. Pays on publication. Credit line given. Buys one-time rights. Simultaneous submissions OK.

Tips: "Exciting air-to-air photos, creative angles and techniques are encouraged. We pay only for the front cover of our magazine and photos used in our calendars. We are a perfect market for photographers that have sailplane photos of excellent quality. Send work dealing with sailplanes only and label all material."

SOCCER AMERICA, Box 23704, Oakland CA 94623. (415)528-5000. Editor-in-Chief: Lynn Berling. Managing Editor: Paul Kennedy. Weekly magazine. Emphasizes soccer news for the knowledgeable soccer fan. "Although we're a small publication, we are growing at a very fast rate. We cover the pros, the international scene, the amateurs, the colleges, women's soccer, etc." Circ. 25,000. Sample copy and photo guidelines available for $1 with 9 × 12 SAE and 85¢ postage. Writer's guidelines free with SASE.

Needs: Uses 10 photos/issue. "We are interested in soccer shots of all types: action, human interest, etc." Reviews photos with or without accompanying ms. Special photo needs include national-level players emerging from youth ranks, shots of college action. "Our only requirement is that they go with our news format." Captions required.

Making Contact & Terms: Query with samples. Send 8×10 glossy b&w prints by mail for consideration. SASE. Reports in 1 month. Pays $12 minimum/b&w photo; $25 minimum/b&w cover photo; $75 minimum/color cover photo; 50¢/inch to $100/ms. Pays on publication. Credit line given. Buys one-time rights. Previously published work OK, "but we must be informed that it has been published."
Tips: "We are rarely interested in how-to's. We are interested in news features that pertain to soccer, particularly anything that involves investigative reporting or in-depth, 'meaty' personality pieces. Our minimum rates are low, but if we get quality material on subjects that are useful to us, we use a lot of material and pay better rates. Our editorial format is similar to *Sporting News*, so newsworthy photos are of particular interest to us. If a soccer news event is coming up in your area, query us."

SOUTHERN CALIFORNIA BUSINESS, 404 S. Bixel St., Los Angeles CA 90017. (213)629-0671. FAX: (213)629-0611. Editor: Christopher Volker. Association publication of L.A. Chamber of Commerce. Monthly newspaper. Emphasizes business. Readers are mostly business owners, male and female, ages 21-65. Circ. 12,000. Estab. 1898. Sample copy for $2. No photo guidelines.
Needs: Uses 10-20 photos/issue; 5-8 supplied by freelance photographers and public relations agencies. Needs photos of events, editorial, technology, business people and new products. Special photo needs include specialty shots on various subjects (mainly business-oriented).
Making Contact & Terms: Interested in receiving work from newer, lesser-known photographers. Query with list of stock photo subjects. Send b&w prints by mail for consideration. Provide resume, business card, brochure, flyer or tearsheets to be kept on file for possible assignments. Will return unsolicited material if a SASE is enclosed. Reports in 3 weeks. Pays $4-5/b&w photo; $100/b&w cover photo; $80-100/hour; $100-150/day; $100-250/photo/text package. Pays on publication. Credit line given. Buys first N.A. serial rights and all rights. Will negotiate with a photographer unwilling to sell all rights. Model release and captions required. Will consider simultaneous submissions.
Tips: In photographer's samples, wants to see "a variety of different subject matter but prefer people shots. Present new ideas, how photography could be more exciting. Send in detailed letter and description of work."

SPECTRUM, The Horace Mann Companies, One Horace Mann Plaza, Springfield IL 62715. Contact: Dave Waugh. Mail number L102. Monthly publication for employees. Includes articles on company programs, monthly employee honors and human interest features on employees and their families.
Needs: Uses about 35 photos/issue; 3-4 supplied by freelancers. "We need photos of our agents at work and with their families." Captions (at least names) preferred.
Making Contact & Terms: Provide resume, business card, brochure, flyer or tearsheets to be kept on file for possible future assignments. SASE. Reports "as soon as we would need a photographer from his/her area of the country." Pays $25-30/hour; $175 maximum/job. Pays on acceptance. Credit line given. Buys all rights and negatives. Simultaneous submissions and previously published work OK.

SPORTS CAR, Suite E, 1371 E. Warner, Tustin CA 92680. (714)259-8240. Editor: Rich McCormack. Publication of the Sports Car Club of America. Monthly magazine. Emphasizes sports car racing and competition activities. Circ. 50,000. Estab. 1944. Sample copy for $2.95.
Needs: Uses 75-100 photos/issue; 75% freelance photography issue come from assignment and 25% from freelance stock. Needs action photos from competitive events, personality portraits and technical photos.
Making Contact & Terms: Query with resume of credits or send 5×7 color or b&w glossy/borders prints or 35mm or 2¼×2¼ transparencies by mail for consideration. Provide resume, business card, brochure, flyer or tearsheets to be kept on file for possible assignments. SASE. Reports in 1 month. Pays $25/color inside photo; $10/b&w inside photo; $250/color cover. Negotiates all other rates. Pays on publication. Credit line given. Buys first N.A. serial rights. Simultaneous submissions OK.
Tips: To break in with this or any magazine, "always send only the absolute best work; try to accommodate the specific needs of your clients. Have a relevant subject, strong action, crystal sharp focus, proper contrast and exposure. We seem to need good candid personality photos of key competitors and officials."

 The double dagger before a listing indicates that the market is located outside the United States and Canada. The symbol is new this year in Photographer's Market.

STATE GOVERNMENT NEWS, Iron Works Pike, Box 11910, Lexington KY 40578. (606)231-1842. Executive Editor: Dag Ryen. Publication of The Council of State Governments. Monthly. Emphasizes state government issues. Readers are state legislators and officials. Circ. 18,000. Estab. 1957. Sample copy free with 9×12 SASE and $1 postage.
Needs: Uses about 12 photos/issue. Model release and captions required. Needs photos of state employees and decision makers in action.
Making Contact & Terms: Interested in receiving work from a newer, lesser-known photographer. Query with list of stock photo subjects. Provide resume, business card, brochure, flyer or tearsheets to be kept on file for possible future assignments. SASE. Pays $150/color cover photo; $25/b&w inside photo. Pays on publication. Credit line not given. Buys one-time rights. Simultaneous submissions OK.
Tips: "Check with us for our current needs. Photograph people that are active and expressive. We may begin using more color."

STUDENT LAWYER, 750 N. Lake Shore Dr., Chicago IL 60611. Editor: Sarah Hoban. Managing Editor: Miriam R. Krasno. Publication of the American Bar Association. Magazine published 9 times/school year. Emphasizes social and legal issues for law students. Circ. 35,000. Sample copy $4.
Needs: Uses about 3-5 photos/issue; all supplied by freelancers. "All photos are assigned, determined by story's subject matter." Model release and captions required.
Making Contact & Terms: Arrange a personal interview to show portfolio or send samples. SASE. Reports in 3 weeks. Pays $300/color cover photo; $75-200/b&w; $100-250/color inside photo. Pays on acceptance. Credit line given. Buys one-time rights. Previously published work OK.

THE SURGICAL TECHNOLOGIST, 7108-C S. Alton Way, Englewood CO 80112. (303)694-9130. Editor: Michelle Armstrong. Publication of the Association of Surgical Technologists. Bimonthly. Emphasizes surgery. Readers are "20-60 years old, operating room professionals, well educated in surgical procedures." Circ. 13,000. Sample copy free with 9×12 SASE and $1.25 postage. Photo guidelines free with SASE.
Needs: Uses 1 photo/issue. Needs "surgical, operating room photos that show members of the surgical team in action." Model release required.
Making Contact & Terms: Query with samples. Submit portfolio for review. Send 5×7 or 8½×11 glossy or matte prints; 35mm, 2¼×2¼ or 4×5 transparencies; b&w or color contact sheets; b&w or color negatives by mail for consideration. Provide resume, business card, brochure, flyer or tearsheets to be kept on file for possible future assignments. SASE. Reports in 4 weeks after review by Editorial Board. Pays $75/b&w cover photo; $150/color cover photo; $25/b&w inside photo; $50/color inside photo. Pays on acceptance. Credit line given. Buys one-time rights. Simultaneous submissions and previously published work OK.

TANK TALK, 570 Oakwood Rd., Lake Zurich IL 60047. (708)438-TANK. FAX: (708)438-8766. Contact: Jim Wisuri. Publication of Steel Tank Institute. Monthly. Emphasizes matters pertaining to the underground storage tank industry. Readers are tank owners, installers, government officials, regulators, manufacturers. Circ. 11,500. Free sample copy with 9×12 SASE and 52¢ postage.
Needs: Uses about 4-6 photos/issue; 50-75% supplied by freelancers. Needs photos of installations, current developments in the industry, i.e., new equipment and features for tanks, author photos, fiberglass tank leaks. Photos purchased with accompanying ms only.
First Contact & Terms: "Call if you have photos of interest to the tank industry." Uses at least 5×7 glossy b&w prints. SASE. Reports in 2 weeks. NPI. Pays on publication. Buys all rights; negotiable. Simultaneous submissions and previously published work OK.

TEAM MAGAZINE, publication of the Young Calvinist Federation, Dept. PM, P.O. Box 7259, Grand Rapids MI 49510. (616)241-5616. FAX: (616)241-5558. Editor: Dale Dièleman. *Team* magazine is a quarterly digest for volunteer church youth leaders. It promotes shared leadership for holistic ministry with high school young people. Contributor's guidelines and sample issue of *Team* for SASE.
Needs: Buys 25-30 photos/year. Photos used in magazines and books—"we produce 1-2 books annually for youth leaders, an additional 5-25 pix." High school young people in groups and as individuals in informal settings—on the street, in the country, at retreats, at school, having fun; racial variety; discussing in two's, three's, small groups; studying the Bible; praying; dating; doing service projects; interacting with children, adults, the elderly.
Making Contact & Terms: Query with samples, query with list of stock photo subjects, send unsolicited photos by mail for consideration. "We like to keep those packages that have potential on file for 2 months. Others (with no potential) returned immediately." Uses 5×7 or 8×10 b&w glossy prints. Also uses color for cover. SASE. Pays $20-50/b&w photo; $50-150/color photo. Credit line given. Buys one-time rights.

Tips: In samples, looks for "more than just faces. We look for activity, unusual situations or settings, symbolic work. No out-of-date fashion or hair." To break in "Send us a selection of photos. We will photocopy and request as needed. We expect good contrast in black and white."

TEXAS ALCALDE MAGAZINE, (formerly *Alcalde Magazine*), P.O. Box 7278, Austin TX 78713. (512)471-3799. FAX: (512)471-8088. Editor: Ernestine Wheelock. Publication of the University of Texas Ex-Students' Association. Bimonthly magazine. Emphasizes University alumni. Readers are graduates, former students and friends who pay dues in the Association. Circ. 52,000. Estab. 1913. Sample copy free with 9 × 12 SASE and $1.30 postage.
Needs: Uses 65 photos/issue; 2-3 supplied by freelance photographers. Needs UT campus shots, professors, students, buildings, city of Austin, UT sports. Will review photos with accompanying ms only. Model release preferred; captions required.
Making Contact & Terms: Interested in receiving work from newer, lesser-known photographers. Query with list of stock photo subjects. Send 5 × 7 or 8 × 10 glossy b&w and color prints; 35mm, 2¼ × 2¼ or 4 × 5 transparencies by mail for consideration. SASE. Reports in 1 month. Fee negotiable. Pays $100/color cover photo; $25/b&w and color inside photo. Pays on publication. Credit line given. Buys one-time rights. Simultaneous submissions and previously published work OK if details of use are supplied.

TEXAS REALTOR MAGAZINE, P.O. Box 2246, Austin TX 78768. (512)480-8200. FAX: (512)370-2390. Editor: Meri Kitchens. Publication of the Texas Association of REALTORS. Monthly magazine. Emphasizes real estate sales and related industries. Readers are male and female realtors, ages 20-70. Circ. 45,000. Estab. 1972. Sample copy free with SASE.
Needs: Uses 10 photos/issue; 100% supplied by freelancers. Needs photos of business, office management, telesales, real estate sales, commercial real estate, nature, sales. Especially wants to see nature and beauty shots of private property for covers.
Making Contact & Terms: NPI.

TEXTILE RENTAL MAGAZINE, Dept. PM, P.O. Box 1283, Hallandale FL 33008. (305)457-7555. Editor: Christine Seaman. Publication of the Textile Rental Services Association of America. Monthly magazine. Emphasizes the "linen supply, industrial and commercial laundering industry." Readers are "heads of companies, general managers of facilities, predominantly male audience; national and international readers." Circ. 6,000.
Needs: Photos "needed on assignment basis only." Model release preferred; captions preferred or required "depending on subject."
Making Contact & Terms: "We contact photographers on an as-needed basis selecting from a directory of photographers." Does not return unsolicited material. Pays $350/color cover plus processing; "depends on the job." Pays on acceptance. Credit line given if requested. Buys all rights. Previously published work OK.
Tips: "Meet deadlines; don't charge more than $100-500 for a series of b&w photos that take less than half a day to shoot."

TOUCH, P.O. Box 7259, Grand Rapids MI 49510. (616)241-5616. Managing Editor: Carol Smith. Publication of Calvinettes. Monthly. Emphasizes "girls 7-14 in action. The magazine is a Christian girls' publication geared to the needs and activities of girls in the above age group." Readers are "Christian girls ages 7-14; multiracial." Circ. 15,500. Estab. 1970. Sample copy and photo guidelines free with 9 × 12 SASE. "Also available is a theme update listing all the themes of the magazine for six months."
Needs: Uses about 5-6 photos/issue; 50-75% from freelancers. Needs photos suitable for illustrating stories and articles: photos of girls aged 7-14 from multi-cultural backgrounds involved in sports, Christian service and other activities young girls would be participating in." Model/property release preferred.
Making Contact & Terms: Interested in receiving work from newer, lesser-known photographers. Send 5 × 7 glossy b&w prints by mail for consideration. SASE. Reports in 2 months. Pays $20-35/ b&w photo; $50/cover. Pays on publication. Credit line given. Buys one-time rights. Simultaneous submissions OK.
Tips: "Make the photos simple. We prefer to get a spec sheet rather than photos and we'd really like to hold photos sent to us on speculation until publication. We select those we might use and send others back. Freelancers should write for our biannual theme update and try to get photos to fit the theme of each issue." Recommends that photographers "be concerned about current trends in fashions and hair styles and that all girls don't belong to 'families.' " To break in, "a freelancer can present a selection of his/her photography of girls, we'll review it and contact him/her on its usability."

TRAFFIC SAFETY, Dept. PM, 1121 Spring Lake Dr., Itasca IL 60143. (708)775-2278. Publisher: Kevin Axe. Editor: Dawn DeLong. Publication of National Safety Council. Bimonthly. Emphasizes highway and traffic safety, accident prevention. Readers are professionals in highway-related fields, including traffic engineers, state officials, driver improvement instructors, trucking executives, licensing officials, community groups, university safety centers. Circ. 20,000. Sample copy free with 8 × 11 SASE.
Needs: Uses about 15-20 photos/issue; 1-2 supplied by freelancers. Needs photos of road scenes, vehicles, accidents; specific needs vary. Photos purchased with accompanying ms only. Model release preferred; captions required.
Making Contact & Terms: Query with b&w prints. SASE. Reports in 2 weeks. NPI; prices decided on individual basis. Pays on publication. Credit line given. Buys all rights but will negotiate.

TRANSPORT TOPICS, 2200 Mill Rd., Alexandria VA 22314. (703)838-1780. FAX: (703)838-1777. Chief Photographer: Michael James. Publication of the American Trucking Association. Weekly tabloid. Emphasizes the trucking industry. Readers are male executives 35-65. Circ. 31,000. Estab. 1935.
Needs: Uses approximately 12 photos/issue; amount supplied by freelancers "depends on need." Needs photos of truck transportation in all modes. Model/property release and photo captions preferred.
Making Contact & Terms: Send unsolicited 35mm or 2¼ × 2¼ transparencies by mail for consideration. Provide resume, business card, brochure, flyer or tearsheets to be kept on file for possible assignments. Does not keep samples on file. SASE. Reports in 2-4 weeks. Pays $200/color cover photo. Pays on acceptance. Credit line given. Buys one-time rights; negotiable. Simultaneous submissions and previously published work OK.
Tips: "Trucks/trucking must be dominant element in the photograph—not an incidental part of an environmental scene."

✴TROT, Dept. PM, 2150 Meadowvale Blvd., Mississauga, ON L5N 6R6 Canada. (416)858-3060. FAX: (416)858-3111. Editor: Harold Howe. Monthly magazine. Emphasizes harness racing. Readers are a cross section of all Canadians. Circ. 21,500. Sample copy available.
Needs: Uses 3-5 photos/issue; 100% supplied by freelance photographers. Uses horse photos from various angles and moods. Photos purchased with accompanying ms only. Looking for Christmas and fall mood shots in particular. Model release preferred; captions required.
Making Contact & Terms: Submit portfolio for review. Uses 8 × 10 glossy color prints. SAE with IRC. Reports in 2 weeks. Pays $100/color cover photo, $50/color inside photo and $25/b&w inside photo. Pays on publication. Credit line given. Buys one-time rights. Simultaneous submissions and previously published work OK.

TROUT, P.O. Box 6225, Bend OR 97708. (503)382-2327. FAX: (503)382-5421. Associate Editor: James A. Yuskavitch. Publication of Trout Unlimited. Quarterly magazine. "Trout is published for the members and supporters of Trout Unlimited. Editorial focus is on trout, salmon and steelhead fishing and conservation in waters throughout North America. Each issue features well-illustrated articles on fishing techniques, famous streams, salmonid species and current coldwater conservation issues. The average reader is male, in his 40s and an avid trout and salmon fisherman. He has a bachelor's degree and works as a white collar professional." Circ. 65,000. Estab. 1959. Sample copy for $4. Photo guidelines free with SASE.
Needs: Uses 15-40 mostly color shots/issue. Nearly all supplied by freelancers; "occasional assignments, usually only when photographer has a good story idea and we know his or her work." Needs "scenics of trout and salmon rivers and streams, anglers fishing in beautiful surroundings, close-ups of trout and salmon, including underwater photography, close-ups of flies, lures and fishing equipment, abstract art and nature photographs related to trout and salmon angling. We feature a 1⅓ page photograph on the table of contents and ad index pages of each issue. The subject matter is open, from realistic to abstract. The only criteria are that it be stunning and relate to trout and salmon. "We're especially interested in seeing large format transparencies for these pages." Model release and captions preferred; "be brief—just the who, what, when, where and why."
Making Contact & Terms: Query with list of stock photo subjects. Send b&w prints or 35mm, 2¼ × 2¼, 4 × 5 or 8 × 10 transparencies by mail for consideration or submit portfolio for review. Provide resume, business card, brochure, flyer or tearsheets to be kept on file for possible assignments. SASE. Reports in 1-3 months. Pays $300/color cover photo; $75-200/color or b&w inside photo; $100-650/photo text package. Negotiates hour and day rate. Pays on publication. Credit line given. Buys one-time and first N.A. serial rights. Previously published work OK.
Tips: In portfolio of samples, "emphasize what you're good at." Trend is more medium and large format use. "We're also beginning to branch out into the posters and calendars which should eventually open additional opportunities to photographers, besides magazine pages. We like to see photographers work. Although most of our photography is assigned or solicited from a small group of photographers, it's a club you can join if you do good work. Send us some of your work and prepare to be rejected.

But how else will we know who you are and what kind of photography you do? If we like you, you'll hear from us. And it isn't rare for us to find a use for an unsolicited photograph that we like."

TURKEY CALL, P.O. Box 530, Edgefield SC 29824. (803)637-3106. Publisher: National Wild Turkey Federation, Inc. (nonprofit). Editor: Gene Smith. Bimonthly magazine. For members of the National Wild Turkey Federation—people interested in conserving the American wild turkey. Circ. 65,000. Estab. 1973. Sample copy $3 with 9 × 12 SASE. Free contributor guidelines for SASE.
Needs: Needs photos of "wild turkeys, wild turkey hunting, wild turkey management techniques (planting food, trapping for relocation), wild turkey habitat." Captions required. Buys at least 50 photos/annually.
Making Contact & Terms: Copyrighted. Send photos to editor for consideration. Send 8 × 10 glossy b&w prints; color transparencies, any format. Uses some horizontal covers. SASE. Reports in 4 weeks. Pays $20/b&w photo; $50-75/inside color photo; cover negotiated. Pays on acceptance. Credit line given.
Tips: Wants no "poorly posed or restaged shots, mounted turkeys representing live birds, domestic turkeys representing wild birds or typical hunter-with-dead-bird shots. Photos of dead turkeys in a tasteful hunt setting are considered."

V.F.W. MAGAZINE, 406 W. 34th St., Kansas City MO 64111. (816)756-3390. FAX: (816)968-1169. Editor: Richard Kolb. Managing Editor: Gary Bloomfield. Monthly magazine. Circ. 2,000,000. For members of the Veterans of Foreign Wars (V.F.W.)—men and women who served overseas—and their families. Sample copy free with SASE and 50¢ postage.
Needs: Photos illustrating accompanying mss on current defense and foreign policy events, veterans issues and , accounts of "military actions of consequence." Photos purchased with accompanying mss. Captions required. Present model release on acceptance of photo.
Making Contact & Terms: Interested in receiving work from newer, lesser-known photographers. Send photos for consideration. Send 8 × 10 glossy b&w prints; glossy color prints or transparencies for cover. "Cover shots must be submitted with a ms. Price for cover shot will be included in payment of manuscript." SASE. Reports in 4 weeks. Pays $250 minimum. Pays $25-50/b&w photo; $35-250/color photo. Pays on acceptance. Buys one-time and all rights; negotiable.
Tips: "Go through an issue or two at the local library (if not a member) to get the flavor of the magazine." When reviewing samples "we look for familiarity with the military and ability to capture its action and people. We encourage military photographers to send us their best work while they're still in the service. Though they can't be paid for official military photos, at least they're getting published by-lines, which is important when they get out and start looking for a job."

VIRGINIA TOWN & CITY, P.O. Box 12164, Richmond VA 23241. (804)649-8471. FAX: (804)343-3758. Editor: Christine Everson. Monthly magazine of Virginia Municipal League concerning Virginia local government. Readers are state and local government officials in Virginia. Circ. 5,000. Estab. 1965. Sample copy $1.50 with 9 × 12 SASE.
Needs: "B&w photos illustrating scenes of local government and some color work for covers." Special photo needs include "illustrations of environmental issues, computer uses, development, transportation, schools, parks and recreation." Photo captions preferred.
Making Contact & Terms: Query with list of stock photo subjects. Send unsolicited photos by mail for consideration. Send b&w prints. Keeps samples on file. SASE. Report "when we can." Pays $60-100/color cover photo; $60-75/b&w cover photo. Pays on publication. Credit line given. Buys all rights; negotiable. Simultaneous submissions and previously published work OK.

VIRGINIA WILDLIFE, Dept. PM, P.O. Box 11104, Richmond VA 23230. (804)367-1000. Art Director: Emily Pels. Monthly magazine. Circ. 55,000. Emphasizes Virginia wildlife, as well as outdoor features in general, fishing, hunting and conservation for sportsmen and conservationists. Free sample copy and photo/writer's guidelines.
Needs: Buys 350 photos/year; about 95% purchased from freelancers. Photos purchased with accompanying ms. Good action shots relating to animals (wildlife indigenous to Virginia); action hunting and fishing shots; photo essay/photo feature; scenic; human interest outdoors; nature; outdoor recreation (especially boating); and wildlife. Photos must relate to Virginia. Accompanying mss: features on wildlife; Virginia travel; first-person outdoors stories. Pays 10¢/printed word. Model release preferred for children, property release preferred for private property; photo captions that identify species and locations required.
Making Contact & Terms: Send 35mm and 2¼ × 2¼ or larger transparencies. Vertical format required for cover. SASE. Reports (letter of acknowledgment) within 30 days; acceptance or rejection within 45 days of acknowledgement. Pays $30-50/color photo; $125/cover photo. Pays on publication. Credit line given. Buys one-time rights.

Tips: "We don't have time to talk with every photographer who submits work to us. We discourage phone calls and visits to our office, since we do have a system for processing submissions by mail. Our art director will not see anyone without an appointment. In portfolio or samples, wants to see a good eye for color and composition and both vertical and horizontal formats. We are seeing higher quality photography from many of our photographers. It is a very competitive field. Show only your best work. Name and address must be on each slide. Plant and wildlife species should also be identified on slide mount. We look for outdoor shots (must relate to Virginia); close-ups of wildlife."

VOCATIONAL EDUCATION JOURNAL, 1410 King St., Alexandria VA 22314. (703)683-3111. FAX: (703)683-7424. Managing Editor: Kathy Leftwich. Monthly magazine for American Vocational Association. Emphasizes vocational education. Readers are teachers and administrators in high school and colleges. Circ. 45,000. Estab. 1926. Sample copy free with 10×13 SASE.
Needs: Uses 15-20 photos/issue, 3-5 supplied by freelancers. "Students in classroom and job training settings; teachers; students in work situations." Model release preferred for children. Photo captions preferred including location, explanation of situation.
Making Contact & Terms: Interested in receiving work from newer, lesser-known photographers. Query with list of stock photo subjects. Send unsolicited photos by mail for consideration. Provide resume, business card, brochure, flyer or tearsheets to be kept on file for possible assignments. Send 5×7 b&w prints and 35mm transparencies. Keeps samples on file. SASE. Reports as needed. Pays $400 up/color cover photo; $50 up/color inside photo; $30 up/b&w inside photo; $250/day; $500-1,000/job. Pays on publication. Credit line given. Buys one-time rights; sometimes buys all rights; negotiable. Simultaneous submissions and previously published work OK.

VOLKSWAGEN WORLD, Volkswagen of America, Mail code 3C03, 3800 Hamlin Rd., Auburn Hills MI 48326. Editor: Marlene Goldsmith. Quarterly magazine. Circ. 250,000. For owners of Volkswagen (VW) automobiles. Free sample copy and contributor's guidelines with 8×10 SASE.
Needs: Buys 25 photos annually. Travel (US, Canada, Mexico), how-to, human interest, humorous, photo essay/photo feature, sport, German high-tech products (how they're made), and celebrity/personality. Photos purchased with accompanying ms; "features are usually purchased on a combination words-and-pictures basis." Submit model release with photo or present model release on acceptance of photo. Captions required.
Making Contact & Terms: Query first with story and/or photo essay idea. Send transparencies or 35mm. Uses vertical format for cover. Reports in 6 weeks. Pays $150/printed page; $300/2-page spread. Pays $350/cover photo. Pay for inside photo is included in total purchase price with ms. Pays on acceptance. Credit line given. Buys first North American rights.

THE WAR CRY, Dept. PM, The Salvation Army, 615 Slaters Lane, Alexandria VA 22313. (703)684-5500. Editor-in-Chief: Colonel Henry Gariepy. Publication of The Salvation Army. Biweekly. Emphasizes the inspirational. Readers are general public and membership. Circ. 300,000. Sample copy free with SASE.
Needs: Uses about 6 photos/issue. Needs "inspirational, scenic, general photos."
Making Contact & Terms: Send color or b&w glossy prints or color slides by mail for consideration. SASE. Reports in 2 weeks. Pays $35/b&w photo; up to $150/color photo; payment varies for text/photo package. Pays on acceptance. Credit line given "if requested." Buys one-time rights. Simultaneous submissions and previously published work OK.

WASTE AGE MAGAZINE, 10th Floor, 1730 Rhode Island Ave. NW, Washington DC 20036. (202)659-4613. Editor-in-Chief: John Aquino. Publication of the National Solid Wastes Management Association. Monthly magazine. Emphasizes management of solid wastes. Readers are sanitation departments, refuse haulers, etc. Circ. 32,000.
Needs: Uses about 12-20 photos/issue; 3-5 supplied by freelance photographers. "Cover shots in color illustrate main story in magazine; inside shots to go with that story. We need names of artists who can take cover photos of quality in various areas of the country."
Making Contact & Terms: Provide resume, business card, brochure, flyer or tearsheets to be kept on file for possible future assignments. SASE. Reports in 3 weeks. Pays $200/color cover. Pays on acceptance. Credit line given. Buys all rights.
Tips: "Print up a cheap brochure, resume or similar item describing experience, covers taken, etc., (maybe include a photocopy, offering sample on request) and price range."

> ■ *The solid, black square before a listing indicates that the market uses various types of audiovisual materials, such as slides, film or videotape.*

*THE WATER SKIER, 799 Overlook Dr., Winter Haven FL 33884. (813)324-4341. FAX: (813)325-8259. Managing Editor: Greg Nixon. Publication of the American Water Ski Association. Bi-monthly magazine. Emphasizes water skiing. Readers are members of American Water Ski Association, active, competitive and recreational water skiers. Circ. 25,000. Sample copy for $1 and 9×12 SASE; photo guidelines free with SASE.
Needs: Uses 40-50 photos/issue; "few" supplied by freelance photographers. Photos purchased with accompanying ms only except for color used on the cover. Model/property releases and captions required.
Making Contact & Terms: Interested in receiving work from a newer, lesser-known photographer. Query with photo story ideas. SASE. Reports in 3 weeks. Pays $10/b&w photo; $15/color photo. Pays on acceptance. Credit line given. Buys all rights.
Tips: "Prefers to see a knowledge of water skiing techniques. We are a very specialized market. Query first."

♦WFCD COMMUNICATOR, Dept. PM, Box 1301, Brandon MB R7A 6N2 Canada. (204)725-4236. Editor: Mike Jubinville. Publication of the Western Fertilizer and Chemical Dealers Association. Quarterly magazine. Emphasizes fertilizer and chemicals, related equipment and products. Audience consists of independent fertilizer and chemical dealers who are primarily male (although this is changing) of various ages. Circ. 2,700. Estab. 1980.
Needs: Uses approximately 10 photos/issue; 20% supplied by freelance photographers. Looking for agricultural shots related to fertilizer and chemical industry, e.g., application equipment and field work in progress. Written release and captions preferred.
Making Contact & Terms: Provide resume, business card, brochure, flyer or tearsheets to be kept on file for possible assignments. SAE and IRC. Reports in 1 month. Pays $25/b&w inside photo. Pays on publication. Credit line given. Buys one-time rights.
Tips: "Be very specific in the shots you take; match them exactly to the requirements of the publication. For example, a picture of a tractor and hay baler is useless to a publication that focuses on chemical application."

WILDLIFE PHOTOGRAPHY, P.O. Box 224, Greenville PA 16125. (412)588-3492. Editor: Bob Noonan. Quarterly. Emphasizes pursuit and capture of wildlife on film. Circ. 3,000. Sample copy $2; writer's guidelines free with SASE.
Needs: Uses about 20 photos/issue; 18 supplied by freelance photographers. Needs photos of wildlife, how-to. Photos purchased with accompanying ms only. Special needs include photographers in action under field conditions. Model release preferred; captions required.
Making Contact & Terms: Preferably submit queried manuscript with photos. SASE. Reports in 6 weeks. Pays $20-75 for text/photo package. "But articles with more thought put into them, better writing, photos shot with us in mind and sidebars and sketches will have a payment ceiling at more than double the previous rate." Pays on publication. Credit line given. Buys one-time rights. Simultaneous submissions and previously published work OK.
Tips: "Select one photo challenge or species of wildlife and give us a ms/photo package which describes the photo target, the challenge and the methods used."

WOMAN BOWLER, 5301 S. 76th St., Greendale WI 53129. (414)421-9000. FAX: (414)421-3013. Editor: Karen Sytsma. Publication of Women's International Bowling Congress. Magazine published 8 times/year. *Woman Bowler* emphasizes women's bowling. Circ. 140,000. Estab. 1936. Sample copy for 10×13 SASE and $2.50 postage. Photo guidelines free with SASE.
Needs: Uses 75 photos/issue; up to 70% supplied by freelancers; 30-50% freelance/issue from assignment. Needs photos of sports action shots, portraits in sports settings, competition and bowling interest shots. Use freelancers nationwide to help fill voids when staff members cannot travel." In near future, needs "available photographers nationwide for assignments in various areas." Model release and photo captions preferred.
Making Contact & Terms: Interested in receiving work from newer, lesser-known photographers. Provide resume, business card, brochure, flyer or tearsheets to be kept on file for possible assignments. Reports in 1-2 weeks. Pays $200-300/color cover photo; $100-300/b&w cover photo; $25/color or b&w inside photo; $75/color page rate; $50/b&w page rate; $75-300/photo/text package. Pays on acceptance. Credit line given (if requested). Buys all rights. Simultaneous submissions and previously published work OK.
Tips: "Looking for '90s look to bowling. New treatments of sports photography welcome. *Woman Bowler* is an excellent opportunity for photographers looking for additional portfolio clips. Use 85-100% color photographs—very limited use of b&w. However, creative use of b&w welcomed. Prefer photographs that make lighting look natural, bowling center lighting poses many problems. Send letter of interest and samples of published work, tearsheets."

WOMENWISE, CFHC, Dept. PM, 38 S. Main St., Concord NH 03104. (603)225-2739. Editor: Carol Porter. Publication of the New Hampshire Federation of Feminist Health Centers. Quarterly tabloid. Emphasizes women's health from a feminist perspective. Readers are women, all ages and occupations. Circ. 3,000+. Estab. 1978. Sample copy for $2.95.
Needs: Varies; 100% supplied by freelancers. Needs photos of primarily women, women's events and demonstrations, etc. Model release required; photo captions preferred.
Making Contact & Terms: Arrange a personal interview to show portfolio. Send b&w prints. Pays $15/b&w cover photo; sub per b&w inside photo. Pays on publication. Credit line given. Buys first N.A. serial rights. Simultaneous submissions and previously published work OK.
Tips: "We don't publish a lot of 'fine-arts' photography now. We want photos which reflect our commitment to empowerment of all women. We prefer work by women."

WOODMEN OF THE WORLD, Dept. PM, 1700 Farnam St., Omaha NE 68102. (402)342-1890, ext. 302. Assistant Editor: Billie Jo Foust. Monthly magazine. Official publication for Woodmen of the World Life Insurance Society. Emphasizes American family life. Circ. 470,000. Estab. 1890. Free sample copy and photo/writer's guidelines.
Needs: Buys 25-30 photos/year. Historic; animal; celebrity/personality; fine art; photo essay/photo feature; scenic; special effects and experimental; how-to; human interest; humorous; nature; still life; travel; and wildlife. Model release required; captions preferred. Accompanying mss: "Material of interest to the average American family."
Making Contact & Terms: Send material by mail for consideration. Uses 8×10 b&w glossy prints; 35mm, 2¼×2¼ and 4×5 transparencies; b&w glossy prints and 4×5 transparencies for cover, vertical format preferred. SASE. Reports in 1 month. Pays $50/b&w inside photo; $50 minimum/cover inside photo; $100-300/cover photo; 10¢/word for ms. Pays on acceptance. Credit line given on request. Buys one-time rights. Previously published work OK.
Tips: "Submit good, sharp pictures that will reproduce well. Our organization has local lodges throughout America. If members of our lodges are in photos, we'll give them more consideration."

YOUNG CHILDREN, 1834 Connecticut Ave., NW, Washington DC 20009-5786. (202)232-8777. Photo Editor: Julie Andrews. Bimonthly journal. Emphasizes education, care and development of young children and promotes education of those who work with children. Read by teachers, administrators, social workers, physicians, college students, professors and parents. Circ. 78,000. Free photo and writer's guidelines.
Needs: Buys photos on continuing basis. Also publishes 8 books/year with photos. Children (from birth to age 8) unposed, with/without adults. Wants on a regular basis "children engaged in educational activities: dramatic play, scribbling/writing, playing with blocks—typical nursery school activities. Especially needs photos of minority children and children with disabilities." No posed, "cute" or stereotyped photos; no "adult interference, sexism, unhealthy food, unsafe situations, old photos, children with workbooks, depressing photos, parties, religious observances. Must provide copies of model releases for all individuals in photos." Accompanying mss: professional discussion of early childhood education and child development topics.
Making Contact & Terms: Interested in receiving work from a newer, lesser-known photographer. Query with samples. Send glossy b&w and color prints; transparencies. SASE. Reports in 2 weeks. Pays $25/inside photo; $75/posters and covers; no payment for ms. Pays on publication. Credit line given. Buys one-time rights; negotiable. Simultaneous submissions and previously published work OK.
Tips: "Write for our guidelines. We are using more photos per issue and using them in more creative ways, such as collages and inside color." Looks for "photos that depict children actively learning through interactions with the world around them; sensitivity to how children grow, learn and feel."

Trade Publications

Just as special interest publications fill a specific need, so too do trade magazines. Most trade publications are directed toward the business community in an effort to keep readers abreast of the everchanging trends and events in their specific professions. For photographers, covering these professions can be financially rewarding and can serve as a stepping stone toward acquiring future jobs.

As often happens with this category, the number of trade publications produced increases or decreases as professions develop or deteriorate. In recent years, for example, many in-flight magazines for airlines corporations have been discontinued due to the industry's financial setbacks. On the flip side, magazines involving computers have flourished as the technology continues to grow. In this year's edition of *Photographer's Market* there are numerous trade publication listings covering a variety of professions.

Primarily, photos in trade publications, as in other publication markets, serve to attract the reader to the articles and illustrate the text in an informative way. Trade publication readers are usually well-educated and very knowledgeable about their businesses or professions. The editors and photo editors, too, are often experts in their particular fields. So, with both the readers and the publications' staffs, you are dealing with a much more discriminating audience. To be taken seriously, your photos must not be merely technically good pictures but also communicate a solid understanding of the subject and reveal greater insights.

In particular, photographers who can communicate their knowledge in both verbal and visual form will often find their work more in demand. If you have such expertise, you may wish to query about submitting a photo/text package that highlights a unique aspect of working in that particular profession or that deals with a current issue of interest to that specific trade or profession.

Many of the photos purchased by these publications come from stock—both that of freelance inventories and of stock photo agencies. Generally, these publications are more conservative with their freelance budgets and use stock as an economical alternative. For this reason, listings in this section will often advise sending a stock list as an initial method of contact. Some of the more established publications with larger circulations and advertising bases will sometimes offer assignments as they become familiar with a particular photographer's work. For the most part, though, stock remains the primary means of breaking in and doing business with this market.

As an editor and corporate photographer, our Close-up subject, Ted Matthews of Charlotte, North Carolina knows what it takes to succeed in the field of trade. Matthews discusses his profession in detail beginning on page 458.

ABA BANKING JOURNAL, 345 Hudson St., New York NY 10014. (212)620-7256. Art Director: Jeff Menges. Monthly magazine. Circ. 42,000. Estab. 1909. Emphasizes "how to manage a bank better. Bankers read it to find out how to keep up with changes in regulations, lending practices, investments, technology, marketing and what other bankers are doing to increase community standing." Photos purchased with accompanying ms or on assignment. Buys 12-24 photos/year; freelance photography is 50% assigned; 50% from stock. Pays $100 minimum/job, or $200/printed page for text/photo package. Credit line given. Pays on acceptance. Buys one-time rights. Query with samples. SASE. Reports in 1 month.
Needs: Personality ("We need candid photos of various bankers who are subjects of articles"), and occasionally photos of unusual bank displays. Also, photos of small-town bank buildings including their surroundings. Captions required.
Making Contact & Terms: For b&w: contact sheet preferred; uses 8 × 10 glossy prints "if prints are ordered." For color: Uses 35mm transparencies and 2¼ × 2¼ transparencies. For cover: Uses color transparencies, square format required. Pays $100-500/photo.
Tips: "I look for the ability to take a portrait shot in a different and exciting way—not just 'look at the camera and smile.' "

ACROSS THE BOARD MAGAZINE, published by The Conference Board, 845 Third Ave., New York NY 10022-6601. (212)759-0900. Picture Editor: Marilyn Stern. Estab. 1974. Trade magazine with 10 monthly issues (January/February and July/August are double issues). Readers are upper-level managers in large corporations. Recent articles have covered pollution in Eastern Europe, working conditions in Korea, U.S. design, healthcare.
Needs: Use 15-20 photos/issue some supplied by freelancers. Wide range of needs, including location portraits, industrial, workplace, social topics, environmental topics, government and corporate projects, foreign business (especially east and west Europe, former USSR and Asia). Need striking, unusual or humorous photos with newsworthy business themes for "Sightings" department. Photo captions required.
Making Contact and Terms: Query *by mail only* with resume of credits, list of stock photo subjects and clients, and brochure or tearsheets to be kept on file. No unsolicited submissions will be returned. "No phone queries please. We buy one-time rights, or six-month exclusive rights if we assign the project. We pay $100-275 inside, up to $500 for cover or $350 per day for assignments."

Tips: "Our style is journalistic. We sometimes assign locally around the USA and internationally. We keep a regional file of photographers."

© Peter Menzel

"(Peter Menzel) has a knack for finding slightly bizarre subjects, or finding a bizarre or unusual aspect to whatever he's covering," says Picture Editor Marilyn Stern, of Across the Board Magazine. *The magazine paid Menzel, of Napa, California, $200 for this "slightly bizarre" shot of Solar-Plant 1 in San Diego County in California. The shot originally was taken on assignment for* Discover Magazine, *but it was never used. Ironically, it has sold over 20 times since then.*

✷ALUMI-NEWS, Dept. PM, P.O. Box 400, Victoria Station, Westmount PQ H3Z 2V8 Canada. (514)489-4941. Editor: Nachmi Artzy. Bimonthly magazine. Emphasizes renovation, construction. Readers are constructors/renovators. Circ. 18,000. Sample copy free with SAE and IRC.
Needs: Uses 20 photos/issue; 25-50% supplied by freelance photographers. Needs photos of construction and renovations. Model release and photo captions preferred.
Making Contact & Terms: Query with list of stock photo subjects. SASE. Reports in 2 weeks. Pays $300/color cover photo, $100-200/color inside photo and $300-500/day. Pays in 30 days. Credit line given. Buys one-time rights; will negotiate. Simultaneous submissions and previously published work OK.
Tips: "We prefer 'people on the job' photos as opposed to products/buildings."

AMERICAN AGRICULTURIST, Suite 202, 2333 N. Triphammer Rd., Ithaca NY 14850. (607)257-8670. FAX: (607)257-8238. Editor: Eleanor Jacobs. Monthly. Emphasizes agriculture in the Northeast—specifically New York, New Jersey and New England. Circ. 53,000. Estab. 1842. Free photo guidelines with SASE.
Needs: Uses 1-2 photos/issue supplied by freelance photographers; 50-75% on assignment, 25-50% from stock. Needs photos of farm equipment, general farm scenes, animals. Geographic location: only New York, New Jersey and New England. Reviews photos with or without accompanying ms. Model release required; captions preferred.

Making Contact & Terms: Interested in receiving work from newer, lesser-known photographers. Query with samples and list of stock photo subjects. Send 35mm transparencies by mail for consideration. SASE. Reports in 3 months. Pays $200/color cover photo and $75-150/inside color photo. Pays on acceptance. Credit line given. Buys one-time rights.
Tips: "We need shots with modern farm equipment with the newer safety features. Also looking for shots of women actively involved in farming and shots of farm activity. We also use scenics. We send out our editorial calendar with our photo needs yearly."

AMERICAN BANKER, Dept. PM, 1 State Street Plaza, New York NY 10004. (212)943-5726. FAX: (212)943-2984. Art Director: Pamela Budz. Daily tabloid. Emphasizes banking industry. "Readers are male and female, senior executives in finance, ages 35-59." Circ. 25,000.
Needs: Uses varying number of photos/issue; 2 supplied by freelancers. Needs environmental portraits. Captions preferred.
Making Contact & Terms: Arrange a personal interview to show portfolio; send unsolicited b&w or color prints by mail for consideration; provide resume, business card, brochure, flyer or tearsheets to be kept on file for possible assignments. Keeps samples on file. SASE. Reports in 1-2 weeks. Pays $900-1,000/color cover photo; $700-900/b&w cover photo; $225/color or b&w inside photo. Pays on acceptance. Credit line given. Buys one-time rights. Simultaneous submissions and previously published work OK.

AMERICAN BEE JOURNAL, Dept. PM, 51 S. 2nd St., Hamilton IL 62341. (217)847-3324. Editor: Joe M. Graham. Monthly trade magazine. Emphasizes beekeeping for hobby and professional beekeepers. Circ. 16,000. Sample copy free with SASE.
Needs: Uses about 100 photos/issue; 1-2 supplied by freelance photographers. Needs photos of beekeeping and related topics, beehive products, honey and cooking with honey. Special needs include color photos of seasonal beekeeping scenes. Model release and captions preferred.
Making Contact & Terms: Query with samples. Send 5×7 or 8½×11 b&w and color prints by mail for consideration. SASE. Reports in 2 weeks. Pays $25/b&w or color cover photo; $5/b&w or color inside photo. Pays on publication. Credit line given. Buys all rights.

AMERICAN BOOKSELLER, Dept. PM, 560 White Plains Rd., Tarrytown NY 10591. (914)631-7800. Editor: Dan Cullen. Art Director: Joan Adelson. Monthly magazine. Circ. 9,000. "*American Bookseller* is a journal for and about booksellers. People who own or manage bookstores read the magazine to learn trends in book selling, how to merchandise books, recommendations on stock, and laws affecting booksellers." Sample copy $5.
Needs: Works with freelance photographers on assignment only. Model release preferred; captions required.
Making Contact & Terms: Uses 5×7 b&w prints; no color used inside. Uses 35mm color transparencies for covers, vertical format preferred. Provide resume, business card, tearsheets and samples to be kept on file for possible assignments. Arrange personal interview to show portfolio. Submit portfolio for review. Query with list of stock photo subjects and samples. SASE. Reports in 5 weeks. Pays $25 minimum/job; $70 minimum for text/photo package, or on a per-photo basis; $25 minimum/b&w inside photo; $600/cover photo. Pays on acceptance. Credit line given. Buys one-time rights, but may negotiate for further use. Previously published work OK.

AMERICAN FARRIERS JOURNAL, P.O. Box 624, Brookfield WI 53008-0624. . (414)782-4480. FAX: (414)782-1252. Editor: Frank Lessiter. Magazine published 7 times/year. Emphasizes horseshoeing and horse health for professional horseshoers. Circ. 7,000 paid. Estab. 1974. Sample copy free with SASE.
Needs: Looking for horseshoeing photos, documentary, how-to (of new procedures in shoeing), photo/ essay feature, product shot and spot news. Photos purchased with or without accompanying ms. Captions required.
Making Contact & Terms: Interested in receiving work from newer, lesser-known photographers. Query with printed samples. SASE. Uses 5×7 or 8×10 semigloss b&w prints, 4-color transparencies for covers. Vertical format. Artistic shots. Pays $25-50/b&w photo; $30-100/color photo. Pays on publication. Credit line given. Buys all rights, but may reassign to photographer after publication.

AMERICAN FIRE JOURNAL, Dept. PM, Suite 7, 9072 Artesia Blvd., Bellflower CA 90706. (213)866-1664. FAX: (213)867-6434. Editor: Carol Carlsen Brooks. Monthly magazine. Emphasizes fire protection and prevention. Circ. 6,000. Estab. 1952. Sample copy $3 with 10×12 SAE and 6 first class stamps. Free photo and writer's guidelines.
Needs: Buys 5 or more photos/issue; 90% supplied by freelancers. Documentary (emergency incidents, showing fire personnel at work); how-to (new techniques for fire service); and spot news (fire personnel at work). Captions required. Seeks short ms describing emergency incident and how it was handled by the agencies involved.

Making Contact & Terms: Query with samples to Lauree Godwin, art director. Provide resume, business card or letter of inquiry. SASE. Reports in 1 month. Uses b&w semigloss prints; for cover uses 35mm color transparencies; covers must be verticals. Pays $4-15/b&w photo, negotiable; $10-30/color photo; $30/cover photo; $1.50-2/inch for ms.

Tips: "Don't be shy! Submit your work. I'm always looking for contributing photographers (especially if they are from outside the L.A. area). I'm looking for good shots of fire scene activity with captions. The action should have a clean composition with little smoke and prominent fire and show good firefighting techniques, i.e., firefighters in full turnouts, etc. It helps if photographers know something about firefighting so as to capture important aspects of fire scene. We like photos that illustrate the drama of firefighting—large flames, equipment and apparatus, fellow firefighters, people in motion. Write suggested captions. Give us as many shots as possible to choose from. Most of our photographers are firefighters or 'fire buffs.' "

AMERICAN OIL & GAS REPORTER, Dept. PM, P.O. Box 343, Derby KS 67037. (316)788-6271. Editor: Bill Campbell. "A monthly business publication serving the domestic exploration, drilling and production markets within the oil/gas industry. The editorial pages are designed to concentrate on the domestic independent oilman. Readers are owners, presidents and other executives." Circ. 12,000. Estab. 1957. Sample copy free with SASE.

Needs: Uses 1 color photo for cover/issue; others are welcome; virtually all from stock. Needs "any photo dealing with the oil and gas industry. We prefer to use only independent oil and gas photos; we discourage anything that would have to do with a major oil company, i.e., Standard, Exxon, Shell, etc." Written release and captions required.

Making Contact & Terms: Send 35mm transparencies and unsolicited photos by mail for consideration. Returns unsolicited material with SASE. Pays $50-100/color cover photo; $10-15/b&w inside photo. Pays on publication. Credit line given. Buys one-time rights. Simultaneous submissions OK.

Tips: Prefers to see "any picture that depicts a typical or picturesque view of the domestic oil and gas industry." Prefers shots depicting "drilling rigs at work and working well sites, not abandoned well sites or equipment 'graveyards.' Wants to show active industry, people in the shots. Do not have special assignments. Need stock photos that match editorial material in issue."

*APARTMENT NEWS PUBLICATIONS, INC., 3220 E. Willow St., Long Beach CA 90806. (310)424-8674. FAX: (213)636-8353. Art Director: Marci Post. Monthly magazine. Emphasizes apartment ownership and management. Readers are male and female apartment owners, ages 35-55. Circ. 60,000. Estab. 1958. Sample copy free. Photo guidelines sheet available.

Needs: Uses 1-5 photos/issue; 1 supplied by freelancers. Needs cover shots of apartment buildings, photos geared toward the apartment owner/manager. Model/property release preferred. Captions preferred.

Making Contact & Terms: Send unsolicited photos by mail for consideration. Provide resume, business card, brochure, flyer or tearsheets to be kept on file for possible assignments. Send 35mm transparencies. Keeps samples on file. Reports if interested. Pays $100/color cover photo. Pays on acceptance. Buys all rights; negotiable. Simultaneous submissions and/or previously published work OK.

Tips: Looks for "clean, balanced work showing ability to shoot outdoor subject matter properly providing depth and vibrant color. We mainly use slides of buildings in different architectural styles and periods, and also prefer blue sky at top of frame and use of flowers."

APPAREL INDUSTRY MAGAZINE, Suite 300 N, 180 Allen Rd., Atlanta GA 30328. (404)252-8831. Editor: Meg Thornton. Monthly magazine. Circ. 18,600. Estab. 1939. Emphasizes production techniques for apparel manufacturing executives; coverage includes cutting edge technology and management of the U.S. apparel manufacturing industry. Sample copy $3.

Needs: Cover photos depicting themes in magazines; feature photos to illustrate articles.

Making Contact & Terms: Works with freelance photographers on assignment only. "Must be an experienced photojournalist." Provide resume, brochure and business card to be kept on file for possible future assignments. Buys 3 photos/issue. Pays $50/b&w photo; $100-200/color photo; $300/complete package. Pays on publication. SASE. Reports on queries in 4-6 weeks.

*AQUATICS INTERNATIONAL, 6255 Barfield Rd., Atlanta GA 30328. (404)256-9800. FAX: (404)256-3116. Associate Editor: Eden Jackson. Bimonthly magazine. Emphasizes commercial aquatic facilities (outdoor, pools, beaches, waterparks). Readers are managers, directors, instructors of aquatic facili-

---

 The asterisk before a listing indicates that the market is new in this edition. New markets are often the most receptive to freelance submissions.

ties. Circ. 30,000+. Estab. 1989. Sample copy $8. Photo guidelines free with SASE.
Needs: Uses 10-12 photos/issue. Needs photos of "aquatic programming and facilities – active!! Must be specific to facilities quoted in the feature article." Reviews photos with or without ms, but need story idea and contact name. Model/property release preferred. Captions required; include name and location of facility, description, ID of persons.
Making Contact & Terms: Send unsolicited color prints and transparencies by mail for consideration. Provide facility/programming leads. Does not keep samples on file. Cannot return material. Reports "upon acceptance (within 3 months, usually)." Pays $50/color cover photo; $25/color inside photo; $10/b&w inside photo. Pays on publication. Credit line given. Buys all rights; negotiable. Simultaneous submissions and previously published work OK; "no submissions to competitors."
Tips: In photo samples looks for "skill, creativity and ability to combine editorial-written content with photography. Find out interesting aquatic programming and facilities in your area."

ART DIRECTION, 6th Floor, 10 E. 39th St., New York NY 10016. (212)889-6500. FAX: (212)889-6504. Monthly magazine. Circ. 11,000. Emphasis is on advertising design for art directors of ad agencies. Buys 5 photos/issue. Sample copy for $4.50 and $1 postage.
Needs: Photos purchased with an accompanying mss only.
Making Contact & Terms: Works with freelance photographers on assignment only basis. Send query to Soshanna Sommer. Provide tearsheets to be kept on file for possible future assignments. SASE. Reports in 2 weeks. Pays $50/b&w photo. Pays on publication. Credit line given. Buys one-time rights.

ATHLETIC BUSINESS, % Athletic Business Publications Inc., Dept. PM, Suite 201, 1842 Hoffman St., Madison WI 53704. (608)249-0186. FAX: (608)249-1153. Art Director: Paul Graff. Monthly magazine. Emphasizes athletics, fitness and recreation. "Readers are mostly male athletic park and recreational directors and club managers, ages 30-65." Circ. 45,000. Estab. 1977. Sample copy $5.
Needs: Uses 4 or 5 photos/issue; 50% supplied by freelancers. Needs photos of sporting shots, athletic equipment, recreational parks and club interiors. Model and/or property release and photo captions preferred.
Making Contact & Terms: Send unsolicited color prints or 35mm transparencies by mail for consideration. Does not keep samples on file. SASE. Reports in 1-2 weeks. Pays $250/color cover photo; $75/color inside photos; $125/color page rate. Pays on publication. Credit line given. Buys all rights; negotiable. Simultaneous submissions and previously published work OK, but should be explained.
Tips: Wants to see ability with subject, high quality and reasonable price. To break in, "shoot a quality and creative shot from more than one angle."

★ATLANTIC SALMON JOURNAL, P.O. Box 429, St. Andrews, NB E0G 2X0 Canada. (514)842-8059. FAX: (514)842-3147. Editor: Harry Bruce, Atlantic Salmon Federation. Quarterly magazine. Readers are avid salmon anglers and conservationists interested in fishing techniques, art and literature, management of the species, scientific discoveries and research and new places to fish. Circ. 20,000. Sample copy and photo guidelines free with SASE.
Needs: Uses 20-25 photos/issue; majority provided with accompanying article. Needs action shots of Atlantic salmon fishing rivers; management techniques; salmon fishing trips to North American or European rivers; Atlantic salmon management, conservation and biology, river restoration and science; Atlantic salmon literature, art, history and politics. Model release and captions required.
Making Contact & Terms: Query with story idea, outline and clips; indicate availability of photos. Will also consider completed mss; send dupes with unsolicited mss. Prefers 8 × 10 b&w, 2¼ × 2¼ color transparencies or 35mm slides. Reports in 4-6 weeks. Pays $300/color cover photo, $50-100/color inside photo, $30/b&w photo. Pays on publication. Credit line given. Buys one-time rights.

AUTOMATED BUILDER, Dept. PM, P.O. Box 120, Carpinteria CA 93014. (805)684-7659. Editor and Publisher: Don Carlson. Monthly. Circ. 26,000. Emphasizes home and apartment construction. Readers are "factory and site builders and dealers of all types of homes, apartments and commercial buildings." Sample copy free with SASE.
Needs: Uses about 40 photos/issue; 10-20% supplied by freelance photographers. Needs in-plant and job site construction photos and photos of completed homes and apartments. Photos purchased with accompanying ms only. Captions required. Will consider dramatic, preferably vertical cover photos. Send color proof or slide.
Making Contact & Terms: "Call to discuss story and photo ideas." Send 35mm or 2¼ × 2¼ transparencies by mail for consideration. SASE. Reports in 2 weeks. Pays $300/text/photo package. Pays $150 for cover photos. Credit line given "if desired." Buys first time reproduction rights.

AVC, Dept. PM, 445 Broad Hollow Rd., Melville NY 11747. (516)845-2700. Editor: Mike McEnaney. Monthly magazine. Emphasizes in-plant industrial, scientific, medical, educational, military and government image-production. Readers include individuals producing images – AV, video, motion pic-

ture, print—for use by non-photographic companies such as Ford, Kraft, Grumman, hospitals, educational institutions, etc. Circ. 35,000. Sample copy $2 with 8½ × 11 SAE. Photo and ms guidelines free with SASE.
Needs: Uses 15 photos/issue, all supplied by freelance photographers. "Covers and inside articles produced by readers. Needs shots produced to fulfill a company need; to help our readers learn their craft." Model release and captions required.
Making Contact & Terms: Query with samples. Send 4 × 5 or larger glossy b&w and color prints; 35mm, 2¼ × 2¼, 4 × 5, 8 × 10 transparencies by mail for consideration. SASE. Reports in 4-6 weeks. NPI. Pays on publication. Credit line given. Buys one-time rights.
Tips: Prefers to see "materials related to our readership—industrial."

BEEF, 3rd Floor, 7900 International Dr., Minneapolis MN 55425. (612)851-4668. Editor: Paul D. Andre. Monthly magazine. Emphasizes beef cattle production and feeding. Readers are feeders, ranchers and stocker operators. Circ. 107,000. Sample copy and photo guidelines free with SASE.
Needs: Uses 35-40 photos/issue; "less than 1%" supplied by freelance photographers. Needs variety of cow-calf and feedlot scenes. Model release and captions required.
Making Contact & Terms: Send 8 × 10 glossy b&w prints and 35mm transparencies by mail for consideration. SASE. Reports in 1 month. Pays $25/b&w inside photo; $50/color inside photo. Pays on acceptance. Buys one-time rights.
Tips: "We buy few photos, since our staff provides most of those needed."

BEEF TODAY, Farm Journal Publishing, Inc., Suite 100, 6205 Earle Brown Dr., Brooklyn Center MN 55430. (612)561-0300. Photo Editor: Greg Lamp. Monthly magazine. Emphasizes American agriculture. Readers are active farmers, ranchers or agribusiness people. Circ. 220,000. Sample copy and photo guidelines free with SASE.
Needs: Uses 20-30 photos/issue; 75% supplied by freelance photographers. We use studio-type portraiture (environmental portraits), technical, details, scenics. Model release preferred; photo captions required.
Making Contact & Terms: Arrange a personal interview to show portfolio or query with resume of credits along with business card, brochure, flyer or tearsheets to be kept on file for possible assignments. SASE. Reports in 2 weeks. NPI. "We pay a cover bonus." Pays on acceptance. Credit line given. Buys one-time rights. Simultaneous submissions OK.
Tips: In portfolio or samples, likes to "see about 20 slides showing photographer's use of lighting and photographer's ability to work with people. Know your intended market. Familiarize yourself with the magazine and keep abreast of how photos are used in the general magazine field."

BEVERAGE DYNAMICS, Dept. PM, 100 Avenue of the Americas, New York NY 10013. (212)274-7000. Editor: Richard Brandes. Nine times/year magazine. Emphasizes distilled spirits, wine and beer. Readers are national—retailers (liquor stores, supermarkets, etc.), wholesalers, distillers, vintners, brewers, ad agencies and media. Circ. 50,000.
Needs: Uses 20 photos/issue; 5 supplied by freelance photographers and photo house (stock). Needs photos of retailers, product shots, concept shots and profiles. Special needs include good retail environments; interesting store settings; special effect wine and beer photos. Model release and captions required.
Making Contact & Terms: Query with samples and list of stock photo subjects. SASE. Reports in 2 weeks. Pays $400/color cover photo; $300/job. Pays on publication. Credit line given. Buys one-time rights or all rights on commissioned photos. Simultaneous submissions OK.

BEVERAGE WORLD, Dept. PM, 150 Great Neck Rd., Great Neck NY 11021. (516)829-9210. FAX: (516)829-5414. Editor: Larry Jabbonsky. Monthly. Circ. 32,000. Estab. 1881. Emphasizes the beverage industry. Readers are "bottlers, wholesalers, distributors of beer, soft drinks, wine and spirits." Sample copy $3.50.
Needs: Uses 25-50 photos/issue; many supplied by freelance photographers. Needs "freelancers in specific regions of the U.S. for occasional assignments."
Making Contact & Terms: Query with samples. Provide resume, business card, brochure, flyer or tearsheets to be kept on file for possible assignments. Pays $100/day; fees paid per assignment; payment range varies according to nature of assignment. Pays on publication or per assignment contract. Rights purchased varies.
Tips: Prefers to see "interesting angles on people, products. Provide affordable quality."

BRAKE & FRONT END, Dept. PM, 11 S. Forge St., Akron OH 44304. (216)535-6117. FAX: (216)535-0874. Editor: Doug Kaufman. Monthly magazine. Circ. 30,000. Estab. 1931. Emphasizes automotive maintenance and repair. Readers are automobile mechanics and repair shop owners.

Needs: Needs "color photos for use on covers. Subjects vary with editorial theme, but basically they deal with automotive or truck parts and service." Wants no "overly commercial photos which emphasize brand names" and no mug shots of prominent people. May buy up to 6 covers annually. Credit line given. Buys first North American serial rights. Submit model release with photos.
Making Contact & Terms: Send contact sheet for consideration. Reports immediately. Pays on publication. SASE. Simultaneous submissions OK. Sample copy $1. Uses 5×7 b&w glossy prints; send contact sheet. Captions required. Pays $8.50 minimum. For cover: Send contact sheet or transparencies. Study magazine, then query. Lead time for cover photos is 2 months before publication date. "Price is negotiable depending on what is needed."
Tips: Send for editorial schedules. Looks for "new, fresh ideas for technical automotive subjects."

BUILDING SUPPLY HOME CENTERS, Dept. PM, 1350 E. Touhy, P.O. Box 5080, Des Plaines IL 60017. FAX: (708)635-8800. Editor: Ed Fitch. Monthly magazine. Emphasizes lumberyards, home center retailing, residential construction. Readers are owners and managers of lumberyards and home centers. Circ. 47,000. Estab. 1917. Sample copy $10.
Needs: Uses 100+ photos/issue; freelance usage varies widely; most is stock, couple issues per year are all assignment. Needs photos of retail and construction. Model release and photo captions preferred.
Making Contact & Terms: Query with list of stock photo subjects. SASE. Report time varies. Pays $100-300/color cover photo; $50-150/color inside photo; $300-600/day. Pays on publication. Credit line given. Buys one-time rights. Simultaneous submissions and previously published work OK.
Tips: Wants to see "application to our industry, uniqueness and clean, sharp look. We're using more symbolic work for covers and lead feature. Make it applicable to market."

BUILDINGS: The Facilities Construction and Management Magazine, 427 6th Ave. SE, P.O. Box 1888, Cedar Rapids IA 52406. (319)364-6167. FAX: (319)365-5421. Editor: Linda Monroe. Monthly magazine. Emphasizes commercial real estate. Readers are building owners and facilities managers. Circ. 42,000. Estab. 1906. Sample copy $5.
Needs: Uses 50 photos/issue; 10% supplied by freelancers. Needs photos of concept, building interiors and exteriors, company personnel and products. Model and/or property release and photo captions preferred.
Making Contact & Terms: Provide resume, business card, brochure, flyer or tearsheets to be kept on file for possible assignments. Send 3×5, 8×10, b&w, color prints; 35mm, 2¼×2¼, 4×5 transparencies. SASE. Reports as needed. Pays $350/color cover photo; $200/color inside photo. Pays on publication. Credit line given. Rights negotiable. Simultaneous submissions OK.

BUSINESS ATLANTA, Dept. PM, 6255 Barfield Rd., Atlanta GA 30328. (404)256-9800. Editor: Ken Anderberg. Managing Editor: John Sequerth. Monthly. Emphasizes "general magazine-style coverage of business and business-related issues in the metro Atlanta area." Readers are "everybody in Atlanta who can buy a house or office building or Rolls Royce." Circ. 36,000. Sample copy $3.25.
Needs: Uses about 40 photos/issue; 35-40 supplied by freelance photographers. Needs "good photos mostly of business-related subjects if keyed to local industry." Model release and captions required.
Making Contact & Terms: Arrange a personal interview to show portfolio. SASE. Reports in 1 month. Pays $75/b&w photo; $500-800/color cover photo; $100-400/color inside photo; $200 minimum/job; $100-1,000/package. Pays on publication. Credit line given. Buys one-time rights and reprint rights.
Tips: "Study the publication for the feel we strive for and don't bring us something either totally off the wall or, at the other extreme, assume that business means boring and bring us something duller than ditchwater. People in the business community are becoming more willing to do unusual things for a photo. We need the ability to work on location with subjects who have little time to spend with a photographer. Anybody can shoot a perfume bottle in a studio. Study *Business Atlanta* to see the types of work we use. Then show me something better."

*BUSINESS NEW HAMPSHIRE MAGAZINE, #201, 404 Chestnut St., Manchester NH 03101. (603)626-6354. FAX: (603)626-6359. Art Director: Nikki Bonenfant. Monthly magazine. Emphasizes business. Readers are male and female—top management, average age 45. Circ. 13,000. Estab. 1984. Sample copy with 9×12 SASE and $1.25.
Needs: Uses 12-20 photos/issue. Needs photos of people, high-tech, software and locations. Photo captions preferred; include names, locations, contact phone number.
Making Contact & Terms: Arrange personal interview to show portfolio. Provide resume, business card, brochure, flyer or tearsheets to be kept on file for possible assignments. Keeps samples on file. SASE. Reports in 3 weeks. Pays $1,000/color cover photo; $60/color inside photo; $40/b&w inside photo. Pays on publication. Credit line given. Buys one-time rights.
Tips: Looks for "people in environment shots, interesting lighting, lots of creative interpretations, a definite personal style."

✸BUTTER FAT MAGAZINE, Dept. PM, Box 9100, Vancouver, BC V6B 4G4 Canada. (604)420-6611. Executive Editor: Carol A. Paulson. Editor: G. Chadsey. Published 4 times/year. Emphasizes dairy farming and marketing for dairy farmers in British Columbia; also emphasizes dairy consumers in British Columbia. Circ. 3,500. Free sample copy.
Needs: Uses 40 photos/issue; 2 are supplied by freelance photographers. Especially needs freelancers throughout the province to work on assignment basis. Needs photos on personalities, locations and events. Special subject needs include abstracted photos related to regulation, government standards and trade economics in the dairy industry. Captions required.
Making Contact & Terms: Arrange personal interview with managing editor to show portfolio. Provide tearsheets to be kept on file for possible future assignments. Pays $10/photo; $50-500 for text/photo package. Pay on color photos and job is negotiable. Credit line given. Payment on acceptance. Simultaneous submissions OK.

CALIFORNIA BUSINESS, Dept. PM, Suite 700, 221 Main St., San Francisco CA 94105. (415)543-8290. FAX: (415)543-8232. Art Director: Gary Suen. Monthly magazine. Emphasizes business. Readers are male and female executives, ages 35-55. Circ. 140,000. Estab. 1965. Sample copy free with SASE.
Needs: Uses 40-45 photos/issue; all supplied by freelancers. Needs photos of "portraiture, on-location accounts for 80% events (news-related). Architecture makes up the other 20%." Model release preferred; photo captions required that include name and title.
Making Contact & Terms: Contact through rep; arrange personal interview to show portfolio; provide resume, business card, brochure, flyer or tearsheets to be kept on file for possible assignments. Cannot return material. Reports in 1-2 weeks. Pays $850/color or b&w cover photo; $375/color or b&w page rate. Pays on acceptance. Credit line given. Buys first N.A. serial rights. Previously published work OK.

CFO MAGAZINE, Dept. PM, 253 Summer St., Boston MA 02210. (617)345-9700. Art Director: Robert Lesser. Monthly. Emphasizes business. Readers are chief financial officers; accountants. Circ. 200,000. Sample copy for 9 × 12 SASE.
Needs: Uses 5-10 photos/issue; 75% supplied by freelance photographers. Needs photos of interesting people, pictures of businessmen, factories, products. Special needs: occasionally need short-notice shots done on assignment in smaller cities and towns. Model release and captions preferred.
Making Contact & Terms: Arrange a personal interview to show portfolio; query with sample or list of stock photo subjects. Send "published clips only; non returnable." Reports only when photographer makes follow-up phone call." Pays $900 maximum (plus expenses)/color cover photo; $200-800/color inside photo, depending on size; $800 maximum including expenses/inside full-page opener, "but we rarely have full-page openers"; $200+ expenses/job. Pays on acceptance. Credit line given. Buys one-time plus reprint rights. Previously published work OK.
Tips: Prefers to see "color samples, preferably tearsheets from other business magazines."

CHEMICAL ENGINEERING, 1221 Avenue of the Americas, New York NY 10020. Phone: (212)512-3377. FAX: (212)512-4762. Art Director: Maureen Gleason. Monthly magazine. Emphasizes equipment and practice of the chemical process industry. Readers are mostly male, median age 38. Circ. 80,000. Estab. 1903. Sample copies available for $7; postage is included.
Needs: Occasionally works with freelancers. Needs composite images; CAD (computer-aided design) images; shots of plant personnel at work; high-tech effects; shots of liquids, tanks, drums, sensors, toxic waste, landfills and remediation. Reviews photos with accompanying captions only. Especially wants to see photos of plant staff handling bulk solids; thermoplastic pumps, cyclone selection; batch process plants; corrosive gases; valves; flowmeters; and strainers. Model/property release required. Photo captions required; include "when, where and whom."
Making Contact & Terms: Interested in receiving work from newer, lesser-known photographers. Submit portfolio for review. Send stock photo list. Provide, resume, business card, brochure, flyer or tearsheets to be kept on file for possible assignments. Keeps samples on file. SASE. Reports in 3 weeks. Pays $450/color cover photo; $200/color inside photo; $100/b&w inside photo; $200/color page rate; $100/b&w page rate. Pays on publication. Credit line given. Buys one-time rights. Simultaneous submissions and previously published work OK.
Tips: "Please respond ONLY if you are familiar with the chemical processing industry." Points out that "after technology, our focus is on engineers at work. We want to feature a diversity of ages, ethnic types, and both men and women in groups and on own. Pictures must show *current* technology, and identify location with permission of subject. Also, photos must be clean, crisp and have good color saturation for excellent reproduction."

CHEMICALWEEK, Dept. PM, 26th Floor, 888 Seventh Ave., New York NY 10106. (212)621-4900. FAX: (212)621-4950. Creative Director: Mitchell F. Holmes. Weekly magazine. Emphasizes chemical R&D, environmental issues, chemical processing, etc. "Most of the readers are corporate executives, CEO's etc." Circ. 50,000. Sample copy $8.

Needs: Uses 2-8 photos/issue; 1-2 supplied by freelancers. Needs photos regarding technology, soaps and detergents, finance, environment, plastics, shipping, transportation, worldwide issues." Model and/or property release required.
Making Contact & Terms: Contact through rep. Submit portfolio for review. Query with list of stock photo subjects. Keeps samples on file. Reports in 1-2 weeks. Pays $300/color cover photo; $150/color inside photo. Pays on publication. Credit line given. Buys one-time or all rights.
Tips: "The subjects for *Chemicalweek* are of a serious nature and cannot be too avant garde due to the audience that we reach; however our subjects are very diversified. Take note of our editorial calendar and approach each issue with the appropriate materials that pertain. We operate on a rapid turnaround; therefore it is very important to stay ahead of our editorial needs."

THE CHRISTIAN MINISTRY, 407 S. Dearborn St., Chicago IL 60605-1111. (312)427-5380. Managing Editor: Mark Halton. Bimonthly magazine. Emphasizes religion—parish clergy. Readers are 30-65 years old; 80% male, 20% female; parish clergy and well-educated. Circ. 12,000. Estab. 1969. Sample copy free for 9×12 SAE and 98¢ postage. Photo guidelines free with SASE.
Needs: Uses 8 photos/issue; 100% supplied by freelancers. Needs photos of clergy (especially female clergy), church gatherings, school classrooms and church symbols. Future photo needs include social gatherings and leaders working with groups. Model release and photo captions preferred.
Making Contact & Terms: Interested in receiving work from newer, lesser-known photographers. Send 8×10 b&w prints by mail for consideration. SASE. Reports in 3 weeks. Pays $50/b&w cover photo; $25/b&w inside photo. Pays on publication. Credit line given. Buys one-time rights. Will consider simultaneous submissions.
Tips: "We're looking for up-to-date photos of clergy, engaged in preaching, teaching, meeting with congregants, working in social activities. We need photos of women, black and Hispanic clergy."

THE CHRONICLE OF PHILANTHROPY, Suite 775, 1255 23rd St. NW, Washington DC 20037. (202)466-1205. Art Director: Sue LaLumia. Biweekly tabloid. Readers come from all aspects of the nonprofit world such as charities (large or small grant maker/giving), foundations, and relief agencies such as the Red Cross. Circ. 20,000. Estab. 1988. Sample copy free.
Needs: Uses 20 photos/issue; 50-75% supplied by freelance photographers. Needs photos of people (profiles) making the news in philanthropy and environmental shots related to person(s)/organization. Most shots arranged with freelancers are specific. Model release and photo captions required.
Making Contact & Terms: Arrange a personal interview to show portfolio. Send unsolicited photos by mail for consideration. Send 35mm, 2¼×2¼, prints by mail for consideration. Provide resume, business card, brochure, flyer or tearsheets to be kept on file for possible assignments. Will send negatives back via certified mail. Reports in 1-2 days. Pays (color and b&w) ½ day: $225+ expenses; full day: $350+ expenses; reprints: $75. Pays on publication. Buys one-time rights. Will consider previously published work.

CITY & STATE, Dept. PM, 740 N. Rush St., Chicago IL 60611. (312)649-5200. FAX: (312)649-5228. Assistant Managing Editor Graphics: Dan Wassmann. Biweekly tabloid. Emphasizes state and local government and current events. Readers are male government executives, average age 44. Circ. 50,000. Estab. 1984. Sample copy $2.50. To request, call (313)446-1634.
Needs: Uses 1-5 photos/issue; 100% supplied by freelancers. Needs personality profiles of government people (mayors, governors), current events photos and "anything relating to the business of government including environmental issues, recycling etc." Especially wants to see "healthcare photos, economic development photos and anything to do with recycling." Photo captions preferred; "who, what, where and when."
Making Contact & Terms: Arrange a personal interview to show portfolio; submit portfolio for review; provide resume, business card, brochure, flyer or tearsheets to be kept on file for possible assignments. Does not keep samples on file. Cannot return material. Pays $150-185/color cover photo; $85-125/b&w cover, color inside or b&w inside photo; $350/day. Pays on publication. Credit line given. Rights negotiable. Simultaneous submissions and previously published work OK.
Tips: Wants to see "good quality, well-thought-out pictures, environmental (people) photos: positioning the subject in an area with good lighting that gives the reader a sense of who that person is and what they do." To break in, "present your work in an organized, professional manner and be willing to take direction."

CLAVIER, Dept. PM, 200 Northfield Rd., Northfield IL 60093. (708)446-5000. Editor: Kingsley Day. Magazine published 10 times/year. Readers are piano and organ teachers. Circ. 20,000. Estab. 1962. Sample copy $2.

Needs: Human interest photos of keyboard instrument students and teachers. Special needs include synthesizer photos, senior citizens performing and children performing.
Making Contact & Terms: Send material by mail for consideration. SASE. Reports in 1 month. Uses b&w glossy prints. Pays $100-150/color cover. For cover: Kodachrome, color glossy prints or 35mm transparencies. Vertical format preferred. Pays $10-25/b&w inside photo. Credit line given. Pays on publication. Buys all rights.
Tips: "We look for sharply focused photographs that show action and for clear color that is bright and true. We need photographs of children and teachers involved in learning music at the piano. We prefer shots that show them deeply involved in their work rather than posed shots. Very little is taken on specific assignment except for the cover. Authors usually include article photographs with their manuscripts. We purchase only one or two items from stock each year."

CLEANING MANAGEMENT MAGAZINE, 13 Century Hill Dr., Latham NY 12110. (518)783-1281. Editor: Tom Williams. Monthly. Emphasizes management of cleaning/custodial/housekeeping operations for commercial buildings, schools, hospitals, shopping malls, airports, etc. Readers are middle to upper-middle managers of in-house cleaning/custodial departments, and managers/owners of contract cleaning companies. Circ. 45,000. Estab. 1963. Sample copy free (limited) with SASE.
Needs: Uses 10-15 photos/issue. Needs photos of cleaning personnel working on carpets, hard floors, tile, windows, restrooms, large buildings, etc. Model release preferred. Photo captions required.
Making Contact & Terms: Provide resume, business card, brochure, flyer or tearsheets to be kept on file for possible assignments; query with specific ideas for photos related to our field. SASE. Reports in 1-2 weeks. Pays $25/b&w inside photo. Credit line given. Will negotiate with a photographer unwilling to sell all rights. Simultaneous submissions and previously published work OK.
Tips: "Query first and shoot what the publication needs."

*CLIMATE BUSINESS MAGAZINE, P.O. Box 13307, Pensacola FL 32501. (904)433-1166. FAX: (904)435-9174. Publisher: Elizabeth A. Burchell. Quarterly magazine. Emphasizes business. Readers are executives, ages 35-54, with average annual income of $68,000. Circ. 24,000. Estab. 1990. Sample copy $4.75.
Needs: Uses 50 photos/issue; 20 supplied by freelancers. Needs photos of Florida topics: technology, government, ecology, global trade, finance, travel and life shots. Model/property release required. Photo captions preferred.
Making Contact & Terms: Send unsolicited photos by mail for consideration. Provide resume, business card, brochure, flyer or tearsheets to be kept on file for possible assignments. Send 5×7 b&w or color prints; 35mm, 2¼×2¼ transparencies. Keeps samples on file. SASE. Reports in 3 weeks. Pays $75/color cover photo; $25/color inside photo; $25/b&w inside photo; $75/color page. Pays on publication. Buys one-time rights.
Tips: "Don't overprice yourself and keep submitting work."

COLLEGE ATHLETIC MANAGEMENT, Dept. PM, 438 W. State S., Ithaca NY 14850. (607)272-0265. FAX: (607)273-0701. Managing Editor: Eleanor Frankel. Bimonthly magazine. Emphasizes college athletics. Readers are managers of college athletic programs. Circ. 14,100. Estab. 1989. Sample copy free with 9×12 SASE.
Needs: Uses 12-15 photos/issue; 100% supplied by freelancers. Needs photos of athletic events and athletic equipment/facility shots. Model release preferred.
Making Contact & Terms: Submit portfolio for review. Keeps samples on file. SASE. Reports in 1-2 weeks. Pays $150-200/color cover photo; $100-150/b&w cover or color inside photo; $35-50/b&w inside photo. Pays on publication. Credit line given. Buys first N.A. serial rights; negotiable. Previously published work OK.

COLLISION, Box M, Franklin MA 02038. Editor: Jay Kruza. Magazine published every 5 weeks. Emphasizes "technical tips and management guidelines" for auto body repairmen and dealership managers in eastern US. Circ. 20,000. Sample copy $3; free photo guidelines with SASE.
Needs: Buys 100 photos/year; 12/issue. Photos of technical repair procedures, association meetings, etc. A regular column called "Stars and Cars" features a national personality with his/her car. Prefer 3+ b&w photos with captions as to why person likes this vehicle. If person has worked on it or customized it, photo is worth more.
Making Contact & Terms: Query with resume of credits and representational samples (not necessarily on subject) or send contact sheet for consideration. Send b&w glossy or matte contact sheet or 5×7 prints. Captions required. SASE. Reports in 3 weeks. Pays $25 for first photo; $10 for each additional photo in the series; pays $50 for first photo and $25 for each additional photo for "Stars and Cars" column. Prefers to buy 5 or 7 photos per series. Extra pay for accompanying mss. Pays on acceptance. Buys all rights, but may reassign to photographer after publication. In created or set-up

photos, which are not direct news, requires photocopy of model release with address and phone number of models for verification. Simultaneous submissions OK.

Tips: "Don't shoot one or two frames; do a sequence or series. It gives us choice, and we'll buy more photos. Often we reject single photo submissions. Capture how the work is done to solve the problem."

COMMERCIAL CARRIER JOURNAL, Chilton Way, Radnor PA 19089. (215)964-4513. Editor-In-Chief: Gerald F. Standley. Managing Editor: Carole A. Smith. Monthly magazine. Emphasizes truck and bus fleet maintenance operations and management. Circ. 79,000. Estab. 1911.

Needs: Spot news (of truck accidents, Teamster activities and highway scenes involving trucks). Photos purchased with or without accompanying ms, or on assignment. Model release and *detailed* captions required. For color photos, uses prints and 35mm transparencies. For covers, uses color transparencies. Uses vertical cover only. Needs accompanying features on truck fleets and news features involving trucking companies.

Making Contact & Terms: Send material by mail for consideration. SASE. Reports in 3 weeks. NPI; payment varies. Pays on a per-job or per-photo basis. Pays on acceptance. Credit line given. Buys all rights.

COMPUTERS IN HEALTHCARE MAGAZINE, Suite 650, 6300 S. Syracuse Way, Englewood CO 80111. (303)220-0600. FAX: (303)773-9716. Editor: Carolyn Dunbar. Monthly magazine. Emphasizes healthcare computing—management focus. Readers are hospital CEO, CFO, MIS directors, physicians, nurses, marketing managers in healthcare, HMD directors and healthcare decision makers. Circ. 17,000. Estab. 1980. Sample copy free for large manila SAE and 10 first-class stamps. No photo guidelines.

Needs: Uses 5-10 photos/issue; 10% supplied by freelancers. Needs photos of very techy—abstract—covers similar to Omni, computer tech focus. "We need to build a stable of highly skilled, competent, reasonably priced freelancers. We will welcome portfolios." Model release and photo captions preferred.

Making Contact & Terms: Query with list of stock photo subjects. Send b&w/color prints by mail for consideration. Submit portfolio for review. Provide resume, business card, brochure, flyer or tearsheets to be kept on file for possible assignments. SASE. Reports in 1-2 weeks. Pays $250/color cover photo. Pays on publication. Credit line given. Buys one-time rights. Simultaneous submissions and previously published work OK.

Tips: "Mostly we are looking for 'hot' cover art. This is a good time for photographers to contact us, because we are planning for next two years. Covers are highly colorful, glitzy, high-end looking with healthcare and computer technology as a theme—but we consider abstract 'futuristic' images. Fit with our style, show an excellent portfolio and make things easy on our end—provide full, speedy service."

CONNSTRUCTION MAGAZINE, Dept. PM, Suite 211, 62 LaSalle Rd., West Hartford CT 06107. (203)523-7518. Editor: Tracy E. McHugh. Quarterly magazine. Emphasizes horizontal construction. Readers are 21-60, male and female, construction company owners and managers. Circ. 5,500. Estab. 1962. Sample copy for 9×12 SASE and 5 first-class stamps. No photo guidelines.

Needs: Uses 80 photos/issue; 10% supplied by freelance photographers. Photo types include trade, on-site and personalities. Model release and photo captions required.

Making Contact & Terms: Query with resume of credits. Provide resume, business card, brochure, flyer or tearsheets to be kept on file for possible assignments. SASE. Reports in 1-2 weeks. Most rates negotiable. Pays $200-400 color cover photo. Pays on publication. Credit line given. Buys first N.A. serial rights.

Tips: "We generally use everything from event coverage to detailed, cover studio shots. But everything is issue specific. Always best to contact us to discuss a shot first."

*✹**CONSTRUCTION COMMENT**, 6th Floor, 920 Yonge St., Toronto ON M4W 3C7 Canada. (416)961-1028. FAX: (416)924-4408. Executive Editor: Gregory Kero. Semiannual magazine. Emphasizes construction and architecture. Readers are builders, contractors, architects and designers. Circ. 5,000. Estab. 1970. Sample copy and photo guidelines available.

Needs: Uses 25 photos/issue; 50% supplied by freelance photographers. Needs "straightforward, descriptive photos of buildings and projects under construction, and interesting people shots of workers at construction sites." Model release and photo captions preferred.

> ✹ *The maple leaf before a listing indicates that the market is Canadian. The symbol is new this year in* Photographer's Market.

Making Contact & Terms: Arrange a personal interview to show portfolio. Query with resume of credits or list of stock photo subjects. Provide resume, business card, brochure, flyer or tearsheets to be kept on file for possible assignments. SASE. Reports in 1 month. Pays $200/color cover photo; $100/b&w cover photo; $25/color or b&w inside photo. Pays on publication. Credit line given. Buys all rights to reprint in our other publications; rights negotiable. Simultaneous submissions and previously published work OK.
Tips: Looks for "representative photos of building projects and interesting construction-site people shots."

CORPORATE CASHFLOW, 6255 Barfield Rd., Atlanta GA 30328. (404)256-9800. Editor: Dick Gamble. Monthly magazine. Emphasizes corporate treasury management. Readers are senior financial officers of large and mid-sized U.S. corporations. Circ. 40,000. Estab. 1980. Sample copy available.
Needs: Uses 1 or 2 photos/issue; 100% supplied by freelancers.
Making Contact & Terms: Provide resume, business card, brochure, flyer or tearsheets to be kept on file for possible assignments. "Atlanta photographers only." Pays $400/color cover photo. Pays on acceptance. Credit line given. Buys one-time rights.

CORPORATE CLEVELAND, Dept. PM, 1720 Euclid Ave., Cleveland OH 44115. (216)621-1644. FAX: (216)621-5918. Art Director: J.R. Weber. Monthly magazine. Emphasizes "all types of business within northeast Ohio." Readers are executives and business owners. Circ. 30,000. Estab. 1977. Sample copy $2.
Needs: Uses 20-25 photos/issue; 95% supplied by freelancers. Needs photos of "people and industrial processes within articles." Captions required.
Making Contact & Terms: Provide resume, business card, brochure, flyer or tearsheets to be kept on file for possible assignments. SASE. Reports in 2 weeks. Pays $200+/color cover photo; $25+/b&w inside photo; $50+/color inside photo. Pays on acceptance. Credit line given. Buys one-time rights. Simultaneous submissions and previously published work OK.

CORPORATE DETROIT MAGAZINE Dept. PM, Suite 303, 26111 Evergreen, Southfield MI 48076. (313)357-8300. FAX: (313)357-8308. Editor: Gary Hoffman. Monthly independent circulated to senior executives. Emphasizes Michigan business. Readers include top-level executives. Circ. 36,000. Free sample copy with 9×12 SASE; call editor for photo guidelines.
Needs: Uses variable number of photographs; most supplied by freelance photographers. Needs photos of business people, environmental, feature story presentation, mug shots, etc. Reviews photos with accompanying ms only. Special needs include photographers based around Michigan for freelance work on job basis. Model release preferred; captions required.
Making Contact & Terms: Arrange a personal interview to show portfolio. Query with resume of credits and samples. SASE. Reports in 2 weeks. NPI; pay individually negotiated. Pays on publication. Credit line given. Buys all rights.

CRANBERRIES, Dept. PM, P.O. Box 858, South Carver MA 02366. (508)866-5055. FAX: (508)866-2970. Publisher/Editor: Carolyn Gilmore. Monthly. Emphasizes cranberry growing, processing, marketing and research. Readers are "primarily cranberry growers but includes anybody associated with the field." Circ. 750. Sample copy free.
Needs: Uses about 10 photos/issue; half supplied by freelance photographers. Needs "portraits of growers, harvesting, manufacturing—anything associated with cranberries." Captions required.
Making Contact & Terms: Send 4×5 or 8×10 b&w or color glossy prints by mail for consideration; "simply query about prospective jobs." SASE. Pays $25-60/b&w cover photo; $15-30/b&w inside photo; $35-100 for text/photo package. Pays on publication. Credit line given. Buys one-time rights. Simultaneous submissions and previously published work OK.
Tips: "Learn about the field."

DAIRY HERD MANAGEMENT, Dept. PM, P.O. Box 2400, Minnetoka MN 55343. (612)931-0211. Editor: Ed Clark. Monthly magazine. Emphasizes dairy management innovations, techniques and practices for dairy producers. Circ. 105,000.
Needs: Animal (natural photos of cows in specific dairy settings), how-to and photo essay/photo feature. Wants on a regular basis photos showing new dairy management techniques. No scenics or dead colors. Model release and captions preferred. Photos purchased with accompanying ms, or on assignment. Wants interesting and practical articles on dairy management innovations, techniques and practices.
Making Contact & Terms: Query with list of stock photo subjects. Uses 5×7 b&w glossy prints; 35mm or 2¼×2¼ transparencies, vertical format required for cover. SASE. Reports in 2 weeks. Pays $100-250 for text/photo package, or on a per-photo basis. Pays $5-25/b&w photo; $25-100/color photo; $50-150/color cover photo; $100-150/ms. Pays on acceptance. Buys one-time rights.

DAIRY TODAY, Farm Journal Publishing, Inc., Suite 100, 6205 Earle Brown Dr., Brooklyn Center MN 55430. (612)561-0300. Photo Editor: Greg Lamp. Monthly magazine. Emphasizes American agriculture. Readers are active farmers, ranchers or agribusiness people. Circ. 111,000. Sample copy and photo guidelines free with SASE.
Needs: Uses 20-30 photos/issue; 75% supplied by freelancers. We use studio-type portraiture (environmental portraits), technical, details, scenics. Model release preferred; photo captions required.
Making Contact & Terms: Arrange a personal interview to show portfolio or query with resume of credits along with business card, brochure, flyer or tearsheets to be kept on file for possible assignments. SASE. Reports in 2 weeks. NPI. "We pay a cover bonus." Pays on acceptance. Credit line given. Buys one-time rights. Simultaneous submissions OK.
Tips: In portfolio or samples, likes to "see about 20 slides showing photographer's use of lighting and ability to work with people. Know your intended market. Familiarize yourself with the magazine and keep abreast of how photos are used in the general magazine field."

*DANCE TEACHER NOW, 3020 Beacon Blvd., W. Sacramento CA 95691-3436. (916)373-0201. FAX: (916)373-0232. Editor: K.C. Patrick. Magazine published 9 times per year. Emphasizes dance, business, health and education. Readers are dance instructors and other related professionals, ages 15-80. Circ. 6,000. Estab. 1979. Sample copy free with 9×12 SASE. Guidelines free with SASE.
Needs: Uses 20 photos/issue; all supplied by freelancers. Needs photos of action shots (teaching, etc.). Reviews photos with accompanying ms only. Model/property release preferred. Photo captions preferred.
Making Contact & Terms: Provide resume, business card, brochure, flyer or tearsheets to be kept on file for possible assignments. Keeps samples on file. SASE. Pays $50+/color cover photo; $20/color inside photo; $20/b&w inside photo. Pays on publication. Credit line given. Buys one-time rights plus publicity rights; negotiable. Simultaneous submissions and/or previously published work OK.

DARKROOM & CREATIVE CAMERA TECHNIQUES, Dept. PM, Preston Publications, 7800 Merrimac Ave., P.O. Box 48312, Niles IL 60648. (708)965-0566. FAX: (708)965-7639. Publisher: Seaton T. Preston. Editor: David Alan Jay. Bimonthly magazine. Covers darkroom techniques, creative camera use, photochemistry and photographic experimentation/innovation—particularly in photographic processing, printing and reproduction—plus general user-oriented photography articles aimed at advanced amateurs and professionals. Lighting and optics are also very important. Circ. 45,500. Estab. 1979. Free photography and writer's guidelines for SASE. Sample copy $4.50.
Needs: "The best way to publish photographs in *Darkroom Techniques* is to write an article on photo or darkroom techniques and illustrate the article. Except for article-related pictures, we publish few single photographs. The two exceptions are: cover photographs—we are looking for strong poster-like images that will make good newsstand covers; and Professional Portfolio—exceptional, professional photographs of an artistic or human nature; most of freelance photography comes from what is currently in a photographer's stock. Model releases are required where appropriate."
Making Contact & Terms: "To submit for cover or Professional Portfolio, please send a selected number of superior photographs of any subject; however, we do not want to receive more than 10 or 20 in any one submission. We ask for submissions on speculative basis only. Except for portfolios, we publish few single photos that are not accompanied by some type of text." Prefer color transparencies over color prints. B&w submissions should be 8×10. For cover submissions, 4×5 transparencies are preferable. Pays $300/covers; $100/page for text/photo package; negotiable. Pays on publication only. Credit line given. Buys one-time rights.
Tips: "We are looking for exceptional photographs with strong, graphically startling images. We look for colorful graphic images with room at top and on one side for covers; technically accurate, crisp, clear images for portfolios. No run-of-the-mill postcard shots please. We are the most technical general-interest photographic publication on the market today. Authors are encouraged to substantiate their conclusions with experimental data. Submit samples, article ideas, etc. It's easier to get photos published with an article."

DATA COMMUNICATIONS MAGAZINE, 41st Floor, 1221 Ave. of the Americas, New York NY 10020. (212)512-2639. Art Director: Ken Surabian. Monthly magazine. Emphasizes data communications. Readers are men in middle management positions. Circ. 70,000.
Needs: Uses 4 photos/issue; 40-50% supplied by freelance photographers. Needs photos of people, still life, industry-related equipment or processes. Model release and photo captions required.
Making Contact & Terms: Provide resume, business card, brochure, flyer or tearsheets to be kept on file for possible assignments. Cannot return material. Reports in 2 weeks. Pays $1,000/color cover photo; $650/color inside photo; $650/color page rate; $250-350/day. Pays on acceptance. Credit line given. Buys one-time and international one-time rights.

DATAMATION MAGAZINE, Dept. PM, 275 Washington St., Newton MA 02158-1630. (617)558-4682. Art Director: Christopher Lewis. Biweekly magazine. Emphasizes data processing for professionals. Readers are professionals in data processing. Circ. 165,000. Sample copy $3.
Needs: Uses 5 photos/issue; all supplied by freelance photographers. Special needs include special effects. Model release required. Also hires photojournalists to take pictures of people in the business.
Making Contact & Terms: Arrange a personal interview to show portfolio; query with samples; submit portfolio for review; provide resume, business card, brochure, flyer or tearsheets to be kept on file for possible future assignments. Pays half-day rates of $200, day rates of $350. Pays $1,000/b&w and color cover photo; $500/b&w and color page. Pays on acceptance. Credit line given. Buys one-time and international rights. Simultaneous submissions OK.
Tips: Prefers to see special effects and still life.

DESIGN & COST DATA, Dept. PM, 8602 N. 40th St., Tampa FL 33604. (813)989-9300. Managing Editor: Melissa Wells. Bimonthly magazine. Covers architecture and architectural design. Readers are architects, specifiers, designers, builders; male and female; students and professionals. Circ. 15,000. Estab. 1958. Sample copy free with 11 × 14 SASE with $2 postage.
Needs: Uses 15-20 photos/issue; 30% supplied by freelancers. Needs architectural photos, including newly completed buildings and newly renovated structures. Permissions and names of architect and building owner required and photo captions required.
Making Contact & Terms: Send unsolicited b&w or color prints, glossy, any format; also send any format transparencies. SASE. Reports in 1 month. Pays $100/color cover photo; $75/color inside photo; $35/b&w inside photo. Pays on publication. Credit line given. Buys one-time rights. Simultaneous submissions and previously published work OK.

DIRECT MARKETING MAGAZINE, Dept. PM, 224 Seventh St., Garden City NY 11530. (516)746-6700. FAX: (516)294-8141. Editor: Mollie Neal. Monthly. Emphasizes direct mail, catalogs, telemarketing, building databases of customers and prospects for all kinds of businesses. Readers are marketers of all kinds—creative (copywriters, designers) and statisticians. Circ. 20,000. Estab. 1938. Sample copy free with 9 × 12 SASE.
Needs: Uses about 20-40 photos/issue; 5-15% supplied by freelancers. Needs portraits for cover stories. Model release and captions preferred.
Making Contact & Terms: Arrange a personal interview to show portfolio. Query with resume of credits. Provide resume, business card, brochure, flyer or tearsheets to be kept on file for possible future assignments. SASE. Reports in 2 weeks. NPI. Credit line given. Buys one-time rights.
Tips: Prefers to see "ability to capture a subject's personality; getting drama into photos; making otherwise dull corporate subjects vital and engaging."

EDUCATION WEEK, Suite 250, 4301 Connecticut Ave. N.W., Washington DC 20008. (202)364-4114. FAX: (202)364-1039. Editor-in-Chief: Ronald A. Wolk. Photo Editor: Benjamin Tice Smith. Weekly. Emphasizes elementary and secondary education. Circ. 65,000. Estab. 1981.
Needs: Uses about 20 photos/issue; all supplied by freelance photographers; 90% on assignment, 10% from stock. Model/property release preferred. Model release usually needed for children (from parents). Photo captions required; include names, ages, what is going on in the picture.
Making Contact & Terms: Interested in receiving work from newer, lesser-known photographers. Query with samples. Provide resume and tearsheets to be kept on file for possible future assignments. Does not return unsolicited material. Reports in 2 weeks. Pays $50-150/b&w photo; $100-300/day; $50-250/job; $50-300 for text/photo package. Pays on acceptance. Credit line given. Buys all rights; negotiable. Simultaneous submissions and previously published work OK.
Tips: "When reviewing samples we look for the ability to make interesting and varied images from what might not seem to be photogenic. Show creativity backed up with technical polish."

ELECTRICAL APPARATUS, Barks Publications, Inc., 400 N. Michigan Ave., Chicago IL 60611-4198. (312)321-9440. Associate Publisher: Elsie Dickson. Monthly magazine. Emphasizes industrial electrical machinery maintenance and repair for the electrical aftermarket. Readers are "persons engaged in the application, maintenance and servicing of industrial and commercial electrical and electronic equipment." Circ. 16,000. Sample copy $4.
Needs: "Assigned materials only. We welcome innovative industrial photography, but most of our material is staff-prepared." Model release required "when requested." Captions preferred.
Making Contact & Terms: Query with resume of credits. Contact sheet or contact sheet with negatives OK. SASE. Reports in 3 weeks. Pays $25-100/b&w or color photo. Pays on publication. Credit line given. Buys all rights, but exceptions are occasionally made. Photos purchased with accompanying ms or on assignment.

ELECTRONIC BUSINESS, 275 Washington St., Newton MA 02158. (617)964-3030. FAX: (617)964-7136. Art Director: Michael Roach. Assistant Art Director: Elizabeth Zisa. Biweekly. Emphasizes the electronic industry. Readers are CEOs, managers and top executives. Circ. 75,000. Estab. 1974.
Needs: Uses 25-30 photos/issue; 25% supplied by freelancers, most on assignment. Needs corporate photos and people shots. Model/property release preferred. Captions required.
Making Contact & Terms: Interested in receiving work from newer, lesser-known photographers. Arrange a personal interview to show portfolio; provide resume, business card, brochure, flyer or tearsheets to be kept on file for possible future assignments. Does not return unsolicited material. Pays $50-250/b&w photo; $200-400/color photo; $50-100/hour; $400-800/day; $200-500/photo/text package. Pays on acceptance. Credit line given. Buys one-time rights. Simultaneous submissions and previously published work OK.
Tips: In photographer's portfolio looks for informal business portrait, corporate atmosphere.

EMERGENCY, The Journal of Emergency Services, 6300 Yarrow Dr., Carlsbad CA 92009. (619)438-2511. FAX: (619)931-5809. Editor: Rhonda Foster. Monthly magazine. Emphasizes pre-hospital emergency medical and rescue services for paramedics, EMTs and firefighters to keep them informed of latest developments in the emergency medical services field. Circ. 26,000. Sample copy $5.
Needs: Buys 50-75 photos/year; 5 photos/issue. Documentary, photo essay/photo feature and spot news dealing with pre-hospital emergency medicine. Needs shots to accompany unillustrated articles submitted and cover photos; year's calendar of themes forwarded on request with #10 SASE. "Try to get close to the action; both patient and emergency personnel should be visible." Photos purchased with or without accompanying ms. Model and property releases preferred. Captions required and should include the name, city and state of the emergency rescue team and medical treatment being rendered in photo. Also needs color transparencies for "Action," a photo department dealing with emergency personnel in action. Accompanying mss: instructional, descriptive or feature articles dealing with emergency medical services.
Making Contact & Terms: Interested in receiving work from newer, lesser-known photographers. Uses 5×7 or 8×10 b&w glossy prints; 35mm or larger transparencies. For cover: Prefers 35mm; 2¼×2¼ transparencies OK. Vertical format preferred. Send material by mail for consideration, especially action shots of EMTs/paramedics in action. SASE. Pays $30/inside photo; $100/color cover photo; $100-300/ms. Pays for mss/photo package, or on a per-photo basis. Pays on acceptance. Credit line given. Buys all rights, "nonexclusive."
Tips: Wants well-composed photos with good overall scenes and clarity that say more than "an accident happened here. We're going toward single-focus uncluttered photos." Looking for more color photos for articles. "Good closeups of actual treatment. Also, sensitive illustrations of the people in EMS — stress, interacting with family/pediatrics etc. We're interested in rescuers, and our readers like to see their peers in action, demonstrating their skills. Make sure photo is presented with treatment rendered and people involved. Prefer model release if possible."

EMPLOYEE ASSISTANCE, Dept. PM, 225 N. New Rd., Waco TX 76710. (817)776-9000. FAX: (817)776-9018. Editor: Stephanie McIntosh. Monthly magazine. Emphasizes problems in the workplace (substance abuse, stress, health issues, AIDS, drug testing). Readers are personnel directors and employee assistance consultants, both men and women, 30-60 years of age. Circ. 25,000. Estab. 1988. Sample copy free upon request.
Needs: Uses approximately 6 photos/issue; 50-75% of all art is freelance. Needs "concept" shots relating to subjects featured, corporate image photos, plus portrait-style photos for featured individuals. Model release required; photo captions preferred.
Making Contact & Terms: Query with list of stock photo subjects or send unsolicited photos by mail for consideration; provide resume, business card, brochure, flyer or tearsheets to be kept on file for possible assignments. Uses 35mm or 2¼×2¼ transparencies. SASE. Reports in 2 weeks. Pays $50-200/b&w photo; $75-200/color photo; $15-50/hour; $250/photo/text package; $400/cover art/photos. Pays on publication. Credit line given. Buys first N.A. serial rights.
Tips: Looks for "health, nursing, counseling, human resources and wellness programs that are people-oriented. Health and wellness promotion is a hot item in our magazine. We look for art to portray this.

ENTERTAINMENT EXPRESS INTERNATIONAL, INC., Dept. PM, P.O. Box 611532, North Miami FL 33261. (305)891-4449. Editor: Evan Resnick. Quarterly magazine. Emphasizes entertainment, party planning, theatrical productions and corporate. Estab. 1989. Sample copy free with SASE.
Needs: Uses 6-12 photos/issue. Needs photos of travel, scenics, personalities, entertainment-related musical groups, celebrities and some animal shots. Especially wants to see shots of "celebrities, musical groups and entertainment-related." Model, property release and photo captions required; include who, what, when, where, why and how.

Making Contact & Terms: Arrange personal interview to show portfolio. Query with resume of credits and list of stock photo subjects. Provide resume, business card, brochure, flyer or tearsheets to be kept on file for possible assignments. Keeps samples on file. Cannot return material. Reports as needed. Pays $25/color or b&w cover or inside photo; $25/color or b&w page rate; $25-50/hour; $100-200/day. Pays on publication. Credit line given. Rights negotiable. Simultaneous submissions and previously published work OK.

Tips: "Our company looks for quality, photo clarity, composition and life! It's also important that the photographer is an amicable person who's easy to do business with and able to respond to specific photo needs." To break in, "nothing ventured, nothing gained . . . always give your work opportunity to exposure whether it be to our publication or anyone else's."

EUROPE MAGAZINE, Dept. PM, Suite 707, 2100 M St. NW, Washington DC 20037. (202)862-9557. Managing Editor: Robert Goodman. Magazine published 10 times/year. Circ. 25,000. Covers the European Common Market with "in-depth news articles on topics such as economics, trade, US-EC relations, industry, development and East-West relations." Readers are "businessmen, professionals, academic, government officials." Free sample copy.

Needs: Uses about 20-30 photos/issue, most of which are supplied by stock houses and freelance photographers. Needs photos of "current news coverage and sectors, such as economics, trade, small business, people, transport, politics, industry, agriculture, fishing, some culture, some travel. Each issue we have an overview article on one of the 12 countries in the Common Market. For this we need a broad spectrum of photos, particularly color, in all sectors. If a photographer queries and lets us know what he has on hand, we might ask him to submit a selection for a particular story. For example, if he has slides or b&w's on a certain European country, if we run a story on that country, we might ask him to submit slides on particular topics, such as industry, transport or small business." Model release and captions not required; identification necessary.

Making Contact & Terms: Send query with list of stock photo subjects. Initially, a list of countries/topics covered will be sufficient. SASE. Reports in 3-4 weeks. Pays on publication. Pays $75-150/b&w photo; $100 minimum/color transparency for inside, $400 for front cover; per job negotiable. Credit line given. Buys one-time rights. Simultaneous submissions and previously published work OK.

Tips: "For certain articles, especially the Member State Reports, we are now using more freelance material than previously. Needs good photo and color quality, but not too touristic a shot. Feature agriculture or industry if possible.

FARM CHEMICALS, Dept. PM, 37733 Euclid Ave., Willoughby OH 44094. (216)942-2000. FAX: (216)942-0662. Editorial Director: Charlotte Sine. Editor: Dale Little. Emphasizes application and marketing of fertilizers and protective chemicals for crops for those in the farm chemical industry. Monthly magazine. Circ. 32,000. Estab. 1896. Free sample copy and photo guidelines with 9 × 12 SAE.

Needs: Buys 6-7 photos/year; 5-30% supplied by freelancers. Photos of agricultural chemical and fertilizer application scenes (of commercial — not farmer — applicators). Model release preferred. Captions required.

Making Contact & Terms: Query first with resume of credits. Uses 8 × 10 b&w and color glossy prints or transparencies. SASE. Reports in 3 weeks. Pays $25-50/b&w photo; $50-100/color photo. Pays on acceptance. Buys one-time rights. Simultaneous submissions and previously published work OK.

FARM JOURNAL, INC., 230 W. Washington Sq., Philadelphia PA 19105. (215)829-4865. Editor: Earl Ainsworth. Photo Editor: Tom Dodge. Monthly magazine. Emphasizes the business of agriculture: "Good farmers want to know what their peers are doing and how to make money marketing their products." Circ. 800,000. Free sample copy upon request.

Needs: Freelancers supply 60% of the photos. Photos having to do with the basics of raising, harvesting and marketing of all the farm commodities. People-oriented shots are encouraged. Also uses human interest and interview photos. All photos must relate to agriculture. Photos purchased with or without accompanying ms. Model release/captions required.

Making Contact & Terms: Arrange a personal interview or send photos by mail. Provide calling card and samples to be kept on file for possible future assignments. Uses 8 × 10 or 11 × 14 b&w glossy or semigloss prints; 35mm or 2¼ × 2¼ transparencies or color prints; transparencies, all sizes for covers. SASE. Reports in 1-4 weeks. Pays by assignment or photo; $25-100/b&w photo; $100-200/color photo, depending on size; pays more for covers. Pays on acceptance. Credit line given. Buys one-time rights, "But this is negotiable." Simultaneous submissions OK.

Tips: "Be original, take time to see with the camera. Be more selective, take more shots to submit. Take as many different angles of subject as possible. Use fill where needed. We also publish five titles — *Farm Journal, Top Producer* (photo editor is Tom Dodge), *Hogs Today, Beef Today, Dairy Today* (photo editor is Greg Lamp — (612)631-3151)."

FARM STORE MERCHANDISING, Dept. PM, Suite 160, 12400 Whitewater Dr., Minnetonka MN 55343. (612)931-0211. Editor: Julie Emnett. Monthly magazine. Emphasizes retailing in agribusiness. Readers are feed, grain, animal health, fertilizer and chemical dealers. Circ. 35,000. Sample copy free with SASE.
Needs: Uses 20 photos/issue; 2 supplied by freelance photographers. Needs photos of marketing, merchandising applications and agribusiness sales shots. Model release preferred; captions required.
Making Contact & Terms: Query with list of stock photo subjects. SASE. Reports in 1 month. Pays $25/b&w inside photo; $50/inside color photo; $25-200/job; $100-300/text/photo package. Pays on publication. Credit line given. Buys one-time rights.

FIREHOUSE MAGAZINE, Suite 21, 445 Broad Hollow Rd., Melville NY 11747. (516)845-2700. FAX: (516)845-7109. Editor-in-Chief: Barbara Dunleavy. Art Director: Tina Sheely. Monthly. Circ. 110,000. Estab. 1973. Emphasizes "firefighting—notable fires, techniques, dramatic fires and rescues, etc." Readers are "paid and volunteer firefighters, EMT's." Sample copy $3 with 9 × 12 SAE and approximately $1.65 postage; photo guidelines free with SASE.
Needs: Uses about 30 photos/issue; 20 supplied by freelance photographers. Needs photos in the above subject areas. Model release preferred.
Making Contact & Terms: Send 8 × 10 matte or glossy b&w or color prints; 35mm, 2¼ × 2¼, 4 × 5, 8 × 10 transparencies or b&w or color negatives with contact sheet by mail for consideration. "Photos must not be more than 30 days old." SASE. Reports ASAP. Pays $200/color cover photo; $15-45/b&w photo; $15-75/color photo. Pays on publication. Credit line given. Buys one-time rights.
Tips: "Mostly we are looking for action-packed photos—the more fire, the better the shot. Show firefighters in full gear, do not show spectators. Fire safety is a big concern. Much of our photo work is freelance. Try to be in the right place at the right time as the fire occurs."

FLEET OWNER MAGAZINE, Dept. PM, Suite 101, 707 Westchester Ave., White Plains NY 10604-3102. (914)949-8500. Art Director: Peggy Navarre. Assistant Art Director: Dan Zeis. Monthly magazine. Covers trucking industry. Readers are male and female executives and managers of trucking companies. Circ, 115,000. Estab. 1941. Sample copies free upon request.
Needs: Uses 25-30 photos/issue; 30% supplied by freelancers. Needs photos of trucks in traffic, on open roads, etc. Also, shots of mechanics working on trucks and so on. Model release preferred "only when person is recognizable." Photo captions preferred.
Making Contact & Terms: Send unsolicited color prints and transparencies by mail for consideration. Provide resume, business card, brochure, flyer or tearsheets to be kept on file for possible assignments. Keeps samples on file. SASE. Reports in 1-2 weeks. Pays $600/color cover photo; $75/color inside photo; $600/day. Pays on publication. Credit line given. Buys one-time rights. Previously published work OK.

FLOORING, 7500 Old Oak Blvd., Cleveland OH 44130. (216)243-8100. FAX: (216)891-2675. Editor: Mark S. Kuhar. Monthly magazine. Emphasizes floor covering and other interior surfacing for floor covering retailers, contractors and distributors. Circ. 25,000. Estab. 1931.
Needs: Uses about 25-30 photos/issue; "a few" supplied by freelance photographers. Stock photos are rarely purchased. Needs photos "to illustrate various articles—mostly showroom shots." Model release and captions preferred.
Making Contact & Terms: Prefers query with samples. Provide resume, business card, brochure, flyer or tearsheets to be kept on file for possible future assignments. SASE. Pay varies; $5/b&w photo; $5-50/color photo or photo/text. Pays on acceptance. Buys all rights.
Tips: "We need to expand our contacts among photographers across the country, especially those available for simple, local assignments (general assignments). Looking for people with demonstrated abilities with 35mm cameras; prefer photojournalists. Want showroom shots emphasizing merchandising, displays, etc. Show me something unique, creative product shots in settings. Get on file. We may need someone in your area soon."

THE FLORIDA SPECIFIER, Dept. PM, Suite 100, 385 W. Fairbanks Ave., Winter Park FL 32789. (407)740-7950. Publisher/President: Mike Eastman. Monthly tabloid. Emphasizes engineering, construction, environmental, wastewater and design-architectural. Readers are ages 40-50's, males, (manager, design-specification). Circ. 38,000. Estab. 1979. Sample copy free for SASE. No photo guidelines.
Needs: Uses 15-25 photos/issue; approximately 20-25% supplied by freelance photographers. Needs photos of technology, construction (highway, building), environmental, water and wastewater. Special photo needs include roofing, pipes and tanks, geosynthetics, asbestos, abatement and stormwater control. Model release and photo captions preferred.
Making Contact & Terms: Query with list of stock photo subjects. SASE. Reports in 1 month. NPI; payment negotiable. Pays on publication. Credit line given. Simultaneous submissions and previously published work OK.

Tips: "Become familiar with publication's format and get a feel for the types of photos they look for and an understanding of subject matter."

FOODSERVICE EQUIPMENT & SUPPLIES SPECIALIST, 1350 E. Touhy Ave., Des Plaines IL 60018. (708)635-8800. Editor: Greg Richards. Monthly magazine. Emphasizes "the foodservice equipment distribution business; stories focus on kitchen design and management profiles. Readers are equipment distributor sales and management personnel, kitchen designers. Circ. 20,000. Sample copy free with 9×12 SASE.
Needs: Uses 8-16 photos/issue. Assigns photos of business management settings, plus restaurant and institutional kitchens. Model release required.
Making Contact & Terms: Provide resume, business card, brochure, flyer or tearsheets to be kept on file for possible assignments. SASE. Reports in 2 weeks. Pays $600-800/day; frequently makes "half-day" assignments. Pays on acceptance. Credit line given. Buys all rights; will negotiate with a photographer unwilling to sell all rights. Previously published work OK.
Tips: "Study the magazine carefully and determine whether you would have both the desire and the ability to shoot the types of photos you see."

FOOTWEAR PLUS, Dept. PM, 225 W. 34th St., New York NY 10122. (212)563-2742. FAX: (212)629-3249. Art Director: Fern Bass. Monthly magazine. Emphasizes shoes and accessories. Readers are male and female, retailers and manufacturers. Circ. 18,000. Estab. 1990. Free sample copy.
Needs: Uses 25 photos/issue; all supplied by freelancers. Needs photos of fashion, still life and people. Reviews photos with or without ms.
Making Contact & Terms: Arrange personal interview to show portfolio. Keeps samples on file. Reports in 1-2 weeks. Pays $800/day for cover and inside pages; $500/day for inside pages minus cover. Rights negotiable.

FORD NEW HOLLAND NEWS, Dept. PM, P.O. Box 1895, New Holland PA 17557. (717)355-1276. Editor: Roseanne Macrina. Published 8 times/year. Emphasizes agriculture. Readers are farm families. Circ. 400,000. Estab. 1960. Sample copy and photo guidelines free with 9×12 SASE.
Needs: Buys 30 photos/year of scenic agriculture relating to the seasons, harvesting, farm animals, farm management and farm people; 50% freelance photography/issue from assignment and 50% freelance stock. Need photo/article combination. Model release and captions required. "Collections viewed and returned quickly."
Making Contact & Terms: "Show us your work." SASE. Reports in 2 weeks. Pays $50-500/color photo, depends on use and quality of photo; $800-$1,500/photo/text package; $500/cover. Payment negotiable. Pays on acceptance. Buys first N.A. serial rights. Previously published work OK.
Tips: Photographers "must see beauty in agriculture and provide meaningful photojournalistic caption material to be successful here. It also helps to team up with a good agricultural writer and query us on a photojournalistic idea."

FURNITURE RETAILER, 1301 Carolina St., Greensboro NC 27401. (919)378-6065. FAX: (919)275-2864. Editor: Patricia Bowling. Monthly magazine. Emphasizes retail home furnishings stores. Readers are primarily male and female retail company executives. Sample copy and photo guidelines free with SASE.
Needs: Uses 15-20 photos/issue; 50% supplied by freelancers. Needs personality photos, shots of store interiors.
Making Contact & Terms: Query with resume of credits. Provide resume, business card, brochure, flyer or tearsheets to be kept on file for possible assignments. Reports only when interested. Pays $500/color cover photo; $250/color inside photo. Pays on acceptance. Credit line given. Buys first N.A. serial rights.
Tips: Looks for "ability to capture personality in business subjects for profiles; ability to handle diverse interiors."

FUTURES MAGAZINE, Dept. PM, Suite 1150, 250 S. Wacker Dr., Chicago IL 60606. (312)977-0999. Editor-in-chief: Darrell Jobman. Editor: Ginger Szala. Monthly magazine. Emphasizes futures and options trading. Readers are individual traders, institutional traders, brokerage firms, exchanges. Circ. 70,000. Sample copy $4.50.
Needs: Uses 12-15 photos/issue; 80% supplied by freelance photographers. Needs mostly personality portraits of story sources, some mug shots, trading floor environment. Model release required; captions preferred.
Making Contact & Terms: Arrange a personal interview to show portfolio. Query with list of stock photo subjects. Provide resume, business card, brochure, flyer or tearsheets to be kept on file for possible future assignments. SASE. Reports in 2 weeks. Pays $150/half day minimum. Pays on publication. Buys all rights.

Tips: All work is on assignment. Be competitive on price. Shoot good work without excessive film use.

GENERAL AVIATION NEWS & FLYER, Dept. PM, P.O. Box 98786, Tacoma WA 98498. (206)588-1743. FAX: (206)588-4005. Managing Editor: Kirk Gormley. Biweekly tabloid. Emphasizes aviation. Readers are pilots and airplane owners and aviation professionals. Estab. 1949. Sample copy $3. Photo guidelines free with SASE.
Needs: Uses 10-20 photos/issue; 10-50% supplied by freelancers. Reviews photos with or without ms, but "strongly prefer with ms." Especially wants to see "travel and destinations, special events."
Making Contact & Terms: Query with resume of credit; send unsolicited prints (up to 8 × 10, b&w or color) or transparencies (35mm or 2¼ × 2¼) by mail for consideration. Does not keep samples on file. SASE. Reports in 1 month. Pays $35-50/color cover photo; $35/color inside photo; $10/b&w inside photo. Pays on publication. Credit line given. Buys one-time rights.
Tips: Wants to see "sharp photos of planes with good color, airshows not generally used."

GOLF INDUSTRY, Dept. PM, Suite 250, 3230 W. Commercial Blvd., Ft. Lauderdale FL 33309. (305)731-0000. Vice President Manufacturing/Editorial: James Kukar. Bimonthly. Emphasizes golf trade. Circ. 21,000. Estab. 1970. Sample copy for $2 and 9 × 12 SAE with 80¢ postage.
Needs: Uses 20-30 photos/issue; all supplied by freelance photographers; 75% from assignment; 25% from stock. Model release preferred; photo captions required.
Making Contact & Terms: Query with list of stock photo subjects. Submit portfolio for review. SASE. Reports in 1 month. Pays $25-150/b&w; $25-500/color; $25-100/hour; $250-1,250/day; and $100-1,500/ photo/text package. Buys one-time rights and all rights; negotiable. Simultaneous submissions and previously published work OK.

GRAIN JOURNAL, 2490 N. Water St., Decatur IL 62526. (217)877-9660. Editor: Mark Avery. Bimonthly. Also produces monthly newsletter. Emphasizes grain industry. Readers are "elevator managers primarily as well as suppliers and others in the industry." Circ. 11,822. Sample copy free with 10 × 12 SAE with 85¢ postage.
Needs: Uses about 6 photos (but we want more)/issue. We need photos concerning industry practices and activities. Captions preferred.
Making Contact & Terms: Query with samples and list of stock photo subjects. SASE. Reports in 1 week. Pays $100/color cover photo; $30/b&w inside photo. Pays on publication. Credit line given. Buys all rights; negotiable.

*GRAPHIS, 141 Lexington Ave., New York NY 10016. (212)532-9387. FAX: (212)213-3229. Associate Art Director: Randell Pearson. Bimonthly publication. Emphasizes applied arts and visual communication. Circ. 20,000. Estab. 1945. Sample copy $14.
Needs: Needs "outstanding photography primarily by those who have established themselves in the applied arts field." Model/property release required. Captions required.
Making Contact & Terms: Submit portfolio for review. Provide resume, business card, brochure, flyer or tearsheets to be kept on file for possible assignments. Keeps samples on file. Reports in 1-2 weeks. NPI. Credit line given. Buys one-time rights. Previously published work OK.
Tips: "Outstanding quality is the only criteria for publication. *Graphis* is distributed to the design community and we feature the work of at least one photographer in each issue. The subjects of these pieces are those whose photography is applied in some form of commercial visual communication."

THE GROWING EDGE, 215 SW 2nd St., P.O. Box 1027, Corvallis OR 97333. (503)757-2511. FAX: (503)757-0028. Editor: Don Parker. Published quarterly. Emphasizes "New and innovative techniques in gardening, indoors, outdoors and in the greenhouse – hydroponics, artificial lighting, greenhouse operations/control, water conservation, new and unusual plant varities." Readers are serious amateurs to small commercial growers. Circ. 40,000. Estab. 1989.
Needs: Uses about 20 photos per issue; most supplied with articles by freelancers. Occasional assignment work (5%); 80% from freelance stock. Model release required; captions preferred including plant types, equipment used.
Making Contact & Terms: Send query with samples. Accepts b&w or color prints; transparencies (any size); b&w or color negatives with contact sheets. SASE. Reports in 4-6 weeks or will notify and keep material on file for future use. Pays $175 for cover photos; $25-50 for inside photos; $75-400 for text/photo package. Pays on publication. Credit line given. Buys first world and one-time anthology rights; negotiable. Simultaneous submissions and previously published work considered.

Tips: "Most photographs are used to illustrate processes and equipment described in text. Some photographs of specimen plants purchased. Many photos are of indoor plants under artificial lighting. The ability to deal with tricky lighting situations is important." Expects more assignment work in the future.

HEARTH AND HOME, Dept. PM, P.O. Box 2008, Laconia NH 03247. (603)528-4285. Editor: Ken Daggett. Monthly magazine. Emphasizes new and industry trends for specialty retailers and manufacturers of solid fuel and gas appliances, hearth accessories and casual furnishings. Circ. 25,000. Sample copy $5.
Needs: Uses about 30 photos/issue; 60% supplied by freelance photographers. Needs "shots of energy and patio furnishings stores (perferably a combination store), retail displays, wood heat installations, fireplaces, wood stoves and lawn and garden shots (installation as well as final design). Assignments available for interviews, conferences and out-of-state stories." Model release required; captions preferred.
Making Contact & Terms: Query with samples or list of stock photo subjects. Send b&w or color glossy prints, transparencies, b&w contact sheets by mail for consideration. SASE. Reports in 2 weeks. Pays $50-100/b&w photo; $75-150/color photo. Pays within 60 days. Credit line given. Buys various rights. Simultaneous and photocopied submissions OK.
Tips: "Call and ask what we need. We're *always* on the lookout for material."

HEAVY DUTY TRUCKING, P.O. Box W, Newport Beach CA 92658-8910. (714)261-1636. Editor: Deborah Whistler. Monthly magazine. Emphasizes trucking. Readers are mostly male—corporate executives, fleet management, supervisors, salesmen and drivers—ages 30-65. Circ. 96,000. Photo guidelines free with SASE.
Needs: Uses 30 photos/issue; 30-100% supplied by freelancers. Needs photos of scenics (trucks on highways), how-to (maintenance snapshots). Model release is "photographer's responsibility." Photo captions preferred.
Making Contact & Terms: Query with resume of credits. Send unsolicited photos by mail for consideration. Send 35mm transparencies. SASE. Sends check when material is used. Pays $150/color cover photo or $75/color or b&w inside photo. Pays on publication. Buys one-time rights.

HEAVY TRUCK SALESMAN, P.O. Box W, Newport Beach CA 92658-8910. (714)261-1636. Managing Editor: Deborah Whistler. Bimonthly magazine. Emphasizes trucking. Readers are mostly male truck dealers and salesmen, ages 30-65. Circ. 15,000. Photo guidelines free with SASE.
Needs: Uses 30 photos/issue; 30-100% supplied by freelancers. Needs photos of truck dealerships, truck salesmen with customers, scenics (trucks on highways), how-to (maintenance snapshots). Model release is "photographer's responsibility." Photo captions preferred.
Making Contact & Terms: Query with resume of credits or send unsolicited photos by mail for consideration. Send 35mm transparencies. SASE. Sends check when material is used. Pays $150/color cover photo; $75/color or b&w inside photo. Pays on publication. Buys one-time rights.

***‡HELICOPTER INTERNATIONAL,** 75 Elm Tree Rd., Locking, Weston-S-Mare, Avon BS248EL England. (934)822524. Editor: E. apRees. Bimonthly magazine. Emphasizes helicopters and autogyros. Readers are helicopter professionals. Circ. 22,000. Sample copy $4.50 and A4 SAE.
Needs: Uses 25-35 photos/issue; 50% supplied by freelance photographers. Needs photos of helicopters, especially newsworthy subjects. Model release preferred; photo captions required.
Making Contact & Terms: Send unsolicited photos by mail for consideration. Send b&w or color 8×10 or 4×5 gloss prints. Cannot return unsolicited material. Reports in 1 month. Pays $20/color cover photo or $5/b&w inside photo. Pays on publication. Credit line given. Buys one-time rights. Simultaneous submissions or previously published work OK.
Tips: Magazine is growing. To break in, submit "newsworthy pictures. No arty-crafty pix; good clear shots of helicopters backed by newsworthy captions, e.g., a new sale/new type/new color scheme/accident, etc."

***HIGH VOLUME PRINTING,** P.O. Box 368, Northbrook IL 60065. (708)564-5940. FAX: (708)564-8361. Editor: Catherine M. Stanulis. Bimonthly. Emphasizes equipment, systems and supplies; large commercial printers: magazine and book printers. Readers are management and production personnel

---

Can't find a listing? Check at the end of each market section for the " '92-'93 Changes" lists. These lists include any market listings from the '92 edition which were either not verified or deleted in this edition.

of high-volume printers and producers of books, magazines and periodicals. Circ. 30,000. Sample copy $5 plus $1.41 postage; free photo guidelines with SASE.

Needs: Uses about 30-35 photos/issue. Model release required; captions preferred.

Making Contact & Terms: Query with samples or with list of stock photo subjects. Send b&w and color prints (any size or finish); 35mm, 2¼ × 2¼, 4 × 5 or 8 × 10 transparencies; b&w or color contact sheet or negatives by mail for consideration. SASE. Reports in 1 month. Pays $200 maximum/color cover photo; $50 maximum/b&w or color inside photo; $200 maximum for text/photo package. Pays on publication. Credit line given. Buys one-time rights with option for future use. Previously published work OK "if previous publication is indicated."

HISPANIC BUSINESS, Suite 300, 360 South Hope Ave., Santa Barbara CA 93105. (805)682-5843. Senior Editor: Rick Mendosa. Monthly publication. Emphasizes Hispanics in business (entrepreneurs and executives), the Hispanic market. Circ. 150,000. Estab. 1979. Sample copy $3.50. Photo guidelines available.

Needs: Uses 25 photos/issue; 10% supplied by freelancers. Needs photos of personalities and action shots. No mug shots. Model and/or property release and photo captions required; name, title.

Making Contact & Terms: Query with resume of credits. Keeps samples on file. Reports in 1-2 weeks. Pays $450/color cover photo; $200/color inside photo; $150/b&w inside photo. Pays on publication. Credit line given. Rights negotiable.

Tips: Wants to see "unusual angles, bright colors, hand activity. Photo tied to profession."

HOGS TODAY, Farm Journal Publishing, Inc., Suite 100, 6205 Earle Brown Dr., Brooklyn Center MN 55430. (612)561-0300. Photo Editor: Greg Lamp. Monthly magazine. Circ. 125,000. Sample copy and photo guidelines free with SASE.

Needs: Uses 20-30 photos/issue; 75% supplied by freelancers. We use studio-type portraiture (environmental portraits), technical, details, scenics. Model release preferred; captions required.

Making Contact & Terms: Arrange a personal interview to show portfolio. Query with resume of credits along with business card, brochure, flyer or tearsheets to be kept on file for possible assignments. SASE. Reports in 2 weeks. NPI. "We pay a cover bonus." Pays on acceptance. Credit line given. Buys one-time rights. Simultaneous submissions OK.

Tips: In portfolio or samples, likes to "see about 20 slides showing photographer's use of lighting and ability to work with people. Know your intended market. Familiarize yourself with the magazine and keep abreast of how photos are used in the general magazine field."

IB (INDEPENDENT BUSINESS): AMERICA'S SMALL BUSINESS MAGAZINE, #211, 875 S. Westlake Blvd., Westlake Village CA 91361. (805)496-6156. FAX: (805)496-5469. Editor: Daniel Kehrer. Editorial Director: Don Phillipson. Bimonthly magazine. Emphasizes small business. All readers are small business owners throughout the US. Circ. 560,000. Estab. 1990. Sample copy $4. Photo guidelines free with SASE.

Needs: Uses 25-35 photos/issue; 100% supplied by freelancers. Needs photos of "exclusively people (men and women) who are small business owners. All pix are by assignment. No spec photos." Special photo needs include dynamic, unusual photos of offbeat businesses and their owners. Model and/or property release and photo captions required; include correct spelling on name, title, business name, location.

Making Contact & Terms: Query with resume of credits. Provide resume, business card, brochure, flyer or tearsheets to be kept on file for possible assignments. Keeps samples on file. SASE. Reports in 6 weeks. Pays $300/color inside photo; $300-700/day. Pays on acceptance. Credit line given. Buys first plus non-exclusive reprint rights.

Tips: "We want colorful, striking photos of small business owners that go well above-and-beyond the usual business magazine. Capture the essence of the business owner's 'native habitat.' "

ILLINOIS LEGAL TIMES, Dept. PM, Suite 1513, 222 Merchandise Mart Plaza, Chicago IL 60654. (312)644-4378. Associate Editor: Kelly Fox. Monthly trade publication, tabloid format. Covers law. Readers are Illinois-based lawyers of various ages and backgrounds. Circ. 17,600. Estab. 1987. Sample copy free with 10 × 13 SASE.

Needs: Uses 30-35 photos/issue; most supplied by freelancers. Needs photos of personalities in the profession.

Making Contact & Terms: Query with resume of credits. Provide resume, business card, brochure, flyer or tearsheets to be kept on file for possible assignment. SASE. Reports in 3 weeks. Pays $100/color or b&w cover photo; $35/b&w or color inside photo. Pays on 15th of month of cover date in which photos appear. Credit line given. Buys all rights; negotiable.

*INDIANA BUSINESS MAGAZINE, 6502 Westfield Blvd., Indianapolis IN 46220. (317)252-2737. FAX: (317)252-2738. Art Director: Andrew Roberts. Monthly magazine. Emphasizes general business in Indiana. Readers are high-level executives of Indiana companies. Circ. 30,000. Estab. 1957. Sample copy $2.

Needs: Uses 15-20 photos/issue; 5 supplied by freelancers. Needs photos of business executives or projects "on assignment basis only." Review photos purchased with accompanying ms only. Model/property release preferred. Captions required; include name and description of activity.

Making Contact & Terms: Query with resume of credits. Provide resume, business card, brochure, flyer or tearsheets to be kept on file for possible assignments. Keeps samples on file. Pays $200/color cover photo; $50/color or b&w inside photo. Pays on publication. Credit line given. Buys one-time rights and all rights; negotiable. Previously published work OK.

INDUSTRIAL PHOTOGRAPHY, PTN Publications, Dept. PM, 445 Broad Hollow Rd., Melville NY 11747. (516)845-2700. Publisher: George Schaub. Managing Editor: Steve Shaw. Monthly magazine. "Our emphasis is on the industrial photographer who produces images (still, cine, video) for a company or organization (including industry, military, government, medical, scientific, educational, institutions, R&D facilities, etc.)." Circ. 46,000. Free sample copy and writer's/photo guidelines.

Needs: All mss and photos must relate to the needs of industrial photographers. Photos purchased with accompanying ms. Seeks mss that offer technical or general information of value to industrial photographers, including applications, techniques, case histories of in-plant departments, etc. Captions and releases required.

Making Contact & Terms: Query with story/photo suggestion. Provide letter of inquiry and samples to be kept on file for possible future assignments. Uses 4×5, 5×7 or 8×10 glossy b&w and color prints or 35mm transparencies; allows other kinds of photos. SASE. Reports in 1 month. Pays $150 minimum/ms, including all photos and other illustrations. Pays on publication. Credit line given. Buys first North American serial rights except photo with text.

Tips: Trend toward "photo-text packages only." In samples wants to see "technical ability, graphic depiction of subject matter and unique application of technique." To break in, "link up with a writer" if not already a writer as well as photographer.

INDUSTRIAL SAFETY AND HYGIENE NEWS, Dept. PM, 1 Chilton Way, Radnor PA 19089. (215)964-4057. Editor: Dave Johnson. Monthly magazine. Emphasizes industrial safety and health for safety and health management personnel in over 36,000 large industrial plants (primarily manufacturing). Circ. 60,000. Free sample copy.

Needs: Occasionally use freelance photography for front covers. Magazine is tabloid size, thus front cover photos must be powerful and graphic with the dramatic impact of a poster.

Making Contact & Terms: Send material by mail for consideration. Uses color, 35mm and $2\frac{1}{4} \times 2\frac{1}{4}$ transparencies. Photographer should request editorial schedule and sample of publication. SASE. Reports in 2 weeks. Pays $300-400/color photo. Credit line given. Pays on publication. Buys all rights on a work-for-hire basis. Previously published work OK.

IN-PLANT PRINTER AND ELECTRONIC PUBLISHER, Dept. PM, P.O. Box 1387, Northbrook IL 60065. (708)564-5940. Editor: Andrea Cody. Bimonthly. Emphasizes "in-plant printing; print and graphic shops housed, supported, and serving larger companies and organizations and electronic publishing applications in those locations." Readers are management and production personnel of such shops. Circ. 41,000. Sample copy $5; free photo guidelines with SASE.

Needs: Uses about 30-35 photos/issue. Needs "working/shop photos, atmosphere, interesting equipment shots, how-to." Model release required; captions preferred.

Making Contact & Terms: Query with samples or with list of stock photo subjects. Send b&w and color (any size or finish) prints; 35mm, $2\frac{1}{4} \times 2\frac{1}{4}$, 4×5, 8×10 slides, b&w and color contact sheet or b&w and color negatives by mail for consideration. SASE. Reports in 1 month. Pays $200 maximum/ b&w or color cover photo; $25 maximum/b&w or color inside photo; and $200 maximum for text/ photo package. Pays on publication. Credit line given. Buys one-time rights with option for future use. Previously published work OK "if previous publication is indicated."

Tips: "Good photos of a case study—such as a printshop, in our case—can lead us to doing a follow-up story by phone and paying more for photos. Photographer should be able to bring out the hidden or overlooked design elements in graphic arts equipment." Trends include artistic representation of common objects found in-plant—equipment, keyboard, etc.

INSTANT AND SMALL COMMERCIAL PRINTER, P.O. Box 1387, Northbrook IL 60065. (708)564-5940. FAX: (708)564-8361. Editor: Stephanie Riefe. Published 10 times/year. Emphasizes the "instant and retail printing industry." Readers are owners, operators and managers of instant and smaller commercial (less than 20 employees) print shops. Circ. 55,000. Estab. 1982. Sample copy $3; photo guidelines free with SASE.

Needs: Uses about 15-20 photos/issue. Needs "working/shop photos, atmosphere, interesting equipment shots, some how-to." Model release required; captions preferred.
Making Contact & Terms: Interested in receiving work from newer, lesser-known photographers. Query with samples or with list of stock photo subjects or send b&w and color (any size or finish) prints; 35mm, 2¼×2¼, 4×5 or 8×10 slides; b&w and color contact sheet or b&w and color negatives by mail for consideration. SASE. Reports in 1 month. Pays $300 maximum/b&w and color cover photo; $50 maximum/b&w and color inside photo; $200 maximum for text/photo package. Pays on publication. Credit line given. Buys one-time rights with option for future use; negotiable. Previously published work OK "if previous publication is indicated."

THE INSTRUMENTALIST, 200 Northfield Rd., Northfield IL 60093. (708)446-5000. FAX: (708)446-6263. Senior Editor: Ann Rohner. Monthly magazine. Emphasizes instrumental music education. Readers are school band and orchestra directors and performers. Circ. 22,500. Estab. 1946. Sample copies $2.50.
Needs: Buys 1-5 photos/issue, mostly color. Needs headshots and human interest photos. "All photos should deal with instrumental music in some way." Especially needs photos for Photo Essay section.
Making Contact & Terms: Send unsolicited photos by mail for consideration. Uses 5×7 or 8×10 b&w and color glossy prints; 35mm and 2¼×2¼ transparencies. Vertical format preferred. SASE. Reports in 2-4 weeks. Pays $15-25/photo. Pays on publication. Credit line given. Buys all rights.
Tips: Request sample copy to review. "We look for shots that capture a natural expression of a player or that zoom in on an instrument to show it in a new perspective. We receive more marching band shots than we can use. We are always looking for closeups of people or classical instruments (no rock or folk instruments). Be sure to take into account logo placement, vertical format and room for cropping. The cover and an occasional inside shot come from assignments. Many covers are provided by freelancers introducing themselves to us for the first time."

INSURANCE WEEK, Dept. PM, Suite 3029, 1001 Fourth Ave. Plaza, Seattle WA 98154. (206)624-6965. Editor: Richard Rambeck. Weekly magazine. Emphasizes timely news for property/casualty insurance industry. Readers are "typically middle-aged male insurance agents or executives." Circ. 9,200. Sample copy free with 9×12 SAE and 3 first-class stamps.
Needs: Uses 1-2 photos/issue; number supplied by freelance photographers varies. Needs "shots of newsmakers, legislators, important meetings, etc. Example: The President addressing national insurance convention." Purchases photos with accompanying ms only. Especially needs more photos of West Coast conventions and legislative hearings. Photo captions required.
Making Contact & Terms: Provide resume and business card. Unsolicited material not returned. Reports in 2 weeks. Pays $25/b&w cover photo or $50-200/photo/text package. Pays on acceptance. Credit line given. Buys one-time rights. Simultaneous submissions OK.
Tips: "Our needs are almost always hard-news related. Good quality b&w. Send letter first—if interested, I'll answer."

JEMS, the Journal of Emergency Medical Services, Dept. PM, P.O. Box 2789, Carlsbad CA 92018. (619)431-9797. Art Director: Kathy Bush. Publication for Ashbeams, NFNA, NFPA. Monthly journal. Emphasizes emergency medical services. Readers are paramedics, emergency physicians, flight nurses, administrators. Circ. 30,000. Estab. 1980. Sample copy free with 10×12 SAE and $2 postage.
Needs: Uses about 6-10 photos/issue; 5-8 supplied by freelance photographers. Needs photos of paramedics in action. Special needs include comunications/extrications, water injuries, hazardous material responses. Model release and captions required.
Making Contact & Terms: Query with samples. Query with list of stock photo subjects. Do not call! Also, don't send originals. SASE. Reports in 1 month. Pays $50-75/b&w cover photo; $150/color cover photo; $25-35/b&w inside photo; and $50-75/color inside photo. Pays on publication. Credit line given. Buys one-time or first North American serial rights.
Tips: "Photos most often published show pre-hospital workers involved in some form of *patient care*. (We do *not* need pictures of smashed cars). Send dupes or originals for our stock files. Photos are selected on quality of image and subject matter needs of each issue." Also publishes *Rescue* magazine(see index)—bimonthly; Circ. 25,000.

The First Markets Index preceding the General Index in the back of this book provides the names of those companies/publications interested in receiving work from newer, lesser-known photographers.

JOBBER RETAILER MAGAZINE, Dept. PM, P.O. Box 3599, Akron OH 44309. (216)867-4401. Editor: Mike Mavrigian. Emphasizes "automotive aftermarket." Readers are "wholesalers, manufacturers, retail distributors of replacement parts." Monthly. Circ. 36,000. Sample copy free with 11 × 14 SAE and $1 postage.
Needs: Uses about 3-20 photos/issue; often needs freelance photographers. Needs automotive feature shots; exterior and interior of auto parts stores. Model release and captions preferred.
Making Contact & Terms: Provide resume, business card, brochure, flyer or tearsheets to be kept on file for possible future assignments. Does not return unsolicited material. Reporting time varies. Pays $50-150/b&w photo; $75-200/color photo. Pays on publication. Credit line given. Buys various rights—"generally all rights." Simultaneous submissions and previously published work OK.
Tips: "Let us know *who* and *where* you are."

♣**THE JOURNAL**, Addiction Research Foundation, 33 Russell St., Toronto, ON M5S 2S1 Canada. (416)964-9235. FAX: (416)595-6036. Editor: Anne MacLennan. Managing Editor: Elda Hauschildt. Monthly tabloid. Readers are professionals in the alcohol and drug abuse field: doctors, teachers, social workers, enforcement officials and government officials. Circ. 12,000. Estab. 1972. Free sample copy and photo guidelines.
Needs: Buys 4-10 photos/issue. Photos relating to alcohol and other drug abuse and smoking. No posed shots. Model release and captions required.
Making Contact & Terms: Send photos or contact sheet for consideration. Send 5 × 7 b&w glossy prints. Not copyrighted. Reports "ASAP." Pays $25 minimum/photo. Pays on publication.
Tips: "We are looking for action shots, street scenes, people of all ages and occupations. Shots should not appear to be posed."

JOURNAL OF EXTENSION, Dept. PM, 432 N. Lake St., Madison WI 53706. (608)262-1974. Assistant Editor: Colleen L. Schuh. Quarterly journal. A professional journal for adult educators. Readers are adult educators, extension personnel. Circ. 12,000. Estab. 1963.
Needs: Uses 1 cover photo/issue; supplied by freelancers. "Each issue we try to highlight the lead article, so the subject matter varies each time." Model release required.
Making Contact & Terms: Send 4 × 6 or 5 × 7 b&w prints by mail for consideration. Call to check on current needs. SASE. Reports in 1 month. Pays $75-100/b&w cover photo. Pays on acceptance. Credit line given. Buys one-time rights.

*JOURNAL OF PROPERTY MANAGEMENT, 7th Floor, 430 N. Michigan Ave., Chicago IL 60611. (312)329-6058. Managing Editor: Marilyn Evans. Bimonthly magazine. Emphasizes real estate management. Readers are mid- and upper-level managers of investment real estate. Circ. 19,600. Estab. 1934. Sample copy free with SASE. Photo guidelines available.
Needs: Uses 6 photos/issue; 50% supplied by freelancers. Needs photos of buildings, building operations and office interaction. Model/property release preferred.

JOURNAL OF PSYCHOACTIVE DRUGS, Dept. PM, 409 Clayton St., San Francisco CA 94117. (415)565-1904. Editor: Jeffrey H. Novey. Quarterly. Emphasizes "psychoactive substances (both legal and illegal)." Readers are "professionals (primarily health) in the drug abuse treatment field." Circ. 1,400. Estab. 1967.
Needs: Uses 1 photo/issue; supplied by freelancers. Needs "full-color abstract, surreal, avant garde or computer graphics."
Making Contact & Terms: Query with samples. Send 4 × 6 color prints or 35mm slides by mail for consideration. SASE. Reports in 2 weeks. Pays $100/color cover photo. Pays on publication. Credit line given. Buys one-time rights. Simultaneous submissions and previously published work OK.

JOURNAL OF PSYCHOSOCIAL NURSING, Dept. PM, 6900 Grove Rd., Thorofare NJ 08086. (609)848-1000. FAX: (609)853-5491. Editor: Dr. Shirley Smoyak. Photo Editor: Mary Jo Krey. Monthly magazine. Covers psychosocial nursing (psychiatric/mental health). Circ. 15,000. Estab. 1962.
Needs: Uses 1 photo/issue; supplied by freelancer. Needs photos of people, abstract concepts. Model release required.
Making Contact & Terms: Query with samples and list of stock photo subjects. Provide resume, business card, brochure, flyer or tearsheets to be kept on file for possible future assignments. SASE. Reports in 1 month. Pays $50-200. Pays on publication. Credit line given. Buys one-time rights. Previously published work OK.
Tips: In samples, wants to see "imagination, unique perspective and knowledge of mental illness." Sees trend toward showing "patient *usually* in sympathetic light." Accordingly, "use a unique perspective, not a trite picture of patients in a mental hospital."

KALIS' SHOPPING CENTER LEASING DIRECTORY, Suite 308, 4900 Leesburg Pike, Alexandria VA 22302-1104. (703)578-3051. FAX: (703)578-3057. Publisher: Nicholas Kalis. Biannual directory. Circ. 1,100. Estab. 1988. Sample copy $25.
Needs: Uses 1 photo/issue. Reviews photos with or without ms. Model/property release required.
Making Contact & Terms: Interested in receiving work from newer, lesser-known photographers. Query with list of stock photo subjects. Reports in 1 month. Pays $50/b&w; $100-300/photo/text package. Credit line given. Buys all rights; negotiable. Simultaneous submissions OK.
Tips: Wants to see examples of shopping center photos. Will accept commission split with photographers who can sell developers on enhanced listings with photos.

LLAMAS MAGAZINE, P.O.Box 100, Herald CA 95638. (916)448-1668. Assistant Editor: Susan Ley. Publication of The International Camelid Journal. Magazine published 8 times/year. Emphasizes llamas, alpacas, vicunas, gunacos and camels. Readers are llama and alpaca owners and ranchers. Circ. 5,500. Estab. 1979. Sample copy $5.75. Photo guidelines free with SASE.
Needs: Uses 30-50 photos/issue; 100% supplied by freelancers. Wants to see "any kind of photo with llamas, alpacas, camels in it. Always need good verticals for the cover. Always need good action shots." Model release and photo captions required.
Making Contact & Terms: Send unsolicited print (b&w or color 35mm) or 35mm transparencies by mail for consideration. Provide resume, business card, brochure, flyer or tearsheets to be kept on file for possible assignments. Reports in 1-2 weeks. Pays $100/color cover photo; $25/color inside photo; $15/b&w inside photo. Pays on publication. Credit line given. Buys one-time rights. Simultaneous submissions and previously published work OK.
Tips: "You must have a good understanding of llamas and alpacas to submit photos to us. It's a very specialized market. Our rates are modest, but our publication is a very slick 4-color magazine and it's a terrific vehicle for getting your work into circulation. We are willing to give photographers a lot of free tearsheets for their portfolios to help publicize their work."

MAINTENANCE SUPPLIES (Including *Building Services Contractor*), Dept. PM, 445 Broad Hollow Rd., Melville NY 11747. Phone: (516)845-2700. FAX: (516)845-7109. Editor: Susan Brady. Monthly magazine. Covers news of maintenance/janitorial supply distribution trade. Circ. 21,000. Sample copies free with 9×12 SASE.
Needs: Typically needs photos of floors, carpets, bathrooms, paper products (towels, etc), plastic products, warehouses and scenics. Especially wants to see photos of environments and restrooms in the coming year. Model/property release required. Photo captions preferred.
Making Contact & Terms: Send stock photo list. Send unsolicited photos, any size or format, by mail for consideration. Provide resume, business card, brochure, flyer or tearsheets to be kept on file for possible future assignments. Keeps samples on file. SASE. Reports in 2 weeks. Pays $200/color cover photo; $150-300/photo-text package; other payment negotiable. Pays on publication. Credit line given. Rights negotiable. Simultaneous submissions OK.

*MARINE BUSINESS JOURNAL, 1766 Bay Rd., Miami Beach FL 33139. (305)538-0700. FAX:(305)532-8657. Editorial Director: Andree Conrad. Bimonthly. Emphasizes recreational marine industry. Readers are people employed in the boating industry, mostly males, age 30-65. Sample copy $5. Photo guidelines free with SASE.
Needs: Uses 5-10 photos/issue supplied by freelancers. "Need photo stringers on-call nationwide for occasional event/product photography." Reviews photos with accompanying ms only. Model release required when appropriate. Photo captions required.
Making Contact & Terms: Query with resume of credits. Query with stock photo list. Provide resume, business card, brochure, flyer or tearsheets to be kept on file for possible assignments. Reports in 1 month. Pays $50/color inside photo; $25/b&w inside photo. Pays on publication. Credit line given. Buys one-time rights.
Tips: "There are too many photographers these days with SLRs."

*MARKETERS FORUM, 383 E. Main St., Centerport NY 11721. (516)754-5000. FAX: (516)754-0630. Publisher: Martin Stevens. Monthly magazine. Readers are entrepreneurs and retail store owners. Circ. 70,000. Estab. 1981. Sample copy $3.
Needs: Uses 3-6 photos/issue; 100% supplied by freelancers. "We publish trade magazines for retail variety goods stores and flea market vendors. Items include: jewelry, cosmetics, novelties, toys, etc. (five and dime type goods). We are interested in creative and abstract impressions—not straight-on product shots. Humor a plus" Model/property release required.
Making Contact & Terms: Send unsolicited photos by mail for consideration. Send color prints; 35mm, 4×5 transparencies. Does not keep samples on file. SASE. Reports in 1-2 weeks. Pays $75/color cover photo; $50/color inside photo. Pays on acceptance. Buys one-time rights. Simultaneous submissions and/or previously published work OK.

MD MAGAZINE, Dept. PM, 55 Fifth Ave., New York NY 10003. (212)989-2100. Picture Editor: Merrill Cason. Monthly magazine. Emphasizes the arts, science, medicine, history and travel; written with the readership (physicians) in mind. For medical doctors. Circ. 160,000.

Needs: A wide variety of photos dealing with history, art, literature, medical history, pharmacology, activities of doctors and sports. Also interested in photo essays. Single pictures require only captions. Picture stories require explanatory text, but not finished ms.

Making Contact & Terms: Arrange a personal interview to show a portfolio. Uses 8 × 10 b&w glossy prints, transparencies. SASE. Reports ASAP. Pays $75-100/¼ page of b&w photos; $150-180/¼ page of color photos; $1,000-1,500/photo-text package. Pays on publication. Simultaneous submissions and previously published work OK.

Tips: "Do not send unsolicited material. Call or write to arrange portfolio interview. Send 80-100 tightly edited slides in sheets or 20-25 prints."

*MEDICAL ECONOMICS MAGAZINE, 5 Paragon Ave., Montvale NJ 07645-1742. Editor: Stephen Murata. Photo Editor: Donna DeAngelis. Biweekly magazine. Emphasizes financial aspects of running a medical practice. Readers are physicians and financial specialists. Circ. 182,000.

Needs: Uses 5 photos/issue; 1-5 supplied by freelance photographers. Needs head and shoulders shots. Day-in-the-life-of shots, indoor and outdoor. Special needs include photos of doctors and their families, homes, and hobbies. Doctors interacting with/examining patients. Model release and captions required.

Making Contact & Terms: Provide resume, business card, flyer or tearsheets to be kept on file for possible assignments, "send to Donna DeAngelis, Art Administrator." Reports only if interested. NPI; negotiable. Pays on acceptance. Credit line given on contents page. Buys one-time rights. Previously published work OK.

Tips: Prefers to see medical and editorial photography, location shots, photomicrography, computer-generated images. "Don't be too pushy. Don't overprice yourself. A good photographer makes a good living."

*MEETING NEWS, 33 Floor, 1515 Broadway, New York NY 10036. (212)626-2227. FAX: (212)302-6273. Art Director: Tara Guild. Monthly tabloid. Emphasizes travel. Readers are male and female executives and staff, ages 35-60. Circ. 75,000. Estab. 1977. Sample copy free with 12 × 16 SASE.

Needs: Uses 20 photos/issue; 50% supplied by freelancers. Needs photos of travel and portraits. Model/property release preferred. Photo captions required.

Making Contact & Terms: Submit portfolio for review. Provide brochure, flyer or tearsheets to be kept on file for possible assignments. Does not keep samples on file. Cannot return material. Pays $600/b&w cover photo; $300/b&w inside photo; $200/color page rate. Pays on publication. Credit line given. Buys one-time rights. Rights negotiable.

Tips: Wants to see straight landscapes or humorous shots. "Portraits should be anything other than 'mug shots.' Don't do shots that look like advertisements. Use your imagination."

*MIDDLE EASTERN DANCER, P.O. Box 181572, Casselberry FL 32718. (407)831-3402. Managing Editor: Jeanette Spencer. Monthly magazine. Emphasizes Middle Eastern dance and culture. Readers are "mostly female, average age 40, but age isn't really a factor. All types of professions; dance is hobby and/or their second profession." Circ. 2500 +. Estab. 1979. Sample copy and photo guidelines free with 9 × 12 SAE and 4 first-class stamps.

Needs: Uses 10-30 photos/issue; most supplied by freelancers; no covers. Needs photos "relating only to the dance or Middle East culture—could be people, clothes, scenery, architecture, etc." Model release and captions required.

Making Contact & Terms: Interested in receiving work from newer, lesser-known photographers. Send unsolicited photos by mail for consideration: preferably b&w prints, any size; 35mm transparencies. SASE. Reports in 2 months. Pays $5/b&w inside photo. Pays on acceptance. Credit line given. Buys first N.A. serial rights. Simultaneous submissions and previously published work OK "as long as not to similiar trade publications."

Tips: Needs photos with "action, good view of subject and costume, if applicable. Avoid anything that dancers will hate you for. Our readership is largely dancers who love the art."

*MINORITY BUSINESS ENTREPRENEUR, 924 N. Market St., Inglewood CA 90302. (310)673-9398. FAX: (310)673-0170. Executive Editor: Jeanie Barnett. Bimonthly magazine. Emphasizes minority, small, disadvantaged businesses. Circ. 35,000. Estab. 1984. Sample copy free with 9½ × 12½ SASE and 5 first-class stamps. "We have editorial guidelines and calendar of upcoming issues available."

Needs: Uses 5-10 photos/issue. Needs "good shots for cover profiles and minority features of our entrepreneurs." Model release required. Photo captions preferred; include name, title and company of subject, and proper photo credit.

Making Contact & Terms: Query with resume of credits. Provide resume, business card, brochure, flyer or tearsheets to be kept on file for possible assigments. "Never submit unsolicited photos." SASE. Reports in 5 weeks. NPI; payment negotiable. Pays on publication. Credit line given. Buys first N.A. serial rights.
Tips: "We're starting to run color photos in our business owner profiles. We want pictures that capture them in the work environment. Especially interested in minority and women photographers working for us. Our cover is an oil painting composed from photos. It's important to have high quality b&ws with shadows on the face to translate easily to oils. Read our publication and have a good understanding of minority business issues. Never submit photos that have nothing to do with the magazine."

MODERN BAKING, Dept. PM, Suite 418, 2700 River Rd., Des Plaines IL 60018. (708)299-4430. Editor: Ed Lee. Monthly. Emphasizes on-premise baking, in supermarkets, foodservice establishments and retail bakeries. Readers are owners, managers and operators. Circ. 27,000. Estab. 1987. Sample copy for 9×12 SAE with $2.90 postage.
Needs: Uses 30 photos/issue; 1-2 supplied by freelancers. Needs photos of on-location photography in above-described facilities. Model release and captions preferred; include company name, location, contact name and telephone number.
Making Contact & Terms: Provide resume, business card, brochure, flyer or tearsheets to be kept on file for possible future assignments. SASE. Reports in 2 weeks. Pays $50 minimum; negotiable. Pays on acceptance. Credit line given. Buys all rights; negotiable.
Tips: Prefers to see "photos that would indicate person's ability to handle on-location, industrial photography."

MODERN OFFICE TECHNOLOGY, 1100 Superior Ave., Cleveland OH 44114. (216)696-7000. FAX: (216)696-7658. Editor: Lura K. Romei. Monthly magazine. Emphasizes office automation, data processing. Readers are middle and upper management and higher in companies of 100 or more employees. Circ. 150,000. Estab. 1957. Sample copy free with 11×14 SAE and 44¢ postage.
Needs: Uses 15 photos/issue; 3 supplied by freelancers. Needs office shots, office interiors, computers, concept shots of office automation and networking. Special photo needs: "any and all office shots are welcome." Model/property release preferred; captions required including non-model names, positions.
Making Contact & Terms: Provide resume, business card, brochure, flyer or tearsheets to be kept on file for possible future assignments. Reports in 3 weeks. Pays $500/color cover photo; $50-100/b&w and color inside photo. Pays on publication. Credit line given. Buys one-time rights.
Tips: "Good conceptual (not vendor-specific) material about the office and office supplies is hard to find. Crack that and you're in business." In reviewing a photographer's samples, looks for "imagination and humor."

MUSHING MAGAZINE, P.O. Box 149, Ester AK 99725. (907)479-0454. Publisher: Todd Hoener. Bimonthly magazine. Readers are dog drivers, all-season mushing enthusiasts, dog lovers, outdoor specialists, innovators and history lovers. Circ. 5,500. Estab. 1987. Sample copy $4 in US. Photo guidelines free with SASE.
Needs: Uses 15 photos/issue; most supplied by freelancers. Needs action photos: all-season and wilderness; also still and close-up photos: specific focus (sledding, carting, equipment, etc). Special photo needs include skijoring, feeding, caring for dogs, summer carting or packing, 1-3 dog-sledding and kids mushing. Model release preferred.
Making Contact & Terms: Send unsolicited photos by mail for consideration. Submit portfolio for review. Reports in 2 months. Pays $175 maximum/color cover photo; $150 maximum/color inside photo; $30 maximum/b&w inside photo. Pays on publication. Credit line given. Buys first N.A. serial rights and second reprint rights. Occasionally buys all rights; will negotiate.
Tips: Wants to see work that shows "the total mushing adventure/lifestyle from environment to dog house." To break in, one's work must show "simplicity, balance and harmony. Strive for unique, provocative shots that lure readers and publishers."

*THE MUSIC & COMPUTER EDUCATOR, 76 N. Broadway, Hicksville NY 11801. (516)681-2922. FAX: (516)681-2926. Art Director: Lorinda Sullivan. Monthly magazine. Emphasizes computer music education. Readers are music teachers/public and private. Circ. 20,000. Estab. 1989.
Needs: Uses 25-35 photos/issue; 2-5 supplied by freelancers. Needs photos of classrooms using music computer technology, children and teachers interacting. Model/property release preferred. Captions preferred.
Making Contact & Terms: Send unsolicited photos by mail for consideration. Send b&w prints; 35mm, 2¼×2¼, 4×5 transparencies. Provide resume, business card, brochure, flyer or tearsheets to be kept on file for possible assignments. Keeps samples on file. Reports in 1-2 weeks. Pays $300+/color cover photo; $200+/b&w cover photo; $250/color inside photo; $100/b&w inside photo. Pays on

Close-up

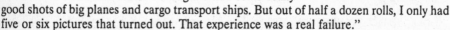

Ted S. Matthews
Corporate Photographer/Editor
Charlotte, North Carolina

Boy Scouts are supposed to live by their motto, "Be Prepared." But Ted Matthews was not prepared to see the handful of bad photographs he took years ago while on a scouting trip to Florida.

"It was a disaster," says Matthews, shaking his head as he recalled his first experience with a camera. "We stopped at air force and naval bases. I thought I had some really good shots of big planes and cargo transport ships. But out of half a dozen rolls, I only had five or six pictures that turned out. That experience was a real failure."

Now an award-winning photographer in Charlotte, North Carolina, Matthews says his photographic skills significantly improved once he learned to use a camera properly in journalism courses at Southern Illinois University. His passion for taking photos grew even more after he landed his first newspaper job in 1980 as a writer/photographer for the *Edwardsville Intelligencer.*

Matthews is a photographer and employee-communications manager at Springs Industries Inc. in nearby Fort Mill, South Carolina. He edits *The Springs Bulletin*, a monthly employee tabloid with 28,000 readers, and shoots most of the photos for the publication. Some, however, are assigned to a network of freelance photographers. To illustrate every issue, he looks for dramatic, unposed photos that tell a story.

"My style is almost strictly photojournalistic," says Matthews. "I prefer to shoot real-life situations. The most rewarding part of photography is capturing emotional moments, making something stop on film and to look at that over and over again."

Matthews excels at shooting candid photos of people, particularly those who work in the textile mills and on the manufacturing lines at Springs. He says that also is a skill he looks for in the freelance photographers he hires.

When it comes to shooting effective portraits, Matthews advises photographers to relate to their subjects, and read them well enough to determine if they are shy, cautious or untrusting. "When you come into most people's lives with a camera, they won't put down a welcome mat, but they won't close the door on you either," he says. "They're thinking, 'Oh, boy! I hope he takes my picture,' because everybody wants some attention.

"And then there are other people who simply won't tolerate it and you need to read that fairly quickly. Usually you can do that just by talking to them, identifying yourself and explaining what you're trying to do. I offer to give them a copy of the print later."

Portraits also work better when subjects are photographed in their natural environment. While shooting, move the camera around, rather than asking them to move for you, says Matthews.

Help your subjects relax by talking to them while you shoot, especially with head shots. "Talk to them about themselves, things that are going on," he says. "Depending on whether they have a sense of humor, you can joke with them."

If your subject still has trouble relaxing, put the camera down a few minutes. This tactic can help the person forget the photo for a moment and concentrate more on the conversation. Once your subject is more relaxed, start shooting, he says.

Since 1985, Matthews has received more than a dozen awards for his photographs, including a prestigious Gold Quill award from the International Association of Business Communicators. The group honored him in London for a photo he shot while at Duke Power Co. of a line employee painting a steel transmission tower 100 feet in the air.

"He had paint all over him, everywhere except his teeth," says Matthews. "We used the shot on the cover to illustrate a story on how Duke extends the life of its transmission towers by coating them with this heavy, rust-resistant paint. I shot very tight shots of him for about an hour in 90-degree heat."

Matthews believes the contest judges were impressed with the photo because it stirred an immediate reaction from viewers. That's one of the qualities he says an award-winning photo should have.

"There should be something about it that makes the viewer react first," says Matthews. "I think you get immediate impact from the Hurricane Hugo picture I took. You may not know what caused the wreckage, but you see a car destroyed, and it's pretty dramatic. Besides that, the best photos should also have all of the technical aspects covered, such as subject matter and composition."

When Matthews makes assignments to freelance photographers, he makes it clear that he doesn't want them to shoot the trite check-passing pictures, what some call the "grip 'n' grins." As he explains, "If I have a grip 'n' grin safety picture of something, I simply won't use it. Grip 'n' grins generally are a waste of space because in most cases you can give the credit where it's due in words, and then use that space for a better photograph."

Matthews says he usually stops and shoots a few frames of check-passings or group shots, and he always sends copies to plant managers who ask for them. But he prefers not to bore readers with such photos in print. Instead, he's found a better way to cover such events. It's a technique he encourages for photographers who are trying to make sales with company publication editors.

"Before they do the check-passing, I'll shoot the people laughing or talking or patting someone on the back," he said. "I'll shoot pictures before and after the event, showing some warmth and camaraderie between the people. I try to show what's really going on."

— *Tyler Cox*

In 1989 Ted Matthews surveyed the ugly scene created by the awesome power of hurricane Hugo. Matthews was researching a story on how the storm affected the operations of Springs Industries Inc., in Lancaster, South Carolina, when he came upon this site with a car sandwiched like an accordian by a falling billboard.

© Ted Matthews

publication. Credit line given. Buys one-time rights. Simultaneous submissions and previously published work OK.

Tips: "Looking for someone who can work on location in music classrooms with computers and show interesting composition."

NATIONAL BUS TRADER, 9698 W. Judson Rd., Polo IL 61064-9049. (815)946-2341. FAX: (815)946-2347. Editor: Larry Plachno. "The Magazine of Bus Equipment for the United States and Canada—covers mainly integral design buses in the United States and Canada." Readers are bus owners, commercial bus operators, bus manufacturers, bus designers. Circ. 5,600. Estab. 1977. Sample copy free (no charge—just write or call).

Needs: Uses about 30 photos/issue; 22 supplied by freelance photographers. Needs photos of "buses; interior, exterior, under construction, in service." Special needs include "photos for future feature articles and conventions our own staff does not attend."

Making Contact & Terms: "Query with specific lists of subject matter that can be provided and mention whether accompanying mss are available." SASE. Reports in 1 week. Pays $3-5/b&w photo; $100-3,000/photo/text package. Pays on acceptance. Credit line given. Buys rights "depending on our need and photographer." Simultaneous submissions and previously published work OK.

Tips: "We don't need samples, merely a list of what freelancers can provide in the way of photos or ms. Write and let us know what you can offer and do. We often use freelance work. We also publish *Bus Tours Magazine*—a bimonthly which uses many photos but not many from freelancers; *The Bus Equipment Guide*—infrequent, which uses many photos; and *The Official Bus Industry Calendar*—annual full-color calendar of bus photos. We also publish historical railroad books and are looking for historical photos on midwest interurban lines and railroads. Due to publication of historical railroad books, we are purchasing many historical photos. In photos looks for subject matter appropriate to current or pending article or book. Send a list of what is available with specific photos, locations, bus/interurban company and fleet number."

NATIONAL FISHERMAN, 120 Tillson Ave., Rockland ME 04841. (207)594-6222. FAX: (207)594-8978. Art Director: Marydale Abernathy. Monthly magazine. Emphasizes commercial fishing, boat building, marketing of fish, fishing techniques and fishing equipment. For amateur and professional boatbuilders, commercial fishermen, armchair sailors, bureaucrats and politicians. Circ. 50,000. Estab. 1960. Free sample copy with 11 × 15 SAE and $2 postage.

Needs: Buys 5-8 photo stories monthly; buys 4-color action cover photo monthly. Action shots of commercial fishing, work boats, traditional sailing fishboats, boat building, deck gear. No recreational, caught-a-trout photos.

Making Contact & Terms: Query. Reports in 8 weeks. Pays $10-25/inside b&w print; $250/color cover transparency. Pays on publication.

Tips: "We seldom use photos unless accompanied by feature stories or short articles—i.e., we don't run a picture for its own sake. Even those accepted for use in photo essays must tell a story—both in themselves and through accompanying cutline information. However, we do use single, stand-alone photos for cover shots. We need sharp b&w glossy photos—5 × 7s are fine. For cover, please send 35mm transparencies; dupes are acceptable. We want high-quality b&w images for inside that will hold detail on newsprint. Send slide samples."

NATION'S BUSINESS, U.S. Chamber of Commerce, 1615 H St. NW, Washington DC 20062. (202)463-5447. Photo Editor: Laurence L. Levin. Assistant Photo Editor: Frances Borchardt. Monthly. Emphasizes business, especially small business. Readers are managers, upper management and business owners. Circ. 850,000. Sample copy free with 9 × 12 SASE.

Needs: Uses about 30-40 photos/issue; 65% supplied by freelancers. Needs portrait-personality photos, business related-oriented-theme pictures relating to the story. Foreign scenics. Model release preferred; captions required.

Making Contact & Terms: Arrange a personal interview to show portfolio. Submit portfolio for review. SASE. Reports in 3 weeks. Pays $200/b&w or color inside photo; $175-300/day. Pays on publication. Credit line given. Buys one-time rights.

Tips: In reviewing a portfolio, "we look for the photographer's ability to light, taking a static situation and turning it into a spontaneous, eye-catching and informative picture."

NEW ENGLAND BUSINESS, Suite 1120, 20 Park Plaza, Boston MA 02116. (617)426-6677. FAX: (617)426-1122. Contact: Art Director. Monthly magazine. Emphasizes businesses based in New England. Readers are male and female business owners and executives. Estab. 1981. Sample copy free with 9 × 12 SASE.

Needs: Uses 20-25 photos/issue; 100% supplied by freelancers. Needs portraits of business people in their environments. Model release preferred; photo captions required.

Making Contact & Terms: Arrange personal interview to show portfolio. Provide resume, business card, brochure, flyer or tearsheets to be kept on file for possible assignments. Keeps samples on file. SASE. Pays $1,000/color cover photo; $500/color inside photo; $100/b&w inside photo. Pays on publication. Credit line given. Buys all rights; negotiable.

Tips: Looks for "business people who don't look stiff or plastic. Eye-catching views of what can be deadly-dull situations."

NEW METHODS, P.O. Box 22605, San Francisco CA 94122-0605. (415)664-3469. Art Director: Ronald S. Lippert, AHT. Monthly. Emphasizes veterinary personnel, animals. Readers are veterinary professionals and interested consumers. Circ. 5,600. Estab. 1976. Sample copy $2; photo guidelines free with SASE.

Needs: Uses 12 photos/issue; 2 supplied by freelance photographers. Assigns 95% of photos. Needs animal, wildlife and technical photos. Most work is b&w. Model and property releases preferred; captions preferred.

Making Contact & Terms: Interested in receiving work from newer, lesser-known photographers. Arrange a personal interview to show portfolio. Query with resume of credits, samples or list of stock photo subjects. Provide resume, business card, brochure, flyer or tearsheets to be kept on file for possible assignments. SASE. Reports in 2 months. Payment is rare, negotiable; will barter. Pays on publication. Credit line given. Buys one-time rights. Simultaneous submissions and previously published work OK.

Tips: Prefers to see "technical photos (human working with animal(s) or animal photos (*not cute*)" in a portfolio or samples. On occasion, needs photographer for shooting new products and local area conventions.

911 MAGAZINE, P.O. Box 11788, Santa Ana CA 92711. (714)544-7776. FAX: (714)838-9233. Editor: Alan Burton. Trade publication. Bimonthly magazine. Emphasizes emergency response—i.e.: police, fire, paramedic, dispatch, utilities, etc. Readers are ages 20-65, mostly male. Circ. 20,000. Estab. 1988. Sample copy free with 9 × 12 SASE and 7 first-class stamps. Photo guidelines free with SASE.

Needs: Uses up to 25 photos/issue; 75% supplied by freelance photographers. "From the Field" department photos are needed of incidents involving two or more emergency agencies in action from law enforcement, fire suppression, paramedics, dispatch, etc., showing proper techniques and attire. Accompany with captions describing incident location by city and state, agencies involved, duration, dollar cost, fatalities and injuries." Model release and photo captions preferred.

Making Contact & Terms: Query with list of stock photo subjects; send unsolicited photos by mail for consideration; provide resume, business card, brochure, flyer or tearsheets to be kept on file for possible assignments. Uses 35mm, 2¼ × 2¼, 4 × 5, 8 × 10 glossy contacts, b&w or color prints; 35mm, 2¼ × 2¼, 4 × 5, 8 × 10 transparencies. SASE. Reports in 3 weeks. Pays $100-200/color cover photo; $50-150/b&w cover photo; $25-75/color inside photo; $20-50/b&w inside photo. Pays on publication. Credit line given. Rights are negotiable. Simultaneous submissions and previously published work OK.

Tips: "We need photos for unillustrated cover stories and features appearing in each issue. Topics include rescue, traffic, communications (dispatch), training, stress, media relations, crime prevention, etc. Calendar available. Assignments possible."

THE NORTHERN LOGGER & TIMBER PROCESSOR, Dept. PM, P.O. Box 69, Old Forge NY 13420. Editor: Eric A. Johnson. Publisher: George F. Mitchell. Monthly magazine. Emphasizes methods, machinery and manufacturing as related to forestry. For loggers, timberland managers and processors of primary forest products in the territory from Maine to Minnesota and from Missouri to West Virginia. Circ. 14,000. Free sample copy.

Needs: Photos purchased with accompanying ms. Buys 3-4 photos/issue. Head shot, how-to, nature, photo essay/photo feature, product shot; mostly b&w. Captions required. "The magazine carries illustrated stories on new methods and machinery for forest management, logging, timber processing, sawmilling and manufacture of other products of northern forests."

Making Contact & Terms: Query with resume of credits. Uses 5 × 7 or 8 × 10 b&w glossy prints; 35mm color transparencies. Vertical format preferred for cover. Copyrighted. SASE. Reports in 2 weeks. Pays $15-20/b&w photo; $35-40/color photo; $35-40/cover photo; $100-250 for text/photo package. Pays on publication. Credit line given. Previously published work OK.

Tips: "Send for a copy of our magazine and look it over before sending in photographs. We're open to new ideas, but naturally are most likely to buy the types of photos that we normally run. An interesting caption can mean as much as a good picture. Often it's an interdependent relationship."

OCEANUS, Woods Hole Oceanographic Institution, Woods Hole MA 02543. (508)457-2000 ext. 2386. FAX: (508)457-2182. Editor: Vicky Cullen. Quarterly. The purpose of *Oceanus* is to serve as a forum for international perspectives on our ocean environment. Circ. 15,000. Estab. 1952.

Needs: Uses about 60 photos/issue; 5-25% supplied by freelancers. "All four issues per year are thematic, covering marine subjects." Captions required.
Making Contact & Terms: Query with resume of credits or with list of stock photo subjects. Provide resume, business card, brochure, flyer or tearsheets to be kept on file for possible assignments. Unsolicited material is not returned. Prefer to trade/negotiate photo use in exchange for caption credits and possible complimentary advertising to our parallel key source market as *Oceanus* is part of a nonprofit research insitition with limited funding.
Tips: "The magazine uses b&w and color photos. Color slides are preferred. Send us high-contrast b&w or color slides with strong narrative element (scientists at work, visible topographic, atmospheric alterations or events). Increasingly we are broadening our scope to cover all aspects of the ocean, from their scientific to artistic perspectives."

OCULAR SURGERY NEWS, Dept. PM, 6900 Grove Rd., Thorofare NJ 08086. (609)848-1000. Editor: Keith Croes. Biweekly newspaper. Emphasizes ophthalmology, medical and eye care. Readers are ophthalmologists in the U.S. Circ. 18,000. Sample copy free with 9 × 12 SASE and 10 first-class stamps.
Needs: Uses 30 photos/issue; less than 10% supplied by freelancers. Needs photos of medical subjects—tie in with special issues. Plans 6 special issues each year; contact for needs. Model release and photo captions preferred.
Making Contact & Terms: Query with list of stock photo subjects. Provide resume, business card, brochure, flyer or tearsheets to be kept on file for possible assignments. SASE. Reports in 2 weeks. Pays $300/color cover photo, $150/color inside photo and $150-250/day. Pays on publication. Credit line given. Buys one-time rights.

✹OH&S CANADA, Dept. PM, 1450 Don Mills Rd., Don Mills ON M3B 2X7 Canada. (416)445-6641. FAX: (416)442-2200. Art Director: Catherine Goard. Bimonthly magazine. Emphasizes occupational health and safety. Readers are health and safety professionals, mostly male, median age of 40. Circ. 7,750. Estab. 1985.
Needs: Uses 3 photos/issue; 70% supplied by freelancers. Primarily uses photos of business, industry on-site, etc. Model release and photo captions preferred.
Making Contact & Terms: Provide resume, business card, brochure, flyer or tearsheets to be kept on file for possible assignments. Pays $800-1,000/color cover photo; $400-600/color inside photo. "Rates of payment vary quite substantially according to photographer experience." Pays on acceptance. Credit line given. Buys one-time rights.
Tips: In portfolio or samples, looking for "industry shots."

OREGON BUSINESS MAGAZINE, Dept. PM, Suite 407, 921 S.W. Morrison, Portland OR 97205. (503)223-0304. Production Manager: Laura Tourin. Monthly. Emphasizes business features. Readers are business executives. Circ. 20,000. Sample copy free with SASE and 90¢ postage.
Needs: Uses about 15 photos/issue; 5 supplied by freelancers. "Usually photos must tie to a story. Query any ideas." Model release and captions required.
Making Contact & Terms: NPI.
Tips: "Query first, also get hooked up with an Oregon writer. Must tie photos to an Oregon business story."

PACIFIC BOATING ALMANAC, Dept. PM, P.O. Box 341668, Los Angeles CA 90034. (213)287-2830. Contact: Peter L. Griffes. Annual publication. Emphasizes West Coast Boating Almanac. Readers are "boat owners who cruise the coast." Circ. 20,000. Estab. 1965. Sample copy $16.95.
Needs: Uses 100 photos/issue; 30% supplied by freelancers. Needs only boating-related photos of the boats and marinas—as well as coastline and aerial scenes. Photo captions preferred.
Making Contact & Terms: Send unsolicited color prints by mail for consideration. Keeps samples on file. SASE. Reports in 3 weeks. Pays $100-200/color cover photo; $20-50/b&w inside photo. Pays on acceptance. Credit line given. Buys all rights "only for use in the Almanac." Simultaneous submissions and previously published work OK.
Tips: Wants to see crisp images.

PACIFIC FISHING, 1515 NW 51st, Seattle WA 98107. (206)789-5333. FAX: (206)784-5545. Editor: Steve Shapiro. Monthly magazine. Emphasizes commercial fishing on West Coast—California to Alaska. Readers are 80% owners of fishing operations, primarily male, ages 25-55; 20% processors, marketers and suppliers. Circ. 11,000. Estab. 1979. Sample copy for 11 × 14 SAE and $2 postage. Photo guidelines free with SASE.
Needs: Uses 15 photos/issue; 10 supplied by freelancers. Needs photos of *all* aspects of commercial fisheries on West Coast of US and Canada. Special needs include "high-quality, active photos and slides of fishing boats and fishermen working their gear, dockside shots and the processing of seafood." Model/property release preferred. Photo captions required that include names and locations.

Making Contact & Terms: Query with resume of credits. Query with list of stock photo subjects. Keeps samples on file. SASE. Reports in 2-4 weeks. Pays $150/color cover photo; $50-100/color inside photo; $25-50/b&w inside photo. Pays on publication. Credit line given. Buys one-time rights, first N.A. serial rights. Previously published work OK "if not previously published in a competing trade journal."
Tips: Wants to see "clear, close-up and active photos."

PEDIATRIC ANNALS, 6900 Grove Rd., Thorofare NJ 08086. (609)848-1000. Editor: Mary L. Jerrell. Monthly journal. Emphasizes "the pediatrics profession." Readers are practicing pediatricians. Circ. 36,000. Sample copy free with SASE.
Needs: Uses 1-4 photos/issue; all supplied by freelance photographers. Needs photos of "children in medical settings, some with adults." Written release required; captions preferred.
Making Contact & Terms: Query with samples. Provide resume, business card, brochure, flyer or tearsheets to be kept on file for possible future assignments. Reports in 6 weeks. Pays $350/color cover photo; $25/inside photo; $50/color inside photo. Pays on publication. Credit line given. Buys all rights. Simultaneous submissions and previously published work OK.

*PET BUSINESS, P.O. Box 2300, Miami FL 33243. Editor: Karen Payne. Monthly news magazine for pet industry professionals. Circ. 17,000. Sample copy $3. Guidelines free with SASE.
Needs: Photos of well-groomed pet animals (preferably purebred) of any age in a variety of situations. Identify subjects. Also, news/action shots related to the pet trade.
Making Contact & Terms: Buys all rights. Payment upon publication; $10 for b&w glossy, $20 for color print or transparency. Credit line given. Submit photos for consideration. Reports within 3 months with SASE.
Tips: Uncluttered background. Portrait-style always welcome. Close-ups best. No humans in photo! News/action shots if timely.

*PETROGRAM, 209 Office Plaza, Tallahassee FL 32301. (904)877-5178. FAX: (904)877-5864. Editor: Tara Boyter. Association publication. Monthly magazine. Emphasizes the wholesale petroleum industry. Readers are predominantly male, increasingly female, ages 30-60. Circ. 700. Estab. mid-1970s. Sample copy free with 9 × 12 SASE and 4 first-class stamps.
Needs: Uses 3-15 photos/issue; 1 supplied by freelancer. Needs photos of petroleum equipment, convenience store settings, traffic situations and environmental protection (Florida specific). Reviews photos with or without a manuscript. Model/property release preferred. Captions preferred; include location and date.
Making Contact & Terms: Submit portfolio for review. Query with stock photo list. Send unsolicited photos by mail for consideration. Provide resume, business card, brochure, flyer or tearsheets to be kept on file for possible assignments. Send 5 × 7, 8 × 10 b&w or color glossy prints. Keeps samples on file. SASE. Reports in 3 weeks. Pays $100/color cover photo; $75/b&w cover photo; $50/color inside photo; $25/b&w inside photo. Pays on publication. Credit line given. Rights negotiable.

PHOTO ELECTRONIC IMAGING, (formerly *Photomethods*), 1090 Executive Way, Des Plaines IL 60018. (708)299-8161. FAX: (708)299-2685. Editor-in-Chief: Kimberly Brady. Senior Editor: Mike Ballai. Art Director: Debbie Todd. Monthly magazine. Emphasizes industrial imagemaking by the in-house (captive) visual communicator and corporate/commercial photographer. Covers all media of visual communications including traditional silver-halide still and motion pictures, still and motion video, audiovisuals, computergraphics, etc. Readers work in industry, military, government, medicine, scientific research, evidence, police departments. Circ. 55,000. Estab. 1957. Photo guidelines with SASE.
Needs: Images must relate to some aspect of "industrial" imaging. Model release and captions required (include technical shooting details).
Making Contact & Terms: Query with resume of credits, samples or dupe photos for consideration. Original photos or slides sent at contributor's risk. Uses glossy, unmounted b&w prints. Also uses color prints or any size transparencies. SASE. Reports in 5 weeks. Pays $250/color cover; NPI for b&w photos. pays on publication. Credit line given. Buys one-time rights for covers.

PIPELINE AND UTILITIES CONSTRUCTION, P.O. Box 22267, Houston TX 77227. (713)662-0676. FAX: (713)722-0676. Editor: Oliver Klinger. Monthly. Emphasizes construction of oil and gas, water and sewer underground pipelines and cable. Readers are contractor key personnel and company construction managers. Circ. 25,000. Estab. 1945. Sample copy $2.
Needs: "Uses photos of pipeline construction but must have editorial material on project with the photos." Will review photos with accompanying ms only.
Making Contact & Terms: Send unsolicited photos by mail for consideration. Uses 4 × 5 or 8 × 10 color or b&w prints. SASE. Reports in 1 month. Pays $100-300 for text/photo package. Buys one-time rights. Simultaneous submissions OK.

Tips: "We rarely use freelance photography. Freelancers are competing with staff as well as complimentary photos supplied by equipment manufacturers. Subject matter must be unique, striking and 'off the beaten track' (i.e., somewhere we wouldn't travel ourselves to get photos)."

PIZZA TODAY, P.O. Box 1347, New Albany IN 47151. Editor: Danny Bolin. Monthly. Emphasizes pizza trade. Readers are pizza shop owner/operators. Circ. 52,000. Estab. 1983. Sample copy for 9½×12½ SAE.
Needs: Uses 80 photos/issue; 20 supplied by freelancers; 100% from assignment. Needs how-tos of pizza making, product shots, profile shots. Special needs include celebrities eating pizza, politicians eating pizza. Photo captions required.
Making Contact & Terms: Provide resume, business card, brochure, flyer or tearsheets to be kept on file for possible assignments. SASE. Reports in 1 month. Pays $5-15/b&w photo; $20-30/color photo (prefer 35mm slides); all fees are negotiated in advance. Pays on publication. Credit line given. Buys all rights. Will negotiate with photographer unwilling to sell all rights. Previously published work OK.
Tips: Accept samples by mail only. "Team up with writer/contributor and supply photos to accompany article. We are not looking for specific food shots—looking for freelancers who can go to pizza shops and take photos which capture the atmosphere, the warmth and humor; 'the human touch.'"

❋PLANT, Sentry Communications, Suite 500, 245 Fairview Mall Dr., Willowdale, ON M2J 4T1 Canada. (416)490-0220. FAX: (416)490-0119. Editor: Ron Richardson. Published 20 times/year. Emphasizes manufacturing. Readers are plant managers and engineers. Circ. 52,000. Sample copy free with SAE and 67¢ Canadian postage.
Needs: Uses about 6-8 photos/issue; 1-2 supplied by freelancers. Needs photos "to illustrate technical subjects featured in a particular issue—many 'concept' or 'theme' shots used on covers." Model release preferred; captions required.
Making Contact & Terms: Query with samples. Provide resume, business card, brochure, flyer or tearsheets to be kept on file for possible assignments. SASE. Reports in 1 month. Pays $150-300/color cover photo; $35-50/b&w inside photo; and $50-200/color inside photo; $100-300/job; $120-600 for text/photo package. Pays on acceptance. Credit line given. Buys first N.A. serial rights.
Tips: Prefers to see "industrial experience, variety (i.e., photos in plants) in samples. Read the magazine. Remember, we're Canadian."

PLANTS SITES & PARKS MAGAZINE, #201, 10240 W. Sample Rd., Coral Springs FL 33065-3938. (800)753-2660. FAX: (305)755-7048. Art Director: David Lepp. Bimonthly magazine. Emphasizes economic development and business. Readers are executives involved in selecting locations for their businesses. Circ. 40,000. Estab. 1973.
Needs: Uses 15-20 photos/issue; 5-10 supplied by freelancers. General business subjects, locations, industrial, food processing and people. Model and/or property release required. Photo captions preferred.
Making Contact & Terms: Query with list of stock photo subjects. Provide resume, business card, brochure, flyer or tearsheets to be kept on file for possible assignments. Keeps samples on file. Reports in 3 weeks. Pays $500/color cover photo; $100-150/color inside photo. Pays on acceptance and publication; negotiable. Buys one-time rights; negotiable. Simultaneous submissions and previously published work OK.
Tips: Wants to see "only very good quality work. Original slides, *no* dupes; no research fees."

PLASTICS TECHNOLOGY, Dept. PM, 633 Third Ave., New York NY 10017. (212)984-2283. FAX: (212)986-3727. Editor: Matthew Naitove. Art Director: Anita Tai. Monthly magazine. Emphasizes plastics product manufacturing. Readers are engineers and managers in manufacturing plants using plastics. Circ. 47,000.
Needs: Uses about 30-35 photos/issue; 1 supplied by freelancer. Needs manufacturing plant shots (mostly interiors) and machine close-ups, product still lifes. Model release required; captions preferred.
Making Contact & Terms: Arrange a personal interview to show portfolio. SASE. Reports in 1 week. Pays $150-300/b&w photo; $250-400/color photo; $700/day; $350/half day. Pays on publication. Credit line given "mainly on covers." Buys one-time rights. Simultaneous submissions and previously published work "if in non-competition medium" OK.
Tips: In portfolio or samples, wants to see "industrial and scientific subjects. Also, creativity and consistent quality with good lighting—especially still life close-ups."

PLUMBING, HEATING, PIPING, (formerly *Domestic Engineering Magazine*), Dept. PM, 400 N. Michigan Ave., Chicago IL 60611. (312)222-2000. Editor: Cari Laird. Monthly magazine. Emphasizes plumbing, heating, air conditioning and piping; also gives information on management marketing and merchandising. For contractors, executives and entrepreneurs. Circ. 40,000.

Needs: "For photos without stories, we could use a few very good shots of mechanical construction—piping, industrial air conditioning, etc.," but most photos purchased are with stories. Buys 5 photos/issue. Captions required.

Making Contact & Terms: Rights purchased are negotiable. Submit model release with photo. Send contact sheet for consideration. Uses 5 × 7 b&w glossy prints; 8 × 10 color glossy prints or transparencies; glossy b&w or color prints or color transparencies for cover; send contact sheet. Pays $10-100/photo; $50-125/cover photo. Pays on acceptance. Reports in 2 weeks. SASE. Simultaneous submissions and previously published work OK.

POLICE MAGAZINE, 6300 Yarrow Dr., Carlsbad CA 92009. (619)438-2511. Managing Editor: Dan Burger. Estab. 1976. Monthly. Emphasizes law enforcement. Readers are various members of the law enforcement community: especially police officers. Sample copy $2 with 9 × 12 SAE and 6 first-class stamps. Photo guidelines free with SASE.

Needs: Uses about 15 photos/issue; 99% supplied by freelance photographers. Needs law-enforcement related photos. Special needs include photos relating to daily police work, crime prevention, international law enforcement, police technology and humor. Model release and captions required.

Making Contact & Terms: Interested in receiving work from newer, lesser-known photographers. Arrange a personal interview to show portfolio. Send b&w prints, 35mm transparencies, b&w contact sheet or color negatives by mail for consideration. SASE. Pays $100/color cover photo; $30/b&w photo; $30 (negotiable)/color inside photo; $150-300/job; $150-300/text/photo package. Pays on acceptance. Buys all rights; rights returned to photographer 45 days after publication. Simultaneous submissions OK.

Tips: "Send for our editorial calendar and submit photos based on our projected needs. If we like your work, we'll consider you for future assignments. Readers don't want the conceptual photo as much as they prefer the picture that teaches them or gives them a better idea of what the author is saying."

POLICE TIMES/CHIEF OF POLICE, 3801 Biscayne Blvd., Miami FL 33137. (305)573-0070. Editor-in-Chief: Jim Gordon. Bimonthly magazines. Readers are law enforcement officers at all levels. Circ. 50,000 + . Sample copy $2.50; free photo guidelines with SASE.

Needs: Photos of police officers in action, civilian volunteers working with the police and group shots of police department personnel. Wants no photos that promote other associations. Buys 60-90 photos/year. Police-oriented cartoons also accepted on spec. Model release and captions preferred.

Making Contact & Terms: Send photos for consideration. Send b&w and color glossy prints. SASE. Reports in 3 weeks. Pays $5-10 upwards/inside photo; $25-50 upwards/cover photo. Pays on acceptance. Credit line given if requested; editor's option. Buys all rights, but may reassign to photographer after publication. Simultaneous submissions and previously published work OK.

Tips: "We are open to new and unknowns in small communities where police are not given publicity."

POLLED HEREFORD WORLD, 11020 N.W. Ambassador Dr., Kansas City MO 64153. (816)891-8400. Editor: Ed Bible. Monthly magazine. Emphasizes Polled Hereford cattle for registered breeders, commercial cattle breeders and agribusinessmen in related fields. Circ. 11,500. Estab. 1947.

Payment & Terms: Pays $5/b&w print; $100/color transparency or print. Pays on publication.

Making Contact: Query. Uses b&w prints and color transparencies and prints. Reports in 2 weeks.

Tips: Wants to see "polled hereford cattle in quantities, in seasonal and/or scenic settings."

THE PREACHER'S MAGAZINE, E. 10814 Broadway, Spokane WA 99206. (509)226-3464. Editor: Randal E. Denny. Quarterly professional journal for ministers. Emphasizes the pastoral ministry. Readers are pastors of large to small churches in 5 denominations; most pastors are male. Circ. 18,000. Estab. 1925. No sample copy available. No photo guidelines.

Needs: Uses 1 photo/issue; 100% supplied by freelancers. Large variety needed for cover, depends on theme of issue. Model release and photo captions preferred.

Making Contact & Terms: Send 35mm b&w/color prints by mail for consideration. Reports ASAP. Pays $60/color cover photo. Pays on acceptance. Credit line given. Buys one-time rights. Simultaneous submissions and previously published work OK.

Tips: In photographer's samples wants to see "a variety of subjects for the front cover of our magazine. We rarely use photos within the magazine itself."

THE PRESS, Dept. PM, 7009 S. Potomac, Englewood CO 80112. (303)397-7600. FAX: (303)397-7619. Art Director: Aggie Kelley. Monthly magazine. Emphasizes screen printing and custom apparel retailing. Readers are "male/female screenprinters—all ages—small to big shops." Circ. 27,500. Estab. 1979.

Needs: Uses approx. 8-10 photos/issue; 100% supplied by freelancers. Needs photos of product shots, how-tos, fashion. Model release required. Photo captions preferred.
Making Contact & Terms: Arrange personal interview to show portfolio. Provide resume, business card, brochure, flyer or tearsheets to be kept on file for possible assignments. Keeps samples on file. Pays $100/color cover photo; $75/b&w cover photo; $100-1,000/day. Pays on publication. Credit line sometimes given. Buys one-time rights. Simultaneous submissions and previously published work OK.

PRO SOUND NEWS, 2 Park Ave., New York NY 10016. (212)213-3444. Editor: Debra Pagan. Managing Editor: Tom Di Nome. Monthly tabloid. Emphasizes professional recording and sound and production industries. Readers are recording engineers, studio owners and equipment manufacturers worldwide. Circ. 21,000. Sample copy free with SASE.
Needs: Uses about 12 photos/issue; all supplied by freelance photographers. Needs photos of recording sessions, sound reinforcement for concert tours, permanent installations. Model release and captions required.
Making Contact & Terms: Query with samples. Send 8 × 10 color glossy prints by mail for consideration. SASE. Reports in 2 weeks. NPI; pays by the job or for text/photo package. Pays on publication. Credit line given. Buys one-time rights. Simultaneous submissions and previously published work OK.

*PROFESSIONAL AGENT, 400 N. Washington St., Alexandria VA 22314. (703)836-9340. FAX: (703)836-1279. Editor: Alan Prochoroff. Monthly. Emphasizes property/casualty insurance. Readers are independent insurance agents. Circ. 32,000. Estab. 1932. Sample copy free with SASE.
Needs: Uses about 20 photos/year supplied by freelancers and stock houses. Model release, property release and captions required.
Making Contact & Terms: Interested in receiving work from newer, lesser-known photographers. "Send copies of portfolio that we can look at during our leisure hours." Query with list of stock photo subjects. Provide resume, business card, brochure, flyer or tearsheets to be kept on file for possible future assignments. Uses minimum 5 × 7 glossy color and b&w prints; 35mm and 2¼ × 2¼ transparencies. SASE. Reporting time varies. Pays $500-900/color cover photo. Pays within 1 month of acceptance. Credit line given. Buys one-time rights or first North American serial rights, exclusive in the insurance industry.

PROFESSIONAL PHOTOGRAPHER, 1090 Executive Way, Des Plaines IL 60018. (708)299-8161. FAX: (708)299-2685. Editor: Alfred DeBat. Senior Editor: Deborah Goldstein. Art Director: Debbie Todd. Monthly. Emphasizes professional photography in the fields of portrait, wedding, commercial/advertising, corporate and industrial. Readers include professional photographers and photographic services and educators. Approximately half the circulation is Professional Photographers of America members. Circ. 32,000+. Estab. 1907. Sample copy $5 postpaid; photo guidelines with SASE.
Needs: Uses 25-30 photos/issue; 100% supplied by freelancers. "We only accept material as illustration that relates directly to photographic articles showing professional studio, location, commercial and portrait techniques. A majority are supplied by Professional Photographers of America members." Reviews photos with accompanying ms only. "We always need commercial/advertising and industrial success stories. How to sell your photography to major accounts, unusual professional photo assignments." Model release preferred; captions required.
Making Contact & Terms: Query with resume of credits. "We want a story query, or complete ms if writer feels subject fits our magazine. Photos will be part of ms package." Uses 8 × 10 glossy unmounted b&w or color prints; 35mm, 2¼ × 2¼, 4 × 5 and 8 × 10 transparencies. SASE. Reports in 8 weeks. NPI. "PPA members submit material unpaid to promote their photo businesses and obtain recognition." Credit line given. Previously published work OK.

PROGRESSIVE ARCHITECTURE, Dept. PM, 600 Summer St., P.O. Box 1361, Stamford CT 06904. (203)348-7531. Editor: John Morris Dixon. Monthly magazine. Emphasizes current information on building design and technology for professional architects. Circ. 75,000.
Needs: Photos purchased with or without accompanying ms and on assignment; 90% assigned. Architectural and interior design. Captions preferred. Accompanying mss: interesting architectural or engineering developments/projects.
Making Contact & Terms: Send material by mail for consideration. Uses 8 × 10 b&w glossy prints; 4 × 5 transparencies. Vertical format preferred for cover. SASE. Reports in 1 month. Pays $500/1-day assignment, $1,000/2-day assignment; $250/half-day assignment or on a per-photo basis. Pays $25

The code NPI (no payment information given) appears in listings that have not given specific payment amounts.

minimum/b&w photo; $50/color photo; $50/color cover photo. NPI for ms.; varies. Pays on publication. Credit line given. Buys one-time rights.

Tips: In samples, wants to see "straightforward architectural presentation."

PROPERTY MANAGEMENT MONTHLY, Suite 400, 8601 Georgia Ave., Silver Spring MD 20910. (301)588-0681. FAX: (301)588-6314. Editor: Ms. Jayson H. Nuhn. Monthly tabloid. Emphasizes management of commercial real estate (offices, apartments, retail, industrial). Readers are males and females involved in the property management/real estate industry. Circ. 12,000+. Estab. 1984. Sample copy free with SASE.

Needs: Uses 30 photos/issue; "almost all" supplied by freelancers. Needs photos of architectural, technical and people. Special photo needs include architectural photos and "grip and grin" people shots at industry functions. Model and/or property release is required. Photo captions preferred; include name and location.

Making Contact & Terms: Query with resume of credits. Provide resume, business card, brochure, flyer or tearsheets to be kept on file for possible assignments. Keeps samples on file. SASE. Reports in 1 month. Pays $250 per half-day; $500 per all day shoot, plus expenses/color cover; $75 per hour, expenses; $6 per print/b&w inside photo. Pays on acceptance. Credit line given. Buys one-time rights.

Tips: Looks for "good use of light/shadows and background shoots. Creativity in posing portrait shots." Photographers "should live in the metropolitan area because our photo needs are met on assignment in this area. Must be able to get names of subjects accurately when photographing industry event."

QUALITY DIGEST, P.O. Box 1503, Red Bluff CA 96080. (916)527-8875. FAX: (916)527-6983. Editor: Scott M. Paton. Monthly digest. Emphasizes quality improvement. Readers are mainly mid-level and senior-level managers in large corporations. Circ. 20,000. Estab. 1981. Sample copy for $6.25. No photo guidelines.

Needs: Uses 10-12 photos/issue; 50% supplied by freelancers. Needs photos of training sessions, meetings in progress, office situations and factory scenes. Special photo needs include service quality. Model release required; photo captions required.

Making Contact & Terms: Send b&w prints by mail for consideration. Reports in 1 month. Pays $300/color cover photo; $50/b&w inside photo. Pays on acceptanc. Credit line given. Buys all rights. Will negotiate with a photographer unwilling to sell all rights. Will consider simultaneous submissions. No previously published work.

QUICK FROZEN FOODS INTERNATIONAL, Suite 305, 2125 Center Ave., Fort Lee NJ 07024-5898. (201)592-7007. FAX: (201)592-7171. Editor: John M. Saulnier. Quarterly magazine. Emphasizes retailing, marketing, processing, packaging and distribution of frozen foods around the world. Readers are international executives involved in the frozen food industry: manufacturers, distributors, retailers, brokers, importers/exporters, warehousemen, etc. Circ. 13,500. Review copy $8.

Needs: Plant exterior shots, step-by-step in-plant processing shots, photos of retail store frozen food cases, head shots of industry executives, product shots, etc. Buys 20-30 photos annually. Captions required.

Making Contact & Terms: Query first with resume of credits. Uses 5×7 b&w glossy prints. SASE. Reports in 1 month. Pays on acceptance. Buys all rights, but may reassign to photographer after publication.

Tips: A file of photographers' names is maintained; if an assignment comes up in an area close to a particular photographer, he may be contacted. "When submitting names, inform us if you are capable of writing a story, if needed."

RADIO-ELECTRONICS MAGAZINE, Dept. PM, 500 B Bi-County Blvd., Farmingdale NY 11735. (516)293-3000. Editor: Brian C. Fenton. Monthly magazine. Emphasizes electronics. Readers are electrical engineers and technicians, both male and female, ages 25-60. Circ. 190,000. Sample copy free with 9×12 SAE.

Needs: Uses 25-50 photos/issue; 2-3 supplied by freelance photographers. Needs photos of how-to, computer screens, test equipment and digital displays. Purchases photos with accompanying ms only. Model release required; photo captions preferred.

Making Contact & Terms: Submit portfolio for review. Provide resume, business card, brochure, flyer or tearsheets to be kept on file for possible assignments. SASE. Reports in 2 weeks. Pays $400/color cover photo. Pays on acceptance. Credit line given. Buys all rights, but willing to negotiate. Simultaneous submissions OK.

THE RANGEFINDER, 1312 Lincoln Blvd., P.O. Box 1703, Santa Monica CA 90406. (213)451-8506. Editor/Photo Editor: Arthur Stern. Monthly journal. Emphasizes topics, developments and products of interest to the professional photographer. Readers are professionals in all phases of photography. Circ. 55,000. Sample copy $2.50. Photo guidelines free with SASE.

Needs: Uses 20-30 photos/issue; 70% supplied by freelancers. Needs all kinds of photos; almost always run in conjunction with articles. Subjects include animal, celebrity/personality, documentary, digital, fashion/beauty, glamour, head shot, photo essay/photo feature, scenics, special effects and experimental, sports, how-to, human interest, nature, still life, travel and wildlife. "We prefer photos accompanying 'how-to' or special interest stories from the photographer." No pictorials. Special needs include seasonal cover shots (vertical format only). Model release required.
Making Contact & Terms: Query with samples. SASE. Reports in 1 month. Pays $40-240 text/photo package only. Credit line given only for cover. Pays on publication. Buys first N.A. serial rights. Previously published work occasionally OK; give details.

RECOMMEND WORLDWIDE, Dept. PM, Suite 120, 5979 N.W. 151st St., Miami Lake FL 33014. (305)828-0123. Art Director: Linda Eouthat. Managing Editor: Roger Vance. Monthly. Emphasizes travel. Readers are travel agents, meeting planners, hoteliers, ad agencies. Sample copy for 8½×11 SASE and 10 first-class stamps.
Needs: Uses about 40 photos/issue; 70% supplied by freelance photographers. "Our publication divides the world up into 7 regions. Every month we use destination-oriented photos of animals, cities, resorts and cruise lines. Features all types of travel photography from all over the world." Model release and captions preferred; identification required.
Making Contact & Terms: "We prefer a resume, stock list and sample card or tearsheets with photo review later." SASE. Pays $150/color cover photo; $25/color inside photo; $50/color page. Pays 30 days upon publication. Credit line given. Buys one-time rights. Simultaneous submissions and previously published work OK.
Tips: Prefers to see "transparencies—either 2¼ or 35mm first quality originals, travel oriented."

REFEREE, P.O. Box 161, Franksville WI 53126. (414)632-8855. FAX: (414)632-5460. Editor: Tom Hammill. Monthly magazine. Readers are mostly male, ages 30-50. Circ. 35,000. Estab. 1976. Sample copy free with 9×12 SAE and 5 first-class stamps. Photo guidelines free with SASE.
Needs: Uses up to 50 photos/issue; 75% supplied by freelancers. Needs action officiating shots—all sports. Photo needs are ongoing. Model release and photo captions preferred.
Making Contact & Terms: Send unsolicited photos by mail for consideration. Any format is accepted. Reports in 1-2 weeks. Pays $100/color cover photo; $75/b&w cover photo; $35/color inside photo; $20/ b&w inside photo. Pays on publication. Credit line given. Rights purchased negotiable. Simultaneous submissions and previously published work OK.
Tips: Prefers photos which bring out the uniqueness of being a sports official. Need photos primarily of officials at high school level in baseball, football, basketball, soccer, volleyball and softball in action. Other sports acceptable, but used less frequently. "When at sporting events, take a few shots with the officials in mind, even though you may be on assignment for another reason." Address all queries to Tom Hammill, editor. "Don't be afraid to give it a try. We're receptive, always looking for new freelance contributors. We are constantly looking for offbeat pictures of officials/umpires. Our needs in this area have increased."

REGISTERED REPRESENTATIVE, Suite 280, 18818 Teller Ave., Irvine CA 92715. (714)851-2220. Art Director: Chuck LaBresh. Monthly magazine. Emphasizes stock brokerage industry. Magazine is "requested and read by 90% of the nation's stock brokers." Circ. 80,000. Sample copy for $2.50.
Needs: Uses about 8 photos/issue; 5 supplied by freelancers. Needs environmental portraits of financial and brokerage personalities, and conceptual shots of financial ideas, all by assignment only. Model release and captions preferred.
Making Contact & Terms: Arrange a personal interview to show portfolio. Provide resume, business card, brochure, flyer or tearsheets to be kept on file for possible future assignments. Does not return unsolicited material. Pays $250-600/b&w or color cover photo; $100-250/b&w or color inside photo. Pays 30 days after publication. Credit line given. Buys one-time rights. Simultaneous submissions or previously published work OK.

REMODELING, 655 15th St. NW, Washington DC 20005. (202)737-0717. Managing Editor: Leslie Ensor. Published 12 times/year. "Business magazine for remodeling contractors." Readers are "small contractors involved in residental and commercial remodeling." Circ. 95,000. Sample copy free with 8×11 SASE.
Needs: Uses 10-15 photos/issue; number supplied by freelancers varies. Needs photos of remodeled residences, both before and after. Reviews photos with "short description of project, including architect's or contractor's name and phone number. We have three regular photo features: *Double Take* is photo caption piece about an architectural photo that fools the eye. *Close Up* is a photo caption showing architectural details. *Before and After* describes a whole-house remodel."

Making Contact & Terms: Provide resume, business card, brochure, flyer or tearsheets to be kept on file for possible future assignments. Reports in 1 month. Pays $100/color cover photo; $25/b&w inside photo; $50/color inside photo; $300 maximum/job. Pays on acceptance. Credit line given. Buys one-time rights.
Tips: Wants "interior and exterior photos of residences that emphasize the architecture over the furnishings."

RESCUE MAGAZINE, Dept. PM, Jems Publishing Co., P.O. Box 2789, Carlsbad CA 92018. (619)431-9797. Art Director: Harriet Wilcox. Bimonthly. Emphasizes techniques, equipment, action stories with unique rescues; paramedics, EMTs, rescue divers, fire fighters, etc. Rescue personnel are most of our readers. Circ. 25,000. Sample copy free with 9×12 SAE and $2 postage. Photo guidelines free with SASE.
Needs: Uses 20-25 photos/issue; 5-10 supplied by freelance photographers. Needs rescue scenes, transport, injured victims, equipment and personnel, training. Special photo needs include strong color shots showing newsworthy rescue operations, including a unique or difficult rescue/extrication, treatment, transport, personnel, etc. Black-and-whites showing same. Model release preferred; captions required.
Making Contact & Terms: Query with samples; or send 5×7 or larger glossy b&w or color prints, 35mm or 2¼×2¼ transparencies or b&w or color contacts sheets by mail for consideration. Don't send originals. SASE. Pays $150-200/color cover photo; $25-35/b&w inside photo; $50-75/color inside photo. Pays on publication. Credit line given. Buys one-time rights. Previously published work OK (must be labeled as such).
Tips: "Ride along with a rescue crew or team. This can be firefighters, paramedics, mountain rescue teams, dive rescue teams, and so on. Get in close." Looks for "photographs that show rescuers in action, using proper techniques and wearing the proper equipment. Submit timely photographs that show the technical aspects of rescue."

RESOURCE RECYCLING, P.O. Box 10540, Portland OR 97210. (503)227-1319. Editor: Meg Lynch. Monthly. Emphasizes "the recycling of post-consumer waste materials (paper, metals, glass, etc.)" Readers are "recycling company managers, local government officials, waste haulers and environmental group executives." Circ. 14,000. Estab. 1982. Sample copy free with $2 postage plus 9×12 SASE.
Needs: Uses about 5-15 photos/issue; 1-5 supplied by freelancers. Needs "photos of recycling facilities, curbside recycling collections, secondary materials (bundles of newspapers, soft drink containers), etc." Model release preferred; photo captions required.
Making Contact & Terms: Send glossy b&w prints and contact sheet. SASE. Reports in 1 month. NPI; payment "varies by experience and photo quality." Pays on publication. Credit line given. Buys first N.A. serial rights. Simultaneous submissions OK.
Tips: "Because *Resource Recycling* is a trade journal for the recycling industry, we are looking only for photos that relate to recycling issues."

RESTAURANT HOSPITALITY, 1100 Superior Ave., Cleveland OH 44114. (216)696-7000. FAX: (216)696-0836. Editor-in-Chief: Michael DeLuca. Monthly. Emphasizes "restaurant management, hotel food service, cooking, interior design." Readers are "restaurant owners, chefs, food service chain executives." Circ. 100,000. Estab. 1919. Sample copy free with 8×10 SAE and $1 postage.
Needs: Uses about 30 photos/issue; 50% supplied by freelancers. "We buy from stock more often than on assignment." Needs "people with food, restaurant and foodservice interiors and occasional food photos." Special needs include "spectacular food and/or beverage shots; query first." Model release and captions preferred.
Making Contact & Terms: Query with resume of credits or samples, or list of stock photo subjects. Provide resume, business card, brochure, flyer or tearsheets to be kept on file for possible future assignments. SASE. Reports in 2 weeks. Pays $50-500/b&w or color photo; $350/half day; $150-450/job plus normal expenses. Pays on acceptance. Credit line given. Buys one-time rights. Previously published work OK "if exclusive to foodservice press."
Tips: "Let us know you exist; we can't assign a story if we don't know you. Send resume, business card, samples, etc. along with query or introductory letter."

ROOFER MAGAZINE, 12120 Amedicus Ln., Ft. Myers FL 33907. (813)275-7663. Associate Publisher: Angela M. Williamson. Art Director: Michael Lopez. Monthly. Emphasizes the roofing industry and all facets of the roofing business. Readers are roofing contractors, manufacturers, architects, specifiers, consultants and distributors. Circ. 17,000. Estab. 1981. Sample copy free with 9×12 SAE and $1.75 postage.
Needs: Uses about 25 photos/issue; few are supplied by freelancers. Needs photos of unusual roofs or those with a humorous slant (once published a photo with a cow stranded on a roof during a flood). Needs several photos of a particular city or country to use in photo essay section. Also, photographs

of buildings after major disasters, showing the destruction to the roof, are especially needed. "Please indicate to us the location, time and date taken, and cause of destruction (i.e., fire, flood, hurricane)." Model release required. Captions preferred, include details about date, location and description of scene.

Making Contact & Terms: Query with samples. Provide resume, brochure and tearsheets to be kept on file for possible future assignments. Does not return unsolicited material. Reports in 1 month. Pays $25 maximum/b&w photo; $50 maximum/color photo. Pays maximum $125 per page for photo essays. Pays on publication. Usually buys one-time rights, "exclusive to our industry."

Tips: "Good lighting is a must. Clear skies, beautiful landscaping around the home or building featured add to the picture. Looking for anything unique, in either the angle of the shot or the type of roof. Humorous photos are given special consideration and should be accompanied by clever captions or a brief, humorous description. No photos of reroofing jobs on your home will be accepted. Most of the photos we publish in each issue are contributed by our authors. Freelance photographers should submit material that would be useful for our photographic essays, depicting particular cities or countries. We've given assignments to freelance photographers before, but most submissions are the ideas of the freelancer."

*SALOME: A JOURNAL FOR THE PERFORMING ARTS, 5548 N. Sawyer, Chicago IL 60625. (312)539-5745. Editor: Effie Mihopoulos. Quarterly. Emphasizes performing arts. Estab. 1975. Sample copy $4. Photo guidelines free with SASE.

Needs: Uses approx. 500 photos/issue; 50% supplied by freelance photographers; 10% freelance assignment; 5-25% stock. Needs photos of performing arts subjects. Model release and photo captions preferred; identification of subject (if person) necessary.

Making Contact & Terms: Send b&w prints by mail for consideration. SASE. Reports in 2 weeks. Pays in copy of magazine. Pays on publication. Credit line given. Buys one-time rights. Simultaneous submissions and previously published work OK (must state with submission).

Tips: Looks for "good composition and a striking image that immediately grabs your attention." There is a trend of "more good photographers creating fiercer competition. Send an overview of photos; examine previous issue of magazine to prepare a sample portfolio."

THE SCIENTIST, Dept. PM, 3501 Market St., Philadelphia PA 19104. (215)386-0100, ext. 1553. Art Director: Catherine Dolan. Biweekly tabloid. Emphasizes science. Readers are mostly male scientists or science administrators. Circ. 30,000.

Needs: Uses 30-40 photos/issue; 30-50% supplied by freelance photographers. Uses photos of "mostly people in labs or with work." Model release and photo captions preferred.

Making Contact & Terms: Provide resume, business card, brochure, flyer or tearsheets to be kept on file for possible assignments. SASE. Reports in 1 month. Pays $125/b&w cover or inside photo. Pays on publication. Credit line given. Buys one-time rights. Previously published work OK.

Tips: "We only use black & white photographs. Since most of our stuff is people oriented, I'm looking for unusual portraits."

SEAFOOD BUSINESS MAGAZINE, Dept. PM, 120 Tillson Ave., Rockland ME 04841. (207)594-6222. FAX: (207)594-8978. Art Director: Michael Schroeder. Bimonthly magazine. Emphasizes seafood, commercial fishing, and prepared seafood. Circ. 16,000. Estab. 1980. Sample copy free with SASE.

Needs: Uses 40 photos/issue; 20 supplied by freelancers. Needs photos of commercial fishing, species shots, i.e. salmon or cod, etc., seafood restaurants, prepared seafood, supermarkets and shots emphasizing international flair. Especially wants to see international seafood shots. Model and/or property release and photo captions preferred.

Making Contact & Terms: Send unsolicited prints or 35mm or 4×5 transparencies by mail for consideration. Provide resume, business card, brochure, flyer or tearsheets to be kept on file for possible assignments. Also, contact by phone. Reports in 1-2 weeks. Pays $200-350/color cover photo; $50-100/color inside photo. Pays on acceptance. Credit line given. Buys one-time rights. Simultaneous submissions and previously published work OK.

Tips: Wants to see creativity. "This is not always easy when photographing fish and seafood." The seafood business is a very big market, and he notes that this is "the industry's leading publication, and it's highly visible. It often leads to other possible opportunities for photographer."

SEAFOOD LEADER, 454 N. 34th St., Seattle WA 98103. (206)547-6030. FAX: (206)548-9346. Assistant to the Editor: Courtney Schrieve. Published bimonthly. Emphasizes seafood industry, commercial fishing. Readers are buyers and brokers of seafood. Circ. 16,000. Estab. 1981. Sample copy $5 with 9×12 SAE.

Needs: Uses about 40 photos/issue; half supplied by freelance photographers, most from stock. Needs photos of international seafood harvesting and farming, supermarkets, restaurants, shrimp, Alaska, many more. Model release preferred. Photo captions preferred including name, place, time.
Making Contact & Terms: Interested in receiving work from newer, lesser-known photographers. Query with list of stock photo subjects. Send photos on subjects we request. SASE. "We only want it on our topics." Reports in 1 month. Pays $100/color cover photo; $50/color inside photo; $25/b&w photo. Pays on publication. Credit line given. Buys one-time rights. Previously published work OK.
Tips: "Send in slides relating to our needs—request editorial calendar." Looks for "aesthetic shots of seafood, shots of people interacting with seafood in which expressions are captured (i.e. not posed shots); artistic shots of seafood emphasizing color and shape. We want clear, creative, original photography of commercial fishing, fish species, not sports fishing."

SECURITY DEALER, Suite 21, 445 Broad Hollow Rd., Melville NY 11747. (516)845-2700. FAX: (516)845-7109. Editor: Susan Brady. Monthly magazines. Emphasizes security subjects. Readers are blue collar businessmen installing alarm, security, CCTV and access control systems. Circ. 22,000. Estab. 1967. Sample copy free with SASE.
Needs: Uses 2-5 photos/issue; none at present supplied by freelance photographers. Needs photos of security-application-equipment. Model release preferred. Captions required.
Making Contact & Terms: Interested in receiving work from newer, lesser-known photographers. Send b&w and color prints by mail for consideration. SASE. Reports "immediately." Pays $25-50/b&w photo; $200/color cover photo; $50-100/inside color photos. Pays 30 days after publication. Credit line given. Buys one-time rights in security trade industry. Simultaneous submissions and previously published work OK.
Tips: "Do not send originals, dupes only, and only after discussion with editor."

SHEEP! MAGAZINE, Dept. PM, W. 2997 Market Rd., Helenville WI 53137. (414)593-8385. FAX (414)593-8384. Editor: Dave Thompson. Monthly tabloid. Emphasizes sheep and wool. Readers are sheep and wool producers across the US and Canada. Circ. 13,000. Estab. 1982. Sample copy for $1. Photo guidelines available.
Needs: Uses 30 photos/issue; 50% supplied by freelancers. Needs photos of sheep, lambs, sheep producers, wool, etc. Model release and photo captions preferred.
Making Contact & Terms: Send unsolicited photos by mail for consideration. Provide resume, business card, brochure, flyer or tearsheets to be kept on file for possible assignments. Uses b&w and color prints; 35mm transparencies. SASE. Reports in 3 weeks. Pays $200/color cover photo; $150/b&w cover photo; $100/color inside photo; $50/b&w inside photo. Credit line given. Buys one-time and all rights; negotiable. Previously published work OK.

SHELTER SENSE, Humane Society of the US, 2100 L St. NW, Washington DC 20037. (202)452-1100. Editor: Geoffrey Handy. Monthly newsletter. Emphasizes animal protection. Readers are animal control and shelter workers, men and women, all ages. Circ. 3,000. Estab. 1978. Sample copy for $1 with 9×12 SAE and 2 first-class stamps.
Needs: Uses 15 photos/issue; 35% supplied by freelance photographers. Needs photos of domestic animals interacting with people/humane workers; animals during the seasons; animal care, obedience; humane society work and functions, other companion animal shots. "We do not pay for manuscripts." Model release required; photo captions preferred.
Making Contact & Terms: Provide resume, business card, brochure, flyer or tearsheets to be kept on file for possible assignments. SASE. Reports in 3 weeks. Pays $45/b&w cover photo; $35/b&w inside photo. Pays on acceptance. Credit line given. Buys one-time rights.
Tips: Keep in mind "much of the material and photos used in *Shelter Sense* are donated by humane society workers/volunteers. However, we will pay for good b&w photos that we think we will be able to use."

*SHOOTER'S RAG-A PRACTICAL PHOTOGRAPHIC GAZETTE, P.O. Box 8509, Asheville NC 28814. (704)254-6700. Editor: Michael Havelin. Quarterly. Emphasizes photographic techniques, practical how-tos and electronic imaging. Readers are male and female professionals, semi-professionals and serious amateurs. Circ. 2,500. Estab. 1992. Sample copy $3 with 10×13 SASE and 75¢ postage. Photo guidelines free with SASE.
Needs: Uses 15-25 photos/issue; 50-75% supplied by freelancers. "Single photos generally not needed. Photos with text and text with photographs should query." Special photo needs include humorous b&w cover shots with photographic theme and detailed description of how the shot was done with accompanying set up shots. Model/property release required. Captions required.
Making Contact & Terms: Query with resume of credits. Query with ideas for text, photo packages. Does not keep samples on file. Does not return unsolicited material. Reports in 1 month. Pays $50/b&w cover photo; $35/color inside photo; $25/b&w inside photo; $50-200/photo text package. Pays

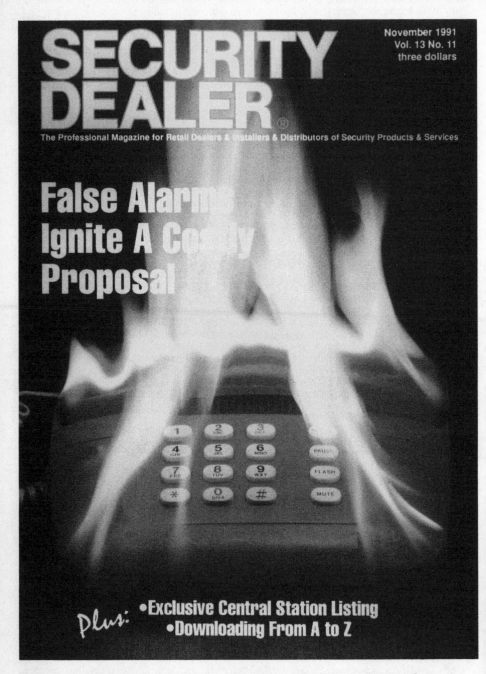

November 1991
Vol. 13 No. 11
three dollars

SECURITY DEALER®

The Professional Magazine for Retail Dealers & Installers & Distributors of Security Products & Services

False Alarms Ignite A Costly Proposal

plus: •Exclusive Central Station Listing
•Downloading From A to Z

Although photographer Paul Prosise, of Gardena, California, had never photographed a burning phone, he certainly was up to the task when approached to shoot the cover for Security Dealer magazine. Prosise had to repaint the phone twice because fire kept burning the paint off and he wanted to try different combustible fluids to see how they would photograph. The piece earned him $300 from the magazine and he used it as a self-promotion piece on a greeting card.

on publication. Credit line given. Buys one-time rights. Simultaneous submissions and/or previously published work OK. Electronic submissions preferred via CIS or Skyland BBS (704)254-7800.
Tips: "Writers who shoot and photographers who write well should query. Don't wait for the world to discover you. Announce your presence."

SIGNCRAFT MAGAZINE, P.O. Box 06031, Fort Myers FL 33906. (813)939-4644. Editor: Tom McIltrot. Bimonthly magazine. Readers are sign artists and sign shop personnel. Circ. 21,000. Estab. 1980. Sample copy $5. Photo guidelines free with SASE.
Needs: Uses over 100 photos/issue; few at present supplied by freelancers. Needs photos of well-designed, effective signs. Model release and captions preferred.
Making Contact & Terms: Query with samples. Send b&w, color prints; 35mm, 2¼ × 2¼ transparencies; b&w, color contact sheet by mail for consideration. SASE. Reports in 1 month. NPI. Pays on publication. Credit line given. Buys first N.A. serial rights. Previously published work possibly OK.
Tips: "If you have some background or past experience with sign making, you may be able to provide photos for us."

SMALL WORLD, Dept. PM, #1212, 225 W. 34th St., New York NY 10022. (212)563-2742. Editor: Elizabeth D. Anbrosio. Monthly magazine. Emphasizes children's products and furniture for retailers and manufactuers. Circ. 8,000. Sample copy free with 10 × 14 SAE and $1 postage.
Needs: Uses about 10 photos/issue; 2-3 supplied by freelancers on assignment. Needs photos of business people and their stores, children's fashion, still-life. Model release required.
Making Contact & Terms: Arrange a personal interview to show portfolio. Submit portfolio for review. Provide resume, business card, brochure, flyer or tearsheets to be kept on file for possible assignments. SASE. Pays $200/color cover photo; $125-200/color inside photo. Usually given as one assignment. Pays on publication. Credit line given. Buys all rights, but will negotiate.
Tips: Prefers to see photos of business people in portfolio. Looks for "energy, versatility, ability to deal with changes on the spot. Do not mail any original work unless specifically requested."

SOCIAL POLICY, Room 620, 25 W. 43rd St., New York NY 10036. (212)642-2929. Managing Editor: Audrey Gartner. Quarterly. Emphasizes "social policy issues—how government and societal actions affect people's lives." Readers are academics, policymakers, lay readers. Circ. 3,500. Estab. 1970. Sample copy $2.50.
Needs: Uses about 9 photos/issue; all supplied by freelance photographers. Needs photos of social consciousness and sensitivity. Model release preferred.
Making Contact & Terms: Arrange a personal interview to show portfolio. Query with samples. Provide resume, business card, brochure, flyer or tearsheets to be kept on file for possible future assignments. Send 8 × 10 b&w glossy prints or b&w contact sheets by mail for consideration. SASE. Reports in 2 weeks. Pays $75/b&w cover photo; $25/b&w inside photo. Pays on publication. Credit line given. Buys one-time rights. Simultaneous submissions and previously published work OK.
Tips: "Be familiar with social issues. We're always looking for relevant photos."

SOUNDINGS TRADE ONLY, 35 Pratt St., Essex CT 06426. (203)767-3200. Editor: David Eastman. Coated-stock tabloid. Monthly national trade paper for the recreational boating industry. Circ. 32,000. Estab. 1978. Sample copy free with 12 × 18 SAE and $2 postage.
Needs: Uses one or two large color photos on page one; 90% by freelance photographers. Subjects: People at work in any setting related to the business (not the sport) of boating—boatyards, marinas, dealerships, boat or accessory manufacturing plants. Captions required: What is going on, where (name of company and location), when, and who (name and title of anyone featured in photo). Answer the "what" in detail.
Making Contact & Terms: Interested in receiving work from newer, lesser-known photographers. Send unsolicited color transparencies by mail for consideration. Prefers large variety to pick from. SASE. Reports in 2 months. Pays $200 for lead photo on page one; $175 for second photo on page one; $125 for color photo used inside. Also uses b&w spot photos inside; pays $50. Credit line given. Buys first-time rights. No stock or file photos. Sometimes makes assignments at $200/half day; send resume for file.
Tips: "Photos are played large as free-standing art elements. Selection is based on vivid color and geometry. High visual impact is more important than subject matter; striking or unusual subject is a bonus."

 The asterisk before a listing indicates that the market is new in this edition. New markets are often the most receptive to freelance submissions.

SOUTHERN LUMBERMAN, Suite 116, 128 Holiday Ct., P.O. Box 681629, Franklin TN 37068-1629. (615)791-1961. FAX: (615)790-6188. Managing Editor: Nanci Gregg. Monthly. Emphasizes forest products industry—sawmills, pallet operations, logging trades. Readers are predominantly owners/operators of midsized sawmill operations nationwide. Estab. 1881. Circ. 12,000. Sample copy $2 with 9×12 SAE and $1.25 postage. Photo guidelines free with SASE.

Needs: Uses about 4-5 photos/issue; 50% supplied by freelancers. "We need black and whites of 'general interest' in the lumber industry. We need photographers from across the country to do an inexpensive b&w shoot in conjunction with a phone interview; we need 'human interest' shots from a sawmill scene—just basic 'folks' shots—a worker sharing lunch with the company dog, sawdust flying as a new piece of equipment is started; face masks as a mill tries to meet OSHA standards, etc." Looking for photo/text packages. Model release and captions required.

Making Contact & Terms: Interested in receiving work from newer, lesser-known photographers. Query with samples. Send 5×7 or 8×10 glossy b&w prints; 35mm, 4×5 transparencies, b&w contact sheets or negatives by mail for consideration. SASE. Reports in 4-6 weeks. Pays a minimum of $20/b&w photos; $25-50/color photo; $125-175/photo/text package. Pays on publication. Credit line given. Buys first N.A. serial rights. No simultaneous or previously published submissions.

Tips: Prefers b&w capture of close-ups in sawmill, pallet, logging scenes. "Try to provide what the editor wants—call and make sure you know what that is, if you're not sure. Don't send things that the editor hasn't asked for. We're all looking for someone who has the imagination/creativity to provide what we need. I'm not interested in 'works of art'—I want and need b&w feature photos capturing essence of employees working at sawmills nationwide. I've never had someone submit anything close to what I state we need—try that. *Read* the description, shoot the pictures, send a contact sheet or a couple 5×7's."

SOYBEAN DIGEST, 540 Maryville Centre Dr., St. Louis MO 63141-1007. (314)576-2788. FAX: (314)576-2786. Editor: Gregg Hillyer. Monthly. Emphasizes production and marketing of soybeans for high-acreage soybean growers. Circ. 230,000. Estab. 1940. Sample copy $3.

Needs: Photos purchased with or without accompanying ms and on assignment. Buys 75 photos/year; 40% from freelance assignment, 10% from freelance stock. Soybean production and marketing photos of modified equipment. Model release required for recognizable persons; property release preferred. Captions preferred; (people: name, phone number, address), location, season. No static, posed or outdated material. Accompanying mss: grower techniques for soybean production and marketing. Prefers photos with ms.

Making Contact & Terms: Interested in receiving work from newer, lesser-known photographers. Send material by mail for consideration. Query with list of stock photo subjects, resume, card, brochure and samples. Uses 5×7 or 8×10 b&w prints; 35mm or 2¼×2¼ transparencies; 35mm, 2¼×2¼, 4×5 and 8×10 transparencies for cover, vertical format preferred. SASE. Reports in 3 weeks. Pays $200-400 for text/photo package or on a per-photo basis. Pays on acceptance. Credit line given. Buys all rights, but may reassign after publication. Previously published work possibly OK.

Tips: "In portfolio or samples we look for soybean, corn and cotton production and related subjects; environmental and conservational corn, soybean and cotton production images; photo journalistic style, saturated color, correct (or bracketed) exposures, a sense of composition, sharp focus, variety of shooting conditions, i.e. weather, light, lenses, formats, angles of view. With continued advances in photographic film and magazine printing we are seeing higher quality images being reproduced. Let us know where you're located. Become familiar with types of photos that are being used in crop production magazines. Be aware that we have a stock photo library ourselves, so you will be 'competing' with a potential client. (Your photography has to be fresh, out of the ordinary with reader-appeal. That's not easy to accomplish.)"

*SPEEDWAY SCENE, P.O. Box 300, North Easton MA 02356. (508)238-7016. Editor: Val LeSieur. Weekly tabloid. Emphasizes auto racing. Circ. 70,000. Estab. 1970. Sample copy free with 8½×11 SAE and 4 first-class stamps.

Needs: Uses 200 photos/issue; 100% supplied by freelancers. Needs photos of oval track auto racing. Reviews photos with or without ms. Photo captions required.

Making Contact & Terms: Send unsolicited photos by mail for consideration. Send b&w, color prints. Reports in 1-2 weeks. NPI. Credit line given. Buys all rights. Simultaneous submissions and/or previously published work OK.

SPORTING GOODS DEALER, 6th Floor, 2 Park Ave., New York NY 10016. (212)779-5556. Editor-in-Chief: Michael Jacobsen. Monthly magazine. Emphasizes news and merchandising ideas for sporting goods dealers. Circ. 29,000. Sample copy $2 with 9×12 SAE and 2 first-class stamps (refunded with first accepted photo).

© Grant Mangold

Soybean Digest *Editor Gregg Hillyer says this photo of a farmer unloading pesticides works well for his magazine because it displays safe techniques for handling such chemicals. The magazine bought the image from Linn Grove, Iowa, photographer Grant Mangold as a 2-page illustration.*

Needs: Photos purchased with or without accompanying ms or on assignment. Spot news relating to the merchandising of sporting goods. Outdoor (fishing, hunting, camping, water sports)-related photos (color preferred). Captions required. Seeks mss on the merchandising of sporting goods through trade channels. Free writer's guidelines.
Making Contact & Terms: Send material by mail for consideration. Uses 5×7 b&w glossy prints; transparencies, standard sizes. Pays $3-6/photo; $200-300/full-page color photo; 2¢/word for ms. Pays on publication. Buys all rights. Simultaneous submissions and previously published work OK if not published in a sporting goods publication.

SPORTS CAR INTERNATIONAL, Dept. PM, #120, 3901 Westerly Pl., Newport Beach CA 92660. (714)851-3044. Art Director: Keith May. Monthly magazine. Emphasizes sports cars. Readers are male, with high income, ages 18-65. Circ. 75,000. Sample copy $8.50.
Needs: Uses 90 photos/issue; 100% supplied by freelance photographers. Needs automotive shots. Also, people shots for profiles. Especially needs more large formal transparencies. Model release required.
Making Contact & Terms: Provide resume, business card, brochure, flyer or tearsheets to be kept on file for possible assignments. SASE. Reports in 2 weeks. Pays $600/color cover photo, $50/color inside photo, $25/b&w inside photo, $200/color page rate, $600/day or $850/photo/text package. Pays on publication. Credit line given. Buys all rights, but willing to negotiate. Simultaneous submissions OK.

SPORTSTYLE, Dept. PM, 7 W 34th St., New York NY 10001. (212)630-3652. FAX: (212)337-3247. Art Director: James Spina or Doug Gottlieb. Biweekly tabloid. Emphasizes sporting goods/apparel. Readers are male and female sports retailers. Sample copy free with SASE.
Needs: Uses 100 photos/issue; 100% supplied by freelancers. Needs photos of sports/fashion, equipment, footwear, retail store profiles, executive profiles (portrait). "All our photography is freelanced. We need *everything!*" Model release and photo captions required.

Making Contact & Terms: Arrange personal interview to show portfolio. Provide resume, business card, brochure, flyer or tearsheets to be kept on file for possible assignments. NPI.

*STAGE DIRECTIONS, 3020 Beacon Blvd., W. Sacramento CA 95691. (916)373-0201. FAX: (916)373-0232. Editor: Stephen Peithman. Ten times per year journal. Emphasizes drama, stage production and theater administration. Circ. 2,000. Estab. 1988. Sample copy free with SASE. Photo guidelines free with SASE.
Needs: Uses 10 photos/issue; all supplied by freelancers. Needs photos of action or close-up product shots. No talking heads. Model/property release preferred. Photo captions preferred.
Making Contact & Terms: Provide resume, business card, brochure, flyer or tearsheets to be kept on file for possible assignments. Keeps samples on file. SASE. Reports in 1 month. Pays $20/color and b&w cover photo; $20/color and b&w inside photo. Pays on publication. Credit line given. Buys one-time rights plus publicity rights; rights negotiable. Simultaneous submissions and/or previously published work OK.

STEP-BY-STEP GRAPHICS, Dept. PM, 6000 N. Forest Park Dr., Peoria IL 61614-3592. (309)688-2300. Managing Editor: Catharine Fishel. Bimonthly. Emphasizes the graphic communications field. Readers are graphic designers, illustrators, art directors, studio owners, photographers. Circ. 45,000. Estab. 1985. Sample copy for $7.50.
Needs: Uses 130 photos/issue; 100% supplied by freelancers. Needs how-to shots taken in artists' workplaces. Assignment only. Model release and captions required; assignment only.
Making Contact & Terms: Query with samples. Provide resume, business card, brochure, flyer or tearsheets to be kept on file for possible future assignments. SASE. Reports in 1 month. NPI; pays by the job on a case-by-case basis. Pays on acceptance. Credit line given. Buys one-time rights or first N.A. serial rights.
Tips: In photographer's samples looking for "color and lighting accuracy particularly for interiors." Recommend letter of inquiry plus samples.

SUCCESSFUL FARMING, Dept. PM, 1716 Locust St., Des Moines IA 50336. (515)284-2579. Art Director: Jim Galbraith. Publishes 14 issues/year. Emphasizes farming production, business, family living and outdoor recreation. Circ. 575,000. Sample copy free with 9×12 SAE and 9 first-class stamps; photo guidelines free with SASE.
Needs: Uses about 64 photos/issue; 55 supplied by freelance photographers: 95% on specific assignments; 5% from stock. Needs photos of farm livestock, farm machinery, buildings, crops (corn, soybeans, wheat, cotton mostly), farming activity, interesting farm people. "We are always looking for good cover shots with unique situations/composition/lighting, etc., farm management and people oriented." Model release required.
Making Contact & Terms: Arrange a personal interview to show portfolio. Query with samples and list of stock photo subjects. Provide resume, business card, brochure, flyer or tearsheets to be kept on file for possible future assignments. Reports in 2 weeks. Pays $450-600/color covers (one-time use); $100-250/color inside photo (one-time use); your daily rate, negotiable plus mileage. Pays on acceptance. Credit line given. Buys all rights on per-day assignments, one-time use on stock photos. No simultaneous submissions or previously published work.
Tips: "We need technically good (lighting, focus, composition) photos. Photographer must remember that his/her pictures must be reproducible by color separation and printing process. More and more of our needs are specific subjects. In other words, more of our photos are taken on assignment. Our needs are fewer in the areas of stock photos and photos taken on speculation. In reviewing a photographer's portfolio or samples, looks for technical excellence plus composition; must have modern agriculture practices."

SUNSHINE ARTISTS USA, 1700 Sunset Dr., Longwood FL 32750-9697. (407)323-5927. Editor: J. Wahl. Monthly. Emphasizes arts and crafts in malls and outdoors. Readers are mainly professional artists and craftsmen making a living at mall and outdoor shows. Circ. 50,000. Sample copy $2.50.
Needs: Uses 25-30 photos/year; mainly submitted by readers. Also 3-4 (35mm slides) of artist's work on cover each month. Needs 5×7 b&w photos of artist's work with article. Photos purchased with accompanying ms only. Special needs include unusual artwork or craft from successful artisans on the show circuit. Model release required; captions preferred.
Making Contact & Terms: Query with resume of credits. Does not return unsolicited material. Reports in 2 weeks. Pays $10/b&w inside photo; $15-35/text/photo package. Pays on publication. Credit line given. Buys first N.A. serial rights.

♣TEACHING TODAY, 49 Primrose Blvd., Sherwood Park, AB T8H-1G1 Canada. (403)467-5273. FAX: (403)467-5273. Editor: Max Coderre. Magazine published 5 times/year. Emphasizes professional development of teachers. Readers are primarily educators, from preschool through university level. Circ.

12,000. Estab. 1983. "Sample copy sent if request accompanied with 9×12 envelope and $3 check or money order. (In US, send US funds.)"
Needs: Uses 3-5 photos/issue; 100% supplied by freelancers; 1% freelance assignment; 99% freelance stock. Needs photos of teachers and/or students in kindergarten to university level to enhance articles. Model release required.
Making Contact & Terms: Interested in receiving work from newer, lesser-known photographers. Send unsolicited photos by mail for consideration. Send b&w or color prints, any size or format. "Enclose envelope with check/money order to cover cost of return mailing or at least 4 IRCs." Reports in 2 months. Pays $5-25/b&w photo; $15-100/color photo. Pays on publication. Credit line given. Buys one-time rights. Simultaneous submissions OK.
Tips: "For color photos for front cover—simple, uncluttered, vivid colors—most photos used are of 1 or 2 people, usually something that we could use pertaining to educational field. B&w or small photographs also used for inside purposes (e.g., to enhance articles). When sending work, give suggestion, reason of where, how, why his/her photos could be (should be) used in educational publication."

TECH DIRECTIONS, (formerly *School Shop/Tech Directions*), P.O. Box 8623, Ann Arbor MI 48107. (313)769-1211. FAX: (313)769-8383. Art, Design and Production Manager: Sharon K. Miller. Monthly except June and July. Magazine for educators and administrators in technical-vocational, industrial and technology education at middle school through community college and university levels. Covers topics related to preparing America's students for their transition to employment and for effective functioning as citizens in our modern technological world. Circ. 45,000. Estab. 1941. Sample copy free with 9×12 SAE with $1 postage.
Needs: Uses 10-15 photos/issue, rarely from freelancers. "We use only photographs depicting activities and projects in industrial/technology and trade and industrial education, and special effects photos from related industries." Special needs include photos that show new developments in the industrial/technology education field. Captions required.
Making Contact & Terms: Interested in receiving work from newer, lesser-known photographers. Send b&w or color prints by mail for consideration. Provide brochure, flyer or tearsheets to be kept on file for possible assignments. NPI; payment depends on usage. Pays on publication. Credit line given. Buys all rights; negotiable.

*TECHNICAL ANALYSIS OF STOCKS & COMMODITIES, 3517 SW Alaska St., Seattle WA 98126-2700. (206)938-0570. Art Director: Christine Morrison. Monthly magazine. Emphasizes stocks, bonds, futures, commodities, options and mutual funds. Circ. 27,500. Estab. 1982. Sample copy $5.
Needs: Uses 6 photos/issue; 100% supplied by freelancers. Needs photos of security instruments (paper) or trading floor. Model/property release preferred. Captions preferred.
Making Contact & Terms: Send unsolicited photos by mail for consideration. Send 5×7 color glossy prints; 35mm, $2\frac{1}{4} \times 2\frac{1}{4}$ or 4×5 transparencies. Keeps samples on file. SASE. Reports in 1 month. Pays $150/color cover photo; $100/color inside photo; $50/b&w inside photo. Pays on publication. Credit line given. Buys one-time and reprint rights; negotiable. Simultaneous submissions and/or previously published work OK.

TECHNOLOGY & LEARNING, Dept. PM, Suite A4, 2169 E. Francisco Blvd, San Rafael CA 94901. (415)457-4333. Editor: Holly Brady. Art Director: Ellen Wright, c/o 2451 E. River Rd., Dayton OH 45439. Monthly. Emphasizes computer in education. Readers are teachers and administrators, grades K-12. Circ. 82,000. Sample copy $3.
Needs: Uses about 7-10 photos/issue; 2 or more supplied by freelance photographers. Photo needs "depend on articles concerned. No general categories. Usually photos used to accompany articles in a conceptual manner. Computer screen shots needed often." Model release required.
Making Contact & Terms: Contact Ellen Wright to arrange a personal interview to show portfolio. Query with nonreturnable samples. Provide resume, business card, brochure, flyer or tearsheets to be kept on file for possible future assignments. SASE. Reports in 3 weeks. Pays $300-700/color cover photo; $50-100/b&w inside photo; $100-300/color inside photo. Pays on acceptance. Credit line given. Buys one-time rights. Previously published work OK.

TELECOMMUNICATIONS, Dept. PM, 685 Canton St., Norwood MA 02062. (617)769-9750. Editor: Tom Valovic. Monthly. Emphasizes "state-of-the-art voice and data communications equipment and services." Readers are "persons involved in communications management/engineering." Circ. 85,000. Sample copy with SAE and 40¢ postage. Runs international also, in Europe.
Needs: Uses about 6 photos/issue; varying number supplied by freelance photographers. Needs "applications-oriented photos of communications systems/equipment." Model release and captions required.
Making Contact & Terms: Query with list of stock photo subjects. Send b&w and color prints, 35mm transparencies by mail for consideration. Provide resume, business card, brochure, flyer or tearsheets to be kept on file for possible assignments. SASE. Reports in 1 week. Pays $250/color cover photo;

$25/b&w and $50/color inside photo. Pays on publication. Credit line given. Buys all rights.

TENNIS INDUSTRY, 1156 Avenue of the Americas., New York NY 10036. (212)921-3786. Vice President, Manufacturing: James Kukar. Published 11 times/year. Emphasizes tennis trade. Circ. 30,000. Sample copy $1 and 9×12 SASE.
Needs: Uses 10-30 photos/issue, all supplied by freelance photographers. Model release preferred; captions required.
Making Contact & Terms: Query with list of stock photo subjects. Submit portfolio for review. SASE. Reports in 1 month. Pays $350/color cover photo; $150/color inside photos. Buys one-time and all rights; negotiable. Simultaneous submissions and previously published work OK.

THOROUGHBRED TIMES, Suite 101, 801 Corporate Dr., Lexington KY 40503. (606)223-9800. Managing Editor: Chuck Manson. Weekly newspaper. Emphasizes thoroughbred breeding and racing. Readers are wide demographic range of industry professionals. Circ. 24,000. Estab. 1985. No photo guidelines.
Needs: Uses 18-20 photos/issue; 40-60% supplied by freelancers. "Looks for photos only from desired trade (thoroughbred breeding and racing)." Needs photos of specific subject features (personality, farm or business). Model release and photo captions preferred.
Making Contact & Terms: Provide resume, business card, brochure, flyer or tearsheets to be kept on file for possible assignments. SASE. Reports in 1 month. Pays $25/b&w cover or inside photo; $25/b&w page rate; $150/day. Pays on publication. Credit line given. Buys one-time rights. No simultaneous submissions. Will consider previously published work.

✿TODAY'S TRUCKING, 452 Attwell Dr.., Etobicoke, ON M9W 5C3 Canada. (416)798-2977. FAX: (416)798-3017. Editor: Rolf Lockwood. Trade publication. Magazine published 10 times/year. Emphasizes heavy trucking. Circ. 30,000. Estab. 1987. Sample copy free with SAE and IRC.
Needs: Uses 35 photos/issue; 15-20% supplied by freelance photographers. Needs photos of trucks, highways, truck drivers, mechanics, etc. Model release preferred; photo captions required.
Making Contact & Terms: Arrange a personal interview to show portfolio, but not required. Send unsolicited transparencies by mail for consideration. SAE and IRC. Reports in 2 weeks. Pays $350/color cover photo; $50+/color inside photo; $35+/b&w inside photo. Pays on acceptance. Credit line not given. Buys one-time rights. Previously published work OK.
Tips: In freelancer's portfolio wants to see "trucks in action, trucking situations, trucks in seasonal situations, dramatic highways, etc." Also looks for "striking color. Prefer extreme lenses—wide, long telephoto."

TOP PRODUCER, Farm Journal Publishing, Inc., 230 W. Washington Square, Philadelphia PA 19105. (215)829-4865. Photo Editor: Tom Dodge. Monthly. Emphasizes American agriculture. Readers are active farmers, ranchers or agribusiness people. Circ. 250,000. Sample copy and photo guidelines free with SASE.
Needs: Uses 20-30 photos/issue; 75% supplied by freelance photographers. "We use studio-type portraiture (environmental portraits), technical, details and scenics." Model release preferred; photo captions required.
Making Contact & Terms: Arrange a personal interview to show portfolio or query with resume of credits along with business card, brochure, flyer or tearsheets to be kept on file for possible assignments. SASE. Reports in 2 weeks. NPI. "We pay a cover bonus." Pays on acceptance. Credit line given. Buys one-time rights. Simultaneous submissions and previously published work OK.
Tips: In portfolio or samples, likes to "see about 20 slides showing photographer's use of lighting and photographer's ability to work with people. Know your intended market. Familiarize yourself with the magazine and keep abreast of how photos are used in the general magazine field."

TRADESWOMAN MAGAZINE, P.O. Box 40664, San Francisco CA 94140. (415)821-7334. Editors: Janet Scoll Johnson and Robin Murphy. Quarterly. Emphasizes women in nontraditional blue collar trades work (carpenters, electricians, etc.). Readers are highly skilled specialized women in crafts jobs with trade unions, and self-employed women such as contractors. Women doing work which is currently considered nontraditional. Circ. 1,500. Estab. 1981. Sample copy $3.

✿ *The maple leaf before a listing indicates that the market is Canadian. The symbol is new this year in* Photographer's Market.

Needs: Uses about 10-15 photos/issue; one-third supplied by freelance photographers. Needs "photos of women doing nontraditional work—either job site photos or inshop photos. Occasionally we just use photos of tools." Special needs include cover quality photos—black and white only.
Making Contact & Terms: Send unsolicited photos by mail for consideration. Send high contrast b&w prints; b&w contact sheet. SASE. Reports in 1 month. Pays $25/b&w photo; payment is negotiable. Pays on acceptance. Credit line given. Rights negotiable. Simultaneous submissions and previously published work OK.
Tips: "We are looking for pictures of strong women whom we consider pioneers in their fields. Since we are nonprofit and do not have a lot of money, we often offer write-ups about authors and photographers in addition to small payments."

TRAVEL AGENT MAGAZINE, Dept. PM, 801 Second Ave., New York NY 10019. Art Director: Curtis Fields. Weekly magazine. Majority of readers are travel professionals ages 21 and up. Circ. 42,000. Estab. 1930. Free sample copy.
Needs: Uses 25 photos/issue; 50% supplied by freelancers. Needs travel photos. Especially interested in various travel and newsweekly-type photos.
Making Contact & Terms: Submit portfolio for review. Query with list of stock photo subjects. Provide resume, business card, brochure, flyer or tearsheets to be kept on file for possible assignments. Keeps samples on file. Reports in 1-2 weeks. Pays $400/color cover photo; $50/color inside photo. Pays on acceptance. Buys one-time rights.

TRUCKERS NEWS, P.O. Box W, Newport Beach CA 92658-8910. (714)261-1636. Managing Editor: Deborah Whistler. Monthly magazine. Emphasizes trucking. Readers are over-the-road truck drivers. Most male, ages 30-65. Circ. 200,000. Photo guidelines free with SASE.
Needs: Uses 20 photos/issue; 50% supplied by freelancers. Needs photos of scenics (trucks on highways), drivers at work. Model release is "photographer's responsibility." Photo captions preferred.
Making Contact & Terms: Query with resume of credits or send unsolicited photos by mail for consideration. Send 35mm transparencies. SASE. Sends check when material is used. Pays $150/color cover photo; $75/color or b&w inside photo. Pays on publication. Buys one-time rights. Does not consider simultaneous submissions or previously published work.

TRUCKSTOP WORLD, P.O. Box W, Newport Beach CA 92658-8910. (714)261-1636. Managing Editor: Deborah Whistler. Bimonthly magazine. Emphasizes trucking. Readers are truckstop managers. Most male, ages 30-65. Circ. 12,000. Photo guidelines free with SASE.
Needs: Uses 10 photos/issue; 30-100% supplied by freelancers. Needs photos of truckstops. Model release is "photographer's responsibility." Photo captions preferred.
Making Contact & Terms: Query with resume of credits or send unsolicited photos by mail for consideration. Send 35mm transparencies. SASE. Sends check when material is used. Pays $150/color cover photo; $75/color or b&w inside photo. Pays on publication. Buys one-time rights.

U.S. NAVAL INSTITUTE PROCEEDINGS, U.S. Naval Institute, Annapolis MD 21402. (301)268-6110. Photo Editor: Linda Cullen. Monthly magazine. Emphasizes matters of current interest in naval, maritime and military affairs—including strategy, tactics, personnel, shipbuilding and equipment. Readers are officers in the Navy, Marine Corps and Coast Guard; also for enlisted personnel of the sea services, members of other military services in this country and abroad and civilians with an interest in naval and maritime affairs. Circ. 119,790. Free sample copy.
Needs: Buys 15 photos/issue. Needs photos of Navy, Coast Guard and merchant ships of all nations; military aircraft; personnel of the Navy, Marine Corps and Coast Guard; and maritime environment and situations. No poor quality photos. Captions required.
Making Contact & Terms: Query first with resume of credits. Pays $200/color cover photo; $50 for article openers; $25/inside editorial. Pays on publication. SASE. Reports in 2 weeks on pictorial feature queries; 6-8 weeks on other materials. Color and b&w: uses 8×10 glossy prints or slides. Pays $10 for official military photos submitted with articles. Pays $250-500 for naval/maritime pictorial features. Buys one-time rights.
Tips: "These features consist of copy, photos and photo captions. The package should be complete, and there should be a query first. In the case of the $25 shots, we like to maintain files on hand so they can be used with articles as the occasion requires. Annual photo contest—write for details."

UNITED ARTS, Suite 6D, 141 Wooster, New York NY 10012. (212)473-6695. Publisher: Larry Qualls. Quarterly journal. Emphasizes theatre, dance and art. Readers are in the university community. Circ. 3,000. Estab. 1988. Sample copy available.
Needs: Needs photos of dance, theatre and art. Special photo needs include art photos of sculpture and theatre production shots. Model release and photo captions required.
Making Contact & Terms: Query with resume of credits. NPI. Reports in 3 weeks. Credit line given. Simultaneous submissions and previously published work OK.

VERMONT BUSINESS MAGAZINE, P.O. Box 6120, Brattleboro VT 05302. (802)257-4100. Editor: Timothy McQuiston. Monthly tabloid. Emphasizes business news. Readers are business owners and managers. Circ. 16,000. Estab. 1972. No sample copies or photo guidelines available.
Needs: Uses 25 photos/issue; 45% supplied by freelancers. Needs photos of business topics. Photos purchased with accompanying ms only. Model release and photo captions preferred.
Making Contact & Terms: Arrange a personal interview to show portfolio. SASE. Reports in 1-2 weeks. Pays $50/b&w cover photo. Pays within 30 days of publication. Credit line given. Buys one-time rights.
Tips: Editor "only needs Vermont-specific photos." Recommends freelancer "call and we'll assign the photos."

VETERINARY ECONOMICS, 9073 Lenexa Dr., Lenexa KS 66215. (913)492-4300. FAX: (913)492-4157. Art Director: Alison J. Fulton. Monthly magazine. Emphasizes management of veterinary practice. Readers are veterinarians of all ages. Circ. 42,000. Estab. 1965. Photo guidelines free with SASE.
Needs: Uses 10 photos/issue; 30% supplied by freelancers. Needs photos of clinics, business and economic subjects. Clinic shots are assigned. Especially wants to see photos to illustrate articles on fees, earnings and expenses. Model and/or property release preferred.
Making Contact & Terms: Query with list of stock photo subjects. Provide resume, business card, brochure, flyer or tearsheets to be kept on file for possible assignments. Samples are kept on file. SASE. Reports in 3 weeks. Pays $350-450/color cover photo; $150/color inside photo; $75/b&w inside photo. Pays on acceptance. Credit line given. Buys one-time rights. Previously published work sometimes OK, but should be explained.
Tips: Wants to see photos with "quality and relevance to stories. Photos must show the concept clearly." To break in, "target your audience carefully. I get too many animal shots that I can't use."

VM & SD (VISUAL MERCHANDISING AND STORE DESIGN), 407 Gilbert Ave., Cincinnati OH 45202. FAX: (513)421-5144. Editor: P.K. Anderson. Monthly magazine. Emphasizes store design and store display (all types of stores). Readers are visual merchandisers and store designers, architects, store owners, presidents and chief executive officers. Circ. 20,000. Estab. 1922. Sample copy free.
Needs: Number of freelance photos used varies considerably. About 20% assigned. Needs architectural shots of stores and photos of displays. Photo captions preferred.
Making Contact & Terms: Query with resume of credits. Provide business card, brochure, flyer or tearsheets to be kept on file for possible assignments. Send unsolicited photos by mail for consideration. Send color 35mm, 2¼ × 2¼ or 4 × 5 photos. SASE. Reports in 3 weeks. Pays $150/color cover photo; $50/color inside photo; $20/b&w inside photo. Pays on publication. Credit line given. Buys one-time rights. Simultaneous submissions and previously published work OK.
Tips: Trend in publication toward "excellent facade shots of stores and more shots concentrating on architectural detail." In samples, wants to see "an excellent sense of composition in interior photographs depicting not only the design of the space, but also the integration of merchandise presentation." To break in, "submit 4 × 5 or 2¼ transparencies showing imaginative window displays as well as unusual store interiors. With interiors, try to convey the store from several vantage points."

WALLS & CEILINGS MAGAZINE, 8602 N. 40th St., Tampa FL 33604. (813)989-9300. Editor: Lee Rector. Monthly magazine. Emphasizes wall and ceiling construction, drywall, lath, plaster, stucco and exterior specialty finishes. Readership consists of 98% male, wall and ceiling contractors. Circ. 19,500. Sample copy $4.
Needs: Uses 15-20 photos/issue. Uses 30% freelance work. Needs photos of interior/exterior architectural shots, contractors and workers on job (installing drywall and stucco). Model release required.
Making Contact & Terms: Query with resume of credits. Send unsolicited photos by mail for consideration. Send b&w or color glossy prints, any size, or 35mm, 2¼ × 2¼ or 4 × 5 transparencies. SASE. Reports in 1 month. Pays $150/color cover photo; $50/color inside photo; $25/b&w inside photo; $50-150/photo/text package. Pays on publication. Credit line given. Buys exclusive, one-time and "our industry" rights. Simultaneous submissions and previously published work OK, provided not submitted to or published by competitors.

WANG IN THE NEWS, 12416 Hymeadow, Austin TX 78750-1896. (512)250-9023. Editor: Larry Storer. Monthly tabloid. Emphasizes computers and related products – specifically Wang and Wang-compatible. Readership is 25-55, 50/50 male/female in occupations ranging from secretaries to lawyers. Basically anyone who uses Wang computers. Circ. 25,000. Sample copy free with 9 × 12 SAE and 2 first-class stamps.
Needs: Uses about 5 photos/issue; 20-30% supplied by freelancers. Usually needs product-oriented shots. Model release and photo captions required.
Making Contact & Terms: Query with resume of credits, business card, brochure, flyer or tearsheets to be kept on file for possible assignments. Query with list of stock photo subjects. Send unsolicited b&w glossy prints, all sizes, by mail for consideration. SASE. Reports in 2 weeks. Pays $25/b&w inside

photo; $100-150/photo/text package. Pays on publication. Credit line given. Buys all rights; negotiable. Does not consider simultaneous submissions or previously published work.
Tips: "Doesn't hurt to try and understand content. Locate Wang installations in area, visit, visualize photo possibilities. Needs photographers in New York area and Boston area from time to time."

WARD'S AUTO WORLD, 28 W. Adams St., Detroit MI 48226. (313)962-4433. FAX: (313)962-4456. Editor-in-Chief: David C. Smith. Monthly. Emphasizes the automotive industry. Circ. 92,000. Estab. 1965. Sample copy free with 9 × 12 SAE and $2 postage.
Needs: Uses about 40 photos/issue, mainly color transparencies; 10-30% supplied by freelancers; 100% assignment. Subject needs vary. "Most photos are assigned. We are a news magazine – the news dictates what we need." Model release preferred; captions required.
Making Contact & Terms: Arrange a personal interview to show portfolio. Query with samples. Provide resume, business card, brochure, flyer or tearsheets to be kept on file for possible future assignments. SASE. Reports in 2 weeks. Pays $50-100/b&w photo; $60-125/color photo; $10-20/hour; $350-500/day. Pays on publication. Credit line given. Buys all rights.
Tips: In reviewing a photographer's portfolio or samples, looks for "creativity, originality and quality." Also looks for "ability to capture news subjects in good candid poses. We need photographers to accompany reporters on interviews, plant tours, etc. More photos are being printed of people; fewer on cars themselves. *Do Not* send us photos of cars. We have all we need. We want freelancers with proven work abilities (who can accompany a reporter on assignment)."

WATER CONDITIONING & PURIFICATION MAGAZINE, Suite 101, 4651 N. First Ave., Tucson AZ 85718. (602)293-5446. FAX: (602)887-2383. Editor: Darlene Scheel. Monthly magazine. Emphasizes water treatment. Readers are water treatment professionals. Circ. 15,446, international. Estab. 1959. Sample copy free with 9 × 12 SASE.
Needs: Uses 20-30 photos/issue; 60% supplied by freelancers. Most photos are used for cover illustrations. "Cover shots vary from water scenes to technology involving water treatment." Wants to see "mainly cover shots" in the coming year. Model, property release and photo captions preferred.
Making Contact & Terms: Send unsolicited color prints or 35mm, 2¼ × 2¼, 4 × 5 or 8 × 10 transparencies by mail for consideration. Provide resume, business card, brochure, flyer or tearsheets to be kept on file for possible assignments. SASE. Reports as needed. Pays $150/color or b&w cover photo; $100/b&w inside photo. Pays on publication. Credit line given. Buys one-time rights.
Tips: "Looking for active water shots – cascading brooks, etc."

WATER WELL JOURNAL, 6375 Riverside Dr., Dublin OH 43017. (614)761-3222. FAX: (614)761-3446. Associate Editor: Gloria Swanson. Monthly. Emphasizes construction of water wells, development of ground water resources and ground water cleanup. Readers are water well drilling contractors, managers, suppliers and ground water scientists. Circ. 36,049. Estab. 1946. Sample copy $1.50.
Needs: Uses 1-3 freelance photos/issue plus cover photos. Needs photos of installations and how-to illustrations. Model release preferred; captions required.
Making Contact & Terms: Contact with resume of credits; inquire about rates. "We'll contact." Pays $10-50/hour; $200/color cover photo; $50/b&w inside photo; "flat rate for assignment." Pays on publication. Credit line given "if requested." Buys all rights.

THE WISCONSIN RESTAURATEUR, 125 W. Doty St., Madison WI 53703. Editor: Jan LaRue. Monthly magazine, except combined issue in November and December. Trade magazine for the Wisconsin Restaurant Association. Emphasizes the restaurant industry. Readers are "restaurateurs, hospitals, schools, institutions, cafeterias, food service students, chefs, etc." Circ. 4,200. Free sample copy and photo guidelines with 9 × 12 SAE and $1.85 postage.
Needs: Photos purchased with or without accompanying ms. Buys 12 photos/year. Animal; celebrity/ personality; photo essay/photo feature; product shot; scenic; special effects/experimental; how-to; human interest; humorous; nature; still life; and wildlife. Wants on a regular basis unusual shots of normal restaurant activities or unusual themes. Photos should relate directly to food service industry or be conceived as potential cover shots. No restaurants outside Wisconsin; national trends OK. No nonmember material except the very unusual. Ask for membership list for specific restaurants. Model release required; captions preferred. Uses accompanying mss related to the food service industry – how-to, unusual concepts, humorous and "a better way." No cynical or off-color material. Writer's guidelines free with SASE.
Making Contact & Terms: Send material by mail for consideration. Provide photocopies of previously submitted work. Uses 5 × 7 b&w glossy prints, vertical format required for cover. SASE. Reports in 1 month. Pays $7.50-15/b&w inside photo; $10-25/b&w cover photo; $15-50 for text/photo package, or on a per-photo basis. Pays on acceptance. Credit line given. Buys one-time rights. Simultaneous submissions and previously published work OK.

WOODSHOP NEWS, 35 Pratt St., Essex CT 06426. (203)767-8227. Senior Editor: Thomas Clark. Monthly tabloid. Emphasizes woodworking. Readers are male, 20's-60's, furniture makers, cabinet-makers, millworkers and hobbyist woodworkers. Circ. 100,000. Estab. 1986. Sample copy and photo guidelines free with 11 × 13 SAE.
Needs: Uses 40 photos/issue; up to 10% supplied by freelancers. Needs photos of people working with wood. Model release and photo captions required.
Making Contact & Terms: Provide resume, business card, brochure, flyer or tearsheets to be kept on file for possible assignments. SASE. Reports in 1 month. Pays $250/color cover photo; $30/b&w inside photo. Pays on publication. Credit line given. Buys one-time rights.

THE WORK BOAT, P.O. Box 1348, Mandeville LA 70470. (504)626-0298. Art Director: Donna Musarra. Bimonthly. Emphasizes news of the work boat industry; all commercial vessels working inland and coastal waters. Readers are executives of towboat, offshore supply, crew boat, dredging and passenger vessel firms, naval architects, leasing companies, equipment companies and shipyards, captains, mates and crews. "Technically minded, balance-sheet conscious." Circ. 13,600. Sample copy $3 with 9 × 12 SAE; photo and writer's guidelines for SASE.
Needs: Uses 10-20 photos/issue; most supplied by freelancers. Buys primarily cover, vertical, of work boats in action, including people. No pleasure boats. Photos should crop 8 × 11 for full-page bleed. Reviews photos with or without ms. "Cover photo corresponds to calendar theme (inside). Submit work 3 months prior to issue at least." Model release preferred; captions required.
Making Contact & Terms: Query with resume of credits and list of stock subjects. Provide resume, business card, brochure, flyer or tearsheets to be kept on file for possible assignments. SASE. Reports and returns slides within 4-6 weeks; cover submissions take 2 months. For cover: Pays $250 on acceptance. Payment varies for color inside photo. Credit line given. Buys one-time rights and first N.A. serial rights. No simultaneous or previously published submissions.
Tips: "We solicit cover submissions—try to secure others from writers. Study the magazine—talk to people in the industry first."

WORLD FENCE NEWS, Suite M, 6301 Manchaca Rd., Austin TX 78745. (800)231-0275. FAX: (512)445-3496. Managing Editor: Rick Henderson. Monthly tabloid. Emphasizes fencing contractors and installers. Readers are mostly male fence company owners and employees, ages 30-60. Circ. 13,000. Estab. 1983. Sample copy free with 10 × 12 SAE.
Needs: Uses 35 photos/issue; 20 supplied by freelancers. Needs photos of scenics, silhouettes, sunsets which include all types of fencing. Also, installation shots of fences of all types. "Cover images are a major area of need." Model and/or property release preferred mostly for people shots. Photo captions required; location, date.
Making Contact & Terms: "If you have suitable subjects, call and describe." SASE. Reports in 3 weeks. Pays $100/color cover photo; $25/b&w inside photo. Pays on acceptance. Credit line given. Buys one-time rights. Previously published work OK.

WORLD TRADE MAGAZINE, Dept. PM, Suite 450, 500 Newport Center Dr., Newport Beach CA 92660. (716)640-7070. Photo Editor: Craig Peterson. Bimonthly magazine. Emphasizes US businesses involved in foreign trade. Readers are male and female executives ages 28-65. Circ. 34,000. Estab. 1987. Sample copy free with 9 × 12 SAE and $2.13 postage. Photo guidelines free with SASE.
Needs: Uses 41 photos/issue; 10-15 supplied by freelancers. Needs photos of personalities (business), technology, locations. Reviews photos with accompanying ms only.
Making Contact & Terms: No phone calls. Send a card instead. Provide resume, business card, brochure, flyer or tearsheets to be kept on file for possible assignments. Keeps samples on file. Cannot return material. Reports as needed. Pays $300/color cover photo; $35-200/color inside photo; $15-30/b&w inside photo. Pays on publication. Credit line given. Buys one-time rights.
Tips: Looks for "ability to photograph business subjects in a way that can *reveal* something about an individual's character and/or corporate lifestyle."

WRITER'S DIGEST/WRITER'S YEARBOOK, 1507 Dana Ave., Cincinnati OH 45207. (513)531-2222. FAX (513)531-4744. Senior Editor: Tom Clark. Monthly magazine. Emphasizes writing and publishing. For "writers and photojournalists of all description: professionals, beginners, students, moonlighters, bestselling authors, editors, etc." Circ. 250,000. Estab. 1921. Buys 15 photos/year. Buys first N.A. serial rights, one-time use only. Submit model release with photo. Query with resume of credits, list of photographed writers, or send contact sheet for consideration. Uses about 10% freelance material each issue. Purchases about 5% of photos from stock or on assignment; 95% of those with accompanying ms. Provide brochure and samples (print samples, not glossy photos) to be kept on file for possible future assignments. "We never run photos without text." Credit line given. Pays on acceptance. Reports in 4 weeks. SASE. Simultaneous submissions OK if editors are advised. Previously published work OK. Sample copy $3; guidelines free with SASE.

Needs: Primarily celebrity/personality ("to accompany profiles"); some how-to, human interest and product shots. All must be writer-related. "We most often use photos with profiles of writers; in fact, we won't buy the profile unless we can get usable photos. The story, however, is always our primary consideration, and we won't buy the pictures unless they can be specifically related to an article we have in the works. We sometimes use humorous shots in our Writing Life column."

Making Contact & Terms: Uses 8×10 glossy prints; send contact sheet. "Do *not* send negatives." Captions required. Pays $50-75. "Freelance work is rarely used on the cover."

Tips: "Shots should not *look* posed, even though they may be. Photos with a sense of place, as well as persona, preferred. Have a mixture of tight and middle-distance shots of the subject. Study a few back issues. Avoid the stereotyped writer-at-typewriter shots; go for an array of settings. Move the subject around, and give us a choice. We're also interested in articles on how a writer earned extra money with photos, or how a photographer works with writers on projects, etc."

Other Publications/'92-'93 changes

The following markets appeared in the 1992 edition of *Photographer's Market* but are not listed in the 1993 edition. They may have been omitted for failing to respond to our request for updates of information, they may have gone out of business or they may no longer wish to receive freelance work.

Consumer Publications

Ambassador (no longer published)
Ambergris (not reviewing work)
Boat Journal (not reviewing work)
Body, Mind & Spirit (did not respond)
Business Traveler International (not reviewing work)
California Magazine (did not respond)
Campus Connection (did not respond)
Canadian Fiction Magazine (did not respond)
Cape Cod Home & Garden (did not respond)
Cape Cod Life Including Martha's Vineyard and Nantucket (did not respond)
Catholic Update (not reviewing work)
Chic Magazine (not reviewing work)
Christian Herald (not reviewing work)
Connection Publication of NJ, Inc., The (did not respond)
Earthtreks Digest (out of business)
Esquire (did not respond)
Event (did not respond)
Florida Home & Garden (merged with South Florida Magazine)
Forerunner, The (did not respond)
Formula Magazine (did not respond)
Georgia Byways Magazine (did not respond)
Golf Illustrated (no longer published)
Guide Magazine (out of business)
Gulfshore Life (did not respond)

Hawaii Magazine (not reviewing work)
Hideaways Guide (not reviewing work)
High School Sports (no longer published)
Home Plan Magazines (not reviewing work)
Hot Truck (out of business)
Inside Magazine (not reviewing work)
International Gymnast (not reviewing work)
Island Grower, The (not reviewing work)
L.A. West (did not respond)
Let's Live (did not respond)
Lifestyle (did not respond)
Lights and Shadows (not reviewing work)
Mother Jones (did not respond)
National Geographic (did not respond)
National Geographic World (did not respond)
New England Living Travel Guide, The (sold)
New Hampshire Life (did not respond)
New Home (out of business)
New Woman (not reviewing work)
New York Alive (did not respond)
North Shore Magazine (not reviewing work)
Northwest Living (out of business)
1001 Home Ideas (did not respond)
Oregon Coast Getaway Guide (no longer published)
Organic Gardening (not reviewing work)
Pacific Northwest Magazine (not reviewing work)
PACIFIC: The Monterey Bay Month (did not respond)

Parents of Teenagers Magazine (sold)
People Magazine (did not respond)
Personal Investor (no longer published)
Playboy Magazine (not reviewing work)
Popular Photography (not reviewing work)
Ranch & Coast Magazine (did not respond)
Rap Express, Heavy Metal Heart Throbs (sold)
Rural Heritage (not reviewing work)
Seventeen (did not respond)
73 Amateur Radio Today (not reviewing work)
Society (did not respond)
Southern Homes Magazine (did not respond)
Tennis Magazine (not reviewing work)
Trains Magazine (out of business)
Treasure (did not respond)
TV Guide (did not respond)
Utne Reader (not reviewing work)
Vail Magazine (not reviewing work)
Victimology: An International Journal (did not respond)
Vision Magazine (no longer publishing)
Water Scooter (did not respond)
Weekly News, The (did not respond)
Yankee Publishing, Inc. (did not respond)

Newspapers & Newsletters

AEA Update (not reviewing work)
Alaska Fisherman's Journal (not reviewing work)

Book Author's Newsletter (did not respond)
Citizen Newspaper Group (not reviewing work)
Cycling U.S.A. (did not respond)
Daily Enterprise-Courier (out of business)
France Today (not reviewing work)
Maryland Farmer, Virginia Farmer, Georgia Farmer, Alabama Farmer, Carolina Farmer, Tennessee Farmer and Kentucky Farmer (did not respond)
Modern Tire Dealer Magazine (not reviewing work)
Northwest Magazine/The Oregonian (out of business)
Sporting News, The (not reviewing work)
Times Journal (not reviewing work)
Townships Sun, The (not reviewing work)
Wichita Falls Times Record News (did not respond)

Special Interest Publications
Arkansas Farm & Country (sold to Southern Farm)
Atlanta Chamber of Commerce (not reviewing work)
Bilans (did not respond)
Bionics (did not respond)
California Monthly (not reviewing work)
Catholic Forester (not reviewing work)
CDA Update (did not respond)
Dimensions in Health Service (not reviewing work)
Dramatics (not reviewing work)
ELCIC Sunday Bulletins (not reviewing work)
Electrical Contractor (not reviewing work)
Explorer International Association of Space Philatelists (did not respond)
Flyfisher (out of business)
Foundation News (did not respond)
Growth Magazine (not reviewing work)
Heartland USA (not reviewing work)
Home & Away Magazine (not reviewing work)
ICF Bugle, The (not reviewing work)

Jaycees Magazine (not reviewing work)
Leadership (not reviewing work)
Lookout, The (not reviewing work)
Mainsheet (did not respond)
Mayo Alumnus, The (not reviewing work)
Nuclear Times (not reviewing work)
Pneumatic Packaging (sold)
Portfolio: A Publication for the Visual Artist (did not respond)
Regards (suspended publication)
Safari Magazine (not reviewing work)
Snack World (not reviewing work)
South American Explorer (did not respond)
Spiritual Life (not reviewing work)
Trailblazer Magazine (did not respond)
United Evangelical Action (not reviewing work)
World Encounter (no longer published)

Trade Publications
Agrichemical Age (no longer published)
American Squaredance (sold)
Asbestos Issues (no longer published)
Biopharm Manufacturing (not reviewing work)
Cabinet Manufacturing & Fabricating (merger)
California Farmer (not reviewing work)
Ceramics Monthly (not reviewing work)
Communications (did not respond)
Delta Design Group, Inc. (did not respond)
Dental Economics (did not respond)
Dixie Contractor (not reviewing work)
Drycleaners News (not reviewing work)
Earnshaw's Review (not reviewing work)
Florida Underwriter (not reviewing work)
Garden Supply Retailer (suspended publication)
Golf Shop Operations (did not

respond)
Ground Water Age (did not respond)
Home Improvement Center (not reviewing work)
IEEE Software (not reviewing work)
IGA Grocergram (did not respond)
Interlit (not reviewing work)
Journal of Family Practice, The (not reviewing work)
Journal of Ophthalmic Nursing & Technology (not reviewing work)
Liquid and Gas Chromatography (not reviewing work)
Manufacturing Engineering (not reviewing work)
Medical World News (sold/not reviewing work)
Music Educators Journal (did not respond)
New Biotech (did not respond)
Personal Selling Power, Inc. (did not respond)
Petroleum Independent (did not respond)
Pharmaceutical Technology (not reviewing work)
Physician and Sportsmedicine, The (not reviewing work)
RDH, The National Magazine for Dental Hygiene Professionals (not reviewing work)
RN Magazine (did not respond)
Southern Beverage Journal (not reviewing work)
Souvenirs & Novelties Magazine (not reviewing work)
Spectroscopy (not reviewing work)
Successful Meetings (did not respond)
Tobacco International (did not respond)
Tourist Attractions and Parks (did not respond)
Utility and Telephone Fleets (did not respond)
Utility Construction and Maintenance (did not respond)
Weingarten Publications (not reviewing work)
Wilson Library Bulletin (did not respond)
Wines & Vines (did not respond)
Wings West (did not respond)
Young Fashions Magazine (no longer published)

Record Companies

Whether shooting an album cover, a self-promotion piece or concert footage, working for record companies can be a gold mine of opportunities. It is a field which searches for quality photos to sell a performer. For those photographers who are persistent and dedicated to their work, record companies can provide a substantial income. At the same time most photographers are allowed to express their artistic vision when shooting music industry assignments.

Many photographers who think of working with record companies dream of shooting record cover and publicity photos for major music stars. But in reality, photographers who go on to long-term, high-profile success often start out working with the smaller, independent music companies, or "indies." Larger companies typically rely on stables of photographers who are either on staff or who work through art studios that deal with music companies. Because of this tendency, it can be quite difficult for a newcomer to break in when these companies already have their pick of talented, reliable photographers.

Currently, about six major companies take in better than 90 percent of all sales in the music industry. The balance is shared among independent companies or subsidiaries of the larger corporations. However, even within this relatively minor segment of the market, there are hundreds of companies competing for very specific music audiences, with many newer labels being born every year.

In light of this prolific growth in the independent market, freelance photographers have reason for optimism. However, for the same reason, freelancers should be alert when dealing with such companies. In most cases, it takes time for recently established companies to learn the various aspects of professionalism and ethics in doing business. In a few cases, companies can be deliberately deceptive and abusive in terms of payment and copyright. Either way, it's best to study a company well before selling stock images to them or working for them on assignment.

It's a good idea to query prospective companies and request copies of their various forms and contracts for photographers; seeing the content and company's image in such materials can tell you a great deal about how organized and professional a company is. In addition, talk to other photographers or network within the music industry to learn more about a prospective company, even if it's listed in this section.

Once you are hired to shoot for a record company, it also doesn't hurt to research the artist's work. Photographer Anthony "Kal" Roberts has found that by listening to an album before he shoots for its cover he gains inspiration and knowledge about the musician. He discusses his approach to shooting for record companies in the Close-up on page 490.

Shooting for the record company market draws upon various skills. There is a need for photographers who can capture good action shots under the adverse, rapidly changing lighting conditions of live performance. Also, there is a tremendous need for photographers with studio-photography skills to coordinate and shoot concept and group shots for cover art as well as promotional photos. A good portfolio for record company prospects shows off the photographer's range of skills or concentration in an imaginative way, but especially illustrates his ability to solve the creative problems facing record company art directors. Such problems may be as "simple" as coming up with a fresh concept for record art, working within the relatively limited visual format of the 5-inch compact disc liner sheet, or assembling a complex finished shot on a limited budget. Even if a photographer has not worked for a record company client previously, he can study the needs of various companies in this section and shoot a series of self-assignments which clearly show his problem-solving abilities.

*ALPHA INTERNATIONAL RECORD CO., 1080 N. Delaware Ave., Philadelphia PA 19125. (215)425-8682. FAX: (215)425-4376. Production Manager: Arthur Stoppe. Estab. 1989. Handles pop, urban, dance and alternative music. Freelancers used for portraits, in-concert shots, studio shots, cover/liner, publicity, posters and print advertising. Works on assignment only. Offers 6-8 assignments annually.
Specs: Uses 8×10 glossy color prints; 35mm and 2¼×2¼ transparencies.
Making Contact: Provide resume, business card, self-promotion piece or tearsheets to be kept on file for future assignments. Samples kept on file. SASE. Reports in 1-2 weeks. Pays $500-1,500/job; $50-250/color photo; $50-250/b&w photo. Pays on acceptance. Credit line given. Buys all rights. Model/property release required.
Tips: Needs "good environmental portraits" (b&w and color) of people for album-cover type use. Also the same but geared for press/publicity use. The types of photos used for record album and single art have a lot more in common with contemporary fashion and even fine art photographs than they may have had in the past.

‡ALPHABEAT, Box 12 01, D-6980 Wertheim/Main, West Germany. Phone: 9342-841 55. Managing Director: Stephan Dehn. Handles disco, dance, pop, soft ballads, wave, synth-pop, electro-disco and funk. Photographers used for portraits, studio shots and special effects for album covers, publicity, brochures, posters and product advertising. Works with freelancers on assignment only.
Specs: Uses color prints.
Making Contact: Send unsolicited photos by mail for consideration. Submit portfolio for review. Provide resume, business card, brochure, flyer or tearsheets to be kept on file for possible future assignments. SASE. Reports in 2 weeks.
Payment & Terms: NPI. Pays according to type of order. Credit line given. Buys all rights; negotiable.

ANTONE'S RECORDS, Dept. PM, 609 B W. 6th St., Austin TX 78701. (512)322-0617. General Manager: Donna McClure. Handles R&B and blues. Photographers used for portraits, in-concert shots and studio shots, album covers, publicity and posters. Works with freelancers on assignment only; offers 5-10 assignments/year.
Specs: Uses 8×10 glossy b&w and color prints.
Making Contact: Provide resume, business card, brochure, flyer or tearsheets to be kept on file for possible future assignments. Cannot return material. Reports in 3 weeks.
Payment & Terms: NPI. Rate of payment varies. Credit line given. Buys all rights, but willing to negotiate.
Tips: To break in, "please submit photographs." There are "good chances" with record companies. More need for "retro lighting, b&w covers."

APON RECORD COMPANY, INC., Steinway Station, Box 3082, Long Island NY 11103. (212)721-5599. President: Andre M. Poncic. Handles classical, folklore and international. Photographers used for portraits and studio shots for album covers and posters. Buys 50+ assignments/year. Provide brochure and samples to be kept on file for possible future assignments.
Specs: Uses b&w prints and 4×5 transparencies.
Making Contact: Send photos by mail for consideration. Cannot return material. Reports in 3 months.
Payment & Terms: NPI; payment negotiable. Credit line given. Buys all rights.

ART ATTACK RECORDS, INC./CARTE BLANCHE RECORDS, Dept. PM, Fort Lowell Station, P.O. Box 31475, Tucson AZ 85751. (602)881-1212. President: William Cashman. Handles rock, pop, country, and jazz. Photographers used for portraits, in-concert shots, studio shots and special effects for album covers, inside album shots, publicity and brochures. Works with freelancers on assignment only; "gives 10-15 assignments/year."
Specs: "Depends on particular project."
Making Contact: Arrange a personal interview to show portfolio. Provide resume, business card, brochure, flyer or tearsheets to be kept on file for possible future assignments. "We will contact only if interested."
Payment & Terms: NPI; payment "negotiable." Credit line given.
Tips: Prefers to see "a definite and original style—unusual photographic techniques, special effects" in a portfolio. "Send us samples to refer to that we may keep on file."

AZRA RECORDS, Dept. PM, P.O. Box 459, Maywood CA 90270. (213)560-4223. Contact: David Richards. Handles rock, heavy metal, novelty and seasonal. Photographers used for special effects and "anything unique and unusual" for picture records and shaped picture records. Works with freelancers on assignment only; "all work is freelance-assigned."
Specs: Uses 8×10 b&w or color glossy prints and 35mm transparencies.
Making Contact: Query with resume of credits or send "anything unique in photo effects" by mail for consideration. SASE. Reports in 2 weeks.
Payment & Terms: NPI; payment "depends on use of photo, either outright pay or percentages." Credit line given. Buys one-time rights.

ROBERT BATOR & ASSOCIATES, Dept. PM, 49 Lakeside Dr., Lake Paradise, Monson MA 01057. (413)267-3537. FAX: (413)267-3538. Art Director: Joan Bator. Estab. 1969. Handles rock and country. Photographers used for in-concert shots and studio shots for album covers, inside album shots, publicity and posters. Works with freelancers on assignment only; offers 400 assignments/year. Buys 5,000 photos/year.
Specs: Uses 4×5 and 8×10 glossy ("mostly color") prints.
Making Contact: Send unsolicited photos by mail for consideration. Provide resume, business card, brochure, flyer or tearsheets to be kept on file for possible future assignments. "You can submit female suggestive photos for sex appeal, or male, but in good taste." SASE. Reports in 1 week.
Payment & Terms: Pays $100-150/b&w photo; $150-250/color photo; $150-189/hour; $400-500/day; $375-495/job. Credit line given. Buys one-time rights; other rights negotiable. Model release preferred. Photo captions preferred.
Tips: Looks "for good clear photos of models. Show some imagination. Would like some sexually-oriented prints—because advertising is geared for it. Also fashion shots—men's and women's apparel: especially swim suits and casual clothing."

BOUQUET-ORCHID ENTERPRISES, Box 11686, Atlanta GA 30355-1686. (404)355-7635. President: Bill Bohannon. Photographers used for live action and studio shots for publicity flyers and brochures. Works with freelancers on assignment only.
Making Contact: Provide brochure and resume to be kept on file for possible future assignments. SASE. Reports in 1 month.
Payment & Terms: NPI.
Tips: "We are just beginning to use freelance photography in our organization. We are looking for material for future reference and future needs."

BRENTWOOD MUSIC, INC., 316 Southgate Ct., Brentwood TN 37027. (615)373-3950. FAX: (615)373-0386. Director of Art Services: Dill Beaty. Estab. 1980. Handles Christian music, children's, sing-along and instrumental. Photographers used for cassette covers, publicity, brochures, posters and product advertising. Works with freelancers on assignment only. Uses some stock photographs of scenics and people.
Specs: Uses color prints or transparencies.
Making Contact: Provide resume, business card, brochure, flyer or tearsheets to be kept on file for possible future assignments. SASE. Reports in 1 month.
Payment & Terms: Pays $25-75/b&w photo; $30-80/hour; $400-1,000/day. Credit line given "most of the time." Buys all rights and one-time rights, depending on needs.
Tips: Prefers to see "warmth, inspiration, character; kids and seasonal shots (especially Christmas)." To break in "submit printed samples. Don't send unsolicited photos."

CAMEX INC., Dept. PM, 535 5th Ave., New York NY 10017. (212)682-8400. President: Victor Benedetto. Handles rock, classical, country, etc. Photographers used for portraits, in-concert shots, studio shots, special effects, album covers, inside album shots, publicity, brochures, posters, event/convention coverage, product advertising. Works with freelance photographers on assignment only; offers "various" assignments/year.
Specs: Uses b&w and color prints (all sizes); 35mm, 2¼×2¼ transparencies.
Making Contact: Send unsolicited photos by mail for consideration. Submit portfolio for review. Does not return unsolicited material. Reports in 1 month.
Payment & Terms: NPI; payment negotiable. Buys one-time rights or all rights.

COSMOTONE RECORDS, P.O. Box 71988, Los Angeles CA 90071-0988. Record Producer: Rafael Brom. Handles all types of records. Photographers used for portraits, studio shots and special effects for album covers, inside album shots, brochures, posters and product advertising. Works on assignment only; offers 1-3 assignments/year.

Specs: Uses all sizes, all finish b&w and color photos.
Making Contact: Cannot return material. Will contact only if interested.
Payment & Terms: Pays $30-200/b&w photo; $50-350/color photo; $30-1,000/job. Credit line given. Buys one-time rights and all rights; negotiable.

*♣DOVentertainment INC.**, Suite 100-159, 2 Bloor St. West, Toronto, ON M4W 3E2 Canada. (416)533-7887. FAX: (416)533-0549. President: Gerald Belanger. Estab. 1990. Handles industrial/experimental/technological. Freelancers used for portraits, in-concert shots, studio shots, special effects and publicity. Works on assignment only.
Specs; Uses color, b&w prints.
Making Contact: Query with stock photo list. Sample kept on file. SASE. Reports in 1-2 weeks.
Payment & Terms: NPI; negotiable. Pays on acceptance. Credit line given. Buys one-time rights. Model/property release preferred.

*DYNAMITE RECORDS,** 5 Aldom Circle W., Caldwell NJ 07006. Contact: Pete Tarlteel. Handles all types of music. Uses photographers for studio shots, publicity, posters.
Specs: Uses b&w prints and 8×10 transparencies.
Making Contact: Query with resume of credits and business card. Does not return unsolicited material. Reports in 1 month.
Payment & Terms: NPI. Credit line given. Buys all rights.

FINER ARTISTS RECORDS, Suite 115, 2170 S. Parker Rd., Denver CO 80231. (303)755-2546. President: R.J. Bernstein. Estab. 1960. Handles rock, classical and country. Uses portraits, in-concert shots, studio shots and special effects for album covers, inside album shots, publicity, brochures and posters. Works with freelancers on assignment only; uses 6 freelancers/year.
Making Contact: Query with resume of credits. Send unsolicited photos by mail for consideration. Submit portfolio for review. Provide resume, business card, brochure, flyer or tearsheets to be kept on file for possible future assignments. Reports in 1 month.
Payment & Terms: NPI; payment negotiable. Credit line given. Buys one-time or all rights; negotiable.

FOUR WINDS RECORD PRODUCTIONS INC., 953 Highway 51, P.O. Box 802, Madison MS 39130-0802. (601)856-7468. A&R: Style Wooten. Handles bluegrass, black gospel, southern gospel and country. Photographers used for portraits, in-concert shots, studio shots and publicity for album covers, inside album covers, publicity, brochures and posters.
Specs: Uses 8×10 glossy color and b&w prints.
Making Contact: Send unsolicited photos by mail for consideration. Looks for "8×10 b&w and color prints of artists they have done." SASE. Reports in 2 weeks.
Payment & Terms: NPI; payment negotiable. Buys one-time rights.
Tips: "We are looking for photographers for Alabama, Georgia, Mississippi, Louisana and Florida."

FOX FARM RECORDING, 2731 Saundersville Ferry Road, Mt. Juliet TN 37122. (615)754-2444. Owner: Kent Fox. Estab. 1970. Handles bluegrass and gospel. Photographers used for portraits, studio shots, special effects for album covers, inside album shots and publicity. Works with freelancers on assignment only.
Specs: Uses b&w/color.
Making Contact: Send unsolicited photos by mail for consideration. SASE. Reports in 1 month.
Payment & Terms: Pays $100-2,000/job. Credit line sometimes given. Buys all rights.

GEFFEN RECORDS, Dept. PM, 9130 Sunset Blvd., Los Angeles CA 90069. (213)285-2780. Art Director: Kevin Reagan. Estab. 1980. Handles rock. Photographers used for portraits, in-concert shots, studio shots and special effects for inside album shots, publicity, posters, event/convention coverage and product advertising. "We use different things all the time." Number of assignments varies.
Specs: Uses 8½×11, b&w, color prints.
Making Contact: Submit portfolio for review. Does not return unsolicited material. "We keep material on file and will make contact when needed.
Payment & Terms: NPI; "Each contract varies." Rights negotiable.

♣ *The maple leaf before a listing indicates that the market is Canadian. The symbol is new this year in* Photographer's Market.

HARD HAT RECORDS & CASSETTES, 519 N. Halifax Ave., Daytona Beach FL 32118. (904)252-0381. President: Bobby Lee Cude. Estab. 1978. Handles country, pop, disco, gospel, MOR. Photographers used for portraits, in-concert shots, studio shots, special effects for album covers, publicity and posters. Works on assignment only; offers varied number of assignments/year. Examples of recent uses: "Daytona Beach's Sand In My Shoes," "There Ain't No Beer in Heaven; That's Why I Drink It Here," and "In-N-Out Urge" all cover montage.
Specs: Uses 8 × 10 glossy b&w prints.
Making Contact: Provide resume, business card, brochure, flyer or tearsheets to be kept on file for possible future assignments. SASE. Does not return unsolicited material. Reports in 1 month.
Payment & Terms: NPI. Pays on a contract basis. Credit line sometimes given. Rights vary.
Tips: "Submit credentials as well as work done for other record companies as a sample; also price, terms. Read *MIX/MUSICIAN* magazines."

INVASION/GNA RECORDS, Dept. PM, 114 Lexington Ave., New York NY 10016. (212)532-1414. FAX: (212)684-0958. Managing Director: Harriette Vidal. Estab. 1985. Photographers used for portraits, in-concert shots and studio shots for album covers, inside album shots, publicity head shots and posters.
Specs: Uses b&w and color prints; uses transparencies.
Making Contact: Provide resume, business card, brochure, flyer or tearsheets to be kept on file for possible future assignments. SASE. Reports in 3 weeks.
Payment & Terms: Pays $100-2,500/b&w photo; $100-2,500/color photo; $100-2,500/job. Credit line given. Buys all rights; negotiable.
Tips: "Be open minded, on time, professional, and as easy as possible to work with. Always looking for new talent and willing to give latitude to innovative photographers."

IRS RECORDS, Dept. PM, 3939 Lankershim Blvd., Universal City CA 91604. (818)508-3130. FAX: (818)373-7173. Creative Director: Hugh Brown. Handles rock, non-lyrical instrumental and folk. Photographers used for portraits and studio shots for cover/liner, inside shots, publicity, posters, print advertising. Buys stock and assigns work, but mostly assigns.
Specs: Uses b&w prints; 35mm, 2¼ × 2¼, 4 × 5 transparencies.
Making Contact: Provide resume, business card, self-promotion piece or tearsheets to be kept on file for possible future assignments. "We like self-promo pieces that show what the photographer is capable of." Keeps samples on file. SASE. Reporting time varies. "If we really like someone's work and have something suitable, we'll call immediately. If something catches our eye, we'll ask for a portfolio to be sent so we can keep the photographer in mind for future use."
Payment & Terms: Payment rates are determined by cover budget and "by how big we think the artist is going to be." Pays $1,000-7,500/cover project; $500-2,000/publicity photo. "We don't differentiate between color and b&w for payment." Pays on usage. Credit line given. Rights negotiable. Model release required.
Tips: "We like to see interaction between photographers and subjects—interesting approaches to standard kinds of shoots, good conceptual skills, and so on." Wants to see more thought, more than just "mere technical proficiency." Points out that "quality work" is appreciated. To break in, "start working with local bands—build a portfolio and a style. Record companies respond to creative approaches and can get away with a lot of stuff that ad agencies can't." Points out the disappearance of LP's and projected elimination of CD 12″ long boxes, so the need for large, detailed photos will also disappear. "We still use photography for close to 95 percent of our covers. And we use *some* photography even when there is illustration on the cover. It's just that now with the smaller packaging format we have less room to work with."

ISLAND RECORDS, 5th Floor, 400 LaFayette St., New York NY 10003. (212)995-0202. Manager of Creative Services: Janet DeMatteis. Uses studio shots for album packages, publicity, posters and product advertising. Works on assignment only. Offers 25 assignments/year.
Specs: Uses b&w and color prints; various sizes and finishes.
Making Contact: Interested in receiving work from newer, lesser-known photographers. Send unsolicited photos by mail for consideration. Provide resume, business card, brochure, flyer or tearsheets to be kept on file for possible future assignments. Send promotional *mailers* for initial contact. SASE. Reports as needed.
Payment & Terms: Pays $1,500-2,500/job. Credit line given. Buys all rights; negotiable. Model/property release required.
Tips: "Our needs change according to the project." To break in, "just keep sending promo pieces. Mostly we have photographers that we use often, however, there are times when we are looking for a different look for whatever recording artist's project we are creating."

Close-up

Anthony "Kal" Roberts
Entertainment Photographer
Nashville, Tennessee

"I have a love affair with the camera," Anthony "Kal" Roberts concedes. "I don't care which side I'm on." True to his statement, Roberts not only has been awarded the Pulitzer Prize for Photography and the National Sigma Delta Chi Society of Professional Journalists award and medal for Distinguished Service to Journalism, he's appeared in over 200 television shows and 40 films.

Has his career in photography, which spans over 25 years, affected his acting career? "Yeah," he says laughing, eyes twinkling, "it helps me steal scenes! I know what the camera is seeing and no one else does, so I get right there in front of it."

Roberts left Oklahoma as a teenager to pursue an acting career in southern California, but soon found the other side of the camera more fun. "I was in a camera store with a friend of mine (Fred Enke), who was a very famous photographer, and fell in love with a Nikon. I didn't know how the devil it worked, I just fell in love with the machinery, the mechanics. I bought it, which was then a very large sum. I said, 'I can't believe I did that. I can't go home and explain to my wife how I just spent all this money on a camera.' And Enke said, 'Don't worry, that's the cheapest thing you'll ever buy in photography.' "

Roberts quickly admits Enke was right. "After I got the camera, I went out and shot a roll of film, the greatest 36 shots ever taken, and gave the roll to (Enke). He developed it, proofed it out and gave (it) to me and I said, 'This isn't what I was seeing.' and he said, 'Then you'd better learn darkroom.' I went back the next week and bought a darkroom. I went in the darkroom and two years later, came out. I just became a fanatic."

In order to learn the craft he was obsessed by, Roberts says he "sat under the feet of every great photographer I could find." After many hours of clicking the shutter and developing his own work, people began offering him money for his images.

Once Roberts accepted photography as a way of life, offers for his work poured in. Hired by Time-Life as a staff photographer, he covered Presidents Kennedy, Nixon, Ford and Carter and took the "last pictures of Robert Kennedy." Roberts eventually dropped politics in favor of entertainment journalism. "I just like entertainment," he explains.

When *Life Magazine* folded, he moved over to newly-created *People Magazine* and developed, wrote and photographed feature articles, including one five-page spread on the last survivor of the Titanic. His work has appeared on over 50 magazine covers and in national advertising campaigns for American Airlines, Datsun, Toyota, Ford, Chrysler and others.

Despite the national acclaim for news photography, Roberts' heart is definitely in entertainment photojournalism. He now concentrates on record albums, video and recording sessions, television and feature films. His credits in this field, however, are no less impressive. He was personal photographer for John Huston and Orson Welles; worked closely with Robert Wise and Alfred Hitchcock and has photographed stars like Frank Sinatra, Johnny Cash, Willie Nelson, Bruce Springsteen, Robert Mitchum, Bob Hope, George Harrison and Charlton Heston.

Roberts admits capturing music on film is trickier than snapping news photos or personality shots. "I won't shoot an album cover unless I listen to the music," he explains. "Then it's what my interpretation of what the music is. An art director (may come in and say), 'This is what we're going to do; we're going to set up here; we're going to have this; this is what it's going to look like.' That's someone who's (just) snapping the shutter. I don't work like that. I listen to the music, I meet the person, talk with him, come up with ideas and capture that."

Roberts' most memorable album cover was for *Heros* by Waylon Jennings and Johnny Cash. "The front of the album had their fronts, the back had their backs." In order to capture the mood for these two "outlaw" musicians, Roberts put the duo in "long dusters," added props, including Steve McQueen's rifle from "Wanted: Dead or Alive" and took them down to an old grave in Tombstone. In addition to the album cover, pictures from that shoot have been used on billboards, posters and magazines.

His 1974 Pulitzer Prize-winning photo happened purely by accident, when he attempted to prevent a newly-released convict from raping and stabbing a woman in a Hollywood parking lot. In the middle of the 45-minute ordeal, after other bystanders had called the police, Roberts ran back to his car and grabbed his camera, "to get some evidence to show the court." He started snapping photos and talking to the ex-con. The man was preparing to stab the woman when Roberts grabbed the man's hand. In the process, Roberts shot another frame, one in which a security guard held his gun in the air after shooting the attacker. The photo appeared on the front page of newspapers around the world. Roberts now considers his heroics "up there on the dumb list," since he was fighting with one hand and taking pictures with the other. He, however, concedes, "I did save her life."

— Marjie McGraw

A rugged cemetery proved to be a marvelous setting for the cover of Heroes, an album by Waylon Jennings and Johnny Cash. Anthony "Kal" Roberts says he prefers to listen to music and gain an understanding of the artist before he takes on an album-cover project. Such research helps him better understand the personality of the image he wants to create.

© Anthony "Kal" Roberts

○ *JODY RECORD INC., 2557 E. 1st St., Brooklyn NY 11223. (718)339-8047. VP-Sales: Tom Bosco. A&R Director: Vince Vallis. Handles rock, jazz, country, pop. Photographers used for portraits, in-concert shots, studio shots and special effects for album covers, publicity, brochures and posters. Works on assignment only.
Specs: Uses b&w prints.
Making Contact: Send unsolicited photos by mail for consideration. Reports in 2 weeks. Buys all rights; negotiable.
Payment & Terms: NPI. Credit line given.
Tips: Looks for something unusual in photos.

KIMBO EDUCATIONAL, P.O. Box 477, 10 N. Third Ave., Long Branch NJ 07740. (908)229-4949. Production Manager: Amy Laufer. Handles educational—early childhood movement oriented records and tapes. General entertainment songs for young children. Physical fitness programs for all ages. Photographers work used for album and catalog covers, brochures and product advertising. Offers 5 assignments/year.
Specs: Uses transparencies.
Making Contact: Provide resume, business card, brochure, flyer or tearsheets to be kept on file for possible future assignments. Cannot return material. "We keep samples on file and contact photographer if in need of their services."
Payment & Terms: "Each job is different. Small advertising job—$75 minimum. Album covers—$200 minimum, $300-400 maximum." Buys all rights; negotiable.
Tips: "We are looking for top quality work but our budgets do not allow us to pay New York City prices (need reasonable quotes). Prefer local photographers—communication easier. We are leaning a little more toward photography, especially in our catalog. In the educational marketplace, it's becoming more prevalent to actually show our products being used by children."

K-TEL INTERNATIONAL (USA), INC., 15535 Medina Rd., Plymouth MN 55447. (612)559-6800. Director of Creative Services: John Dittrich. Estab. 1969. Handles rock, classical, country, jazz, rap, oldies and gospel. Photographers used for portraits, studio shots and special effects for album covers, inside album shots, publicity, brochures, posters, event/convention coverage, and product advertising. Assigns 12 jobs/year. Examples of recent uses: Gary Lemel, "How Fast Forever Goes" (CD and cassette cover); Celestial Navigations III (CD and cassette inside, back cover), and Chris Boardman, "Tu Do Bem" (CD and cassette cover).
Specs: Uses b&w and color.
Making Contact: Interested in receiving work from newer, lesser-known photographers. Query with resume of credits. Send by mail for consideration promotional pieces that can be filed for future reference. Provide resume, business card, brochure, flyer or tearsheets to be kept on file for possible future assignments. Cannot return material. Reports in 1 month.
Payment & Terms: NPI; negotiable according to project budget. Credit line given. Buys all rights; negotiable. Model release required.
Tips: In reviewing samples looks for "creativity, dramatic lighting and unusual contemporary techniques."

L.R.J. RECORDS, 1700 Plunkett Ct., Box 3, Belen NM 87002. (505)864-7441. FAX: (505)864-7441. President: Little Richie Johnson. Handles country and bilingual records. Estab. 1959. Photographers used for record album photos.
Making Contact: Send material by mail for consideration.
Payment & Terms: NPI; payment negotiable. Pays on receipt of completed job. Credit line given. Buys all rights, but may reassign to photographer.

LANDMARK COMMUNICATIONS GROUP, P.O. Box 148296, Nashville TN 37214. President: Bill Anderson, Jr. Handles country/gospel. Photographers used for in-concert shots, studio shots and special effects for album covers and product advertising. Works with freelancers on assignment only; offers 2-3 assignments/year. Buys 2 photos/year.
Specs: Uses color and b&w prints.
Making Contact: Provide resume, business card, brochure, flyer or tearsheets to be kept on file for possible future assignments. SASE. Reports in 1 month.
Payment & Terms: NPI; payment depends on project. Credit line given. Buys one-time rights.

***‡LASER RECORDS & MUSIC PTY LTD,** Box 38, Balmain, 2041 N.S.W. Australia. (02)8182590. Publicity Manager: Kymberlie Harrison. Handles jazz, big band, Broadway, 50's, 60's rock. Photographers used for portraits, in-concert shots, studio shots, special effects "reconstruction of antique photos and memorabilia" for album covers/CD's, inside album shots, publicity, brochures, posters and product advertising. Offers 40-60 assignments/year; buys 70-150 photos/year.

Specs: Uses 8×10 b&w glossy prints; 2¼×2¼ and 35mm transparencies.
Making Contact: Send unsolicited photos by mail for consideration. Submit portfolio for review. Provide business card, brochure, flyer or tearsheets to be kept on file for possible future assignments. Looks for "8×10 or proof sheets color or b&w of nostalgia artists and bands. Also stills of beautiful scenery for New Age audio products." SASE. Reports in 3 weeks.
Payment & Terms: Pays $80-150/b&w photo; $125 minimum/hour; $250/3 hour session. Credit line given. Buys all rights; negotiable.

*LEGS RECORDS—A.J. PROMOTIONS, 825 5th St., Menasha WI 54952. (414)725-4467. Executive President: Lori Lee Woods (artist). Manager: Jean M. Wilson. Handles rock, country, MOR, gospel. Photographers used for studio shots and special effects for publicity and posters. Works with freelance photographers on assignment only.
Specs: Uses 8×10 glossy b&w and color prints, and 35mm transparencies.
Making Contact: Submit portfolio for review. Provide resume, business card, brochure, flyer or tearsheets to be kept on file for possible future assignments. Does not return unsolicited material. Reports in 3 weeks.
Payment & Terms: NPI. Credit line given. Buys all rights.
Tips: Prefers to see sexy but conservative, different, down to earth photos.

LIN'S LINES, Suite 434, 156 Fifth Ave., New York NY 10010. (212)691-5630. FAX: (212)645-5038. President: Linda K. Jacobson. Estab. 1983. Handles all types of records. Uses photographers for portraits, in-concert shots, studio shots for album covers, inside album shots, publicity, brochures, posters and product advertising. Works an assignment only; gives 6 assignments/year.
Specs: Uses 8×10 prints; 35mm transparencies.
Making Contact: Query with resume of credits. Provide resume, business card, brochure, flyer or tearsheets to be kept on file for possible future assignments. "Do not send unsolicited photos." SASE. Reports in 1 month.
Payment & Terms: Pays $50-500/b&w photo; $75-750/color photo; $10-50/hour; $100-1,500/day; $75-3,000/job. Credit line given. Buys one-time rights; all rights, but may reassign to photographer.
Tips: Prefers unusual and exciting photographs such as holograms and 3-D images. "Send *interesting* material, initially in postcard form."

*LOCONTO PRODUCTIONS & RECORDING STUDIOS, Box 16540, Plantation FL 33318. (305)741-7766. Executive Vice President: Phyllis Loconto. Handles "all types" of records. Photographers used for portraits, studio shots, for album covers, inside album shots, publicity, brochures, posters, event/convention coverage and product advertising.
Specs: Varied.
Payment & Terms: NPI. Pays/job; negotiated. Credit line given. Buys all rights.
Tips: "I manage 'events' promotions—always interested in creative photography."

♣LONE WOLF, 1235 Lambeth Rd., Oakville ON L6H 2E2 Canada. (416)849-0244. FAX: (416)849-9715. Contact: Jill Heath. Estab. 1986. Handles alternative music. Photographers used for portraits, in-concert shots, studio shots and special effects for covers art, innersleeves, publicity and posters.
Making Contact: SASE. Reports in 1 month.
Payment & Terms: NPI. Credit line given. Buys all rights. "Photos may be used for t-shirts, posters, etc."
Tips: "I think photographers may be successful contacting bands individually. I've found that bands tend to hang on to pictures they like that they've received. As a sometimes photographer myself, with a handful of 'jacket' innersleeve credits to my name, this method exclusively is what has helped me get these credits." Observes that "photography (and artwork) may have to become simpler to accommodate the 5×5 CD format, rather than the 12×12 LP format."

LUCIFER RECORDS, INC., Box 263, Brigantine NJ 08203. (609)266-2623. President: Ron Luciano. Photographers used for portraits, live action shots and studio shots for album covers, publicity flyers, brochures and posters. Freelancers supply 50% of photos.
Making Contact: Provide brochure, calling card, flyer, resume and samples. Purchases photos for album covers and record sleeves. Submit portfolio for review. SASE. Reports in 2-6 weeks.
Payment & Terms: NPI; payment negotiable. Buys all rights.

JACK LYNCH MUSIC GROUP, (Nashville Country Productions/Nashville Bluegrass/Jalyn & Nashville Country Recording Companies), 306 Millwood Dr., Nashville TN 37217-1609. (615)366-9999. CEO: Col. Jack Lynch. Estab. 1963. Handles country, bluegrass and gospel. Uses photographers for portraits, in-concert shots and studio shots for album covers. Works with freelancers on assignment only; offers 1-10 assignments/year.

Specs: Uses various size b&w and color prints/transparencies.
Making Contact: Provide resume, business card, brochure, flyer or tearsheets to be kept on file for possible future assignments. SASE. Reports in 1 month.
Payment & Terms: Pays variable rates; $50-100/b&w photo; $100-200/color photo; $50-100/hour; $500-1,000/day; and $500-1,000/job. Credit line usually given. Buys exclusive product rights.
Tips: Call or write for information. Looks for good service, quality work and reasonable fees.

LEE MAGID, Box 532, Malibu CA 90265. (213)463-5998. President: Lee Magid. Operates under Grass Roots Records label. Handles R&B, jazz, C&W, gospel, rock, blues, pop. Photographers used for portraits, in-concert shots, studio shots, and candid photos for album covers, publicity, brochures, posters and event/convention coverage. Works with freelancers on assignment only; offers about 10 assignments/year.
Specs: Uses 8×10 buff or glossy b&w or color prints and 2¼×2¼ transparencies.
Making Contact: Send print copies by mail for consideration. SASE. Reports in 2 weeks.
Payment & Terms: NPI. Credit line given. Buys all rights.

MARICAO RECORDS/HARD HAT RECORDS, 519 N. Halifax Ave., Daytona Beach FL 32118. (904)252-0381. President: Bobby Lee Cude. Handles country, MOR, pop, disco and gospel. Photographers used for portraits, in-concert shots, studio shots and special effects for album covers, inside album shots, publicity, brochures, posters, event/convention coverage and product advertising. Works with freelancers on assignment only; offers 12 assignments/year.
Specs: Uses b&w and color photos.
Making Contact: Submit portfolio for review. Provide resume, business card, brochure, flyer, tearsheets or samples to be kept on file for possible future assignments. SASE. Reports in 2 weeks.
Payment & Terms: NPI; pays "standard fees." Credit line sometimes given. Rights negotiable.
Tips: "Submit sample photo with SASE along with introductory letter stating fees, etc. Read *Mix Music* magazine."

MR. WONDERFUL PRODUCTIONS, INC., Dept. PM, 1730 Kennedy Rd., Louisville KY 40216-5110. (502)774-1066. President: Ronald C. Lewis. Estab. 1984. Handles R&B, gospel and rock. Uses portraits and in-concert shots for publicity and posters. Works on assignment only. Works with 3 freelance photographers/year.
Specs: Uses 8×10 b&w prints.
Making Contact: Send unsolicited photos by mail for consideration. Provide resume, business card, brochure, flyer or tearsheets to be kept on file for possible future assignments. SASE. Reports in 2 weeks.
Payment & Terms: Pays $40 minimum/b&w and color photos; $100/complete job. Credit line given. Buys exclusive product rights.

*NEXT PLATEAU RECORDS, INC., Suite 1103, 1650 Broadway, New York NY 10019. (212)541-7640. Vice President: Jenniene LeClerq. Handles R&B, dance, rap and crossover/pop. Photographers used for portraits, in-concert shots, studio shots and video shoot shots for album covers, publicity and posters. Works with freelance photographers on assignment basis only; gives 8-12 assignments/year.
Specs: Uses 8×10 glossy b&w prints.
Making Contact: Send unsolicited photos by mail for consideration. "Once initial contact is made, and there is interest, we arrange for meeting." Wants to see "photos which could easily translate to an album cover (musicians/conceptual)." Cannot return unsolicited material. Photographers should follow up in 2-4 weeks.
Payment & Terms: Pays $800-1200/job for album work; pays less for promo shots.
Tips: "We want to see photos which work well in a square (album) form." Photographers "should possess the ability not only to take good photos but to creatively bring a concept to life. Independent labels frequently work with freelancers since few have staff photographers. If we're particularly pleased with one photographer's work, we tend to stick with them over a series of projects. One new use for photographers now is to get live shots taken at a video shoot for future promotion of the record and video."

Can't find a listing? Check at the end of each market section for the " '92-'93 Changes" lists. These lists include any market listings from the '92 edition which were either not verified or deleted in this edition.

NIGHTSTAR RECORDS, INC., Dept. PM, P.O. Box 602, Yarmouthport MA 02675. (508)362-3601. President: David M. Robbins. Estab. 1990. Handles New Age and easy listening. Photographers used for portraits, studio shots, special effects and landscape for album covers, inside album shots, publicity and brochures. Works on assignment only. Gives 4-6 freelance assignments/year.
Specs: Uses any, glossy, b&w and color prints.
Making Contact: Send unsolicited photos by mail for consideration; provide resume, business card, brochure, flyer or tearsheets to be kept on file for possible future assignments. Wants to see panoramic shots of natural scene subjects such as mountains, plains, rivers and ocean/beach scenes. Does not return unsolicited material. Reports in 1 month.
Payment & Terms: NPI. "Payment depends on usage. Album covers pay more than brochures." Credit line given in liner notes. Buys all rights.
Tips: "If you live in the general area of Massachusetts, we would also be interested in your portfolio work. Submit photos that you would consider your best. If we feel we can use a photo, you will be contacted. We would never use any photo without written consent and making payment." To break in, realize that "beautiful photos speak for themselves. If you have what people want, then they will use it. Nightstar uses photos quite frequently on album covers as opposed to artwork."

NORTHEASTERN RECORDS, P.O. Box 3589, Saxonville MA 01701-0605. (508)820-4440. FAX: (508)820-7769. General Manager: Lynn Joiner. Estab. 1988. Handles classical and folk, country, jazz and world music. Uses portraits, scenery/landscape for album covers, inside album shots and product advertising. Gives freelancers assignments 3-4 times/year; buys from freelancers 3-4 times/year.
Specs: Uses 8 × 10 glossy prints; 35mm, 2¼ × 2¼ transparencies.
Making Contact: Query with resume of credits. Provide resume, business card, brochure, flyer or tearsheets to be kept on file for possible future assignments. Does not return unsolicited material. Reports as needed.
Payment & Terms: NPI. Cover credits usually inside on credit page. Buys one-time rights for album use plus use in related promotional materials.
Tips: "Some photographers develop a reputation for doing covers for the record industry and consequently are in great demand and can charge high fees. Others, who may be equally as good, remain unknown to us. Market your service—have a card or brochure *printed* with examples of your best work."

NUCLEUS RECORDS, P.O. Box 111, Sea Bright NJ 07760. President: Robert Bowden. Estab. 1979. Handles rock, country. Photographers used for portraits, studio shots for publicity, posters and product advertising. Works with freelance photographers on assignment basis only.
Making Contact: Interested in receiving work from newer, lesser-known photographers. Send still photos of people for consideration. SASE. Reports in 3 weeks.
Payment & Terms: Pays $25-50/b&w photo; $75-100/color photo; $50-75/hour; $100-200/day; $500-1,000/job. Credit line given. Buys one-time rights and all rights; negotiable. Model release required; captions preferred.

*ORIGINAL SOUND RECORD CO., INC., 7120 Sunset Blvd., Hollywood CA 90046. (213)851-2500. FAX: (213)851-8162. Vice President: Paul Politi. Estab. 1959. Handles rock and oldies. Freelancers used for portraits, in-concert shots, studio shots, special effects for cover/liner, inside shots, publicity, brochures, posters and print advertising. Works on assignment only.
Specs: Uses b&w, color prints; 2¼ × 2¼, 4 × 5 and 8 × 10 transparencies.
Making Contact: Provide resume, business card, self-promotion piece or tearsheets to be kept on file for possible future assignments. Samples kept on file. SASE. Reports in 1 month.
Payment & Terms: NPI; payment negotiable. Pays on usage. Credit line given. Buys all rights. Model/property release required.

○ **THE PRESCRIPTION CO.**, 70 Murray Ave., Port Washington NY 11050. (516)767-1929. President: David F. Gasman. VP (A&R): Kirk Nordstrom. Tour Coordinator: Bill Fearn. Secretary: Debbie Fearn. Handles rock, soul and country & western. Photographers used for portraits, in-concert/studio shots and special effects for album covers, inside album shots, publicity flyers, brochures, posters, event/convention coverage and product advertising. Works on assignment only.
Specs: Uses b&w/color prints.
Making Contact: To arrange interview to show portfolio, "send us a flyer or tearsheets for our files." Cannot return material. "We want no original photos submitted."
Payment & Terms: NPI; payment negotiable. Rights negotiable.
Tips: "Send us a flyer or some photos for our files. We're only a small company with sporadic needs. If interested we will set up an in-person meeting. There is always need for good photography in our business, but like most fields today, competition is growing stiffer. Art and technique are important, of course, but so is a professional demeanor when doing business."

PRO/CREATIVES, 25 W. Burda Pl., New City NY 10956-7116. President: David Rapp. Handles pop and classical. Photographers used for record album photos, men's magazines, sports, advertising illustrations, posters and brochures.
Making Contact: Query with examples, resume of credits and business card. Reports in 1 month. SASE.
Payment & Terms: NPI. Buys all rights.

RAPP PRODUCTIONS including RR & R Records, Rapp Records and Rapture and Ready Records, 9305 Dogwood Pl., Gainesville GA 30506. (404)889-8624. Publicity Coordinators: Marci Wheeler and Gini Hammel. Estab. 1966. Handles Rapp Records, commercial all types; RR & R, all categories; Rapture Records, Christian music, all categories and Ready Records, promotional. Photographers used for portraits, in-concert shots, studio shots, special effects for album covers, publicity, brochures, posters, event/convention, product advertising. Number of photos bought from freelancers per year varies.
Specs: Uses all formats and sizes.
Making Contact: Send unsolicited photos by mail for consideration. Submit portfolio for review. SASE. Reports in 1 month.
Payment & Terms: NPI. Payment varies according to usage; negotiable. Credit line given. Buys all rights; negotiable.
Tips: In photographer's portfolio or samples wants to see "originality, feeling and remembrance." Sees trend toward "less sex, violence and culture shock. More publicity or promotional shots and advertisements."

RELATIVITY RECORDS, INC., 187-07 Henderson Ave., Hollis NY 11423. (718)217-3600. Art Director: David Bett. Estab. 1979. Handles rock, heavy metal, hardcore, pop and jazz. Photographers used for portraits, in-concert shots, studio shots and special effects for album covers, inside album shots, publicity, posters and event/convention. Works on assignment only; offers approx. 20-25 assignments/year. Examples of recent uses: "Second Coming," by Shotgun Messiah; "The Fabulous Chi-Ali," by Chi Ali. In both cases, photos used for album covers, posters, ads and print publicity.
Specs: Uses 8×10 b&w prints, 35mm or 2¼×2¼ color transparencies.
Making Contact: Submit portfolio for review. Provide resume, business card, brochure, flyer or tearsheets to be kept on file for possible future assignments. Contact by phone to arrange submission of portfolio or send card to be kept on file. SASE. Reports when we want to hire photographer.
Payment & Terms: Pays $50-1,500/b&w photo; $50-1,500/color photo; publicity photos $50-150 per shot; album cover photo $500-2,500; back cover $150-500. Credit line given. Buys one-time rights.
Tips: In photographer's portfolio wants to see "music-oriented photos: portraits of musicians; photos used on albums, posters, or for publicity or photos that could work as album covers. We have bands all over the U.S., though mainly in NYC & LA areas. Always looking for photographers with imagination and good rapport with musicians. We use freelancers exclusively, a core group of about 10-12, but willing to add good photographers to our roster. We probably use photography on about 60% of our covers, and somewhere on all our albums. Photo must have good concept or look to be on cover."

ROBBINS RECORDS, INC., HC80, Box 5B, Leesville LA 71446. National Representative: Sherree Angel. Estab. 1972. Handles religious, gospel and country. Photographers used for studio shots and special effects for album covers and publicity. Works on assignment only; offers variable assignments/year.
Specs: Uses various size b&w or color prints.
Making Contact: Send religious or gospel album cover material by mail for consideration. Provide resume, business card, brochure, flyer or tearsheets to be kept on file for possible future assignments. Cannot return material. Report time varies.
Payment & Terms: NPI; pays agreed amount/job. Buys all rights; negotiable.
Tips: "Freelancers have a fair chance of working with record companies. Some special effects photography is being used."

*ROCKIT RECORDS/SATELLITE MODELING STUDIOS, Suite 306, 35918 Union Lake Rd., Mt. Clemens MI 48043. (313)792-8452. Marketing Director: Joseph Trupiano. Estab. 1981. Handles rock, pop, pop/rock, country, heavy metal, r&b, rap, new age, jazz, dance. Freelancers used for portraits, in-concert shots, studio shots, special effects, seascape and landscape with female models for inside album shots, publicity, brochures, posters, event/convention coverage, product advertising, creative set. Examples of recent uses: "Staying Power Vol 2" CD (photo used in insert); "Power Source Vol 3" CD (photo used in insert) and "RCM Magazine" (cover shot).

Specs: Uses 8 × 10 glossy b&w and color prints.
Making Contact: Send samples of best work, resume, portfolio if possible. SASE. Reports in 1 month.
Payment & Terms: NPI; pays by the job, amount depends on client negotiation. Credit line given. Buys one-time rights; negotiable. Model release required. Property release preferred. Photo captions preferred.
Tips: "We solicit poster companies, record companies, advertisers, magazines. Our requirements are that of female models in: tropical scenes, beach scenes, exotic scenes, sensual looks, etc. Be creative with your set design. Use lots of satin backdrops, floor coverings (satin), pillows (African props such as zebra, leopard, tiger, type of pillows and fabrics). Color up your lighting by using yellows, reds, greens, etc. More and more uses for innovative and creative shots are in demand. These type photos will always assist in the sales of our products. The more appealing it is to the consumer the better the chances of making that sale. We presently are accepting photos of female models for our record company products (Compact Disc inserts) released by our affiliate record label, Rockit Records, Inc. Should your photo be accepted it will gain recognition for the photographer on a worldwide level."

ROCKWELL RECORDS, Box 1600, Haverhill MA 01831. (617)373-6011. President: Bill Macek. Produces top 40 and rock and roll records. Photographers used for live action shots, studio shots and special effects for album covers, inside album shots, publicity, brochures and posters. Photos used for jacket design and artist shots. Buys 4-6 photos and offers 4-6 assignments/year. Freelancers supply 100% of photos.
Making Contact: Interested in seeing all types of photos. "No restrictions. I may see something in a portfolio I really like and hadn't thought about using." Arrange a personal interview. Submit b&w and color sample photos by mail for consideration. Submit portfolio for review. Provide brochure, calling card, flyer or resume to be kept on file for possible future assignments. SASE. Local photographers preferred, but will review work of photographers from anywhere.
Payment & Terms: NPI; payment varies.

ROLL ON RECORDS®, 112 Widmar Pl., Clayton CA 94517. (510)672-8201. Owner: Edgar J. Brincat. Estab. 1986. Handles country, rock, r&b, pop/soul, gospel, middle of the road, easy listening. Photographers used for portraits, in-concert shots, studio shots and special effects for album covers, inside album shots and publicity. Works with freelancers on assignment only; offers 2-4 assignments/year.
Specs: Uses various sizes, glossy b&w or color prints.
Making Contact: Query with resume of credits. Provide resume, business card, brochure, flyer or tearsheets to be kept on file for possible future assignments. SASE. Reports in 2 weeks.
Payment & Terms: Pays $300-1,500/b&w photo; $400-2,000/color photo; negotiable. Credit line given. Buys all rights.
Tips: "We expect an itemized contract and a price that does not change" when working with freelancers. The future outlook is "very good" for freelancers.

SIRR RODD RECORD & PUBLISHING CO., P.O. Box 58116, Philadelphia PA 19102-8116. President/A&R: Rodney Jerome Keitt. Handles R&B, jazz, top 40, rap, pop, gospel and soul. Uses photographers for portraits, in-concert shots, studio shots and special effects for album covers, inside album shots, publicity, posters, event/convention and product advertising. Buys 10 (minimum) photos/year.
Specs: Uses 8 × 10 glossy b&w or color prints.
Making Contact: Submit portfolio for review. Provide resume, business card, brochure, flyer or tearsheets to be kept on file for possible future assignments. SASE. Reports in 1 month.
Payment & Terms: Pays $40-200/b&w photo; $60-250/color photo; $75-450/job. Credit line given. Buys all rights, negotiable.
Tips: "We look for the total versatility of the photographer. Of course, you can show us the more common group photos, but we like to see new concepts in group photography. Remember that you are freelancing. You do not have the name, studio, or reputation of 'Big Time' photographers, so we both are working for the same thing—exposure! If your pieces are good and the quality is equally good, your chances of working with record companies are excellent. Show your originality, ability to present the unusual, and what 'effects' you have to offer."

SOLAR RECORDS, Dept. PM, 1635 N. Cahuenga Blvd., Hollywood CA 90028. (213)461-0390. Production Coordinator: Brenda Patrick. Handles R&B. Uses portraits, in-concert shots, studio shots for album covers, inside album shots, publicity and posters. Works on assignment only; uses 10-12 freelance photographers/year.
Specs: Uses b&w and color prints.
Making Contact: Arrange a personal interview to show portfolio. Submit portfolio for review. Provide resume, business card, brochure, flyer or tearsheets to be kept on file for possible future assignments. SASE. Reports in 2 weeks.
Payment & Terms: Pays $1,000-4,000/assignment. Buys all rights.

Edgar Brincat, owner of Roll on Records in Clayton, California, worked with a photographer on this shot in an effort to find the right angle for a cassette cover. The photo was chosen from about 35 shots and the photographer earned $75 for his efforts.

© Roll on Records

*THE SOUND ACHIEVEMENT GROUP, Box 24625, Nashville TN 37202. (615)883-2600. President: Royce Gray. Estab. 1984. Handles all forms of gospel. Photographers used for in-concert shots, studio shots and location shots for album covers, publicity, brochures, posters, event/convention and product advertising. Works on assignment only; offers 10-15 assignments/year.

Specs: Uses b&w prints; 2¼ × 2¼ color transparencies.

Making Contact: Arrange a personal interview to show portfolio. Provide resume, business card, brochure, flyer or tearsheets to be kept on file for possible future assignments. SASE. Reports in 1 month.

Payment & Terms: Pays $15-35/hour; $75-300/job. Credit line given. Buys all rights; negotiable.

Tips: In photographer's portfolio, wants to see "album and promo shots of artists. We're a custom company, our budgets vary from job to job. Your chances are good providing you're flexible with your budget."

THE SPARROW CORPORATION, Dept. PM, P.O. Box 5010, Brentwood TN 37024-5010. (615)371-6800. Contact: Director of Creative Services. Handles Christian, worship, and children's albums. Uses photographers for portraits, studio shots for album covers, inside album shots, publicity, brochures, posters, event/convention coverage, product advertising, cassette inserts and mobiles. Works with freelancers on assignment only; gives 10 assignments/year.

Specs: Uses 8 × 10 color prints; 2¼ × 2¼ transparencies.

Making Contact: Provide resume, business card, brochure, flyer or tearsheets to be kept on file for possible future assignments. SASE. Reports "if artist calls for feedback or when we decide to use the photos."

Payment & Terms: Pays $300-1,000/job. Credit line given. Buys all rights.

Tips: "Prefer to see people shots, close-up faces, nice graphic design and elements included. Send clean-cut samples with wholesome images. No nude models, etc. Be friendly, but not pushy or over-bearing. Freelancers have very good chances. We are moving toward more detailed photo sets and designs that can carry a theme and using elements which can be used separately or together according to need. We have incorporated a new instrumental series and are always looking for mood shots."

*‡STORYVILLE RECORDS AB, Dortheavej 39, Copenhagen NV DK 2400 Denmark. (01)260757. President/Owner: Karl Emil Knudsen. Handles jazz and blues. Uses portraits, in-concert shots, studio shots, special effects for album covers, inside album shots, publicity. "We also publish books and are working on a series of picture books on jazz."
Specs: Uses b&w and color transparencies.
Making Contact: Send unsolicited photos by mail for consideration. Provide resume, business card, brochure, flyer or tearsheets to be kept on file for possible future assignments. Wants to see portraits or in-concert/live shots for books only. SASE. Reports in 1 month.
Payment & Terms: Pays $40-100/b&w photo; $75-200/color photo; $200-300/assignment. Credit line given. Buys all rights; negotiable.
Tips: "99% of all covers show/use photos. We issue 25-40 LP/CDs per year. Since most artists perform in New York, Los Angeles, San Francisco he should be from/live in those areas. Someone who has done this work for 20-30 years with a backlog of material has a good chance for our forthcoming books."

SUSAN RECORDS, P.O. Box 1622, Hendersonville TN 37077-1622. Manager: S.D. Neal. Estab. 1970. Handles rock and country. Uses in-concert shots, studio shots and special effects for album covers, inside album shots, publicity, brochures, posters, event/convention coverage and product advertising. Works with freelance photographers on assignment only.
Specs: Uses any size or format b&w/color.
Making Contact: Send unsolicited photos by mail for consideration. Submit portfolio for review. SASE. Reports in 3 weeks.
Payment & Terms: NPI; payment negotiable. Pays per b&w photo and per color photo. Credit line given. Buys one-time rights.
Tips: Observes that opportunities are good. Sees trend toward use of many concert shots.

‡SWOOP RECORDS, Stewart House, Hill Bottom Rd., Sands-IND-EST, Highwycombe, Bucks, HP124HJ England. (063)064-7374. FAX: (063)064-7612. Owner: Ron Lee. Estab. 1970. Uses portraits, in-concert shots, studio shots and special effects for album covers, inside album shots, publicity, brochures, posters, event/convention coverage and product advertising. Examples of recent uses: "Nightmare" (front cover); "Daniel Boone" (front/back cover); and "Orphan" (front cover).
Specs: Uses 8×10 glossy/matte b&w/color.
Making Contact: Interested in receiving work from newer, lesser-known photographers. Wants to see all types. SASE. Reports in 3 weeks.
Payment & Terms: NPI. Credit line given. Buys all rights. Model release required. Photo captions required.
Tips: Depending on the photographer's originality. "Prospects can be very good."

TEROCK RECORDS, P.O. Box 1622, Hendersonville TN 37077. Secretary: S.D. Neal. Handles rock, soul and country records. Uses photographers for in-concert and studio shots for album covers, inside album shots, publicity flyers, brochures, posters and product advertising.
Making Contact: Send material by mail for consideration. SASE. Reports in 3 weeks.
Payment & Terms: NPI. Pays per job. "Photographers have to set a price." Credit line given.

TRANSWORLD RECORDS, Suite 115, 2170 S. Parker Rd., Denver CO 80231. (303)755-2546. President: R.J. Bernstein. Estab. 1960. Handles rock, classical and country. Uses portraits, in-concert shots, studio shots and special effects for album covers, inside album shots, publicity, brochures and posters. Works with freelancers on assignment only; gives 6 assignments/year.
Making Contact: Query with resume of credits. Send unsolicited photos by mail for consideration. Submit portfolio for review. Provide resume, business card, brochure, flyer or tearsheets to be kept on file for possible future assignments. Does not return unsolicited material. Reports in 1 month.
Payment & Terms: NPI; payment negotiable. Credit line given. Buys all rights; negotiable.

MIKE VACCARO PRODUCTIONS INC., Dept. PM, P.O. Box 7991, Long Beach CA 90807. (213)424-4958 Contact: Mike Vaccaro. Handles classical. Photographers used for portraits, in-concert shots, studio shots, special effects for album covers, publicity, brochures, event/convention coverage and product advertising. Works on assignment only; gives 2-3 assignments/year.

Making Contact: Arrange a personal interview to show portfolio. Query with resume of credits. Send unsolicited photos by mail for consideration or submit portfolio for review. Provide resume, business card, brochure, flyer or tearsheets to be kept on file for possible future assignments. Does not return unsolicited material. Reports as needed.

Payment & Terms: NPI; payment, credit line and rights purchased are negotiable.

Tips: "Flexibility in many styles and special effects" is advisable.

WINDHAM HILL PRODUCTIONS, INC., 831 High St., Palo Alto CA 94301. (415)329-0647. Art Director: Candace Upman. Handles mostly jazz-oriented, acoustic and electronic music. Uses freelance photographers for portraits, art shots for covers, inside album shots, posters. Buys 20-30 freelance photos/year.

Specs: Uses 35mm, 2¼×2¼, 4×5 and 8×10 transparencies. "Please send dupes. If we want more accurate version we will ask for original."

Making Contact: Submit portfolio for review. SASE. Reports in 1 month.

Payment & Terms: NPI; payment varies. Credit line given. Buys one-time rights or all rights, "depends on the nature of the product."

Tips: "I am not looking for variations of shots we have already used. I am looking for unusual points of view, generally of natural subjects, without people or animals. Become acquainted with our covers before submitting materials. Send materials that have personal significance. I am not merely looking for technically excellent work. I want work with heart."

Record Companies/'92-'93 changes

The following markets appeared in the 1992 edition of *Photographer's Market* but are not listed in the 1993 edition. They may have been omitted for failing to respond to our request for updates of information, they may have gone out of business or they may no longer wish to receive freelance work.

Barnett Productions Inc. (did not respond)

Charta Records/Delux Records (did not respond)

Current Records (not reviewing work)

EFA-MEDIEN-GMBH (did not respond)

Narada Productions (not reviewing work)

Northwest International Enter

tainment (not reviewing work)

Orinda Records (did not respond)

Plankton Records (did not respond)

Public Library Services (out of business)

Rammit Records (not reviewing work)

Ripsaw Record Co. (did not re-

spond)

Shaolin Film & Records (late verification)

Sound Ceremony Records (did not respond)

Sounds of WinchesterTriple X Management (did not respond)

Williamson, Alix B. (not reviewing work)

Stock Photo Agencies

Without a doubt, the fastest growing aspect of photography is the stock industry. Stock photo agencies represent photographers of all skills and specialties and they market images to virtually every other market segment. More and more photographers are moving into stock as a way of selling their work and agencies are sprouting like wildflowers all over the globe. Photographers find that stock agencies are better at marketing photos on a world-wide scale, which give the photographers more time to practice their craft.

Most agencies operate by offering reprint rights on the same images to various clients. Typically, they split the usage fee with the photographer according to an agreed-upon percentage. While some agencies will buy single photos or small inventories of needed subject matter, many will work only with photographers who can initially deliver a large quantity of photos—200, 500 or 1,000 images—and who will continue to submit large quantities on a regular basis. So you must be very attentive to which agencies welcome the casual submission and which ones expect a major commitment for new work.

It's best to study agencies very carefully and to shop around. In the listings in this section, in particular, it's especially important to review the category, Payment & Terms, and compare the policies against the ethical guidelines chart on the next page.

Stock agencies will often specialize in certain subject matters—for instance, sports, fashion or science—or deal with particular types of clients, such as advertising, editorial or corporate. In particular, there has been a visible increase in the number of agencies marketing audiovisual materials.

Some agencies which are developing their AV market are primarily looking for stock transparencies to be used in audiovisual productions, while others are seeking stock film or videotape footage of a range of subjects. Stock agencies with these kinds of audiovisual needs have been marked with a special AV symbol—a solid, black square—before the listing's name for easier recognition.

As a way of evaluating the professionalism of various agencies, request copies of their guidelines, contracts and other materials before doing business with them. Most firms are reputable, but some are either unethical in their practices or have not yet acquired proper organization and professionalism. An agency's materials will tell you a great deal about how the firm will handle your work and cooperate with you.

Generally, for your own protection, you should strive to work only with agencies that work on a contract basis. Whether you choose to accept an exclusive contract, one that's nonexclusive or one that offers limited exclusivity will depend upon many of your personal marketing goals. Also, before signing any contracts, you should have the terms reviewed by an attorney as well as individuals knowledgeable about stock photography terms.

Some agencies will market your images through other agencies, or sub-agents. This is especially true for international stock firms. In contract terms, you should also look closely for any terms that apply to geographic availability and the compensation for offering such rights.

The standards of most stock agencies are quickly being upgraded since they seek to do business with top clients and expect high multiple resales of a given image. There is little or no room for amateurish work, leftover shots or images that otherwise lack a strong ability to communicate visually. Every photo that a stock agency markets must be of the utmost quality—at least comparable to the caliber of work which they are already presenting. Accordingly, every image a photographer submits must also be top-notch. Among the

Ethical guidelines for stock

Before a photographer signs a contract with a stock photo agency, he needs some guarantee of fair treatment. The Picture Agency Council of America (PACA) has established a set of ethical guidelines to which all members in the council must adhere in order to retain their memberships. These guidelines are a good check list for the photographer to use when prospecting for an agency or negotiating his contract.

PACA members will openly and freely discuss with photographers:
● *Ownership of agency, and/or change thereof.*
● *Editing, inventory and refiling procedures.*
● *Disposition of any suit or settlement pertaining to a specific photographer's work, including documentation if requested.*
● *International representation policies.*
● *Policies regarding free or reduced rate usages for charitable organizations.*
● *Sub agency or franchise representation policies.*

Membership agencies should also offer photographers a fair and straightforward written contract, which should address such items as:
● *Payment schedule.*
● *Right to inspect agency records as they pertain to the individual photographer.*
● *Contract period and renewal.*
● *Charges, deductions or assessments related to the photographer's account.*
● *Procedure and schedule for return of photographs upon termination of contract.*

Also royalty statements should include:
● *An adequate photo description.*
● *A description or code for the usage.*
● *The amount of the photographer's share.*
● *An itemization of any deductions that are made.*

---

best ways to learn what goes into highly marketable stock images are to study agency catalogs and stock industry references such as the *Stock Workbook*, as well as the listings in this section.

Besides shooting high-quality images, photographers must strive for professionalism in all aspects of their business. To work successfully in the stock field, you must know how stock agencies do business, how to do business with agencies, how to gear your images for them and their clients, and how to make the most of the marketing opportunities stock agencies provide. The "Tips" paragraphs in many of the listings in this section offer insight into the industry's practices and requirements.

What's ahead

In the last year, rapid technological advances have occurred, specifically with CD-Rom. This technology allows a photographer's images to be digitized and then encoded onto compact disks. The disks, containing around 100 images, are then sold as a package to advertising firms, corporations or whomever. Once a disk is purchased photos on it can be used over and over at no extra cost.

The issue has placed the industry in a state of flux as proponents and opponents to such technology have rallied in opposite corners. Those favoring compact disks see them as a way to open up new markets and generate additional sales for photographers.

On the other side of the coin, opponents say the disks will make it easier for copyrights to be infringed and they worry that photographers will not get their just due when it comes to payment. Allstock Inc., in Seattle, Washington, has even operated a campaign against clip art disks.

The American Society of Magazine Photographers (ASMP) has used the controversy as a focal point in its efforts to form a collective for photographers. ASMP Executive Director Richard Weisgrau says one aspect of the collective will be to take requests from CD-Rom producers who are searching for certain photo topics. The collective will notify its members of subjects being sought. In turn, members will send their photos of the subject to the collective which gathers all images and submits them to disk producers. The producers choose images from the package and then they pay the collective for the photos. The collective then doles out checks to those photographers whose work was bought. Most importantly the collective also will make sure no copyright laws are violated.

Several stock agencies aren't happy with the concept because they fear photographers will leave stock houses to join the collective. Weisgrau hopes the idea will make some sloppy stock agencies clean up their acts in order to keep photographers.

There also has been a battle line drawn over last year's purchase of The Image Bank (TIB) by Eastman Kodak. Most agencies seem to be taking a wait-and-see attitude toward the purchase. However, stock agencies throughout the world fear that the industry could suffer by giving TIB an unfair technological advantage. Smaller agencies feel they may not be able to compete with the CD-Rom and other technological advances Kodak has to offer.

Others are happy with the purchase because of the advances in technology that can be made. They also see Kodak as a past friend of the photo industry and they don't expect the relationship to change.

When examining this year's stock agency section be on the lookout for our Close-up subject, Gerry Boudrias, of Photo Search Ltd., Edmonton Canada. In the feature on page 544 Boudrias talks about the industry and servicing clients and he explains what agencies look for when they examine images.

There are a number of helpful references and organizations that will assist you in learning more about the stock industry and its standard practices. These sources also can help you stay in touch with industry trends. These include: *Stock Photo Letter*, a quarterly newsletter published by stock photo expert Jim Pickerell, (301)251-0720; the *ASMP Stock Photography Handbook*, published by the American Society of Magazine Photographers, (212)889-9144; and the Picture Agency Council of America, (414)765-9442.

*AAA STOCK PHOTOGRAPHY, 32 Spring St., Wallington NJ 07057. (201)773-7966. FAX: (201)773-7966. "Call before faxing." Reviewer: Jeff Greenberg. Estab. 1988. Picture library. Has 100,000 photos. Clients include: textbook publishers, magazine publishers, religious publishing houses and travel industry.
Subject Needs: Images used by travel industry, textbook publishers, magazine publishers and religious publishing houses.
Specs: Uses 35mm transparencies.
Payment & Terms: Buys photos/film outright. Average price per image (to clients): $25-100/color. Statements issued "whenever photographers call." Payment made "at time of outright purchase." Buys all rights. Informs photographer and allows him to negotiate when client requests all rights. Photo captions required.
Making Contact: Send dupes only. Without SASE materials will not be returned. Expects minimum initial submission of 20 images. Reports in 1-2 weeks.
Tips: "By sending images you are offering them for outright purchase."

■‡ACE PHOTO AGENCY, 22 Maddox St., Mayfair, London WIR 9PG United Kingdom. (01)629-0303. FAX: (01)495-6100. Chief Editor: John Panton. Stock photo agency. Has approximately 300,000 photos. Clients include: ad agencies, audiovisual firms, businesses, book/encyclopedia publishers, magazine publishers, postcard companies, calendar companies, greeting card companies, design companies and direct mail companies.

Subject Needs: People, sport, corporate, industrial, travel (world), seas and skies, still life and humor.
Specs: Uses 35mm, 2¼×2¼, 4×5 and 8×10 transparencies.
Payment & Terms: Pays 50% commission on color photos, 30% (overseas sales). General price range: $135-1,800. Works on contract basis only; offers limited regional exclusivity and contracts. Contracts renew automatically for 2 years with each submission. Charges catalog insertion fee, $100 deducted from first sale. Statements issued quarterly. Payment made quarterly. Photographers permitted to review sales records with 4 weeks written notice. Offers one-time rights, first rights or mostly non-exclusive rights. Informs photographers when client requests to buy all rights, but agency negotiates for photographer. Model/property release required for people and buildings. Photo captions required; include place, date and function.
Making Contact: Arrange a personal interview to show portfolio. Query with samples. SASE. Reports in 2 weeks. Photo guidelines free with SASE. Distributes tips sheet twice yearly to "ace photographers under contract."
Tips: Prefers to see "total range of subjects in collection. Must be commercial work, not personal favorites. Must show command of color, composition and general rules of stock photography. All people must be mid-Atlantic to sell in U.K. Must be sharp and also original. No dupes. Be professional and patient."

*‡ACTION PRESS, Geschwister-Scholl-Str. 33, 2000 Hamburg 20 Germany. (40)46-040-64. FAX: (40)46-26-14. Contact: Renate Meier. Estab. 1970. Stock photo agency. News/feature syndicate. Has 8 million photos. Has branch office in 3 other cities. Clients include: book/encyclopedia publishers, magazine publishers and newspapers.
Subject Needs: Actual events, people, movies, show-biz and landscapes.
Specs: Uses 35mm transparencies.
Payment & Terms: Pays 40-60% commission on color photos. Average price per image (to clients): $80-100/b&w; $100-200/color. Negotiates fees below standard minimum prices. Offers volume discounts to customers; inquire about specific terms. Photographer can choose not to sell images on discount terms. Works with or without a contract; limited regional exclusivity. Statements issued monthly. Payment made monthly. Offers one-time rights. Model/property release required. Captions required.
Making Contact: Query with samples. Query with stock photo list. Samples kept on file. Expects minimum initial submission of 100 images with periodic submission of about 400-800 images/month. Reports in 1 month. Market tips sheet distributed quarterly upon request.

ADVENTURE PHOTO, Suite 202, 56 E. Main St., Ventura CA 93001. (805)643-7751. FAX: (805)643-4423. Estab. 1987. Stock agency. Member of Picture Agency Council of America (PACA). Has 125,000 photos. Clients include: advertising agencies, public relations firms, businesses, magazine publishers, calendar and greeting card companies.
Subject Needs: Adventure Photo offers its clients 5 principle types of images: Adventure Sports (sailing, windsurfing, rock climbing, skiing, mountaineering, mountain biking, etc.), Adventure Travel (All fifty states as well as third world and exotic locations.), Landscapes, Environmental and Wildlife.
Specs: Uses 35mm, 2¼×2¼ and 4×5 transparencies.
Payment & Terms: Pays 50% commission on color photos. Works on contract basis only. Offers nonexclusive contract. Contracts renew automatically with each submission; time period not specified. Statements issued monthly. Payment made monthly. Photographers allowed to review sales figures. Offers one-time rights; occasionally negotiates exclusive and unlimited use rights. "We notify photographers and work to settle on acceptable fee when client requests all rights." Model release and photo captions required. With captions, include description of subjects, locations and persons.
Making Contact: Write to photo editor for copy of submission guidelines. SASE. Reports in 1 month. Photo guidelines free with SASE.
Tips: In freelancer's portfolio or samples, wants to see "well-exposed, well-lit transparencies (reproduction quality)." Unique outdoor sports, travel and wilderness images. "We love to see shots of this subject matter that portray metaphors commonly used in ad business ("risk taking," "teamwork," etc.)." To break in, "we request new photographers send us 2-4, 20-image sheets they feel are representative of their work. Then when we sign a photographer, we pass ideas to them regularly about the kinds of shots our clients are requesting, and we pass them any ideas we get too. Then we counsel our

The double dagger before a listing indicates that the market is located outside the United States and Canada. The symbol is new this year in Photographer's Market.

photographers always to look at magazines and advertisements to stay current on the kinds of images art directors and agencies are using."

■**AMERICAN STOCK PHOTOGRAPHY,** Dept. PM, Suite 716, 6255 Sunset Blvd., Hollywood CA 90028. (213)469-3900. President: Christopher C. Johnson. Manager: Darrell Presho. Stock photo agency. Has 2 + million photos. Clients include: advertising agencies, public relations firms, audiovisual firms, businesses, book/encyclopedia publishers, magazine publishers, newspapers, postcard companies, calendar companies, greeting card companies and TV and movie production companies.
Subject Needs: General stock, all categories. Special emphasis upon California scenics and lifestyles.
Specs: Uses 35mm, 2¼ × 2¼, 4 × 5 transparencies; b&w contact sheets; b&w negatives.
Payment & Terms: Buys photos outright; pays $5-20. Pays 50% commission. General price range: $100-750. Offers one-time rights. Model release and photo captions required.
Making Contact: Contact Camerique Inc., 1701 Skippack Pk., P.O. Box 175, Blue Bell, PA 19422. (215)272-4000. SASE. Reports in 1 week. Photo guidelines free with SASE. Tips sheet distributed quarterly to all active photographers with agency; free with SASE.

AMWEST PICTURE AGENCY, 15922 E. Princeton Ave., Aurora CO 80013. (303)699-8776. FAX: (303)693-1443. Owner: Marla A. Murphy. Manager: John Eickhorn. Clients include: ad agencies, brochures, textbooks, magazines and calendar companies.
Subject Needs: Couples and singles in everyday activity, leisure and working. Teens and active seniors in positive situations, sports or upbeat, happy settings. Some need for "problem" shots but people interacting is paramount. Handicapped people coping and learning. All kinds of sports, business and high-tech office settings—all the preceding in b&w and color. Needs more coverage of the western U.S./recreation areas, people enjoying the western life.
Specs: Uses 8 × 10 b&w prints; 35mm, 2¼ × 2¼ and 4 × 5 transparencies.
Payment & Terms: Pays 50% commission. Works on contract basis only. Offers nonexclusive contract. "A four-year contract must be signed." Contracts renew automatically with each submission for four years. Will charge duping fee in near future. Payment made monthly. Offers one-time and electronic media rights; other rights and sales negotiable. Sometimes considers offering all rights to clients; "depends on what is offered." Model release preferred. Model released photography should be marked "MR." Photo captions required; include "all details you can add. Some photo requests are very specific." Model released photography should be marked "MR."
Making Contact: "A SASE must be enclosed with your letter of inquiry and submissions, or we cannot return our packet of information to you."
Tips: Edit down tightly. Well shot, completely focused and perfect exposure get the most attention and sell best. "We are looking for more photographers in Idaho, Montana, Wyoming, California, Colorado, Arizona and central states. Also looking for new ideas in photography, especially of people. Be very specific in captioning your work."

■‡**THE ANCIENT ART & ARCHITECTURE COLLECTION,** 6 Kenton Rd., Harrow-on-the-Hill, Middlesex HA1 2BL London, England. (81)422-1214. Contact: The Librarian. Picture library. Has 200,000 photos. Clients include: public relations firms, audiovisual firms, book/encyclopedia publishers, magazine publishers and newspapers.
Specs: Uses 35mm, 2¼ × 2¼, 4 × 5 or 8 × 10 transparencies.
Payment & Terms: Pays 50% commission. Offers one-time rights. Fully detailed captions required.
Making Contact: Query with samples and list of stock photo subjects. SASE. Reporting time not specified.
Tips: "Material must be suitable for our specialist requirements. We cover historical and archeological periods from 25,000 BC to the 19th century AD, worldwide. All civilizations, cultures, religions, objects and artifacts as well as art are includable. Pictures with tourists, cars, TV aerials, and other modern intrusions not accepted."

■‡**ANDES PRESS AGENCY,** 26 Padbury Ct., London E2 England. (071)739-3159. Director: Carlos Reyes. Picture library and news/feature syndicate. Has 500,000 photos. Clients include: audiovisual firms, book/encyclopedia publishers, magazine publishers and newspapers.

■ *The solid, black square before a listing indicates that the market uses various types of audiovisual materials, such as slides, film or videotape.*

Subject Needs: "We have a large collection of photographs on social, political and economic aspects of Latin America, Africa, Asia, Europe and Britain, specializing in contemporary world religions."
Specs: Uses 8 × 10 glossy b&w prints; 35mm and 2¼ × 2¼ transparencies; b&w contact sheets and negatives.
Payment & Terms: Pays 50% commission for b&w and color photos. General price range: £50-200/b&w photo; £50-300/color photo; (British currency). Enforces minimum prices. Works on contract basis only. Offers non-exclusive contract. Statements issued quarterly. Payment made quarterly. Photographers allowed to review account records to verify sales figures. Offers one-time rights. Informs photographer and allows him to negotiage when client requests all rights. "We never sell all rights, photographer has to negotiate if interested." Model/property release preferred. Captions required.
Making Contact: Interested in receiving work from newer, lesser-known photographers. Query with samples. Send stock photo list. SASE. Reports in 1 week. Photo guidelines free with SASE.
Tips: "We want to see that the photographer has mastered one subject in depth. Also, we have a greater market for photo-features as opposed to stock photos only."

■**ANIMALS ANIMALS/EARTH SCENES,** 17 Railroad Ave., Chatham NY 12037. (518)392-5500. Branch office: Suite 1111, 580 Broadway, New York NY 10012. (212)925-2110. President: Eve Kloepper. Member of Picture Agency Council of America (PACA). Has 850,000 photos. Clients include: ad agencies, public relations firms, businesses, audiovisual firms, book publishers, magazine publishers, encyclopedia publishers, newspapers, postcard companies, calendar and greeting card companies.
Subject Needs: "We specialize in nature photography with an emphasis on all animal life."
Specs: Uses 8 × 10 glossy or matte b&w prints; 35mm and some larger format color transparencies.
Payment & Terms: Pays 50% commission. Offers one-time rights; other uses negotiable. Model release required if used for advertising. Captions required.
Making Contact: Send material by mail for consideration. SASE. Reports in 1-2 months. Free photo guidelines with SASE. Tips sheet distributed regularly to established contributors.
Tips: "First, pre-edit your material. Second, know your subject. We need captions, including Latin names, and they must be correct!"

ANTHRO – PHOTO FILE, 33 Hurlbut St., Cambridge MA 02138. (617)868-4784, 497-7227. President/Owner: Nancy S. DeVore. Stock photo agency. Has approximately 10,000 color photos, 2,000 b&w photos. Clients include: book/encyclopedia publishers, magazine publishers and newspapers, *Primate Societies* by Smuts, U.Chicago Press (photos of monkeys and apes); *Discover* magazine, article on chimpanzees; and *Cultural Anthropology*, by Haviland, Holt, Rinehart, Winston (photos of various peoples).
Subject Needs: Anthropology and biology.
Specs: Uses 8 × 10 glossy b&w prints; 35mm and 2¼ × 2¼ transparencies.
Payment & Terms: Pays 40% commission to agency, 60% to photographer. Pays $125-600/b&w photo; $160-800/color photo. Works with or without signed contract, negotiable. Offers guaranteed subject exclusivity within files. Contracts renew automatically with each submission; time period not specified. Charges duping fee at cost/image. Statements issued annually. Payment made annually, within one month of end of cycle. Photographers allowed to review account records to verify sales figures. Buys one-time rights. Informs photographer and allows him to negotiate when client requests all rights. Model/property release preferred for U.S.A. people close-up. Photo captions required; include description of action, people and place.
Making Contact: Query with samples; "send 25 dupes labeled with name and caption." SASE.
Tips: Prefers to see behavioral/anthropological emphasis. "Send duplicates or prints labeled and captioned with emphasis on the important topics for anthrotexts and biology texts; sociology texts; geography and social studies texts. Look at the current best selling texts. There is an increasing need for illustratiing culture change and environmental pollution."

*‡**ARQUIVO INTERNACIONAL DE COR, COMUNICAÇÃO PELA IMAGEM, LDA.,** R.D. Cristovão da Gama, 138, 4100 Porto Portugal. (2)610 39 67. FAX: (2)610 39 67. Contact Manager: Maria Guimaraes. Estab. 1986. Stock photo agency. Has 20,000 photos. Clients include: advertising agencies, public relations firms, audiovisual firms, businesses, magazines publishers, newspapers, postcard publishers, calendars companies, greeting card companies and packaging companies.
Subject Needs: "As a stock photo agency, we deal with general subjects. We are, however, deeply interested in starting to work on representing video and films."
Specs: Uses b&w, color prints; 35mm, 2¼ × 2¼, 4 × 5, 8 × 10 transparencies; European PAL System videotape.
Payment & Terms: Pays 40-60% commission on b&w and color photos. Average price per image (to clients): $330/b&w or color photo depending on usage. Works with or without a signed contract, negotiable; offers exclusive contracts. Contracts renew automatically with additional submissions every year. Statements issued quarterly. Payment made quarterly. Photographers permitted to review account

records to verify sales figures or account for various deductions "whenever they want to check." Offers one-time rights or non-exclusive rights. Informs photographer and allows him to negotiate when client requests all rights. Model/property release required. Captions required.

Making Contact: Submit portfolio for review. Query with samples. Query with stock photo list. Samples kept on file. SASE. Expects minimum initial submission of 50-100 images. Reports in 1-2 months. Photo guidelines available. Market tips sheet distributed infrequently.

Tips: "As a stock photo agency, we should be prepared to provide any kind of image. Therefore we do have interest on general themes such as: men, architecture and art, economy, industry, traffic, science, technology and nature (animal and geography)."

ATLANTA STOCK ASSOCIATES, P.O. Box 723093, Atlanta GA 30339. (404)434-8363. President: Betsy Harbison. Photo Editor: Don Holebrooks. Estab. 1987. Southeastern regional stock photo agency. Has over 45,000 slides. Clients include: ad agencies, public relations firms, audiovisual firms, corporate clients, book/encyclopedia publishers, magazine publishers, trade show/exhibit manufacturers.

Subject Needs: Specializes in Southeastern images, however, "general practitioner." Wants to see a photographer's view of the world around him. Scenics, people and their lifestyles, occupations, industry, transportation, plants and animals, travel destinations, abstracts and still lifes. "Each image must be able to stand alone if necessary." Especially needs shots of ordinary people, all ages, all races in a variety of daily activities as a single, in family structure, and in peer group. Critical need for ethnics, including, black, hispanic, oriental. Issues include wellness, health, nutrition, ecology, pollution and recyclying worldwide, city skylines, historic locations, area festivals, education and holiday scenics.

Specs: "Tack sharp" images, simple backgrounds void of unrelated material. Successful shots have proper placement in frame for subject and space for copy. Needs horizontal and verticals with various angles and distances from subject. Uses 35mm transparencies as base format; larger formats acceptable, "but must be individually mounted."

Payment & Terms: Pays 50% commission on use fees ranging from $125 and up. Offers exclusivity within 400 mile radius of agency's Atlanta office. Statement issues quarterly. Payment made quarterly if under $300, at time of sale if over $300. Offers one-time rights; CD-ROM rights and exclusivity "only on photographer's written permission." Model/property release preferred; captions required. Wants 300 acceptable original images as minimum to start contract and 300 each succeeding year. Contracts renew for three years with additional submissions.

Making Contact: Query letter requesting guidelines. SASE for return invitation to submit portfolio for review. "When you have been invited to send a submission you must remit $5 for administrative fees, 100 slides for review and return postage and shipping materials for your submission. While professional status is not required for acceptance, materials must compete with other agency material for the client's choice. We are looking for strong shooters and volume. If the 300 minimum taxes your capacity then save yourself and don't respond."

Tips: "ASA has a very close working relationship with its photographers. You will be one of maximum 50-75 photographers in our files. We are not concerned with your professional status, but your work must meet our standards."

*‡AUSTRALIAN PICTURE LIBRARY, 12 Falcon St., Crows Nest NSW 2065 Australia, (02)438-3011. FAX: (02)439-6527. Managing Director: Jane Symons. Estab. 1979. Stock photo agency and news/feature syndicate. Has 750,000 photos. Clients include: advertising agencies, public relations firms, audiovisual firms, businesses, book/encyclopedia publishers, magazine publishers, newspapers, postcard publishers, calendar companies and greeting card companies.

Subject Needs: Australia, world travel, sports, people, industry, personalities, music industry.

Specs: Uses 8×10 b&w prints; 35mm, 2¼×2¼ and 6×7cm transparencies.

Payment & Terms: Pays 50% commission. Offers volume discounts to customers. Discount sales terms not negotiable. Works on contract basis only; offers exclusive contracts. Statements issued quarterly. Payment made quarterly. Offers one-time rights. Informs photographer and allows him to negotiate when client requests all rights. Model/property release required. Captions required.

Making Contact: Submit portfolio for review. Expects minimum initial submission of 400 images with minimum yearly submissions of at least 1000 images. Reports in 1 month. Photo guidelines free with SASE. Catalog available. Market tips sheet distributed quarterly to agency photographers.

Tips: Looks for formats larger than 35mm in travel, landscapes and scenics with excellent quality. "There must be a need within the library that doesn't conflict with existing photographers too greatly. Stock is a business. Photographers must have a long-term plan, not just the immediate view."

The asterisk before a listing indicates that the market is new in this edition. New markets are often the most receptive to freelance submissions.

*■‡BARNABY'S PICTURE LIBRARY, Barnaby House, 19 Rathbone St., London WIP 1AF England. 071-636-6128. FAX: 071-637-4317. Contact: Mrs. Ruth Turner. Stock photo agency and picture library. Has 4,000,000 photos. Clients include: ad agencies, public relations firms, audiovisual firms, businesses, book/encyclopedia publishers, magazine publishers, newspapers, film production companies, BBC, all TV companies, record companies, etc.
Specs: Uses 8×10 b&w prints; 35mm, 2¼×2¼, 4×5 and 8×10 transparencies.
Payment & Terms: Pays 50% commission on b&w and color photos. Model release and captions required.
Making Contact & Terms: Arrange a personal interview to show portfolio. Send unsolicited photos by mail for consideration. Submit portfolio for review. SASE. Reports in 3 weeks. Photo guidelines free with SASE. Tips sheet distributed yearly to anyone for SASE.

*‡BAVARIA BILDAGENTUR GMBH, Postfach 1160, 8035 Gauting, West Germany. (089)850-8044. FAX: (089)850-8043. Director: Anton Dentler. Stock photo agency and picture library. Has 800,000 photos. Clients include: ad agencies, public relations firms, audiovisual firms, businesses, book/encyclopedia publishers, magazine publishers, newspapers, postcard companies, calendar companies and greeting card companies.
Subject Needs: All kinds.
Specs: Uses 35mm, 2¼×2¼, 4×5 and 8×10 transparencies.
Payment & Terms: Pays 50% commission on color photos. Offers one-time rights and first rights. Model release preferred; captions required.
Making Contact: Query with samples. Send unsolicited photos by mail for consideration. Submit portfolio for review. SASE. Reports in 2 weeks. Photo guidelines sheet for SASE.

■ROBERT J. BENNETT, INC., 310 Edgewood St., Bridgeville DE 19933. (302)337-3347, 270-0326. FAX: (302)337-3444. President: Robert Bennett. Estab. 1947. Stock photo agency.
Subject Needs: General subject matter.
Specs: Uses 8×10 glossy b&w prints; 35mm, 2¼×2¼ and 4×5 transparencies.
Payment & Terms: Pays 50% commission US; 40-60% foreign. Pays $5-50/hour; $40-400/day. Pays on publication. Offers non-exclusive contract. Statements issued monthly. Payment made monthly. Photographers allowed to review account records to verify sales figures. Buys one-time rights. Informs photographer and allows him to negotiate when client requests all rights. Model/property release and photo captions required.
Making Contact: Interested in receiving work from newer, lesser-known photographers. Query with resume of credits. Query with stock photo list. Provide resume, business card, brochure or tearsheet to be kept on file for possible future assignments. Works on assignment only. Keeps samples on file. Reports in 1 month.

BIOLOGICAL PHOTO SERVICE, P.O. Box 490, Moss Beach CA 94038. (415)726-6244. Photo Agent: Carl W. May. Stock photo agency. Has 80,000 photos. Clients include: ad agencies, businesses, book/encyclopedia publishers and magazine publishers.
Subject Needs: All subjects in the life sciences, including agriculture, natural history and medicine. "Stock photographers must be scientists." Subject needs include: "color enhanced scanning electron micrographs; photographic coverage of contemporary medical problems; modern medical imaging; minor phyla of invertebrates; animal behavior; and biological conservation. All aspects of general and pathogenic microbiology. All aspects of normal human biology and the basic medical sciences, including anatomy, histology, human embryology and human genetics. Computer-generated images.
Specs: Uses 4×5−11×14 glossy, high-contrast b&w prints; 35mm, 2¼×2¼, 4×5, 8×10 transparencies. "Dupes acceptable for rare and unusual subjects, but we prefer originals."
Payment & Terms: Pays 50% commission on b&w and color photos. General price range: $90-500, sometimes higher for advertising uses. Statements issued quarterly. Payment made quarterly; "one month after end of quarter." Photographers allowed to review account records to verify sales figures "by appointment at any time." Offers one-time rights; negotiable. Informs photographer and allows him to negotiate when client requests all rights. "Photographer is consulted during negotiations for 'buyouts,' etc." Model release required for photos used in advertising and other commercial areas. Photo captions required; include complete identification of subject and location.
Making Contact: Query with list of stock subjects and resume of scientific and photographic background. SASE. Reports in 2 weeks. Photo guidelines free with query, resume and SASE. Tips sheet distributed intermittently to stock photographers only.
Tips: "When samples are requested, we look for proper exposure, maximum depth of field, adequate visual information and composition, and adequate technical and general information in captions. Requests fresh light and electron micrographs of traditional textbook subjects; applied biology such as bioengineering, agriculture, industrial microbiology, and medical research; biological careers; field research. We avoid excessive overlap among our photographer/scientists. We are experiencing an ever-

growing demand for photos covering environmental problems of all sorts—local to global, domestic and foreign. Tropical biology, marine biology, and forestry are hot subjects. Our three greatest problems with potential photographers are: 1) Inadequate captions. 2) Inadequate quantites of *good* and *diverse* photos. 3) Poor sharpness/depth of field/grain/composition in photos."

BLACK STAR PUBLISHING CO., INC., 116 E. 27th St., New York NY 10016. (212)679-3288. Director of Creative Servies: Lois Wadler. Stock agency. Has 4 million color transparencies, 1 million b&w prints. Clients include: magazines, ad agencies, book/encyclopedia publishers, corporations, poster companies, graphic design firms, TV and card companies.
Specs: Send at least 300 color transparencies. All formats accepted. "Our tastes and needs are eclectic. We do not know from day to day what our clients will request. Submissions should be made on a trial and error basis. Our only demand is top quality. Mark slides with 'MR' for those that are model released."
Payment & Terms: Pays 50% commission. Offers first North American serial rights; "other rights can be procured on negotiated fees." Model release, if available, should be submitted with photos. "Especially need model-released photos of buisness lifestyle and medicine."
Making Contact: Call to arrange an appointment or to get additional info. Also send submissions or porfolios with SASE. Reports in 1-2 weeks sooner if requested. SASE. Free photo guidelines.
Tips: Black Star's files are international and topical, and also include a broad-based, model-released subject file for sales to advertising agencies. Requires exclusive worldwide contracts.

‡JOHN BLAKE PICTURE LIBRARY, The Georgian House, 6 The Plain, Thornbury, Bristol BS12 2AG United Kingdom. (0454)418321/413240. FAX: (0454)416636. Proprietor: John Blake. Picture library. Has 50,000 photos. Clients include: ad agencies, businesses, book/encyclopedia publishers, magazine publishers, postcard companies and calendar companies.
Subject Needs: "The general topography of Britain, Europe and the rest of the world, in all format transparencies and b&w. Constantly expanding stock includes landscapes, countryside, churches, architecture, cities, towns, villages, gardens, people at work and play. Comprehensive collection on the Cotswolds."
Specs: Uses 6×8 glossy b&w prints; 2¼×2¼ and 4×5 transparencies.
Payment & Terms: Pays 50% commission for b&w and color photos. General price range: $50-250. Works with or without a signed contract, negotiable. Offers nonexclusive contract. Statements issued monthly. Payment made monthly. Photographers allowed to review account records to verify sales figures. Offers one-time rights. Informs photographer and allows him to negotiate when client requests all rights. Model release and captions required.
Making Contact: Query with list of stock photo subjects. Solicits photos by assignment only. SASE. Reports in 1 month. Photo guidelines free for SASE.
Tips: Prefers to see "sharp and accurate focusing, good composition, good color saturation: ability to take less then obvious view of a commonly-seen tourist attraction. We require color shots of businesses, office situations, where VDTs, keyboards, faxes etc. are in use. Business people meeting, ancillary services such as secretarial needs are always in demand. We are always on the lookout for topical features on the USA (crime, environmental issues, etc.) which we would also need copy for. Good composition is becoming less important as ad agencies and publishers seek to achieve eye-catching effects with logos and graphics in pictures. We often need to find images with blank areas to one side to get this effect for clients."

■D. DONNE BRYANT STOCK PHOTOGRAPHY, P.O. Box 80155, Baton Rouge LA 70898. (504)387-1620. FAX: (504)383-2951. President: Douglas D. Bryant. Stock photo agency. Has 250,000 photos. Clients include: ad agencies, audiovisual firms, book/encyclopedia publishers and magazine publishers. Currently represents 60 professional photographers.
Subject Needs: Specializes in picture coverage of Latin America with emphasis on Mexico, Central America, South America, the Caribbean Basin and the Southern USA. Eighty percent of picture rentals are for editorial usage. Important subjects include agriculture, anthropology/archeology, art, commerce and industry, crafts, education, festivals and ritual, geography, history, indigenous people and culture, museums, parks, religion, scenics, sports and recreation, subsistence, tourism, transportation, travel and urban centers.

> 🍁 *The maple leaf before a listing indicates that the market is Canadian. The symbol is new this year in* Photographer's Market.

Specs: Uses 8×10 glossy b&w; 35mm, 2¼×2¼ and 4×5 color transparencies.

Payment & Terms: Pays 50% commission on b&w and color photos. General price range: $85-1,600. Works with or without a signed contract, negotiable. Offers nonexclusive contracts. Contracts do not contain automatic renewal clauses. Statements issued monthly. Payment made monthly. Does not allow photographers to review account records to verify sales figures. Offers one-time rights and electronic media rights. Offers $1,500 per image for all rights. Model release preferred for people. Captions required; include location and brief description.

Making Contact: Query with resume of credits and list of stock photo subjects. SASE. Reports in 1 month. Photo guidelines free with SASE. Tips sheet distributed every 3 months to agency photographers.

Tips: Prefers to see "developed picture stories related to one of the subject interests listed above. Would like to see more coverage of commerce and industry, as well as better coverage of the modern urban environment in Latin American countries. There is a decreasing interest in Latin American Indians and ruins and an increasing interest in the modern and dynamic urban Latin culture. A photographer interested in shooting Latin scenics will make sales through the DDB Stock Agency, but a photographer who is willing to photograph inside modern schools, factories and hospitals will make far more. We would like to improve our coverage of Mexico, especially Mexico City and the other larger cities. We also want to increase coverage of Cuba, the Dominican Republic, Lima, Caribbean Isles, tropical rainforest destruction/colonization and illegal aliens/INS activity along the US/Mexico border. We are seeing an increased demand for Hispanic culture in the US. All these areas are receiving increasing interest and our files are weak in these subject areas. Freelancers interested in working successfully with DDB Stock should visit Latin America two or more times a year to shoot stock pictures. These self assignments should be co-ordinated with the agency to assure saleable subjects. Successful agency photographers submit 500-1,000 new images each year. Most successful agency photographers speak Spanish and understand Latin culture. The photographers who earn the most money at DDB Stock are those who would rather tour a Mexican steel mill or hospital than relax on the beach at Cancun. Our ideal photographer is a cultural geographer with an artist's eye and world class photography talent. We have several of these individuals and value them highly."

✦**BRYCE FINLEY, INC.,** P.O. Box 553, Christina Lake BC V0H1E0 Canada. (604)447-6106. CEO: Bryce Finley. Estab. 1987. Stock photo agency. Has 5,000,000 photos. Clients include: advertising agencies, public relations firms, book/encyclopedia publishers, magazine publishers, postcard companies, calendar companies and greeting card companies.

Subject Needs: Handles all subjects, expecially model-released people engaged in all activities, for advertising. Especially needs work from foreign photographers, pornographic sets, nudes, sports, leisure.

Specs: Uses 35mm transparencies and larger formats.

Payment & Terms: Pays 50% commission. Enforces minimum prices. Works on contract basis only. Offers limited regional exclusive, non-exclusive and guaranteed subject exclusive contracts. Statements issued quarterly. Payment made quarterly. Offers one-time rights. Model/property release and photo captions required.

Making Contact: Interested in receiving work from newer, lesser-known photographers. Query with samples. SASE. Reports in 2 weeks.

■**CALIFORNIA VIEWS/Pat Hathaway Historical Collection,** 171 Forest Ave., Pacific Grove CA 93990. (408)373-3811. Photo Archivist: Pat Hathaway. Picture library; historical collection. Has 60,000 b&w images, 2,000 35mm color. Clients include: ad agencies, public relations firms, audiovisual firms, businesses, book/encyclopedia publishers, magazine publishers, newspapers, postcard companies, calendar companies, greeting card companies, television and video and historical exhibition.

Subject Needs: Historical photos of California from 1860-1990s.

Specs: Uses 8×10 b&w prints.

Payment & Terms: Buys photos outright; pays $10-100 per b&w photo. General price range: $100-150, $175-200. Offers one-time rights.

Making Contact: Deals with local freelancers only. Buys only historical photos. Does not return unsolicited material. Reports in 1 month.

■**CAMERIQUE INC. INTERNATIONAL,** Main office: Dept. PM, 1701 Skippack Pike, P.O. Box 175, Blue Bell PA 19422. (215)272-4000. FAX: (215)272-7651. Representatives in Boston, Los Angeles, Chicago, New York City, Toronto, Sarasota FL, and Tokyo. Photo Director: Christopher C. Johnson. Estab. 1973. Has 300,000 photos. Clients include: advertising agencies, public relations firms, audiovisual firms, businesses, book/encyclopedia publishers, magazine publishers, newspapers, postcard companies, calendar companies, greeting-card companies.

Subject Needs: General stock photos, all categories. Emphasizes people activities all seasons. Always need large format color scenics from all over the world. No fashion shots; all people shots, including celebrities must have releases.

Specs: Uses 35mm, 2¼, 4×5 transparencies; b&w contact sheets; b&w negatives; "35mm accepted if of unusual interest or outstanding quality."

Payment & Terms: Sometimes buys photos outright; pays $10-25/photo. Also pays 50% commission on b&w/color. General price range: $150-500. Works on contract basis only. Offers limited regional exclusivity and nonexclusive contracts. Contracts are valid "indefinitely until cancelled in writing." Charges $100-150 catalog insertion fee; $30 duping fee. Also charges advertising fees; not specified. Statements issued monthly. Payment made monthly; within 10 days of end of month. Offers one-time rights. Model/property release required for people, houses, pets. Photo captions are required; "any descriptive information that would help to market photos."

Making Contact: Query with list of stock photo subjects; send unsolicited photos by mail for consideration; "send letter first we'll send our questionnaire and spec sheet." SASE. Reports in 2 weeks. Will return material with SASE. Tips sheet distributed periodically to established contributors.

Tips: Prefers to see "well-selected, edited color on a variety of subjects. Well-composed, well-lighted shots, featuring contemporary styles and clothes. Be creative, selective, professional and loyal. Communicate openly and often."

CATHOLIC NEWS SERVICE, 3211 Fourth St. NE, Washington DC 20017-1100. (202)541-3252. Photos/ Graphics Manager: Barbara Stephenson. Photos/Graphics Researcher: Sarah Davis. Wire service transmitting news, features and photos to Catholic newspapers.

Subject Needs: News or feature material related to the Catholic Church or Catholics; head shots of Catholic newsmakers; close-up shots of news events, religious activities. Especially interested in photos aimed toward a general family audience and photos depicting modern lifestyles, e.g., family life, human interest, teens, poverty, active senior citizens, families in conflict, unusual ministries, seasonal and humor.

Specs: Uses 8×10 glossy prints.

Payment & Terms: Pays $25/photo; $75-200/job. Offers one-time rights. Captions required.

Making Contact: Send material by mail for consideration. SASE.

Tips: Submit 10-20 good quality prints covering a variety of subjects. Some prints should have relevance to a religious audience. "Knowledge of Catholic religion and issues is helpful. Read a Diocesan newspaper for ideas of the kind of photos used. Caption information should accompany photos. Photos should be up-to-date and appeal to a general family audience. No flowers, no scenics, no animals. As we use more than 1,000 photos a year, chances for frequent sales are good. Send only your best photos."

‡CEPHAS PICTURE LIBRARY, 20 Bedster Gardens, East Molesey, Surrey KT8 9SZ United Kingdom. Tel. & Fax: (081)979-8647. Director: Mick Rock. Picture library. Has 50,000 photos. Clients include: ad agencies, public relations firms, businesses, book/encyclopedia publishers, magazine publishers, postcard companies and calendar companies.

Subject Needs: "We are a general picture library covering all aspects of all countries. Wine and vineyards a major speciality."

Specs: Uses 35mm and 2¼×2¼ transparencies.

Payment & Terms: Pays 50% commission for color photos. General price range: £40-400+ (English currency). Offers one-time rights. Model release preferred; captions required.

Making Contact: Send unsolicited photos by mail for consideration. SASE. Reports in 1 week. Photo guidelines for SASE.

Tips: Looks for "transparencies in white card mounts with informative captions and names on front of mounts. Only top-quality, eye-catching transparencies required. Our sales of transparencies relating to wine and vineyards are expanding rapidly. We need more from the USA, the less well-known areas, as well as California; Mexico, Chile, Argentina and Brazil. Show us more city scenes and National Parks. Also required are pictures of Americans in everyday situations, showing the American way of life, etc. — especially teenagers."

BRUCE COLEMAN PHOTO LIBRARY, 117 E. 24th St., New York NY 10010. (212)979-6252. FAX: (212)979-5468. Photo Director: Marta Serra-Jovenich. Estab. 1970. Stock photo agency. Member of Picture Agency Council of America (PACA). Has 900,000 photos. Clients include: advertising agencies, public relations firms, audiovisual firms, businesses, book/encyclopedia publishers, magazine publishers, newspapers, postcard publishers, calendar companies, greeting card companies, zoos (installations), T.V.

Subject Needs: Nature, travel, science, people, industry.
Specs: Uses 35mm, 2¼×2¼, 4×5 color transparencies.
Payment & Terms: Pays 50% commission on color film. Average price per image (to clients): color $175-975. Works on exclusive contract basis only. Renews automatically for 5 years. Statements issued quarterly. Payment made quarterly. Does not allow photographer to review account records; any deductions are itemized. Offers one-time rights. Informs photographer and allows him to negotiate when client requests all rights. Model/property release preferred for people, private property. Captions required; location, species, genus name, Latin name, points of interest.
Making Contact: Query with resume of credits. Works with local freelancers only. Samples kept on file. SASE. Expects minimum initial submission of 300 images with annual submission of 2,000. Reports in 3 months on completed submission; 1 week acknowledgement. Photo guidelines free with SASE. Catalog available. Markets tips sheet distributed bi-monthly to most active photographers. Also quarterly newsletter, "Norman's News," given to all current photographers.
Tips: "We look for strong dramatic angles, beautiful light, sharpness. No gimmicks (prism, color, starburst filters, etc.). We like photos that express moods/feelings and show us a unique eye/style. We like to work to be properly captioned. Caption labels should be typed or computer generated and they should contain all vital information regarding the photograph." Sees a trend "towards a journalistic style of stock photos. We are asked for natural settings, dramatic use of light and/or angles. Photographs should not be contrived and should express strong feelings toward the subject. We advise photographers to shoot a lot of film, photograph what they really love and follow our want lists."

*‡**COLORIFIC PHOTO LIBRARY,** Visual House, 1 Mastmaker Rd., London E14 9WT England. (71)723-5031. FAX: (71)262-6870. Editorial Director: Christopher Angeloglou. Estab. 1970. Picture library, news/feature syndicate. Has 300,000+ photos. Clients include: advertising agencies, public relations firms, audiovisual firms, book/encyclopedia publishers, magazine publishers, newspapers, calendar companies.
Specs: Uses 35mm, 2¼×2¼ transparencies.
Payment & Terms: Pays 50% commission on color photos. Average price per image (to clients): $150-350/color photo. Enforces minimum prices. "Prices vary according to type of market." Photographers have option of not allowing their work to be discounted. Works with or without contract. Offers limited regional exlusivity and non-exclusive contracts. Contracts renew automatically with additional submissions every three-five years. Statements issued quarterly. Payment made quarterly. Offers one-time rights. Informs photographer and allows him to negotiate when client requests all rights. Model/property release preferred. Captions required.
Making Contact: Query with resume of credits. SASE. Expects minimum initial submission of 250 images. Review held after first submission received." Reports as needed. Photo guidelines free with SASE.

■‡**COLOTHEQUE S.P.R.L.,** Avenue Paul Hymans, 103 (bte 23), 1200 Brussels Belgium. (02)762-48-07. FAX: (02)770-39-67. Manager: René J. Mertens von der Becke. Stock photo agency and picture library. Has 200,000 photos. Clients include: advertising agencies, public relations firms, audiovisual firms, businesses, book/encyclopedia publishers, magazine publishers, postcard companies, calendar and greeting card companies, and tour operators.
Specs: Uses 35mm, 2¼×2¼ and 4×5 transparencies.
Payment & Terms: Pays 60% commission on color photos. General price range: 3,000-60,000 (Belgian currency). Enforces minimum prices. Offers volume discounts to customers; terms specified in photographer's contract. Photographers can choose not to sell images on discount terms. Works on contract basis only. Offers limited regional exclusivity. Contracts renew automatically for unlimited time period. Statements issued monthly or quarterly depending on sales. Payments made monthly or quarterly. Photographers allowed to review account records to verify sales figures. Offers one-time rights. Model/property release and captions required.
Making Contact: Interested in receiving work from newer, lesser-known phtographers. Arrange a personal interview to show a portfolio. Send unsolicited photos by mail for consideration. SASE.
Tips: Stock photography business is "growing in quality and quantity." To break in, "furnish excellent material."

‡**EDUARDO COMESANA-AGENCIA DE PRENSA,** Casilla de Correo 178 (Suc.26), Buenos Aires 1426 Argentina. (541)776-2959, 773-5943. FAX: (541)776-2959, 313-7267. Director: Eduardo Comesana. Stock photo agency, picture library and news/feature syndicate. Has 300,000 photos. Clients include: ad agencies, book/encyclopedia publishers, magazine publishers and newspapers.
Subject Needs: Personalities, entertainment, politics, science and technology, expeditions, archeology, travel, industry, nature, human interest, education, medicine, foreign countries, agriculture, space, ecology, leisure and recreation, couples, families and landscapes. "We have a strong demand for science-related subjects like shown in *Discover*, *Smithsonian* and *National Geographic* magazines.

Specs: Uses 8×10 glossy b&w prints; 35mm, 2¼×2¼ and 4×5 transparencies.
Payment & Terms: Pays $80/b&w photo; $100-300/color photo; 60% commission. Works with or without contract; negotiable. Offers limited regional exclusivity. Contracts continue "indefinitely unless terminated by either party with not less than 90 days written notice." Statements issued quarterly. Payment made quarterly. Photographers allowed to review account records to verify sales figures. Offers one-time and electronic media rights. Informs photographer and allows him to negotiate when client requests all rights. Model/property release preferred. Photo captions required; include "who, what, where, when, why and how."
Making Contact: "Send introductory letter or fax stating what photographer wants to syndicate. Do not send unsolicited material without previous approval." We would like to know as much as possible about the prospective contributor. A complete list of subjects will be appreciated." Include IRCs or check for postage in US dollars. Reports in 1 month.
Tips: Represents Black Star in South America; Woodfin Camp & Associates, Outline Press Syndicate from New York City; and Shooting Star from Los Angeles. "We would like to review magazine-oriented stories with a well-written text and clear captions. In case of hot-news material, please fax or phone before sending anything. Freelancers should send us an introductory letter stating the type of photography he intends to sell through us. In our reply we will request him to send at least five stories of 10 to 20 colors each, for review. We would like to have some clippings of his photography."

■**COMSTOCK, INC.**, 30 Irving Place, New York NY 10003. (212)353-8600. President: Henry Scanlon. Member of Picture Agency Council of America (PACA). Has 4,000,000 photos. Clients include: ad agencies, public relations and audiovisual firms, businesses, book/encyclopedia and magazine publishers, newspapers, and postcard, calendar and greeting card companies.
Subject Needs: Write for subject guidelines.
Specs: Uses 35mm (preferred), 2¼×2¼, 4×5 or 8×10 transparencies; 8×10 b&w double-weight fiber-based prints.
Payment & Terms: Pays 50% of stock sale; 25% commission to agency on assignments. General price range: $150-20,000. Works on contract basis only. Offers exclusive contract only. Contracts renew automatically with each submission for one year after first 5-year base period. Charges filing fee of $2/image. Charges duping fee of $3.50 per 4×5; $1.75 per 35mm. Statements issued monthly. Payment made monthly. Photographers allowed to review account records to verify sales figures or account for various deductions, but "during normal business hours, and for their accounts only." Offers one-time rights and nonexclusive rights. "We do not sell all rights and discourage the practice. If subject does ask, the photographer is informed." Model and/or property release preferred; "must have model releases for commercial files." Photo captions required; include "who, what, when, where, why."
Making Contact: Contact Jane Kinne, editorial director. Query with resume of credits or list of stock photo subjects. SASE. Reports in 3 weeks.
Tips: "We represent very few photographers all of whom are extremely productive, most of whom make their living from stock photography. We could use more coverage in the science and hi-tech areas and in child-development from birth to full adulthood. We look for creativity, originality, a recognizable point of view, consistent technical excellence. Have an area of specialty and expertise. Present a scrupulously *edited* portfolio. Know and understand what stock is and what competition is out there; have a specialty that you care about passionately."

■**CUSTOM MEDICAL STOCK PHOTO**, 3819 N. Southport Ave., Chicago IL 60613. (312)248-3200 or (800)373-2677. FAX: (312)248-7427. Medical Archivist: Mike Fisher. Member of Picture Agency Council of America (PACA). Clients include: ad agencies, magazines, textbook publishers, design firms, audiovisual firms and hospitals. All commercial and editorial markets that express interest in medical and scientific subject area. Clients include: Scott, Foresman & Co., editorial, drug abuse, psychological testing, pathology; Foote, Cone, Belding, commerical.
Subject Needs: Biomedical, scientific, healthcare environmentals and general biology for advertising illustrations, textbook and journal articles, annual reports, editorial use and patient education.
Specs: Uses 35mm, 2¼×2¼ and 4×5 transparencies. Negatives for electron microscopy. 4×5 copy transparencies of medical illustrations.
Payment & Terms: Pays per shot or commission. Per-shot rate depends on usage. Commission: 50% - domestic leases; 30-40% - foreign leases. Works on contract basis only. Credit line given if applicable, client discretion. Offers one-time rights; other rights negotiable.

Making Contact: Query with list of stock photo subjects and request current want list and submission packet. "PC captioning disk available for database inclusion, please request. Do not send uncaptioned unsolicited photos by mail. SASE. Reports in average 4 weeks. Monthly want list available by U.S. Mail, and by FAX. Model and property release copies required.

Tips: "Our past want lists are a valuable guide to the types of images requested by our clients. Past want lists are available. Environmentals of researchers hi-tech biomedicine, physicians, nurses and patients of all ages in situations from neonatal care to mature adults are requested frequently. Almost any image can qualify to be medical if it touches an area of life: breakfast, sports, etc. Trends also follow newsworthy events found on newswires. Photos should be good clean images that portray a single idea whether it is biological, medical or scientific; the ability to recognize the newsworthiness of subjects. Put together a minimum of 100 images for submission. Call before shipping to receive computer disk and caption information and return information. Contributing to our agency can be very profitable if a solid commitment can exist."

■**CYR COLOR PHOTO AGENCY,** Box 2148, Norwalk CT 06852. (203)838-8230. Contact: Judith A. Cyr. Has 125,000 transparencies. Clients include: ad agencies, businesses, book publishers, magazine publishers, encyclopedia publishers, calendar companies, greeting card companies, poster companies and record companies.

Subject Needs: "As a stock agency, we are looking for all types. There has been a recent interest in family shots (with parents and children) and people in day-to-day activities. Also modern offices with high-tech equipment and general business/professional settings. Mood shots, unusual activities, etc. are always popular—anything not completely 'standard' and common. Photos must be well-exposed and sharp, unless mood shots."

Specs: Uses 35mm to 8×10 transparencies.

Payment & Terms: Pays 50% commission. Works on contract basis only. Offers nonexclusive contract. Payment made upon payment from client. Offers one-time rights, all rights, first rights or outright purchase; price depending upon rights and usage. Informs photographer and allows him to negotiate when client requests all rights. Model release and captions preferred.

Making Contact: Send material by mail for consideration. SASE. "Include postage for manner of return desired." Reports in 4 weeks. Distributes tips sheet periodically to active contributors; "usually when returning rejects."

Tips: Each submission should be accompanied by an identification sheet listing subject matter, location, etc. for each photo included in the submission. All photos should be properly numbered, with photographer's initials; also using vinyl sheets is a great time-saver in reviewing photos. "We have received more requests from clients to use 35mm in a slide presentation only (i.e. one time) and/or in a video presentation. Thus, there are more uses of a photo with limited copyright agreements."

■‡**DAS PHOTO,** Domaine de Bellevue, 181, Septon 6940 Belgium. (086)32 24 26. Director: David Simson. Stock photo agency. Has 50,000 photos. Clients include: advertising agencies, public relations firms, audiovisual firms, book/encyclopedia publishers, magazine publishers, calendar companies and greeting card companies. Previous/current clients include: Stern and Oggi, both features and Oxford University Press, book commission; *Vogue*; Geographical Magazine (GB); Spectator; Guardian; and BBC.

Subject Needs: Handles "mainly reportage—suitable for publishers and magazines although we do deal with most subjects. We are specialists in selling photo material in all European countries."

Specs: Uses 8×10 glossy b&w prints; 35mm, 2¼×2¼, 4×5 and 8×10 transparencies.

Payment & Terms: Pays 50% commission. Pays $40-500/b&w photo; $60-1000/color photo; $350/day plus expenses. Works on contract basis only. Offers limited regional exclusivity contract. Guarantees subject exclusivity within files. Contracts renew automatically with additional submissions. Charges duping fee of 100%/image. Statements issued quarterly. Payment made quarterly, when sales are made. Photographers allowed to review account records to verify sales figures. Rights negotiable. Informs photographers and allows them to negotiate when a client requests all rights. Model release preferred. Photo captions preferred; include description of location, country and subject matter.

Making Contact: Interested in receiving work from newer, lesser-known photographers. Query with samples, send unsolicited photos by mail for consideration. SASE. Reports in 1 week. Photo guideline sheet and tips sheet free with SASE."

Tips: "We take a large variety of material but it has to be saleable, sharp and good color saturation. Send 100-500 good saleable images for selection.

■**LEO DE WYS INC.,** 1170 Broadway, New York NY 10001. (212)689-5580. FAX: (212)545-1185. President: Leo De Wys. Office Manager: Laura Diez. Member of Picture Agency Council of America (PACA). Has 350,000 photos. Clients include: ad agencies, public relations and AV firms, business, book, magazine and encyclopedia publishers, newspapers, calendar and greeting card companies, textile firms, travel agencies and poster companies.

Subject Needs: Travel and destination (over 2,000 categories); and released people pictures in foreign countries (i.e., Japanese business people, German stockbrokers, English nurses, Mexican dancers, exotic markets in Asia, etc.).
Specs: Uses 35mm, medium format and 4×5 transparencies.
Payment & Terms: Price depends on quality and quantity. Usually pays 50% commission; 33⅓% for foreign sales. General price range: $125-6,500. Works with photographers on contract basis only. Offers exclusive and limited regional exclusive contracts; prefers to offer exclusive contract. Contracts renew automatically for five years. Offers to clients "any rights they want to have; payment is calculated accordingly." Charges 50% catalog insertion fee. "Company advances duping cost and deducts after sale has been made." Statements issued bimonthly and quarterly. Payment made bimonthly and quarterly. Photographers allowed to review account records to verify their sales figures. Offers one-time rights. Informs photographers and permits him to negotiate when client requests all rights; some conditions. Model release required; "depends on subject matter." Captions preferred.
Making Contact: Query with samples—"(about 40 pix) is the best way." Query with list of stock photo subjects or submit portfolio for review. SASE. Reporting time depends; often the same day. Photo guidelines free with SASE.
Tips: "Photos should show what the photographer is all about. They should show his technical competence—photos that are sharp, well-composed, have impact, if color they should show color. Company now uses bar coded computerized filing system." Seeing trend toward more use of food shots tied in with travel such as "key lime pie for Key West and Bavarian beer for Germany. Also more shots of people—photo-released and in local costumes. Currently, the destinations most in demand are the USA, Canada, Mexico and the Caribbean."

DEVANEY STOCK PHOTOS, Suite 306, 755 New York Ave., Huntington NY 11743. (516)673-4477. FAX: (516)673-4440. President: William Hagerty. Photo Editor: Ruth Fahlbusch. Has over 1 million photos. Clients include: ad agencies, book publishers, magazines, corporations and newspapers. Previous/current clients: Young & Rubicam, BBD&O, Hallmark Cards, *Parade* Magazine, MacMillan Publishing, Harcourt Brace & Jovanovich, *Newsday*.
Subject Needs: Accidents, animals, education, medical, artists, elderly, scenics, assembly lines—auto and other, entertainers, schools, astronomy, factory, science, automobiles, family groups, aviation, finance, babies, fires, shipping, movies, shopping, flowers, food, beaches, oceans, skylines, foreign, office, birds, sports, gardens, operations, still life, pets, business, graduation, health, police, teenagers, pollution, television, children, history, hobbies, travel, churches, holidays, cities, weddings, communications, houses, women, writing, zoos, computers, housework, recreation, religion, couples, crime, crowds, dams, industry, laboratories, law, lawns lumbering, restaurants, retirement, romance, etc.—virtually all subjects.
Specs: Uses 8×10 glossy b&w prints; uses all sizes of transparencies.
Payment & Terms: Does not buy photos outright. Pays 50% commission on color; 30% on b&w. Works with photographers with or without a signed contract, negotiable. Contracts automatically renew for a 3-year period. Offers nonexclusive contract. Statements issued upon sale. Payment made monthly. Photographers not allowed to review account records to verify sales figures. Offers one-time rights. Model release preferred. Captions required.
Making Contact: Interested in receiving work from newer, lesser-known photographers. Query with list of stock photo subjects or send material by mail for consideration. SASE. Reports in 1 month. Free photo guidelines with SASE. Distributes monthly tips sheet free to any photographer. Model/property release preferred; captions required. "Releases from individuals and homeowners are most always required if photos are used in advertisements."
Tips: "An original submission of 200 original transparencies in vinyl sheets is required. We will coach."

*‡DIANA PHOTO PRESS AB, Box 6266, S-102 34, Stockholm Sweden. (46)8 6651945. FAX: (46)8 6653295. Manager: Diana Schwarcz. Estab. 1973. Clients include: magazine publishers and newspapers.
Subject Needs: Personalities and portraits of well-known people.
Specs: Uses 18×24 b&w prints; 35mm transparencies.
Payment & Terms: Pays 30% commission on b&w and color photos. Average price per image (to clients): $150/b&w and color image. Enforces minimum prices. Works on contract basis only. Statements issued monthly. Payment made in 60-90 days. Offers one-time rights. Informs photographer and allows him to negotiate when client requests all rights. Captions required.
Making Contact: Query with samples. Samples kept on file. SASE. Does not report; "Wait for sales report."

‡DINODIA PICTURE AGENCY, 13 Vithoba Ln., Vithalwadi, Kalbadevi, Bombay India 400 002. (91)22-318572. FAX: (91)22-2863406. Owner: Jagdish Agarwal. Estab. 1987. Stock photo agency. Has 200,000 photos. Clients include: advertising agencies, public relations firms, audiovisual firms, businesses,

book/encyclopedia publishers, magazine publishers, newspapers, postcard companies, calendar companies and greeting card companies.
Subject Needs: "We specialize in photos on India—people and places; fairs and festivals; scenic and sports; animals and agriculture."
Specs: Uses 35mm, 2¼ × 2¼ and 4 × 5 transparencies.
Payment & Terms: Does not buy photos outright. Pays 50% commission on b&w and color photos. General price range: US $50-250. Negotiate fees below stated minimum prices. Offers volume discounts to customers; inquire about specific terms. Discount sales terms not negotiable. Works on contract basis only. Offers limited regional exclusivity. "Prefers exclusive for India." Contracts renew automatically with additional submissions for 5 years. Statement issued monthly. Payment made monthly. Photographers permitted to review sales figures. Informs photographer allows him to negotiate when client request all rights. Offers one-time rights. Model release preferred, photo captions required.
Making Contact: Interested in receiving work from newer, lesser-known photographers. Query with resume of credits, samples and list of stock photo subjects. SASE. Reports in 1 month. Photo guidelines free with SASE. Market tips sheet distributed monthly to contracted photographers.
Tips: "We look for style, maybe in color, composition, mood, subject-matter; whatever, but the photos should have above average appeal." Sees trend that "market is saturated with standard documentary-type photos. Buyers are looking more often for stock that appears to have been shot on assignment."

DR. STOCK INC., #320, 1939 NE Loop 410, San Antonio TX 78217. (512)829-7733. CEO: Peter Berndt MD. Estab. 1990. Stock photo agency. Has 5,000 photos. Clients include: advertising agencies, public relations firms, businesses, book/encyclopedia pubilshers, magazine publishers, newspapers.
Subject Needs: Handles biomedical, biological, scientific images only.
Specs: Uses 35mm, 2¼ × 2¼ transparencies.
Payment & Terms: Pays 40% commission on color photos. General price range: $50 up. Statements issued quarterly. Payment made monthly on receipt of our payment. Photographers allowed to review account records to verify sales figures. Offers one-time rights. Model release required for recognizable subjects. Photo captions required.
Making Contact: Interested in receiving work from newer, lesser-known photographers. Query with samples. Query with list of stock photo subjects. SASE. Reports in 1 month. Photo guidelines free with SASE. Market tips sheets free with SASE.
Tips: This firm is in a heavy recruitment stage and seeks new photographers; recruiting very selectively. "We need a steady supply of high quality medical, biological, scientific subjects; prefer the images on slow (fine grained film). We see an increasing demand for scientific images of all kinds. The market seems unlimited, but competition is certainly noticeable."

■FRANK DRIGGS COLLECTION, Dept. PM, 1235 E. 40 St., Brooklyn NY 11210. (718)338-2245. Owner: Frank Driggs. Stock photo agency. Has 100,000 photos. Clients include: ad agencies, public relations firms, audiovisual firms, businesses, book/encyclopedia publishers, magazine publishers, newspapers, motion pictures.
Subject Needs: All aspects of music.
Payment & Terms: Buys and leases photos. Pays 50% commission on b&w and color photos; 50% commission on film. General price range: $75-100/photo. Works with photographers with or without signed contract, negotiable. Offers non-exclusive contract. Buys one-time rights. Informs photographer and allows him to negotiate when client requests all rights. Photo captions preferred; include dates and location of photos.
Making Contact: Query with samples and list of stock photo subjects. Works on assignment only. SASE. Reports in 1 month.
Tips: To break in, show "clear action or off-stage shots, b&w and color."

■DRK PHOTO, 265 Verde Valley School Rd., Sedona AZ 86336. (602)284-9808. FAX: (602)284-9096. President: Daniel R. Krasemann. "We handle only the personal best of a select few photographers—not hundreds. This allows us to do a better job aggressively marketing the work of these photographers." Member of Picture Agency Council of America (PACA) and A.S.P.P. Clients include: ad agencies; PR and AV firms; businesses; book, magazine, textbook and encyclopedia publishers; newspapers; postcard, calendar and greeting card companies; branches of the government; and nearly every facet of the publishing industry, both domestic and foreign.
Subject Needs: "Especially needs marine and underwater coverage. Also interested in S.E.M.'s, African, European and Far East wildlife; and good rainforest coverage.
Specs: Uses 35mm, 2¼ × 2¼ and 4 × 5 transparencies.
Payment & Terms: Pays 50% commission on color photos. General price range: $75-"into thousands." Offers one-time rights; "other rights negotiable between agency/photographer and client." Model release preferred; captions required.

Making Contact: "With the exception of established professional photographers shooting enough volume to support an agency relationship, we are not soliciting open submissions at this time. Those professionals wishing to contact us in regards to representation should query with a brief letter of introduction and tearsheets."

DYNAMIC GRAPHICS INC., CLIPPER & PRINT MEDIA SERVICE, 6000 N. Forrest Park Dr., Peoria IL 61614. (309)688-8800. Photo Editor: Samantha M. Wick. Clients include: ad agencies, printers, newspapers, companies, publishers, visual aid departments, TV stations, etc.
Subject Needs: Generic stock photos (all kinds). "Our needs are somewhat ambiguous and require that a large number of photos be submitted for consideration. We will send a 'photo needs list' and additional information if requested."
Specs: Majority of purchases are b&w. Send 8×10s, contact sheets and high contrast conversions. Minimal use of 35mm and 4×5 transparencies.
Payment & Terms: Pays $50 and up/b&w photo; $100 and up/color photo. Pays on acceptance. Rights are specified in contract. Model release required.
Making Contact: Send tearsheets or folio of 8×10 b&w photos by mail for consideration; supply phone number where photographer may be reached during working hours. Reports in 6-8 weeks.

■**ELITE PHOTOGRAPHY, INC.,** Box 2789, Toledo OH 43606. Director: David Thompson. Clients include: advertising agencies, public relations firms, audiovisual firms, businesses, magazine publishers, postcard companies, calendar and greeting card companies, book/encyclopedia publishers, video distributors.
Subject Needs: "We are a stock agency that is specializing in photography of women, be it pretty pictures, cheesecake, nude, exotic, or erotic. Although we are strict on such rules as focusing and exposures, our needs are as varied as the marketplace — if it is salable, we will sell it."
Specs: Uses 35mm and 2¼×2¼ transparencies. "Don't send larger transparencies or b&w unless she is a special subject."
Payment & Terms: Rarely buys photos/film outright. Pays 50% commission on b&w and color photos. General price range: $150-1,500, complete sets higher. Works on contract basis only. Contracts renew automatically with additional submissions; all for one-year extensions. Statements issued after sales within 45 days of receiving payment. Buys "any rights the photographers will sell." Model release required; captions preferred.
Making Contact & Terms: Interested in receiving work from newer, lesser-known photographers. Query with samples. Send unsolicited photos by mail for consideration. "Send a professional looking package certified to us. Make sure it is sent requesting a return receipt." SASE. Reports in 2 weeks. Photo guidelines, tip sheet free with SASE *and* samples. (No phone calls please.)
Tips: "Be able to compose, focus and expose a photograph properly. Remember that we specialize in photographs of women, with cheesecake and nude/erotic the biggest and fastest sales. Show us you can produce marketable images, and we'll do the rest. Almost all of our magazine buyers are screaming for cover shots — shoot them! In addition, we also direct market sets overseas to publishers. This creates a very lucrative market for those with sets that have already sold in the US. We can still market them to the rest of the world. For those with such talent, Elite now deals in video and is interested in seeing sample VHS tapes that fall within our subject guidelines. We are very interested in seeing much more photography involving women working in all career fields and in various forms of play such as sports and other leisure activities. We also want more mother and child photography."

■**ENVISION,** 220 W. 19th St., New York NY 10011. (212)243-0415. Director: Sue Pashko. Estab. 1986. Stock photo agency. Has 100,000 photos. Clients include: advertising agencies, audiovisual firms, book/encyclopedia publishers, magazine publishers, postcard companies, calendar and greeting card companies and graphic design firms.
Subject Needs: Professional quality photos of food, commercial food processing, fine dining, American cities especially the Midwest, crops, Third World lifestyles, marine mammals, European landmarks, tourists in Europe and Europe in winter looking lovely with snow, and anything on Africa and African-Americans.
Specs: Uses 35mm, 2¼×2¼, 4×5 or 8×10 transparencies.
Payment & Terms: Pays 50% commission on b&w and color photos. General price range: $125 and up. Offers one-time rights; "Each sale individually negotiated — usually one-time rights." Model release required; captions required.
Making Contact: Query with resume of credits "on company/professional stationery." SASE. Reports in 1 month.
Tips: "We are looking for the *very* best quality photographs. Clients expect the very best in professional quality material. Photos that are unique taken with a very individual style — demands for traditional subjects *but* with a different point of view — African and Hispanic-American lifestyle photos are in great demand."

■‡GREG EVANS PHOTO LIBRARY, 91 Charlotte St., London W1P ILB England. (071)636-8238. FAX: (071)637-1439. Manager: Greg Evans. Picture library. Has 250,000 photos. Clients include: ad agencies, public relations firms, audiovisual firms, businesses, book/encyclopedia publishers, magazine publishers, newspapers, postcard companies, calendar companies and greeting card companies and travel companies.
Specs: Uses 35mm, 2¼ × 2¼, 4 × 5, 2¼ × 2¾ and 8 × 10 transparencies.
Payment & Terms: Pays 50% commission on color photos. Offers one-time rights and also buys outright. Model release required.
Making Contact: Arrange a personal interview to show portfolio. Send unsolicited photos by mail for consideration. SASE. Reports in 1 week. Quarterly tips sheet free with SASE.
Tips: Wants to see "creativity, sharpness, clarity, perfect exposure, precise captions" in work submitted.

■EWING GALLOWAY, 100 Merrick Rd., Rockville Centre NY 11570. (516)764-8620. Photo Editor: Tom McGeough. Estab. 1920. Stock photo agency. Member of Picture Agency Council of America (PACA). Has 3,000,000 photos. Clients include: advertising agencies, public relations firms, audiovisual firms, businesses, book/encyclopedia publishers, magazine publishers, newspapers, postcard companies, calendar companies, greeting card companies and religious organizations.
Subject Needs: General subject library. Does not carry personalities or news items. Lifestyle shots (model released) are most in demand.
Specs: Uses 8 × 10 glossy b&w prints; 35mm, 2¼ × 2¼ and 4 × 5 transparencies.
Payment & Terms: Pays 30% commission on b&w photos; 50% on color photos. General price range: $400-450. Charges catalog insertion fee of $400/photo. Statements issued monthly. Payment made monthly. Offers one-time rights; also unlimited rights for specific media. Model/property release required. Photo captions required; include location, specific industry, etc.
Making Contact: Interested in receiving work from newer, lesser-known photographers. Query with samples. Send unsolicited photos by mail for consideration; must include return postage. SASE. Reports in 3 weeks. Photo guidelines free with SASE. Market tips sheet distributed monthly; free with SASE.
Tips: Wants to see "high quality—sharpness, subjects released, shot only on best days—bright sky and clouds." Medical and educational material is currently in demand. We see a trend toward photography related to health and fitness, high-tech industry, and mixed race in business and leisure.

■FASHIONS IN STOCK, Dept. PM, 23-68 Steinway St., Long Island City NY 11105. (718)721-1373. President: Nicasio Sanchez. Estab. 1987. Stock photo agency. Has 60,000 photos. Clients include: advertising agencies, public relations firms, businesses, magazine publishers and calendar companies.
Subject Needs: "We specialize in stock photos that tell a story, illustrate a scenario, be it in the area of business, leisure, family, friendships, etc. Many of our stock photos are fashion-oriented. Our photos also deal with current controversial issues. The photos all include people against a backdrop of unique regional interest or interesting architecture, exotic locales. People also shown participating in sports of all kinds, in business settings, at family holidays, shopping, and in academic environments."
Specs: Uses 8 × 10 fiber base, b&w prints; 35mm, 2¼ × 2¼, 4 × 5 transparencies; b&w contact sheets; b&w negatives; 16mm film; VHS videotape.
Payment & Terms: Pays 50% commission on b&w/color photos. Offers one-time rights; other rights negotiable. Model release required; photo captions preferred.
Making Contact: Arrange a personal interview to show portfolio "if photographer's location is permanent." Submit portfolio for review. SASE. Reports in 1 week. Tips sheet distributed to photographers with fashions in stock.
Tips: "We are looking for current, fashionable stock photography that can convey an idea or sell a product or service. The photos must have flexibility, universality, a keen insight into people's feelings. We also look for unique locations in different areas of the United States as a background. Our focus is mostly on commercial print advertising." Stock is being used instead of assignment work by many advertising agencies. "They are looking for casual, upscale types of people of all ages. I notice a large request for young women (20s to early 30s) in professional scenarios, different ethnic groups (Asian, African-American, Hispanic) working and playing together, and elderly people involved in work or exercise. The photographer working with FIS would grow rapidly and would save considerable processing and model expenses. We also push for assignment work for our photographers. We are currently establishing an office in Manhattan."

FERN-WOOD DESIGNS AND PHOTO MARKETING AGENCY, (A Division of Fern-Wood Enterprises, Inc.), P.O. Box 948, Wrightsville Beach NC 28480. (919)256-2897. FAX: (919)256-3299. Vice President and Secretary: Carol G. Wood. President and Treasurer: Mary C. Fernandez de Castro. Estab. 1990. Stock photo agency and greeting card publisher. Clients include: advertising agencies, public relations firms, businesses, postcard companies and calendar companies.

Subject Needs: "Coastal beach scenes, boats, birds, flowers, historical landmarks, old barns and buildings, landscapes and people worldwide, specializes in photos with natural settings rather than posed settings, unusual and interesting subject matter."
Specs: Uses 4×6 glossy b&w or color prints; 35mm, 2¼×2¼ and 4×5 transparencies.
Payment & Terms: Buys photos outright. Pays $50 minimum; higher fees negotiable. Pays 50% commission on color photos. General price range: average $250. Offers volume discounts to customers; terms specified in photographer's contract. Photographers can choose not to sell images on discount terms. Works on contract basis only; offers limited regional exclusivity and guaranteed subject exclusivity. Contracts renew automatically for one year. Charges $25 filing fee with contract. Statements issued quarterly. Payment made monthly. Photographers permitted to review account records to verify sales figures or account for various deductions. Offers one-time rights; rights negotiated depending on photographer. Informs photographers and allows him to negotiate when client requests all rights. Model release required if subject is identifiable; photo captions preferred.
Making Contact: Interested in receiving work from newer, lesser-known photographers. Arrange a personal interview to show portfolio. Query with list of stock photo subjects. Send unsolicited photos by mail for consideration. Keeps samples on file. SASE. Reports in 3 weeks. Market tips sheet distributed monthly to photographers and clients; free with SASE.
Tips: Looks for style, composition, subject matter and originality. Sees trend toward natural shots of coastal regions, golf courses, candid shots of people in their own environment, historical landmarks and environmental subject matter.

■**FINE PRESS SYNDICATE**, Box 22323, Ft Lauderdale FL 33335. Vice President: R. Allen. Has 49,000 photos and 100+ films. Clients include: ad agencies, public relations firms, businesses, audiovisual firms, book publishers, magazine publishers, postcard companies and calendar companies worldwide.
Subject Needs: Nudes; figure work, seminudes and erotic subjects (female only).
Specs: Uses color glossy prints; 35mm, 2¼×2¼ transparencies; 16mm film; videocasettes: VHS and Beta.
Payment & Terms: Pays 50% commission on color photos and film. Price range "varies according to use and quality." Enforces minimum prices. Works on contract basis only. Offers exclusivity only. Statements issued monthly. Payment made monthly. Offers one-time rights. Does not inform photographer or permit him to negotiate when client requests all rights. Model/property release preferred.
Making Contact: Interested in receiving work from newer, lesser-known photographers. Send unsolicited material by mail for consideration or submit portfolio for review. SASE. Reports in 2 weeks.
Tips: Prefers to see a "good selection of explicit work. Currently have European and Japanese magazine publishers paying high prices for very explicit nudes and 'X-rated' materials. Clients prefer 'American-looking' female subjects. Send as many samples as possible. Foreign magazine publishers are buying more American work as the value of the dollar makes American photography a bargain. More explicit poses are requested."

■✹**FIRST LIGHT ASSOCIATED PHOTOGRAPHERS**, 1 Atlantic Ave., Suite 204, Toronto ON M6K 3E7 Canada. (416)532-6108. President: Pierre Guevremont. Estab. 1984. Stock and assignment agency. Has 450,000 photos. Clients include: advertising agencies, public relations firms, audiovisual firms, businesses, book/encyclopedia publishers, magazine publishers, newspapers, postcard companies, calendar companies and greeting card companies.
Subject Needs: Natural history, international travel, commercial imagery in all categories. Special emphasis upon model-released people, high tech, industry, and business. "Our broad files require variety of subjects."
Specs: Uses 35mm, 2¼×2¼ and 4×5 transparencies.
Payment & Terms: Pays 50% commission. General price range: $150-5,000. Works on contract basis only. Offers limited regional exclusivity. Charges variable catalog insertion fees. Statements issued monthly. Payment made monthly. Offers one-time rights. Informs photographers and permits them to negotiate when client requests all rights. Model release preferred; photo captions required.
Making Contact: Query with list of stock photo subjects. SASE. Reports in 1 month. Photo guidelines free with SASE. Tips sheet distributed every 6 weeks.
Tips: Wants to see "tight, quality edit and description of goals and shooting plans."

■✹**FOCUS TONY STONE WORLDWIDE**, 5th Floor, 161 Eglinton Ave. East, Toronto ON M4P 1J5 Canada. (416)488-9495. FAX: (416)488-9448. Estab. 1985. Stock photo agency. Has 100,000+ photos. Clients include: advertising agencies, public relations firms, book/encyclopedia/magazine publishers, calendar publishers and record companies.
Specs: Uses 35mm, 2¼×2¼, 4×5 and 8×10 transparencies.
Payment & Terms: Pays 50% commission. General price range: $350-4,500. "We maintain strong pricing to solidify the industry." Works on contract basis only. Offers exclusive and non-exclusive contracts. Charges fee "only from future sales/doesn't sell, photograph doesn't pay." Statements issued

monthly. Payment made monthly. "All account records on computer; can be verified in minutes." Offers one-time rights; other rights negotiable. "We do not offer buy-outs—the trade off on future sales is unrealistic. Rights are controlled through our international rights control system." Model/property release and photo captions required.

Making Contact: Submit portfolio for review. SASE. Reports in 2 weeks. Photo guidelines free with SASE. Tips sheet distributed quarterly to contract photographers. "Please call or write for our extensive photographer's submission guide."

Tips: "We work with a very select file of images. We do not have millions and from our knowledge we earn the largest per image income of any agency through our worldwide sales network of 15 offices. Our goal is simple: provide enough income for our photographers to enable them to dedicate 100% of their time shooting stock. Please direct inquiries to Andrea Sproule, Creative Department."

*‡FOCUS—STOCK FOTOGRAFICO, Santa Fe 3192, #5 "A", Buenos Aires 1425 Argentina. (1)83-3905. Director: Carlos Goldin. Has 150,000 photos. Clients include: advertising agencies, audiovisual firms, businesses, book/encyclopedia and magazine publishers, calendar companies.

Subject Needs: People in general for advertising—at work, jogging, mature couples, in the office, in meetings, beside the corporate jet, at ease during relaxing hours, in restaurants and bars, having a drink, with children. Families in general, in all situations. Everyday scenes and specially produced stock shots.

Specs: Uses 35mm, 2¼×2¼, and 4×5 transparencies; prefers Kodachrome, but will accept other good quality slides. Works only with originals.

Payment & Terms: Sometimes buys photos/film outright. Pays $50-1,000 US/photo; pays 50% commission/color. General price range $50-300. Enforces minimum prices. Offers volume discounts to customers; inquire about specific terms. Discount sale terms not negotiable. Works on contract basis only. Offers limited regional exclusivity. Contracts renew automatically with additional submission for one year. Charges duping fee. Statements issued semi-annually. Payment made semi-annually. Photographers allowed to review account records to verify sales figures or account for various deductions. Offers one-time rights or all rights. Informs photographer and allows him to negotiate when client requests all rights. Model release preferred. Captions required.

Making Contact: Interested in receiving work from newer, lesser-known photographers. Query with samples. Send unsolicited photos by mail for consideration. SASE, IRCs. Reports in 1 month. Photo guidelines free with SASE, IRCs. Distributes tip sheet every six months "to our photographers"; free with SASE, IRCs.

Tips: "We are interested in opening our stock agency for a few good North American photographers who wish to open up their markets."

■❋FOTO EXPRESSION INTERNATIONAL (Toronto), Box 1268, Station "Q" Toronto, ON M4T 2P4 Canada. (416)841-9788. FAX: (416)841-2283. Photo Editor: Mrs. Veronika Kubik. Selective archive of photo, film and audiovisual materials. Clients include: ad agencies, public relations and audiovisual firms, TV stations, networks, film distributors, businesses, book, encyclopedia and trade magazine publishers, newspapers and news magazines. Also, postcard, calendar and greeting card companies.

Subject Needs: City views, aerial, travel, wildlife, nature/natural phenomena and disasters, underwater, aerospace, weapons, warfare, industry, research, computers, educational, religions, art, antique, abstract, models, sports. Worldwide news and features, personalities and celebrities.

Specs: Uses 8×10 b&w; 35mm and larger transparencies; 16mm, 35mm film; VHS, Beta and commercial videotapes (AV). Motion Picture, news film, film strip and homemade video.

Payment & Terms: Sometimes buys transparencies outright. 40% for b&w; 50% for color and 16mm, 35mm films and AV (if not otherwise negotiated). Offers one-time rights. Model release and captions required for photos.

Making Contact: Submit portfolio for review. The ideal portfolio for 8×10 b&w prints includes 10 prints; for transparencies include 60 selections in plastic slide pages. With portfolio you must send SASE with return postage (out of Canada—either money-order or International Postal Coupon). Photo guidelines free with SASE. Reports in 3 weeks. Tips sheet distributed twice a year only "on approved portfolio."

Tips: "We require photos, slides, motion picture films, news film, homemade video and AV that can fulfill the demand of our clientele." Quality and content therefore is essential. Photographers, cameramen, reporters, writers, correspondents and representatives are required worldwide by FOTO-PRESS, Independent News Service International, (416-841-4486/FAX: 416-841-2283), a division of the FOTO ex-PRESS-ion in Toronto. Contact Mr. Milan J. Kubik, Director, International section.

FOTOCONCEPT INC., Dept. PM, 18020 SW 66th St., Ft. Lauderdale FL 33331. (305)680-1771. FAX: (305)680-8996. Vice President: Aida Bertsch. Estab. 1985. Stock photo agency. Member of Picture Agency Council of America (PACA). Has 150,000 photos. Clients include: magazines, advertising agencies, newspapers and publishers.

Subject Needs: General worldwide travel, medical and industrial.
Specs: Uses 35mm, 2¼×2¼, 4×5 transparencies.
Payment & Terms: Pays 50-55% commission for color photos. Works on contract basis only. Offers nonexclusive contract. Contracts renew automatically with each submission for one year. Statements issued quarterly. Payment made quarterly. Photographers allowed to review account records to verify sales figures. Offers one-time rights. Informs photographer and allows him to negotiate when client requests all rights. Model release and photo captions required.
Making Contact: Query with samples; query with list of stock photo subjects. SASE. Reports in 1 month. Photo guidelines free with SASE. Tips sheet distributed annually to all photographers.
Tips: Wants to see "clear, bright colors and graphic style." Points out that they are "looking for photographs with people of all ages with good composition, lighting and color in any material for stock use. Send 200 transparencies which best represents work with a SASE, for consideration."

■‡FOTO-PRESS TIMMERMANN, Speckweg 34A, D-8521 Moehrendorf, West Germany. 9131/42801. FAX 9131/450528. Contact: Wolfgang Timmermann. Stock photo agency. Has 100,000 slides. Clients include: ad agencies, audiovisual firms, businesses, book/encyclopedia publishers, magazine publishers, newspapers and calendar companies.
Subject Needs: All themes: landscapes, countries, towns, people, animals, nature.
Specs: Uses 35mm, 2¼×2¼, 4×5 and 8×10 transparencies.
Payment & Terms: Pays 50% commission on color prints. Average price per image to clients: $130-300. Enforces strict minimum prices. Works on non-exclusive contract basis only. First period: three years, automatically renewed for one year. Offers one-time rights. Model/property release preferred, captions required including state, country, city, subject, etc.
Making Contact: Interested in receiving work from newer, lesser-known photographers. Query with list of stock photo subjects. Send unsolicited photos by mail for consideration. SASE. Reports in 2 weeks.

■FOTOS INTERNATIONAL, 4230 Ben Ave., Studio City CA 91604. (818)508-6400. FAX: (818)762-2181. Manager: Max B. Miller. Has 4 million photos. Clients include: ad agencies, public relations firms, businesses, book publishers, magazine publishers, encyclopedia publishers, newspapers, calendar companies, TV and posters.
Subject Needs: "We are the world's largest entertainment photo agency. We specialize exclusively in motion picture, TV and popular music subjects. We want color only! The subjects can include scenes from productions, candid photos, rock, popular or classical, concerts, etc., and must be accompanied by full caption information."
Specs: Uses 35mm color transparencies only.
Payment & Terms: Buys photos outright; no commission offered. Pays $5-200/photo. Offers one-time rights and first rights. Model release optional; captions required.
Making Contact: Query with list of stock photo subjects. SASE. Reports in 1 month.

FPG INTERNATIONAL CORP., 32 Union Square E., New York NY 10003. (212)777-4210. Director of Photography: Rebecca Taylor. A full service agency with emphasis on images for the advertising, corporate, design and travel markets. Member of Picture Agency Council of America (PACA).
Subject Needs: High-tech industry, model released human interest, foreign and domestic scenics in large formats, still life, animals, architectural interiors/exteriors with property releases.
Specs: Minimum submission requirement per year—1,000 original color transparencies, exceptions for large format, 500 b&w full-frame 8×10 glossy prints.
Payment & Terms: Pays 50% commission upon licensing of reproduction rights. Works on contract basis only. Offers exclusive contract only. Contracts renew automatically upon contract date; 5-year contract. Charges catalog insertion fee; rate not specified. Statements issued monthly. Payment made monthly. Photographers allowed to review account records to verify sales figures. Licenses one-time rights; other rights negotiable. "We sell various rights as required by the client." When client requests all rights, "we will contact a photographer and get their permission;" some conditions.
Making Contact: "Initial approach should be by mail. Tell us what kind of material you have, what your plans are for producing stock and what kind of commercial work you do. Enclose reprints of published work." Photo guidelines and tip sheets provided for affiliated photographers. Model/property releases required and must be indicated on photograph; photo captions required.

■ *The solid, black square before a listing indicates that the market uses various types of audiovisual materials, such as slides, film or videotape.*

Tips: "Submit regularly; we're interested in committed, high-caliber photographers only. Be selective and send only first-rate work. Our files are highly competitive."

FRANKLIN PHOTO AGENCY, 85 James Otis Ave., Centerville MA 02632. (508)428-4378. President: Nelson Groffman. Has 35,000 transparencies. Clients include: publishers, advertising and industrial.
Subject Needs: Scenics, animals, horticultural subjects, dogs, cats, fish, horses, antique and classic cars, and insects.
Specs: Uses 35mm, 2¼×2¼ and 4×5 color transparencies. "More interest now in medium size format—2¼×2¼.
Payment & Terms: Does not buy outright; pays 50% commission. General price range: $100-300; $60/b&w photo; $100/color photo. Works with or without contract, negotiable. Offers nonexclusive contract. Statements issued semi-annually. Payment made when client pays. Photographers not allowed to review account records to verify sales figures. Offers one-time and one-year exclusive rights. Informs photographer and allows him to negotiate when client requests all rights. Model/property release required for people, houses; present release on acceptance of photo. Photo captions preferred.
Making Contact: Interested in receiving work from newer, lesser-known photographers. Query first with resume of credits. Reports in 1 month. SASE.
Tips: Wants to see "clear, creative pictures—dramatically recorded."

■**FROZEN IMAGES, INC.**, Suite 512, 400 First Ave. N., Minneapolis MN 55401. (612)339-3191. Director: Lonnie Schroeder. Stock photo agency. Has approximately 150,000 photos. Clients include: ad agencies, public relations firms, audiovisual firms, graphic designers, businesses, book/encyclopedia publishers, magazine publishers, newspapers and calendar companies.
Subject Needs: All subjects including abstracts, scenics, industry, agriculture, US and foreign cities, high tech, businesses, sports, people and families.
Specs: Uses transparencies.
Payment & Terms: Pays 50% commission on color photos. Works on contract basis only. Offers limited regional exclusivity. Contracts renew automatically with each submission; time period not specified. Charges catalog insertion fee; rate not specified. Statements issued monthly. Payment made monthly; within 5 days of end of month. Photographers allowed to review account records to verify sales figures "with notice and by appointment." Offers one-time rights. Informs photographers when client requests all rights, but agency negotiates terms. Model/property release required for people and private property. Photo captions required.
Making Contact: Query with resume of credits. Query with list of stock photo subjects. SASE. Reports in 1 month or ASAP (sometimes 6 weeks). Photo guidelines free with SASE. Tip sheet distributed quarterly to photographers in the collection.
Tips: Wants to see "technical perfection, graphically strong, released (when necessary) images in all subject areas."

F/STOP PICTURES INC., P.O. Box 359, Springfield VT 05156. (802)885-5261. President: John Wood. Estab. 1984. Stock photo agency. Member of Picture Agency Council of America (PACA). Has 135,000 photos. Clients include: advertising agencies, public relations firms, audiovisual firms, businesses, book/encyclopedia publishers, magazine publishers, newspapers, postcard companies, calendar companies and greeting card companies.
Subject Needs: "We specialize in New England and rural America, but we also need worldwide travel photos and model-released people and families."
Specs: Uses 35mm, 2¼×2¼, 4×5, 8×10 transparencies.
Payment & Terms: Pays 50% commission on color photos. Average price per image: $225. Enforces minimum prices, minimum of $100, exceptions for reuses. Works on contract basis only. Offers nonexclusive contract, exclusive contract for some images only. Contracts renew automatically for four years. Statements issued monthly. Payment made monthly by 31st of statement month. Photographers allowed to review account records to verify sales figures. Offers one-time rights. Informs photographer and allows him to negotiate when client requests all rights. Model/property release required for recognizable people and private property. Captions required; include complete location data and complete identification (including scientific names) for natural history subjects.
Making Contact: Arrange a personal interview to show portfolio. Query with list of stock photo subjects. Submit portfolio for review. SASE. Reports in 2 weeks. Photo guidelines free with SASE. Market tips sheet distributed quarterly to contracted photographers only. Not currently accepting new photographs.
Tips: Especially wants to work with "professional full-time photographers willing to shoot what we need." Send minimum of 500 usable photos in initial shipment, and 500 usable per quarter thereafter." Sees trend toward "more realistic people situations, fewer staged looking shots; more use of electronic manipulation of images,."

FUNDAMENTAL PHOTOGRAPHS, Dept. PM, 210 Forsyth St., New York NY 10002. (212)473-5770. Partners: Kip Peticolas and Richard Megna. Stock photo agency. Clients include: book/encyclopedia publishers.
Subject Needs: Science illustration—from rainbows to nuclear reactors; scientific/technical (physics, chemistry, photomicrographs and industrial illustrations). . .basic science to high technology.
Specs: Uses color: 35mm, 2¼×2¼, 4×5 and 8×10 transparencies; b&w: 8×10 prints.
Payment & Terms: Pays on commission basis; b&w 40%, color 50%. General price range $150-2,000. Offers one-time rights. Model release and captions required.
Making Contact: Arrange a personal interview to show portfolio. Query with resume of credits, samples or list of stock photo subjects. SASE. Reports in 1 month. Photo guidelines free with SASE. "Tips sheet distributed to photographers we use."
Tips: "We look for excellent technical quality, an imaginative and knowledgeable approach to science illustration and good clean graphic imagery. Overall, there is a demand for high quality in images and a need for ways to communicate and illustrate the concepts of a high-tech society."

■**GAMMA/LIAISON,** Dept. PM, 11 E. 26th St., New York NY 10010. (212)447-2500. Executive Vice President/Director: Jennifer Coley. Has 5 million plus photographs. Extensive stock files include news (reportage), human interest stories, movie stills, personalities/celebrities. Clients include: newspapers and magazines, book publishers, audiovisual producers, encyclopedia publishers and corporation/graphic designers.
Subject Needs: People, sports, scenics, travel, industry, medical, special effects, food and still life.
Specs: Uses 35mm or 2¼×2¼ transparencies.
Payment & Terms: Pays 50% commission. Works on contract basis only. Offers exclusive and non-exclusive contracts. Contracts renew automatically with each submission; time period not specified. Statements issued monthly. Payment made monthly. Buys one-time rights. Model release and photo captions required.
Making Contact: Submit portfolio with description of past experience and publication credits.
Tips: Involves a "rigorous trial period for first 6 months of association with photographer." Prefers previous involvement in publishing industry. Also has second division, Liaison International, which specializes in corporate and stock assignment work (see listing, this section).

■**MARILYN GARTMAN AGENCY, INC.,** Dept. PM, Suite 612, 731 S. Plymouth Ct., Chicago IL 60605. (312)987-0078. FAX: (312)987-0134. President/Manager: John Ford. Stock photo agency. Has 500,000 photos. Clients include: ad agencies, public relations firms, audiovisual firms, businesses, book/encyclopedia publishers, magazine publishers and calendar companies.
Subject Needs: Geographic (world wide) general categories going from subjects like abstracts to zoos.
Specs: Uses b&w prints, 35mm, 2¼×2¼ and 4×5 and 8×10 transparencies.
Payment & Terms: Pays 50% commission for b&w and color photos. Offers one-time rights. Model release and captions required.
Making Contact: Query with resume of credits, samples and list of stock photo subjects; do not send unsolicited material. Distributes tips sheet every few months to contracted photographers.
Tips: "We will speak to the individual photographer and request portfolio or samples—at that time we will tell the photographer what we desire to see."

■‡**GEOSCIENCE FEATURES PICTURE LIBRARY,** 6 Orchard Dr., WYE, Kent TN25 5AU United Kingdom. (0233)812707 (UK). FAX: (0233)812707. Contact: Dr. Basil Booth. Stock photo agency, picture library, earth sciences and natural history picture library. Has 140,000+ photos; approximately 10,000 feet 16mm film, mainly volcanic eruptions. Clients include: ad agencies, public relations firms, audiovisual firms, businesses, book/encyclopedia publishers, magazine publishers, newspapers, calendar companies and television companies.
Subject Needs: Zoology (all aspects, particularly animal behavior, portrait shots of mammals, birds, reptiles, etc. are required but action pictures are being requested more these days; no zoo shots). Botany (all aspects, plants, for example, should include flower close-up, entire flower head and entire plant, plant adaptations, trees, etc.). Microbiology. Earth sciences, particularly violent weather (tornados), volcanic eruptions and northern lights. General subjects.
Specs: Uses 8×10 glossy b&w prints; 35mm, 2¼×2¼, 6×7cm, 4×5 and 8×10 transparencies; b&w and color contact sheets, 16mm film, and VHS videotape. "No filtration material; we will add at duping stage."
Payment & Terms: Pays 55% commission for b&w photos; 60% commission for color photos; 50% for film. General price range: £20-50/b&w photo; £30-500/color photo. Offers one-year exclusive and occasionally 3-year exclusive rights; mostly nonexclusive, one-time only, one-edition and territory rights. Model release preferred; captions required (brief).

Making Contact: Arrange a personal interview to show portfolio. Query with resume of credits, samples and list of stock photo subjects. SASE. Reports in 2 weeks to 1 month, depending on work load. Photo guidelines free with SASE. Distributes tips sheet twice a year to all our photographers. "Concentrate in fields most familiar to you—i.e., bird photographers should specialize in birds, and so on, and improve technique, especially with difficult subjects."
Tips: Prefers to see "images that are razor sharp. Full color saturation. No filter gimmicks. Good composition (artistic where relevant). Where possible each picture should tell a story (except landscape, etc). Action shots. High speed flash. No posed wild animals. No domestic animals. Several themes to show photographer's versatility. Subjects required include moods, skys, volcanic eruptions, weather, earthquakes, natural history, geology, geography, peoples, communications, sports, (no glamour). Images should be factual and well-composed, but not arty."

■‡GEOSLIDES (Photography), 4 Christian Fields, London SW16 3JZ England. (081) 764-6292. Library Director: John Douglas. Picture library. Has approximately 100,000 photos. Clients include: ad agencies, public relations firms, audiovisual firms, businesses, book/encyclopedia publishers, magazine publishers, newspapers, calendar companies and television.
Subject Needs: Only from: Africa (South of Sahara); Asia; Arctic and Sub-Arctic; Antarctic. Anything to illustrate these areas. Accent on travel/geography.
Specs: Uses 8×10 glossy b&w prints; 35mm and 2¼×2¼ transparencies.
Payment & Terms: Pays 50% commission. General price range $70-1,000. Works with or without contract; negotiable. Offers nonexclusive contract. Statements issued monthly. Payment made upon receipt of client's fees. Photographers not allowed to review account records to verify sales figures. Offers one-time rights and first rights. Does not inform photographer and allow him to negotiate when client requests all rights. Model release required. Photo captions required; include description of location, subject matter and sometimes the date.
Making Contact: Query with resume of credits and list of stock photo subjects. SASE. Reports in 1 month. Photo guidelines for SASE (International Reply Coupon). No samples until called for. Leaflets available.
Tips: Looks for "technical perfection, detailed captions, must suit lists (especially in areas). Increasingly competitive on an international scale. Quality is important. Need for large stocks with frequent renewals." To break in, "build up a comprehensive (i.e. in subject or geographical area) collection of photographs which are well documented."

○ JOEL GORDON PHOTOGRAPHY, 112 4th Ave., New York NY 10003. (212)254-1688. Picture Agent: Elaine Abrams. Stock photo agency. Clients include: ad agencies, designers and textbook/encyclopedia publishers.
Specs: Uses 8×10 b&w prints, 35mm transparencies, b&w contact sheets and b&w negatives.
Payment & Terms: "Usually" pays 50% commission on b&w and color photos. Offers volume discounts to customers; terms specified in contract. Photographers can choose not to sell images on discount terms. Offers nonexclusive contract. Payment made after customer's check clears. Photographers allowed to review account records to verify sales figures. Does not inform photographer and allow him to negotiate when client requests all rights. Offers one-time rights. Model/property release and photo captions preferred.
Making Contact: Interested in receiving work from newer, lesser-known photographers.

■HAVELIN COMMUNICATIONS, Box 8509, Asheville NC 28814. Contact: Michael F. Havelin. Has 20,000 b&w and color photos. Clients include: advertising agencies, public relation firms, audiovisuals firms, businesses, book/encyclopedia publishers, magazine publishers, newspapers, postcard companies, calendar companies and greeting card companies.
Subject Needs: "We stock photos of pollution and its effects; animals, insects, spiders, reptiles and amphibians; solar power and alternative energy sources; and guns and hunting."
Specs: Uses b&w prints; 35mm, 2¼×2¼, 8×10 and 4×5 transparencies.
Payment & Terms: Pays 50% commission. General price range: highly variable. Offers nonexclusive contract. Statements issued after sales. Payment made quarterly upon sales and receipt of client payment. Photographers allowed to review account records to verify sales figures upon request. Offers one-time rights. Informs photographer and allows him to negotiate when client requests all rights. Model release preferred for recognizable people. Photo captions required; include who, what, where, when, why and how.
Making Contact: Interested in receiving work from newer, lesser-known photographers. Query with list of stock photo subjects. Photo guidelines free with SASE. Tips sheet distributed intermittently; free with SASE.
Tips: "We are always interested in well-exposed, informative images that have impact, as well as photo essays or images which tell a story on their own, and photo illustrated articles. Slicker work is selling better than isolated 'record' shots." To break in, "act professionally. People who work in visual media

still need to write coherent business letters and intelligent, informative captions. Don't take rejection personally. It may not be the right time for the editor to use your material. Don't give up. Be flexible."

■**HIGH COUNTRY IMAGES,** 631 Lupfer Ave., Whitefish MT 59937. (406)862-6622 or (406)862-6617. Manager: Alan T. Thompson. Estab. 1990. Stock photo agency. Has 6,000-10,000 slides; 8,000-12,000 negatives. Clients include: advertising agencies, businesses, book/encyclopedia publishers, magazine publishers, calendar companies, greeting card companies.
Subject Needs: "All subject matter except nude or obscene. Prefer shots of people doing things, mixed races, travel, hobbies, pets, children, farm, etc."
Specs: Uses 8×10 glossy b&w or color prints; 35mm or 2¼×2¼ transparencies; 8mm, super 8, 16mm, 35mm film; VHS videotape.
Payment & Terms: Pays 50% commission on b&w and color photos; 80% commission on films and videos. General price range: $75-100 b&w; $100-300 color. Photographers can choose not to sell images or discount terms. Works on contract basis only. Contracts renew automatically with additional submissions. Charges $100 filing fee; $2 catalog insertion fee. Statements issued quarterly. Payment made monthly. Photographers permitted to review account records to verify sales figures or account for various deductions. Offers one-time rights. Informs photographer and allows him to negotiate when client requests all rights. Model release required. Photo captions required; include "when, what, where, etc."
Making Contact: Interested in receiving work from newer, lesser known photographers. Send for free information. SASE. Reports in 1 month. Photo guidelines free with SASE. Market tips sheet distributed quarterly to contracted photographers; details free with SASE.
Tips: Query first, then send best work (3×5) print sample. Do not send originals or negatives. "We use a lot of people doing things and mixed races working together."

High Country Images photographer Wayne Mumford shoots strong wildlife and scenic photos. This is a shot of the Montana Flathead Valley and Glacier National Park in winter. The photo ran on the cover of Montana Magazine and has increased requests from other markets for similar images from the agency.

© Wayne Mumford

■**HILLSTROM STOCK PHOTO, INC.,** 5483 N. Northwest Hwy., (Box 31100), Chicago IL 60630 (60631 for Box No.). (312)775-4090, 775-3557. President: Ray F. Hillstrom, Jr. Stock photo agency. Has 1 million color transparencies; 50,000 b&w prints. "We have a 22-agency network." Clients include: ad agencies, public relations firms, audiovisual firms, businesses, book/encyclopedia publishers, magazine publishers, newspapers, calendar companies, greeting card companies and sales promotion agencies.

Subject Needs: "We need hundreds of 35mm color model-released sports shots (all types); panoramic 120mm format worldwide images. Model-released: heavy industry, medical, high-tech industry, computer-related subjects, family-oriented subjects, foreign travel, adventure sports and high-risk recreation, Midwest festivals (country fairs, parades, etc.), the Midwest. We need more color model released family, occupation, sport, student, senior citizen, high tech and on-the-job shots."
Specs: Uses 8 × 10 b&w prints; 35mm, 2¼ × 2¼ and 4 × 5 transparencies.
Payment & Terms: Pays $50-5,000/b&w and color photo; pays 50% commission on b&w and color photos. Works with or without contract, negotiable. Offers limited regional exclusivity. Statements issued periodically; time period not specified. Payment made monthly; within 30 days. Photographers allowed to review account records to verify sales figures. Offers one-time rights. Informs photographer and allows him to negotiate when client requests all rights. Model/property release required for people and private property. Photo captions required; include location, subject and description of function.
Making Contact: Send unsolicited photos by mail for consideration. Include three business cards and detailed stock photo list. SASE and check for postage for return of submitted material; make check to pay Hillstrom Stock Photo. Reports in 3 weeks. Photo guidelines free with SASE.
Tips: Prefers to see good professional images, proper exposure, mounted, and name IDs on mount. In photographer's samples, looks for "large format, model and property release, high-tech, people on the job, worldwide travel and environment. Show us at least 200 different images with 200 different subjects."

■HISTORICAL PICTURES, Dept. PM, Room 201, 921 W. Van Buren, Chicago IL 60607. (312)733-3239. FAX: (312)733-2844. Sales Research: Shirley Neiman. Picture library. Clients include: ad agencies, audiovisual firms, book/encyclopedia publishers and magazine publishers and corporate clients.
Subject Needs: Topics from pre-history through current, worldwide.
Specs: Uses any size, any finish b&w and color prints; also transparencies and b&w negatives.
Payment & Terms: Buys photos outright; pays 50% commission. Works on contract basis only (nonexclusive). Offers one-time rights. Photo captions required.
Making Contact: Query with list of stock photo subjects. Will return material submitted for review. Reports in 1 month.
Tips: Most sales are to editorial clients such as book and magazine publishers and corporate clients.

■‡HOLT STUDIOS LTD., The Courtyard, 24 High St., Hungerford, Berkshire, RG17 0NF United Kingdom. 0488-683523. Director: Nigel D. Cattlin. Picture library. Has 40,000 photos. Clients include: ad agencies, public relations firms, audiovisual firms, businesses, book/encyclopedia publishers, magazine publishers and newspapers.
Subject Needs: Photographs of world agriculture associated with crop production and crop protection including healthy crops and relevant weeds, pests, diseases and deficiencies. Farming, people and machines throughout the year including good landscapes. Livestock and livestock management. Worldwide assignments undertaken.
Specs: Uses 35mm, 2¼ × 2¼ and 4 × 5 transparencies.
Payment & Terms: Occasionally buys photos outright. Pays 50% commission. General price range: $100-1,500. Offers one-time rights. Captions required.
Making Contact: Send unsolicited photos by mail for consideration. SASE. Reports in 1 week. Photo guidelines for SASE. Distributes tips sheets every 3 months to all associates.
Tips: "Holt Studios looks for high quality technically well-informed and fully labeled color transparencies of subjects of agricultural interest." Currently sees "expanding interest particularly conservation and the environment."

■✻HOT SHOTS STOCK SHOTS, INC., 309 Lesmill Rd., Toronto ON M3B 2V1 Canada. (416)441-3281. FAX: (416)441-1468. Attention: Editor. Member of Picture Agency Council of America (PACA). Clients include: advertising and design agencies, publishers, major printing houses and product manufacturers. Previous/current clients include: McLaren: Lintas, child skating, television ad; Reidmore Books, industrial, education, historical, textbook; and Postcard Factory, Atlantic scenics, postcards, keychains and placemats.
Subject Needs: People and human interest/lifestyles, commerce and industry, wildlife, historic and symbolic Canadian.
Specs: Color transparency material any size, b&w contacts only.
Payment & Terms: Pays 50% commission, quarterly upon collection; 30% for foreign sales through sub-agents. Price ranges: $200-2,000. Pays $100-500/b&w photo; $100-3,000/color photo. Works on contract basis only. Offers exclusive, limited regional exclusivity and nonexclusive contracts. Most contracts renew automatically for 3-year period with each submission. Charges catalog insertion fee of 50% of separation costs. Statements issued quarterly. Payment made quarterly. Photographers allowed to review account to verify sales figures. Offers one-time, electronic media, and other rights to clients. Allows photographer to negotiate when client requests all rights. Requests agency promo-

tion rights. Model release preferred (include people, property). Photo captions required (include where, when, what, who, etc.).

Making Contact: Photo guidelines free with business SASE, reply in 1 week. Must send a minimum of 300 images. Unsolicited submissions must have return postage.

Tips: "Submit colorful, creative, current, technically strong images with negative space in composition." Looks for people, lifestyles, variety, bold composition, style, flexibility and productivity. "People should be model released for top sales." Prefer Kodachrome and medium format. Photographers should "shoot for business, not for artistic gratification; tightly edited, good technical points (exposure, sharpness etc.) professionally mounted, captioned/labeled and good detail."

■‡THE HUTCHISON LIBRARY, 118B Holland Park Ave., London W11 4UA England. (071)229-2743. Director: Michael Lee. Stock photo agency, picture library. Has around 500,000 photos. Clients include: ad agencies; public relations firms; audiovisual firms; businesses, book/encyclopedia publishers; magazine publishers; newspapers; postcard, calendar, television and film companies.

Subject Needs: "We are a general, documentary library (no news or personalities, no modeled 'set-up' shots). We file by country and aim to have coverage of every country in the world. Within each country we cover such subjects as industry, agriculture, people, customs, urban, landscapes, etc. We have special files on many subjects such as medical (traditional, alternative, hospital etc.), energy, environmental issues, human relations (relationships, childbirth, young children, etc. but all *real people*, not models). We are principally a color library though we hold a very small collection of b&w 'back-up.' "

Specs: Uses 8×10 b&w prints and 35mm transparencies.

Payment & Terms: Pays 50% commission for b&w and color photos. Statements issued and payment made semi-annually. Sends statement with check in June and January. Photographers not allowed to review account records to verify sales figures. Offers one-time rights. Model release preferred; captions required.

Making Contact: Arrange a personal interview to show portfolio. Send letter with brief description of collection and photographic intentions. Reports in 2 weeks, depends on backlog of material to be reviewed; as soon as possible. We have letters outlining working practices and lists of particular needs (they change). Distributes tips sheets to photographers who already have a relationship with the library.

Tips: Looks for "collections of reasonable size (never less than 500 transparencies) and variety, well captioned (or at least well indicated picture subjects, captions can be added to mounts later) sharp pictures (an out of focus tree branch or whatever the photographer thinks adds mood is not acceptable, clients must not be relied on to cut out difficult areas of any picture), good color, composition and informative pictures, prettiness is rarely enough . . . our clients want information, whether it is about what a landscape looks like or how people live, etc."

*‡I.C.P. INTERNATIONAL COLOUR PRESS, Via Alberto Da Giussano 15, Milano Italy 20145. (02)4696459 or 48008493. FAX: (02)48195625. Marketing Assistant: Alessandro Bissocoli. Estab. 1970. Stock photo agency. Has 1,200,000 transparencies. Clients include: advertising agencies, public relations firms, audiovisual firms, businesses, book/encyclopedia publishers, magazine publishers, postcard publishers, calendar companies and greeting card companies.

Specs: Uses 35mm, 2¼×2¼, 4×5 and 8×10 transparencies only.

Payment & Terms: Pays 50% commission on color photos. Average price per image (to clients): $400/color image. Offers volume discounts to customers; terms specified in photographer's contract. Discount sales terms not negotiable. Works on exclusive contract basis only. Contracts renew automatically with additional submissions, for three years. Charges 100% duping, postage and packing fees. Statements issued monthly. Payment made monthly. Photographers permitted to review account records to verify sales figures or account for various deductions. Offers one-time, first and sectorial exclusive rights. Model/property release required. Captions required.

Making Contact: Arrange personal interview to show portfolio. Query with samples and stock photo list. Works on assignment only. SASE. No fixed minimum for initial submission. Reports in 3 weeks. SASE.

■THE IMAGE BANK/WEST, 4526 Wilshire Blvd., Los Angeles CA 90010. (213)930-0797. General Manager: Lilly Filipow. Maintains over 1,000,000 stock photographs and illustrations in Los Angeles and 3,000,000 in New York. Clients include: ad agencies, design and public relations firms, corpora-

tions, audiovisual firms, publishers, retailers, and film/TV. Also, postcard, calendar and greeting card companies.
Specs: Uses 35mm color transparencies; "some larger formats."
Payment & Terms: Pays 50% commission for photos. Works with photographers on exclusive contract basis only. Statements issued quarterly. Payment made quarterly. Photographers allowed to review account records to verify sales figures. Offers one-time electronic media and agency promotion rights; negotiable, "however, photographers do not negotiate directly with the client." Model/property release and captions required. Photo captions are required; include date, location, description of image, especially for hi-tech imagery.
Making Contact: Interested in receiving work from newer, lesser-known photographers. When reviewing freelancer's portfolio and/or demos, looks for people, industry and an awareness of what's currently selling in the stock industry.
Tips: "Study the stock marketplace—present work which is currently relevant and present a vision for future work. All images must be originals."

■☀**IMAGE FINDERS PHOTO AGENCY, INC.,** 7th Floor, 134 Abbott St., Vancouver BC V6B 2K4 Canada. (604)688-9818. General Manager: Pindar Azad. Has 300,000 photos of all subjects. Clients include: ad agencies, graphic designers, public relations firms, businesses, audiovisual firms, book publishers, magazine publishers, encyclopedia publishers, newspapers, postcard companies, calendar companies and greeting card companies.
Subject Needs: Business, education, medical, hospitality, service and industrial, and general worldwide stock.
Specs: Uses transparencies only.
Payment & Terms: Does not buy outright; pays 50% commission. General price range: $200+, more for ad campaigns. Works on contract basis only. Offers limited regional exclusivity. Some contracts renew automatically with each submission; time periods of 1 and 2 years according to contract. Charges duping fee of 50%/image; takes out of commissions. Charges variable catalog insertion fee; takes out of commissions. Statements issued quarterly. Payment made quarterly. Offers one-time rights, all rights or first rights. Informs photographer and allows him to negotiate when client requests all rights; "requires photographer's written approval." Model/property release required for people and houses. Photo captions required; include description, technical data, etc.
Making Contact: "Send SASE for questionnaire and description of agency. Please do not send unsolicited material. Tearsheets OK." Photo guidelines free with SASE and International Reply Coupons. "(*Please no* foreign stamps—*stamps must be Canadian*)." Distributes quarterly want list to established contributors.
Tips: "Show the very best work. Ask lots of questions, and review monthly magazine and stock catalogs."

■**THE IMAGE WORKS,** P.O. Box 443, Woodstock NY 12498. (914)246-8800. Directors: Mark Antman and Alan Carey. Stock photo agency. Member of Picture Agency Council of America (PACA). Has 350,000 photos. Clients include: ad agencies, audiovisual firms, book/encyclopedia publishers, magazine publishers and newspapers.
Subject Needs: "We specialize in documentary style photography of worldwide subject matter. People in real life situations that reflect their social, economic, political, leisure time and cultural lives." Topic areas include health care, education, business, family life and travel locations.
Specs: Uses 8×10 glossy/semi-glossy b&w prints; 35mm and 2¼×2¼ transparencies.
Payment & Terms: Pays 50% commission on b&w and color photos. General price range: $135-900. Works on contract basis only. Offers nonexclusive contract. Charges duping fee of $1.75. Charges catalog insertion fee of 50%. Statements issued monthly. Payment made monthly. Photographers allowed to review account records to verify sales figures by appointment. Photographer must also pay for accounting time. Offers one-time and electronic media rights. Informs photographer and allows him to negotiate when client requests all rights. Model release preferred; captions required.
Making Contact: Query with list of stock photo subjects or samples. SASE. Reports in 1 month. Tips sheet distributed monthly to contributing photographers.
Tips: "We want to see photographs that have been carefully edited, that show technical control and a good understanding of the subject matter. All photos should be thoroughly captioned and indicate if they are model released. More and more there is a need for photos shot specifically for stock. These pictures illustrate real-life situations but are more controlled than newspaper-style shooting. Still they must not look contrived. They must have strong graphic impact and can be used both editorially and for commercial markets. Stock photographers must be aware of the need to meet deadlines and they should shoot their subjects to fit various layout shapes. Quite often layouts are pre-determined and editors/art directors are looking for the right pictures to fill a space. The use of stock photography increases every year. The markets are world-wide. Once New York City was the only place you could sell photos. With overnight delivery services, publishers and photo agencies can be anywhere. Free-

lancers who work with us must be hard workers. They have to want to make money at their photography and do it fulltime. Freelancers have to have a high degree of self-motivation to succeed."

■IMAGERY UNLIMITED, P.O. Box 2878, Alameda CA 94501. (510)769-9766. President: Jordan Coonrad. Estab. 1981. Stock photo agency. Has 50,000+ photos. Clients include: advertising agencies, public relations firms, designers, audiovisual firms, businesses, book/encyclopedia publishers, magazine publishers, newspapers, and postcard and calendar companies.
Subject Needs: Needs photos of "military, aviation, aerials, computers, business situations, travel and high-tech industry."
Specs: Uses 35mm, 2¼×2¼, 4×5, 8×10 transparencies.
Payment & Terms: Sometimes buys photos outright. Pays 30-60%; "50% is average." General price range: $200-5,000. Works with or without contract, negotiable. Charges various fees; types and amounts not specified. Statements issued monthly. Payment made monthly. Photographers allowed to review account records to verify sales figures. Offers one-time rights, electronic media rights and various negotiable rights. "Rights are negotiated based on client needs." Informs photographer and allows him to negotiate when client requests all rights. Model release preferred for "people in advertising or corporate use." Photo captions are required; include description of subject and noteworthy facts.
Making Contact: Query with resume of credits. Query with samples. Send stock photo list. Also "send photos when requested after initial contact." SASE. Reports in 1 month. Photo guidelines not available. Tips sheet sometimes distributed.
Tips: In freelancer's samples, wants to see high quality, sharp, graphic images. "Prefer Kocachrome. Other film OK in 2¼ and larger formats. Submit 100-200 well-edited images in pages. *No yellow boxes.*" Confirms trend toward "increased use of stock photos."

IMAGES PRESS SERVICE CORP., Dept. PM, 7 E. 17th St., New York NY 10003. (212)675-3707. FAX: (212)243-2308. Managers: Peter Gould and Barbara Rosen. Has 100,000+ photos. Clients include: public relations firms, book publishers, magazine publishers and newspapers.
Subject Needs: Current events, celebrities, feature stories, pop music, pin-ups and travel.
Specs: Uses b&w prints, 35mm transparencies, b&w contact sheets and b&w negatives.
Payment & Terms: Pays 50% commission on b&w and color photos. General price range: $50-1,000. Offers one-time rights or first rights. Captions required.
Making Contact: Query with resume of credits or with list of stock photo subjects. Also send tearsheets or photocopies of "already published material, original story ideas, gallery shows, etc." SASE. Reports in 2 weeks.
Tips: Prefers to see "material of wide appeal with commercial value to publication market; original material similar to what is being published by magazines sold on newsstands. We are interested in ideas from freelancers that can be marketed and assignments arranged with our clients and subagents." Wants to see "features that might be of interest to the European or Japanese press, and that have already been published in local media. Send copy of publication and advise rights available." To break in, be persistent and offer fresh perspective.

■IMPACT VISUALS PHOTO & GRAPHIC, INC., Suite 901, 28 W. 27th St., New York NY 10001. (212)683-9688. Co-Editor: Michael Kaufman and Donna Binder. News/feature syndicate. Has 100,000 photos. Clients include: public relations firms, audiovisual firms, businesses, book/encyclopedia publishers, magazine publishers, newspapers, progressive organizations, churches, unions and nonprofit organizations.
Subject Needs: Needs "b&w and color transparency work . . . news and documentary photos on issues of social concern: especially poverty, workers, environment, racism, gay/lesbian, anti-intervention, government, Latin America, Africa, Asia; also economics, education, health, etc.
Specs: Uses 8×10 glossy or matte b&w prints; 35mm transparencies.
Payment & Terms: Does not buy outright. Pays 50% commission on b&w and color photos to members, 40% to contributors. Pays $25-2,500; most in $75-225 range. Works with or without contract; negotiable. Offers exclusive contract only. Contracts renew automatically with each submission for 1 year period after initial term of 2 years. Charges duping fee of 100%/image. Statements issued bimonthly. Payment made bimonthly. Photographers allowed to review account records to verify sales figures; "by appointment for full members." Offers one-time rights; other rights negotiable. Informs photographer and allows him to negotiate when client requests all rights; "handled through the agency on a separate percentage." Model release preferred. Photo captions required; include "date, place, who and what."

Making Contact: Write for intro brochure for "new members." SASE. Reports in 1 month. Photo guidelines free with SASE. Tip sheet distributed bi-monthly to members only.

Tips: In portfolio or samples, especially looks for "20-30 b&w prints, captioned, and/or 40-60 color slides, captioned. Should show news or documentary from a progressive perspective, with strong composition and excellent technique on "issues of social concern." Also include resume and note about interests and political perspectives broadly speaking."

■**INDEX STOCK PHOTOGRAPHY**, 126 Fifth Ave., New York NY 10011. (212)929-4644. FAX: (212)633-1914. Manager: Pamela Ostrow. Has 500,000 tightly edited photos. Clients include: ad agencies, corporate design firms, graphic design agencies, inhouse agencies, direct mail production houses, magazine publishers, audiovisual firms, calendar, postcard and greeting card companies.

Subject Needs: Up-to-date, model-released, people photos. Also: business executives and activities in general, industry, technology (science & research) and computers, family, mature adults, sports, US and general scenics, major cities and local color, foreign/travel, and animals.

Specs: Uses 35mm, 2¼×2¼, 4×5 and 8×10 transparencies. "All 35mm must be Kodachrome."

Payment & Terms: Pays 50% commission on back-up material; 25% on catalog shots. General price range: $125-5,000. Sells one-time rights plus some limited buyouts (all rights) and exclusives. Model/property releases and captions required.

Making Contact: Query with list of stock photo subjects. Reports in 2 weeks with submission guidelines and general information.

Tips: "We have expanded our foreign representation to include Korea, Australia, Hong Kong and Italy. Educate yourself to the demands and realities of the stock photography marketplace, find out where your own particular style and expertise fit in, and edit unmercifully. The demands for new images increase daily as more ad people become comfortable using stock images that rival assignment work." Looks for "technically perfect samples of that photographer's personal expertise; different examples/compositions of the same subject. Submit 200-500 originals (in person or by mail) that are representative of your work. We have opened a branch office at 6500 Wilshire Blvd., Suite 500, Los Angeles, CA (213)658-7707. FAX: (213)651-4975. Manager: Chris Ferrone."

INTERNATIONAL COLOR STOCK, INC., Suite 1502, 555 NE 34th St., Miami FL 33137. (305)573-5200. Contact: Dagmar Fabricius or Randy Taylor. Estab. 1989. Stock photo syndicate. Clients include: foreign agencies distributing to all markets.

Subject Needs: "We serve as a conduit, passing top-grade, model-released production stock to foreign agencies. We have no US sales and no US archives."

Specs: Uses 35mm, 2¼×2¼ transparencies.

Payment & Terms: Pays 80% commission. Works on contract basis only. Offers exclusive foreign contract only. Contracts renew automatically on annual basis. Charges duping fee of 100%/image. Also charges catalog insertion fee of 100%/image. Statements issued monthly. Payment made monthly. Photographers allowed to review account records to verify sales figures "upon reasonable notice, during normal business hours." Offers one-time rights. Requests agency promotion rights. Informs photographer and allows him to negotiate when client requests all rights; "if notified by subagents." Model/property release required. Photo captions preferred; include "who, what, where, when, why and how."

Making Contact: Query with resume of credits. Reports "only when photographer is of interest" to them. Photo guidelines sheet not available. Tips sheet not distributed.

Tips: Has strong preference for experienced photographers. "Our percentages are extremely low. Because of this, we deal only with top shooters seeking long-term success. If you are not published 20 times a month or have not worked on contract for two or more photo agencies or have less than 15 years experience, please do not call us."

INTERNATIONAL PHOTO NEWS, 193 Sandpiper Ave., Royal Palm Beach FL 33411. (407)793-3424. Photo Editor: Jay Kravetz. News/feature syndicate. Has 50,000 photos. Clients include: newspapers, magazines and book publishers. Previous/current clients include: *Lake Worth Herald*, *S. Florida. Entertainment Guide* and *Prime-Time*; all three celebrity photos with story.

Subject Needs: Celebrities of politics, movies, music and television at work or play.

Specs: Uses 5×7, 8×10 glossy b&w prints.

Payment & Terms: General price range: $5. Pays $5/b&w photo; $10/color photo; 25% commission. Offers one-time rights. Captions required.

Making Contact: Query with resume of credits. Solicits photos by assignment only. SASE. Reports in 1 week.

Tips: "We use celebrity photographs to coincide with our syndicated columns. Must be approved by the celebrity."

INTERNATIONAL STOCK, Dept. PM, 113 E. 31st St., New York NY 10016. (212)696-4666. FAX: (212)725-1241. Managing Director: Donna Macfie. Estab. 1982. Stock photo agency. Member of Picture Agency Council of America (PACA). Has 1 million photos. Clients include: advertising agencies, public relations firms, audiovisual firms, businesses, book/encyclopedia publishers, magazine publishers, newspapers, postcard companies, calendar companies, greeting card companies.
Subject Needs: Model-released people/lifestyle photos for advertising; worldwide travel; industry; corporate and computer scenes; medicine and health; food; fashion; special effects; sports; scenics and animals.
Specs: Uses b&w and color prints; also 35mm, 2¼×2¼, 4×5 and 8×10 transparencies.
Payment & Terms: Pays 50% commission on b&w and color photos. General price range: $350-500. Offers one-time rights and all rights. Model release preferred; photo captions required.
Making Contact: Query with list of stock photo subjects. SASE. Reports in 2 weeks. Photo guidelines free with SASE. Market tips sheet distrubuted to contracted photographers.

INTERPRESS OF LONDON AND NEW YORK, 400 Madison Ave., New York NY 10017. Editor: Jeffrey Blyth. Has 5,000 photos. Clients include: magazine publishers and newspapers.
Subject Needs: Offbeat news and feature stories of interest to European editors. Captions required.
Specs: Uses 8×10 b&w prints and 35mm color transparencies.
Payment & Terms: NPI. Offers one-time rights.
Making Contact: Send material by mail for consideration. SASE. Reports in 1 week.

JEROBOAM, INC., 120-D 27th St., San Francisco CA 94110. (415)824-8085. Contact: Ellen Bunning. Has 150,000 b&w photos, 100,000 color slides. Clients include: text and trade books, magazine and encyclopedia publishers and editorial. Previous/current clients include: textbook publishers of marriage and family, psychology and Spanish; Harper & Collins, John Wiley, Harcourt Brace, D.C. Heath, West Publishing, Benjamin Cummings, Wadsworth, Addison Wesley, Mayfield and Holt.
Subject Needs: "We want people interacting, relating photos, artistic/documentary/photojournalistic images, especially minorities and handicapped. Images must have excellent print quality—contextually interesting and exciting, and artistically stimulating." Need shots of school, family, career and other living situations. Child development, growth and therapy, medical situations. No nature or studio shots.
Specs: Uses 8×10 double weight glossy b&w prints with a ¼" border. Also uses 35mm transparencies.
Payment & Terms: Works on consignment only; does not buy outright; pays 50% commission. Works without a signed contract. Statements issued monthly. Payment made monthly. Photographers allowed to review account records to verify sales figures. Offers one-time rights. Informs photographer and allows him to negotiate when client requests all rights. Model release required for people in contexts of special education, sexuality, etc. Photo captions preferred; include "age of subject, location, etc."
Making Contact: Interested in receiving work from newer, lesser-known photographers. Call if in the Bay area; if not, query with samples, query with list of stock photo subjects, send material by mail for consideration or submit portfolio for review. "We look at portfolios the first Wednesday of every month." SASE. Reports in 2 weeks.
Tips: "The Jeroboam photographers have shot professionally a minimum of 5 years, have experienced some success in marketing their talent and care about their craft excellence and their own creative vision. Jeroboam images are clear statements of single moments with graphic or emotional tension. We look for people interacting, well exposed and printed with a moment of interaction. New trends are toward more intimate, action shots even more ethnic images needed. Be honest in regards to subject matter (what he/she *likes* to shoot)."

JOURNALISM SERVICES, INC., 118 E. Second St., Lockport IL 60441. (815)838-6486. FAX: (815)838-6523. President: John Patsch. Estab. 1978. Stock photo agency. Member of Picture Agency Council of America (PACA). Has 100,000 photos. Clients include: advertising agencies, public relations firms, businesses, book/encyclopedia publishers, magazine publishers, calendar companies.
Subject Needs: Model released people (medium format only).
Specs: Uses 35mm, 2¼×2¼, 4×5, transparencies.
Payment & Terms: Pays 50% commission on color photos. Average price per image (to clients): color $295. Works on contract basis only. Offers non-exclusive contract. Issues monthly statements. Payment made monthly. Offers one-time rights; negotiable. Does not inform photographer or allow him to negotiate when client requests all rights. Model/property release required. Captions required.
Making Contact: Query with stock photo list. Samples kept on file. SASE. Expects minimum initial submission of 40 images with additional submission annually. Reports in 1 month. Photo guidelines free with SASE. Market tips sheet distributed 3 times a year.
Tips: Wants to see images of model-released people; excellent use of color and subject. "The trend is toward more diversified model-released business subjects."

■‡KEYSTONE PRESSEDIENST GMBH, Kleine Reichenstr. 1, 2000 Hamburg 11, 2 162 408 Germany. (040)33 66 97-99. FAX: (040)324036. President: Dieter Boldt. Stock photo agency, picture library and news/feature syndicate. Has 3.5 million color transparencies and b&w photos. Clients include: ad agencies, public relations firms, audiovisual firms, businesses, book/encyclopedia publishers, magazine publishers, newspapers, postcard companies, calendar companies, greeting card companies and TV stations.
Subject Needs: All subjects excluding sports events.
Specs: Uses b&w prints; 35mm, 2¼×2¼, 4×5 and 8×10 transparencies.
Payment & Terms: Pays 50% commission on b&w and 60% for color photos. General price range: $30-1,000. Offers one-time and first rights. Model release preferred; photo captions required.
Making Contact: Send unsolicited photos by mail for consideration. Deals with local freelancers by assignment only. SASE. Reports in 2 weeks. Distributes a monthly tip sheet.
Tips: Prefers to see "American way of life—people, cities, general features—human and animal, current events—political, show business, scenics from the USA—travel, touristic, personalities—politics, TV. An advantage of working with KEYSTONE is our wide circle of clients and very close connections to all leading German photo users." Especially wants to see skylines of all U.S. cities. Send only highest quality works.

■JOAN KRAMER AND ASSOCIATES, INC., Suite 605, 10490 Wilshire Blvd., Los Angeles CA 90024. (310)446-1866. FAX: (310)446-1856. President: Joan Kramer. Member of Picture Agency Council of America (PACA). Has 1 million b&w and color photos dealing with travel, cities, personalities, animals, flowers, lifestyles, underwater, scenics, sports and couples. Clients include: ad agencies, magazines, recording companies, photo researchers, book publishers, greeting card companies, promotional companies and AV producers.
Subject Needs: "We use any and all subjects! Stock slides must be of professional quality."
Specs: Uses 8×10 glossy b&w prints; any size transparencies.
Payment & Terms: Does not buy outright; pays 50% commission. Offers all rights. Model release required.
Making Contact: Query or call to arrange an appointment. SASE. Do not send photos before calling.

HAROLD M. LAMBERT STUDIOS, INC., Dept. PM, P.O. Box 27310, Philadelphia PA 19150. (215)885-3355. Vice President: Raymond W. Lambert. Has 1.5 million b&w photos and 400,000 transparencies of all subjects. Clients include: ad agencies, publishers and religious organizations.
Subject Needs: Farm, family, industry, sports, robotics in industry, scenics, travel and people activities. No flowers, zoo shots or nudes.
Specs: Send 35mm, 2¼×2¼ or 4×5 transparencies.
Payment & Terms: Buys photos outright—"rates depend on subject matter, picture quality and film size"; or pays 50% commission on color. Works on contract basis only. Offers nonexclusive contract. Photographers not allowed to review account records to verify sales figures. Offers one-time rights. Under some conditions, informs photographer and allows him to negotiate when client requests all rights. Model/property release required for people (single person and very small groups), domestic animals and real property. Photo captions preferred. Present model release on acceptance of photo. Submit material by mail for consideration. Reports in 2 weeks. SASE. Free photo guidelines.
Making Contact: Send negatives or contact sheet. Photos should be submitted in blocks of 100.
Tips: "We return unaccepted material, advise of material held for our file, and supply our photo number." Also, "We have 7 selling offices throughout the US and Canada."

*LANDMARK STOCK EXCHANGE, 51 Digital Dr., Novato CA 94949. (415)883-1600. 1-800-288-5170. FAX: (415)883-6725. Contact: Director. Estab. 1989. Stock photo agency and licensing agents. Clients include: advertising agencies, design firms, book publishers, magazine, postcard, greeting card, poster publishers, T-shirts, design firms and "many" gift manufacturers.
Subject Needs: Scenics, model-released people (women/men in swimsuits, children), cars, still-life, illustration, unique photographs i.e. abstracts, hand-colored, b&w images.
Specs: Uses 35mm, 2¼×2¼, 4×5 transparencies.
Payment & Terms: Pays 50% commission for licensed photos. Enforces minimum prices. "Prices are based on usage." Payment made monthly. Offers one-time rights. Model/property release required. Captions preferred for scenics and animals.
Making Contact: Arrange personal interview to show portfolio. Submit portfolio for review. Query with samples. Query with stock photo list or phone call. Samples kept on file. SASE. Photo guidelines free on request.
Tips: "We are always looking for innovative, creative, images in all subject areas, and strive to set trends in the photo industry. Many of our clients are gift manufacturers. We look for images that are suitable for publication on posters, greeting cards, etc. We consistently get photo requests for outstanding scenics, swimsuit shots (men and women) and wildlife."

■**LGI PHOTO AGENCY**, Dept. PM, 241 W. 36th St., New York NY 10018. (212)736-4602. Vice President: Laura Giammarco. Estab. 1978. Stock photo agency and news/feature syndicate. Has 1 million photos. Clients include: advertising agencies, public relations firms, audiovisual firms, book/encyclopedia publishers, magazine publishers, newspapers and calendar companies.
Subject Needs: "We handle news events which relate to personalities in TV, music, film, sports, politics etc. We also represent special studio and at-home sessions with these people."
Specs: Uses mostly photos, some film.
Payment & Terms: Pays 50% commission on b&w/color photos; percentage on film varies. General price range: minimum $125/b&w, $175/color. Offers one-time rights.
Making Contact: Arrange a personal interview to show portfolio. Non-local photographers can phone for advice submitting work for review. Works on assignment only. Cannot return material. Reports as needed.

LIAISON INTERNATIONAL, 11 E. 26th St., New York NY 10010. (212)447-2500. Vice President: Lisa Papel. Corporate and stock division of Gamma/Liaison. Extensive stock material, with the following categories: People, scenic/nature, animals, food, sports, travel, industry and abstract/art. Clients include: corporations and graphic designers.
Specs: Uses 35mm or 2¼×2¼ transparencies.
Payment & Terms: Pays 50% commission. Works on contract basis only. Offers exclusive contract only; works on assignment. Contracts renew automatically with each submission; time period not specified. Statements issued monthly. Payment made monthly. Offers all rights on assigned stock.
Making Contact: Submit portfolio with description of past experience and publication credits.
Tips: Involves a "rigorous trial period for first 6 months of association with photographer." Prefers previous involvement in publishing industry. (For general stock, see also listing for parent company, Gamma/Liaison, in this section).

*****LIFESTYLES STOCK PHOTO AGENCY**, P.O. Box 4280, Santa Barbara CA 93140. (805)684-9544. FAX: (805)684-1627. Owners: Kent Fleming or Shawn Weimer. Estab. 1991. Stock photo agency. Has 50,000 photos. Clients include: advertising agencies, public relations firms, businesses, book/encyclopedia publishers, magazine, calendar comapnies, health care industry.
Subject Needs: "Model-released people images only; seniors and ethnics are our specialty."
Specs: Uses 35mm, 2¼×2¼, 4×5, 8×10 transparencies.
Payment & Terms: Pays 50% commission. Average price per image (to clients): $300-500/color image. Offers volume discounts to customers; terms specified in photographer's contract. Discount sales terms not negotiable. Works on non-exclusive contract basis only. Statements issued quarterly. Payment made quarterly. Photographers permitted to review account records to verify sales figures or account for various deductions "under supervision." Offers one-time or electronic media rights. Informs photographer and allows him to negotiate when client requests all rights. Model/property release required. Captions required.
Making Contact: Query for submission guidelines. Reports within 2 weeks. Photo guidelines available. Catalog available for $25 plus shipping. Market tips sheet distributed.
Tips: "We like to see new directions in lighting and composition with advertising quality and editorial impace, all this while depicting everyday life."

*****LIGHT SOURCES STOCK**, 23 Drydock Ave., Boston MA 02210. (617)261-0346. FAX: (617)261-0358. Editor: Sonja L. Rodrigue. Estab. 1989. Stock photo agency. Has 35,000 photos. Clients include: advertising agencies, book/encyclopedia publishers, magazine publishers, calendar companies, greeting card companies.
Subject Needs: Children, families, educational, medical and scenics (travel).
Specs: Uses 35mm and 2¼×2¼ transparencies.
Payment & Terms: Average price per image (to clients): $100-250/b&w photo; $100-450/ color photo. Enforces minimum prices. Offers volume discounts to customers; inquire about specific terms. Photographers can choose not to sell images on discount terms." Works on non-exclusive contract basis only. Contracts renew automatically with additional submissions. Statements issued semiannually. "Payment is made when agency is paid by the client." Model/property release preferred. Captions required.
Making Contact: Arrange personal interview to show portfolio. Samples kept on file. SASE. Expects minimum initial submission of 200 images with periodic submission of at least 100 images every six months. Reports in 1-2 weeks. Photo guidelines available.

LIGHTWAVE, Suite 306-114, 1430 Massachusetts Ave., Cambridge MA 02138. (617)628-1052. (800)628-6809 (outside 617 area code). FAX: (617)623-7568. Contact: Paul Light. Has 250,000 photos. Clients include: ad agencies and textbook publishers. "Our files consist of people in everyday activities."

Subject Needs: Candid photos of people in everyday activities in the U.S., France, Japan and Spain.
Specs: Uses color transparencies.
Payment & Terms: Pays $190/photo; 50% commission. Works on contract basis only. Offers nonexclusive contract. Contracts renew automatically with each submission for one year. Statements issued annually. Payment made "after each usage." Offers one-time rights. Informs photographer and allows him to negotiate when client requests all rights. Model/property release preferred. Photo captions are required.
Making Contact: Interested in receiving work from newer, lesser-known photographers. Send SASE for guidelines.
Tips: "Photographers should enjoy photographing people in everyday activities. Work should be carefully edited before submission. Shoot constantly and watch what is being published. We are looking for photographers who can photograph daily life with compassion and originality."

✹MACH 2 STOCK EXCHANGE LTD., #204-1409 Edmonton Tr NE, Calgary AB T2E 3K8 Canada. (403)230-9363. FAX: (403)230-5855. Assistant Manager: Donna Shannon. Estab. 1986. Stock photo agency. Member of Picture Agency Council of America (PACA). Clients include: advertising agencies, public relations firms, audiovisual firms and businesses.
Subject Needs: Corporate, high-tech, lifestyle, industry. In all cases, prefer people-oriented images.
Specs: Uses 35mm, 2¼×2¼, 4×5, 8×10 transparencies.
Payment & Terms: Pays 50% commission on color photos. Average sale $300. Works on contract basis only. Offers limited regional exclusivity. Contracts renew automatically with additional submissions. Charges 50% duping and catalog insertion fees. Statements issued monthly. Payment made monthly. "All photographers statements are itemized in detail, anything concerning their account they may ask us." Offers one-time and 1-year exclusive rights; no electronic media rights for clip art type CD's. Informs photographers and allows him to negotiate when client requests all rights. "We generally do not sell buy-out." Model/property release and photo captions required.
Making Contact: Query with samples and list of stock photo subjects. SASE. Reports in 1 month. Market tips sheet distributed monthly to contracted photographers.
Tips: "Please call first. We will then send a basic information package out. If terms are agreeable between the two parties then original images can be submitted pre-paid." Sees trend toward more photo requests for families, women in business, the environment and waste management. Active vibrant seniors. High-tech and computer-generated or manipulated images.

‡MAURITIUS DIE BILDAGENTUR GMBH, Postfach 2 09, 8102 Mittenwald Germany. Phone: 08823/40-0. FAX: 08823/8881. President: Hans-Jorg Zwez. Stock photo agency. Has 1.2 million photos. Has 5 branch offices in Germany, Belgium and Austria. Clients include: advertising agencies, businesses, book/encyclopedia publishers, magazine publishers, postcard companies, calendar companies and greeting card companies.
Subject Needs: All kinds of contemporary themes: geography, people, animals, plants, science, economy.
Specs: Uses 2¼×2¼, 4×5 and 8×10 transparencies.
Payment & Terms: Pays 50% commission for color photos. Offers one-time rights. Model release and captions preferred.
Making Contact: Query with samples. Submit portfolio for review. SASE. Reports in 2 weeks. Tips sheet distributed once a year.
Tips: Prefers to see "people in all situations, from baby to grandparents, new technologies, transportation."

MEDICAL IMAGES INC., 26 West Shore Pl., Salisbury CT 06068. (203)824-7858. President: Anne Darden. Estab. 1990. Stock photo agency. Has 30,000 photos. Clients include: advertising agencies, public relations firms, corporate accounts, book/encyclopedia publishers, magazine publishers and newspapers.
Subject Needs: Medical and health-related material, including commercial-looking photography of generic doctor's office scenes, hospital scenarios and still life shots. Also, technical close-ups of surgical procedures, diseases, high-tech colorized diagnostic imaging, microphotography, nutrition, exercise and preventive medicine.

Can't find a listing? Check at the end of each market section for the " '92-'93 Changes" lists. These lists include any market listings from the '92 edition which were either not verified or deleted in this edition.

Specs: Uses 8×10 glossy b&w prints; 35mm, 2¼×2¼, 4×5 and 8×10 transparencies.
Payment & Terms: Pays 50% commission on b&w and color photos. Average price per image: $175-3,500. Enforces minimum prices. Works with or without contract. Offers non-exclusive contract. Contracts renew automatically. Statements issued quarterly. Payment made bimonthly. "If client pays within same period, photographer gets check right away; otherwise, in next payment period." Photographer's accountant may review records with prior appointment. Offers one-time rights. Model/property release preferred; photo captions required; include medical procedures, diagnosis when applicable, whether model released or not, etc.
Making Contact: Interested in receiving work from newer, lesser-known photographers. Query with list of stock photo subjects or telephone with list of subject matter. SASE. Reports in 2 weeks. Photo guidelines available. Market tips sheet distributed quarterly to contracted photographers.
Tips: Looks for "quality of photograph—focus, exposure, composition, interesting angles; scientific value; and subject matter being right for our markets." Sees trend toward "more emphasis on editorial or realistic looking medical situations. Anything too 'canned' is much less marketable."

■**MEDICHROME**, 232 Madison Ave., New York NY 10016. (212)679-8480. Manager: Sharon Rembi. Has 500,000 photos. Clients include: publications firms, businesses, book/encyclopedia and magazine publishers, newspapers and pharmaceutical companies.
Subject Needs: Needs "everything that is considered medical or health-related, such as: stock photos of doctors with patients and other general photos to very specific medical shots of diseases and surgical procedures; high-tech shots of the most modern diagnostic equipment; exercise and diet also." Special needs include organ transplants, home health care, counseling services and use of computers by medical personnel.
Specs: Uses 8×10 b&w prints; and 35mm, 2¼×2¼, 4×5 and 8×10 transparencies.
Payment & Terms: Pays 50% commission on b&w and color photos. General price range: "$150 for comp and AV. All brochures are based on size and print run. Ads are based on exposure and length of campaign." Offers one-time or first rights; all rights are rarely needed—very costly. Model release preferred; captions required.
Making Contact: Query by "letter or phone call explaining how many photos you have and their subject matter." SASE. Reports in 2 weeks. Distributes tips sheet every 6 months to Medichrome photographers only.
Tips: Prefers to see "loose prints and slides in 20-up sheets. All printed samples welcome; no carousel, please. Lots of need for medical stock. Very specialized and unusual area of emphasis, very costly/difficult to shoot, therefore buyers are using more stock."

■**MEGA PRODUCTIONS, INC.**, 1714 N. Wilton Pl., Los Angeles CA 90028. (213)462-6342. FAX: (213)462-7572. Director: Michele Mattei. Estab. 1974. Stock photo agency and news/feature syndicate. Has "several million" photos. Clients include: book/encyclopedia publishers, magazine publishers, television, film and newspapers.
Subject Needs: Needs "television, film, studio, celebrity, paparazzi, feature stories (sports, national and international interest events, current news stories). Written information to accompany stories appreciated. We do not wish to see fashion and greeting card-type scenics."
Specs: Uses 35mm, 2¼×2¼ transparencies.
Payment & Terms: Pays 50% commission on color photos. General price range: $100-20,000; 50% commission of sale. Offers one-time rights. Model release preferred; photo captions required.
Making Contact: Query with resume of credits. Query with samples. Query with list of stock photo subjects. Works with local freelancers only. Occasionally assigns work. Reports in 1 week.
Tips: "Studio shots of celebrities, and home/family stories are frequently requested." In samples, looking for "marketability, high quality, recognizable personalities and current newsmaking material. Also, looks for paparazzi celebrity at local and national events. We deal mostly in Hollywood entertainment stories. We are interested mostly in celebrity photography and current events. Written material on personality or event helps us to distribute material faster and more efficiently."

*****MOTION PICTURE AND TV PHOTO ARCHIVE**, 11821 Mississippi Ave., Los Angeles CA 90025. (310)478-2379. FAX: (310)477-4864. President: Ron Avery. Estab. 1988. Stock photo agency. Member of Picture Agency Council of America. Has 60,000 photos. Has eight branch offices. Clients include: advertising agencies, book/encyclopedia publishers, magazine publishers, newspapers, postcard publishers, calendar companies, greeting card companies.
Subject Needs: Color shots of current stars.
Specs: Uses 8×10 b&w/color prints; 35mm, 2¼×2¼, 4×5 and 8×10 transparencies.
Payment & Terms: Buys photos/film outright. Pays 50% commission on b&w and color photos. Average price per image (to clients): $180-1,000/b&w image; $180-1,500/color image. Enforces minimum prices. Offers volume discounts to customers; terms specified in photographer's contract. Works

with or without a signed contract, negotiable with limited regional exclusivity. Contracts renew automatically with additional submissions.
Making Contact: Reports in 1-2 weeks.

*MOUNTAIN STOCK PHOTO & FILM, P.O. Box 1910, Tahoe City CA 96145. (916)583-6646. FAX: (916)583-5935. Manager: Meg deVré. Estab. 1986. Stock photo agency. Member of Picture Agency Council of America (PACA). Has 60,000+ photos; minimal films/videos. Clients include: advertising agencies, public relations firms, audiovisual firms, businesses, book/encyclopedia publishers, magazine publishers, newspapers, calendar companies, greeting card companies.
Subject Needs: "We specialize in and always need action sports, scenic and lifestyle images."
Specs: Uses 35mm, 2¼×2¼, 4×5, transparencies.
Payment & Terms: Pays 50% commission on color photos. Enforces minimum prices. "We have a $100 minimum fee." Offers volume discounts to customers; inquire about specific terms. Discount sales terms not negotiable. Works on contract basis only. Offers guaranteed subject exclusivity (within files). Some contracts renew automatically. Charges 50% catalog insertion fee. Statements issued quarterly. Payment made quarterly. Photographers are allowed to review account records with due notice. Offers unlimited and limited exclusive rights. Informs photographer and allows him to negotiate when client requests all rights. Model/property release required. Captions required.
Making Contact: Interested in receiving work from newer, lesser-known photographers. Query with resume of credits. Query with samples. Query with stock photo list. Samples kept on file. SASE. Expects minimum initial submission of 500 images. Reports in 1 month. Photo guidelines free with SASE. Market tips sheet distributed quarterly to contracted photographers; upon request.
Tips: "I see the need for images, whether action or just scenic, that evoke a feeling or emotion."

■NATIONAL BASEBALL LIBRARY, Box 590, Cooperstown NY 13326. (607)547-9988. Photo Collection Manager: Patricia Kelly. Picture library. Has 175,000 photos. Clients include: ad agencies, public relations and audiovisual firms, businesses, book/encyclopedia publishers, magazine publishers, newspapers, postcard companies, calendar companies, ball clubs, baseball fans and educational/college/high school.
Subject Needs: Uses "baseball related photos from the late 1800's to present day. Includes photos of all Hall of Famers, players not in the Hall of Fame, teams, stadiums, world series and many more, action, portraits and group photos.
Payment & Terms: "We accept donations only. We will honor copyright ownership. We refer client to photographer for permission to use and to negotiate a price for use." General price range: $20-50. Offers one-time rights.
Making Contact: Query with samples. Send unsolicited photos by mail for consideration. SASE. Reports in 2 weeks.
Tips: "Our clients want good action photos of players whether modern day or turn-of-the century players in uniform."

NATIONAL NEWS BUREAU, P.O. Box 5628, Philadelphia PA 19129. (215)546-8088. Photo Editor: Andy Edelman. Clients include: book and magazine publishers, and newspapers. Distributes/syndicates to 1,100 publications.
Subject Needs: "All feature materials; fashion; celebrity."
Specs: Uses 8×10 b&w and color prints, and b&w and color contact sheets.
Payment & Terms: Buys photos outright; pays $15-500. Offers all rights. Model release and captions required.
Making Contact: Query with samples. Send photos by mail for consideration. Submit portfolio for review. SASE. Reports in 2 weeks.
Tips: Needs photos of "new talent—particularly undiscovered female models." Points out that "European magazine market is a major outlet for female photos."

*‡NATURAL SCIENCE PHOTOS, 33 Woodland Dr., Watford, Hertfordshire WD1 3BY England. 0923-245265. FAX: 0923-246067. Partners: Peter and Sondra Ward. Estab. 1969. Stock photo agency and picture library. Members of British Association of Picture Libraries and Agencies. Has 100,000 photos. Clients include ad agencies, public relations firms, audiovisual firms, businesses, book/encyclopedia publishers, magazine publishers, newspapers, postcard companies, calendar companies, greeting card companies and television. Current clients: International Masters Publishing, Wildlife fact file; Salamander Books Ltc, *The Illustrated Encyclopedia of Elephants* (34 photos), *Explore the World of Snakes* (16 photos) and 202 photographs reproduced by Colour Library Books in their six book series on *Nature Facts*.
Subject Needs: Natural science of all types, including wildlife (terrestrial and aquatic), habitats (including destruction and reclamation), botany (including horticulture, agriculture, pests, diseases, treatments and effects), ecology, pollution, geology, primitive peoples, astronomy, scenics (mostly

without artifacts), climate and effects, e.g. hurricane damage and etc., creatures of economic importance, e.g. disease carriers and domestic animals and fowl. "We need all areas of natural history, habitat and environment from South and Central America, also high quality marine organisms.
Specs: Uses 35mm, 2¼ × 2¼ original color transparencies.
Payment & Terms: Pays 66% commission for color photos. General price range: $55-1,400. "We have minimum fees for small numbers, but negotiate bulk deals sometimes involving up to 200 photos at a time." Works on contract basis only; offers non-exclusivity contract. Statements issued quarterly or semiannually depending on volume of sales made (if large, pay more frequently). Offers one-time rights, exclusive on calendars. Informs photographers and permits them to negotiate when a client requests all rights. Copyright not sold without written permission. Model release preferred; captions required.
Making Contact: Arrange a personal interview to show a portfolio. Submit portfolio for review, Query with samples. Samples kept on file. Send unsolicited photos by mail for consideration. SASE. Reports in 1-4 weeks, according to pressure on time.
Tips: "We look for all kinds of living organisms, accurately identified and documented, also habitats, environment, weather and effects, primitive peoples, horticulture, agriculture, pests, diseases and etc. Animals, birds and etc. showing action or behavior particularly welcome. We are not looking for 'arty' presentation, just straightforward graphic images, only exceptions being 'moody' scenics. There has been a marked increase in demand for really good images with good colour and fine grain with good lighting. Pictures that would have sold a few years ago that were a little 'soft' or grainy are now rejected, particularly where advertising clients are concerned."

*NATURAL SELECTION STOCK PHOTOGRAPHY INC., 183 St. Paul St., Rochester NY 14604. (716)232-1502. FAX: (716)232-6325. Manager: Deborah Free. Estab. 1987. Stock photo agency. Member of Picture Agency Council of America (PACA). Has 120,000+ photos. Clients include: advertising agencies, public relations firms, businesses, book/encyclopedia publishers, magazine publishers, newspapers, postcard publishers, calendar companies, greeting card companies.
Subject Needs: Anything pertaining to nature in US and abroad.
Specs: Uses 35mm, 2¼ × 2¼, 4 × 5, 8 × 10, transparencies.
Payment & Terms: Pays 50% commission on b&w and color photos. Works with or without a signed contract, negotiable. Works with or without a signed contract, negotiable. Offers non-exclusive contract. Some contracts have 3-year renewal clauses. Issues quarterly statements. Payment made monthly. Offers one-time rights. Informs photographers when client requests all rights. "We do all negotiations." Model/property release required. Captions required. Include subject, state, country, location in state.
Making Contact: Submit portfolio for review. Query with samples. SASE. Expects minimum initial submission of 100-200 photos with regular updates of 500-1,000. Reports in 1 week to 1 month. Photo guidelines free with SASE. Catalog available.
Editors Note: *Natural Selection* expects to change some of its submission requirements and contract terms. Check with the agency before submitting work.

NAWROCKI STOCK PHOTO, P.O. Box 16565, Chicago IL 60616. (312)427-8625. FAX: (312)427-0178. Director: William S. Nawrocki. Stock photo agency, picture library. Member of Picture Agency Council of America (PACA). Has over 300,000 photos and 500,000 historical photos. Clients include: ad agencies, public relations firms, editorial, businesses, book/encyclopedia publishers, magazine publishers, newspapers, postcard companies, calendar companies and greeting card companies.
Subject Needs: Model-released people, all age groups, all types of activities, families, couples, relationships, updated travel, domestic and international, food.
Specs: Uses 35mm, 2¼, 2¼ × 2¾, 4 × 5 and 8 × 10 transparencies. "We look for good composition, exposure and subject matter; good color." Also, finds large format work "in great demand." Medium format and professional photographers preferred.
Payment & Terms: Buys only historical photos outright. Pays variable percentage on commission according to use/press run. Commission depends on agent-foreign or domestic 50%/40%/35%. Works on contract basis only. Offers limited regional exclusivity and non-exclusivity. Charges duping and catalog insertion fee; rates not specified. Statements issued monthly. Payment made monthly. Offers one-time media rights; other rights negotiable. Requests agency promotion rights. Informs photographer and allows him to negotiate when client requests all rights. Model release and photo captions required.
Making Contact: Interested in receiving work from newer, lesser-known photographers. Arrange a personal interview to show portfolio. Query with resume of credits, samples and list of stock photo subjects. Submit portfolio for review. SASE. Reports ASAP. Photo guidelines free with SASE. Tips sheet distributed "to our photographers." Suggest that you call first—discuss your photography with the agency, your goals, etc. "NSP prefers to help photographers develop their skills. We tend to give direction and offer advice to our photographers. We don't take photographers on just for their images."

NSP prefers to treat photographers as individuals and likes to work with them." Provide return Federal Express. Allow 2 weeks for review. Label and caption images. Has network with domestic and international agencies.

Tips: "A stock agency uses just about everything. We are using more people images, all types—family, couples, relationships, leisure, the over 40's and 50's group. Looking for large format—variety and quality. More images are being custom shot for stock with model releases. Model releases are very, very important—a key to a photographer's success and income. Model releases are the most requested for ads/brochures."

NEW ENGLAND STOCK PHOTO, Box 815, Old Saybrook CT 06475. (203)388-1741. President: Betty Rogers Johansen. Stock photo agency. Has 100,000 photos in files. Clients include: ad agencies, public relations firms, businesses, book/encyclopedia publishers, magazine publishers, postcard, calendar and greeting card companies.

Subject Needs: "We are a general interest agency with a wide variety of clients and subject matter. Always looking for good people shots—workplace, school, families, couples, children, senior citizens—engaged in everyday life situations, including recreational sports, home life, vacation and outdoor activities. We also get many requests for animal shots—horses, dogs, cats and wildlife (natural habitat). Special emphasis on New England—specific places, lifestyle and scenics, but have growing need for other US and international subject matter. Also use setup shots of flowers, food, nostalgia."

Specs: Uses 8×10 glossy b&w prints; 35mm, 2¼×2¼, 4×5 transparencies. "We are especially interested in more commercial/studio photography, such as food and interiors, which can be used for stock purposes. Also, we get many requests for particular historical sites, annual events, and need more coverage of towns/cities, mainstreets and museums."

Payment & Terms: Pays 50% commission for b&w and color photos. Average price per image: $100-1,000/b&w photo; $100-3,000/color photo. Works with photographers on contract basis only. Offers non-exclusive contract. Charges 50% catalog insertion fee. Satements issued monthly. Payments made monthly. Photographers allowed to review account records to verify sales figures. Offers one-time rights; postcard, calendar and greeting card rights. Informs photographer and allows him to negotiate when client requests all rights. Model/property release preferred (people and private property); captions required.

Making Contact: Interested in receiving work from newer, lesser-known photographers. Query with list of stock photo subjects or send unsolicited photos by mail for consideration. SASE. Reports in 3 weeks. Guidelines free with SASE. Distributes monthly tip sheet to contributing photographers.

Tips: "Quality, not quantity, is the key. We look for images with a clear message or mood, good depth of field, and dramatic scenics with good captions. We look for technically excellent images with good captions—who, what, where. We are not interested in bodies of work concentrated on generic scenics and nature. The need is for people involved in daily life, environmental and social issues, travel, education, specific locations, etc. People and animal shots should usually be closeup, active and vital images. We do get assignment requests for photographers, so it is helpful to get a good sense of a photographer's special skills and interests. Our clients expect us to have just about any subject—from angry bears to a man having a haircut or a retired couple playing golf. We are getting more requests for specific locations so we advise our photographers to carry a notebook or cassette recorder to gather information while shooting. There are fewer calls for so-called 'generic' scenics, so we are rejecting a lot of good images for lack of geographic location. Also see more of a trend for model-released images in editorial and textbook usage—so get that release! Also become aware of issues of today; concerns about our environment, aging, health and fitness, education and drugs are subjects we are hearing more and more about. There are constant demands for images depicting them. Also, ethnic mix in people shots is more essential. We are not just looking for pretty pictures but those showing our relationship with each other and our world."

■**THE NEW IMAGE STOCK PHOTO AGENCY INC.,** Suite 200, 38 Quail Ct., Walnut Creek CA 94596. (415)934-2405. President: Tracey Prever. Estab. 1986. Stock photo agency. Has 50,000 photos. Clients include: advertising agencies, public relations firms, audiovisual firms, businesses, book/encyclopedia publishers, magazine publishers, newspapers, calendar companies and greeting card companies.

Subject Needs: "We mainly deal with commercial clients in advertising. We look for model-released people images in all different situations . . . lifestyles, corporate, people working, etc. Also, industry, travel, technology and medical."

Payment & Terms: Pays 50% commission on color photos. General price range: $200-1,000. Offers limited regional exclusivity contract. Statements issued bimonthly. Payment made bimonthly. Offers one-time rights. Informs photographer and allows him to negotiate when client requests all rights. Model release and photo captions required.

Making Contact: Arrange a personal interview to show portfolio. SASE. Reports in 1 month. Photo guidelines free with SASE. Tips sheet distributed quarterly to contracted photographers.
Tips: Wants to see "technical quality as well as salable subject matter, variety, model-released people images." Individual style is especially desired.

‡OKAPIA K.G., Michael Grzimek & Co., 6 Frankfurt/Main, Roderbergweg 168 Germany; or Constanze Presse Haus, Kurfürstenstr. 72 -74 D1000 Berlin 30 Germany. 030 2640018 1. FAX: 030 2640018 2. President: Grzimek. Stock photo agency and picture library. Has 350,000 photos. Clients include: ad agencies, book/encyclopedia publishers, magazine publishers, newspapers, postcard companies, calendar companies, greeting card companies and school book publishers.
Subject Needs: Natural history, science and technology, and general interest.
Specs: Uses 13×18cm minimum b&w prints; 35mm, 2¼×2¼, 4×5 and 8×10 transparencies.
Payment & Terms: Buys photos outright $40. Pays 50% commission on b&w and color photos. Offers one-time rights. Model release and captions required.
Making Contact: Send unsolicited material by mail for consideration. SASE. Distributes "tips" sheets on request.
Tips: "We need every theme which can be photographed." Looks for minimum of 200 slides in submission. For best results, "send pictures continuously." Work must be of "high standard quality."

OMEGA NEWS GROUP/USA, P.O. Box 30167, Philadelphia PA 19103-8167. (215)985-9200. FAX: (215)763-4015. Managing Editor: A.S. Rubel. Stock photo and press agency. Clients include: ad agencies, public relations firms, businesses, book publishers, magazine publishers, encyclopedia publishers, newspapers, calendar and poster companies.
Subject Needs: "All major news, sports, features, society shots, shots of film sets, national and international personalities and celebrities in the news as well as international conflicts and wars."
Specs: Uses 8×10 glossy b&w prints; 35mm, 2¼×2¼ or 4×5 transparencies. Photos must be stamped with name only on mounts and back of prints; prints may be on single or double weight but unmounted.
Payment & Terms: Pays 50% commission. NPI; price depends upon usage (cover, inside photo, etc.). Offers first North American serial rights; other rights can be procured on negotiated fees. Releases required on most subjects; captions a must.
Making Contact: Submit material by mail for consideration. SASE. Send resume, including experience, present activities and interests, and range of equipment. Supply phone number where photographer may be reached during working hours.
Tips: Should have experience in news and/or commercial work on location. "We always welcome the opportunity to see new work. We are interested in quality and content, not quantity. Comprehensive story material welcomed."

*OMNI-PHOTO COMMUNICATIONS, 5 E. 22nd St., New York NY 10010. (212)995-0805. FAX: (212)995-0895. President: Roberta Guerette. Estab. 1979. Stock photo agency. Has 15,000 photos. Clients include: advertising agencies, public relations firms, audiovisual firms, businesses, book/encyclopedia publishers, magazine publishers, postcard publishers, calendar companies, greeting card companies.
Subject Needs: Travel, multicultural and people.
Specs: Uses 8×10 b&w prints; 35mm, 2¼×2¼, 4×5, 8×10 transparencies.
Payment & Terms: Pays 50% commission on b&w and color photos. Works on contract basis only. Contracts renew automatically with additional submissions. Model/property release required. Captions required.
Making Contact: Query with resume of credits. Query with samples. SASE. Expects minimum initial submission of 200-300 images. Photo guidelines free with SASE.
Tips: "Spontaneous-looking, yet professional quality photos of people interacting with each other. Carefully thought out backgrounds, props and composition, commanding use of color. Stock photographers must produce a high quality, work at an abundant rate. Self-assignment is very important, as is a willingness to obtain model releases, caption thoroughly and make submissions regularly."

*‡ORION PRESS, 1-13 Kanda-Jimbocho, Chiyoda-ku, Tokyo Japan 101. (03)3295-1400. FAX: (03)3295-0227. Manager: Mr. Mitsuo Nagamitsu. Estab. 1952. Stock photo agency. Has 700,000 photos. Has 3 branch offices. Clients include: advertising agencies, public relations firms, businesses, book/encyclopedia publishers, magazine publishers, newspapers, postcard publishers, calendar companies, greeting card companies.
Subject Needs: All subjects wish to have images of people, especially.
Specs: Uses 35mm, 2¼×2¼, 4×5, 8×10 transparencies.
Payment & Terms: Pays 50% commission on b&w and color photos. Average price per image (to clients): $175-290/b&w photo; $290-500/color photo. Negotiates fees below standard minimum prices. Offers volume discounts to customers; inquire about specific terms. Photographers can choose not to

sell images on discount terms. Works with limited regional exclusivity with or without a signed contract, negotiable. Contracts renew automatically with additional submissions. Statements issued monthy. Payment made 2½ months after sales report. Offers one-time rights. Model/property release required. Captions required.
Making Contact: Query with samples. SASE. Expects minimum initial submission of 100 images with periodic submission of at least 100-200 images. Photo guidelines free on request.

*OUT OF THIS WORLD PHOTOGRAPHY, 329 Rochford Dr., Easley SC 29642. (803)269-8618. FAX: (803)269-7677. Sole Proprietor: Bruce Hansel, Ph.D. Estab. 1986. Stock photo agency. Has 50 photos. Clients include: magazine, postcard, poster publishers and calendar companies.
Subject Needs: Astrophotographs of Messier and New General Catalog objects, planets, comets, asteroids, eclipses and occultations. "High magnification lunarshots OK, but no full moon or sunsets, please! Southern declination objects needed in particular."
Specs: Uses 3×5, 8×10 glossy color and b&w prints; 35mm, 2¼×2¼, 4×5, transparencies.
Payment & Terms: Pays 50% commission on b&w and color photos; 50% commission on films. Average price per image (to clients): b&w $25-200; color $50-400. Enforces minimum prices.Works with or without a signed contract, negotiable. Offers non-exclusive contract. Issues statements on request. Payment made "whenever an image is sold as soon as paid by purchasor." Rights negotiable. Informs photographer and allows him to negotiate when client requests all rights. Captions preferred including details on object, exposure, film type and telescope used.
Making Contact & Terms: Interested in receiving work from newer, lesser-known photographers. Samples kept on file. SASE. Expects minimum initial submission of 1 image. "Volume is not an issue, perfection is." Reports in 1-2 weeks. Photo guidelines free with SASE.
Tips: Wants to see "excellent shots of less commonly photographed objects. I look at three things mainly—focus, guiding and contrast."

*■OUTLINE PRESS SYNDICATE INC., 11th Floor, 596 Broadway, New York NY 10012. (212)226-8790. President: Jim Roehrig. Personality/Portrait. Has 250,000 photos. Clients include: advertising agencies, public relations firms, magazine publishers, newspapers and production/film co.
Subject Needs: Heavy emphasis on personalities, film, TV, political feature stories.
Payment & Terms: General price range: negotiable. Rights negotiable. Model release preferred; captions required.
Making Contact: Query with resume of credits. Works with local freelancers by assignment only. Does not return unsolicited material. Reports in 3 weeks.
Tips: Prefers a photographer that can create situations out of nothing. "The market seems to have a non-ending need for celebrities and the highest quality material will always be in demand."

*■‡OXFORD SCIENTIFIC FILMS, Lower Road, Long Hanborough, Witney, Oxfordshire OX8 8LL England. (0993)881881. Photo Library Manager: Sandra Berry. Film Library: Jane Mulleneux. Film unit and stills and film libraries. Has 250,000 photos; over one million feet of stock footage on 16mm, and 40,000 feet on 35mm. Clients include: ad agencies, design companies, audiovisual firms, book/encyclopedia publishers, magazine and newspaper publishers, calendar, postcard and greeting card companies.
Subject Needs: Natural history: animals, plants, behavior, close-ups, life-histories, histology, embryology, electron microscopy. Scenics, geology, weather, conservation, country practices, ecological techniques, pollution, special-effects, high speed, time-lapse.
Specs: Uses 35mm and larger transparencies; 16 and 35mm film and videotapes.
Payment & Terms: Pays 50% commission on b&w and color photos. Enforces minimum prices. Offers volume discounts to customers; inquire about specific terms. Discount sale terms not negotiable. Works on contract basis only; prefers exclusivity, but negotiable by territory. Contracts renew automatically with additional submissions. "All contracts reviewed after 24 months initially, either party may then terminate contract, giving 3 months notice in writing." Statements issued quarters. Payment made quarterly. Photographers permitted to review sales figures. Photo captions required. Informs photographer and allows him to negotiate when client rquests all rights.
Making Contact: Interested in receiving work from newer, lesser-known photographers. Query with list of stock photo subjects. SASE. Reports in 1 month. Distributes wants list quarterly to all photographers.
Tips: Prefers to see "good focus, composition, exposure. Rare or unusual natural history subjects."

■PACIFIC STOCK, P.O. Box 90517, Honolulu HI 96835. (808)735-5665. FAX: (808)735-7801. Owner/President: Barbara Brundage. Estab. 1987. Stock photo agency. Member of Picture Agency Council of America (PACA). Has 100,000+ photos; 100+ films. Clients include advertising agencies, public relations firms, audiovisual firms, businesses, book/encyclopedia publishers, magazine publishers, postcard companies, calendar companies and greeting card companies. Previous/current clients:

American Airlines, *Life* magazine (cover), Eveready Battery (TV commercial).
Subject Needs: "Pacific Stock is the *only* stock photo agency worldwide specializing in Pacific-related photography (both still and motion picture). Locations include North American West Coast, Hawaii, Pacific Islands, Australia, New Zealand, Far East, etc. Subjects include: people, travel, culture, sports, marine science and industrial."
Specs: Uses 35mm, 2¼ × 2¼, 4 × 5 and 8 × 10 (all formats) transparencies; Super 8, 16mm and 35mm film; ¾" Betacam, 1" videotape, D2 original format videotape.
Payment & Terms: Pays 50% commission on color photos; 50% on films. Works on contract basis only. Offers limited regional exclusivity. Charges catalog insertion rate of 50%/image. Statements issued monthly. Payment made monthly. Photographers allowed to review account records to verify sales figures. Offers one-time or first rights; additional rights with photographer's permission. Informs photographer and allows him to negotiate when client requests all rights. Model and property release required for all people and certain properties, i.e. homes and boats. Photo captions are required; include: "who, what, where."
Making Contact: Query with resume of credits and list of stock photo subjects. SASE. Reports in 2 weeks. Photo guidelines free with SASE. Tips sheet distributed quarterly to interested photographers; free with SASE.
Tips: Looks for "highly edited shots preferrably captioned in archival slide pages. Photographer must be able to supply minimum of 1,000 slides (must be model released) for initial entry and must make quarterly submissions of fresh material from Pacific area destinations from areas outside Hawaii." Major trends to be aware of include: "Increased requests for 'assignment style' photography so it will be resellable as stock. The two general areas (subject) requested are: tourism usage and economic development. Looks for focus, composition and color. As the Pacific region expands, more people are choosing to travel to various Pacific destinations, while greater development occurs, i.e. construction, banking, trade, etc. Increased requests for film, particularly 35mm format of Pacific region scenery, aerials and ocean. Be interested in working with our agency to supply what is on our want lists."

■**PANORAMIC IMAGES,** (formerly Panoramic Stock Images), #3700, 230 N. Michigan Ave., Chicago IL 60601. (312)236-8545. FAX: (312)704-4077. Photo Editors: Kathy Arp/Doug Segal. Estab. 1986. Stock photo agency. Member of Picture Agency Council of America (PACA). Has 50,000 photos. Clients include: advertising agencies, audiovisual firms, businesses, magazine publishers, newspapers, postcard companies, calendar companies, corporate design firms, graphic designers and corporate art consultants.
Subject Needs: Works only with *panoramic formats* (2:1 aspect ratio or greater). Subject include: cityscapes/skylines, landscape/scenics, travel, conceptual and backgrounds (puffy clouds, sunrises/sunsets, water, trees, etc.) Also accepts medium and large formats. "No 35mm."
Specs: Uses 2¼ × 5, 2¼ × 7 and 2¼ × 10 (6 × 12cm, 6 × 17cm and 6 × 24cm). "2¼ formats (chromes only) preferred; will accept 70mm pans, 5 × 7, 4 × 10, 4 × 5 and 8 × 10 horizontals and verticals."
Payment & Terms: Pays 50% commission on color photos. Average price: $700. Offers one-time rights and limited exclusive usage. Model release preferred "and/or property release, if necessary." Photo captions required. Please read our submission guidelines before sending photos.
Making Contact: Arrange a personal interview to show portfolio. Query with samples. Query with list of stock photo subjects. SASE. Reports in 1 month; also sends "response postcard immediately to all photo submissions." Photo guidelines free with SASE. Tips sheet distributed 3-4 times yearly to agencies and prospective photographers, free with SASE.
Tips: Wants to see "well-exposed chromes. Panoramic portraiture of well-known locations nationwide and worldwide. Also, generic beauty panoramics. Use of panoramic point of view is exponentially increasing in lucrative advertising and corporate design areas. PSI has doubled in gross sales, staff and number of contributing photographers over the past months and we expect strong growth to continue. We are the only stock agency dedicated to panoramic photography."

DOUGLAS PEEBLES PHOTOGRAPHY, 445 Iliwahi Loop, Kailua, Oahu HI 96734. (808)254-1082. FAX: (808)254-1267. Owner: Douglas Peebles. Estab. 1975. Stock photo agency. Has 50,000 photos. Clients include: advertising agencies, public relations firms, businesses, magazine publishers, newspapers, postcard companies and calendar companies. Previous/current clients: *Travel Holiday*, magazine; GTE, book; and Hill & Knowton, brochure–all scenics of Hawaii.
Subject Needs: South Pacific and Hawaii.
Specs: Uses 35mm, 2¼ × 2¼, 4 × 5 color transparencies.
Payment & Terms: Pays 50% commission on color photos. General price range: $100-5,000; $100-5,000/color photo. Works on contract basis only. Offers non-exclusive contract. Charges 50% duping fee. Statements issued quarterly. Payment made quarterly. Photographers allowed to review account records to verify sales figures. Offers one-time rights. Model/property release required; photo captions preferred.

Making Contact: Interested in receiving work from newer, lesser-known photographers. Contact by telephone. SASE. Reports in 1 month. Photo guideline sheet not available.
Tips: Looks for "strong color, people in activities and model released. Call first."

*PHOTO ASSOCIATES NEWS SERVICE, #1636, 3421 M. St. NW, Washington DC 20007. (202)965-4428. FAX: (202)337-1969 or (703)659-0896. Bureau Manager: Peter Heimsath. Estab. 1970. News/feature syndicate. Has 15,000 photos. Clients include: public relations firms, book/encyclopedia publishers, magazine publishers, newspapers.
Subject Needs: Needs feature and immediate news for worldwide distribution, also celebrities doing unusual things.
Specs: Uses 8×10 glossy or matte b&w or color prints; 35mm transparencies.
Payment & Terms: Pays $100-750/color photo; $50-100/b&w photo. Pays 50% commission on b&w and color photos. Average price per image (to clients): $75-100/b&w photo; $100-300/color photo. Negotiates fees at standard minimum prices depending on subject matter and need, reflects monies to be charged. Offers volume discounts to customers; terms specified in photographer's contract. Photographers can choose not to sell images on discount terms. Works with or without a signed non-exclusive contract, negotiable. Statements issued monthly. Payment made monthly. "Photographers may review records to verify sales, but don't make a habit of it. Must be a written request." Offers one-time rights. Informs photographer and allows him to negotiate when client requests all rights. Photo Associates News Service will negotiate with client request of all rights purchase. Model/property release preferred. Captions required that included name of subject, when taken, where taken, competition and process instructions.
Making Contact: Query with resume of credits, samples or stock photo list. Samples kept on file. SASE. Expects minimum initial submission of 100 images with periodic submission of at least 100 images every two months. Reports in 1 month. Photo guidelines free with SASE. Market tips sheet distributed to those who make serious inquiries with SASE.
Tips: "Put yourself on the opposite side of the camera, to grasp what the moment has to say. Are you satisfied with your material before you submit it? More and more companies seem to take the short route to achieve their visual goals. They don't want to spend real money to obtain a new approach to a possible old idea. Too many times, photographs loose there freshness, because the process isn't thought out correctly."

*‡PHOTO IMAGES, SDN BHD, P.O. Box 6617, Kampong Tunku 47308 Petaling Jaya Malaysia. (3)342-7801 or (3)342-7802. FAX: (3)342-7803. Managing Director: Peter Anderson. Photo Editor: Justina Singaraju. Has 100,000+ color transparencies mainly of Southeast Asia. Clients include: advertising agencies, travel agencies, book and magazine publishers, corporations, calendar and postcard companies.
Subject Needs: Lifestyle shots, everyday activities, tourist scenes, glamour, scenics, nature and sports in the U.S., Europe, South America and Africa.
Specs: Uses b&w glossy prints; 35mm, 2¼×2¼, 6×7, 4×5, 8×10 color transparencies.
Payment & Terms: Pays 50% commission. Offers all rights.
Making Contact: Send captioned samples and present interest and range of equipment. Market tips sheet distributed 2-3 times/year.
Tips: "Only send sharp-focused and well-composed images. We look for quality not quantity."

*‡PHOTO INDEX, 2 Prowse St., West Perth Western Australia 6005. (09)481-0375. FAX: (09)481-6547. Manager: Lyn Woldendorp. Estab. 1979. Stock photo agency. Has 80,000 photos. Clients include: advertising agencies, public relations firms, audiovisual firms, businesses, book/encyclopedia publishers, magazine publishers, postcard publishers, calendar companies.
Subject Needs: Needs generic stock photos, especially lifestyle, sport and business with people.
Specs: Uses 35mm, 2¼×2¼, 4×5 transparencies.
Payment & Terms: Pays 50% commission on color photos. Average price per image (to clients): $150-200/color photo. Offers volume discounts to customers; inquire about specific terms. Discount terms not negotiable. Works on exclusive contract basis only. Five-year contract renewed automatically. Statements issued quarterly. Payment made quarterly. Photographers permitted to review account records to verify sales figures or account for various deductions "within reason." Offers one-time rights. Informs photographer and allows him to negotiate when client requests all rights. Model/property release preferred. Captions preferred that include what industry and work.
Making Contact: Query with samples. Expects minimum initial submission of 1,000 images with periodic submission of at least several hundred, quarterly. Reports in 1-2 weeks. Photo guidelines free with SASE. Catalog available. Market tips sheet distributed quarterly to contributing photographers.
Tips: "A photographer working in the stock industry. Should treat it professionally. Observe what sells of his work in each agency he puts into as one agencies market can be very different to anothers. Take agencies photo needs lists seriously. Treat it as a business."

‡**THE PHOTO LIBRARY** (Photographic Library of Australia, Ltd.), Suite 1, No. 7 Ridge St., North Sydney 2060 N.S.W. Australia. (02)929-8511. Editor: Lucette Moore. Picture library. Has over 400,000 photos. Clients include: advertising agencies, public relations firms, magazines, businesses, book/encyclopedia publishers, postcard companies, calendar companies, greeting card companies, designers and government departments.
Subject Needs: From abstracts to zoos. "We especially are looking for people pictures (families, couples, business), industrial and high tech."
Specs: Uses 35mm, 2¼×2¼, and 4×5 transparencies.
Payment & Terms: Pays 50% commission for color photos. Offers limited regional exclusivity contract following expiry of agreement: continues until photographer wants to withdraw images. Statements issued quarterly. Payment made quarterly; 10 days after end of quarter. Photographer allowed to review his own account, once per year to verify sales figures. Offers one-time rights, all rights and limited rights. Informs photographer and allows him to negotiate when client requests all rights. Requires model release (held by photographer) and photo captions.
Making Contact: Interested in receiving work from newer, lesser-known photographers. Send unsolicited photos by mail for consideration to Lucette Moore, Box 121, Cammeray N.S.W. Works with local and overseas freelancers. SASE. Reports in 10 days. Guidelines free with SASE. Distributes tip sheet quarterly to photographers on file.
Tips: Prefers to see top quality commercial usage and good graphic images. "We see an increase in stock usage by advertising agents as they recognize a higher level of creative excellence in stock compared to previous years."

■**PHOTO NETWORK**, 1541J Parkway Loop, Tustin CA 92680. (714)259-1244. Owner: Cathy Aron. Stock photo agency. Member of Picture Agency Council of America (PACA). Has 500,000 photos. Clients include: ad agencies, AV producers, textbook companies, graphic artists, public relations firms, newspapers, corporations, magazines, calendar companies and greeting card companies.
Subject Needs: Needs shots of personal sports and recreation, industrial/commercial, high-tech, families, couples (all ages), animals, travel and lifestyles. Special subject needs include people over 55 enjoying life, medical shots (patients and professionals), children and animals.
Specs: Uses 35mm, 2¼×2¼, 4×5 transparencies.
Payment & Terms: Pays 50% commission. Works on contract basis only. Offers limited regional exclusivity. Contracts automatically renew with each submission for 3 years. Charges catalog insertion fee; rate not specified. Statements issued monthly. Payment made monthly. Photographers allowed to review account records to verify sales figures. Offers one-time rights. Informs photographer and allows him to negotiate when client requests all rights. Model/property release preferred. Photo captions preferred; include places—parks, cities, buildings, etc. "No need to describe the obvious, i.e., mother with child."
Making Contact: Interested in receiving work from newer, lesser-known photographers. Query with list of stock photo subjects. SASE. Reports in 1 month.
Tips: Wants to see a portfolio "neat and well-organized and including a sampling of photographer's favorite photos." Looks for "clear, sharp focus, strong colors and good composition. We'd rather have many very good photos rather than one great piece of art. Would like to see photographers with a specialty or specialties and have it covered thoroughly. You need to supply new photos on a regular basis and be responsive to current trends in photo needs. Contract photographers are supplied with quarterly 'want' lists and information about current trends."

*****PHOTO OPTIONS STOCK AGENCY**, 2206 Gill St., Huntsville AL 35801. (205)533-4331, (205)979-8412. President: Elaine Fredericksen. Estab. 1983. Stock photo agency. Has 40,000 photos. Clients include: advertising agencies, public relations firms, businesses, book/encyclopedia publishers, magazine publishers.
Subject Needs: "Our specialty is photos of the Southeast, but we also stock all general areas: corporate, life style, sports, etc."
Specs: Uses 35mm, 2¼×2¼, 4×5, 8×10, transparencies.
Payment & Terms: Pays 50% commission on color photos. Works on contract basis only. Offers nonexclusive contract. Issues statement with each check. Payment made monthly at end of month payment is received. Photographer is allowed to review account records. Offers one-time rights. Informs photographer and allows him to negotiate when client requests all rights. Property release preferred; Model release required for people, especially children; captions required. "Good captions sell photos."
Making Contact: Arrange a personal interview to show portfolio. Submit portfolio for review. Query with samples. Samples not kept on file. Expects minimum initial submission of 200-500 images. "Regular submissions of photos increase sales." Reports in 3 weeks. Photo guidelines free with SASE. Market tips sheet distributed quarterly to agency photographers; free with SASE. Samples available upon request.

Close-up

Gerry Boudrias
Photo Editor
Photo Search Ltd.
Edmonton, Canada

© Harry Korol

Gerry Boudrias says he has an obligation as a new stock agency owner to fulfill the needs of his clients. In order to do that he must maintain an assortment of photographs from which a client can choose. "Having gone through a fine arts program, I understand a photographer's desire to be creative," says Boudrias, who graduated in 1988 from Concordia University in Montreal, Quebec. "I guess I was one of the renegades in school because my motto was always, 'It's not art until somebody pays for it.' "

Boudrias believes many photographers ignore such a basic understanding of the field. They shoot for artistic images and often fail to capture photos a client might purchase. "I've seen work turned down, fine work, amazing work sometimes, and the client says, 'It's a beautiful image, but it doesn't do what we're trying to say here,' " he says. "A good photographer is one who has a creative sensibility, but understands why he is there in the first place, and that's to help the client."

In order for stock photographers to fulfill such obligations they must follow the advice of their agency, says Boudrias, who opened his agency in 1991 with partner Gerard Vaillancourt. As a matter of course, the agency periodically supplies its freelancers with "hit lists" that explain the needs of the clients. Photographers interested in selling their work should review the lists and make those suggested shots a priority the next time they pick up their cameras.

"Shoot the stuff the agency asks you for," suggests Boudrias, a former stock photographer. "When I send out a hit list, I'm not asking for it because I'm bored and I'm trying to figure out things for people to do. I'm asking for this stuff because somebody has called up and is looking for it."

Photo Search represents 16 photographers and maintains a growing stock portfolio containing over 60,000 images. Because the hit lists are sent to all photographers who work with the agency, Boudrias tries to convince the freelancers to work together whenever possible. By communicating, the photographers can divide up the shooting assignments amongst themselves without overlapping. This keeps them from shooting the same images and provides the agency with more diverse photos from which clients can choose, he says. Such an attitude not only helps the agency and the client, but it makes more money for the photographers because there are saleable images.

Boudrias hastens to add that, while stock photographers should want to make money off their work, they should not expect to see returns overnight. "Don't look at stock as a get-rich-quick scheme and don't look at stock as something that's going to create something for you if you're looking for a job right now. What you have to do when you consider stock is look at the long-term," he says. One of the freelancers who works with Photo Search is actually using his stock images as a retirement fund. The photographer, who is around 40, works as a stringer for an Edmonton newspaper. Over the next 10 or 15 years he hopes to build a large enough portfolio to go into semi-retirement and live comfortably off what he makes through the stock agency, said Boudrias.

Another downside to the early years of stock is that it may actually cost the photographer money. When Boudrias began working as a stock photographer he often found himself spending more than he earned. "You have to get beyond that initial phase," he says. "Put it this way, you can't send your material off to a stock agency and then a week later start standing by the mailbox waiting for the check to come in. It just doesn't happen."

—Michael Willins

© Mufty

The popularity of stock photography has resulted in stock agencies cropping up all over the world. In 1991, Gerry Boudrias and a partner opened their agency, Photo Search Ltd. in Edmonton, Canada, as a result of the growth of the western portion of his country. The man's appearance in this sea of bleacher seats makes this photo by Mufty an extremely marketable one to advertising firms and other corporate clients. It is one of over 60,000 the stock agency has to offer.

Tips: In samples looks for "dynamic, professional-quality images, commercial as well as artistic; good, thorough captions and appropriate model releases. Best sellers are photos of the Southeast and images of people, especially business, corporate, medical situations. Commit yourself to providing a continuous supply of stock to an agency. Fresh images sell. If you are not friendly and cooperative, don't call us. We're a down-home, personal service agency."

PHOTO RESEARCHERS, INC., 60 E. 56th St., New York NY 10022. (212)758-3420. FAX: (212)355-0731. President: Robert Zentmaier. Stock agency representing hundreds of photographers. Includes the National Audubon Society and Science Source Collection. Member of Picture Agency Council of America (PACA). Clients include: ad agencies and publishers of textbooks, encyclopedias, filmstrips, trade books, magazines, newspapers, calendars, greeting cards, posters, and annual reports in US and foreign markets.

Subject Needs: All aspects of natural history and science; human nature (especially children and young adults 6-18 engaged in everyday activity); industry; "people doing what they do"; and pretty scenics to informational photos, particularly needs model released people photos and property photos such as houses, cars and boats.

Specs: Uses 8×10 matte doubleweight b&w prints and any size transparencies.

Payment & Terms: Rarely buys outright; works on 50% stock sales and 30% assignments. General price range: $150-7,500. Indicate model release on photo. Offers one-time and one-year exclusive rights.

Making Contact: Query with description of work, type of equipment used and subject matter available. Send to Bug Sutton, Creative Director. Follow up to arrange a personal interview to show portfolio; or submit portfolio for review. Reports in 1 month maximum. SASE.

Tips: "When a photographer is accepted, we analyze his portfolio and have consultations to give the photographer direction and leads for making sales of reproduction rights. We seek the photographer who is highly imaginative, or into a specialty, enthusiastic and dedicated to technical accuracy. We are taking very few photographers—unlike the old days. We are looking for serious photographers who have many hundreds of photographs to offer for a first submission and who are able to contribute often. More advertisers are using stock. Many editorial textbook publishers are turning to color only. Electronic imaging systems for showing and selling stock will be in place before we know it."

*❋PHOTO SEARCH LTD., #2002, 9909 104 St., Edmonton, Alberta T5K 2G5 Canada. (403)425-3766. FAX: (403)425-3766. Photo Editor: Gerry Boudrias. Estab. 1991. Stock photo agency. Has 60,000+ photos. Clients include: advertising agencies, public relations firms, audiovisual firms, businesses, book/encyclopedia publishers, magazine publishers, newspapers, postcard publishers, calendar companies, graphic designers, government agencies.

Subject Needs: "We always need good people photos showing, among other things, multi-culturalism, seniors leading active, healthy lives, and women in non-traditional work roles. Especially needed for next year will be: environmental issues, natives, lifestyle photos of couples, high-tech industrial, business people, travel in Southeast Asia, wildlife, nightlife, and outdoor recreation activities."

Specs: Uses 35mm, 2¼×2¼, 4×5 color transparencies.

Payment & Terms: Pays 50% commission on color photos. Average price per image (to clients): $80-400/color photo; editorial work ranges from $80-200; advertising work ranges from $200-500. Negotiates fees below standard minimum prices. Offers volume discounts to customers; terms specified in photographer's contract. Photographers can choose not to sell images on discount terms. Works on limited regional exclusivity contract basis only. "All contracts are automatically renewed for a one-year period, unless either party provides written notice." Payment made quarterly. Photographers permitted to review account records to verify sales figures or account for various deductions. Offers one-time and electronic media rights. Informs photographer and allows him to negotiate when client requests all rights. "While we reserve the right to final judgment, we confer with photographers about all-right sales. We insist on doing what we feel is right for the agency and the photographer." Model/property release required. "Model releases are imperative for photographers who wish to make sales in the advertising field." Captions required. "Point out information that could be important that may not be evident in the image."

The double dagger before a listing indicates that the market is located outside the United States and Canada. The symbol is new this year in Photographer's Market.

Making Contact: Submit portfolio for review. Query with samples. Query with stock photo list. SASE. Expects minimum initial submission of 200 images. Reports in 1 month. Photo guidelines free with SASE. Send international postage for mailings to U.S. "General list for anybody on request."

■**PHOTOBANK,** Suite B, 17952 Skypark Circle, Irvine CA 92714. (714)250-4480. FAX: (714)752-5495. Photo Editor: Kristi Bressert. Stock photo agency. Has 750,000 transparencies. Clients include: ad agencies, public relations firms, audiovisual firms, book/encyclopedia publishers, magazine publishers, postcard companies, calendar publishers and greeting card companies.
Subject Needs: Emphasis on active couples, lifestyle, medical, family and business. High-tech shots are always needed. These subjects are highly marketable, but model releases are a must.
Specs: Uses all formats: 35mm, 2¼×2¼, 4×5, 6×7 and 8×10; color only.
Payment & Terms: Pays 50% commission. Average price per image: $275-500/color photo. Negotiates fees below minimum prices. Offers volume discounts to customers; terms specified in photographer's contract. Photographers can choose not to sell images on discount terms. Works with or without contract. Offers exclusive, limited regional exclusive non-exclusive and guaranteed subject exclusivity contracts. Contracts renew automatically with additional submissions. Statements issued quarterly. Payment made quarterly. Photographers permitted to review account records to verify sales figures or account for various deductions. Offers one-time rights, electronic media rights and agency promotion rights. Informs photographer and allows him to negotiate when client requests all rights. Offers one-time rights. Model/property release required for people and property. Photo captions preferred.
Making Contact: Interested in receiving work from newer, lesser-known photographers. Query with samples and list of stock photos. SASE. Reports in 2 weeks. Photo guidelines free with SASE.
Tips: Prefers to see "The 3 'C's: clarity, color, composition. Clients are looking for assignment quality and are very discerning with their selections. Only your best should be considered for submission. Please tightly edit your work before submitting. Model released people shots in lifestyle situations (picnic, golf, tennis, etc.) sell."

***PHOTOEDIT,** 6056 Corbin Ave., Tarzana CA 91356. (818)342-2811. FAX: (818)343-9548. President: Leslye Borden. Estab. 1987. Stock photo agency. Member of Picture Agency Council of America (PACA). Has 250,000 photos. Clients include: advertising, public relations firms, businesses, book/encyclopedia publishers, magazine publishers.
Subject Needs: People—seniors, teens, children, families, minorities.
Specs: Uses 35mm transparencies.
Payment & Terms: Pays 50% commission on color photos. Average price per image (to clients): $185. Works on contract basis only. Offers non-exclusive contract. Charges catalog insertion fee of $400/per image. Statements issued or quarterly; monthly if earn over $1,000 per month. Payment made monthly or quarterly at time of statement. Photographers are allowed to review account records. Offers one-time rights; limited time use. Consults photographer when client requests all rights. Model preferred for people.
Making Contact: Arrange a personal interview to show portfolio. Submit portfolio for review. Query with samples. Samples not kept on file. SASE. Expects minimum initial submission of 1,000 images with additional submission of 1,000 per year. Reports in 1 month. Photo guidelines free with SASE.
Tips: In samples looks for "drama, color, social relevance, inter-relationships, current (*not* dated material), tight editing. We want photographers who have easy access to models (not professional) and will shoot actively and on spec."

■‡**THE PHOTOGRAPHIC GAME,** Box 233, Forestville, Sydney NSW 2087, Australia. (61)(2)451-2739. FAX: (61)(2)975-4457. Contact: Malcolm Thomas. Keeps 300,000 photos on file. Specializes in the Australian and Japanese markets. Clients include: magazine, book publishers, audiovisual and record companies, public relations firms, calendars, corporate clients and ad agencies.
Subject Needs: Human interest, business-oriented shots, sport, glamour, humor and portraits. Submissions accepted from anywhere in the world.
Specs: Uses 35mm and larger format transparencies, "unless b&w is outstanding."
Payment & Terms: Pays 50% commission. General price range: $25-2,000.
Making Contact: "Send us a few samples (10-100) so we can judge quality and a list of what you have available. Very prompt replies."
Tips: "Sharpness, color, action and impact are what sell photos. Your shots should have 1, 2, 3 or all of these in them."

***PHOTOLINK STOCK PHOTOGRAPHY,** 141 The Commons, Ithaca NY 14850. (607)272-0642. FAX: (607)272-8634. Director: Jon Reis. Estab. 1988. Stock photo agency. Has 50,000 photos. Clients include: advertising agencies, public relations firms, businesses, book/encyclopedia publishers, magazine publishers.

Subject Needs: Up-to-date model released photos of families, children, business people; recreational sports; aviation; travel/scenics including upstate New York.
Specs: Uses 8×10 (off-beat pics), b&w prints; 35mm transparencies.
Payment & Terms: Pays 50% commission on b&w and color photos. Average price per image (to clients): b&w $150-200; color $150-200. Works on contract basis only. Offers guaranteed subject exclusivity (within files). Issues annual statements. Payment made bimonthly. Photographers are allowed to review account records. Offers one-time rights. Informs photographer and allows him to negotiate when client requests all rights. Model/property release preferred. Captions required; include what, where.
Making Contact: Interested in receiving work from newer, lesser-known photographers. Query with stock photo list. Samples not kept on file. SASE. Expects minimum initial submission of 80 images with additional submissions of at least 30-40 every 3 months. Reports in 1-2 weeks. Photo guidelines free with SASE. Market tips sheet distributed quarterly to contracted photographers.
Tips: Looks for "diversity of work with 3-5 subjects extensively covered; strong initial editing before we see the work—just your best. It's hard to sell photos which are unreleased or uncaptioned. Get out there with model releases and then clearly caption your slides!"

■**PHOTO/NATS, INC.**, 33 Aspen Ave., Newton MA 02166. (617)969-9531. President: Marilyn Wood. Estab. 1984. Stock photo agency. Has 100,000 photos. Clients include: agencies, audiovisual firms, book/text/encyclopedia publishers, magazine publishers, postcard companies, calendar companies, greeting card companies and businesses.
Subject Needs: The natural world: environmental issues, animal behavior, 4-season series, conservation and waste, biking, running, crops, gardening, endangered species, garden pests.
Specs: Uses 8×10 glossy b&w prints; 35mm, 2¼×2¼, 4×5 color transparencies.
Payment & Terms: Pays 50% commission on b&w and color photos. General price range: $75-1,000. Enforces minimum prices. Offers volume discounts to customers; inquire about specific terms. Discount sales terms not negotiable. Works on non-exclusive contract only. Contracts renew on voluntary basis. Statements issued monthly. Payment made monthly. Offers one-time and other rights. Informs photographer and allows him to negotiate when client requests all rights. Model/property release required for advertising. Photo captions required include subject, place, binomials in plants.
Making Contact: Interested in receiving work from newer, lesser-known photographers. Query with list of stock photo subjects. "Do not send unsolicited transparencies." Cannot return material. Reports in 1 month. Photo guidelines free with SASE. Market tips sheet distributed every 2 months to contracted photographers.
Tips: "We're looking for only your best action shots of the natrual world, i.e., animals and insects plus gorgeous gardens and gardening 'how-tos.' We expect to receive submissions on a regular basis."

■**PHOTOPHILE**, Dept. PM, Suite B-203, 6150 Lusk Blvd., San Diego CA 92121. (619)453-3050. FAX: (619)452-0994. Director: Kelly Nelson. Clients include: publishers (trade, text, reference, periodical, etc.), advertisers, broadcasters, etc. Write with SASE for photographer's information. "Professionals only, please."
Subject Needs: Lifestyle, vocations, sports, industry, entertainment, business and computer graphics.
Specs: Uses 35mm, 2¼×2¼, 4×5 and 6×7 original transparencies.
Payment & Terms: Does not buy outright; pays 50% commission. NPI. Works on contract basis only. Offers limited regional exclusivity. Charges variable fee for catalog insertion. Statements issued monthly. Payment made monthly; upon payment from client. Photographers are allowed to review account records to verify sales figures. "We periodically send copies of a photographer's account records automatically." Rights negotiable; usually offers one-time rights. Informs photographer and allows him to negotiate when client requests all rights. Model and property release preferred; photo captions preferred, include location or description of obscure subjects.
Tips: "Specialize, and shoot for the broadest possible sales potential. Get releases!" Points out that the "greatest need is for model-released people subjects; sharp-focus and good composition is important; a minimum submission of 500 salable images required and a photographer must be continuously shooting to add new images to our files." If photographer's work is salable, "it will sell itself."

*****PHOTOREPORTERS, INC.**, 875 6th Ave., New York NY 10001. General Manager: Roberta Boehm. Estab. 1958. Stock photo agency, news/feature syndicate. Clients include: public relations firms, book/encyclopedia publishers, magazine publishers and newspapers.

The asterisk before a listing indicates that the market is new in this edition. New markets are often the most receptive to freelance submissions.

Subject Needs: Celebrities, politics and photo stories such as human interest.
Specs: Uses 35mm transparencies.
Payment & Terms: Pays 50% commission on b&w and color photos. General price range: $175/¼ page color; $125/¼ page b&w. Enforces minimum prices. Photographers can choose not to sell images on discount terms. Works with or without contract. Statements issued monthly. Payment made monthly. Offers one-time and electronic media rights. Model release and photo captions preferred.
Making Contact: Contact by telephone. SASE. Reports in 3 weeks.

*■PHOTOTAKE, INC., 4523 Broadway, New York NY 10040. (212)942-8185. FAX: (212)942-8186. Director: Leila Levy. Stock photo agency; "fully computerized photo agency specializing in science and technology in stock and on assignment." Has 200,000 photos. Clients include: ad agencies, businesses, newspapers, public relations and AV firms, book/encyclopedia and magazine publishers, and postcard, calendar and greeting card companies.
Subject Needs: General science and technology photographs, medical, high-tech, computer graphics, special effects for general purposes, health-oriented photographs, natural history, people and careers.
Specs: Uses 8×10 prints; 35mm, 2¼×2¼, 4×5 or 8×10 transparencies; contact sheets or negatives.
Payment & Terms: Pays 50% commission on b&w and color photos. Offers one-time or first rights (world rights in English language, etc.). Model release and captions required.
Making Contact: Arrange a personal interview to show portfolio. Query with samples or with list of stock photo subjects. Submit portfolio for review. *SASE.* Reports in 1 month. Photo guidelines "given on the phone only." Tips sheet distributed monthly to "photographers that have contracted with us at least for a minimum of 500 photos."
Tips: Prefers to see "at least 100 color photos on general photojournalism or studio photography and at least 5 tearsheets — this, to evaluate photographer for assignment. If photographer has enough in medical, science, general technology photos, send these also for stock consideration." Using more "illustration type of photography. Topics we currently see as hot are: general health, computers, news on science. Photographers should always look for new ways to illustrate concepts generally."

■PHOTRI INC., Suite C2 North, 3701 South George Maxon Dr., Falls Church VA 22041. (703)836-4439. President: Jack Novak. Member of Picture Agency Council of America (PACA). Has 400,000 b&w photos and color transparencies of all subjects. Clients include: book and encyclopedia publishers, ad agencies, record companies, calendar companies, and "various media for AV presentations."
Subject Needs: Military, space, science, technology, romantic couples, people doing things, humor, picture stories. Special needs include calendar and poster subjects. Needs ethnic mix in photos. Has subagents in 10 foreign countries interested in photos of USA in general.
Specs: Uses 8×10 glossy b&w prints; 35mm and larger transparencies.
Payment & Terms: Seldom buys outright; pays 50% commission. Pays: $45-65/b&w photo; $100-1,500/color photo; $50-100/film/ft. Negotiates fees below standard minimums. Offers volume discounts to customers; term's specified in photographer's contract. Discount sale terms not negotiable. Work with or without contract; offers non-exclusivity. Charges $75 catalog insertion fee. Statements issued quarterly. Payments made quarterly. Photographers allowed to review records to verify sales figures or account for various deductions. Offers one-time rights. Model release required if available and if photo is to be used for advertising purposes. Property release and photo captions required.
Making Contact: Call to arrange an appointment or query with resume of credits. Reports in 2-4 weeks. SASE.
Tips: "Respond to current needs with good quality photos. Take other than sciences, i.e., people and situations useful to illustrate processes and professions. Send photos on energy and environmental subjects. Also need any good creative 'computer graphics.' Subject needs include major sports events."

■‡PICTOR INTERNATIONAL, LTD., Twyman House, 31-39 Camden Rd., London NW1 9LR England. (071)482-0478. FAX: (071)267-1396. Managing Director: Alberto Sciama. Stock photo agency and picture library with offices in London, Paris, Munich, Milan, New York and Washington DC. Has 750,000 photos. Clients include: advertising agencies, public relations firms, audiovisual firms, businesses, book/encyclopedia publishers, magazine publishers, postcard companies, calendar companies, greeting card companies and travel plus decorative posters; jigsaw companies.
Subject Needs: "Pictor is a general stock agency. We accept *all* subjects. Needs primarily people shots (released): business, families, couples, children, etc. Criteria for acceptance: photos which are technically and aesthetically excellent."
Specs: Uses 35mm, 2¼×2¼, 4×5 and 8×10 transparencies.
Payment & Terms: Pays 50% commission for color photos. General price range: $100 to $15,000. Statements issued monthly. Offers one-time rights, first rights and all rights. Requires model release and photo captions. Buys photos outright depending on subject.

Making Contact: Arrange a personal interview to show portfolio. Query with list of stock photo subjects. Send unsolicited photos by mail for consideration. Photo guidelines sheet available for SASE. Publishes annual catalog. Tips sheet for "photographers we represent only."
Tips: Looks for "photographs covering all subjects. Criteria: technically and aesthetically excellent. Clients are getting more demanding and expect to receive only excellent material. Through our marketing techniques and PR, we advertise widely the economic advantages of using more stock photos. Through this technique we're attracting 'new' clients who require a whole different set of subjects."

■**THE PICTURE CUBE INC.**, Suite 1131, 89 Broad St., Boston MA 02110. (617)367-1532. FAX: (617)482-9266. President: Sheri Blaney. Member of Picture Agency Council of America (PACA). Has 300,000 photos. Clients include: ad agencies, public relations firms, businesses, audiovisual firms, textbook publishers, magazine publishers, encyclopedia publishers, newspapers, postcard companies, calendar companies, greeting card companies and TV. Guidelines available with SASE.
Subject Needs: US and foreign coverage, contemporary images, agriculture, industry, energy, high technology, religion, family life, multicultural, animals, transportation, work, leisure, travel, ethnicity, communications, people of all ages, psychology and sociology subjects. "We need lifestyle, model-released images of families, couples, technology and work situations. We emphasize New England/Boston subjects for our ad/design and corporate clients."
Specs: Uses 8×10 prints and 35mm, 2¼×2¼, 4×5 and larger slides. "Our clients use both color and b&w photography."
Payment & Terms: Pays 50% commission. General price range: $125-300/b&w; $160-400/color photo. "We negotiate special rates for nonprofit organizations." Offers volume discounts to customers; inquire about specific terms. Discount sales terms not negotiable. Works on nonexclusive contract basis only. Contracts renew automatically for three years. Charges catalog insertion fee. Statements issued monthly. Payment made bimonthly. Photographers allowed to review account records to verify sales figures. Offers one-time rights. Informs photographer and allows him to negotiate when a client requests all rights. Model/property release preferred; captions required including event, location, desctiption, if model released..
Making Contact: Request guidelines before sending any materials. Arrange a personal interview to show portfolio. SASE. Reports in 1 month.
Tips: "B&w photography is being used more and we will continue to stock it. Serious freelance photographers "must supply a good amount (at least a thousand images per year, sales-oriented subject matter) of material, in order to produce steady sales. All photography submitted must be high quality, with needle-sharp focus, strong composition, correctly exposed. All of our advertising clients require model releases on all photos of people, and, often on property (real estate)."

PICTURE GROUP, INC., 830 Eddy St., Providence RI 02905. (401)461-9333. Managing Editor: Philip Hawthorne. Estab. 1979. Stock photo agency, news/feature syndicate. Has 500,000+ photos. Clients include: book/encyclopedia publishers and magazine publishers.
Subject Needs: Needs photos of "topical, contemporary issues and news, including industry, science, health, environment, politics, lifestyles and people in the news."
Specs: Uses b&w prints; 35mm and 2¼×2¼ transparencies.
Payment & Terms: NPI; commission negotiable. Offers one-time rights. Model release preferred; photo captions required.
Making Contact: Contact by phone before sending work. SASE. Reports ASAP. Photo guidelines available to contract photographers. Tips distributed occasionally to contract photographers.
Tips: In freelancer's samples, wants to see professionalism, originality, intelligence, relevance, integrity and hard work. "The demand for released material is growing, also for most up-to-date, distinctive, well-informed material with complete captions."

*****PICTURE PERFECT STOCK PHOTOS**, 159 Main St., P.O. Box 15760, Stamford CT 06901-0760. (203)967-2512. FAX: (203)323-8362. Director: Andres Aquino. Stock photo agency, picture library. Has 300,000+ photos. Clients include: advertising agencies, public relations firms, audiovisual firms, businesses, book/encyclopedia publishers, magazine publishers, newspapers, postcard publishers, calendar companies, greeting card companies.
Subject Needs: Photos of all subjects; heavy on people, travel, glamour, beauty, fashion, medical, science, business and technology.
Specs: Uses b&w prints; 35mm, 2¼×2¼, 4×5, 8×10 transparencies; VHS and ¾", videotape.
Payment & Terms: Pays 50% commission on b&w and color photos. Average price per image (to clients): b&w $150-2,000; and color $150-3,000. Enforces minimum prices. Offers volume discounts to customers; terms specified in photographers contract. Photographers can choose not to sell images on discount terms. Works on contract basis only. Offers exclusive and non-exclusive contracts. Contracts renew automatically. Charges catalog insert fee of $100/photo. Statements issued quarterly. Payment made monthly. Photographer is allowed to review account records pertaining to his/her sales

only. Offers one-time rights. Informs photographer and permits him to negotiate when client requests all rights. Model/property release required; captions required.
Making Contact: Interested in receiving work from newer, lesser-known photographers. Query with samples. Query with stock photo list. Samples kept on file. SASE. Expects minimum initial submission of 20-100 images, with additional submission of 20/month or more. Reports in 3 weeks. Photo guidelines free with SASE. Market tips sheet distributed from time to time in the form of newsletter. Specific requests weekly via telephone: 1-900-73PHOTO.
Tips: "We prefer sharp, carefully edited images in your area of specialization. Trends: images with specific commercial applications; images with senior citizens enjoying outdoor activities or engaged in activities with younger people; and images that evoke emotions and intellectual responses."

PICTURE THAT, INC., Dept. PM, 880 Briarwood Rd., Newtown Square PA 19073. (215)353-8833. Stock Librarian: Lili Etezady. Estab. 1978. Stock photo agency. Clients include: advertising agencies, public relations firms, businesses, book/encyclopedia publishers, magazine publishers, postcard companies, calendar companies and greeting card companies.
Subject Needs: Handles all subjects: nature, scenics, sports, people of all types and activities, animals, some abstracts and art, and travel (especially East Coast and Pennsylvania).
Specs: Uses 35mm and 2¼×2¼ transparencies.
Payment & Terms: Pays 50% commission on photos. General price range: varies with usage and circulation. Offers one-time rights. Model release and photo captions preferred.
Making Contact: Query with list of stock photo subjects; SASE. Call for info.
Tips: Likes to see good color and good exposure. Send images in plastic sheets with captions and photographer's name on slides. "We encourage new photographers as we build our stock. We are receiving more and more requests for lifestyle photos, people in all situations, especially active and sports shots; also senior citizens. They must be model-released."

PICTURES INTERNATIONAL, P.O. Box 470685, Tulsa OK 74147-0685. (918)664-1339. Picture Editor: Jim Wray. Has 50,000 images. Clients include: ad agencies, public relations firms, magazine publishers, and paper product (calendars, postcards, greeting cards) companies.
Specs: Uses 2¼×2¼ and larger transparencies; also 8×10 glossy b&w and color prints. Will consider stereo (3-D) images; see separate listing under "Advertising in 3-D."
Payment & Terms: Pays 50% commission on b&w and color photos. Model releases and photo captions required.
Making Contact: Submit photos by mail for consideration. Photo guidelines and tip sheet free upon request. SASE.

■PICTURESQUE STOCK PHOTOS, 1520 Brookside Drive #3, Raleigh NC 27604. (919)828-0023. Manager: Syd Jeffrey. Estab. 1987. Stock photo agency. Member of Picture Agency Council of America (PACA). Has 300,000 photos. Clients include: advertising agencies, public relations firms, design firms, businesses, book/encyclopedia publishers and magazine publishers.
Subject Needs: Travel/destination, model-released people, lifestyle, business, industry and general topics.
Specs: Uses 35mm, 2¼×2¼, 4×5 and 8×10 transparencies.
Payment & Terms: Pays 50% commission on color photos. Offers various rights depending on client needs. Model releases and photo captions required.
Making Contact: Contact by telephone for submissions guidelines. SASE. Reports in 1 month. Tips sheet distributed quarterly to member photographers.
Tips: Submission requirements include 200-300 original transparencies; wide range of subjects.

■‡PLANET EARTH PICTURES/SEAPHOT LTD, 4 Harcourt St., London W1H IDS England. 071-262-4427. FAX: 071-706-4042. Managing Director: Gillian Lythgoe. Has 200,000 photos. Clients include: ad agencies, public relations and audiovisual firms, businesses, book/encyclopedia and magazine publishers, and postcard and calendar companies.
Subject Needs: "Marine—surface and underwater photos covering all marine subjects, including water sports, marine natural history, seascapes, ships, natural history. All animals and plants: (interrelationships and behavior), landscapes, natural environments, pollution and convervation." Special subject needs: polar and rainforest animals and scenery.
Specs: Uses any size transparencies.
Payment & Terms: Pays 50% commission on color photos. General price range: £50 (1 picture/1 AV showing), to over £1,000 for advertising use. Prices negotiable according to use. Works with or without a signed contract, negotiable. Statements issued quarterly. Payment made quarterly. Photographers allowed to review account records to verify sales figures. Offers one-time rights. Informs photographer and allows him to negotiate when client requests all rights. Model release preferred; photo captions required.

Making Contact: Arrange a personal interview to show portfolio. Send photos by mail for consideration. SASE. Reports ASAP. Distributes tips sheet every 6 months to photographers.

Tips: "We like photographers to have received our photographer's booklet that gives details about photos and captions. In reviewing a portfolio, we look for a range of photographs on any subject—important for the magazine market—the quality. Trends change rapidly. There is a strong emphasis that photos taken in the wild are preferable to studio pictures. Advertising clients still like larger format photographs. Exciting and artistic photographs used even for wildlife photography, protection of environment."

‡**PRO-FILE**, 2B Winner Commercial Building, 401-403 Lockhart Rd., Wanchai Hong Kong. (852)574-7788. FAX: (852)574-8884. Director: Neil Farrin. Stock photo agency. Has 100,000+ photos. Clients include: advertising agencies, public relations firms, audiovisual firms, businesses, book/encyclopedia publishers, magazine publishers and calendar companies.

Subject Needs: General stock, worldwide, emphasis on Asia.

Specs: Uses 35mm, 2¼×2¼ and 4×5 transparencies.

Payment & Terms: Pays 50% commission. Works on contract basis only. Guarantees subject exclusivity within files and limited regional exclusivity. Charges duping and catalog insertion fees. Statements issued quarterly. Payment made quarterly. Photographers allowed to review account records to verify sales figures. Offers one-time and electronic media rights. Requests agency promotion rights. Informs photographer and allows him to negotiate when client requests all rights. Model and property releases required. Photo captions required.

Making Contact: Interested in receiving work from newer, lesser-known photographers. Query with resume of credits and list of stock photo subjects. SASE. Reports in 3 months. Distributes tips sheet "as necessary" to current photographers on file.

Tips: Has second office in Singapore; contact main office for information.

■**PROFILES WEST**, Dept. PM, 210 E. Main St., P.O. Box 1199, Buena Vista CO 81211. (719)395-8671. FAX: (719)395-8840. President, Photographer Representative: Allen Russell. Estab. 1987. Stock photo agency. Member of Picture Agency Council of America (PACA). Has 200,000 photos. Clients include: advertising agencies, public relations firms, audiovisual firms, businesses, book/encyclopedia publishers, magazine publishers, postcard companies, calendar companies and greeting card companies.

Subject Needs: "Our specialty is the American West and its people at work and play. We are very strong in leisure sports and lifestyles, people at work and Western scenes."

Specs: Uses 35mm, medium and large format transparencies.

Payment & Terms: Pays 50% commission on color photos. General price range: $125+. Works on contract basis only. Offers nonexclusive contract and guarantees subject exclusivity within files. Contracts renew automatically with each submission for 1 year. Charges catalog insertion of varying rate. Statements issued bimonthly. Payment made bimonthly. Photographers allowed to review account records to verify sales figures or account for various deductions. Offers one-time and electronic media rights. "A wide range of rights is offered but one-time dominates." Informs photographer and allows him to negotiate when client requests all rights. Model and/or property release preferred.

Making Contact: Query with list of stock photo subjects. Submit portfolio for review. SASE. Photo guidelines free with SASE. Tips sheet distributed to contract photographers.

Tips: In photographer's portfolio, wants to see "an organized style which shows people and their environment in a manner which looks unposed, even when it often is. A commitment to developing a series of subjects rather than only random shots." The trend is towards "a desire for images which go beyond the limits of what has come to be expected from stock: more emotion, realism, etc. There is a tremendous need for stock photographers to accept that they are small business people and act accordingly. Most need to tighten their scope of subject and find where they can best compete."

■**RAINBOW**, Dept. PM, P.O. Box 573, Housatonic MA 01236. (413)274-6211. FAX: (413)274-6689. Director: Coco McCoy. Estab. 1976. Stock photo agency. Member of Picture Agency Council of America (PACA). Has 100,000 photos. Clients include: public relations firms, design agencies, audiovisual firms, book/encyclopedia publishers, magazine publishers and calendar companies. 20% of sales come from overseas.

Subject Needs: Although Rainbow is a general coverage agency, it specializes in high technology images and is continually looking for talented coverage in fields such as computer graphics, robotics, subatomic research, medicine, DNA, communications, lasers and space. We are also looking for graphically strong and colorful images in such areas as macro and microphotography, illustrations of physics, biology and earth science concepts; also active children, teenagers and elderly people. Worldwide travel locations are always in demand."

Specs: Uses 35mm and larger transparences.
Payment & Terms: Pays 50% commission. General price range: $165-$1000. Works with or without contract, negotiable. Offers limited regional exclusivity contract. Contracts renew automatically with each submission; no time limit. Charges duping fee of 50%/image. Statements issued quarterly. Payment made quarterly. Photographers allowed to review account records to verify sales figures. Offers one-time rights. Informs photographer and allows him to negotiate when client requests all rights. Model release is required for advertising, book covers or calendar sales. Photo captions required for scientific photos or geographic locations, etc.; include simple description if not evident from photo.
Making Contact: Photographers may write or call us for more information. We may ask for an initial submission of 150-300 chromes. Arrange a personal interview to show portfolio or query with samples. SASE. Published professionals only. Reports in 2 weeks. Guidelines sheet for SASE. Distributes a tips sheets twice a year.
Tips: Looks for well-composed, well-lit, sharp focused images with either a concept well illustrated or a mood conveyed by beauty or light. "Clear captions help our researchers choose wisely and ultimately improve sales. As far as trends in subject matter goes, strong, simple images conveying the American Spirit. . .families together, farming, scientific research, winning marathons, hikers reaching the top, are the winners. And include females doing 'male' jobs, black scientists, Hispanic professionals, Oriental children with a blend of others at play, etc. The importance of model releases for editorial covers, selected magazine usage and always for advertising/corporate clients cannot be stressed enough!"

■✹**REFLEXION PHOTOTHEQUE,** Suite 1000, 1255 Square Phillips, Montreal PQ H3B 3G1 Canada. (514)876-1620. President: Michel Gagne. Estab. 1981. Stock photo agency. Has 100,000 photos. Clients include: advertising agencies, public relations firms, audiovisual firms, businesses, book/encyclopedia publishers, magazine publishers, newspapers, postcard companies, calendar companies and greeting card companies.
Subject Needs: Model-released people of all ages in various activities. Also, beautiful homes, recreational sports, North American wildlife, industries, U.S. cities, antique cars, hunting and fishing scenes, food, and dogs and cats in studio setting.
Specs: Uses 35mm, 2¼×2¼, 4×5, 8×10 transparencies.
Payment & Terms: Pays 50% commission on color photos. Average price per image: $150-500. Enforces minimum prices. Offers volume discounts to customers; inquire about specific terms. Discount sales terms not negotiable. Works on contract basis only. Offers limited regional exclusive and non-exclusive contracts. Contracts renew automatically for five years. Charges 100% duping fee and 75% catalog insertion fee. Statements issued quarterly. Payment made monthly. Photographers allowed to review account records to verify sales figures. Offers one-time rights. Informs photographer and allows him to negotiate when client requests all rights. Model/property release preferred. Photo captions required; include country, place, city, or activity..
Making Contact: Interested in receiving work from newer, lesser-known photographers. Arrange a personal interview to show portfolio. Query with list of stock photo subjects. Submit portfolio for review. "We deal with local freelancers only." SASE. Reports in 1 month. Photo guidelines available.
Tips: "Limit your selection to 100 images. Images must be sharp and well exposed. Send only if you have high quality material on the listed subjects."

■**REX USA LTD (incorporating RDR),** 351 W. 54th St., New York NY 10019. (212)586-4432. FAX: (212)541-5724. Bureau Chief: April Sandmeyer. Estab. 1935. Stock photo agency, news/feature syndicate. Affiliated with Rex Features in London. Member of Picture Agency Council of America (PACA). Has 1,500,000 photos. Clients include: advertising agencies, public relations firms, audiovisual firms, businesses, book/encyclopedia publishers, magazine publishers, newspapers, postcard companies, calendar companies, greeting card companies and TV, film and record companies.
Subject Needs: Primarily editorial material: celebrities, personalities (studio portraits, candid, paparazzi), human interest, news features, movie stills, glamour, historical, geographic, general stock, sports and scientific.
Specs: Uses all sizes and finishes of b&w and color prints; 35mm, 2¼×2¼, 4×5, and 8×10 transparencies; b&w and color contact sheets; b&w and color negatives; VHS videotape.
Payment & Terms: NPI; varies depending on quality of subject matter and exclusivity. Pays 50% commission on b&w and color photos. Offers one-time rights, first rights and all rights. Model release and photo captions preferred.
Making Contact: Arrange a personal interview to show portfolio. Query with samples. Query with list of stock photo subjects. SASE. Reports in 1-2 weeks.

■**H. ARMSTRONG ROBERTS,** Dept. PM, 4203 Locust St., Philadelphia PA 19104. (215)386-6300. FAX: (215)386-5521. President: Bob Roberts. Estab. 1920. Stock photo agency. Member of the Picture Agency Council of America (PACA). Has 1 million + photos. Has branch offices, number not specified. Clients include: advertising agencies, public relations firms, audiovisual firms, businesses, book/

encyclopedia publishers, magazine publishers, newspapers, postcard publishers, calendar companies and greeting card companies.

Subject Needs: Uses images on all subjects in depth except personalities and news.

Specs: Uses b&w negatives only; 35mm, 2¼×2¼, 4×5 and 8×10 transparencies.

Payment & Terms: Buys only b&w negatives outright. NPI; rate varies. Pays 35% commission on b&w photos; 45-50% on color photos. Works with or without a signed contract, negotiable. Offers various contracts including exclusive, limited regional exclusivity, and nonexclusive. Guarantees subject exclusivity within files. Charges duping fee 5%/image. Charges .5%/image for catalog insertion. Statements issued monthly. Payment made monthly. Payment sent with statement. Photographers allowed to review account records to verify sales figures "upon advance notice." Offers one-time rights. Informs photographer and allows him to negotiate when client requests all rights. Model release and captions required.

Making Contact: Query with resume of credits; query with stock photo list. Does not keep samples on file. SASE. Reports in 1-2 weeks. Photo guidelines free with SASE. Catalog available "as supplies last." Market tips sheet free to contract photographers.

CHRIS ROBERTS REPRESENTS, P.O. Box 7218, Missoula MT 59807. (406)728-2180. Owner/Art Director: Chris Roberts. Photographer's representative company, stock photo agency. Has 3,000 photos.

Subject Needs: "We are building a specialty in images from the Western and Southwestern U.S., people, animals, nature, scenics, architecture, industry and livelihoods (cowboys, Indians, loggers, fishermen).

Specs: Uses 35mm and 4×5 transparencies.

Payment & Terms: Pays 50% on color photos. General price range: $45 minimum. Works on contract basis only. Offers non-exclusive contract. Payment made upon receipt of payment from client. Photographers allowed to review account records to verify sales figures. Offers one-time and limited rights. Informs photographer and allows him to negotiate when client requests all rights. Model releases (for recognizable faces) and photo captions required.

Making Contact: Interested in receiving work from newer, lesser-known photographers. Query with SASE. Arrange a personal interview to show portfolio. Send unsolicited photos by mail for consideration. Submit portfolio for review. Provide resume, business card, brochure, flyer or tearsheets to be kept on file for possible future assignments. SASE. Reports in 3 weeks. Submission guidelines available.

Tips: "If you've got a scenic or good location spot, put people doing something in it. Stock images 'want' people." In reviewing portfolio looks for "simplicity, composition, clarity, technical expertise."

*‡ROCA-SASTRE, AGENCIA ACI, Passeig de Gràcia, 92, Barcelona 08008 Spain. (93)487-2662 or (93)487-0534. FAX: (93)487-0538. Director: Elvira Roca-Sastre. Estab. 1980. Stock photo agency, news/feature syndicate. Has 1 million photos. Clients include: advertising agencies, public relations firms, audiovisual firms, book/encyclopedia publishers, magazine publishers, newspapers, postcard publishers, calendar companies, greeting card companies.

Subject Needs: General subjects, personalities and news features.

Specs: Uses 35mm, 2¼×2¼, 4×5, 8×10 transparencies.

Payment & Terms: Pays 60/40% commission on b&w and color photos. Offers volume discounts to customers. Works with or without a signed exclusive only contract. Statements issued monthly. Payment made monthly. Offers one-time rights. Informs photographer and allows him to negotiate when client requests all rights. Model/property release preferred. Captions preferred.

Making Contact: Arrange personal interview to show portfolio.

■RO-MA STOCK, 3101 W. Riverside Dr., Burbank CA 91505. (818)842-3777. FAX: (818)566-7380. Owner: Robert Marien. Estab. 1989. Stock photo agency. Member of Picture Agency Council of America (PACA). Has 30,000 photos. Clients include: advertising agencies, public relations firms, audiovisual firms, businesses, book/encyclopedia publishers, magazine publishers, postcard, calendar, greeting card and design companies.

Subject Needs: People involved with nature, leisure, family, children and sports. Also, nature, including animals, plants landscapes (macro/micro) and the environment.

Specs: Primarily uses 35mm, 2¼×2¼, 4×5, 8×10 and 70mm dupes. Also 8×10 b&w prints, contact sheets and negatives. Also b&w contact sheets and negatives.

Payment & Terms: Pays 30% commission on b&w photos; 50% commission on color photos. General price range: corporate $500-1,500; editorial $175-1,500; misc. $200-900; direct ad $500-2,500; advertising $250-3,000. Minimum price $100. Offers volume discounts to customers; terms specified in photog-

---

The code NPI (no payment information given) appears in listings that have not given specific payment amounts.

rapher's contract. Photographers can choose not to sell images on discount terms. Works on contract basis only. Offers limited regional exclusivity. Charges 100% uping fees, 50% catalog insertion fee. Statements issued quarterly. Payment made as soon as agency gets paid. Offers one-time rights. Informs photographer and allows him to negotiate when client requests all rights. Model/property release required for people, buildings houses, racing cars, motorcylces. Photo captions required for animals/plants, include common name, scientific name, habitat photographer's name; for others include subject, vocation, photographer's name.

Making Contact: Interested in receiving work from newer, lesser-known photographers. Arrange a personal interview to show portfolio. Query with resume of credits. "We deal with local freelancers only." SASE. Reports in 2 weeks. Photo guidelines $1. Market tips sheet distributed upon request to contracted photographers.

Tips: Wants to see "well-composed subject, high sharpness and color saturation." Sees strong demand for "family and children orientation, also good and healthy senior citizen situations. More people involved in outdoors activities and environment, details of architecture etc. More exotic food and travel. More high-tech and computer graphics. Patterns in nature also welcome."

■‡**SCIENCE PHOTO LIBRARY, LTD.**, 112 Westbourne Grove, London W2 5RU England. (071)727-4712. FAX: (071)727-6041. Research Director: Rosemary Taylor. Stock photo agency. Has 100,000 photos. Clients include: ad agencies, public relations firms, audiovisual firms, businesses, book/encyclopedia publishers, magazine publishers, newspapers, postcard companies, calendar companies and greeting card companies.

Subject Needs: SPL specializes in all aspects of science, medicine and technology. "Our interpretation of these areas is broad. We include earth sciences, landscape, and sky pictures; animals up to the size of insects (but not natural history pictures of birds, mammals etc.). We have a major and continuing need of high-quality photographs showing science, technology and medicine *at work*: laboratories, high-technology equipment, computers, lasers, robots, surgery, hospitals, etc. We are especially keen to sign up American freelance photographers who take a wide range of photographs in the fields of medicine and technology. We like to work closely with photographers, suggesting subject matter to them and developing photo features with them. We can only work with photographers who agree to us distributing their pictures throughout Europe, and preferably elsewhere. We duplicate selected pictures and syndicate them to our agents around the world."

Specs: Uses color prints; and 35mm, 2¼×2¼, 4×5, 6×7, 6×5 and 6×9 transparencies.

Payment & Terms: Pays 50% commission for b&w and color photos. General price range: $80-1,000; varies according to use. Only discount below minimum for volume or education. Offers volume discounts to customers; inquire about specific terms. Discount sales terms not negotiable. Works on contract basis only. Offers limited regional exclusivity; exceptions are made; subject to negotiation. Agreement made for four years; general continuation is assured unless otherwise advised. Statements issued quarterly. Payment made quarterly. Photographers allowed to review account records to verify sales figures; fully computerized accounts/commission handling system. Offers one-time rights. Model release and photo captions are required.

Making Contact: Interested in receiving work from newer, lesser-known photographers. Query with samples or query with list of stock photo subjects. Send unsolicited photos by mail for consideration. Returns material submitted for review. Reports in 3 weeks. Photo guidelines sheet for SASE. Distributes a tip sheet to our photographers.

Tips: Prefers to see "a small (20-50) selection showing the range of subjects covered and the *quality*, style and approach of the photographer's work. Our best-selling areas in the last 2 years have been medicine and technology. We see a continuing trend in the European market towards very high-quality, carefully-lit photographs. This is combined with a trend towards increasing use of medium and large-format photographs and decreasing use of 35mm (we make medium-format duplicates of some of our best 35mm); impact of digital storage/manipulation; problems of copyright and unpaid usage. The emphasis is on an increasingly professional approach to photography."

SHARPSHOOTERS, INC., #114, 4950 SW 72 Ave., Miami FL 33155. (305)666-1266. Manager, Photographer Relations: Edie Tobias. Estab. 1984. Stock photo agency. Member of Picture Agency Council of America (PACA). Has 300,000 photos. Clients include: advertising agencies.

Subject Needs: Model-released people for advertising use. Well-designed, styled photographs that capture the essence of life: children, families, couples at home, at work and at play.

Specs: Uses transparencies only, all formats.

Payment & Terms: Pays 50% commission on color photos. General price range: $250-10,000. Works on contract basis only. Offers exclusive contract only. Statements issued monthly. Payments made monthly. Offers one-time rights usually, "but if clients pay more they get more usage rights. We never offer all rights on photos." Model/property release required. Photo captions preferred.

Making Contact: Interested in receiving work from newer, lesser-known photographers. Query along with nonreturnable printed promotion pieces. Cannot return unsolicited material. Reports in 1 week.
Tips: Wants to see "technical excellence, originality, creativity and design sense, excellent ability to cast and direct talent, and commitment to shooting stock." Observes that "photographer should be in control of all elements of his/her production: casting, styling, props, location, etc., but be able to make a photograph that looks natural and spontaneous."

SILVER IMAGE PHOTO AGENCY, INC., 5128 NW 58th Court, Gainesville FL 32606. (904)373-5771. President/Owner: Carla Hotvedt. Estab. 1988. Stock photo agency. Assignments in Florida/S. Georgia. Has 20,000 color/b&w photos. Clients include: public relations firms, book/encyclopedia publishers, magazine publishers and newspapers.
Subject Needs: Florida-based travel/tourism, Florida cityscapes and people, nationally oriented topics such as drugs, environment, recycling, pollution, etc. Humorous people and animal photos.
Specs: Uses 8×10 glossy b&w prints; 35mm transparencies.
Payment & Terms: Pays 50% commission on b&w/color photos. General price range: $25-600. Works on contract basis only. Offers nonexclusive contract. Statements issued monthly. Payment made monthly. Offers one-time rights. Informs photographer and allows him to negotiate when client requests all rights. Model release preferred. Photo captions required: include name, year shot, city, state, etc.
Making Contact: Query with list of stock photo subjects. SASE; will return if query first. Reports on queries in 2 weeks; material—up to 2 months. Photo guidelines free with SASE. Tips sheets distributed as needed. SASE. Do not submit material unless requested first.
Tips: Looks for ability to tell a story in one photo. "I will look at photographer's work if they seem to have images outlined on my stock needs list which I will send out after receiving a query letter with SASE. Because of my photojournalistic approach my clients want to see people-oriented photos, not just pretty scenics. I also get many calls for drug-related photos and unique shots from Florida."

SILVER VISIONS, P.O. Box 2679, Aspen CO 81612. (313)923-3137. Owner: Joanne M. Johnson. Estab. 1987. Stock photo agency. Has 4,000 photos. Clients include: book/encyclopedia publishers, magazine publishers, postcard companies, calendar companies and greeting card companies.
Subject Needs: Emphasizes lifestyles—people, families, children, couples involved in work, sports, family outings, pets, etc. Also scenics of mountains and deserts, horses, dogs, cats, cityscapes—Denver, L.A., Chicago, Baltimore, NYC.
Specs: Uses 8×10 or 5×7 glossy or semigloss b&w prints; 35mm, 2¼×2¼ or 4×5 transparencies.
Payment & Terms: Pays 50% commission on b&w and color photos. General price range: $35-750. Offers one-time rights and English language rights. Model release and photo captions preferred.
Making Contact: Query with samples. SASE. Reports in 2 weeks. Photo guidelines free with SASE.
Tips: Wants to see "emotional impact or design impact created by composition and lighting. Photos must evoke a universal human interest appeal. Sharpness and good exposures—needless to say." Sees growing demand for "minority groups, senior citizens, fitness."

‡THE SLIDE FILE, 79 Merrion Square, Dublin 2 Ireland. (0001)766850. FAX: (0001)608332. Director/Photographer: George Munday. Stock photo agency and picture library. Has 50,000 photos. Clients include: ad agencies, public relations firms, businesses, book/encyclopedia publishers, magazine publishers, newspapers and designers.
Subject Needs: Overriding consideration is given to Irish or Irish-connected subjects. Has limited need for overseas locations, but is happy to accept material depicting other subjects, particularly people.
Specs: Uses 35mm, 2¼×2¼ and 4×5 transparencies.
Payment & Terms: Pays 50% commission on color photos. General price range: £60-1,000 English currency ($75-900). Offers one-time rights. Model release preferred; captions required.
Making Contact: Query with list of stock photo subjects. Works with local freelancers only. Does not return unsolicited material. Reports in 1 month.
Tips: "Apart from growing sales of Irish-oriented material, the trend seems to indicate increasing use of people shots—executives, families, couples, etc. particularly on medium format."

*SOUFOTO/EASTFOTO, INC., Suite 1505, 225 W 34th St., New York NY 10122. (212)564-5485. FAX: (212)564-4249. Director: Victoria Edwards. Estab. 1935. Stock photo agency. Has 800,000 photos. Clients include: audiovisual firms, book/encyclopedia publishers, magazine publishers, newspapers.
Subject Needs: Interested in photos of Eastern Europe, Russia, China.
Specs: Uses 8×10 glossy b&w and color prints; 35mm, 2¼×2¼ transparencies.
Payment & Terms: Pays 50% commission. Average price per image to clients $150-250/b&w photo; $150-250/color photo. Negotiates fees below standard minimum prices. "Bulk sales are negotiable." Offers volume discounts to customers. Offers exclusive contracts, limited regional exclusivity and non-

exclusivity. Statements issued quarterly. Payment made quarterly. Photographers permitted to review account records to verify sales figures or account for various deductions. Offers one-time, electronic media and non-exclusive rights. Informs photographer and allows him to negotiate when client requests all rights. Model/property release preferred. Captions required.

Making Contact: Arrange personal interview to show portfolio. Query with samples. Query with stock photo list. Samples kept on file. SASE. Expects minimum initial submission of 50-100 images. Reports in 1-2 weeks.

Tips: Looks for "news and general interest photos (color) with human element."

■**SOUTHERN STOCK PHOTO AGENCY,** Suite 33, 3601 W. Commercial Blvd., Ft. Lauderdale FL 33309. (305)486-7117. FAX: (305)486-7118. Contact: Marketing Director. Estab. 1976. Stock photo agency. Member of Picture Agency Council of America (PACA). Has 750,000 photos. Clients include: advertising agencies, design firms, businesses, book/encyclopedia publishers, magazine publishers, newspapers, calendar companies and greeting card companies.

Subject Needs: Needs photos of "southern U.S. cities, Bahamas, Caribbean, South America, and model-released lifestyle photos with young families and active seniors."

Specs: Uses color, 35mm, 2¼×2¼, 4×5 transparencies.

Payment & Terms: Pays 50% commission on color photos. General price range: $225-5,000. Offers contract. Statements issued bimonthly. Payment made bimonthly. Photographers not allowed to review account records to verify sales figures. Offers one-time rights, first time rights and all rights. Informs photographer and allows him to negotiate when client requests all rights. Model release and photo captions required.

Making Contact: Interested in receiving work from newer, lesser-known photographers. Query with samples. SASE. Reports in 1 month. Photo guidelines free with SASE.

Tips: In portfolio or samples, wants to see approximately 200 transparencies of a cross section of their work. Photographers "must be willing to submit regular new work."

SPECTRUM PHOTO, 3127 W. 12 Mile Rd., Berkley MI 48072. Phone: (313)398-3630. FAX: (313)398-3997. Manager: Corinne Bolton. Estab. 1990. Stock photo agency. Has 150,000 images. Clients include: ad agencies, public relations firms, businesses, magazine publishers, postcard publishers, calendar companies and display companies.

Subject Needs: All subjects, but especially "high-tech, business, industry, people, food, glamour and backgrounds."

Specs: Uses 8×10 glossy b&w prints; 35mm, 2¼×2¼ and 4×5 transparencies.

Payment & Terms: Pays 50% commission on b&w and color film. General price range: $50-300/b&w photo; $75-1,500/color photo. Works on contract basis only. Offers limited regional exclusivity. Contracts renew automatically with each submission; time period not specified. Charges duping fee of 50%/image. Statements issued monthly. Payment made bimonthly. Photographers allowed to review account records to verify sales figures. Offers one-time and electronic media rights. Requires agency promotion rights. Informs photographer and permits negotiation when client requests all rights, with some conditions. Model/property release and photo captions required.

Making Contact: Query with samples. Does not keep samples on file. SASE. Submit minimum of 50-100 images in initial query. Expects periodic submissions of 300-600 images each year. Reports in 3 weeks. Photo guidelines sheet free with SASE. Tips sheet available semiannually to contracted photographers.

Tips: Wants to see "creativity, technical excellence and marketability" in submitted images. "We have many requests for business-related images, high-tech, and people photos. Shoot as much as possible and send it to us."

*■‡**SPORTING PICTURES (UK), LTD.,** 7A Lambs Conduit Passage, London, WC1R 4RG England. (071)405-4500. FAX: (071)831-7991. Picture Editor: Steve Brown. Estab. 1972. Stock photo agency, picture library. Has 3 million photos. Clients include: advertising agencies, public relations firms, audiovisual firms, businesses, book/encyclopedia publishers, magazine publishers, newspapers, postcard companies, calendar companies and greeting card companies.

Subject Needs: Sport photos: gridiron, basketball, baseball, ice hockey, boxing and athletics.

Specs: Uses 35mm transparencies.

Payment & Terms: Enforces minimum prices. Works with or without a signed contract, negotiable. Statements issued quarterly. Payment made quarterly.

Making Contact: Submit portfolio for review. Samples kept on file "if pictures are suitable." SASE. Expects minimum initial submission of 50 images. Reports ASAP.

***SPORTS LENS, INC.,** 570 H Grand St.-H-1102, New York NY 10002. (212)979-0873. President: Tony Furnari. Stock photo agency. Has 50,000 photos. Clients include: advertising agencies, public relations firms, audiovisual firms, businesses, book/encyclopedia publishers, magazine publishers, newspapers, calendar companies, greeting card companies, sports related companies.

Subject Needs: All sports: pro golf, strobed basketball and track and field.

Specs: Uses 35mm, 2¼×2¼ transparencies.

Payment & Terms: Pays 50% commission on b&w and color photos. Average price per image (to clients): $75-150/b&w photo; $125-500/color photo. Enforces minimum prices. Offers volume discounts to customers; terms specified in photographer's contract. Discount sales terms not negotiable. Works with or without a signed contract, negotiable. Statements issued per usage of slide. Payment made ASAP, pending client payment. Photographers permitted to review account records to verify sales figures or account for various deductions "upon request." Offers one-time rights. Model/property release preferred with generic sports photos. Captions required.

Making Contact: Query with resume of credits. Expects minimum initial submission of 100 slides. Reports in 1-2 weeks. Market tips sheet free on request distributed when needed to Sports Lens, Inc. photographers only.

Tips: Looks for "Professional quality, sharp images, action, head shots. No dupes ever used. Originals only."

SPORTSLIGHT PHOTO, Suite 800, 127 W. 26 St., New York NY 10001. (212)727-9727. Director: Roderick Beebe. Stock photo agency. Has 250,000 photos. Clients include: ad agencies, public relations firms, businesses, book/encyclopedia publishers, magazine publishers, newspapers, postcard companies, calendar companies, greeting card companies and design firms.

Subject Needs: "We specialize in every sport in the world. We deal primarily in the recreational sports such as skiing, golf, tennis, running, canoeing, etc., but are expanding into pro sports, and have needs for all pro sports, action and candid close-ups of top athletes. We also handle adventure-travel photos, e.g., rafting in Chile, trekking in Nepal, dogsledding in the Arctic, etc."

Specs: Uses 35mm transparencies.

Payment & Terms: Pays 50% commission. General price range: $70-3,000. Contract negotiable. Offers limited regional exclusivity. Contract is of indefinite length until either party (agency or photographer) seeks termination. Statements issued quarterly. Payment made quarterly. Photographers allowed to review account records to verify sales figures "when discrepancy occurs." Offers one-time rights, rights depend on client, sometimes exclusive rights for a period of time. Informs photographer and allows him to negotiate when client requests all rights. Model release required for corporate and advertising usage; captions required. (Obtain releases whenever possible). Strong need for model-released "pro-type" sports.

Making Contact: Interested in receiving work from newer, lesser-known photographers. Query with list of stock photo subjects, "send samples *after* our response." SASE must be included. Cannot return unsolicited material. In reviewing work looks for "range of sports subjects that show photographer's grasp of the action, drama, color and intensity of sports, as well as capability of capturing great shots under all conditions in all sports." Reports in 2-4 weeks. Photo guideline sheet free with SASE.

Tips: "Well edited, perfect exposure and sharpness, good composition and lighting in all photos. Seeking photographers with strong interests in particular sports. Shoot variety of action, singles and groups, youths, male/female—all combinations. Plus leisure, relaxing after tennis, lunch on the ski slope, golf's 19th hole, etc. Clients are looking for all sports these days. All ages, also. Sports fashions change rapidly, so that is a factor. Art direction of photo shoots is important. Avoid brand names and minor flaws in the look of clothing. Attention to detail is very important. Shoot with concepts/ideas such as teamwork, determination, success, lifestyle, leisure, cooperation and more in mind. Clients look not only for individual sports, but for photos to illustrate a mood or idea. There is a trend toward use of real-life action photos in advertising as opposed to the set-up slick ad look. More unusual shots are being used to express feeling, attitude, etc."

■TOM STACK & ASSOCIATES, Suite 212, 3645 Jeannine Dr., Colorado Springs CO 80917. (719)570-1000. Contact: Jamie Stack. Member: Picture Agency Council of America (PACA). Has 1.5 million photos. Clients include: ad agencies, public relations firms, businesses, audiovisual firms, book publishers, magazine publishers, encyclopedia publishers, postcard companies, calendar companies and greeting card companies.

Subject Needs: Wildlife, endangered species, marine-life, landscapes, foreign geography, people and customs, children, sports, abstract/arty and moody shots, plants and flowers, photomicrography, scientific research, current events and political figures, Indians, etc. Especially needs women in "men's" occupations; whales; solar heating; up-to-date transparencies of foreign countries and people; smaller mammals such as weasels, moles, shrews, fisher, marten, etc.; extremely rare endangered wildlife; wildlife behavior photos; current sports; lightning and tornadoes; hurricane damage. Sharp images, dramatic and unusual angles and approach to composition, creative and original photography with impact. Especially needs photos on life science flora and fauna and photomicrography. No run-of-the-mill travel or vacation shots. Special needs include photos of energy-related topics—solar and

The athletic power of these two hurdlers at the New York Games coupled with sharp focus and tight cropping make this an awesome image for photographer Roderick Beebe, of Sportslight. The New York City agency sold the shot for $400 to Mita Copystar which ran the image in a corporate newsletter. The photo accompanied a story on the New York Games, which the company sponsored.

wind generators, recycling, nuclear power and coal burning plants, waste disposal and landfills, oil and gas drilling, supertankers, electric cars, geo-thermal energy.
Specs: Uses 35mm transparencies.
Payment & Terms: Does not buy outright; pays 60% commission. General price range: $150-200/color; as high as $7,000. Offers one-time rights, all rights or first rights. Model release and captions preferred.
Making Contact: Query with list of stock photo subjects or send at least 800 transparencies for consideration. SASE or mailer for photos. Reports in 2 weeks. Photo guidelines with SASE.
Tips: "Strive to be original, creative and take an unusual approach to the commonplace; do it in a different and fresh way." Have need for "more action and behavioral requests for wildlife. We are large enough to market worldwide and yet small enough to be personable. Don't get lost in the 'New York' crunch—try us. Shoot quantity. We try harder to keep our photographers happy. We attempt to turn new submissions around within 2 weeks. We take on only the best, and so that we can continue to give more effective service."

*■THE STOCK ADVANTAGE, 213 N 12th St., Allentown PA 18102. (215)776-7381. FAX: (215)776-1831. Director of Marketing: James Gallucci. Estab. 1986. Stock photo agency. Has 100,000 photos; 3,500 feet of film. Clients include: advertising agencies, public relations firms, businesses, book/encyclopedia publishers, magazine publishers, newspapers and TV, video/film producers.
Subject Needs: Regional, lifestyle and business photos.
Specs: Uses 35mm, 2¼×2¼, 4×5 transparencies; all types of film/video.
Payment & Terms: Pays 50% commission. Average price per image to clients $350-500/color photo. Enforces minimum prices. Offers volume discounts to customers; inquire about specific terms. Discount sales terms not negotiable. Works on contract basis only; offers non-exclusive contracts. Contracts renew automatically after two-year period has elapsed. Charges shipping and handling. Statements issued monthly. Payment made monthly. Offers one-time and electronic media rights; negotiable. Model/property release preferred. Captions required.
Making Contact: Arrange personal interview to show portfolio. Query with samples. SASE. Expects minimum initial submission of 500 images with bi-monthly submissions of at least 200. Reports in 1-2 weeks. Photo guidelines free with SASE. Free catalog available. Market tips sheet distributed to agency members and non-members upon request.

Tips: "Subjects vary based on photographer's interests. Images are accepted on most formats, all must be of good composition, high resolution, film of little grain and correct exposures."

■**STOCK BOSTON INC.**, Dept. PM, 36 Gloucester St., Boston MA 02115. (617)266-2300. Manager of Editing: Jean Howard. Estab. 1970. Stock photo agency. Member of Picture Agency Council of America (PACA). Clients include: advertising agencies, public relations firms, audiovisual firms, businesses, book/encyclopedia publishers, magazine publishers, newspapers, postcard companies, calendar companies and greeting card companies.
Subject Needs: "We seek pictures of real people in their everyday lives. Technical quality must be excellent, model releases are preferred."
Specs: Uses 8×10 b&w prints; 35mm, 2¼×2¼, 4×5, 8×10 transparencies.
Payment & Terms: Pays 50% on b&w and color photos. General price range: $175-up. Offers one-time rights. Model release and photo captions preferred.
Making Contact: Send SASE for information. Reports in 1 week. Photo guidelines available on acceptance. Tips sheet distributed quarterly to contributors.
Tips: In freelancers' portfolios or samples, wants to see "a representative sample of the type of work they typically shoot: 50-100 b&w prints, 100-200 transparencies. Please request more information." Trends in stock include "a swing away from the bland, over-lit studio set-up and move towards a realistic approach. B&w still does quite well at Stock Boston, particularly in the editorial market."

■**THE STOCK BROKER**, Dept. PM, Suite 110, 450 Lincoln St., Denver CO 80203. (303)698-1734. Contact: Jeff Cook. Estab. 1981. Stock photo agency. Member of Picture Agency Council of America (PACA). Has 200,000 photos. Clients include: advertising agencies, public relations firms, audiovisual firms, businesses, book/encyclopedia publishers, magazine publishers and calendar companies.
Subject Needs: Recreational and adventure sports, travel, nature, business/industry and people.
Specs: Uses 8×10 glossy b&w prints; 35mm, 2¼×2¼, 4×5 or 8×10 transparencies.
Payment & Terms: Pays 50% commission on color and b&w photos. General price range: $200-4,000. Offers one-time rights. Model release required.
Making Contact: Query with samples. SASE. Reports in 1 month. Photo guidelines free with SASE. Market tips sheet distributed to contract photographers.
Tips: "Since we rarely add new photographers we look for outstanding work both asthetically and technically. Photos that are conceptual, simple, graphic, and bright and work well for advertising are selected over those that are simply documentary, busy or subtle. Clients are getting more daring and creative and expect better quality. Each year this has caused our standards to go up and our view of what a stock photo is to expand."

*****STOCK IMAGERY, INC.**, 711 Kalamath, Denver CO 80204. (303)592-1091. FAX: (303)592-1278. President: Garry Adams. Estab. 1980. Stock photo agency. Members of Picture Agency Council of America (PACA). Has 100,000+ photos. "We also deal with a network of sub-agents in 15 countries around the world." Clients include: advertising agencies, public relations firms, audiovisual firms, businesses, book/encyclopedia publishers, magazine publishers, newspapers, postcard publishers, calendar companies, greeting card companies, TV.
Subject Needs: All subjects.
Specs: Uses 35mm, 2¼×2¼, 4×5, 8×10, transparencies.
Payment & Terms: Pays 50% commission on color photos. Average price per image (to clients): color $175+. "We have set prices, but under special circumstances we contact photographer prior to negotiations." Works on contract basis only; exclusive or nonexclusive. Contracts run 5 years and renew for 3 additional years. Charges vary for promotions/catalogs; 100% for file dupes. "Duplicates and catalog fees are deducted from photographer's resulting commissions at a rate not to exceed 50% in any one quarter." Payment made quarterly. Photographers are allowed to review account records by appointment only. Offers one-time rights or unlimited, exclusive rights (1 year). Informs photographer and allows him to negotiate when client requests all rights. Model/property release is required. Captions required.
Making Contact: Arrange personal interview to show portfolio. Query with samples. Query with stock photo list. Samples kept on file. SASE. Minimum number of images in initial submission varies. "Photographer must have 250 images on file to be put under contract." Photo guidelines free with SASE. Market tips sheet distributed quarterly. Sent with photographer's commission reports or free with SASE.
Tips: In samples looks for "high-caliber, natural style of work. Growing trend in environmental photography (pro and con), and natural, 'average' people instead of slickly posed models. Abstract and computer-graphics-type work growing also."

■**THE STOCK MARKET**, 360 Park Ave. South, New York NY 10010. (212)684-7878. Contact: Sally Lloyd/Kelly Foster. Estab. 1981. Stock photo agency. Member of Picture Agency Council of America (PACA). Has 1,600,000 photos. Clients include: advertising agencies, public relations firms, corporate design firms, book/encyclopedia publishers, magazine publishers, newspapers, postcard companies, calendar companies and greeting card companies.

Subject Needs: Topics include lifestyle, corporate, industry, nature and travel.

Specs: Uses color, all formats.

Payment & Terms: Pays 50% gross sale on color photos. Works on exclusive contract basis only. Charges catalog insertion fee of 50%/image for U.S. edition only. Statements issued bimonthly. Payment made bimonthly. Photographers allowed to review account records to verify sales figures. Offers one-time rights and first rights. When client requests to buy all rights, "we ask permission of photographer, then we negotiate." Model and property release preferred for all people, private homes, boats, cars, property. Photo captions are required; include: "what and where."

Making Contact: Arrange a personal interview to show portfolio. Query with samples. Submit portfolio of 250 transparencies in vinyl sheets. SASE. Reports in 2-3 weeks. Tips sheet distributed as needed to contract photographers only.

■**STOCK OPTIONS,** 4602 East Side Ave., Dallas TX 75226. (214)826-6262. FAX: (214)826-6263. Owner: Karen Hughes. Estab. 1985. Stock photo agency. Member of Picture Agency Council of America (PACA). Has 50,000 photos. Clients include: advertising agencies, public relations firms, audiovisual firms, corporations, book/encyclopedia, magazine publishers, newspapers, postcard companies, calendar and greeting card companies. "We are a subsidiary for Camerarique Ave. Int'l."

Subject Needs: Emphasizes the southern US. Files include Gulf Coast scenics, wildlife, fishing, festivals, food, industry, business, people, etc. Also western folklore.

Specs: Uses 35mm, 2¼×2¼ and 4×5 transparencies and 70mm.

Payment & Terms: Pays 50% commission on b&w or color photos. General price range: $300-1,500. Works on contract basis only. Offers nonexclusive contract. Contract automatically renews with each submission to 5 years from expiration date. Charges catalog insertion fee of $300/image and marketing fee of $5/hour. Statements issued upon receipt of payment. Payment made immediately. Photographers allowed to review account records to verify sales figures. Offers one-time and electronic media rights. "We will inform photographers for their consent only when a client requests all rights, but we will handle all negotiations." Model and property release is preferred, people, some properties, all models. Photo captions are required; include subject and location.

Making Contact: Interested in receiving work from newer, lesser-known photographers. Arrange a personal interview to show portfolio. Query with list of stock photo subjects. Contact by "query and submit 200 sample photos." Works with local freelancers only. SASE. Reports in 1 month. Tips sheet distributed annually to all photographers.

Tips: Wants to see "clean, in focus, relevant and current materials." Current stock requests include: industry, environmental subjects, people in up-beat situations, food, Texas cities and rural scenics.

■‡**STOCK PHOTOS,** Carbonero y Sol, 30, Madrid 28006 Spain. (1)564-4095. FAX: (1)564-4353. Director: Marcelo Brodsky. Estab. 1988. Stock photo agency and news/feature syndicate. Has 150,000 photos. Clients include: advertising agencies, audiovisual firms, businesses, book/encyclopedia publishers, magazine publishers and newspapers.

Subject Needs: Stock photography for advertising with model-released people, top quality magazine stories with short text and people.

Specs: "We specialize in advertising in our ad section and we also handle magazine photography in our editorial section." Uses 35mm b&w prints; 35mm, 2¼×2¼, 4×5, 8×10 transparencies.

Payment & Terms: Pays 50% commission on color photos. General price range: Minimum $90-1,500. Offers one-time rights. Model release required for advertising materials.

Making Contact: Query with samples. Reports in 3 weeks. Tips sheet distributed once a year to working photographers; free with SASE.

Tips: Looks for "transparencies of technical excellence, professionalism in producing stock and knowledge of the needs of this market, whether editorial or advertising. We need high-tech imagery, high-tech stories/reportage for magazines, pictures with models, teenagers, people consuming, people doing their professions, medicine, etc. Portraits of celebrities have another area of the market and we also sell them very well in Spain."

■**STOCK PILE, INC.,** Main office: Dept. PM, 2404 N. Charles St., Baltimore MD 21218. (301)889-4243. Branch: Box 15384, Rio Rancho NM 87174. (505)892-7288. Vice President: D.B. Cooper. Picture library. Has 28,000 photos. Clients include: ad agencies, art studios, slide show producers, etc.

Subject Needs: General agency looking for well-lit, properly composed images that will attract attention. Also, people, places and things that lend themselves to an advertising-oriented marketplace.
Specs: Transparencies, all formats. Some black and white, 8 × 10 glossies.
Payment & Terms: Pays 50% commission on b&w and color photos. Offers one-time rights. Model release preferred; captions required.
Making Contact: Inquire for guidelines, submit directly (minimum 100) or call for personal interview. All inquiries and submissions must be accompanied by SASE. *Send all submissions to New Mexico address.*
Tips: Periodic newsletter sent to all regular contributing photographers.

THE STOCK SHOP, 232 Madison Ave., New York NY 10016. (212)679-8480. FAX: (212)532-1934. President: Barbara Gottlieb. Estab. 1975. Member of Picture Agency Council of America (PACA). Has 2,000,000 photos. Clients include: advertising agencies, public relations firms, businesses, book/encyclopedia publishers, magazine publishers, postcard companies, calendar companies and greeting card companies.
Subject Needs: Needs photos of travel, industry and medicine. Also model released life-style including old age, couples, babies, men, women, families.
Specs: Uses 35mm, 2¼ × 2¼, 4 × 5 and 8 × 10 transparencies.
Payment & Terms: Pays 50% commission on color photos. General price range: $150 and up. Works on exclusive contract basis only. Contracts renew automatically with each submission for length of original contract. Charges catalog insertion fee of 7½%/image. Statements issued monthly. Payment made monthly. Offers one-time rights. Does not inform photographer of clients request for all rights. Model release and photo captions required.
Making Contact: Arrange a personal interview to show portfolio. Submit portfolio for review. SASE. Tips sheet distributed as needed to contract photographers only.
Tips: Wants to see "a cross section of the style and subjects the photographer has in his library. 200-300 samples should tell the story. Photographers should have at least 1,000 in their library. Photographers should not photograph people *before* getting a model release. The day of the 'grab shot' is over."

THE STOCK SOLUTION, 307 W. 200 South, #3004, Salt Lake City UT 84101. (801)363-9700. FAX: (801)363-9707. President: Royce Bair. Stock photo agency. Member of Picture Agency Council of America (PACA). Has 150,000 photos. Clients include: ad agencies, businesses, book/encyclopedia and magazine publishers, calendar companies and design studios. Also operates newsletter (twice/month) called "Expressline" which provides want lists for photographers.
Subject Needs: Leisure, outdoor recreation, business, finance, industry, health/medical, education, family/children, national parks, major cities, commerce, transportation. Nature and scenics only on a limited basis.
Specs: Uses 35mm, 2¼ × 2¼, 4 × 5 and 8 × 10 transparencies; also 8 × 10 b&w prints.
Payment & Terms: Pays 50% commission on color photos. General price range: $250-500; "minimum usually $150, maximum is unlimited." Works on contract basis only. Offers nonexclusive contract. Statements issued quarterly. Payment made periodically. "Photos with net sales of $500/month or more are paid monthly." Photographers may review account records to verify sales. Offers one-time rights; occasionally, one-year exclusives for advertising or calendar. Informs photographer and allows him to negotiate when client requests all rights. Model/property release is preferred, "but required for advertising use sales." Photo captions are preferred; include: "who (I.D. person(s) in photo and give model release info.), and *where* (state or country and city or what mountain range or what national park, etc.)"
Making Contact: Query with resume of credits, samples, list of stock photo subjects. Submit portfolio for review. SASE. Reports in 2 weeks. Photo guidelines free with SASE. Tips sheet sent quarterly free to contract photographers; $3 for inquiring, noncontract photographers.
Tips: "We can usually determine with a portfolio of only 100 slides if we want to represent a photographer. We actively seek photographers who photograph people in real-life situations of home, family and work, but who are willing to make the extra effort necessary to prop and light the scene in order to make it more salable to today's demanding clients in advertising and publishing." Does not require exclusive contract, but offers worldwide representation if requested. Recommends reading the *ASMP Stock Photography Handbook.*

■**STOCK SOUTH,** Suite K-2, 75 Bennett St. NW, Atlanta GA 30309. (404)352-0538. FAX: (404)352-0563. President: David Perdew. Estab. 1989. Stock photo agency. Has 150,000 photos; color and b&w. Clients include: advertising agencies, public relations firms, audiovisual firms, businesses, book/encyclopedia publishers, magazine publishers and newspapers. Holds photographs on consignment.

© Lance Beeny

The photo-listing newsletter "Expressline," published by The Stock Solution, helped photographer Lance Beeny, of Sandy, Utah, capitalize on the needs of Inbound/Out-bound Magazine. The layout of the shot worked well for the cover of the publication and earned Beeny $500. The image of the keyhole with the skeleton key leaves the viewer wondering what lies on the other side of the door. The lighting of the subject makes the photo a success.

Subject Needs: Lifestyles, corporate, leisure, travel (southeastern particularly). All should be model- and property-released.
Specs: Uses 8×10 glossy b&w prints; 35mm, 2¼×2¼, and 4×5 transparencies.
Payment & Terms: Pays 50% commission on b&w and color photos. General price range: $250-1,000. Rights negotiable. Model release required.
Making Contact: Query with samples. SASE. Reports in 3 weeks. Photo guidelines free with SASE. Market tips sheet distributed monthly to contracted photographers.
Tips: Wants to see photos that are "model-released, clean, dramatic and graphic. In all situations, we're looking for outstanding photographs that are better than anything we've seen. Edit tightly."

■**THE STOCKHOUSE, INC.**, Box 741008, Houston TX 77274. (713)796-8400. FAX: (713)796-8047. Sales and Marketing Director: Celia Jumonville. Stock photo agency. Member of Picture Agency Council of America (PACA). Has 500,000 photos. Clients include: advertising agencies, public relations firms, audiovisual firms, businesses, book/encyclopedia publishers, magazine publishers, newspapers, postcard companies, calendar companies and greeting card companies.
Subject Needs: Needs photos of general topics from travel to industry, lifestyles, nature, US and foreign countries. Especially interested in Texas and petroleum and medical.
Specs: Uses 35mm, 2¼×2¼, 4×5, 8×10 transparencies; "originals only."
Payment & Terms: Pays 50% commission on color photos. General price range: $150-1,000. Works on contract basis only. Offers limited regional exclusivity. Statements issued monthly. Payment made following month after payment by client. Photographers allowed to review account records to verify sales figures by appointment. Offers one-time rights; other rights negotiable. Informs photographer and allows him to negotiate when client requests all rights; must be handled through the agency only. Model/property release preferred for people and personal property for advertising use; photographer retains written release. Photo captions required; include location, date and description of activity or process.
Making Contact: Interested in receiving work from newer, lesser-known photographers. Query with samples; request guidelines and tipsheet. SASE. Photo guidelines free with SASE. Tips sheet distributed quarterly to contract photographers.
Tips: In freelancers' samples, wants to see "quality of photos—color saturation, focus and composition. Also variety of subjects and 200-300 transparencies on the first submission. Trends in stock vary depending on the economy and who is needing photos. Quality is the first consideration and subject second. We do not limit the subjects submitted since we never know what will be requested next. Industry and lifestyles and current skylines are always good choices." (Submissions send to 9261 Kirby Dr. Houston TX 77054.)

■**TONY STONE WORLDWIDE LTD.**, #240, 6100 Wilshire Blvd., Los Angeles CA 90048. (213)938-1700. Tony Stone Worldwide Ltd. (offices in 15 locations worldwide). Creative Manager: Sarah Stone. Estab. in U.S. 1988, Worldwide 1968. Stock photo agency. Member of Picture Agency Council of America (PACA). Clients include: advertising agencies, public relations firms, audiovisual firms, businesses, book/encyclopedia publishers, magazine publishers, newspapers, calendar, greeting card and travel companies.
Subject Needs: Very high quality, technically and creatively excellent stock imagery on all general subjects for worldwide and US distribution.
Specs: Uses b&w prints; 35mm, 2¼×2¼, 4×5 and 8×10 transparencies.
Payment & Terms: Pays 50% commission on b&w and color photos. General price range: $150-24,000. "Minimum price is $100 unless very exceptional circumstances, e.g., very specialized, low-level usage or limited exposure of imagery." Offers volume discounts to customers, "but *maximum* 10% and then rarely;" inquire about specific terms. Works on contract basis only. "We have *seven* levels of exclusivity." Charges catalog insertion fee. Statements issued monthly. Payment made quarterly. Access to records only allowed in case of suspicion of fraud or definite variance between payments and sales statements. Offers various rights. "When client requests all rights, we ask photographer's permission and negotiate accordingly." Model/property release required. Photo captions required with as much detail as possible.
Making Contact: Query with resume of credits. Query with samples; "never send unsolicited photos by mail for consideration." Reports in 2 weeks. Photo guidelines free with SASE. Market tips sheet distributed quarterly to contracted photographers.
Tips: Wants to see "technical ability, creativity. Commitment to high standards." Sees increased demand for high quality. "If you can't shoot better imagery than that already available, don't bother at all."

■**SUPERSTOCK INC./SUPERSTOCK CATALOG**, Dept. PM, 11 W. 19th St., New York NY 10011. (212)633-0708. Director of Photographer Relations: Jane Stoffo. Stock photo agency. Has more than 300,000 photos in file. Clients include: ad agencies, public relations firms, audiovisual firms, businesses,

book/encyclopedia publishers, magazine publishers, newspapers, postcard companies, calendar companies, greeting card companies and major corporations.
Subject Needs: "We are a general stock agency involved in all markets, our files are comprised of all subject matter."
Specs: Uses 35mm, 2¼×2¼, 4×5 and 8×10 transparencies.
Payment & Terms: "We work on a contract basis." Contracts renew automatically with each submission for five years. Statements issued monthly. Payment made monthly. Photographers allowed to review account records to verify sales figures. Rights offered "varies, depending on client's request." Informs photographer and allows him to negotiate when client requests all rights. Model release and photo captions required.
Making Contact: Query with resume of credits; query with tearsheets only; query with list of stock photo subjects; submit portfolio for review "when requested." SASE. Reports in 3 weeks. Photo guidelines sheet free with SASE or sent if requested via phone. Newsletter distributed monthly to contracted photographers.
Tips: "The use of catalogs as a buying source is a very effective means of promoting photographs, and a continuing trend in the industry is the importance of bigger, comprehensive catalogs. We produce the SuperStock Photo Catalog in the US. Space is available to professional photographers regardless of any of their other photographic affiliations. Participation in this catalog provides an excellent opportunity for photographers to take advantage of the growing international market for stock, and receive the highest royalty percentage for internationally distributed photographs."

■✤**TAKE STOCK INC.**, 705, 603 7th Ave. SW, Calgary AB T2P 2T5 Canada. (403)233-7487. FAX: (403)265-4061. Vice President: Helen Grenon. Estab. 1987. Stock photo agency. Clients include: advertising agencies, public relations firms, audiovisual firms, corporate, book/encyclopedia publishers, magazine publishers, newspapers, postcard companies, calendar companies and greeting card companies.
Subject Needs: Model-released people (all ages), Canadian images, arts/recreation, industry/occupation, business, high-tech.
Specs: Uses 35mm, 2¼×2¼, 4×5, 8×10 transparencies. Prefer medium to large format.
Payment & Terms: Pays 50% commission on transparencies. General price range: $80-600. Works on contract basis only. Offers limited regional exclusivity. Contracts renew automatically with additional submissions with "1-year review then every 3 years." Charges 100% duping fees. Statements issued monthly. Payment made monthly. Photographers allowed to review account records to verify sales figures, "anytime by appointment." Offers one-time rights, exclusive rights. Informs photographer and allows him to negotiate when client requests all rights. Model/property release and photo caption required.
Making Contact: Query with list of stock photo subjects. SASE. Reports in 3 weeks. Photo guidelines free with SASE. Tips sheet distributed monthly to photographers on file.

■‡**TANK INCORPORATED**, Box 212, Shinjuku, Tokyo 160-91, Japan. (03)239-1431. Telex: 26347 PHT-PRESS. FAX: 03230-3668. President: Masayoshi Seki. Has 500,000 slides. Clients include advertising agencies, encyclopedia/book publishers, magazine publishers and newspapers.
Subject Needs: "Women in various situations, families, special effect and abstract, nudes, scenic, sports, animal, celebrities, flowers, picture stories with texts, humorous photos, etc."
Specs: Uses 8×10 b&w prints; 35mm, 2¼×2¼ and 4×5 slides; b&w contact sheets; videotape.
Payment & Terms: Pays 40% commission on b&w and color photos. "As for video, we negotiate at case by case basis." General price range: $70-1,000. Works with or without a signed contract; negotiable. Offers guaranteed subject exclusivity within files. Contracts renew automatically with each submission for 3 years. Statements issued monthly. Payment made monthly; within 45 days. Photographers not allowed to review account records to verify sales figures. Offers one-time rights. Informs photographer and allows him to negotiate when client requests all rights. Model and property release is required for glamour/nude sets. Photo captions required.
Making Contact: Interested in receiving work from newer, lesser-known photographers. Query with samples, with list of stock photo subjects or send unsolicited material by mail for consideration. SASE. Reports in 1 month. Photo guidelines free with International Reply Coupons.
Tips: "We need some pictures or subjects which strike viewers. Pop or rock musicians are very much in demand. If you want to make quick sales, give us some story ideas with sample pictures which show quality, and we will respond to you very quickly. Also, give us brief bio. Color transparencies with

---

✤ *The maple leaf before a listing indicates that the market is Canadian. The symbol is new this year in* Photographer's Market.

sample stories to accompany—no color prints at all. Stock photography business requires patience. Try to find some other subjects than your competitors. Keep a fresh mind to see salable subjects." Remarks that "photographers should have eyes of photo editor. Try to take photos which make editors use them easily. Also, give a little back ground of these photos."

TERRAPHOTOGRAPHICS/BPS, Box 490, Moss Beach CA 94038. (415)726-6244. Photo Agent: Carl May. Stock photo agency. Has 25,000 photos on hand; 70,000 on short notice. Clients include: ad agencies, businesses, book/encyclopedia publishers and magazine publishers.
Subject Needs: All subjects in the Earth sciences: paleontology, volcanology, seismology, petrology, oceanography, climatology, mining, petroleum industry, civil engineering, meteorology, astronomy. Stock photographers must be scientists. "Currently, we need more on energy resource conservation, natural and cut gems, economic minerals, recent natural disasters and severe weather." Environmental issues are hot topics. Much more needed from the Third World, formerly Communist countries and the Middle East.
Specs: Uses 8×10 glossy b&w prints; 35mm, 2¼×2¼, 4×5 and 8×10 transparencies.
Payment & Terms: Pays 50% commission on all photos. General price range: $90-500. Works with or without a signed contract, negotiable. Offers exclusive contract only. Contracts have automatic renewal clauses; time period not specified. Statements issued quarterly. Payment quarterly within one month of end of quarter. Photographers allowed to review account records to verify sales figures. Offers one-time rights; other rights negotiable. However, "this rarely happens at our agency." Informs photographer and allows him to negotiate when client requests all rights. Model release required for any commercial use, but not purely editorial. Photo captions required; include "all information necessary to identify subject matter and give geographical location."
Making Contact: Query with list, and resume of scientific and photographic background. SASE. Reports in 2 weeks. Photo guidelines free with query, resume and SASE. Tips sheet distributed intermittently only to stock photographers.
Tips: Prefers to see proper exposure, maximum depth of field, interesting composition, good technical and general information in caption. Natural disasters of all sorts, especially volcanic eruptions, storms and earthquakes; scientists at work using modern equipment. "We are a suitable agency only for those with both photographic skills and sufficient technical expertise to identify subject matter. We only respond to those who provide a rundown of their scientific and photographic background and at least a brief description of coverage. Captions must be neat and contain precise information on geographical locations. Don't waste your time submitting images on grainy film. Our photographers should be able to distinguish between dramatic, compelling examples of phenomena and run-of-the-mill images in the earth and environmental sciences. We need more on all sorts of weather phenomena; the petroleum and mining industries from exploration through refinement; problems and management of toxic wastes; environmental problems associated with resource development; natural areas threatened by development; and oceanography."

■**THIRD COAST STOCK SOURCE,** P.O. Box 92397, Milwaukee WI 53202. (414)765-9442. Director: Paul Henning. Managing Editor: Mary Ann Platts. Research Manager: Paul Butterbrodt. Editorial Manager: J.P. Slater. Member of Picture Agency Council of America (PACA). Has over 100,000 photos. Clients include: ad agencies, public relations firms, audiovisual firms, corporations, book/encyclopedia publishers, magazine publishers, newspapers, calendar companies and greeting card companies.
Subject Needs: People in lifestyle situations, business, industry, medium format scenics (domestic and foreign), traditional stock photo themes with a new spin.
Specs: Uses 35mm, 2¼×2¼, 4×5 and 8×10 transparencies (slow and medium speed color tranparency film preferred).
Payment & Terms: Pays 50% commission on b&w and color photos. General price range: $200 and up. Enforces minimum prices. Works on contract basis only. Offers limited regional exclusivity. Contracts with photographers renew automatically for 5 years. Charges duping and catalog insertion fee. Statements issued quarterly. Payment made quarterly. Photographers allowed to review account records to verify sales figures. Offers one-time rights. Informs photographer and allows him to negotiate when client requests all rights. Model release required in most cases; captions required.
Making Contact: Interested in receiving work from newer, lesser-known photographers. Submit 200-300 images for review. SASE. Reports in 1 month. Photo guidelines free with SASE. Tips sheet distributed 4 times/year to "photographers currently working with us."
Tips: "We are looking for technical expertise; outstanding, dramatic and emotional appeal. We are anxious to look at new work. Learn what stock photography is all about. Our biggest need is for photos of model-released people: couples, seniors, business situations, recreational situations, etc. Also, we find it very difficult to get great winter activity scenes (again, with people) and photos which illustrate holidays: Christmas, Thanksgiving, Easter, etc."

■THE TRAVEL IMAGE, Dept. PM, 5335 McConnell Ave., Los Angeles CA 90066. (213)823-3439. President: Greg Wenger. Has 300,000 photos and growing. Clients include: ad agencies, editorial, public relations and audiovisual firms, businesses, book/encyclopedia and magazine publishers, newspapers and wholesale tour operators. Previous/current clients: SFA Adv. Conn., travel photos, Europe, UK, travel books; Halsey Publications, inflight magazines, travel articles; and Zaner, Bloser Publishers, text books, China Mongolia, Silk Route.

Subject Needs: "Travel photos—popular tourist destinations, leisure activities and geographic locations."

Specs: Original color; 35mm, 2¼×2¼ and 4×5 transparencies.

Payment & Terms: Pays 50% commission on sale. Works on contract basis only. Payment made monthly. Model release, captions and subject ID required. Offers one time rights.

Making Contact: By mail, request "guidelines"; must include SASE. "Submit your strongest suit of images, fully identified as to subject and location. Include a stock list."

Tips: "Best-sellers are strong in color and composition. Looks for quality images in volume of popular destinations worldwide on an ongoing basis. People-oriented subjects, scenics and activities. The US has become a travel destination for more countries. Good photos of US vacation spots are in demand, as well as the Orient, Southeast Asia, Oceana, South America, Europe, Eastern Europe, former USSR and Caribbean. Be prepared to commit to a great deal of time, energy, creativity—and film. Submit samples by mail after requesting our guidelines."

‡TROPIX PHOTOGRAPHIC LIBRARY, 156 Meols Parade, Meols, Merseyside L47 6AN England. 51 632 1698. FAX: 51 632 1698. Director: Veronica Birley. Picture library specialist. Has 25,000 transparencies. Clients include: book/encyclopedia publishers, magazine publishers, newspapers, ad agencies, public relations firms, audiovisual firms, businesses, television/film companies and travel agents.

Subject Needs: "All aspects of the developing world and the natural environment. Detailed and accurate captioning is essential. Tropix documents the Third World from its power stations to its peanut growers, from its rain forests to its refugees. Education, medicine, agriculture, industry, technology and other Third World topics. Plus environmental topics worldwide."

Specs: Uses 35mm, 2¼×2¼, 4×5, 8×10 transparencies and rarely 8×10 b&w glossy (with borders) prints.

Payment & Terms: Pays 50% commission. General price range: £50-175 (English currency). Works on contract basis only. Guarantees subject exclusivity within files. Charges cost of returning photographs by insured/registered post, if required. Statements issued quarterly. Payment made quarterly. Photographers allowed to have qualified auditor review account records to verify sales figures in the event of a dispute but not as routine procedure. Offers one-time rights. Other rights only by special written agreement. Informs photographer when a client requests all rights; but agency handles negotiation. Model release preferred. Photo captions required; include accurate, detailed data, preferably on disk. Guidelines are available from agency.

Making Contact: Interested in receiving work from newer, lesser-known photographers. Query with list of stock photo subjects; *no* unsolicited photographs, please. Photo guidelines free with SASE. "On receipt of our leaflets, a very detailed reply should be made by letter. Photographs are requested after receipt of this letter, if they appear suitable. When sumbitting photographs, always screen out those which are technically imperfect." Reports in 1 month; sooner if material is topical.

Tips: Looks for "special interest topics, accurate and informative captioning, sharp focus always, correct exposure, strong images and an understanding of involvement with specific subject matters. Travellers' scene, views and impressions, however artistic, are not required except as part of an informed, detailed collection. Not less than 200 salable transparencies per country photographed should be available." Sees a trend toward electronic image grabbing and development of a pictorial data base.

UNICORN STOCK PHOTO LIBRARY, 5400 NW 86th Terrace, Kansas City MO 64154. (816)587-4131. FAX: (816)741-0632. President/Owner: Betts Anderson. Has 150,000 color slides. Clients include: ad agencies, corporate accounts, textbooks, magazines, calendars and religious publishers.

Subject Needs: Ordinary people of all ages and races doing everyday things: at home, school, work and play. Current skylines of all major cities; tourist attractions, historical; wildlife; seasonal/holiday; and religious subjects. "We particularly need images showing 2 or more races represented in one photo and family scenes with BOTH parents. There is a critical need for more minority shots including hispanics, orientals and blacks. We also need ecology illustrations such as recycling, pollution and people cleaning up the earth."

Specs: Uses 35mm color slides.

Payment & Terms: Pays 50% commission. General price range: $50-400. Works on contract basis only. Offers nonexclusive contract. Contracts renew automatically with additional submissions for 3 years. Charges duping fee; rate not specified. Statement issued monthly. Payment made monthly. Offers one-time rights. Informs photographer and allows him to negotiate when client requests all rights. Model release preferred; increases sales potential considerably. Photo captions required; include: location; ages of people; dates on skylines.

Making Contact & Terms: Write first for guidelines. "We are looking for professionals who understand this business and will provide a steady supply of top-quality images. At least 300 images are required to open a file. Contact us by letter including $10 for our 'Information for Photographers' package."

Tips: "We keep in close, personal contact with all our photographers. Our monthly newsletter is a very popular medium for doing this. Our biggest need is for minorities and interracial shots. If you can supply us with this subject, we can supply you with checks. Because UNICORN is in the Midwest, we have many requests for framing/gardening/agriculture/winter and general scenics of the Midwest."

*‡UNIVERSAL-STOCK AGENCY, Friedrich Lau Str. 26, 4000 Düsseldorf 30 Germany. (211)43 1557. FAX: (211)454 1631. Director: Ralf Dietrich. Estab. 1953. Stock photo agency. Has 1 million photos. Clients include: advertising agencies, public relations firms, businesses, book/encyclopedia publishers, magazine publishers, newspapers, postcard publishers, calendar companies, greeting card companies, TV industry.

Subject Needs: "We handle all topics apart from well known personalities and politics. Our needs are: people, business, industry and geography worldwide.

Specs: Uses 35mm, $2\frac{1}{4} \times 2\frac{1}{4}$, 4×5, 8×10 transparencies.

Payment & Terms: Pays 50% commission color photos. Average price per image (to clients): $100-150. Negotiates fees below standard minimum prices. Offers volume slide discounts to customers; terms specified in photographer's contract. Discount sales terms not negotiable. Works with or without signed, non-exclusive, guaranteed subject exclusivity contract, negotiable. Statements issued quarterly. Payment made quarterly. Offers one-time rights. Informs photographer and allows him to negotiate when client requests all rights. Model/property release required. Captions required.

Making Contact: Submit portfolio for review. Samples kept on file. SASE. Expects minimum initial submission of not less than 100 images with about 600 to 1,000 slides annually. Reports in 4 months. Photo guidelines free with SASE. Market tips sheet distributed upon request.

Tips: "Look at the way advertisements are made in magazines. Sales are more likely in mid-size formats. Read books with motives of cities, landscapes, etc. Look for postcards to get an idea of how to take photos and what to take photos of."

VISUAL IMAGES WEST, INC., 600 East Baseline B6, Tempe AZ 85283. (602)820-5403. Photo Director: Jude Westlake Moyer. Estab. 1985. Stock photo agency. Member of Picture Agency Council of America (PACA). Clients include: advertising agencies, public relations firms, businesses, book/encyclopedia publishers, magazine publishers, and newspapers. Clients include Bank of America, Wrangler Jeans, Jeep, America West Airlines.

Subject Needs: Needs photos of southwestern lifestyles and scenics. Also general travel and model-released lifestyles.

Specs: Uses $2\frac{1}{4}$ up to 4×5 transparencies; "scenics in large format only."

Payment & Terms: Pays 50% commission on domestic photos. General price range: editorial, $185 and up; advertising, $230 base rate. Works on contract basis only. Offers limited regional exclusive and catalog exclusive contracts. Statements issued when payment is due. Payment made monthly. Photographers are allowed to review account records to verify sales figures. Offers one-time rights and specific print and/or time usages. When client requests all rights, "we inform photographer and get approval of 'buyout' but agency is sole negotiator with client." Model/property release required for people, homes, vehicles, animals; photo captions required.

Making Contact: Contact by telephone for photographer's package. SASE. Reports in 1 month. Photo guidelines free with SASE. Tips sheet distributed quarterly to contract photographers.

Tips: Trend among clients is "toward medium and large format. Looks for "professional quality, sharp focus; proper exposure, simple design and a direct message. When sending work to review make sure the submission is tightly edited. Include subject list of what work is available."

■VISUALS UNLIMITED, P.O. Box 146, Hale Hill Rd., East Swanzey NH 03446-0146. (603)352-6436. President: Dr. John D. Cunningham. Stock photo agency and photo research service. Has over 500,000 photos. Clients include: ad agencies, public relations firms, audiovisual firms, businesses, book/encyclopedia publishers, magazine publishers, postcard companies, calendar companies and greeting card companies.

Subject Needs: All fields: (biology, environmental, medical, natural history, geography, history, scenics, chemistry, geology, physics, industrial, astronomy and "general."

Specs: Uses 5×7 or larger b&w prints; 35mm, $2\frac{1}{4} \times 2\frac{1}{4}$, 4×5 and 8×10 transparencies; b&w contact sheets; and b&w negatives.

Payment & Terms: Pays 50% commission for b&w and color photos. Negotiates fees based on use, type of publication, user (e.g., nonprofit group vs. publisher). Average price per image (to clients): $30-90/b&w photo; $50-190/color photo. Offers volume discounts to customers; terms specified in contract. Photographers can choose not to sell images on discount terms. Works on contract basis only. Offers non-exclusive contract. Contracts renew automatically for an indefinite time unless return of photos is requested. Statements issued per project. Payment made 1-2 days after completion of project. Photographers not allowed to review account records to verify sales figures; "All payments are exactly 50% of fees generated." Offers one-time rights. Informs photographer and allows him to negotiate when client requests all rights. Model release preferred; captions required..

Making Contact: Interested in receiving work from newer, lesser-known photographers. Query with samples or send unsolicited photos for consideration. Submit portfolio for review. SASE. Reports in 1 week. Photo guidelines sheet is free with SASE. Distributes a tip sheet several times/year as deadlines allow, to all people with files.

Tips: Looks for "focus, composition, and contrast, of course. Instructional potential (e.g., behavior, anatomical detail, habitat, example of problem, living conditions, human interest). Increasing need for exact identification, behavior, and methodology in scientific photos; some return to b&w as color costs rise. Edit carefully for focus and distracting details; submit anything and everything from everywhere that is geographical, biological, geological, environmental, and people oriented."

■**WEATHERSTOCK,** P.O. Box 44124, Tucson AZ 85733. (602)325-4207. Director/Photographer: Warren Faidley. Estab. 1987. Stock photo agency. Has basic inventory of 20,000 images with an additional collection of 50,000 images representing the work of 20 photographers. Clients include: advertising agencies, public relations firms, audiovisual firms, businesses, book/encyclopedia publishers, magazine publishers, postcard companies, calendar companies, greeting card companies and scientific.

Subject Needs: "We are *only* accepting the following images at this time: tornadoes, hurricanes, and avalanches, in progress only. No damage photos please. We are also accepting images of rain forest cutting and burning, storms at sea and major flooding in progress. Our video department needs footage of tornadoes in progress."

Specs: Uses 5×7, 8×10 b&w/color prints; 35mm, $2\frac{1}{4} \times 2\frac{1}{4}$, 4×5, 8×10 transparencies. "We prefer transparencies, for most subjects, but will consider prints of dramatic weather shots."

Payment & Terms: Buys photos/videotape outright; pays $10-1,000/color photo; $10-1,000/b&w photo; $5-5,000/minute of videotape footage. Pays 50% commission on color photos. Average price per image (to clients): $150-1,000/b&w and color photo; $500-10,000 videotape. Negotiates fees below stated minimums, bulk sales may be lower. Offers volume discounts to customers; inquire about specific terms. Photographers can choose not to sell images on discount terms. Works on contract basis only. Offers non-exclusive contract. Contracts renew automatically for 6 months. Statements issued monthly. Payment made monthly following receipt of payment by clients. Photographers allowed to review account records to verify sales figures. Informs photographer and allows him to negotiate when client requests all rights. Offers one-time rights, first rights electronic media rights, all rights and other negotiated rights. Any exclusive uages "are approved by represented photographers." Model/property release required on non-editorial type images; photo captions required.

Making Contact: Interested in receiving work from newer, lesser-known photographers. "*Do not send* photos with first contact." SASE. Reports in 2 weeks. Photo guidelines free with SASE. Tips sheet distributed quarterly to contract photographers.

Tips: "Since we are the world's first and only stock agency which specializes in weather and related images, we can offer clients a more detailed and quality selection than the general interest agencies, including even the biggest ones. We are able to fill everything from greeting card scenics for the client that demands super scenic quality to the advertiser or scientific client who has a very specific request. If we don't have the image, we can almost always locate it through our vast collection of weather references. If a photographer is interested in being represented by Weatherstock, the transparencies must be of very high quality. We are completely nonexclusive in our representation. Many photographers that we represent have similar images that they sell on their own or photos that they file with other agencies. The stock photography business is becoming *very* competitive. Only the best images will sell."

WEST STOCK, INC., Suite 520, 83 S. King St., Seattle WA 98104. (206)621-1611. FAX: (206)223-1545. Chairman: Mark Karras. President: Rick Groman. Project Director: Stephanie Webb. Files contain over 500,000 transparencies. Clients include: ad agencies, design firms, major corporations, magazines, book publishers, calendar and greeting card companies.

Subject Needs: "Our files are targeted to meet the needs of advertising, corporate communications and publishing. We need strong imagery of virtually all subjects, especially people involved in business, leisure activities, sports and recreation. Model-released people and property essential."

Specs: Only original transparencies accepted, 35mm and larger.

Payment & Terms: Pays 50% commission. General price range: $200-15,000. Excepting slide shows and multi-media presentations, we generally do not go below $200/range. Works on contract basis only. Offers non-exclusivity. Standard contract is 3 yrs with automatic renewal for additional 3 years. Charges 50% catalog insertion fee. Statements issued monthly. Payment made monthly. "Our contracts have an audit provision." Offers one-time electronic media, agency promotion and other rights. Informs photographer and allows him to negotiate when client requests all rights. Model/property releases and captions required.

Making Contact: Very interested in receiving work from newer, lesser-known photographers. Send letter outlining qualifications along with tearsheets to receive guidelines. "Please, no telephone calls or portfolios sent without our request."

Tips: "We expect photographers to have a thorough understanding of stock photography prior to contacting us. We do not represent amateur photographers. The stock photography market is competitive and sophisticated. In order to stay ahead of the crowd we demand nothing but the finest in professional photography. We see a trend toward more and more photography. Electronics in the photo business is here to stay."

■WESTLIGHT, 2223 S. Carmelina Ave., Los Angeles CA 90064. (213)820-7077. Owner: Craig Aurness. Estab. 1978. Stock photo agency. Member of Picture Agency Council of America (PACA). Has 2,000,000 photos. Clients include: advertising agencies, public relations firms, audiovisual firms, corporations, book/encyclopedia publishers, magazine publishers, newspapers, postcard companies, calendar companies, greeting card companies and TV.

Subject Needs: Needs photos of all top quality subjects.

Specs: Uses 35mm, 2¼ × 2¼, 4 × 5 transparencies.

Payment & Terms: Pays 50% commission; international sales, 40% of gross. General price range: $600 + . Offers exclusive contract and some guaranteed subject exclusivity within files. Contracts renew automatically with each submission for one year. Charges duping fees of 100%/image. Also charges catalog insertion fee 50%/image. Statements issued quarterly. Payment made quarterly; within 30 days of end of quarter. Photographers allowed to review account records to verify sales figures. Offers one-time rights and first rights. Informs photographer and allows him to negotiate when client requests all rights. Model and property release required for recognizable people and private places. Photo captions rquired.

Making Contact: Query with resume of credits. Query with tearsheet samples. Query with list of stock photo subjects; show a specialty. Cannot return material. Reports in 1 month. Photo guidelines free with SASE. Tips sheet distributed monthly to contract photographers. Send tearsheets only, no unsolicited photos.

Tips: Photographer must have "ability to regularly produce the best possible photographs on a specialized subject, willingness to learn, listen and fill agency file needs."

■‡DEREK G. WIDDICOMBE, Worldwide Photographic Library, Oldfield, High Street, Clayton West, Huddersfield, Great Britain HD8 9NS. (011)44 484 862638. FAX: (011)44 484 862638. Proprietor: Derek G. Widdicombe. Picture library. Has over 100,000 photos. Clients include: ad agencies, public relations firms, audiovisual firms, businesses, book/encyclopedia publishers, magazine publishers, newspapers, postcard companies, calendar companies, greeting card companies, television, packaging, exhibition and display material, posters, etc.

Subject Needs: "The library covers many thousands of different subjects from landscape, architecture, social situations, industrial, people, moods and seasons, religious services, animals, natural history, travel subjects and many others. We have some archival material. These subjects are from worldwide sources."

Specs: Uses 20.3 × 24.4 cm. glossy b&w prints. Also, all formats of transparencies; 35mm preferred.

Payment & Terms: Pays 50% commission for b&w and color photos. General price range: reproduction fees in the range of £25-200 (English currency); pays $52-333 or higher/b&w photo; $73-500 or higher/color photo. Works with or without contract; negotiable. Offers limited regional exclusivity and nonexclusive contract. Statements issued quarterly. Payment made quarterly. Photographers not allowed to review account records to verify sales figures. Offers one-time and electronic media rights. Requests agency promotion rights. Does not inform photographer or allow him to negotiate when client requests all rights. Model/property release required for portraits of people and house interiors. Photo captions required.

Making Contact: "Send letter first with details on what you have to offer." Send small selection at own risk with return postage/packing. SASE.

Tips: Looks for "technical suitability (correct exposure, sharpness, good tonal range, freedom from defects, color rendering [saturation] etc.). Subject matter well portrayed without any superfluous objects in picture. Commercial suitability (people in pictures in suitable dress, up-to-date cars – or none, clear-top portions for magazine/book cover titles). Our subject range is so wide that we are offering the whole spectrum from very traditional (almost archival) pictures to abstract, moody, out-of-focus shots. Send material in small batches – normally a hundred images at a time, and let us know what you have to send."

THE WILDLIFE COLLECTION, 69 Cranberry St., Brooklyn NY 11201. (718)935-9600. FAX: (718)935-9031. Director: Sharon Cohen. Estab. 1987. Stock photo agency. Has 150,000 photos. Clients include: advertising agencies, public relations firms, businesses, book/encyclopedia publishers, magazine publishers, newspapers, postcard companies, calendar companies, greeting card companies, zoos and aquariums.

Subject Needs: "We handle anything to do with nature—animals, scenics, vegetation, underwater. We are in particular need of coverage from the Galapagos, Everglades, India, South America and Europe."

Specs: Uses 35mm, 2¼×2¼, 4×5, transparencies.

Payment & Terms: Pays 50% commission on color photos. General price range: $100-6,000. Works on contract basis only. Offers limited regional exclusivity. Contracts renew automatically "until either party wishes to terminate." Statements issued monthly. Payment made monthly. Photographers permitted to review sales figures. Offers one-time rights. Informs photographers and allows them to negotiate when client requests all rights, "but they can only negotiate through us—not directly." Model release "not necessary with nature subjects." Photo captions required; include common, scientific name and region found.

Making Contact: Interested in receiving work from newer, lesser-known photographers. Query with samples. Printed samples kept on file. SASE. Expects minimum initial submission of 200 images. "We would like 2,000 images/year; this will vary." Reports in 2 weeks. Photo guidelines and free catalog with 6½×9½″ SASE with 75¢ postage. Market tips sheet distributed quarterly to signed photographers only.

Tips: In samples wants to see "great lighting, extreme sharpness; *non-stressed* animals; large range of subjects; excellent captioning; general presentation. Care of work makes a large impression. The effect of humans on the environment is being requested more often as are unusual and engangered animals."

The gentle moment of a man and woman viewing their new baby is a perfect stock photo for any photographer wanting to sell to an advertising firm. Although the shot was set up, photographer Melanie Carr makes the most of the lighting and the models. Carr actually is married to the "father" in the photo, Leo Gradinger, and the two operate Zephyr Pictures in Del Mar, California. The shot has sold around 10 times.

© Melanie Carr

*‡WILDLIGHT PHOTO AGENCY, 1/165 Hastings Parade, North Bondi, NSW 2026 Australia. (02)301-737. (02)302-466. Contact: Manager. Estab. 1985. Stock photo agency, picture library. Has 300,000 photos. Clients include: advertising agencies, public relations firms, audiovisual firms, businesses, book/encyclopedia publishers, magazine publishers, newspapers, postcard publishers, calendar companies, greeting card companies.

Specs: Uses 35mm, 2¼×2¼, 4×5, 8×10 transparencies.
Payment & Terms: Pays 50% commission on color photos. Works on exclusive contract basis only. Statements issued monthly. Payment made monthly. Offers one-time rights. Model/property release required. Captions required.
Making Contact: Arrange personal interview to show portfolio. Expects minimum initial submission of 1,000 images with periodic submission of at least 250/month. Reports in 1-2 weeks. Photo guidelines available.

■‡S & I WILLIAMS POWER PIX, Castle Lodge, Wenvoe, Cardiff CF5 6AD Wales, United Kingdom. (0222) 595163. FAX: (0222)593905. President: Steven Williams. Picture library. Has 100,000 photos. Clients include: ad agencies, public relations firms, audiovisual firms, businesses, book/encyclopedia publishers, magazine publishers, postcard companies, calendar companies, greeting card companies and music business, i.e. records, cassettes and CDs.
Specs: Uses 35mm, 2¼×2¼, 4×5 and 8×10 transparencies.
Payment & Terms: Pays 50% commission on b&w and color photos. General price range:£50-£500 (English currency). Written model release and captions are required.
Making Contact: Arrange a personal interview to show portfolio. Query with resume of credits, samples or stock photo list. SASE. Reports in 1-2 weeks. Photo guidelines available for SASE. Distributes a tips sheet every 3-6 months to photographers on books.
Tips: Prefers to see "a photographer who knows his subject and has done his market research by looking at pictures used in magazines, record covers, books, etc.—bright colorful images and an eye for something just that little bit special."

■‡WORLD VIEW-FOTOTHEEK BV, A.J. Ernststraat 1S1, Amsterdam, Holland 1083 GV. 31-20-420224. FAX: 31-20-6420224. Managing Director: Bert Blokhuis. Estab. 1985. Stock photo agency. Has over 100,000 transparencies. Clients include: advertising agencies, audiovisual firms, businesses, calendar companies and corporations.
Subject Needs: Wants to see "sizes bigger then 35mm, only model-released commercial subjects."
Specs: Uses 2¼×2¼, 4×5, 8×10 transparencies only.
Payment & Terms: Pays 40-60% commission on transparencies. General price range: US $300/color photos, minimum $100. Offers volume discounts to customers; inquire about specific terms. Discount sales terms not negotiable. Works on contract basis only. Offers limited regional exclusivity. Contracts renew automatically for 4 years. Statements issued monthly. Payment made quarterly. Photographers permitted to review sales figures. Offers one-time rights. Informs photographer and allows him to negotiate when client requests all rights. Model release and photo captions required.
Making Contact: Interested in receiving work from newer, lesser-known photographers. Query with samples. SASE. Reports in 3 weeks.
Tips: In freelancer's samples, wants to see "small amount of pictures (20 or 30) plus a list of subjects available and list of agents." Work must show quality.

WORLDWIDE PHOTO IMAGES, (formerly N.E.B. Stock Photo Agency), Suite 112, 805 E St., San Rafael CA 94901. (415)883-0305. Owner: Norman Buller. Estab. 1988. Stock photo agency. Has 4,000 photos. Clients include: advertising agencies, businesses, book/encyclopedia publishers, magazine publishers, postcard companies, calendar companies, greeting card companies and men's magazines, foreign and domestic. Previous/current clients include: *Playboy; Baseball Cards* magazine, 1958 original Dodgers team, 2¼×2¼ transparencies; Augsberg Fortress, Trees in Mist.
Subject Needs: Nudes, animals, people, celebrity nudes and all pro sports.
Specs: Uses b&w and color prints; also 35mm, 2¼×2¼ transparencies.
Payment & Terms: Pays 50% commission on all sales. Works with or without a signed contract, negotiable. Offers nonexclusive contract. Payment made immediately upon payment from client. Photographers allowed to review account records to verify sales figures. Offers one-time or first rights and all rights. Handles all negotiation. Model release required.
Making Contact: Interested in receiving work from newer, lesser-known photographers. Query with samples and list of stock photo subjects. Send unsolicited photos by mail for consideration. Reports immediately.
Tips: "Work must be good. Buyers are incredibly picky! Getting harder to please everyday. We have worldwide clientele, don't edit too tightly, let me see 90% of your material on hand and critique it from there!"

‡WORLDWIDE PRESS AGENCY, Box 579, 1000 Buenos Aires, Argentina. 962-3182 and 952-9927. Director: Victor Polanco. Stock photo agency and picture library. Clients include: ad agencies, book/ encyclopedia publishers, magazine publishers, newspapers, postcard companies, calendar companies and greeting card companies.

Subject Needs: Handles picture stories, fashion photos, human interest, pets, wildlife, film and TV stars, pop and rock singers, classic musicians and conductors, sports, interior design, architectural and opera singers.

Specs: Uses 8×12 glossy b&w prints; 35mm and 2¼×2¼ transparencies.

Payment & Terms: Pays 40% commission for b&w and color photos. General price range: "The Argentine market is very peculiar. We try to obtain the best price for each pic. Sometimes we consult the photographer needs." Offers one-time rights. Prefers written model release and photo captions.

Making Contact: Query with list of stock photo subjects. Does not return unsolicited material. Reports "as soon as possible."

■**ZEPHYR PICTURES**, Suites D & U, 2120 Jimmy Durante Blvd., Del Mar CA 92014. (619)755-1200. FAX: (619)755-3723. Owner: Leo Gradinger. Estab. 1982. Stock photo agency. Member of Picture Agency Council of America (PACA). Also commercial photo studio. Has 200,000+ photos. Clients include: advertising agencies, public relations firms, audiovisual firms, businesses, book/encyclopedia publishers, magazine publishers, newspapers, postcard and calendar companies, developers, corporate, finance, education, design studios and TV stations.

Subject Needs: "We handle everything from A to Z. We specialize in people (model-released) for advertising. New material is shot on a weekly basis. We also have lots of great material for the textbook and editorial markets."

Specs: Uses 35mm, 2¼×2¼, 4×5, 8×10, 6×7 transparencies.

Payment & Terms: Pays 50% commission for b&w and color photos. Average price per image: $250-650. Enforces minimum prices. Sub agency agreement 50-50 domestic, 40% to photographer on foreign sales. Offers volume discounts to customers; inquire about specific terms. Discount sales terms not negotiable. Works on contract basis only. Offers limited regional exclusivity. Contracts renew automatically for three years, auto-renewal each year thereafter. Charges 25% catalog insertion fee. Statements issued monthly. Payment made monthly. Photographers allowed to review account records to verify sales figures. Offers one-time rights; other rights negotiable. Model/property release and photo captions required.

Making Contact: Interested in receiving work from newer, lesser-known photographers. Arrange a personal interview to show portfolio. Query with list of stock photo subjects. SASE. Reports in 2-3 weeks, according to time demands. Photo guidelines available occasionally. Tips sheet distributed twice a year to any photographers who are contracted for submissions.

Tips: "I am looking for a photographer who *specializes* in one maybe two areas of expertise. Be professional. Call or write to let us know who you are and what you specialize in. If we are interested, we ask you to send 20 to 40 of your very best images with a SASE and return postage. We are shooting at the highest level of sophistication for stock since our beginning 10 years ago. The market demands it. and we will continue to try and provide a high level of creativity in our images."

Stock Photo Agencies/'92-'93 changes

The following markets appeared in the 1992 edition of *Photographer's Market* but are not listed in the 1993 edition.

Adams Picture Library (did not respond)

Berg & Associates (sold to Picture Perfect Stock Photos, see index)

Bernsen's International Press Service Ltd. (BIPS) (did not respond)

Christmas Archives International (did not respond)

Davis Travel Photography, James (not reviewing work)

DMI Photo Agency (not accepting new work)

Earth Images (no longer using freelance work)

Folio, Inc. (did not respond)

Haas Photo Library, Robert (did not respond)

Harding Picture Library, Robert (did not respond)

Horizon International Pty. Ltd. (did not respond)

Image Bank, The (did not respond)

Image Merchants (did not respond)

Image Quest Inc. (did not respond)

Lewis Stock Photos, Frederic (merged, now Archive Photos)

Light Images, Inc. (did not respond)

Miller Comstock Inc. (not reviewing work)

Natural History Photographic Agency (NHPA) (did not respond)

News Flash International, Inc. (did not respond)

Photo Gems (not reviewing work)

Pictorial Parade (merged, now Archive Photos)

Pictorial Press (did not respond)

Preferred Stock Photography (out of business)

Retna Ltd. (did not respond)

Scenic Photo Imagery (out of business)

Scoopix Photo Library (did not respond)

Stills (did not respond)

Stock Photos Brasil (did not respond)

Stockphotos Inc. (did not respond)

Stone Worldwide/Los Angeles, Ltd., Tony (not reviewing work)

Summit Photofile (not reviewing work)

Suomen Kuvapalvelu Oy (did not respond)

Telegraph Colour Library (did not respond)

Telephoto (sold)

Travel Photo International (did not respond)

Visions Photo, Inc. (did not respond)

Zefa Zentrale Farbbild Agentur GmbH (did not respond)

Resources

Contests

Almost everyone has heard the expression, "It's not whether you win or lose, but how you play the game." The same phrase holds true for contests in the photo world, with one amendment: "Don't be afraid of criticism."

Everyone likes to win. You wouldn't enter a contest if you didn't think you had a chance to finish on top. But that doesn't always happen and photographers who can learn from those losses will be better for it in the long run. Contests are an excellent way for aspiring artists to measure their talent and progress. Also, the publicity and awards connected with some of the more prestigious contests can go a long way in actually helping you advance your career.

The 66 listings in this section cover a wide range of styles — such as fine art photography and photojournalism — and photographic media, including film and videotape. In particular, listings with various kinds of audiovisual, film or video needs have been marked with a special AV symbol — a solid, black square — before the listing's name for easier recognition.

The listings contain only the basic information needed to make contact with the sponsoring organization and a brief description of the styles or media open to consideration. It's recommended that you read through the listings first to get an idea of the ones for which your work would likely be eligible, then write to them requesting complete, up-to-date entry information.

When entering contests, be especially alert for any which require the surrender or transfer of "all rights" to images either upon entry or upon winning the contest. Protection of your copyright is one of your main responsibilities as a photographer (see Copyright/ rights in the Business of Photography, on page 11.) , and contests are one way in which photographers have sometimes lost, unknowingly, their copyrights to valuable images. Granting limited rights for publicity purposes is reasonable, but you should never assign rights of any kind without adequate financial compensation or without a written agreement. In your request for entry guidelines, be sure to request clear information about all such terms.

In the meantime, enter any competition and as many as you wish. And by the way, best of luck!

*■AMERICAN INTERNATIONAL FILM/VIDEO FESTIVAL, (formerly Ten Best of the West), P.O. Box 4034, Long Beach CA 90804. Festival Chairman: George Cushman. Sponsored by the American Motion Picture Society. Sponsors worldwide annual competition in its 63rd consecutive year for film and videotape. Closing date September 30, 1992.

*ANACORTES ARTS & CRAFTS FESTIVAL, P.O. Box 6, Anacortes WA 98221. (206)293-6211. Director: Judith Nebot. Two-day festival, first weekend in August. Over 225 booths plus juried show with prizes.

ART ON THE GREEN, P.O. Box 901, Coeur d'Alene ID 83814. (208)667-9346. Outdoor art & crafts festival including juried show first August weekend each year.

*ART SHOW AT THE DOG SHOW, 11301 West 37 North, Wichita KS 67205. (316)722-6181. Chairman: Joe Miller. A national juried fine arts competition devoted to canine art. All entries must include a dog.

ARTIST FELLOWSHIP GRANTS, c/o Oregon Arts Commission, 550 Airport Rd. SE, Salem OR 97310. (503)378-3625. Assistant Director: Vincent Dunn. Offers cash grants to Oregon photographers in odd-numbered years..

■BALTIMORE ANNUAL INDEPENDENT FILM & VIDEO MAKERS' COMPETITION, % The Baltimore Film Forum, 10 Art Museum Dr., Baltimore MD 21218. (410)889-1993. Annual international competition. Applications available in summer, due in fall. Winners screened in April during International Film Festival.

BEVERLY ART CENTER ART FAIR & FESTIVAL, 2153 W. 111th St., Chicago IL 60643. (312)445-3838. Chairman: Pat McGrail. Annual event for still photos and all fine art held in June in Chicago. March deadline.

CAMERA BUG INTERNATIONAL, Camera Bug Club Headquarters, 2106 Hoffnagle St., Philadelphia PA 19152. (215)742-5515. Contest Chairman: Nicholas M. Friedman. Annual contest open to all photographers. Provide SASE or 29¢ postage for submission guidelines.

*COUNCIL ON FINE ART PHOTOGRAPHY, 5613 Johnson Avenue, West Bethesda MD 20817-3503. (301)897-0083. CEO: Lowell Anson Kenyon. Conducts talent search and exhibits outstanding work (in the Nation's Capital and environs) by emerging and serious fine art photographers. Exhibitors share gallery fees which average $25 per show. Send #10 SASE for particulars on forthcoming exhibitions.

*COUNTERPOINT: ANNUAL NATIONAL JURIED PHOTOGRAPHY, PRINTMAKING AND DRAWING EXHIBITION, P.O. Box 176, Ingram TX 78025. Art Director: Betty Vernon. Send SASE to Hill Country Arts Foundation, P.O. Box 176PM, Ingram TX 78025 for prospectus. Awards $2,200.

■THE CREATIVITY AWARDS SHOW, 6th Floor, 10 E. 39th St., New York NY 10016. (212)889-6500. Show Director: Dan Barron. Sponsor: *Art Direction* magazine. Annual show for photos and films published for worldwide distribution.

■DANCE ON CAMERA FESTIVAL, Sponsored by Dance Films Association, Inc., Room 507, 1133 Broadway, New York NY 10010. (212)727-0764. Executive Director: Susan Braun. Annual festival competition for 16mm films with optical soundtrack and ¾-inch videotapes in NTSC format, on all aspects of dance.

*ECLIPSE AWARDS, Thoroughbred Racing Association, Suite 1, 420 Fair Hill Dr., Elkton MD 21921. (410)392-9200. FAX: (410)398-1366. Director of Services Bureau: Kennith R. Knelly. Sponsor: Thoroughbred Racing Associations, Daily Racing Form and National Turf Writers Association. Annual event for photographers.

*FINE ARTS WORK CENTER IN PROVINCETOWN, P.O. Box 565, Provincetown MA 02657. (508)487-9960. Contact: Visual Coordinator. Seven-month residency program for artists and writers. Housing, monthly stipend and materials allowance provided from October 1 through May 1. Send SASE for application. Deadline February 1.

43rd INTERNATIONAL EXHIBITION OF PHOTOGRAPHY, 2260 Jimmy Durante Blvd., Del Mar CA 92014-2216. (619)755-1161. Sponsor: Del Mar Fair (22nd District Agricultural Association). Annual event for still photos/prints. May 3rd deadline. Send #10 SASE for brochure.

14TH ANNUAL GAZETTE PHOTOGRAPHY CONTEST, *Pure-Bred Dogs/American Kennel Gazette,* 51 Madison Ave., New York NY 10010. (212)696-8332. Sponsor: The American Kennel Club. Annual competition for photos (prints) of pure-bred dogs.

GALLERY MAGAZINE, 401 Park Ave. S., New York NY 10016-8802. Contest Editor: Judy Linden. Sponsors monthly event for still photos of nudes. Offers monthly and annual grand prizes. Write for details or buy magazine.

GEORGIA COUNCIL FOR THE ARTS INDIVIDUAL ARTISTS GRANT PROGRAM, 530 Means St. NW, Suite 115, Atlanta GA 30318. (404)651-7926. Visual Arts Coordinator: Richard Waterhouse. Open to individual artists, who must have been legal residents of Georgia for at least one year prior to the application date. To be eligible for funding, the artist must submit a specific project proposal for completion during the 1994 fiscal year. Deadline: April 1, 1993.

GOLDEN ISLES ARTS FESTIVAL, Box 673, Saint Simons Island GA 31522. (912)638-8770. Contact: Registration Chairman, Coastal Center for the Arts. Sponsor: Coastal Alliance for the Arts. Annual competition for still photos/prints; all fine art and craft.

GREATER MIDWEST INTERNATIONAL VIII, CMSU Art Center Gallery, Warrensburg MO 64093. (816)543-4498. Gallery Director: Billi R.S. Rothove. Sponsor: CMSU Art Center Gallery/Missouri Arts Council. Sponsors annual competition for all media. Send SASE for current prospectus.

*IDAHO WILDLIFE, Box 25, Boise ID 83707. (208)334-3748. Editor: Diane Ronayne. Annual contest; pays cash prizes of $20-150. Rules in summer and fall issues of *Idaho Wildlife* magazine. Deadline October 1. Winners published.

INDIVIDUAL ARTIST FELLOWSHIP PROGRAM, % Montana Arts Council, 48 N. Last Chance Gulch, Helena MT 59620. (406)444-6430. Director of Artists Services: Martha Sprague. Offers several annual awards of $2,000 in all visual arts, including photography. Open to Montana residents only.

‡INTERNATIONAL DIAPORAMA FESTIVAL, Auwegemvaart 79, B-2800 Mechelen, Belgium. President: J. Denis. Sponsor: Koninklijke Mechelse Fotokring. Competition held every other year (even years) for slide/sound sequences.

*INTERNATIONAL WEDDING PHOTOGRAPHY AWARDS, 1312 Lincoln Blvd., Santa Monica CA 90401. (310)451-0090. Membership Director: Irene Cairns. Accepts 8×10 prints from Wedding Photographers International members only; contest split into two semi-annual competitions. Winner is named International Wedding Photographer of the year. Also sponsors annual album and 16×20 print competition open to non-members.

INTERNATIONAL WILDLIFE PHOTO COMPETITION, 280 E. Front St., Missoula MT 59807. (406)728-9380. Chairman: Dale Rivers. Professional and amateur catagories, color and b&w prints, color slides accepted; $1,700 in cash and prizes. Entry deadline mid-March 1993. Co-sponsored by the 16th Annual International Wildlife Film Festival and the Rocky Mountain School of Photography.

*LASSEN COUNTY ARTS COUNCIL'S ANNUAL JURIED PHOTOGRAPHY SHOW, P.O. Box 91, Susanville CA 96130. (916)257-5222. Program Director: Lori Collier. Outdoor photography contest with an emphasis on "Rails and Trails." Cash prizes. Works to be exhibited throughout September. Work must be submitted by July 15th.

*LEADING AMERICAN PHOTOGRAPHY COMPETITION, Art Horizons Photography Department PM, P.O. Box 1046, Hackensack NJ 07602. (201)487-7277. Director: Nora Smith. Winners receive thousands of dollars in prizes, "free publicity."

*MAYFAIR 1993 JURIED PHOTOGRAPHY EXHIBITION, 2020 Hamilton St., Allentown PA 18104. (215)437-6900. May juried exhibition open to all types of original photographs, by artists within 75 mile radius of Allentown. Maximum 3 entries, $10 non-refundable fee to enter. Send for prospectus; entry deadline March 1.

■THE "MOBIUS"™ ADVERTISING AWARDS, 841 N. Addison Ave., Elmhurst IL 60126-1291. (708)834-7773. FAX: (708)834-5565. Chairman: J.W. Anderson. Executive Director: Patricia Meyer. Sponsor: The United States Festivals Association. Annual international awards competition for print advertising, package design, TV and radio commericals.

*NATURAL WORLD PHOTOGRAPHIC COMPETITION & EXHIBITON, The Carnegie Museum of Natural History, 4400 Forbes Ave., Pittsburgh PA 15213. (412)622-3283. Contact: Division of Education. Held each fall, contest accepts color and b&w prints depicting the "natural world." Prizes totalling $1,300 are awarded and a juried show is selected for exhibition in the museum.

The asterisk before a listing indicates that the market is new in this edition. New markets are often the most receptive to freelance submissions.

*NEW YORK STATE FAIR PHOTOGRAPHY COMPETITION AND SHOW, New York State Fair, Syracuse NY 13209. (315)487-7711. Program Manager: Janet J. Edison. Open to amateurs and professionals in both b&w and color. Two prints may be entered per person. Prints only, no transparencies. Entry deadline August 1.

NEW YORK STATE YOUTH MEDIA ARTS SHOWS, New York State Summer Institutes, The State Education Department, Room 685 EBA, Albany NY 12234. (518)474-8773. Funded by the state legislature and administered by the New York State Education Department. Annual exhibition for still photos, film, videotape, creative sound, computer arts and holography. Open to New York state elementary and secondary grade students only.

*NIKON SMALL WORLD COMPETITION, 1300 Walt Whitman Rd., Melville New York 11747. (516)547-8500. Advertising Manager: B. Loechner. International contest for photography through the microscope, 35mm — limit 3 entries. First prize $4,000.

1993 PHOTOGRAPHY ANNUAL, 410 Sherman, Box 10300, Palo Alto CA 94303. (415)326-6040. Executive Editor: Jean A. Coyne. Sponsor: *Communication Arts* magazine. Annual competition for still photos/prints. Deadline March 16, 1993.

■NORTH AMERICAN OUTDOOR FILM/VIDEO AWARDS, Suite 101, 2017 Cato Ave., State College PA 16801. (814)234-1011. Sponsor: Outdoor Writers Association of America. Annual competition for films/videos on conservation and outdoor recreation subjects. Two categories: Recreation/Promotion and Conservation. $50 fee/entry.

*PHOTO EXHIBIT '93, P.O. Box 614, Park Forest IL 60466-0614. (708)474-9194. Exhibit Director: Kare Lindell. Sponsor: Park Forest Photography Club. Annual competition held April 24-25 for still photos/prints and slides. Open to amateur photographers residing in the United States. March 6th deadline.

*PHOTO METRO MAGAZINE ANNUAL CONTEST, 6 Rodgers #207C, San Francisco CA 94103. (415)861-6453. Photography contest with cash prizes and publication. Send SASE for information. Address will change in fall 1992.

*PHOTOGRAPHIC ALLIANCE U.S.A., 1864 61st St., Brooklyn NY 11204-2352. President: Henry Mass. Represents the International Federation of Photographic Art. Furnishes members with entry forms for international salons and other information regarding upcoming photographic events.

PHOTOGRAPHIC COMPETITION ASSOCIATION QUARTERLY CONTEST, P.O. Box 53550-B, Philadelphia PA 19105. (215)279-2193. Contact: Competition Committee. Sponsor: Photographic Competition Association (PCAA). Quarterly competition for still photos/prints.

PHOTOGRAPHY NOW, % the Center for Photography at Woodstock, 59 Tinker St., Woodstock NY 12498. (914)679-9957. Sponsors annual competition. Call for entries. Juried annually by renowned photographers, critics, museums. Call or write for prospectus in early spring.

*PHOTOSPIVA 93, Spiva Art Center, 3950 Newman Rd., Joplin MO 64801. (417)623-0183. Director: V.A. Christensen. National photography competition. Send SASE for prospectus.

PHOTOWORK 93, Barrett House Galleries, 55 Noxon St., Poughkeepsie NY 12601. (914)471-2550. Associate Director: Fran Smulcheski. National photography exhibition judged by New York City curator. Deadline for submissions December 1992. Send SASE in September for prospectus.

PICTURE PERFECT, P.O. Box 15760, Stamford CT 06901. (203)967-2512. Publisher: Andres Aquino. Ongoing photo contest in 31 subjects. Offers publishing opportunities, cash prizes and outlet for potential stock sales.

*PICTURES OF THE YEAR, 27 Neff Annex, 9th and Elm, Columbia MO 65201. (314)882-4442. Coordinator: Marilyn Upton. Photography competition for professional magazine, newspaper and freelance photographers.

*THE PRINT CLUB, 1614 Latimer St., Philadelphia PA 19103. (215)735-6090. Contact: Director. Sponsor: The Print Club. Annual international competition of prints (even years) and photos (odd years); juried selections. Entrants must be members of The Print Club; $30 membership is open to all interested. Over $2,000 in prize awards. Sponsor assumes right to exhibit if selected and right to reproduce in show catalog if award-winning. Write for complete information, send SASE.

PRO FOOTBALL HALL OF FAME PHOTO CONTEST, 2121 George Halas Dr. NW, Canton OH 44708. (216)456-8207. Curator/ Director of Research Information: Joe Horrigan. Sponsor: Canon USA, Inc. Annual event for still photos. Open to professional photographers on NFL coverage assignments only.

PULITZER PRIZES, 702 Journalism, Columbia University, New York NY 10027. (212)854-3841 or 3842. Administrator: Robert C. Christopher. Annual competition for still photos/prints published in American newspapers. February deadline for work published in the previous year.

‡SALON INTERNACIONAL DE ARTE FOTOGRAFICO, Foto Club Buenos Aires, Box 5377, 1000 Buenos Aires, Argentina. Salon Chairman: Ismael Rusconi. Annual competition for still photography since 1946; monochrome and color prints, photojournalism prints and pictorial, nature and photojournalism slides. Open to anyone. Conducted according to PSA "exhibition standards" and FIAP regulations, with PSA, FIAP and FCSA medals. Closing date by the middle of June every year, exhibition in July. Fees are fixed at $8/section with a supplement for air mail return. Photo clubs sponsoring international salons can send entries without any fee, provided a similar right is granted for the FCBA.

*SAN FRANCISCO SPCA PHOTO CONTEST, SF/SPCA, 2500 16th St., San Francisco CA 94103. (415)554-3000. Coordinator: Frank Burtnett. Entry fee $5 per image, no limit. Photos of pet(s) with or without people. Color slides, color or b&w prints, no larger than 8×12 (matte limit 11×14). Make check payable to SF/SPCA. Three best images win prizes. Deadline for entry Jan. 15 each year, include return postage and phone number.

*SCHOLASTIC ART AND WRITING AWARDS, Scholastic, Inc., 730 Broadway, New York NY 10003. For photographers. Purpose is to provide scholarship grants to college-bound high school seniors; program open to students in the 7th-12th grades.

SELECTIONS, 1151 Mission St., San Francisco CA 94103. Executive Director: Lynette Molnar. Offers annual juried photography exhibition from April to May. March deadline. Send SASE with requests for information.

■SINKING CREEK FILM/VIDEO FESTIVAL, Creekside Farm, 1250 Old Shiloh Rd., Greeneville TN 37743. (615)638-6524. Director: Mary Jane Coleman. Sponsors annual competition for 16mm film and ¾" videotape. Offers workshops in film and video production and seminars in media analysis. Holds screening of winners from its national film/video competition. Festival held in June at Vanderbilt University, Nashville, TN. April deadline; $8,000 in cash awards.

SPRINGFIELD INTERNATIONAL COLOR SLIDE EXHIBIT, Box 255, Wilbraham MA 01095. Sponsor: Springfield Photographic Society. Sponsors annual event for 35mm color slides.

*TAYLOR COUNTY FAIR PHOTO CONTEST, P.O. Box 613, Grafton WV 26354-0613. Co-Chairman: K.M. Bolyard.

*30TH ANNUAL INTERNATIONAL UNDERWATER PHOTOGRAPHIC COMPETITION, P.O. Box 2401, Culver City CA 90231. (310)278-4527; (213)262-6076. Competition Chairperson: Esther Chao. Offers annual competition in 8 categories (7 underwater, 1 ocean related). Deadline November 14, 1992.

32ND ANNUAL NAVAL AND MARITIME PHOTO CONTEST, U.S. Naval Institute, 118 Maryland Ave., Annapolis MD 21402. (410)268-6110. Photo Editor: Linda Cullen. Sponsors annual competition for still photos/prints and 35mm slides. December deadline.

*U.S. INDUSTRIAL FILM & VIDEO FESTIVAL, 841 N. Addison Ave., Elmhurst IL 60126-1291. (708)834-7773. FAX: (708)834-5565. Chairman: J.W. Anderson. Executive Director: Patricia Meyer. Sponsor: The United States Festivals Association. Annual international festival for film and video.

■ *The solid, black square before a listing indicates that the market uses various types of audiovisual materials, such as slides, film or videotape.*

UNLIMITED EDITIONS INTERNATIONAL JURIED PHOTOGRAPHY COMPETITIONS, % Competition Chairman, Box 4144, Friendly Station, Greensboro NC 27404-4144. (704)696-3269. President/Owner: Gregory Hugh Leng. Sponsors juried photography contests offering cash and prizes. Also offers opportunity to sell work to Unlimited Editions.

*■VISIONS OF U.S. HOME VIDEO COMPETITION, 2021 North Western Ave., Los Angeles CA 90027. (213)856-7787. Contact: Lee Arnone-Briggs. Annual competition for home videos shot on 8mm video, Beta or VHS.

*WESTCHESTER INTERNATIONAL SALON, P.O. Box 248, Larchmont NY 10538. (914)834-1555. Color slide competition worldwide, pictorial, nature, photo-travel, photo-journalism divisions, March 1993.

*WESTERN HERITAGE AWARDS, 1700 NE 63rd St., Oklahoma City OK 73111. (405)478-2250. Public Relations Director: Dana Sullivant. Sponsor: National Cowboy Hall of Fame. Annual competition for film and videotape held the 3rd week of March in Oklahoma City.

*WORLD IMAGE PHOTOGRAPHERS ASSOCIATION, P.O. Box 361, Mesa AZ 85211. Director: Bernie Wilt. Monthly contest for still photos and slides. Provide SASE for entry form.

*‡WORLD PRESS PHOTO, Van Baerlestraat 144, Amsterdam The Netherlands 1071 BE. (31)20 67660G6. Annual contest open to photojournalists. Covers press photographs in b&w and color taken during 1992. Deadline January 31, 1993.

■WORLDFEST—HOUSTON INTERNATIONAL FILM & TV FESTIVAL AND FILM MARKET, Box 56566, Houston TX 77256. (713)965-9955. Executive Director: J.H. Todd. Sponsor: city of Houston, others. Annual festival for film, videotape and screenplays held in April in Houston. Request entry fee and additional information by mail or phone. All winning entries are automatically submitted to more than 200 international film festivals.

*YOSEMITE RENAISSANCE, P.O. Box 313, Yosemite CA 95389. (209)372-4775. Director: Kay Pitts. Annual all media exhibit. Cash awards of $4,500. September 12 deadline for slide entry. Send for entry form.

YOUR BEST SHOT, %*Popular Photography* magazine 1633 Broadway, New York NY 10019. Monthly photo contest, 2-page spread featuring 5 pictures: first ($300), second ($200), third ($100) and two honorable mention ($50 each).

Workshops

The popularity of photography throughout the world has led to many changes in the field, both in equipment and in continuing education. Colleges throughout the United States are adopting photography classes as part of their regular curriculum and some are offering photo degrees. As photography climbs in popularity so do the number of workshops offered. There are around 140 workshops listed in this year's edition of *Photographer's Market* and they cover a wide range of styles and techniques.

The current emphasis in workshops appears to be on scenic locations and photo tours. The tours feature special experiences such as cruises, river raft trips and backpacking into remote areas combined with photographic opportunities or training.

When considering the possibility of attending a workshop a photographer must take a good look at the quality of the tour and the type of colleagues who also will attend. It is important to know if the workshop is for beginners, advanced amateurs or professionals and information from the workshop organizer can help you make that determination. Nothing is worse for a professional than attending a workshop that deals with the basics of capturing images. On the other end of the spectrum, a beginner does not want to attend a workshop in which everyone is talking way over his head. Know what you want to get out of the workshop and know what will be covered while you are there.

These workshop listings contain only the basic information needed to make contact with the sponsor and a brief description of the styles or media covered in the programs. The workshop experience can be whatever the photographer wishes it to be — a holiday from his working routine, or an exciting introduction to new skills and perspectives on the craft. Some photographers who start out by attending someone else's workshops come away so inspired that sooner or later they establish their own.

Conventional photography is still the primary focus of most of these programs. However, there is increasing interest from photographers in film and video, too. Accordingly, workshops that offer programs relating to film, video or other audiovisual skills have been marked with a special AV symbol — a solid, black square — before the listing's name for easier recognition.

ANSEL ADAMS GALLERY PHOTOGRAPHY WORKSHOPS, P.O. Box 455, Yosemite National Park CA 95389. (209)372-4413. Contact: Workshop Coordinator. Offers workshops in fine art photography within Yosemite National Park.

ALASKA ADVENTURES, P.O. Box 11309, Anchorage AK 99511. (907)345-4597. Contact: Chuck Miknich. Offers photo opportunities for Alaska wildlife and scenery on remote fishing/float trips and remote fish camp.

ALASKA UP CLOSE, P.O. Box 32666, Juneau AK 99803. (907)789-9544. Contact: Judy Shuler. Offers photography tours and workshops in nature and wildlife subjects.

*AMBIENT LIGHT WORKSHOPS, 5 Tartan Ridge Rd., Burr Ridge IL 60521. (708)325-5464. Contact: John J. Mariana.

*AMERICAN SOUTHWEST PHOTOGRAPHY WORKSHOP, P.O. Box 220450, El Paso TX 79913. (915)581-7959. Director: Geo. B. Drennan. Offers intense field workshops for the serious black and white photographer.

✿AMPRO PHOTO WORKSHOPS, 636 E. Broadway, Vancouver BC V5T 1X6 Canada. (604)876-5501. Fax: (604)876-5502. Approved trade school. Offers part-time and full-time career courses in commercial photography and photofinishing technician. "Twenty-nine different courses in camera, darkroom and studio lighting—from basic to advanced levels. Special seminars with top professional photographers. Course tuition ranges from under $100 for part-time to $5,500 for full-time."

ANCHELL PHOTOGRAPHY WORKSHOPS, 1411 N. Catalina St., Los Angeles CA 90027. (213)465-8777. Director: Steve Anchell. Offers workshops in fine arts photography and landscape techniques. Tuition: $395-525.

*ANDERSON RANCH ARTS CENTER, Box 5598, Snowmass Village CO 81615. (303)923-3181. Photography Director: James Baker. Offers 25 intensive weekend to two-week photo workshops for personal growth and professional development. Workshops take place on historical campus near the resort community of Aspen, Colorado.

*ANNUAL INTERNATIONAL MAIL ART SHOW, 220 S. 4th Ave., Kent WA 98032. (206)859-3991. Visual Arts Coordinator: Liz Gasper. 500-700 artists from over 40 countries send art (5 × 8 or smaller). All work shown, no jury, no returns, documentation (show poster and mailing list) is sent to all who send work.

*ARIZONA SHUTTERBUG ADVENTURES, 7016 E. Rivercrest Rd., Tucson AZ 85715. (602)721-2445 from 6am to sunset. Photo and video safaris to Arizona ghost towns and backroads, canyons, mountains, desert scenes, cacti and Arizona Wildlife with professional photographers as guides.

*BALLENGER-TULLEY PHOTO WORKSHOPS, P.O. Box 457, La Canada CA 91012. (818)954-0933 or (818)564-9086. Contact: Noella Ballenger or Jalien Tulley. Three-day travel and nature photo workshops in California. Individual instruction in small groups emphasizes visual awareness and problem solving in the field.

*AL BELSON PHOTOGRAPHY WORKSHOPS, 3701 W. Moore Ave., Santa Ana CA 92704. (714)432-7070 ext 603. Director: Al Belson. Workshops throughout the year covering portraiture, landscape and fine art.

BIG SUR SEMINARS, P.O. Box 222333, Carmel CA 93922. (408)384-4644. Director: Jane Murray. Offers workshops in developing personal vision for beginning and intermediate photographers.

BIXEMINARS, 919 Clinton Ave. SW, Canton OH 44706-5196. (216)455-0135. Founder/Instructor: R.C. Bixler. Offers three-day, weekend seminars for beginners through advanced amateurs. Usually held third weekend of February, June and October. Covers composition, lighting, location work and macro.

BLOCK ISLAND PHOTOGRAPHY WORKSHOPS, 319 Pheasant Dr., Rocky Hill CT 06067. (203)563-9156. Director: Stephen Sherman. Workshops take place on Block Island Rhode Island and also in the deserts of California and the canyons of Arizona. Offers workshop programs in black and white zone system, portraiture and landscapes.

*MATT BRADLEY PHOTOGRAPHY WORKSHOPS, 15 Butterfield Ln., Little Rock AR 72212. (501)224-0692. Workshop Director: Marcia Hartmann. *National Geographic* photographer teaches his "Creative Image" workshop three times a year at various Arkansas state parks.

*THE BROOKFIELD/SOHO PHOTOGRAPHIC WORKSHOP, 127 Washington St., Norwalk CT 06854 (203)853-6155. Director: John Russell. Community darkroom with school offering classes and workshops for all levels and interests.

CALIFORNIA REDWOODS PHOTOGRAPHY TOUR, 1516 5th St., Berkeley CA 94710. (800)245-3874. Marketing Coordinator: Elizabeth Gignilliat. Offers five-day workshop on location through redwood country; includes lodging in coastal inns.

🍁 *The maple leaf before a listing indicates that the market is Canadian. The symbol is new this year in* Photographer's Market.

CALIFORNIA WILDLIFE PHOTOGRAPHIC SAFARIS, P.O. Box 30694, Santa Barbara CA 93130. (805)569-3731. Contact: Sharon Peterson. Offers 4-day and weekend photo safaris to photograph and study the biology of California's unspoiled wildplaces and treasured wildlife. Five-person limit per safari. Photographic instructor: B. "Moose" Peterson.

*THE CAMERA OF NEW YORK, Second Floor, 853 Broadway, New York NY 10003. (212)260-7077. President: Tony Troncale. Offers workshops, classes, lectures and exhibitions covering all aspects of the medium of photography. Call for latest program listings.

CAMERA-IMAGE WORKSHOPS, P.O. Box 1501, Downey CA 90240. Instructors: Craig Fucile and Jan Pietrzak. Offers workshops in winter, spring and fall in California and Utah. Instruction in color, b&w techniques, exposure, filtration, equipment use, Cibachrome and hand-coated print making.

CAPE MAY PHOTO WORKSHOP INC., (formerly Art Kane Photo Workshop, Inc.) 1511 New York Ave., Cape May NJ 08204. (609)884-7117. Contact: Bill Deering. Offers workshops (including international workshops) in wide range of disciplines for beginners to advanced photographers, including: fashion, photojournalism, portrait, advertising, fine art, documentary design, still life, corporate and stock. Also offers training in studio lighting and printing.

VERONICA CASS ACADEMY OF PHOTOGRAPHIC ARTS, 7506 New Jersey Ave., Hudson FL 34667. (813)863-2738. President: Marilynn deChant. Offers 8 one-week workshops in photo retouching techniques. Price per week ranges from $450-525.

CENTER FOR PHOTOGRAPHY, 59 Tinker St., Woodstock NY 12498. (914)679-9957. Contact: Director. Offers monthly exhibitions, a summer workshop series, annual call for entry shows, library, darkroom, fellowships, and photography magazine, classes, lectures.

CHINA PHOTO WORKSHOP TOURS, #211, 22111 Cleveland, Dearborn MI 48124-3461. (313)561-1842. Director: D.E. Cox. Offers annual photo tours to China's major cities and scenic countryside; includes meetings with top Chinese photographers.

*CLOSE-UP EXPEDITIONS, 1031 Ardmore Ave., Oakland CA 94610. (510)465-8955. Guide and Outfitter: Donald Lyon. Worldwide, year-round travel and nature photography expeditions, 10-25 days. Professional photographer guides put you in the right place at the right time to create unique marketable images.

*CORY NATURE PHOTOGRAPHY WORKSHOPS, 1629 Rustic Homes Ln., Signal Mountain TN 37377. (615)886-1004. Contact: Tom or Pat Cory. Small workshops featuring individual attention in the Smoky Mountains of Tennessee, the Blue Ridge area of North Carolina and the High Sierras of California.

*CREATIVE ADVENTURES, 67 Maple St., Newburgh NY 12550. (914)561-5866. Contact: Richie Suraci. Photographic adventures into "exotic, sensual, beautiful international locations." Send SASE.

CREATIVE VISION WORKSHOPS IN COLORADO HIGH COUNTRY, 317 E. Winter Ave., Danville IL 61832-1857. (217)442-3075. Director: Orvil Stokes. Offers workshops in the color zone system, previsualization, contrast control, image design, selling your photographs and modified b&w zone system for roll film.

CUMMINGTON COMMUNITY OF THE ARTS, Cummington Community of the Arts, RR#1, Box 145, Cummington MA 01026. (413)634-2172. Contact: Executive Director. Residences for artists of all disciplines from 1-3 months.

DEERFIELD AT STONINGTON, 701 Elm Street, Essexville MI 48732. (800)882-8458. Director: Chuck McMartin. Offers wildlife photo workshops in the Hiawatha National Forest in Michigan's Upper Pennisula.

*FAMILY PHOTO WEEKEND, Mystic Seaport Museum, 50 Greenmanville Ave., P.O. Box 6000, Mystic CT 06355-0990. (203)572-5315. Models in 19th century costumes pose for amateur photographers. Sponsored by Eastman Kodak Co., features photo contests, with cash prizes for children and adults.

CHARLENE FARIS WORKSHOPS, #A, 9524 Guilford Dr., Indianapolis IN 46240. (317)848-2634. Director: Charlene Faris. Offers two-day programs for beginners in marketing and learning to shoot marketable photos. Also conducts week-long seminars at sea.

■**FILM IN THE CITIES/LIGHTWORKS,** 2388 University Ave., St. Paul MN 55114. (612)646-6104. Director: Ruth Williams. Offers basics through advanced level courses in photography, film/video production, screenwriting and electronic sound composition.

FINE ART WORKSHOP SERIES, (formerly Bodie Fine Art Workshop Series/Global Preservation Projects), P.O. Box 30866, Santa Barbara CA 93105. (805)682-3398. Director: Thomas I. Morse. Offers workshops promoting the preservation of environmental and historic treasures. Produces international photographic exhibitions and publications.

*****FOCUS ADVENTURES,** P.O. Box 771640, Steamboat Springs CO 80477. (303)879-2244. FAX: (303)879-9022. Owner: Karen Schulman. Workshops in the art of seeing, nature photography, hand coloring photographs, light, creativity and self promotion. Photographic trips to the Native American areas of the Southwest and The Sioux Reservation in South Dakota.

*****FOCUS SEMINAR IN HYBRID IMAGING AND NEW TECHNOLOGIES,** 5210 Photo/Lansing Community College, Box 40010, Lansing MI 48901-7210. (517)483-1673. A three-day series of workshops, seminars, forums and demonstrations related to hybrid imaging, new technologies in photography, imaging and computer graphics.

*****FOUR SEASONS NATURE PHOTOGRAPHY,** Box 620132, Littleton CO 80162. (303)972-1893. Co-directors: Daniel Poleschook, Jr. and Joseph K. Lange. Specializes in small-group nature-photography tours to nature's finest locations in the western United States, Alaska, Florida, Canada and Africa. Features wildlife and scenery photography with instructional slide shows included.

FRIENDS OF ARIZONA HIGHWAYS PHOTO ADVENTURES, P.O. Box 6106, Phoenix AZ 85005-6106. (602)271-5904. Sales Supervisor: Shannon Rosenblatt. Offers photo adventures to Arizona's spectacular locations with top professional photographers whose work routinely appears in *Arizona Highways.*

OLIVER GAGLIANI ZONE SYSTEM WORKSHOP, 35 Yosemite Rd., San Rafael CA 94903. (415)472-4010. Contact: Barry Lee Marris. Offers two-week workshop in Zone System techniques in Virginia City, Nevada.

*****GETTING & HAVING A SUCCESSFUL EXHIBITION,** # 201, 163 Amsterdam Ave., New York NY 10023. (212)838-8640. Speaker: Bob Persky. A 1-day seminar.

GOLDEN GATE SCHOOL OF PROFESSIONAL PHOTOGRAPHY, P.O. Box 187, Fairfield CA 94533. (707)422-0319. Director: Jim Inks. Offers short courses in photography annually.

GREAT SMOKY MOUNTAINS PHOTOGRAPHY WORKSHOPS, 205 Wayah Road, Franklin NC 28734. (704)369-6044. Instructors: Tim Black/Bill Lea. Offers programs which emphasize the use of natural light in creating quality scenic, wildflower and wildlife images.

HALLMARK INSTITUTE OF PHOTOGRAPHY, P.O. Box 308, Turner's Falls MA 01376. (413)863-2478. Director: Paul Turnbull. Offers workshops in commercial and professional portrait photography, 10-month resident professional photography studio management program.

*****HEART OF NATURE INSPIRATIONAL WORKSHOPS,** 14618 Tyler Fte Rd., Nevada City CA 95959. (916)292-3839. Contact: Robert Frutos. "Explores your personal vision, offers discovery techniques for visualizing and creating powerful images and the technical skills to render your unique vision."

HORIZONS: The New England Craft Program, 374 Old Montague Rd., Amherst MA 01002. (413)549-4841. Director: Jane Sinauer. Two 3-week summer sessions in b&w for high school students each summer plus 1-week adult workshop in Oaxaca, Mexico in February 1993.

*****IMAGE MASTER WORKSHOPS AND SEMINARS,** 74 Fifth Ave., New York NY 10011. (212)229-1260. Coordinator: Jennifer Nay. Workshops and seminars for advertising and commercial photographers, given year-round in cities across the country."

*****INFRARED WORKSHOP,** Photocentral/H.A.R.D., 1099 "E" St., Hayward CA 94541. (510)881-6735. Coordinators: Geir and Kate Jordahl. Workshops dedicated to seeing more through photography.

*****INTERNATIONAL CENTER OF PHOTOGRAPHY,** 1130 5th Ave. at 94th St., New York NY 10128. (212)860-1776. Contact: Education Department. Offers programs in b&w photography, non-silver printing processes, color photography, still life, photographing people, large format, studio, color printing, editorial concepts in photography, zone system, the freelance photographer, etc.

*INTERNATIONAL PHOTO TOURS (VOYAGERS INTERNATIONAL), Box 915, Ithaca NY 14851. (607)257-3091. Managing Director: David Blanton. Emphasizes techniques of nature photography.

*IRISH PHOTOGRAPHIC WORKSHOP, Voyagers, P.O. Box 915, Ithaca NY 14851. (607)257-3091. Director: Dave Blanton. Offers two-week workshop in the West of Ireland. Cost: $1790; airfare not included.

*THE LATENT IMAGE WORKSHOP AND WILDERNESS WORKSHOPS IN PHOTOGRAPHY, 5613 Johnson Ave., West Bethesda MD 20817-3503. Director: Lowell Anson Kenyon, FCFAP. Special indepth workshops for serious fine art photographers.

*THE LIGHT FACTORY, P.O. Box 32815, Arlington Street at South Boulevard, Charlotte NC 28232. (704)333-9755. Director: Linda Foard. Gallery and non-profit organization dedicated to fine art photography since 1972. Offers classes and workshops including a series of travel photography workshops to various destinations.

JOE McDONALD'S WILDLIFE PHOTOGRAPHY WORKSHOPS AND TOURS, Rt. 2, Box 1095., McClure PA 17841. (717)543-6423. (215)433-7025, answering machine and messages. Owner: Joe McDonald. Offers small groups, quality instruction with emphasis on wildlife.

*McNUTT FARM II/OUTDOOR WORKSHOP, 6120 Cutler Lake Rd., Blue Rock OH 43720. (614)674-4555. Director: Patty L. McNutt. Outdoor shooting of livestock, pets, wildlife and scenes in all types of weather.

■THE MAINE PHOTOGRAPHIC WORKSHOPS, Rockport ME 04856. (207)236-8581. Fax: (207)236-2885. Director: David H. Lyman. Offers more than 200 one-week workshops for professionals and serious amateurs in photography, film and television, digital imaging from May through October. Also professional year-round resident programs in photography and film and video production. Request materials by mail, phone or fax. Specify primary area of interest.

*MAKING A LIVING IN PHOTOGRAPHY, P.O. Box 151232, San Rafael CA 94915. (415)459-1495. Contact: Jay Daniel. Day-long seminars given twice a year on skills for professional photographers.

*MENDOCINO COAST PHOTOGRAPHY SEMINARS, P.O. Box 1629, Mendocino CA 95460. (707)937-2805. Program Director: Hannes Krebs. Offers a variety of workshops, including a foreign expedition to Chile.

MESSANA PHOTO WORKSHOP, 22500 Rio Vista, St. Clair Shores MI 48081. (313)773-5815. Joseph P. Messana. Offers on-location photographic workshops – architecture, nature, scenics, models and sculpture. Fall color trip in October; spring trip to Chicago; weekly area classes held in Detroit, suburbs and Canada.

*MICHIGAN PHOTOGRAPHY WORKSHOPS, MPW INTERNATIONAL, 28830 W. 8 Mile Rd., Farmington Hills MI 48336. FAX: (313)542-3441. Directors/Instructors: Alan Lowy and C.J. Elfont. Workshops, seminars and lectures dealing with Classical Nude Figures (Victorian House), Nude Figure in the Environment (Ludington Dunes), Boudoir and Fashion photography, Nature photography on location, and Still-life and Product photography.

*MISSOURI PHOTOJOURNALISM WORKSHOP, 27 Neff Annex, 9th and Elm, Columbia MO 65201. (314)882-4442. Coordinator: Marilyn Upton. Workshop for photojournalists. Participants learn the fundamentals of documentary photo research, shooting editing and layout.

Market conditions are constantly changing! If you're still using this book and it's 1994 or later, buy the newest edition of Photographer's Market *at your favorite bookstore or order directly from* Writer's Digest Books.

NATURE IMAGES, INC., P.O. Box 2037, West Palm Beach FL 33402. (407)586-7332. Director: Helen Longest-Slaughter. Photo workshops offered in Yellowstone National Park and Wisconsin's northwoods.

*NEW ENGLAND SCHOOL OF PHOTOGRAPHY, 537 Commonwealth Ave., Boston MA 02215. (617)437-1868. Administrative Director: Peter Forrest. Instruction in professional and creative photography.

*NEW SCHOOL/PARSONS INTERNATIONAL PHOTO WORKSHOPS, 66 5th Ave., Photo Department, New York NY 10011. (212)229-8923. Assistant Chairperson: Janet Grunwald. Workshops in New York City, France, Germany and Russia bring together diverse groups of photography students and professionals in a variety of fields, including photojournalism, fashion and electronic imaging.

NEW YORK CITY COLOR PRINTING WORKSHOPS, 230 W. 107th St., New York NY 10025. (212)316-1825. Contact: Joyce Culver. Offers two-day weekend, color print workshop making prints from color negatives or internegatives in a professional New York City lab. Call or write for brochure.

*1993 PHOTOGRAPHIC EDUCATION SERIES, St. Charles Parks & Recreation, 1900 West Randolph, St. Charles MO 63301. (314)949-3372. Program Administrator: Patrick Zarrick. Comprehensive photography series featuring out-of-state photo tours and workshops, regional weekend field workshops and seminars featuring "finest photographers" in U.S. and weekly "how-to" programs.

THE OGUNQUIT PHOTOGRAPHY SCHOOL, Box 2234, Ogunquit ME 03907. (207)646-7055. Director: Stuart Nudelman. Offers programs in photographic sensitivity, marketing photos, photodocumentation and creativity, and nature photography with guest instructors, AV symposiums for educators and traveling workshops.

■**OHIO INSTITUTE OF PHOTOGRAPHY AND TECHNOLOGY,** 2029 Edgefield Rd., Dayton OH 45439. (513)294-6155. Education Coordinator: Helen Morris. Eight workshops during July and August cover black & white and color darkroom techniques, location shooting with large format equipment, techniques for improving everyday photography of people, fashion and glamour, advanced black and white printing, and creating special effects. Workshops run Monday through Thursday, 6:30-9:30 p.m. and Saturday, 9:00 a.m.-6:00 p.m.. Two-day workshops designed especially for high school photo instructors will be offered and qualify for approved CEU credits.

OKLAHOMA ARTS INSTITUTES, P.O. Box 18154, Oklahoma City OK 73154. (405)842-0890. Fax: (405)848-4538. October photography workshop at Quartz Mountain Resort in Southwest Oklahoma.

*OREGON PHOTO TOURS, 745 E. 8th, Coquille OR 97423. (503)396-5792. Owner: Tony Mason. Offers one-on-one photographic tours throughout Oregon and the American West.

OREGON SCHOOL OF ARTS AND CRAFTS, 8245 SW Barnes Rd., Portland OR 97225. (503)297-5544. Admissions Counselor: Valorie Hadley. Offers workshops and classes in photography throughout year.

OUTBACK RANCH OUTFITTERS, P.O Box 384, Joseph OR 97846. (503)426-4037. Owner: Ken Wick. Offers photography trips by horseback or river raft into Oregon wilderness areas.

OZARK PHOTOGRAPHY WORKSHOP FIELDTRIP, 40 Kyle St., Batesville AR 72501. (501)793-4552. Conductor: Barney Sellers. Offers opportunities for all-day outdoor subject shooting. No slides shown, fast moving, looking at subjects through the camera lens.

*PACIFIC NORTHWEST FIELD SEMINARS, #212, 83 S. King, Seattle WA 98104. (206)553-2636. Coordinator: Jean Tobin. Nature photography seminars of 2-4 days, from May to October, in areas such as Mt. Rainier National Park, Crater Lake National Park, Mount St. Helens, Oregon Dunes and the Columbia Gorge.

THE PALO ALTO PHOTOGRAPHIC WORKSHOPS, 854 Rorke Way, Palo Alto CA 94303. (415)424-0105. Co-Directors: Douglas Peck and Stacy Geiken. Offers one-day classes in beginning photography, nature photography, 4×5 view camera and lighting techniques.

PERSONAL WORKSHOP SERIES BY DAVID M. STONE, 207 Granston Way, Buzzards Bay MA 02532. (508)759-9666. Contact: David M. Stone. Offers individualized workshops in nature photography, marketing your photographs, etc. scheduled at photographer's convenience. Send SASE for complete brochure.

*PETERS VALLEY CRAFT CENTER, 19 Kuhn Rd., Layton NJ 07851. (201)948-5200. Offers workshops June-August, 2-5 days long. Write or call for brochure.

PHOTO ADVENTURE TOURS, 2035 Park St., Atlantic Beach NY 11509-1236. (516)371-0067. Manager: Pamela Makaea. Offers photographic tours to Iceland, India, Nepal, Russia, China, Scandinavia and domestic locations such as New Mexico, Navajo Indian regions, Hawaiian Islands, Michigan, Albuquerque Balloon Festival and New York.

PHOTO ADVENTURES, P.O. Box 591291, San Francisco CA 94159. (415)221-3171. Instructor: Jo-Ann Ordano. Offers practical workshops covering creative and documentary photo technique in California nature subjects and San Francisco by moonlight.

*PHOTO FOCUS/COUPEVILLE ARTS CENTER, P.O. Box 171 MP, Coupeville WA 98239. (206)678-3396. Director: Judy Lynn. Offers variety of workshops with nationally recognized instructors.

PHOTO TOURS: IN FOCUS WITH MICHELE BURGESS, 20741 Catamaran Lane, Huntington Beach, CA 92646. (714)536-6104. President: Michele Burgess. Offers overseas tours to photogenic areas with expert photography consultation, at a leisurely pace and in small groups (maximum group size 20).

PHOTOGRAPHIC ARTS WORKSHOPS, P.O. Box 1791, Granite Falls WA 98252. (206)691-4105. Director: Bruce Barnbaum. Offers wide range of workshops across US and Canada. Workshops feature instruction in composition, exposure, development, printing and photographic philosophy. Includes critiques of student portfolios. Sessions held in field, darkroom and classroom with various instructors.

*PHOTOGRAPHY AT THE SUMMIT, 2305 Mt. Werner Circle, Steamboat Springs CO 80487. (303)879-6111 Ext: 472. Workshop Assistant: Heidi Barbee. A weeklong workshop with *National Geographic* staff.

*PHOTOGRAPHY BEFORE 1900, Box A-1, State Road 68, Pilar NM 87531. (800)678-7586. Instructor: Joe Zimmerman. Make pinhole cameras, explore various processes (cyanotype, vandyke brown, photoj-printing on fabric, kallitype).

PHOTOGRAPHY WORKSHOPS, % Pocono Environmental Education Center, RD2, Box 1010, Dingmans Ferry PA 18328. (717)828-2319. Attention: Dan Hendey. Offers weekend workshops throughout the year focusing on subjects in the natural world.

PHOTOGRAPHY WORKSHOPS, (formerly Nature Photography Workshops), 8410 Madeline Drive, St. Louis MO 63114. (314)427-6311. Instructors: Ed and Lee Mason. Offers customized workshops for one, three or five days, and for 3 weeks at your location.

PHOTO-NATURALIST WORKSHOPS, Box 377, Terlingua TX 79852. (800)359-4138. President: Steve Harris. Offers rafting/photo tours with Jim Bones through various canyons in the Southwest.

PORTRAITURE WITH WAH LUI, % Daytona Beach Community College, P.O. Box 2811, Daytona Beach FL 32120-2811. (904)254-4475. Museum Director: Alison Nordstrom. Offers spring workshops at the Southeast Museum of Photography.

*PRATT MANHATTAN, 295 Lafayette Ave., New York NY 10012. (212)925-8481. Assistant Dean (School of Professional Studies): Karen Miletsky. Offers courses on photographic lighting and beginner through advanced photography. Tuition ranges from $190-$290.

PROFESSIONAL PHOTOGRAPHER'S SOCIETY OF NEW YORK PHOTO WORKSHOPS, 121 Genesee St., Avon NY 14414. (716)226-8351. Director: Lois Miller. Offers week-long, specialized, hands-on workshops for professional photographers.

 The double dagger before a listing indicates that the market is located outside the United States and Canada. The symbol is new this year in **Photographer's Market.**

*PUBLISHING YOUR PHOTOS AS CARDS & POSTERS, #201, 163 Amsterdam Ave., New York NY 10023. (212)362-6637. Lecturer: Harold Davis. A one-day workshop.

*REDWOOD NATIONAL PARK FIELD SEMINARS, 1111 Second St., Crescent City CA 95531. (707)464-6101. Contact: Field Seminar Coordinator. One-to five-day workshops in the redwoods and along coastline, beginning and advanced seminars.

ROCKY MOUNTAIN PHOTO WORKSHOPS, % Latigo Ranch, Box 237, Kremmling CO 80459. (800)227-9655. (303)724-9008. Director: Jim Yost. Offers workshops in photography featuring western cattle round-ups and wildflowers.

ROCKY MOUNTAIN SCHOOL OF PHOTOGRAPHY, P.O. Box 7605, Missoula MT 59807. (406)543-0171. Vice President: Jeanne Chaput. Offers workshops throughout US and abroad.

SAN JUAN MAJESTY WORKSHOP, 412 Main St., Grand Junction CO 81501. (303)245-6700. Director: Steve Traudt. Offers annual photography workshops in the scenic Rocky Mountain area of Ouray, Colorado in late July.

*RON SANFORD, P.O. Box 248, Gridley CA 95948. (916)846-4687. Contact: Ron or Nancy Sanford. Travel and wildlife workshops and tours.

SANTA FE PHOTOGRAPHIC WORKSHOPS, P.O. Box 9916, Santa Fe NM 87504. (505)983-1400. FAX: (505)989-8604. Director: Reid Callanan. Offers 40 one-week, summer workshops with many of today's top photographers.

*PETER SCHREYER PHOTOGRAPHIC TOURS, P.O. Box 533, Winter Park FL 32790. (407)671-1886. Tour Director: Peter Schreyer. Specialty photographic tours to the American west, Europe and the backroads of Florida. Travel in small groups of 10-15 participants.

JOHN SEXTON PHOTOGRAPHY WORKSHOPS, 291 Los Agrinemsors, Carmel Valley CA 93924. (408)659-3130. Director: John Sexton. Managing Director: Victoria Bell Sexton. Offers a selection of intensive workshops with master photographers.

SIERRA PHOTOGRAPHIC WORKSHOPS, 3251 Lassen Way, Sacramento CA 95821. (800)925-2596. Contact: Sierra Photographic Workshops. Offers week-long workshops in various scenic locations for "personalized instruction in outdoor photography, technical knowledge useful in learning to develop a personal style, learning to convey ideas through photographs."

*BOB SISSON'S MACRO/NATURE PHOTOGRAPHY, %Katherine L. Rowland, P.O. Box 35187, Sarasota FL 34242-5187. (813)349-1714. Coordinator: Katherine L. Rowland. "You will be encouraged to take a closer look at nature through the lens, to learn the techniques of using nature's light correctly and to think before exposing film."

*SISTER KENNY INSTITUTE INTERNATIONAL ART SHOW BY DISABLED ARTISTS, 800 E. 28th St., Minneapolis MN 55407-3799. (612)863-4482. Director: Nanette Boudreau. Show is held once a year usually in April and May for disabled artists only. Deadline for entries, Feb. 28.

*THE 63 RANCH PHOTO WORKSHOPS, P.O. Box 979, Livingston MT 59047. (406)222-0570. Director: Laurance B. Aiuppy. Contact: Sandra Cahill. Workshop in June and September including field day in Yellowstone National Park for intermediate to advanced amateur (or beginning professional) photographers.

SOUTH FLORIDA PHOTOGRAPHIC WORKSHOPS, P.O. Box 811045, Boca Raton FL 33481-1045. (407)997-9879. Director: Anita Starkoff. Offers number of photographic workshops.

SOUTHWEST PHOTOGRAPHIC WORKSHOPS, P.O. Box 19272, Houston TX 77224. (713)496-2905. Contact: Jay Forrest. On-location photographic workshops in Texas and New Mexico.

SPIRIT WALKER EXPEDITIONS, P.O. Box 240, Gustavus AK 99826. (907)697-2266. President: Nathan Borson. Offers guided wilderness sea kayaking tours in Southeastern Alaska.

SPLIT ROCK ARTS PROGRAM, University of Minnesota, 306 Wesbrook Hall, 77 Pleasant St. SE, Minneapolis MN 55455. (612)624-6800. Registrar: Vivien Oja. One-week, intensive summer residential workshops; nature and documentary photography as well as other arts. Duluth campus on Lake Superior.

*STONE CELLAR DARKROOM WORKSHOPS, 51 Hickory Flat Rd., Buckhannon WV 26201. (304)472-1669. Photography/Printmaker: Jim Stansbury. Master color printing and color field work, small classes with Jim Stansbury. Work at entry-level or experienced-level.

*SUMMIT PHOTOGRAPHIC WORKSHOPS, P.O. Box 24571, San Jose CA 95154. (408)265-7217. Owner and Instructor: Barbara Brundege. Nature, wildlife and outdoor photographic seminars and tours lasting up to one week in California, U.S. National Parks and wilderness areas.

SUPERIOR/GUNFLINT PHOTOGRAPHY WORKSHOPS, P.O. Box 19286, Minneapolis MN 55419. (800)328-3325 (summer). Director: Layne Kennedy. Offers wilderness adventure photo workshops twice yearly. Winter session includes dogsledding. Write for details. Summer session involves canoe trips. Prices range from $485-585, includes food, lodging, outfitting and workshop.

*TECHNIQUES FOR THE NATURE PHOTOGRAPHER, 207 Granston Way, Buzzards Bay MA 02532. (508)759-9666. Contact: David M. Stone. Custom designed for up to 3 participants. Highly intense half-day workshops as varied topics as decided by participants. Dates as scheduled for mutual convenience.

THOMPSON PHOTO PRODUCTS PHOTO WORKSHOPS, 2019 University Ave., Knoxville TN 37921. (615)637-0215. General Manager: Michael Ellison. Offers 5 workshops in outdoor, nature and wildlife photography.

TRAVEL PHOTOGRAPHY WORKSHOP in Santa Fe with Lisl Dennis, Box 2847, Santa Fe NM 87504-2847. (505)982-4979. Photographer Dennis offers one-week workshops in 35mm color photography in May and September.

TRINITY ALPS PHOTOGRAPHY WORKSHOPS, 216 Marquis Place, Santa Maria CA 93454. (805)928-3386. Director: Mary Ellen Schultz. Offers programs in all aspects of nature photography. Makes trips to California, Washington, Maine and Canada.

*UC-BERKELEY EXTENSION PHOTOGRAPHY PROGRAM,% University of California Berkeley Extension, 55 Laguna St., San Francisco CA 94102. (415)642-8840. Director, Photography Program: Michael Lesser. Offers courses and workshops for beginning, advanced and professional photographers.

*UNIVERSITY OF WISCONSIN SCHOOL OF THE ARTS AT RHINELANDER, 727 Lowell Hall, 610 Langdon St., Madison WI 53703. (608)263-3494. Coordinator: Kathy Berigan. One-week interdisciplinary arts program held during July in northern Wisconsin.

USC ADVENTURE PHOTOGRAPHY, % University of Southern California, Los Angeles CA 90089-7791. (213)743-7084. Director: Dave Wyman. Offers photo workshops in nature and adventure travel.

JOSEPH VAN OS PHOTO SAFARIS, INC., P.O. Box 655, Vashon Island WA 98070. (206)463-5383. Director: Randy Green. Offers photo tours and workshops worldwide.

VENTURE WEST, P.O. Box 7543, Missoula MT 59807. (406)825-6200. Owner: Cathy Ream. Offers various photographic opportunities, including wilderness pack and raft trips, ranches, and fishing and hunting.

✸VISIONQUEST PHOTOGRAPHIC ADVENTURES, Box 572, Duncan BC V9L 3X9 Canada. (604)746-4341. Owner: Paul Fletcher. Offers weekend/weeklong photo workshops on Vancouver Islands' West Coast and on the Queen Charlotte Islands.

*VISUAL DEPARTURES PHOTOGRAPHIC WORKSHOPS, P.O. Box 1653, Ross CA 94957. President: Brenda Tharp. Offers multi-day photography tours and workshops in exciting locations worldwide. Specializes in creative outdoor and travel photography with emphasis on low-impact travel and unique cultural experiences.

PETE VOGEL PHOTO WORKSHOPS, P.O. Box 229, Winchester OR 97495. (503)672-2453. Instructor: Pete Vogel. Offers 3-day workshops at Wildlife Safari, a 600-acre drive-thru wild animal park.

MARK WARNER NATURE PHOTO WORKSHOPS, Box 142, Ledyard CT 06339. (203)376-6115. Offers 1-7 day workshops on nature and wildlife photography by nationally published photographer and writer at various East Coast and Western locations.

*WFC ENTERPRISES, P.O. Box 5054, Largo FL 34649. (813)581-5906. Owner: Wayne F. Collins. Photoworkshops (glamour), January through November, all on weekend. Free brochure on request.

WHITE MAGIC UNLIMITED, P.O. Box 5506, Mill Valley CA 94942-5506. (415)381-8889. President: Jack Morison. Offers specialty travel and photo safaris worldwide.

WILD HORIZONS, INC., P.O. Box 5118-PM, Tucson AZ 85703. (602)622-0672. President: Thomas A. Wiewandt. Offers workshops in field techniques in nature/travel photography at vacation destinations in the American Southwest selected for their outstanding natural beauty and wealth of photographic opportunities. Customized learning vacations for small groups are also offered in E. Africa and Ecuador/Galápagos.

WILDERNESS PHOTOGRAPHY EXPEDITIONS, 402 S. 5th, Livingston MT 59047. (406)222-2302. President: Tom Murphy. Offers programs in wildlife and landscape photography in Yellowstone Park and Montana.

WOODSTOCK PHOTOGRAPHY WORKSHOPS, 59 Tinker, Woodstock NY 12498. (914)679-9957. Offers annual lectures and workshops in creative photography from July through September. Faculty includes numerous top professionals.

*WORKSHOPS IN THE WEST, P.O. Box 13496, Austin TX 78711. (512)295-3348. Contact: Joe Englander. Photographic instruction in beautiful locations, all formats, color and b&w, darkroom instruction.

YELLOWSTONE INSTITUTE, Box 117, Yellowstone National Park WY 82190. (307)344-7381, ext. 2384. Registrar: Jeanne Peterman. Offers workshops in nature, wildlife and close-up photography.

YOSEMITE FIELD SEMINARS, P.O. Box 230, El Portal CA 95318. (209)379-2646. Seminar Coordinator: Penny Otwell. Offers workshops in outdoor field photography throughout the year.

YOUR WORLD IN COLOR, % Stone Cellar Darkroom, P.O. Box 253, Buckhannon WV 26201. (304)472-1669. Director: Jim Stansbury. Offers workshops in color processing, printing and related techniques. Also arranges scenic field trips.

*JOSEPH ZAIA PHOTOVISION WORKSHOPS, 275 Maybury Avenue, Staten Island NY 10308. (718)356-8968. Director/Instructor: Joseph J. Zaia. Offers personalized instruction for individuals or small groups; locally or on locations to: Cape Ann, Massachusetts; Boothbay Harbor, Maine; Vermont and within New York. Workshops may consist of classes and one to six days, depending on individual or group desires. Worshops are suitable for beginner and seasoned photographers. Cost based on location and conditions. Consider approximately $100 per day plus expenses. Advance planning is strongly suggested.

Recommended Books
& Publications

Photographer's Market recommends the following additional reading material to stay informed of market trends as well as to find additional names and addresses of photo buyers. Most are available either in a library or bookstore or from the publisher. To insure accuracy of information, use copies of these resources that are no older than a year.

ADVERTISING AGE, *740 Rush St., Chicago IL 60611-2590. Weekly advertising and marketing tabloid.*

ADWEEK, *A/S/M Communications,Inc., 49 E. 21st St., New York NY 10160-0625. Weekly advertising and marketing magazine.*

AMERICAN PHOTO, *43rd Floor, 1633 Broadway, New York NY 10019. Monthly magazine, formerly* American Photographer, *now emphasizing the craft and philosophy of photography.*

ART CALENDAR, *Rt. 2, Box 273-C, Sterling VA 22170. Monthly magazine listing galleries reviewing portfolios, juried shows, percent-for-art programs, scholarships and art colonies, among other art-related topics.*

ART DIRECTION, *6th Floor, 10 E. 39th St., New York NY 10016-0199. Monthly magazine featuring art directors' views on advertising and photography.*

ART DIRECTORS ANNUAL, *Art Directors Club, 250 Park Ave. South, New York NY 10003. Annual showcase of work selected by the organization.*

ASMP BULLETIN, *monthly newsletter of the American Society of Magazine Photographers, 419 Park Ave. South, New York NY 10016. Subscription comes with membership in ASMP.*

COMMUNICATION ARTS, *410 Sherman Ave., Box 10300, Palo Alto CA 94303. Magazine covering design, illustration and photography. Published 8 times a year.*

THE DESIGN FIRM DIRECTORY, *Wefler & Associates, Inc., Box 1167, Evanston IL 60204. Annual directory of design firms.*

EDITOR & PUBLISHER, *The Editor & Publisher Co., Inc., 11 W. 19th St., New York NY 10011. Weekly magazine covering latest developments in journalism and newspaper production. Publishes an annual directory issue listing syndicates and another directory listing newspapers.*

ENCYCLOPEDIA OF ASSOCIATIONS, *Gale Research Co., 835 Penobscot Building, Detroit MI 48226-4094. Annual directory listing active organizations.*

FOLIO, *Box 4949, Stamford CT 06907-0949. Monthly magazine featuring trends in magazine circulation, production and editorial.*

GREEN BOOK, *% AG Editions, 142 Bank St., New York NY 10014. Annual directory of nature and stock photographers for use by photo editors and researchers.*

GREETINGS MAGAZINE, *MacKay Publishing Corp., 309 Fifth Ave., New York NY 10016. Monthly magazine featuring updates on the greeting card and stationery industry.*

GUIDE TO TRAVEL WRITING & PHOTOGRAPHY, *by Ann and Carl Purcell, published by Writer's Digest Books, 1507 Dana Ave., Cincinnati OH 45207.*

GUILFOYLE REPORT, *% AG Editions, 142 Bank St., New York NY 10014. Quarterly market tips newsletter for nature and stock photographers.*

HOW TO SHOOT STOCK PHOTOS THAT SELL, *by Michal Heron, published by Allworth Press, distributed by Writer's Digest Books, 1507 Dana Ave., Cincinnati OH 45207.*

HOW YOU CAN MAKE $25,000 A YEAR WITH YOUR CAMERA, *by Larry Cribb, published by Writer's Digest Books, 1507 Dana Ave., Cincinnati OH 45207. Newly revised edition of the popular book on finding photo opportunities in your own hometown.*

INDUSTRIAL PHOTOGRAPHY, *% PTN Publishing, 445 Broad Hollow Rd., Melville NY 11747. (516)845-2700. Monthly magazine for photographers in various types of staff positions in industry, education and other institutions.*

INTERNATIONAL STOCK PHOTOGRAPHY REPORT, *by Craig Aurness, % Westlight Stock Photo Agency, 2223 S. Carmelina Ave., Los Angeles CA 90064. Annual report on trends and issues affecting photographers and agencies in the stock photo industry.*

LIGHTING SECRETS FOR THE PROFESSIONAL PHOTOGRAPHER, *by Alan Brown, Tim Grondin and Joe Braun, published by Writer's Digest Books, 1507 Dana Ave., Cincinnati OH 45207.*

LITERARY MARKET PLACE, *R.R. Bowker Company, 121 Chanlon Rd. New Providence NJ 07974.*

MADISON AVENUE HANDBOOK, *Peter Glenn Publications, 17 E. 48th St., New York NY 10017. Annual directory listing advertising agencies, audiovisual firms and design studios in the New York area.*

NEGOTIATING STOCK PHOTO PRICES, *by Jim Pickerell. Available through American Society of Magazine Photographers, 419 Park Ave. South, New York NY 10016. Hardbound book which offers pricing guidelines for selling photos through stock photo agencies.*

NEWS PHOTOGRAPHER, *Suite 306, 3200 Croasdaile Dr., Durham NC 27705. (919)383-7246. Monthly news tabloid published by the National Press Photographers Association.*

NEWSLETTERS IN PRINT, *Gale Research Co., 835 Penobscot Building, Detroit MI 48226-4094. Annual directory listing newsletters.*

1993 GUIDE TO LITERARY AGENTS & ART/PHOTO REPS, *published by Writer's Digest Books, 1507 Dana Ave., Cincinnati OH 45207.*

O'DWYER DIRECTORY OF PUBLIC RELATIONS FIRMS, *J.R. O'Dwyer Company, Inc., 271 Madison Ave., New York NY 10016. Annual directory listing public relations firms, indexed by specialties.*

OUTDOOR PHOTOGRAPHER, *Suite 1220, 12121 Wilshire Blvd., Los Angeles CA 90025. Monthly magazine emphasizing equipment and techniques for shooting in outdoor conditions.*

THE PERFECT PORTFOLIO, *by Henrietta Brackman, published by Amphoto Books, % Watson-Guptill Publishing, 1515 Broadway, New York NY 10036.*

PETERSEN'S PHOTOGRAPHIC MAGAZINE, *8490 Sunset Blvd., Los Angeles CA 90069. Monthly magazine for beginning and semi-professional photographers in all phases of still photography.*

PHOTO/DESIGN, *1515 Broadway, New York NY 10036. Monthly magazine emphasizing photography in the advertising/design fields.*

PHOTO DISTRICT NEWS, *49 East 21st St., New York NY 10010. Monthly trade magazine for the photography industry.*

THE PHOTOGRAPHER'S BUSINESS & LEGAL HANDBOOK, *by Leonard Duboff, published by Images Press, distributed by Writer's Digest Books, 1507 Dana Ave., Cincinnati OH 45207. A guide to copyright, trademarks, libel law and other legal concerns for photographers.*

PHOTOGRAPHER'S GUIDE TO MARKETING AND SELF-PROMOTION, *by Maria Piscopo, published by Writer's Digest Books, 1507 Dana Ave., Cincinnati, Ohio 45207.*

PHOTOGRAPHER'S SOURCE, *by Henry Horenstein, published by Fireside Books, % Simon & Schuster Publishing, Rockefeller Center, 1230 Avenue of the Americas, New York NY 10020.*

PRINT, *9th Floor, 104 Fifth Ave., New York NY 10011. Bimonthly magazine focusing on creative trends and technological advances in illustration, design, photography and printing.*

PROFESSIONAL PHOTOGRAPHER, *published by Professional Photographers of America (PPA), 1090*

Executive Way, Des Plaines IL 60018. Monthly magazine, emphasizing technique and equipment for working photographers.

PROFESSIONAL PHOTOGRAPHER'S GUIDE TO SHOOTING & SELLING NATURE & WILDLIFE PHOTOS, *by Jim Zuckerman, published by Writer's Digest Books, 1507 Dana Ave., Cincinnati OH 45207.*

PROFESSIONAL PHOTOGRAPHER'S SURVIVAL GUIDE, *by Charles E. Rotkin, published by Writer's Digest Books, 1507 Dana Ave., Cincinnati OH 45207. A guide to becoming a professional photographer, making the first sale, completing assignments and earning the most from photographs.*

PUBLISHERS WEEKLY, *205 W. 42nd St., New York NY 10017. Weekly magazine covering industry trends and news in book publishing, book reviews and interviews.*

PUBLISHING NEWS, *Hanson Publishing Group, Box 4949, Stamford CT 06907-0949. Bimonthly newsmagazine of the publishing industry.*

THE RANGEFINDER, *1312 Lincoln Blvd., Santa Monica CA 90404. Monthly magazine on photography technique, products and business practices.*

SELL & RESELL YOUR PHOTOS, *by Rohn Engh, published by Writer's Digest Books, 1507 Dana Ave., Cincinnati OH 45207. Newly revised edition of the classic volume on marketing your own stock images.*

SHUTTERBUG, *Box 1209 Titusville FL 32781. Monthly magazine of photography news and equipment reviews.*

STANDARD DIRECTORY OF ADVERTISING AGENCIES, *National Register Publishing Co., Inc., 3004 Glenview Rd., Wilmette IL 60091. Annual directory listing advertising agencies.*

STANDARD RATE AND DATA SERVICE, *3004 Glenview Rd., Wilmette IL 60091. Annual directory listing magazines, plus their advertising rates.*

STOCK PHOTOGRAPHY HANDBOOK, *by Michal Heron, published by Ameican Society of Magazine Phototgraphers, 419 Park Ave. South, New York NY 10016.*

THE STOCK WORKBOOK, *published by Scott & Daughters Publishing, Inc., Suite A, 940 N. Highland Ave., Los Angeles CA 90038. (213)856-0008. Annual directory of stock photo agencies.*

SUCCESSFUL FINE ART PHOTOGRAPHY, *by Harold Davis, published by Images Press, distributed by Writer's Digest Books, 1507 Dana Ave., Cincinnati OH 45207.*

TAKING STOCK, *published by Jim Pickerell, Suite A, 110 Frederick Ave., Rockville MD 20850. Newsletter for stock phtographers; includes coverage of trends in business practices such as pricing and contract terms.*

WRITER'S MARKET, *Writer's Digest Books, 1507 Dana Ave., Cincinnati OH 45207. Annual directory listing markets for freelance writers. Lists names, addresses, contact people and marketing information for book publishers, magazines, greeting card companies and syndicates. Many listings also list photo needs and payment rates.*

Glossary

Absolute-released images. Any images for which signed model or property releases are on file and immediately available. For working with stock photo agencies that deal with advertising agencies, corporations and other commercial clients, such images are absolutely necessary to sell usage of images. Also see Model release, Property release.

Acceptance (payment on). The buyer pays for certain rights to publish a picture at the time he accepts it, prior to its publication.

Agency promotion rights. In stock photography, these are the rights that the agency requests in order to reproduce a photographer's images in any promotional materials such as catalogs, brochures and advertising.

Agent. A person who calls upon potential buyers to present and sell existing work or obtain assignments for his client. A commission is usually charged. Such a person may also be called a *photographer's rep.*

All rights. A form of rights often confused with work for hire. Identical to a buyout, this typically applies when the client buys all rights or claim to ownership of copyright, usually for a lump sum payment. This entitles the client to unlimited, exclusive usage and usually with no further compensation to the creator. Unlike work for hire, the transfer of copyright is not permanent. A time limit can be negotiated, or the copyright ownership can run to the maximum of 35 years. Also see Copyright/rights in the Business of Photography section.

All reproduction rights. See all rights.

All subsidiary rights. See all rights.

ASMP member pricing survey. These statistics are the result of a national survey of the American Society of Magazine Photographer's (ASMP) compiled to give an overview of various specialties comprising the photography market. Though erroneously referred to as "ASMP rates", this survey is not intended to suggest rates or to establish minimum or maximum fees.

Assignment. A definite OK to take photos for a specific client with mutual understanding as to the provisions and terms involved.

Assignment of copyright, rights. The photographer transfers claim to ownership of copyright over to another party in a written contract signed by both parties. Terms are almost always exclusive, but can be negotiated for a limited time period or as a permanent transfer. Also see Copyright/rights in the Business of Photography section.

Assign (designated recipient). A third-party person or business to which a client assigns or designates ownership of copyrights that the client purchased originally from a creator, such as a photographer.

Audiovisual. Materials such as filmstrips, motion pictures and overhead transparencies which use audio backup for visual material.

Automatic renewal clause. In contracts with stock photo agencies, this clause works on the concept that every time the photographer delivers an image, the contract is automatically renewed for a specified number of years. The drawback is that a photographer can be bound by the contract terms beyond the contract's termination and be blocked from marketing the same images to other clients for an extended period of time.

AV. See Audiovisual.

Betacam. A videotape mastering format typically used for documentary/location work. Because of its compact equipment design allowing mobility and its extremely high-quality for its size, it has become an accepted standard among TV stations for news coverage.

Bimonthly. Every two months.

Biweekly. Every two weeks.

Bleed. In a mounted photograph it refers to an image that extends to the boundaries of the board.

Blurb. Written material appearing on a magazine's cover describing its contents.

Body copy. Text used in a printed ad.

Bounce light. Light that is directed away from the subject toward a reflective surface.

Bracket. To make a number of different exposures of the same subject in the same lighting conditions.

Buyout. A form of work for hire where the client buys all rights or claim to ownership of copyright, usually for a lump sum payment. Also see All rights, Work for hire.

Capabilities brochure. In advertising and design firms, this type of brochure—similar to an annual report—is a frequent request from many corporate clients. This brochure outlines for prospective clients the nature of a company's business and the range of products or services it provides.

Caption. The words printed with a photo (usually directly beneath it) describing the scene or action. Synonymous with *cutline.*

Catalog work. The design of sales catalogs is a type of print work that many art/design studios and advertising agencies do for retail clients on a regular basis. Because the emphasis in catalogs is upon selling merchandise, photography is used heavily in catalog design. Also there is a great demand for such work, so many designers, art directors and photographers consider this to be "bread and butter" work, or reliable source or income.

Cibachrome. A photo printing process that produces fade-resistant color prints directly from color slides.

Clips. See Tearsheets.

Collateral materials. In advertising and design work, these are any materials or methods used to communicate a client's marketing identity or promote its product or service. For instance, in corporate identity designing, everything from the company's trademark to labels and packaging to print ads and marketing brochures is often designed at the same time. In this sense, collateral design—which uses photography at least as much as straight advertising does—is not separate from advertising but supportive to an overall marketing concept.

Commission. The fee (usually a percentage of the total price received for a picture) charged by a photo agency or agent for finding a buyer and attending to the details of billing, collecting, etc.

Composition. The visual arrangement of all elements in a photograph.

Copyright. The exclusive legal right to reproduce, publish and sell the matter and form of a literary or artistic work. Also see Copyright/rights in the Business of Photography section.

C-print. Any enlargement printed from a negative. Any enlargement from a transparency is called an R-print.

Credit line. The byline of a photographer or organization that appears below or beside published photos.

Crop. To omit unnecessary parts of an image when making a print or copy negative in order to focus attention on the important part of the image.

Cutline. See Caption.

Day rate. A minimum fee which many photographers charge for a day's work, whether a full day is spent on a shoot or not. Some photographer's offer a half-day rate for projects involving up to a half-day of work. This rate typically includes mark-up but not additional expenses, which are usually billed to the customer.

Demo(s). A sample reel of film or sample videocassette which includes excerpts of a filmmaker's or videographer's production work for clients.

Disclaimer. A denial of legal claim used in ads and on products.

Dry mounting. A method of mounting prints on cardboard or similar materials by means of heat, pressure, and tissue impregnated with shellac.

EFP. Abbreviation for Electronic Field Processing equipment. Trade jargon in the news/video production industry for a video recording system that is several steps above ENG in quality. Typically, this is employed when film-like sharpness and color saturation are desirable in a video format. It requires a high degree of lighting, set-up and post-production. Also see ENG.

ENG. Abbreviation for Electronic News Gathering equipment. Trade jargon in the news/video production industry for professional-quality video news cameras which can record images on videotape or transmit them by microwave to a TV station's receiver.

Exclusive property rights. A type of exclusive rights in which the client owns the physical image, such as a print, slide, film reel or videotape. A good example is when a portrait which is shot for a person to keep, while the photographer retains the copyright. Also see Copyright/rights in the Business of Photography section.

Exclusive rights. A type of rights in which the client purchases exclusive usage of the image for a negotiated time period, such as one, three or five years. Can also be permanent. Also see All rights, Work for Hire.

Fee-plus basis. An arrangement whereby a photographer is given a certain fee for an assignment—plus reimbursement for travel costs, model fees, props and other related expenses incurred in filling the assignment.

First rights. The photographer gives the purchaser the right to reproduce the work for the first time. The photographer agrees not to permit any prior publication of the work elsewhere for a specified amount of time. Also see Copyright/rights in the Business of Photography section.

Format. The size, shape and other traits giving identity to a periodical.

Four-color printing, four-color process. A printing process in which four primary printing inks are run in four separate passes on the press to create the visual effect of a full-color photo, as in magazines, posters and various other print media. Four separate negatives of the color photo—shot through filters—are placed identically (stripped) and exposed onto printing plates, and the images are printed from the plates in four ink colors.

Gaffer. In motion pictures, the person who is responsible for positioning and operating lighting equipment, including generators and electrical cables.

Grip. A member of a motion picture camera crew who is responsible for transporting, setting up, operating, and removing support equipment for the camera and related activities.

Holography. Recording on a photographic material the interference pattern between a direct coherent light beam and one reflected or transmitted by the subject. The resulting hologram gives the appearance of three dimensions, and, within limits, changing the viewpoint from which a hologram is observed shows the subject as seen from different angles.

In perpetuity. A term used in business contracts which means that once a photographer has sold his copyrights to a client, the client has claim to ownership of the image or images forever. Also see All rights, Work for hire.

Internegative. An intermediate image used to convert a color transparency to a black-and-white print.

IRC. Abbreviation for International Reply Coupon. IRCs are used instead of stamps when submitting material to foreign buyers.

Leasing. A term used in reference to the repeated selling of one-time rights to a photo; also known as *renting.*

Logo. The distinctive nameplate of a publication which appears on its cover.

Model release. Written permission to use a person's photo in publications or for commercial use.

Ms, mss. Manuscript and manuscripts, respectively. Their abbreviations are used in *Photographer's Market* listings.

Multi-image. A type of slide show which uses more than one projector to create greater visual impact with the subject. In more sophisticated multi-image shows, the projectors can be programmed to run by computer for split-second timing and animated effects.

Multimedia. A generic term used by advertising, public relations and audiovisual firms to describe productions using more than one medium together—such as slides and full-motion, color video—to create a variety of visual effects. Usually such productions are used in sales meetings and similar kinds of public events.

News Release. See Press release.

No right of reversion. A term in business contracts which specifies once a photographer sells his copyrights to an image or images, he has surrendered his claim to ownership. This may be unenforceable, though, in light of the 1989 Supreme Court decision on copyright law. Also see All rights, Work for hire.

NPI. An abbreviation used within listings in *Photographer's Market* that means "no payment information given." Even though we request specific dollar amounts for payment information in each listing, the information is not always provided.

Offset. A printing process using flat plates. The plate is treated to accept ink in image areas and to reject it in nonimage areas. The inking is transferred to a rubber roller and then to the paper.

One-time rights. The photographer sells the right to use a photo one time only in any medium. The rights transfer back to the photographer on his request after the photo's use. Also see Copyright/rights in the Business of Photography section.

On spec. Abbreviation for "on speculation." Also see Speculation, Assignment.

PACA. See Picture Agency Council of America.

Page rate. An arrangement in which a photographer is paid at a standard rate per page. A page consists of both illustrations and text.

Panoramic Format. A camera format which creates the impression of peripheral vision for the viewer. It was first developed for use in motion pictures and later adapted to still formats. In still work, this format requires a very specialized camera and lens system.

Pans. See Panoramic format.

Picture Agency Council of America. A trade organization consisting of stock photo agency professionals established to promote fair business practices in the stock photo industry. The organization monitors its member agencies and serves as a resource for stock agencies and stock photographers. Also see listing under Professional Organizations, on page 597.

Point-of-purchase, point-of-sale. A generic term used in the advertising industry to describe in-store marketing displays which promote a product. Typically, these colorful and highly-illustrated displays are placed near check out lanes or counters, and offer tear-off discount coupons or trial samples of the product.

P-O-P, P-O-S. See Point-of-purchase.

Portfolio. A group of photographs assembled to demonstrate a photographer's talent and abilities, often presented to buyers.

Press Release. A form of publicity announcement which public relations agencies and corporate communications staff people send out to newspapers and TV stations to generate news coverage. Usually this is sent in typewritten form with accompanying photos or videotape materials. Also see Video News Release.

Property release. Written permission to use a photo of private property and public or government facilities in publications or commercial use.

Publication (payment on). The buyer does not pay for rights to publish a photo until it is actually published, as opposed to payment on acceptance.

Release. See Model release, Property release.

Rep. Trade jargon for sales representative. Also see Agent.

Query. A letter of inquiry to an editor or potential buyer soliciting his interest in a possible photo assignment or photos that the photographer may already have.

Resume. A short written account of one's career, qualifications and accomplishments.

Royalty. A percentage payment made to a photographer/filmmaker for each copy of his work sold.

R-print. Any enlargement made from a transparency. Any enlargement from a negative is called a C-print.

SAE. Self-addressed envelope. Rather than requesting a self-addressed, stamped envelope, market listings may advise sending a SAE with the proper amount of postage to guarantee safe return of sample copies.

SASE. Abbreviation for self-addressed stamped envelope. Most buyers require SASE if a photographer wishes unused photos returned to him, especially unsolicited materials.

Self-assignment. Any photography project which a photographer shoots to show his abilities to prospective clients. This can be used by beginning photographers who want to build a portfolio or by photographers wanting to make a transition into a new market.

Self-promotion piece. A printed piece which photographers use for advertising and promoting their businesses. These pieces usually use one or more examples of the photographers' best work, and are professionally designed and printed to make the best impression.

Semigloss. A paper surface with a texture between glossy and matte, but closer to glossy.

Semimonthly. Twice a month.

Serial rights. The photographer sells the right to use a photo in a periodical. Rights usually transfer back to the photographer on his request after the photo's use.

Simultaneous submissions. Submission of the same photo or group of photos to more than one potential buyer at the same time.

Speculation. The photographer takes photos on his own with no assurance that the buyer will either purchase them or reimburse his expenses in any way, as opposed to taking photos on assignment.

Stock photo agency. A business that maintains a large collection of photos which it makes available to a variety of clients such as advertising agencies, calendar firms, and periodicals. Agencies usually retain 40-60 percent of the sales price they collect, and remit the balance to the photographers whose photo rights they've sold.

Stock Photography. Primarily the selling of reprint rights to existing photographs rather than shooting on assignment for a client. Some stock photos are sold outright, but most are rented for a limited time period. Individuals can market and sell stock images to individual clients from their personal inventory, or stock photo agencies can market a photographer's work for them. Many stock agencies hire photographers to shoot new work on assignment which then becomes the inventory of the stock agency.

Stringer. A freelancer who works part-time for a newspaper, handling spot news and assignments in his area.

Stripping. A process in printing production where negatives are put together to make a composite image or prepared for making the final printing plates, especially in four-color printing work. Also see Four-color printing.

Subagent. See Subsidiary agent.

Subsidiary agent. In stock photography, this is a stock photo agent which handles marketing of stock images for a primary stock agency in certain US or foreign markets. These are usually affiliated with the primary agency by a contractual agreement rather than by direct ownership, as in the case of an agency which has its own branch offices.

SVHS. Abbreviation for Super VHS. A videotape equipment format utilizing standard VHS format tape but which is a step above consumer quality in resolution. The camera system separates the elements of the video signal into two main components of sharpness and color which can be further enhanced in post-production and used for TV broadcast.

Table-top. Still-life photography; also the use of miniature props or models constructed to simulate reality.

Tabloid. A newspaper that is about half the page size of an ordinary newspaper, and which contains many photos and news in condensed form.

Tearsheet. An actual sample of a published work from a publication.

Trade journal. A publication devoted strictly to the interests of readers involved in a specific trade or profession, such as doctors, writers, or druggists, and generally available only by subscription.

Transparency. A color film with positive image, also referred to as a slide.

Tungsten light. Artificial illumination as opposed to daylight.

U-Matic. A trade name for a particular videotape format produced by the Sony Corporation.

Unlimited use. A type of rights in which the client has total control over both how and how many times an image will be used. Also see All rights, Exclusive rights, Work for hire.

VHS. Abbreviation for Video Home System. A standard videotape format for recording consumer-quality videotape. This is the format most commonly used in home videocassette recording and portable camcorders.

Video news release. A videocassette recording containing a brief news segment specially prepared for broadcast on TV new programs. Usually, public relations firms hire AV firms or filmmaker/videographers to shoot and produce these recordings for publicity purposes of their clients.

Videotape. Magnetic recording tape similar to that used for recording sound but which also records moving images, especially for broadcast on television.

Videowall. An elaborate installation of computer-controlled television screens in which several screens create a much larger moving image. For example, with 8 screens, each of the screens may hold a portion of a larger scene, or two images can be shown side by side, or one image can be set in the middle of a surrounding image.

VNR. See Video news release.

Work for hire, Work made for hire. Any work that is assigned by an employer and the employer becomes the owner of the copyright. Copyright law clearly defines the types of photography which come under the work-for-hire definition. An employer can claim ownership to the copyright only in cases where the photographer is a fulltime staff person for the employer or in special cases where the photographer negotiates and assigns ownership of the copyright in writing to the employer for a limited time period. Stock images cannot be purchased under work-for-hire terms. Also see Copyright/rights, in the Business of Photography section.

World rights. A type of rights in which the client buys usage of an image in the international marketplace. Also see All rights.

Worldwide exclusive rights. A form of world rights in which the client buys exclusive usage of an image in the international marketplace. Also see All rights.

Zone System. A system of exposure which allows the photographer to previsualize the print, based on a gray scale containing nine zones. Many workshops offer classes in Zone System.

Zoom lens. A type of lens with a range of various focal lengths.

First Markets Index

The following index contains over 600 markets which are interested in receiving work from newer, lesser-known photographers. While some of these listings are lower paying markets, many are at the top-end of the pay scale. The index has been divided up into categories which coincide with the categories in this book. Please refer to the General Index for the page number of each market.

Orange Coast Magazine
Oregon Coast Magazine
Other Side, The
Outlook
Paint Horse Journal
Palm Beach Life
Palm Springs Life Magazine
Parents Magazine
Pennsylvania
Pennsylvania Game News
Pets Magazine
Practical Horseman
Primal Voices
Prime Time Sports & Fitness
Profitable Games
Radiance
Rag Mag
Ranger Rick
Relix Magazine
Reminisce
Reptile & Amphibian Magazine
Road King Magazine
Roanoker, The
Rock & Ice
Sail Magazine
Salt Water Sportsman
Science of Mind Magazine
Scuba Times Magazine
Sea, The Magazine of Western Boating
Seek
Sheet Music Magazine
Single Profile Magazine
Sinister Wisdom
Skiing Magazine
Sky
Snow Week
Snowmobile West
Southern Accents
Southern Boating
Southern Exposure
Sport Fishing
Spur
State, The
Stock Car Racing Magazine
Straight
Strain, The
Summit
Sun, The
Sunday School Counselor
Surfing Magazine
Swank
Tampa Review
Teens Today
Tennis Week
Texas Fish & Game
Texas Gardener
Track and Field News
Trailer Boats Magazine
Trajectories
Transitions Abroad
Tropical Fish Hobbyist Magazine
True West
Turn-Ons, Turn-On Letters, Options, BeauTwins Magazine

Vermont Life
Waterway Guide
Wetern Horseman
Western Outdoors
Western Sportsman
Wheelings
Where Magazine
White Review, The James
WIN Magazine
Windsurfing
With
Woman Engineer
Wordsmith
Your Health
Your Home
Your Money Magazine

Publications/Newspapers & Newsletters
Anchorage Daily News
AVSC News
Baja Times
Banjo Newsletter
Bear Essential News for Kids
California School Employee
Capital, The
Capper's
Columbus Times Newspaper
Fishing & Hunting News
Florida Grower & Rancher
General Aviation News & Flyer
Guardian Newsweekly
Inside Texas Running
Jazz Times
Kane County Chronicle
Mercury, The
Mom Guess What Newspaper
National Masters News
North Island News
On Track
Patriot Ledger, The
Produce News, The
Senior Voice of Florida
Sentinel, The
Singer Media Corporation
Southern Motoracing
Star Newspapers, The
Travel News
Traverse City Record-Eagle
U-The National College Newspaper
VeloNews
Ventura County & Coast Reporter
Voyager International
Washington Blade, The
Watertown Public Opinion
Writer's Forum

Publications/Special Interest
AI Magazine
Alabama Municipal Journal
Alfa Owner
American Fitness
American Forests Magazine
American Hunter
American Motorcyclist

Anchor News
Appalachian Trailway News
Army Reserve Magazine
Auto Trim News
BC Professional Engineer, The
Bible Advocate, The
Bicycle USA
Black Writer, The
Bowling Magazine
Bulletin of the Atomic Scientists
California Nurse
Canada Lutheran
CEA Advisor
Chess Life
Civitan Magazine
Computer Magazine
Confident Living
Currents
Cycling: BC
Discovery Magazine
Elks Magazine, The
Fellowship
FFA New Horizons
Florida Wildlife
Ford Times
Greyhound Review, The
Hicall
Hoof Beats
Horse Show Magazine
"In the Fast Lane"
International Olympic Lifter
ITE Journal
Jet Sports
Journal of Physical Education, Recreation & Dance
Journal of Soil & Water Conservation
Journal of the National Technical Association
Judicature
LACMA Physician
Lutheran, The
Magazine for Christian Youth!, The
Mainstream-Animal Protection Inc.
Manitoba Teacher, The
Mennonite Brethren Herald
Midwest Motorist, The
Morgan Horse, The
NACLA Report on the Americas
Network
Nevada Farm Bureau Agriculture and Livestock Journal
North American Whitetail Magazine
Oklahoma Today
Ontario Technologist, The
Pennsylvania Angler
Pennsylvania Heritage
Pennsylvanian Magazine
Pentecostal Evangel
Pentecostal Messenger, The
Persimmon Hill
Population Bulletin
Presbyterian Record, The

Preservation News
Princeton Alumni Weekly
Proceedings/Naval History
Relay Magazine
Retired Officer Magazine, The
Rockford Review & Tributary
Science Teacher, The
Secretary, The
Signpost Magazine
Single Parent, The
Southern California Business
Sports Car
State Government News
Team Magazine
Texas Alcalde Magazine
Touch
Trot
Turkey Call
V.F.W. Magazine
Vocational Education Journal
Water Skier, The
WFCD Communicator
Wildlife Photography
Woman Bowler
Womenwise
Young Children

Publications/Trade
American Agriculturist
American Bee Journal
American Bookseller
American Farriers Journal
American Fire Journal
American Oil & Gas Reporter
Aquatics International
Butter Fat Magazine
Chemical Engineering
Christian Ministry, The
Clavier
Cleaning Management Magazine
Climate Business Magazine
Collision
Construction Comment
Corporate Cleveland
Cranberries
Dairy Herd Management
Dance Teacher Now
Education Week
Electrical Apparatus
Electronic Business
Emergency
Entertainment Express International, Inc.
Farm Chemicals
Farm Journal, Inc.
Farm Store Merchandising
Firehouse Magazine
Flooring
General Aviation News & Flyer
Golf Industry

Growing Edge, The
Helicopter International
In-Plant Printer and Electronic Publisher
Instant and Small Commercial Printer
Instrumentalist, The
Insurance Week
JEMS
Journal, The
Kalis' Shopping Center Leasing Directory
Llamas Magazine
Marine Business Journal
Middle Eastern Dancer
National Bus Trader
National Fisherman
New Methods
911 Magazine
Northern Logger & Timber Processor, The
Pacific Boating Almanac
Pacific Fishing
Pediatric Annals
Pet Business
Pizza Today
Plumbing, Heating, Piping
Police Magazine
Police Times/Chief of Police
Polled Hereford World
Professional Agent
Progressive Architecture
Recommend Worldwide
Referee
Remodeling
Rescue Magazine
Roofer Magazine
Salome Seafood Leader
Shooter's Rag
Social Policy
Soundings Trade Only
Southern Lumberman
Soybean Digest
Sporting Goods Dealer, The
Sports Car International
Stage Directions
Sunshine Artists USA
Teaching Today
Tech Directions
Telecommunications
Thoroughbred Times
Tradeswoman Magazine
U.S. Naval Institute Proceedings
VM & SD (Visual Merchandising and Store Design)
Walls & Ceilings Magazine
Wang in the News
Ward's Auto World
Water Well Journal
Wisconsin Restaurateur, The
World Fence News
World Trade Magazine

Record Companies
Island Records
Nucleus Records
Swoop Records

Stock Photo Agencies
Andes Press Agency
Atlanta Stock Associates
Bennett Inc., Robert J.
Bryce Finley, Inc.
Colotheque S.P.R.L.
DAS Photo
Devaney Stock Photos
Dr. Stock Inc.
Elite Photography Inc.
Ewing Galloway
Fern-Wood Designs and Photo Marketing Agency
Fine Press Syndicate
Focus Stock Photografico
Foto-Press Timmerman
Franklin Photo Agency
Gordon Photography, Joel
Havelin Communications
Image Bank/West, The
Jeroboam, Inc.
Lightwave
Medical Images Inc.
Mountain Stock Photo & Film
Nawrocki Stock Photo
New England Stock Photo
Omega News Group/USA
Out of This World
Oxford Scientific Films
Peebles Photography, Douglas
Photo Library
Photobank
Photolink Stock Photography
Photo/Nats
Picture Perfect Stock Photos
Pro-File
Reflexion Phototheque
Roberts Represents, Chris
Ro-Ma Stock
Science Photo Library, Ltd.
Sharpshooters, Inc.
Southern Stock Photo Agency
Sportslight Photo
Stock Options
Stockhouse Inc., The
Tank Incorporated
Third Coast Stock Source
Tropix Photographic Library
Visuals Unlimited
Weatherstock
West Stock, Inc.
Wildlife Collection, The
World View-Fototheek
Worldwide Photo Images
Zephyr Pictures

Index

If the specific market you are looking for is not listed in this General Index, check the '92-93 Changes at the end of the appropriate section. Any listings which have had a name change will be cross-referenced in this index.

If the specific market you are looking for is not listed in this General Index, check the '92-93 Changes at the end of the appropriate section. Any listings which have had a name change will be cross-referenced in this index.

If the specific market you are looking for is not listed in this General Index, check the '92-93 Changes at the end of the appropriate section. Any listings which have had a name change will be cross-referenced in this index.

If the specific market you are looking for is not listed in this General Index, check the '92-93 Changes at the end of the appropriate section. Any listings which have had a name change will be cross-referenced in this index.

**If the specific market you are looking for is not listed in this General Index, check the
'92-93 Changes at the end of the appropriate section. Any listings which have had a
name change will be cross-referenced in this index.**

If the specific market you are looking for is not listed in this General Index, check the '92-93 Changes at the end of the appropriate section. Any listings which have had a name change will be cross-referenced in this index.

If the specific market you are looking for is not listed in this General Index, check the '92-93 Changes at the end of the appropriate section. Any listings which have had a name change will be cross-referenced in this index.

Other Photography Books Of Interest

Professional Photographer's Survival Guide, by Charles E. Rotkin—A comprehensive guide on becoming a professional photographer, making the first sale, successfully completing assignments and earning the most from your photographs. 368 pages/$16.95/paperback

Achieving Photographic Style, by Michael Freeman—You'll learn how to achieve the same special effects the pros use by examining the work of 100 great professionals, including Cartier-Bresson and Ansel Adams. 224 pages/$21.95/paperback

APA #2: Japanese Photography—A comprehensive collection of over 1,200 color photographs, representing the work of Japan's top commercial photographers. 616 pages/$69.95/hardcover

Guide to Literary Agents & Art/Photo Reps—This new directory provides thorough and accurate listings of 400 reps and agents across North America. 240 pages/$15.95/hardcover

Expert Techniques for Creative Photography, by Michael Busselle—Top photographer and author of more than 20 books Michael Busselle shows you how to achieve professional photographic results by applying some traditional—and some not-so-traditional—photographic techniques. 192 pages/95 color, 37 b&w illus./$24.95/paperback

Profitable Model Photography, by Art Ketchum—Any photographer—from beginner to experienced—will learn how to set up a model photography business, and how to keep his business growing. 128 pages/$18.95/paperback

Successful Fine Art Photography, by Harold Davis—This book will turn your dream of making a living as a fine art photographer into a reality by showing you the step-by-step process of creating—and successfully marketing—fine art photography prints. 160 pages/$21.95/paperback

How to Start & Run a Successful Photography Business, by Gerry Kopelow—In this practical, easy-to-implement guide aspiring professional photographers will find everything they need to start and run their own successful photography business. 160 pages/$19.95/paperback

Sell & Re-Sell Your Photos, by Rohn Engh—This consistent bestseller—now in its tenth year of publication—has been revised and updated to continue helping you sell your photos, again and again, to nationwide markets by phone and mail. 368 pages/40 b&w illus/$14.95/paperback

A Guide to Travel Writing & Photography, by Ann & Carl Purcell—This book introduces you to the colorful and appealing opportunities that allow you to explore your interest in travel while making a living. 144 pages/80 color photos/$22.95/paperback

The Professional Photographer's Guide to Shooting & Selling Nature & Wildlife Photos, by Jim Zuckerman—A professional photographer shows you how to take fabulous wildlife and nature photos—and the best ways to reach the right markets for those photos. 144 pages/250 color photos/$22.95/paperback

Photo Gallery & Workshop Handbook, by Jeff Cason—This book offers the most current, accurate and up-to-date U.S. and international and workshop info. 192 pages/$19.95/paperback

Nikon System Handbook, by Moose Peterson—You'll find everything "you ever needed to know" about the Nikon system, from lenses to flashes. 144 pages/$19.95/paperback

Photographer's Publishing Handbook, by Harold Davis—This book provides insight into the variety of options for selling your photos and/or getting them published, including self-publishing. 160 pages/$19.95/paperback

Winning Photo Contests, by Jeanne Stallman—This is the only book available that focuses specifically on how you can enter and win a photo contest. 128 pages/$14.95/paperback

The Photographer's Business & Legal Handbook, by Leonard Duboff—This book deals with all of the legal and business questions for the working photographer. 134 pages/$18.95/paperback

Photo Marketing Handbook, by Jeff Cason—The perfect *international* companion to *Photographer's Market!* Now you sell your photos worldwide! 160 pages/$21.95/paperback.

Lighting Secrets for the Professional Photographer, by Alan Brown, Tim Grondin, & Joe Braun—A "problems/solutions" approach to special lighting tricks and techniques for creating more dynamic photographs, complete with 4-color illustrations and step-by-step explanations. 144 pages/300 color illus/$22.95, paperback

How to Shoot Stock Photos That Sell, by Michal Heron—Includes 25 step-by-step assignments to help photographers build an integrated file of stock subjects that fill the current gaps in stock. 192 pages/30 b&w illus/$16.95, paperback

How to Sell Your Photographs & Illustrations, by Elliott & Barbara Gordon—This book offers proven techniques, procedures, and formulas to help photographers and illustrators increase their freelance income. 128 pages/24 b&w illus/$5.99, paperback

How You Can Make $25,000 a Year with Your Camera (No Matter Where You Live), by Larry Cribb—Revised and Updated! Scores of ideas for photographers who want to sell photographs in their own communities. 224 pages/Illustrated/$12.95, paperback

The Photographer's Guide to Marketing & Self-Promotion, by Maria Piscopo—Here's everything you need to know to plan and execute your own personalized self-promotion campaign and sell more of your photos. 128 pages/29 color, 12 b&w photos/$7.99, paperback

To order books directly from the publisher, include $3.00 postage and handling for one book, $1.00 for each additional book. Allow 30 days for delivery. Send to: Writer's Digest Books, 1507 Dana Avenue, Cincinnati, Ohio 45207. Credit card orders call TOLL-FREE 1-800-289-0963. Prices subject to change without notice.

Clues for Spotting Unethical Clients _____

There are indicators as to a client's ethics hidden in the way they have handled photographs returned as "unused," and therefore unpaid. Here are a few things to look for:

☐ *New, grease-pencil marks on slide pages, especially where such might indicate selection of specific images.*

☐ *Any new notations or marks made on the slide frames or in the borders of prints.*

☐ *Evidence of newly applied wax, tape or other temporary adhesives anywhere on slides or prints.*

☐ *Fingerprints, smears or scratches on photos.*

☐ *Slide mounts that have been opened (slits in the mounts; cracked plastic mounts; exchanged mounts; slides upside down, off center or reversed in mounts).*